2. Identification and analysis of the financial reporting issues

a. Issue identification

Read the case and look for potential financial reporting issues. To do this, you need to know the accounting principles and rules and have an understanding of the business and the business transactions. Issues are usually about deciding whether or not to **recognize** something (revenues, liabilities etc.), deciding how to **measure** financial statement elements (leave them as they are or write them down or off), or how to **present/disclose** these items in the financial statements (treat them as current or long-term, debt or equity, discontinued or continuing operations, etc.).

b. Ranking issues

Focus on the more important issues. In other words, focus first on the issues that are material to the users of the information (those that are more complex and/or those that affect any of the key numbers or ratios identified above). You should identify right away what you consider to be material.

c. Analysis

The analysis should consider both qualitative and quantitative aspects. It should also look at the issue from different perspectives. For example, in a revenue recognition issue, should the revenue be recognized now or later? Consider only the relevant alternatives.

Qualitative:
- Each perspective must be supported by making reference to GAAP and accounting theory (including the conceptual framework). For example, recognize the revenue now because... or recognize it later because...

- Make sure the analysis is case specific—i.e., that it refers to the facts of the specific case.

- Make strong arguments for both sides of the discussion. If the issue is a real issue, there is often more than one way to account for the transaction or event.

- Make sure that the analysis considers the substance of the transaction from a business and economic perspective.

Quantitative:
- Calculate the impact of the different perspectives on key financial statement numbers/ratios. Would this decision be relevant to users?

- Calculate what the numbers might look like under different accounting methods, if they are relevant.

3. Recommendations

After each issue is analyzed, conclude on how the items should be accounted for. Your conclusion should be based on your role and the financial reporting objective that you identified earlier.

WileyPLUS

WileyPLUS is a research-based, online environment for effective teaching and learning.

The market-leading homework experience in *WileyPLUS* offers:

A Blank Sheet of Paper Effect

The *WileyPLUS* homework experience, which includes type-ahead for account title entry, imitates a blank sheet of paper format so that students use recall memory when doing homework and will do better in class, on exams, and in their professions.

A Professional Worksheet Style

The professional, worksheet-style problem layouts help students master accounting skills while doing homework that directly applies to the classroom and the real world.

The Opportunity to Catch Mistakes Earlier

Multi-part problems further help students focus by providing feedback at the part-level. Students can catch their mistakes earlier and access content-specific resources at the point of learning.

WileyPLUS includes a full ebook, interactive tutorials, assessment capabilities, and Blackboard integration.

STARR COMPANY
Trial Balance
June 30, 2014

	Debit	Credit
cal	$	

Cash
Owner's Capital

Type-ahead feature for account title entry replaces drop-down menus.

$ $

WileyPLUS

ALL THE HELP, RESOURCES, AND PERSONAL SUPPORT YOU AND YOUR STUDENTS NEED!

www.wileyplus.com/resources

1st DAY OF CLASS ...AND BEYOND!

2-Minute Tutorials and all of the resources you and your students need to get started

WileyPLUS

Student Partner Program

Student support from an experienced student user

Wiley Faculty Network

Collaborate with your colleagues, find a mentor, attend virtual and live events, and view resources
www.WhereFacultyConnect.com

WileyPLUS

Quick Start

Pre-loaded, ready-to-use assignments and presentations created by subject matter experts

Technical Support 24/7
FAQs, online chat, and phone support
www.wileyplus.com/support

Your *WileyPLUS* Account Manager, providing personal training and support

INTERMEDIATE ACCOUNTING

TENTH CANADIAN EDITION

INTERMEDIATE ACCOUNTING

Donald E. Kieso, PhD, CPA
KPMG Peat Marwick Emeritus Professor of Accounting
Northern Illinois University
DeKalb, Illinois

Jerry J. Weygandt, PhD, CPA
Arthur Andersen Alumni Professor of Accounting
University of Wisconsin
Madison, Wisconsin

Terry D. Warfield, PhD
Associate Professor
University of Wisconsin
Madison, Wisconsin

Nicola M. Young, MBA, FCA
Saint Mary's University
Halifax, Nova Scotia

Irene M. Wiecek, FCPA, FCA
University of Toronto
Toronto, Ontario

Bruce J. McConomy, PhD, CPA, CA
Wilfrid Laurier University
Waterloo, Ontario

Library and Archives Canada Cataloguing in Publication

Intermediate accounting / Donald E. Kieso ... [et al.]. — 10th Canadian ed.

Includes index.
ISBN 978-1-118-30084-8 (v. 1).—ISBN 978-1-118-30085-5 (v. 2)

1. Accounting—Textbooks. I. Kieso, Donald E.

HF5636.I56 2013   657'.044   C2012-906693-1

Production Credits
Acquisitions Editor: Zoë Craig
Vice President and Publisher: Veronica Visentin
Vice President, Marketing: Carolyn Wells
Marketing Manager: Anita Osborne
Editorial Manager: Karen Staudinger
Production Manager: Tegan Wallace
Developmental Editor: Daleara Jamasji Hirjikaka
Media Editor: Channade Fenandoe
Editorial Assistant: Luisa Begani
Design & Typesetting: Lakeside Group Inc. (Gail Ferreira Ng-A-Kien)
Cover Design: Lakeside Group Inc. (John Lightfoot)
Cover Photo: ©istockphoto.com/bagi998
Printing and Binding: Courier

References to the *CICA Handbook—Accounting* are reprinted (or adapted) with permission from the Canadian Institute of Chartered Accountants (CICA), Toronto, Canada. Any changes to the original material are the sole responsibility of the author (and/or publisher) and have not been reviewed or endorsed by the CICA.

Questions adapted from (Financial Accounting: Assets (FA2) Exams or Financial Accounting: Liabilities & Equities (FA3) Exams) published by the Certified General Accountants Association of Canada, © CGA-Canada, (2012), reproduced with permission. All rights reserved. Because of regular Tax Act updates, changes to IFRS and the *CICA Handbook*, the contents of these examinations may be out of date; therefore the accuracy of the contents is the sole responsibility of the user.

Printed and bound in the United States of America

1 2 3 4 5 CC 17 16 15 14 13

Dedicated to accounting educators in Canada
and to the students in their intermediate financial accounting courses.
Embracing continuing change as standards evolve
in a multiple-GAAP world.

About the Authors

Canadian Edition

Nicola (Nickie) M. Young, MBA, FCA, is a Professor of Accounting in the Sobey School of Business at Saint Mary's University in Halifax, Nova Scotia, where her teaching responsibilities have varied from introductory to advanced financial accounting courses to the survey course in the Executive MBA program. She is the recipient of teaching awards, and has contributed to the academic and administrative life of the university through chairing the Department of Accounting and membership on the Board of Governors and on the pension and other committees. Nickie was associated with the Atlantic School of Chartered Accountancy for over 25 years in a variety of roles, including program and course development, teaching, and program reform. In addition to contributions to the accounting profession at the provincial level, Nickie has served on national boards of the Canadian Institute of Chartered Accountants (CICA) dealing with licensure and education. She has worked with the CICA's Public Sector Accounting Board (PSAB) for many years as an associate, as a member and chair of the Board, and as a chair and member of PSAB task forces. Nickie recently served on the Board of Directors of the CICA and on its Education and Qualifications Committee. She and Irene Wiecek co-authored the *IFRS Primer: International GAAP Basics* (Canadian and U.S. editions).

Irene M. Wiecek, FCPA, FCA, is a Senior Lecturer in Accounting at the University of Toronto where she is cross-appointed to the Joseph L. Rotman School of Management. She teaches financial reporting in various programs, including the Commerce Program (Accounting Specialist) and the Master of Management & Professional Accounting Program (MMPA). The Associate Director of the MMPA Program for many years, she co-founded and is Director of the CA/Rotman Centre for Innovation in Accounting Education, which supports and facilitates innovation in accounting education. Irene has been involved in professional accounting education for over 25 years, sitting on various provincial and national professional accounting organization committees as well as developing and directing the CICA IFRS Immersion Programs for practising accountants. She was appointed a member of the E&Y Academic Resource Center where she helped to author a new IFRS curriculum for the Americas. In the area of standard setting, she has chaired the CAAA CICA Financial Reporting Exposure Draft Response Committee. Irene co-authored the *IFRS Primer: International GAAP Basics* (Canadian and U.S. editions) and was the co-editor and contributor for the book *Leveraging Change—The New Pillars of Accounting Education.*

Bruce J. McConomy, Ph.D., CPA, CA, is a Professor of Accounting at Wilfrid Laurier University in Waterloo, Ontario. He was a Senior Audit Manager with Deloitte and Touche before returning to Queen's University to obtain his Ph.D. in accounting. Bruce has been the Director of the CA/Laurier Centre for the Advancement of Accounting Research and Education since it was created in 2005, and is the CA Ontario Professor of Accounting at Laurier. He has been teaching intermediate financial accounting since the mid-1990s to undergraduates, and since the start of Laurier's CMA/MBA program to graduate students. He taught for several years at the ICAO School of Accountancy, taught in the CMA Entrance Examination Preparation program, and is involved with the education activities of CGA – Canada. He has published articles in *Contemporary Accounting Research, Journal of Accounting, Auditing and Finance, Journal of Business, Finance and Accounting,* and *Accounting Perspectives.* He also has articles published in *Issues in Accounting Education, Journal of Accounting Case Research, CA Magazine,* and *CMA Management.* Bruce was elected to and served on Council at the Institute of Chartered Accountants of Ontario from 2006 to 2010. Bruce is an Associate Editor of *Accounting Perspectives.*

U.S. Edition

Donald E. Kieso, Ph.D., CPA., received his bachelor's degree from Aurora University and his doctorate in accounting from the University of Illinois. He has served as chairman of the Department of Accountancy and is currently the KPMG Emeritus Professor of Accountancy at Northern Illinois University. He has public accounting experience with Price Waterhouse & Co. (San Francisco and Chicago) and Arthur Andersen & Co. (Chicago) and research experience with the Research Division of the American Institute of Certified Public Accountants (New York). He has done post-doctorate work as a Visiting Scholar at the University of California at Berkeley and is a recipient of NIU's Teaching Excellence Award and four Golden Apple Teaching Awards. Professor Kieso is the author of other accounting and business books and is a member of the American Accounting Association, the American Institute of Certified Public Accountants, and the Illinois CPA Society. He is the recipient of the Outstanding Accounting Educator Award from the Illinois CPA Society, the FSA's Joseph A. Silvoso Award of Merit, the NIU Foundation's Humanitarian Award for Service to Higher Education, the Distinguished Service Award from the Illinois CPA Society, and in 2003 received an honorary doctorate from Aurora University.

Jerry J. Weygandt, Ph.D., CPA., is Arthur Andersen Alumni Professor of Accounting at the University of Wisconsin-Madison. He holds a Ph.D. in accounting from the University of Illinois. His articles have appeared in *Accounting Review, Journal of Accounting Research, Accounting Horizons, Journal of Accountancy*, and other academic and professional journals. Professor Weygandt is the author of other accounting and financial reporting books and is a member of the American Accounting Association, the American Institute of Certified Public Accountants, and the Wisconsin Society of Certified Public Accountants. He has been actively involved with the American Institute of Certified Public Accountants and has been a member of the Accounting Standards Executive Committee (AcSEC) of that organization. He also served on the FASB task force that examined the reporting issues related to accounting for income taxes. He is the recipient of the Wisconsin Institute of CPAs' Outstanding Educator's Award and the Lifetime Achievement Award. In 2001, he received the American Accounting Association's Outstanding Accounting Educator Award.

Terry D. Warfield, Ph.D., is the Robert and Monica Beyer Professor of Accounting at the University of Wisconsin-Madison. He received a B.S. and M.B.A. from Indiana University and a Ph.D. in accounting from the University of Iowa. Professor Warfield's area of expertise is financial reporting, and prior to his academic career, he worked for five years in the banking industry. He served as the Academic Accounting Fellow in the Office of the Chief Accountant at the U.S. Securities and Exchange Commission in Washington, D.C., from 1995–1996. Professor Warfield's primary research interests concern financial accounting standards and disclosure policies. He has published scholarly articles in *The Accounting Review, Journal of Accounting and Economics, Research in Accounting Regulation*, and *Accounting Horizons*, and he has served on the editorial boards of *The Accounting Review, Accounting Horizons*, and *Issues in Accounting Education*. Professor Warfield has served on the Financial Accounting Standards Committee of the American Accounting Association (Chair 1995–1996) and the AAA-FASB Research Conference Committee. He currently serves on the Financial Accounting Standards Advisory Council of the Financial Accounting Standards Board. Professor Warfield has received teaching awards at both the University of Iowa and the University of Wisconsin, and he was named to the Teaching Academy at the University of Wisconsin in 1995. Professor Warfield has developed and published several case studies based on his research for use in accounting classes. These cases have been selected for the AICPA Professor-Practitioner Case Development Program and have been published in *Issues in Accounting Education*.

We have come through a period of unprecedented change in the area of accounting standards. Standard setters are conscious of the standard-setting fatigue that is setting in. The pace of change looks to be slowing; however, uncertainty continues regarding whether the United States will move to International Financial Reporting Standards (IFRS).

The year 2011 was a banner year for change, with most Canadian publicly accountable entities moving to IFRS and private entities constrained by generally accepted accounting principles moving to either IFRS or Accounting Standards for Private Enterprises (ASPE). What a very rich data set to study. For public companies, all have restated their 2010 financial statements to follow IFRS, so we have both IFRS and pre-changeover GAAP information. This is exciting!

Now that the dust is settling and we have survived the transition to IFRS and ASPE, where does that leave us in the education arena? In the accounting classroom, many of us have struggled with the rise of the multiple GAAP environments, while trying to sort out whether and how to teach and learn IFRS and ASPE (one, the other, or both?). Should we look at what has been, what is there now, or what will be there when our students graduate? It is apparent that we cannot do it all. So what should we do?

This whole process is quite liberating as it brings the focus back to what is important. It is not necessarily about simplifying things. Financial reporting is a complex and messy process. In essence, accountants take multi-dimensional things such as people, events, and businesses and convert them into two-dimensional financial statements. This distillation is huge, and the responsibility to be transparent and true to the people, places, and business models that underlie the financial statements can be daunting. It is not simple, but therein lie the rewards and the challenges of financial reporting.

How do we produce better accountants? We can help students to think critically and independently: to help them master foundational skills and equip them with tools for more complex tasks. We can help foster the mindset to do the right thing: to act ethically and professionally and to think of the greater good. Finally, we can help them to respect and embrace complex standards and decision-making as part of being a professional. The basics are an extremely important foundation, but there is so much more to learn.

This edition is about consolidating knowledge. We have done our best to emphasize the following:

1. **Foundations**: Ensuring that good foundations are being laid in terms of the basics (theory and principles) and mechanics (numbers, journal entries, calculations, methods). We have a new *WileyPLUS* platform, a standardized chart of accounts, and the highest quality and widest variety of end-of-chapter material.

2. **Uncertainty**: Helping students to understand that good and ethical judgements need to be made. Accrual accounting requires that accountants be able to deal with business uncertainty. Things are rarely black and white, and decision-making is complicated by the fact that individuals with competing wants and needs are making the decisions. We continue to emphasize ethical decision-making and dealing with uncertainty through the use of open-ended questions in the end-of-chapter material.

3. **Perspectives**: Acknowledging and embracing differing perspectives. People see things differently. The multiple GAAP world is evidence of this. We have included side-by-side chapter illustrations showing ASPE versus IFRS journal entries, and we have included more comparative end-of-chapter material that focuses on different ways to view and account for the same information.

4. **Business**: Making sure that students understand business events and transactions. Accounting is communicating a story about the business. We start each chapter with a business-focused feature story and a discussion of the business perspective of the key issues in the chapter so students can better understand a business.

New Features

As noted above, several new features have been added to this edition.

Emphasis on Business

The focus of the feature story that starts each chapter in this edition is on the business models of various companies and industries, along with accounting issues that affect them. The first section of most chapters focuses on **Understanding the Business**, which introduces the accounting topic in the context of everyday business.

Emphasis on IFRS and ASPE

Icons: Individual IFRS and ASPE icons call attention to items treated differently by the two sets of standards. The joint IFRS-ASPE icon indicates a direct comparison between the two approaches.

Side-by-side journal entries: Indicated with a green background, these journal entries illustrate differences in treatment between IFRS and ASPE.

Enhanced comparison charts: The end-of-chapter charts that identify the major differences between IFRS and ASPE have now been augmented with a column that provides cross-references to relevant illustrations and brief exercises that describe the differences outlined in the comparison chart. As before, where there is a new standard being proposed, we have added a column to the end-of-chapter charts so that you understand what may be in store in the near future, or provided a Looking Ahead feature to alert you to upcoming changes expected.

Augmented end-of-chapter material: End-of-chapter material has been expanded such that numerous questions require students to prepare the solution using both IFRS and ASPE.

Emphasis on Readability

The readability of the text has been improved by using fewer abbreviations, plainer language, and shorter sentences. **A new end-of-book glossary** provides definitions of key terms highlighted in the text. **Alternative Terminology** notes within the chapter familiarize the students with other commonly used terms.

Grounding in Accounting Research and Theory

Theory

We have always emphasized concepts and principles, including those that span other disciplines, such as law and finance. In addition to this, the new **Accounting Theory** icon calls attention to accounting theory that underpins much of the accounting body of knowledge, introducing students to an accounting research perspective.

Continuing Features

Many things have contributed to the success of this Kieso textbook over the years. The following points outline just a few.

Real World
Emphasis

Finance

Law

What Do
the Numbers
Mean?

Underlying
Concept

Ethics

Digging
Deeper

Real-World Emphasis

Since intermediate accounting is a course in which students must understand the application of accounting principles and techniques in practice, we strive to include as many real-world examples as possible.

In order to help you integrate your knowledge of economics, finance, and law with accounting, we have included finance and law icons. We have developed the material so that you gain an appreciation for these fundamentals before trying to account for them.

Many chapters have a **business transactions example box**. In most business transactions, you give something up and receive something. These boxes are meant to help you understand what has been given up and what has been received in the transaction. As noted earlier, this is tremendously helpful when you are trying to decide how to account for a transaction or economic event.

Reinforcement of the Concepts

Throughout each chapter you are asked What Do the Numbers Mean? and are presented with discussions applying accounting concepts to business contexts. This feature builds on the opening feature stories in making the accounting concepts relevant to you. Through current examples of how accounting is applied, you will be better able to relate to and understand the material. The underlying concepts icons in each chapter alert you to remember that the issue under discussion draws on concepts identified in Chapter 2 as part of the conceptual framework. More emphasis has been placed on measuring fair values using the new IFRS 13 standard. In addition, an Analysis section is present in most chapters. This section discusses the effect on the financial statements of many of the accounting choices made by corporate management, alerting you to look behind the numbers. Finally, the accounting equation appears in the margin next to key journal entries to help you understand the impact of each transaction on the financial position and cash flows of the company.

Integration of Ethics Coverage

Rather than featuring ethics coverage and problem material in isolation, we use an ethics icon to highlight ethical issues as they are discussed within each chapter. This icon also appears beside exercises, problems, or cases where ethical issues must be dealt with in relation to all kinds of accounting situations. A Writing Assignment featuring the "ethical accountant" has been added to each chapter to help students reflect on ethical situations that an accountant typically confronts.

Helping Students Practise

The end-of-chapter material is comprehensive. Brief exercises, exercises, and problems focus on quantitative material. Case material allows you to analyze business transactions and apply both IFRS and ASPE. Research and Writing Assignment questions allow you to explore the nature of GAAP differences and understand how different accounting standard setters can arrive at different solutions in terms of standards. Comprehensive coverage problems after chapters 5, 9, 12, 14, 17, and 23 combine material from the current chapter with previous chapters so that you understand how it all fits together.

A summary guiding you through the case study method appears inside the front cover of this text. This is in addition to the full Case Study Primer available on *WileyPLUS* and the Student Website.

Analysis doesn't have to be just part of the cases. Our Digging Deeper feature asks you to look more closely at the results you obtain in the problems and exercises. For instance, you might be asked to comment on results or determine how things might be different if one of the original variables were to change. Digging Deeper questions are identified using the icon shown here.

WileyPLUS is an innovative, research-based on-line environment for effective teaching and learning.

WileyPLUS

WileyPLUS builds students' confidence because it takes the guesswork out of studying by providing students with a clear roadmap: **what to do, how to do it, and if they did it right.** Students will take more initiative so you'll have greater impact on their achievement in the classroom and beyond.

Among its many features, this on-line learning interface allows students to study and practise using the digital textbook, quizzes, and algorithmic exercises. The immediate feedback helps students understand where they need to focus their study efforts. As noted earlier, we have standardized the chart of accounts to reduce complexity and to facilitate on-line practice.

Currency and Accuracy

Significant Change

As in past editions, we have endeavoured to make this edition the most current and accurate text available. Everywhere there has been a significant change in the accounting standard or how it is applied, it has been highlighted with a significant change icon. Where change is on the horizon, we have noted this at the end of each chapter under the Looking Ahead section. We are also committed to issuing brief update supplements on *WileyPLUS* when new standards are issued.

The following list outlines the revisions and improvements made to this text.

Chapter 2   Conceptual Framework Underlying Financial Reporting

- More emphasis has been placed on ASPE versus IFRS.
- Information asymmetry is discussed.
- The material on the proposed changes in the conceptual framework has been moved to the end of the chapter.
- The fair value principle material has been augmented and updated.
- More practical examples have been added linking the concepts and theory to real life.

Chapter 3   The Accounting Information System

- The worksheet example has been extended to include the impact of IFRS (a company with FV-OCI investments).
- A statement of changes in equity has been included as part of the key example in the chapter, rather than a statement of retained earnings.

Chapter 4   Reporting Financial Performance

- More material has been added explaining function versus nature.
- The chapter has been restructured for better flow.
- Extraordinary items material has been removed.
- Additional financial statement excerpts are presented to show the diversity of different presentations.
- Additional material has been added explaining the concept of recycling versus not recycling other comprehensive income.

Chapter 5   Financial Position and Cash Flows

- More emphasis has been placed on presentation under IFRS (for example, using Canadian companies that have recently adopted IFRS).
- More comprehensive examples have been added of the preparation of the statement of cash flows (under the indirect method) and there is more discussion of items such as contingencies and subsequent events.

Chapter 6   Revenue Recognition

- The chapter has been reorganized for better flow.
- The re-exposure draft material on the contract-based revenue recognition method has been updated and moved to the end of chapter and journal entries related to the proposed standards have been de-emphasized. (An update will be provided on the companion website and in *WileyPLUS* once the standard is issued.)

- Additional examples and journal entries are presented in the body of the chapter.
- Side-by-side comparisons have been added.

Chapter 7   Cash and Receivables

- A side-by-side example has been added of the effective interest rate amortization method versus straight-line.
- Changes to derecognition requirements under IFRS and ASPE have been clarified (including a discussion of changes made by Canadian Tire in 2011 during its transition to IFRS).

Chapter 8   Inventory

- The chapter has been refreshed and streamlined.
- A side-by-side comparison of IFRS and ASPE has been added for biological assets.

Chapter 9   Investments

- Additional charts show ASPE versus IAS 39 versus IFRS 9 for recognition, measurement, and impairment.
- Side-by-side examples were added comparing IFRS and ASPE treatment of the following:
  - Effective interest versus straight-line amortization
  - Reporting interest separately versus combined with changes in fair value
  - IAS 39, IFRS 9, and ASPE 3856 measurement
  - IAS 39, IFRS 9, and ASPE 3856 impairment
  - Significant influence investments
  - Recycling versus not
- Additional requirements are included in the end-of-chapter material for students to apply both ASPE and IFRS.
- Proposed changes to IFRS 9 are noted under Looking Ahead. An update will be provided on the companion website and in *WileyPLUS* once the standards are finalized.

Chapter 10   Property, Plant, and Equipment: Accounting Model Basics

- An appendix was added. Appendix 10B—Revaluation: The Proportionate Method is a new detailed numerical example of this method.
- More examples in the problem material are focused on IFRS versus ASPE differences (such as recognition of separate components of property, plant, and equipment; capitalization of interest; and acquisition of property, plant, and equipment with share based payments).

Chapter 11   Depreciation, Impairment, and Disposition

- A side-by-side example has been added of minimum depreciation under IFRS versus ASPE.
- The comparison of impairment under IFRS versus ASPE has been made clearer (including a side-by-side example and references to exercise material illustrating differences).

Chapter 12   Intangible Assets and Goodwill

- Exercises and problem material have been strengthened so that they focuses on IFRS/ASPE differences in areas such as impairment of limited life intangibles, indefinite life intangibles, and goodwill.

Chapter 13   Non-Financial and Current Liabilities

- Side-by-side examples have been added of differences in accounting for asset retirement obligation liabilities and premiums and rebates under IFRS versus ASPE.
- Clarification has been provided of the differences between IFRS and ASPE (and further changes that are being considered under IFRS) regarding terminology and accounting for items such as "contingencies" and "provisions."

Chapter 14 *Long-Term Financial Liabilities*
- References have been made to the fair value standard, IFRS 13.
- A discussion and side-by-side example have been added dealing with accounting for credit risk under the fair value option for liabilities under IFRS 9 and IAS 39.

Chapter 15 *Shareholders' Equity*
- Excerpts have been updated emphasizing statement of changes in shareholders' equity and capital disclosures under IFRS.

Chapter 16 *Complex Financial Instruments*
- The chapter and appendix have been streamlined.
- Side-by-side examples have been added of IFRS and ASPE treatment for the following:
  - Bifurcation of convertible debt
  - Fair value hedges
  - Cash flow hedges
  - Recycling gains and losses on hedges
- A brief update on the new hedging standards once finalized will be provided on the companion website and in *WileyPLUS*.

Chapter 17 *Earnings Per Share*
- Chapter learning objectives have been condensed.
- Summary steps have been added for calculating earnings per share.
- End-of-chapter material has been added to bridge simple concepts with more complex ones.

Chapter 18 *Income Taxes*
- The focus has been changed from ASPE to IFRS, but both sets of standards are still discussed.
- The drop in Canadian tax rates has been reflected in the examples in this chapter (and the other chapters in text); most examples now use tax rates in the 20%–30% range.

Chapter 19 *Pensions and Other Employee Future Benefits*
- The chapter now focuses on the immediate recognition approach and compares and contrasts ASPE and IFRS.
- The worksheet approach has been updated to take into account changes to IAS 19.
- A discussion has been added regarding the net employee benefit liability or asset to be reported on the statement of financial position under IAS 19.
- The defer and amortize approach has been moved to Appendix 19B.

Chapter 20 *Leases*
- The chapter focuses on existing GAAP under IFRS/ASPE, while outlining the impact of exposure draft proposals. Once a new standard is issued, more details will be provided on the companion website and in *WileyPLUS*.

Chapter 21 *Accounting Changes and Error Analysis*
- The chapter has been updated for transition year.
- Examples showing the change to IFRS have been included.

Chapter 22 *Statement of Cash Flows*
- The chapter builds on Chapter 5 and starts with a more comprehensive example of the preparation of the statement of cash flows under the indirect method, followed by the direct method.

Chapter 23 *Other Measurement and Disclosure Issues*
- The chapter has been refreshed and streamlined.

- A new section on financial statement analysis has been added to pull together the ratio analysis and related material from earlier chapters.
- More financial statement analysis and ratio analysis questions have been added to the end-of-chapter material.

Special Student Supplements

The *Study Guide to Accompany Intermediate Accounting*, Tenth Canadian Edition, prepared by Michelle Lum, provides a solid review of the concepts presented in the intermediate accounting course, and gives students strategies for dealing with the complexities of applying those concepts. The following are included in this guide to help you make your way through each chapter.

To Help Gain a Solid Understanding of the Concepts

- A chapter **Overview** introduces the reader to the topics covered and their importance.

- **Study Steps** review the business transaction under discussion; show how to recognize, measure, and disclose issues related to that transaction; and demonstrate how to then make the appropriate calculations and apply the appropriate accounting methods.

- **Tips** alert learners to common pitfalls and misconceptions and to remind students of important terminology, concepts, and relationships.

- A **Toolkit** printed on cards can be detached from the guide and referred to throughout the course. These cards present material such as a review of the conceptual triangle from the book, a glossary of definitions, and summary of key ratios.

To Aid in Applying Concepts Successfully

- **Exercises and Multiple-Choice Questions** allow students to practise using material that is representative of homework assignments and exam questions they are likely to encounter.

- **Purposes** identify the essence of each exercise or question and link it to the text material.

- **Solutions** show students the appropriate worked-out solutions for each exercise and multiple-choice question.

- **Explanations** give users the details of how selected solutions were derived and explain why things are done as shown.

- **Approaches** coach students on the particular model, computational format, or other strategy to be used to solve particular problems.

The *Intermediate Accounting Simulation Practice Set* by Fred Pries will help students see how the individual topics they study in intermediate accounting are related to the accounting systems of an organization and to the financial statements as a whole. Students play the role of a newly hired accountant for Woodlawn Engineering, an owner-managed company, and prepare a full set of financial statements starting from an unadjusted trial balance. Each module of the simulation is linked to a particular topic covered in the intermediate accounting course and introduces new information. Students analyze this information, recommend what adjustments are needed to the books and financial statements of the company, and write reports to the chief financial officer explaining the basis for their recommendations.

Canadian Financial Accounting Cases by Camillo Lento and Jo-Anne Ryan provides additional cases at the intermediate level that may be used either for assignment purposes or for in-class discussion. The cases are keyed to various topics covered by the two volumes of *Intermediate Accounting* and have been developed using IFRS and ASPE.

Acknowledgements

We thank the users of our ninth edition, including the many instructors, faculty, and students who contributed to this revision through their comments and instructive criticism. In addition, special thanks are extended to contributors to our tenth edition manuscript and supplements.

Reviewers

Peter Alpaugh, George Brown College

Karen Baker, Loyalist College

Maria Belanger, Algonquin College

Stephen Bergstrom, SAIT Polytechnic

Carla Carnaghan, University of Lethbridge

Brian Conheady, University of Ottawa

Angela Davis, Booth University College

Kristie Dewald, University of Alberta

Allan Foerster, Wilfrid Laurier Univesity

Trevor Hagyard, Concordia University

Helmut Hauke, University of Calgary

Karel Hrazdil, Simon Fraser University

Don Jones, University of Windsor

Michael Kaine, Sheridan Institute of Technology and Advanced Learning

Duane Kennedy, University of Waterloo

Gerry La Rocca, Vanier College

Cécile Laurin, Algonquin College

Barb Lee, College of New Caledonia

Camillo Lento, Lakehead University

Marie Madill-Payne, George Brown College

Ron Naraine, Fanshawe College

Dal Pirot, Grant MacEwan University

David Sale, Kwantlen Polytechnic University

Ramesh Saxena, University of Guelph—Humber

Wendy Schultz, University of Manitoba

John Siambanopoulos, King's University College

Zvi Singer, McGill University

Rikard Smistad, Mount Royal University

Rhian Stewart, Mount Allison University

Dragan Stojanovic, University of Toronto

Ruth Ann Strickland, Western University

Joe Toste, Centennial College

Desmond Tsang, McGill University

Appreciation is also extended to colleagues at the Rotman School of Management, University of Toronto and the School of Business and Economics, Wilfrid Laurier University, who provided input, suggestions, and support, especially Peter Thomas, for his professionalism and wisdom.

It takes many people and co-ordinated efforts to get an edition off the ground. Many thanks to the team at John Wiley & Sons Canada, Ltd., who are superb: Zoë Craig, Acquisitions Editor; Daleara Hirjikaka, Developmental Editor, Veronica Visentin, Publisher; Karen Staudinger, Editorial Manager, who has been an integral part of the last five editions; Channade Fenandoe, Media Editor, for managing this increasingly important aspect of the text; Deanna Durnford, Supplements Coordinator; and Anita Osborne, Marketing Manager. Their enthusiasm and support have been invaluable. The design and editorial contributions of Gail Ferreira Ng-A-Kien, Laurel Hyatt, Ruth Wilson, and Belle Wong are also very much appreciated.

We are particularly grateful to Mustafa Beg-Mohamed, Kristie Dewald, Jocelyn King, Michelle Lum, Irene Plavcic, and Pamela Ritchie for all their help with the end-of-chapter material and solutions. Thanks also go to Vida Barker, Laura Cumming, Robert Ducharme, Elizabeth Hicks, Stacey Hann, Helmut Hauke, Cécile Laurin, Richard Michalski, Marie Sinnot, Rikard Smistad, Ruth Ann Strickland, and Dragan Stojanovic, who contributed so much to the related supplements.

We appreciate the continuing co-operation of the accounting standards group at the Canadian Institute of Chartered Accountants and of Ron Salole, Vice-President of Standards. They have been as open and helpful as possible in all our dealings with them. We also thank the CICA, Accounting Standards Board and the IASB for allowing us to quote from their materials and Shoppers Drug Mart for permitting us to use its 2011 financial statements prepared under IFRS for our specimen financial statements.

We appreciate the opportunity to reach out to so many colleagues and students through this book. Your conversations and input have greatly helped shape the book and make it all it can be. We are thankful to be part of a group of such dedicated educators! Let's keep the conversation going.

Suggestions and comments are always appreciated. We have striven to produce an error-free text, but if anything has slipped through the variety of checks undertaken, please let us know so that corrections can be made to subsequent printings.

Irene M. Wiecek
TORONTO, ONTARIO
wiecek@rotman.utoronto.ca

Bruce McConomy
WATERLOO, ONTARIO
bmcconom@wlu.ca

December 2012

I would like to say a special thank you to Nickie who transitions off this book as Bruce transitions on. You are an amazing analytical thinker, Nickie, and this text exists today largely through your significant contributions. I will miss our lengthy technical and theoretical conversations that always seemed to start innocently enough with "one quick question…". I have learned so much from you and it has been a privilege and pleasure working with you.

–Irene

Brief Contents

VOLUME ONE

CHAPTER 1
The Canadian Financial Reporting Environment

CHAPTER 2
Conceptual Framework Underlying Financial Reporting

CHAPTER 3
The Accounting Information System

CHAPTER 4
Reporting Financial Performance

CHAPTER 5
Financial Position and Cash Flows

CHAPTER 6
Revenue Recognition

CHAPTER 7
Cash and Receivables

CHAPTER 8
Inventory

CHAPTER 9
Investments

CHAPTER 10
Property, Plant, and Equipment: Accounting Model Basics

CHAPTER 11
Depreciation, Impairment, and Disposition

CHAPTER 12
Intangible Assets and Goodwill

TABLES

VOLUME TWO

CHAPTER 13
Non-Financial and Current Liabilities

CHAPTER 14
Long-Term Financial Liabilities

CHAPTER 15
Shareholders' Equity

CHAPTER 16
Complex Financial Instruments

CHAPTER 17
Earnings Per Share

CHAPTER 18
Income Taxes

CHAPTER 19
Pensions and Other Employee Future Benefits

CHAPTER 20
Leases

CHAPTER 21
Accounting Changes and Error Analysis

CHAPTER 22
Statement of Cash Flows

CHAPTER 23
Other Measurement and Disclosure Issues

SPECIMEN FINANCIAL STATEMENTS
Shoppers Drug Mart

TABLES

Contents

CHAPTER 1 The Canadian Financial Reporting Environment   p. 3

FINANCIAL STATEMENTS AND FINANCIAL REPORTING   **p. 4**
Accounting and Capital Allocation   p. 5
Stakeholders   p. 6
Objective of Financial Reporting   p. 8
Information Asymmetry   p. 10

STANDARD SETTING   **p. 12**
Need for Standards   p. 12
Parties Involved in Standard Setting   p. 12

GENERALLY ACCEPTED ACCOUNTING PRINCIPLES   **p. 17**
GAAP Hierarchy   p. 17
Professional Judgement   p. 18

CHALLENGES AND OPPORTUNITIES FOR THE ACCOUNTING PROFESSION   **p. 18**
Oversight in the Capital Marketplace   p. 18
Centrality of Ethics   p. 19
Standard Setting in a Political Environment   p. 20
Principles versus Rules   p. 21
Impact of Technology   p. 22
Integrated Reporting   p. 23
Conclusion   p. 23

CHAPTER 2 Conceptual Framework Underlying Financial Reporting   p. 37

CONCEPTUAL FRAMEWORK   **p. 38**
Rationale for Conceptual Framework   p. 38
Development of the Conceptual Framework   p. 39
Information Asymmetry Revisited   p. 40

OBJECTIVE OF FINANCIAL REPORTING   **p. 40**
Qualitative Characteristics of Useful Information   p. 40
Elements of Financial Statements   p. 45

FOUNDATION PRINCIPLES   **p. 48**
Recognition/Derecognition   p. 48
Measurement   p. 51
Presentation and Disclosure   p. 56

FINANCIAL REPORTING ISSUES   **p. 58**
Principles-Based Approach   p. 58
Financial Engineering   p. 59
Fraudulent Financial Reporting   p. 59

IFRS/ASPE COMPARISON   **p. 61**
Looking Ahead   p. 61

APPENDIX 2A—FAIR VALUE MEASUREMENTS   **p. 67**
Income Models for Measuring Fair Value   p. 69

CHAPTER 3 The Accounting Information System   p. 89

ACCOUNTING INFORMATION SYSTEM   **p. 90**
Basic Terminology   p. 90
Debits and Credits   p. 92
Accounting Equation   p. 92

THE ACCOUNTING CYCLE AND THE RECORDING PROCESS   **p. 94**
Identifying and Recording Transactions and Other Events   p. 94
Journalizing   p. 96
Posting   p. 96
Trial Balance   p. 98

ADJUSTING ENTRIES   **p. 99**
Adjusting Entries for Prepayments   p. 100
Adjusting Entries for Accruals   p. 105
Adjusting Entries for Estimated Items   p. 108
Unrealized Holding Gains or Losses (NI and OCI)   p. 110

FINANCIAL STATEMENTS AND OWNERSHIP STRUCTURE   **p. 111**

THE CLOSING PROCESS   **p. 112**
Preparing Closing Entries   p. 112
Reversing Entries   p. 115
The Accounting Cycle Summarized   p. 116

USING A WORK SHEET   **p. 116**
Adjustments Entered on the Work Sheet   p. 116
Work Sheet Columns   p. 117
Preparing Financial Statements from a Work Sheet   p. 119
Closing Entries   p. 122
Monthly Statements, Yearly Closing   p. 122

APPENDIX 3A—USING REVERSING ENTRIES   **p. 124**
Illustration of Reversing Entries—Accruals   p. 124
Illustration of Reversing Entries—Prepayments   p. 125
Summary of Reversing Entries   p. 126

CHAPTER 4 Reporting Financial Performance   p. 155

PERFORMANCE   p. 156
  Business Models and Industries   p. 156
  Communicating Information about
    Performance   p. 159
  Quality of Earnings/Information   p. 160

THE STATEMENT OF INCOME AND THE STATEMENT OF COMPREHENSIVE INCOME   p. 163
  Measurement   p. 163
  Discontinued Operations   p. 165
  Presentation   p. 169

STATEMENT OF RETAINED EARNINGS AND THE STATEMENT OF CHANGES IN EQUITY   p. 182
  Presentation of the Statement of Retained
    Earnings   p. 182
  Presentation of the Statement of Changes in
    Equity   p. 184

DISCLOSURE AND ANALYSIS   p. 185
  Disclosures   p. 185
  Analysis   p. 185

IFRS/ASPE COMPARISON   p. 186
  A Comparison of IFRS and ASPE   p. 186
  Looking Ahead   p. 186

APPENDIX 4A—CASH BASIS VERSUS ACCRUAL BASIS EARNINGS   p. 190
  Differences between Cash and Accrual
    Bases   p. 190
  Conversion from Cash Basis to Accrual
    Basis   p. 192
  Theoretical Weaknesses of the Cash Basis
    p. 194

CHAPTER 5 Financial Position and Cash Flows   p. 221

USEFULNESS OF THE STATEMENTS OF FINANCIAL POSITION AND CASH FLOWS FROM A BUSINESS PERSPECTIVE   p. 222
  Analyzing a Statement of Financial
    Position   p. 222
  Assessing Earnings Quality   p. 223
  Assessing the Creditworthiness of
    Companies   p. 223

STATEMENT OF FINANCIAL POSITION   p. 223
  Usefulness of the Statement of Financial
    Position   p. 223
  Limitations of the Statement of Financial
    Position   p. 225
  Classification in the Statement of Financial
    Position   p. 225

Preparation of the Classified Statement of Financial
    Position (Balance Sheet)   p. 228
  Additional Information Reported   p. 239
  Techniques of Disclosure   p. 240

STATEMENT OF CASH FLOWS   p. 243
  Purpose, Content, and Format of a Cash Flow
    Statement   p. 243
  Preparation of the Statement of Cash Flows   p. 245
  Usefulness of the Statement of Cash Flows   p. 248
  Perspectives   p. 250

IFRS/ASPE COMPARISON   p. 252
  A Comparison of IFRS and ASPE   p. 252
  Looking Ahead   p. 252

APPENDIX 5A—RATIO ANALYSIS: A REFERENCE   p. 255

APPENDIX 5B—SPECIMEN FINANCIAL STATEMENTS   p. 259
  Shoppers Drug Mart   p. 259

CUMULATIVE COVERAGE: CHAPTERS 3 TO 5   p. 312

CHAPTER 6 Revenue Recognition   p. 315

UNDERSTANDING THE NATURE OF SALES TRANSACTIONS FROM A BUSINESS PERSPECTIVE   p. 316
  Economics of Business Transactions   p. 317
  Legalities   p. 321
  Information for Decision-Making   p. 322

RECOGNITION AND MEASUREMENT   p. 322
  Earnings Process   p. 323
  Measurability   p. 327
  Collectibility   p. 331
  Mechanics   p. 334

PRESENTATION AND DISCLOSURE   p. 344
  Presentation   p. 344
  Disclosure   p. 346

CONTRACT-BASED REVENUE RECOGNITION MODEL   p.346
  Core Principle   p. 346
  Five Steps   p. 346
  Other Issues Regarding the Contract-Based
    Approach   p. 349

IFRS/ASPE COMPARISON   p. 350
  A Comparison of IFRS and ASPE   p. 350
  Looking Ahead   p. 352

CHAPTER 7 Cash and Receivables   p. 373

UNDERSTANDING CASH AND ACCOUNTS RECEIVABLE p. 374

How Do Companies Manage and Control
Cash?   p. 374
What Types of Companies Have Extensive Accounts
Receivable?   p. 375
Accounts Receivable Categories   p. 375
Accounts Receivable Planning and Control   p. 375

CASH RECOGNITION AND MEASUREMENT   p. 376
What Is Cash?   p. 377
Reporting Cash   p. 377
Summary of Cash-Related Items   p. 379

**RECEIVABLES—RECOGNITION AND
MEASUREMENT   p. 380**
Definition and Types   p. 380
Recognition and Measurement of Accounts
Receivable   p. 382
Impairment of Accounts Receivable   p. 385
Recognition and Measurement of Short-Term Notes
and Loans Receivable   p. 391
Recognition and Measurement of Long-Term Notes
and Loans Receivable   p. 392
Derecognition of Receivables   p. 399

**PRESENTATION, DISCLOSURE, AND ANALYSIS OF
RECEIVABLES   p. 406**
Presentation and Disclosure   p. 406
Analysis   p. 408

IFRS/ASPE COMPARISON   p. 409
A Comparison of IFRS and ASPE   p. 409
Looking Ahead   p. 410

APPENDIX 7A—CASH CONTROLS   p. 413
Management and Control of Cash   p. 413
Using Bank Accounts   p. 414
The Imprest Petty Cash System   p. 414
Physical Protection of Cash Balances   p. 415
Reconciliation of Bank Balances   p. 416

CHAPTER 8 Inventory p. 447

UNDERSTANDING INVENTORY   p. 448
What Types of Companies Have Inventory?
p. 448
Inventory Categories   p. 449
Inventory Planning and Control   p. 449
Information for Decision-Making   p. 450

RECOGNITION   p. 451
Accounting Definition   p. 451
Physical Goods Included in Inventory   p. 452
Inventory Errors   p. 458

MEASUREMENT   p. 460
Costs Included in Inventory   p. 460
Inventory Accounting Systems   p. 464
Cost Formulas   p. 467
Lower of Cost and Net Realizable Value   p. 473

Exceptions to Lower of Cost and Net Realizable
Value Model   p. 477
Estimating Inventory   p. 480

**PRESENTATION, DISCLOSURE, AND
ANALYSIS   p. 482**
Presentation and Disclosure of Inventories   p. 482
Analysis   p. 483

IFRS/ASPE COMPARISON   p. 485
A Comparison of IFRS and ASPE   p. 485
Looking Ahead   p. 485

**APPENDIX 8A—THE RETAIL INVENTORY METHOD
OF ESTIMATING INVENTORY COST   p. 488**

**APPENDIX 8B—ACCOUNTING GUIDANCE FOR
SPECIFIC INVENTORY   p. 495**

CHAPTER 9 Investments   p. 525

UNDERSTANDING INVESTMENTS   p. 527
Types of Investments   p. 527
Types of Companies That Have Investments   p. 527
Information for Decision-Making   p. 529

MEASUREMENT   p. 530
Cost/Amortized Cost Model   p. 531
Fair Value through Net Income (FV-NI)
Model   p. 536
Fair Value through Other Comprehensive Income
(FV-OCI) Model   p. 541
Impairment Models   p. 545

STRATEGIC INVESTMENTS   p. 548
Investments in Associates   p. 549
Investments in Subsidiaries   p. 554

**PRESENTATION, DISCLOSURE, AND
ANALYSIS   p. 557**
Presentation and Disclosure   p. 557
Analysis   p. 561
IFRS/ASPE Comparison   p. 561
A Comparison of IFRS and ASPE   p. 561
Looking Ahead   p. 563

**CUMULATIVE COVERAGE: CHAPTERS
6 TO 9   p. 594**

**CHAPTER 10 Property, Plant, and
Equipment: Accounting Model
Basics   p. 597**

**THE IMPORTANCE OF PROPERTY, PLANT,
AND EQUIPMENT FROM A BUSINESS
PERSPECTIVE   p. 598**

DEFINITION AND COST ELEMENTS   p. 599
Property, Plant, and Equipment Assets   p. 599

Recognition Principle   p. 600
Cost Elements   p. 601

MEASUREMENT OF COST   p. 604
Determining Asset Cost when Cash Is Not
Exchanged at Acquisition   p. 604
Costs Associated with Specific Assets   p. 613

MEASUREMENT AFTER ACQUISITION   p. 615
Cost Model   p. 616
Revaluation Model   p. 616
Fair Value Model   p. 619
Costs Incurred after Acquisition   p. 621

IFRS/ASPE COMPARISON   p. 626
A Comparison of IFRS and ASPE   p. 626
Looking Ahead   p. 628

APPENDIX 10A—CAPITALIZATION OF BORROWING COSTS   p. 631
Qualifying Assets   p. 632
Capitalization Period   p. 632
Avoidable Borrowing Costs   p. 632
Disclosures   p. 636

APPENDIX 10B—REVALUATION: THE PROPORTIONATE METHOD   p. 637

CHAPTER 11   Depreciation, Impairment, and Disposition   p. 669

THE IMPORTANCE OF DEPRECIATION, IMPAIRMENT, AND DISPOSITION FROM A BUSINESS PERSPECTIVE   p. 670

DEPRECIATION—A METHOD OF ALLOCATION   p. 671
Factors Considered in the Depreciation
Process   p. 672
Methods of Allocation (Depreciation)   p. 674
Depreciation—Methods of Calculation   p. 675
Depletion of Mineral Resources   p. 678
Other Depreciation Issues   p. 681

IMPAIRMENT   p. 684
Indicators of Impairment   p. 684
Impairment—Recognition and Measurement
Models   p. 685
Asset Groups and Cash-Generating Units   p. 689

HELD FOR SALE AND DERECOGNITION   p. 691
Long-Lived Assets to Be Disposed of by Sale   p. 691
Derecognition   p. 691

PRESENTATION, DISCLOSURE, AND ANALYSIS   p. 693
Presentation and Disclosure   p. 693

Analysis   p. 695

IFRS/ASPE COMPARISON   p. 698
A Comparison of IFRS and ASPE   p. 698
Looking Ahead   p. 699

APPENDIX 11A—DEPRECIATION AND INCOME TAX   p. 702
Capital Cost Allowance Method   p. 702

CHAPTER 12   Intangible Assets and Goodwill   p. 735

THE IMPORTANCE OF INTANGIBLE ASSETS AND GOODWILL FROM A BUSINESS PERSPECTIVE   p. 736

DEFINITION, RECOGNITION, AND MEASUREMENT OF INTANGIBLE ASSETS   p. 737
Characteristics   p. 737
Recognition and Measurement at
Acquisition   p. 738
Recognition and Measurement of Internally
Developed Intangible Assets   p. 740
Recognition and Measurement after
Acquisition   p. 743
Specific Intangibles   p. 746

IMPAIRMENT AND DERECOGNITION   p. 751
Impairment of Limited-Life Intangibles   p. 751
Impairment of Indefinite-Life Intangibles   p. 752
Derecognition   p. 753

GOODWILL   p. 753
Definition of Goodwill   p. 753
Recognition and Measurement of Goodwill   p. 754
Bargain Purchase   p. 756
Valuation after Acquisition   p. 757
Impairment of Goodwill   p. 757

PRESENTATION, DISCLOSURE, AND ANALYSIS   p. 759
Presentation and Disclosure   p. 760
Analysis   p. 765

IFRS/ASPE COMPARISON   p. 766
A Comparison of IFRS and ASPE   p. 766
Looking Ahead   p. 767

APPENDIX 12A—VALUING GOODWILL   p. 770
Excess-Earnings Approach   p. 770
Total-Earnings Approach   p. 773
Other Valuation Methods   p. 774

CUMULATIVE COVERAGE: CHAPTERS 10 TO 12   p. 800

A New Accounting World Order

STARTING WITH THEIR 2011 FISCAL YEAR, Canadian publicly accountable companies have joined their counterparts in many parts of the world in using International Financial Reporting Standards (IFRS) for their financial statements. Many made the transition from Canadian generally accepted accounting principles (GAAP) quite smoothly, says Cameron McInnis, chief accountant of the Ontario Securities Commission (OSC), which regulates public companies in Ontario.

OSC staff reviewed interim financial reports filed by companies for quarters in 2011. "Overall, compliance with IFRS was quite good," Mr. McInnis says. "Canadian securities regulators and other stakeholder groups did a good job trying to get public companies to mobilize early" and come up with IFRS transition plans several years before the 2011 mandatory changeover.

But there were some growing pains. "We reviewed areas that were 'new' to Canada as a result of IFRS having different requirements than old Canadian GAAP," Mr. McInnis says. For example, the OSC found that some companies did not comply with all of the requirements for business combinations, which among other things require much greater disclosures to help investors understand the reasons for the business acquisition. Companies could do a better job in the application of disclosure requirements for critical judgements and sources of estimation uncertainty, areas where IFRS requires additional discussion compared with old Canadian GAAP.

"We also found certain presentation issues that caused us concern," says Mr. McInnis. For example, some financial reports included subtotals in the statement of comprehensive income that should not be presented. Non-GAAP measures, such as "EBITDA" (earnings before income taxes, depreciation, and amortization), as well as other subtotals with "inappropriate" labels, were found in the financial reports. The OSC was concerned that investors could be confused or even misled by some of these presentations.

The OSC has issued bulletins alerting companies to the problems found during 2011 and 2012, informing them how to handle the new standards in future. The OSC planned to look for specific items in 2012 annual statements, including how companies handle impairment of assets—another significant change under IFRS.

Prior to 2011, very few companies adopted IFRS early. The OSC also didn't see an increase in cross-listed companies (those that also trade on foreign stock exchanges) wanting to use U.S. GAAP—probably because U.S. GAAP requirements are quite complex, he says. However, many companies in rate-regulated industries such as power generation have been given permission to temporarily use U.S. GAAP since IFRS does not yet have a standard in that area.

While Canadian companies are still adjusting to IFRS, the standards do much to improve the clarity and comparability of financial statements. "It's a major step forward," Mr. McInnis says.

1 | The Canadian Financial Reporting Environment

LEARNING OBJECTIVES

After studying this chapter, you should be able to:

1. Explain how accounting makes it possible to use scarce resources more efficiently.

2. Explain the meaning of "stakeholder" and identify key stakeholders in financial reporting, explaining what is at stake for each one.

3. Identify the objective of financial reporting.

4. Explain how information asymmetry and bias interfere with the objective of financial reporting.

5. Explain the need for accounting standards.

6. Identify the major entities that influence the standard-setting process and explain how they influence financial reporting.

7. Explain the meaning of generally accepted accounting principles (GAAP).

8. Explain the significance of professional judgement in applying GAAP.

9. Discuss some of the challenges and opportunities for accounting.

North American financial reporting systems are among the best in the world. Our commitment to keeping our financial reporting systems strong is as intense as ever, because in this changing business world, information must be relevant and reliable for our capital markets to work efficiently. This chapter explains the environment of financial reporting and the many factors that affect it.

The chapter is organized as follows:

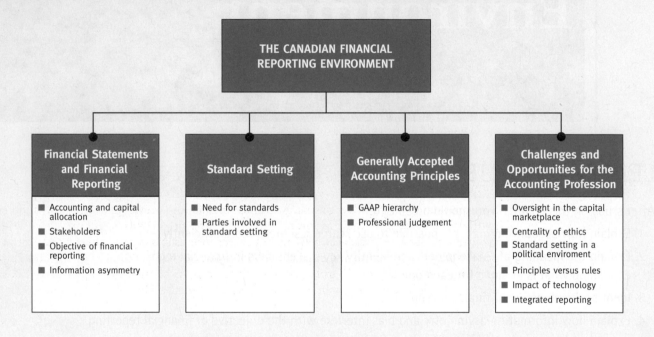

FINANCIAL STATEMENTS AND FINANCIAL REPORTING

Like other human activities and disciplines, accounting is largely a product of its environment. This environment includes conditions, constraints, and influences that are social, economic, political, and legal, all of which change over time. As a result, accounting theory and practices have always evolved and need to continue to evolve in order to remain relevant.

Over the past decade or so, the accounting landscape has changed dramatically, being shaped by many things—some good and some not so good. These include:

- spectacular business failures, including **WorldCom Inc.**, **Enron**, and **Arthur Andersen**,
- capital market failures, including the subprime lending crisis and bank failures,
- near bankruptcies of several countries,
- globalization of capital and other markets,
- increasing use of more sophisticated technology, and
- increasing access to information.[1]

All of these factors, as well as many others, provide accountants with great challenges but also great opportunities!

Accounting is defined best by describing its three essential characteristics. Accounting is (1) the identification, measurement, and communication of financial information (2) about economic entities (3) to interested persons.

Financial accounting (financial reporting) is the process that culminates in the preparation of financial reports that cover all of the enterprise's business activities and that are used by both **internal and external** parties. Users of these financial reports include investors, creditors, and others. In contrast, **managerial accounting** is the process of identifying, measuring, analyzing, and **communicating financial information** to **internal** decision-makers. This information may take varied forms, such as cost-benefit analyses and forecasts that management uses to plan, evaluate, and control an organization's operations.

Financial statements are the principal way of communicating financial information to those who are outside an enterprise. These statements give the firm's history, quantified in terms of money. The most frequently provided financial statements are the:

1. **statement of financial position,**
2. **statement of income/comprehensive income,**
3. **statement of cash flows,** and
4. **statement of changes in equity**.

In addition, **note disclosures** are an important part of each financial statement.

Some financial information cannot be expressed in the financial statements or is better expressed through other means. Examples include the president's letter and supplementary schedules in the corporate annual report, prospectuses, reports filed with government agencies, news releases, management forecasts, and descriptions of an enterprise's social or environmental impact. Such information may be required by a pronouncement by an authority or a regulatory rule[2] or custom, or because management wants to disclose it voluntarily. The main focus of this textbook is the basic financial statements.

Accounting and Capital Allocation

Because **resources** are limited, people try to conserve them, use them effectively, and identify and encourage those who can make efficient use of them. Through an **efficient use of resources**, our standard of living increases.

Markets, free enterprise, and competition determine whether a business will succeed and thrive. The accounting profession has the important responsibility of **measuring company performance** accurately and fairly on a timely basis. The information provided by accounting enables investors and creditors to **compare** the income and assets of companies and thus **assess the relative risks and returns** of different investment opportunities. Based on their assessments, investors and creditors can then channel their resources (that is, invest in these companies or lend them money) more effectively. Illustration 1-1 shows the process of **capital allocation**.

Illustration 1-1
Capital Allocation Process

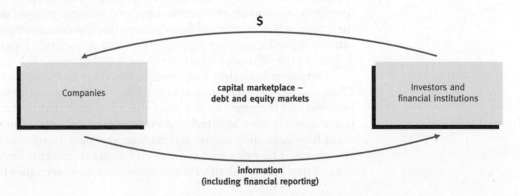

In Canada, the primary exchange mechanisms for allocating resources are **debt and equity markets,**[3] as well as **financial institutions** such as banks.[4] The debt and equity marketplace includes both public stock markets/exchanges and private sources.

Illustration 1-2 shows the sources of capital in Canada for various stages of company growth.

Illustration 1-2

Sources of Capital

Financing Growth Companies

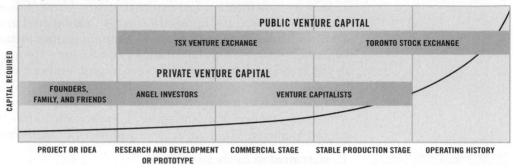

Copyright TSX Inc., 2012. All rights reserved.

Providing an effective system to facilitate capital allocation is critical to a healthy economy. Efficient capital markets promote productivity, encourage innovation, and provide a platform for buying and selling securities and obtaining and granting credit.[5] Unreliable and irrelevant information leads to **poor capital allocation**, which hurts the securities markets and economic growth. The accounting numbers that companies report affect the **transfer of resources** among companies and individuals. Consider the fact that stock prices generally rise when positive news (including financial information) is expected or released. In addition, **credit rating agencies** use accounting and other information to rate companies' financial stability.[6] This gives investors and creditors **additional independent information** to use when making decisions. For companies, a good rating can mean greater access to capital and at lower costs.

Stakeholders

Objective 2

Explain the meaning of "stakeholder" and identify key stakeholders in financial reporting, explaining what is at stake for each one.

Stakeholders are parties who have something at risk in the financial reporting environment, such as their salary, job, investment, or reputation. Key stakeholders in the financial reporting environment include **traditional users** of financial information as well as others. In the stakeholder context, **users** may be more broadly defined to include not only parties who are relying directly on the financial information for resource allocation (such as investors and creditors) but also others who help in the efficient allocation of resources (such as financial analysts and regulators).

The broader definition of users includes anyone who **prepares, relies on, reviews, audits, or monitors financial information**. It includes investors, creditors, analysts, managers, employees, customers, suppliers, industry groups, unions, government departments and ministers, the public in general (such as consumer groups), regulatory agencies, other companies, and standard setters, as well as auditors, lawyers, and others. Illustration 1-3 shows the relationships among these stakeholders.

Various stakeholders have specific functions in the financial reporting environment. Company management **prepares** the financial statements. It has the best insight into the business and therefore knows what should be included in the financial statements. The statements are then **audited and reviewed** by auditors, who may discuss with management how economic events and transactions have been communicated in the financial statements. The value that auditors add to the statements lies in the auditors' independence. They act on behalf of the shareholders to ensure that management is accounting

Illustration 1-3

Selected Key Stakeholders in the Financial Reporting Environment

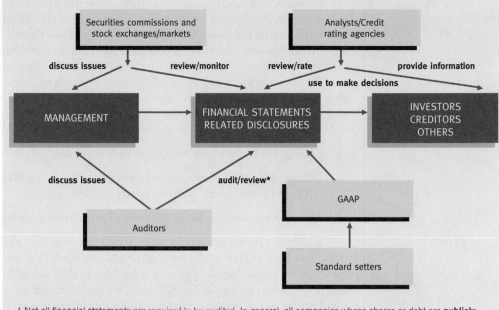

* Not all financial statements are required to be audited. In general, all companies whose shares or debt are **publicly traded** must have an audit and therefore comply with generally accepted accounting principles (GAAP). Private companies may decide not to have an audit but must have unanimous shareholder consent according to the Canada Business Corporations Act. For private companies, the decision to have an audit or not may depend on whether the statements' users would find audited GAAP statements more useful.

properly for the economic transactions. The auditors also **review** the information to ensure that it reflects sound accounting choices.

Investors and creditors **rely on** the financial statements to make decisions. It is up to these parties to carefully examine the information given. Standard setters **set generally accepted accounting principles (GAAP)**. Securities commissions and stock exchanges **monitor** the financial statements to ensure full and plain disclosure of material information and to determine whether the companies may continue to list their shares on stock exchanges. Finally, the credit rating agencies and analysts **monitor and analyze** the information produced by the company, looking for signs of change; that is, an improved or weakened financial condition.

Illustration 1-4 identifies what is at stake for each stakeholder. This is not meant to be a complete list. Rather, it identifies the major stakeholder groups.

Illustration 1-4

What Is at Stake for Each Stakeholder?

STAKEHOLDER	WHAT IS AT STAKE?
Investors/creditors	Investment/loan
Management	Job, bonus, reputation, salary increase, access to capital markets by company
Securities commissions and stock exchanges	Reputation, effective and efficient capital marketplace
Analysts and credit rating agencies	Reputation, profits
Auditors	Reputation, profits (companies are their clients)
Standard setters	Reputation
Others	Various

As noted in Illustration 1-3, the system provides **checks and balances** to ensure that the people with capital—the investors and creditors—have good information to use when deciding where best to invest or allocate their capital. The system does not always work, however. Because the system involves people, human behaviour is often a key unpredictable variable. People often act in their own **self-interest** rather than in the **best interest of the capital marketplace, and by extension, the economy.**

What Do the Numbers Mean?

Consider the much-publicized crisis that arose when large numbers of borrowers with lower-quality, "subprime" mortgages defaulted, which was partly responsible for destabilizing the capital markets and the economy. What was this all about and how did it trigger a global recession? Much has to do with individuals and entities acting in their own self-interest and a lack of transparency or lack of understanding of the true risks involved.

Financial institutions regularly securitize pools of assets in order to access the cash that is tied up in the assets. As a general rule, the securitization involves selling the assets to a separate entity, often for cash. The entity then sells units or shares in the pool of assets to investors. The following are the steps in a normal securitization of mortgage assets.

1. Lender lends money to customers to buy homes.

2. Lender sells pool of mortgage assets from the above loans to a separate entity (often referred to as a special purpose entity or SPE).

3. SPE sells units or shares in the pool of mortgages to investors.

Ethics

There is nothing inherently wrong with this structure and it can work very well for all parties as long as they understand the risks involved. It is good for borrowers as it makes funds more accessible. It is good for lenders as they are able to get their cash out of the mortgage assets. It is good for SPEs as they earn interest on the pool of assets. Finally, it is good for investors as they earn a return on their investment. What went wrong in the subprime lending situation, then?

First, the lenders or their designated mortgage brokers loaned money aggressively, in the hopes of higher profits, to borrowers who may not have been creditworthy. Second, many of the loans were adjustable-rate notes, which meant that, initially, the interest rates were low—often below the prime lending rate, which is where the term "subprime" comes from. But subsequently, the rates reset themselves according to the loan agreement, often becoming significantly higher. Therefore, even though the borrower may have been able to afford the loan payments initially, many could no longer afford them once the interest rates went higher. The borrowers borrowed the funds anyway because they wanted to buy houses even though they knew or should have known that they might not be able to keep up with the loan payments in future. Third, many investors in the SPE did not understand the risks they were taking on by investing in this type of pool of assets, which was systemically risky due to the creditworthiness of the borrowers and the mortgages' interest rate reset feature.

Things began to unwind when the mortgages' interest rates were set higher. This caused many borrowers to default on the mortgages and lose their homes. These homes were repossessed and flooded the market, driving house prices down. Many borrowers found that the amounts of their mortgages were now higher than the value of their homes and they walked away from their debt, causing more homes to go on sale in an already depressed market. The investors in the SPE suffered large losses due to the defaulted loans. All this contributed to a depressed economy.

From a financial reporting perspective, a few lessons were learned:

1. Many capital market participants act in their own self-interest to the potential harm of others.

2. The amount and nature of risk is not always properly communicated to investors.

3. Investors do not always understand what they are investing in.

Stakeholders in the capital marketplace are working to ensure that this type of situation does not happen again.

Objective of Financial Reporting

Objective 3
Identify the objective of financial reporting.

What is the **objective of financial reporting**? The objective of general-purpose financial reporting is to **provide financial information about the reporting entity that is useful to present and potential equity investors, lenders, and other creditors in making**

decisions in their capacity as capital providers. (This is referred to as the **decision-usefulness approach** to financial reporting.) Information that is decision-useful to capital providers may also be useful to other users of financial reporting who are not investors and creditors. Let's examine each of the elements of this objective.[7]

What Do the Numbers Mean?

General-purpose financial statements provide financial reporting information to a wide variety of users. For example, when **George Weston Limited** issues its financial statements, these statements help investors, shareholders, creditors, suppliers, employees, and regulators to better understand its financial position and related performance. Weston users need this type of information to make effective decisions. To be cost-effective in providing this information, general-purpose financial statements are most appropriate. In other words, general-purpose financial statements provide at the **least cost the most useful information possible**.

When Weston issues its financial statements, its primary focus is on investors and creditors because they have the most critical and immediate need for information in financial reports. They need this financial information to assess Weston's ability to generate net cash inflows and to understand management's ability to protect and enhance the company's assets (which will be used to generate future net cash inflows).

In addition to providing decision-useful information about future cash flows, management is also accountable to investors for the custody and safekeeping of the company's economic resources and for their efficient and profitable use. This is referred to as **stewardship**. For example, the management of George Weston Limited has the responsibility for protecting its economic resources from unfavourable effects of economic factors, such as price changes, and technological and social changes. Because how Weston discharges its responsibilities usually affects its ability to generate net cash inflows, financial reporting may also provide decision-useful information to assess management performance in this role.[8]

Theory

As part of the objective of general-purpose financial reporting, an **entity perspective** is adopted. Companies are viewed as separate and distinct from their owners (present shareholders) using this perspective. The assets of Weston are viewed as assets of the company and not of a specific creditor or shareholder. Investors and creditors have claims on Weston's assets in the form of liability or equity claims. The entity perspective is common today, because most companies that report their financial information have substance distinct from their investors (both shareholders and creditors). Thus, a perspective that financial reporting should be focused only on the needs of shareholders—often referred to as the **proprietary perspective**—is not considered appropriate.

As mentioned earlier, investors are interested in assessing (1) the company's ability to generate net cash inflows and (2) management's ability to protect and enhance the capital providers' investments. Financial reporting should therefore help investors assess the amounts, timing, and uncertainty of prospective cash inflows from dividends or interest, and the proceeds from the sale, redemption, or maturity of securities or loans. In order for investors to make these assessments, they must understand the economic resources of an enterprise, the claims to those resources, and the changes in them. Financial statements and related explanations should be a primary source for determining this information.

The emphasis on "assessing cash flow prospects" does not mean that the cash basis is preferred over the accrual basis of accounting. Information based on accrual accounting generally better indicates a company's present and future ability to generate favourable cash flows than does information limited to the financial effects of cash receipts and payments. Recall from your first accounting course the objective of **accrual-basis accounting**. It ensures that a company records events that change its financial statements in the periods in which the events occur, rather than only in the periods in which it receives or pays cash. Using the accrual basis to determine net income means that a company recognizes revenues when it provides the goods or services rather than when it receives cash. Similarly, it recognizes expenses when it incurs them rather than when it pays them. Under accrual accounting, a company generally recognizes revenues when it makes sales. The company can then relate the revenues to the economic environment of the period in which they occurred. Over the long run, trends in revenues and expenses are generally more meaningful than trends in cash receipts and disbursements.

Providing information that is useful to users is a challenging task since they have **different needs and levels of knowledge**. **Institutional investors**[9] hold an increasing percentage of equity share holdings[10] and generally put a lot of their resources into managing their investment portfolios. Can those who prepare financial information therefore assume that the average individual investor has the same needs and knowledge level as an institutional investor when it comes to business and financial reporting? Likely not. This issue will be discussed further in Chapter 2.

Information Asymmetry

Objective 4
Explain how information asymmetry and bias interfere with the objective of financial reporting.

Ideally, to facilitate the flow of capital in the most efficient and effective manner, all stakeholders should have equal access to all relevant information. In other words, there should be symmetry of access to information (**information symmetry**). This is nice in theory but it does not always work in practice. Management may feel that disclosure of all information may hurt the company's competitive advantage or position. For instance, if the company were in the middle of a lawsuit, management would want to be careful about how much information was disclosed as it might affect the outcome of the lawsuit. In cases such as this, the company must weigh the costs and benefits of sharing information. On the one hand, if the company is known to be open and forthright, revealing information may facilitate the flow of capital to the company and perhaps lower the cost of capital. On the other hand, if the company is too open, it might give away proprietary information that might cause profits to be less. For this reason, perfect information symmetry does not exist and as a general rule, management rightly has access to more information than others since they run the company. In other words, there is **information asymmetry**.

Despite the above, there are other reasons why information asymmetry exists in the marketplace. This might be due to the way the markets operate or due to human nature. Some issues are as follows:

1. Capital markets such as stock exchanges are not necessarily fully efficient; that is, not all information is incorporated into the stock prices of companies. The problem of course is that the prices may not reflect hidden or insider information. This may be due to reasons noted above or other reasons as in point 2 below.

2. Human behaviour sometimes results in individuals and companies acting in ways that will maximize their own well-being at the cost of other capital market participants. For instance, management may wish to show only positive information about a company in order to ensure access to capital markets or maximize their own personal bonus.

Accounting and economic theory tries to help us understand these issues. The **efficient markets hypothesis** proposes that market prices reflect all information about a company.[11]

In addition to research on whether market mechanisms are efficient or not, accounting theorists also look at the issue of information asymmetry from other perspectives. There are two common types of information asymmetry problems that are studied by academics. These are identified and briefly explained below. Basically these theories argue that information asymmetry results in a suboptimal or inefficient capital marketplace. In markets where this phenomenon is observed, investors may discount share prices, may require higher costs of capital (as a penalty for having to deal with the lack of information), or may choose not to invest in the market. In the extreme, information asymmetry may interfere with a company's ability to access capital and/or minimize cost of capital.

Theory

We will refer back to these concepts throughout the text. Since these concepts are also studied in other disciplines, the examples below look at them from a financial reporting and capital marketplace perspective.

Adverse selection—Basically, this means that where information asymmetry exists, the capital marketplace may attract the wrong type of company; that is, those companies that have the most to gain from not disclosing information. In addition, those that fully disclose information may choose not to enter the capital marketplace knowing that share prices may be discounted due to the known existence of information asymmetry.

Moral hazard—This concept refers to human nature and notes that people will often shirk their responsibilities if they think that no one is watching. For instance, if a manager of a pharmaceutical company knows that he can get away with it, and is willing and able to shirk his stewardship responsibilities, he may choose not to disclose negative information about ongoing drug trials, knowing that it will result in a decline in share prices and perhaps his bonus. Accountants sometimes refer to this as **management bias**. Managers may decide to downplay the negative and focus on the positive (referred to as **aggressive accounting**). This bias might take the form of overstated assets and/or net income, understated liabilities and/or expenses, or carefully selected note disclosures that emphasize only positive events.[12] **Conservative accounting** would be the opposite.[13] Any bias in financial reporting results in less useful information.

There are many reasons why management may present biased information in the financial statements. Illustration 1-5 examines these possible motivations. The issue of bias will be revisited in Chapter 2 and throughout the text.

Illustration 1-5

Possible Motivations for Management Bias

MOTIVATION TO BIAS INFORMATION	EXPLANATION
Evaluation of management performance	Financial statements provide evidence to investors about how well management has discharged its stewardship function.
Compensation structures	Management remuneration may be based on financial statements directly (for example, bonus based on net income) or indirectly (stock options based on the value of the shares that may be affected by reported net income).
Access to capital markets and meeting financial analyst expectations	There is a strong desire to meet financial analysts' expectations as this may affect a company's cost of capital or access to capital markets.[14] In addition, there may be a concern that share prices and therefore management compensation may drop.
Contractual obligations	Many lending agreements and contracts require that certain financial benchmarks be met, and these often relate to financial stability or liquidity. For instance, a debt covenant (a term in a loan agreement) may state that the company must maintain certain minimum financial ratios or the loan may be called (demanded to be repaid).

What Do the Numbers Mean?

In their book *Freakonomics*, Levitt and Dubner acknowledge that it is very common in most transactions for one party to have more or better information than the other. Often, in a transaction, one party is an expert and the other not. In the capital marketplace, experts including accountants, bankers, institutional investors, and company managers all have more and better information than the average consumer or investor. Levitt and Dubner go on to argue, however, that the Internet allows information to pass very freely from experts to non-experts. Levitt and Dubner argue that the Internet has "vastly shrunk the gap between experts and the public."

Shifting to another discipline, for example, consider your own relationship with your family doctor. Several decades ago, if something was wrong with you, you would have made an appointment and sat passively in the doctor's office while he or she analyzed your symptoms and made a diagnosis. At that point in time, the doctor may have shared the analysis and diagnosis with you and may have handed you an illegible prescription to fill.

The Internet has changed this. Now, most people do a bit of research before they go to the doctor. By doing a quick search on the Internet, patients are able to get information so that they know what questions to ask and what options are available for treatment. Patients can now freely access information about side effects and new drugs. Many people keep their own medical histories. Doctors understand that their role is to help their patients navigate the significant amount of information that is available, not necessarily to dictate a diagnosis and treatment.

The real question is: As people turn more and more to the Internet and the information there becomes more and more robust, what is the role of experts in the capital marketplace and how will the issue of information asymmetry evolve?

Source: Steven Levitt and Stephen Dubner, *Freakonomics*, HarperCollins Publishers, New York, 2005.

STANDARD SETTING

Need for Standards

Objective 5
Explain the need for accounting standards.

Accounting standards help reduce the information asymmetry problem in financial reporting. They do this by requiring that transactions and events be recognized, measured, presented, and disclosed in a specific way. But the main controversy in financial reporting is this: Whose rules should we play by, and what should they be? The answer is not immediately clear. This is because the users of financial statements have both similar and conflicting needs for information of various types.

Accounting professions in various countries have tried to develop a set of standards that are generally accepted and universally practised. Without these standards, each enterprise would have to develop its own standards, and readers of financial statements would have to become familiar with every company's particular accounting and reporting practices. It would be almost impossible to prepare statements that could be compared.

This common set of standards and procedures is called **generally accepted accounting principles (GAAP)**. The term "generally accepted" means either that an authoritative rule-making body in accounting has created a reporting principle in a particular area or that, over time, a specific practice has been accepted as appropriate because it is used universally.[15] Although principles and practices have resulted in both debate and criticism, most members of the financial community recognize them as the standards that over time have proven to be most useful. A more detailed discussion of GAAP is presented later in this chapter.

Parties Involved in Standard Setting

Objective 6
Identify the major entities that influence the standard-setting process and explain how they influence financial reporting.

Before 1900, single ownership was the most common form of business organization in our economy. Financial reports emphasized **solvency and liquidity** and were only for **internal use** or for banks and other lending institutions to examine. From 1900 to 1929, the growth of large corporations and their absentee ownership led to **increasing investment and speculation** in corporate stock. When the stock market crashed in 1929, this contributed to the Great Depression. These events emphasized the need for **standardized and increased corporate disclosures** that would allow shareholders to make informed decisions.

Several organizations play a role in developing financial reporting standards in Canada. The major organizations are:

1. Canadian Accounting Standards Board (AcSB): *www.frascanada.ca*

2. International Accounting Standards Board (IASB): *www.ifrs.org*

3. The Financial Accounting Standards Board (FASB): *www.fasb.org* and the U.S. Securities and Exchange Commission (SEC): *www.sec.gov*

4. Provincial securities commissions such as the Ontario Securities Commission (OSC): *www.osc.gov.on.ca*

Significant Change

Illustration 1-6 shows how these organizations influence GAAP for Canadian entities. Each will be discussed in greater detail below.

Standard-Setting Body	GAAP Development	How GAAP Applies to Canadian Entities
AcSB	GAAP for Canadian private companies (referred to as **Accounting Standards for Private Enterprises or ASPE),** pension plans, and not-for-profit entities	ASPE is effective for periods beginning on or after January 1, 2011. Not-for-profit entities in the public sector may have to follow public sector GAAP, which is the responsibility of the Public Sector Accounting Board (PSAB).
IASB	GAAP for public companies, referred to as **International Financial Reporting Standards (IFRS)**	IFRS is effective for periods beginning on or after January 1, 2011. Private companies and not-for-profit entities may choose to use IFRS.
FASB	GAAP for U.S. entities (referred to as U.S. GAAP)	The FASB is working with the IASB toward convergence of standards. Canadian public companies may choose to follow U.S. GAAP (see text directly below under Securities commissions).
Securities commissions	Not responsible for GAAP but often require additional disclosures for public companies	The Ontario Securities Commission requires that public companies follow IFRS or U.S. GAAP (where public companies list on U.S. stock exchanges or markets and choose to follow U.S. GAAP instead of IFRS) for periods beginning on or after January 1, 2011.

Illustration 1-6

Various Entities Responsible for GAAP

Canadian Accounting Standards Board (AcSB)

The first official recommendations on standards of financial statement disclosure were published in 1946 by the **Canadian Institute of Chartered Accountants (CICA)**. Today, the **Accounting Standards Board (AcSB)** has primary responsibility for setting GAAP in Canada and produces a variety of authoritative material, including the most important source of GAAP, the *CICA Handbook*.[16] The *CICA Handbook* was originally published in 1968[17] and now consists of several volumes of accounting and assurance guidance.[18]

The objectives of the AcSB are as follows:

a. To establish financial reporting standards and guidance that improve the quality of information reported by Canadian entities, principally annual and interim general purpose financial statements, with due consideration for the costs and the benefits to the preparers and users of financial statements of different categories of reporting entity, and changes in the economic environment.

b. To facilitate the capital allocation process in both the business and not-for-profit sectors through improved information.

c. To participate with other standard setters in the development of a single set of high quality internationally accepted financial reporting standards.

d. To support the implementation of financial reporting standards and the resolution of emerging application issues.[19]

Two basic premises underlie the process of establishing financial accounting standards:

1. The AcSB should **respond to the needs and viewpoints** of the **entire economic community**, not just the public accounting profession.

2. The AcSB should **operate in full public view** through a **due process** system that gives interested persons enough opportunity to make their views known.

The **Accounting Standards Oversight Council (AcSOC)** oversees AcSB activities. Its duties include providing input to AcSB activities and reporting to the public, among other things. Members of the AcSB and the AcSOC come from a wide range of groups that are interested or involved in the financial reporting process.[20]

The AcSB is responsible for setting standards for public and private entities as well as not-for-profit entities (including some profit-oriented government entities). As noted in Illustration 1-6, from 2011 onward, the AcSB is responsible for developing standards for private enterprises, not-for-profit entities, and pension plans only. Standards for publicly accountable entities (public companies) will be developed by the International Accounting Standards Board even though still adopted into Canadian GAAP by the AcSB. This approach makes sense for a number of reasons, including the following:

1. Public companies operate globally and often raise funds in global capital markets; therefore, it makes sense to have a common language for reporting financial position and performance so that users can compare companies.

2. Private companies often operate locally, have less complex business models and fewer users who are often close to the company, and can gain other information about the business first hand. Therefore, it makes sense to have a separate GAAP that is less complicated, has fewer disclosures, and is geared toward fewer users who have access to additional information about the company.

Note that there are some private companies that are global and complex. These entities have the option to use IFRS. Private entities that are looking to go public may find it easier to follow IFRS right from the beginning.[21]

International Accounting Standards Board (IASB)

Most countries agree that more uniform standards are needed. As a result, the International Accounting Standards Committee (IASC) was formed in 1973 to try to lessen the areas of difference among countries' own standards. The IASC's objective in standard setting was to work generally to improve and harmonize regulations, accounting standards, and procedures relating to the presentation of financial statements. Eliminating differences is not easy: the financial reporting objectives in each country are different, the institutional structures are often not comparable, and there are strong national tendencies in most countries. Nevertheless, much progress has been made since the IASC's early days. In 2001, a new **International Accounting Standards Board (IASB)** was created.

According to the IASB website, its aims are as follows:

- to develop a single set of high quality, understandable, enforceable and globally accepted international financial reporting standards (IFRSs) through its standard-setting body, the IASB;

- to promote the use and rigorous application of those standards;

- to take account of the financial reporting needs of emerging economies and small and medium-sized entities (SMEs); and

- to bring about convergence of national accounting standards and IFRSs to high quality solutions.[22]

Illustration 1-7 shows the governing structure of the IASB. As shown in the diagram, the **IFRS Foundation** monitors, reviews the effectiveness of, appoints members to, and funds the IASB. The **International Financial Reporting Interpretation Committee (IFRIC)** studies issues where guidance in IASB is insufficient or non-existent. If necessary, it produces additional guidance in the form of IFRIC interpretations, which are part of IFRS.

The **IFRS Advisory Council** is composed of various user groups, such as preparers of financial statements, analysts, auditors, regulators, professional accounting bodies, and academics. As its name suggests, it provides guidance and feedback to the IASB.

Illustration 1-7

How the IASB Is Set Up[23]

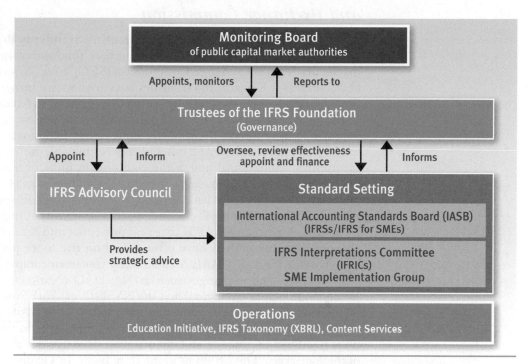

Illustration 1-8 shows the various stages in producing an international standard.

Illustration 1-8

Evolution of a New or Revised IFRS[24]

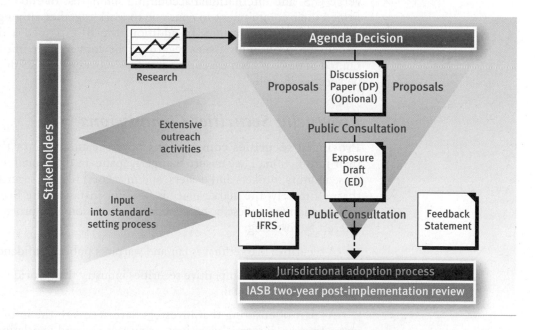

The process is very similar to the Canadian and U.S. processes. One difference is the increased and more common use of discussion papers (DPs). DPs are often the predecessors of exposure drafts (EDs). When IFRS are being formulated, the IASB may issue a DP and ask for comment letters just as it does for EDs. Therefore, by the time the proposed standard gets to the ED stage, many key decisions have already been made.[25]

The IASB is quickly becoming the dominant standard-setting body in the world. As of December 2011, over 122 countries required or allowed the use of IFRS (with 92 of these countries requiring IFRS for all domestic listed companies).[26]

Financial Accounting Standards Board and the Securities and Exchange Commission

In the United States, the **Financial Accounting Standards Board (FASB)** is the major standard-setting body, although it does not have final authority over standards—instead, the **Securities and Exchange Commission (SEC)** does. (Note that the SEC is a national body whereas in Canada, the securities commissions are provincial.) The SEC has confirmed its support for the FASB by stating that financial statements that conform to FASB standards will be presumed to have substantial authoritative support. The SEC has also indicated in its reports to the U.S. government that it continues to believe that the private sector (for example the FASB) should stay responsible for establishing and improving accounting standards, although the commission must oversee any changes. Like the Canadian securities commissions, the SEC also indicates its position on various financial reporting issues through what it calls financial reporting releases.

U.S. GAAP has and will continue to have a significant impact on GAAP in Canada. First, since Canadian GAAP is based on principles and is fairly open to interpretation, **accounting professionals have often relied on the more prescriptive, specific guidance** provided in U.S. GAAP. Second, many Canadian companies are also listed on U.S. stock markets and exchanges such as NASDAQ (National Association of Securities Dealers Automated Quotation) and the NYSE (New York Stock Exchange). To be listed on a U.S. exchange, these companies must follow U.S. GAAP[27] or IFRS.[28] As we move toward international harmonization in accounting standards, the U.S. standards will continue to influence Canadian and international standards due to the significant capital pool of these markets. This brings us to the third point. In October 2002, the FASB and IASB signed an agreement (the Norwalk Agreement) that formalized their commitment to converge U.S. and international accounting standards. In 2008, FASB and the IASB reaffirmed their commitment to continue to work together although it is not clear that this relationship will continue. In addition, the SEC issued a document known as the "Roadmap"[29] outlining issues regarding the convergence initiative. More recently, the United States has been examining just how moving to IFRS might work from a practical perspective if at all.

Provincial Securities Commissions

Provincial securities commissions[30] oversee and monitor the capital marketplace in their jurisdiction. They ensure that participants in the capital markets (including companies, auditors, brokers and dealers, and investors) respect securities law and legislation so that, ultimately, the marketplace is fair. For instance, the British Columbia Securities Commission (www.bcsc.bc.ca) states that its mission is to protect and promote the public interest by fostering:

- A securities market that is fair and warrants public confidence

- A dynamic and competitive securities industry that provides investment opportunities and access to capital

As part of ensuring that investors have access to the information that they need in order to make informed decisions, securities law and legislation require that companies that issue shares to the public and whose shares trade on a Canadian stock exchange or stock market produce GAAP financial statements.

Ontario is home to the largest stock exchange in Canada, the **Toronto Stock Exchange (TSX)**, and most large Canadian public companies are therefore registered with the **Ontario Securities Commission (OSC)**. The OSC reviews and monitors the financial statements of companies whose shares are publicly traded on the TSX so that it can judge whether the statements present the financial position and results of operations of these companies fairly.[31] It also issues its own MD & A disclosure requirements.[32] Stock exchanges, as well as securities commissions, have the ability to fine a company and/or delist the company's shares from the stock exchange, which removes a company's access to capital markets.

GENERALLY ACCEPTED ACCOUNTING PRINCIPLES

Objective 7
Explain the meaning of generally accepted accounting principles (GAAP).

GAAP includes **not only specific rules**, **practices**, **and procedures** for particular circumstances but also **broad principles and conventions that apply generally**, including underlying concepts.

GAAP Hierarchy

The **GAAP hierarchy** identifies the sources of GAAP and lets users know which ones should be consulted first in asking the question: What is GAAP?

Under ASPE, GAAP is divided into **primary sources** and **other sources**. Based on the *CICA Handbook*, Part II, Section 1100, the **primary** sources of GAAP (in descending order of authority) are as follows:

- *Handbook* Sections 1400 to 3870, including Appendices; and

- **Accounting guidelines**, including Appendices.

Other sources of GAAP noted in Section 1100 include:

- **Background information and basis for conclusion documents issued by the AcSB**

- **Pronouncements** by accounting standard-setting bodies in other jurisdictions, although it is not necessary to comply with guidance in IFRS or other GAAP in order to comply with Canadian GAAP for private entities[33]

- **Approved drafts of primary sources** of GAAP where no primary sources apply (such as exposure drafts)

- **Research studies**

- Accounting **textbooks, journals, studies, and articles**

- Other sources, including industry practice

In general, primary sources must be looked at **first** for how to treat an issue. If primary sources do not deal with the specific issue, the entity should use accounting policies that are **consistent with the primary sources** as well as developed through use of professional judgement in accordance with the concepts in Section 1000 (the **conceptual framework**). As business is constantly changing and new business transactions and contracts are regularly being entered into, the other listed sources are also important sources of GAAP.

Under IFRS, GAAP incorporates:[34]

- IFRS

- International Accounting Standards (IAS) (standards that were issued by the IASB's predecessor)[35]

- Interpretations (IFRIC or the former Standards Interpretation Committee [SIC]).

Where the above do not specifically apply, management uses professional judgement (in considering the applicability of similar IFRS in similar situations in applying the conceptual framework) as long as the resulting information is relevant and reliable. The following sources would be considered, in descending order:

- Pronouncements of other standard-setting bodies

- Other accounting literature

- Accepted industry practices

In essence, although the wording is different, both hierarchies are similar, as follows:

- They provide guidance that helps answer the question "What is GAAP?"

- They rank sources and consider certain sources as more important.

- They are grounded in the conceptual framework.

- They establish the value of and expect the use of professional judgement.

Professional Judgement

Objective 8
Explain the significance of professional judgement in applying GAAP.

Professional judgement plays an especially important role in ASPE and IFRS.[36] This is due to the basic philosophy of Canadian and international accountants on standard setting: **there cannot be a rule for every situation**. ASPE and IFRS are therefore based primarily on **general principles** rather than **specific rules**. The basic premise is that professional accountants with significant education and experience will be able to apply these principles appropriately to any situation.

In a principles-based standard-setting system, the conceptual framework underlies the standards. Therefore, accountants either apply specific standards that are based on the conceptual framework, or, if no specific standard exists, the accountant uses the conceptual framework and professional judgement to reason through to an answer, as noted previously as part of the GAAP hierarchy.[37] Chapter 2 examines the conceptual framework in greater detail. As can be seen from the previous discussion, the conceptual framework is the foundation of financial reporting.

CHALLENGES AND OPPORTUNITIES FOR THE ACCOUNTING PROFESSION

Objective 9
Discuss some of the challenges and opportunities for accounting.

During 2001 and 2002, the future of the capital market system was challenged by several major corporate scandals, as mentioned earlier in this chapter. This was followed by the subprime lending and banking crisis, which triggered a period of significant global economic instability. The resulting turmoil has given stakeholders a chance to re-examine their roles in the capital marketplace and to question if and how they add value to the system. Advancements in technology and the way we view information are also having a profound impact on accounting. It is useful to continually review the role accountants play in the capital markets in light of constant change. Are we doing what we should? Can we do better? Do others understand what we do?

Oversight in the Capital Marketplace

Ethics

While most stakeholders fulfill their roles in the capital marketplace in a very positive and productive manner, some do not. Should the markets be self-regulating? Accounting scandals at companies such as **Enron, Cendant, Sunbeam, Rite-Aid,** and **Livent** have prompted the government to increase regulation in the capital marketplace. In the U.S., the Sarbanes-Oxley Act **(SOX)**, enacted in 2002, gave more resources to the SEC to fight fraud and poor business practices.[38] The SEC was able to increase its policing efforts and approve new auditor independence rules and materiality guidelines for financial reporting.

In addition, SOX introduced sweeping changes to the institutional structure of the accounting profession. The following are some of the legislation's key provisions:

- An **accounting oversight board** was established and given oversight and enforcement authority. It was mandated to establish auditing, quality control, and independence standards and rules, and is known as the **Public Company Accounting Oversight Board (PCAOB)**.

- Stronger **independence rules** were made for auditors. Audit partners, for example, are required to rotate every five years.

- CEOs and CFOs are required to **certify** that the financial statements and company disclosures are appropriate and fairly presented and they must **forfeit bonuses and profits** if there is a restatement of their companies' accounting disclosures.

- Company management must **report on the effectiveness of the financial reporting internal control systems** and the auditors must assess and report on these internal controls.

- Audit committees must have **independent members** and members with financial expertise.

- Companies must disclose whether they have a **code of ethics** for their senior financial officers.

Stakeholders in Canada were faced with the question of whether similar reforms should be put in place in our capital markets. Companies that issue shares in the United States are bound by SOX[39] and these companies therefore have no choice. Many stakeholders felt that unless Canada matched the standard set by SOX, Canadian capital markets would be seen as inferior. As a result, many of the SOX requirements have now been put in place in Canada as follows:

- The **Canadian Public Accountability Board (CPAB)**[40] was formed to look after similar issues as the PCAOB.

- The **Canadian Securities Administrators** has issued rules that, among other things, require company management to take **responsibility for the appropriateness and fairness of the financial statements**, public companies to have **independent audit committees**, and public accounting firms to be subject to the Canadian Public Accountability Board.[41]

- The **CSA** has issued a harmonized statement that requires much **greater disclosures**, including ratings from rating agencies, payments by companies to stock promoters, legal proceedings, and details about directors, including their previous involvement with bankrupt companies.[42]

- The **Province of Ontario** has made amendments to its Securities Act.

The impact of these reforms on North American capital markets has been to put more emphasis on government regulation and less on self-regulation. Do we have the balance right? At a minimum, there is greater understanding of the roles that the various stakeholders play. However, stakeholders should be doing things because they are the right things to do, not because they must do so by law.

Centrality of Ethics

Ethics

Accountants play significant roles in the capital marketplace. Illustration 1-3 shows that they are part of every stakeholder group, including preparers, auditors, regulators, investors, and others. They are therefore central in making the capital marketplace efficient and effective. However, decision-making is a complicated and human process. In accounting, as in other areas of business, **ethical dilemmas** are common. Some of these dilemmas are simple and easy to resolve. Many, however, are complex, and solutions are not obvious. Management biases—either internally prompted (by the desire to maximize bonuses, for example) or externally prompted (by the desire to meet analysts' earnings expectations, for example)—are the starting point of many ethical dilemmas. These biases sometimes lead to an emphasis on short-term results over long-term results and place accountants (both inside and outside the company) in an environment of conflict and pressure. Basic questions such as "Is this way of communicating financial information transparent?", "Does it provide useful information?", and "What should I do in this circumstance?" cannot always be answered by simply following GAAP or the rules of the profession. Technical competence is not enough when decisions have an ethical side.

Doing the **right thing** and making the right decision is not always easy. What is right is not always evident and the pressures to "bend the rules," "play the game," or "just ignore it" can be considerable. In these cases, self-interest must be balanced with the interests of others. The decision is more difficult because no consensus has emerged among business professionals as to what constitutes a comprehensive ethical system.

This process of **ethical sensitivity** and choosing among alternatives can also be complicated by time pressures, job pressures, client pressures, personal pressures, and peer pressures. Throughout this textbook, ethical considerations are presented to make you aware of the types of situations that you may encounter in your professional responsibility. Many believe that accountants play the role of a conscience in the capital marketplace. That is our challenge and opportunity. Throughout the text, we will refer to specific ethics-related issues with an ethics icon. The cases at the end of each chapter focus on professional judgement and accounting policy choices. Ethical considerations will be considered in these cases.

Standard Setting in a Political Environment

When it comes to influencing the development of accounting standards, the most powerful force may be the stakeholder. **Accounting standards result as much from political action as they do from careful logic or research findings.** As part of their mandate, standard setters include all stakeholders as members, giving them a **formal voice** in the process. Furthermore, through due process, all interested parties can comment on proposed changes or new standards. This is a good thing.

However, stakeholders may want particular economic events to be accounted for or reported in a particular way, and they may fight hard to get what they want. They know that the most effective way to influence the standards that dictate accounting practice is to participate in formulating them or to try to influence or persuade the formulator. This is not necessarily optimal since stakeholders who makes themselves heard the loudest may get their way to the detriment of others.

Should politics play a role in setting financial accounting and reporting standards? The AcSB and IASB do not exist in isolation. Standard setting is part of the real world, and it cannot escape politics and political pressures. That is not to say that politics in standard setting is necessarily bad. Since many accounting standards do have economic consequences,[43] it is not surprising that special interest groups become vocal and critical (some supporting, some opposing) when standards are being formulated. Given this reality, a standard-setting body must pay attention to the economic consequences of its actions; at the same time, however, it should not issue pronouncements that are motivated mainly by politics. While paying attention to its constituencies, standard setters should base their standards on sound research and a conceptual framework that is grounded in economic reality. Recent work by the European Financial Reporting Advisory Group has resulted in some widely supported conclusions that standard setters should undertake an effects analysis during the standard-setting process.

The standard-setting process is difficult enough when a standard setter is a national one such as the AcSB. The political nature of standard setting has increased as more and more countries have adopted IFRS. The IASB, for instance, has 16 members from many countries. It must consider the needs of all users when creating or changing standards. These user needs become more diverse as we consider the different political, cultural, economic, social, and legal settings of an increasing number of countries.

One political factor is how the standard-setting bodies are financed. The IASB has committed to four principles to ensure that the nature and amount of funding for standard setting does not result in politicization of standard setting. The principles are as follows per the IASB website:

Funding should be:

1. Broad-based: It should not rely on one or a few sources.

2. Compelling: Constituents should not be allowed to benefit from the standards without contributing to the process of standard setting.

3. Open-ended: Financial commitments for funding should not be contingent upon any particular outcomes that may infringe upon independence in the standard-setting process.

4. Country-specific: Funding should be shared by the major economies on a proportionate basis.[44]

The challenge for standard setters is to find a balance between letting stakeholders have a voice while not bowing to undue political pressures. You might find it very interesting to follow along as a standard is being set. Information such as IASB minutes, presentations to the IASB, exposure drafts, discussion papers, and comment letters are all available on the IASB website (www.iasb.org). You will see that some spirited discussion takes place and there are many dissenting views.

Principles versus Rules

As mentioned in this chapter, Canadian, U.S., and international accounting standards are becoming increasingly interrelated. All parties are committed to converging toward a high quality set of standards, but there are still many issues that standard setters must deal with. One key issue is the **principles versus rules** debate regarding GAAP.

U.S. GAAP has historically been more prescriptive (even though it is based on principles) and thus has leaned toward the rules-based approach. **In a rules-based approach— much like the Canadian tax system**—there is a rule for most things (even though the rule may be based on a principle). The result is that the body of knowledge is significantly larger. There is also a tendency for companies to interpret the rules literally. Many companies take the view that if there is no rule for a particular situation, they are free to choose whatever treatment they think is appropriate (within reason). Similarly, many believe that as long as they comply with a rule, even in a narrow sense, they are in accordance with GAAP. Some accountants, auditors, lawyers, and companies favour a GAAP body of knowledge that is more prescriptive because it may be easier to **defend** how to account for a particular item.

Unfortunately, the rules-based approach does not always emphasize the importance of communicating the **best** information for users. Just because a practice is defensible does not mean it provides the best information. This particular issue is a significant one for the United States as it decides whether to adopt IFRS.[45]

IFRS and ASPE are more principles-based. The body of knowledge is smaller and the idea is that one or more principles form the basis for decision-making in many differing scenarios. In addition, professional judgement is fundamental. There is less emphasis on right and wrong answers. Rather, the financial reporting is a result of carefully reasoned application of the principle to the business facts. In a principles-based body of knowledge, bright-line tests are minimized. **Bright-line tests** are numeric benchmarks for determining accounting. For instance, when determining how to account for a lease under Section 3065 (ASPE), there is a test that looks at whether the lease term is greater than 75% of the economic life of the asset. The trouble with bright-line tests is that they create a distinctive threshold that is either met or not. In reality it is not so clear-cut.

The challenge is for standard setters to ensure that the body of knowledge:

1. rests on a cohesive set of principles and conceptual framework that are consistently applied,

2. is sufficiently flexible to be of use in many differing business situations and industries, and

3. is sufficiently detailed to provide good guidance but not so big as to be unwieldy.

Throughout the text, we will focus on the development of professional judgement within a principles-based GAAP system (IFRS and ASPE). The cases at the end of each chapter are particularly good for helping to understand how to apply GAAP and deal with choice and ambiguity.

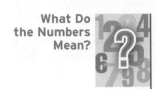

What Do the Numbers Mean?

Will the United States migrate to IFRS? That is a big question. As mentioned previously, there is a significant difference philosophically between IFRS, which is a high-level, principles-based system, and U.S. GAAP, which is a more detailed, prescriptive system of GAAP. While IFRS consists of between 2,000 and 3,000 pages, prior to 2009, U.S. GAAP had more than 2,000 separate standards, many containing multiple pages. The bodies of knowledge are different in size and level of detailed guidance. FASB has since restructured the U.S. body of knowledge, reorganizing the separate standards into one large set of U.S. GAAP. This initiative is known as the codification project and it brings all of U.S. GAAP under one roof. This is a giant move forward in helping to make U.S. GAAP more accessible and user friendly.

Prior to the codification, FASB surveyed more than 1,400 people who use U.S. GAAP. Some 80% felt it was confusing and 85% felt the required level of research to determine how to account for something was excessive.

While the codification project makes U.S. GAAP more user friendly, it is still fundamentally different from IFRS. For a number of years FASB and the IASB have been working together to harmonize various specific standards so that they are worded essentially the same. Moving from a prescriptive, detailed body of knowledge to a more high-level principles-based body of knowledge may not be so easy, however. In a speech in December 2010, the deputy chief accountant of the SEC, Paul Beswick, asked what a reasonable approach would be for the United States to move over to IFRS. Mr. Beswick proposed what he called a "condorsement" approach: part endorsement and part convergence. Under this approach, U.S. GAAP would continue to exist and FASB would continue to work through each IFRS standard to ensure it was suitable for the U.S. capital market. (This is the convergence aspect.) In addition, FASB would consider new IASB standards and make a decision whether to endorse them or not. Whether U.S. companies will ever be able to use IFRS remains to be seen.

(*Source:* Financial Accounting Foundation, FASB Accounting Standards Codification, 2011.)

Impact of Technology

As **providers of information**, accountants **identify, measure, and communicate useful information to users**. Technology affects this process in many profound ways. Information is becoming increasingly abundant and available through technology. Companies now file required disclosures electronically with securities commissions. Investors can tap into conversations, including earnings calls, briefings with analysts, and interviews with senior management and market regulators. This gives stakeholders easy access to a significant amount of very timely company information. The Internet's flexibility allows users to take advantage of tools such as search engines and hyperlinks and quickly find related information about a company. The Internet allows companies to disclose more detail, which the user can then aggregate and analyze. From the company's perspective, providing information over the Internet gives the company access to a much larger group of users. Information can also be targeted to specific users, and costs are greatly reduced as well.

Some of the main drawbacks concern accessibility: Will all users have the knowledge and ability to access the information? Equal access is certainly important to ensure fairness for all stakeholders. Another issue is the quality and reliability of the information, especially since the information may not be audited. Are certain sites and content more reliable than others? Finally, will making increasing amounts of information available in this way leave companies open to information theft or manipulation?

As technology advances at a dramatic pace, will this lead to on-line real-time and/or continuous reporting with access for all users? The industry is experimenting with the use of extensible business reporting language (XBRL). This system allows a company to tag its information so that users can more easily extract it for analyzing and other use. Will this make users rely less on traditional annual audited financial statements? Will this change the role of the public accountant? This issue will be discussed further in Chapter 3.

The challenge is to embrace technological opportunities without losing the quality and content of traditional financial reporting.

Integrated Reporting

Financial performance is rooted in a company's business model (that is, the earnings process, how companies finance the process, and what resources companies invest in). While historically, this has not always been the focus of financial accounting, a company's ability to articulate its strategic vision and carry out that vision affects financial performance. The accounting information system is also part of a larger system of information management—a system that contains a significant amount of non-financial information.

Institutional investors are increasingly looking for more information about how the company deals with environmental, social, and governance issues.[46]

The **International Integrated Reporting Committee (IIRC)** has been established to look at this broader view of reporting and includes in its membership corporations, investors, accountants, regulators, academics, standard setters, and others. Their goal is to work toward a more integrated framework for business reporting that includes management information, governance and compensation, and financial and sustainability reporting.[47]

The opportunity is to view financial reporting as part of a larger integrated "ecosystem" and not in isolation.

Conclusion

Financial reporting is standing at the threshold of some significant changes. Is the accounting profession up to the challenge? We believe that the profession is reacting responsibly and effectively to correct the shortcomings that have been identified and to move forward with a new vision. Because of its great resources and expertise, the profession should be able to develop and maintain high standards. This is and will continue to be a difficult process that requires time, logic, and diplomacy. Through a well-chosen mix of these three ingredients, however, the accounting profession will continue to be a leader on the global business stage.

Quiz

SUMMARY OF LEARNING OBJECTIVES

1 Explain how accounting makes it possible to use scarce resources more efficiently.

Accounting provides reliable, relevant, and timely information to managers, investors, and creditors so that resources are allocated to the most efficient enterprises. Accounting also provides measurements of efficiency (profitability) and financial soundness.

2 Explain the meaning of "stakeholder" and identify key stakeholders in financial reporting, explaining what is at stake for each one.

Investors, creditors, management, securities commissions, stock exchanges, analysts, credit rating agencies, auditors, and standard setters are some of the major stakeholders. See Illustration 1-3.

3 **Identify the objective of financial reporting.**

The objective of financial reporting is to communicate information that is useful to key decision-makers such as investors and creditors in making resource allocation decisions (including assessing management stewardship) about the resources and claims to resources of an entity and how these are changing.

4 **Explain how information asymmetry and bias interfere with the objective of financial reporting.**

Ideally, all stakeholders should have access to the same information in order to ensure that good decisions are made in the capital marketplace. (This is known as information symmetry.) However, this is not the case—there is often information asymmetry. Of necessity, management has access to more information so that it can run the company. It must also make sure that it does not give away information that might harm the company, such as in a lawsuit where disclosure might cause the company to lose. Aside from this, information asymmetry exists because of management bias whereby management acts in its own self-interest, such as wanting to maximize management bonuses. This is known as moral hazard in accounting theory. Information asymmetry causes markets to be less efficient. It may cause stock prices to be discounted or costs of capital to increase. In addition, it might detract good companies from raising capital in the particular market where relevant information is not available (referred to as adverse selection in accounting theory). The efficient markets hypothesis is felt to exist only in a semi-strong form, meaning that only publicly available information is assimilated into stock prices.

5 **Explain the need for accounting standards.**

The accounting profession has tried to develop a set of standards that is generally accepted and universally practised. This is known as GAAP (generally accepted accounting principles). Without this set of standards, each enterprise would have to develop its own standards, and readers of financial statements would have to become familiar with every company's particular accounting and reporting practices. As a result, it would be almost impossible to prepare statements that could be compared. In addition, accounting standards help deal with the information asymmetry problem.

6 **Identify the major entities that influence the standard-setting process and explain how they influence financial reporting.**

The Canadian Accounting Standards Board (AcSB) is the main standard-setting body in Canada for private companies, pension plans, and not-for-profit entities. Its mandate comes from the Canada Business Corporations Act and Regulations as well as provincial acts of incorporation. For public companies, GAAP is International Financial Reporting Standards (IFRS) as established by the International Accounting Standards Board (IASB). Public companies are required to follow GAAP in order to access capital markets, which are monitored by provincial securities commissions. The Financial Accounting Standards Board (FASB) is also important as it influences IFRS standard setting. Private companies may choose to follow IFRS. Public companies that list on U.S. stock exchanges may choose to follow U.S. GAAP.

7 **Explain the meaning of generally accepted accounting principles (GAAP).**

Generally accepted accounting principles are either principles that have substantial authoritative support, such as the *CICA Handbook*, or those arrived at through the use of professional judgement and the conceptual framework.

8 **Explain the significance of professional judgement in applying GAAP.**

Professional judgement plays an important role in Accounting Standards for Private Enterprises (ASPE) and IFRS since much of GAAP is based on general principles, which need to be interpreted.

9 **Discuss some of the challenges and opportunities for accounting.**

Some of the challenges facing accounting are oversight in the capital markets, centrality of ethics, standard setting in a political environment, principles-versus rules-based standard setting, the impact of technology, and integrated reporting. All of these require the accounting profession to continue to strive for excellence and to understand how accounting adds value in the capital marketplace.

KEY TERMS

Accounting Standards Board (AcSB), p. 13

Accounting Standards for Private Enterprises (ASPE), p. 13

Accounting Standards Oversight Council (AcSOC), p. 14

accrual-basis accounting, p. 9

adverse selection, p. 11

aggressive accounting, p. 11

bright-line tests, p. 21

Canadian Institute of Chartered Accountants (CICA), p. 13

Canadian Public Accountability Board (CPAB), p. 19
capital allocation, p. 5
CICA Handbook, p. 13
conservative accounting, p. 11
decision-usefulness approach, p. 9
due process, p. 14
efficient markets hypothesis, p. 10
entity perspective, p. 9
ethical dilemmas, p. 9
financial accounting, p. 5
Financial Accounting Standards Board (FASB), p. 16
financial reporting, p. 5
financial statements, p. 5
GAAP hierarchy, p. 17
generally accepted accounting principles (GAAP), p. 12

general-purpose financial statements, p. 9
IFRS Advisory Council, p. 15
IFRS Foundation, p. 14
information asymmetry, p. 10
information symmetry, p. 10
institutional investors, p. 10
International Accounting Standards Board (IASB), p. 14
International Financial Reporting Interpretation Committee (IFRIC), p. 14
International Financial Reporting Standards (IFRS), p. 13
International Integrated Reporting Committee (IIRC), p. 23
management bias, p. 11
managerial accounting, p. 5

moral hazard, p. 11
objective of financial reporting, p. 8
Ontario Securities Commission (OSC), p. 16
professional judgement, p. 18
proprietary perspective, p. 9
provincial securities commissions, p. 16
Public Company Accounting Oversight Board (PCAOB), p. 19
Securities and Exchange Commission (SEC), p. 16
stakeholders, p. 6
stewardship, p. 9
Toronto Stock Exchange (TSX), p. 16

Brief Exercises

(LO 1) BE1-1 How does accounting help the capital allocation process?

(LO 2) BE1-2 Identify at least three major stakeholders that use financial accounting information and briefly explain how these stakeholders might use the information from financial statements.

(LO 3) BE1-3 What are the major objectives of financial reporting?

(LO 4) BE1-4 Describe what is meant by information asymmetry.

(LO 4) BE1-5 How does information asymmetry hurt investors in the capital marketplace?

(LO 5) BE1-6 What is the value of having a common set of standards in financial accounting and reporting?

(LO 5) BE1-7 What is the likely limitation on "general-purpose financial statements"?

(LO 6) BE1-8 What are some of the developments or events that occurred between 1900 and 1930 that helped bring about changes in accounting theory or practice?

(LO 6) BE1-9 Which organization is currently dominant in the world for setting accounting standards?

(LO 6) BE1-10 Explain the role of the Canadian Accounting Standards Board (AcSB) in establishing generally accepted accounting principles.

(LO 6) BE1-11 What is the role of the Ontario Securities Commission (OSC) in standard setting?

(LO 6) BE1-12 What are some possible reasons why another organization, such as the OSC or the Securities and Exchange Commission (SEC), should not issue financial reporting standards?

(LO 6) BE1-13 What are the sources of pressure that change and influence the development of accounting principles and standards?

(LO 6) BE1-14 Some individuals have argued that the AcSB and the International Accounting Standards Board (IASB) need to be aware of the economic consequences of their pronouncements. What is meant by "economic consequences"? What are some of the dangers if politics play too much of a role in the development of financial reporting standards?

(LO 6) BE1-15 Some individuals have argued that all Canadian companies should follow the same set of accounting principles. Explain why there are multiple sets of standards in Canada.

(LO 6) BE1-16 If you were given complete authority to decide this, how would you propose that accounting principles or standards be developed and enforced?

(LO 7) BE1-17   If you had to explain or define "generally accepted accounting principles," what essential characteristics would you include in your explanation?

(LO 7) BE1-18   Explain the difference between primary and other sources of GAAP.

(LO 8) BE1-19   The chairman of the Financial Accounting Standards Board (FASB) at one time noted that "the flow of standards can only be slowed if (1) producers focus less on quarterly earnings per share and tax benefits and more on quality products, and (2) accountants and lawyers rely less on rules and law and more on professional judgement and conduct." Explain his comment.

(LO 8, 9) BE1-20   What is the difference between principles-based and rules-based accounting standards? In which category does IFRS belong? ASPE? Explain.

(LO 9) BE1-21   One writer recently noted that 99.4% of all companies prepare statements that are in accordance with GAAP. Why then is there such concern about fraudulent financial reporting?

(LO 9) BE1-22   Some foreign countries have reporting standards that are different from standards in Canada. What are some of the main reasons why reporting standards are often different among countries?

(LO 9) BE1-23   How are financial accountants pressured when they need to make ethical decisions in their work? Is having technical mastery of GAAP enough to practise financial accounting?

(LO 9) BE1-24   What are some of the major challenges facing the accounting profession?

(LO 9) BE1-25   The Sarbanes-Oxley Act was enacted to combat fraud and curb poor reporting practices. What are some key provisions of this legislation? Are these provisions in effect in Canada?

Cases

Refer to the Case Primer to help you answer these cases.

Ethics

CA1-1   When the AcSB issues new standards, the implementation date is usually 12 months after the issue date, but early implementation is encouraged. In this case, Paula Popov, controller, is discussing with her financial vice-president the need for early implementation of a standard that would result in a fairer presentation of the company's financial condition and earnings. When the financial vice-president determines that early implementation of the standard will lower the reported net income for the year, he discourages Popov from implementing the standard until it is required.

Instructions
Discuss the ethical issues.

(CMA adapted. Used with permission.)

CA1-2   Boston Clothing Limited was a private company that experienced cash flow difficulties and hired new management to turn the company around. The company then went public and the shares sold at $15 per share. Within months, however, the share price plummeted and Beatle Clothing Inc. acquired the company for $1 per share when it was on the threshold of bankruptcy.

Instructions
Who were the stakeholders in this situation? Explain what was at stake and why and how they were affected when the share price plummeted.

CA1-3   The national credit rating agency downgraded the credit rating of Grand Limited by two levels from BB to B+. The credit rating agency was concerned about the company's ability to refinance portions of its debt. Both BB and B+ are considered "junk" bonds and are below the BBB− category, which is the lowest grade that many pension and mutual funds are allowed to hold.

Financial statement analysts said the company's financial profile had weakened due to tight debt covenants and resulting cash flow restrictions.

Instructions
(a) Discuss whether the credit rating agency is a stakeholder from Grand Limited's perspective.

(b) Discuss any bias that Grand might have when it issues its financial statements.

Writing Assignments

WA1-1   Some critics argue that having different organizations establish accounting principles is wasteful and ineffi-cient. Instead of mandating accounting standards, each company could voluntarily disclose the type of information it considered important. In addition, if an investor wanted additional information, the investor could contact the company and pay to receive the desired information.

Instructions

Comment on the appropriateness of this viewpoint.

WA1-2   Some accountants have said that the development and acceptance of generally accepted accounting principles (that is, standard setting) is undergoing a "politicization." Some use the term "politicization" in a narrow sense to mean the influence by government agencies, particularly the securities commissions, on the development of generally accepted accounting principles. Others use it more broadly to mean the compromise that results when the bodies that are responsible for developing generally accepted accounting principles are pressured by interest groups (securities commissions, stock exchanges, businesses through their various organizations, financial analysts, bankers, lawyers, etc.).

Instructions

(a) What are the arguments in favour of the politicization of accounting standard setting?

(b) What are the arguments against the politicization of accounting standard setting?

(CMA adapted. Used with permission.)

WA1-3   Three models for setting accounting standards follow:

1. The purely political approach, where national legislative action decrees accounting standards

2. The private, professional approach, where financial accounting standards are set and enforced by private, profes-sional actions only

3. The public/private mixed approach, where standards are set by private sector bodies that behave as though they were public agencies and the standards are mostly enforced through government agencies

Instructions

(a) Which of these three models best describes standard setting in Canada? Explain your choice.

(b) Why are companies, financial analysts, labour unions, industry trade associations, and others actively interested in standard setting?

(c) Cite an example of a group other than the AcSB that tries to establish accounting standards. Speculate on why such a group might want to set its own standards.

WA1-4   The increased availability and accessibility of information has had a major impact on the process of financial reporting. Most companies have websites and make available to stakeholders a significant amount of financial informa-tion, including annual reports and other financial data. This has sparked the question of whether companies should use a continuous reporting model instead of the current discrete model where financial statements are generally issued only quarterly and annually. Under a continuous reporting model, the company would make more information available to users in real time or perhaps on a "delayed" real-time basis (such as weekly).

Instructions

What are the pros and cons of a continuous reporting model? Consider the various stakeholders in the capital market-place.

WA1-5   **Nortel Networks Inc.**, the former telecommunications giant, was accused of misstating its financial state-ments. The auditors for the company signed audit reports in which they stated that the financial statements of the com-pany were fairly presented.

Instructions

Real World Emphasis   How is it possible that a company can misrepresent its financial statements and still receive a "clean" audit opinion from its auditors?

WA1-6   As mentioned in the chapter, the capital marketplace's reaction to recent corporate failures has been to increase the amount of government regulation.

Instructions

(a) Identify what steps Canada and the United States have taken to increase government regulation.

(b) What other options to strengthen the capital marketplace might have been available to stakeholders?

(c) What are the strengths and weaknesses of government regulation?

WA1-7   Effective 2011, Canada now has a two-tiered system for determining GAAP for private versus public companies. Private companies will follow ASPE as prepared by the AcSB, and public companies will have to follow IFRS. Private companies will be allowed to use IFRS if they choose.

Instructions

Discuss, noting the pros and cons of having this type of system versus a system where there is one set of GAAP for private and public entities. Consider in your response the differences between private and public entities, including the users and type of financial information each report.

WA1-8   Financial statements can be a valuable tool for many interested parties in the performance of a company. Consider a public company in Alberta that drills oil and sells it to refineries in the United States. The company prepares its financial statements using IFRS and publishes the statements on its website.

Instructions

Explain who the stakeholders are that would be interested in the financial reporting of the company and what information would be most relevant to these stakeholders.

WA1-9   There are many situations in which management of a company may want to disclose more or less information about their operations. In a situation where a manufacturer is preparing for the launch of a new product line, the information available to management may include the projected release date of the product, the associated costs, the price at which the product will be sold, and the results of any market research performed as to the expected sales.

Instructions

Why might management want to share the information above with the public? Why might they try to keep this information private? Also consider the impact of management's decision on those outside of the organization.

Ethics

WA1-10   While it is a goal of standard setters to develop accounting standards that will provide comparability across organizations and over time, there are instances when professional judgement must be used in determining the correct amount of disclosure. Assume the role of the ethical accountant working as an advisor for ABC Inc., a toy manufacturer. ABC Inc. has received reports that a particular toy may have led to injuries for the users. At this point in time the information available is inconclusive as to whether the toy actually caused the injury or whether it was a result of user error. Management must now decide whether to communicate the potential malfunction to the public or to wait for additional information.

Instructions

(a) Describe the reasons for management to await additional information before making a public statement about the safety of the toy.

(b) Describe the reasons management might communicate the potential defect to the public immediately.

(c) In your role as the ethical accountant, what course of action would you recommend and why?

WA1-11   The integrated reporting initiative discussed in this chapter focuses on extending the disclosure of financial statements to include more information about a company and its objectives and performance.

Instructions

Discuss what type of users of the financial statements would be in favour of the additional disclosure required for integrated reporting.

WA1-12   The IASB has instituted four principles related to its funding to ensure that funding does not lead to politicization of standard setting. The standards specify that funding should be broad-based, compelling, open-ended, and country-specific. This differs from the funding process for AcSB and FASB.

Instructions

(a) Discuss the four principles and what impact they have on the standard-setting process.

(b) What issues might arise if these principles did not exist?

(c) AcSB and FASB do not have the same principles in place. Why might the same principles not work for AcSB and FASB?

RESEARCH AND FINANCIAL ANALYSIS

RA1-1 Annual Improvements to IFRSs

The IASB released an Exposure Draft (ED) in May 2012 titled *Annual Improvements to IFRSs: 2010 – 2012 Cycle*. This IASB publication is intended to invite comment on changes that might improve various standards. The ED is available on the IASB website.

Instructions

Read the ED and respond to the following questions:

(a) What are the general questions raised by the ED? Why might these questions add value to the development of Canadian GAAP?

(b) Discuss the amendments proposed for IFRS 8 *Operating Segments*.

(c) Do the changes to IFRS 8 result in standards that are more easily used? Without these changes could the same treatment be achieved? What would the process be for determining the correct treatment?

RA1-2 IASB

Michael Sharpe, then deputy chairman of the International Accounting Standards Committee, made the following comments before the Financial Executives International 63rd Annual Conference:

There is an irreversible movement toward the harmonization of financial reporting throughout the world. The international capital markets require an end to:

1. The confusion caused by international companies announcing different results depending on the set of accounting standards applied. Recent announcements by Daimler-Benz (now DaimlerChrysler) highlight the confusion that this causes.

2. Companies in some countries obtaining unfair commercial advantages from the use of particular national accounting standards.

3. The complications in negotiating commercial arrangements for international joint ventures caused by different accounting requirements.

4. The inefficiency of international companies having to understand and use myriad accounting standards depending on the countries in which they operate and the countries in which they raise capital and debt. Executive talent is wasted on keeping up to date with numerous sets of accounting standards and the never-ending changes to them.

5. The inefficiency of investment managers, bankers, and financial analysts as they seek to compare financial reporting drawn up in accordance with different sets of accounting standards.

6. Failure of many stock exchanges and regulators to require companies subject to their jurisdiction to provide comparable, comprehensive, and transparent financial reporting frameworks giving international comparability.

7. Difficulty for developing countries and countries entering the free market economy, such as China and Russia, in accessing foreign capital markets because of the complexity of and differences between national standards.

8. The restriction on the mobility of financial service providers across the world as a result of different accounting standards.

Clearly, eliminating these inefficiencies by having comparable high-quality financial reporting used across the world would benefit international businesses.

Instructions

Research the issue using the Internet and answer the following questions:

(a) What is the International Accounting Standards Board and what is its relationship with the International Accounting Standards Committee?

(b) Which stakeholders might benefit from the use of international accounting standards?

(c) What do you believe are some of the major obstacles to harmonization?

RA1-3 Canadian Coalition for Good Governance

**Real World
Emphasis**

The **Canadian Coalition for Good Governance** was formed in 2002 and represents a significant number of institutional investors in Canada.

Instructions

(a) How does an institutional investor differ from other investors?

(b) In your opinion, what impact would the presence of a large number of investors have on management's financial reporting decisions?

(c) Go to the coalition's website (www.ccgg.ca) and identify the coalition's three largest member companies.

(d) Go to these member companies' websites and identify their major investments.

RA1-4 SOX

In 2002, the *Sarbanes-Oxley Act* was passed in the United States to strengthen the capital marketplace. In the following year, there were many debates in Canada about whether the securities commissions in Canada should adopt the same regulations. In the end, Canada did adopt a similar level of regulation.

Instructions

(a) Why was the Act issued and what are its key components?

(b) What impact do you think the Act had on the U.S. capital marketplace?

(c) Do you think there were any spillover effects in the Canadian marketplace? (*Hint:* look on the websites of the provincial securities commissions, the Canadian Institute of Chartered Accountants, the TSX, and the *Globe and Mail* and *Financial Post*. Key words might be "SOX," "corporate accountability," and "post Enron.")

(d) Changes to the Sarbanes-Oxley Act were proposed in 2012 under Bill S1933. The bill would allow lower earning private companies to become public without full SOX compliance. One example is that companies earning less than $1 billion annually can defer adoption of certain SOX requirements, an example of which is auditing standards. This change would mean that new public companies deemed to be emerging growth companies can avoid requirements related to mandatory firm rotation and auditor discussion and analysis. Research and discuss two potential benefits and two possible weaknesses of the new bill.

RA1-5 Convergence of IASB and FASB

Find the FASB website and locate the "Update Report to the FSB Plenary on Accounting Convergence" that was issued in 2012. Convergence between the standards in the United States and IFRS is an ongoing topic of discussion among standard setters. Some of the significant differences between U.S. GAAP and IFRS are related to the perceived rules-based approach taken by the United States compared with the principles-based approach of IFRS.

Instructions

Review the report and respond to the following questions:

(a) Refer to the section related to revenue recognition. What are the reasons provided for the convergence of standards? Explain in your own words how these reasons highlight the differences between IFRS and U.S. GAAP.

(b) Compare the comments on the impairment model between the two standards and discuss, in your own words, whether the proposed amendments will result in more transparency for users.

(c) In your own words, state the differences between a rules-based approach and a principles-based approach.

(d) Comment on which approach you believe would be better, noting your thoughts on whether this issue will be a significant impediment to the United States moving to IFRS.

RA1-6 Financial Reporting Pressures

What follows is part of the testimony from Troy Normand in the **WorldCom** case. He was a manager in the corporate reporting department and is one of five individuals who pleaded guilty. He testified in the hope of receiving no prison time when he was ultimately sentenced.

Q: Mr. Normand, if you could just describe for the jury how the meeting started and what was said during the meeting?

A: I can't recall exactly who initiated the discussion, but right away Scott Sullivan acknowledged that he was aware we had problems with the entries, David Myers had informed him, and we were considering resigning.

He said that he respected our concerns but that we weren't being asked to do anything that he believed was wrong. He mentioned that he acknowledged that the company had lost focus quite a bit due to the preparations for the Sprint merger, and that he was putting plans in place and projects in place to try to determine where the problems were, why the costs were so high.

He did say he believed that the initial statements that we produced, that the line costs in those statements could not have been as high as they were, that he believed something was wrong and there was no way that the costs were that high.

I informed him that I didn't believe the entry we were being asked to do was right, that I was scared, and I didn't want to put myself in a position of going to jail for him or the company. He responded that he didn't believe anything was wrong, nobody was going to be going to jail, but that if it later was found to be wrong, that he would be the person going to jail, not me.

He asked that I stay, don't jump off the plane, let him land softly, that's basically how he put it. And he mentioned that he had a discussion with Bernie Ebbers asking Bernie to reduce projections going forward and Bernie had refused.

Q: Mr. Normand, you said that Mr. Sullivan said something about don't jump out of the plane. What did you understand him to mean when he said that?

A: Not to quit.

Q: During this meeting, did Mr. Sullivan say anything about whether you would be asked to make entries like this in the future?

A: Yes, he made a comment that from that point going forward we wouldn't be asked to record any entries, high-level late adjustments, that the numbers would be the numbers.

Q: What did you understand that to mean, the numbers would be the numbers?

A: That after the preliminary statements were issued, with the exception of any normal transactions, valid transactions, we wouldn't be asked to be recording any more late entries.

Q: I believe you testified that Mr. Sullivan said something about the line cost numbers not being accurate. Did he ask you to conduct any analysis to determine whether the line cost numbers were accurate?

A: No, he did not.

Q: Did anyone ever ask you to do that?

A: No.

Q: Did you ever conduct any such analysis?

A: No, I didn't.

Q: During this meeting, did Mr. Sullivan ever provide any accounting justification for the entry you were asked to make?

A: No, he did not.

Q: Did anything else happen during the meeting?

A: I don't recall anything else.

Q: How did you feel after this meeting?

A: Not much better actually. I left his office not convinced in any way that what we were asked to do was right. However, I did question myself to some degree after talking with him wondering whether I was making something more out of what was really there.

Instructions

Answer the following questions:

(a) What appears to be the ethical issue in this case?

(b) Was Troy Normand acting improperly or immorally?

(c) What would you do if you were Troy Normand?

(d) Who are the major stakeholders in this case?

RA1-7 Prudence

In 2012, Hans Hoogervorst, Chairman of the IASB, gave a speech at the FEE Conference on Corporate Reporting of the Future entitled "The Concept of Prudence: Dead or Alive?". The speech can be found on the IFRS website at: www.ifrs.org.

Instructions

(a) Hoogervorst indicated in his speech that there are many instances that demonstrate that IFRS implementation has not led to a loss of prudence. Discuss some specific examples Hoogervorst provides in which the revised conceptual framework of IFRS continues to instill the concept of prudence, although in practice not definition, in financial reporting.

(b) How does professional judgement impact the application of the areas discussed above?

(c) In your opinion, does IFRS result in the loss of prudence? Does this affect the value of financial reporting under the new standards?

ENDNOTES

[1] Julia Christensen Hughes and Joy Mighty, in their book entitled *Taking Stock* (Queen's School of Policy Studies, Kingston, 2010), refer to this as the ubiquity of information, meaning that information is now more freely, openly, and readily available. In the book, Christensen Hughes and Mighty discuss the impact of this phenomenon on education; however, it applies equally to the capital marketplace.

[2] All public companies must disclose certain information under provincial securities law. This information is collected by the provincial securities commissions under the Canadian umbrella organization, the Canadian Securities Administrators (CSA), and is available electronically at www.sedar.com.

[3] The largest, most senior equity market in Canada is the Toronto Stock Exchange (TSX). The junior market—the TSX Venture Exchange (formerly the CDNX Stock Market)—was created in 2001 to handle start-up companies. The Montreal Exchange (TMX), known also as the Canadian Derivatives Exchange, is the main market for derivatives and futures trading.

[4] According to the Canadian Bankers Association website, based on total assets as at October 31, 2010, the six largest banks in Canada, from largest to smallest, based on assets, were Royal Bank of Canada, Toronto Dominion Bank, Scotiabank, Bank of Montreal, Canadian Imperial Bank of Commerce, and Desjardins Group. Note that the Royal Bank is the 36th largest bank in the world.

[5] AICPA Special Committee on Financial Reporting, "Improving Business Reporting: A Customer Focus," supplement in *Journal of Accountancy* (October 1994).

[6] For example, institutions such as Dominion Bond Rating Service, Moody's, and Standard & Poor's rate issuers of bonds and preferred shares in the Canadian and global marketplaces.

[7] IASB *Conceptual Framework*, Chapter 1 and *CICA Handbook–Accounting*, Part II, Section 1000.12.

[8] Management's duty to manage assets with care and trust is referred to as its fiduciary responsibility.

[9] Institutional investors are corporate investors such as insurance companies, pension plans, mutual funds, and others. They are considered a separate class of investors because of their size and financial expertise, and the large size of the investments that they hold in other companies. In general, for the reasons just mentioned, institutional investors have greater power than the average investor.

[10] The Canadian Coalition for Good Governance (CCGG) is a group of institutional investors that controls over $2 trillion in investments (including investments in private and public equities and

bonds). Its members include many significant pension funds in Canada, such as Alberta Teachers' Retirement Fund, Ontario Teachers' Pension Plan, OPSEU Pension Trust, and Ontario Municipal Employees Retirement System, as well as many significant mutual funds and financial institutions, such as Mackenzie Financial Corp., RBC Asset Management Inc., and TD Asset Management Inc. According to its website (www.ccgg.ca), CCGG was started in 2002 "to represent Canadian institutional shareholders in the promotion of corporate governance practices that best align the interests of boards and management with those of the shareholder." As a comparison point, the estimated total market capitalization of the TSX is currently estimated at $2 trillion.

[11] There are three forms of the efficient markets hypothesis: (1) the weak form (market prices incorporate all historic publicly available information), (2) the semi-strong form (market prices incorporate all public information), and (3) the strong form (market prices incorporate all information whether public or not). Historically, economists have argued that North American markets are less than perfectly efficient and that they are efficient in the semi-strong form only. This hypothesis has come under attack in the last couple of years. Many feel that we have put too much faith in the belief that markets are efficient and may need other mechanisms to deal with information asymmetry.

[12] This is not a new problem. David Brown, chairman of the Ontario Securities Commission (OSC), spoke at length on this topic in a speech in 1999 entitled "Public Accounting at a Crossroads." Arthur Levitt, chair of the Securities and Exchange Commission (SEC), discussed his concerns over this issue in "Numbers Game," a major address to New York University in 1998. Both the OSC and the SEC review financial statements and financial reporting practices to ensure that investors have "full and plain disclosure" of all material facts that are needed to make investment decisions. In their speeches, Mr. Brown and Mr. Levitt both cited specific cases where they felt that financial reporting practices were problematic.

[13] As noted earlier, conservative accounting would generally result in ensuring assets and income are not overstated and all relevant information disclosed.

[14] Financial analysts monitor earnings announcements carefully and compare them with their earlier expectations. They and others (including certain stock markets) post what they refer to as **earnings surprises** each day on their websites. Earnings surprises occur when a company reports net income figures that are different from what the market expected. The focus is on net income or earnings. If net income is higher than expected, this is a positive earnings surprise. If net income is lower than expected, this is a negative earnings surprise and the market will generally react unfavourably, resulting in declining share prices. For quarterly earnings numbers released on May 24, 2012, the NASDAQ website noted that there were 14 positive earnings surprises and 13 negative earnings surprises. Positive earnings surprises included the Toronto Dominion Bank, H.J. Heinz Company, and Verifone Systems Inc. Selected negative earnings surprises noted for the same day included Royal Bank of Canada and Tiffany & Co.

[15] The terms "principle" and "standard" are used interchangeably in practice and throughout this textbook.

[16] The Canada Business Corporations Act and Regulations (CBCA) Part XIV Financial Disclosure and Part 8 (paras. 70 and 71), as well as provincial corporations acts, require that most companies incorporated under these acts prepare financial statements in accordance with GAAP per the *CICA Handbook–Accounting*.

[17] The *Handbook* is also available to students and members on-line. With the rapid pace of change in standard setting, most members use the on-line version as their main source of GAAP.

[18] Technically, IFRS is considered to be part of the Canadian *CICA Handbook–Accounting* for legal reasons although the *CICA Handbook–Accounting* as it relates to IFRS will exactly mirror the IASB standards. This was done as an interim measure as many Canadian laws refer to Canadian GAAP. At some point, these laws will be amended to reflect the fact that GAAP for public companies in Canada is IFRS according to the IASB.

[19] AcSB Due Process (Adopted by the AcSB on March 20, 2012 and endorsed by AcSOC on June 21, 2012). Accounting Standards Board, www.frascanada.ca, 2012.

[20] According to the CICA website, AcSOC membership consists of senior members from business, finance, government, academe, the accounting and legal professions, regulators, and the financial analyst community. The members have a broad perspective on the complex issues facing standard setters. The goal is to achieve full representation across the spectrum of stakeholders.

[21] Actually, there are at least seven sets of GAAP in Canada. The *CICA Handbook–Accounting* is divided into five parts: Part I—IFRS (for publicly accountable enterprises), Part II—Accounting Standards for Private Enterprises, Part III—Accounting Standards for Not-for-profit Organizations, Part IV—Accounting Standards for Pension Plans, and Part V—Pre-changeover Canadian GAAP (pre-2011). In addition, the *Public Sector Accounting Standards Handbook* contains GAAP for governments. Finally, as mentioned earlier, the Ontario Securities Commission allows Canadian public companies that are U.S. reporting issuers to use U.S. GAAP.

[22] www.ifrs.org. Copyright © 2012 IFRS Foundation. All rights reserved. Note that the IASB also establishes standards for small and medium-sized private entities (referred to as IFRS for SMEs). Since

AcSB produces separate standards for Canadian private entities, Canadian companies do not follow IFRS for SMEs.

[23] IFRS, *Who We Are and What We Do*, November 2011, p. 2. Copyright © 2012 IFRS Foundation. All rights reserved.

[24] IFRS, *Who We Are and What We Do*, November 2011, p. 5. Copyright © 2012 IFRS Foundation. All rights reserved.

[25] For instance, the IASB issued a DP for revenue recognition, financial statement presentation, and fair value measurement and received 221, 227, and 136 comment letters, respectively. These comment letters were used to draft the subsequent ED.

[26] www.iasplus.com, "Use of IFRSs by Jurisdiction." A complete up-to-date list is on the website. Some of these countries allow companies to alter IFRS (i.e. not follow certain standards or follow alternate standards). The IASB is currently conducting its own survey to gain a better understanding.

[27] U.S. GAAP is a mixture of more than 2,000 documents that have developed over the past 60 years or so. It includes items such as FASB Standards (SFAS), Interpretations, and Staff Positions; APB Opinions; and AICPA Research Bulletins. The body of knowledge is very prescriptive and detailed and therefore very complex and difficult to follow. In the past several years, the FASB has undertaken a process whereby all the standards have been collected in one database. The database has been resorted, reorganized, and the standards cross-referenced. This project is generally referred to as the codification project. All standards have been renumbered under this new system and it is hoped that the body of knowledge will now be easier to access, research, and understand.

[28] Before 2007, Canadian companies that were listed on U.S. exchanges could use IFRS or pre-changeover Canadian GAAP but had to reconcile their reporting to U.S. GAAP. This reconciliation was difficult and cumbersome and many Canadian entities decided to just use U.S. GAAP for their U.S. filings. The OSC allows Canadian reporting issuers who list on U.S. stock exchanges/markets to use U.S. GAAP or IFRS according to Canadian Securities Administrators National Instrument 52-107.

[29] SEC, *Roadmap for the Potential Use of Financial Statements Prepared in Accordance with International Financial Reporting Standards by U.S. Issuers*, November 2008.

[30] In Canada, securities regulation is carried out by each province, with each of the 10 provinces and three territories being responsible for the companies in its jurisdiction. Many critics feel that this is cumbersome and costly, and are therefore lobbying for a national securities commission. There has been some movement in this direction. The provincial and territorial regulators have formed the Canadian Securities Administrators (CSA). The CSA is mainly responsible for developing a harmonized approach to securities regulation across the country (www.csa-acvm.ca). For now, the CSA collects and archives all filings that are required under the securities regulations of each province and territory (www.sedar.com).

[31] The OSC has a Continuous Disclosure Team that regularly reviews public companies' financial statements and other regulatory findings. The team plans to review each company at least every four years. Results of the review are published on the OSC website.

[32] For instance, in 2002, Staff Accounting Notice 52-303 on "Non-GAAP Earnings Measures" was issued.

[33] *CICA Handbook–Accounting*, Part II, Section 1100.20.

[34] IAS 8. Copyright © 2012 IFRS Foundation. All rights reserved. Reproduced by Wiley Canada with the permission of the IFRS Foundation ®. No permission granted to third parties to reproduce or distribute.

[35] The IASB decided to retain the old numbering system for these standards for familiarity and to signal that these standards are older and originated from the IASB's predecessor, the IASC.

[36] As mentioned earlier, U.S. GAAP is often said to be more prescriptive, and provides significantly more detailed guidance than IFRS and ASPE.

[37] Neither ASPE nor IFRS is a perfect principles-based system. The conceptual frameworks for both were written after many of the other standards were written. Therefore, there may be inconsistencies. Standard setters are working to get rid of these inconsistencies in the standards.

[38] Sarbanes-Oxley Act of 2002, H. R. Rep. No. 107-610 (2002).

[39] Sarbanes-Oxley Act of 2002, Section 106 (2002).

[40] www.cpab-ccrc.ca.

[41] CSA Multilateral Instrument 52-109, 52-110, and 52-108. A multilateral instrument is an instrument that has been adopted by one or more CSA jurisdictions.

[42] CSA revised National Instrument 51-102, "Continuous Disclosure Obligations." A national instrument is an instrument that has been adopted by all CSA jurisdictions.

[43] "Economic consequences" in this context means the impact of accounting reports on the wealth positions of issuers and users of financial information and the decision-making behaviour resulting

from that impact. The resulting behaviour of these individuals and groups could have harmful financial effects on the providers of the financial information (enterprises). For a more detailed discussion of this phenomenon, see Stephen A. Zeff, "The Rise of Economic Consequences," *Journal of Accountancy* (December 1978), pp. 56–63.

[44] These principles were established in 2008. The IASB's 2010 revenue including contributions was 22.8 million pounds sterling.

[45] Note that adoption of IFRS is not necessarily the same as convergence with IFRS. Under convergence, the two sets of standards might still exist side by side and have differing aspects.

[46] The CICA has issued a Discussion Brief entitled *Environmental, Social and Governance (ESG) Issues in Institutional Investor Decision Making*. It is published by the CICA's Canadian Performance Reporting Board and is available on-line (www.cica.ca/cpr).

[47] The IIRC has issued a discussion paper published in 2011 entitled *Towards Integrated Reporting – Communicating Value in the 21st Century* (available at www.theiirc.org).

© istockphoto.com/wsfurian

How Much Is a Tree Worth?

HOW TO VALUE A COMPANY'S ASSETS in its financial statements has long been debated. Standard setters and corporations are increasingly favouring the fair value principle, which measures an asset based on what a company could expect to sell it for on the market today.

One of the most challenging types of assets to measure are natural resources, partly because the prices they fetch can vary widely over short periods. Take the forestry industry as an example. How do you measure the value of trees, especially when newly planted ones take years before they can be harvested?

Sino-Forest Corporation was a leading forestry company. As of 2010, it owned approximately 800,000 hectares of forest in China. Timber holdings represented over 50% of its more than U.S. $5.7 billion in reported assets. Because Sino-Forest traded on the Toronto Stock Exchange (TSX), it followed pre-changeover Canadian GAAP. In 2010, the company accounted for its plantations on the cost basis.

For 2011, however, the company had to switch to IFRS. For its plantations that it purchased, Sino-Forest held the trees for only a brief period of their lifespan, during which they underwent minimal growth. It earned revenue by parcelling the plantations for resale as standing timber or for sale as harvested logs. The company determined that these purchased plantations fell under IAS 2 *Inventories*, since it held them for sale in the ordinary course of business or sold them as harvested logs. Therefore, it intended to measure those trees at the lower of cost and net realizable value.

For its timber holdings that it planted itself, Sino-Forest intended to follow IAS 41 *Agriculture* and measure their value at their fair value less costs to sell. The company used a third-party valuator that measured the timber holdings at fair value. Only trees older than three or four years were valued at fair value; trees younger than that were not saleable and were measured at cost (as a default estimate of fair value). The valuator calculated an average yield of timber per hectare and multiplied the total number of hectares by the average prices expected for logs and other forest products minus any increases in harvesting costs.

At the time the text went to press, it was not known what accounting policies Sino-Forest actually used in 2011, as it filed for bankruptcy in early 2012. Its shares were delisted from the TSX for failing to produce financial statements for audit.

Sources: Sino-Forest Corporation 2010 Annual Report; "Summary of Sino-Forest's China Forest Asset 2010 Valuation Reports," company report released May 27, 2011; The Canadian Press, "Sino-Forest to Be Delisted from TSX," CBC News online, April 6, 2012.

2 | Conceptual Framework Underlying Financial Reporting

LEARNING OBJECTIVES

After studying this chapter, you should be able to:

1. Indicate the usefulness and describe the main components of a conceptual framework for financial reporting.

2. Identify the qualitative characteristics of accounting information.

3. Define the basic elements of financial statements.

4. Describe the foundational principles of accounting.

5. Explain the factors that contribute to choice and/or bias in financial reporting decisions.

6. Discuss current trends in standard setting for the conceptual framework.

After studying Appendix 2A, you should be able to:

7. Understand in greater detail how fair value is measured.

Users of financial statements need relevant and reliable information. To help develop this type of financial information, accountants use a conceptual framework that guides financial accounting and reporting. In this chapter, we discuss the basic concepts that underlie this conceptual framework.

The chapter is organized as follows:

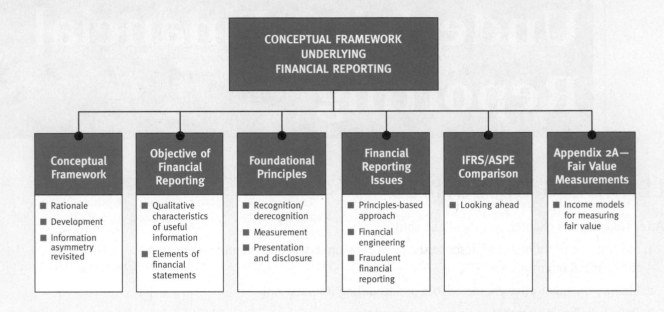

CONCEPTUAL FRAMEWORK

Objective 1
Indicate the usefulness and describe the main components of a conceptual framework for financial reporting.

A **conceptual framework** is like a constitution: it is a "coherent system of interrelated objectives and fundamentals that can lead to consistent standards and that prescribes the nature, function, and limits of financial accounting and financial statements."[1] Many observers believe that the real contribution of standard-setting bodies, and even their continued existence, depends on the quality and usefulness of the conceptual framework.

Rationale for Conceptual Framework

Why is a conceptual framework necessary? First, to be useful, **standard setting should build on an established body of concepts and objectives**. Having a soundly developed conceptual framework as their starting point, standard setters are then able to issue additional **useful and consistent** standards over time. The result is a **coherent** set of standards and rules, as they have all been built upon the same foundation. It is important that such a framework **increase** financial statement users' **understanding** of and **confidence** in financial reporting, and that it **enhance the comparability** of different companies' financial statements.

Second, by referring to an existing framework of basic theory, it should be possible to solve **new and emerging practical problems** more quickly. It is difficult, if not impossible, for standard setters to quickly state the proper accounting treatment for highly complex situations. Practising accountants, however, must solve such problems on a day-to-day basis. By using **good judgement**, and with the help of a **universally accepted conceptual framework**, it is hoped that accountants will be able to decide against certain alternatives quickly and to focus instead on a logical and acceptable treatment.

Development of the Conceptual Framework

Over the years, many organizations, committees, and interested individuals have developed and published their own conceptual frameworks, but no single framework has been universally accepted and relied on in practice. Realizing there was a need for a generally accepted framework, in 1976 the FASB issued a three-part discussion memorandum entitled "Conceptual Framework for Financial Accounting and Reporting: Elements of Financial Statements and Their Measurement." It stated the major issues that would need to be addressed in establishing a conceptual framework for setting accounting standards and resolving financial reporting controversies. Based on this, six Statements of Financial Accounting Concepts were then published. A seventh statement, on accounting measurement, was added in 2000.

The AcSB and IASB followed the FASB's example and issued their own respective frameworks. At the time this text was going to press, the IASB and FASB were continuing to work on a joint conceptual framework to promote global consistency and comparability. The first part of the new joint framework has been issued by both the IASB and FASB dealing with the objective of general-purpose financial reporting and the qualitative characteristics of useful information. This chapter incorporates ideas from the newly emerging framework. The AcSB has signalled that it will likely adopt the framework for private entities as well.

Illustration 2-1 shows an overview of a conceptual framework.[2] At the first level, the objectives identify accounting's **goals and purposes**: these are the conceptual framework's

Illustration **2-1**

Conceptual Framework for Financial Reporting

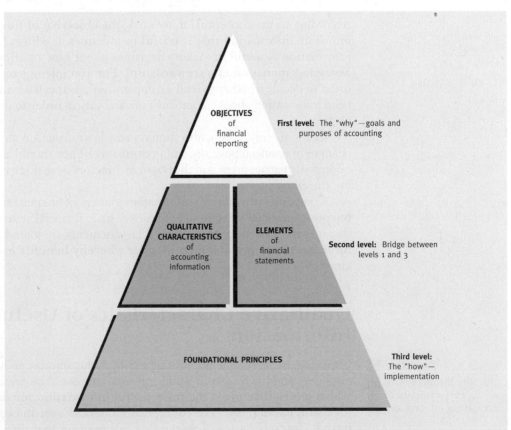

building blocks. At the second level are the **qualitative characteristics** that make accounting information useful and the **elements of financial statements** (assets, liabilities, equity, revenues, expenses, gains, and losses).[3] At the third and final level are the **foundational principles** used in establishing and applying accounting standards.

Information Asymmetry Revisited

Theory

As discussed in Chapter 1, investors and creditors need information in order to make sound resource allocation decisions. However, information in the capital marketplace is not always evenly accessible or available to investors and creditors. Stock markets and regulators go to great lengths to ensure information symmetry for all capital market participants so that no one is at a disadvantage. Despite this, various stakeholders often do not have the same information. This can be a problem as stakeholders may make suboptimal decisions because they are lacking good or complete information.

Financial statements play a large part in helping to ensure that investors, creditors, and others have access to information they need to make decisions. However, because of **adverse selection** and/or **moral hazard** (see Chapter 1), problems may arise. The moral hazard issue is worse where certain stakeholders such as accountants and bankers have expert knowledge that the rest of the capital marketplace does not. They may use this expertise to act in their own self-interest to the detriment of other capital marketplace participants such as investors.

A well-written conceptual framework based on sound principles may help address these information asymmetry concerns.

OBJECTIVE OF FINANCIAL REPORTING

According to the conceptual framework, the **objective of financial reporting** is to communicate information that is **useful** to investors, creditors, and other users. Financial information is useful in making decisions about how to **allocate resources** (including **assessing management stewardship**). For example, a bank may need information in order to decide whether to lend a company money or call a loan. Similarly, an investor may need information about a company's profitability in order to decide whether to invest in it or divest.

Consequently, companies should provide information about their financial position, changes in financial position, and performance. They should also show how efficiently and effectively management and the board of directors have discharged their responsibilities to use the entity's resources.[4]

Companies provide this information to users of financial statements through **general-purpose financial statements**. These are basic financial statements that give information that meets the needs of **key users**.[5] The statements are intended to provide the most **useful information possible in a manner whereby benefits exceed costs** to the different kinds of users.

Qualitative Characteristics of Useful Information

Choosing an acceptable accounting method, the amount and types of information to be disclosed, and the format in which information should be presented involves determining **which alternative gives the most useful information for decision-making purposes** (**decision usefulness**). The conceptual framework's second level has identified the **qualitative characteristics** of accounting information that distinguish information that is better (more useful) for making decisions from information that is inferior (less useful). These characteristics are explained next.

Fundamental Qualitative Characteristics

Relevance and **representational faithfulness** (sometimes referred to as faithful representation) are fundamental qualities that make accounting information useful for decision-making. Above all else, these two characteristics must be present.

Relevance. To be relevant, accounting information must be capable of **making a difference in a decision**. If a piece of information has no impact on a decision, it is irrelevant to that decision. Care should be taken to ensure that relevant information is included in financial reporting. Relevant information helps users make predictions about the final outcome of past, present, and future events; that is, it has **predictive value**. For example, separating income from continuing operations from that of operations that have been discontinued may help users predict future income. Relevant information also helps users confirm or correct their previous expectations; it has **feedback/confirmatory value**. For instance, providing information about rental income and the value of the investment in rental properties might help users assess how well management is managing the investment in rental properties.

When discussing relevance, the notion of materiality is often referred to. **Materiality** refers to how important a piece of information is. It is generally thought to be material if it would make a difference to the decision-maker. For instance, a major product defect would be of interest to a potential investor. All material information is relevant and should be included in the financial statements. When making the determination whether something is material or not, the amount in question is often compared with the entity's amounts of other revenues and expenses, assets and liabilities, or net income.

It is hard to give firm guidelines to decide when an item is or is not material because materiality depends on both a relative amount and relative importance.

For example, the two sets of numbers in Illustration 2-2 show relative size.

Illustration 2-2

Materiality Comparison

	Company A	Company B
Sales	$10,000,000	$100,000
Costs and expenses	9,000,000	90,000
Income from operations	1,000,000	10,000
Unusual gain	20,000	5,000

During the particular period, the revenues and expenses, and therefore the net incomes, of Company A and Company B are proportional. That is, the amounts for Company A are 10 times larger than those for Company B. Each has an unusual gain.

In looking at the abbreviated income figures for Company A, it does not appear significant whether the amount of the unusual gain is presented separately or is merged with the regular operating income. It is only 2% of the operating income and, if merged, would not seriously distort the income figure. Company B has had an unusual gain of only $5,000, but it is relatively much more significant than the larger gain recognized by A. For Company B, an item of $5,000 amounts to 50% of its operating income. Obviously, including such an item in ordinary operating income would affect the amount of that income materially. In this example, we can therefore see the importance of an item's relative size in determining its materiality.

Current auditing standards (CAS 320) use as a benchmark example, 5% of pretax income from continuing operations for manufacturing companies and 1% of revenues for not-for-profit entities. This is not a definitive rule and is a fairly simplistic view of materiality. We need to consider the item's impact on other factors, such as on key financial statement ratios and management compensation; in other words, on **any sensitive number on the financial statements**. In addition, both **quantitative** and **qualitative** factors must be considered in determining whether an item is material.

Qualitative factors might include illegal acts, failure to comply with regulations, or inadequate or inappropriate description of an accounting policy. Materiality is also a factor in a large number of internal accounting decisions. The amount of classification required in a subsidiary expense ledger, the degree of accuracy required in prorating expenses among the departments of a business, and the extent to which adjustments should be made for accrued and deferred items are examples of judgements that should finally be determined based on reasonableness and practicability. In other words, the materiality constraint must be sensibly applied. Only by exercising good judgement and professional expertise can reasonable and appropriate answers be found.

Representational Faithfulness.   Accounting information is representationally faithful to the extent that it reflects the underlying **economic substance** of an event or transaction. This notion of representing economic reality is sometimes referred to as **transparency**. If financial statement users read the financial statements, can they see what lies beneath the numbers? This is critical since the statements are meant to tell a story about the business. Is this a risky business? Is it a mature business? Is it capital intensive? How do we ensure that this information is appropriately presented? Information that is representationally faithful is **complete, neutral,** and **free from material error**.

Completeness refers to the fact that the statements should include all information necessary to portray the underlying events and transactions. Care must be taken to ensure that pertinent information is included since it is possible to misrepresent something by not including all pertinent information. Often this is a question of the amount of details to be presented. For instance, it is important to note the nature of capital assets that an entity has under its control, including property, plant, and equipment. But presenting the amortized cost of such investment might not be sufficient if some of these assets are leased. The presumption about most property, plant, and equipment that is reported on a statement of financial position is that the company has legal title to the property. Therefore, if this is not the case—in other words, the assets are leased—this additional information should be presented.

Neutrality means that information cannot be selected to **favour one set of interested parties over another**. The information should not be manipulated in any way. Factual, truthful, unbiased information needs to be the overriding consideration when preparing financial information.

What Do the Numbers Mean?

Livent Inc. was a Canadian company that produced and presented large Broadway-style musicals. In 1993, the company went public, listing its shares on the TSX. By 1998, it filed for bankruptcy protection while it was being accused of accounting irregularities, and in 2001 it was investigated by the Ontario Securities Commission (OSC). The following excerpt is from the OSC Notice of Hearing and Allegation about manipulation of the financial statements. The Respondents mentioned below were company management including Garth Drabinsky, Myron Gottlieb, Gordon Eckstein, and Robert Topol.

Real World Emphasis

> … at the end of each financial reporting period, Livent accounting staff circulated to the Respondents a management summary reflecting actual results (including net income, on a show-by-show basis, compared to budget), as well as any improper adjustments carried forward from a prior financial period in connection with each show. Having regard to the actual results, the Respondents then provided instructions, directly or indirectly, to the Livent accounting staff specifying changes to be made to the actual results reflected in the company's books and records. In order to give effect to the Respondents' instructions, Livent accounting staff manipulated Livent's books and records by various means which did not accord with GAAP. The effect of the manipulations was to improve the presentation of Livent's financial results for the reporting period. Draft financial statements would then be generated for the reporting period incorporating the manipulations. These draft financial statements were then distributed to the Livent audit committee and, thereafter the Livent board of directors, for their review and approval. The Respondents attended meetings of the audit committee and the board of directors where these draft financial statements were discussed and ultimately approved. The Respondents did not disclose to the

audit committee or the board of directors that, to their knowledge, the financial statements were false or misleading.

Among other things, management was charged with deliberately and systematically biasing the information. This contributed to the company's eventual downfall. Garth Drabinsky and Myron Gottlieb, co-founders of Livent, were found guilty in 2009 of two counts of fraud and one of forgery. Drabinsky's lawyers argued that he was not motivated by personal greed but rather by a desire to save the company.

Ethics

In practice, management needs to use many assumptions because of uncertainty in financial reporting, such as uncertainty caused by accrual accounting. For instance, revenues are recorded when earned and not necessarily when cash is received. Thus, companies must estimate the amount of revenue that will be realized or eventually collected. When choosing these assumptions, management must use its best estimates (**management best estimate**) in order to portray the economic reality. Management best estimate assumptions are unbiased, and involve management making diligent efforts to obtain and use all information that it has access to in order to come up with the best quality information.[6]

As we can see in the Livent example, producing financial statements with biased information can have significant negative consequences, not only for investors and creditors, but also for financial statement preparers and company management.

There is also another aspect to neutrality: neutrality in standard setting. Some observers argue that standards should not be issued if they cause undesirable economic effects on an industry or company (the **economic consequences argument**, which was mentioned in Chapter 1). Standards must be free from bias, however, or we will no longer have **credible financial statements**. Standard setters must therefore choose the best standards regardless of economic consequences. If the accounting results in users changing their decisions, then by definition, the information is decision-relevant.[7]

Freedom from material error means that the information must be reliable. The task of converting economic events (which are constantly changing and difficult to measure) to numbers in a set of financial statements is complex. Management must make estimates and use judgement in determining how to portray events and transactions. This does not mean that information must be "perfectly accurate in all respects."[8] Often, there is no correct or single right way to portray economic reality. For instance, how does a company portray the impact of a major ecological disaster such as an oil spill? Significant assumptions must be made about cleanup activities in order to estimate potential costs and liabilities.

How much effort should be put into obtaining information? Do we need to incur costs such as hiring engineers to help estimate? When is a mismeasurement an error? Information is more useful if it is free from material error, so every attempt must be made to achieve this. Companies must ensure that they invest in good information systems so that they can capture necessary information and must also have strong internal controls to ensure that errors and omissions are minimized.

Enhancing Qualitative Characteristics

Enhancing qualitative characteristics include **comparability**, **verifiability**, **timeliness**, and **understandability**.

Comparability.   Information that has been measured and reported in a similar way (both company to company and consistently from year to year) is considered comparable. **Comparability** enables users to **identify the real similarities and differences in economic phenomena** because these have not been obscured by accounting methods that cannot be compared. For example, the accounting for inventory is different under IFRS and FASB. FASB allows the use of last-in, first-out (LIFO) accounting, for instance, whereas IFRS does not. The result is that in times of rising prices, companies using LIFO, such as **Walmart Stores Inc.**, will have a net income that is lower than companies not using LIFO, such as **Loblaw Companies Limited**.

It is important to remember that **resource allocation decisions involve evaluations of alternatives** and it is easier to make a valid evaluation if comparable information is available. Although it is not a substitute for comparable information, a full disclosure of information sometimes allows users to overcome inconsistencies in how information is presented.

Verifiability.   **Verifiability** exists when knowledgeable, independent users achieve similar results or reach consensus regarding the accounting for a particular transaction. Some numbers are more easily verified than others; for example, cash can be verified by confirming with the bank where the deposit is held. Other numbers—such as accruals for future pension liabilities—are more difficult (although not necessarily impossible) to verify, as many assumptions are made to arrive at an estimate. Numbers that are easy to verify with a reasonable degree of accuracy are often referred to as "hard" numbers. Those that have more measurement uncertainty are called "soft" numbers.

Timeliness.   **Timeliness** is also important. Information should be available to decision-makers before it loses its ability to influence their decisions. Quarterly reporting (involving the issuance of financial information every three months) provides information on a more timely basis. Thus, users have information throughout the year as opposed to having to wait until after the year end for the annual financial statements.

Understandability.   Users need to have **reasonable knowledge** of business and financial accounting matters in order to understand the information in financial statements. However, financial information must also be of sufficient quality and clarity that it allows reasonably informed users to see its significance. This is the information's **understandability**. In addition, standard setters assume that users have the responsibility to review and analyze the information with reasonable diligence. This point is important: it means that the onus to prepare understandable statements and to be able to understand them rests with both the financial statement preparer and the user. This characteristic affects both how information is reported and how much is reported.

Where the underlying transactions or economic events are more complex, the assumption is that users will seek the aid of an advisor.[9] The preparer must also have a clear understanding of the legalities and economics of transactions in order to be able to portray them in the most meaningful way to users.

What Do the Numbers Mean?

Real World Emphasis

An excerpt follows from the notes to the financial statements of **Enron Corp.** for the year ended December 31, 2000 (all figures are in U.S. dollars). The complexity of the business arrangements makes it difficult to understand the nature of the underlying transactions. It contributes to a set of financial statements that lack transparency. The choice of words also makes the note difficult to read.

> In 2000 and 1999, Enron sold approximately $632 million and $192 million, respectively, of merchant investments and other assets to Whitewing. Enron recognized no gains or losses in connection with these transactions. Additionally, in 2000, ECT Merchant Investments Corp., a wholly owned Enron subsidiary, contributed two pools of merchant investments to a limited partnership that is a subsidiary of Enron. Subsequent to the contributions, the partnership issued partnership interests representing 100% of the beneficial, economic interests in the two asset pools, and such interests were sold for a total of $545 million to a limited liability company that is a subsidiary of Whitewing. See Note 3. These entities are separate legal entities from Enron and have separate assets and liabilities. In 2000 and 1999, the Related Party, as described in Note 16, contributed $33 million and $15 million, respectively, of equity to Whitewing. In 2000, Whitewing contributed $7.1 million to a partnership formed by Enron, Whitewing, and a third party. Subsequently, Enron sold a portion of its interest in the partnership through a securitization. See Note 3.[10]

Trade-Offs

In general, preparers of financial information should identify all **relevant** information, then consider how best to ensure that the financial statements are presented such that they reflect the economic substance **(representational faithfulness)**. Both characteristics must be present in order to ensure the information is decision-relevant.

However, it is not always possible for financial information to have all the enhancing qualities of useful information. Trade-offs may exist. For instance, in the interest of providing more relevant information, a new standard may be applied prospectively. In this case, comparability (or **consistency** year to year) is temporarily sacrificed for better information in the future.

The accounting profession is constantly striving to produce financial information that meets all of the qualitative characteristics of useful information.

Cost Versus Benefits.   Too often, users assume that information is a cost-free commodity. But preparers and providers of accounting information know this is not true. This is why the **cost-benefit relationship** must be considered: the costs of providing the information must be weighed against the benefits that can be had from using the information. In order to justify requiring a particular measurement or disclosure, the costs must be justified by the benefits. In other words, the benefits must outweigh the costs.

The difficulty in cost-benefit analysis is that the costs and, especially, the benefits are not always evident or measurable. There are several kinds of costs, including the costs of:

- Collecting and processing
- Distributing
- Auditing
- Potential litigation
- Disclosure of proprietary information to competitors
- Analysis and interpretation

The benefits are enjoyed by both preparers (in terms of greater management control and access to capital) and users (in terms of allocation of resources, tax assessment, and rate regulation). Benefits are generally more difficult to quantify than costs.

The AcSB has taken some steps to reduce the cost of providing information by developing separate standards for private entities that are less onerous and costly. This model allows these companies to follow a simplified version of GAAP based on cost-benefit considerations. In many cases, the shareholders and creditors of private companies have greater access to information and do not necessarily rely solely on the external financial statements. In addition, for smaller private companies, the business and business model are not so complicated and therefore less complex accounting standards are required. Private entities have the option to use IFRS if they wish.

Elements of Financial Statements

Objective 3
Define the basic elements of financial statements.

At present, accounting uses many terms that have specific meanings. These terms make up the **language of accounting and business**. There are many **elements** that users expect to find on the financial statements, including **assets, liabilities, equity, revenues, expenses, gains,** and **losses**. In addition, within each of these categories there are many subcategories, such as current and non-current assets, cash, inventory, and so on. The conceptual framework's second level defines the basic elements so that users have a common understanding of the main items presented on the financial statements.

The **basic elements** of financial statements that are most directly related to measuring an enterprise's performance and financial status are listed below. Each of these elements will be explained and examined in more detail in later chapters.[11]

Assets

Assets have three essential characteristics:

1. There is some economic benefit to the entity.

2. The entity has control over that benefit.

3. The benefits result from a past transaction or event.[12]

For instance, consider a manufacturing plant that is owned by a company. The economic benefits are represented by the cash flows that the plant will generate. The entity has access to (control over) those benefits through legal ownership of the property itself (a tangible asset), thus allowing the company to decide whether to sell it or use it in order to generate cash flows. The transaction giving rise to the benefits would have been the acquisition of the asset.

An asset may also be represented by a contractual or other right. For instance, a purchased patent has value because it gives the holder access to future cash flows from sale of the patented product. Another example of an asset generated through contractual rights is a leased machine. The lease contract gives the company contractual rights to use the asset despite the fact that the company does not have legal title to the machine.

Law

When determining if a present economic resource exists, care must be taken to review not only items such as inventory, cash, land, and patents (which represent both tangible and intangible properties) but also contractual and other rights (such as forward contracts, insurance, and others).

Liabilities

Liabilities have three essential characteristics:

1. They represent a present duty or responsibility.

2. The duty or responsibility obligates the entity, leaving it little or no discretion to avoid it.

3. The transaction or event results from a past transaction or event.[13]

Similar but opposite to an asset, a liability has a negative economic value and requires that the entity give up economic resources to settle the obligation. For instance, assume that a company hires employees and agrees to pay them a salary for services provided. Once the employee accepts the offer of employment and starts to provide services, a liability is created. The company has a duty to pay the salary according to the predetermined employment arrangement with the employee once the employee has rendered services. The entity must pay the salary, otherwise there will be negative consequences. For example, the employee will quit and may sue the company for unpaid wages.

Liabilities may arise through contractual obligations as noted in the case above, or through statutory requirements, such as for illegally polluting. In addition, they may arise through other means including constructive and equitable obligations. **Constructive obligations** are obligations that arise through past or present practice that signals that the company acknowledges a potential economic burden. For instance, the entity might make a statement that it stands behind its products. Therefore, if a product is defective, even though the entity might not be required to replace it under the terms of the sales contract, the expectation is that the entity will replace it because of the policy to stand behind its products. **Equitable obligations** arise due to moral or ethical considerations. For instance, a company might feel a moral obligation to retrain an employee who is being downsized. Care should be taken to ensure that all obligations are identified and properly accounted for. These will be discussed further in subsequent chapters, including Chapters 13, 14, and 16.

Liabilities may be further categorized by standard setters as financial (as defined in IAS 32 regarding contractual obligations to deliver cash or other financial assets) or non-financial (everything else).[14]

Equity

Equity is a **residual interest** in an entity that remains after deducting its liabilities from its assets. This is also known as its net worth. In a business enterprise, the equity is the **ownership** interest.[15] Equity would normally consist of common or ordinary shares, preferred shares, retained earnings, and, under IFRS, accumulated other comprehensive income.

Revenues

Revenues are increases in economic resources, either by inflows or other enhancements of an entity's assets or by settlement of its liabilities, which result from an entity's **ordinary activities**. For instance, assume that a real estate company owns 10 buildings and leases them out under long-term leases. For this company, revenues would include rental income.

Expenses

Expenses are decreases in economic resources, either by outflows or reductions of assets or by the incurrence of liabilities that result from an entity's **ordinary revenue-generating activities**. For instance, for the real estate company above, this would include heating and property taxes.

Gains/Losses

Gains are increases in equity (net assets) from an entity's **peripheral or incidental transactions** and from all other transactions and other events and circumstances affecting the entity during a period, except those that result from revenues or investments by owners.[16]

Losses are decreases in equity (net assets) from an entity's **peripheral or incidental transactions** and from all other transactions and other events and circumstances affecting the entity during a period, except those that result from expenses or distributions to owners.

For the same real estate company, this might include gains and losses on the sale of the buildings. As noted in the above example, the company's business model includes purchasing buildings and renting them out on a long-term basis, not buying and selling buildings.

The financial statements include the following items:

1. Income statement and/or statement of comprehensive income (IFRS only)

2. Statement of financial position

3. Statement of retained earnings or changes in shareholders' equity (IFRS only)

4. Statement of cash flows

The term **comprehensive income** is a relatively new income concept and includes more than the traditional notion of net income. It includes net income and **other comprehensive income** (all other changes in equity except for owners' investments and distributions). Other comprehensive income is made up of revenues, expenses, gains, and losses that, in accordance with primary sources of GAAP, are recognized in comprehensive income, but excluded from net income. For example, the following would be included as other comprehensive income in the comprehensive income statement:

• Unrealized holding gains and losses on certain securities and property, plant, and equipment (revaluation method)

• Certain gains and losses related to foreign exchange instruments, foreign operations, and certain types of hedges

- Certain gains and losses related to remeasurement of defined benefit plans and liabilities measured at fair value

Note that IFRS does not require companies to use the terms "comprehensive income" or "other comprehensive income." This will be discussed further in Chapter 4. The concepts of comprehensive income and other comprehensive income do not exist under ASPE. Items would either be booked through net income or straight to shareholders' equity.

FOUNDATIONAL PRINCIPLES

Objective 4
Describe the foundational principles of accounting.

The conceptual framework's third level consists of **foundational principles** that implement the basic objectives of the first level. These concepts help explain which, when, and how financial elements and events should be **recognized, measured,** and **presented/disclosed** by the accounting system. They act as guidelines for developing rational responses to controversial financial reporting issues. They have evolved over time, and the specific accounting standards issued by standard setters are based on these concepts in a fundamental way.

Basic **foundational principles** underlying the financial accounting structure also include assumptions and conventions. It is often difficult to put a label onto the items noted below and accounting practices vary, and so we have grouped them together. The label is not important—it is the substance of the concept and how it provides a solid foundation for accounting standard setting that is important. We will discuss the 10 foundational principles and assumptions under the groupings of recognition/derecognition, measurement, and presentation and disclosure, as follows:

Recognition/Derecognition	Measurement	Presentation and Disclosure
1. Economic entity assumption	5. Periodicity assumption	10. Full disclosure principle
2. Control	6. Monetary unit assumption	
3. Revenue recognition and realization principles	7. Going concern assumption	
4. Matching principle	8. Historical cost principle	
	9. Fair value principle	

Recognition/Derecognition

Recognition deals with the act of including something on the entity's statement of financial position or income statement. At a macro level, decisions need to be made whether to consolidate investments in other entities. At a micro level, decisions need to be made whether and when to include assets, liabilities, revenues, expenses, gains, and losses in the financial statements. In addition, once recognized, decisions need to be made when to derecognize these elements (remove them from the financial statements). These are significant decisions.

The conceptual framework provides general recognition and measurement criteria, and underlying principles may be used to justify whether something should be reflected in the financial statements or not.

Historically, elements of financial statements have been recognized when:

- they meet the definition of an element (for example, a liability),

- they are probable, and

- they are reliably measurable.

For instance, an entity must use all information to make a neutral decision as to whether the liability or asset exists or not (that is, whether the definition is met). It must then decide whether it is probable that an outflow or inflow of resources will occur and whether it is measurable. We will discuss measurement in greater detail in the next section.

The term "probable" may have differing meanings under IFRS and ASPE when dealing with recognition of losses and liabilities. Under IFRS, "probable" is defined as "more likely than not" (often interpreted to mean a greater than 50% chance).[17] Under ASPE, it is defined as "likely" (that is, there is a high chance of occurrence).[18] Note that this may cause more losses and liabilities to be recognized under IFRS due to a perceived lower threshold.

Derecognition is the act of taking something off the statement of financial position or income statement. In the past, derecognition criteria have been discussed in the context of financial instruments only, and primarily focused on financial assets. We will discuss derecognition as it pertains to financial instruments in Chapters 7 and 14. Having said this, just as the conceptual framework includes general recognition criteria for all elements, it makes sense that it should include general derecognition criteria for all elements. The standard setters plan to discuss the inclusion of derecognition criteria in the framework as a future project.[19]

Several additional underlying principles help determine whether something should be recognized or not. A discussion of these follows.

Economic Entity Assumption and Control

The **economic entity assumption** (or entity concept) allows us to **identify an economic activity** with a particular **unit of accountability** (for example, a company, division, or individual). If all the economic events that occur could not be separated in a meaningful way, there would be no basis for accounting. This concept helps accountants determine what to include or recognize in a particular set of financial statements (as well as what not to recognize).

For tax and legal purposes, the **legal entity** is the relevant unit for a company. Taxes are paid based on taxable income for each legal entity. GAAP, however, considers a broader definition when preparing consolidated financial statements. A parent and its subsidiaries are separate **legal entities**, but merging their activities for accounting and reporting purposes gives more meaningful information. Thus, the consolidated financial statements are prepared from the perspective of the **economic entity**. This allows the company to recognize and group together the assets, liabilities, and other financial statement elements that are under the parent's **control** into one set of statements. Historically, the definition of control has been anchored in the number of common shares held in most cases.[20] However, the concept is changing.[21] The IASB and FASB have an ongoing project on defining the reporting entity.[22]

In the meantime, the IASB has issued a new standard[23] dealing with consolidation that defines **control**. The standard notes that an investor has control over an investee when it has the following:

1. power over the investee;
2. exposure, or rights, to variable returns from its involvement with the investee; and
3. the ability to use its power over the investee to affect the amount of the investors' returns.

This new standard is principles-based and broadens the concept so that control is assessed not only through ownership of common shares but through other means as well, including exposure to the risks and rewards of the entity.

Under ASPE, control is defined as the continuing power to determine strategic decisions without the co-operation of others—a similarly broad concept.[24] For situations where control is exercised through voting shares, the ASPE standards are similar. However, in other situations, the ASPE standards are significantly different. ASPE focuses more on whether the investee is "demonstrably distinct" from the company. In assessing this, the company looks at the following (as well as other factors):

- whether the entity in question can be unilaterally dissolved by the company and
- whether others have more than a 10% ownership interest.[25]

Consolidation of financial statements is generally covered in advanced accounting courses and will not be dealt with further here for that reason. It is important, however, to have a high-level view of which entities are included as part of the economic entity for financial reporting purposes. As mentioned earlier, this will also have an impact on accounting for derecognition of financial instruments in situations where assets are transferred.[26]

Many companies use what are known as special purpose entities (SPEs). SPEs are sometimes referred to as variable interest entities or structured entities. They are often separate legal entities set up for a specific purpose, such as to hold leases, pension funds, or perhaps certain investments and/or to create investment opportunities for investors. Are SPEs part of the economic entity for consolidated financial reporting purposes? This was the centre of much of the controversy surrounding the Enron scandal. Enron created many SPEs that it did not consolidate. It sold assets to these SPEs, often at a profit. As it turned out, Enron should have consolidated them since the liabilities and losses of these SPEs ended up being liabilities and losses of Enron. In other words, Enron was exposed to the risks of ownership.

Enron's accounting had the impact of understating liabilities as well as overstating income in its consolidated financial statements. Most of the activity involving generating new standards for consolidation as well as new principles for defining the economic entity are meant to address non-transparency and off–balance sheet items.

Revenue Recognition and Realization Principles

A crucial question for many enterprises is when revenue should be recognized. This is governed loosely by what is known as the **revenue recognition principle**. Although this is a principle in transition, historically, revenue has generally been recognized when the following three conditions are met:

1. **risks and rewards** have passed and/or the **earnings process is substantially complete (significant acts have been performed and there is no continuing involvement);**

2. **the revenue is measurable**; and

3. **the revenue is collectible** (realized or realizable).[27]

Revenues are **realized** when products (goods or services), merchandise, or other assets are **exchanged** for cash or claims to cash. Revenues are **realizable** if the assets received or held can be readily converted into cash or claims to cash. Assets are readily convertible if they can be sold or interchanged in an active market at prices that are readily determinable and there is no significant additional cost.

As we will see in Chapter 6, an alternative contract-based approach to revenue recognition is being developed under IFRS. This approach is a **balance sheet approach** and recognizes that a transaction has occurred when the entity enters into a contract. Under this proposed model, the entity has rights and performance obligations under the contract. Collectible revenues are recognized when **performance obligations are settled** (when control over goods/services pass to the customer). There is a presumption that the contract is measurable.

Matching Principle

Assets such as property, plant, and equipment contribute to a company's ability to generate revenues. Therefore, accounting attempts to match these costs with the revenues that they produce. This practice is called **matching** because it dictates that effort (expenditures) be matched with accomplishment (revenues) whenever this is reasonable and can be done. It also illustrates the **cause and effect relationship** between the money spent to earn revenues and the revenues themselves.

It may be difficult to establish exactly how much of a contribution is made to each period, however, and so often an estimation technique must be used. GAAP requires that a **rational and systematic** allocation policy be used that will approximate the asset's contribution to the revenue stream. Selection of a rational and systematic allocation technique involves making assumptions about the benefits that are being received as well as the costs associated with those benefits. The cost of a long-lived asset, for example, must be allocated over all accounting periods during which the asset is used because the asset contributes to revenue generation throughout its useful life.

Assets such as inventory similarly contribute to a company's ability to generate revenues, but in a different way. While property, plant, and equipment are normally used up in generating revenues, inventory is sold to generate revenues. Operating expenditures incurred during the year are often classified into two groups depending on whether they are seen to be part of the inventory production process or not. These two groups are labelled **product costs** and **period costs**.

Product costs such as material, labour, and overhead attach to the product and are carried into future periods as inventory (if not sold) since they are seen to be part of the inventory production process and because inventory meets the definition of an asset. Period costs such as officers' salaries and other administrative expenses are recognized immediately—even though the benefits associated with these costs occur in the future. This is because they are not seen as part of the production process and therefore are not inventory costs and because the costs do not meet the definition of an asset by themselves. Period costs are seen to be a normal ongoing annual expense of running the business as opposed to part of the inventory production process. This same analysis occurs for self-constructed or internally generated assets other than inventory.

What Do the Numbers Mean?

Livent Inc., mentioned earlier, followed the policy of deferring preproduction costs for the creation of each separate show until the show was opened. The company felt that this was acceptable as it was creating an asset: the show. On opening night, the show would start to produce revenues and then the costs were amortized and matched with those revenues. Such costs included advertising, publicity and promotions, set construction, props, costumes, and salaries paid to the cast, crew, musicians, and creative workers during rehearsal. In short, anything to do with the production was deferred.

Ethics

On the one hand, one might argue that this was a bit aggressive. One could also argue that this treatment was acceptable because of the direct and incremental nature of these costs in terms of future production revenues. The trouble began when Livent started to reclassify some of these costs as fixed assets and also to reallocate these costs to different and unrelated shows that had higher revenue. The company even had spreadsheets to keep track of actual results as compared with those that were publicly reported.[28] As noted earlier, there was more going on than a simple accounting policy choice.

While in the past, it may have been acceptable to capitalize certain costs on the basis of matching, there are no grounds for recognizing assets and liabilities that do not specifically meet the definitions of these elements under the current conceptual framework. If a cost or expenditure does not meet the definition of an asset, it is expensed (matching notwithstanding). Care should be taken also to ensure that only costs directly related with the creation of assets such as inventory or property, plant, and equipment are included. Similarly, there are no grounds for deferral of revenues as liabilities in the name of matching.[29]

Measurement

Finance

Because **accrual accounting** is followed, many estimates must be used when preparing financial statements. Most numbers on a statement of financial position and income statement are in fact quite "soft" and inexact. In order to communicate information about economic events, accountants must convert the economic events into the language of business: numbers. Some things are easy to measure, such as cash in the bank. Others are not so easy to measure. For instance, how do you measure the potential cost of selling what later proves to be a dangerous product?

Too much uncertainty may make it inappropriate to recognize a financial statement element. As a general rule, **elements cannot be recognized** in the financial statements if they cannot be **measured**. We will first discuss a few underlying concepts, such as periodicity, unit of measure, and going concern. Then we will look at basic measurement choices. The key for accountants is to **determine an acceptable level of uncertainty**, use **measurement tools** that help deal with the uncertainty, and **disclose enough information** to signal the uncertainty.

Measurability is a big issue for many financial statement elements. When there is a **variance** between the recognized amount and another reasonably possible amount, this is called **measurement uncertainty**. Accountants are continually working to develop and make use of **measurement tools** such as option pricing and discounted cash flow models, as well as others. When observable values are not available (such as market prices and cost), these models are used as a way of dealing with measurement uncertainty. There is a trade-off with uncertainty. Too much measurement uncertainty undermines the reliability of the financial statements. However, if the element is not recognized at all in the financial statements, then all relevant information has not been included and the statements are incomplete. A compromise is to measure and recognize the elements in the body of the financial statements and to disclose the measurement uncertainty and its significance in the notes to the financial statements.

Appendix 2A looks in greater detail at measurement models that incorporate uncertainty.

Periodicity Assumption

The most accurate way to measure the results of an enterprise's activity would be to do the measurement at the time of the enterprise's eventual liquidation. At that point, there is complete certainty about all of the company's cash flows. Business, government, investors, and various other user groups, however, cannot wait that long for such information. Users need to be informed about performance and economic status on a **timely basis** so that they can evaluate and compare firms. For this reason, information must be reported periodically. The **periodicity assumption** (or time period assumption) implies that an enterprise's economic activities can be divided into **artificial time periods**. These time periods vary, but the most common are one month, one quarter, and one year.

The shorter the time period, the more difficult it becomes to **determine the proper net income** for the period. A month's results are usually less reliable than a quarter's results, and a quarter's results are likely less reliable than a year's results. This is because more estimates are needed to accrue costs and revenues in accrual accounting when the time period is shorter. Investors want and demand information that has been quickly processed and distributed, yet the more quickly the information is released, the more likely errors become.

The question of what time period is appropriate is becoming more serious because product cycles are shorter and products become obsolete more quickly. Many observers believe that, given the advances in technology, more on-line, **real-time financial information** needs to be provided to ensure that relevant information is available. The issue of continuous financial reporting was introduced in Chapter 1.

Monetary Unit Assumption

The **monetary unit assumption** means that money is the common denominator of economic activity and is an appropriate **basis for accounting measurement** and analysis. This assumption implies that the monetary unit is the most effective way of expressing to interested parties changes in capital and exchanges of goods and services. The monetary unit is relevant, simple, universally available, understandable, and useful. Applying this assumption depends on the even more basic assumption that **quantitative data** are useful in communicating economic information and in making rational economic decisions.

In Canada and the United States, accountants have chosen generally to ignore the phenomenon of **price-level change** (inflation and deflation) by assuming that the unit of measure, the dollar, remains reasonably **stable**. This assumption about the monetary unit has been used to justify adding 1970 dollars to 2013 dollars without any adjustment. Only if circumstances change dramatically (such as if Canada or the United States were to experience extremely high inflation) would the standard setters consider "inflation accounting." IAS 29 deals with hyperinflation. There is no comparable standard under ASPE.

Going Concern Assumption

Most accounting methods are based on the **going concern assumption**. This is the assumption that a business enterprise will **continue to operate for the foreseeable future**; that is, it will not be forced to end its operations. Although there are many business failures, experience indicates that companies do have a fairly high continuance rate. While accountants do not believe that business firms will last indefinitely, they do expect them to last long enough to fulfill their commitments. Management must assess the company's ability to continue as a going concern and take into account all available information, looking out at least 12 months from the date of the statement of financial position.

The implications of this assumption are profound. The **historical cost principle** would have limited usefulness if **liquidation** were assumed to be likely. Under a liquidation approach, for example, asset values are better stated at **net realizable value** (sales price less costs of disposal) than at **acquisition cost**. Amortization and amortization policies are justifiable and appropriate only if we assume some permanence to the enterprise; this is what justifies allocating the costs of the amortized assets to future periods to match them against future revenues. If a liquidation approach were adopted, the **current versus non-current classification** of assets and liabilities would lose much of its significance. Labelling anything a **fixed or long-term** asset would be difficult to justify. Indeed, listing liabilities according to their likely liquidation would be more reasonable.

The going concern assumption applies in most business situations. The only time when the assumption does not apply is when **there is intent to liquidate the company's net assets and cease operations or cease trading in the company's shares or when the company has no realistic alternative but to liquidate or cease operations**. In these cases, a total revaluation of assets and liabilities can provide information that closely approximates the entity's **net realizable value**. The accounting problems that arise when an enterprise is in liquidation are presented in advanced accounting courses. In order to illustrate the going concern concept and the question of liquidation, consider the situation of Air Canada.

What Do the Numbers Mean?

On April 1, 2003, Air Canada filed for bankruptcy protection under the Companies' Creditors Arrangement Act (CCAA) due to cash flow difficulties. The CCAA provides a "safe harbour" for companies in distress, giving them the opportunity to reorganize their financial affairs in a systematic manner while at the same time holding off creditors. Air Canada's protection was granted for the period ending June 30. This was subsequently extended to September 30, 2003. In the meantime, the company issued its first quarter results.

Real World Emphasis

Should the statements have been prepared on a **liquidation basis** or a **going concern basis**? Air Canada prepared the statements on a going concern basis using the assumption that:

- management was in the process of developing a plan to restructure operations under the CCAA,

- it had been able to obtain "debtor in possession" financing from General Electric Canada Finance Inc., and

- it expected the company to continue operating as a going concern.

The financial statements fully disclosed these facts. Companies are required to disclose any material uncertainties that may cast doubt upon their ability to continue as a going concern. As it turns out, the company successfully emerged from bankruptcy protection in 2004 but in 2009 was in the news once again, deliberating whether it needed to apply for protection under CCAA. In 2010, the airline was able to generate a profit and so was on more stable ground.

How do we measure things when we assume the entity is a going concern? Management must continually assess the likelihood of outcomes (such as whether the company will lose a lawsuit) based on history and supporting evidence. Often, companies rely on specialists such as lawyers and engineers for help with such assessments.

Historical Cost Principle

Transactions are initially measured at the amount of cash (or cash equivalents) that was paid or received or the fair value that was ascribed to the transactions when they took place. This is often called the **historical cost principle**. The historical cost principle has three underlying assumptions that support its value and usefulness:

1. It represents a value at a **point in time**.

2. It results from a **reciprocal exchange** (in other words, a two-way exchange).

3. The exchange includes **an outside arm's-length party**.

Initial Recognition. For non-financial assets, the value includes any **laid-down costs**; that is, any cost that is incurred to get the asset ready (whether for sale or for generating income by using it). Inventory, for instance, might include the **cost of material, labour, and a reasonable allocation of overhead**. Similarly, for a self-constructed asset, cost would include any expenditure made to get the asset **ready for its intended use**, including transportation and installation costs.

Sometimes it is not possible or not appropriate to determine a value using the historical cost principle. Transactions that have some or all of the following characteristics present challenges:

• **Nonmonetary** or **barter transactions** where **no cash or monetary consideration** is exchanged. Here it may be more difficult to determine the value of the assets exchanged.

• **Nonmonetary, non-reciprocal transactions** where there is **no exchange**, such as donations.

• **Related party transactions** where the parties to the transaction are not acting at arm's length (in other words, there is **no outside party**). In these cases, the exchange price may not reflect the true value of the assets exchanged.

As a default, an attempt may be made to estimate the **fair value** if possible, and this may become the cost basis going forward.

The historical cost principle also applies to financial instruments. Bonds, notes, and accounts payable and receivable are issued by a business enterprise in exchange for assets, or perhaps services. This price, established by the exchange transaction, is the "cost" of the financial instrument and gives the figure at which the instrument should be recognized in the financial statements as long as it is equal to fair value of the financial instrument issued. Where the instruments are issued in exchange for cash, the cost is straightforward but where they are issued for goods or services, the value may be more difficult to determine. Measurement techniques such as discounting are used to measure the fair value.

Subsequent Remeasurement. Historical cost has an important advantage over other valuation methods. Because it generally comes from an **arm's-length transaction** or exchange, it represents a bargained, fairly arrived-at value at a specific point in time. When it is first recognized, cost usually represents fair value. Over time, however, it often becomes irrelevant in terms of **predictive value**.

Later remeasurements also have limitations, however. They can be based on different measurement values, such as fair value, and give information that is more relevant, but they often involve **measurement uncertainty**. Furthermore, because there is often no external exchange (exchange with an outside party), the values may be **subjective**. Despite these limitations, the trend is toward an increasingly **mixed valuation model**. What used to be primarily a **historical cost-based model**, modified by the application of conservatism (that is, revaluations occurred if the asset's value declined below cost), is moving more toward a **market valuation model**. The use of fair value will be discussed below.

Fair Value Principle

IFRS has increasingly called for the use of standardized fair value measurements in the financial statements. This is an emerging principle that we will call the **fair value principle**. Fair value information may be more useful than historical cost for certain types of assets and liabilities and in certain industries. For example, companies report many financial instruments, including derivatives, at fair value. Brokerage houses and mutual funds prepare their financial statements using fair value.

Fair value is defined under IFRS as "the price that would be received to **sell** an asset or paid to transfer a liability in an orderly transaction between market participants at the measurement date."[30] Accordingly, fair value is an **exit price**. Exit price refers to a selling price, as opposed to an "entry price," which reflects the entity's purchase price. According to the definition, fair value is also a **market-based measure**, as opposed to an **entity-specific measure**. As such, it is meant to be more objective. It seeks to determine value by looking at how market participants would value the item in question. It does not look at value from the perspective of the entity itself and as such it does not consider company-specific synergies.[31]

Illustration 2-3 illustrates the various ways to define "value" or price.

Illustration **2-3**

Defining Value or Price

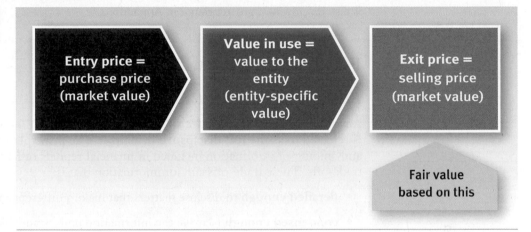

For instance, assume that a restaurant has a fully integrated industrial kitchen, and the grills are built in but are now broken. The restaurant may attribute a higher value to the grills since they are an integrated part of the kitchen and already in place. This value represents an entity-specific value. Market participants might view the value of broken, used equipment as being lower – perhaps at scrap value – especially if the grills are too costly to fix. This latter value is the fair value under IFRS. Where a liquid market does not exist, the entity may use a model such as a discounted cash flow model to estimate fair value.

Which value is better for use in the financial statements? Good question. There is a trade-off. Entity-specific value may be more relevant for operating assets where the entity plans to hold on to them and use them to produce revenues, but it is more subjective. As noted above, the market-based view is more objective and verifiable and thus, where fair value is called for under IFRS, the market-based view must be applied.

At initial acquisition, historical cost generally equals fair value. In subsequent periods, as market and economic conditions change, historical cost and fair value often diverge. These fair value measures or estimates often provide more relevant information about the expected cash flows related to the asset or liability. For example, when a long-lived asset declines in value, a fair value measure may be used to help determine a potential impairment loss.

In order to encourage increased use of fair value and to simplify accounting, standard setters have given companies the option to use fair value for most financial instruments (such as cash, receivables, non-strategic investments, and payables) as an accounting policy choice. This is referred to as the **fair value option** under both IFRS and ASPE. Standard setters feel that fair value is more relevant for most financial instruments as it reflects the current cash equivalent value. In addition, markets exist for many financial instruments, thereby providing independent, objective evidence of value. Under the fair value option, financial instruments are measured at fair value with gains and losses being booked to income. IFRS requires certain criteria be met in order for the fair value option to be used.

Certain standards under IFRS explicitly allow the use of fair value for non-financial assets (such as investment properties and property, plant, and equipment) or require it for others (such as biological assets). ASPE does not make reference to the use of fair value for these items although it does acknowledge that fair value measures might be used in certain industries including the agricultural and mineral industries.[32] Note that ASPE has defined fair value as the "amount of consideration that would be agreed upon in an arm's length transaction between knowledgeable, willing parties who are under no compulsion to act."[33]

There are some subtle differences here including the fact that the ASPE definition does not refer to an orderly market nor does it stipulate that the price is an exit price.

The use of the fair value principle will be expanded upon in future chapters. Fair value is also discussed in greater detail in Appendix 2A.

Presentation and Disclosure

Full Disclosure Principle

Anything that is relevant to decisions should be included in the financial statements. This is referred to as the **full disclosure principle**. The principle recognizes that the nature and amount of information included in financial reports reflects a series of judgemental trade-offs. These trade-offs aim for information that is:

- **detailed enough** to disclose matters that make a difference to users, but

- **condensed enough** to make the information understandable, and also appropriate in terms of the costs of preparing and using it.

More information is not always better. Too much information may result in the user being unable to digest or process the information. This is called **information overload**. Information about a company's financial position, income, cash flows, and investments can be found in one of three places:

1. The **main body of financial statements**

2. The **notes to the financial statements**

3. As supplementary information, including the **Management Discussion and Analysis** (MD&A)

The financial statements are a **formalized, structured way of communicating financial information**. Disclosure is not a substitute for proper accounting.[34] Certain numbers, such as earnings per share, send signals to the capital marketplace. For example, cash basis accounting for cost of goods sold is misleading, even if accrual-based amounts have been disclosed in the notes to the financial statements. As mentioned in Chapter 1, the market watches and listens for signals about earnings in particular and does not usually react well to negative earnings surprises.

The **notes to financial statements** generally **amplify or explain** the items presented in the main body of the statements. If the information in the main body of the statements gives an incomplete picture of the enterprise's performance and position, additional information that is needed to complete the picture should be included in the notes.

Information in the notes does not have to be quantifiable, nor does it need to qualify as an element. Notes can be partially or totally narrative. Examples of notes are:

- **Descriptions** of the accounting policies and methods used in measuring the elements reported in the statements

- **Explanations** of uncertainties and contingencies

- **Details** that are too voluminous to include in the statements

The notes are not only helpful to understanding the enterprise's performance and position, they are essential.

Supplementary information may include details or amounts that present a different perspective from what appears in the financial statements. They may include quantifiable information that is high in relevance but low in reliability, or information that is helpful but not essential. One example of supplementary information is the data and schedules provided by oil and gas companies: typically they give information on proven reserves as well as the related discounted cash flows.

Supplementary information also includes management's explanation of the financial information and a discussion of its significance in the **MD&A**. The CICA's publication *MD&A: Guidance on Preparation and Disclosure* lays out six general disclosure principles.

MD&As should:

- enable readers to view the entity through management's eyes;

- supplement and complement the information in the financial statements;

- be complete, fair and balanced, and provide information that is material to the decision-making needs of users;

- have a forward-looking orientation;

- focus on management's strategy for generating value over time; and

- be understandable, relevant, and comparable.[35]

Thus, the MD&A is a step toward a more broadly based business reporting model that also contains forward-looking information. The guidance also includes a framework that identifies five key elements that should be included in the MD&A:

1. The company's **vision, core businesses, and strategy**

2. **Key performance drivers**

3. **Capabilities** (capital and other resources) to achieve the desired results

4. **Results** (historical and prospective)

5. **Risks** that may shape and/or affect the achievement of results

It is hoped that these additional disclosures will give users of the financial information a greater insight into the company's business.[36]

The content, arrangement, and display of financial statements, along with other facets of full disclosure, are discussed specifically in Chapters 4, 5, and 23, and more generally throughout the text. Note that under IFRS there is a general trend toward increased disclosures in a bid for greater transparency.

Illustration 2-4 presents the conceptual framework discussed in this chapter. It is similar to Illustration 2-1, except that it gives additional information for each level. We cannot overemphasize the usefulness of this conceptual framework in helping to understand many of the problem areas that are examined in later chapters.

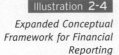

Expanded Conceptual Framework for Financial Reporting

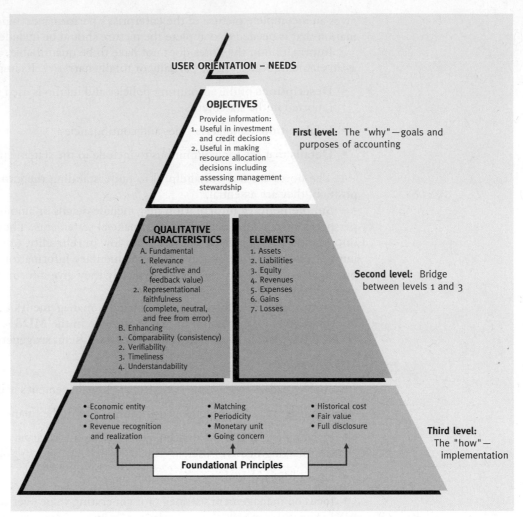

FINANCIAL REPORTING ISSUES

Objective 5
Explain the factors that contribute to choice and/or bias in financial reporting decisions.

Making financial reporting decisions is complex. This section examines the factors that make this process challenging. As mentioned earlier in the chapter, the main objective of financial reporting is to **provide reliable**, **decision-relevant financial information** to users so that they can make well-informed capital allocation decisions. Capital that is invested in good investments fuels the economy and encourages job growth and wealth creation. To achieve this objective, well-judged choices must be made between alternative accounting concepts, methods, and means of disclosure. Accounting principles and rules must be **selected and interpreted and professional judgement must be applied**.

As mentioned, accounting is **influenced by its environment** (in many cases in a negative way) and by decisions made by individuals who often act in **self-interest** or in the interests of the company (at the expense of other stakeholders). Because of this, it is unrealistic to believe that the financial reporting system will always work properly. Instead of wealth creation in the capital markets and the economy, financial reporting decisions sometimes lead to wealth and value destruction. Bias may exist and this is not a good thing.

Principles-Based Approach

IFRS and ASPE are **principles-based**; that is, they are based on a few foundational principles and concepts like those in the conceptual framework noted earlier in the chapter.

Ethics

The benefit of this approach is that all decisions should theoretically be **consistent** if they start from the same foundational reasoning.[37] Another benefit is that principles-based GAAP is **flexible**. The most appropriate accounting for any new situation or novel business transaction may be arrived at through reason by going back to these principles (sometimes referred to as **first principles**). However, principles-based GAAP is sometimes criticized for being too flexible. Some critics feel that it allows too much choice and therefore results in **lack of comparability**.

Care should therefore be taken to ensure that this flexibility is not abused. The key foundational concept of **neutrality** is of the greatest importance. **The conceptual framework developed in this chapter is the anchor that should ground all financial reporting decisions.** In the absence of specific GAAP guidance, an entity should adopt accounting policies that are:

1. consistent with specific GAAP guidance and

2. **developed** through exercising professional judgement and applying the conceptual framework.[38]

Financial Engineering

A practice known as **financial engineering** became more visible during the past two decades. Financial engineering is the process of legally structuring a business arrangement or transaction so that it meets the company's financial reporting objective (such as maximizing earnings or minimizing a debt to equity ratio). This is often done by creating complex legal arrangements and financial instruments. These arrangements and instruments are created so that the resulting accounting meets the desired objective within GAAP. For example, a company that is raising debt financing might want the instrument structured so that it meets the GAAP definition of equity rather than debt. In this way, the debt to equity ratio is not negatively affected.

Ethics

Many financial institutions develop and market these financial instruments to their clients. These arrangements are often called **structured financings**. Since Enron, this practice has been reduced. Are financial engineering and the practice of structured financings ethically acceptable? Financial engineering has moved from being an accepted practice and commodity to a potentially fraudulent activity.

Illustration 2-5 looks at the various shades of grey in accounting for transactions.

Illustration 2-5

Choice in Accounting Decision-Making

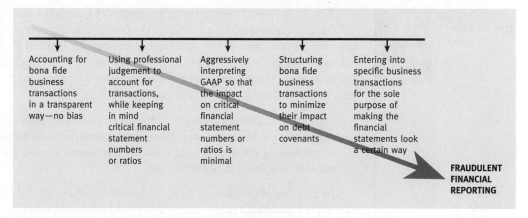

Fraudulent Financial Reporting

The role of accountants who are responsible for preparing a company's financial records is to capture business and economic events and transactions as they occur and communicate them to interested parties. They should not use the financial statements to portray

Ethics

something that is not there. Similarly, good financial reporting should be a result of **well-reasoned and supported analysis** that is grounded in a conceptual framework. It should not be influenced by external pressures. Pressures in the capital marketplace are everywhere, however, and their potentially negative impact on financial reporting must be acknowledged. Pressures may arise from various sources, including the ones discussed below.

Economic or Business Environment

Sometimes a company experiences sudden drops in revenue or market share. The underlying reason may be unique to the company and due to some poor strategic and business decisions or it may result from an industry or economic downturn. This may put pressure on a company to "prop up" its revenues. There may be pressure to recognize revenues before they should be recognized or to defer the recognition of some expenses.

Some companies use an industry or economic downturn as an opportunity to "clean up" their financial statements and generally take large writedowns on assets such as inventory or goodwill.

The markets expect a loss and the company's share price is therefore not overly affected in a negative way. This "purging" of the statement of financial position has the positive impact of making future earnings look better.

Other Pressures

Budgets put tremendous pressure on company management. Since bonuses and even jobs depend on meeting budgets, sometimes this negative influence leaks inappropriately into accounting decisions. Other pressures were discussed in Chapter 1.

If these and other pressures are not monitored and controlled properly, they are a major problem. In order to lessen the chances of fraudulent financial reporting, various controls and a solid governance structure may be put in place by a company. These could include:

- Vigilant, knowledgeable top management

- An independent audit committee

- An internal audit function

- Other internal controls at lower levels

What Do the Numbers Mean?

The U.S.-based Committee of Sponsoring Organizations of the Treadway Commission (COSO) is composed of professional accounting organizations such as the American Accounting Association, the American Institute of Certified Public Accountants (AICPA), Financial Executives International, the Institute of Internal Auditors, and the National Association of Accountants (now the Institute of Management Accountants). COSO's mandate, according to its website (www.coso.org), is as follows:

> ...to provide thought leadership through the development of comprehensive frameworks and guidance on enterprise risk management, internal control and fraud deterrence designed to improve organizational performance and governance and to reduce the extent of fraud in organizations.

In 2010 COSO released a report entitled *Fraudulent Financial Reporting: 1998–2007*. The report updated a prior report that it had released looking at fraud for the period 1987 to 1997. The 2010 report found that there were 347 alleged cases of fraud that were investigated by the SEC from 1998 to 2007 (as compared with 294 cases for the prior 10-year period). COSO calculated the dollar amount of the misappropriations to be in the area of U.S. $120 billion.

The most common area of fraud involved revenue recognition (alleged in 61% of the frauds). This was followed by overstatement of assets including overcapitalization of expenses (51% of the cases). Understatement of liabilities was much lower (31% of the cases). Approximately 26% of the firms allegedly involved in fraud changed auditors. The average period the alleged frauds took place was 31 months.

Although the report stated that more study was needed to determine why the frauds were committed, it noted that the SEC identified in its proceedings the following motivations for fraud:

- the need to meet internal or external earnings expectations,

- an attempt to conceal the company's deteriorating financial condition,

- the need to increase the stock price,

- the need to bolster financial performance for pending equity or debt financing, or

- the desire to increase management compensation based on financial results.

It will be interesting to see what the next decade brings.

Source: M.S. Beasley, J. V. Carcello, D. R. Hermanson, and T. L. Neal, *Fraudulent Financial Reporting: 1998–2007, An Analysis of U.S. Public Companies*, Committee of Sponsoring Organizations of the Treadway Commission, 2010.

IFRS/ASPE COMPARISON

Objective 6
Discuss current trends in standard setting for the conceptual framework.

ASPE and IFRS are fundamentally similar since they are both principles-based. The IASB and FASB are continuing to work on a joint project to complete a common conceptual framework. As mentioned earlier, it is the intent to use this framework in Canada for private entities as well. This chapter includes the work produced to date. So far, the IASB has issued new guidance on the objectives of financial reporting and qualitative characteristics of useful information. We have noted some differences throughout the chapter but these will be looked at in more detail in subsequent chapters.

Looking Ahead

The standard setters continue to work on definitions for financial statement elements and recognition/derecognition and measurement criteria. They also plan to work on issues related to presentation and disclosure and the status of the framework itself.

Below is a brief overview of the latest thinking on these parts of the conceptual framework. This is a work in progress.

Proposed Financial Statement Elements Definitions

The proposed framework project attempts to redefine major elements such as assets and liabilities. The intent is not to change the substance of how we define these elements but more to tweak the wording to provide more clarity in complex situations. In most cases, for basic transactions, the proposed definitions will not change the accounting. It is worthwhile to study the proposed definitions since they provide added insights into how we view assets and liabilities. According to the proposed definitions, **assets** have two essential characteristics:

1. They involve **present economic resources**.

2. The entity has a right or access to these resources where others do not.

In order for something to be an asset, the entity must provide evidence that it represents an economic resource and then link itself to that resource. In other words, the entity must first prove that the item has economic value and then that the entity may lay claim to or access that value.

Economic resources are defined to include things that are **scarce and capable of producing cash flows** (and therefore have economic value) where the **right to access is an enforceable right** (by law or other means). The economic resource is the thing itself (such as a building or the right to use it) and not the future cash flows that will be generated by it, although potential future cash flows generally drive the value.

For instance, if a company owns a parcel of land on which it builds a manufacturing facility, the land and manufacturing facility are considered assets for the following reasons:

- **Present economic resource**: The land and plant represent a present resource; in other words, the entity may sell or use the property now. In addition, the property is not freely available to all, so it has economic value: someone would pay something to acquire the property.

- Right or access that others do not have: If the land were freely available to all, it would not be considered to have **specific economic value to the entity**. For instance, consider the air we breathe. It is freely available to everyone and although it has value in that we need it to survive, it is not considered to be an asset specific or unique to the entity.

In terms of the land and plant, the entity has sole ownership of the property since it holds legal title. It therefore is connected to this specific economic resource and may lay claim to it. If everyone owns or has access to the land (such as public parklands), then no single entity or individual (except perhaps the government itself) can lay claim to it as an asset on their statement of financial position even though they may derive benefit from using the land. If the entity has legal title, access is enforceable under law.

Illustration 2-6 depicts the essence of an asset.

Illustration 2-6

The Essence of an Asset

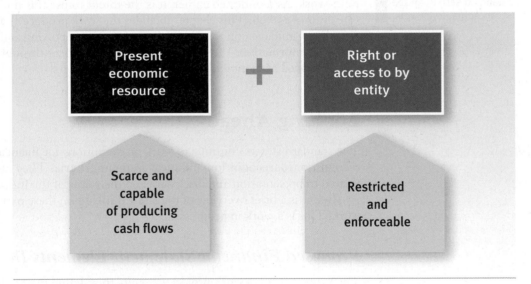

As another example, an insurance contract gives the insured party an **unconditional right** to recover insured losses from the insurance company. This contract has value even if no loss is suffered. Insurance transfers risk to the insurance company and the insured party is willing to pay a premium for that. This unconditional right is therefore a present economic resource.

In addition to this unconditional right, the insurance contract **also gives** the insured party a specific **conditional right** to receive compensation if a loss occurs. This is not a present economic resource since it does not exist until a loss occurs in the future. Therefore, although the contract contains both conditional and unconditional rights, only the unconditional rights represent economic resources (unless and until a loss occurs). The two rights are intertwined, however, since the conditional right can only legally be accessed by virtue of the unconditional right. Both are taken into account when measuring the value of the asset. The premium on the insurance contract provides a good measure of the value of the contract.

A summary of selected economic resources follows in Illustration 2-7.[39]

Item	Example	What Is the Economic Resource?	Explanation
Tangible non-monetary assets	Land	The land itself is a **present** economic resource. It may be sold or used currently.	The **future** cash flows are not the economic resource although they are considered in valuing the **present** economic resource.
Intangible assets	Patents	The patent itself is a **present** economic resource. It may be sold or used currently.	Same as above
Financial assets	Accounts receivable	The existing contractual right to receive the cash flows is the **present** economic resource. The receivable may be sold or retained (and cash collected).	Same as above
Other, for example, insurance contracts	Fire insurance contract (contains both an unconditional right to insurance coverage over a period of time and a conditional right to receive cash equal to the loss should a loss event occur).	The unconditional promise by the insurance company to provide coverage over the term of the insurance is a **present** economic resource to the insured party (who has paid for this right).	The unconditional promise exists (and is enforceable through contract law) even though there may never be a loss from fire. The promise to pay a certain amount of money equal to the insured loss (if a fire occurs) is a conditional promise. This specific amount may or may not be paid out depending on if there is a fire. It would only become a **present** economic resource when and if a fire occurs and the entity is entitled to a payout.

Illustration 2-7

Present and Potential Economic Resources

Obligations may be conditional, unconditional, or both (just like contractual and other rights). **Unconditional obligations** are sometimes referred to as **stand-ready obligations**. That is, the obligor "stands ready" to do whatever is required under the terms of the contract, agreement, or law. They are obligated. For instance, with an insurance contract, the insurer stands ready to pay out an amount equal to a loss that is covered under the insurance contract should the loss occur. Other examples include guarantees and warranties. Obligations where the entity agrees to provide a future service or deliver something in future are often referred to as **performance obligations**.

A **liability** is defined as:

1. a present economic obligation that is an unconditional promise or other requirement to provide or forego economic resources, and

2. where the entity is the obligor.

Illustration 2-8 depicts the essence of a liability.

Entities must follow laws and/or regulations in the legal jurisdiction in which they operate. This duty for companies (and all citizens) to abide by the law may be seen by some as an unconditional obligation. Often it is not clear if a law has been violated and therefore, there are legal systems (courts, lawyers, judges, juries) that will help establish whether it has. The potential breaking of a law and/or regulation may be seen as a contingency and a **conditional obligation** may exist. If the law is violated, the company has an economic burden, which results in a present obligation that is enforceable under law. Note that the proposed definition includes **enforceability**. This is an important aspect since if

Illustration 2-8

The Essence of a Liability

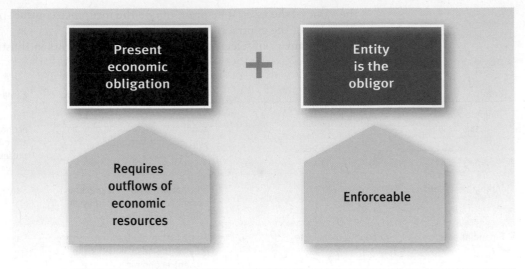

Law

Illustration 2-9

Present and Potential Economic Obligations

an obligation is not enforceable (for instance under contract or other law), perhaps it is not an obligation.

The uncertainty regarding whether a law has been broken and whether the company must pay a fine or settle a lawsuit is taken into account when measuring the liability (which results from the unconditional obligation). Note that it may be that the unconditional obligation, and hence the liability, is measured at an amount that is close to zero even when taking into account the conditional obligation. Illustration 2-9 looks at some potential economic obligations.

Item	Example	What Is the Economic Obligation?	Explanation
Financial obligations	Accounts payable	The existing contractual obligation to pay cash flows is the present economic obligation.	The entity owes the money and payment is enforceable under contract law. There is an unconditional promise to pay.
Non-financial obligations	Lawsuit – court ruling against the company	There exists a stand-ready obligation (unconditional) to abide by society's rules. The company owes the settlement because it lost the court case. The only potential contingency relates to whether the company plans to appeal the ruling.	The settlement is enforceable through the court system.
Non-financial obligations	Lawsuit – court case in progress	There is a stand-ready obligation (unconditional) to abide by society's rules. The company may have a conditional obligation depending on the outcome of the court case.	The settlement (if any) depends upon the outcome of the court case. The uncertainty would be taken into account through measurement (the company and lawyers would assess likely outcomes and their respective probabilities).
Constructive obligations	Responsibility for environmental cleanup not mandated by law (but where the company has a published policy stating that it will be responsible for the cleanup). No one has sued the company yet (and may never).	There is a stand-ready obligation created (under IFRS) through the company's published policy to be responsible for the cleanup.	The obligation would presumably be enforceable through common or other law depending on the jurisdiction (that is through someone suing the company).

Comparison of Definitions

Illustration 2-10 compares the definitions that exist now with the proposed definitions for assets and liabilities. The proposed definitions include many of the same characteristics as the existing standards but the new wording is meant to provide additional guidance and reduce inconsistencies between the various standards. As noted earlier, for most assets and liabilities, applying the new definitions will yield the same accounting result.

Illustration 2-10

Comparison of Definitions

Significant Change

Definitions	Existing Standards	Current Proposed Definitions (as discussed earlier in the chapter)
Assets	**Assets** are economic resources that have been obtained or are controlled by a particular entity as a result of past transactions or events from which future economic benefits may be obtained. They have three essential characteristics: 1. They embody a **future benefit**. 2. The entity can **control access** to this benefit. 3. The **transaction** or event that gives the entity access to this benefit **has occurred**.	**Assets** have two essential characteristics: 1. they involve **present economic resources** 2. to which the entity has a **right or access** where others do not.
Liabilities	**Liabilities** are obligations that arise from past transactions or events, which may result in a transfer of assets. Liabilities also have three essential characteristics: 1. They embody a **duty or responsibility**. 2. The entity has **little or no discretion to avoid** the duty. 3. The **transaction** or event that obligates the entity **has occurred**.	**Liabilities** have two essential characteristics: 1. they represent a **present economic obligation** 2. for which the entity is the obligator **(which is enforceable)**.

Presently under discussion is a model that requires recognition of these elements when (a) they meet the respective definitions, and (b) they are measurable.

Under this newer view, probability is incorporated through measurement. That is, the dollar value assigned to the element considers the riskiness and uncertainties of any related cash flows.

SUMMARY OF LEARNING OBJECTIVES

1 Indicate the usefulness and describe the main components of a conceptual framework for financial reporting.

A conceptual framework is needed to (1) create standards that build on an established body of concepts and objectives, (2) provide a framework for solving new and emerging practical problems, (3) increase financial statement users' understanding of and confidence in financial reporting, and (4) enhance comparability among different companies' financial statements.

The first level deals with the objective of financial reporting. The second level includes the qualitative characteristics of useful information and elements of financial statements. The third level includes foundational principles and conventions.

2 Identify the qualitative characteristics of accounting information.

The overriding criterion by which accounting choices can be judged is decision usefulness; that is, the goal is to provide the information that is the most useful for decision-making. Fundamental characteristics include relevance and faithful representation. These two characteristics must be present. Enhancing characteristics include comparability, verifiability, timeliness, and understandability. There may be trade-offs.

3   Define the basic elements of financial statements.

The basic elements of financial statements are (1) assets, (2) liabilities, (3) equity, (4) revenues, (5) expenses, (6) gains, and (7) losses.

4   Describe the foundational principles of accounting.

(1) Economic entity: the assumption that the activity of a business enterprise can be kept separate and distinct from its owners and any other business unit. (2) Control: the entity has the power to make decisions and reap the benefits or be exposed to the losses (which are variable). (3) Revenue recognition: revenue is generally recognized when it is (a) earned, (b) measurable, and (c) collectible (realizable). (4) Matching: the assumption assists in the measurement of income by ensuring that costs (relating to long-lived assets) incurred in earning revenues are booked in the same period as the revenues earned. (5) Periodicity: the assumption that an enterprise's economic activities can be divided into artificial time periods to facilitate timely reporting. (6) Monetary unit: the assumption that money is the common denominator by which economic activity is conducted, and that the monetary unit gives an appropriate basis for measurement and analysis. (7) Going concern: the assumption that the business enterprise will have a long life. (8) Historical cost principle: existing GAAP requires that many assets and liabilities be accounted for and reported based on their acquisition price. (9) Fair value principle: assets and liabilities are valued at fair value—that is, an exit price—and viewed

from a market participant perspective. (10) Full disclosure principle: accountants follow the general practice of providing information that is important enough to influence an informed user's judgement and decisions.

5   Explain the factors that contribute to choice and/or bias in financial reporting decisions.

Choice is the result of many things, including principles-based standards, measurement uncertainty, and increasingly complex business transactions. The conceptual framework is the foundation that GAAP is built on. If there is no primary source of GAAP for a specific decision, then professional judgement must be used, making sure that the accounting policies chosen are consistent with the primary sources of GAAP and the conceptual framework.

Financial engineering is the process of legally structuring a business arrangement or transaction so that it meets the company's financial reporting objective. This can be a dangerous practice since it often results in biased information.

Fraudulent financial reporting often results from pressures on individuals or the company. These pressures may come from various sources, including worsening company, industry, or economic conditions; unrealistic internal budgets; and financial statement focal points related to contractual, regulatory, or capital market expectations. Weak internal controls and governance also contribute to fraudulent financial reporting.

6   Discuss current trends in standard setting for the conceptual framework.

The IASB and FASB will continue to work toward a common conceptual framework. The project on objectives and qualitative characteristics is complete. The boards are focusing on defining elements and the recognition/measurement frameworks.

KEY TERMS

assets, p. 46
basic elements, p. 46
comparability, p. 43
completeness, p. 42
comprehensive income, p. 47
conceptual framework, p. 38
conservatism, p. 86
consistency, p. 45
constructive obligations, p. 46
control, p. 49
cost-benefit relationship, p. 45
decision usefulness, p. 40

derecognition, p. 49
economic entity assumption, p. 49
economic substance, p. 42
elements of financial statements, p. 40
equitable obligations, p. 46
equity, p. 47
exit price, p. 55
expenses, p. 47
fair value option, p. 56
fair value principle, p. 55
feedback/confirmatory value, p. 41
financial engineering, p. 59

first principles, p. 59
freedom from material error, p. 43
full disclosure principle, p. 56
gains, p. 47
general-purpose financial statements, p. 40
going concern assumption, p. 52
historical cost principle, p. 54
information overload, p. 56
laid-down costs, p. 54
liabilities, p. 46
losses, p. 47

management best estimate, p. 43

matching, p. 50

materiality, p. 41

measurement uncertainty, p. 52

monetary unit assumption, p. 52

neutrality, p. 42

nonmonetary/barter transactions, p. 54

nonmonetary, non-reciprocal
   transactions, p. 54

notes to financial statements, p. 56

objective of financial reporting, p. 40

other comprehensive income, p. 47

performance obligation, p. 63

periodicity assumption, p. 52

predictive value, p. 41

present economic resources, p. 62

qualitative characteristics, p. 40

realizable (revenue), p. 50

realized (revenue), p. 50

reciprocal exchange, p. 54

recognition, p. 48

related party transactions, p. 54

relevance, p. 41

representational faithfulness, p. 41

revenue recognition principle, p. 50

revenues, p. 47

stand-ready obligations, p. 63

supplementary information, p. 57

timeliness, p. 44

transparency, p. 42

understandability, p. 44

verifiability, p. 44

APPENDIX 2A

FAIR VALUE MEASUREMENTS

Objective 7
Understand in greater detail how fair value is measured.

Fair value as a basis for measurement was introduced in Chapter 2. This appendix goes into a bit more detail regarding the IFRS fair value model. Although the use of fair value may introduce greater relevance into the financial statements in many cases, it may also introduce more measurement uncertainty and subjectivity, especially where liquid markets are not available to provide evidence of fair value.

Per IFRS 13, in order to measure fair value, an entity must determine the item being measured, how the item would be or could be used by market participants, the market that the item would be (or was) bought and sold in, and finally, if a model is being used to measure fair value, which model it is. These items are looked at in more detail below.[40]

- The particular asset being measured: Consider the specific nature, condition, and location of the asset being measured. Is it old, damaged, obsolete?

- The valuation premise (if dealing with non-financial assets): Many non-financial assets are used for different purposes. For instance, a building may be rented out, used as part of a manufacturing facility, or held for capital appreciation purposes. The perceived value of the building might be different depending on what we might use it for. Generally, the asset is valued based on what is referred to as its **highest and best use** in the market **regardless of how the entity is actually using the asset**. The highest and best use concept values the asset based on the highest value that the market would place on the asset considering all possible uses that are physically possible, legally permissible, and financially feasible. For example, in trying to measure the fair value of a piece of land zoned as residential, you would not consider a value that assumed that the land was zoned as a commercial property (since commercial development is not legally permissible at the measurement date).

- The **principal market**: The measurement would consider the value based on the market that the entity normally buys and sells in. This would usually also be the **most advantageous market**, that is, the market in which the price would be the highest. Many entities buy and sell in different markets so this concept looks at the main market that the company deals in. For instance, if a company buys and sells shares for investment purposes through the TSX, then the company would use market values as quoted by the TSX.

- The valuation technique: In many cases, a liquid market for the item being measured will be available and this best represents fair value. (Think of a situation such as valuing common shares that trade on the TSX.) In other cases, however, a valuation technique or model would be used to value the item. Any time that pure market values are not used, you are essentially estimating the value using a model. If a model is used, then the entity must determine inputs to use (including things such as discount rates and future cash flows to be generated by the asset). Illustration 2A-1 looks at this. Inputs that are observable in the market (for instance, the prime interest rate) are better than those that are not, as the observable inputs are more objective. Observable inputs provide higher quality measurements because they are objective.

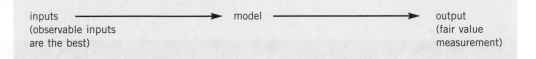

Since estimating a fair value using a model introduces measurement uncertainty, we try to offset this by using solid input information. Inputs are classified into three categories depending on their quality (level 1 inputs, level 2 inputs, and level 3 inputs). Level 1 inputs are the highest quality inputs and will produce the best quality fair value measurement. Level 3 inputs are at the other end and are used where level 1 and/or 2 inputs are not available.

This categorization of inputs is often referred to as the fair value hierarchy. Level 1 and 2 inputs are generally observable in various markets and are therefore more objective, whereas level 3 inputs are generally not observable and hence more subjective. Level 1 inputs essentially require the existence of liquid markets that generate good solid information that may be used as the inputs. A company must disclose information about which models and input levels are used. The lower the level of input (for instance level 3), the greater the required disclosures. This gives additional information to financial statement users about the measurement uncertainty.

Valuation models may be roughly categorized into three groups:

1. Market models: These use prices and other information generated from market transactions involving identical or similar transactions. An example is the earnings multiples model. Under this example, a company may be valued using publicly available earnings numbers for similar companies as well as multiples that are generated by comparing publicly available earnings numbers with share prices.

2. Income models: These convert future amounts (such as future cash flows to be generated by an asset) to current amounts (that is, amounts adjusted for the time value of money). Examples include discounted cash flows and options pricing models.

3. Cost models: These attempt to reflect the amount that would be required to replace the asset's *service capacity*. These models are used for older non-financial assets where the item being valued is no longer bought and sold; perhaps it is obsolete. The value is benchmarked against similar items (that are currently sold), focusing for instance on service capacity.

Fair value measures may be calculated using any of these models and using different types of inputs. Illustration 2A-2 describes the various levels of inputs and different models in the fair value hierarchy. A piece of manufacturing equipment is used as an example for purposes of the illustration. Assume we are trying to determine the fair value of a piece of equipment in order to determine if an impairment loss needs to be recognized.

	Market Model	Income Model	Cost Model
Level 1 inputs	Quoted prices in active market for identical machine (would only be applicable if the machine were fairly new or a well-established second-hand market existed)	Risk-free interest rate	Quoted market price to replace the **exact same** *service capacity* of the asset (note that it may be very difficult to get this type of information where the equipment is older or technology has changed)
Level 2 inputs	Quoted prices for similar machine or for the identical machine in a market that is not very active or liquid (that is, there is not much volume)	Risk-adjusted interest rate recently charged by a creditor for a recent loan	Quoted prices to replace a **similar** *service capacity*. May not be able to acquire an asset in the exact same condition or with the exact same service capacity.
Level 3 inputs	Management estimate of what a potential purchaser would pay for the machine (absence of an active, liquid market)	Management estimates of future cash flows that are expected to be generated by an asset and internally generated estimate of incremental interest rate	Management estimates of prices for similar assets with similar service capacity

Illustration 2A-2

The Fair Value Hierarchy: Trying to Estimate the Fair Value of a Machine that Manufactures Inventory

Which model should be used? You should use the one that provides the best quality fair value measure. This is a judgement call and depends on the characteristics of the asset itself and available information. In most cases, only one model may work, but in some cases, more than one may be applicable.

In the example above, if the machinery is older and obsolete, the market model will not suffice because you will likely not be able to get any market information for the exact or similar machine, especially if the machines are no longer produced. Nor would it make sense for management to try to estimate market values for the exact or similar machine as too much judgement is involved. In this case, an income model might be used or alternatively, a cost model (which looks at valuing the service capacity as opposed to the asset). Inputs from various level might be needed to do the calculation. As noted above, the lower the level of the inputs, the greater the disclosures required.

However, if valuing a company that is going public, you may be able to use both the market and income models. You might use the income model to measure the value by focusing on the discounted cash flows. Alternatively you might look at recent market transactions for similar companies (or perhaps earnings multiples). There is no right or wrong answer, just better or worse information. If you are able to measure fair value by using more than one model, this will help because you can compare the estimates to see if they are both reasonable or not. However, keep in mind that more effort is expended.

Income Models for Measuring Fair Value

Finance

The second column in the illustration looks at income models. These are very commonly used models and will be explained further here. Valuation models include discounted cash flow (discussed below) and options pricing models (discussed in Chapter 16).

Fair value estimates arrived at by using discounted cash flow models incorporate one or more of the following components:[41]

1. Estimates of cash flows: Management makes its best estimates of expected cash flows incorporating contractual cash flows as well as estimated cash flows.

2. Time value of money: An interest rate is used to discount the cash flows. This rate may be the risk-free rate or it may be a risk-adjusted rate (see next point).

3. Uncertainty or risk: Since not all cash flows are the same in terms of amount, timing, and riskiness, discounted cash flow models reflect the risk or uncertainty by adjusting either the cash flows or the discount rate but generally not both in the same calculation. Uncertainty may be reflected in the numerator by applying probabilities to various cash flow scenarios. It may be incorporated in the discount rate by applying a risk premium such that the rate exceeds the risk-free rate.

Discounted Cash Flow Models

The **discounted cash flow model** is a very robust, widely accepted tool for dealing with uncertainty and the time value of money.

Two approaches are generally accepted:

1. Traditional approach: The discount rate reflects all risks in the cash flows but the cash flows are assumed to be certain.

2. Expected cash flow approach: A risk-free discount rate is used to discount cash flows that have been adjusted for uncertainty.

Traditional Approach

Under the **traditional discounted cash flow approach**, the stream of contracted cash flows is discounted, and the discount rate is adjusted to accommodate the riskiness of the cash flows. This model is best used where the cash flows are otherwise fairly certain. The discount rate would be adjusted for the credit risk that is associated with the party that is paying the cash flows. This method is useful for instruments where the cash flows are specified in the contract, such as fixed interest and principal payments. It is not very useful for more complex instruments where the cash flows may be variable for other reasons than the credit risk.

Assume that Company A has issued a 10% bond that is due in 10 years and has a face value of $100. Assume further that the risk-adjusted market rate that reflects the credit risk of Company A is 10%. This rate would be the rate that the market would demand of Company A, given the specific credit risk. The bond's present value would be calculated as follows:

> PV $1 at 10% × Principal (10 years) + PV of an annuity of $10 for 10 years at 10%
> (All discounted at 10%) = $100

Expected Cash Flow Approach

Under the **expected cash flow approach**, the discount rate is the risk-free rate and the cash flow uncertainty is dealt with by using probabilities. The projected cash flows reflect the uncertainty in terms of amount and timing using probability weighting. This model is more flexible and is useful where the financial instruments have variable cash flows.

In this case, assume that the instrument has a variable cash flow. Assume that there is a 20% chance of a payment in three years of $30 and an 80% chance of a payment in three years of $60. If the risk-free rate is 5%, the expected cash flows (incorporating the credit risk) are as follows:

> 20% × $30 + 80% × $60 = $54
> PV $54 at 5% (3 years) = $54 × 0.86384 = $46.65

What Do the Numbers Mean?

Note that these methods may be used for valuing items at fair value, estimating liabilities, or conducting impairment tests. Subsequent chapters will examine these uses in greater detail.

When fair values are used to value a company's own debt, interesting results may arise. Where the company's own risk of not being able to repay the debt has increased, using fair value to revalue the debt results in a gain!

For instance, assume a company that is normally profitable has suffered losses in the current year. As a result of being less profitable, it has less cash and is now cash squeezed. Its ability to repay its own debt may now be called into question. The company's liquidity risk has increased. From a creditor perspective, the credit risk for this company has increased. In other words, there is a greater risk that the company will not repay the amount owed. If the company uses amortized cost to value the liability, the debt is not revalued in the financial statements. However, if fair value is used to measure the liability, the debt must be revalued. Where the fair value is measured using discounted cash flow, the entity must now use a higher discount rate to reflect the increased risk. The higher discount rate means a lower present value.

Therefore, the debt is written down with the following journal entry: debit liability and credit gain. This results in a better debt to equity ratio and higher income even though the company is worse off. The IASB has implemented a change in the current accounting standard. IFRS 9 requires that any gains resulting from the revaluation of a company's own debt (that are due to deteriorating ability to repay the debt) must be booked through other comprehensive income. Note that they do not increase EPS, but they still increase comprehensive income.

SUMMARY OF LEARNING OBJECTIVE FOR APPENDIX 2A

7 Understand in greater detail how fair value is measured.

Fair value measurement is a market-based approach that incorporates the specific attributes of the asset/liability being measured, the valuation premise (how the asset/liability is to be used), the principal market, and the valuation technique. Since market prices are not always available, valuation models are used to measure the value. Inputs to these models are either observable in the market or not. Observable inputs are most useful since they are more objective. The fair value hierarchy establishes three levels of inputs, with level 1 being the highest and best type of input (based on observable market prices). Because level 3 inputs are more subjective, additional disclosures are required. Valuation models include discounted cash flow and options pricing models.

KEY TERMS

discounted cash flow model, p. 70
expected cash flow approach, p. 70
fair value hierarchy, p. 68

highest and best use, p. 67
most advantageous market, p. 67
principal market, p. 67

traditional discounted cash flow
  approach, p. 70

Quiz

Note: All assignment material with an asterisk (*) relates to the appendix to the chapter.

Brief Exercises

(LO 2) BE2-1   Indicate the qualitative characteristic of financial information being described in each item below:

(a) Financial statements should include all information necessary to portray the underlying transactions.

(b) Financial information should make a difference in a user's decision-making.

(c) Financial information should not favour one user or stakeholder over another.

(d) Financial information should reflect the economic substance of business events or transactions.

(e) Financial information should help users assess the impact of past, present, or future events.

(f) Financial information must be reliable and without errors or omissions.

(g) Financial information should help users confirm or correct their previous expectations.

(h) Financial information should be reported and measured in a similar way within a company and between different companies.

(i) Financial information should be of sufficient quality and clarity to permit reasonably informed users to assess the information's significance.

(j) Financial information should be available to users before it loses its ability to be decision-useful.

(k) Knowledgeable, independent users should be able to achieve similar results and consensus when accounting for a particular financial transaction.

(LO 2) BE2-2   Identify which qualitative characteristic of accounting information is best described in each item below. (Do not simply use relevance and representational faithfulness.)

(a) The annual reports of Melissa Corp. are audited by public accountants.

(b) Able Corp. and Mona, Inc. both use the straight-line depreciation method.

(c) Swedish Corp. issues its quarterly reports within five days after each quarter ends.

(d) Philips Inc. segregates information that relates to one of its two subsidiaries that was disposed of in the year but was included in its consolidated statements for prior years.

(e) The CFO of WebDesign stresses that factual, truthful, unbiased information is the overriding consideration when preparing WebDesign's financial information.

(f) EB Energy Inc. appreciates that financial information may be misrepresented or misinterpreted if all pertinent information is not included.

(g) Wright Industries exercises due care and professional judgement in developing all estimates and assumptions used to prepare its financial information.

(LO 2, 4) BE2-3   What principle(s) from the conceptual framework does Henday Limited use in each of the following situations?

(a) Henday includes the activities of its subsidiaries in its financial statements.

(b) Henday was involved in litigation with Kinshasa Ltd. over a product malfunction. This litigation is disclosed in the financial statements.

(c) Henday allocates the cost of its tangible assets over the period when it expects to receive revenue from these assets.

(d) Henday records the purchase of a new packaging machine at its cash equivalent price.

(e) Henday prepares quarterly financial statements for its users.

(f) In preparing its financial statements, Henday assesses its ability to continue to operate for the foreseeable future.

(g) Henday records revenue when risks and rewards are passed to the purchaser.

(h) Henday records its agricultural inventory at fair value. The company feels that this market-based value is more relevant, objective, and verifiable.

(LO 3) BE2-4   Discuss whether the following items would meet the definition of an asset using the IFRS definitions currently in place. If so, explain with reference to the appropriate criteria.

(a) Maxwell Ltd. owns a corporate fleet of cars for senior management's use in performing work duties.

(b) A franchisee has a licence to operate a Tim Hortons restaurant.

  (c) Customized manufacturing machinery can only be used for one product line and has a small and limited customer market.

  (d) The parent company has guaranteed the operating line of credit of its subsidiary, which resulted in the subsidiary obtaining a lower interest rate than it would otherwise receive. Is the guarantee an asset for the subsidiary?

  (e) FreshWater Inc. bottles and sells the spring water from a natural spring near its property. Is the natural spring an asset of the company?

  (f) Mountain Ski Resort Ltd. often has to use its snow-making machine to make snow for its hills and trails when there is not enough natural snowfall. Is the snow an asset for Mountain Ski?

(LO 3) BE2-5   Refer to BE2-4. Discuss whether the items identified would be considered assets if the definition proposed by IFRS were applied.

(LO 3) BE2-6   Discuss whether the following items would meet the definition of a liability using the criteria currently in place under IFRS. If so, explain with reference to the appropriate criteria.

  (a) Environmental remediation when a chemical spill has occurred. This spill has violated an existing law and statute. Does a liability for cleanup exist?

  (b) Environmental remediation after a chemical spill has occurred. No existing law or statute has been broken. Does a liability for cleanup exist?

  (c) As part of its contract with the government, a logging company must replant one tree for each tree it cuts. Does a liability for replanting exist?

  (d) A logging company has a corporate policy of always replanting trees and advertises this fact in its corporate and marketing brochures. Does a liability for replanting exist?

(LO 3) BE2-7   Repeat BE2-6 but apply the definition of a liability proposed by the IASB and FASB.

(LO 3, 4) BE2-8   Assets are the cornerstone of financial reporting; often it is unclear whether an expenditure is an asset or an expense. For each of the transactions described below, consider if the expenditure should be recorded as an asset or as an expense. Be sure to include a discussion of the specific criteria in your response. Assume all items are material.

  (a) Akamu Corp. pays legal fees of $2,500 in purchasing land to be used as a parking lot.

  (b) Luca, Inc. pays $7,000 to pave the driveway to its office building.

  (c) On January 1, Alan & Cheng, Chartered Accountants, pays six months' office rent to cover the month of January and the next five months.

  (d) Mattamy Inc. pays $190,000 to workers for construction of a building to be used as its corporate headquarters.

  (e) Pharma Inc. incurs legal fees of $5,500 for registering a patent for its product.

  (f) Delhi's Florists pays wages of $2,100 for November to an employee who drives its delivery truck.

  (g) Delhi's Florists pays $4,500 for flowers to be delivered to its premises.

(LO 3) BE2-9   For each item that follows, indicate which element of the financial statements it belongs to:

(a) Retained earnings	(f) Loss on sale of equipment
(b) Sales Revenue	(g) Interest payable
(c) Acquired goodwill	(h) Dividends
(d) Inventory	(i) Issuance of common shares
(e) Depreciation	

(LO 4) BE2-10   For each item that follows, identify the foundational principle of accounting that best describes it.

  (a) For its annual reports, Sumsong Corp. divides its economic activities into 12-month periods.

  (b) Sullivan, Inc. does not adjust amounts in its financial statements for the effects of inflation.

  (c) Kiran Ltd. reports current and non-current classifications in its statement of financial position.

  (d) In preparing its consolidated financial statements, Paddy Corporation assesses if it has the power to direct the other entity's activities.

  (e) Jaspreet Corporation reports revenue in its income statement when it is earned even if cash has not been collected.

  (f) Duong Enterprises normally includes business transactions in its general ledger when the item meets the definition of an element (as defined in the conceptual framework) and the item is measurable.

(g) Gomez, Inc. provides information about pending lawsuits in the notes to its financial statements.

(h) Douglas Farms reports land on its statement of financial position at the amount paid to acquire it, even though the estimated fair value is higher.

(i) King Corporation uses fair value measurements for its financial instruments portfolio.

(j) Magnificent Inc. assumes that it will continue to operate into the foreseeable future.

(LO 1, 2, 5) BE2-11 What is the objective of financial reporting? For each of the situations discussed below, explain the qualitative characteristics of financial information that help provide decision-useful information to users.

(a) Marcus Corp. has a management bonus plan based on net income. Marcus records revenue only after the risks and rewards of ownership of the goods it sells have passed to the customer.

(b) Sosa Ltd. is a real estate company that holds land for eventual sale to developers. Sosa provides fair value information on its property holdings to its users.

(c) Mohawk Inc. has entered into a rental agreement that will eventually transfer ownership of the manufacturing equipment to Mohawk at the end of three years. Irrespective of the legal documentation, Mohawk will account for this transaction based on its economic impact to the company.

(d) Standard setters must ensure that accounting standards do not favour one set of users over another or one industry over another.

(LO 7) *BE2-12 Medici Patriarchs purchased the following investments during 2014:

(a) 1,000 shares of Private Limited, a start-up company. The value of this investment was based on an internally developed model.

(b) 5,000 shares of CIBC, a public company listed on the TSX.

(c) $15,000 of corporate bonds. Although these bonds do not trade in an active market, their value closely resembles movements in the Bank of Canada bond rate.

Based on the discussion in Appendix 2A, indicate at which level in the fair value hierarchy these investment values will fall.

(LO 7) *BE2-13 Lucky Enterprises is using a discounted cash flow model. Identify which model Lucky might use to estimate discounted fair value under each scenario, and calculate the fair value:

Scenario 1: Cash flows are fairly certain
$100/year for 5 years
Risk-adjusted discount rate is 6%
Risk-free discount rate is 3%

Scenario 2: Cash flows are uncertain
75% probability that cash flows will be $100 in 5 years
25% probability that cash flows will be $75 in 5 years
Risk-adjusted discount rate is 6%
Risk-free discount rate is 3%

Exercises

(LO 2, 5) E2-1 (Qualitative Characteristics) The conceptual framework identifies the fundamental and enhancing qualitative characteristics that make accounting information useful.

Instructions

Answer the following questions related to these qualitative characteristics.

(a) Which quality of financial information makes it possible for users to confirm or correct prior expectations?

(b) Identify some of the trade-offs and constraints in financial reporting.

(c) The U.S. Securities and Exchange Commission chairman once noted that if it becomes accepted or expected that accounting principles are determined or modified in order to achieve goals that do not involve economic measurement, we risk a serious loss in confidence in the credibility of our financial information system. Which qualitative characteristic of accounting information should ensure that this situation will not occur?

(d) Owens Corp. chooses to account for a transaction based simply on its legal form. Is this acceptable?

(e) Companies in the mining industry defer losses on their properties because recognizing such losses immediately could have adverse economic consequences for the industry. Which qualitative characteristic of accounting information is not followed?

(f) Only Once Ltd. provides overly complicated descriptions and explanations in its statement notes and provides only aggregated totals on the face of its financial statements. Which qualitative characteristic of accounting information is not followed?

(g) Baskins does not issue its first-quarter report until after the second quarter's results are reported. Which qualitative characteristic of accounting information is not followed?

(h) Predictive value is an ingredient of which qualitative characteristics of useful information?

(i) Vittorio Inc. is the only company in its industry to depreciate its plant assets on a straight-line basis. Which qualitative characteristic is not present?

(j) Green Gable Corp. has tried to determine the replacement cost of its inventory. Three different appraisers arrive at substantially different amounts for this value. The president then decides to use the middle value for external reports. Which qualitative characteristic of information is lacking in these data? (Do not use reliability or representational faithfulness.)

(k) The controller at Owens Inc. noticed that a material transaction was not included in the year-end financial results. Which qualitative characteristic is not present?

(LO 3) E2-2 (Elements of Financial Statements) The elements that are most directly related to measuring an enterprise's performance and financial status follow:

Assets	Expenses	Liabilities
Gains	Equity	Revenues
Losses		

Instructions

(a) Indicate which element is being described below. For any item that is an asset or liability, consider if the item qualifies under both the definition currently in place and that proposed under IFRS:

1. Arises from peripheral or incidental transactions.

2. Obliges a transfer of resources because of a present, enforceable obligation.

3. Increases in the ownership interest through issuance of shares.

4. Cash dividends to owners (declared and paid).

5. An expenditure that has future economic benefit.

6. Decreases in assets during the period for the payment of taxes.

7. Arises from income-generating activities that are the entity's ongoing major or central operations.

8. Is the residual interest in the enterprise's assets after deducting its liabilities.

9. Increases assets during the period through the sale of a product.

10. Decreases assets during the period by purchasing the company's own shares.

(b) Indicate which element listed above is being illustrated in the examples that follow. Consider both the current and proposed definitions of assets and liabilities.

1. NotesCo. has a written contract to receive money from the sale of copies of future recordings of music yet to be written.

2. ReadyMart Inc. has inventory out on consignment at a local retailer waiting for sale to the final customer.

3. Music Corp. has a written contract to deliver a percentage of future music revenues (royalties) from the sale of existing recordings.

(LO 4) E2-3 (Foundational Principles) The foundational principles of accounting are as follows:

Recognition/Derecognition	Measurement	Presentation and Disclosure
1. Economic entity	5. Periodicity	10. Full disclosure
2. Control	6. Monetary unit	
3. Revenue recognition and realization	7. Going concern	
4. Matching	8. Historical cost	
	9. Fair value	

Instructions

For each situation that follows, identify by its number the foundational principle above that best describes it.

(a) Allocates expenses to revenues in the proper period.

(b) Indicates that market value changes after the purchase are not recorded in the accounts unless impairment exists. (Do not use the revenue recognition principle.)

(c) Ensures that all relevant financial information is reported.

(d) Is why plant assets are not reported at their liquidation value. (Do not use the historical cost principle.)

(e) Related to the economic entity principle, defines the entities that should be consolidated in the financial statements.

(f) Indicates that personal and business record keeping should be separately maintained.

(g) Separates financial information into time periods for reporting purposes.

(h) Permits the use of market value valuation in certain specific situations.

(i) Requires passing of risks and rewards, measurability, and collectibility before recording the transaction.

(j) Assumes that the dollar is the measuring unit for reporting on financial performance.

(LO 4) **E2-4** **(Foundational Principles)** The following are operational guidelines and practices that have developed over time for financial reporting.

1. Price-level changes (inflation and deflation) are not recognized in the accounting records.

2. Financial information is presented so that reasonably prudent investors will not be misled.

3. Property, plant, and equipment are capitalized and depreciated over the periods that they benefit.

4. There is no intent to liquidate the company's operations or activities.

5. Market value is used by companies for the valuation of certain securities that are regularly bought and sold.

6. After initial acquisition, the entity values land at its original transaction price.

7. All significant post–balance sheet events are reported.

8. Revenue is recorded at the point of sale.

9. All important aspects of bond indentures are presented in financial statements.

10. The rationale for accrual accounting is stated.

11. The use of consolidated statements is justified.

12. Reporting must be done at defined time intervals.

13. An allowance for doubtful accounts is established.

14. Goodwill is recorded only at the time of a business combination.

15. Sales commission costs are charged to expense.

Instructions

Select the foundational principle that best justifies each of these procedures and practices.

(LO 1, 2, 4) **E2-5** **(Foundational Principles)** Examples of some operational guidelines used by accountants follow.

1. The treasurer of Sweet Grapes Corp. would like to prepare financial statements only during downturns in the company's wine production, which occur periodically when the grape crop fails. He states that it is at such times that the statements could be most easily prepared. The company would never allow more than 30 months to pass without statements being prepared.

2. Tower Manufacturing Ltd. decided to manufacture its own widgets because it would be cheaper than buying them from an outside supplier. In an attempt to make its statements more comparable with those of its competitors, Tower charged its inventory account for what it felt the widgets would have cost if they had been purchased from an outside supplier. (Do not use the revenue recognition principle.)

3. Cargo Discount Centres buys its merchandise by the truckload and train carload. Cargo does not include any transportation costs in calculating the cost of its ending inventory. Such costs, although they vary from period to period, are always material in amount.

4. Quick & Healthy, a fast-food company, sells franchises for $100,000, accepting a $5,000 down payment and a 25-year note for the remainder. Quick & Healthy promises for three years to assist in site selection, building, and management training. Quick & Healthy records the full $100,000 franchise fee as revenue when the contract is signed.

5. Mustafa Corp. faces a possible government expropriation (i.e., takeover) of its foreign facilities and possible losses on sums that are owed by various customers who are almost bankrupt. The company president has decided that these possibilities should not be noted on the financial statements because Mustafa still hopes that these events will not take place.

6. Maurice Morris, owner of Rare Bookstore, Inc., bought a computer for his own use. He paid for the computer by writing a cheque on the bookstore chequing account and charged the Office Equipment account.

7. Brock Inc. decides that it will be selling its subsidiary, Breck Inc., in a few years. Brock has excluded Breck's activities from its consolidated financial results.

8. Wilhelm Corporation expensed the purchase of new manufacturing equipment.

9. A large lawsuit has been filed against Mahoney Corp. Mahoney has recorded a loss and related estimated liability that is equal to the maximum possible amount that it feels it might lose. Mahoney is confident, however, that either it will win the suit or it will owe a much smaller amount.

Instructions

(a) Discuss the usefulness of a conceptual framework.

(b) For each of the situations above, list the foundational principle or qualitative characteristic of financial information that has been violated.

E2-6 (Qualitative Characteristics) In general, financial information should include all relevant information that faithfully represents the economic substance of business transactions.

Instructions

Discuss whether it is possible for financial information to have all of the qualitative characteristics.

(LO 2, **E2-7 (Conceptual Framework—Comprehensive)** The following are transactions recorded by Bounce Corporation
3, 4) during the current year.

1. Ordinary operating maintenance on equipment was recorded as follows:

Equipment	2,000	
Accounts Payable		2,000

2. The company received an advance on a custom order for merchandise that will be shipped during the next accounting year.

Cash	18,000	
Sales Revenue		18,000

3. Bounce Corporation is holding inventory on consignment for Rubber Ltd. Bounce will only pay Rubber when a sale is made to a customer. It has made the following entry for the inventory:

Inventory	15,000	
Accounts Payable		15,000

4. On the last day of the accounting period, a 12-month insurance policy was purchased. The insurance coverage is for the next accounting year.

Insurance Expense	4,000	
Cash		4,000

Instructions

For each transaction, determine which component of the conceptual framework (i.e., qualitative characteristic, element, or principle) was violated, if any, and give the entry that should have been recorded if there was a violation.

(Adapted from CGA-Canada Examination.)

(LO 4) **E2-8 (Full Disclosure Principle)** The following information is for Brittany, Inc.

1. To be more concise, the company decided that only net income should be reported on the income statement. Details on revenues, cost of goods sold, and expenses were also omitted from the notes.

2. Equipment purchases of $270,000 were partly financed during the year by issuing a $110,000 note payable. The company offset the equipment against the note payable and reported plant assets at $160,000. No information has been provided in the notes.

3. During the year, an assistant controller for the company embezzled $50,000. Brittany's net income for the year was $2.3 million. Neither the assistant controller nor the money has been found. No information has been provided in the notes.

4. Brittany has reported its ending inventory at $2.7 million in the financial statements. No other information on inventories is presented in the financial statements and related notes.

5. The company changed its method of amortizing equipment from the double-declining balance to the straight-line method. This change is not mentioned anywhere in the financial statements.

Instructions

(a) Explain the meaning and implications of the full disclosure principle and how such information may be provided to users.

(b) For each of the situations above, discuss whether Brittany has followed acceptable accounting and disclosure practices.

(LO 4) E2-9   (Going Concern Assumption)

Instructions

(a) Explain the meaning and implications of the going concern assumption in financial accounting.

(b) If the going concern assumption did not apply in accounting, how would this affect the amounts shown in the financial statements for the following items?

1. Land
2. Unamortized bond premium
3. Depreciation expense
4. Inventory
5. Prepaid insurance

(LO 4, 6) E2-10   (Revenue Recognition Principle) The following independent situations require professional judgement for determining when to recognize revenue from the transactions.

1. Air Yukon sells you an advance purchase airline ticket in September for your flight home at Christmas.

2. Better Buy Ltd. sells you a home theatre on a "no money down, no interest, and no payments for one year" promotional deal.

3. The Centurions baseball team sells season tickets to games on-line. Fans can purchase the tickets at any time, although the season doesn't officially begin until April. It runs from April through October.

4. Designers End Ltd. sells you a sweater. In August, you placed the order using Designers' on-line catalogue. The sweater arrives in September and you charge it to your Designers End credit card. You receive and pay the credit card bill in October.

Instructions

(a) Explain when revenue is historically recognized under the current revenue recognition principle.

(b) Identify when revenue should be recognized in each of the situations under the current revenue recognition model.

(LO 7) *E2-11   (Fair Value Principle) Meerkat Industries would like to determine the fair value of its manufacturing facility in London, Ontario. The facility consists of land, building, and manufacturing equipment.

Instructions

(a) Identify some of the considerations that are involved in a fair value measurement.

(b) Explain the various levels of input in the fair value hierarchy.

(c) Using the fair value hierarchy, discuss the level 1, 2, and 3 types of inputs that Meerkat could use to value each asset as well as its facility altogether.

*E2-12   (Discounted Cash Flow Models) Hoda Inc. owns 25% of the common shares of Willard Corp. The other 75% are owned by the Willard family. Hoda acquired the shares eight years ago through a financing transaction. Each year, Hoda has received a dividend from Willard. Willard has been in business for 60 years, and continues to have strong operations and cash flows. Hoda must determine the fair value of this investment at its year end. Since there is no market on which the shares are traded, Hoda must use a discounted cash flow model to determine fair value.

Hoda management intends to hold the shares for five more years, at which time, they will sell the shares to the Willard family under an existing agreement for $1 million. There is no uncertainty in this amount. Management expects to receive dividends of $80,000 for each of the five years, although there is a 20% chance that dividends could be $50,000 each year. The risk-free rate is 4% and the risk-adjusted rate is 6%.

Instructions

(a) Identify some of the items Hoda will need to consider in determining the fair value of the investment.

(b) Calculate the fair value of the investment in Willard using the traditional approach.

(c) Calculate the fair value of the investment using the expected cash flow approach.

(d) In this case, which discounted cash flow model is the best and why?

Problems

P2-1 Foundational principles of financial reporting may be grouped into four categories: recognition/derecognition, measurement, presentation, and disclosure.

Instructions

Briefly describe what is meant by these terms.

P2-2 Fusters, Inc. issues audited financial statements to its creditors and is required to maintain certain covenants based on its debt to equity ratio and return on assets. In addition, management of Fusters receives a bonus partially based on revenues for the year. Information related to Fusters, Inc. follows.

1. Depreciation expense on the building for the year was $45,000. Because the building was increasing in value during the year, the controller decided not to record any depreciation expense in the current year.

2. New legislation was discussed by the government that would require new pollution control technology for companies such as Fusters. Prior to this, Fusters had been complying with all current requirements and otherwise believed that it was acting in an environmentally responsible manner. In anticipation of this legislation being passed next year, Fusters expects it will need to upgrade its equipment and has booked the following entry:

Equipment	21,000	
Accounts Payable		21,000

3. During the year, the company sold certain equipment for $285,000, recognizing a gain of $69,000. Because the controller believed that new equipment would be needed in the near future, the controller decided to defer the gain and amortize it over the life of the new equipment that would soon be purchased.

4. An order for $61,500 has been received from a customer on January 2, 2014, for products on hand. This order was shipped f.o.b. shipping point on January 9, 2014. The company made the following entry in 2013:

Accounts Receivable	61,500	
Sales Revenue		61,500

Instructions

(a) Discuss the reporting objectives of the users of Fusters' financial statements.

(b) Comment on the appropriateness of Fusters, Inc.'s accounting procedures and their impact on the company's financial statement users. Use the current conceptual framework (as opposed to the proposed conceptual framework).

(c) Discuss whether there are alternatives available under IFRS to provide the reporting desired by Fusters' management.

P2-3 Transactions from Lucky Bamboo, Inc.'s current year follow.

1. Lucky Bamboo, Inc. thinks it should dispose of its excess land. While the book value is $50,000, current market prices are depressed and only $25,000 is expected upon disposal. The following journal entry was made:

Loss on Disposal of Land	25,000	
Land		25,000

2. Merchandise inventory that cost $630,000 was reported on the statement of financial position at $690,000, which is the expected selling price less estimated selling costs. The following entry was made to record this increase in value:

Inventory	60,000	
Sales Revenue		60,000

3. The company is being sued for $500,000 by a customer who claims damages for personal injury that was allegedly caused by a defective product. Company lawyers feel extremely confident that the company will have no liability for damages resulting from the situation. Nevertheless, the company decides to make the following entry:

Litigation Expense	450,000	
Litigation Liability		450,000

4. Because the general level of prices increased during the current year, Lucky Bamboo, Inc. determined that there was a $16,000 understatement of depreciation expense on its equipment and decided to record it in its accounts. The following entry was made:

Depreciation Expense	16,000	
Accumulated Depreciation—Equipment		16,000

5. Lucky Bamboo, Inc. has been concerned about whether intangible assets could generate cash in case of liquidation. As a result, goodwill arising from a business acquisition during the current year and recorded at $800,000 was written off as follows:

Retained Earnings	800,000	
Goodwill		800,000

6. Because of a "fire sale," equipment that was obviously worth $200,000 was acquired at a bargain price of $155,000. The following entry was made:

Equipment	200,000	
Cash		155,000
Revenue		45,000

Digging Deeper

Instructions

In each of the above situations, discuss the appropriateness of the journal entries in terms of generally accepted accounting principles. For purposes of your discussion, assume that the financial statements, particularly net income, will be used by the court in a divorce settlement for the company president's wife.

P2-4 Accounting information provides useful data about business transactions and events. The people who provide and use financial reports must often select and evaluate accounting alternatives. The conceptual framework that was discussed in this chapter examines the characteristics of accounting information that make it useful for decision-making. It also points out that various limitations that are part of the measurement and reporting process can make it necessary to trade off or sacrifice some of the characteristics of useful information.

Instructions

(a) For each of the following pairs of qualitative characteristics, give an example of a situation in which one of the characteristics may be sacrificed for a gain in the other:

1. Relevance and verifiability
2. Relevance and comparability
3. Relevance and timeliness
4. Relevance and understandability

(b) What criterion should be used to evaluate trade-offs between information characteristics?

P2-5 You are hired to review the accounting records of Sheridan Corporation (a public corporation) before it closes its revenue and expense accounts as at December 31, 2014, the end of its current fiscal year. The following information comes to your attention.

1. During the current year, Sheridan Corporation changed its shipment policy from f.o.b. destination to f.o.b shipping point. This would result in an additional $50,000 of revenue being recorded for fiscal 2014.

2. The estimated useful life of its manufacturing equipment was reviewed by management and increased by five years. This reduced depreciation expense by $50,000 during fiscal 2014.

3. When the statement of financial position was prepared, detailed information about the amount of cash on deposit in each of several banks was omitted. Only the total amount of cash under a caption "Cash in banks" was presented.

4. During the current year, Sheridan Corporation purchased an undeveloped piece of land for $320,000. The company spent $80,000 on subdividing the land and getting it ready for sale. A property appraisal at the end of the year indicated that the land was now worth $500,000. Although none of the lots was sold, the company recognized revenue of $180,000, less related expenses of $80,000, for a net income on the project of $100,000. The company has historically used the cost model for this type of property.

5. For several years, the company used the FIFO method for inventory valuation purposes. During the current year, the president noted that all the other companies in the industry had switched to the moving average method. The company decided not to switch to moving average because net income would decrease by $830,000.

6. During fiscal 2014, new government legislation was passed requiring companies like Sheridan to install additional health and safety devices in their offices by 2019. Although Sheridan does not intend to retrofit the required new devices until 2019, an accrual for $375,500 has been established in the year-end financial statements for the future installation costs.

7. To maintain customer goodwill, Sheridan voluntarily recalled some products during the year. Sheridan has not established an accrual and is recording the returns as they happen.

Instructions

State whether or not you agree with each of the accounting decisions made by Sheridan Corporation. Explain your reasoning and, wherever possible, support your answers by referring to the generally accepted accounting principles that apply to the circumstances.

P2-6 The following transactions fall somewhere in the continuum of the choices in accounting decision-making that are shown in Illustration 2-5.

1. The company president approaches one of the company's creditors to ask for a modification of the repayment terms so that they extend beyond the current year. This would make the liabilities long-term rather than short-term and would improve the company's current ratio.

2. The controller determines that significant amounts of capital assets are impaired and should be written off. Coincidentally, the company is currently showing lower levels of net income, but expects better results in the following years.

3. The company management decides to use FIFO as opposed to weighted average since it more closely approximates the flow of costs.

4. The vice-president of finance decides to capitalize interest during the self-construction of only one of its properties. This policy will increase net income and several profitability ratios.

5. The business owner enters into an arrangement with a business associate whereby they will buy each other's merchandise before year end. The merchandise will then be shipped to customers after year end from the holding company's warehouse.

6. The assets and liabilities of an investment have been consolidated into Maher Company's annual financial statements. Maher Company does not have the power to direct the investee's activities.

Instructions

For each situation, state where it falls in the continuum of choices in decision-making.

P2-7 A Special Committee on Financial Reporting proposed the following constraints related to financial reporting.

1. Business reporting should exclude information outside of management's expertise or for which management is not the best source, such as information about competitors.

2. Management should not be required to report information that would significantly harm the company's competitive position.

3. Management should not be required to provide forecast financial statements. Rather, management should provide information that helps users forecast for themselves the company's financial future.

4. Other than for financial statements, management need report only the information it knows. That is, management should be under no obligation to gather information it does not have, or does not need, in order to manage the business.

5. Companies should present certain elements of business reporting only if users and management agree they should be reported—a concept of flexible reporting.

Instructions

For each item, briefly discuss how the proposed constraint addresses concerns about the costs and benefits of financial reporting.

P2-8 Recently, your Uncle Warren, who knows that you always have your eye out for a profitable investment, has discussed the possibility of your purchasing some corporate bonds that he just learned of. He suggests that you may wish to get in on the ground floor of this deal. The bonds being issued by Jingle Corp. are 10-year debentures, which promise a 40% rate of return. Jingle manufactures novelty and party items.

You have told Uncle Warren that unless you can take a look at Jingle's financial statements, you would not feel comfortable about such an investment. Thinking that this is the chance of a lifetime, Uncle Warren has obtained a copy of Jingle's most recent, unaudited financial statements, which are a year old. These statements were prepared by Mrs. Jingle. You look over these statements, and they are quite impressive.

The statement of financial position showed a debt to equity ratio of 1:10 and, for the year shown, the company reported net income of $2,424,240.

The financial statements are not shown in comparison with amounts from other years. In addition, there are no significant note disclosures about inventory valuation, depreciation methods, loan agreements, and so on.

Instructions

Write a letter to Uncle Warren explaining why it would be unwise to base an investment decision on the financial statements that he has given you. Refer to the concepts developed in this chapter.

Cases

Refer to the Case Primer to help you answer these cases.

Real World Emphasis

CA2-1   Bre-X Minerals (Bre-X), a small mining company, announced in the early 1990s that it had discovered a fairly significant gold deposit in Indonesia. The company's shares skyrocketed from pennies a share to over $280 per share. Subsequently, it was discovered that the company had been "salting the samples" [42] and that there was little, if any, gold there. This information was not disclosed to the market until long after it was discovered that there was no gold. Certain parties who had access to this information benefited; however, many investors lost a significant amount of money.

Many investors lost millions of dollars, including the Ontario Municipal Employees Retirement System and the Ontario Teachers' Pension Plan. Investors sued the company and its management for providing misleading information.

Instructions

Using the conceptual framework, identify and analyze the financial reporting issues.

Ethics

CA2-2   Bennett Environmental Inc. operates in North America. Its basic business is high-temperature treatment services for contaminated soil. In its 2011 financial statements, the company had a loss of $9.3 million (and an accumulated deficit of $43.7 million).

In the notes to the financial statements, the company stated that it deferred certain transportation costs and recorded them as assets. These costs relate to shipping contaminated materials to the treatment plant. They are reimbursable under the terms of the contract. Per note 19, the company can only run efficiently when it operates continuously for extended periods; however, demand for the services is sporadic. Therefore, the company's business model is structured such that it shuts down operations and otherwise stockpiles inventory. These shutdown periods are followed by active periods during which it processes the stockpiled inventory. Revenues for 2011, a shutdown period, were $0.

In addition, the company received a subpoena from the U.S. Department of Justice regarding conspiracy to commit fraud with respect to the bidding process on a government process. During 2009, the courts stayed proceedings, essentially halting the proceedings for the time being.

Real World Emphasis

Instructions

Assume that the financial statements must be issued prior to the resolution of the lawsuit. Discuss the financial reporting issues.

CA2-3   The statement that follows about Timber Company appeared in a financial magazine:

> The land and timber holdings are now carried on the company's books at a mere $100 million (U.S.). The value of the timber alone is variously estimated at $1 billion to $3 billion and is rising all the time. The understatement is pretty severe, conceded company management, who noted, "We have a whole stream of profit nobody sees and there is no way to show it on our books."

Instructions

Act as an analyst and discuss the financial reporting issues. Assume that this is a public company.

Writing Assignments

WA2-1   Roger Chang has some questions about the theoretical framework in which standards are set. He knows that standard setters are continually striving to develop a conceptual framework for the formulation of accounting theory. Yet Roger's supervisors have said that these theoretical frameworks have little value in the practical sense—in the real world. Roger did notice that accounting standards seem to be established after the fact rather than before—in other words, after problems occur. He thought this meant the theory could be poorly structured but he never really questioned the process at school because he was too busy doing the homework. He also noted that the conceptual framework for IFRS is worded differently from the one for ASPE and that some of the concepts are different.

Roger thinks that he might feel less anxious about accounting theory and accounting terminology if he could identify the basic concepts and definitions that are accepted by the profession and then consider them in light of his current work. By doing this, he hopes to develop an appropriate connection between theory and practice. He also wonders if everyone should use the same framework.

Instructions

Explain to Roger the purpose and benefit of a conceptual framework.

WA2-2 In the IASB standard-setting conceptual framework, the word "reliability" has been replaced with "faithful representation." This has caused much discussion among preparers of financial information. This change has led to other implications related to substance over form, neutrality, conservatism, and the ability of entities to "override" a standard in very rare circumstances.

Instructions

Discuss the following questions. (You may find the IASB's *Basis for Conclusions to the Exposure Draft: Conceptual Framework for Financial Reporting: The Objective of Financial Reporting and Qualitative Characteristics and Constraints of Decision-Useful Financial Reporting Information*, of May 29, 2008, helpful in your discussion. It is available on the IASB website at: www.ifrs.org.)

(a) "Faithful representation" has replaced the term "reliability" as a fundamental qualitative characteristic of financial information. What does faithful representation mean and how does this differ from reliability? Why was the term "reliability" replaced?

(b) What does "substance over form" mean? Give examples of where this might be relevant.

(c) How does "conservatism" conflict with the meaning of "faithful representation"?

(d) In IAS 1, a company is allowed, in rare circumstances, to override an accounting standard if applying the standard would not result in a "true and fair view." How does this support faithful representation? Are there any enhancing characteristics that might be violated by this? If you were a financial statement user of a company that had decided to use this override, what information would you like to have disclosed in the financial statements? Why?

WA2-3 An accountant must be familiar with the concepts involved in determining the earnings of a business entity. The amount of earnings that is reported for a business entity depends on the proper recognition, in general, of revenues and expenses for a specific time period. In some situations, costs are recognized as expenses at the time of product sale; in other situations, guidelines have been developed for recognizing costs as expenses or losses by other criteria.

Instructions

(a) Explain the rationale for recognizing costs as expenses at the time of product sale.

(b) Explain how the matching principle might contradict the definition of an asset. Give examples of where this might arise. What should take precedence: the matching principle or the asset definition?

(c) What is the rationale that makes it appropriate to treat costs as expenses of a period instead of assigning them to an asset? Explain.

(d) In what general circumstances would it be appropriate to treat a cost as an asset instead of as an expense? Explain.

(e) Some expenses are assigned to specific accounting periods based on a systematic and rational allocation of asset cost. Explain the rationale for recognizing expenses in this way.

(f) Identify the conditions in which it would be appropriate to treat a cost as a loss.

(AICPA adapted)

*WA2-4 The fair value hierarchy establishes three levels of input, with level one being the best type, because it uses the most objective inputs, and level three using the most subjective inputs.

Instructions

For each of the following scenarios, identify the level of fair value input and the method that has been used and what disclosure should be provided to assist the user's understanding.

(a) A company uses the fair value method for reporting its investment property. The company hired a building appraiser who reviewed prices for sales of similar buildings in the neighbourhood to determine the property's fair market value.

(b) A company recently purchased a trademark from another company. The trademark was valued using the royalty-based approach. This approach involves estimating the amount of royalties that would have had to be paid on future sales forecasts, if the company did not own the trademark itself. Sales are estimated for the year, then royalty costs are estimated based on these sales and discounted to determine the present value of the trademark.

(c) The company owns 1,000 shares in RX Limited, a publicly traded company. The RX Limited shares were valued by looking at their closing price at the reporting date.

(d) The equipment's fair value was determined using details from a supplier price list for the replacement equipment.

(e) The company valued one of its brand names using the discounted cash flow method. The sales and costs were forecast for the next five years based on management's plans. The terminal value was determined to be 3% based on market growth rates anticipated for North America. All of the future cash flows were discounted using the company's weighted average cost of capital.

WA2-5   The proposed definition of a liability is a "present economic obligation for which the entity is the obligor." These terms can be further expanded as follows (as taken from IASB Board meeting minutes):

"Present" means at the report date that an economic obligation exists.

"Economic obligation" is an unconditional promise to incur an economic burden and is enforceable by legal or equivalent means.

Instructions

Using the definition of a liability, discuss whether or not the following scenarios would result in the recognition of a liability. (The following situations are adapted from examples provided in FASB board meetings on the Conceptual Framework—Elements Phase of June 25, 2008, and May 7, 2008.) Also explain how you might use probabilities in each scenario.

(a) Silverstrike Mines has purchased the right to mine for silver in two countries. In Country X, the environmental regulations require the company to completely fill in mining shafts greater than 15 metres when the mining operations cease or pay a fine of 250,000 euros per shaft. In Country Y, there are no environmental laws, but Silverstrike has signed a contract to fill in any mine shafts greater than 15 metres, in return for which the local government would grant it exploration rights within a 200-kilometre radius of the existing mine. It is December 31, 2014, and the company now has four operating mining shafts in Country X that are 17 metres deep. In Country Y, the company has six shafts that are only 10 metres deep. However, the company will have to dig down to 17 metres in Country Y to hit silver, and this should be completed by December 2015 with 95% certainty.

(b) Zion Limited has an employee benefit plan that will pay for medical and dental coverage after an employee leaves the company, provided the employee has worked for 15 years for the company. If the employee is terminated or leaves voluntarily before the 15 years is completed, then the company will not pay for any benefits. Historically, the company has found that only 15% of employees leave before the 15 years has passed. At the reporting date of December 31, 2014, there is one employee who is still currently employed and has been with the company for 11 years. How would the liability for this employee's benefits be determined?

(c) Beatonville's soccer team has just finished building a new soccer stadium and is now trying to raise corporate funds to help pay for the centre. The team has recently signed a contract with Masonry Limited, a large employer in the area, for sponsorship. The agreement states that in return for $2 million to be paid today, the team will allow Masonry to have its corporate name and logo on the building for eight years. At the end of eight years, the contract can be renewed, or the team will seek another sponsor.

RESEARCH AND FINANCIAL ANALYSIS

RA2-1 Teck Resources Limited

Real World Emphasis

Obtain the 2011 financial statements of **Teck Resources Limited** from SEDAR (www.sedar.com).

Instructions

(a) Using the notes to the consolidated financial statements, determine the company's revenue recognition policy. Comment on whether the company uses an aggressive or conservative method for reporting revenue.

(b) Give two examples of where historical cost information is reported in the financial statements and related notes. Give two examples where fair value information is reported in either the financial statements or related notes.

(c) When the company transitioned to IFRS, it had to restate its 2010 financial statements. Comment on the pros and cons of restating the financial statements.

(d) The company adopted IFRS in 2011. Did the move to IFRS cause comprehensive income for 2010 to increase or decrease? Why did this happen? Briefly identify the main adjustments required to move to IFRS.

RA2-2 Air Canada

Real World Emphasis

In its 2011 financial statements (Note 4), **Air Canada** has disclosed its critical estimates and judgements used in preparation of the financial statements.

Instructions

Access the 2011 annual report for Air Canada for the year ended December 31, 2011, from the company's website or SEDAR (www.sedar.com). Read Note 4 and related notes and answer the following questions.

(a) What are the main critical accounting estimates and judgements that the company discloses? Briefly outline.

(b) Why is it important that the company disclose these types of things? Consider this question from a user perspective.

(c) How significant are the related financial statement elements?

RA2-3 Retrieval of Information on Public Company

There are several commonly available indexes and reference products that help individuals locate articles that have appeared in business publications and periodicals. Articles can generally be searched by company or by subject matter. Several common sources are *Canadian Business and Current Affairs (CBCA Fulltext Business)*, *Investex Plus*, *The Wall Street Journal Index*, *Business Abstracts* (formerly the *Business Periodical Index*), and *ABI/Inform*.

Instructions

Use one of these resources to find an article about a company that interests you. Read the article and answer the following questions. (*Note:* Your library may have hard copy or CD-ROM versions of these sources or they may be available through your library's electronic database.)

(a) What is the article about?

(b) What specific information about the company is included in the article?

(c) Identify any accounting-related issues that are discussed in the article.

RA2-4 Fair Values

Using fair values came under attack in light of the credit crunch of the last decade and the related financial crisis. Some have even accused fair value accounting of exacerbating the crisis. Access the following articles:

"Discussing the Credit Crunch," *IASB INSIGHT Journal*, Q1 and Q2 (from www.iasb.co.uk), and "Fair Values: When the Engine Overheats, Don't Blame the Oil Light," by Paul Cherry and Ian Hague, *CA Magazine*, June/July 2009 (from www.camagazine.com).

Instructions

Using the articles, address the following questions:

(a) What impact does using fair values to report assets and liabilities have on the financial statements?

(b) Why do some believe that using fair values is not appropriate for financial reporting? Discuss this in light of the financial crisis that began in 2007.

(c) What are the arguments to support using fair values in financial reporting?

(d) Do you think fair value accounting should be used in the preparation of financial statements?

(e) Does IFRS allow for greater use of fair values? Discuss giving examples.

ENDNOTES

[1] "Conceptual Framework for Financial Accounting and Reporting: Elements of Financial Statements and Their Measurement," FASB discussion memorandum (Stamford, CT: FASB, 1976), p. 1 of the "Scope and Implications of the Conceptual Framework Project" section.

[2] Adapted from William C. Norby, *The Financial Analysts Journal*, March/April 1982, p. 22.

[3] IFRS does not define other comprehensive income as a separate element of the financial statements as it simply contains other elements such as revenues, expenses, gains, and losses. It is considered to be a subclassification of the income statement. In addition, IFRS defines income as including both revenues and gains in paragraph 4.29 of the Conceptual Framework. It defines expenses as also including losses (4.33).

[4] IASB *IFRS Conceptual Framework* Chapter 1 OB4.

[5] Investors and creditors are assumed to be the primary or key users. For not-for-profit entities, key users include members and contributors rather than investors.

[6] How does the concept of **neutrality** fit with the notion of **conservatism**? Few conventions in accounting are as misunderstood as conservatism. In situations involving uncertainty and professional judgement, historically, the concept of conservatism has meant that **net assets and net income would not be overstated**. Conservatism acknowledges a **pre-existing tendency** of companies to overstate net assets and net income and acts to counterbalance this tendency. Users of financial statements are more tolerant of understated net assets and net income than overstated balances. Does the use of conservatism represent a bias? Many believe that it does. The trend in financial reporting is away from any bias, including conservatism. The concept of conservatism is currently being downplayed in the conceptual framework in favour of neutrality. Having said that, there are many existing standards, both in IFRS and ASPE, where conservatism is embedded. For instance, where cost is used as a measurement basis (as opposed to fair value), accountants feel quite justified and even compelled to override the historical cost principle and write down the carrying value of an impaired asset. However, accountants are not always so quick to recognize an increase in the asset's value.

[7] As a matter of fact, when the IASB issued its new standards on Joint Arrangements in July 2011, it produced a document that assessed the effects of the standard (*IASB Effect Analysis*). In the document the IASB noted the following: "We expect our standards to have economic effects, and we expect those effects to be beneficial for some entities and detrimental to others. For example, a change in financial reporting requirements might affect the cost of capital for individual entities by changing the absolute or relative level of information asymmetry associated with those entities."

[8] IASB, *IFRS Conceptual Framework*, Chapter 3 QC15.

[9] IASB, *IFRS Conceptual Framework*, Chapter 3 QC32. This represents a subtle shift in the level of knowledge required. Prior to the joint IASB/FASB conceptual framework project, users were expected to have only a reasonable understanding of business and a willingness to study the statements.

[10] Consolidated financial statements of Enron Corp. for the year ended December 31, 2000.

[11] The elements are defined in the respective conceptual frameworks under IFRS and ASPE and even though the wording differs, they are essentially very close in meaning.

[12] *CICA Handbook–Accounting*, Part II, Section 1000.25 and IFRS *Conceptual Framework* 4.4 and 4.8-4.14.

[13] *CICA Handbook–Accounting*, Part II, Section 1000.29 and IFRS *Conceptual Framework* 4.4 and 4.15-4.19.

[14] The terms "financial" and "non-financial" are somewhat vague and are meant to draw a line between liabilities that represent financial instruments (financial liabilities) and all other liabilities. Therefore, the term "non-financial" includes items such as contractual nonmonetary performance obligations (such as warranties to fix assets or provide services) and non-contractual monetary obligations (such as lawsuits).

[15] The IASB and FASB are currently looking at the definition of "equity" since the line between liabilities and equity is not well defined for complex financial instruments and business structures.

[16] Under IFRS, revenues and gains are grouped together under the heading of Income in the framework. Similarly, expenses and losses are grouped together under the heading of Expenses. Thus, although acknowledging the existence of and the potential for separate disclosure of gains and losses, IFRS defines fewer elements. ASPE defines these items separately.

[17] IFRS 37.16 and .23.

[18] *CICA Handbook–Accounting*, Part II, Section 3290.06.

[19] As we will see later in the text, derecognition is linked with how we define the entity, especially where the entity is transferring or selling assets to another entity that it may control. For instance, if an entity transfers investments to another entity that it controls, there is essentially no derecognition since the entity will end up consolidating the combined entity and the entity is just seen to be transferring things between the two.

[20] That is, if the parent owns more than 50% of the (voting) common shares, it can exercise voting control.

[21] For example, it is now harder to define the boundaries of companies. There are public companies with multiple public subsidiaries, each with joint ventures, licensing arrangements, and other affiliations and strategic alliances. Increasingly, loose affiliations of enterprises in joint ventures or customer-supplier relationships are formed and dissolved in a matter of months or weeks. These virtual companies raise accounting issues about how to account for the entity.

[22] See joint IASB/FASB project on the conceptual framework (reporting entity).

[23] IFRS 10 *Consolidated Financial Statements*. This standard was issued in 2011 and is effective for years beginning on or after January 1, 2013. It will replace SIC 12, the previous standard dealing with special purpose entities.

[24] *CICA Handbook–Accounting*, Part II, Section 1590.03 and *Accounting Guideline* 15.

[25] The 10% test is an example of a bright-line test discussed in Chapter 1. IASB is, in principle, trying to purge bright-line tests from IFRS due the fact that in most cases, the "line drawn" is an arbitrary one.

[26] For instance, this may be the case where entity A transfers an asset to entity B and entity A controls entity B. Entity A may be able to derecognize the asset and perhaps recognize a gain/loss but when the consolidated statements are prepared, the asset will be included in the consolidated financial statements and any gain/loss eliminated.

[27] *CICA Handbook–Accounting*, Part II, Section 3400.04 - .06 and IAS 18.14.

[28] OSC Notice of Hearing and Statement of Allegations concerning Livent Inc., July 3, 2001.

[29] Many would argue that accounting standard setters are migrating toward a balance sheet emphasis. Thus the concept of matching is not as central as it would be if the statement of comprehensive income were the main focus. In addition, the use of fair value in measuring assets renders the concept of matching—as historically defined—useless.

[30] IFRS 13.9. The term "market" refers to any mechanism whereby parties objectively determine price, usually through bargaining and supply and demand. IFRS 13 includes the following as examples: exchange markets (such as the London Stock Exchange), dealer markets (such as commodities markets and used-equipment markets), brokered markets (such as real estate markets), and others.

[31] This is different from the way accountants have historically viewed fair values, which often considered the value from the entity's perspective, including any company-specific synergies. The objective of moving to a market-based fair value measure is to reduce subjectivity. For instance, an entity may believe that the asset is worth more than the market thinks it is worth and often attributes this to past entity-specific synergies, which are difficult to prove.

[32] *CICA Handbook–Accounting*, Part II, Section 3031.04. The standard acknowledges that certain assets may be held at net realizable value or fair value less cost to sell. These assets are excluded from the requirements of Section 3031 which essentially requires the use of historical cost for unimpaired inventory.

[33] *CICA Handbook–Accounting*, Part II, various sections including Sections 1582, 3055, 3063, 3064, 3065, 3461 and others.

[34] According to GAAP, recognition means including an item in one or more individual statements and does not mean disclosure in the notes to the financial statements. Some critics might argue, however, that if markets are assumed to be efficient, then as long as the information is disclosed, the market will absorb and use the information in pricing the shares. Whether the markets are fully efficient or not is a question that researchers seek to answer. There is evidence that efficient markets exist at least in a semi-strong form.

[35] CICA Canadian Performance Reporting Board, *MD&A: Guidance on Preparation and Disclosure*. This material is part of CICA Standards and Guidance Collection.

[36] Although MD&A disclosures are mandated for public companies, the *CICA Guidance*, in its executive summary, notes that the MD&A can also be used by other organizations to communicate more effectively.

[37] Because the framework was developed after many of the standards were created, there may be some standards that are inconsistent with the framework. Note that the framework does not override any specific standard. The standard setters are working to get rid of inconsistencies between the older standards and the framework.

[38] The IASB and FASB continue to work on the new joint conceptual framework. It is an iterative process since the boards must continually test the concepts against the existing and constantly changing body of knowledge to ensure the concepts stand up to current practice and needs.

[39] The ideas were taken from the IASB *Information for Observers Paper* dated February 2007.

[40] Ideas and concepts taken from IFRS 13 *Fair Value Measurement*.

[41] Recall that these estimates should reflect market participant assumptions (not entity specific ones).

[42] The term "salting" refers to the practice of tampering with the samples (and adding in some, or more, gold).

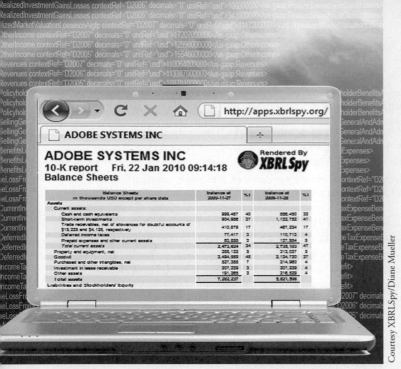

Extensive Innovations in Accounting Information Systems

THE ELECTRONIC COMMUNICATION language XBRL, or Extensible Business Reporting Language, is revolutionizing how businesses report their accounting information. Developed by XBRL International, a non-profit consortium, XBRL is an open standard, without any licence fees.

Instead of treating financial information as a block of text, XBRL provides a unique identifying tag for each item of data, such as company net profit. These XBRL tags allow for automated data processing. Computers can treat XBRL information "intelligently"—they can select it, analyze it, store it, and exchange it with other computers. XBRL thus increases the speed with which financial data are used, reduces the possibility for error, and permits automated checking of information. It can handle data in different languages and with different accounting standards.

XBRL Canada's role is to create and maintain XBRL taxonomies based on Canadian reporting standards and to increase awareness and understanding of XBRL and its uses in Canada. Taxonomies are the dictionaries that define the specific tags for individual items of data. XBRL Canada has created two taxonomies designed to enable preparation of XBRL-based financial statements that conform to Canadian GAAP: the Primary Financial Statements taxonomy, which covers the balance sheet, income statement, and statement of cash flows; and the Notes taxonomy, for preparing the notes to the financial statements. XBRL Canada is also working on a project to help companies with the convergence with IFRS, which will result in a taxonomy that conforms to IFRS as used in Canada, along with tools that will cross-reference pre-existing Canadian GAAP and IFRS.

With XBRL, companies can save costs and streamline financial information collecting and reporting, while consumers of financial data— investors, analysts, financial institutions, and regulators—can receive, find, compare, and analyze data more quickly and efficiently.

In fact, the Canadian Securities Administrators (CSA) is considering whether to make filing in XBRL format a requirement. Until it does, XBRL financial statements will not be a substitute for financial statements required to be filed under Canadian securities legislation; issuers must continue to file in PDF format.

Sources: www.securities-administrators.ca/industry_resources.aspx?id=54

The Accounting Information System

LEARNING OBJECTIVES

After studying this chapter, you should be able to:

1. Understand basic accounting terminology.
2. Explain double-entry rules.
3. Explain how transactions affect the accounting equation.
4. Identify the steps in the accounting cycle and the steps in the recording process.
5. Explain the reasons for and prepare adjusting entries.
6. Explain how the type of ownership structure affects the financial statements.
7. Prepare closing entries and consider other matters relating to the closing process.
8. Prepare a 10-column work sheet and financial statements.

After studying Appendix 3A, you should be able to:

9. Identify adjusting entries that may be reversed.

PREVIEW OF CHAPTER 3

It is important to understand how companies record transactions, update their accounting records, and prepare financial statements. The purpose of this chapter is to explain and illustrate the features of an accounting information system. Even though most companies have sophisticated computerized accounting systems, it is still important to understand the mechanics of bookkeeping. How do transactions get captured in the accounting system? How do the accounting records get updated at the end of each period? How and when are the financial statements produced? At the end of the fiscal year, what do we do to ready the books of account to start a new fiscal year and a new accounting cycle? This chapter addresses these questions.

The chapter is organized as follows:

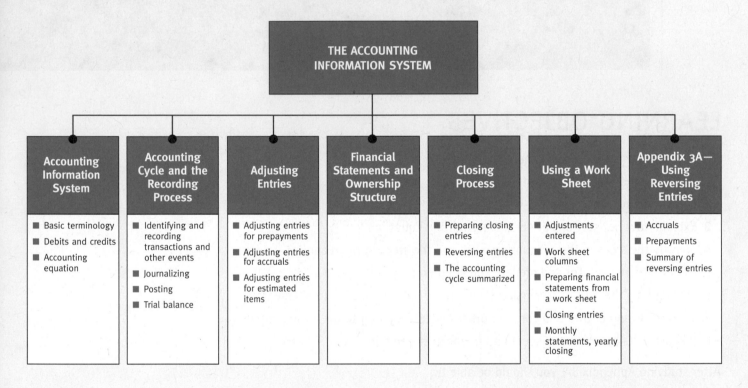

ACCOUNTING INFORMATION SYSTEM

The system of collecting and processing transaction data to make financial information available to interested parties is known as the **accounting information system**.

Accounting information systems can be very different from one business to another. Many factors shape these systems, including the type of business and the kinds of transactions it engages in, the firm's size, the amount of data handled, and the kind of information that management and others need to get from the system.

Basic Terminology

Objective 1
Understand basic accounting terminology.

Financial accounting is built on a set of concepts (discussed in Chapters 1 and 2) for identifying, recording, classifying, and interpreting transactions and other events relating to enterprises. It is important to understand the **basic terminology** that is used in collecting accounting data.

BASIC TERMINOLOGY

Event. Something of consequence that happens. An **event** generally is the source or cause of changes in assets, liabilities, and equity. Events can be external or internal.

Transaction. An **external event** involving a transfer or exchange between two or more entities or parties.

Account. A systematic arrangement that accumulates transactions and other events. A separate **account** is kept for each asset, liability, revenue, and expense, and for gains, losses, and capital (owners' equity).

Permanent and temporary accounts. **Permanent** (real) **accounts** are asset, liability, and equity accounts; they appear on the statement of financial position. **Temporary** (nominal) **accounts** are revenue, expense, and dividend accounts; except for dividends, they appear on the statement of comprehensive income. Temporary accounts are closed at the end of each fiscal year; permanent accounts are left open.

Ledger.[1] The book (or electronic database) containing the accounts. Each account usually has a separate page. A **general ledger** is a collection of all the asset, liability, owners' equity, revenue, and expense accounts. A **subsidiary ledger** contains the details of a specific general ledger account.

Journal. The book of original entry where transactions and other selected events are first recorded. Various amounts are transferred to the ledger from the book of original entry, the **journal**.

Posting. The process of transferring the essential facts and figures from the book of original entry to the ledger accounts.

Trial balance. A list of all open accounts in the ledger and their balances. A **trial balance** that is taken immediately after all adjustments have been posted is called an **adjusted trial balance**. A trial balance taken immediately after closing entries have been posted is known as a **post-closing** or **after-closing trial balance**. A trial balance can be prepared at any time.

Adjusting entries. Entries that are made at the end of an accounting period to bring all accounts up to date on an accrual accounting basis so that correct financial statements can be prepared.

Financial statements. Statements that reflect the collecting, tabulating, and final summarizing of the accounting data. Four **financial statements** are involved: (1) the **statement of financial position** (or **balance sheet** under ASPE), which shows the enterprise's financial condition at the end of a period; (2) the **statement of comprehensive income** (or **income statement** under ASPE), which measures the results of operations during the period; (3) the **statement of cash flows**, which reports the cash provided and used by operating, investing, and financing activities during the period; and (4) the **statement of changes in shareholders' equity** (or **statement of retained earnings** under ASPE), which reconciles the balance of the retained earnings and other equity accounts from the beginning to the end of the period. These financial statements are discussed further in Chapters 4 and 5.

Closing entries. The formal process for reducing temporary accounts to zero and then determining net income or net loss and transferring it to an owners' equity account. Using **closing entries** is also known as "closing the ledger," "closing the books," or merely "closing."

Reversing entries. Entries made to reverse some of the adjusting entries prior to recording the next period's transactions. These entries are optional (as discussed in Appendix 3A).

Debits and Credits

Objective 2
Explain double-entry rules.

The terms **debit** and **credit** refer to the left and right sides of a general ledger account, respectively. They are commonly abbreviated as Dr. for debit and Cr. for credit. These terms do not mean "increase" or "decrease." The terms "debit" and "credit" are used repeatedly in the recording process to describe where entries are made. For example, the act of entering an amount on the left side of an account is called **debiting** the account. Making an entry on the right side is **crediting** the account. When the totals of the two sides are compared, an account will have a debit balance if the total of the debit amounts is more than the credits. Conversely, an account will have a credit balance if the credit amounts exceed the debits. The procedure of having debits on the left and credits on the right is an accounting custom. We could function just as well if debits and credits were reversed. However, the custom of having debits on the left side of an account and credits on the right side (like the custom of driving on the right-hand side of the road) has been adopted in Canada. This rule applies to all accounts.

The equality of debits and credits is the basis for the double-entry system of recording transactions (also sometimes called double-entry bookkeeping). Under the **double-entry accounting** system, which is used for accounting around the world, the two-sided (dual) effect of each transaction is recorded in appropriate accounts. This system gives a logical method for recording transactions. It also offers a way of proving the accuracy of the recorded amounts. Every transaction is recorded with total debits equal to total credits, so the sum of all the debits posted to the accounts must equal the sum of all the credits.

All **asset** and **expense** accounts are increased on the left (or debit side) and decreased on the right (or credit side). Conversely, all **liability** and **revenue** accounts are increased on the right (or credit side) and decreased on the left (or debit side). Shareholders' equity accounts, such as Common Shares, and Retained Earnings, are increased on the credit side, whereas Dividends is increased on the debit side. The basic guidelines for an accounting system are presented in Illustration 3-1.

Illustration 3-1

Double-Entry (Debit and Credit) Accounting System

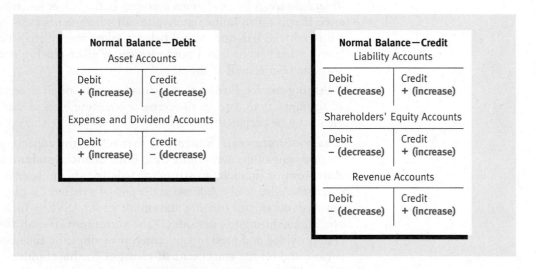

Objective 3
Explain how transactions affect the accounting equation.

Accounting Equation

In a double-entry system, for every debit there must be a credit, and vice versa. This leads us to the basic accounting equation for corporations shown in Illustration 3-2.

Illustration 3-2

The Basic Accounting Equation

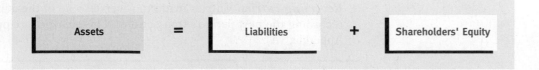

Illustration 3-3 expands this equation to show the accounts that compose shareholders' equity. In addition, the debit/credit rules and effects on each type of account are shown. Study this diagram carefully. It will help you understand the fundamentals of the double-entry system. Like the basic equation, the expanded basic equation must balance (total debits **must** equal total credits).[2]

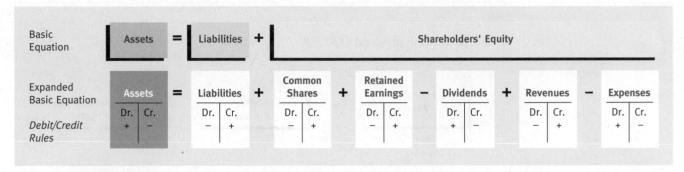

Illustration **3-3**

Expanded Basic Equation Debit/Credit Rules and Effects

Every time a transaction occurs, the elements in the equation change, but the basic equality of the two sides remains. To illustrate, here are eight different transactions for Perez Inc.:

1. Owners invest $40,000 in exchange for common shares:

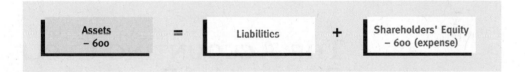

2. Disburses $600 cash for secretarial wages:

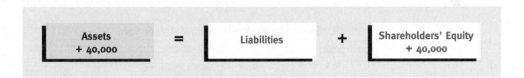

3. Purchases office equipment priced at $5,200, giving a 10% promissory note in exchange:

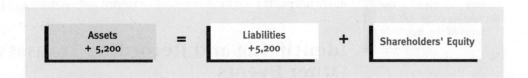

4. Services are rendered for cash of $4,000:

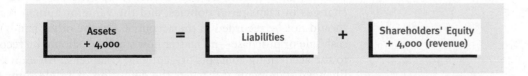

5. Pays off a short-term liability of $7,000:

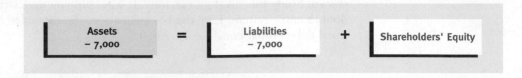

6. Declares a cash dividend of $5,000:

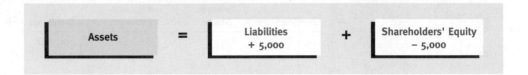

7. Pays off a long-term liability of $80,000 by issuing common shares:

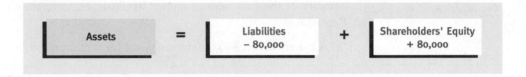

8. Pays $16,000 cash for a delivery van:

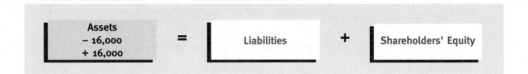

THE ACCOUNTING CYCLE AND THE RECORDING PROCESS

Objective 4
Identify the steps in the accounting cycle and the steps in the recording process.

Illustration 3-4 charts the steps in the **accounting cycle.** These are the accounting procedures normally used by enterprises to record transactions and prepare financial statements.

Identifying and Recording Transactions and Other Events

The first step in the accounting cycle is to **analyze transactions** and other selected **events.** The problem is determining what to **record.** There are no simple rules for whether an event should be recorded. It is generally agreed that changes in personnel, changes in managerial policies, and the value of human resources, though important, should not be recorded in the accounts. On the other hand, when the company makes a cash sale or purchase—no matter how small—it should be recorded. The treatment relates to the accounting concepts presented in Chapter 2. An item should be **recognized** in the financial statements if it meets the definition of an **element** (such as a liability or asset), and is **measurable.** Where there is uncertainty about the future event occurring or not (such as the potential loss from a lawsuit), the entity must use all available information to

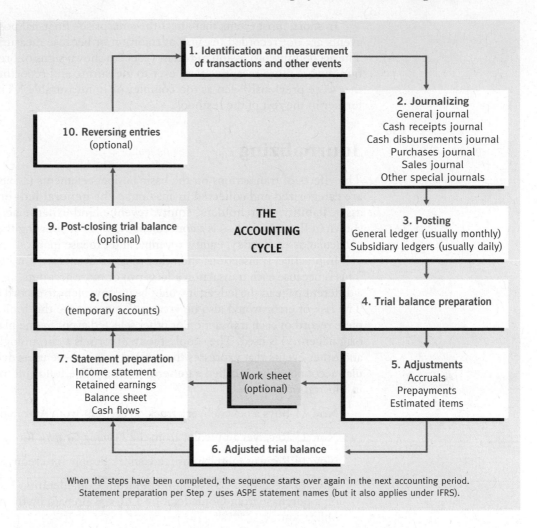

1. **Identification and measurement of transactions and other events**

2. **Journalizing**
General journal
Cash receipts journal
Cash disbursements journal
Purchases journal
Sales journal
Other special journals

10. **Reversing entries** (optional)

THE ACCOUNTING CYCLE

3. **Posting**
General ledger (usually monthly)
Subsidiary ledgers (usually daily)

9. **Post-closing trial balance** (optional)

4. **Trial balance preparation**

8. **Closing** (temporary accounts)

7. **Statement preparation**
Income statement
Retained earnings
Balance sheet
Cash flows

Work sheet (optional)

5. **Adjustments**
Accruals
Prepayments
Estimated items

6. **Adjusted trial balance**

When the steps have been completed, the sequence starts over again in the next accounting period.
Statement preparation per Step 7 uses ASPE statement names (but it also applies under IFRS).

make a neutral decision as to whether the liability/asset exists or not. The uncertainty would be taken into account when the element is measured. Recognition and measurement criteria were discussed in Chapter 2.

Information about transactions and other events and circumstances is captured and recorded in the financial statements. Events are of two types:

- **External events** involve interaction between an entity and its environment, such as a **transaction** with another company, a change in the price of a product or service that a company buys or sells, or a flood or earthquake.

- **Internal events** occur within an entity, such as using buildings and machinery in its operations, or transferring or consuming raw materials in production processes.

Many events have external **and** internal elements. For example, acquiring the services of employees or others involves exchange transactions that are external events. The employee provides services and the company pays the employee. Using those services (labour), is part of production, which is internal. Events may be initiated and controlled by an entity, such as the purchase of merchandise or the use of a machine, or they may be beyond its control, such as an interest rate change, a theft or vandalism, or a change in tax rates.

As a particular kind of **external event**, a **transaction** can be an exchange in which each entity both receives and gives up value, such as a purchase or sale of goods or services. Alternatively, a transaction can be a transfer in one direction in which an entity incurs a liability or transfers an asset to another entity without directly receiving value in exchange. (In other words, the transaction is non-reciprocal.) Examples include distributions to owners, the payment of taxes, gifts, charitable contributions, uninsured losses, and thefts.

In short, most events that affect the enterprise's financial position are recorded. Some events are not recorded because of tradition or because measuring them is too complex. The accounting profession in recent years has shown signs of breaking with age-old traditions and is more receptive than ever to measuring and reporting events and other items that were previously seen as too complex or immeasurable.[3] These areas will be studied further in the rest of the textbook.

Journalizing

The effects of transactions on the basic business elements (assets, liabilities, and equities) are categorized and collected in accounts. The **general ledger** is a collection of all the asset, liability, shareholders' equity, revenue, and expense accounts. A **T account** (as shown in Illustration 3-6) is a convenient method for showing the effect of transactions on particular asset, liability, equity, revenue, and expense items.

In practice, transactions and other selected events are not first recorded in the ledger. This is because each transaction affects two or more accounts, and since each account is on a different page in the ledger, it would be inconvenient to record each transaction this way. The risk of error would also be greater.[4] To overcome this limitation and to have a complete record of each transaction or other selected event in one place, a journal (the book of original entry) is used. The simplest journal form is a chronological listing of transactions and other events that expresses the transactions and events as debits and credits to particular accounts. This is called a **general journal**. The following transactions are presented in Illustration 3-5:

Nov. 11 Buys a new delivery truck on account from Auto Sales Inc., $22,400.

Nov. 13 Receives an invoice from the *Evening Graphic* for advertising, $280.

Nov. 14 Returns merchandise to Canuck Supply for credit, $175.

Nov. 15 Receives a $95 debit memo from Confederation Ltd., indicating that freight on a purchase from Confederation Ltd. was prepaid by the supplier but is the buyer's obligation.

Each general journal entry has four parts:

1. The accounts and amounts to be debited (Dr.)

2. The accounts and amounts to be credited (Cr.)

3. A date

4. An explanation

Debits are entered first, followed by the credits, which are slightly indented. The explanation begins below the name of the last account to be credited and may take one or more lines. The Reference column is completed when the accounts are posted.

In some cases, businesses use **special journals** in addition to the general journal. Special journals summarize transactions that have a common characteristic (such as cash receipts, sales, purchases, and cash payments), which saves time in doing the various bookkeeping tasks.

Posting

The items entered in a general journal must be transferred to the general ledger. This procedure is called **posting** and is part of the summarizing and classifying process.

For example, the November 11 entry in the general journal in Illustration 3-5 shows a debit to Trucks of $22,400 and a credit to Accounts Payable of $22,400. The amount in the debit column is posted from the journal to the debit side of the general ledger (GL) account Trucks. The amount in the credit column is posted from the journal to the credit side of the GL account Accounts Payable.

Illustration 3-5

General Journal with Sample Entries

GENERAL JOURNAL PAGE 12

Date 2014	Account Title and Explanation	Ref.	Debit	Credit
Nov. 11	Trucks	8	22,400	
	Accounts Payable	34		22,400
	(Purchased delivery truck on account)			
Nov. 13	Advertising Expense	65	280	
	Accounts Payable	34		280
	(Received invoice for advertising)			
Nov. 14	Accounts Payable	34	175	
	Purchase Returns and Allowances	53		175
	(Returned merchandise for credit)			
Nov. 15	Freight-In	55	95	
	Accounts Payable	34		95
	(Received debit memo for freight on merchandise purchased)			

The numbers in the Ref. column of the general journal refer to the GL accounts to which the items are posted. For example, the 34 placed in the column to the right of Accounts Payable indicates that this $22,400 item was posted to Account No. 34 in the ledger.

The general journal posting is completed when all the posting reference numbers have been recorded opposite the account titles in the journal. This means that the number in the posting reference column serves two purposes: (1) it indicates the ledger account number of the account involved, and (2) it indicates that the posting has been completed for that item. Each business enterprise chooses its own numbering system for its ledger accounts. One practice is to begin numbering with asset accounts and to follow with liabilities, shareholders' equity, revenue, and expense accounts, in that order.

The various ledger accounts in Illustration 3-6 are shown after the posting process is completed. The source of the data that have been transferred to the ledger account is indicated by the reference GJ 12 (General Journal, page 12).

Illustration 3-6

Ledger Accounts, in T Account Format

Trucks No. 8

Nov. 11 GJ 12   22,400 |

Accounts Payable No. 34

Nov. 14 GJ 12   175 | Nov. 11 GJ 12   22,400
  | 13 GJ 12   280
  | 15 GJ 12   95

Purchase Returns and Allowances No. 53

  | Nov. 14 GJ 12   175

Freight-In No. 55

Nov. 15 GJ 12   95 |

Advertising Expense No. 65

Nov. 13 GJ 12   280 |

Trial Balance

A trial balance is a list of general ledger accounts and their balances at a specific time. Customarily, a trial balance is prepared at the end of an accounting period. The accounts are listed in the order in which they appear in the general ledger, with debit balances listed in the left column and credit balances in the right column. The totals of the two columns must agree.

The main purpose of a trial balance is to prove the mathematical equality of debits and credits after posting. Under the double-entry system, this equality will occur when the sum of the debit account balances equals the sum of the credit account balances. A trial balance also uncovers errors in journalizing and posting. In addition, it is useful when preparing financial statements. The procedures for preparing a trial balance consist of:

1. Listing the account titles and their balances

2. Totalling the debit and credit columns

3. Proving the equality of the two columns

Illustration 3-7 shows the trial balance prepared from the ledger of Pioneer Advertising Agency Inc. at the end of its first month of operations.

Illustration 3-7

Trial Balance (Unadjusted)

PIONEER ADVERTISING AGENCY INC.
Unadjusted Trial Balance
October 31, 2014

	Debit	Credit
Cash	$ 80,000	
Accounts receivable	72,000	
Supplies	25,000	
Prepaid insurance	6,000	
Fair value – NI investments	10,000	
Office equipment	50,000	
Notes payable		$ 50,000
Accounts payable		35,000
Unearned revenue		12,000
Common shares		100,000
Dividends	5,000	
Service revenue		100,000
Salaries and wages expense	40,000	
Rent expense	9,000	
	$297,000	$297,000

Note that the total debits, $297,000, equal the total credits, $297,000. In the trial balance, the account numbers of the account titles are also often shown to the left of the titles.

A trial balance does not prove that all transactions have been recorded or that the ledger is correct. Even though the totals in the trial balance columns agree, there can still be many errors. For example, the trial balance may still balance when:

1. a transaction is not journalized,

2. a correct journal entry is not posted,

3. a journal entry is posted twice,

4. incorrect accounts are used in journalizing or posting, or

5. offsetting errors are made in recording a transaction amount.

In other words, as long as equal debits and credits are posted, even to the wrong account or in the wrong amount, the total debits will equal the total credits.

ADJUSTING ENTRIES

Objective 5
Explain the reasons for and prepare adjusting entries.

In order for revenues to be recorded in the period in which they are earned, and for expenses to be recognized in the period in which they are incurred, **adjusting entries** are made at the end of the accounting period. In short, **adjustments are needed to ensure that the revenue recognition principle is followed and that proper matching occurs.**

The use of adjusting entries makes it possible to report on the statement of financial position the appropriate assets, liabilities, and owners' equity at the statement date and to report on the statement of comprehensive income the proper net income (or loss) and comprehensive income for the period. However, the trial balance—the first pulling together of the transaction data—may not contain up-to-date and complete data. This is true for the following reasons:

1. Some events are **not journalized daily** because it is not efficient to do so. Examples are the consumption of supplies and the earning of wages by employees.

2. Some costs are not journalized during the accounting period because these costs **expire with the passage of time** rather than as a result of recurring daily transactions. Examples of such costs are building and equipment deterioration, rent, and insurance.

3. Some items may be **unrecorded**. An example is a utility service bill that will not be received until the next accounting period.

Adjusting entries are required every time financial statements are prepared. The starting point is to analyze each trial balance account to determine whether it is complete and up to date for financial statement purposes. The analysis requires a thorough understanding of the company's operations and the relationships between its accounts. Preparing adjusting entries is often a complicated process that requires the services of a skilled professional. In accumulating the adjustment data, the company may need to take inventory counts of supplies and repair parts. It may also be desirable to prepare supporting schedules of insurance policies, rental agreements, and other contractual commitments. Adjustments are often prepared after the end of the period, but the entries are dated as at the statement of financial position date.

Adjusting entries can be classified as **prepayments, accruals,** or **estimated items** (including fair value estimates).[5] Each of these classes has subcategories as follows:

PREPAYMENTS

1. **Prepaid Expenses.** Expenses paid in cash and recorded as assets before they are used or consumed.
2. **Unearned Revenues.** Revenues received in cash and recorded as liabilities before they are earned.

ACCRUALS

3. **Accrued Revenues.** Revenues earned but not yet received in cash or recorded.
4. **Accrued Expenses.** Expenses incurred but not yet paid in cash or recorded.

ESTIMATED ITEMS

5. **Bad Debts.** Expenses for impaired accounts receivable estimated in the period the related revenue is earned.
6. **Unrealized Holding Gain or Loss.** Gain (or loss) on fair value—NI investments is estimated at the end of an accounting period and recorded as an increase (or decrease) to the investment account with a corresponding gain (or loss) in the Statement of Comprehensive Income.
7. **Unrealized Holding Gain or Loss—OCI.** Gain (or loss) on fair value—OCI investments estimated at the end of an accounting period and recorded as an increase (or decrease) to the investment account with a corresponding gain (or loss) in OCI on the Statement of Comprehensive Income.

Specific examples and explanations of each type of adjustment are given later in this chapter. Each example is based on the October 31 trial balance of Pioneer Advertising Agency Inc. (Illustration 3-7). We assume that Pioneer Advertising uses an accounting period of one month. Thus, monthly adjusting entries will be made. The entries will be dated October 31.

Adjusting Entries for Prepayments

As mentioned above, prepayments are either **prepaid expenses** or **unearned revenues**. Adjusting entries for prepayments are required at the statement date to record the portion of the prepaid expense or unearned revenue that was actually incurred or earned in the current accounting period. Assuming an adjustment is needed for both types of prepayments, the asset and liability involved are overstated and the related expense and revenue are understated. For example, in the trial balance, the balance in the asset account Supplies shows only supplies purchased. This balance is overstated; the related expense account, Supplies Expense, is understated because the cost of supplies used has not been recognized. Thus, the adjusting entry for prepayments will decrease a statement of financial position account and increase a statement of comprehensive income account. Illustration 3-8 shows the effects of adjusting entries for prepayments.

Illustration 3-8

Adjusting Entries for Prepayments

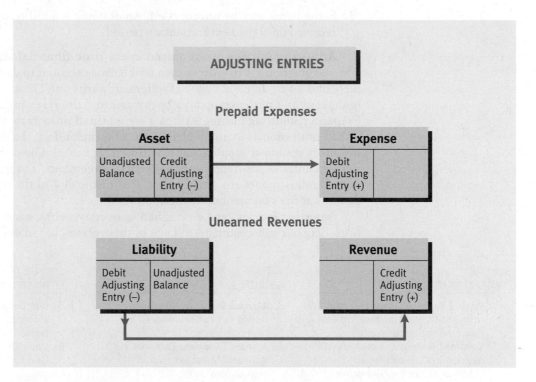

Prepaid Expenses

As previously stated, expenses that have been paid in cash and recorded as assets before they are used or consumed are identified as **prepaid expenses**. When a cost is incurred, an asset account is debited to show the service or benefit that will be received in the future. Prepayments often occur for such things as insurance, supplies, advertising, and rent.

Prepaid expenses expire either with the passage of time (such as rent and insurance) or by being used and consumed (such as supplies). The expiration of these costs does not require an entry each day, which would be unnecessary and impractical. Instead, it is customary to postpone the recognition of such cost expirations until financial statements are prepared. At each statement date, adjusting entries are made to record the expenses that apply to the current accounting period and to show the remaining unexpired costs in the asset accounts.

Supplies

Oct. 5

Supplies purchased; record asset

Oct. 31

Supplies used; record supplies expense

Before adjustment, assets are overstated and expenses are understated. **Thus, the prepaid expense adjusting entry results in a debit to an expense account and a credit to an asset account.**

Supplies. Several different types of supplies are used in businesses. For example, a CA firm will have office supplies such as stationery, envelopes, and paper. In contrast, an advertising firm will have advertising supplies such as graph paper, colour ink cartridges, and poster paper. Supplies are generally debited to an asset account when they are acquired. During the course of operations, supplies are partly or entirely consumed. However, recognition of the used-up supplies is deferred until the adjustment process when a physical inventory (a count) of supplies is taken. The difference between the balance in the Supplies account (the asset) and the cost of supplies on hand represents the supplies used up for the period (the expense).

Pioneer Advertising Agency purchased advertising supplies costing $25,000 on October 5. The debit was made to the asset Supplies, and this account shows a balance of $25,000 in the October 31 trial balance. An inventory count at the close of business on October 31 reveals that $10,000 of supplies is still on hand. Thus, the cost of supplies used is $15,000 ($25,000 – $10,000), and the following adjusting entry is made:

A = L + SE
−15,000   −15,000

Cash flows: No effect

	Oct. 31		
Supplies Expense		15,000	
Supplies			15,000
(To record supplies used)			

After the adjusting entry is posted, the two supplies accounts, in T account form, are as shown in Illustration 3-9.

Illustration 3-9

Supplies Accounts After Adjustment

Supplies				Supplies Expense	
10/5	25,000	10/31 Adj.	15,000	10/31 Adj. 15,000	
10/31 Bal.	10,000				

The asset account Supplies now shows a balance of $10,000, which is equal to the cost of supplies on hand at the statement date. In addition, Supplies Expense shows a balance of $15,000, which equals the cost of supplies used up in October. **If the adjusting entry is not made, October expenses will be understated and net income overstated by $15,000. Moreover, both assets and shareholders' equity will be overstated by $15,000 on the October 31 statement of financial position.**

Insurance. Most companies have fire and theft insurance on inventory and equipment, personal liability insurance for accidents suffered by customers, and automobile insurance on company cars and trucks. The cost of insurance protection is the amount paid as insurance premiums. The term (duration) and coverage (what the company is insured against) are specified in the insurance policy. The minimum term is usually one year, but three- to five-year terms may be available and offer lower annual premiums. Insurance premiums are normally charged to the asset account Prepaid Insurance when they are paid. At the financial statement date, it is necessary to debit Insurance Expense and credit Prepaid Insurance for the cost that has expired during the period.

On October 4, Pioneer Advertising Agency Inc. paid $6,000 for a one-year fire insurance policy. The coverage began as of October 1. The premium was charged to Prepaid Insurance when it was paid, and this account shows a balance of $6,000 in the October 31 trial balance. An analysis of the policy reveals that $500 of insurance expires each month ($6,000/12). Thus, the following adjusting entry is made:

Insurance

Oct. 4

Insurance purchased; record asset

Insurance Policy			
Oct. $500	Nov. $500	Dec. $500	Jan. $500
Feb. $500	March $500	April $500	May $500
June $500	July $500	Aug. $500	Sept. $500
1 YEAR $6,000			

Oct. 31

Insurance expired; record insurance expense

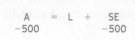

A = L + SE
−500   −500

Cash flows: No effect

Oct. 31		
Insurance Expense	500	
Prepaid Insurance		500
(To record insurance expired)		

After the adjusting entry is posted, the accounts are as in Illustration 3-10.

Illustration 3-10

Insurance Accounts After Adjustment

Prepaid Insurance				Insurance Expense		
10/4	6,000	10/31 Adj.	500	10/31 Adj.	500	
10/31 Bal.	5,500					

The asset Prepaid Insurance shows a balance of $5,500, which represents the unexpired cost of the 11 months of remaining coverage. At the same time, the balance in Insurance Expense is equal to the insurance cost that has expired in October. **If this adjustment is not made, October expenses will be understated by $500 and net income overstated by $500. Moreover, both assets and owners' equity also will be overstated by $500 on the October 31 statement of financial position.**

Depreciation/Amortization. Companies typically own a variety of productive facilities such as buildings, equipment, and motor vehicles. These assets provide a service for many years. The term of service is commonly referred to as the asset's **useful life**. **Because an asset such as a building is expected to provide service for many years, it is recorded as an asset, rather than an expense, in the year it is acquired.** Such assets are recorded at cost, as required by the cost principle.

In order to match the cost of the asset with the revenues that it is generating, a portion of the cost of a long-lived asset should be reported as an expense during each period of the asset's useful life. **Depreciation/amortization** is the process of **allocating the cost of an asset** to expense over its useful life in a rational and systematic manner.

From an accounting standpoint, when productive facilities are acquired, the transaction is viewed essentially as a long-term prepayment for services. Periodic adjusting entries for depreciation are therefore needed for the same reasons described earlier for other prepaid expenses. In other words, it is necessary to recognize the cost that has expired during the period (the expense) and to report the unexpired cost at the end of the period (the asset).

In determining a productive facility's useful life, there are three main causes of depreciation:

- Actual use

- Deterioration due to the elements

- Obsolescence

When an asset is acquired, the effects of these factors cannot be known with certainty, so they must instead be estimated. Thus, depreciation is an estimate rather than an exact measurement of the cost that has expired. A common procedure in calculating depreciation expense is to divide the asset's cost by its useful life. For example, if the cost is $10,000 and the useful life is expected to be 10 years, annual depreciation is $1,000.

For Pioneer Advertising, depreciation on the office equipment is estimated at $4,800 a year (cost of $50,000 less a salvage value of $2,000 divided by a useful life of 10 years), or $400 per month. Accordingly, depreciation for October is recognized by the following adjusting entry:

Underlying Concept

The historical cost principle requires that depreciable assets be recorded at cost. Matching allows this cost to be allocated to periods of use.

Depreciation

Oct. 1

Office equipment purchased; record asset ($50,000)

Office Equipment

Oct. $400	Nov. $400	Dec. $400	Jan. $400
Feb. $400	March $400	April $400	May $400
June $400	July $400	Aug. $400	Sept. $400

Depreciation=$4,800/year

Oct. 31
Depreciation recognized; record depreciation expense

	Oct. 31		
Depreciation Expense		400	
Accumulated Depreciation—Office Equipment			400
(To record monthly depreciation)			

A = L + SE
-400   -400

Cash flows: No effect

After the adjusting entry is posted, the accounts show that the balance in the accumulated depreciation account will increase by $400 each month, as shown in Illustration 3-11.

Illustration 3-11

Accounts After Adjustment for Depreciation

Office Equipment	
10/1 50,000	

Accumulated Depreciation—Office Equipment		Depreciation Expense	
	10/31 400	10/31 Adj. 400	

Therefore, after journalizing and posting the adjusting entry at November 30, the balance will then be $800 in the accumulated depreciation account.

Accumulated Depreciation—Office Equipment is a contra asset account. A **contra asset account** is an account that is offset against an asset account on the statement of financial position. In the case of accumulated depreciation, this account is offset against Office Equipment on the statement of financial position and its normal balance is therefore a credit. This account is used instead of crediting Office Equipment so that the equipment's original cost and the total cost that has expired to date can both be disclosed. In the statement of financial position, Accumulated Depreciation—Office Equipment is deducted from the related asset account (which is normally a debit), as shown in Illustration 3-12.

Illustration 3-12

Statement of Financial Position Presentation of Accumulated Depreciation

Office equipment	$50,000	
Less: Accumulated depreciation—office equipment	400	$49,600

The difference between any depreciable asset's cost and its related accumulated depreciation is known as its **book value**. In Illustration 3-12, the equipment's book value or **carrying amount** at the statement of financial position date is $49,600. It is important to realize that the asset's **book value and market value are generally two different values**.

Note also that depreciation expense identifies that portion of the asset's cost that has expired in October. As in the case of other prepaid adjustments, **if this adjusting entry is not made, then total shareholders' equity and net income will be overstated and the expense will be understated**.

If additional equipment is involved, such as delivery or store equipment, or if the company has buildings, depreciation expense is recorded on each of these items. Related accumulated depreciation accounts also are created. These accumulated depreciation accounts would be described in the ledger as follows: Accumulated Depreciation—Trucks, Accumulated Depreciation—Office Equipment, and Accumulated Depreciation—Buildings.

Unearned Revenues

As stated earlier, revenues that have been received in cash and recorded as liabilities before they are earned are called **unearned revenues**. Items such as rent, magazine subscriptions, and customer deposits for further service may result in unearned revenues.

Airlines such as **Air Canada** and **WestJet** treat receipts from the sale of tickets as unearned revenue until the flight service is provided. (For example, "Advance Ticket Sales" totalled $308 million on WestJet's December 31, 2010 financial statements.) The growth in Advance Ticket Sales of $21.6 million (or 7.5% as compared to 2009) was part of the reason WestJet's cash and cash equivalents increased significantly in 2010. In fact, one of the ratios that WestJet tracks is cash on hand divided by advance tickets sales which increased from 3.51 in 2009 to 3.86 in 2010. This is a key indicator that the company has sufficient cash on hand to meet its liabilities as they come due.

Source: Based on WestJet's Annual Report for the year 2010.

**Real World
Emphasis**

Tuition fees received by a university before the start of a semester are also considered unearned revenue. Unearned revenues are the opposite of prepaid expenses. Indeed, unearned revenue on the books of one company is likely to be a prepayment on the books of the company that has made the advance payment. For example, if identical accounting periods are assumed, a landlord will have unearned rent revenue when a tenant has prepaid rent.

When the payment is received for services that will be provided in a future accounting period, an unearned revenue account (a liability) should be credited to recognize the obligation that exists. Unearned revenues are later earned by performing the service for the customer (which discharges the liability). During the accounting period, it may not be practical to make an entry each day as the revenue is earned. In such cases, the recognition of earned revenue is delayed until the adjustment process. At that time, an adjusting entry is then made to record the revenue that has been earned and to show the liability that remains. In the typical case, liabilities are overstated and revenues are understated prior to adjustment. Thus, the adjusting entry for unearned revenues results in a debit (decrease) to a liability account and a credit (increase) to a revenue account.

Pioneer Advertising Agency received $12,000 on October 2 from R. Knox for advertising services that are expected to be completed by December 31. The payment was credited to Unearned Revenue, and this account shows a balance of $12,000 in the October 31 trial balance. When analysis reveals that $4,000 of these services have been earned in October, the following adjusting entry is made:

A = L + SE
      −4,000 +4,000

Cash flows: No effect

Oct. 31		
Unearned Revenue	4,000	
Service Revenue		4,000
(To record revenue for services provided)		

After the adjusting entry is posted, the accounts are as shown in Illustration 3-13.

Illustration 3-13
Service Revenue Accounts After Prepayments Adjustment

Unearned Revenue				Service Revenue		
10/31 Adj.	4,000	10/2	12,000		10/31 Bal.	100,000
		10/31 Bal.	8,000		10/31 Adj.	4,000
					10/31 Bal.	104,000

The account Unearned Revenue now shows a balance of $8,000, which represents the remaining advertising services that are expected to be performed in the future. At the same time, Service Revenue shows total revenue earned in October of $104,000. **If this adjustment is not made, revenues and net income will be understated by $4,000 in the statement of comprehensive income. Moreover, liabilities will be overstated and shareholders' equity will be understated by $4,000 on the October 31 statement of financial position.**

Alternative Method for Adjusting Prepayments

So far, the assumption has been that an asset (such as prepaid rent) or liability (such as unearned revenue) is recorded when the company initially pays or receives the cash. An alternative treatment is to record the initial entry through the related income statement account and adjust it later. For example, if Pioneer Advertising Agency Inc. paid $6,000 for a one-year fire insurance policy on October 1, it could initially have recorded the whole amount in Insurance Expense. Thus at October 31, the adjusting entry would be as follows:

$$A = L + SE$$
$$+5,500 \qquad +5,500$$

Cash flows: No effect

Oct. 31		
Prepaid Insurance	5,500	
Insurance Expense		5,500
(To record unexpired insurance)		

The same could be done for other prepayments, such as supplies and rent.

Adjusting Entries for Accruals

The second category of adjusting entries is **accruals**. Adjusting entries for accruals are required in order to record revenues earned and expenses incurred in the current accounting period that have not been recognized through daily entries. If an accrual adjustment is needed, the revenue account (and the related asset account) and/or the expense account (and the related liability account) are understated. Thus, the adjusting entry for accruals will increase both a statement of financial position and a statement of comprehensive income account. Adjusting entries for accruals are shown in Illustration 3-14.

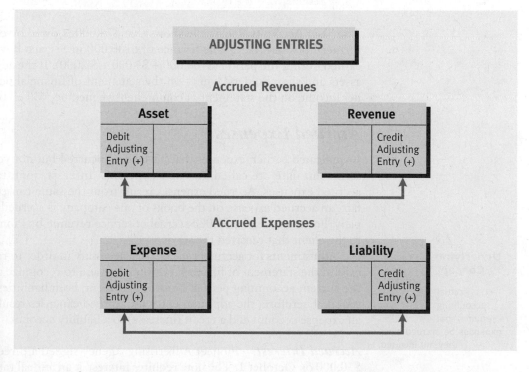

Accrued Revenues

As explained earlier, revenues that have been **earned but not yet received** in cash or recorded at the statement date are **accrued revenues**. Accrued revenues may **accumulate (accrue) with the passing of time,** as in the case of interest income and rent revenue. These types of accrued revenues are unrecorded because earning interest and rent does not involve daily transactions. Accrued revenues may also result from services that have been performed but neither billed nor collected, as in the case of commissions and fees. These types of accrued revenues may be unrecorded because only a portion of the total service has been provided.

An adjusting entry is required to show the receivable that exists at the statement of financial position date and to record the revenue that has been earned during the period. Before adjustment, both assets and revenues are understated. Accordingly, an adjusting entry for accrued revenues results in a debit (increase) to an asset account and a credit (increase) to a revenue account.

In October, Pioneer Advertising Agency earned $2,000 for advertising services that were not billed to clients before October 31. Because these services have not yet been billed, they have not been recorded in any way. Thus, the following adjusting entry is made:

A   = L +   SE
+2,000   +2,000

Cash flows: No effect

Oct. 31		
Accounts Receivable	2,000	
Service Revenue		2,000
(To record revenue for services provided)		

Illustration 3-15 shows the accounts after the adjusting entry is posted.

Illustration 3-15

Receivable and Revenue Accounts After Accrual Adjustment

Accounts Receivable			Service Revenue		
10/31	72,000		10/31	100,000	
10/31 Adj.	2,000		10/31	4,000	
10/31 Bal.	74,000		10/31 Adj.	2,000	
			10/31 Bal.	106,000	

The asset Accounts Receivable shows that $74,000 is owed by clients at the statement of financial position date. The balance of $106,000 in Service Revenue is the total revenue earned during the period ($100,000 + $4,000 + $2,000). If the adjusting entry is not made, assets and shareholders' equity on the statement of financial position, and revenues and net income on the statement of comprehensive income, will all be understated.

Accrued Expenses

As indicated earlier, expenses that have been incurred but not yet paid or recorded at the statement date are called **accrued expenses**. Interest, rent, taxes, and salaries can be accrued expenses. Accrued expenses result from the same causes as accrued revenues. In fact, an accrued expense on the books of one company is accrued revenue to another company. For example, the $2,000 accrual of service revenue by Pioneer is an accrued expense to the client that received the service.

Adjustments for accrued expenses are necessary in order to record the obligations that exist at the statement of financial position date and to recognize the expenses that apply to the current accounting period. Before adjustment, both liabilities and expenses are understated. Therefore, the adjusting entry for accrued expenses results in a debit (increase) to an expense account and a credit (increase) to a liability account.

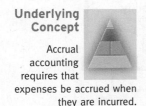

Underlying Concept

Accrual accounting requires that expenses be accrued when they are incurred.

Accrued Interest.   Pioneer Advertising Agency signed a three-month note payable for $50,000 on October 1. The note requires interest at an annual rate of 12%. The interest to be paid is determined by three factors:

- The note's face value

- The interest rate, which is always expressed as an annual rate

- The length of time the note is outstanding

The total interest due on the $50,000 note at its due date three months later is $1,500 ($50,000 × 12% × ³/₁₂), or $500 for one month. The formula for calculating interest and how it applies to Pioneer Advertising for the month of October are shown in Illustration 3-16.

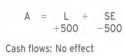

Formula for Calculating Interest

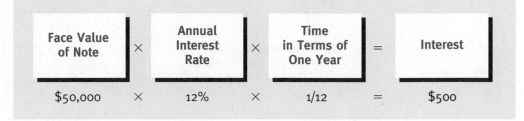

Note that the time period is expressed as a fraction of a year. The accrued expense adjusting entry at October 31 is as follows:

A = L + SE
+500 −500

Cash flows: No effect

	Oct. 31		
Interest Expense		500	
Interest Payable			500
(To record interest on notes payable)			

After this adjusting entry is posted, the accounts are as shown in Illustration 3-17.

Illustration 3-17

Interest Accounts After Adjustments

Interest Expense			Interest Payable	
10/31	$500		10/31	$500

Interest Expense shows the interest charges that apply to the month of October. The amount of interest owed at the statement date is shown in Interest Payable. It will not be paid until the note comes due at the end of three months. The Interest Payable account is used instead of crediting Notes Payable in order to disclose the two types of obligations (interest and principal) in the accounts and statements. **If this adjusting entry is not made, liabilities and interest expense will be understated, and net income and shareholders' equity will be overstated.**

Accrued Salaries. Some types of expenses, such as employee salaries and commissions, are paid for after the services have been performed. At Pioneer Advertising, salaries were last paid on October 24; the next payment of salaries will not occur until November 7. As shown in the calendar that follows, five working days remain in October (October 27, 28, 29, 30, and 31).

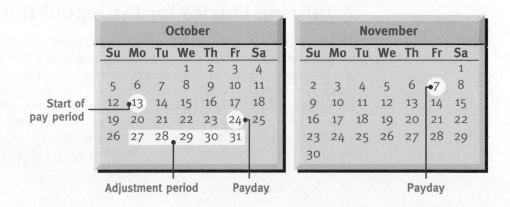

At October 31, the salaries for these days represent an accrued expense and a related liability to Pioneer Advertising. The employees receive total salaries of $10,000 for a five-day workweek, or $2,000 per day. Thus, accrued salaries at October 31 are $10,000 ($2,000 × 5), and the adjusting entry is:

A = L + SE
+10,000 −10,000

Cash flows: No effect

Oct. 31		
Salaries and Wages Expense	10,000	
Salaries and Wages Payable		10,000
(To record accrued salaries)		

After this adjusting entry is posted, the accounts are as shown in Illustration 3-18.

Illustration 3-18

Salary Accounts After Adjustment

Salaries and Wages Expense			Salaries and Wages Payable	
10/27	36,000			10/31 Adj. 10,000
10/31 Adj.	10,000			
10/31 Bal.	46,000			

After this adjustment, the balance in Salaries and Wages Expense of $46,000 (23 days × $2,000) is the actual salary expense for October. The balance in Salaries and Wages Payable of $10,000 is the amount of liability for salaries owed as at October 31. **If the $10,000 adjustment for salaries is not recorded, Pioneer's expenses will be understated by $10,000, and its liabilities will be understated by $10,000.**

At Pioneer Advertising, salaries are payable every two weeks. Consequently, the next payday is November 7, when total salaries of $20,000 will again be paid. The payment consists of $10,000 of salaries and wages payable at October 31 plus $10,000 of salaries and wages expense for November (5 working days as shown in the November calendar × $2,000). Therefore, the following entry is made on November 7:

A = L + SE
−20,000 −10,000 −10,000

Cash flows: ↓ 20,000 outflow

Nov. 7		
Salaries and Wages Payable	10,000	
Salaries and Wages Expense	10,000	
Cash		20,000
(To record November 7 payroll)		

This entry eliminates the liability for Salaries and Wages Payable that was recorded in the October 31 adjusting entry and records the proper amount of Salaries and Wages Expense for the period November 1 to November 7.

Adjusting Entries for Estimated Items

The third category of adjusting entries is **estimated items**. Adjusting entries for estimated items are required in order to record expenses, gains, and losses incurred in the current accounting period that have not been recognized through daily entries. If an estimated adjustment is needed for anticipated bad debts, the expense account is understated. So, the adjusting entry will typically increase both a contra account on the statement of financial position and an income statement account. Similarly, an adjusting entry for an unrealized gain would increase an investment account and affect unrealized gains on the statement of comprehensive income. Adjusting entries for estimated items are shown in Illustration 3-19.

Illustration 3-19

Adjusting Entries for Estimated Items

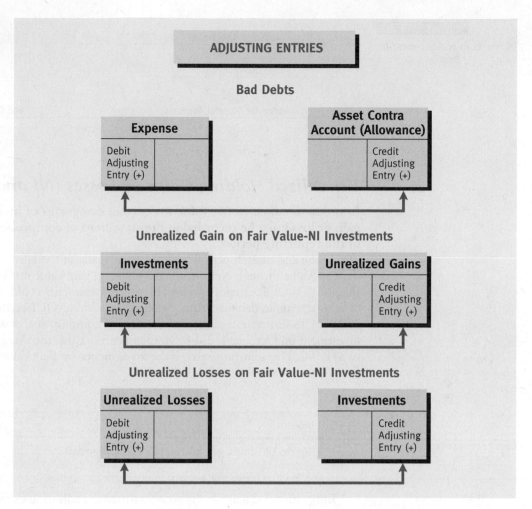

ADJUSTING ENTRIES

Bad Debts

Expense		**Asset Contra Account (Allowance)**	
Debit Adjusting Entry (+)			Credit Adjusting Entry (+)

Unrealized Gain on Fair Value-NI Investments

Investments		**Unrealized Gains**	
Debit Adjusting Entry (+)			Credit Adjusting Entry (+)

Unrealized Losses on Fair Value-NI Investments

Unrealized Losses		**Investments**	
Debit Adjusting Entry (+)			Credit Adjusting Entry (+)

Bad Debts

Oct. 31

Uncollectible accounts; reduce net receivables

Bad Debts

In order to properly match revenues with expenses, an estimate of bad debts must be recorded as an expense of the period in which the revenue was earned instead of being recorded in the period when the accounts or notes are written off. So that the receivable balance shows its proper value, estimated uncollectible receivables must be recognized. Proper matching and valuation therefore require an adjusting entry.

At the end of each period, an estimate is made of the amount of current period revenue on account that will later be uncollectible. The estimate is based on the amount of bad debts experienced in past years, general economic conditions, how long the receivables are past due, and other factors that indicate the likelihood of collection. Often the estimate is expressed as a percentage of revenue each month, followed by a detailed analysis at the end of the fiscal year. As we will see in Chapter 7, the Allowance for Doubtful Accounts may be calculated by applying different percentages to the aged trade accounts receivable and trade notes receivable balances at the end of the period.

To illustrate, assume that experience shows that a reasonable estimate for bad debt expense for the month is $1,600. The adjusting entry for bad debts is:

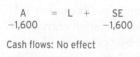

A   = L +   SE
−1,600   −1,600

Cash flows: No effect

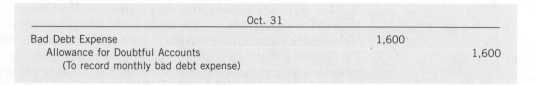

Oct. 31		
Bad Debt Expense	1,600	
Allowance for Doubtful Accounts		1,600
(To record monthly bad debt expense)		

Illustration 3-20 shows the accounts after the adjusting entry is posted.

Illustration 3-20

Accounts After Adjustment for Bad Debt Expense

Accounts Receivable		
10/1	72,000	
10/31	2,000	
10/31 Bal.	74,000	

Allowance for Doubtful Accounts				Bad Debt Expense		
		10/31 Adj.	1,600	10/31 Adj.	1,600	

Unrealized Holding Gains or Losses (NI and OCI)

In order to adjust to fair value for certain categories of investments, an unrealized gain or loss must be recorded in the statement of comprehensive income at the end of the reporting period.

At the end of each period, an estimate is made of the fair value of investments held in the Fair Value through Net Income (FV-NI) and Fair Value through Other Comprehensive Income (FV-OCI) categories. Fair Value-NI investments could include equity investments or investments in debt securities, whereas Fair Value-OCI excludes debt securities under IFRS 9.[6] To illustrate, assume that $10,000 of common shares were acquired as an equity investment on October 1, 2014. On October 31, 2014, the shares' fair value had increased to $11,500. The adjusting entry, if the investments are Fair Value-NI, is:

A   =   L   +   SE
+1,500   +1,500

Cash flows: No effect

	Oct. 31		
FV-NI Investments		1,500	
Unrealized Holding Gain or Loss			1,500
(To record holding gain on Fair Value-NI investment)			

Illustration 3-21 shows the accounts after the adjusting entry is posted.

Illustration 3-21

Accounts After Adjustment for Holding Gain on Fair Value-NI Investment

FV-NI Investments				Unrealized Holding Gain or Loss		
10/1	10,000			10/31 Adj.	1,500	
10/31 Adj.	1,500					
10/31 Bal.	11,500					

Alternatively, if the investment was being held in the Fair Value-OCI category, the adjusting entry would be:

A   =   L   +   SE
+1,500   +1,500

Cash flows: No effect

	Oct. 31		
FV-OCI Investments		1,500	
Unrealized Holding Gain or Loss – OCI			1,500
(To record holding gain on Fair Value-OCI investments)			

The impact on the basic accounting equation and cash flows would be the same as the Fair Value-NI example above, and the impact on the accounts would be similar to Illustration 3-21 (although the account names would change to correspond to the adjusting journal entry).

Assuming that the investments held by Pioneer Advertising are best categorized as fair value through net income (rather than Fair Value-OCI), the adjusted trial balance of the company is provided in Illustration 3-22.

Illustration 3-22

Trial Balance (Adjusted)

PIONEER ADVERTISING AGENCY, INC.
Adjusted Trial Balance
October 31, 2014

	Debit	Credit
Cash	$ 84,000	
Accounts receivable	74,000	
Allowance for doubtful accounts		$ 1,600
Supplies	10,000	
Prepaid insurance	5,500	
FV—NI Investments	11,500	
Office equipment	50,000	
Accumulated depreciation—office equipment		400
Notes payable		50,000
Accounts payable		35,000
Interest payable		500
Unearned revenue		8,000
Salaries and wages payable		10,000
Common shares		100,000
Dividends	5,000	
Service revenue		106,000
Unrealized holding gain or loss		1,500
Salaries and wages expense	46,000	
Supplies expense	15,000	
Rent expense	9,000	
Insurance expense	500	
Interest expense	500	
Depreciation expense	400	
Bad debt expense	1,600	
	$313,000	$313,000

FINANCIAL STATEMENTS AND OWNERSHIP STRUCTURE

Objective 6

Explain how the type of ownership structure affects the financial statements.

After the adjusting entries have been prepared and posted, an adjusted trial balance is prepared. The adjusted trial balance greatly helps in the preparation of the financial statements. Assets and liabilities are reported on the statement of financial position, often grouped into current and non-current classifications. Common shares, retained earnings, and accumulated other comprehensive income are reported in the shareholders' equity section of the statement of financial position. Dividends are reported on the statement of changes in shareholders' equity. Revenues and expenses are reported on the statement of comprehensive income. Revenues and expenses are eventually transferred to retained earnings at the end of the period while other comprehensive income is transferred to **accumulated other comprehensive income**.[7] As a result, a change in any one of these items affects shareholders' equity. The relationships within shareholders' equity are shown in Illustration 3-23.

The type of ownership structure that a business enterprise uses determines the types of accounts that are part of the equity section or that affect it. In a **corporation**,[8] **Common Shares, Contributed Surplus, Dividends, Retained Earnings**, and **Accumulated Other Comprehensive Income** are commonly used accounts. In a **proprietorship** or **partnership**, a **Capital** account is used to indicate the investment in the company by the owner(s). An Owner's **Drawings** or withdrawal account may be used to indicate withdrawals by the owner(s). These two accounts are grouped or netted under **Owners' Equity**.

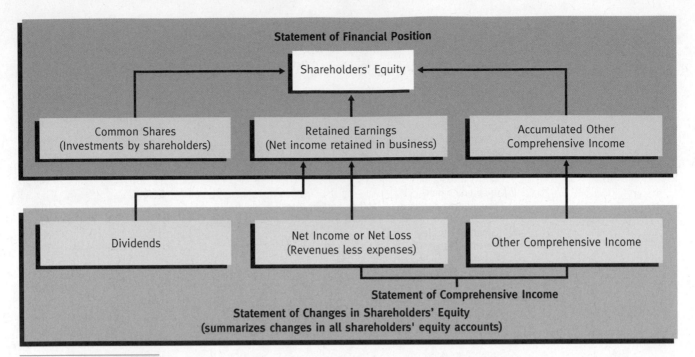

Illustration 3-23

Financial Statements and Shareholders' Equity Classifications

Illustration 3-24 summarizes the transactions that affect owners' equity and relates them to the temporary and permanent account classifications and to the types of business ownership. The OCI and AOCI accounts relate only to companies following IFRS.

Illustration 3-24

Effects of Transactions on Owners' or Shareholders' Equity Accounts

		Ownership Structure			
		Proprietorships and Partnerships		Corporations	
Transactions Affecting Owners' Equity	Impact on Owners' Equity	Temporary Accounts	Permanent Accounts	Temporary Accounts	Permanent Accounts
Investment by owner(s)	Increase		Owner's Capital		Common Shares and related accounts
Revenues earned	Increase	Revenue ⎫		Revenue ⎫	Retained Earnings/ AOCI
Expenses incurred	Decrease	Expense ⎬	Owner's Capital	Expense ⎬	
Withdrawal by owner(s)	Decrease	Owner's Drawings ⎭		Dividends ⎬	
OCI				OCI ⎭	

THE CLOSING PROCESS

Preparing Closing Entries

Objective 7
Prepare closing entries and consider other matters relating to the closing process.

The **closing process** reduces the balance of temporary accounts to zero in order to prepare the accounts for the next period's transactions. In the closing process, all of the revenue and expense account balances (the statement of comprehensive income items) are transferred to a clearing account called **Income Summary**, which is used only at year end. Revenues and expenses are matched in the Income Summary account. The net result of this matching is the net income or net loss for the period. This is then transferred to an owners' equity account. For a corporation, this would be the Retained Earnings or, for OCI items, an AOCI account. For proprietorships and partnerships, this would normally be the capital accounts or owners' equity account. All **closing entries** are posted to the appropriate general ledger accounts.

For example, assume that the revenue accounts of Collegiate Apparel Shop Inc. (CASI) have the following balances, after adjustments, at year end:

Sales revenue	$280,000
Rent revenue	27,000
Interest income	5,000

These revenue accounts would be closed and the balances transferred by the following closing journal entry:

A = L + SE
−312,000
+312,000

Cash flows: No effect

Sales Revenue	280,000	
Rent Revenue	27,000	
Interest Income	5,000	
Income Summary		312,000
(To close revenue accounts to Income Summary)		

Assume that the expense accounts, including Cost of Goods Sold, have the following balances, after adjustments, at year end:

Cost of goods sold	$206,000
Selling expenses	25,000
Administrative expenses	40,600
Interest expense	4,400
Income tax expense	13,000

These expense accounts would be closed and the balances transferred through the following closing journal entry:

A = L + SE
−289,000
+289,000

Cash flows: No effect

Income Summary	289,000	
Cost of Goods Sold		206,000
Selling Expenses		25,000
Administrative Expenses		40,600
Interest Expense		4,400
Income Tax Expense		13,000
(To close expense accounts to Income Summary)		

The Income Summary account now has a credit balance of $23,000, which is net income. **The net income is then transferred to retained earnings by closing the Income Summary account to Retained Earnings,** as follows:

A = L + SE
−23,000
+23,000

Cash flows: No effect

Income Summary	23,000	
Retained Earnings		23,000
(To close Income Summary to Retained Earnings)		

Any items posted to Other Comprehensive Income would similarly be closed out to Accumulated Other Comprehensive Income, which acts like a second retained earnings account for certain gains and losses booked to Other Comprehensive Income. Assuming

CASI had holding gains on Fair Value through Other Comprehensive Income investments of $12,000, the holding gain would be closed to as follows:

A = L + SE
         −12,000
         +12,000
 	
Cash flows: No effect
	Unrealized Holding Gain or Loss-OCI
	   Accumulated Other Comprehensive Income
	     (To close holding gains on Fair Value-OCI investments
	     to Accumulated Other Comprehensive Income)
		12,000
		
		              12,000

Assuming that dividends of $7,000 were declared and distributed during the year, the Dividends account is closed directly to Retained Earnings, as follows:

A = L + SE
        −7,000
        +7,000
 	
Cash flows: No effect
	Retained Earnings
	   Dividends
	     (To close Dividends to Retained Earnings)
		7,000
		
		          7,000

After the closing process is completed, each statement of comprehensive income account is balanced out to zero and is ready to be used in the next accounting period. Illustration 3-25 shows the closing process in T account form.

Illustration **3-25**

The Closing Process

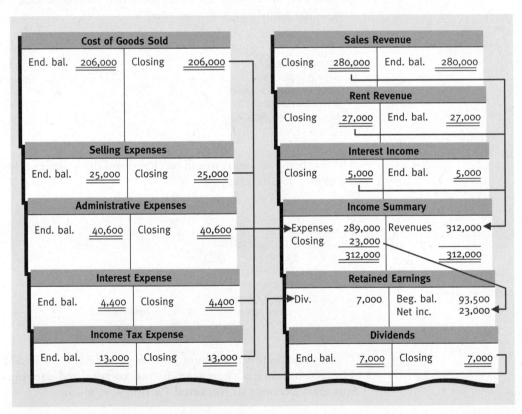

Inventory and Cost of Goods Sold

The closing procedures just shown assume that a perpetual inventory system is being used. With a **perpetual inventory system**, purchases and sales are recorded directly in the inventory account as they occur. Therefore, the balance in Inventory should represent the ending inventory amount, and no adjusting entries are needed to update the inventory account. To be sure that the inventory amount is accurate, a **physical count** of the items in the inventory is generally done each year.

In the perpetual inventory system, since all purchases are debited directly to the Inventory account, there is no separate Purchases account. However, a Cost of Goods Sold account is used to accumulate what is issued from inventory. That is, when inventory items are sold, the cost of the sold goods is credited to Inventory and debited to Cost of Goods Sold.

With a **periodic inventory system**, a Purchases account is used, and the Inventory account is unchanged during the period. The Inventory account therefore represents the beginning inventory amount throughout the period. At the end of the accounting period, the Inventory account must be adjusted by **closing out the beginning inventory amount and recording the ending inventory amount**. The ending inventory is determined by physically counting the items on hand and valuing them at cost or at the lower of cost or market. Under the periodic inventory system, cost of goods sold is therefore determined by adding the beginning inventory to net purchases and deducting the ending inventory.

To illustrate how cost of goods sold is calculated with a periodic inventory system, assume that Collegiate Apparel Shop has a beginning inventory of $30,000, purchases of $200,000, Freight-in of $6,000, purchase returns and allowances of $1,000, purchase discounts of $3,000, and ending inventory of $26,000. Each of these accounts would be closed out to cost of goods sold (as illustrated in Chapter 8) and then the cost of goods sold account would be closed to the income summary account. The calculation of cost of goods sold is shown in Illustration 3-26.

Illustration 3-26

Calculation of Cost of Goods Sold

Beginning inventory			$30,000
Purchases		$200,000	
Less: Purchase returns and allowances	$1,000		
Less: Purchase discounts	3,000	4,000	
Net purchases		196,000	
Plus: Freight-in		6,000	
Cost of goods purchased			202,000
Cost of goods available for sale			232,000
Less: Ending inventory			26,000
Cost of goods sold			$206,000

Cost of goods sold will be the same whether using the perpetual or periodic method.

Post-Closing Trial Balance

We already mentioned that a trial balance is taken after the period's regular transactions have been entered and that a second trial balance (the adjusted trial balance) is taken after the adjusting entries have been posted. A third trial balance may be taken after posting the closing entries. The trial balance after closing, often called the **post-closing trial balance**, shows that equal debits and credits have been posted to the Income Summary account. The post-closing trial balance consists only of asset, liability, and owners' equity accounts (that is, the permanent accounts).

Reversing Entries

After the financial statements have been prepared and the books have been closed, it is often helpful to reverse some of the adjusting entries before recording the next period's regular transactions. Such entries are called **reversing entries**. A reversing entry is made at the beginning of the next accounting period and is the exact opposite of the related adjusting entry made in the previous period. The recording of reversing entries is an optional step in the accounting cycle that may be done at the beginning of the next accounting period. Appendix 3A discusses reversing entries in more detail.

The Accounting Cycle Summarized

The steps in the accounting cycle are summarized in Illustration 3-27.

Illustration 3-27

The Accounting Cycle Summarized

The procedures that form the complete accounting cycle normally performed for each annual fiscal period is summarized below.

1. Enter the period's transactions in appropriate journals.
2. Post from the journals to the ledger (or ledgers).
3. Take an unadjusted trial balance (trial balance).
4. Prepare adjusting journal entries and post to the ledger(s).
5. Take a trial balance after adjusting (adjusted trial balance).
6. Prepare the financial statements from the second (adjusted) trial balance.
7. Prepare closing journal entries and post to the ledger(s).
8. Take a trial balance after closing (post-closing trial balance).
9. Prepare reversing entries (optional) and post to the ledger(s).

USING A WORK SHEET

To make the end-of-period (monthly, quarterly, or annually) accounting and reporting process easier, a work sheet is often used. A **work sheet** is a spreadsheet that is used to adjust the account balances and prepare the financial statements. Using a work sheet helps accountants prepare financial statements on a timelier basis. It is not necessary to delay preparing the financial statements until the adjusting and closing entries are journalized and posted. The **10-column work sheet** shown later in this chapter (Illustration 3-28) has columns for the first trial balance, adjustments, adjusted trial balance, statement of comprehensive income, and statement of financial position.

The work sheet does not replace the financial statements. Instead, it is an informal device for accumulating and sorting the information that is needed for the financial statements. Completing the work sheet makes it more certain that all of the details of the end-of-period accounting and statement preparation have been brought together properly.

Adjustments Entered on the Work Sheet

The following items, (a) through (g), are the basis for the adjusting entries made in the work sheet in Illustration 3-28:

(a) Office equipment is amortized at the rate of 10% per year based on an original cost of $67,000.

(b) Estimated bad debts are 0.25% of sales ($400,000).

(c) Insurance of $360 expired during the year.

(d) Interest of $800 accrued on notes receivable as at December 31.

(e) The Rent Expense account contains $500 of rent paid in advance, which is applicable to next year.

(f) Property taxes of $2,000 accrued to December 31.

(g) The fair value through other comprehensive income (FV-OCI) investments account is based on the original cost of an equity investment acquired on July 1. On December 31, the fair value of the investment is $15,000. Tax calculations for OCI items will be covered in Chapter 18. To simplify matters for Chapter 3, assume that changes in fair value for FV-OCI investments are non-taxable.

The adjusting entries shown on the December 31, 2014 work sheet are as follows:

(a) Depreciation Expense—Office Equipment	6,700	
Accumulated Depreciation—Office Equipment		6,700
(b) Bad Debt Expense	1,000	
Allowance for Doubtful Accounts		1,000
(c) Insurance Expense	360	
Prepaid Insurance		360
(d) Interest Receivable	800	
Interest Income		800
(e) Prepaid Rent	500	
Rent Expense		500
(f) Property Tax Expense	2,000	
Property Tax Payable		2,000
(g) FV-OCI Investments	3,000	
Unrealized Holding Gain or Loss-OCI		3,000

These adjusting entries are transferred to the work sheet's Adjustments columns and each adjustment can be named by letter. The accounts that are set up from the adjusting entries and that are not already in the trial balance are listed below the totals of the trial balance, as shown on the work sheet. The Adjustments columns are then totalled and balanced.

Work Sheet Columns

The 10-column work sheet for Uptown Cabinet Corp. is shown in Illustration 3-28. Each of the columns is explained below.

Trial Balance Columns

Data for the trial balance are obtained from the ledger balances of Uptown Cabinet Corp. at December 31. The amount for Inventory, $40,000, is the year-end inventory amount under a perpetual inventory system.

Adjustments Columns

After all adjustment data are entered on the work sheet, the equality of the adjustment columns is established. The balances in all accounts are then extended to the adjusted trial balance columns.

Adjusted Trial Balance

The adjusted trial balance shows the balance of all accounts after adjustment at the end of the accounting period. For example, the $2,000 shown opposite Allowance for Doubtful Accounts in the Trial Balance Cr. column is added to the $1,000 in the Adjustments Cr. column. The $3,000 total is then extended to the Adjusted Trial Balance Cr. column.

Similarly, the $900 debit opposite Prepaid Insurance is reduced by the $360 credit in the Adjustments column. The result, $540, is shown in the Adjusted Trial Balance Dr. column.

Statement of Comprehensive Income and Statement of Financial Position Columns

All the debit items in the Adjusted Trial Balance columns are extended into the Statement of Comprehensive Income or Statement of Financial Position columns to the right. All the credit items are also extended. The next step is to total the Statement of Comprehensive

Income columns; the amount that is needed in order to balance the debit and credit columns is the total of the pre-tax income or loss for the period and OCI. The income (before tax and OCI) of $18,640 is shown in the Statement of Comprehensive Income Dr. column because revenues and gains exceeded expenses and losses by that amount. The unrealized holding gain or loss-OCI would eventually be closed out to Accumulated Other Comprehensive Income, whereas all other revenue and expense accounts would be closed to Retained Earnings.

Illustration 3-28

Work Sheet

	A	B		C		D		E		F	
1		UPTOWN CABINET CORP. Ten-Column Work Sheet For the Year Ended December 31, 2014									
	Accounts	Trial Balance		Adjustments		Adjusted Trial Balance		Statement of Comp. Income		Statement of Financial Position	
2		Dr.	Cr.	Dr.	Cr.	Dr.	Cr.	Dr.	Cr.	Dr.	Cr.
3	Cash	1,200				1,200				1,200	
4	Notes receivable	16,000				16,000				16,000	
5	Accounts receivable	41,000				41,000				41,000	
6	Allowance for doubtful accounts		2,000		(b)1,000		3,000				3,000
7	Inventory	40,000				40,000				40,000	
8	Prepaid insurance	900			(c)360	540				540	
9	FV-OCI investments	12,000		(g)3,000		15,000				15,000	
10	Office equipment	67,000				67,000				67,000	
11	Accumulated depreciation— office equipment		12,000		(a)6,700		18,700				18,700
12	Notes payable		20,000				20,000				20,000
13	Accounts payable		13,500				13,500				13,500
14	Bonds payable		30,000				30,000				30,000
15	Common shares		50,000				50,000				50,000
16	Retained earnings, Jan. 1, 2014		26,200				26,200				26,200
17	Sales revenue		400,000				400,000		400,000		
18	Cost of goods sold	316,000				316,000		316,000			
19	Salaries and wages expense	20,000				20,000		20,000			
20	Advertising expense	2,200				2,200		2,200			
21	Travel expense	8,000				8,000		8,000			
22	Office expense	19,000				19,000		19,000			
23	Telephone and internet expense	600				600		600			
24	Rent expense	4,800			(e)500	4,300		4,300			
25	Property tax expense	3,300		(f)2,000		5,300		5,300			
26	Interest expense	1,700				1,700		1,700			
27	**Totals**	**553,700**	**553,700**								
28	Depreciation expense			(a)6,700		6,700		6,700			
29	Bad debt expense			(b)1,000		1,000		1,000			
30	Insurance expense			(c)360		360		360			
31	Interest receivable			(d)800		800				800	
32	Interest income				(d)800		800		800		
33	Prepaid rent			(e)500		500				500	
34	Property tax payable				(f)2,000		2,000				2,000
35	Unrealized holding gain or loss-OCI				(g) 3,000		3,000		3,000		
36	**Totals**			**14,360**	**14,360**	567,200	567,200	385,160	403,800		
37	Income (before tax) and OCI							18,640			
38	**Totals**							**403,800**	**403,800**		
39	Income (before tax) and OCI								18,640		
40	Income tax expense			(h)3,440		3,440		3,440			
41	Income tax payable				(h)3,440		3,440				3,440
42	Net income and OCI							15,200			15,200
43	**Totals**					**570,640**	**570,640**	**18,640**	**18,640**	**182,040**	**182,040**

Income Taxes and Net Income

The federal and provincial income tax expense and related tax liability are calculated next (item [h] in Illustration 3-28). The company is assumed to use a tax rate of 22% to arrive at $3,440 (no allocation is made for deferred taxes on Other Comprehensive Income to simplify the example). This adjustment is entered in the Statement of Comprehensive Income Dr. column as Income Tax Expense and in the Statement of Financial Position Cr. column as Income Tax Payable. The following adjusting journal entry is recorded on December 31, 2014, posted to the general ledger, and then entered on the work sheet:

(h) Income Tax Expense	3,440	
Income Tax Payable		3,440
(To record income tax expense on income before tax)		

Next, the Statement of Comprehensive Income columns are balanced with the income taxes included. The $15,200 difference between the debit and credit columns in this illustration represents the total of net income plus OCI, or comprehensive income. The comprehensive income of $15,200 is entered in the Statement of Comprehensive Income Dr. column to achieve equality and in the Statement of Financial Position Cr. column.

Preparing Financial Statements from a Work Sheet

The work sheet gives the information that is needed to prepare financial statements without referring to the ledger or other records. In addition, the data have been sorted into appropriate columns, which makes it easier to prepare the statements.

The financial statements prepared from the 10-column work sheet are as follows: **Statement of Comprehensive Income for the Year Ended December 31, 2014 (Illustration 3-29), Statement of Changes in Shareholders' Equity for the Year Ended December 31, 2014 (Illustration 3-30), and Statement of Financial Position as at December 31, 2014 (Illustration 3-31).**

Statement of Comprehensive Income

The statement of comprehensive income in the illustration is for a trading or merchandising (retailing) business. If it were a manufacturing business, it would use three inventory accounts: raw materials, work-in-process, and finished goods. Salaries and wages are assumed to relate to selling. Earnings per share is based on net income (not comprehensive income), which will be covered in more detail in Chapter 4.

Statement of Changes in Shareholders' Equity

The net income earned by a corporation may be retained in the business or distributed to shareholders by paying dividends. In Illustration 3-30, the net income earned during the year was added to the balance of Retained Earnings on January 1, increasing the balance to $38,400 on December 31. No dividends were declared during the year. A statement of changes in shareholders' equity is required for public companies instead of a statement of changes in retained earnings (for companies following ASPE, for instance). The statement of changes in shareholders' equity includes changes in all equity accounts, including Accumulated Other Comprehensive Income, Retained Earnings, and Common Shares. This statement will be covered in more detail in Chapter 4.

Illustration 3-29

Statement of Comprehensive Income

UPTOWN CABINET CORP.
Statement of Comprehensive Income
For the Year Ended December 31, 2014

Sales revenue			$400,000
Cost of goods sold			316,000
Gross profit on sales			84,000
Selling expenses			
Salaries and wages expense		$20,000	
Advertising expense		2,200	
Travel expense		8,000	
Total selling expenses		30,200	
Administrative expenses			
Office expense	$19,000		
Telephone and internet expense	600		
Rent expense	4,300		
Property tax expense	5,300		
Depreciation expense—office equipment	6,700		
Bad debt expense	1,000		
Insurance expense	360		
Total administrative expenses		37,260	
Total selling and administrative expenses			67,460
Income from operations			16,540
Other revenues and gains			
Interest income			800
			17,340
Other expenses and losses			
Interest expense			1,700
Income before income taxes			15,640
Income tax expense			3,440
Net income			12,200
Other comprehensive income			3,000
Comprehensive income			$ 15,200
Earnings per share			$ 1.22

UPTOWN CABINET CORP.
Statement of Changes in Shareholders' Equity
For the Year Ended December 31, 2014

	Total	Common Shares	Comprehensive Income	Retained Earnings	Accumulated OCI
Beginning, Jan. 1, 2014	$76,200	$50,000	$ –0–	$26,200	$ –0–
Net income for 2014	12,200		12,200	12,200	
Other comprehensive income	3,000		3,000		3,000
Comprehensive income			$15,200		
Ending balance, Dec. 31, 2014	$91,400	$50,000		$38,400	$3,000

Illustration 3-30

Statement of Changes in Shareholders' Equity

Statement of Financial Position

The statement of financial position prepared from the 10-column work sheet has new items such as interest receivable created by year-end adjusting entries. Interest receivable, prepaid insurance, and prepaid rent are included as current assets. These assets are considered current because they will be converted into cash or consumed in the ordinary routine of the business in a relatively short period of time. The amount of Allowance for Doubtful

Accounts is deducted from the total of accounts, notes, and interest receivable because it is estimated that only $54,800 of the $57,800 will be collected in cash. If the allowance relates only to Accounts Receivable, it could be set up as a contra account for just Accounts Receivable. The Fair Value-OCI Investments are typically considered a non-current (or long-term) asset, as discussed in Chapter 9.

In the property, plant, and equipment section, the accumulated depreciation is deducted from the cost of the office equipment; the difference in the two amounts is the book value or carrying amount of the office equipment.

Illustration 3-31

Statement of Financial Position

UPTOWN CABINET CORP.
Statement of Financial Position
As at December 31, 2014

Assets

Current assets			
Cash			$ 1,200
Notes receivable	$16,000		
Accounts receivable	41,000		
Interest receivable	800	$57,800	
Less: Allowance for doubtful accounts		3,000	54,800
Inventory			40,000
Prepaid insurance			540
Prepaid rent			500
Total current assets			97,040
Non-current assets			
Long-term investments			
Fair Value-OCI investments			15,000
Property, plant, and equipment			
Office equipment		67,000	
Less: Accumulated depreciation		18,700	
Total property, plant, and equipment			48,300
Total assets			$160,340

Liabilities and Shareholders' Equity

Current liabilities			
Notes payable			$ 20,000
Accounts payable			13,500
Property tax payable			2,000
Income tax payable			3,440
Total current liabilities			38,940
Non-current liabilities			
Bonds payable, due June 30, 2018			30,000
Total liabilities			68,940
Shareholders' equity			
Common shares, issued and outstanding,			
10,000 shares		$50,000	
Retained earnings		38,400	
Accumulated other comprehensive income		3,000	
Total shareholders' equity			91,400
Total liabilities and shareholders' equity			$160,340

Property tax payable is shown as a current liability because it is an obligation that is payable within a year. Other short-term accrued liabilities would also be shown as current liabilities.

The bonds payable, due in 2018, are non-current liabilities and are shown in a separate section. (Interest on the bonds was paid on December 31.) Accumulated Other Comprehensive Income is included in the shareholders' equity section.

Closing Entries

The entries for the closing process are as follows:

GENERAL JOURNAL
December 31, 2014

Interest Income	800	
Sales Revenue	400,000	
Cost of Goods Sold		316,000
Salaries and Wages Expense		20,000
Advertising Expense		2,200
Travel Expense		8,000
Office Expense		19,000
Telephone and Internet Expense		600
Rent Expense		4,300
Property Tax Expense		5,300
Depreciation Expense—Office Equipment		6,700
Bad Debt Expense		1,000
Insurance Expense		360
Interest Expense		1,700
Income Tax Expense		3,440
Income Summary		12,200
(To close revenues and expenses to Income Summary)		
Income Summary	12,200	
Retained Earnings		12,200
(To close Income Summary to Retained Earnings)		
Unrealized Holding Gain or Loss–OCI	3,000	
Accumulated Other Comprehensive Income		3,000
(To close other comprehensive income items to		
Accumulated Other Comprehensive Income)		

Monthly Statements, Yearly Closing

Using a work sheet at the end of each month or quarter makes it possible to prepare interim financial statements even though the books are closed only at the end of each year. For example, assume that a business that closes its books on December 31 wants monthly financial statements. At the end of January, a work sheet similar to the one illustrated in this chapter can be prepared to supply the information that is needed for the statements for January. At the end of February, a work sheet can be used again. Note that because the accounts were not closed at the end of January, the statement of comprehensive income taken from the work sheet on February 28 will present the net income for two months. To obtain a statement of comprehensive income for only the month of February, the items in the January statement are simply subtracted from the same items in the statement of comprehensive income for the months of January and February together.

The March work sheet would show the revenues and expenses for three months, and the revenues and expenses for the first two months could be subtracted to supply the amounts needed for a statement of comprehensive income for the month of March only, and so on throughout the year.

SUMMARY OF LEARNING OBJECTIVES

1 Understand basic accounting terminology.

It is important to understand the following terms: (1) event, (2) transaction, (3) account, (4) permanent and temporary accounts, (5) ledger, (6) journal, (7) posting, (8) trial balance, (9) adjusting entries, (10) financial statements, and (11) closing entries.

2 Explain double-entry rules.

The left side of any account is the debit side; the right side is the credit side. All asset and expense accounts are increased on the left or debit side and decreased on the right or credit side. Conversely, all liability and revenue accounts are increased on the right or credit side and decreased on the left or debit side. Shareholders' equity accounts, Common Stock, and Retained Earnings are increased on the credit side, whereas Dividends is increased on the debit side.

3 Explain how transactions affect the accounting equation.

In a double-entry accounting system, for every debit there must be a credit, and vice versa. This leads us to the basic accounting equation for corporations: Assets = Liabilities + Shareholders' Equity. The effect of individual transactions on the statement of financial position can be explained using the basic accounting equation. The shareholders' equity portion of the equation can also be expanded to illustrate the effect of transactions on components of equity such as common shares and retained earnings. Whenever a transaction occurs, the elements of the equation change, but the equality of the two sides of the equation remains unaffected.

4 Identify the steps in the accounting cycle and the steps in the recording process.

The basic steps in the accounting cycle are (1) identification and measurement of transactions and other events, (2) journalizing, (3) posting, (4) the unadjusted trial balance, (5) adjustments, (6) the adjusted trial balance, (7) statement preparation, and (8) closing. The first three steps in the accounting cycle form the basis of the recording process used by most medium-sized companies on a daily basis. The simplest journal form is a chronological listing of transactions and events that are expressed as debits and credits to particular accounts. The items entered in a general journal must then be transferred (posted) to the general ledger.

To help prepare financial statements, an unadjusted trial balance should be prepared at the end of a specific period (usually a month, quarter, or year) after the entries have been recorded in the journals and posted to the general ledger.

5 Explain the reasons for and prepare adjusting entries.

Adjustments achieve a proper matching of revenues and expenses, which is needed to determine the correct net income for the current period and to achieve an accurate statement of the end-of-the-period balances in assets, liabilities, and owners' equity accounts. When preparing adjusting journal entries, you must first determine how the original transaction was recorded. For example, was an asset created earlier in the fiscal year (such as prepaid rent) when the initial payment was made? If so, an adjustment for the related expense is required. Alternatively, if a statement of comprehensive income account was used initially, an adjustment may be required to set up the proper statement of financial position account at the end of the period.

6 Explain how the type of ownership structure affects the financial statements.

The type of ownership structure that a business enterprise uses determines the types of accounts that are part of the equity section. In a corporation, ordinary or common shares, contributed surplus, retained earnings, and accumulated other comprehensive income are commonly shown separately on the statement of financial position. In a proprietorship or partnership, an owner's capital account is used to indicate the investment in the company by the owner(s). An owner's drawings or withdrawal account may be used to indicate withdrawals by the owner(s). These two accounts are grouped or netted under owners' equity.

7 Prepare closing entries and consider other matters relating to the closing process.

In the closing process, all of the revenue and expense account balances (income statement items) are transferred to a clearing account called Income Summary, which is used only at the end of the fiscal year. Revenues and expenses are matched in the Income Summary account. The net result of this matching, which represents the net income or net loss for the period, is then transferred to a shareholders' equity account (retained earnings for a corporation and capital accounts for proprietorships and partnerships).

Under a perpetual inventory system there are a few additional items to consider. For example, the balance in the inventory account should represent the ending inventory amount. When the inventory records are maintained in a periodic inventory system, a purchases account is used; the inventory account is unchanged during the period. The inventory account balance represents the beginning inventory amount throughout the period. At the end of the accounting period, the inventory account must be adjusted by closing out the beginning inventory amount and recording the ending inventory amount.

8 Prepare a 10-column work sheet and financial statements.

The 10-column work sheet provides columns for the first trial balance, adjustments, adjusted trial balance, statement of comprehensive income, and statement of financial position. The work sheet does not replace the financial statements. Instead, it is the accountant's informal device for accumulating and sorting the information that is needed for the financial statements.

KEY TERMS

account, p. 91
accounting cycle, p. 94
accounting information system, p. 90
accrued expenses, p. 106
accrued revenues, p. 105
accumulated other comprehensive
  income, p. 111
adjusted trial balance, p. 91
adjusting entries, p. 91
balance sheet, p. 91
book value, p. 103
carrying amount, p. 103
closing entries, p. 91
closing process, p. 112
contra asset account, p. 103
credit, p. 92

debit, p. 92
depreciation/amortization, p. 102
double-entry accounting, p. 92
event, p. 91
financial statements, p. 91
general journal, p. 96
general ledger, p. 91
income statement, p. 91
journal, p. 91
periodic inventory system, p. 115
permanent accounts, p. 91
perpetual inventory system, p. 114
post-closing trial balance, p. 115
posting, p. 91
prepaid expenses, p. 100
reversing entries, p. 91

special journals, p. 96
statement of cash flows, p. 91
statement of changes in shareholders'
  equity, p. 91
statement of comprehensive
  income, p. 91
statement of financial position, p. 91
statement of retained earnings, p. 91
subsidiary ledger, p. 91
T account, p. 96
temporary accounts, p. 91
transaction, p. 91
trial balance, p. 91
unearned revenues, p. 100
useful life, p. 102
work sheet, p. 116

APPENDIX 3A

USING REVERSING ENTRIES

Objective 9
Identify adjusting entries that may be reversed.

The purpose of reversing entries is to make it easier to record transactions in the next accounting period. The use of reversing entries does not change the amounts reported in the previous period's financial statements.

Illustration of Reversing Entries—Accruals

Reversing entries are usually used for reversing two types of adjusting entries: accrued revenues and accrued expenses. To illustrate the optional use of reversing entries for accrued expenses, we will use the following transaction and adjustment data:

1. October 24 (initial salary entry): $4,000 of salaries and wages expense incurred between October 1 and October 24 is paid.

2. October 31 (adjusting entry): $1,200 of salaries and wages expense is incurred between October 25 and October 31. This will be paid in the November 7 payroll.

3. November 7 (subsequent salary entry): $2,500 of salaries and wages expense is paid. Of this amount, $1,200 applies to accrued salaries and wages payable at October 31 and $1,300 was incurred between November 1 and November 7.

The comparative entries are shown in Illustration 3A-1.

Reversing Entries Not Used				Reversing Entries Used			
Initial Salary Entry				**Initial Salary Entry**			
Oct. 24	Salaries and Wages Expense	4,000		Oct. 24	Salaries and Wages Expense	4,000	
	Cash		4,000		Cash		4,000
Adjusting Entry				**Adjusting Entry**			
Oct. 31	Salaries and Wages Expense	1,200		Oct. 31	Salaries and Wages Expense	1,200	
	Salaries and Wages Payable		1,200		Salaries and Wages Payable		1,200
Closing Entry				**Closing Entry**			
Oct. 31	Income Summary	5,200		Oct. 31	Income Summary	5,200	
	Salaries and Wages Expense		5,200		Salaries and Wages Expense		5,200
Reversing Entry				**Reversing Entry**			
Nov. 1	No entry is made.			Nov. 1	Salaries and Wages Payable	1,200	
					Salaries and Wages Expense		1,200
Subsequent Salary Entry				**Subsequent Salary Entry**			
Nov. 7	Salaries and Wages Payable	1,200		Nov. 7	Salaries and Wages Expense	2,500	
	Salaries and Wages Expense	1,300			Cash		2,500
	Cash		2,500				

Illustration 3A-1

Comparison of Entries for Accruals, with and Without Reversing Entries

The illustration shows that the first three entries are the same whether or not reversing entries are used. The last two entries, however, are different. The November 1 reversing entry eliminates the $1,200 balance in Salaries and Wages Payable that was created by the October 31 adjusting entry. The reversing entry also creates a $1,200 credit balance in the Salaries and Wages Expense account. As you know, it is unusual for an expense account to have a credit balance; however, the balance is correct in this instance. It is correct because the entire amount of the first salary payment in the new accounting period will be debited to Salaries and Wages Expense. This debit will eliminate the credit balance, and the resulting debit balance in the expense account will equal the salaries and wages expense incurred in the new accounting period ($1,300 in this example).

When reversing entries are made, all cash payments of expenses can be debited to the expense account. This means that on November 7 (and every payday), Salaries and Wages Expense can be debited for the amount paid without having to consider any accrued salaries and wages payable. Being able to make the same entry each time simplifies the recording process in an accounting system.

Illustration of Reversing Entries—Prepayments

Up to this point, we have assumed that all prepayments are recorded as prepaid expenses or unearned revenues. In some cases, prepayments are recorded directly in expense or revenue accounts. When this occurs, prepayments may also be reversed. To illustrate the use of reversing entries for prepaid expenses, we will use the following transaction and adjustment data:

December 10 (initial entry): $20,000 of office supplies is purchased for cash.

December 31 (adjusting entry): $5,000 of office supplies is on hand.

The comparative entries are shown in Illustration 3A-2.

Reversing Entries Not Used				Reversing Entries Used		
Initial Purchase of Supplies Entry				**Initial Purchase of Supplies Entry**		
Dec. 10	Supplies	20,000		Dec. 10	Supplies Expense	20,000
	Cash		20,000		Cash		20,000
Adjusting Entry				**Adjusting Entry**		
Dec. 31	Supplies Expense	15,000		Dec. 31	Supplies	5,000
	Supplies		15,000		Supplies Expense		5,000
Closing Entry				**Closing Entry**		
Dec. 31	Income Summary	15,000		Dec. 31	Income Summary	15,000
	Supplies Expense		15,000		Supplies Expense		15,000
Reversing Entry				**Reversing Entry**		
Jan. 1	No entry			Jan. 1	Supplies Expense	5,000
					Supplies		5,000

Illustration 3A-2

Comparison of Entries for Prepayments, with and Without Reversing Entries

After the adjusting entry on December 31 (with or without reversing entries), the asset account Supplies shows a balance of $5,000 and Supplies Expense shows a balance of $15,000. If Supplies Expense was debited when the supplies were first purchased, a reversing entry is made to return to the expense account the cost of the still unused supplies. The company then continues to debit Supplies Expense for additional purchases of office supplies during the next period.

It could be asked why all prepaid items are not simply entered originally into real accounts (assets and liabilities), as this would make reversing entries unnecessary. Sometimes this practice is followed. Doing this is particularly useful for items that need to be allocated over several periods (such as supplies and parts inventories). However, items that do not follow this regular pattern and that may or may not involve two or more periods are usually first entered in revenue or expense accounts. The revenue and expense accounts may not require adjusting and are systematically closed to Income Summary. Using the reversing accounts adds consistency to the accounting system and makes the recording simpler, especially when a large number of such transactions occur during the year. For example, the bookkeeper knows that when an invoice is received for anything except a capital asset acquisition, the amount is expensed. This way, when the invoice is received, the bookkeeper does not have to worry about whether or not the item will result in a prepaid expense at the end of the period, because adjustments will be made at that time.

Summary of Reversing Entries

The guidelines for using reversing entries can be summarized as follows:

1. All accrued items should be reversed.

2. All prepaid items for which the original cash transaction was debited or credited to an expense or revenue account should be reversed.

3. Adjusting entries for estimated items such as depreciation and bad debts are not reversed.

Although reversing entries reduce potential errors and are therefore often used, they do not have to be used. Many accountants avoid them entirely. Reversing entries add an extra step to the bookkeeping process. Also there may be instances where it does not

Quiz

make sense to use them. As an example, assume a company with a December 31 year end has accrued six months' worth of interest on a bond that pays interest annually (June 30 interest payment date) at year end. If the company releases financial information monthly, it would not make sense to reverse the entry in January since this would show a credit balance when the monthly reports are prepared.

SUMMARY OF LEARNING OBJECTIVES FOR APPENDIX 3A

9 Identify adjusting entries that may be reversed.

Reversing entries are usually used for reversing two types of adjusting entries: accrued revenues and

accrued expenses. Prepayments may also be reversed if the initial entry to record the transaction is made to an expense or revenue account.

Note: All assignment material with an asterisk (*) relates to the appendix to the chapter. All references to balance sheet and statement of financial position refer to the same financial statement. If not otherwise specified, depreciation expense should be calculated for the portion of the accounting period the asset is used.

Brief Exercises

(LO 1) BE3-1 Plant Inc. uses the following accounts in its trial balance:

1. Sales
2. Investment Loss
3. Dividends
4. Salaries and Wages Payable
5. Fair Value-OCI Investment
6. Cost of Goods Sold
7. Accumulated Other Comprehensive Income
8. Allowance for Doubtful Accounts
9. Fair Value—Net Income Investments
10. Retained Earnings
11. Interest Receivable
12. Unrealized Gain or Loss-OCI

Indicate whether each account is (a) a permanent account or a temporary account and (b) an asset, contra-asset, liability, revenue, expense, gain, loss, or shareholders' equity account.

(LO 2) BE3-2 Moosa Corp. has the following accounts:

1. Accounts Receivable
2. Income Tax Expense
3. Rent Revenue
4. Retained Earnings
5. Bank Loans

6. Unrealized Gain or Loss-OCI

7. Accumulated Other Comprehensive Income

For each account, indicate (a) whether a $100 debit to the account would increase or decrease the account, and (b) whether the account balance at the end of the fiscal year would be adjusted during the closing process.

(LO 3)   BE3-3   Kothari Ltd. made the following transactions:

1. Payment of a $200 invoice on account

2. Increase in the fair value of a Fair Value—Net Income Investment by $250

3. Sale on account for $100

4. Purchase of equipment paid for with $500 cash and a $1,000 note payable

5. Increase in the fair value of a Fair Value-OCI Investment by $150

6. Repayment of a $2,000 bank loan

Indicate the effect of each of the transactions on (a) the basic accounting equation and (b) the expanded basic accounting equation.

(LO 4)   BE3-4   The following transactions for Juan More Taco Inc. (JMT) occurred in the month of May. Prepare journal entries for each transaction.

May	1	Owners invest $12,000 cash in exchange for common shares of JMT Inc., a small chain of fast food outlets.
	3	Buy ovens and computers on account for $4,500.
	13	Pay $800 to landlord for May rent.
	21	Bill $750 to Sub's Away for a staff function, for which JMT provided food and beverages.

(LO 4)   BE3-5   One Wiser Corp. had the following transactions during the first month of business. Journalize the transactions.

August	2	Invested $12,000 cash and $2,500 of equipment in the business in exchange for common shares.
	7	Purchased supplies on account for $600. (Debit asset account.)
	12	Performed services for clients, collecting $1,300 in cash and billing the clients $670 for the remainder.
	15	Paid August rent, $600.
	19	Counted supplies and determined that only $270 of the supplies purchased on August 7 were still on hand.

(LO 4, 5)   BE3-6   On July 1, 2014, Blondie Ltd. pays $18,000 to No Claims Insurance Ltd. for a three-year insurance contract. Both companies have fiscal years ending December 31. Prepare two sets of journal entries for Blondie, with each set of journal entries recording the July 1, 2014 entry and the December 31, 2014 adjusting entry. Treat the expenditure as an asset in the first set of journal entries, and treat the expenditure as an expense in the second set of journal entries.

(LO 4, 5)   BE3-7   Using the data in BE3-6, prepare two sets of journal entries for No Claims Insurance, with each set of journal entries recording the July 1, 2014 entry and the December 31, 2014 adjusting entry. No Claims uses an Unearned Revenue account and an Insurance Revenue account. Treat the receipt of cash as a liability in the first set of journal entries, and treat the receipt of cash as revenue in the second set of journal entries.

(LO 4, 5)   BE3-8   On August 1, Secret Sauce Technologies Inc. paid $12,600 in advance for two years' membership in a global technology association. Prepare two sets of journal entries for Secret Sauce, with each set of journal entries recording the August 1 journal entry and the December 31 adjusting entry. Treat the expenditure as an asset in the first set of journal entries, and treat the expenditure as an expense in the second set of journal entries.

(LO 4, 5)   BE3-9   Store-it-Here owns a warehouse. On September 1, it rented storage space to a lessee (tenant) for six months for a total cash payment of $12,000 received in advance. Prepare two sets of journal entries for Store-it-Here, with each set of journal entries recording the September 1 journal entry and the December 31 adjusting entry. Treat the receipt of cash as a liability in the first set of journal entries, and treat the receipt of cash as a revenue in the second set of journal entries.

(LO 4, 5)   BE3-10   ABC Commerce Corp.'s weekly payroll totals $20,000 and is paid every two weeks. The final payroll for the year was for the week ended December 24. ABC pays full payroll during the holiday season. The next payroll was paid on January 7. To prepare for year end, employees were expected to return to work on December 28. Prepare ABC's adjusting entry on December 31, and the journal entry to record the $40,000 cash payment on January 7.

(LO 5) BE3-11   Included in Carville Corp.'s December 31, 2014 trial balance is a note payable of $20,000. The note is an eight-month, 12% note dated October 1, 2014. Prepare Carville's December 31, 2014 adjusting entry to record the accrued interest, and June 1, 2015 journal entry to record payment of principal and interest due to the lender.

(LO 5) BE3-12   Prepare the following adjusting entries at December 31 for Karpai Ltd:

1. Interest on notes receivable of $600 is accrued.

2. Fees earned but unbilled total $1,800.

3. Salaries earned of $1,200 have not been recorded.

4. Bad debt expense for the year is $900.

Use the following account titles: Service Revenue, Accounts Receivable, Interest Income, Interest Receivable, Salaries and Wages Expense, Salaries and Wages Payable, Allowance for Doubtful Accounts, and Bad Debt Expense.

(LO 5) BE3-13   At the end of Rafael Limited's first year of operations, its trial balance shows Equipment $20,000; Accumulated Depreciation—Equipment $0; and Depreciation Expense $0. Depreciation for the year is estimated to be $4,000. Prepare the adjusting entry for depreciation at December 31, and provide the balance sheet presentation for the equipment at December 31.

(LO 5) BE3-14   Yeliw Enterprises purchases inventory amounting to $12,000, and records the expenditure as a debit to Office Equipment. What would be the effect of this error on the balance sheet and income statement in the period of the purchase, assuming the inventory is sold during the year? (Assume the sale and related accounts receivable were correctly recorded when the inventory was sold.)

(LO 5) BE3-15   On May 1, Bashir and Hendricks (B&H), Accountants, pays $1,200 to a landlord for one month's rent in advance for the month of May.

(a) Assuming that B&H records all prepayments in (permanent) balance sheet accounts:
1. Prepare the journal entry B&H should record when it pays the rent on May 1.
2. Prepare the adjusting entry B&H should record at the end of May, when the month's rent has expired.

(b) Assuming that B&H records all prepayments in (temporary) income statement accounts:
1. Prepare the journal entry B&H should record when it pays the rent on May 1.
2. Prepare the adjusting entry B&H should record at the end of May, when the month's rent has expired.

(c) Compare and comment on the ending balances of each account, for each alternative in parts (a) and (b).

(LO 5) BE3-16   Jerry Holiday is the maintenance supervisor for Ray's Insurance Co. and has recently purchased a riding lawn mower and accessories that will be used in caring for the grounds around corporate headquarters. He sent the following information to the accounting department:

Cost of mower and accessories	$9,600	Date purchased	July 1, 2014
Estimated useful life	8 years	Monthly salary of groundskeeper	$1,100
		Estimated annual fuel cost	$150

Calculate the amount of depreciation expense (for the mower and accessories) that should be reported on Ray's Insurance Co.'s December 31, 2014 income statement. Assume straight-line depreciation.

(LO 7) BE3-17   Willis Corporation has Beginning Inventory $76,000; Purchases $486,000; Freight-in $16,200; Purchase Returns $5,800; Purchase Discounts $5,000; and Ending Inventory $69,500. Calculate Willis's cost of goods sold.

(LO 7) BE3-18   Tiger Inc. has the following year-end account balances: Sales Revenue $928,900; Interest Income $17,500; Cost of Goods Sold $406,200; Operating Expenses $129,000; Income Tax Expense $55,100; and Dividends $15,900. Prepare the year-end closing entries.

(LO 9) *BE3-19   Pelican Inc. made a December 31 adjusting entry to debit Salaries and Wages Expense and credit Salaries and Wages Payable for $2,700. On January 2, Pelican paid the weekly payroll of $5,000. Prepare Pelican's (a) January 1 reversing entry, (b) January 2 entry (assuming the reversing entry was prepared), and (c) January 2 entry (assuming the reversing entry was not prepared).

Exercises

(LO 4) E3-1 (Transaction Analysis—Service Company) Bill Rosenberg recently opened his legal practice. During the first month of operations of his business (a sole proprietorship), the following events and transactions occurred:

April	2	Invested $15,000 cash along with equipment valued at $10,000 in the business.
	2	Hired a secretary-receptionist at a salary of $480 per week payable monthly.
	3	Purchased $1,200 of supplies on account. (Debit an asset account.)
	7	Paid office rent of $750 for the month.
	11	Completed the preparation of a will and billed the client $1,500 for services rendered. (Use the Service Revenue account.)
	12	Received a $4,200 retainer for future services.
	17	Received cash of $2,900 for services completed for Botticelli Limited.
	21	Paid insurance expense of $180.
	30	Paid the secretary-receptionist $1,920 for the month.
	30	A count of supplies indicated that $220 of supplies had been consumed.
	30	Purchased a new computer for $4,100 paid for with personal funds. (The computer will be used only for business purposes.)

Instructions

Journalize the transactions in the general journal. (Omit explanations.)

(LO 4) E3-2 (Corrected Trial Balance) The April 30, 2014 trial balance below of Many Happy Returns Company, a sole proprietorship, does not balance. Your review of the ledger reveals the following:

1. Each account has a normal balance.

2. The debit footings (totals) in Prepaid Insurance, Accounts Payable, and Property Tax Expense were each understated by $200.

3. Transposition errors were made in Accounts Receivable and Service Revenue, and the correct balances are $3,290 and $8,860, respectively.

4. A debit posting to Advertising Expense of $300 was omitted.

5. A $1,500 cash drawing by the owner was debited to Happy Tremblay's Owner's Capital, and credited to Cash.

	Debit	Credit
Cash	$ 4,800	
Accounts receivable	3,920	
Prepaid insurance	700	
Equipment		$ 8,000
Accounts payable		4,500
Property tax payable	560	
Owner's capital		11,200
Service revenue	8,680	
Salaries and wages expense	4,200	
Advertising expense	1,100	
Supplies expense		1,330
Property tax expense		800
	$23,960	$25,830

Instructions

Prepare a correct trial balance.

(LO 4) E3-3 (Corrected Trial Balance) Below is the April 30 trial balance of Blues Around the Corner Corporation:

	Debit	Credit
Cash	$ 3,238	
Accounts receivable	15,799	
Supplies	1,122	
Equipment	9,650	
Accumulated depreciation—equipment		$ 1,250
Accounts payable		3,212
Salaries and wages payable		850
Common shares		6,000

	Debit	Credit
Retained earnings		13,185
Service revenue		10,722
Salaries and wages expense	3,000	
Office expense	2,410	
	$35,219	$35,219

An examination of the ledger shows these errors:

1. Salaries and Wages Payable include $300 of salaries and wages accrued in April, which are related to employee services provided in May.

2. Supplies on hand amounting to $325 on April 30 are included in Office Expense.

3. Sales of $500 related to a concert recording performed in April are not yet billed or included in income as of April 30.

4. Equipment purchased for $1,200 cash was recorded as an Office Expense.

5. Payment from a customer collected on April 15 was recorded as follows:

	Debit	Credit
Accounts Receivable	1,800	
Cash		1,800

Instructions

Use the information above and T accounts to record the required changes to the accounts and to prepare a corrected trial balance.

(LO 4) E3-4 **(Trial Balance)** The trial balance of Mis-Match Inc. on June 30, 2014, is as follows:

	Debit	Credit
Cash	$ 2,870	
Accounts receivable	3,231	
Supplies	800	
Equipment	3,800	
Accounts payable		$ 2,666
Unearned revenue		1,200
Common shares		6,000
Retained earnings		2,795
Service revenue		2,380
Salaries and wages expense	3,400	
Office expense	940	
	$15,041	$15,041

The following transactions took place in July 2014:

1. Payments received from customers on account amounted to $1,320.

2. A computer printer was purchased on account for $500.

3. Services provided to clients and billed on account amounted to $3,890.

4. $400 of supplies was purchased on account in July, and a physical count on July 31 showed that there was $475 of supplies on hand on July 31.

5. When the Unearned Revenue account was reviewed, it was found that $825 of the balance was earned in July.

6. Salaries and Wages Expense of $670 related to employee services provided in July was not yet recorded as of July 31.

7. Payments to suppliers on account amounted to $2,125.

8. Received invoices totalling $1,160 related to office expenses incurred in July.

9. Declared a dividend of $575 on July 31.

Instructions

Prepare the trial balance as at July 31, 2014, assuming that Mis-Match did not record closing entries at the end of June 2014. (*Note:* It may be necessary to add one or more accounts to the trial balance.)

(LO 4, 5) E3-5   (Transactions of a Corporation, Including Investment and Dividend) LD Driving Range Inc. was opened on March 1 by Phil Woods. The following selected events and transactions occurred during March:

March	1	Invested $80,000 cash in the business in exchange for common shares.
	3	Purchased Mickey Mickelson's Golf Land for $70,500 cash. The price consists of $2,500 for March rent that was already paid; land, $20,000; building, $32,000; and equipment, $16,000.
	5	LD sponsored and paid for an open house costing $6,800.
	6	Paid $2,400 cash for a one-year insurance policy.
	10	Purchased golf equipment for $5,500 from VJ Ltd., payable in 30 days.
	18	Earned fees of $3,700, which were billed on account.
	25	Declared and paid a $1,500 cash dividend.
	30	Incurred and paid salaries and wages expense of $1,900.
	30	Paid rent for the month of April in the amount of $2,500.
	31	Received fees of $750 related to a golf tournament that will take place in April.

Woods uses the following accounts for his company: Cash; Prepaid Insurance; Prepaid Rent; Land; Buildings; Equipment; Accounts Payable; Unearned Revenue; Common Shares; Dividends; Service Revenue; Advertising Expense; Rent Expense; and Salaries and Wages Expense.

Instructions

(a) Journalize the March transactions.

(b) Identify any adjusting entries that should be recorded before preparing financial statements for the month of March.

(LO 4, 5) E3-6   (Alternative Treatment of Prepayment) At Sugarland Ltd., prepaid costs are debited to expense when cash is paid and unearned revenues are credited to revenue when the cash is received. During January of the current year, the following transactions occurred.

Jan.	2	Received $11,100 for services to be performed in the future.
	2	Paid $3,600 for casualty insurance protection for the year.
	10	Paid $5,700 for supplies.

On January 31, it is determined that $3,500 of the service revenue has been earned and that there is $2,800 of supplies on hand.

Instructions

(a) Journalize and post the January transactions. Use T accounts.

(b) Journalize and post the adjusting entries at January 31.

(c) Determine the ending balance in each of the accounts.

(d) How would account balances on January 31 be affected if Sugarland records prepayments by debiting an asset when prepaid costs are paid in cash, and crediting a liability when unearned revenues are collected in advance?

(LO 4, 5) E3-7   (Alternative Treatment of Prepayment) Black-Eyed Pears Ltd. initially records all prepaid costs as expenses and all revenue collected in advance as revenues. The following information is available for the year ended December 31, 2014.

1. Purchased a one-year insurance policy on May 1, 2014, for $9,600 cash.

2. On October 1, 2014, paid $9,200 for five months' rent in advance.

3. On October 15, 2014, purchased 36 advertising spots on a local radio station at a cost of $9,000. The advertising spots were to be used over the next six months. At December 31, the company had used 18 spots.

4. Signed a contract for legal services starting December 1, 2014, for $4,500 per month. Paid for the first three months on December 1, 2014.

5. During the year, sold $1,500 of gift certificates. Determined that on December 31, 2014, $475 of these gift certificates had not been redeemed.

Instructions

(a) For each of the above, prepare a journal entry to record the initial transaction.

(b) Post each of the above transactions. Use T accounts (ignore the Cash account).

(c) Journalize and post the adjusting entries at December 31, 2014.

(d) Determine the ending balance in each of the accounts.

(e) Would the adjusting entries and accounts be affected if Black-Eyed Pears records prepayments by debiting an asset when prepaid costs are paid in cash, and crediting a liability when unearned revenues are collected in advance?

(LO 5) **E3-8** **(Adjusting Entries)** The ledger of Rainy Day Umbrella Ltd. on March 31 of the current year includes the following selected accounts before adjusting entries have been prepared:

	Debit	Credit
Prepaid Insurance	$ 3,600	
Supplies	2,800	
Equipment	25,000	
Accumulated Depreciation—Equipment		$ 8,400
Notes Payable		20,000
Unearned Rent Revenue		9,300
Rent Revenue		60,000
Interest Expense	–0–	
Salaries and Wages Expense	14,000	

An analysis of the accounts shows the following:

1. The equipment depreciation is $350 per month.

2. One half of the unearned rent was earned during the quarter.

3. Interest of $300 has accrued on the notes payable.

4. Supplies on hand total $950.

5. Insurance expires at the rate of $300 per month.

Instructions

(a) Prepare the adjusting entries at March 31, assuming that adjusting entries are made quarterly. Additional accounts are Depreciation Expense; Insurance Expense; Interest Payable; and Supplies Expense.

(b) If the notes payable have been outstanding since January 1 of the current year, what is the annual interest rate on the note payable?

(LO 5) **E3-9** **(Adjusting Entries)** Suli Mani opened a legal practice on January 1, 2014. During the first month of operations, the following transactions occurred.

1. Performed services for clients represented by insurance companies. At January 31, $6,000 of such services was earned but not yet billed to the insurance companies.

2. Membership fees for the year to the law society, which were incurred but not paid before January 31, totalled $720.

3. Purchased computer equipment on January 1 for $8,400, paying $2,000 in cash and signing a $6,400, one-year note payable. The equipment depreciation is $350 per month. Interest is $50 per month.

4. Purchased a one-year malpractice insurance policy on January 1 for $12,000. (Suli Mani records prepayments in an appropriate asset account.)

5. Purchased $3,800 of office supplies in January. On January 31, determined that $500 of the office supplies had been used.

Instructions

(a) Prepare the adjusting entries on January 31. Account titles are Accumulated Depreciation—Equipment; Depreciation Expense; Service Revenue; Accounts Receivable; Insurance Expense; Interest Expense; Interest Payable; Prepaid Insurance; Supplies; Supplies Expense; Operating Expenses; and Accounts Payable.

(b) Prepare the adjusting entries on January 31 assuming that the law firm first records prepayments through the related income statement accounts (in other words, it uses the alternate method).

(LO 5) **E3-10** **(Analyze Adjusted Data)** A partial adjusted trial balance of Joy Limited at January 31, 2014, shows the following:

JOY LIMITED
Adjusted Trial Balance
January 31, 2014

	Debit	Credit
Supplies	$ 600	
Prepaid insurance	2,400	
Salaries and wages payable		$ 800
Unearned revenue		1,000
Service revenue		3,000
Supplies expense	950	
Insurance expense	2,400	
Salaries and wages expense	1,800	

Instructions

Answer the following questions, assuming the company's fiscal year begins January 1:

(a) If the amount in Supplies Expense is the January 31 adjusting entry, and $650 of supplies was purchased in January, what was the balance in Supplies on January 1?

(b) If the amount in Insurance Expense is the January 31 adjusting entry for one month of insurance expense, and the original insurance premium had been paid for one year of coverage, what was the total 12-month premium and when was the policy purchased?

(c) If $2,500 of salaries and wages was paid in January, what was the balance in Salaries and Wages Payable at December 31, 2013?

(d) If $1,600 was received in January for services performed in January, what was the balance in Unearned Revenue at December 31, 2013?

(LO 5) E3-11 (Adjusting Entries) Alberto Rock is the new owner of Summer Computer Services Inc. At the end of August 2014, his first month of ownership, Alberto is trying to prepare monthly financial statements. Information follows for transactions that occurred in August:

1. At August 31, Alberto owed his employees $6,000 in wages that would be paid on September 1.

2. At the end of the month, he had not yet received the month's utility bill. Based on previous experience, he estimated the bill would be $900.

3. On August 1, Alberto invested $60,000 of the company's funds with a local bank in a 180-day guaranteed investment certificate. The annual interest rate is 3%.

4. Rent of $1,200 for September was paid on August 31 and charged to rent expense.

Instructions

Use the information to prepare the adjusting entries as at August 31, 2014.

(LO 5) E3-12 (Adjusting Entries) Selected accounts of Bang Bang Boom Fireworks Limited follow:

Supplies			
Beg. Bal.	800	08/31	470

Accounts Receivable			
08/17	2,400		
08/31	1,650		

FV-NI Investments			
Beg. Bal.	3,450	08/31	800

FV-OCI Investments			
08/16	6,000		
08/31	720		

Salaries and Wages Payable			
		08/31	600

Unearned Revenue			
08/31	400	08/20	650

Service Revenue			
		08/17	2,400
		08/31	1,650
		08/31	400

Salaries and Wages Expense			
08/15	800		
08/31	600		

Supplies Expense				Investment Income or Loss	
08/31	470			08/31	800

Unrealized Gain or Loss (OCI)	
08/31	720

Instructions

From an analysis of the T accounts, reconstruct (a) the August transaction entries, and (b) the adjusting entries that were recorded on August 31.

(LO 5) E3-13 (Adjusting Entries) The trial balance for Hanna Resort Limited on August 31 is as follows:

HANNA RESORT LIMITED
Trial Balance
August 31, 2014

	Debit	Credit
Cash	$ 6,700	
Prepaid rent	3,500	
Supplies	1,800	
Land	20,000	
Buildings	142,000	
Accumulated depreciation—buildings		$ 20,448
Equipment	16,000	
Accumulated depreciation—equipment		4,320
Accounts payable		4,800
Unearned rent revenue		4,600
Notes payable		77,000
Common shares		81,000
Retained earnings		4,680
Dividends	5,000	
Rent revenue		68,002
Salaries and wages expense	43,200	
Rent expense	12,250	
Interest expense	1,600	
Utilities expense	9,200	
Maintenance and repairs expense	3,600	
	$264,850	$264,850

Additional information:

1. The balance in Prepaid Rent includes payment of the final month's rent and rent for August 2014.

2. An inventory count on August 31 shows $650 of supplies on hand.

3. Buildings and equipment are depreciated straight-line. From date of purchase, the buildings have an estimated useful life of 25 years, and the equipment has an estimated useful life of 10 years. For both asset categories, residual value is estimated to be 10% of cost.

4. Rent revenue includes amounts received for September rentals in the amount of $8,000. Of the unadjusted Unearned Rent Revenue of $4,600, one half was earned prior to August 31.

5. Salaries of $375 were unpaid at August 31.

6. Rental fees of $800 were due from tenants at August 31.

7. The note payable interest rate is 8% per year, and the note has been outstanding since December 1, 2013.

Instructions

(a) Journalize the adjusting entries on August 31 for the three-month period June 1 to August 31.

(b) Prepare an adjusted trial balance as at August 31.

(LO 7) E3-14   (Closing Entries) The adjusted trial balance of Serious Limited shows the following sales data at the end of its fiscal year on October 31, 2014: Sales $1,250,000; Freight-out $18,000; Sales Returns and Allowances $4,000; and Sales Discounts $15,000.

Instructions

(a) Prepare the sales revenue section of the statement of comprehensive income.

(b) Prepare separate closing entries for (1) sales and (2) the contra accounts to sales.

(LO 8) E3-15   (Closing Entries) Information follows for Shakira Corporation for the month of January:

Cost of Goods Sold	$228,000	Salary and Wages Expense	$ 61,000
Cash	62,000	Inventory	16,000
Advertising Expense	3,200	Interest Expense	1,200
Note Payable	33,000	Sales Discounts	7,000
Freight-out	9,000	Sales Returns and Allowances	1,000
Insurance Expense	12,000	Sales Revenue	364,000
Rent Expense	20,000	Retained Earnings	14,000

Instructions

Prepare the necessary closing entries.

(LO 7) E3-16   (Closing Entries) Selected accounts for Winslow Inc. as at December 31, 2014, are as follows:

Inventory	$ 60,000	Sales Discounts	$ 5,000
FV-NI Investments	22,000	Sales Returns and Allowances	2,000
FV-OCI Investments	11,000	Cost of Goods Sold	222,700
Retained Earnings	45,000	Administrative Expenses	31,000
Dividends	18,000	Income Tax Expense	30,000
Accumulated Other Comprehensive Income	17,000	Investment Income	3,000
Sales Revenue	390,000	Unrealized Gain or Loss – OCI	1,500

Instructions

Prepare closing entries for Winslow Inc. on December 31, 2014.

(LO 7) E3-17   (Missing Amounts) Financial information follows for two different companies:

	Bessembinder Ltd.	Doberman Inc.
Sales Revenue	$192,000	(d)
Sales Returns and Allowances	(a)	$16,000
Net Sales Revenue	162,000	65,000
Cost of Goods Sold	55,500	(e)
Gross Profit	(b)	37,000
Operating Expenses	35,000	23,000
Net Income	(c)	14,000

Instructions

Calculate the missing amounts.

(LO 7) E3-18   (Find Missing Amounts—Periodic Inventory) Financial information follows for four different companies:

	Pamela's Cosmetics Inc.	Scheibli Grocery Inc.	Berthault Wholesalers Ltd.	Kaiserman Supply Ltd.
Sales Revenue	$98,000	(c)	$144,000	$120,000
Sales Returns and Allowances	(a)	$ 5,000	12,000	9,000
Net Sales Revenue	74,000	101,000	132,000	(g)
Beginning Inventory	21,000	(d)	44,000	24,000
Purchases	63,000	105,000	(e)	90,000
Purchase Returns and Allowances	6,000	10,000	8,000	(h)
Ending Inventory	(b)	48,000	30,000	28,000
Cost of Goods Sold	64,000	72,000	(f)	72,000
Gross Profit	10,000	29,000	18,000	(i)

Instructions

Determine the missing amounts for (a) to (i). Show all calculations.

(LO 7) **E3-19** **(Cost of Goods Sold Section—Periodic Inventory)** The trial balance of Jangles Corporation at the end of its fiscal year, August 31, 2014, includes the following accounts: Purchases $151,600; Sales Revenue $250,000; Freight-in $4,000; Sales Returns and Allowances $4,000; Freight-out $1,000; and Purchase Returns and Allowances $21,000. Inventory on September 1, 2013, was $22,800 and ending inventory on August 31, 2014, is $21,500.

Instructions

Prepare the cost of goods sold section of the statement of comprehensive income for the year ending August 31.

(LO 8) **E3-20** **(Work Sheet)** Selected accounts follow for Kings Inc., as reported in the work sheet at the end of May 2014:

Accounts	Adjusted Trial Balance		Income Statement		Balance Sheet	
	Dr.	Cr.	Dr.	Cr.	Dr.	Cr.
Cash	9,000					
Inventory	80,000					
Accounts payable		26,000				
Sales revenue		480,000				
Sales returns and allowances	10,000					
Sales discounts	5,000					
Cost of goods sold	290,000					
Salaries and wages expense	62,000					
Interest income		12,000				

Instructions

Extend the amounts reported in the adjusted trial balance to the appropriate columns in the work sheet. Do not total individual columns.

(LO 8) **E3-21** **(Work Sheet Preparation)** The trial balance of Airbourne Travel Inc. on March 31, 2014, is as follows:

AIRBOURNE TRAVEL INC.
Trial Balance
March 31, 2014

	Debit	Credit
Cash	$ 1,800	
Accounts receivable	2,600	
Supplies	600	
Equipment	6,000	
Accumulated depreciation—equipment		$ 400
Accounts payable		1,100
Unearned revenue		500
Common shares		6,400
Retained earnings		600
Sales revenue		2,600
Salaries and wages expense	500	
Miscellaneous expense	100	
	$11,600	$11,600

Additional information:

1. A physical count reveals only $520 of supplies on hand.

2. Equipment is depreciated at a rate of $100 per month.

3. Unearned ticket revenue amounted to $100 on March 31.

4. Accrued salaries are $850.

Instructions

Enter the trial balance on a work sheet and complete the work sheet, assuming that the adjustments relate only to the month of March. (Ignore income taxes.)

(LO 8) **E3-22** **(Work Sheet and Balance Sheet Presentation)** The adjusted trial balance of West Kayne Consulting is provided in the following work sheet for the month ended April 30, 2014.

WEST KAYNE CONSULTING
Work Sheet (Partial)
For the Month Ended April 30, 2014

Account Titles	Adjusted Trial Balance Dr.	Cr.	Income Statement Dr.	Cr.	Balance Sheet Dr.	Cr.
Cash	$17,672					
Accounts receivable	8,520					
Prepaid rent	3,280					
Equipment	18,050					
Accumulated depreciation—equipment		$ 4,895				
Accounts payable		4,472				
Notes payable		6,700				
Owner's capital		34,960				
Owner's drawings	6,250					
Service revenue		13,190				
Salaries and wages expense	8,040					
Rent expense	2,260					
Depreciation expense	145					
Interest expense	83					
Interest payable		83				

Instructions

(a) Complete the work sheet and prepare a balance sheet as illustrated in this chapter.

(b) How would the balance sheet differ if West Kayne was a corporation instead of a sole proprietorship?

(LO 8) E3-23   (Work Sheet and Statement of Financial Position Presentation) The adjusted trial balance of North Bay Corporation is provided in the following work sheet for the year ended December 31, 2014.

NORTH BAY CORPORATION
Work Sheet (Partial)
For the Year Ended December 31, 2014

Account Titles	Adjusted Trial Balance Dr.	Cr.	Statement of Comprehensive Income Dr.	Cr.	Statement of Financial Position Dr.	Cr.
Cash	$117,600					
FV-NI investments	42,150					
Accounts receivable	56,720					
Prepaid rent	11.000					
FV-OCI investments	33,990					
Equipment	219,000					
Accumulated depreciation—equipment		$ 81,000				
Accounts payable		54,470				
Interest payable		4,800				
Notes payable		60,000				
Common shares		100,000				
Retained earnings		133,440				
Service revenue		211,190				
Salaries and wages expense	73,090					
Rent expense	66,000					
Depreciation expense	27,000					
Bad debt expense	5,250					
Interest expense	5,100					
Investment income		5,800				
Unrealized gain or loss—OCI		6,200				

Instructions

The note payable is due in four months. Complete the work sheet and prepare a statement of financial position as illustrated in this chapter.

(LO 8) E3-24 (Partial Work Sheet Preparation) Lazy Dog Inc. is a small private company that prepares monthly financial statements from a work sheet. Selected parts of the February work sheet showed the following data:

LAZY DOG INC.
Work Sheet (Partial)
For the Month Ended February 28, 2014

Account Titles	Trial Balance Dr.	Cr.	Adjustments Dr.	Cr.	Adjusted Trial Balance Dr.	Cr.
Supplies	3,256		(a)	1,500	1,756	
Accumulated depreciation		6,682	(b)	257		6,939
Interest payable		100	(c)	50		150
Supplies expense			(a) 1,500		1,500	
Depreciation expense			(b) 257		257	
Interest expense			(c) 50		50	

During February, no events occurred that affected these accounts. At the end of February, the following information is available and relates to the adjustments identified by letter in the work sheet:

1. Supplies on hand, $1,756
2. Monthly depreciation, $257
3. Accrued interest, $50

Instructions

Reproduce the data that would appear in the February work sheet and indicate the amounts that would be shown in the February income statement and balance sheet.

(LO 5, 9) *E3-25 (Adjusting and Reversing Entries) On December 31, adjusting information for Big & Rich Corporation is as follows:

1. Estimated depreciation on equipment is $3,400.
2. Property taxes amounting to $2,525 have been incurred but are unrecorded and unpaid.
3. Employee wages that are earned by employees but are unpaid and unrecorded amount to $3,900.
4. The Revenue account includes amounts that have been paid by customers for services that have not yet been completed. The amount has been determined to be $5,500.
5. Interest of $200 on a $25,000 note payable has not been recorded or paid.

Instructions

(a) Prepare the adjusting entries.
(b) Prepare the reversing entries, where appropriate.

(LO 5, 9) *E3-26 (Closing and Reversing Entries) On December 31, the adjusted trial balance of Domino Inc. shows the following selected data:

Accounts Receivable	$ 9,700	Service Revenue	$110,000
Interest Expense	12,800	Interest Payable	6,400

Analysis shows that adjusting entries had been made, and included above, for (1) $9,700 of services performed but not billed, and (2) $6,400 of accrued but unpaid interest.

Instructions

(a) Prepare the closing entries for the temporary accounts at December 31.
(b) Prepare the reversing entries on January 1.
(c) Enter the adjusted trial balance data in the four accounts using T accounts, and post the entries in (a) and (b).
(d) Prepare the entries to record (1) collection of the service revenue on January 10, and (2) the payment of all interest due (that is, $6,400) on January 15.
(e) Post the entries in (d) to the temporary accounts.

(LO 5, 9) *****E3-27** **(Adjusting and Reversing Entries)** A review of the accounts of Tucker and Wu Pan Accountants reflected the following transactions, which may or may not require adjustment at the year ended December 31, 2014.

1. The Prepaid Rent account shows a debit of $7,200 paid October 1, 2014, for a one-year lease that started on that day. The payment was for the last month's rent plus five months' rent starting on October 1, 2014.

2. On November 1, 2014, Services Revenue was credited $2,400 for an amount paid by a client for audit services to be performed in January.

3. On June 1, 2014, a cheque in the amount of $6,000 was issued for a two-year subscription to a trade publication starting on June 1, 2014. The amount was charged to Operating Expenses.

4. Interest of $1,270 has accrued on notes payable.

Instructions

Prepare (a) the adjusting entry for each item and (b) the reversing entry for each item, where appropriate.

Problems

P3-1 Transactions follow for Emily Cain, D.D.S., for the month of September:

Sept.	1	Cain begins practice as a dentist and invests $32,000 cash.
	2	Purchases dental equipment on account from Dig Deep Drill Limited for $12,500.
	4	Pays rent for office space, $1,300 in total for the months of September and October (i.e., $650 per month).
	4	Employs a receptionist, Wanda Phillips.
	5	Purchases dental supplies for cash, $900.
	8	Receives cash of $1,960 from patients for services performed and $1,600 for referrals to specialists.
	10	Pays miscellaneous expenses, $680.
	14	Bills patients $4,740 for services performed.
	18	Pays Dig Deep Drill Limited on account, $6,300.
	19	Withdraws $2,000 cash from the business for personal use.
	20	Receives $2,100 from patients on account.
	25	Bills patients $2,780 for services performed.
	30	Pays the following expenses in cash: salaries and wages, $1,400; and miscellaneous expense, $85.
	30	Dental supplies used during September amount to $330.

Instructions

(a) Enter the transactions in appropriate ledger accounts, using the following account titles: Cash; Accounts Receivable; Prepaid Rent; Supplies; Equipment; Accumulated Depreciation—Equipment; Accounts Payable; Emily Cain's Owner's Drawings; Service Revenue; Rent Expense; Miscellaneous Expense; Salaries and Wages Expense; Supplies Expense; Depreciation Expense; Income Summary; and Emily Cain's Owner's Capital. Allow 10 lines for the Cash and Income Summary accounts, and five lines for each of the other accounts that are needed. Record depreciation on the equipment using the straight-line method, five-year useful life, and no residual value.

(b) Prepare an adjusted trial balance.

(c) Prepare an income statement, balance sheet, and statement of owners' equity.

(d) Prepare a post-closing trial balance at September 30.

P3-2 Yancy Advertising Agency Limited was founded by Tang Min in January 2010. Presented below are both the adjusted and unadjusted trial balances as at December 31, 2014:

YANCY ADVERTISING AGENCY LIMITED
Trial Balance
December 31, 2014

	Unadjusted Dr.	Unadjusted Cr.	Adjusted Dr.	Adjusted Cr.
Cash	$ 10,750		$ 10,750	
Accounts receivable	30,000		35,000	
Supplies	10,400		5,000	

	Unadjusted		Adjusted	
	Dr.	Cr.	Dr.	Cr.
Prepaid insurance	11,600		2,200	
Equipment	60,000		60,000	
Accumulated depreciation—equipment		$ 28,000		$ 39,500
Accounts payable		5,000		11,000
Interest payable		–0–		650
Notes payable		5,000		5,000
Unearned revenue		17,800		20,600
Salaries and wages payable		–0–		9,600
Common shares		10,000		10,000
Retained earnings		3,500		3,500
Sales revenue		67,800		70,000
Salaries and wages expense	10,000		19,600	
Insurance expense			9,400	
Interest expense	350		1,000	
Depreciation expense			11,500	
Supplies expense			11,400	
Rent expense	4,000		4,000	
	$137,100	$137,100	$169,850	$169,850

Instructions

(a) Journalize the annual adjusting entries that were made.

(b) Prepare an income statement and a statement of retained earnings for the year ending December 31, and a balance sheet at December 31.

P3-3 A review of the ledger of Rolling Resort Inc. at December 31 produces the following data for the preparation of annual adjusting entries:

1. Salaries and Wages Payable, $0. There are eight salaried employees. Five employees receive a salary of $1,200 each per week, and three employees earn $800 each per week. Employees do not work weekends. All employees worked two days after the last pay period and before December 31.

2. Unearned Rent Revenue, $415,200. The company began subleasing condos in its new building on November 1. Each tenant has to make a $5,000 security deposit that is not refundable until occupancy is ended. At December 31, the company had the following rental contracts that are paid in full for the entire term of the lease:

Date	Term (in months)	Monthly Rent	Number of Leases
Nov. 1	6	$ 4,100	5
Dec. 1	6	$10,300	4

3. Prepaid Advertising, $16,200. This balance consists of payments on two advertising contracts. The contracts provide for monthly advertising in two trade magazines. The terms of the contracts are as follows:

Contract	Date	Amount	Number of Magazine Issues
A650	May 1	$7,200	12
B974	Oct. 1	9,000	24

The first advertisement runs in the month in which the contract is signed.

4. Notes Payable, $80,000. This balance consists of a note for one year at an annual interest rate of 9%, dated June 1.

Instructions

(a) Prepare the adjusting entries at December 31. (Show all calculations.)

(b) Rolling Resort is preparing for a meeting with potential investors. What is the net effect of the adjusting entries on net income? Explain why Rolling Resort's potential investors should be willing to wait for Rolling Resort to complete its year-end adjustment process before deciding whether or not to invest in the company.

Digging
Deeper

P3-4   Below are the completed financial statement columns of the work sheet for Canned Heat Limited:

CANNED HEAT LIMITED
Work Sheet
For the Year Ended December 31, 2014

Account No.	Account Titles	Statement of Comprehensive Income Dr.	Statement of Comprehensive Income Cr.	Statement of Financial Position Dr.	Statement of Financial Position Cr.
101	Cash			18,000	
112	Accounts receivable			42,000	
130	Prepaid insurance			1,800	
140	FV-OCI investments			25,500	
157	Equipment			98,000	
167	Accumulated depreciation—equipment				28,600
201	Accounts payable				31,600
212	Salaries and wages payable				7,200
301	Common shares				80,000
306	Retained earnings				60,000
400	Service revenue		142,000		
622	Maintenance and repairs expense	13,200			
711	Depreciation expense	38,800			
722	Insurance expense	8,800			
726	Salaries and wages expense	106,600			
732	Utilities expense	3,500			
801	Unrealized gain or loss—OCI		6,800		
	Totals	170,900	148,800	185,300	207,400
	Net Loss and OCI		22,100	22,100	
		170,900	170,900	207,400	207,400

Instructions

(a) Prepare a statement of comprehensive income, statement of changes in shareholders' equity, and statement of financial position. Canned Heat's shareholders invested $24,000 in exchange for common shares. Accumulated other comprehensive income had a balance of $0 on January 1, 2014.

(b) Prepare closing entries for the year ended December 31, 2014, and a post-closing trial balance.

P3-5   Noah's Foods has a fiscal year ending on September 30. Selected data from the September 30 work sheet follow:

NOAH'S FOODS
Work Sheet
For the Year Ended September 30, 2014

	Trial Balance Dr.	Trial Balance Cr.	Adjusted Trial Balance Dr.	Adjusted Trial Balance Cr.
Cash	37,400		37,400	
Supplies	18,600		1,500	
Prepaid insurance	31,900		3,600	
FV-OCI investments	17,200		13,500	
Land	62,800		62,800	
Equipment	120,000		120,000	
Accumulated depreciation—equipment		36,200		41,000
Accounts payable		14,600		14,600
Unearned revenue		2,700		1,700
Mortgage payable		50,000		50,000
Common shares		50,000		50,000
Retained earnings		59,700		59,700
Dividends	14,000		14,000	
Sales revenue		278,500		279,500
Salaries and wages expense	109,000		109,000	
Maintenance and repairs expense	30,500		30,500	
Utilities expense	26,300		26,300	

	Trial Balance		Adjusted Trial Balance	
	Dr.	Cr.	Dr.	Cr.
Property tax expense	18,000		21,000	
Interest expense	6,000		12,200	
Totals	491,700	491,700		
Insurance expense			28,300	
Supplies expense			17,100	
Interest payable				6,200
Depreciation expense			4,800	
Property tax payable				3,000
Unrealized gain or loss—OCI			3,700	
Totals			505,700	505,700

Instructions

(a) Prepare a complete work sheet.

(b) Prepare a statement of financial position. (*Note:* In the next fiscal year, $10,000 of the mortgage payable is due for payment.)

(c) Journalize the adjusting entries, using data in the work sheet.

(d) Journalize the closing entries, using data in the work sheet.

(e) Prepare a post-closing trial balance.

P3-6 The trial balance of Slum Dog Fashion Centre Inc. contained the following accounts at November 30, the company's fiscal year end:

SLUM DOG FASHION CENTRE INC.
Trial Balance
November 30, 2014

	Debit	Credit
Cash	$ 29,200	
Accounts receivable	82,000	
Inventory	105,000	
Supplies	8,600	
Equipment	225,000	
Accumulated depreciation—equipment		$ 86,000
Trucks	128,000	
Accumulated depreciation—trucks		39,000
Notes payable		85,000
Accounts payable		78,500
Common shares		300,000
Retained earnings		38,000
Sales revenue		950,200
Sales returns and allowances	24,200	
Cost of goods sold	611,500	
Salaries and wages expense	150,000	
Advertising expense	46,400	
Utilities expense	24,000	
Maintenance and repairs expense	32,100	
Delivery expense	46,700	
Rent expense	64,000	
	$1,576,700	$1,576,700

Adjustment data:

1. Store supplies on hand totalled $3,100.

2. Depreciation is $40,000 on the store equipment and $30,000 on the delivery trucks.

3. Interest of $9,000 is accrued on notes payable at November 30.

Additional information:

1. Salaries and wages expense is 60% selling and 40% administrative.

2. Rent expense and utilities expense are 90% selling and 10% administrative.

3. Of the notes payable, $35,000 is due for payment next year.

4. Maintenance and repairs expense is 100% administrative.

Instructions

(a) Enter the trial balance on a work sheet and complete the work sheet.

(b) Prepare a multiple-step income statement, and statement of retained earnings for the year; and a classified balance sheet as at November 30, 2014. (Hint: look ahead to Chapter 4 to see what a multiple-step income statement is.)

P3-7 Second-Hand Almost New Department Store Inc. is located near the shopping mall. At the end of the company's fiscal year on December 31, 2014, the following accounts appeared in two of its trial balances:

	Unadjusted	Adjusted
Accounts payable	$ 79,300	$ 79,300
Accounts receivable	95,300	95,300
Accumulated depreciation—building	42,100	52,500
Accumulated depreciation—equipment	29,600	42,900
Building	190,000	190,000
Cash	68,000	68,000
Common shares	160,000	160,000
Retained earnings	16,600	16,600
Cost of goods sold	412,700	412,700
Depreciation expense—building	–0–	10,400
Depreciation expense—equipment	–0–	13,300
Dividends	28,000	28,000
Equipment	110,000	110,000
Insurance expense	–0–	7,200
Interest expense	3,000	11,000
Interest payable	–0–	8,000
Interest income	4,000	4,000
Inventory	75,000	75,000
Mortgage payable	80,000	80,000
Prepaid insurance	9,600	2,400
Property tax expense	–0–	4,800
Property tax payable	–0–	4,800
Salaries and wages expense	108,000	108,000
Sales revenue	718,000	718,000
Sales commission expense	11,000	14,500
Sales commission payable	–0–	3,500
Sales returns and allowances	8,000	8,000
Utilities expense	11,000	11,000

Analysis reveals the following additional information:

1. Insurance expense and utilities expense are 60% selling and 40% administrative.

2. In the next year, $20,000 of the mortgage payable will be due for payment.

3. Property tax expense and depreciation on the building are administrative expenses; depreciation on the equipment is a selling expense; $32,000 of the salaries and wages expense related to office salaries and the remainder related to sales salaries.

Instructions

(a) Prepare a multiple-step income statement, statement of retained earnings, and classified balance sheet. (Hint: Look ahead to Chapter 4 to see what a multiple-step income statement is.)

(b) Journalize the adjusting entries that were made.

(c) Journalize the closing entries that are necessary.

P3-8 The following accounts appeared in the December 31 trial balance of the Majestic Theatre:

	Debit	Credit
Equipment	$960,000	
Accumulated depreciation—equipment		$120,000
Notes payable		186,000
Sales revenue		750,000
Advertising expense	62,000	
Salaries and wages expense	80,000	
Interest expense	9,000	

Instructions

(a) From the account balances above and the information that follows, prepare the annual adjusting entries necessary on December 31:

1. The equipment has an estimated life of 16 years and a residual value of $40,000. (Use the straight-line method.)

2. The note payable is a 90-day note given to the bank on October 20 and bearing interest at 10%.

3. In December, 2,000 coupon admission books were sold at $25 each; they can be used for admission any time after January 1.

4. Of the Advertising Expense balance, $1,100 is paid in advance.

5. Salaries accrued but unpaid are $11,800.

(b) What amounts should be shown for each of the following on the income statement for the year?

1. Interest expense   3. Advertising expense

2. Sales revenue   4. Salaries and wages expense

P3-9 The trial balance and the other information for consulting engineers Mustang Rovers Consulting Limited follow:

MUSTANG ROVERS CONSULTING LIMITED
Trial Balance
December 31, 2014

	Debit	Credit
Cash	$83,700	
Accounts receivable	81,100	
Allowance for doubtful accounts		$ 750
Supplies	1,960	
Prepaid insurance	0	
Equipment	85,000	
Accumulated depreciation—equipment		6,250
Notes payable		7,200
Common shares		35,010
Retained earnings		161,100
Service revenue		100,000
Rent expense	9,750	
Salaries and wages expense	28,500	
Insurance expense	18,500	
Utilities expense	1,080	
Miscellaneous expense	720	
	$310,310	$310,310

Additional information:

1. Fees received in advance from clients were $6,900.

2. Services performed for clients that were not recorded by December 31 were $7,300.

3. Bad debt expense for the year was $6,300.

4. Insurance expense included a premium paid on December 31 in the amount of $6,000 for the period starting on January 1, 2015.

5. Equipment, net of accumulated depreciation, is being depreciated at 9% per year.

6. Mustang gave the bank a 90-day, 12% note for $7,200 on December 1, 2014.

7. Rent is $750 per month. The rent for 2014 and for January 2015 has been paid.

8. Salaries and wages earned but unpaid at December 31, 2014, were $2,510.

9. Dividends of $80,000 were declared for payment on February 1, 2015.

Instructions

(a) From the trial balance and other information given, prepare annual adjusting entries as at December 31, 2014.

(b) Prepare an income statement for 2014, a balance sheet as at December 31, 2014, and a statement of retained earnings for 2014.

P3-10   Brook Corporation was founded by Ronnie Brook in January 2003. The adjusted and unadjusted trial balances as at December 31, 2014, follow:

BROOK CORPORATION
Trial Balance
December 31, 2014

	Unadjusted		Adjusted	
	Dr.	Cr.	Dr.	Cr.
Cash	$ 7,000		$ 8,000	
Accounts receivable	13,000		25,800	
Note receivable	10,000		10,000	
Supplies	8,500		5,500	
Prepaid insurance	3,250		2,500	
Prepaid rent	6,000		4,000	
Equipment	50,000		50,000	
Accumulated depreciation—equipment		$ 27,000		$33,750
Accounts payable		5,000		5,150
Unearned revenue		7,000		5,600
Salaries and wages payable				1,500
Common shares		15,000		15,000
Retained earnings		4,500		4,500
Service revenue		58,600		72,800
Interest income				1,000
Salaries and wages expense	10,350		11,850	
Insurance expense			750	
Depreciation expense			6,750	
Supplies expense	5,000		8,150	
Rent expense	4,000		6,000	
	$117,100	$117,100	$139,300	$139,300

Instructions

(a) Journalize the annual adjusting entries that were made.

(b) Prepare an income statement and statement of retained earnings for the year ending December 31, 2014, and a balance sheet at December 31, 2014.

P3-11   The following information relates to Joachim Anderson, Realtor, at the close of the fiscal year ending December 31:

1. Joachim paid the local newspaper $335 for an advertisement to be run in January of the next year, and charged it to Advertising Expense.

2. On November 1, Joachim signed a three-month, 10% note to borrow $15,000 from Yorkville Bank.

3. The following salaries and wages are due and unpaid at December 31: sales, $1,420; office clerks, $1,060.

4. Interest of $500 has accrued to date on a note that Joachim holds from Grant Muldaur.

5. The estimated loss on bad debts for the period is $1,560.

6. Stamps and stationery are charged to the Office Expense account when purchased; $110 of these supplies remain on hand.

7. Joachim has not yet paid the December rent of $1,000 on the building his business uses.

8. Insurance was paid on November 1 for one year and charged to Prepaid Insurance, $1,170.

9. Property tax accrued, $1,670.

10. On December 1, Joachim accepted Alana Palmer's two-month, 15% note in settlement of her $6,000 account receivable.

11. On October 31, Joachim received $2,580 from Tareq Giza in payment of six months' rent for Giza's office space in the building and credited Unearned Rent Revenue.

12. On September 1, Joachim paid six months' rent in advance on a warehouse, $8,300, and debited the asset account Prepaid Rent.

13. The bill from Light & Power Limited for December has been received but not yet entered or paid, $510.

14. The estimated depreciation on equipment is $1,400.

Instructions

Prepare annual adjusting entries as at December 31.

P3-12 The trial balance follows of the Masters Golf Club, Inc. as at December 31. The books are closed annually on December 31.

MASTERS GOLF CLUB, INC.
Trial Balance
December 31

	Debit	Credit
Cash	$ 115,000	
Accounts receivable	63,000	
Allowance for doubtful accounts		$ 9,000
Land	350,000	
Buildings	600,000	
Accumulated depreciation—buildings		40,000
Equipment	300,000	
Accumulated depreciation—equipment		120,000
Prepaid insurance	12,000	
Common shares		880,000
Retained earnings		152,000
Sales revenue		413,000
Rent revenue		44,000
Utilities expense	74,000	
Salaries and wages expense	90,000	
Maintenance and repairs expense	54,000	
	$1,658,000	$1,658,000

Instructions

(a) Enter the balances in ledger accounts. Allow five lines for each account.

(b) From the trial balance and the information that follows, prepare annual adjusting entries and post to the ledger accounts:

1. The buildings have an estimated life of 30 years with no residual value (the company uses the straight-line method).

2. The equipment is depreciated at 10% of its year-end carrying value per year.

3. Insurance expired during the year was $5,300.

4. The rental revenue is the amount received for 11 months for dining facilities. The December rent of $4,000 has not yet been received.

5. It is estimated that 24% of the accounts receivable will be uncollectible.

6. Salaries and wages earned but not paid by December 31 amounted to $3,600.

7. Sales revenue included dues paid in advance by members and totalled $9,900.

(c) Prepare an adjusted trial balance.

(d) Prepare closing entries and post to the ledger.

P3-13   The December 31 trial balance of Red Roses Boutique Inc. follows:

RED ROSES BOUTIQUE INC.
Trial Balance
December 31

	Debit	Credit
Cash	$ 18,500	
Accounts receivable	42,000	
Allowance for doubtful accounts		$ 700
Inventory, December 31	80,000	
Equipment	84,000	
Accumulated depreciation—equipment		35,000
Prepaid insurance	5,100	
Notes payable		28,000
Common shares		80,600
Retained earnings		10,000
Sales revenue		600,000
Cost of goods sold	398,000	
Salaries and wages expense	115,000	
Advertising expense	6,700	
Office expense	5,000	
	$754,300	$754,300

Instructions

(a) Create T accounts and enter the balances shown.

(b) Prepare adjusting entries for the following and post to the T accounts. Open additional T accounts as necessary. (The books are closed yearly on December 31.)

　　1. Bad debts are estimated to be $3,800 (the percentage of sales method is used).

　　2. Equipment is depreciated based on a 10-year life and no residual value.

　　3. Insurance expired during the year is $2,100.

　　4. Interest accrued on notes payable is $6,420.

　　5. Sales salaries and wages earned but not paid are $8,000.

　　6. Advertising paid in advance is $750.

　　7. Office supplies on hand total $3,500 and were charged to Office Expense when they were purchased.

(c) Prepare closing entries and post to the accounts.

P3-14   The unadjusted trial balance of Clancy Inc. at December 31, 2014, is as follows:

	Debit	Credit
Cash	$ 17,740	
Accounts receivable	103,000	
Allowance for doubtful accounts		$ 3,500
Inventory	60,000	
Prepaid insurance	4,620	
Bond Investment at Amortized Cost	40,000	
Land	30,000	
Building	154,000	
Accumulated depreciation—building		12,400
Equipment	33,600	
Accumulated depreciation—equipment		5,600
Goodwill	16,600	
Accounts payable		101,050
Bonds payable (20-year, 7%)		180,000
Common shares		121,000
Retained earnings		21,360
Sales revenue		200,000
Rent revenue		10,800
Advertising expense	22,500	
Supplies expense	10,800	
Purchases	98,000	

	Debit	Credit
Purchase discounts		900
Salaries and wages expense	53,500	
Interest expense	12,250	
	$656,610	$656,610

Additional information:

1. Actual advertising costs amounted to $1,500 per month. The company has already paid for advertisements in *Montezuma Magazine* for the first quarter of 2015.

2. The building was purchased and occupied on January 1, 2012, with an estimated useful life of 20 years, and residual value of $30,000. (The company uses straight-line depreciation.)

3. Prepaid insurance contains the premium costs of several policies including Policy A, cost of $2,640, one-year term, taken out on September 1, 2014; and Policy B, cost of $1,980, three-year term, taken out on April 1, 2014.

4. A portion of Clancy's building has been converted into a snack bar that has been rented to the Ono Food Corp. since July 1, 2013, at a rate of $7,200 per year payable each July 1.

5. One of the company's customers declared bankruptcy on December 30, 2014. It is now certain that the $2,700 the customer owes will never be collected. This fact has not been recorded. In addition, Clancy estimates that 4% of the Accounts Receivable balance on December 31, 2014, will become uncollectible.

6. An advance of $600 to a salesperson on December 31, 2014, was charged to Salaries and Wages Expense.

7. On November 1, 2012, Clancy issued 180 $1,000 bonds at par value. Interest is paid semi-annually on April 30 and October 31.

8. The equipment was purchased on January 1, 2012, with an estimated useful life of 12 years, and no residual value. (The company uses straight-line depreciation.)

9. On August 1, 2014, Clancy purchased at par value 40 $1,000, 9% bonds maturing on July 31, 2016. Interest is paid on July 31 and January 31.

10. The inventory on hand at December 31, 2014, was $90,000 after a physical inventory count.

Instructions

(a) Prepare adjusting and correcting entries for December 31, 2014, using the information given. Record the adjusting entry for inventory using a Cost of Goods Sold account.

(b) Indicate which of the adjusting entries could be reversed.

P3-15 The unadjusted trial balance of Imagine Ltd. at December 31, 2014, is as follows:

	Debit	Credit
Cash	$ 10,850	
Accounts receivable	56,500	
Allowance for doubtful accounts		$ 750
FV-NI investments	8,600	
Inventory	58,000	
Prepaid insurance	2,940	
Prepaid rent	13,200	
FV-OCI investments	14,000	
Bond Investment at Amortized Cost	18,000	
Land	10,000	
Equipment	104,000	
Accumulated depreciation		18,000
Accounts payable		9,310
Bonds payable		50,000
Common shares		100,000
Retained earnings		103,260
Sales revenue		223,310
Rent revenue		10,200
Purchases	170,000	
Purchase discounts		2,400
Freight-out	9,000	
Freight-in	3,500	
Salaries and wages expense	31,000	

	Debit	Credit
Interest expense	6,750	
Miscellaneous expense	890	
	$517,230	$517,230

Additional information:

1. On November 1, 2014, Imagine received $10,200 rent from its lessee for a 12-month lease beginning on that date. This was credited to Rent Revenue.

2. Imagine estimates that 7% of the Accounts Receivable balances on December 31, 2014, will be uncollectible. On December 28, 2014, the bookkeeper incorrectly credited Sales Revenue for a receipt of $1,000 on account. This error had not yet been corrected on December 31.

3. After a physical count, inventory on hand at December 31, 2014, was $77,000.

4. Prepaid insurance contains the premium costs of two policies: Policy A, cost of $1,320, two-year term, taken out on September 1, 2014; Policy B, cost of $1,620, three-year term, taken out on April 1, 2014.

5. The regular rate of depreciation is 10% of cost per year. Acquisitions and retirements during a year are depreciated at half this rate. There were no retirements during the year. On December 31, 2013, the balance of Equipment was $90,000.

6. On April 1, 2014, Imagine issued at par value 50 $1,000, 11% bonds maturing on April 1, 2017. Interest is paid on April 1 and October 1.

7. On August 1, 2014, Imagine purchased at par value 18 $1,000, 12% Legume Inc. bonds, maturing on July 31, 2016. Interest is paid on July 31 and January 31.

8. On May 30, 2014, Imagine rented a warehouse for $1,100 per month and debited Prepaid Rent for an advance payment of $13,200.

9. Imagine's FV-NI investments consist of shares with total market value of $9,400 as of December 31, 2014.

10. The FV-OCI investment is an investment of 500 shares in Yop Inc., with current market value of $25 per share as of December 31, 2014.

Instructions

(a) Prepare the year-end adjusting and correcting entries for December 31, 2014, using the information given. Record the adjusting entry for inventory using a Cost of Goods Sold account.

(b) Indicate which of the adjusting entries could be reversed.

P3-16 Mona Kamaka, CGA, was retained by Downtown TV Repair Ltd. to prepare financial statements for the month of March 2014. Mona accumulated all the ledger balances from the business records and found the following:

DOWNTOWN TV REPAIR LTD.
Trial Balance
March 31, 2014

	Debit	Credit
Cash	$ 7,200	
Accounts receivable	3,500	
Supplies	900	
Equipment	15,000	
Accumulated depreciation—equipment		$ 3,000
Accounts payable		5,950
Salaries and wages payable		600
Unearned revenue		1,500
Common shares		10,000
Retained earnings		4,160
Service revenue		8,000
Salaries and wages expense	3,600	
Advertising expense	800	
Utilities expense	310	
Depreciation expense	700	
Maintenance and repairs expense	1,200	
	$33,210	$33,210

Mona reviewed the records and found the following errors:

1. Cash received from a customer on account was recorded as $570 instead of $750.

2. The purchase, on account, of a scanner that cost $900 was recorded as a debit to Supplies and a credit to Accounts Payable for $900.

3. A payment of $30 for advertising expense was entered as a debit to Utilities Expense, $30 and a credit to Cash, $30.

4. The first salary payment this month was for $1,800, which included $600 of salaries and wages payable on February 28. The payment was recorded as a debit to Salaries and Wages Expense, $1,800 and a credit to Cash of $1,800. The business does not use reversing entries.

5. A cash payment for maintenance and repairs expense on equipment for $90 was recorded as a debit to Equipment, $90, and a credit to Cash, $90.

Instructions

(a) Prepare an analysis of each error that shows (1) the incorrect entry, (2) the correct entry, and (3) the correcting entry.

(b) Prepare a corrected trial balance.

P3-17   Samuels Corp. began operations on January 1, 2014. Its fiscal year end is December 31. Samuels has decided that prepaid costs are debited to an asset account when paid, and all revenues are credited to revenue when the cash is received. During 2014, the following transactions occurred.

1. On January 1, 2014, Samuels bought office supplies for $4,100 cash. A physical count at December 31, 2014, revealed $1,900 of supplies still on hand.

2. Samuels bought a $6,000, one-year insurance policy for cash on August 1, 2014. The policy came into effect on this date.

3. On November 15, 2014, Samuels received a $1,200 advance cash payment from a client for architectural services to be provided in the future. As at December 31, 2014, one third of these services had not been performed.

4. On December 1, 2014, Samuels rented out excess office space for a six-month period starting on this date, and received a $1,100 cheque for the first and last month's rent.

Instructions

(a) For each of the above transactions, prepare the journal entry for the original transaction and any adjusting entry required at December 31, 2014.

(b) In a business where there are several divisions or office locations where accounting is performed, is it possible that prepayments would be treated as assets in some offices and as expenses in others when initially recorded? Why or why not? Does the business have to have a consistent approach in all of its offices?

Digging
Deeper

RESEARCH AND FINANCIAL ANALYSIS

Real World
Emphasis

RA3-1 Shoppers Drug Mart

The financial statements of **Shoppers Drug Mart** are presented in Appendix 5B. Complete the following instructions by referring to these financial statements and the accompanying notes.

Instructions

(a) What were the company's total assets at the end of the two periods that are presented?

(b) How much cash (and cash equivalents) did the company have at December 31, 2011?

(c) What were the company's revenues for the current and preceding year? What are the main sources of revenues?

(d) Using the financial statements and related notes, identify the items that may result in adjusting entries for "prepaid expenses and deposits" and "accounts payable and accrued liabilities."

(e) Identify three major adjustments that the company made to its financial statements relating to the transition to IFRS.

(f) Briefly summarize the content of the Management's Responsibility for Financial Reporting and the Auditors' Report. How much responsibility does senior management have for the creation and monitoring of the accounting information systems that produce the financial information?

RA3-2 Financial Statement Dates

Companies normally issue their annual financial statements within weeks of year end.

Instructions

(a) Identify the top five Canadian companies (by revenue) in the following industries:

1. Banking

2. Insurance

3. Real estate

4. Biotechnology and pharmaceuticals

(b) For each company, identify its year-end date and the date that the financial statements were finalized (look at the auditor's report). Go to the company websites or SEDAR to find the statements.

(c) What is the likely reason that the banks have a different year end than the other companies?

(d) How many days does it take for the companies to produce the statements after their fiscal year ends? Look at the average time period for each industry. Within each industry, how close are the issue dates among companies? Comment on your findings.

Ethics

(e) The ethical accountant has just finalized her company's financial statements, which indicate that net income will be less than analyst expectations by several cents per share. The CEO has suggested that the company delay releasing its financial statements by a week as he is about to cash some stock options, and does not want any bad news to affect share price. Discuss.

RA3-3 Enterprise Resource Planning (ERP)

ERP software systems include bookkeeping systems as well as systems to monitor and manage human resource functions, quality control functions, and many other aspects of business. The software runs off a centralized database that services all company departments and functions.

Instructions

Research and write a one- to two-page summary that gives details about what ERPs are and why they have gained so much attention. Why do companies find them so useful? What are the pros and cons of these systems? (*Hint:* Search "enterprise resource planning" on the Internet.)

RA3-4 Extensible Business Reporting Language

Extensible business reporting language (XBRL) is a financial reporting system that allows a company to "tag" each piece of financial information as it is input into the company's books of account. Information is tagged in the database according to a standardized tagging system (taxonomy). Users are then able to find and extract information about companies.

In the United States, use of XBRL will be mandatory for all public company filings with the Securities Exchange Commission. In Canada, the Ontario Securities Commission is discussing whether to make the use of XBRL mandatory for public companies.

The following is an excerpt from the XBRL Canada website (www.xbrl.ca):

XBRL Canada is a not-for-profit consortium of leading Canadian companies and organisations, whose role is to create and maintain XBRL taxonomies based on Canadian reporting standards, to increase the awareness, knowledge and understanding of XBRL and its uses in Canada and to stimulate and promote the adoption of XBRL in Canada. XBRL Canada is a jurisdiction of XBRL International.

Initially, XBRL Canada created two taxonomies designed to enable preparation of XBRL based financial statements that conformed to Canadian Generally Accepted Accounting Principles (GAAP) prior to the adoption of IFRS. The first is referred to as the Primary Financial Statements (PFS) taxonomy, and covers the Balance Sheet, Income Statement and Statement of Cash Flow. The second, the Notes taxonomy, is for the preparation of the Notes to the Financial Statements. Both taxonomies have been "acknowledged" by XBRL International and are available on this website for free download.

Subsequently, XBRL Canada created a single Canadian GAAP taxonomy, for preparation of the primary financial statements and the notes. This taxonomy is a combination of the previous two taxonomies, with some updates to reflect new standards. While Canadian publically accountable companies will be using IFRS beginning in 2011, non-publically accountable companies will largely be using the Canadian GAAP accounting standards reflected in Part 11 of the CICA Accounting Handbook. The new combined taxonomy can be used to prepare XBRL financial statements in accordance with the standards for non-publically accountable companies.

Instructions

Discuss the following.

(a) What is XBRL? Provide an overview of how the XBRL system works and how information "tagged" using XBRL might be utilized by users such as investors. (*Note:* You may want to refer to the opening vignette and the XBRL website for further details.)

(b) What are the pros and cons of mandating the use of XBRL for public filings with securities commissions?

ENDNOTES

[1] Most companies use accounting software systems instead of manual systems. The software allows the data to be entered into a database and various reports can then be generated, such as journals, trial balances, ledgers, and financial statements.

[2] Accumulated Other Comprehensive Income (AOCI) would also be part of the expanded basic equation if the company had Fair Value-OCI Investments (or other items affecting Other Comprehensive Income and Accumulated Other Comprehensive Income). If the AOCI balance represented accumulated gains, it would be added in the equation similar to retained earnings. If AOCI represented accumulated losses, it would be subtracted.

[3] Examples of these include accounting for post-retirement health care plans and stock-based employee compensation. These will be covered in Chapters 19 and 16, respectively.

[4] The transition to electronic bookkeeping systems and databases has dramatically changed the way bookkeeping is carried out. Much of the terminology and visual layout of the reports has been retained, however.

[5] Other, less common adjustments, such as revaluation of property, plant, and equipment at the end of an accounting period, are discussed in later chapters.

[6] Fair Value-OCI investments are not permitted under ASPE. See Chapter 9 for a full discussion of accounting for investments, including considerations in the determination of fair value.

[7] Accumulated other comprehensive income is a balance sheet account that is the total of all past charges and credits to OCI to the balance sheet date. It is similar to the retained earnings account.

[8] Corporations are incorporated under a government act such as the Canada Business Corporations Act. The main reason for incorporation is to limit the liability for the owners if the corporation gets sued or goes bankrupt. When companies are incorporated, shares are issued to owners and the company becomes a separate legal entity (that is, it is distinct from its owners).

Courtesy Zipcar

Zipping the Way to Reduced Car Ownership

FOR MOST COMPANIES, profitability is the "gold standard" measurement of performance. But when a business is more focused on social goals that may take decades to achieve, quarterly profit is not the performance measure it most looks up to.

This is the case with Zipcar, the world's largest car-sharing company. Its mission is "to enable simple and responsible urban living" by reducing the number of cars in major cities across North America, including Toronto and Vancouver, along with the United Kingdom and Spain. Unlike a car rental company, Zipcar's business model is based on membership. Members pay a monthly or yearly fee to belong, and then pay by the hour or day to borrow from its fleets in urban areas as well as on college and university campuses. Zipcar estimates its members save about $600 a month over car ownership, and it claims that each of its vehicles takes about 15 personal automobiles off the road.

Zipcar, which started in 2000 in Cambridge, Mass., didn't turn a profit until the third quarter of 2011, shortly after it became a public company. On the first page of its first annual report, Zipcar stresses growth in its revenues (which increased every year from U.S. $58 million in 2007 to $242 million in 2011) and its members (who numbered 140,000 in 2007 and rose every year to 673,000 in 2011). While it continues to expand through new locations, mergers, and acquisitions, the company knows that its new shareholders need to see long-term profitability. "We realize that revenue growth in and of itself does not deliver shareholder value unless it translates into strong bottom line returns. It is our plan to continue to invest substantially in new opportunities while retaining an important focus on the operational excellence that will drive improved margins and profitability every year," its 2011 annual report states.

With a fleet of more than 9,000 cars that is growing, fleet operations is Zipcar's biggest expense, costing more than U.S. $159 million in 2011. One way it tries to lower vehicle carrying costs is by negotiating favourable financing with lenders. "Given our ongoing growth ambitions in existing and new markets, access to attractive fleet financing is integral to our success," said Zipcar CFO Ed Goldfinger. Cutting costs will be even more important as Zipcar faces competition from traditional car rental companies such as Hertz, which recently announced its decision to retrofit its fleet to accept last-minute hourly bookings without a membership fee.

Zipcar has its eye on what it says is a potential annual U.S. $10-billion global car-sharing market. With rising fuel prices and environmental concerns, more people living in cities, and the fact that the average urban car sits idle for an estimated 90% of the time, Zipcar expects that private car ownership in cities will eventually become a thing of the past.

Sources: Mark Clothier, "Can Hertz Outrun Zipcar in Hourly Car Rentals?", *Bloomberg Businessweek*, March 29, 2012; " "Zipcar Doubles its Asset Backed Securitization Facility to $100m to Support Fleet Growth," Zipcar news release, January 4, 2012; Zipcar Annual Report, 2011; Evelyn M. Rusli, "Zipcar Soars in Market Debut," *New York Times*, April 14, 2011.

CHAPTER
4 | Reporting Financial Performance

LEARNING OBJECTIVES

After studying this chapter, you should be able to:

1. Understand how firms create value and manage performance.

2. Understand how users use information about performance to make decisions.

3. Understand the concept of and be able to assess quality of earnings/information.

4. Understand the differing perspectives on how to measure income.

5. Measure and report results of discontinued operations.

6. Measure income and prepare the income statement and the statement of comprehensive income using various formats.

7. Prepare the statement of retained earnings and the statement of changes in equity.

8. Understand how disclosures and analysis help users of financial statements assess performance.

9. Identify differences in accounting between IFRS and ASPE and potential changes.

After studying Appendix 4A, you should be able to:

10. Explain the differences between the cash basis of accounting and the accrual basis of accounting.

The way items are reported in the statement of income/comprehensive income can affect how useful it is to users. Although the net income number (the bottom line) is a key focal point for many users, the other elements in the income statement have significant information content as well. This chapter examines the many different types of revenues, expenses, gains, and losses that are represented in the income statement and related information.

The chapter is organized as follows:

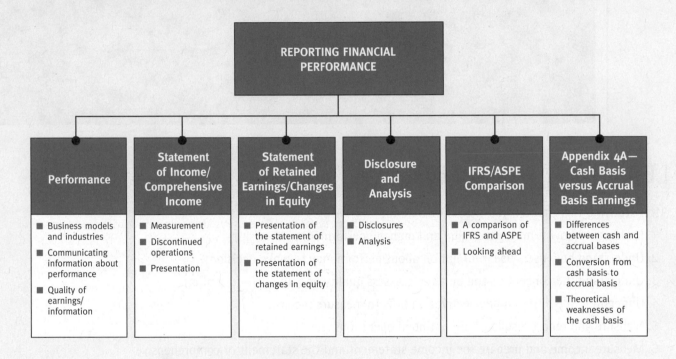

PERFORMANCE

The **income statement**, often called the **statement of income/earnings** or **comprehensive income**, is the report that measures the success of a company's operations for a specific time period. It is a key statement.

All income statements are not the same, however. This is partly due to underlying differences in business models and/or industry, and partly because of how this information is communicated. We will look at business models and industries first.

Business Models and Industries

Objective 1
Understand how firms create value and manage performance.

The basic **business model** consists of getting cash, investing it in resources, and then using these resources to generate profits. This model can be broken down into three distinct types of activities:

1. **Financing:** Obtaining cash funding, often by borrowing, issuing shares, or (in established companies) retaining profits. Financing activities also involve the repayment of debt and/or repurchase of shares.

2. **Investing:** Using the funding to buy assets and invest in people. Investing activities also include divestitures.

3. **Operating:** Using the assets to earn profits.

In performing these three types of activities, companies are exposed to different levels of **risk** and are given different **opportunities**. Some industries are riskier than others. Take, for instance, a small corner pizzeria, owned by a chef who makes and sells fresh pizzas to the local neighbourhood versus a big multinational chemical company that transports and sells chemicals. The biggest business risks the pizzeria has may be to ensure that the pizza ingredients are fresh and that there are sufficient cash flows. The multinational company faces many risks, including the risk of lawsuits due to pollution, risk of fraud given the fact that many employees work for the company, the risk of workplace accidents, and many others.

Finance

Managing risks takes money. There is an area of study devoted to this called **risk management**. It involves identifying risks, deciding if and how to manage risks, and monitoring risks. Companies can use various techniques to manage risks, such as educating their employees, buying insurance, and installing safety equipment. This all costs money, however. So the riskier the business, the more decisions need to be made about how to manage the risks, keeping in mind that the decisions made will affect profits. The market demands a greater return when there is greater risk. This is referred to as the **risk/return tradeoff**.[1]

On the opportunities side, some industries have greater opportunities. Consider the potential for companies where there are emerging markets or technologies. Companies must make decisions about which opportunities to take and when. Value creation is central in any business model. It refers to the act of finding an optimal balance between managing risks and taking the right opportunities such that the firm's net assets and potential are maximized. Well-run companies develop strategies that will allow them to react to the best opportunities in order to maximize shareholder value and maintain risks at an acceptable level.

Underlying Concept

The concept of representational faithfulness requires the financial statements to reflect the economic reality of running a business, including how it creates and sustains value.

Illustration 4-1 presents an overview of the business model.

Different industries have different business models, and within industries different companies have different business models. Consider the two statements of income in Illustration 4-2. **Walmart Stores Inc.** is in the retail business. It buys large quantities of inventory in bulk wholesale and then sells them at the retail level through its stores at a markup. That is how it creates value for its investors. **Nexen Inc.** is in the oil and gas

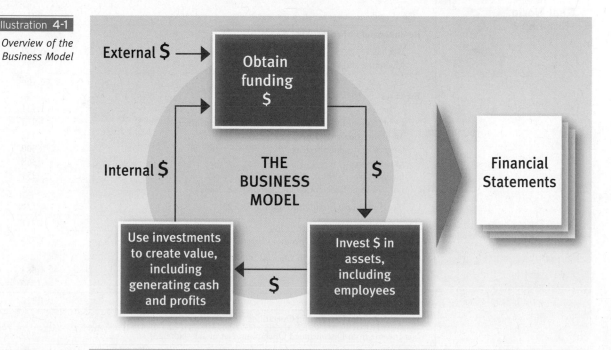

Walmart: Consolidated Statements of Income

(Amounts in millions except per share data)	2011	2010 As Adjusted	2009 As Adjusted
		Fiscal Years Ended January 31,	
Revenues:			
Net sales	$418,952	$405,132	$401,087
Membership and other income	2,897	2,953	3,167
	421,849	408,085	404,254
Costs and expenses:			
Cost of sales	315,287	304,444	303,941
Operating, selling, general and administrative expenses	81,020	79,639	77,546
Operating income	25,542	24,002	22,767
Interest:			
Debt	1,928	1,787	1,896
Capital leases	277	278	288
Interest income	(201)	(181)	(284)
Interest, net	2,004	1,884	1,900
Income from continuing operations before income taxes	23,538	22,118	20,867
Provision for income taxes:			
Current	6,703	7,643	6,564
Deferred	876	(487)	569
	7,579	7,156	7,133
Income from continuing operations	15,959	14,962	13,734
Income (loss) from discontinued operations, net of tax	1,034	(79)	146
Consolidated net income	16,993	14,883	13,880
Less consolidated net income attributable to noncontrolling interest	(604)	(513)	(499)
Consolidated net income attributable to Walmart	$ 16,389	$ 14,370	$ 13,381

Illustration 4-2

Statements of Income—
Walmart Versus Nexen

Real World
Emphasis

NEXEN INC.
Consolidated Statement of Income for the years ended December 31

(Cdn $ millions, except per-share amounts)	2011	2010
Revenues and Other Income		
Net Sales	6,169	5,496
Marketing and Other Income (Note 20)	295	323
	6,464	5,819
Expenses		
Operating	1,431	1,336
Depreciation, Depletion, Amortization, and Impairment (Note 5)	1,913	1,628
Transportation and Other	425	566
General and Administrative	300	428
Exploration	368	328
Finance (Note 12)	251	362
Loss on Debt Redemption and Repurchase (Note 11)	91	–
Net (Gain) Loss from Dispositions (Note 23)	(38)	41
	4,741	4,689
Income from Continuing Operations before Provision for Income Taxes	1,723	1,130
Provision for (Recovery of) Income Taxes (Note 21)		
Current	1,584	1,125
Deferred	(256)	(449)
	1,328	676
Net Income from Continuing Operations	395	454
Net Income from Discontinued Operations, Net of Tax (Note 23)	302	673
Net Income Attributable to Nexen Inc. Shareholders	**697**	**1,127**

exploration business. Any oil and gas that it sells is discovered, usually after spending a significant amount of time, effort, and money to find and develop the oil and gas. This is how Nexen creates value for its shareholders.

Because of these different business models and industries, Nexen's cost structure is different than Walmart's. We can see from the statements for Wal-Mart that 75 cents out of every dollar of sales is for cost of goods sold ($315,287/$421,849). Its main cost relates to the inventory that it has sold. For Nexen, the largest cost is depreciation, depletion, amortization, and impairment, which account for 30 cents out of every dollar of sales ($1,913/$6,464). Its main cost relates to the depletion of its wells and natural resource properties.

Now let's look at another retailer, **Macy's, Inc.** The statement of operations for Macy's (in U.S. $) is shown in Illustration 4-3.

CONSOLIDATED STATEMENTS OF OPERATIONS
(millions, except per share data)

	2011	2010	2009
Net sales	$ 26, 405	$ 25,003	$ 23,489
Cost of sales	(15,738)	(14,824)	(13,973)
Gross margin	10,667	10,179	9,516
Selling, general and administrative expenses	(8,281)	(8,260)	(8,062)
Gain on sale of properties, impairments, store closing costs, and division consolidation costs	25	(25)	(391)
Operating income	2,411	1,894	1,063
Interest expense	(447)	(579)	(562)
Interest income	4	5	6
Income before income taxes	1,968	1,320	507
Federal, state, and local income tax expense	(712)	(473)	(178)
Net income	$ 1,256	$ 847	$ 329
Basic earnings per share	$ 2.96	$ 2.00	$ 0.78
Diluted earnings per share	$ 2.92	$ 1.98	$ 0.78

The accompanying notes are an integral part of these Consolidated Financial Statements.

Illustration 4-3

Consolidated Statement of Operations—Macy's, Inc.

Real World Emphasis

Note that even though Macy's is in the same industry as Walmart, because it buys wholesale and sells retail, its cost structure is a bit different. Only 60 cents out of every dollar goes toward cost of goods sold ($15,738/26,405). What is the difference between Macy's and Walmart? The numbers are different primarily because of a different business strategy. Walmart prices it goods lower to attract more customers and get higher volumes of sales. It follows what is known as a **low cost/high volume strategy**. Macy's, on the other hand, is able to attract higher prices because it sells more unique and higher end products. This is referred to as a **cost differentiation strategy**. The purpose of this discussion is not to teach you everything you need to know about different industries, business models, and strategies. Rather, the goal is to introduce you to these ideas and get you thinking about how the financial statements might best reflect these factors in the interest of transparency. It is important to think about the nature of the industry as well as the business model and strategy when preparing and using financial statements. The statements should tell users about the business.

Objective 2

Understand how users use information about performance to make decisions.

Communicating Information about Performance

There are several ways in which the income statement helps financial statement users decide where to invest their resources and evaluate how well management is using a company's resources.

For example, investors and creditors can use the information in the income statement to:

1. **Evaluate the enterprise's past performance and profitability.** By examining revenues, expenses, gains, and losses, users can see how the company (and management) performed and compare the company's performance with that of its competitors. (Balance sheet information is also useful in assessing profitability, such as by calculating return on assets. See Appendix 5A.)

2. **Provide a basis for predicting future performance.** Information about business risk and past performance can be used to determine important trends that, if they continue, provide information about future performance. However, success in the past does not necessarily mean the company will have success in the future.

3. **Help assess the risk of not achieving future net cash inflows.** Information on the various components of income—revenues, expenses, gains, and losses—highlights the relationships among them and can be used to assess the risk of not achieving a particular level of cash flows in the future. For example, segregating a company's recurring **operating** income (results from continuing operations) from nonrecurring income sources (discontinued operations) is useful because **operations are usually the primary way to generate revenues and cash**. Thus, results from continuing operations usually have greater significance for predicting future performance than do results from nonrecurring activities.

In summary, a well-prepared statement of income/comprehensive income provides feedback and predictive value, which help stakeholders understand the business.

Quality of Earnings/Information

Not all information is created equal. Some information is high quality and some is poor quality. For instance, information that is complete and unbiased is better than incomplete and biased information. Financial statements can be of a higher or lower quality also. Some statements better represent the underlying business and industry than others and it is important to understand why. Let's look at some of the things that make a statement of income/comprehensive income less useful.

The statement of income/comprehensive income and other key financial statements are presented as a series of point estimates. For instance, in Illustration 4-3, the net sales for Macy's for the year ended 2011 were presented as U.S. $26,405 million. It is important to understand that even though the statements show elements such as net sales as point estimates, revenues, expenses, gains, and losses are rarely exact dollar values. Rather, they represent a range of possible values. This is because the numbers included in financial statements are based on numerous assumptions.

By definition, accrual accounting requires **estimates** of such things as sales and expenses. The income statement includes a mix of **hard** numbers (which are easily measured with a reasonable level of certainty, such as cash sales) and **soft** numbers (which are more difficult to measure, such as provision for bad debt). With soft numbers, there is significant measurement uncertainty.

Specifically, the statement of income/comprehensive income has the following shortcomings:

1. **Items that cannot be measured reliably are not reported in the income statement.** Currently, companies are not allowed to include certain items in the determination of income even though these items arguably affect an entity's performance from one point in time to another. For example, contingent gains cannot be recorded in income, as there is uncertainty about whether the gains will ever be realized. Note that if items are material, in general, they should be disclosed in the notes.

2. **Income numbers are affected by the accounting methods that are used.** For example, one company may choose to depreciate or amortize its plant assets on an accelerated basis; another may choose straight-line amortization. Assuming all other

factors are equal, the first company's income will be lower even though the two companies are essentially the same. The result is that we are comparing "apples and oranges." GAAP requires that information about accounting methods be disclosed.

3. **Income measurement involves the use of estimates.** For example, one company may estimate in good faith that an asset's useful life is 20 years while another company uses a 15-year estimate for the same type of asset. Similarly, some companies may make overly optimistic estimates of future warranty returns and bad debt writeoffs, which would result in lower expenses and higher income. As mentioned above, when there is significant measurement uncertainty, the resulting numbers that are captured in the financial statements are sometimes called "soft numbers." GAAP requires that where there is significant measurement uncertainty, additional disclosures be made.

Ethics

4. **Financial reporting bias.** Chapter 1 discussed the importance of ethics. Chapter 2 discussed how pressures on financial reporting can lead to financial engineering and fraud. Bias exists and it degrades the quality of the financial statements.

5. **GAAP.** Because the process of standard setting is political, GAAP is not always optimal. For instance, historically, most leases were not recorded on the balance sheet. Similarly, certain pension surpluses and deficits were excluded as well. Although the standard setters are systematically working their way through the standards to fix issues such as these, care should be taken to look for items that may not be properly represented in the financial statements.

Let's look specifically at the concept of **quality of earnings**. Quality of earnings refers to how solid the earnings numbers are. The concept of quality of earnings is used by analysts and investors to assess how well the reported income reflects the underlying business and future potential. If the quality is assessed as low, then the numbers are discounted. If the quality is assessed as high, then the numbers are accepted as is. Users start with the statement of income/comprehensive income and supplement that information with the other statements, notes to the statements, and other facts that they know about the company (perhaps from company announcements, news reports, or information in the MD&A).

When analyzing the quality of earnings, two aspects are generally considered:

1. **Content**, which includes:

    (a) the **integrity of the information**, including whether it is unbiased and reflects the underlying business fundamentals, and

    (b) the **sustainability of the earnings**.

Underlying Concept

Higher quality earnings have greater predictive value.

2. **Presentation**, which means the earnings are presented in a clear, concise manner that makes the information easy to use and understandable.

Since quality of earnings analysis is often done to assess future earnings potential, sustainability of income is important. Sustainability of income refers to whether the company is able to continue to generate or sustain these earnings in the future given its current business model, the industry, and the economy. This can be difficult to assess. Note that well-prepared statements send a signal by attempting to segregate income that is recurring from income that is not. For instance, where a company has sold part of its operations, the income statement segregates earnings from the part of the business that has been sold.

The statements may reflect the nature and source of the income on a historical basis but they cannot and do not make any promises about the future. Even though the underlying business might be accurately and appropriately reflected in GAAP financial statements, the quality of the earnings might be judged to be low because the earnings are felt to be unsustainable.[2]

Higher quality earnings provide higher quality information and have a lower margin of potential misstatement. They are more representative of the underlying business and economic reality. The shares of companies with higher quality earnings are valued higher in the capital markets, all other things being equal. Earnings that cannot be replicated and/or appear significantly biased are discounted by the markets.

Illustration 4-4 presents some attributes of high-quality earnings.

Illustration 4-4

Some Attributes of High-Quality Earnings

High-quality earnings have the following characteristics:

1. Content
   - **Unbiased**, as numbers are not manipulated, and **objectively determined**. Consider the need to estimate, the accounting choices, and the use of professional judgement.
   - **Reflect the economic reality** as all transactions and events are appropriately captured.
   - **Reflect primarily the earnings generated from ongoing core business activities** instead of earnings from one-time gains or losses.
   - **Closely correlate with cash flows from operations.** Earnings that convert to cash more quickly provide a better measure of real earnings as there is little or no uncertainty about whether they will be realized.
   - **Based on sound business strategy and business model.** Consider the riskiness of the business, business strategy, industry, and the economic and political environments. Identify the effect of these on earnings stability, volatility, and sustainability. Consider also the cost structure of the company including fixed versus variable costs (high fixed costs can make the company riskier in times of falling sellig prices).

2. Presentation
   - **Transparent**, as no attempt is made to disguise or mislead. It reflects the underlying business fundamentals.
   - **Understandable**

Ethics

Earnings management may be defined as the process of **targeting certain earnings levels** (whether current or future) or desired earnings trends and then **working backwards to determine what has to be done to ensure that these targets are met**. This can involve the selection of accounting and other company policies, the use of estimates, and even the execution of transactions. In many cases, earnings management is used to increase income in the current year by reducing income in future years. For example, companies may prematurely recognize sales before they are complete in order to boost earnings. Some companies may enter into transactions only so that the statements look better, and thus incur unnecessary transaction costs.

Theory

Earnings management can also be used to decrease current earnings in order to increase future income. Reserves may be established by using aggressive assumptions to estimate items such as sales returns, loan losses, and warranty returns. These reserves can then be reduced in the future to increase income. Earnings management activities have a negative effect on the quality of earnings. As long as there is full disclosure, an efficient market should see through these attempts to mask the underlying economic reality. Unfortunately, companies do not always disclose all important information and markets do not always operate efficiently.

Although many users do not believe that management intentionally misrepresents accounting results, there is concern that much of the information that companies distribute is too promotional and that troubled companies take great pains to present their results in the best light. Preparers of financial statements must strive to present information that is of the highest quality. Users of this information must assess the quality of earnings before making their decisions.

What Do the Numbers Mean?

Public companies are required to fully disclose material changes during the year. They therefore issue not only annual financial statements but also quarterly ones. Investors, creditors, analysts, shareholders, regulators, and others monitor this information. Analysts in particular will start to formulate opinions as to what the income or sales number will be, even before the company issues its quarterly or annual statements. This sets up an expectation. Recall the discussion regarding earnings surprises from Chapter 1. Many companies feel pressure to meet analysts' expectations and may be tempted to ensure that there are no negative earnings surprises.

Real World Emphasis

Nortel Networks Corp., once the biggest maker of telecommunications equipment in North America, succumbed to this. In early 2000, the company was concerned that projected revenues would not be met because of a slump in the technology industry. According to U.S. Securities and Exchange Commission (SEC) documents:

Nortel Networks Corporation ("Nortel" or "the Company") engaged in two fraudulent accounting schemes, one involving revenue fraud and the other involving earnings management fraud, which enabled Nortel to meet the unrealistic revenue and earnings guidance that it had provided to Wall Street in 2000 and again in 2002 and 2003. The first scheme accelerated material amounts of revenues into 2000 and created the false appearance that Nortel was weathering an economic downturn better than its competitors. The second scheme reduced or increased Nortel's earnings as necessary to create the false appearance that Nortel had stabilized its operations and returned to profitability.

In 2006, Nortel agreed to pay $2.4 billion in a shareholder lawsuit, and in 2007 it settled with the SEC for $35 million. The RCMP charged three former top executives in 2008 with several counts of fraud including falsifying the books and the case went to trial in 2012. The executives were fired from the company in 2004 and the company declared bankruptcy in 2009, with the remaining operations being bought out by others.

Source: Ian Austen. "Nortel Offers $2.4 Billion to Settle Lawsuits," *New York Times*, February 9, 2006; David Scheer, "Nortel Pays $35 Million to End SEC Accounting Probe," Bloomberg, October 15, 2007; "Timeline of Events Leading up to Nortel Trial," Postmedia, January 13, 2012; Securities Exchange Commission Civil Action No. 07-CV-8851.

As mentioned at the beginning of the chapter, the main statement that gives information about performance is the statement of income/comprehensive income. The statement of retained earnings and the statement of changes in equity show the accumulated and retained income over time. We will first look at the statement of income/comprehensive income and then the statement of retained earnings/changes in equity.

THE STATEMENT OF INCOME AND THE STATEMENT OF COMPREHENSIVE INCOME

Measurement

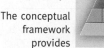
Objective 4
Understand the differing perspectives on how to measure income.

Underlying Concept

The conceptual framework provides definitions for the elements revenues, expenses, gains, and losses in Chapter 2.

The big question is how do we measure income? Is it **net income** or is it comprehensive income or is it something else, such as operating income? This is very important since many users focus on income and treat it as one of the most important numbers on the income statement, if not the most important. Earnings per share (EPS) numbers are generally based on net income.

Net income represents revenues and gains less expenses and losses both from continuing and discontinued operations. **Comprehensive income** is net income plus/minus other comprehensive income/loss. The concept of **operating income** is not defined by GAAP but is generally seen to be ongoing revenues less expenses. It represents a measure of regular income before any irregular items[3] such as gains/losses, discontinued operations, and other comprehensive income.

Net income has been around for many years and therefore is well understood. Earnings per share are calculated based on net income. ASPE currently uses this view of income.

More recently, the concept of comprehensive income has emerged in GAAP.[4] Essentially, this newer measure of income includes all changes in equity aside from shareholder transactions and is therefore more "comprehensive," as its name suggests. This notion of earnings is sometimes referred to as the **all-inclusive approach** to measuring income. IFRS generally supports this view of income.

Some users support a **current operating performance approach** to income reporting. They argue that the most useful income measures are the ones that reflect only regular and recurring revenue and expense elements; that is, normalized, sustainable earnings. Irregular items do not reflect an enterprise's future earning power since, by definition, they are irregular and atypical or nonrecurring. Operating income supporters believe that including one-time items such as writeoffs and restructuring charges reduces the income measure's basic **predictive value**.

In contrast, others warn that a focus on operating income potentially misses important information about a firm's performance. Any gain or loss that is experienced by the firm, whether it is directly or indirectly related to operations, contributes to the firm's long-run profitability. As one analyst notes, "write-offs matter. They speak to the volatility of (past) earnings."[5] In other words, they have **feedback value**. As a result, some non-operating items can be used to assess the riskiness of future earnings—and therefore they have **predictive value**. Furthermore, determining which items are (regular) **operating** items and which are **irregular** requires judgement and this could lead to differences in the treatment of irregular items and to possible manipulation of income measures.

Other comprehensive income (OCI) is made up of certain specific gains or losses including unrealized gains and losses on certain securities, certain foreign exchange gains or losses, and other gains and losses as defined by IFRS.[6] Some items are "recycled." This means that they are recognized first in OCI and then reclassified later to net income. For instance, under IAS 39 gains and losses on investments classified as fair value through other comprehensive income (FV-OCI) are first booked to OCI and then booked to net income later, when the investment is impaired or sold. This will be examined in Chapter 9. Some items—such as gains on revaluing property, plant, and equipment under the revaluation method—are not recycled. They are recognized once in OCI. This will be revisited in Chapter 10.

Illustration 4-5 shows some items included in OCI and notes how these are dealt with under ASPE. An asterisk (*) shows which items are recycled.

Illustration 4-5

How OCI Items Are Treated Under IFRS and ASPE

Items Defined as OCI under IFRS	ASPE Treatment
Changes in revaluation surplus under the revaluation method for property, plant, and equipment	Revaluation method not allowed.
Certain gains and losses on remeasurement of defined benefit pension plans	Off-balance sheet (not directly recognized) under the deferral and amortization approach. Recognized in net income under the immediate recognition approach.
Gains and losses arising from translating the financial statements of certain foreign operations*	Recognized directly in Equity.
Gains and losses on hedging instruments for certain hedges*	Hedging instruments are generally not recognized until maturity, and related gains and losses are generally recognized in net income when the hedged item is recognized in net income.
Gains and losses on remeasuring FV-OCI Investments**	FV-OCI Investment category not applicable.

*subsequently recycled to net income.
** subsequently recycled to net income under IAS 39 (not IFRS 9)

Other comprehensive income is closed out to a balance sheet account that is often referred to as **Accumulated Other Comprehensive Income**, which acts as a type of retained earnings account. Accumulated Other Comprehensive Income is an equity account on the balance sheet. We will come back to this item later in the chapter.

Having these multiple views of income may confuse the marketplace. For instance, should EPS be based on comprehensive income instead of net income? Why does IFRS use the comprehensive income concept but ASPE does not?

What Do the Numbers Mean?

Analysts focus on EPS, which is based on net income. It raises the interesting question as to whether the analysts don't understand the concept of comprehensive income or whether they really believe that the "real number" is net income. Some argue that OCI represents only unrealized gains and losses and this is why it should be segregated. When looking at the items included in OCI, they generally include unrealized gains and losses. However, there are many unrealized gains and losses that are included in net income.

Consider for instance the revaluation of a U.S. dollar receivable or a provision for obsolete inventory. These unrealized gains and losses are booked to net income.

The idea of comprehensive income is a sound one because it takes an all-inclusive view of income, defining it as all changes in equity other than shareholder transactions. Hopefully, as we move forward, OCI will disappear as a separate income statement classification.

Objective 5
Measure and report results of discontinued operations.

What Do the Numbers Mean?

Discontinued Operations

One of the most common types of irregular items relates to **discontinued operations**. Discontinued operations include **components of an enterprise** that have been **disposed of** (by sale, abandonment, or spinoff) or are classified as held for sale.[7]

Industry and business are continually evolving, especially where technology is concerned. Companies might discontinue operations as part of a downsizing strategy to improve their operating results, to focus on core operations, or even to generate cash flows. For example, **Napster Inc.** (formerly Roxio Inc.), whose shares were traded on NASDAQ, was the subject of much controversy for helping music lovers swap music for free. Napster helped pioneer what is referred to as peer-to-peer file sharing of music. Until December 17, 2004, the company had two divisions: the consumer software division and the on-line music distribution division. The consumer software division was sold so that the company could focus solely on the on-line music distribution business. Its goal was to become a leading global provider of consumer digital music services. In 2008, Napster was acquired by **Best Buy** for U.S. $121 million. In 2011, **Rhapsody International Inc.**, a private company and the largest on-demand music service in the United States, struck a deal with Best Buy to purchase the Napster subscribers and assets, leaving Best Buy with a minority interest.

Source: John Borland, "Roxio Sells Software Division, Focuses on Napster," CNET, August 9, 2004; Yinka Adegoke, "Best Buy to Buy Napster for $121 Million," Reuters, September 15, 2008; Julianne Pepitone, "Today Is Napster's Last Day of Existence, CNNMoneyTech, November 30, 2011.

Separate Component

In order to qualify for separate presentation on the income statement, the discontinued business must be a **component of an entity** (a business component) where the **operations, cash flows, and financial elements are clearly distinguishable** from the rest of the enterprise. A component can be any one of the following as indicated in Illustration 4-6:[8]

Illustration 4-6

Business Components under ASPE and IFRS

Considered a Component under ASPE	Considered a Component under IFRS
• An **operating segment**. Operating segments engage in business activities, have their performance reviewed by management (specifically the chief operating decision-maker), and have discrete accounting information available.	• A separate major **line of business or geographical area of operations.**
• A **reporting unit** as defined in *CICA Handbook*, Part II, Section 3064, which deals with goodwill and intangible assets. A reporting unit is equal to an operating segment or one level below, the difference being that performance is reviewed by a lower level of management.	• A **business** that meets the criteria to be accounted for as held for sale upon acquisition.
• A **subsidiary** as defined in *CICA Handbook*, Part II, Section 1590. Subsidiaries are separate legal entities.	
• An **asset group** as defined in *CICA Handbook*, Part II, Section 3063 for impairment of long-lived assets. An asset group has cash flows that are largely independent of other cash flows from the business.	
• Operations without long-lived or other assets.	

ASPE is less restrictive, as IFRS generally allows only major lines of business or geographical areas to be included. Therefore, more items will likely be categorized as discontinued under ASPE.

Depending on which GAAP is being followed, a component consists of a **unit of operation**, which may be as small as a hotel or an apartment building that is being rented out, or as large as a major subsidiary or geographical area. In terms of discontinued operations, when does the **disposal of an asset** constitute a **disposal of a component?** **The key elements are that the asset or group of assets generates its own net cash flows** (is a cash-generating unit) **and is operationally distinct (that is, it operates as a separate unit)**.

Illustration 4-7 gives a conceptual view of what constitutes a component in terms of discontinued operations under ASPE.

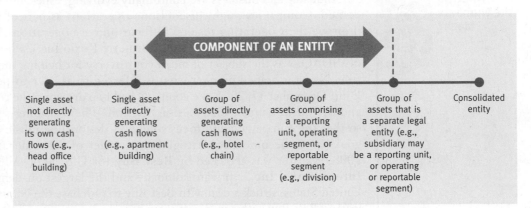

Under ASPE, in order to be presented as discontinued operations, the operations and cash flows from the component must be eliminated from the ongoing operations and the entity must not have continuing involvement. Generally, this will be the case in a straightforward sale.[9]

Assets Held for Sale

If the component is not yet disposed of, an additional condition must be met before the transaction can be given a different presentation on the income statement. This condition is that the assets relating to the component must be considered to be **held for sale** by the company. Assets are considered to be held for sale when all of the following criteria are met:

- There is an **authorized plan** to sell.
- The asset is **available for immediate sale** in its current state.
- There is an **active program** to find a buyer.
- Sale is **probable** within one year.
- The asset is **reasonably priced** and actively marketed.
- **Changes** to the plan are **unlikely**.[10]

In summary, for accounting purposes, assets may be considered as held for sale when there is a **formal plan** to dispose of the component. This ensures that only assets or asset groups for which management has a detailed, approved plan for disposal get measured and presented as held for sale.

Note that assets that are held for sale might not (and do not need to) meet the definition of discontinued operations. Where this is the case, these assets, as noted below, would be measured and presented the same way (similar to discontinued operations) **on the balance sheet**, but any related gains or losses on remeasurement would be recorded as part of income from continuing operations.[11]

Measurement and Presentation

Let's turn to the balance sheet side of things and look at the measurement and presentation of the assets that are held for sale. When an asset is held for sale, regardless of whether it meets the definition of a discontinued operation, the asset is **remeasured** to the lower of its carrying value and fair value less its cost to sell.[12] Note that if the value of an asset that has been written down later increases, **the gain can be recognized up to the amount of the original loss**. Once an asset has been classified as held for sale, **no further depreciation is recognized**.

Assets and related liabilities that are classified in this way are **presented** separately as held for sale in the balance sheet (if material), and retain their original classification as assets (or liabilities) that are current or noncurrent under ASPE.[13] Under IFRS, assets held for sale are generally classified as current assets.[14] If the asset meets the definition of a discontinued operation, the results of operations are shown separately on the income statement, net of tax for both the current and prior periods.[15] Comparative information is required for prior years on the income statement but not on the balance sheet.[16] Otherwise, the writedown is treated like any other asset impairment charge on the income statement (as part of income from continuing operations and pre-tax). The example that follows illustrates accounting concepts related to discontinued operations.

On November 1, 2014, top management of DeGrootes Corporation approves a detailed plan to discontinue its electronics division (a major line of business) at December 31, 2014. The plan, among other things, identifies steps to find a buyer and includes a timeline for disposition, along with a calculation of the expected gain or loss on disposition. The business is available for sale immediately.

As top management has approved the disposal and has stated in reasonable detail which assets are to be disposed of and how, a **formal plan** exists. The division is a separate business (being a division) that is therefore operationally distinct, with separate cash flows. Since it is a division, it will also have separate financial information and is thus a business component. Separate financial information is critical so that the gain or loss from discontinued operations can be properly **measured**. The company will have no continuing involvement in the electronics division after it is sold.

During the current year, the electronics division lost $300,000 (net of tax). DeGrootes estimates that it can sell the business at a loss of $500,000 (net of tax). The assets and liabilities relating to the division would be segregated on the balance sheet as follows under ASPE, according to their nature:

- Current assets: as "current assets held for sale/related to discontinued operations"

- Noncurrent assets: as "noncurrent assets held for sale/related to discontinued operations"

- Current liabilities: as "current liabilities related to assets held for sale/discontinued"

- Long-term liabilities: as "long-term liabilities related to assets held for sale/discontinued"

Under IFRS, the assets and liabilities would be presented as held for sale and classified as current assets and liabilities.

The information would be shown as follows on the current year's annual income statement (assuming $20 million of income before discontinued operations).

Income from continuing operations		$20,000,000
Discontinued operations		
Loss from operation of discontinued electronics division		
(net of tax)	$300,000	
Loss from disposal of electronics division (net of tax)	500,000	800,000
Net income		$19,200,000

The company would stop recording depreciation on the division's assets and, in the following year, would show any operating losses or profits and/or revised gain or loss on disposal as discontinued operations. Estimated future losses would not be included in the loss from operations since they would already be implied (and therefore included) in the fair value estimate of the assets held for sale or sold. The company would, in addition to the detail shown on the income statement, make additional note disclosures including a description of the disposal. The detail shown on the face of the income statement (breakdown between earnings/loss from operations and gain/loss from sale) could also be shown in the notes.[17] Illustration 4-8 shows how Canadian-based **Cameco Corporation**, one of the world's largest uranium producers, presented its discontinued operation in its 2010 statements. The statement of earnings is supplemented by notes 18 and 24, reproduced in the illustration below the statement of earnings. By the end of 2009, the assets had been disposed of.

Illustration 4-8

Presentation of a Discontinued Operation— Cameco Corporation

Real World Emphasis

For the years ended December 31 ($Cdn thousands, except per share amounts)	2010	2009
Revenue from		
Products and services	$2,123,655	$2,314,985
Expenses		
Products and services sold	1,127,879	1,324,278
Depreciation, depletion and reclamation	251,547	240,643
Administration	155,810	135,558
Exploration	95,796	49,061
Research and development	4,794	630
Interest and other [note 15]	3,474	(12,470)
Gains on derivatives [note 26]	(75,183)	(243,804)
Cigar Lake remediation	16,633	17,884
Loss (gain) on sale of assets [note 16]	107	(566)
	1,580,857	1,511,214
Earnings from continuing operations	542,798	803,771
Other expense [note 17]	(11,150)	(36,912)
Earnings before income taxes and minority interest	531,648	766,859
Income tax expense [note 18]	27,251	52,897
Minority interest	(10,352)	(3,035)
Earnings from continuing operations	**$ 514,749**	**$ 716,997**
Earnings from discontinued operations [note 24]	–	382,425
Net earnings	**$ 514,749**	**$1,099,422**
Net earnings per share [note 27]		
Basic		
Continuing operations	$ 1.31	$ 1.84
Discontinued operations	–	0.99
Total basic earnings per share	$ 1.31	$ 2.83
Diluted		
Continuing operations	$ 1.30	$ 1.84
Discontinued operations	–	0.98
Total diluted earnings per share	$ 1.30	$ 2.82

24. Restructuring of the Gold Business
The assets and liabilities related to discontinued operations have been reclassified as assets or liabilities of discontinued operations on the consolidated balance sheets. Operating results related to the discontinued operations have been included in earnings from discontinued operations on the consolidated statements of earnings. Comparative period balances have been restated.

(a) Sale of Centerra Gold Inc. (Centerra)
On December 30, 2009, Cameco completed a public offering of 88,618,472 common shares of Centerra for net proceeds of approximately $871,000,000 and recorded a net gain of $374,000,000. Concurrent with this offering, Cameco transferred an additional 25,300,000 common shares of Centerra to Kyrgyzaltyn pursuant to the agreement that Cameco entered into with the Government of the Kyrgyz Republic on April 24, 2009. As a result of the closing of the public offering, and the transfer of the Centerra common shares to Kyrgyzaltyn, Cameco has disposed of its entire interest in Centerra.

(continued)

(b) Kyrgyz Share Transfer

In 2007, the Parliament of the Kyrgyz Republic challenged the legal validity of Kumtor Gold Company (Kumtor) agreements with the Kyrgyz Republic. As a result, Cameco and Centerra entered into discussions with Kyrgyzaltyn, culminating in the signing of two agreements in August 2007 providing for the transfer of a certain number of Centerra shares to Kyrgyzaltyn, subject to certain conditions. These agreements, however, were never ratified by the Kyrgyz parliament.

On April 24, 2009, Cameco, Centerra, the Kyrgyz government and other parties signed a new agreement to resolve all the issues related to the Kumtor mine. On April 30, 2009, the Kyrgyz parliament ratified the agreement and enacted legislation authorizing implementation of the agreement. On June 11, 2009, closing occurred and Centerra issued 18,232,615 treasury shares to Kyrgyzaltyn and Cameco transferred 25,300,000 shares of its 113,918,000 Centerra common shares to a custodian, to be held in escrow, for ultimate release to Kyrgyzaltyn, subject to certain conditions. Cameco retained its voting rights over these shares while they were held in escrow. As a result of the public offering concluded on December 30, 2009, Cameco released the shares held in escrow to Kyrgyzaltyn.

The total amount of the after-tax loss related to this agreement is $179,000,000, of which an expense of $46,000,000 was recorded in 2009, a recovery of $20,000,000 in 2008 and an expense of $153,000,000 in 2007.

(c) Financial Results of Discontinued Operations

The results of the operations of Centerra are presented under "discontinued operations" on the consolidated statements of earnings. The following table presents the components of the discontinued operations amounts, net of future income tax expenses [note 18]:

(Millions)	2010	2009
Sale of Centerra	–	$374.2
Kyrgyz share transfer	–	(45.9)
Operating earnings	–	54.1
Earnings from discontinued operations	–	$382.4

The following table presents the components of the operating results of Centerra:

(Millions)	2010	2009
Revenue	–	$770.2
Expenses		
Products and services sold	–	440.4
Depreciation, depletion and reclamation	–	122.4
Exploration	–	28.5
Other	–	37.3
Earnings before income taxes and minority interest	–	141.6
Income tax expense	–	33.4
Minority interest	–	54.1
Operating earnings	–	$54.1

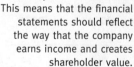

Underlying Concept

The business model should be transparent. This means that the financial statements should reflect the way that the company earns income and creates shareholder value.

Presentation

Objective 6

Measure income and prepare the income statement and the statement of comprehensive income using various formats.

There are many different ways to present performance information. Some involve formatting only and some involve signalling information about core ongoing operations versus peripheral or discontinued operations. Income can be further classified by customer, product line, nature or function, or by operating and non-operating, continuing and discontinued, and regular and irregular categories. Recall that the objective of financial reporting is to communicate information to users about the company and give them the information that they need to make decisions. Items should not be offset except in very limited situations; for example gains and losses should generally be shown separately and not as a net item.

We have already looked at discontinued operations and other comprehensive income as unique items. Next let's look at items that are reflected in continuing operations on the statement of income/comprehensive income. We will then look at different ways to present the whole statement of income/comprehensive income.

Ordinary versus Peripheral Activities

What is the difference between revenues/expenses and gains/losses? Should they be shown separately? The importance of properly presenting these elements should not be underestimated. For many decision-makers, the parts of a financial statement may be more useful than the whole. From a business perspective, a company must be able to generate positive net cash flows from its normal ongoing core (regular) business activities (revenues minus expenses) in order to survive and prosper.[18] Having income statement elements shown in some detail and in a format that shows the data from prior years allows decision-makers to better assess whether a company does indeed generate cash flows from its normal ongoing core business activities and whether it is getting better or worse at it.

The **distinction** between revenues and gains (and expenses and losses) depends to a great extent on how the enterprise's **ordinary** or **typical business activities** are defined. It is therefore critical to understand an enterprise's typical business activities. For example, when McDonald's sells a hamburger, the selling price is recorded as **revenue**. However, when McDonald's sells a deep fryer machine, any excess of the selling price over the book value would be recorded as a **gain**. This difference in treatment results because the hamburger sale is part of the company's regular operations while the deep fryer sale is not. Only when a manufacturer of deep fryers sells a fryer, therefore, would the sale proceeds be recorded as **revenue**.

Unusual gains and losses are items that by their nature are not typical of everyday business activities or do not occur frequently. They include such items as writedowns of inventories and gains and losses from fluctuations of foreign exchange. However, they are generally presented as part of normal, recurring revenues, expenses, gains, and losses (as part of income from continuing operations). If they are not material in amount, they are combined with other items in the income statement. If they are material, they are disclosed separately. This separate presentation allows for greater transparency as the users are able to see the cause of major gains and losses.

If the same types of gains/losses recur each year, then they are not really unusual and care must be taken to classify them with other gains and losses as normal transactions. Otherwise, it is misleading.[19] Illustration 4-9 shows how **Air Canada** presents some gains and losses, including a reversal of a provision (estimated liability) for a fine related to carrying cargo. The explanation included in the note is also shown.

Illustration 4-9

Presentation of Gains and Losses for Air Canada

Real World Emphasis

CONSOLIDATED STATEMENT OF OPERATIONS

For the year ended December 31

(Canadian dollars in millions except per share figures)		2011	2010
Operating revenues			
Passenger	Note 21	$10,208	$ 9,427
Cargo	Note 21	481	466
Other		923	893
Total revenues		**11,612**	**10,786**
Operating expenses			
Aircraft fuel		3,375	2,652
Wages, salaries and benefits		1,991	1,913
Airport and navigation fees		1,007	961
Capacity purchase agreements	Note 22	1,003	971
Depreciation, amortization and impairment		728	801
Aircraft maintenance		681	654
Sales and distribution costs		612	581
Food, beverages and supplies		278	279
Communications and information technology		193	195
Aircraft rent		335	353
Other		1,230	1,194

(continued)

Total operating expenses		**11,433**	**10,554**
Operating income before exceptional item		**179**	**232**
Provision adjustment for cargo investigations, net	Note 19	–	46
Operating income		**179**	**278**
Non-operating income (expense)			
Foreign exchange gain (loss)		(54)	184
Interest income		36	19
Interest expense		(320)	(397)
Net financing expense relating to employee benefits	Note 10	(16)	(75)
Loss on financial instruments recorded at fair value	Note 18	(63)	(3)
Other		(12)	(31)
		(429)	**(303)**
Loss before income taxes		**(250)**	**(25)**
Recovery of income taxes	Note 13	1	1
Net loss		**$ (249)**	**$ (24)**
Net income (loss) attributable to:			
Shareholders of Air Canada		(255)	(33)
Non-controlling interests		6	9
		$ (249)	**$ (24)**
Net loss per share			
Basic and diluted	Note 16	$ (0.92)	$ (0.12)

The accompanying notes are an integral part of the consolidated financial statements.

3. SUMMARY OF SIGNIFICANT ACCOUNTING POLICIES

D) CAPACITY PURCHASE AGREEMENTS

Air Canada has capacity purchase agreements with Jazz and certain other regional carriers, including those operating aircraft of 18 seats or less, some of which are referred to as Tier III carriers. Under these agreements, Air Canada markets, tickets and enters into other commercial arrangements relating to these flights and records the revenue it earns under Passenger revenue. Operating expenses under capacity purchase agreements include the capacity purchase fees, which, under the capacity purchase agreement between the Corporation and Jazz (the "Jazz CPA"), are based on variable and fixed rates ("CPA Rates") plus mark-up and pass-through costs. The CPA Rates are periodically set by the parties for rate periods of three years. The parties set the rates through negotiations based on Jazz's forecasted costs for the applicable rate period and an operating plan for the applicable rate period provided by Air Canada. Pass-through costs are non-marked-up costs charged to the Corporation and include fuel, airport and user fees and other costs. These expenses are recorded in the applicable category within Operating expenses.

19. CONTINGENCIES, GUARANTEES AND INDEMNITIES

Contingencies and Litigation Provisions

Investigations by Competition Authorities Relating to Cargo

The European Commission, the United States Department of Justice and the Competition Bureau in Canada have investigated or are investigating alleged anti-competitive cargo pricing activities, including the levying of certain fuel surcharges, of a number of airlines and cargo operators, including Air Canada. Competition authorities have sought or requested information from Air Canada as part of their investigations. Air Canada has been cooperating with these investigations, which are likely to lead, or have led, to proceedings against Air Canada and a number of airlines and other cargo operators in certain jurisdictions. Air Canada is also named as a defendant, and may otherwise become implicated, in a number of class action lawsuits and other proceedings that have been filed before the United States District Court, in Canada and Europe in connection with these allegations. In the United States, the investigation by the US Department of Justice has concluded with no proceedings having been instituted against the Corporation.

On November 9, 2010, Air Canada announced that the European Commission issued a decision finding that 12 air cargo carriers (including groups of related carriers) had infringed European Union competition law in the setting of certain cargo charges and rates for various periods between 1999 and 2006. Air Canada was among the carriers subject to the decision and a fine of

(continued)

21 Euros (approximately C$29 at an exchange rate of $1.3970) was imposed on Air Canada. Air Canada is appealing this decision and filed an application for appeal before the European General Court. In the first quarter of 2011, Air Canada paid the fine, as required, pending the outcome of its appeal. Following the decision by the European Commission and a review of proceedings and investigations in other jurisdictions, Air Canada recorded a net reduction to the provision for cargo investigations of $46 in 2010.

As at December 31, 2011, Air Canada has a provision of $37 relating to outstanding claims in this matter, which is recorded in Accounts payable and accrued liabilities. This provision is an estimate based upon the status of investigations and proceedings at this time and Air Canada's assessment as to the potential outcome for certain of them. The provision does not address the proceedings and investigations in all jurisdictions, but only where there is sufficient information to do so. Air Canada has determined it is not possible at this time to predict with any degree of certainty the outcome of all proceedings and investigations. As stated above, Air Canada is appealing the decision issued by the European Commission and, if and as appropriate, based on the outcome of any updates regarding this appeal as well as developments regarding proceedings and investigations in other jurisdictions, may adjust the provision in its results for subsequent periods as required.

Underlying Concept

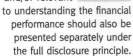

Any items that are material and/or relevant to understanding the financial performance should also be presented separately under the full disclosure principle.

Basic Presentation Requirements

Companies are required to include all elements in the financial statements as long as they are measurable and probable. In addition, the following items are specifically required to be presented separately in the statement of income/comprehensive income. Judgement may be used to determine where additional items are best presented (that is, in the income statement or notes).[20]

Illustration 4-10 shows the basic items that need to be presented in the statements of income/comprehensive income under ASPE and IFRS.

Illustration 4-10

Items Required in the Statement of Income/Comprehensive Income under GAAP

ASPE per Section 1520*	IFRS as per IAS 1*
• Revenue	• Revenue
• Income from investments	• Gains/losses from derecognition of financial asset measured at amortized cost
• Income tax expense (before discontinued operations)	• Gains/losses on reclassification of financial assets
• Income or loss before discontinued operations	• Finance costs
• Results of discontinued operations	• Share of profit/loss for investments accounted for using the equity method
• Net income or loss	• Tax expense
	• Results of discontinued operations
	• Profit or loss
	• Other comprehensive income classified by nature showing which will be recycled and which will not
	• Share of other comprehensive income of investments accounted for using the equity method
	• Comprehensive income
	• Profit or loss and comprehensive income attributable to non-controlling interest and owners

*some of the requirements noted here are from recent standards updates and so may not be reflected in the financial statement exhibits throughout the text.

Combined Statement of Income/Comprehensive Income

Under IFRS, the statement of comprehensive income is presented either:[21]

1. in a single combined statement including revenues, expenses, gains, losses, net income, other comprehensive income, and comprehensive income, or

2. in two separate statements showing the traditional income statement in one and a second statement beginning with net income and displaying the components of other comprehensive income, as well as comprehensive income.

Alternative Terminology

Note that a company is not required to use the terms "Other comprehensive income" or "Comprehensive income" under IFRS. Other terminology may be used.

By providing information on the components of comprehensive income, the company communicates information about all changes in net assets. With this information, users will be better able to understand the quality of the company's earnings. This information should help users predict the amounts, timing, and uncertainty of future cash flows.

A combined income statement format is shown in Illustration 4-11 for **Southgobi Resources Ltd.**, a Canadian company whose shares list on the TSX. The company chose to adopt IFRS early.

Real World Emphasis

By convention, income statements may be presented using one of a number of formats, including what are referred to as the single-step, multiple-step, and condensed formats. These are not GAAP-required formats. Companies choose which format that they think best presents the performance information. In addition, expenses may be grouped in different ways, perhaps emphasizing activities or functions (such as selling, production, research, and development) versus the nature of the expense (payroll, depreciation, and so on). These formats will be discussed next.

Illustration 4-11

Combined Income and Comprehensive Income Statement

Consolidated Statement of Comprehensive Income

(expressed in thousands of U.S. dollars, except for share and per share amounts)

		Year ended December 31,	
	Notes	2011	2010
Revenue		$ 179,049	$ 79,777
Cost of sales	2.3, 5	(127,343)	(69,904)
Gross profit		51,706	9,873
Other operating expenses	2.3, 6	(29,189)	(12,643)
Administration expenses	2.3, 7	(28,749)	(25,438)
Evaluation and exploration expenses	8	(31,768)	(18,769)
Loss from operations		(38,000)	(46,977)
Finance costs	9	(12,765)	(175,855)
Finance income	9	107,732	103,948
Income/(loss) before tax		56,967	(118,884)
Current income tax expense	10	(7,340)	(1,806)
Deferred income tax recovery	10	8,118	4,495
Net income/(loss) attributable to equity holders of the Company		57,745	(116,195)
OTHER COMPREHENSIVE INCOME			
(Loss)/gain on available-for-sale assets, net of tax	13	(11,202)	27,761
Net comprehensive income/(loss) attributable to equity holders of the Company		$ 46,543	$ (88,434)
BASIC INCOME/(LOSS) PER SHARE	11	$ 0.32	$ (0.66)
DILUTED LOSS PER SHARE	11	$ (0.19)	$ (0.66)

The accompanying notes are an integral part of these consolidated financial statements.

Single-Step Income Statements

In reporting revenues, gains, expenses, and losses, a format known as the **single-step income statement** is often used. In the single-step statement, only two main groupings are used: **revenues** and **expenses**. Expenses and losses are deducted from revenues and gains to arrive at net income. The expression "single-step" comes from the single subtraction that is needed to arrive at net income before discontinued operations. Frequently, income tax is reported separately as the last item before net income before discontinued operations to indicate its relationship to income before income tax.

Illustration 4-12 shows the single-step income statement of Dan Deines Corporation. Note that Dan Deines does not have any other comprehensive income numbers and so net income is equal to comprehensive income.

The single-step form of income statement is widely used in financial reporting in smaller private companies. The **multiple-step** form described below is used almost exclusively by public companies.

The main advantages of the single-step format are that the **presentation is simple** and **no one type of revenue or expense item is implied to have priority over any other**. Potential classification problems are thus eliminated. The main disadvantage of the single-step format is over-simplification and less detail.

Illustration 4-12

Single-Step Income Statement

DAN DEINES CORPORATION
Income Statement
For the Year Ended December 31, 2014

Revenues	
Net sales	$2,972,413
Dividend revenue	98,500
Rental revenue	72,910
Total revenues	3,143,823
Expenses	
Cost of goods sold	1,982,541
Selling expenses	453,028
Administrative expenses	350,771
Interest expense	126,060
Total expenses	2,912,400
Net income before tax	231,423
Income tax expense	66,934
Net income	$ 164,489
Earnings per common share	$1.74

Multiple-Step Income Statements

Some users argue that **presenting other important revenue and expense data separately** makes the income statement more informative and more useful. For instance, additional information is communicated if there is separation between the company's operating and non-operating activities such as **other revenues and gains** and **other expenses and losses**. These other categories include interest revenue and expense, gains or losses from sales of miscellaneous items, and dividends received.

A **multiple-step income statement** separates **operating** transactions from the **non-operating** transactions and **matches** costs and expenses with related revenues. It also highlights certain intermediate components of income that are used to calculate ratios for assessing the enterprise's performance (that is, gross profit/margin).

To illustrate, Dan Deines Corporation's multiple-step income statement is presented in Illustration 4-13. Note, for example, that at least three main subtotals are presented that deal with operating activities: net sales revenue, gross profit, and income from operations.

DAN DEINES CORPORATION
Income Statement
For the Year Ended December 31, 2014

Sales revenue			
Sales			$3,053,081
Less: Sales discounts	$ 24,241		
Sales returns and allowances	56,427		80,668
Net sales revenue			2,972,413
Cost of goods sold			1,982,541
Gross profit			989,872
Operating expenses			
Selling expenses			
Sales salaries and commissions	202,644		
Sales office salaries	59,200		
Travel and entertainment	48,940		
Advertising expense	38,315		
Freight and transportation-out	41,209		
Shipping supplies and expense	24,712		
Postage and stationery	16,788		
Telephone and Internet expense	12,215		
Depreciation of sales equipment	9,005	453,028	
Administrative expenses			
Officers' salaries	186,000		
Office salaries	61,200		
Legal and professional services	23,721		
Utilities expense	23,275		
Insurance expense	17,029		
Depreciation of building	18,059		
Depreciation of office equipment	16,000		
Stationery, supplies, and postage	2,875		
Miscellaneous office expenses	2,612	350,771	803,799
Income from operations			186,073
Other revenues and gains			
Dividend revenue		98,500	
Rental revenue		72,910	171,410
			357,483
Other expenses and losses			
Interest on bonds and notes			126,060
Income before income tax			231,423
Income tax			66,934
Net income for the year			$ 164,489
Earnings per common share			$1.74

The disclosure of net sales revenue is useful because regular revenues are reported as a separate item. Irregular or incidental revenues are disclosed elsewhere in the income statement. As a result, trends in revenue from continuing operations (typical business activities) should be easier to identify, understand, and analyze. Similarly, the reporting of gross profit provides a useful number for evaluating performance and assessing future earnings. A study of the trend in gross profits may show **how successfully a company uses its resources** (prices paid for inventory, costs accumulated, wastage); it may also be a basis for **understanding how profit margins have changed** as a result of competitive pressure (which may limit the prices that the company is able to charge for its products and services). Gross profit percentage is a very important ratio in the retail business.

Finally, disclosing income from operations **highlights the difference between regular and irregular or incidental activities**. Disclosure of operating earnings may help in comparing different companies and assessing their operating efficiencies. Note that if Dan Deines had **discontinued operations or other comprehensive income**, these would be added to the bottom of the statement and shown separately. Discontinued operations would be presented before net income. Other comprehensive income would be presented after net income. Income/losses from discontinued operations are by definition **nonrecurring** and therefore have **little predictive value**. They do, however, give **feedback value** on past decisions made by management. Net income that consists mainly of net income from continuing operations would be viewed as **higher quality**.

When a multiple-step income statement is used, some or all of the following sections or subsections may be presented:

INCOME STATEMENT SECTIONS

1. *Continuing Operations*
   (a) **Operating** Section. A report of the **revenues and expenses** of the company's principal operations.
      i. **Sales or Revenue** Section. A subsection presenting sales, discounts, allowances, returns, and other related information. Its purpose is to arrive at the net amount of sales revenue.
      ii. **Cost of Goods Sold** Section. A subsection that shows the cost of goods that were sold to produce the sales.
      iii. **Selling Expenses.** A subsection that lists expenses resulting from the company's efforts to make sales.
      iv. **Administrative or General Expenses.** A subsection reporting expenses for general administration.
   (b) **Non-Operating** Section. A report of revenues and expenses resulting from the company's secondary or auxiliary activities. In addition, special gains and losses that are infrequent and/or unusual are normally reported in this section. Generally these items break down into two main subsections:
      i. **Other Revenues and Gains.** A list of the revenues earned or gains incurred from non-operating transactions, and generally net of related expenses.
      ii. **Other Expenses and Losses.** A list of the expenses or losses incurred from non-operating transactions, and generally net of any related income.
   (c) **Income Tax.** A short section reporting income taxes on income from continuing operations.
2. *Discontinued Operations.* Material gains or losses resulting from the disposition of a part of the business (net of taxes).
3. *Other Comprehensive Income.* Other gains/losses that are not required by primary sources of GAAP to be included in net income. This section includes all other changes in equity that do not relate to shareholder transactions (net of taxes).

Although the **content** of the operating section is generally the same, the **presentation** or organization of the material does not need to be as described above. Sometimes the expenses are grouped by nature instead of function. This is discussed below.

Usually, financial statements that are provided to external users have **less detail** than internal management reports. The latter tend to have more expense categories, and they are usually grouped along lines of responsibility. This detail allows top management to judge staff performance.

Whether a single-step or multiple-step income statement is used, **irregular transactions** such as discontinued operations and other comprehensive income are **required to be reported separately**, following income from continuing operations.

Condensed Financial Statements

In some cases, it is impossible to present all the desired expense detail in a single income statement of convenient size. This problem is solved by including only the totals of expense groups in the statement of income and preparing **supplementary schedules** of expenses to support the totals. With this format, the income statement itself may be reduced to a few lines on a single sheet. In such instances, readers who want to study all the reported data on operations must give their attention to the supporting schedules.

The income statement shown in Illustration 4-14 for Dan Deines Corporation is a condensed version of the more detailed multiple-step statement presented earlier and is more typical of what is done in actual practice.

An example of a supporting schedule, cross-referenced as Note D and detailing the selling expenses, is shown in Illustration 4-15.

Deciding **how much detail** to include in the income statement is always a problem. On the one hand, a simple, summarized statement allows a reader to quickly discover important factors. On the other hand, disclosure of the results of all activities provides users with detailed relevant information. Earlier, we looked at the basic presentation requirements under GAAP. As long as these requirements are met, there is a significant amount of flexibility in how to present the information.

Illustration 4-14

Condensed Income Statement

DAN DEINES CORPORATION
Income Statement
For the Year Ended December 31, 2014

Net sales		$2,972,413
Cost of goods sold		1,982,541
Gross profit		989,872
Selling expenses (see Note D)	$453,028	
Administrative expenses	350,771	803,799
Income from operations		186,073
Other revenues and gains		171,410
		357,483
Other expenses and losses		126,060
Income before income tax		231,423
Income tax		66,934
Net income for the year		$ 164,489
Earnings per share		$1.74

Illustration 4-15

Sample Supporting Schedule

Note D: Selling expenses

Sales salaries and commissions	$202,644
Sales office salaries	59,200
Travel and entertainment	48,940
Advertising expense	38,315
Freight and transportation-out	41,209
Shipping supplies and expense	24,712
Postage and stationery	16,788
Telephone and Internet expense	12,215
Depreciation of sales equipment	9,005
Total selling expenses	$453,028

Presentation of Expenses: Nature versus Function

Whether the single-step or multiple-step method is used, consideration should be given to providing additional details about expenses. This helps ensure transparency. IFRS requires an entity to present an analysis of expenses based on either nature or function, as follows:

1. **Nature** Nature refers to the type of expense (such as depreciation, purchases of materials, transport costs, and employee benefits). This method tends to be more straightforward since no allocation of costs is required between functions.

2. **Function** Function refers to business function or activity. Most businesses are structured around activities. For instance, a manufacturing business will have a production function, a selling function, and a head office function that supports the other two functions. Therefore a statement that shows expenses by function for the manufacturing business would group costs by production, selling, and administration. These might be presented as cost of sales (production), distribution costs (selling), and administrative costs (administration). This method requires more judgement since costs such as payroll and amortization are allocated between functions. At a minimum, this method requires that cost of sales be presented separately from other costs. This presentation gives more insight into the various phases of operations (such as production and distribution).

Under IFRS, entities are encouraged to present this in the income statement; however, it may be presented elsewhere. Under ASPE, although this is not mandated, an entity may choose to make such disclosures if it feels that the information is decision relevant. Which method is better? That depends on the nature of the business and industry. For instance, it is useful in the retail and manufacturing industries to focus on cost of sales and gross profit. Gross profit margins give important information about pricing and costs. Therefore, manufacturing and retail companies may wish to present costs by function. Similarly, entities that are heavily involved in research and development may wish to present costs by function to highlight this. Since research and development costs may be largely composed of payroll costs, they would otherwise be lumped with payroll or salary expenses if the expenses were presented by nature and not by function.

Real World Emphasis

Because information about the nature of expense is useful for predicting cash flows, additional information, including amortization, depreciation, and employee benefits expenses, must also be disclosed when the income statement presents expenses by function. Illustration 4-16 shows an income statement for **Air Liquide** with expenses presented by nature. Air Liquide produces and sells gases such as oxygen and hydrogen. According to the company, natural gas is a significant raw material required to produce hydrogen. Since natural gas is a commodity, its price varies depending on supply and demand. Thus, the cost of gases will vary. Air Liquide might choose to show the expenses by nature to emphasize the significance of gas purchases.

Illustration 4-16

Air Liquide Income Statement Classified by Nature of Expense

Consolidated income statements (summarized)

For the year ended December 31

In millions of euros	Notes	2010	2011
Revenue		13,488.0	14,456.9
Purchases		(5,240.0)	(5,761.6)
Personnel expenses		(2,378.3)	(2,481.5)
Other income and expenses		(2,495.4)	(2,650.2)
Operating Income Recurring before depreciation and amortization		**3,374.3**	**3,563.6**
Depreciation and amortization expense		(1,122.1)	(1,154.9)
Operating Income Recurring		**2,252.2**	**2,408.7**

(continued)

For the year ended December 31

In millions of euros	Notes	2010	2011
Other non-recurring operating income and expenses		2.0	27.8
Operating income		**2,254.2**	**2,436.5**
Net finance costs		(228.9)	(235.5)
Other financial income and expenses		(82.3)	(62.7)
Income taxes		(512.7)	(576.4)
Share of profit of associates		27.8	32.8
Profit for the period		1,458.1	1,594.7
Minority interests		54.5	59.8
Net Profit (Group share)		1,403.6	1,534.9
Basic earnings per share (in euros)		**4.99**	**5.43**
Diluted earnings per share (in euros)		**4.97**	**5.41**

Real World Emphasis

Illustration 4-17 shows the consolidated income statements for **EADS N.V.**. The company divides its business into four segments, which are operated through four companies—Airbus, Astrium, Eurocopter and Cassidian. EADS manufactures commercial and military aircraft through Airbus including the A380 and A400M aircraft. EADS produces satellite systems through Astrium and helicopters through Eurocopter. EADS also provides solutions for armed forces and civil security through Cassidian which owns MBDA, a missile and missile system provider. Note that EADS has prepared the statements in two parts: a statement of income and a statement of comprehensive income that begins with net income. As discussed earlier, this is an option under IFRS. The illustration includes additional note disclosures regarding the expenses by nature as required under IFRS. Since EADS is primarily a manufacturing company, it makes sense that it would like to show its expenses by areas (function), highlighting the cost of sales and gross margins.

Illustration 4-17

EADS Income Statement Classified by Function

EADS N.V.—Consolidated Income Statements (IFRS) for the years ended 31 December 2011, 2010, and 2009

(In € million)	Note	2011	2010	2009
Revenues	5, 6	**49,128**	**45,752**	**42,822**
Cost of sales	7	(42,285)	(39,528)	(38,383)
Gross margin		**6,843**	**6,224**	**4,439**
Selling expenses		(981)	(1,024)	(924)
Administrative expenses		(1,427)	(1,288)	(1,272)
Research and development expenses	8	(3,152)	(2,939)	(2,825)
Other income	9	359	171	170
Other expenses	10	(221)	(102)	(102)
Share of profit from associates accounted for under the equity method	11	164	127	115
Other income from investments	11	28	18	19
Profit (loss) before finance costs and income taxes	5	**1,613**	**1,187**	**(380)**
Interest income		377	316	356
Interest expense		(364)	(415)	(503)
Other financial result		(233)	(272)	(445)
Total finance costs	12	(220)	(371)	(592)

(continued)

Income taxes	13	(356)	(244)	220
Profit (loss) for the period		**1,037**	**572**	**(752)**
Attributable to:				
Equity owners of the parent (Net income (loss))		1,033	553	(763)
Non-controlling interests		4	19	11
Earnings per share		€	€	€
Basic	38	1.27	0.68	(0.94)
Diluted	38	1.27	0.68	(0.94)

The accompanying notes are an integral part of these Consolidated Financial Statements (IFRS).

EADS N.V.—Consolidated Statements of Comprehensive Income (IFRS) for the years ended 31 December 2011, 2010, and 2009

(In € million)	2011	2010	2009
Profit (loss) for the period	**1,037**	**572**	**(752)**
Currency translation adjustments for foreign operations	(25)	119	(279)
Effective portion of changes in fair value of cash flow hedges	(365)	(2,983)	2,948
Net change in fair value of cash flow hedges transferred to profit or loss	(171)	(201)	(1,456)
Net change in fair value of available-for-sale financial assets	(20)	12	136
Actuarial gains (losses) on defined benefit plans	(747)	(127)	(594)
Unrealized gains (losses) from investments accounted for using the equity method	129	(161)	33
Tax on income and expense recognized directly in equity	331	1,096	(381)
Other comprehensive income, net of tax	**(868)**	**(2,245)**	**407**
Total comprehensive income of the period	**169**	**(1,673)**	**(345)**
Attributable to:			
Equity owners of the parent	163	(1,679)	(354)
Non-controlling interests	6	6	9

The accompanying notes are an integral part of these Consolidated Financial Statements (IFRS).

7. Functional costs

Inventories recognised as an expense during the period amount to € 35,036 million (2010: € 32,840 million; 2009: € 30,274 million).

Further included in cost of sales are amortisation expenses of fair value adjustments of non-current assets in the amount of € 40 million (2010: € 44 million; 2009: € 56 million; these are related to the EADS merger, the Airbus Combination.

Personnel expenses are:

(In € million)	2011	2010	2009
Wages, salaries and social contributions	10,286	9,625	9,094
Net periodic pension cost (see Note 25b)	424	452	424
Total	**10,710**	**10,077**	**9,518**

The **Gross Margin** increases by € 619 million to € 6,843 million compared to € 6,224 million in 2010. This improvement is mainly related to better performance of legacy programmes at Airbus Commercial. The operational improvement at Airbus (including better pricing and positive volume/mix effects) and Eurocopter is partly compensated by unfavourable foreign exchange rate effects at Airbus Commercial and onerous contract charges for the A350XWB.

Intraperiod Tax Allocation

As previously noted, certain irregular items are shown on the income statement net of tax, which is a more informative disclosure to statement users. This procedure of allocating tax balances within a period is called **intraperiod tax allocation**. Intraperiod tax allocation relates the income tax expense or benefit of the fiscal period to the underlying income statement items and events that are being taxed. Intraperiod tax allocation is used for the following items: (1) income from continuing operations, (2) discontinued operations, and (3) other comprehensive income. Companies pay taxes at the federal and provincial level in Canada and rates are dictated by the Canada Revenue Agency.[22]

In applying the concept of intraperiod tax allocation, assume that Schindler Corp. has income before income tax and discontinued operations of $250,000 and a gain from the sale of one of its operations of $100,000. If the income tax rate is assumed to be 25%, the information in Illustration 4-18 is presented on the income statement.

Illustration 4-18

Intraperiod Tax Allocation, Discontinued Operations

Income before income tax and discontinued operations	$250,000
Income tax	62,500
Income before discontinued operations	187,500
Gain from sale of discontinued operations net of applicable taxes of ($25,000)	75,000
Net income	$262,500

The income tax of $62,500 ($250,000 × 25%) that is attributed to income before income tax and discontinued operations is determined from the revenue and expense transactions related to this income. In this income tax calculation, the tax consequences of items excluded from the determination of income before income tax and discontinued operations are not considered. The "gain from sale of discontinued operation" then shows a separate tax effect of $25,000.

Earnings per Share

Typically, the results of a company's operations are summed up in one important figure: net income. As if this simplification were not enough, the financial world has widely accepted an even more distilled and compact figure as its most significant business indicator: **earnings per share** (EPS). Many users focus primarily on the earnings per share number (rightly or wrongly) as a key indicator of the company's performance. While the earnings per share number yields significant information, it does not tell the whole story. This undue emphasis on earnings per share makes it a very sensitive number for companies. Note further that when comprehensive income is presented, it begs the questions as to why EPS is not based on this more "comprehensive" measurement of income.

The calculation of earnings per share is usually straightforward. The calculation is: Net income minus preferred dividends (income available to common shareholders) divided by the weighted average number of common shares outstanding. To illustrate, assume that Lancer Inc. reports net income of $350,000 and declares and pays preferred dividends of $50,000 for the year. The weighted average number of common shares outstanding during the year is 100,000 shares. Earnings per share is $3.00, as calculated in Illustration 4-19.

Illustration 4-19

Sample Calculation of Earnings per Share

$$\frac{\text{Net Income} - \text{Preferred Dividends}}{\text{Weighted Average Number of Common Shares Outstanding}}$$

$$= \text{Earnings per Share (EPS)}$$

$$= \frac{\$350,000 - \$50,000}{100,000}$$

$$= \$3.00$$

Note that the EPS figure measures the number of dollars earned by each common share but not the dollar amount paid to shareholders in the form of dividends.

"Net income per share" or "earnings per share" is a ratio that commonly appears in prospectuses, proxy material, and annual reports to shareholders. It is also highlighted in the financial press, by statistical services like Standard & Poor's, and by Bay Street securities analysts. Because of its importance, public companies are required to disclose earnings per share on the face of their income statement. In addition, a company that reports a discontinued operation must report earnings per share for income before discontinued operations as well as per share amounts for discontinued operations either on the face of the income statement or in the notes to the financial statements.[23] Throughout the chapter, we have included numerous sample income statements that include EPS. Earnings per share information related to comprehensive income is not required.

Many corporations have simple capital structures that include only common shares. For these companies, a presentation such as earnings per common share is appropriate on the income statement. In many instances, however, companies' earnings per share are subject to dilution (reduction) in the future because existing contingencies allow future issues of additional common shares. These corporations would present both basic EPS and fully diluted EPS.[24]

In summary, the simplicity and availability of figures for per share earnings mean that they are used widely. Because of the excessive importance that the public—even the well-informed public—attaches to earnings per share, this information must be made as meaningful as possible. Note that this area is of lesser relevance to private entities as most have shares that are closely held. Therefore, companies following ASPE are not required to include EPS.

STATEMENT OF RETAINED EARNINGS AND THE STATEMENT OF CHANGES IN EQUITY

Objective 7
Prepare the statement of retained earnings and the statement of changes in equity.

Net income is closed out to retained earnings at the end of the period. Retained earnings show the company's accumulated earnings (or deficit in the case of losses). Under ASPE, the **statement of retained earnings** shows this accumulated income (or deficit) as well as how much has been paid out as dividends.

Recall that OCI only exists under IFRS and that OCI is closed out to accumulated other comprehensive income (AOCI). Therefore, under IFRS we need an expanded statement that shows the changes in retained earnings and AOCI. Under IFRS, instead of a statement of retained earnings, we use a **statement of changes in equity** and show all changes in all equity accounts including retained earnings and AOCI.

Presentation of the Statement of Retained Earnings

Retained earnings are affected by many variables and can be presented in many different ways. Net income increases retained earnings and a net loss decreases retained earnings. Both cash and share dividends decrease retained earnings. Retroactively applied changes in accounting principles and corrections of errors may either increase or decrease retained earnings. Information on retained earnings, including the changes it has undergone, can be shown in different ways. For example, companies following ASPE usually prepare a separate retained earnings statement, as shown in Illustration 4-20.

Illustration 4-20

Retained Earnings Statement

STATEMENT OF RETAINED EARNINGS
For the Year Ended December 31, 2014

Balance, January 1, as reported		$1,050,000
Correction for understatement of net income in prior period		
(inventory error) (net of taxes of $35,000)		50,000
Balance, January 1, as adjusted		1,100,000
Add: Net income		360,000
		1,460,000
Less: Cash dividends	$100,000	
Less: Stock dividends	200,000	300,000
Balance, December 31		$1,160,000

Underlying Concept

The retrospective application ensures consistency.

The reconciliation of the beginning to the ending balance in retained earnings provides information about why net assets increased or decreased during the year. The association of dividend distributions with net income for the period indicates what management is doing with earnings: it may be putting part or all of the earnings back into the business, distributing all current income, or distributing current income plus the accumulated earnings of prior years. Note that the retained earnings statement may be combined with the income statement by adding it to the bottom of the income statement. Changes in accounting occur frequently in practice, because important events or conditions may be in dispute or uncertain at the statement date. One type of accounting change occurs when a different accounting principle is adopted to replace the one previously used. **Changes in accounting principle** would include, for example, a change in the method of inventory pricing from FIFO to average cost. Accounting changes are only allowed if they are required by a primary source of GAAP or if they result in reliable and more relevant information. Under ASPE, there are some exceptions to this principle. For instance, where ASPE allows a choice of accounting policies such as accounting for income taxes, significant influence investment, or development costs, an accounting policy change may be made without having to prove that the new policy is reliable and more relevant. This is because, in principle, ASPE is meant to be more flexible and adaptable.

Changes in accounting principle are generally recognized through **retrospective restatement,** which involves determining the effect of the policy change on the income of prior periods that are affected. The financial statements for all prior periods that are presented for comparative purposes should be restated except when the effect cannot be determined reasonably. If all comparative years are not disclosed, a cumulative amount would instead be calculated and adjusted through the opening retained earnings amount.

To illustrate, Gaubert Inc. decided in March 2014 to change from the FIFO method of valuing inventory to the weighted average method. If prices are rising, cost of sales would be higher and ending inventory lower for the preceding period.

Illustration 4-21 shows what should be presented in the 2014 financial statements.

Illustration 4-21

Income Statement Presentation of a Change in Accounting Principle

Retained earnings, January 1, 2014, as previously reported	$120,000
Cumulative effect on prior years of retrospective application	
of new inventory costing method (net of $9,000 tax)	14,000
Adjusted balance of retained earnings, January 1, 2014	$106,000

The journal entry would be:

A = L + SE
−14,000   −14,000

Cash flows: No effect

Income Tax Receivable	9,000	
Retained Earnings	14,000	
Inventory		23,000

The example in the illustration assumes that no comparative data for prior years are shown. A note describing the change and its impact would also be required. Another type of change is a change in accounting estimate which is accounted for prospectively with no catch-up adjustment. Accounting changes will be revisited in Chapter 21.

Presentation of the Statement of Changes in Equity

The statement of changes in equity reports the changes in each shareholders' equity account and in total shareholders' equity during the year, including comprehensive income. The statement of shareholders' equity is often **prepared in columnar form** with columns for each account and for total shareholders' equity. This is a required statement under IFRS.

To illustrate the presentation of the statement of changes in shareholders' equity, assume the company had Net Income of $110,000 and Other Comprehensive Income of $30,000. Assume further that the company had the following shareholders' equity account balances at the beginning of 2014: Common Shares $300,000; Retained Earnings $50,000; and Accumulated Other Comprehensive Income $60,000. No changes in the Common Shares account occurred during the year. A statement of changes in equity for V. Gill Inc. is shown in Illustration 4-22.

Illustration 4-22
Presentation of Comprehensive Income Items in the Changes in Equity Statement

V. GILL INC.
Statement of Changes in Equity
For the Year Ended December 31, 2014

	Total	Common Shares	Comprehensive Income	Retained Earnings	Accumulated Other Comprehensive Income
Beginning balance	$410,000	$300,000		$ 50,000	$60,000
Net income	110,000		$110,000	110,000	
Other comprehensive income[25]	30,000		30,000		30,000
Comprehensive income			$140,000		
Ending balance	$550,000	$300,000		$160,000	$90,000

Note that other comprehensive income is accumulated in an account called Accumulated Other Comprehensive Income, as shown in Illustration 4-23. This account acts like a second Retained Earnings account. Amounts in Accumulated Other Comprehensive Income will either be recycled through net income when realized or may be transferred directly to retained earnings.

Regardless of the display format chosen, the **accumulated other comprehensive income** of $90,000 is reported in the shareholders' equity section of the balance sheet of V. Gill Inc., as shown in Illustration 4-23.

Illustration 4-23
Presentation of Accumulated Other Comprehensive Income in the Statement of Financial Position

V. GILL INC.
Statement of Financial Position as at December 31, 2014
(Shareholders' Equity Section)

Shareholders' equity	
Common shares	$300,000
Retained earnings	160,000
Accumulated other comprehensive income	90,000
Total shareholders' equity	$550,000

DISCLOSURE AND ANALYSIS

Disclosures

In addition to disclosures on the face of the financial statements, the notes to the financial statements provide a great source of background and explanatory information. The notes supplement the main statements. They should be presented in a systematic manner and cross-referenced to the main financial statements. The notes should include the following:

1. Accounting policies

2. Sources of estimation uncertainty

3. Information about the capital of the company (including how the company manages its capital and any changes)

4. Information including dividends, the legal form of the entity, its country of incorporation, description of business name of the parent company, and information required under the full disclosure principle including the basis of preparation where the financial statements were not prepared on a going concern basis.

Analysis

As noted earlier, **financial analysts and investors** assess quality of earnings and factor it into their resource allocation decisions.

Some attributes of high-quality earnings were expressed in Illustration 4-4. To assess the quality of earnings, you must look at the whole set of financial statements including the notes. In addition, the MD&A provides valuable insights into the nature of the business and industry and what is happening. Newspaper articles and analysts' reports are also good sources of information. When analyzing the health of a company and its quality of earnings, look for and analyze the following:

* **Accounting policies**—aggressive accounting policies, soft numbers

* **Notes to financial statements**—unrecognized liabilities and asset overstatement

* **Measurement uncertainty**—how hard/soft are the numbers? How risky is the business?

* **Financial statements** as a whole—complexity of presentation or language (which may obscure the company's performance or financial position)

* **Income statement**—percentage of net income derived from ongoing operations, to see whether the company can produce profits mainly from its core business

* **Cash flow statement**—cash from operating activities versus net income, to get a sense of whether net income is backed by cash or not

* **Statement of Financial Position**—to see how the company is financed and what the revenue-generating assets are

* **Other**—environmental factors such as the industry and economy. How is the company doing compared with its competitors? How is it positioning itself to take advantage of opportunities and manage risk? Where is the industry going? Are current earnings likely to be repeated in the future?

Companies often try to help users assess the results of operations and their financial position by providing modified GAAP information such as **non-GAAP earnings**. Non-GAAP earnings start with GAAP net income and add back or deduct nonrecurring or non-operating items to arrive at an adjusted net income number. Non-GAAP earnings are not bad as such. If the calculation of the non-GAAP earnings is **clearly disclosed and explained**, and is also reconciled to net income, it hopefully adds value to the decision-making process. The danger with these numbers is that there are no standards to ensure that the calculation is **consistently** prepared and **comparable** between companies.

The OSC has issued a Staff Notice on these disclosures.[26] Its concern is that the additional information presented may mislead people. The OSC has therefore set out certain principles. An excerpt from the Staff Notice follows:

Specifically, an issuer should:

1. state explicitly that the non-GAAP financial measure does not have any standardized meaning prescribed by the issuer's GAAP and is therefore unlikely to be comparable to similar measures presented by other issuers;

2. present with equal or greater prominence to that of the non-GAAP financial measure, the most directly comparable measure calculated in accordance with the issuer's GAAP and presented in its financial statements;

3. explain why the non-GAAP financial measure provides useful information to investors and the additional purposes, if any, for which management uses the non-GAAP financial measure;

4. provide a clear quantitative reconciliation from the non-GAAP financial measure to the most directly comparable measure calculated in accordance with the issuer's GAAP and presented in its financial statements, referencing to the reconciliation when the non-GAAP financial measure first appears in the document, or in the case of content on a website, in a manner that meets this objective (for example, by providing a link to the reconciliation);

5. explain any changes in the composition of the non-GAAP financial measure when compared to previously disclosed measures.

In staff's view, non-GAAP financial measures generally should not describe adjustments as non-recurring, infrequent or unusual, when a similar loss or gain is reasonably likely to occur within the next two years or occurred during the prior two years.

It is interesting to see how the OSC has defined the term "unusual items" as noted above in the excerpt—that is if an item is reasonably likely to occur in the next two years, it is recurring.

IFRS/ASPE COMPARISON

A Comparison of IFRS and ASPE

Objective 9
Identify differences in accounting between IFRS and ASPE and potential changes.

Illustration 4-24 sets out the major differences between GAAP for private entities and international accounting standards for publicly accountable enterprises.

	Accounting Standards for Private Enterprises (ASPE)—*CICA Handbook*, Part II, Sections 1400, 1506, 1520, 1521, 3251, and 3475	IFRS—IAS 1, 8, and IFRS 5	References to related illustrations and select brief exercises
Required presentation on face of income statement	As noted earlier in the chapter, ASPE mandates a list of required items that must be presented.	As noted earlier in the chapter, IFRS mandates a list of required items that must be presented.	Illustration 4-10
Guidance on how to classify expenses (nature versus function)	There is no guidance on how or when to present expenses according to their nature or function. Entities are free, however, to present their income statements in a manner that is most transparent as long as they adhere to the required disclosures noted above.	IFRS requires that the entity present an analysis of expenses based either on their nature or function.	Illustration 4-16 and 4-17
Discontinued operations	Held-for-sale assets and liabilities are classified as current or non-current depending on the nature of the assets/liabilities unless the assets have been sold prior to the completion of the financial statements. The definition of a discontinued operation component includes operating segments, reporting units, subsidiaries, asset groups, and operations with no assets. Additional guidance is provided noting that the operations and cash flows must have been or will be eliminated and the enterprise must have no significant continuing involvement.	Held-for-sale assets and liabilities are reclassified as current assets/liabilities. The definition of a discontinued operation component includes major lines of business or geographical areas and businesses acquired with an intent to resell.	Illustration 4-6 BE 4-7 and BE 4-8
Other comprehensive income/comprehensive income	Not recognized. Transactions are either booked through net income or directly to a separate component of shareholders' equity (such as certain foreign currency gains/losses).	Certain items must be classified as either comprehensive income or net income. In addition, entities must prepare a statement of comprehensive income.	Illustration 4-5 BE 4-5
Earnings per share	Not mentioned since many private entities have closely held shareholdings by definition.	Basic and diluted EPS must be presented in the statements.	
Statement of retained earnings versus statement of changes in shareholders' equity	The statement of retained earnings is one of the core financial statements. There is no requirement to present a statement of changes in shareholders' equity, although changes in shareholder equity accounts must be disclosed.	The statement of changes in equity is a required statement.	Illustration 4-20 and 4-22
Accounting changes	Certain accounting policy choice changes do not have to meet the "must be reliable and more relevant" test.	For all accounting policy changes, new policy must be reliable and more relevant.	

Illustration 4-24

IFRS and ASPE Comparison Chart

Looking Ahead

The IASB has been working on its "Performance Reporting" project since September 2001. In October 2001, the FASB also began to work on a similar project. There was concern that the two projects were diverging in focus, and so, in April 2004, the IASB and FASB decided to work together to come up with a joint, converged standard. In March 2006, the name of the project was changed to "Financial Statement Presentation" and it now consists of three phases:

Phase A—What constitutes a complete set of financial statements

Phase B—Presentation of information on the face of the statements

Phase C—Interim financial reporting

Phase A is complete and embedded in IAS 1. Working principles for Phase B, which have been agreed upon, state that the financial statements should:

- provide a cohesive financial picture of an entity,
- provide information to help users assess the liquidity of an entity,
- separate the financing activities from other activities,
- provide information about the measurement of assets and liabilities, and
- disaggregate information and present subtotals and totals.

The following was taken from a presentation of the preliminary views document issued by the IASB in 2008. The chart illustrates how information regarding various aspects might be presented on the various statements. The work on the project is on hold, because the IASB is focusing on other projects including leases, revenues, and financial instruments.

Proposed format for the presentation of financial statements

Statement of financial position	Statement of comprehensive income	Statement of cash flows
Business • Operating assets and liabilities • Investing assets and liabilities	Business • Operating income and expenses • Investing income and expenses	Business • Operating cash flows • Investing cash flows
Financing • Financing assets • Financing liabilities	Financing • Financing asset income • Financing liability expenses	Financing • Financing asset cash flows • Financing liability cash flows
Income taxes	Income taxes on continuing operations (business and financing)	Income taxes
Discontinued operations	Discontinued operations net of tax	Discontinued operations
	Other comprehensive income, net of tax	
Equity		Equity

On a final note, the IASB and AcSB are working together to redefine the meaning of "component" for discontinued operations in the hopes of harmonizing the definition between ASPE and IFRS. At the time of writing of this chapter, the AcSB had issued an ED to propose that component be defined the same way under ASPE as for IFRS.

SUMMARY OF LEARNING OBJECTIVES

1 Understand how firms create value and manage performance.

A business is based on a basic model of obtaining financing, investing in assets, and using those assets to generate profits. Different industries have different business models. Even within an industry, different businesses may have different strategies for generating revenues. Some businesses and industries are riskier than others. Companies must decide how and whether to manage these risks. Managing risks costs money, which reduces profits. Capital markets demand greater returns for riskier businesses.

2 Understand how users use information about performance to make decisions.

Users use information about performance to evaluate past performance and profitability and to provide a basis for predicting future performance. They also use the information to help assess risk and uncertainty regarding future cash flows.

3 Understand the concept of and be able to assess quality of earnings/information.

The concept of quality of earnings is used by analysts and investors to assess how well the reported income reflects the underlying business and future potential. When assessing quality of earnings, consider all information about a company. High-quality earnings have various attributes, as noted in Illustration 4-4. Where the information is biased, this degrades the quality.

4 Understand the differing perspectives on how to measure income.

There are various ways to measure income, including operating income, net income, and comprehensive income. IFRS recognizes the concept of comprehensive income but this is not included under ASPE. Other comprehensive income consists of a set list of items identified under IFRS essentially dealing with certain unrealized gains/losses. Under IFRS, some of these items are recycled (reclassified) to net income and some are not.

5 Measure and report results of discontinued operations.

The gain or loss on disposal of a business component involves the sum of: (1) the income or loss from operations to the financial statement date, and (2) the gain or loss on the disposal of the business component. These items are reported net of tax among the irregular items in the income statement. Related assets are identified on the balance sheet where material. Under IFRS, non-current assets are reclassified to current assets.

6 Measure income and prepare the income statement and the statement of comprehensive income using various formats.

There are many ways to present the income statement and the statement of comprehensive income. GAAP lays out certain minimum requirements but beyond that, a company has some leeway to present the information as it wishes. The goal is to ensure that the statements present information about performance in a transparent manner, including presenting items such that the users can see which are ordinary versus peripheral activities. IFRS allows the statement of comprehensive income to be presented in a combined statement or two separate statements.

By convention, companies use what is known as a single-step method or a multiple-step method (or a variation of the two).

IFRS requires entities to provide information about either the nature or function of expenses. When information is presented using function, additional disclosures should be made regarding the breakdown of the nature of expenses as the latter has good cash flow predictive value. The entity should choose the method that best reflects the nature of the business and industry.

7 Prepare the statement of retained earnings and the statement of changes in equity.

The retained earnings statement should disclose net income (loss), dividends, prior period adjustments, and transfers to and from retained earnings (appropriations). This statement is required under ASPE.

The statement of changes in equity is a required statement under IFRS and takes the place of the statement of changes in retained earnings. It shows all changes in all equity accounts including accumulated other comprehensive income.

8 Understand how disclosures and analysis help users of financial statements assess performance.

Disclosures include notes and supplementary information. They provide background and explanatory information necessary to understand the business. Investors and analysts use quality of earnings analysis to help determine a company's value.

9 Identify differences in accounting between IFRS and ASPE and potential changes.

The chart in Illustration 4-24 outlines the major differences. The IASB may eventually change the way financial statements are presented. The major statements, including balance sheet, income state- ment, and statement of cash flows, would be classified according to business and financing activities. The IASB is also working to harmonize the definition of "component" for purposes of discontinued operations.

KEY TERMS

all-inclusive approach, p. 163
business component, p. 165
business model, p. 156
capital maintenance theory, p. 219
changes in accounting principle, p. 183
current operating performance
    approach, p. 163
discontinued operations, p. 165
earnings management, p. 162
earnings per share, p. 181

function, p. 178
held for sale, p. 166
income statement, p. 156
intraperiod tax allocation, p. 181
multiple-step income statement, p. 174
nature, p. 178
net income, p. 163
non-GAAP earnings, p. 185
operating income, p. 163
quality of earnings, p. 161

risk management, p. 157
risk/return tradeoff, p. 157
single-step income statement, p. 174
statement of changes in equity, p. 182
statement of comprehensive income,
    p. 156
statement of income/earnings, p. 156
statement of retained earnings, p. 182

APPENDIX 4A

CASH BASIS VERSUS ACCRUAL BASIS EARNINGS

Differences Between Cash and Accrual Bases

Objective 10

Explain the differences between the cash basis of accounting and the accrual basis of accounting.

Most companies use the **accrual basis** of accounting: they recognize revenue when it is earned and recognize expenses in the period when they are incurred, which means that the time when cash is received or paid is not a factor in recognizing the transaction. Some small enterprises and the average individual taxpayer, however, use a strict or modified cash basis approach. Under the **strict cash basis**, revenue is recorded only when the cash is received, and expenses are recorded only when the cash is paid. On the cash basis, income is determined based on the actual collection of revenues and payment of expenses, and the revenue recognition and matching principles are ignored. Consequently, cash basis financial statements do not conform with generally accepted accounting principles.

To illustrate and contrast accrual basis accounting and cash basis accounting, assume that Quality Contractor signs an agreement to build a garage for $22,000. In January, Quality Contractor begins construction, incurs costs of $18,000 on credit, and by the end of January delivers a finished garage to the buyer. In February, Quality Contractor collects $22,000 cash from the customer. In March, Quality pays the $18,000 that is owed to the creditors. Illustrations 4A-1 and 4A-2 show the net income for each month under cash basis accounting and accrual basis accounting.

Illustration **4A-1**

Income Statement—Cash Basis

QUALITY CONTRACTOR
Income Statement Cash Basis
For the Month of

	January	February	March	Total
Cash receipts	$-0-	$22,000	$ -0-	$22,000
Cash payments	-0-	-0-	18,000	18,000
Net income (loss)	$-0-	$22,000	$(18,000)	$ 4,000

Illustration **4A-2**

Income Statement—Accrual Basis

QUALITY CONTRACTOR
Income Statement Accrual Basis
For the Month of

	January	February	March	Total
Revenues	$22,000	$-0-	$-0-	$22,000
Expenses	18,000	-0-	-0-	18,000
Net income (loss)	$ 4,000	$-0-	$-0-	$ 4,000

For the three months combined, total net income is the same under both cash basis accounting and accrual basis accounting; the difference is in the timing of net income. The balance sheet is also affected by the basis of accounting. For instance, if cash basis accounting were used, Quality Contractor's balance sheets at each month end would appear as in Illustration 4A-3.

Illustration **4A-3**

Balance Sheets—Cash Basis

QUALITY CONTRACTOR
Balance Sheets Cash Basis
As at

	Jan. 31	Feb. 28	Mar. 31
Assets			
Cash	$-0-	$22,000	$4,000
Total assets	$-0-	$22,000	$4,000
Liabilities and Owners' Equity			
Owners' equity	$-0-	$22,000	$4,000
Total liabilities and owners' equity	$-0-	$22,000	$4,000

Illustration 4A-4 shows what Quality Contractor's balance sheets at each month end would look like if accrual basis accounting were used.

Illustration **4A-4**

Balance Sheets—Accrual Basis

QUALITY CONTRACTOR
Balance Sheets Accrual Basis
As at

	Jan. 31	Feb. 28	Mar. 31
Assets			
Cash	$ -0-	$22,000	$4,000
Accounts receivable	22,000	-0-	-0-
Total assets	$22,000	$22,000	$4,000
Liabilities and Owners' Equity			
Accounts payable	$18,000	$18,000	$ -0-
Owners' equity	4,000	4,000	4,000
Total liabilities and owners' equity	$22,000	$22,000	$4,000

An analysis of the preceding income statements and balance sheets shows the following ways in which cash basis accounting is inconsistent with basic accounting theory:

1. The cash basis understates revenues and assets from the construction and delivery of the garage in January. It ignores the $22,000 of accounts receivable, which is a near-term future cash inflow.

2. The cash basis understates the expenses incurred with the construction of the garage and the liability outstanding at the end of January. It ignores the $18,000 of accounts payable, which is a near-term future cash outflow.

3. The cash basis understates owners' equity in January by not recognizing the revenues and the asset until February, and it overstates owners' equity in February by not recognizing the expenses and liability until March.

In short, cash basis accounting violates the theory underlying the elements of financial statements.

The **modified cash basis**, a mixture of cash basis and accrual basis, is the method often followed by professional services firms (doctors, lawyers, accountants, consultants) and by retail, real estate, and agricultural operations. It is the pure cash basis of accounting with modifications that have substantial support, such as capitalizing and amortizing plant assets or recording inventory.[27]

Conversion from Cash Basis to Accrual Basis

Fairly often, a cash basis or a modified cash basis set of financial statements needs to be converted to the accrual basis so it can be presented to investors and creditors. To illustrate this conversion, assume that Dr. Diane Windsor keeps her accounting records on a cash basis. In the year 2014, Dr. Windsor received $300,000 from her dental patients and paid $170,000 for operating expenses, resulting in an excess of cash receipts over disbursements of $130,000 ($300,000 – $170,000). At January 1 and December 31, 2014, she has the accounts receivable, unearned service revenue, accrued liabilities, and prepaid expenses shown in Illustration 4A-5.

Illustration 4A-5		
Excerpt from General Ledger	Jan. 1, 2014	Dec. 31, 2014
Accounts receivable	$12,000	$9,000
Unearned revenue	–0–	4,000
Accrued liabilities	2,000	5,500
Prepaid expenses	1,800	2,700

Service Revenue Calculation

To convert the amount of cash received from patients to service revenue on an accrual basis, changes in accounts receivable and unearned revenue during the year must be considered. Accounts receivable at the beginning of the year represent revenues earned last year that are collected this year. Ending accounts receivable indicate revenues earned this year that are not yet collected. Therefore, beginning accounts receivable are subtracted and ending accounts receivable added to arrive at revenue on an accrual basis, as shown in Illustration 4A-6.

Illustration 4A-6		
Conversion of Cash Receipts to Revenue—Accounts Receivable	Cash receipts from customers	(– Beginning accounts receivable) (+ Ending accounts receivable) = Revenue on an accrual basis

Using similar analysis, beginning unearned service revenue represents cash received last year for revenues earned this year. Ending unearned service revenue results from collections this year that will be recognized as revenue next year. Therefore, beginning unearned service revenue is added and ending unearned service revenue is subtracted to arrive at revenue on an accrual basis, as shown in Illustration 4A-7.

Illustration 4A-7

Conversion of Cash Receipts to Revenue—Unearned Service Revenue

Cash receipts from customers	(+ Beginning unearned revenue) (− Ending unearned revenue)	=	Revenue on an accrual basis

Cash collected from customers, therefore, is converted to service revenue on an accrual basis, as Illustration 4A-8 shows.

Illustration 4A-8

Conversion of Cash Receipts to Service Revenue

Cash receipts from customers		$300,000
Beginning accounts receivable	$(12,000)	
Ending accounts receivable	9,000	
Beginning unearned revenue	–0–	
Ending unearned revenue	(4,000)	(7,000)
Service revenue (accrual)		$293,000

Operating Expense Calculation

To convert cash paid for operating expenses during the year to operating expenses on an accrual basis, you must consider changes in prepaid expenses and accrued liabilities during the year. Beginning prepaid expenses should be recognized as expenses this year. (The cash payment occurred last year.) Therefore, the beginning prepaid expenses balance is added to cash paid for operating expenses to arrive at operating expense on an accrual basis.

Conversely, ending prepaid expenses result from cash payments made this year for expenses to be reported next year. (The expense recognition is deferred to a future period.) As a result, ending prepaid expenses are deducted from cash paid for expenses, as shown in Illustration 4A-9.

Illustration 4A-9

Conversion of Cash Payments to Expenses—Prepaid Expenses

Cash paid for operating expenses	(+ Beginning prepaid expenses) (− Ending prepaid expenses)	=	Expenses on an accrual basis

Using similar analysis, beginning accrued liabilities result from expenses recognized last year that require cash payments this year. Ending accrued liabilities relate to expenses recognized this year that have not been paid. Beginning accrued liabilities, therefore, are deducted and ending accrued liabilities are added to cash paid for expenses to arrive at expenses on an accrual basis, as shown in Illustration 4A-10.

Illustration 4A-10

Conversion of Cash Payments to Expenses—Accrued Liabilities

Cash paid for operating expenses	(− Beginning accrued liabilities) (+ Ending accrued liabilities)	=	Expenses on an accrual basis

For Dr. Diane Windsor, therefore, cash paid for operating expenses is converted to operating expenses on an accrual basis as in Illustration 4A-11.

Cash paid for operating expenses		$170,000
Beginning prepaid expense	$ 1,800	
Ending prepaid expense	(2,700)	
Beginning accrued liabilities	(2,000)	
Ending accrued liabilities	5,500	2,600
Operating expenses (accrual)		$172,600

Illustration 4A-12 shows how this entire conversion can be presented in a work sheet.

DIANE WINDSOR, D.D.S.
Conversion of Income Statement Data from Cash Basis to Accrual Basis
For the Year 2014

	Cash Basis	Add	Deduct	Accrual Basis
			Adjustments	
Collections from customers	$300,000			
– Accounts receivable, Jan. 1			$12,000	
+ Accounts receivable, Dec. 31		$9,000		
+ Unearned revenue, Jan. 1		—		
– Unearned revenue, Dec. 31			4,000	
Service revenue				$293,000
Disbursement for expenses	170,000			
+ Prepaid expenses, Jan. 1		1,800		
– Prepaid expenses, Dec. 31			2,700	
– Accrued liabilities, Jan. 1			2,000	
+ Accrued liabilities, Dec. 31		5,500		
Operating expenses				172,600
Excess of cash collections over disbursements—cash basis	$130,000			
Net income—accrual basis				$120,400

Using this approach, collections and disbursements on a cash basis are adjusted to revenue and expenses on an accrual basis to arrive at accrued net income. In any conversion from the cash basis to the accrual basis, depreciation or amortization expense is an expense in arriving at net income on an accrual basis.

Theoretical Weaknesses of the Cash Basis

Underlying Concept

Accrual-based net income is a good predictor of future cash flows.

Quiz

The cash basis does report exactly when cash is received and when cash is disbursed. To many people, that information represents something solid, something concrete. Isn't cash what it's all about? Does it make sense to invent something, design it, produce it, market it, and sell it, if you aren't going to get cash for it in the end? If so, then what is the merit of accrual accounting?

Today's economy is based more on credit than cash. And the accrual basis, not the cash basis, recognizes all aspects of credit. Investors, creditors, and other decision-makers seek timely information about an enterprise's future cash flows. Accrual basis accounting provides this information by reporting the cash inflows and outflows associated with earnings activities as soon as these cash flows can be estimated with an acceptable degree of certainty. Receivables and payables are forecasters of future cash inflows and outflows. In other words, accrual basis accounting aids in predicting future cash flows by reporting transactions and other events with cash consequences at the time the transactions and events occur, rather than when the cash is received and paid.

SUMMARY OF LEARNING OBJECTIVE FOR APPENDIX 4A

10 Explain the differences between the cash basis of accounting and the accrual basis of accounting.

Accrual basis accounting provides information about cash inflows and outflows associated with earnings activities as soon as these cash flows can be estimated with an acceptable degree of certainty. That is, accrual basis accounting aids in predicting future cash flows by reporting transactions and events with cash consequences at the time the transactions and events occur, rather than when the cash is received and paid. The cash basis focuses on when the cash is received or dispersed, and therefore it is not the best predictor of future cash flows if the company has irregular cash flow patterns.

KEY TERMS

accrual basis, p. 190   modified cash basis, p. 192   strict cash basis, p. 190

Note: All assignment material with an asterisk (*) relates to the appendix to the chapter.

Brief Exercises

(LO 1) BE4-1 Sunmart Inc. is a discount retailer with 1,000 stores located across North America. Sunmart purchases bulk quantities of groceries and household goods, and then sells the goods directly to retail customers at a markup. Pharmedical Inc. is a pharmaceutical company that develops medications to prevent and treat diseases. Pharmedical develops, produces, and markets medications for purchase by patients of healthcare professionals and customers of retail pharmacies and stores. Referring to each company's business model, which company would have (a) a higher gross profit percentage, (b) a higher selling expense as a percentage of sales, (c) a higher research and development expense as a percentage of sales, and (d) higher net income?

(LO 2) BE4-2 Several of Jae Corporation's major customers experienced cash flow problems in 2014, mainly due to their increasing labour and production costs in 2013 and 2014. As a result, Jae's accounts receivable turnover ratio (net sales revenue/average trade receivables [net]) decreased significantly in 2014. However, Jae believes that its customers' cash flow problems are temporary. In estimating uncollectible accounts receivable as at December 31, 2014, Jae decreased the estimated percentage of its outstanding accounts receivable that will become uncollectible (a lower percentage was applied in 2014 than was applied in the previous five years). Jae's bad debt expense as a percentage of sales for the year ended December 31, 2014, was lower than the percentage reported in the previous five years, and no additional note disclosure regarding potentially higher risk of uncollectible accounts was reported. Based only on the information above, (a) evaluate the quality of information provided by Jae and (b) indicate whether the earnings reported by Jae will be discounted in the capital markets.

(LO 3) BE4-3 Environmental Corporation specializes in the production and sale of eco-friendly packaging. In 2014, Environmental reported net income (earnings) in excess of analyst expectations. This included a significant gain on sale of investments in the year and lower depreciation expense due to the company's change from the declining balance method (used by competitors) to the straight-line method for depreciating its equipment. Answer the following questions based only on the information provided. (a) From the perspective of an investor, does Environmental have high-quality earnings? (b) Will the earnings reported by Environmental be discounted in the capital markets?

(LO 3) BE4-4 Faz Corporation is a manufacturer of paints and specialty coatings. In March 2014, Beck Inc. filed a lawsuit against Faz Corporation for alleged patent infringement, claiming $1.1 million in damages. Faz's lawyer disputed the claim, but in December 2014, Faz's lawyer informed management that Faz will likely lose the dispute and have to pay between $900,000 and $1.1 million. Dissatisfied with this estimate and its potential impact on 2014 net income, Faz's management sought a second legal opinion in December 2014. The lawyer who provided the second opinion suggested that Faz will likely have to pay between $400,000 and $600,000. In its financial statements for the year ended December 31, 2014, Faz recorded a provision for a loss on the lawsuit and a liability in the amount of $500,000. Answer the following questions based only on the information provided. (a) Does Faz have high-quality earnings? (b) Will the earnings reported by Faz be discounted in the capital markets?

(LO 4) BE4-5 Delray Inc. follows IFRS and has the following amounts for the year ended December 31, 2014: gain on sale of FV-NI investments (before tax) $1,000; loss from operation of discontinued division (net of tax) $3,000; income from operations (before tax) $15,000; unrealized holding gain-OCI (net of tax) $1,000; income tax on income from continuing operations $4,000; loss from disposal of discontinued division (net of tax) $5,000. The unrealized holding gain-OCI relates to investments that are not quoted in an active market. (a) Calculate income from continuing operations. (b) Calculate net income. (c) Calculate other comprehensive income. (d) Calculate comprehensive income. (e) How would your answers to parts (a) to (d) be different if Delray followed ASPE?

(LO 4) BE4-6 On January 1, 2014, Rocket Corp. had cash and common shares of $60,000. At that date, the company had no other asset, liability, or shareholders' equity balances. On January 2, 2014, Rocket paid $40,000 cash for equity securities that it designated as fair value through other comprehensive income (FV-OCI) investments. During the year, Rocket received non-taxable cash dividends of $18,000 and had an unrealized holding gain of $25,000 (net of tax) on these securities. Determine the following amounts for 2014: (a) net income, (b) other comprehensive income, (c) comprehensive income, and (d) accumulated other comprehensive income (as at the end of 2014).

(LO 5) BE4-7 Billy's Burgers (BB) is a franchisor that operates several corporate-owned restaurants as well as several franchised restaurants. The franchisees pay 3% of their sales revenues to BB in return for advertising and support. During the year, BB sold its corporate-owned stores to a franchisee. BB continues to monitor quality in its franchised operations and franchisees must buy all products from it. The corporate-owned stores are not considered a separate major line of business. (a) Would the sale qualify for discontinued operations treatment under IFRS? (b) Would the sale qualify for discontinued operations treatment if BB prepared financial statements in accordance with ASPE?

(LO 5) BE4-8 Mega Inc.'s manufacturing division lost $100,000 (net of tax) for the year ended December 31, 2014, and Mega estimates that it can sell the division at a loss of $200,000 (net of tax). The division qualifies for treatment as a discontinued operation. (a) Explain how the discontinued operation would be measured and presented on the income statement and balance sheet under ASPE. (b) Explain how your answer to part (a) would be different if Mega prepared financial statements in accordance with IFRS.

(LO 6, 8) BE4-9 Taylor Corporation had net sales revenue of $2,780,000 and investment revenue of $103,000 in 2014. Other items pertaining to 2014 were as follows:

Cost of merchandise sold	$2,190,000
Salaries and wages	175,000
Advertising and promotion	60,000
Entertainment	37,000
Selling expenses	272,000
Salaries and wages	142,000
Rent	48,000
Utilities	21,000
Administrative expenses	211,000
Increase in value of company reputation	35,000
Unrealized gain on value of patents	17,000
Interest expense	76,000
Income tax expense	40,000

Taylor has 10,000 common shares outstanding. Prepare a single-step income statement showing expenses by nature. Include calculation of EPS.

(LO 6, 8) BE4-10 Use the information in BE4-9 to prepare a multiple-step income statement for Taylor Corporation, showing expenses by function.

(LO 6, 8) BE4-11 The Blue Collar Corporation had income from continuing operations of $12.6 million in 2014. During 2014, it disposed of its restaurant division at an after-tax loss of $89,000. Before the disposal, the division operated at a loss of $315,000 (net of tax) in 2014. Blue Collar also had an unrealized gain-OCI of $43,000 (net of tax) related to its fair value-OCI investments. Blue Collar had 10 million common shares outstanding during 2014. Blue Collar accounts for its investments in accordance with IAS 39. Prepare a partial statement of comprehensive income for Blue Collar beginning with income from continuing operations. Include calculation of EPS.

(LO 6, 8) BE4-12 The Big and Rich Corporation had income from operations before tax for 2014 of $7.3 million. In addition, it suffered an unusual and infrequent loss of $1,770,000 from a tornado. Of this amount, $500,000 was insured. In addition, the company realized a loss from the sale of a building amounting to $250,000. The corporation's tax rate is 30%. Prepare a partial income statement for Big and Rich beginning with income from operations. The corporation had five million common shares outstanding during 2014. Include calculation of EPS.

(LO 7) BE4-13 Your Pal Postcard Company Limited reports the following for 2014: sales revenue $900,000; cost of sales $750,000; operating expenses $100,000; and unrealized gain on fair value-OCI investments $60,000. The company had January 1, 2014 balances as follows: common shares $600,000; accumulated other comprehensive income $250,000; and retained earnings $900,000. The company did not issue any shares during 2014. On December 15, 2014, the board of directors declared a $300,000 dividend payable on January 31, 2015. The company accounts for its investments in accordance with IAS 39. Prepare a statement of changes in equity. Ignore income tax.

(LO 7) BE4-14 Global Corporation prepares financial statements in accordance with ASPE. At January 1, 2014, the company had retained earnings of $529,000. In 2014, net income was $1,646,000, and cash dividends of $660,000 were declared and paid. Prepare a 2014 statement of retained earnings for Global Corporation.

(LO 8) BE4-15 Use the information in BE4-14 to prepare a statement of retained earnings for Global Corporation, assuming that in 2014, Global discovered that it had overstated 2011 depreciation by $25,000 (net of tax).

(LO 8) BE4-16 Turner Limited had 40,000 common shares on January 1, 2014. On April 1, 8,000 shares were repurchased. On August 31, 12,000 shares were issued. Calculate the number of shares outstanding at December 31, 2014, and the weighted average number of shares for 2014.

(LO 8) BE4-17 In 2014, I & T Corporation reported net income of $1.6 million, and declared and paid preferred share dividends of $400,000. During 2014, I & T had a weighted average of 120,000 common shares outstanding. Calculate I & T's 2014 earnings per share.

(LO 10) *BE4-18 In 2014, Renato Corp. had cash receipts from customers of $152,000 and cash payments for operating expenses of $97,000. At January 1, 2014, accounts receivable was $13,000 and total prepaid expenses was $17,500. At December 31, 2014, accounts receivable was $18,600 and total prepaid expenses was $23,200. Calculate (a) total service revenue and (b) total operating expenses.

Exercises

(LO 4, 6) E4-1 **(Comprehensive Income)** Reach Out Card Company Limited reported the following for 2014: net sales revenue $1.2 million; cost of goods sold $750,000; selling and administrative expenses $320,000; gain on disposal of building $250,000; and unrealized gain-OCI (related to fair value through OCI investments) $18,000. The company accounts for its investments in accordance with IAS 39.

Instructions

Prepare a statement of comprehensive income. Ignore income tax and EPS.

(LO 4, 6) E4-2 **(Comprehensive Income)** Pike Corporation, a clothing retailer, had income from operations (before tax) of $375,000, and recorded the following before tax gains/(losses) for the year ended December 31, 2014:

Gain on sale of equipment	27,000
Unrealized (loss)/gain on fair value-net income investments	(54,000)
(Loss)/gain on disposal of building	(68,000)
Gain on sale of fair value-net income investments	33,000

Pike also had the following account balances as of January 1, 2014:

Retained earnings	$410,000
Accumulated other comprehensive income (this was due to a revaluation surplus on land)	74,000
Accumulated other comprehensive income (this was due to gains on fair value through OCI investments)	55,000

As of January 1, 2014, Pike had one piece of land that it accounted for using the revaluation model. It was most recently revalued to fair value on December 31, 2013, when its carrying amount was adjusted to fair value of $215,000. In January 2014, the piece of land was sold for proceeds of $216,000. In applying the revaluation model, Pike maintains the balance in the Revaluation Surplus (OCI) account until the asset is retired or disposed of.

In 2009, Pike purchased a portfolio of investments that the company intended to hold for longer term strategic purposes, and classified the portfolio of investments as fair value through other comprehensive income (FV-OCI). The investments in the portfolio are traded in an active market. Pike records unrealized gains and losses on these investments as OCI, and then books these gains and losses to net income when they are impaired or sold. The portfolio's carrying amount on December 31, 2013, was $110,000. The entire portfolio was sold in November 2014 for proceeds of $126,000.

Pike's income tax expense for 2014 was $99,000. Pike prepares financial statements in accordance with IFRS.

Instructions

(a) Calculate net income for the year ended December 31, 2014.

(b) Calculate retained earnings as at December 31, 2014.

(c) Explain the change in accumulated other comprehensive income in 2014.

(d) Calculate net income for the year ended December 31, 2014, and retained earnings as at December 31, 2014, if Pike prepares financial statements in accordance with ASPE. Assume that under ASPE, Pike's retained earnings at January 1, 2014, would be $465,000, and that Pike's income tax expense would not change.

(LO 5) **E4-3 (Discontinued Operations)** Assume that PAC Inc. decided to sell SBTV, a subsidiary, on September 30, 2014. There is a formal plan to dispose of the business component, and the sale qualifies for discontinued operations treatment. Pertinent data on the operations of the TV subsidiary are as follows: loss from operations from beginning of year to September 30, $1.9 million (net of tax); loss from operations from September 30 to end of 2014, $700,000 (net of tax); estimated loss on sale of net assets to December 31, 2014 (net of tax), $150,000. The year end is December 31. PAC prepares financial statements in accordance with IFRS.

Instructions

(a) What is the net income/loss from discontinued operations reported in 2014?

(b) Prepare the discontinued operations section of the income statement for the year ended 2014.

(c) If the amount reported in 2014 as a gain or loss from disposal of the subsidiary becomes materially incorrect, when and how is the correction reported, if at all?

(d) How would the discontinued operation be presented on the balance sheet?

(e) How would your answer to part (d) be different if PAC prepared financial statements in accordance with ASPE?

(LO 5) **E4-4 (Discontinued Operations)** On October 5, 2014, Diamond in the Rough Recruiting Group Inc.'s board of directors decided to dispose of the Blue Division. A formal plan was approved. Diamond derives approximately 75% of its income from its human resources management practice. The Blue Division gets contracts to perform human resources management on an outsourced basis. The board decided to dispose of the division because of unfavourable operating results.

Net income for Diamond was $91,000 for the fiscal year ended December 31, 2014 (after a charge for tax at 30% and after a writedown for the Blue assets). Income from operations of the Blue Division accounted for $4,200 (after tax) of this amount.

Because of the unfavourable results and the extreme competition, the board believes that it cannot sell the business intact. Its final decision is to auction off the office equipment. The equipment is the division's only asset and has a carrying value of $25,000 at October 5, 2014. The board believes that proceeds from the sale will be approximately $5,000 after the auction expenses. Currently, the estimated fair value of the equipment is $8,000. The Blue Division qualifies for treatment as a discontinued operation. Diamond prepares financial statements in accordance with ASPE.

Instructions

(a) Prepare a partial income statement for Diamond in the Rough Recruiting Group and the appropriate footnote that relates to the Blue Division for 2014. The income statement should begin with income from continuing operations before income tax.

(b) Explain how the assets would be valued and presented on the balance sheet.

(c) Explain how the assets would be valued and presented on the balance sheet if Diamond prepared financial statements in accordance with IFRS.

Digging Deeper

(d) From the perspective of an investor, comment on Diamond's quality of earnings if Diamond presented the Blue Division as a discontinued operation, but did not have a formal plan in place to dispose of the division.

(LO 6) **E4-5 (Calculation of Net Income)** The following are all changes in the account balances of Bravar Company Ltd. during the current year, except for Retained Earnings:

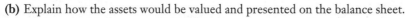

	Increase (Decrease)		Increase (Decrease)
Cash	$90,000	Accounts payable	$ (76,000)
Accounts receivable (net)	70,000	Unearned revenue	22,000
Inventory	167,000	Bonds payable	82,000
Investments in FV-NI securities	(27,000)	Common shares	125,000
		Contributed surplus	75,000

Instructions

Calculate the net income for the current year, assuming that there were no entries in the Retained Earnings account except for net income and a dividend declaration of $19,000, which was paid in the current year.

(LO 6) **E4-6** **(Calculation of Net Income)** Videohound Video Company, a sole proprietorship, had the following information for 2014:

Cash balance, January 1	$ 23,000	Total assets, December 31	$101,000
Accounts receivable, January 1	19,000	Cash balance, December 31	20,000
Collections from customers during year	200,000	Accounts receivable, December 31	36,000
Capital account balance, January 1	38,000	Merchandise taken for personal use	11,000
Total assets, January 1	75,000	Total liabilities, December 31	41,000
Cash investment added by sole			
proprietor, July 1	5,000		

Instructions

Calculate the net income for 2014.

(LO 6) **E4-7** **(Income Statement Items)** Certain account balances follow for Vincenti Products Corp.:

Rental revenue	$ 8,500	Sales discounts	$ 17,800
Interest expense	2,700	Selling expenses	79,400
Beginning retained earnings	114,400	Sales revenue	490,000
Ending retained earnings	74,000	Income tax expense	100
Dividends revenue	91,000	Cost of goods sold	384,400
Sales returns and allowances	22,400	Administrative expenses	82,500

Instructions

Based on the balances, calculate the following:

(a) total net revenue,

(b) net income or loss, and

(c) dividends declared during the current year.

(LO 6) **E4-8** **(Multiple-Step and Single-Step—Periodic Inventory Method)** Income statement information for Flett Tire Repair Corporation for the year 2014 follows:

Administrative expenses:		Freight-in	$ 14,000
Salaries and wages expense	$ 39,000	Purchase discounts	10,000
Depreciation expense—building	28,500	Dividend revenue	20,000
Office supplies expense	9,500	Inventory (beginning)	120,000
Inventory (ending)	137,000	Sales returns and allowances	15,000
Loss—other (due to flood damage)	50,000	Selling expenses:	
Gain on the sale of equipment	5,500	Salaries and wages	71,000
Purchases	600,000	Depreciation expense—store equipment	18,000
Sales revenue	930,000	Store supplies expense	9,000
Interest expense	9,000		

The effective tax rate on all income is 25%, and Flett applies ASPE.

Instructions

(a) Prepare a multiple-step income statement for 2014, showing expenses by function.

(b) Prepare a single-step income statement for 2014, showing expenses by nature.

(c) Discuss the merits of the two income statements, compared with each other.

(LO 6) **E4-9** **(Combined Single-Step)** The following information was taken from the records of Presley Inc. for the year 2014:

Gain—other (due to expropriation)	$ 95,000	Cash dividends declared	$ 70,000
Loss from operation of discontinued		Retained earnings, January 1, 2014	600,000
Ace Division	75,000	Cost of goods sold	850,000
Administrative expenses	240,000	Selling expenses	300,000
Rent revenue	40,000	Sales revenue	1,900,000
Loss—other (due to flood)	60,000		

The following additional information was also available: income tax applicable to income from continuing operations, $187,000; income tax applicable to loss from operation of discontinued Ace Division, $25,000.

The company has elected to adopt ASPE.

Instructions

(a) Prepare a single-step income statement for 2014, showing expenses by function.

(b) Prepare a combined single-step income and statement of retained earnings.

(LO 6, 7) E4-10 (Multiple-Step Statement, Statement of Comprehensive Income, and Statement of Changes in Equity) The following is information for Gottlieb Corp. for the year ended December 31, 2014:

Net sales revenue	$1,300,000	Loss on inventory due to decline in net	
Unrealized gain on fair value		realizable value (NRV)	$ 80,000
through OCI investments	42,000	Loss on sale of equipment	35,000
Interest income	7,000	Depreciation expense related to buildings	
Cost of goods sold	780,000	omitted by mistake in 2013	55,000
Selling expenses	65,000	Retained earnings at December 31, 2013	980,000
Administrative expenses	48,000	Loss—other (due to expropriation of land)	60,000
Dividend revenue	20,000	Dividends declared	45,000

The effective tax rate is 25% on all items. Gottlieb prepares financial statements in accordance with IFRS, and accounts for its investments in accordance with IAS 39. The FV-OCI investments trade on the stock exchange.

Instructions

(a) Prepare a multiple-step statement of comprehensive income for 2014, showing expenses by function. Ignore calculation of EPS.

(b) Prepare the retained earnings section of the statement of changes in equity for 2014.

(c) Prepare the journal entry to record the depreciation expense omitted by mistake in 2013.

(d) How should Gottlieb account for the unrealized gain on fair value through OCI investments if it prepares financial statements in accordance with ASPE? How would Gottlieb's retained earnings balance at December 31, 2013, be different if financial statements in all previous years were prepared in accordance with ASPE?

(LO 6, 8) E4-11 (Single-Step Income Statement) The financial records of Geneva Inc. were destroyed by fire at the end of 2014. Fortunately, the controller had kept the following statistical data related to the income statement:

1. The beginning merchandise inventory was $84,000 and it decreased by 20% during the current year.

2. Sales discounts amounted to $15,000.

3. There were 15,000 common shares outstanding for the entire year.

4. Interest expense was $20,000.

5. The income tax rate was 25%.

6. Cost of goods sold amounted to $420,000.

7. Administrative expenses were 20% of cost of goods sold but only 4% of gross sales.

8. Selling expenses were four fifths of cost of goods sold.

Instructions

Based on the available data, prepare a single-step income statement for the year ended December 31, 2014, including calculation of EPS. Expenses should be shown by function.

(LO 6, 8) E4-12 (Multiple-Step and Single-Step) Two accountants, Yuan Tsui and Sergio Aragon, are arguing about the merits of presenting an income statement in the multiple-step versus the single-step format, and presenting expenses in the nature or function of expense format. The discussion involves the following 2014 information for Singh Corp. (in thousands):

Administrative expenses		Selling expenses	
Salaries and wages	$ 3,900	Freight-out	$ 2,290
Depreciation of office furniture		Salaries and wages	67,280
and equipment	3,560	Depreciation of sales equipment	6,480
Rent	16,200	Advertising	42,500
Cost of goods sold	58,570	Sales revenue	306,500
Rental revenue	15,230	Interest expense on bonds payable	1,860

Common shares outstanding for 2014 total 30,550,000. The effective tax rate on all income is 30%.

Instructions

Digging Deeper

(a) Prepare an income statement for the year ended December 31, 2014, using the multiple-step format, showing expenses by function. Include calculation of EPS.

(b) Prepare an income statement for the year ended December 31, 2014, using the single-step format, showing expenses by nature. Include calculation of EPS.

(c) From the perspective of an investor who is interested in information about operating versus non-operating items and the various areas of the company's operations, which format and classification of expenses is preferred? Explain why.

(LO 6, 8) E4-13 (Multiple-Step and Unusual Items) The following balances were taken from the books of the Big Track Trucking Company Limited on December 31, 2014:

Interest income	$ 86,000	Accumulated depreciation—equipment	$ 40,000
Cash	51,000	Accumulated depreciation—buildings	28,000
Sales revenue	1,380,000	Notes receivable	155,000
Accounts receivable	150,000	Selling expenses	194,000
Prepaid insurance	20,000	Accounts payable	170,000
Sales returns and allowances	150,000	Bonds payable	100,000
Allowance for doubtful accounts	7,000	Administrative expenses	97,000
Sales discounts	45,000	Accrued liabilities	32,000
Land	100,000	Interest expense	60,000
Equipment	200,000	Notes payable	100,000
Building	140,000	Loss—other (due to storm damage)	150,000
Cost of goods sold	621,000	Depreciation expense	60,000

Assume the total effective tax rate on all items is 25%.

Instructions

Prepare a multiple-step income statement showing expenses by function. Assume that 150,000 common shares were outstanding during the year. Include calculation of EPS.

(LO 6, 8) E4-14 (Condensed Income Statement—Periodic Inventory Method) The following are selected ledger accounts of Holland Rose Corporation at December 31, 2014:

Cash	$ 185,000	Entertainment expense	$ 69,000
Inventory (as of Jan. 1, 2014)	535,000	Office expense	33,000
Sales revenue	4,275,000	Insurance expense	24,000
Unearned revenue	117,000	Advertising expense	54,000
Purchases	2,786,000	Freight-out	93,000
Sales discounts	34,000	Depreciation of office equipment	48,000
Purchase discounts	27,000	Depreciation of sales equipment	36,000
Salaries and wages (sales)	284,000	Telephone and Internet expense (sales)	17,000
Salaries and wages (administrative)	346,000	Utilities expense (administrative)	32,000
Purchase returns and allowances	15,000	Miscellaneous expense	8,000
Sales returns and allowances	79,000	Rental revenue	240,000
Freight-in	72,000	Loss on disposal of equipment	70,000
Accounts receivable	142,500	Interest expense	176,000
Sales commission expense	83,000	Common shares	900,000

Holland's effective tax rate on all items is 25%. A physical inventory indicates that the ending inventory is $686,000. The number of common shares outstanding is 90,000.

Instructions

Prepare a multi-step 2014 income statement for Holland Rose Corporation, showing expenses by function. Include calculation of EPS.

(LO 7) E4-15 (Statement of Retained Earnings) The Holiday Corporation, a private company, began operations on January 1, 2011. During its first three years of operations, Holiday reported net income and declared dividends as follows:

	Net income	Dividends declared
2011	$ 55,000	$ –0–
2012	135,000	30,000
2013	160,000	50,000

The following information is for 2014:

Income before income tax	$440,000
Prior period adjustment: understatement of 2011 depreciation expense (before tax)	57,000
Cumulative increase in prior years' income from change in inventory method (before tax)	37,000
Dividends declared (of this amount, $25,000 will be paid on January 15, 2015)	100,000
Effective tax rate	25%

Instructions

Prepare a 2014 statement of retained earnings for Holiday Corporation. The company follows ASPE.

(LO 7) E4-16   (Comprehensive Income) Rainy Day Umbrella Corporation had the following balances at December 31, 2013 (all amounts in thousands): preferred shares $2,006; common shares $5,291; contributed surplus $2,225; retained earnings $13,692; and accumulated other comprehensive income $1,526.

During the year ended December 31, 2014, the company earned net income of $4,352,000, generated an unrealized holding gain on fair value through OCI investments of $348,000, sold common shares of $170,000, and paid out dividends of $23,000 and $7,000 to preferred and common shareholders, respectively. The company accounts for its investments in accordance with IAS 39.

Instructions

Prepare a statement of changes in equity for the year ended December 31, 2014, as well as the shareholders' equity section of the Rainy Day Umbrella Corporation balance sheet as at December 31, 2014.

(LO 8) E4-17   (Earnings per Share) The shareholders' equity section of Emerson Corporation as at December 31, 2014, follows:

8% cumulative preferred shares, 100,000 shares authorized, 80,000 shares outstanding	$ 4,500,000
Common shares, 10 million shares authorized and issued	10,000,000
Contributed surplus	10,500,000
	25,000,000
Retained earnings	177,000,000
	$202,000,000

Net income of $24 million for 2014 reflects a total effective tax rate of 25%. Included in the net income figure is a loss of $15 million (before tax) relating to the operations of a business segment that is to be discontinued.

Instructions

Calculate earnings per share information as it should appear in the financial statements of Emerson Corporation for the year ended December 31, 2014.

(LO 8) E4-18   (Earnings per Share) At December 31, 2014, Tres Hombres Corporation had the following shares outstanding:

10% cumulative preferred shares, 107,500 shares outstanding	$10,750,000
Common shares, 4,000,000 shares outstanding	20,000,000

During 2014, the corporation's only share transaction was the issuance of 400,000 common shares on April 1. During 2014, the following also occurred:

Income from continuing operations before tax	$23,650,000
Discontinued operations (loss before tax)	3,225,000
Preferred dividends declared	1,075,000
Common dividends declared	2,200,000
Effective tax rate	30%

Instructions

Calculate earnings per share information as it should appear in the financial statements of Tres Hombres Corporation for the year ended December 31, 2014.

(LO 10) *E4-19   (Cash and Accrual Basis) Portmann Corp. maintains its financial records using the cash basis of accounting. As it would like to secure a long-term loan from its bank, the company asks you, as an independent CA, to convert its cash basis income statement information to accrual basis. You are provided with the following summarized data for 2012, 2013, and 2014:

	2012	2013	2014
Cash receipts from sales:			
On 2012 sales	$320,000	$160,000	$ 30,000
On 2013 sales	-0-	355,000	90,000
On 2014 sales	-0-	-0-	408,000
Cash payments for expenses:			
On 2012 expenses	185,000	67,000	25,000
On 2013 expenses	40,000ª	135,000	55,000
On 2014 expenses	-0-	45,000ᵇ	218,000

ªPrepayments of 2013 expense
ᵇPrepayments of 2014 expense

Instructions

Using the information above, prepare abbreviated income statements for the years 2012 and 2013 using:

(a) The cash basis of accounting

(b) The accrual basis of accounting

Problems

P4-1 In recent years, Grace Inc. has reported steadily increasing income. The company reported income of $20,000 in 2011, $25,000 in 2012, and $30,000 in 2013. Several market analysts have recommended that investors buy Grace Inc. shares because they expect the steady growth in income to continue. Grace is approaching the end of its 2014 fiscal year, and it looks to be a good year once again. However, it has not yet recorded warranty expense.

Based on prior experience, this year's warranty expense should be around $5,000, but some of top management has approached the controller to suggest that a larger, more conservative warranty expense should be recorded this year. Income before warranty expense is $43,000. Specifically, by recording an $8,000 warranty accrual this year, Grace could report an income increase for this year and still be in a position to cover its warranty costs in future years.

Digging Deeper

Instructions

(a) What is earnings management?

(b) What would be the effect of the proposed accounting in 2014? In 2015?

(c) What is the appropriate accounting in this situation?

(d) Discuss the effect of the proposed accounting on a potential investor's decision to invest in the company.

P4-2 On November 1, 2013, Campbell Corporation management decided to discontinue operation of its Rocketeer Division and approved a formal plan to dispose of the division. Campbell is a successful corporation with earnings of $150 million or more before tax for each of the past five years. The Rocketeer Division, a major part of Campbell's operations, is being discontinued because it has not contributed to this profitable performance.

The division's main assets are the land, building, and equipment used to manufacture engine components. The land, building, and equipment had a net book value of $96 million on November 1, 2013.

Campbell's management has entered into negotiations for a cash sale of the division for $87 million (net of costs to sell). The expected sale date and final disposal date of the division is expected to be July 1, 2014. Campbell Corporation has a fiscal year ending May 31. The results of operations for the Rocketeer Division for the 2013–14 fiscal year and the estimated results for June 2014 are presented below. The before-tax losses after October 31, 2013, are calculated without depreciation on the building and equipment.

Period	Before-Tax Loss
June 1, 2013, to October 31, 2013	$(6,100,000)
November 1, 2013, to May 31, 2014	(3,900,000)
June 1 to 30, 2014 (estimated)	(700,000)

The Rocketeer Division will be accounted for as a discontinued operation on Campbell's financial statements for the year ended May 31, 2014. Campbell's tax rate is 25% on operating income and all gains and losses. Campbell prepares financial statements in accordance with IFRS.

Instructions

(a) Explain how the Rocketeer Division's assets would be reported on Campbell Corporation's balance sheet as at May 31, 2014.

(b) Explain how the discontinued operations and pending sale of the Rocketeer Division would be reported on Campbell Corporation's income statement for the year ended May 31, 2014.

(c) On July 5, 2014, Campbell Corporation disposes of the division assets at an adjusted price of $84 million. Explain how the discontinued operations and sale of the Rocketeer Division would be reported on Campbell Corporation's income statement for the year ended May 31, 2015. Assume the June 2014 operating loss is the same as estimated.

(d) Assume that Campbell Corporation management was debating whether the sale of the Rocketeer Division qualified for discontinued operations accounting treatment under IFRS. List specific factors or arguments that management would use to suggest that the Rocketeer Division should be treated as a discontinued operation. Why might management have a particular preference about which treatment is given? From an external user's perspective, what relevance does the presentation of the discontinued operation have when interpreting the financial results?

(CMA adapted. Used with permission.)

P4-3   Information for 2014 follows for Rolling Thunder Corp.:

Retained earnings, January 1, 2014	$ 1,980,000
Sales revenue	36,500,000
Cost of goods sold	28,500,000
Interest income	170,000
Selling and administrative expenses	4,700,000
Unrealized gain on fair value-OCI investments	320,000
Loss on impairment of goodwill (not tax deductible)	520,000
Income tax on continuing operations for 2014 (assume this is correct)	797,500
Assessment for additional income tax for 2012 (normal, recurring)	500,000
Gain on sale of fair value-net income investments (normal, recurring)	110,000
Loss—other (due to flood damage)	390,000
Loss from disposal of discontinued division (net of tax of $87,500)	262,500
Loss from operation of discontinued division (net of tax of $55,000)	165,000
Dividends declared on common shares	250,000
Dividends declared on preferred shares	70,000

Rolling Thunder decided to discontinue its entire wholesale division (a major line of business) and to keep its manufacturing division. On September 15, it sold the wholesale division to Dylane Corp. During 2014, there were 800,000 common shares outstanding all year. Rolling Thunder's tax rate is 25% on operating income and all gains and losses (use this rate where the tax provisions are not given). Rolling Thunder prepares financial statements in accordance with IFRS, and accounts for its investments in accordance with IAS 39.

Instructions

Prepare a multiple-step statement of comprehensive income showing expenses by function. Include calculation of EPS.

P4-4   Lanestar Inc. reported income from continuing operations before tax of $1,790,000 during 2014. Additional transactions occurring in 2014 but not included in the $1,790,000 are as follows:

1. The corporation experienced an insured flood loss of $80,000 during the year.

2. At the beginning of 2012, the corporation purchased a machine for $54,000 (residual value of $9,000) that had a useful life of six years. The bookkeeper used straight-line depreciation for 2012, 2013, and 2014, but failed to deduct the residual value in calculating the depreciable amount.

3. The sale of fair value-net income investments resulted in a loss of $107,000.

4. When its president died, the corporation gained $100,000 from an insurance policy. The cash surrender value of this policy had been carried on the books as an investment in the amount of $46,000 (the gain is non-taxable).

5. The corporation disposed of its recreational division at a loss of $115,000 before tax. Assume that this transaction meets the criteria for accounting treatment as discontinued operations.

6. The corporation decided to change its method of inventory pricing from average cost to the FIFO method. The effect of this change on prior years is to increase 2012 income by $60,000 and decrease 2013 income by $20,000 before taxes. The FIFO method has been used for 2014.

Instructions

(a) Prepare an income statement for the year 2014 starting with income from continuing operations before income tax. Calculate earnings per share as required under IFRS. There were 80,000 common shares outstanding during the year. (Assume a tax rate of 30% on all items, unless they are noted as being non-taxable.)

(b) Assume that beginning retained earnings for 2014 is $2,540,000 and that dividends of $175,000 were declared during the year. Prepare the retained earnings portion of the statement of changes in equity for 2014.

(c) Discuss how proper classification and disclosure of items on the income statement help users in making their investment and credit decisions.

Digging Deeper

P4-5   The trial balance follows for McLean Corporation at December 31, 2014:

MCLEAN CORPORATION
Trial Balance
Year Ended December 31, 2014

	Debits	Credits
Purchase discounts		$ 10,000
Cash	$ 218,600	
Accounts receivable	105,000	
Rent revenue		18,000
Retained earnings		260,000
Salaries and wages payable		18,000
Sales revenue		1,400,000
Notes receivable	110,000	
Accounts payable		49,000
Accumulated depreciation—equipment		28,000
Sales discounts	14,500	
Sales returns and allowances	17,500	
Notes payable		70,000
Selling expenses	432,000	
Administrative expenses	99,000	
Common shares		300,000
Income tax expense	25,000	
Dividends	45,000	
Allowance for doubtful accounts		5,000
Supplies	14,000	
Freight-in	20,000	
Land	70,000	
Equipment	140,000	
Bonds payable		100,000
Gain on sale of land		30,000
Accumulated depreciation—building		19,600
Inventory	89,000	
Buildings	98,000	
Purchases	810,000	
Totals	$2,307,600	$2,307,600

A physical count of inventory on December 31 showed that there was $124,000 of inventory on hand.

Instructions

Prepare a single-step income statement and a statement of retained earnings assuming that McLean is a private company that prepares financial statements in accordance with ASPE. Assume that the only changes in retained earnings during the current year were from net income and dividends.

P4-6   Veselin Komel, vice-president of finance for Hand Corp., has recently been asked to conduct a seminar for the company's division controllers. He would discuss the proper accounting for items that are large but do not typify normal business transactions (due to either the nature or frequency of the transaction). Komel prepared the situations that follow to use as examples in the discussion. He understands that accounting standards mandate separate presentation of certain items, that these standards change over time, and that different standards may have different requirements. He has decided to focus on general principles.

1. An earthquake destroys one of the oil refineries owned by a large multinational oil company. Earthquakes are rare in this location.

2. A publicly held company has incurred a substantial loss in the unsuccessful registration of a bond issue. The company accesses capital markets very frequently.

3. A large portion of a farmer's crops is destroyed by a hailstorm. Severe damage from hailstorms is rare in this area.

4. A large diversified company sells a block of shares from its portfolio of investments. The shares are currently treated as fair value-OCI investments.

5. A company sells a block of common shares of a publicly traded company. The block of shares, which represents less than 10% of the publicly held company, is the only share investment that the company has ever owned. The shares are accounted for as fair value-OCI investments.

6. A company that operates a chain of warehouses sells the extra land surrounding one of its warehouses. When the company buys property for a new warehouse, it usually buys more land than it needs for the warehouse because it expects the land to increase in value. Twice during the past five years, the company sold excess land.

7. A textile manufacturer with only one plant moves to another location and incurs relocation costs of $725,000. Prior to the move, the company had been in the same location for 100 years.

8. A company experiences a material loss in the repurchase of a large bond issue that has been outstanding for three years. The company regularly repurchases bonds of this type.

9. A railroad experiences an unusual flood loss to part of its track system. Flood losses normally occur every three or four years. How would this be different if the company were to insure itself against this loss?

10. A machine tool company sells the only land it owns. The land was acquired 10 years ago for future expansion, but shortly after the purchase, the company abandoned all plans for expansion and decided to keep the land as an investment that would appreciate in value.

Instructions

For each situation, determine whether the item should be classified as unusual. Explain the reasons for your position. Assume that the company follows IFRS, and that the company accounts for its investments in accordance with IAS 39.

P4-7   The following financial statement was prepared by employees of Klein Corporation:

KLEIN CORPORATION
Income Statement
Year Ended December 31, 2014

Sales revenue	
Gross sales revenue, including sales taxes	$1,044,300
Less: Sales returns, and allowances	56,200
Net sales revenue	988,100
Dividend revenue, interest income, and purchase discounts	30,250
Recoveries of accounts written off in prior years	13,850
Total revenues	1,032,200
Operating expenses	
Cost of goods sold	465,900
Salaries and wages expense	60,500
Rent	19,100
Freight-in and freight-out	3,400
Bad debt expense	24,000
Appropriation of retained earnings for possible inventory losses	3,800
Total operating expenses	576,700
Income before unusual items	455,500
Unusual items	
Loss on discontinued styles (Note 1)	37,000
Loss on sale of fair value-net income investments (Note 2)	39,050
Loss on sale of warehouse (Note 3)	86,350
Tax assessments for 2013 and 2012 (Note 4)	34,500
Total unusual items	196,900
Net income	$ 258,600
Net income per common share	$ 2.30

Note 1: New styles and rapidly changing consumer preferences resulted in a $37,000 loss on the disposal of discontinued styles and related accessories.

Note 2: The corporation sold an investment in trading securities at a loss of $39,050. The corporation normally sells securities of this type.

Note 3: The corporation sold one of its warehouses at an $86,350 loss (net of taxes).

Note 4: The corporation was charged $34,500 for additional income taxes resulting from a settlement in 2014. Of this amount, $17,000 was for 2013, and the balance was for 2012. This type of litigation recurs frequently at Klein Corporation.

Instructions

Identify and discuss the weaknesses in classification and disclosure in the single-step income statement above. You should explain why these treatments are weaknesses and what the proper presentation of the items would be in accordance with recent professional pronouncements.

P4-8 The following account balances were included in the trial balance of Reid Corporation at June 30, 2014:

Sales revenue	$1,928,500	Telephone and Internet expense (office)	$ 2,820
Sales discounts	31,150	Salaries and wages (office)	7,320
Cost of goods sold	1,071,770	Supplies expense (sales)	4,850
Salaries and wages (sales)	56,260	Maintenance and repairs expense (office)	9,130
Sales commission expense	97,600	Depreciation understatement due to	
Advertising expense (sales)	28,930	error—2012 (net of tax)	17,700
Freight-out	21,400	Miscellaneous expense (office)	6,000
Entertainment expense (sales)	14,820	Sales returns and allowances	62,300
Telephone and Internet expense (sales)	9,030	Dividend revenue	38,000
Depreciation of sales equipment	4,980	Interest expense	18,000
Maintenance and repairs expense (sales)	6,200	Income tax	133,000
Miscellaneous expenses (sales)	4,715	Dividends declared on preferred shares	9,000
Supplies expense (office)	3,450	Dividends declared on common shares	32,000
Depreciation of office furniture and equipment	7,250		

During 2014, Reid incurred production salary and wage costs of $710,000, consumed raw materials and other production supplies of $474,670, and had an increase in work-in-process and finished goods inventories of $112,900. The Retained Earnings account had a balance of $292,000 at June 30, 2014, before closing. There are 180,000 common shares outstanding. Assume Reid has elected to adopt IFRS. (*Hint:* Production payroll and materials costs reduced by the increase in ending work-in-process and finished goods inventories = the cost of goods sold.)

Instructions

(a) Prepare an income statement for the year ended June 30, 2014, using the multiple-step format and showing expenses by function.

(b) Prepare the retained earnings portion of the statement of changes in equity for the year ended June 30, 2014.

(c) Prepare an income statement for the year ended June 30, 2014, using the single-step format and showing expenses by nature.

P4-9 A combined single-step income and statement of retained earnings for California Tanning Salon Corp. follows for 2014 (amounts in thousands):

Net sales revenue		$640,000
Operating expenses		
Cost of goods sold		500,000
Selling, general, and administrative expenses		66,000
Other, net		17,000
		583,000
Income before income tax		57,000
Income tax		19,400
Net income		37,600
Retained earnings at beginning of period, as previously reported	141,000	
Adjustment required for correction of error	(7,000)	
Retained earnings at beginning of period, as restated		134,000
Dividends on common shares		(12,200)
Retained earnings at end of period		$159,400

Additional facts are as follows:

1. Selling, general, and administrative expenses for 2014 included a usual but infrequently occurring charge of $10.5 million for a loss on inventory due to decline in NRV.

2. Other, net for 2014 included the results of an identified component of the business that management had determined would be eliminated from the future operations of the business ($9 million). If the decision had not been made to discontinue the operation, income tax for 2014 would have been $22.4 million instead of $19.4 million.

The component has one asset, a piece of equipment with a carrying value of $3.2 million, which is included on the company's balance sheet under property, plant, and equipment.

3. "Adjustment required for correction of an error" resulted from a change in estimate as the useful life of certain assets was reduced to eight years and a catch-up adjustment was made.

4. The company disclosed earnings per common share for net income in the notes to the financial statements. The company has elected to adopt ASPE.

Instructions

(a) Discuss the appropriate presentation of the facts in the California Tanning Salon Corp. income statement and statement of retained earnings, and discuss the theory that supports the presentation.

(b) Prepare a revised combined statement of income and retained earnings for California Tanning Salon Corp.

P4-10 A combined statement of income and retained earnings for DC 5 Ltd. for the year ended December 31, 2014, follows. (As a private company, DC 5 has elected to follow ASPE.) Also presented are three unrelated situations involving accounting changes and the classification of certain items as ordinary or unusual. Each situation is based on the combined statement of income and retained earnings of DC 5 Ltd.

DC 5 LTD.
Combined Statement of Income and Retained Earnings
For the Year Ended December 31, 2014

Sales revenue	$5,700,000
Cost of goods sold	2,900,000
Gross profit	2,800,000
Selling, general, and administrative expenses	1,800,000
Income before income tax	1,000,000
Income tax	300,000
Income before unusual item	700,000
Loss from tornado (net of taxes)	490,000
Net income	210,000
Retained earnings, January 1	700,000
Retained earnings, December 31	$ 910,000

Situation 1. In late 2014, the company discontinued its apparel fabric division. The loss on the sale of this discontinued division amounted to $620,000. This amount was included as part of selling, general, and administrative expenses. Before its disposal, the division reported the following for 2014: sales revenue of $1.2 million; cost of goods sold of $600,000; and selling, general, and administrative expenses of $450,000.

Situation 2. At the end of 2014, the company's management decided that the estimated loss rate on uncollectible accounts receivable was too low. The loss rate used for the years 2013 and 2014 was 1.2% of total sales revenue, and owing to an increase in the writeoff of uncollectible accounts, the rate was raised to 3% of total sales revenue. The amount recorded in Bad Debt Expense under the heading Selling, General, and Administrative Expenses for 2014 was $68,400 and for 2013 it was $75,000.

Situation 3. On January 1, 2012, the company acquired machinery at a cost of $500,000. The company adopted the declining-balance method of depreciation at a rate of 20% for this machinery, and had been recording depreciation over an estimated life of 10 years, with no residual value. At the beginning of 2014, a decision was made to adopt the straight-line method of depreciation for this machinery. Depreciation for 2014, based on the straight-line method, was included in selling, general, and administrative expenses. (*Hint:* a change in depreciation method is considered a change in estimate, not a change in accounting policy.)

Instructions

For each of the three unrelated situations, prepare a revised combined statement of income and retained earnings for DC 5 Ltd. The company has a 30% income tax rate.

P4-11 Hamad Corporation began operations on January 1, 2011. Recently the corporation has had several unusual accounting problems related to the presentation of its income statement for financial reporting purposes. The company follows ASPE.

You are the CA for Hamad and have been asked to examine the following data:

HAMAD CORPORATION
Income Statement
For the Year Ended December 31, 2014

Sales revenue	$9,500,000
Cost of goods sold	5,900,000
Gross profit	3,600,000
Selling and administrative expense	1,300,000
Income before income tax	2,300,000
Income tax (30%)	690,000
Net income	$1,610,000

This additional information was also provided:

1. The controller mentioned that the corporation has had difficulty collecting certain receivables. For this reason, the bad debt accrual was increased from 1% to 2% of sales revenue. The controller estimates that if this rate had been used in past periods, an additional $83,000 worth of expense would have been charged. The bad debt expense for the current period was calculated using the new rate and is part of selling and administrative expense.

2. There were 400,000 common shares outstanding at the end of 2014. No additional shares were purchased or sold in 2014.

3. The following items were not included in the income statement:
   - Inventory in the amount of $112,000 was obsolete.
   - The company announced plans to dispose of a recognized segment. For 2014, the segment had a loss, net of tax, of $162,000.

4. Retained earnings as at January 1, 2014, were $2.8 million. Cash dividends of $700,000 were paid in 2014.

5. In January 2014, Hamad changed its method of accounting for plant assets from the straight-line method to the diminishing balance method. The controller has prepared a schedule that shows what the depreciation expense would have been in previous periods if the diminishing balance method had been used.

	Depreciation Expense under Straight-Line	Depreciation Expense under Diminishing Balance	Difference
2011	$ 75,000	$150,000	$ 75,000
2012	75,000	112,500	37,500
2013	75,000	84,375	9,375
	$225,000	$346,875	$121,875

6. In 2014, Hamad discovered that in 2013 it had failed to record $20,000 as an expense for sales commissions. The sales commissions for 2013 were included in the 2014 expenses.

Instructions

(a) Prepare the income statement for Hamad Corporation. Do not prepare notes to the financial statements. The effective tax rate for past years was 30%. (*Hint:* a change in depreciation method is considered a change in estimate, not a change in accounting policy.)

(b) Prepare a combined statement of net income and retained earnings.

Digging Deeper

(c) From the perspective of the reader of the financial statements, what is the purpose of intraperiod tax allocation for the statements of income and retained earnings?

P4-12 Joe Schreiner, controller for On Time Clock Company Inc., recently prepared the company's income statement and statement of changes in equity for 2014. Schreiner believes that the statements are a fair presentation of the company's financial progress during the current period, but he also admits that he has not examined any recent professional pronouncements on accounting.

ON TIME CLOCK COMPANY INC.
Income Statement
For the Year Ended December 31, 2014

Sales revenues			$377,852
Less: Sales returns and allowances			16,320
Net sales revenue			361,532
Cost of goods sold:			
Inventory, January 1, 2014		$ 50,235	
Purchases	$192,143		
Less: Purchase discounts	3,142	189,001	
Cost of goods available for sale		239,236	
Inventory, December 31, 2014		41,124	
Cost of goods sold			198,112
Gross profit			163,420
Selling expenses		41,850	
Administrative expenses		32,142	73,992
Income before income tax			89,428
Other revenues and gains			
Unrealized gain on fair value-OCI investments			36,000
Dividend revenue			40,000
			165,428
Income tax			56,900
Net income			$108,528

ON TIME CLOCK COMPANY INC.
Excerpt from Statement of Changes in Equity
For the Year Ended December 31, 2014

Retained earnings, January 1, 2014			$216,000
Add:			
Net income for 2014	$108,528		
Gain on sale of long-term investments	31,400	$139,928	
Deduct:			
Loss on expropriation	13,000		
Correction of mathematical error (net of tax)	17,186	(30,186)	109,742
Retained earnings, December 31, 2014			$325,742

Instructions

(a) Assume that On Time Clock Company follows IFRS, and that the company accounts for its investments in accordance with IAS 39. Prepare a statement of comprehensive income showing expenses by function. Ignore calculation of EPS.

(b) Prepare the retained earnings and accumulated other comprehensive income portion of the statement of changes in equity. Assume an opening balance of $120,000 in accumulated other comprehensive income.

P4-13 Faldo Corp. is a public company and has 100,000 common shares outstanding. In 2014, the company reported income from continuing operations before income tax of $2,710,000. Additional transactions not considered in the $2,710,000 are as follows:

1. In 2014, Faldo Corp. sold equipment for $140,000. The machine had originally cost $80,000 and had accumulated depreciation to date of $36,000. The gain or loss is considered ordinary.

2. The company discontinued operations of one of its subsidiaries during the current year at a loss of $290,000 before tax. Assume that this transaction meets the criteria for discontinued operations. The loss on operation of the discontinued subsidiary was $90,000 before tax. The loss from disposal of the subsidiary was $200,000 before tax.

3. The sum of $520,000 was received as a result of a lawsuit for a breached 2011 contract. Before the decision, legal counsel was uncertain about the outcome of the suit and had not established a receivable.

4. In 2014, the company reviewed its accounts receivable and determined that $54,000 of accounts receivable that had been carried for years appeared unlikely to be collected. No allowance for doubtful accounts was previously set up.

5. An internal audit discovered that amortization of intangible assets was understated by $35,000 (net of tax) in a prior period. The amount was charged against retained earnings.

Instructions

Analyze the above information and prepare an income statement for the year 2014, starting with income from continuing operations before income tax. Calculate earnings per share as it should be shown on the face of the income statement. (Assume a total effective tax rate of 25% on all items, unless otherwise indicated.)

P4-14 Amos Corporation was incorporated and began business on January 1, 2014. It has been successful and now requires a bank loan for additional working capital to finance an expansion. The bank has requested an audited income statement for the year 2014 using IFRS. The accountant for Amos Corporation provides you with the following income statement, which Amos plans to submit to the bank:

AMOS CORPORATION
Income Statement

Sales revenue		$850,000
Dividend revenue		32,300
Gain on recovery of insurance proceeds from earthquake loss (unusual)		27,300
Unrealized holding gain on fair value-OCI investments		5,000
		914,600
Less:		
Selling expenses	$100,100	
Cost of goods sold	510,000	
Advertising expense	13,700	
Loss on inventory due to decline in NRV	34,000	
Loss on discontinued operations	48,600	
Administrative expenses	73,400	779,800
Income before income tax		134,800
Income tax		33,700
Net income		$101,100

Amos had 100,000 common shares outstanding during the year. Amos accounts for its investments in accordance with IAS 39.

Instructions

(a) Indicate the deficiencies in the income statement as it currently is. Assume that the corporation prepares a single-step income statement.

(b) Prepare a revised single-step statement of comprehensive income.

P4-15 The equity accounts of Feeling Alright Vitamin Limited as at January 1, 2014, were as follows:

Retained earnings, January 1, 2014	$257,600
Common shares	600,000
Preferred shares	250,000
Contributed surplus	300,000
Accumulated other comprehensive income	525,000

During 2014, the following transactions took place:

Adjustment to correct error in prior years (gain net of tax)	$ 48,000
Unrealized gains on fair value-OCI investments (net of tax)	82,000
Dividends:	
Common shares	120,000
Preferred shares	62,000
Issue of equity:	
Common shares	300,000
Preferred shares	5,000
Net income	325,000

Instructions

Prepare a statement of changes in equity for the year ended December 31, 2014. The company follows IFRS and accounts for its investments in accordance with IAS 39.

P4-16 The following is from a recent income statement for Baring Corp (a public company):

Sales revenue	$21,924,000,000
Costs and expenses	20,773,000,000
Income from operations	1,151,000,000
Other income	22,000,000
Interest and debt expense	(130,000,000)
Earnings before income tax	1,043,000,000
Income tax	(287,000,000)
Net income	$ 756,000,000

It includes only five separate numbers, two subtotals, and the net earnings figure.

Digging Deeper

Instructions

(a) Indicate the deficiencies in the income statement.

(b) What recommendations would you make to the company to improve the usefulness of its income statement?

(c) Why do some businesses provide only a minimal disclosure of financial statement elements on their income statement?

*P4-17 On January 1, 2014, Caroline Lampron and Jenni Meno formed a computer sales and service enterprise in Montreal by investing $90,000 cash. The new company, Razorback Sales and Service, has the following transactions in January:

1. Paid $6,000 in advance for three months' rent of office, showroom, and repair space.

2. Purchased 40 personal computers at a cost of $1,500 each, six graphics computers at a cost of $3,000 each, and 25 printers at a cost of $450 each, paying cash on delivery.

3. Sales, repair, and office employees earned $12,600 in salaries during January, of which $3,000 was still payable at the end of January.

4. Sold 30 personal computers for $2,550 each, four graphics computers for $4,500 each, and 15 printers for $750 each. Of the sales amounts, $75,000 was received in cash in January and $30,750 was sold on a deferred payment plan.

5. Other operating expenses of $8,400 were incurred and paid for during January; $2,000 of incurred expenses were payable at January 31.

Instructions

(a) Using the transaction data above, prepare (1) a cash basis income statement and (2) an accrual basis income statement for the month of January.

(b) Using the transaction data above, prepare (1) a cash basis balance sheet and (2) an accrual basis balance sheet as at January 31, 2014.

(c) Identify the items in the cash basis financial statements that make cash basis accounting inconsistent with the theory underlying the elements of financial statements.

*P4-18 Dr. John Gleason, M.D., maintains the accounting records of Bones Clinic on a cash basis. During 2014, Dr. Gleason collected $146,000 in revenues and paid $55,470 in expenses. At January 1, 2014, and December 31, 2014, he had accounts receivable, unearned revenue, accrued liabilities, and prepaid expenses as follows (all long-lived assets are rented):

	January 1	December 31
Accounts receivable	$9,250	$16,100
Unearned revenue	2,840	1,620
Accrued liabilities	3,435	2,200
Prepaid expenses	2,000	1,775

Instructions

Last week, Dr. Gleason asked you, his CA, to help him determine his income on the accrual basis. Write a letter to him explaining what you did to calculate net income on the accrual basis. Be sure to state net income on the accrual basis and to include a schedule of your calculations.

Cases

Refer to the Case Primer to help you answer these cases.

CA4-1   As a reviewer for the Ontario Securities Commission, you are in the process of reviewing the financial statements of public companies. The following items have come to your attention:

1. A merchandising company overstated its ending inventory two years ago by a material amount. Inventory for all other periods is correctly calculated.

2. An automobile dealer sells for $137,000 an extremely rare 1930 S type Invicta, which it purchased for $21,000 10 years ago. The Invicta is the only such display item that the dealer owns.

3. During the current year, a drilling company extended the estimated useful life of certain drilling equipment from 9 to 15 years. As a result, amortization for the current year was materially lowered.

4. A retail outlet changed its calculation for bad debt expense from 1% to 0.5% of sales because of changes in its clientele.

5. A mining company sells a foreign subsidiary that does uranium mining, although the company continues to mine uranium in other countries.

6. A steel company changes from straight-line amortization to accelerated amortization in accounting for its plant assets stating that the expected pattern of consumption of the future economic benefits has changed.

7. A construction company, at great expense to itself, prepares a major proposal for a government loan. The loan is not approved.

8. A water pump manufacturer has had large losses resulting from a strike by its employees early in the year.

9. Amortization for a prior period was incorrectly understated by $950,000. The error was discovered in the current year.

10. A large sheep rancher suffered a major loss because the provincial government required that all sheep in the province be killed to halt the spread of a rare disease. Such a situation has not occurred in the province for 20 years.

11. A food distributor that sells wholesale to supermarket chains and to fast food restaurants (two major classes of customers) decides to discontinue the division that sells to one of the two classes of customers.

Instructions

Discuss the financial reporting issues.

Integrated Case

(*Hint*: If there are issues here that are new, use the conceptual framework to help you support your analysis with solid reasoning.)

IC4-1   United Manufacturing Company (UMC) recently filed for bankruptcy protection. The company manufactures downhill skis and its shares trade on the TSX. With the increased popularity of such alternative winter sports as snowboarding and tubing, sales of skis are sagging. The company has decided to start a new line of products that focuses on the growing industry surrounding snow tubing and snowboarding. At present, however, the company needs interim financing to pay suppliers and its payroll. It also needs a significant amount of cash so that it can reposition itself in the marketplace. Management is planning to go to the bank with draft financial statements to discuss additional financing. The company's year end is December 31, 2013, and it is now January 15, 2014. Current interest rates for loans are 5%, but because it is in bankruptcy protection, UMC feels that it will likely have to pay at least 15% on any loan. There is concern that the bank will turn the company down.

At a recent management meeting, the company decided to convert its ski manufacturing facilities into snowboard manufacturing facilities. It will no longer produce skis. Management is unsure if the company will be able to recover the cost of the ski inventory. Although the conversion will result in significant expenditures, the company feels that this is justified if UMC wants to remain a viable business. The shift in strategic positioning will not result in any layoffs as most employees will work in the retrofitted plant. The remaining employees will be trained in the new business.

The conversion to snowboard manufacturing facilities would not require selling the ski manufacturing machines as these machines can be used to produce snowboards. The company estimates the results and cash flows from its operation of selling skis to be a $20-million loss.

On December 15, 2013, the company entered into an agreement with LKT to sell its entire inventory in ski bindings to LKT. Under the terms of the deal, LKT paid $10 million cash for the inventory (its regular selling price at the time). The cost to UMC of this inventory was $6 million and so a profit of $4 million was booked pre-tax. In a separate deal, UMC agreed to buy back the inventory in January for $10,125,000.

NON-GAAP FINANCIAL MEASURES

This section describes the non-GAAP financial measures we use in this MD&A to explain our financial results. It also provides reconciliations of the non-GAAP financial measures to the most comparable IFRS financial measures.

EBITDA

The term EBITDA does not have any standardized meaning under IFRS. Therefore, it is unlikely to be comparable to similar measures presented by other companies. We define EBITDA as operating revenues less operating costs, as shown in BCE's consolidated income statements. EBITDA for BCE's segments is the same as segment profit as reported in Note 3 to BCE's 2011 consolidated financial statements.

We use EBITDA to evaluate the performance of our businesses as it reflects their ongoing profitability. We believe that certain investors and analysts use EBITDA to measure a company's ability to service debt and to meet other payment obligations or as a common measurement to value companies in the telecommunications industry. EBITDA also is one component in the determination of short-term incentive compensation for all management employees. EBITDA has no directly comparable IFRS financial measure. Alternatively, the following table provides a reconciliation of net earnings to EBITDA.

	2011	2010
Net earnings	2,574	2,190
Severance, acquisition and other costs	409	262
Depreciation	2,538	2,388
Amortization	723	737
Finance costs		
Interest expense	842	685
Interest on employee benefit obligations	984	992
Interest on fund unit liability	—	370
Expected return on pension plan assets	(1,032)	(898)
Other income	(129)	(173)
Income taxes	720	632
EBITDA	7,629	7,185

Adjusted net earnings also excludes the fair value adjustments on the fund unit liability and adjusts earnings to reflect the interest on the fund unit liability as non-controlling interest. We define Adjusted EPS as Adjusted net earnings per BCE common share.

We use Adjusted net earnings and Adjusted EPS, among other measures, to assess the performance of our businesses without the effects of severance, acquisition and other costs, and net (gains) losses on investments, net of tax and non-controlling interest. We exclude these items because they affect the comparability of our financial results and could potentially distort the analysis of trends in business performance. Excluding these items does not imply they are non-recurring.

FREE CASH FLOW

The term free cash flow does not have any standardized meaning according to IFRS. It is therefore unlikely to be comparable to similar measures presented by other companies.

We define free cash flow as cash flows from operating activities, excluding acquisition costs paid, and dividends/distributions received from Bell Aliant, less capital expenditures, preferred share dividends, dividends/distributions paid by subsidiaries to non-controlling interest and Bell Aliant free cash flow.

We consider free cash flow to be an important indicator of the financial strength and performance of our business because it shows how much cash is available to repay debt and reinvest in our company. We present free cash flow consistently from period to period, which allows us to compare our financial performance on a consistent basis.

We believe that certain investors and analysts use free cash flow to value a business and its underlying assets.

The most comparable IFRS financial measure is cash flows from operating activities. The following table is a reconciliation

	2011		2010	
	TOTAL	PER SHARE	TOTAL	PER SHARE
Net earnings attributable to common shareholders	2,221	2.88	2,083	2.74
Severance, acquisition and other costs	282	0.37	189	0.25
Net gains on investments	(89)	(0.12)	(133)	(0.18)
Fair value adjustment of fund unit liability	—	—	(49)	(0.06)
Adjustment to reflect interest on fund unit liability as non-controlling interest	—	—	29	0.04
Adjusted net earnings	2,414	3.13	2,119	2.79

The most comparable IFRS financial measures are net earnings attributable to common shareholders and EPS. The ... table is a reconciliation of net earnings attributable to common shareholders and earnings per share to Adjusted net earnings on a consolidated basis and per BCE common share (Adjusted EPS), respectively.

ADJUSTED NET EARNINGS AND ADJUSTED EPS

The terms Adjusted net earnings and Adjusted EPS do not have any standardized meaning according to IFRS. They are therefore unlikely to be comparable to similar measures presented by other companies.

We define Adjusted net earnings as net earnings attributable to common shareholders before severance, acquisition and other costs, and net (gains) losses on investments. For 2010,

of cash flows from operating activities to free cash flow on a consolidated basis.

	2011	2010
Cash flows from operating activities	4,869	4,367
Bell Aliant dividends / distributions to BCE	214	291
Capital expenditures	(3,256)	(2,998)
Cash dividends paid on preferred shares	(118)	(108)
Cash dividends/distributions paid by subsidiaries to non-controlling interest	(315)	—
Acquisition costs paid	70	24
Bell Aliant free cash flow	47	(139)
Free cash flow	1,511	1,437

ENDNOTES

1 For instance, if a risky company borrows from the bank, it will have to be charged at a higher interest rate than a less risky company.

2 In assessing whether earnings are sustainable, a strategic analysis of the company's positioning within the industry must be performed, as well as an assessment of the business model's viability. This is beyond the scope of this course.

3 The term "irregular" is used for transactions and other events that come from developments that are outside the normal business operations.

4 In actuality, this concept has its roots in **capital maintenance theory**, which says that as long as capital is maintained from year to year, the rest is assumed to be income. Capital may be defined as financial (in terms of amount of dollars invested in the business) or physical (earnings potential of the income-generating assets).

5 D. McDermott, "Latest Profit Data Stir Old Debate Between Net and Operating Income," *The Wall Street Journal*, May 3, 1999.

6 These items will be discussed in greater detail in subsequent chapters.

7 *CICA Handbook–Accounting*, Part II, Section 3475.27 and IFRS 5.32.

8 *CICA Handbook–Accounting*, Part II, Section 3475.28 and IFRS 5.31.

9 Cash flows might not be seen to be eliminated, for instance, where the entity continues to sell products to the disposed component or to its customers. Continuing involvement might be evidenced where the entity retains an ownership interest in the disposed component or where it provides management services. Consideration would be given to the significance of the cash flows or continuing involvement.

10 *CICA Handbook–Accounting*, Part II, Section 3475.08 and IFRS 5.7 and .8.

11 The term "income from continuing operations" is a financial statement subtotal often used. Its use is not mandated nor required by GAAP but companies use it where there are discontinued operations.

12 *CICA Handbook–Accounting*, Part II, Section 3475.13 and IFRS 5.15.

13 *CICA Handbook–Accounting*, Part II, Section 3475.33-.35. These assets and liabilities would be classified as current only if they have been sold prior to the completion of the financial statements and the proceeds are expected to be received within the year.

14 IFRS 5.3.

15 *CICA Handbook–Accounting*, Part II, Section 3475.30.

16 IFRS 5.40 and *CICA Handbook–Accounting*, Part II, Section 3475.35.

17 *CICA Handbook–Accounting*, Part II, Sections 3475.36 and .37; IFRS 5.41 and .42.

18 In addition, these cash flows must be sufficient to cover other things such as cost of capital.

19 Some companies report items such as restructuring charges every year as unusual items. Research on the market reaction to income containing one-time items indicates that the market discounts the earnings of companies that report a series of nonrecurring items. Such evidence supports the argument that these elements reduce the quality of earnings. See J. Elliot and D. Hanna, "Repeat Accounting Write-Offs and the Information Content of Earnings," *Journal of Accounting Research* (Supplement, 1996).

20 *CICA Handbook–Accounting*, Part II, Section 1520.04 and IAS 1.97 – .105. ASPE notes that where these items may be set out "more readily" in the notes or in a schedule, this should be noted on the income statement.

21 IAS 1.81.

22 Corporate tax rates in Canada have been declining over the past several years. As a general note, the federal rate is 15% and the provincial rate averages about 10%, for a total of 25%.

23 IAS 33.68.

24 Earnings per share will be covered in significant detail in Chapter 17.

25 Details of other comprehensive income are presented in the income statement and are also shown in the statements of shareholders' equity or in the notes.

26 OSC Staff Notice 52-306.

27 A cash or modified cash basis might be used in the following situations:

   1. A company that is primarily interested in cash flows (for example, a group of physicians that distributes cash-basis earnings for salaries and bonuses)
   2. A company that has a limited number of financial statement users (a small, closely held company with little or no debt)
   3. A company that has operations that are relatively straightforward (small amounts of inventory, long-term assets, or long-term debt)

Courtesy Shoppers Drug Mart Corporation

"Pointing" the Way to Increased Customer Loyalty

STARTED BY TORONTO pharmacist Murray Koffler in 1962, Shoppers Drug Mart Corporation has grown to more than 1,250 stores across the country, reaching 9 out of 10 Canadians. In addition to its Shoppers Drug Mart and Pharmaprix stores, the company also operates Shoppers Home Health Care stores, which sell assistive-living devices such as wheelchairs. With sales in 2011 of about $10.5 billion, Shoppers is the largest retail drug store chain in Canada.

As competition increased, Shoppers decided to launch a loyalty program to reward returning customers. In 2000, the Shoppers Optimum program was born, and signed up six million members in the first year. It now has close to 10 million members, making it one of the largest retail loyalty card programs in Canada.

Loyalty programs encourage customers to shop at one store over another, as they accumulate points for every dollar they spend and bonus points during special promotions. Customers can then redeem points for free merchandise. In addition to increasing traffic at stores and building brand loyalty, these programs allow retailers to collect information on customers' shopping habits, and market special promotions directly to targeted groups.

Loyalty programs do come at a price. When sales are made that earn points for customers,

Shoppers defers a portion of the revenue from the sale representing the retail value of the points earned. In 2011, Shoppers deferred more than $183 million of sales in relation to Optimum. However, it feels it was money well invested, with management calling Optimum "a key component of our value proposition." It's one way to differentiate Shoppers from the competition, the company says. "With today's consumer being ever more value conscious, it is also imperative that we optimize our promotional effectiveness and leverage the strengths of our Shoppers Optimum program in order to drive sales, gain share and enhance margins," it states in its 2011 annual report. Optimum members visit Shoppers stores more often and spend almost twice as much in each visit as non-members, making cardholders "our most valuable customers," the company says.

In 2012, Shoppers teamed up with the Royal Bank of Canada to offer the co-branded RBC Shoppers Optimum bank account and debit card. It provides even more Optimum points for purchases, not only in Shoppers stores but at other retailers. In addition, customers can convert their points from RBC's own loyalty program, RBC Rewards, to Shoppers Optimum points. Shoppers also planned to install 300 RBC automatic teller machines in its stores for customer convenience.

Sources: Shoppers Drug Mart Corporation, 2011 Annual Report; "RBC and Shoppers Drug Mart Launch Innovative National Program," RBC news release, January 17, 2012; Christine Dobby, "RBC and Shoppers Drug Mart to Offer New Debit and Loyalty Card," *National Post*, January 17, 2012.

5 Financial Position and Cash Flows

LEARNING OBJECTIVES

After studying this chapter, you should be able to:

1. Understand the statement of financial position and statement of cash flows from a business perspective.

2. Identify the uses and limitations of a statement of financial position.

3. Identify the major classifications of a statement of financial position.

4. Prepare a classified statement of financial position.

5. Identify statement of financial position information that requires supplemental disclosure.

6. Identify major disclosure techniques for the statement of financial position.

7. Indicate the purpose and identify the content of the statement of cash flows.

8. Prepare a statement of cash flows using the indirect method.

9. Understand the usefulness of the statement of cash flows.

10. Identify differences in accounting between ASPE and IFRS.

11. Identify the significant changes planned by the IASB regarding financial statement presentation.

After studying Appendix 5A, you should be able to:

12. Identify the major types of financial ratios and what they measure.

PREVIEW OF CHAPTER 5

The statement of financial position and statement of cash flows complement the income statement, offering information about the company's financial position and how the firm generates and uses cash. This chapter examines the many different types of assets, liabilities, and shareholders' equity items that affect the statement of financial position and the statement of cash flows.

The chapter is organized as follows:

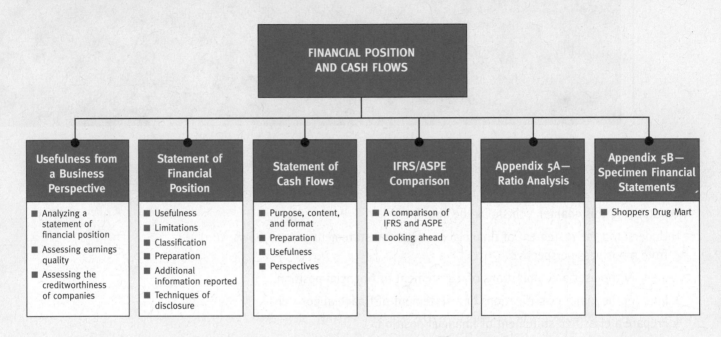

FINANCIAL POSITION AND CASH FLOWS					
Usefulness from a Business Perspective	**Statement of Financial Position**	**Statement of Cash Flows**	**IFRS/ASPE Comparison**	**Appendix 5A— Ratio Analysis**	**Appendix 5B— Specimen Financial Statements**
■ Analyzing a statement of financial position ■ Assessing earnings quality ■ Assessing the creditworthiness of companies	■ Usefulness ■ Limitations ■ Classification ■ Preparation ■ Additional information reported ■ Techniques of disclosure	■ Purpose, content, and format ■ Preparation ■ Usefulness ■ Perspectives	■ A comparison of IFRS and ASPE ■ Looking ahead		■ Shoppers Drug Mart

USEFULNESS OF THE STATEMENTS OF FINANCIAL POSITION AND CASH FLOWS FROM A BUSINESS PERSPECTIVE

Objective 1
Understand the statement of financial position and statement of cash flows from a business perspective.

It is important to understand how the users of financial statements use the statement of financial position and the statement of cash flows. For example, what might potential investors in a company focus on when analyzing a statement of financial position? What aspects of the statement of cash flows do financial analysts focus on when they are assessing earnings quality? How do creditors use financial statements to assess the creditworthiness of companies that have requested a loan? These questions will be answered below.

Analyzing a Statement of Financial Position

The statement of financial position (SFP) provides information about a company's liquidity and solvency in order to assess the risk of investing (or increasing the investment) in the company. In addition, the SFP provides details about the company's financial structure, such as whether it is financed primarily by debt or equity. If a company is heavily indebted, it may not be able to make the most of opportunities that occur as the economy improves. On the other hand, as discussed later in this chapter, companies with more financial flexibility are typically better able to survive economic downturns and to take advantage of opportunities to invest and expand. Investors can use the SFP and related notes to the financial statements to assess companies' financial flexibility and their risk of business failure.

Assessing Earnings Quality

Theory

It is important to understand how financial analysts and other users of the cash flow statement use it to assess earnings quality. One concern of users of financial statements is that company insiders might manipulate information to make earnings look better or worse than they are, for strategic reasons. For example, if managers are trying to increase their bonus or prevent the company from violating the terms of a loan, they may be tempted to artificially increase earnings. They could do this by reducing the allowance for doubtful accounts or reducing the provision for inventory obsolescence. Likewise, managers might try to lower earnings in a year when they have missed their bonuses, so that they can more easily increase earnings and their bonuses the next year. Analyzing the cash flow statement is often done to assess earnings quality. For example, if net income is significantly higher than cash flows from operations, this is a sign of poor earnings quality that may require further analysis. Similarly, if a company relies on the issuance of shares or other financing activities to offset repeated negative cash flow from operations, the financial statement users would be concerned.

Assessing the Creditworthiness of Companies

Creditors often rely on the statement of financial position to assess a company's liquidity and its ability to service debt. Similarly, a review of a company's long-term debt and shareholders' equity section helps to determine its solvency level. For example, when a company has a high debt-to-total-assets ratio, it is at higher risk of bankruptcy. Companies that use a higher proportion of debt are typically at higher risk and require higher cash flow from operations to ensure that they are able to make interest and principal payments as they come due. The preparation and use of the SFP and statement of cash flows are discussed in more detail below.

STATEMENT OF FINANCIAL POSITION

Objective 2
Identify the uses and limitations of a statement of financial position.

The **statement of financial position**, often referred to as the **balance sheet**, reports a business enterprise's assets, liabilities, and shareholders' equity at a specific date. This financial statement provides information about the nature and amounts of investments in enterprise resources, obligations to creditors, and the owners' equity in net resources. It therefore helps in predicting the amounts, timing, and uncertainty of future cash flows.

How quickly will my assets convert to cash?

Usefulness of the Statement of Financial Position

The SFP contains information about assets, liabilities, and shareholders' equity. As such, it becomes a basis for calculating rates of return on invested assets and for evaluating the enterprise's capital structure. Information in the SFP is also used to assess business risk[1] and future cash flows. In this regard, **the SFP is useful for analyzing a company's liquidity, solvency**, and **financial flexibility**, as described below. It also helps in analyzing profitability (even though this is not the main focus of the statement).

Obligation Ocean

We are drowning in a
sea of debt!

Can we afford the high
payoff investment?

**What Do
the Numbers
Mean?**

**Real World
Emphasis**

Liquidity depends on the amount of time that is expected to pass until an asset is realized (converted into cash or other monetary asset) or until a liability has to be paid. Does the company have enough cash on hand and cash coming in to cover its short-term liabilities? Certain ratios help assess overall liquidity, including the **current ratio, quick or acid test ratio**, and **current cash debt coverage ratio**. The liquidity of certain assets, such as receivables and inventory, is assessed through **turnover ratios**.[2] These ratios look at how fast the receivables or inventories are being collected or sold. Creditors are interested in **short-term** liquidity ratios, because these ratios indicate whether the enterprise will have the resources to pay its current and maturing obligations. Similarly, shareholders assess liquidity to evaluate the possibility of future cash dividends or the buyback of shares. In general, the greater the liquidity, the lower the risk of enterprise or business failure.[3]

Solvency reflects an **enterprise's ability to pay its debts and related interest**. For example, when a company carries a high level of long-term debt compared with its assets, it is at higher risk for insolvency than a similar company with less long-term debt. Companies with higher debt are riskier because more of their assets will be required to meet these fixed obligations (such as interest and principal payments). Certain ratios help assess solvency. These are often called "coverage" ratios as they refer to a company's ability to cover its interest and long-term debt payments.

Liquidity and solvency affect an entity's **financial flexibility**, which measures the **"ability of an enterprise to take effective actions to alter the amounts and timing of cash flows so it can respond to unexpected needs and opportunities."[4]** For example, a company may become so loaded with debt—so financially inflexible—that its cash sources to finance expansion or to pay off maturing debt are limited or non-existent. An enterprise with a high degree of financial flexibility is better able to survive bad times, to recover from unexpected setbacks, and to take advantage of profitable and unexpected investment opportunities. Generally, the greater the financial flexibility, the lower the risk of enterprise or business failure.

Air Canada filed for bankruptcy protection in April 2003. Factors such as outbreaks of severe acute respiratory syndrome (SARS), the Iraq war, and terrorism threats had severely reduced airline travel, and therefore airlines' cash inflows. At that time, Air Canada's total debt exceeded its total assets by $2,558 million, leaving it very little flexibility to react to changes in its environment. It was therefore very vulnerable to the decreasing demand for its services. Its current liabilities exceeded its current assets by $1,386 million, resulting in an inability to cover its day-to-day operating costs. By the end of the second quarter, the company had taken steps, while under bankruptcy protection, to ease the cash flow problems and increase flexibility. These included:

- arranging for interim financing (called debtor in possession financing) with General Electric Capital Canada Inc. (GE),

- restructuring union contracts, and

- renegotiating aircraft leases for 106 planes (with GE).

This debtor in possession financing provided the company with an additional $700-million line of credit while the other two significant renegotiations helped reduce immediate cash needs for salaries and lease/rent payments. Note that the line of credit, while providing short-term relief, increases total debt when it is used. The company announced that it hoped to emerge from bankruptcy protection by the end of 2003. It did not quite meet this target but did eventually emerge from bankruptcy protection on September 30, 2004. With a new strategy that included a competitive cost structure, a redesigned network, a new revenue model, and a new corporate structure, the company managed to turn a $258-million profit for its 2005 year end despite the increase in fuel prices. As at December 31, 2005, the long-term debt to equity ratio was still high at 6.6:1; however, this was a significant improvement over the previous year when the ratio was 32:1.

By 2008, Air Canada's long-term debt to equity ratio had risen to 8.6:1 and the company acknowledged the negative impact of weakening demand (again) from a recessionary environment, pension deficits, and volatile fuel prices as potential issues contributing to its significantly leveraged position. The company continued to actively manage its exposures by doing the following:

- ensuring that it had cash balances on hand, and access to additional capital if needed,
- hedging fuel prices, and
- controlling costs.

The liquidity risk is and will always be an ongoing concern for the company given the nature of the industry. More recently, Air Canada's liquidity and solvency were being challenged by a requirement to resume payments for its registered pension plans, by rising fuel prices, and by labour unrest. This is examined further below as part our discussion of the SFP and the calculation of free cash flow.

Limitations of the Statement of Financial Position

Because the income statement and the statement of financial position are interrelated, it is not surprising that the statement of financial position has many of the same limitations as the income statement. Here are some of the major limitations of the SFP:

1. Many assets and liabilities are stated at their historical cost. As a result, the information that is reported in the SFP has higher reliability but it can be criticized as being less relevant than the current fair value would be. Use of historical cost and other valuation methods was discussed in Chapter 2. As noted there, as a general trend, we are moving toward greater use of fair value, specifically for things such as investments and biological assets.

2. Judgements and estimates are used in determining many of the items reported in the SFP. This recalls the issue identified in Chapter 4 when discussing income statement limitations. As was stated there, the financial statements include many "soft" numbers; that is, numbers that are significantly uncertain.

3. The SFP necessarily **leaves out many items** that are of relevance to the business but cannot be recorded objectively.[5] These may be either assets or liabilities. Recall again the discussion from Chapter 4. Because liquidity and solvency ratios worsen when liabilities are recognized, a company may be biased against including liabilities in the financial statements. Knowing this, analysts habitually look for and capitalize[6] many liabilities that may be "off–balance sheet" before they calculate key liquidity and solvency ratios. For example, when reviewing a company, analysts consider off–balance sheet liabilities such as certain types of leases. The information that is disclosed in the notes to the financial statements and the analyst's knowledge of the business and industry become critical in this context, as they make it possible to identify and measure off–balance sheet items that often represent either additional risk to the company or unrecognized assets.

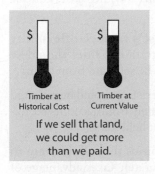

Timber at Historical Cost **Timber at Current Value**

If we sell that land, we could get more than we paid.

Underlying Concept

"Soft" numbers are less reliable than "hard" numbers and have less predictive value because they are likely to change.

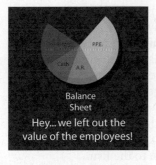

P.P.E.

Cash A.R.

Balance Sheet

Hey… we left out the value of the employees!

Classification in the Statement of Financial Position

Objective 3
Identify the major classifications of a statement of financial position.

SFP accounts are **classified** (like the income statement) so that **similar items are grouped together** to arrive at significant subtotals. The material is also arranged so that important relationships are shown.

As is true of the income statement, the statement of financial position's parts and subsections can be more informative than the whole. Individual items should be separately reported and classified in enough detail so that users can assess the amounts, timing, and uncertainty of future cash flows, and evaluate the company's liquidity and financial flexibility, profitability, and risk.

Classification in financial statements helps analysts and other financial statement users by **grouping items with similar characteristics** and **separating items with different characteristics**. In this regard, the SFP has additional information. Recall that many users use the information in financial statements to assess risk, including the company's financial flexibility, as noted earlier. Consider how the following groupings of assets and liabilities provide additional insight:

1. Assets that are of a different type or that have a different **function** in the company's activities should be reported as separate items. For example, merchandise inventories should be reported separately from property, plant, and equipment. Inventory will be sold and property, plant, and equipment will be used. In this way, investors can see how fast inventory is turning over or being sold.

2. Liabilities with **different implications for the enterprise's financial flexibility** should be reported as separate items. For example, long-term liabilities should be reported separately from current liabilities, and debt should be separate from equity.

3. Assets and liabilities with different **general liquidity characteristics** should be reported as separate items. For example, cash should be reported separately from accounts receivable and property held for use is reported separately from that held for sale.

4. Certain assets, liabilities, and equity instruments have **attributes that allow them to be measured or valued more easily**. Reporting these separately takes advantage of this characteristic. Monetary assets, and liabilities and financial instruments are two such groupings. Each will be discussed separately below.

Monetary versus Nonmonetary Assets and Liabilities

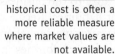

Underlying Concept

With nonmonetary assets, historical cost is often a more reliable measure where market values are not available.

Monetary assets represent either money itself **or claims to future cash flows that are fixed and determinable in amounts and timing**.[7] Because of these characteristics, they are said to be easier to measure, and they generally are. In addition, their carrying values (which approximate net realizable value) are more representative of reality as they normally are close to the amount of cash that the company will receive in the future. Examples are accounts and notes receivable. Likewise, liabilities that require **future cash outflows that are fixed and determinable in amounts and timing** are also considered to be monetary and thus easier to measure.[8] Accounts and notes payable and long-term debt are examples. In contrast, other assets—such as inventory; property, plant, and equipment; certain investments; and intangibles—are **nonmonetary assets** because their value in terms of a monetary unit such as dollars is not fixed. There is therefore additional measurement uncertainty. These assets are frequently recorded at their historical cost (or amortized cost), which often does not reflect the economic value to the firm.

Financial Instruments

Law

Financial instruments are contracts between two or more parties that create financial assets for one party and a financial liability or equity instrument for the other. They are often marketable or tradable, and therefore easy to measure.[9] Many financial instruments are also monetary assets or liabilities. Financial assets include the following:

- **Cash**

- **Contractual rights to receive cash or another financial instrument**

- Equity **investments in other companies**[10]

Contractual rights to **receive** cash or other financial instruments are assets, whereas contractual obligations to **pay** are liabilities. Cash, accounts receivable, and all payables are examples of financial instruments. These instruments are all monetary. Shares are also financial instruments. Current accounting standards on financial instruments require fair value accounting for certain types of financial instruments, including certain types of investments, especially where market values are readily available. This is due to the fact that fair value (often market value) is fairly easy to obtain and represents an objective view of the measurement of the instrument. In addition, IFRS and ASPE generally allow an entity to choose to value financial instruments in certain situations at fair value as an accounting policy choice (with gains and losses booked through net income). This is referred to as the fair value option. Financial instruments should not be offset against each other on the SFP except under limited circumstances. The accounting and reporting of financial instruments is discussed more extensively in Chapters 7, 9, 13, 14, 15, and 16. Derivatives, a more complex type of financial instrument, will be covered in Chapter 16. Most monetary assets and liabilities are financial instruments.

The three general classes of items that are included in the SFP are assets, liabilities, and equity. They are defined below.

ELEMENTS OF THE STATEMENT OF FINANCIAL POSITION

1. *Assets.* **Present economic benefits** that are controlled by an entity as a result of past transactions or events.
2. *Liabilities.* **Present obligations that arise from past transactions or events.**
3. *Equity/Net assets.* The **residual interest** in an entity's assets that remains after deducting its liabilities. In a business enterprise, the equity is the ownership interest.

Significant Change

These are the same definitions from Chapter 2 and the conceptual framework, but as discussed in Illustration 2-10 there have been proposed changes to these definitions. Illustration 5-1 shows a standard format for presenting the SFP for many companies.

Illustration 5-1

Statement of Financial Position Classifications

Assets	Liabilities and Shareholders' Equity
Current assets	Current liabilities
Long-term investments	Long-term debt
Property, plant, and equipment	Shareholders' equity
Intangible assets	Capital shares
Other assets	Contributed surplus
	Retained earnings
	Accumulated other comprehensive income/other surplus

Although the SFP can be classified or presented in other ways, in actual practice the major subdivisions noted in Illustration 5-1 are closely followed, with exceptions in certain industries. When the SFP is for a proprietorship or partnership, the classifications in the owners' equity section are presented a little differently, as will be shown later in the chapter. In addition, some companies following IFRS, such as British Airways plc, choose to invert the order of items in their SFP (listing non-current assets first, and current assets last; and similarly, listing shareholders' equity first, followed by non-current liabilities and then current liabilities).

These standard classifications make it easier to calculate important ratios, such as the current ratio for assessing liquidity and debt to equity ratios for assessing solvency. Because total assets are broken down into categories, users can easily calculate which assets are more significant than others and how these relationships change over time.[11] This gives insight into management's strategy and stewardship. Illustration 5-2 shows a classified statement of financial position for Air Canada.

Illustration 5-2

Classified Statement of Financial Position—Excerpt from Air Canada's December 31, 2011 Financial Statements

CONSOLIDATED STATEMENT OF FINANCIAL POSITION
As at December 31
(Canadian dollars in millions)

		2011	2010
ASSETS			
Current			
Cash and cash equivalents	Note 3P	$ 848	$ 1,090
Short-term investments	Note 3Q	1,251	1,102
		2,099	2,192
Restricted cash	Note 3R	76	80
Accounts receivable		712	641
Aircraft fuel inventory		92	67
Spare parts and supplies inventory	Note 3S	93	88
Prepaid expenses and other current assets		255	279
		3,327	3,347
Property and equipment	Note 5	5,088	5,629
Intangible assets	Note 6	312	317
Goodwill	Note 7	311	311
Deposits and other assets	Note 8	595	549
		$ 9,633	$10,153
LIABILITIES			
Current			
Accounts payable and accrued liabilities		$ 1,175	$ 1,182
Advance ticket sales		1,554	1,375
Current portion of long-term debt and capital leases	Note 9	424	567
		3,153	3,124
Long-term debt and capital leases	Note 9	3,906	4,028
Pension and other benefit liabilities	Note 10	5,563	3,328
Maintenance provisions	Note 11	548	493
Other long-term liabilities	Note 12	469	468
		13,639	11,441
EQUITY			
Shareholders' equity			
Share capital	Note 14	840	846
Contributed surplus		58	54
Deficit		(4,983)	(2,344)
		(4,085)	(1,434)
Non-controlling interest		79	146
		$ 9,633	$10,153

The accompanying notes are an integral part of the consolidated financial statements.

Note that the total shareholders' equity position changed significantly from 2010 to 2011. Shareholders' equity (in millions) decreased from –$1,434 to –$4,085 during the year. Just a few years earlier, Air Canada was in a positive equity position, with shareholders' equity of +$762 at the end of 2008.

The worsening equity position is partly due, as previously discussed, to a dramatic increase in fuel costs.

Preparation of the Classified Statement of Financial Position (Balance Sheet)

Objective 4
Prepare a classified statement of financial position.

Current Assets

Current assets include cash and other assets that will ordinarily be realized within one year from the date of the statement of financial position or within the normal

operating cycle if the cycle is longer than a year.[12] The operating cycle is the average time between the acquisition of assets for processing and the realization in cash or cash equivalents. Cash is realized through sales of the product that is created from the materials and supplies. The cycle begins with cash and then moves through inventory, production, and receivables, and back to cash. When there are several operating cycles within one year, the one-year period is used. If the operating cycle is more than one year, the longer period is used. Illustration 5-3 shows the operating cycle for manufacturing companies.

Illustration 5-3

The Business Operating Cycle for Manufacturing Companies

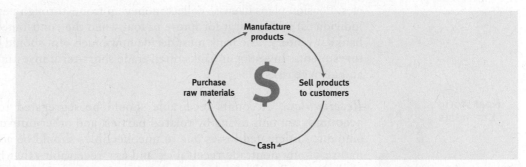

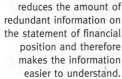

Underlying Concept

Grouping these similar items together reduces the amount of redundant information on the statement of financial position and therefore makes the information easier to understand.

For most industries, current assets are generally segregated and presented in the SFP in order according to their liquidity.[13] The five major items that are found in the current assets section are cash, short-term investments (including derivatives), receivables, inventories, and prepayments. These items are valued as follows:

1. Cash: at its stated value

2. Investments: at cost/amortized cost or fair value

3. Accounts receivable: at the estimated amount that is collectible

4. Inventories: generally at the lower of cost and net realizable value

5. Prepaid items: at cost

Cash. Cash is often grouped with other cash-like liquid assets and reported as **cash and cash equivalents**. Cash and cash equivalents are defined as **cash, demand deposits**, and **short-term, highly liquid investments that are readily convertible into known amounts of cash and have an insignificant risk of changing in value.**[14] Illustration 5-4 details the cash and cash equivalents for Canadian-based pharmaceutical company **AstraZeneca**.

Illustration 5-4

Balance Sheet Presentation of Cash and Cash Equivalents— Excerpt from AstraZeneca December 31, 2011 Financial Statements

Cash and Cash Equivalents

Cash and cash equivalents comprise cash in hand, current balances with banks and similar institutions and highly liquid investments with maturities of three months or less when acquired. They are readily convertible into known amounts of cash and are held at amortised cost.

Any restrictions on the general availability of cash or any commitments regarding how it is likely to be used must be disclosed and may affect whether the items are presented as current.

How much cash should a company hold? In general, a company needs enough liquid assets, including cash, to be able to settle its current liabilities in a timely manner; however, it must also ensure that its assets do not sit idle. Cash itself is generally non–interest-bearing and so does not contribute to net income. Too much cash can make a company a more likely target for a takeover bid if it is publicly traded.

Real World Emphasis

Short-Term Investments. Investments in debt and equity securities are presented separately and valued at cost/amortized cost or fair value. Those measured at cost are written down when impaired. Companies that have excess cash often have significant amounts of short-term investments. While deciding what to do with the money, they will temporarily invest it to generate some profits (instead of letting the funds sit idle as non–interest-bearing cash). In addition, the way a company does business can result in higher levels of investments. For instance, the business models of insurance companies, pension funds, and banks result in significant amounts of temporary as well as long-term investments. Insurance companies collect premiums up front and invest the money so that they have funds available to pay out future claims that arise under the insurance policies. Pension plans likewise collect money up front (through pension contributions from individuals) and invest it for future payout when the contributors retire. Money is like a bank's inventory. The bank must decide how much of it should be invested and in which investments. Investment banks often trade short-term investments to maximize profits and manage risks.

Real World Emphasis

Receivables.   Accounts receivable should be segregated to show **ordinary trade accounts**, amounts owing by **related parties**, and other **unusual items** of a substantial amount. Anticipated losses due to uncollectibles should be accrued. The amount and nature of any nontrade receivables and any receivables that have been designated or pledged as collateral should be disclosed. Accounts receivable are valued at their net realizable value. Illustration 5-5 shows how **QLT Inc.**, a Canadian biotechnology company, reported its receivables in Note 4 to its financial statements.

Illustration 5-5

Balance Sheet Presentation of Securities—Excerpt from QLT Inc.'s December 31, 2011 Financial Statements

4. ACCOUNTS RECEIVABLE

(In thousands of U.S. dollars)	2011	2010
Visudyne	$8,877	$10,139
Trade and other	1,108	520
	$9,985	$10,659

At December 31, 2011 and 2010, accounts receivable related to Visudyne represents amounts due from our distributors in the U.S. for sale of bulk Visudyne to them, and amounts due from Novartis relating to the 20% royalties due on net sales outside the U.S. as well as reimbursement of specified royalty and other costs. Our principal U.S. wholesale distributor of Visudyne is ASD Speciality Healthcare, Inc. and our other distributor is Priority Healthcare Distribution, Inc.

What Do the Numbers Mean?

QLT is a biotechnology company that specializes in the discovery, development, and commercialization of drugs, including light-activated drugs such as Visudyne. Visudyne is marketed through **Novartis Ophthalmics** (Novartis), the company's co-development partner. The companies share the earnings from distribution of the drug, which is also distributed via ASD Specialty Healthcare, Inc. and Priority Healthcare Distribution, Inc. Because of the relationship between QLT and Novartis, Novartis is considered a related party and the accounts receivable are therefore disclosed separately.[15] Note also that because the company markets and distributes its main product through Novartis and the two other distributors, almost all of its receivables come from these three sources. This creates a credit risk concentration. This is important information and is thus highlighted in Note 16 of the financial statements, which deals with financial instruments and concentration of credit risk. Ordinary trade and other receivables represent a very small part of QLT's total receivables.

Inventories.   "Inventories are assets:

1. **held for sale in the ordinary course of business,**

2. **in the process of production for such sale, or**

3. **in the form of materials or supplies to be consumed in the production process or in the rendering of service."**[16]

They are valued at the lower of cost and net realizable value, with cost being determined using a **cost formula** such as first-in, first-out (FIFO), weighted average cost, or specific identification (where items are not ordinarily interchangeable). It is important to disclose these details as this information helps users understand the amount of judgement that was used in measuring this asset. For a manufacturer, the stage of the inventories' completion is also indicated (raw materials, work in process, and finished goods). Illustration 5-6 shows the breakdown of QLT's inventory.

Illustration 5-6

Balance Sheet Presentation of Inventories—Excerpt from QLT Inc.'s December 31, 2011 Financial Statements

5. INVENTORIES

(In thousands of U.S. dollars)	2011	2010
Raw materials and supplies	$ 50	$ 74
Work-in-process	26,098	28,045
Finished goods	171	274
Provision for excess inventory	$(11,077)	(11,077)
Provision for non-completion of product inventory	(2,185)	(2,185)
	13,057	15,131
Less: Long-term inventory (see Note 9)	11,119	11,807
Current inventory	$ 1,938	$ 3,324

Our provision for excess inventory of $11.1 million, which was substantially applied against our long-term inventory, has been determined based on our forecast of future Visudyne demand. During the year ended December 31, 2011, there was no charge against this provision.

During the years ended December 31, 2011 and 2010, there were no charges against the provision for non-completion of product inventory.

What Do the Numbers Mean?

QLT also discloses the following in its significant accounting policy note:

Inventory and Cost of Sales

For periods after 2009, Visudyne cost of sales, consisting of expenses related to the production of bulk Visudyne, royalty expense on Visudyne sales and ongoing damages related to the Massachusetts Eye and Ear Infirmary judgment (See Note 19 – Contingencies), are charged against earnings in the period that we sell to distributors in the U.S. and to Novartis outside the U.S. Through December 31, 2009, Visudyne cost of sales were charged against earnings in the period that Novartis sold to end customers.

We utilize a standard costing system, which includes a reasonable allocation of overhead expenses, to account for inventory and cost of sales, with adjustments being made periodically to reflect current conditions. Losses on manufacturing purchase commitments are immediately charged to cost of sales. Our standard costs are estimated based on management's best estimate of annual production volumes and material costs. Overhead expenses comprise direct and indirect support activities related to manufacturing and involve costs associated with activities such as quality inspection, quality assurance, supply chain management, safety and regulatory. Overhead expenses are allocated to inventory at various stages of the manufacturing process under a standard costing system. Unallocated overheads are recognized as cost of sales in the period in which they are incurred. For periods after 2009, overhead was allocated to cost of sales as Visudyne was sold to our distributors in the U.S. and to Novartis outside the U.S. Through December 31, 2009, overhead was allocated to cost of sales as Visudyne was sold by Novartis to third parties.

The **nature of the inventory is important in assessing value**. QLT's inventory consists mainly of manufactured pharmaceuticals, which must be made according to very high standards and demanding specifications. Because of this, QLT acknowledges the risk that the manufactured batches might not pass quality inspection. The company also has a provision for obsolescence since products may become "off-code"; that is, they are unusable due to their age. Retailers would consider theft and out-of-date stock in assessing the value of their inventory. High-tech companies would consider obsolescence.

Finally, QLT classifies some of its inventory as long-term. Inventory is generally presented as a current asset since it will usually be sold within the year. Where QLT does not feel it will be able to convert the inventory to cash within the following year due to the specific nature of the inventory or market conditions, it has decided that it makes more sense to present it as long-term.

Which types of companies are likely to have significant inventory? Companies that sell and manufacture goods will normally carry inventory (as compared with companies that offer services only). How much inventory is enough or, conversely, how much inventory is too much? Companies must have at least enough inventory to meet customer demands. On the other hand, inventory ties up significant amounts of cash flows, creates storage costs, and subjects the company to risk of theft, obsolescence, and so on. Many companies operate on a just-in-time philosophy, meaning that they streamline their production and supply channels so that they can order the raw materials and produce the product in a very short time. Car manufacturers often follow this philosophy, thus freeing up working capital and reducing the need for storing inventory.

Prepaid Expenses.   **Prepaid expenses** included in current assets are **expenditures already made for benefits (usually services) that will be received within one year or the operating cycle**, whichever is longer. These items are current assets because cash does not need to be used for them again in the current year or operating cycle as they have already been paid for. A common example is the payment in advance for an insurance policy. It is classified as a prepaid expense at the time of the expenditure because the payment occurs before the coverage benefit is received. Prepaid expenses are reported at the amount of the unexpired or unconsumed cost. Other common prepaid expenses include rent, advertising, property taxes, and office or operating supplies.

Companies often include insurance and other prepayments for two or three years in current assets even though part of the advance payment applies to periods beyond one year or the current operating cycle. This is done by convention even though it is inconsistent with the definition of current assets.

Non-current Investments

Non-current investments normally consist of one of the types shown in Illustration 5-7.

Illustration 5-7

Types of Non-current Investments

TYPES OF NON-CURRENT INVESTMENTS	MEASUREMENT
Debt Securities	
Held to maturity	Amortized cost
Equity Securities	
Investments in associates (significant influence investments)	Equity method
Subsidiaries	Consolidated
Non-consolidated subsidiaries	Fair value or at cost
Where no influence or control	Fair value or at cost
Other	
Sinking funds, tangible assets held as investments, other	Generally at cost

Long-term investments are usually presented on the SFP just below current assets in a separate section called "Investments." Many securities that are properly shown among long-term investments are, in fact, readily marketable. They are not included as current assets unless management intends to convert them to cash in the short term; that is, within a year or the operating cycle, whichever is longer.

Management may be holding some of these investments for strategic reasons (such as for significant influence investments or non-consolidated subsidiaries). Investments that are held for strategic reasons are generally held for longer periods of time and are consolidated (subsidiaries) or accounted for using the equity method (significant influence investments in associates). This will be examined in greater detail in Chapter 9.

Long-term investments carried at other than fair value must be written down when impaired.

Real World Emphasis

Property, Plant, and Equipment

Property, plant, and equipment are tangible capital assets—that is, properties of a durable nature—that are **used in ongoing business operations to generate income**. These assets consist of physical or tangible property, such as land, buildings, machinery, furniture, tools, and wasting resources (for example, timberland and minerals). They are generally carried at their cost or amortized cost. With the exception of land, most assets are either depreciable (such as buildings) or depletable (such as timberlands or oil reserves). IFRS allows an option to carry them at fair value using a revaluation or fair value method. Like all other assets, property, plant, and equipment are written down when impaired.

ClubLink Enterprises Limited has significant capital assets. In fact, in 2011, property, plant, and equipment and intangible assets represented 92.8% of the corporation's total assets. This is not surprising as the company is one of Canada's largest golf club developers and operators. The bulk of these assets are in land (golf courses) and buildings and land improvements. Illustration 5-8 shows the detailed breakdown of these assets, as presented in Note 7 to ClubLink's financial statements.

Illustration 5-8

Statement of Financial Position Presentation of Property, Plant, and Equipment—Excerpt from ClubLink Enterprises Limited's December 31, 2011 Financial Statements

PROPERTY, PLANT AND EQUIPMENT

Property, plant and equipment consist of the following:

(thousands of Canadian dollars)	Land	Building and Land Improvements	Docks	Bunkers, Cart Paths and Irrigation	Rolling stocks and Equipment	Total
Cost						
At January 1, 2010	$280,681	$178,401	$58,708	$87,765	$ 97,936	**$703,491**
Business combinations	6,222	3,346	—	3,045	1,468	**14,081**
Additions	460	1,992	307	1,430	9,724	**13,913**
Exchange difference	(721)	(2,053)	(3,159)	(166)	(2,956)	**(9,055)**
At December 31, 2010	286,642	181,686	55,856	92,074	106,172	**722,430**
Additions	2,020	2,101	72	790	10,143	**15,126**
Business combinations	3,950	3,468	—	3,466	973	**11,857**
Disposals	—	—	—	—	(920)	**(920)**
Impairment	—	(469)	—	(201)	(47)	**(717)**
Exchange difference	495	817	1,259	129	1,121	**3,821**
At December 31, 2011	$293,107	$187,603	$57,187	$96,258	$117,442	**$751,597**
Accumulated Depreciation						
At January 1, 2010	$ —	$ 42,344	$ —	$32,782	$ 43,920	**$119,046**
Depreciation	—	5,550	3,280	4,729	8,978	**22,537**
Exchange difference	—	(554)	(44)	(26)	(1,442)	**(2,066)**
At December 31, 2010	—	47,340	3,236	37,485	51,456	**139,517**
Depreciation	—	5,278	3,245	5,019	8,639	**22,181**
Disposals	—	—	—	—	(778)	**(778)**
Exchange difference	—	256	165	22	358	**801**
At December 31, 2011	$ —	$ 52,874	$ 6,646	$42,526	$ 59,675	**$161,721**
Net book value at January 1, 2010	$280,681	$136,057	$58,708	$54,983	$ 54,016	**$584,445**
Net book value at December 31, 2010	$286,642	$134,346	$52,620	$54,589	$ 54,716	**$582,913**
Net book value at December 31, 2011	$293,107	$134,729	$50,541	$53,732	$ 57,767	**$589,876**

Certain property, plant and equipment have been assigned as collateral for borrowings (note 11).

(continued)

Illustration 5-8

*Excerpt from
ClubLink Enterprise Limited's
December 31, 2011
Financial Statements
(continued)*

ClubLink is committed to spend $1,837,000 as at December 31, 2011 to complete certain rolling stock improvements.

During the year, management determined a golf club was impaired since it accepted an offer to purchase the property which was less than its book value. This proposed sale did not proceed and management has recorded an impairment loss of $717,000 to other income in the statement of earnings and comprehensive earnings. The resulting carrying value represents management's estimate of fair value less costs to sell.

As at December 31, 2011, ClubLink had equipment under finance lease with a net book value of $9,704,000 (2010 – $11,493,000).

**What Do
the Numbers
Mean?**

Note that in its statement of cash flows ClubLink further segregates its spending into **operating** and **development** expenditures. This helps users understand which expenditures are made to maintain existing operations and which ones will be coming on stream to expand operations, and are therefore enhancing the company's growth potential. The basis of measuring the property, plant, and equipment; any liens against the properties; and accumulated depreciation should be disclosed, usually in notes to the statements. Under IFRS, a reconciliation is provided, reconciling the capital assets from the beginning to end of the period, showing items such as additions, disposals, impairment, and depreciation (IAS 16.73).

Aside from companies in the golf club business, those based in real estate, manufacturing, resources, or pharmaceuticals also have large amounts of capital assets on their statements of financial position. These types of companies are often referred to as being **capital-intensive** since they require large amounts of capital to invest in their long-term revenue-generating assets.

Intangible Assets

Intangible assets are capital assets that have no physical substance and usually have a higher degree of uncertainty about their future benefits. They include patents, copyrights, franchises, goodwill, trademarks, trade names, and secret processes. These intangibles are initially recorded at cost and are divided into two groups for accounting purposes:

- those with finite lives and
- those with indefinite lives.

Those with finite lives are amortized to expense over their useful lives. Those with indefinite lives are not amortized. Both are tested for impairment.

Intangibles can amount to significant economic resources, yet financial analysts often ignore them. This is because their **valuation and measurement are difficult**. Many intangible assets, especially those that are **internally generated** (such as goodwill), are never recognized at all on the SFP.

As Illustration 5-9 shows, a significant portion of **Valeant Pharmaceuticals International**'s total assets (after the company merged with **Biovail Corporation**) is composed of goodwill and intangibles.

Illustration 5-9

*Balance Sheet Presentation of
Goodwill and Intangible
Assets—Excerpt from Valeant
Pharmaceuticals International
Inc.'s Financial Statements
(amounts in thousands
of U.S. dollars)*

**Real World
Emphasis**

| | At December 31 | |
	2011	2010
ASSETS		
Current		
Cash and cash equivalents	$ 164,111	$ 394,269
Marketable securities	6,338	6,083
Accounts receivable, net	569,268	274,819
Inventories, net	355,212	229,582
Prepaid expenses and other current assets	33,651	26,088
Assets held for sale	72,239	4,014
Income taxes receivable	8,233	8,243
Deferred income taxes, net	148,454	77,068
	1,357,506	1,020,166

(continued)

	At December 31	
	2011	2010
Marketable securities	—	2,083
Property, plant and equipment, net	414,242	281,752
Intangible assets, net	7,657,798	6,372,780
Goodwill	3,598,786	3,001,376
Deferred tax assets, net	54,681	80,085
Other long-term assets, net	58,700	36,875
	$13,141,713	$10,795,117

What Do the Numbers Mean?

A further look at the detail behind the amount for intangibles shows that Valeant's intangibles include trademarks and product rights for several pharmaceutical products. It makes sense that the company would have a large amount of money invested in intangibles since Valeant is in the business of developing pharmaceutical products. The drugs are patented by the company and become main revenue generators. However, the true value of **internally generated** patents is generally not reflected in the SFP. Instead, it is most often the **purchased** rights to drugs that show up as intangible assets since the value of these rights is measured through their acquisition.

Other Assets

The items included in the **other assets** section vary widely in practice. Some of the items that are commonly included (if they are not included anywhere else) are non-current receivables, intangible assets, assets in special funds, deferred income tax assets, property held for sale, and advances to subsidiaries. The company should be careful to disclose these assets in enough detail for users to get a better idea of their nature.

Alternative Terminology

Deferred income taxes under IFRS are referred to as future income taxes under ASPE.

Deferred income tax assets (called "**future income tax assets**" under ASPE) represent the taxes that may be avoided or saved due to deductions that a company may take when it prepares its **future** tax returns. These accounts are mainly a result of temporary differences between what has been recognized in the accounts as revenues and expenses under GAAP and what has been recognized on the tax return under the provisions of the Income Tax Act. Deferred (or future) income taxes will be discussed in greater detail in Chapter 18.

Current Liabilities

Current liabilities are the **obligations that are due within one year from the date of the statement of financial position or within the operating cycle, where this is longer.**[17] This concept includes:

1. Payables resulting from the acquisition of goods and services: trade accounts payable, wages payable, taxes payable

2. Collections received in advance for the delivery of goods or the performance of services, such as unearned rent revenue or unearned subscriptions revenue

3. Other liabilities whose liquidation will take place within the operating cycle, such as the portion of long-term bonds to be paid in the current period, or short-term obligations arising from a purchase of equipment

4. Short-term financing that is payable on demand (such as a bank overdraft)

5. Derivative financial instruments

At times, a liability that is payable within the year may not be included in the current liabilities section. This may occur either when the debt will be refinanced through another long-term issue, or when the debt is retired out of non-current assets.[18] This approach is justified because the liquidation of the liability does not result from the use of current assets or the creation of other current liabilities.

Current liabilities are not reported in any consistent order. The items that are most commonly listed first are bank indebtedness, accounts payable, or accrued liabilities; those that are most commonly listed last are income taxes payable, current maturities of long-term debt, or other current liabilities. Any secured liability—for example, notes payable that have shares held as collateral for them—is fully described in the notes so that the assets providing the security can be identified.

The excess of total current assets over total current liabilities is referred to as working capital (sometimes called "net working capital"). Working capital is thus the net amount of a company's relatively liquid resources. That is, it is the liquid buffer (or cushion) that is available to meet the operating cycle's financial demands. Working capital, as an amount, is rarely disclosed on the SFP, but it is calculated by bankers and other creditors as an indicator of a company's short-run liquidity. To determine the actual liquidity and availability of working capital to meet current obligations, however, one must analyze the current assets' composition and their nearness to cash.

Long-Term Debt and Liabilities

Underlying Concept

Information about covenants and restrictions gives insight into the entity's financial flexibility and is therefore disclosed in respect of the full disclosure principle.

Long-term liabilities are obligations that are not reasonably expected to be liquidated within the normal operating cycle but instead are payable at some later date. Bonds payable, notes payable, some deferred (future) income tax liabilities, lease obligations, and pension obligations are the most common examples. Generally, extensive supplementary disclosure is needed for this section, because most long-term debt is subject to various covenants and restrictions in order to protect lenders.[19] Long-term liabilities that mature within the current operating cycle are classified as current liabilities if current assets will be used to liquidate them.

Generally, long-term liabilities are of three types:

1. Obligations arising from **specific financing situations**, such as the issuance of bonds, long-term lease obligations, and long-term notes payable

2. Obligations arising from **ordinary enterprise operations**, such as pension obligations, deferred income tax liabilities, and deferred or unearned revenues

3. Obligations that **depend on the occurrence or non-occurrence of one or more future events to confirm the amount payable**, the payee, or the date payable, such as service or product warranties and other contingencies

It is desirable to report any premium or discount as an addition to, or subtraction from, the bonds payable. The terms of all long-term liability agreements (including the maturity date or dates, interest rates, nature of the obligation, and any security pledged to support the debt) are frequently described in notes to the financial statements. **Deferred income tax liabilities (future income tax liabilities)** are future amounts that are expected to be owed by the company to the government for income taxes. Deferred or unearned revenues are often treated as liabilities because a service or product is owed to the customer (performance obligation). They may be classified as long-term or current.

The excerpt from **Empire Company Limited** in Illustration 5-10 is an example of the liabilities section of the balance sheet. It also shows the treatment of shareholders' equity by Empire, which is discussed in the Owner's Equity section of this chapter. The company owns Sobeys Inc. food stores.

Illustration 5-10

Balance Sheet Presentation of Liabilities and Shareholders' Equity—Excerpt from Empire Company Limited's 2011 Balance Sheet (in millions of dollars)

Liabilities		
Current	May 7, 2011	May 1, 2010
Bank indebtedness	$ 8.1	$ 17.8
Accounts payable and accrued liabilities	1,689.0	1,621.6
Income taxes payable	—	19.5
Long-term debt due within one year	49.7	379.4
Liabilities relating to assets held for sale	12.7	—
Future tax liabilities	46.6	50.9
	1,806.1	2,089.2

(continued)

	May 7, 2011	May 1, 2010
Long-term debt	1,095.4	829.0
Other long-term liabilities	143.2	130.6
Future tax liabilities	95.9	86.4
Employee future benefits obligation	130.0	125.1
Minority interest	35.8	35.6
	3,306.4	3,295.9
Shareholders' Equity		
Capital stock	320.5	325.1
Contributed surplus	4.7	3.2
Retained earnings	2,944.2	2,652.2
Accumulated other comprehensive loss	(20.4)	(28.1)
	3,249.0	2,952.4
	$6,555.4	$6,248.3

Note that the company's long-term debt is mainly comprised of notes payable and credit facilities.

Owners' Equity

Law

The **owners' equity** (shareholders' equity) section is one of the most difficult sections to prepare and understand. This is due to the complexity of capital share agreements and the various restrictions on residual equity that are imposed by corporation laws, liability agreements, and boards of directors. As shown for Empire Company Limited in Illustration 5-10, the section is usually divided into four parts:

1. **Capital shares**, which represents the exchange value of shares that have been issued

2. **Contributed surplus**, which may include items such as gains from certain related party transactions

3. **Retained earnings**, which includes undistributed earnings, and is sometimes referred to as "earned surplus"

4. **Accumulated other comprehensive income**, which may include unrealized gains and losses on certain investments; certain gains or losses from hedging activities; gains or losses on revalued property, plant, and equipment; and other. This does not need to be called "accumulated other comprehensive income."

The major disclosure requirements for capital shares (or stock) are their authorized, issued, and outstanding amounts. Contributed surplus is usually presented as one amount. Retained earnings, also presented as one amount, is positive if the company has undistributed accumulated profits. Otherwise, it will be a negative number and labelled "deficit." Any capital shares that have been reacquired by the company (treasury stock) are shown as a reduction of shareholders' equity.[20]

A corporation's ownership or shareholders' equity accounts are quite different from the equivalent accounts in a partnership or proprietorship. Partners' permanent capital accounts and the balances in their temporary accounts (drawings accounts) are shown separately. Proprietorships ordinarily use a single capital account that handles all of the owner's equity transactions.

Illustration 5-11 presents the shareholders' equity section from **Talisman Energy Inc.**

Illustration 5-11

Balance Sheet Presentation of Shareholders' Equity— Excerpt from Talisman Energy Inc.'s December 31, 2011 Balance Sheet (in millions of dollars)

Shareholders' equity	2011	2010
Common shares (note 20)	$ 1,561	$1,480
Preferred shares	191	—
Contributed surplus	186	108
Retained earnings	7,292	6,819
Accumulated other comprehensive income (note 21)	788	788
	10,018	9,195

Real World
Emphasis

Note that the company has chosen to show the details on the number of shares issued and authorized in the notes to the financial statements. Common shares are also referred to as "ordinary shares" under IFRS.

Statement of Financial Position Format

One method of presenting a classified SFP is to list assets by sections on the left side and liabilities and shareholders' equity by sections on the right side. The main disadvantage of this format is that it requires two facing pages. To avoid the use of facing pages, another format, shown in Illustration 5-12, lists liabilities and shareholders' equity directly below assets on the same page.

Illustration 5-12

Classified Statement of Financial Position

SCIENTIFIC INNOVATION PRODUCTS, INC.
Statement of Financial Position
December 31, 2014

Assets

Current assets			
Cash		$ 42,485	
Investments—trading		28,250	
Accounts receivable	$165,824		
Less: Allowance for doubtful accounts	1,850	163,974	
Notes receivable		23,000	
Inventory (at lower of average cost and NRV)		489,713	
Supplies on hand		9,780	
Prepaid expenses		16,252	
Total current assets			$ 773,454
Long-term investments			87,500
Property, plant, and equipment			
Land (at cost)		125,000	
Buildings (at cost)	975,800		
Less: Accumulated depreciation	341,200	634,600	
Total property, plant, and equipment			759,600
Intangible assets, net of accumulated amortization			80,000
Goodwill			20,000
Total assets			$1,720,554

Liabilities and Shareholders' Equity

Current liabilities			
Accounts payable		$247,532	
Accrued interest		500	
Income taxes payable		62,520	
Accrued salaries, wages, and other liabilities		9,500	
Deposits received from customers		420	
Total current liabilities			$ 320,472
Long-term debt			
(Twenty-year 12% debentures, due January 1, 2018)			500,000
Total liabilities			820,472
Shareholders' equity			
Paid in on capital shares			
Preferred, (7%, cumulative—authorized,			
issued, and outstanding, 30,000 shares)	$300,000		
Common (authorized, 500,000 shares;			
issued and outstanding, 400,000 shares)	400,000		
Contributed surplus	37,500	737,500	
Retained earnings	102,333		
Accumulated other comprehensive income	60,249	162,582	
Total shareholders' equity			900,082
Total liabilities and shareholders' equity			$1,720,554

Additional Information Reported

Objective 5
Identify statement of
financial position
information that requires
supplemental disclosure.

SUPPLEMENTAL STATEMENT OF FINANCIAL POSITION INFORMATION

1. *Contingencies.* Material events that have an uncertain outcome.

2. *Accounting policies.* Explanations of the valuation methods that are used or the basic assumptions that are made for inventory valuations, amortization methods, investments in subsidiaries, etc.

3. *Contractual situations.* Explanations of certain restrictions or covenants that are attached to specific assets or, more likely, to liabilities.

4. *Additional detail.* Expanded details on specific statement of financial position line items.

5. *Subsequent events.* Events that happened after the statement of financial position data were compiled.

Contingencies

A **contingency** is an **existing situation in which there is uncertainty about whether a gain or loss will occur and that will finally be resolved when one or more future events occur or fail to occur.**[21] In short, contingencies are material (or potentially material) events that have an uncertain future. Examples of gain contingencies are tax operating loss carry-forwards or unsettled company litigation against another party. Typical loss contingencies relate to litigation against the company, environmental issues, or possible tax assessments. Contingencies are not recognized unless they meet the definition of an asset/liability.

In general terms, a liability is recognized when it is probable/likely and measurable under both IFRS and ASPE. Additional note disclosures are required. Under IFRS, probable is defined as more likely than not whereas under ASPE the threshold for recognition is higher, requiring a high chance of occurrence. **Contingent gains** are not recognized under IFRS or ASPE, but are **disclosed where** an inflow of economic benefits is seen as probable.[22] The accounting and reporting requirements for contingencies are examined fully in Chapter 13.

Accounting Policies

Accounting standards recommend disclosure for all significant accounting principles and methods that management has chosen from among alternatives or that are peculiar to a particular industry. For instance, inventories can be calculated under different cost formulas (such as weighted average and FIFO); plant and equipment can be amortized under several accepted methods of cost allocation (such as double-declining-balance and straight-line); and investments can be carried at different valuations (such as cost, fair value, or the equity method). Users of financial statements who are more informed know of these possibilities and examine the statements closely to determine the methods that are used and their impact on net income and key ratios.

Companies are also required to disclose information about their use of estimates in preparing the financial statements when the related measurement uncertainty is material.[23] The disclosure of significant accounting principles and methods and of risks and uncertainties is particularly useful when this information is given as the first note or when it is presented in a separate summary that precedes the notes to the financial statements.

Contractual Situations

In addition to contingencies and different valuation methods, contractual obligations should also be disclosed in the notes to the financial statements when they are significant.[24] It is mandatory, for example, that the essential provisions of guarantees, lease contracts, pension obligations, and stock option plans be clearly stated in the notes. The analyst who examines a set of financial statements wants to know not only the liability amounts but also how the different contractual provisions (that is, the terms and conditions) are affecting the company now, and will affect it in the future.

Commitments that oblige a company to maintain a certain amount of working capital, limit its payment of dividends, restrict its use of assets, or require it to maintain certain financial ratios must all be disclosed if they are material. Considerable judgement is needed to determine whether leaving out such information is misleading. The principle in this situation is, "When in doubt, disclose." It is better to disclose a little too much information than not enough.

The accountant's judgement should include ethical considerations, because the way of disclosing the accounting principles, methods, and other items that have important effects on the enterprise may reflect the interests of a particular stakeholder in subtle ways that are at the expense of other stakeholders. A reader, for example, may benefit from having certain information highlighted in comprehensive notes, whereas the company—not wanting to emphasize that information—may choose to provide limited (rather than comprehensive) information in its notes.

Additional Detail

For many SFP items, further detail is disclosed to make it clearer. This has already been discussed under the various headings of the SFP: assets, liabilities, and equity.

Subsequent Events

Several weeks or months may pass after the end of the year before the financial statements are issued. This time is used to count and price inventory, reconcile subsidiary ledgers with controlling accounts, prepare necessary adjusting entries, ensure that all transactions for the period have been entered, and obtain an audit of the financial statements.

During this period, important transactions and events may occur that materially affect the company's financial position or operating situation. These events are known as **subsequent events**.[25] Notes to the financial statements should explain any significant financial events that occur after the formal date of the SFP but before the financial statements have been issued.

Subsequent events fall into two types:

1. Events that provide further evidence of **conditions that existed** at the date of the SFP

2. Events that indicate **conditions that occurred after** the financial statement date

In the first type, the financial statements must be adjusted for the events reflecting conditions that existed at the date of the SFP. In the second type, the events reflecting conditions that occurred after the financial statements date must be disclosed in notes if the condition causes a significant change to assets or liabilities, and/or it will have a significant impact on future operations. These issues will be covered in further detail in Chapter 23.

Techniques of Disclosure

The additional information that is reported should be disclosed as completely and as intelligently as possible. The following methods of disclosing pertinent information are available: explanations in parentheses, notes, cross-references and contra items, and supporting schedules, as will be explained next.

Underlying Concept

The basis for including additional information is the full disclosure principle; that is, the information needs to be important enough to influence the decisions of an informed user.

Ethics

Underlying Concept

There is a trade-off here. Timely information is more relevant but may not be as reliable because it takes time to verify the information to ensure that it is complete and accurate.

Objective 6

Identify major disclosure techniques for the statement of financial position.

Parenthetical Explanations

Additional information is often provided by explanations in parentheses that follow the item. For example, shareholders' equity may be shown as it is in Illustration 5-12 in the financial statements of Scientific Innovation Products.

Using parentheses makes it possible to disclose relevant additional SFP information that adds clarity and completeness. It has an advantage over a note because it brings the additional information into the body of the statement where it is less likely to be missed. Of course, lengthy parenthetical explanations that might distract the reader from the SFP information must be used carefully.

Notes

Notes are used if additional explanations cannot be shown conveniently as parenthetical explanations or to reduce the amount of detail on the face of the statement. For example, the details for property, plant, and equipment of Air Canada are shown in Note 5 to its financial statements rather than on the face of the statement, as Illustration 5-13 shows. Including this level of detail on the face of the SFP would make it more difficult to read and to focus on the main groupings of assets.

Illustration 5-13

Notes Disclosure—Excerpt from Notes to Air Canada's Financial Statements (in thousands of dollars)

5. PROPERTY AND EQUIPMENT

	Aircraft and flight equipment	Buildings, and leasehold improvements	Ground and other equipment	Purchase deposits, including capitalized interest	Total
Year ended December 31, 2011					
At January 1, 2011	$ 4,928	$ 545	$ 121	$ 35	$ 5,629
Additions	64	5	14	77	160
Reclassifications	(20)	8	28	(16)	—
Disposals	(4)	(9)	—	—	(13)
Depreciation	(622)	(43)	(23)	—	(688)
At December 31, 2011	$ 4,346	$ 506	$ 140	$ 96	$ 5,088
At December 31, 2011					
Cost	$ 5,929	$ 794	$ 295	$ 96	$ 7,114
Accumulated depreciation	(1,583)	(288)	(155)	—	(2,026)
	$ 4,346	$ 506	$ 140	$ 96	$ 5,088

As at December 31, 2011, property and equipment includes finance leased assets including 19 aircraft (2010 – 19) with a cost of $396 (2010 – $400) less accumulated depreciation of $158 (2010 – $83) for a net book value of $238 (2010 – $317) and facilities with a cost of $66 (2010 – $66) less accumulated depreciation $16 (2010 – $13) for a net book value of $50 (2010 – $53).

Included in flight equipment as at December 31, 2011 are rotable parts, including spare engines with a cost of $339 (2010 – $328) less accumulated depreciation of $94 (2010 – $48) for a net book value of $245 (2010 – $280). Also included in flight equipment are 38 aircraft and 11 spare engines (2010 – 42 aircraft and 11 spare engines) which are leased to Jazz (Note 17) and third parties with a cost of $463 (2010 – $477) less accumulated depreciation of $124 (2010 – $80) including accumulated impairment losses of $46 related to its fleet of A340-300 as described below (2010 – $46) for a net book value of $339 (2010 – $397). Depreciation expense for 2011 for this flight equipment amounted to $46 (2010 – $80 including an impairment charge of $46).

As at December 31, 2011, flight equipment included 21 aircraft (2010 – 17) that are retired from active service with a net carrying value of $12 (2010 – $4). In 2010, the Corporation recorded an impairment charge of $49 in Depreciation, amortization and impairment on its fleet of A340-300 and retired B767-200 aircraft due to the carrying value exceeding the estimated recoverable amount.

Interest capitalized during 2011 amounted to $4 at an interest rate of 12.16% (2010 $1 at an interest rate of 12.16%).

The notes must present all essential facts as completely and concisely as possible. Loose wording can mislead readers instead of helping them. Notes should add to the total information that is made available in the financial statements, not raise unanswered questions or contradict other parts of the statements. For example, the property and equipment note for Air Canada provides users with additional information about changes in the major classifications of property and equipment items during the year. The original Air Canada Note 5 also provides further details of flight equipment, leased equipment, etc., not reproduced here in the interest of brevity.

Cross-References and Contra Items

When there is a direct relationship between an asset and a liability, this can be cross-referenced on the SFP. For example, among the current assets section of an SFP dated as at December 31, 2014, this might be shown as follows:

Cash on deposit with sinking fund trustee for redemption of bonds payable—see Current liabilities	$800,000

In the same SFP, in the current liabilities section would be the amount of bonds payable to be redeemed within one year:

Bonds payable to be redeemed in 2015—see Current assets	$2,300,000

This cross-reference points out that $2.3 million of bonds payable are to be redeemed currently, and thus far only $800,000 in cash has been set aside for the redemption. This means, therefore, that the additional cash will need to come from unrestricted cash, from sales of investments, from profits, or from some other source. The same information can be shown in parentheses if this technique is preferred.

Another common procedure is to establish contra or adjunct accounts. A **contra account** on an SFP is an item that reduces an asset, liability, or owners' equity account. Examples include Accumulated Depreciation and Allowance for Doubtful Accounts. Contra accounts provide some flexibility in presenting the financial information. Use of the Accumulated Depreciation account, for example, allows a statement reader to see the asset's original cost and its amortization to date.

An **adjunct account**, on the other hand, increases an asset, liability, or owners' equity account. An example is Premium on Bonds Payable, which, when added to the Bonds Payable account, describes the enterprise's total bond liability.

Supporting Schedules

Often a separate schedule is needed to present more detailed information about certain assets or liabilities because the SFP only provides a single summary item.

Terminology

Account titles in the general ledger often use terms that are not the most helpful ones for an SFP. Account titles are often brief and include technical terms that are understood only by accountants. Statements of financial position, meanwhile, are examined by many people who are not familiar with the technical vocabulary of accounting. Thus, statements of financial position should contain descriptions that will be generally understood and are less likely to be misinterpreted.

STATEMENT OF CASH FLOWS

The statement of financial position, the income statement, and the statement of changes in shareholders' equity each present information about an enterprise's cash flows during a period, but they do this to a limited extent and in a fragmented manner. For instance, comparative statements of financial position might show what new assets have been acquired or disposed of and what liabilities have been incurred or liquidated. The income statement presents information about the resources provided by operations, but not the details of the cash that has been provided. The statement of changes in shareholders' equity shows the amount of dividends declared. None of these statements presents a detailed summary of all the cash inflows and outflows, or the sources and uses of cash during the period. To satisfy this need, the **statement of cash flows** (also called the cash flow statement) is required.[26]

The statement's value is that it helps users evaluate liquidity, solvency, and financial flexibility, as previously defined. The material in Chapter 5 is introductory as it reviews the statement of cash flows' existence, usefulness, the mechanics of calculating cash flows from operations and preparing the statement using the indirect method. Note that Chapter 22 deals with the preparation and content of the statement of cash flows in greater detail.

Purpose, Content, and Format of a Cash Flow Statement

Objective 7
Indicate the purpose and identify the content of the statement of cash flows.

The main purpose of a statement of cash flows is to allow users to **assess the enterprise's capacity to generate cash and cash equivalents and to enable users to compare cash flows of different entities.**[27]

Reporting the sources, uses, and net increase or decrease in cash helps investors, creditors, and others know what is happening to a company's most liquid resource. Because most people maintain their chequebook and prepare their tax return on a cash basis, they can relate to and understand the statement of cash flows as it shows the causes and effects of cash inflows and outflows and the net increase or decrease in cash. The statement of cash flows answers the following simple but important questions:

1. Where did cash come from during the period?

2. What was cash used for during the period?

3. What was the change in the cash balance during the period?

Cash receipts and cash payments during a period are classified in the statement of cash flows into three different activities: **operating**, **investing**, and **financing** activities. These are the main types of activities that companies engage in. These classifications are defined as follows:

1. **Operating activities** are the enterprise's main revenue-producing activities and all other activities that are not related to investing or financing.

2. **Investing activities** are the acquisitions and disposals of long-term assets and other investments that are not included in cash equivalents.

3. **Financing activities** are activities that result in changes in the size and composition of the enterprise's equity capital and borrowings.[28]

With cash flows classified into each of these categories, the statement of cash flows has assumed the basic format shown in Illustration 5-14.

Illustration 5-14

*Basic Format of Cash
Flow Statement*

Statement of Cash Flows	
Cash flows from operating activities	$XXX
Cash flows from investing activities	XXX
Cash flows from financing activities	XXX
Net increase (decrease) in cash	XXX
Cash at beginning of year	XXX
Cash at end of year	$XXX

Illustration 5-15 shows examples of cash inflows and outflows by activity when using the indirect method.

Illustration 5-15

Cash Inflows and Outflows

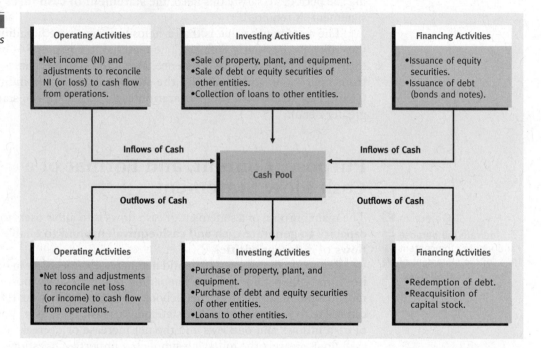

The following excerpt from the statement of cash flows for **Loblaw Companies Limited** highlights the operating activities section of the statement. This example provides a summary of typical adjustments found in the reconciliation of earnings to cash flows from operations.

Consolidated Statements of Cash Flow

For the years ended December 31, 2011 and January 1, 2011 (millions of Canadian dollars)	2011 (52 weeks)	2010 (52 weeks)
Operating Activities		
Net earnings	$ 769	$ 675
Income taxes (note 4)	288	319
Net interest expense and other financing charges (note 3)	327	353
Depreciation and amortization	699	628
Income taxes paid	(216)	(298)
Interest received	60	52
Settlement of equity forward contracts (note 25)	(7)	—
Net (increase) decrease in credit card receivables	(104)	98
Change in non-cash working capital	8	151
Fixed assets and other related impairments	5	27
(Gain)/loss on disposal of assets	(18)	8
Other	-3	16
Cash Flows from Operating Activities	1,814	2,029

Preparation of the Statement of Cash Flows

Companies can prepare their statements of cash flows by using either the direct or indirect methods. Only the operating activities section of the statement differs between the two methods. In this chapter we introduce the statement and concentrate on preparing a basic statement using the indirect method. More complex aspects of the statement, including preparation of the statement of cash flows using the direct method, are covered in Volume 2.

Companies obtain the information to prepare a statement of cash flows from a variety of sources. These include the SFP, income statement, and selected transaction data—normally data in the general ledger Cash account. Because the statement is intended to include all cash transactions, the Cash account is an important source of information. Preparation of the statement requires the following steps:

1. Determine the cash provided by or used in operating, investing, and financing activities by analyzing changes in SFP balances, related income statement balances, and other selected transaction information.

2. Determine the change (increase or decrease) in cash during the period.

3. Reconcile the change in cash with the beginning and ending cash and cash equivalents balances.

In this chapter, we use the following simple example to prepare a statement of cash flows using the indirect method. We first look briefly at how to calculate the cash provided by or used in operating activities. Assume that on January 1, 2014, in its second year of operations, Telemarketing Inc. expanded its business. First it issued 50,000 shares for $50,000 cash. The company then rented additional office space, purchased additional furniture and telecommunications equipment, and performed marketing services throughout the year. On December 31, 2014, the company also purchased land with fair value of $150,000, which was financed partially by the issuance of bonds. Finally, it paid cash dividends of $15,000 during the year. Illustration 5-16 shows the company's comparative statements of financial position at the beginning and end of 2014.

Illustration 5-16

Comparative Statements of Financial Position for Telemarketing Inc.

TELEMARKETING INC.
Statements of Financial Position

Assets	Dec. 31, 2014	Dec. 31, 2013	Increase/Decrease
Cash	$ 61,000	$ 30,000	$ 31,000 increase
Accounts receivable	86,000	45,000	41,000 increase
Land	150,000	–0–	150,000 increase
Property, plant, and equipment	300,000	200,000	100,000 increase
Total	$597,000	$275,000	
Liabilities and Shareholders' Equity			
Accounts payable	$ 62,000	$50,000	12,000 increase
Bonds payable	200,000	–0–	200,000 increase
Common shares	180,000	130,000	50,000 increase
Retained earnings	155,000	95,000	60,000 increase
Total	$597,000	$275,000	

Illustration 5-17 shows the company's income statement.

Illustration 5-17

*Income Statement Data for
Telemarketing Inc.*

TELEMARKETING INC.
Income Statement
For the Year Ended December 31, 2014

Revenues	$250,000
Operating expenses	120,000
Depreciation expense	30,000
Income before income tax	100,000
Income tax	25,000
Net income	$ 75,000

Additional information:

Dividends of $15,000 were paid during the year. The bonds were issued on December 31, 2014, to help finance the acquisition of the land. Specifically, $100,000 worth of the land was acquired in exchange for $100,000 of bonds, with the remainder of the bonds being issued for cash.

Cash provided by operating activities is the excess of cash receipts over cash payments for operating activities. Companies determine this amount by converting net income on an accrual basis to a cash basis. To do this, they add to or deduct from net income those items in the income statement that do not affect cash, such as depreciation expense and noncash gains or losses. They then adjust net income for the items that are affected by changes in current asset or liability account balances. For example, increases in accounts receivable between years would reflect the fact that more sales remain uncollected at the end of the current year compared with the prior year. Similarly, a decrease in accounts payable would suggest that the current year's purchases have been paid off more quickly than similar purchases in the prior year. Determination of cash provided by (or used for) operating activities requires that a company analyze not only the current year's income statement but also the comparative SFP and selected transaction data (especially items affecting the Cash account). This analysis is important since, for instance, credit sales from last year that are collected this year (and were previously recorded as accounts receivable) will increase cash.

Analysis of Telemarketing Inc.'s comparative statements of financial position reveals two items that will affect the calculation of net cash provided by operating activities:

1. The increase in accounts receivable is a noncash increase of $41,000 in revenues from uncollected credit sales. This amount would have been included in net income as sales revenue and so must be deducted in arriving at cash from operations. In short, the company has to reduce cash flow from operations by $41,000, as it has fewer cash resources available to it due to a higher accounts receivable balance in 2014.

2. The increase in accounts payable is a noncash increase of $12,000 in expenses accrued but not yet paid. This amount would have been deducted in arriving at net income but, since these expenses did not require a cash outlay, they will be added back in arriving at cash from operations. The company has conserved some of its cash resources by not paying off its accounts payable as quickly in 2014 as it did in 2013.

A review of the income statement indicates that depreciation expense totalling $30,000 was deducted in arriving at net income. Because depreciation is a noncash item that has been deducted as an expense, it must be added back to net income to arrive at cash from operations. In addition, to obtain cash from operations, Telemarketing Inc. deducts from net income the increase in accounts receivable ($41,000) and it adds back to net income the increase in accounts payable ($12,000) as discussed above. Note that since there were no sales of property, plant, and equipment during the year, there is no need to adjust for noncash gains or losses. As a result of these adjustments, the company determines that cash provided by operations amounted to $76,000, as calculated in Illustration 5-18.

Net income		$75,000
Adjustments to reconcile net income to net cash provided by operating activities:		
Depreciation expense	$ 30,000	
Increase in accounts receivable	(41,000)	
Increase in accounts payable	12,000	1,000
Net cash provided by operating activities		$76,000

Telemarketing Inc.'s only investing activities were the land and property, plant, and equipment purchases. From the analysis of changes in SFP balances, it can be seen that land increased by $150,000. However, other available information states that $100,000 of the land purchased was paid for via an exchange for bonds. Since this is a noncash exchange, the $100,000 increase in land (and the related $100,000 increase in bonds payable) is not included on the statement of cash flows. Details of the exchange would be disclosed via a note to the financial statements. The remaining increase to land ($50,000) was cash based and must be disclosed on the statement of cash flows. There was also an increase to (net) property, plant, and equipment (PPE) of $100,000 on the SFP requires further analysis. Since PPE is shown on a net basis on the SFP, it is net of related accumulated depreciation. From our analysis of operating activities and the income statement, we know that depreciation expense was $30,000 for the year. So the increase in PPE must have been $130,000 prior to recording of depreciation expense ($130,000 − 30,000 = $100,000 [net] increase to PPE). The purchase of PPE of $130,000 is shown as part of investing activities.

Telemarketing Inc. has three financing activities: (1) the increase of $50,000 in common shares resulting from the issuance of these shares, (2) the cash portion of the increase in bonds payable as discussed above, and (3) the payment of $15,000 in cash dividends. Illustration 5-19 presents Telemarketing Inc.'s statement of cash flows for 2014.

TELEMARKETING INC.
Statement of Cash Flows
For the Year Ended December 31, 2014

Cash flows from operating activities		
Net income		$ 75,000
Adjustments to reconcile net income to net cash provided by operating activities:		
Depreciation expense	$ 30,000	
Increase in accounts receivable	(41,000)	
Increase in accounts payable	12,000	1,000
Net cash provided by operating activities		76,000
Cash flows from investing activities		
Purchase of land	(50,000)	
Purchase of property, plant, and equipment	(130,000)	
Net cash used by investing activities		(180,000)
Cash flows from financing activities		
Issuance of common shares	50,000	
Issuance of bonds payable	100,000	
Payment of cash dividends	(15,000)	
Net cash provided by financing activities		135,000
Net increase in cash		31,000
Cash at beginning of year		30,000
Cash at end of year		$ 61,000

Note: During 2014, the company issued $100,000 of bonds payable in exchange for land.

The increase in cash of $31,000 that is reported in the statement of cash flows agrees with the increase in cash that was calculated from the comparative statements of financial position. Note that in addition to the exchange of bonds payable for land, other examples of a company's activities not involving cash would include the conversion of bonds to shares, an issuance of debt to purchase assets, and other nonmonetary exchanges. These activities should not be included in the body of the cash flow statement but should be disclosed elsewhere in the financial statements.

Note that the net cash provided by operating activities section begins with net income and reconciles to cash. This presentation is called the indirect method of presenting cash flows from operating activities. Another option is the direct method. The direct method normally presents the following information in the operations portion of the statement:

- Cash received from customers

- Cash paid to suppliers and employees

- Interest paid or received

- Taxes paid

- Other

The rest of the statement remains the same in both methods.

Under IFRS and ASPE, either method is acceptable, although the direct method is preferred by standard setters. See Chapter 22 for a more detailed discussion.

Usefulness of the Statement of Cash Flows

Objective 9
Understand the usefulness of the statement of cash flows.

Although net income provides a long-term measure of a company's success or failure, cash is a company's lifeblood. Without cash, a company will not survive. For small and newly developing companies, cash flow is often the single most important element of survival. Even medium and large companies indicate that controlling cash flow is a major concern.

Creditors examine the statement of cash flows carefully because they are concerned about being paid. A good starting point in their examination is to find **net cash provided by operating activities**. A high amount of net cash provided by operating activities indicates that a company was able to generate enough cash internally from operations in the most recent period to pay its bills without further borrowing. Conversely, a low or negative amount of net cash provided by operating activities indicates that a company did not generate enough cash internally from its operations and, therefore, may have had to borrow or issue equity securities to acquire additional cash.

Just because a company was able to generate cash flows from operating activities in the most recent period, however, does not mean that it will be able to do so again in future periods. Consequently, creditors look for answers to the following questions in the company's statement of cash flows:

- How successful is the company in generating net cash provided by operating activities?

- What are the trends in net cash flow provided by operating activities over time?

- What are the major reasons for the positive or negative net cash provided by operating activities?

- Are the cash flows sustainable or renewable? In other words, can they be repeated over time?

It is important to recognize that companies can fail even though they are profitable. The difference between net income and net cash provided by operating activities can be substantial. One of the main reasons for the difference between a positive net income and negative net cash provided by operating activities is major increases in receivables and/or inventory. To illustrate, assume that in its first year of operations, Hinchcliff Inc. reported net income of $80,000. Its net cash provided by operating activities, however, was a negative $95,000, as shown in Illustration 5-20.

HINCHCLIFF INC.
Net Cash Flow from Operating Activities

Net income		$ 80,000
Adjustments to reconcile net income to net cash provided by operating activities:		
Increase in receivables	$ (75,000)	
Increase in inventory	(100,000)	(175,000)
Net cash provided by operating activities		$ (95,000)

Note that the negative net cash provided by operating activities occurred for Hinchcliff even though it reported a positive net income. The company could easily experience a "cash crunch" because it has tied up its cash in receivables and inventory. If problems in collecting receivables occur or inventory is slow-moving or becomes obsolete, the company's creditors may have difficulty collecting on their loans.

Companies that are expanding often experience this type of "cash crunch" as they must buy increasing inventory amounts to meet increasing sales demands. This means that the cash outflow to purchase the inventory occurs before the cash inflow from the customer for sale of that product. This is often referred to as a "lead-lag" factor. The cash outflow leads (occurs first) and the cash inflow from sales lags (occurs later). The lead-lag factor requires the company to use up any excess cash that it has on hand or to borrow more funds. Refer back to Illustration 5-3 on the business operating cycle.

As mentioned earlier in the chapter, financial flexibility may be assessed by using information from the financial statements. The cash flow statement is especially good for providing this type of information.

Financial Liquidity

One ratio that is used to assess liquidity is the **current cash debt coverage ratio**. It indicates whether the company can pay off its current liabilities for the year from its operations. The formula for this ratio is shown in Illustration 5-21.

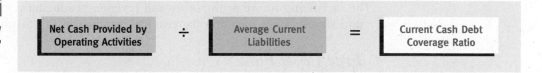

| Net Cash Provided by Operating Activities | ÷ | Average Current Liabilities | = | Current Cash Debt Coverage Ratio |

The higher this ratio, the less likely a company will have liquidity problems. For example, a ratio of at least 1:1 is good because it indicates that the company can meet all of its current obligations from internally generated cash flow. To compare this ratio with a benchmark number, it can be compared with the ratios for similar companies in the industry (or with the ratios of prior years for the company itself).

Financial Flexibility

A more long-run measure that provides information on financial flexibility is the **cash debt coverage ratio**. This ratio indicates a company's ability to repay its liabilities from net cash provided by operating activities without having to liquidate the assets that it uses in its operations. Illustration 5-22 presents the formula for this ratio.

| Net Cash Provided by Operating Activities | ÷ | Average Total Liabilities | = | Cash Debt Coverage Ratio |

The higher this ratio, the less likely a company will experience difficulty in meeting its obligations as they come due. As a result, this ratio signals whether the company can pay its debts and survive if external sources of funds become limited or too expensive.

Perspectives

Cash Flow Patterns

Refer to Illustration 5-19 showing the full statement of cash flows for Telemarketing Inc. The cash flow statement can yield some interesting results when users look at the various patterns between cash inflows and outflows for the following subtotals on the statement: operating, investing, and financing cash flows. For instance, Telemarketing Inc. has positive cash flows (cash inflows; "+") from operating activities of $76,000, negative cash flows (cash outflows; "−") from investing activities of $180,000, and positive cash flows (cash inflows; "+") from financing activities of $135,000. Together these numbers thus yield a "+" "−" "+" pattern.

Interpreting this, the company is getting its cash from operations (which is a very good sign) and also from the issuance of common shares and long-term debt. It is investing this cash to expand the business. The fact that the company is able to raise funds in the capital markets by issuing shares indicates that the capital markets have faith in the company's ability to prosper. As the company expands, it may be able to move to having the bulk of the money used to finance purchases of capital assets being generated from operations. This would mean that the company would not have to increase its solvency risk by issuing debt or further diluting its shareholders' equity by issuing more shares. Telemarketing Inc. appears to be a successful company in an expansionary mode.

Companies that generate cash from investing activities may be selling off long-term assets. This pattern generally goes with a company that is downsizing or restructuring. If the assets that are being disposed of are not needed, then it makes sense to free up the capital that is tied up. Similarly, if the assets being disposed of relate to operations that are not profitable, disposal reflects a good management decision. However, if the company is in a position where it **must** sell off core income-producing assets to generate cash, then it may be sacrificing future profitability and revenue-producing potential. This is obviously undesirable. Thus, cash flow patterns have significant information content.

Free Cash Flow

A more sophisticated way to examine a company's financial flexibility is to develop a **free cash flow** analysis. This analysis starts with net cash provided by operating activities and ends with free cash flow, which is calculated as net cash provided by operating activities less capital expenditures and dividends.[29] Free cash flow is the amount of discretionary cash flow that a company has for purchasing additional investments, retiring its debt, purchasing treasury stock, or simply adding to its liquidity. This measure indicates a company's level of financial flexibility. A free cash flow analysis can answer questions such as these:

- Is the company able to pay its dividends without the help of external financing?

- If business operations decline, will the company be able to maintain its needed capital investment?

- What is the free cash flow that can be used for additional investments, retirement of debt, purchases of treasury stock, or additions to liquidity?

Illustration 5-23 shows a free cash flow analysis for Nestor Corporation.

Illustration **5-23**

Free Cash Flow Analysis

NESTOR CORPORATION
Free Cash Flow Analysis

Net cash provided by operating activities	$ 411,750
Less: Capital expenditures	(252,500)
Dividends	(19,800)
Free cash flow	$ 139,450

This analysis shows that Nestor has positive, and substantial, net cash provided by operating activities of $411,750. Nestor reports on its statement of cash flows that it purchased equipment of $182,500 and land of $70,000 for total capital spending of $252,500. This amount is subtracted from net cash provided by operating activities because, without continued efforts to maintain and expand its facilities, it is unlikely that Nestor can continue to maintain its competitive position. Capital spending is deducted first on the analysis above to indicate it is generally the least discretionary expenditure that a company makes. Dividends are then deducted to arrive at free cash flow.

Nestor has more than enough cash flow to meet its dividend payment and therefore has satisfactory financial flexibility. Nestor used its free cash flow to redeem bonds and add to its liquidity. If it finds additional investments that are profitable, it can increase its spending without putting its dividend or basic capital spending in jeopardy. Companies that have strong financial flexibility can take advantage of profitable investments even in tough times. In addition, strong financial flexibility frees companies from worry about survival in poor economic times. In fact, those with strong financial flexibility often do better in poor economic times because they can take advantage of opportunities that other companies cannot.

Real World Emphasis

In 2011, Air Canada found itself under pressure with respect to its free cash flow, due in part to payments required for its registered pension plans. Although Air Canada's cash, cash equivalents, and short-term investments totalled almost $2.3 billion as of June 30, 2011, in the second quarter of 2011, free cash flow of $241 million decreased $56 million from the second quarter of 2010.[30] The drop in free cash flow was largely attributed to pension contributions in 2011. Air Canada had been able to avoid making past contributions to its pension plans for several years based on the terms of the Air Canada 2009 Pension Regulations, which had been passed by the federal government in 2009. However, these payments resumed in 2011.[31] Overall, the legislation provided funding relief in two parts: a moratorium on special payments until December 31, 2010, and a set schedule of payments for 2011, 2012, and 2013. Air Canada, therefore, can expect to feel additional pressure on its free cash flows relating to its pension plans in 2014, making pensions a continuing issue between the company and its unions.

Caution

As more and more complex financial instruments are created, more presentation issues arise for financial statement preparers. Many instruments have attributes of both debt and equity. This is significant for analysts since a misclassification will affect key ratios. Note disclosure of the details of the instruments helps analysts and other users in assessing a company's liquidity and solvency. This issue will be discussed further in subsequent chapters on liabilities and equities.

IFRS/ASPE COMPARISON

A Comparison of IFRS and ASPE

Objective 10

Identify differences in
accounting between
ASPE and IFRS.

The differences between the IFRS and ASPE sets of standards in how assets, liabilities, and shareholders' equity are accounted for and presented on the SFP and how cash activity is reported on the statement of cash flows are set out in Illustration 5-24.

	Accounting Standards for Private Enterprises (ASPE)—*CICA Handbook*, Part II, Sections 1400, 1510, 1521, 1540, and 3251	IFRS—IAS 1, 7, and 40	References to related illustrations and select brief exercises
Specific items to be presented in the balance sheet/SFP	For the most part, IFRS and ASPE require essentially the same items to be presented.	The following items are required to be presented under IFRS: • Investment property • Biological assets • Provisions	Illustration 10-8 Illustration 8-26 Illustration 8-27 Illustration 8-28
Current versus non-current liabilities	If company has refinanced debt by the issue date of the financial statements, may present as non-current.	If no unconditional right to defer payment of financial liability beyond one year as at the balance sheet date, must show as current (including situations where the company has refinanced the debt after the balance sheet date but before issue).	BE5-8 and BE5-9
Cash flow statement	Equity investments are excluded from cash and cash equivalents. Interest and dividends included in net income are treated as operating activities and those booked through retained earnings are treated as financing activities.	Certain preferred shares acquired within a short period of maturity date may be classified as cash and cash equivalents. IFRS allows flexibility in how to treat interest and dividends (may be classified as operating, investing, or financing activities).	BE5-15
Cash flow per share information	Prohibited—may not be disclosed	No prohibition on disclosure of this number.	BE5-17
Disclosure of date financial statements authorized for issue	No requirement to disclose.	Must disclose date that the financial statements were authorized for issue.	

Illustration 5-24

IFRS and ASPE Comparison Chart

Objective 11

Identify the significant
changes planned by
the IASB regarding
financial statement
presentation.

Looking Ahead

As noted in Chapter 4, the IASB and FASB are working on financial statement presentation as a major project. The idea is to present the main financial statements so as to highlight major business and financing activities. In July 2010, the IASB published a "staff draft" of an exposure draft on financial statement presentation. On March 1, 2011, IASB staff presented the results and findings of its outreach activities. However, the project was then paused as the IASB and FASB decided to conduct more outreach activities before issuing an exposure draft on financial statement presentation, which could ultimately result in the replacement of IAS 1 and IAS 7. The outreach activities focus primarily on (1) the perceived cost or benefits of staff proposals and (2) the implications of the proposals for financial reporting by financial services entities.[32] The stated main goal of the IASB and FASB proposals is to "improve the comparability and understandability of information presented in financial statements, by imposing some degree of standardisation in the way that information is presented in the financial statements, particularly regarding how information is classified, and the degree to which it is disaggregated."

SUMMARY OF LEARNING OBJECTIVES

1 Understand the statement of financial position and statement of cash flows from a business perspective.

It is important to understand how users of financial statements use the SFP and the cash flow statement. For example, potential investors in a company may use the SFP to analyze a company's liquidity and solvency in order to assess risk of investing. In addition, the SFP provides details about the company's financial structure. Users may use a company's statement of cash flows to assess its earnings quality and obtain information about its operating, investing, and financing activities.

2 Identify the uses and limitations of a statement of financial position.

The SFP provides information about the nature and amounts of investments in enterprise resources, obligations to creditors, and the owners' equity in net resources. The SFP contributes to financial reporting by providing a basis for (1) calculating rates of return, (2) evaluating the enterprise's capital structure, and (3) assessing the enterprise's liquidity, solvency, and financial flexibility. The limitations of an SFP are as follows: (1) The SFP often does not reflect current value, because accountants have adopted a historical cost basis in valuing and reporting many assets and liabilities. (2) Judgements and estimates must be used in preparing an SFP. The collectibility of receivables, the saleability of inventory, and the useful life of long-term tangible and intangible assets are difficult to determine. (3) The SFP leaves out many items that are of financial value to the business but cannot be recorded objectively, such as its human resources, customer base, and reputation.

3 Identify the major classifications of a statement of financial position.

The SFP's general elements are assets, liabilities, and equity. The major classifications within the SFP on the asset side are current assets; investments; property, plant, and equipment; intangible assets; and other assets. The major classifications of liabilities are current and long-term liabilities. In a corporation, owners' equity is generally classified as shares, contributed surplus, retained earnings, and accumulated other comprehensive income.

4 Prepare a classified statement of financial position.

The most common format lists liabilities and shareholders' equity directly below assets on the same page.

5 Identify statement of financial position information that requires supplemental disclosure.

Five types of information are normally supplemental to account titles and amounts presented in the SFP. (1) Contingencies: Material events that have an uncertain outcome. (2) Accounting policies: Explanations of the valuation methods that are used or the basic assumptions that are made for inventory valuation, amortization methods, investments in subsidiaries, and so on. (3) Contractual situations: Explanations of certain restrictions or covenants that are attached to specific assets or, more likely, to liabilities. (4) Additional information: Clarification by giving more detail about the composition of SFP items. (5) Subsequent events: Events that happen after the date of the SFP.

6 Identify major disclosure techniques for the statement of financial position.

There are four methods of disclosing pertinent information in the SFP: (1) Parenthetical explanations: Additional information or description is often provided by giving explanations in parentheses that follow the item. (2) Notes: Notes are used if additional explanations or descriptions cannot be shown conveniently as parenthetical explanations. (3) Cross-reference and contra items: A direct relationship between an asset and a liability is cross-referenced on the SFP. (4) Supporting schedules: Often a separate schedule is needed to present more detailed information about certain assets or liabilities because the SFP provides just a single summary item.

7 Indicate the purpose and identify the content of the statement of cash flows.

The main purpose of a statement of cash flows is to provide relevant information about an enterprise's cash receipts and cash payments during a period. Reporting the sources, uses, and net increase or decrease in cash lets investors, creditors, and others know what is happening to a company's most liquid resource. Cash receipts and cash payments during a period are classified in the statement of cash flows into three different activities: (1) Operating activities: Involve the cash effects of transactions that enter into the determination of net income. (2) Investing activities: Include making and collecting loans and acquiring and disposing of investments (both debt and equity) and property, plant, and equipment. (3) Financing activities: Involve liability and owners' equity items and include (a) obtaining capital from owners and providing them with a return on their investment and (b) borrowing money from creditors and repaying the amounts borrowed.

8 Prepare a statement of cash flows using the indirect method.

This involves determining cash flows from operations by starting with net income and adjusting it for noncash activities, such as changes in accounts receivable (and other current asset/liability) balances, depreciation, and gains/losses. It is important to look carefully at prior years' operating activities that might affect cash this year, such as cash collected this year from last year's credit sales and cash spent this year for last year's accrued expenses. The cash flows from investing and financing activities can then be determined by analyzing changes in SFP accounts and the cash account.

9 Understand the usefulness of the statement of cash flows.

Creditors examine the statement of cash flows carefully because they are concerned about being paid. The amount of net cash flow provided by operating activities in relation to the company's liabilities is helpful in making this assessment. In addition, measures such as a free cash flow analysis provide creditors and shareholders with a better picture of the company's financial flexibility.

10 Identify differences in accounting between ASPE and IFRS.

Illustration 5-24 outlines the major differences in how both sets of standards account for and present items on the SFP and statement of cash flows. Both sets of standards largely require that the same SFP elements be presented. In addition, IFRS requires presentation of biological assets, investment properties, and provisions. The statement of cash flow presentation requirements are similar.

11 Identify the significant changes planned by the IASB regarding financial statement presentation.

The IASB has been planning to change the way financial statements are presented by issuing a new standard. However, the project was paused in 2011 "until the IASB concludes its ongoing deliberations about its future work plan." The major statements, including SFP, income statement, and statement of cash flows, are eventually expected to be classified according to business and financing activities.

KEY TERMS

adjunct account, p. 242
cash and cash equivalents, p. 229
cash debt coverage ratio, p. 249
contingency, p. 239
contra account, p. 242
current assets, p. 228
current cash debt coverage ratio, p. 249
current liabilities, p. 235
deferred income tax assets, p. 235
deferred income tax liabilities, p. 236
financial flexibility, p. 224

financial instruments, p. 226
financing activities, p. 243
free cash flow, p. 250
future income tax assets, p. 235
future income tax liabilities, p. 236
intangible assets, p. 234
investing activities, p. 243
liquidity, p. 224
long-term liabilities, p. 236
monetary assets, p. 226
non-current investments, p. 232

nonmonetary assets, p. 226
operating activities, p. 243
other assets, p. 235
owners' equity, p. 237
prepaid expenses, p. 232
property, plant, and equipment, p. 233
solvency, p. 224
statement of cash flows, p. 243
statement of financial position, p. 223
subsequent events, p. 240
working capital, p. 236

RATIO ANALYSIS: A REFERENCE

Objective 12
Identify the major types of financial ratios and what they measure.

Companies expose themselves to many risks in doing business. Strategically, the goal is to identify these risks and then manage them in order to take advantage of opportunities and maximize shareholder value. How do users know whether a company is managing its risks in a way that will create the most shareholder value? Illustration 5A-1 shows the business model that was originally introduced in Chapter 4. Now risks have been added to the model, along with the key management personnel responsible for managing the risks.[33]

Illustration 5A-1

The Business Model and Various Related Risks that a Company Must Manage

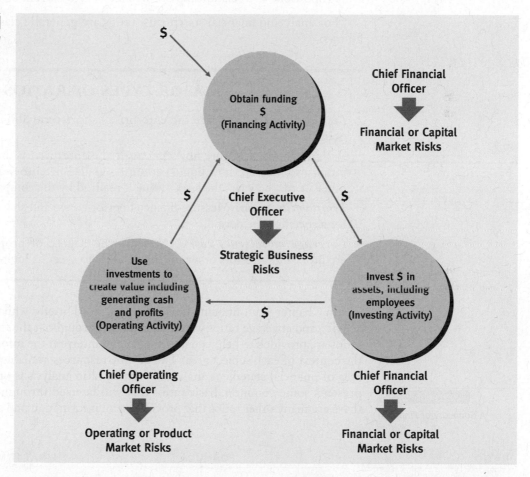

Financial or capital market risks are related to financing and investing activities. For example, when a company borrows funds, it might increase its solvency and liquidity risk. **Operating or product market risks** are related to operating activities. For instance, when it manufactures a drug, there is a risk that a company might not be able to produce quality products on time or successfully target the appropriate market for sale of the drug.

Information about risks is useful and much of this information is included in the annual report, both within the financial statements and in other parts. The financial statements give information about financing, investing, and operating activities and therefore provide indirect feedback on how related risks are being managed and how this in turn affects performance. A solvent company that constantly generates cash from operations has a solid business model where risks and opportunities are well managed to create value. Companies usually disclose explicit information about risks and risk management policies in the Management Discussion and Analysis section of the annual report.

Ratio analysis helps in assessing operating and financial risks by **expressing the relationship between selected financial statement data**. Qualitative information from financial statements is gathered by **examining relationships** between items on the statements and **identifying trends** in these relationships. Relationships are often expressed in terms of a percentage, a rate, or a simple proportion.

Real World Emphasis

To illustrate, recently **Shoppers Drug Mart Corporation** had current assets of $2,695.6 million and current liabilities of $1,776.2 million, as you can see in their financial statements, which are reproduced in Appendix 5B. The relationship is determined by dividing current assets by current liabilities. The alternative means of expression are:

Percentage: Current assets are 152% of current liabilities.

Rate: Current assets are 1.52 times as great as current liabilities.

Proportion: The relationship of current assets to current liabilities is 1.52:1.

For analyzing financial statements, ratios are generally classified into four types, as follows:

MAJOR TYPES OF RATIOS

Liquidity ratios. Measure the enterprise's short-term ability to pay its maturing obligations.

Activity ratios. Measure how effectively the enterprise is using its assets. Activity ratios also measure how liquid certain assets like inventory and receivables are; in other words, how fast the asset's value is realized by the company.

Profitability ratios. Measure financial performance and shareholder value creation for a specific time period.

Coverage or solvency ratios. Measure the degree of protection for long-term creditors and investors or a company's ability to meet its long-term obligations.

In Chapter 4, profitability ratios were discussed briefly, while in this chapter, liquidity, activity, and coverage ratios were touched on. Throughout the remainder of the textbook, ratios are provided to help you understand and interpret the information presented within the context of each subject area. The on-line resources available with this text look at the area of financial statement analysis, of which ratio analysis is one part. Illustration 5A-2 presents some common, basic ratios that will be used throughout the text. In practice, there are many other ratios that provide useful information and are therefore also used.

Illustration 5A-2

A Summary of Financial Ratios

RATIO	FORMULA	WHAT IT MEASURES
I. Liquidity		
1. Current ratio	$\dfrac{\text{Current assets}}{\text{Current liabilities}}$	Short-term debt-paying ability
2. Quick or acid-test ratio	$\dfrac{\text{Cash, marketable securities, and receivables (net)}}{\text{Current liabilities}}$	Immediate short-term liquidity
3. Current cash debt coverage ratio	$\dfrac{\text{Net cash provided by operating activities}}{\text{Average current liabilities}}$	Company's ability to pay off its current liabilities in a specific year from its operations

(continued)

RATIO	FORMULA	WHAT IT MEASURES
II. Activity		
4. Receivables turnover	$\dfrac{\text{Net sales}}{\text{Average trade receivables (net)}}$	Liquidity of receivables
5. Inventory turnover	$\dfrac{\text{Cost of goods sold}}{\text{Average inventory}}$	Liquidity of inventory
6. Asset turnover	$\dfrac{\text{Net sales}}{\text{Average total assets}}$	How efficiently assets are used to generate sales
III. Profitability		
7. Profit margin on sales	$\dfrac{\text{Net income}}{\text{Net sales}}$	Net income generated by each dollar of sales
8. Rate of return on assets	$\dfrac{\text{Net income}}{\text{Average total assets}}$	Overall profitability of assets
9. Rate of return on common share equity	$\dfrac{\text{Net income minus preferred dividends}}{\text{Average common shareholders' equity}}$	Profitability of owners' investment
10. Earnings per share	$\dfrac{\text{Net income minus preferred dividends}}{\text{Weighted average shares outstanding}}$	Net income earned on each common share
11. Price earnings ratio	$\dfrac{\text{Market price of shares}}{\text{Earnings per share}}$	Ratio of the market price per share to earnings per share
12. Payout ratio	$\dfrac{\text{Cash dividends}}{\text{Net income}}$	Percentage of earnings distributed as cash dividends
IV. Coverage		
13. Debt to total assets	$\dfrac{\text{Total debt}}{\text{Total assets}}$	Percentage of total assets provided by creditors
14. Times interest earned	$\dfrac{\text{Income before interest charges and taxes}}{\text{Interest charges}}$	Ability to meet interest payments as they come due
15. Cash debt coverage ratio	$\dfrac{\text{Net cash provided by operating activities}}{\text{Average total liabilities}}$	Company's ability to repay its total liabilities in a specific year from its operations
16. Book value per share	$\dfrac{\text{Common shareholders' equity}}{\text{Outstanding shares}}$	Amount each share would receive if the company were liquidated at the amounts reported on the balance sheet

Illustration 5A-2

A Summary of Financial Ratios (continued)

The key to a refined, information-rich analysis is having a good **understanding of the business, business risks, and industry** before calculating and interpreting any ratios. Specialized industries focus on different ratios depending on the critical success factors in their business. As discussed throughout the chapter, different companies and businesses would be expected to have different types of assets and capital structures. Furthermore, they would be expected to have different types of costs, revenue streams, and business models.

Success in the retail industry, for instance, comes from the ability to set prices and target customers in a way that gets maximum market penetration. Also critical is the ability to minimize inventory shrinkage (because there is a high risk of theft) and keep inventory moving so that it does not become obsolete or out of fashion. A company's ability to achieve this, or its failure to do so, is reflected in the gross profit margin (a ratio). This is calculated by dividing gross profit by revenues. Companies must achieve a gross profit that is high enough to cover other costs. A stable gross profit margin is a positive sign that management is dealing with all of the above issues.

Once ratios are calculated, they must then be examined and the information interpreted. Examining ratios by themselves provides very little insight. Instead, the **ratios must be compared with or benchmarked against similar ratios, perhaps for the same company from prior periods or, alternatively, for similar companies in the same industry**.

When benchmarking is done against industry numbers, it may be necessary to create industry benchmarks if they are not available. To do this, select several companies that have a similar business model and are in the same industry. Companies that are the same size are better comparators.

Note that average amounts may be approximated by taking opening and closing balances and dividing by two.

SUMMARY OF LEARNING OBJECTIVE FOR APPENDIX 5A

13 Identify the major types of financial ratios and what they measure.

Ratios express the mathematical relationship between one quantity and another, in terms of a percentage, a rate, or a proportion. Liquidity ratios measure the short-term ability to pay maturing obligations. Activity ratios measure how effectively assets are being used. Profitability ratios measure an enterprise's success or failure. Coverage ratios measure the degree of protection for long-term creditors and investors.

KEY TERMS

activity ratios, p. 256	liquidity ratios, p. 256	ratio analysis, p. 256
coverage ratios, p. 256	profitability ratios, p. 256	solvency ratios, p. 256

SPECIMEN FINANCIAL STATEMENTS

Shoppers Drug Mart

The following pages contain the financial statements, accompanying notes, and other information from the 2011 annual financial statements of Shoppers Drug Mart. Note 30 has been reproduced partially in the interest of brevity. The text of the full note and other financial information that is not reproduced here is available on WileyPLUS and the student website. The corporate profile below is taken from the company annual report.

Corporate profile

Shoppers Drug Mart Corporation is the licensor of full-service retail drug stores operating under the names Shoppers Drug Mart® and Pharmaprix®. Founded in 1962 by Toronto pharmacist Murray Koffler, the Company has grown to a network of more than 1,200 stores across Canada. These conveniently located stores are owned and operated by licensed Associate-owners, who have helped build a brand that is synonymous with exceptional service, value and trust. The Company also licenses or owns 58 medical clinic pharmacies operating under the names Shoppers Simply Pharmacy® and Pharmaprix Simplement Santé®, as well as eight luxury beauty destinations operating as Murale™.

With fiscal 2011 sales of approximately $10.5 billion, the Company is the leader in Canada's retail drug store marketplace and is the number one provider of pharmacy products and services. Shoppers Drug Mart has successfully leveraged its leadership position in pharmacy and its convenient store locations to capture a significant share of the market in front store merchandise, including over-the-counter medications, health and beauty aids, cosmetics and fragrances, seasonal products and everyday household essentials. The Company offers a broad range of high-quality private label products including Life Brand®, Quo®, Etival Laboratoire®, Baléa®, Everyday Market®, Simply Food®, Nativa® and Bio-Life®, among others, and value-added services such as the Healthwatch® program, which offers patient counselling and advice on medications, disease management and health and wellness, and the Shoppers Optimum® program, one of the largest retail loyalty card programs in Canada.

As well, the Company owns and operates 63 Shoppers Home Health Care® stores, which are engaged in the sale and service of assisted-living devices and equipment to institutional and retail customers. In addition to its retail network, the Company owns Shoppers Drug Mart Specialty Health Network Inc., a provider of specialty drug distribution, pharmacy and comprehensive patient support services, and Medi-System Technologies Inc., a provider of pharmaceutical products and services to long-term care facilities in Ontario and Alberta.

At this point, we recommend that you take 20 to 30 minutes to scan the statements and notes to familiarize yourself with the contents and accounting elements. Throughout the following chapters, when you are asked to refer to specific parts of Shoppers' financials, do so. Then, when you have completed reading this book, we challenge you to reread Shoppers' financials to see how much greater and more sophisticated your understanding of them has become.

Management's Responsibility for Financial Statements

Management is responsible for the preparation and presentation of the accompanying consolidated financial statements and all other information in the Annual Report. This responsibility includes the selection and consistent application of appropriate accounting principles and methods in addition to making the estimates, judgements and assumptions necessary to prepare the consolidated financial statements in accordance with Canadian generally accepted accounting principles, which complies with International Financial Reporting Standards. It also includes ensuring that the financial information presented elsewhere in the Annual Report is consistent with the consolidated financial statements.

In fulfilling its responsibilities, management has established and maintains systems of internal controls. Although no cost-effective system of internal controls will prevent or detect all errors and irregularities, these systems are designed to provide reasonable assurance regarding the reliability of the Company's financial reporting and preparation of the financial statements in accordance with Canadian generally accepted accounting principles. These systems include controls to provide reasonable assurance that resources are safeguarded from material loss or inappropriate use, that transactions are authorized, recorded and reported properly and that financial records are reliable for preparing the consolidated financial statements. Internal auditors, who are employees of the Company, review and evaluate internal controls on management's behalf. The consolidated financial statements have been audited by the independent auditors, Deloitte & Touche LLP, in accordance with generally accepted auditing standards. Their report follows.

The Board of Directors, acting through an Audit Committee which is comprised solely of directors who are not employees of the Company, is responsible for determining that management fulfils its responsibility for financial reporting and internal control. This responsibility is carried out through periodic meetings with senior officers, financial management, internal audit and the independent auditors to discuss audit activities, the adequacy of internal financial controls and financial reporting matters. The Audit Committee has reviewed these consolidated financial statements and the Management's Discussion and Analysis and has recommended their approval by the Board of Directors prior to their inclusion in this Annual Report.

Domenic Pilla
President and Chief Executive Officer

TORONTO, ONTARIO
FEBRUARY 9, 2012

Brad Lukow
Executive Vice-President and Chief Financial Officer

To the Shareholders of Shoppers Drug Mart Corporation

We have audited the accompanying consolidated financial statements of Shoppers Drug Mart Corporation, which comprise the consolidated balance sheets as at December 31, 2011, January 1, 2011, and January 3, 2010 and the consolidated statements of earnings, consolidated statements of comprehensive income, consolidated statements of changes in shareholders' equity and consolidated statements of cash flows for the 52 week periods ended December 31, 2011 and January 1, 2011, and a summary of significant accounting policies and other explanatory information.

Management's Responsibility for the Consolidated Financial Statements

Management is responsible for the preparation and fair presentation of these consolidated financial statements in accordance with International Financial Reporting Standards, and for such internal control as management determines is necessary to enable the preparation of consolidated financial statements that are free from material misstatement, whether due to fraud or error.

Auditor's Responsibility

Our responsibility is to express an opinion on these consolidated financial statements based on our audits. We conducted our audits in accordance with Canadian generally accepted auditing standards. Those standards require that we comply with ethical requirements and plan and perform the audit to obtain reasonable assurance about whether the consolidated financial statements are free from material misstatement.

An audit involves performing procedures to obtain audit evidence about the amounts and disclosures in the consolidated financial statements. The procedures selected depend on the auditor's judgment, including the assessment of the risks of material misstatement of the consolidated financial statements, whether due to fraud or error. In making those risk assessments, the auditor considers internal control relevant to the entity's preparation and fair presentation of the consolidated financial statements in order to design audit procedures that are appropriate in the circumstances, but not for the purpose of expressing an opinion on the effectiveness of the entity's internal control. An audit also includes evaluating the appropriateness of accounting policies used and the reasonableness of accounting estimates made by management, as well as evaluating the overall presentation of the consolidated financial statements.

We believe that the audit evidence we have obtained in our audits is sufficient and appropriate to provide a basis for our audit opinion.

Opinion

In our opinion, the consolidated financial statements present fairly, in all material respects, the financial position of Shoppers Drug Mart Corporation as at December 31, 2011, January 1, 2011 and January 3, 2010 and its financial performance and its cash flows for the 52 week periods ended December 31, 2011 and January 1, 2011 in accordance with International Financial Reporting Standards.

Deloitte & Touche LLP

Chartered Accountants,
Licensed Public Accountants

FEBRUARY 9, 2012
TORONTO, ONTARIO

Consolidated Statements of Earnings

For the 52 weeks ended December 31, 2011 and January 1, 2011
(in thousands of Canadian dollars, except per share amounts)

	Note	2011	2010[1]
Sales		$ 10,458,652	$ 10,192,714
Cost of goods sold	9	(6,416,208)	(6,283,634)
Gross profit		4,042,444	3,909,080
Operating and administrative expenses	10, 11, 13	(3,131,539)	(3,011,758)
Operating income		910,905	897,322
Finance expenses	12	(64,038)	(60,633)
Earnings before income taxes		846,867	836,689
Income taxes	14		
Current		(208,696)	(238,779)
Deferred		(24,237)	(6,059)
		(232,933)	(244,838)
Net earnings		$ 613,934	$ 591,851
Net earnings per common share			
Basic	25	$ 2.84	$ 2.72
Diluted	25	$ 2.84	$ 2.72
Weighted average common shares outstanding (millions):			
Basic	25	216.4	217.4
Diluted	25	216.5	217.5
Actual common shares outstanding (millions)	24	212.5	217.5

[1] In preparing its 2010 comparative information, the Company has adjusted amounts reported previously in financial statements prepared in accordance with Canadian Generally Accepted Accounting Principles ("previous Canadian GAAP"). See Note 30 to these consolidated financial statements for an explanation of the transition to International Financial Reporting Standards ("IFRS").

The accompanying notes are an integral part of these consolidated financial statements.

Consolidated Statements of Comprehensive Income

For the 52 weeks ended December 31, 2011 and January 1, 2011
(in thousands of Canadian dollars)

	Note	2011	2010[1]
Net earnings		$ 613,934	$ 591,851
Other comprehensive income (loss), net of tax			
Effective portion of changes in fair value of hedges on interest rate derivatives (net of tax of $nil (2010: $525))	18	–	1,120
Effective portion of changes in fair value of hedges on equity forward derivatives (net of tax of $12 (2010: $205))	18	(39)	(521)
Net change in fair value of hedges on interest rate and equity forward derivatives transferred to earnings (net of tax of $163 (2010: $13))	18	411	33
Retirement benefit obligations actuarial losses (net of tax of $7,433 (2010: $2,905))	21	(21,943)	(8,150)
Other comprehensive loss, net of tax	7	(21,571)	(7,518)
Total comprehensive income		$ 592,363	$ 584,333

[1] In preparing its 2010 comparative information, the Company has adjusted amounts reported previously in financial statements prepared in accordance with previous Canadian GAAP. See Note 30 to these consolidated financial statements for an explanation of the transition to IFRS.

The accompanying notes are an integral part of these consolidated financial statements.

Consolidated Balance Sheets

As at December 31, 2011, January 1, 2011 and January 3, 2010
(in thousands of Canadian dollars)

	Note	December 31, 2011	January 1, 2011[1]	January 3, 2010[1]
Current assets				
Cash		$ 118,566	$ 64,354	$ 44,391
Accounts receivable		493,338	432,089	470,935
Inventory		2,042,302	1,957,525	1,852,441
Income taxes recoverable		–	20,384	–
Prepaid expenses and deposits		41,441	68,468	74,206
Total current assets		2,695,647	2,542,820	2,441,973
Non-current assets				
Property and equipment	15	1,767,543	1,677,340	1,541,841
Investment property	15	16,372	12,770	5,884
Goodwill	16	2,499,722	2,493,108	2,483,430
Intangible assets	17	281,737	272,217	258,766
Other assets		18,214	19,678	16,716
Deferred tax assets	14	21,075	26,264	28,456
Total non-current assets		4,604,663	4,501,377	4,335,093
Total assets		$ 7,300,310	$ 7,044,197	$ 6,777,066
Liabilities				
Bank indebtedness	19	$ 172,262	$ 209,013	$ 270,332
Commercial paper	19	–	127,828	260,386
Accounts payable and accrued liabilities	18	1,109,444	990,244	970,831
Income taxes payable		26,538	–	17,046
Dividends payable	24	53,119	48,927	46,748
Current portion of long-term debt	20	249,971	–	–
Provisions	22	12,024	12,562	11,009
Associate interest		152,880	138,993	130,189
Total current liabilities		1,776,238	1,527,567	1,706,541
Long-term debt	20	695,675	943,412	946,098
Other long-term liabilities	23	520,188	442,124	386,262
Provisions	22	1,701	1,852	1,062
Deferred tax liabilities	14	38,678	26,607	25,219
Total long-term liabilities		1,256,242	1,413,995	1,358,641
Total liabilities		3,032,480	2,941,562	3,065,182
Shareholders' equity				
Share capital	24	1,486,455	1,520,558	1,519,870
Treasury shares	24	(4,735)	–	–
Contributed surplus	26	10,246	11,702	10,274
Accumulated other comprehensive loss	7	(30,214)	(8,643)	(1,125)
Retained earnings		2,806,078	2,579,018	2,182,865
Total shareholders' equity		4,267,830	4,102,635	3,711,884
Total liabilities and shareholders' equity		$ 7,300,310	$ 7,044,197	$ 6,777,066

[1] In preparing its 2010 comparative information, the Company has adjusted amounts reported previously in financial statements prepared in accordance with previous Canadian GAAP. See Note 30 to these consolidated financial statements for an explanation of the transition to IFRS.

The accompanying notes are an integral part of these consolidated financial statements

On behalf of the Board of Directors:

Domenic Pilla
Director

Holger Kluge
Director

Consolidated Statements of Changes in Shareholders' Equity

For the 52 weeks ended December 31, 2011 and January 1, 2011
(in thousands of Canadian dollars)

	Note	Share Capital	Treasury Shares	Contributed Surplus	Accumulated Other Comprehensive Loss (Notes 18 and 21)	Retained Earnings	Total
Balance as at January 1, 2011[1]		$ 1,520,558	$ –	$ 11,702	$ (8,643)	$ 2,579,018	$ 4,102,635
Total comprehensive income		–	–	–	(21,571)	613,934	592,363
Dividends	24	–	–	–	–	(215,671)	(215,671)
Share repurchases	24	(35,576)	(4,735)	–	–	(171,203)	(211,514)
Share-based payments	26	–	–	(1,210)	–	–	(1,210)
Share options exercised	26	1,466	–	(246)	–	–	1,220
Repayment of share-purchase loans		7	–	–	–	–	7
Balance as at December 31, 2011		$ 1,486,455	$ (4,735)	$ 10,246	$ (30,214)	$ 2,806,078	$ 4,267,830
Balance as at January 3, 2010[1]		$ 1,519,870	$ –	$ 10,274	$ (1,125)	$ 2,182,865	$ 3,711,884
Total comprehensive income		–	–	–	(7,518)	591,851	584,333
Dividends	24	–	–	–	–	(195,698)	(195,698)
Share-based payments	26	–	–	1,592	–	–	1,592
Share options exercised	26	655	–	(164)	–	–	491
Repayment of share-purchase loans		33	–	–	–	–	33
Balance as at January 1, 2011[1]		$ 1,520,558	$ –	$ 11,702	$ (8,643)	$ 2,579,018	$ 4,102,635

[1] In preparing its 2010 comparative information, the Company has adjusted amounts reported previously in financial statements prepared in accordance with previous Canadian GAAP. See Note 30 to these consolidated financial statements for an explanation of the transition to IFRS.

The accompanying notes are an integral part of these consolidated financial statements.

Consolidated Statements of Cash Flows

For the 52 weeks ended December 31, 2011 and January 1, 2011
(in thousands of Canadian dollars)

	Note	2011	2010[1]
Cash flows from operating activities			
Net earnings		$ 613,934	$ 591,851
Adjustments for:			
Depreciation and amortization	13, 15, 17	296,464	278,421
Finance expenses	12	64,038	60,633
Loss on sale or disposal of property and equipment, including impairments	15, 17	2,015	3,880
Share-based payment transactions	26	(1,210)	1,592
Recognition and reversal of provisions, net	22	9,218	12,160
Other long-term liabilities	23	296	18,491
Income tax expense	14	232,933	244,838
		1,217,688	1,211,866
Net change in non-cash working capital balances	27	32,166	(34,824)
Provisions used	22	(9,907)	(9,817)
Interest paid		(63,853)	(62,916)
Income taxes paid		(202,256)	(276,108)
Net cash from operating activities		973,838	828,201
Cash flows from investing activities			
Proceeds from disposition of property and equipment and investment property		55,459	60,538
Business acquisitions	8	(10,496)	(11,779)
Deposits		105	1,534
Acquisition or development of property and equipment	15	(341,868)	(415,094)
Acquisition or development of intangible assets	17	(53,836)	(56,625)
Other assets		1,464	(3,249)
Net cash used in investing activities		(349,172)	(424,675)
Cash flows from financing activities			
Repurchase of own shares	24	(206,779)	–
Proceeds from exercise of share options	26	1,220	491
Repayment of share-purchase loans	24	7	33
Repayment of bank indebtedness, net	19	(36,714)	(61,319)
Repayment of commercial paper, net	19	(128,000)	(133,000)
Revolving term debt, net	20	152	(1,298)
Payment of transaction costs for debt refinancing	20	(575)	(2,792)
Repayment of financing lease obligations	23	(2,173)	(1,436)
Associate interest		13,887	9,277
Dividends paid	24	(211,479)	(193,519)
Net cash used in financing activities		(570,454)	(383,563)
Net increase in cash		54,212	19,963
Cash, beginning of the year		64,354	44,391
Cash, end of the year		$ 118,566	$ 64,354

[1] In preparing its 2010 comparative information, the Company has adjusted amounts reported previously in financial statements prepared in accordance with previous Canadian GAAP. See Note 30 to these consolidated financial statements for an explanation of the transition to IFRS.

The accompanying notes are an integral part of these consolidated financial statements.

1. GENERAL INFORMATION

Shoppers Drug Mart Corporation (the "Company") is a public company incorporated and domiciled in Canada, whose shares are publicly traded on the Toronto Stock Exchange. The Company's registered address is 243 Consumers Road, Toronto, Ontario M2J 4W8, Canada.

The Company is a licensor of 1,199 Shoppers Drug Mart®/Pharmaprix® full-service retail drug stores across Canada. The Shoppers Drug Mart®/Pharmaprix® stores are licensed to corporations owned by pharmacists ("Associates"). The Company also licenses or owns 58 Shoppers Simply Pharmacy®/Pharmaprix Simplement Santé® medical clinic pharmacies and eight Murale™ beauty stores. In addition, the Company owns and operates 63 Shoppers Home Health Care® stores. In addition to its store network, the Company owns Shoppers Drug Mart Specialty Health Network Inc., a provider of specialty drug distribution, pharmacy and comprehensive patient support services, and MediSystem Technologies Inc., a provider of pharmaceutical products and services to long-term care facilities in Ontario and Alberta.

The majority of the Company's sales are generated from the Shoppers Drug Mart®/Pharmaprix® full-service retail drug stores and the majority of the Company's assets are used in the operations of these stores. As such, the Company presents one operating segment in its consolidated financial statement disclosures. The revenue generated by Shoppers Drug Mart®/Pharmaprix Simplement Santé®, MediSystem Technologies Inc. and Shoppers Drug Mart Specialty Health Network Inc. is included with prescription sales of the Company's retail drug stores. The revenue generated by Shoppers Home Health Care® and Murale™ is included with the front store sales of the Company's retail drug stores.

These consolidated financial statements of the Company as at and for the financial year ended December 31, 2011 include the accounts of Shoppers Drug Mart Corporation, its subsidiaries, and the Associate-owned stores that comprise the majority of the Company's store network. The financial year of the Company consists of a 52 or 53 week period ending on the Saturday closest to December 31. The current financial year is the 52 weeks ended December 31, 2011. The comparative financial year is the 52 weeks ended January 1, 2011. The Company has also presented the consolidated balance sheet as at January 3, 2010, the Company's date of transition to International Financial Reporting Standards ("IFRS").

2. BASIS OF PREPARATION

(a) Statement of Compliance

These consolidated financial statements have been prepared in accordance with Canadian Generally Accepted Accounting Principles ("Canadian GAAP"). These consolidated financial statements also comply with International Financial Reporting Standards ("IFRS") as issued by the International Accounting Standards Board ("IASB").

These are the Company's first consolidated financial statements prepared in accordance with IFRS. IFRS 1, "First-time Adoption of International Financial Reporting Standards", has been applied in the preparation of these financial statements. Consolidated financial statements of the Company had been prepared under previous Canadian GAAP, which differs in certain respects from IFRS. When preparing the Company's 2011 consolidated financial statements, management has amended certain accounting methods in order to comply with IFRS. The comparative consolidated financial statements reflect the adoption of IFRS.

An explanation of how the transition from previous Canadian GAAP to IFRS has affected the reported financial position, financial performance and cash flows of the Company is provided in Note 30 to these consolidated financial statements.

These consolidated financial statements were authorized for issuance by the Board of Directors of the Company on February 9, 2012.

(b) Use of Estimates and Judgements

The preparation of these consolidated financial statements in conformity with IFRS requires management to make certain judgements, estimates and assumptions that affect the application of accounting policies and the reported amounts of assets and liabilities and disclosure of contingent assets and liabilities at the date of these consolidated financial statements and the reported amounts of revenues and expenses during the reporting period.

Notes to the Consolidated Financial Statements (continued)

December 31, 2011 and January 1, 2011 (in thousands of Canadian dollars, except per share data)

2. BASIS OF PREPARATION (continued)

Judgement is commonly used in determining whether a balance or transaction should be recognized in the consolidated financial statements and estimates and assumptions are more commonly used in determining the measurement of recognized transactions and balances. However, judgement and estimates are often interrelated.

The Company has applied judgement in its assessment of the appropriateness of the consolidation of the Associate-owned stores, classification of items such as leases and financial instruments, the recognition of tax losses and provisions, determining the tax rates used for measuring deferred taxes, determining cash-generating units, identifying the indicators of impairment for property and equipment and intangible assets with finite useful lives, and the level of componentization of property and equipment.

Estimates are used when estimating the useful lives of property and equipment and intangible assets for the purpose of depreciation and amortization, when accounting for or measuring items such as inventory provisions, Shoppers Optimum® loyalty card program deferred revenue, assumptions underlying the actuarial determination of retirement benefit obligations, income and other taxes, provisions, certain fair value measures including those related to the valuation of business combinations, share-based payments and financial instruments and when testing goodwill, indefinite useful life intangible assets and other assets for impairment. Actual results may differ from these estimates.

Estimates and underlying assumptions are reviewed on an ongoing basis. Revisions to accounting estimates are recognized in the period in which the estimates are revised and in any future periods affected.

3. SIGNIFICANT ACCOUNTING POLICIES

The accounting policies set out in these consolidated financial statements have been applied consistently to all periods presented in these consolidated financial statements.

(a) Basis of Consolidation

(i) Subsidiaries

Subsidiaries are entities controlled by the Company. Control exists where the Company has the power to govern the financial and operating policies of an entity so as to obtain benefits from its activities. All of the Company's subsidiaries are wholly-owned. The financial statements of subsidiaries are included in the Company's consolidated financial statements from the date that control commences until the date that control ceases.

(ii) Associate-owned Stores

Associate-owned stores comprise the majority of the Company's store network. The Company does not have any direct or indirect shareholdings in these Associates' corporations. The Associates' corporations remain separate legal entities. The Company consolidates the Associate-owned stores under IAS 27, "Consolidated and Separate Financial Statements" ("IAS 27"). The consolidation of the stores under IAS 27 was determined based on the concept of control under IAS 27 and determined primarily through the agreements with Associates ("Associate Agreements") that govern the relationship between the Company and the Associates.

(iii) Transactions Eliminated on Consolidation

Intra-company balances and transactions and any unrealized earnings and expenses arising from intra-company transactions, including those of the Associate-owned stores, are eliminated in preparing the consolidated financial statements.

(b) Basis of Measurement

These consolidated financial statements have been prepared on the historical cost basis except for certain financial instruments, deferred revenue related to the Shoppers Optimum® loyalty card program and the liabilities for the Company's long-term incentive plan and restricted share unit plan, which are measured at fair value (see Note 26 to these consolidated financial statements for further information on the long-term incentive plan and the restricted share unit plan). Any recognized impairment losses will also impact the historical cost of certain balances.

The methods used to measure fair values are discussed further in Note 4 to these consolidated financial statements.

(c) Revenue

(i) Sale of Goods and Services

Revenue is comprised primarily of retail sales, including prescription sales. Retail sales are recognized as revenue when the goods are sold to the customer. Revenue is net of returns and amounts deferred related to the issuance of points under the Shoppers Optimum® Loyalty Card Program (the "Program"). Where a sales transaction includes points awarded under the Program, revenue allocated to the Program points is deferred based on the fair value of the awards and recognized as revenue when the Program points are redeemed and the Company fulfills its obligations to supply the awards.

Revenue is measured at the fair value of the consideration received or receivable from the customer for products sold or services supplied.

(ii) Shoppers Optimum® Loyalty Card Program

The Shoppers Optimum® Loyalty Card Program allows members to earn points on their purchases in Shoppers Drug Mart®, Pharmaprix®, Shoppers Simply Pharmacy®, Pharmaprix Simplement Santé®, Shoppers Home Health Care® and Murale™ stores at a rate of 10 points for each dollar spent on eligible products and services, plus any applicable bonus points. Members can then redeem points, in accordance with the Program rewards schedule or other offers, for qualifying merchandise at the time of a future purchase transaction.

When points are earned by Program members, the Company defers revenue equal to the fair value of the awards. The Program's deferred revenue is recognized within accounts payable and accrued liabilities in the Company's consolidated balance sheets. When awards are redeemed by Program members, the redemption value of the awards is charged against the deferred revenue balance and recognized as revenue.

The estimated fair value per point is determined based on the expected weighted average redemption levels for future redemptions based on the program reward schedule, including special redemption events. The trends in redemption rates (points redeemed as a percentage of points issued) are reviewed on an ongoing basis and the estimated fair value per point is adjusted based upon expected future activity.

(d) Vendor Rebates

The Company classifies rebates and other consideration received from vendors as a reduction to the cost of inventory. These amounts are recognized in cost of goods sold when the associated inventory is sold. Certain exceptions apply where the consideration received from the vendor is a reimbursement of a selling cost or a payment for services delivered to the vendor, in which case the consideration is reflected in cost of goods sold or operating and administrative expenses dependent on where the related expenses are recorded.

(e) Finance Expenses

Finance expenses are comprised of interest expense on borrowings and the amortization of transaction costs incurred in conjunction with debt transactions. All borrowing costs are recognized in earnings on an accrual basis using the effective interest method, net of amounts capitalized as part of the cost of qualifying property and equipment.

The Company's finance income is not significant.

(f) Borrowing Costs

Borrowing costs that are directly attributable to the acquisition, construction or development of a qualifying asset are recognized as part of the cost of that asset. Qualifying assets are those that require a substantial period of time to prepare for their intended use. All other borrowing costs are recognized as finance expenses in the period in which they are incurred.

The Company capitalizes borrowing costs at the weighted average interest rate on borrowings outstanding for the period. The Company commences capitalization of borrowing costs as part of the cost of a qualifying asset when activities are undertaken to prepare the asset for its intended use and when expenditures, including borrowing costs, are incurred for the asset. Capitalization of borrowing costs ceases when substantially all of the activities necessary to prepare the asset for its intended use are complete.

The Company's financial instruments are classified and measured as follows:

Financial Asset/Liability	Category	Measurement
Cash	Loans and receivables	Amortized cost
Accounts receivable	Loans and receivables	Amortized cost
Deposits[1]	Loans and receivables	Amortized cost
Long-term receivables[2]	Loans and receivables	Amortized cost
Bank indebtedness	Financial liabilities	Amortized cost
Commercial paper	Financial liabilities	Amortized cost
Accounts payable and accrued liabilities	Financial liabilities	Amortized cost
Dividends payable	Financial liabilities	Amortized cost
Long-term debt	Financial liabilities	Amortized cost
Other long-term liabilities	Financial liabilities	Amortized cost

Derivatives	Classification	Measurement
Interest rate derivatives[3]	Effective cash flow hedge	Fair value through other comprehensive income (loss)
Equity forward derivatives[3][4]	Derivative financial instrument	Fair value through earnings
Equity forward derivatives[3][4]	Effective cash flow hedge	Fair value through other comprehensive income (loss)

(1) The carrying value of deposits is recognized within prepaid expenses and deposits in the consolidated balance sheets.

(2) The carrying value of long-term receivables is recognized within other assets in the consolidated balance sheets.

(3) The carrying values of the Company's derivatives are recognized within other assets, accounts payable and accrued liabilities and other long-term liabilities in the consolidated balance sheets.

(4) The portion of the equity forward derivative agreements relating to the earned long-term incentive plan units and earned restricted share unit plan units is considered a derivative financial instrument. The portion of the equity forward derivative agreements relating to the unearned long-term incentive plan units and unearned restricted share unit plan units is considered an effective cash flow hedge. See Note 26 to these consolidated financial statements for further discussion of the long-term incentive plan and the restricted share unit plan.

Financial instruments measured at amortized cost are initially recognized at fair value and then subsequently at amortized cost using the effective interest method, less any impairment losses, with gains and losses recognized in earnings in the period in which the gain or loss occurs. Changes in the fair value of the Company's derivative instruments designated as effective cash flow hedges are recognized in other comprehensive income (loss) and changes in derivative instruments not designated as effective hedges are recognized within operating and administrative expenses in the Company's consolidated statements of earnings in the period of the change.

The Company categorizes its financial assets and financial liabilities that are recognized in the consolidated balance sheets at fair value using the fair value hierarchy. The fair value hierarchy has the following levels:

• Level 1 – quoted market prices in active markets for identical assets or liabilities;

• Level 2 – inputs other than quoted market prices included in Level 1 that are observable for the asset or liability, either directly (as prices) or indirectly (derived from prices); and

• Level 3 – unobservable inputs such as inputs for the asset or liability that are not based on observable market data.

The level in the fair value hierarchy within which the fair value measurement is categorized in its entirety is determined on the basis of the lowest level input that is significant to the fair value measurement in its entirety.

Notes to the Consolidated Financial Statements (continued)
December 31, 2011 and January 1, 2011 (in thousands of Canadian dollars, except per share data)

3. SIGNIFICANT ACCOUNTING POLICIES (continued)

(g) Income Taxes

Income tax expense is comprised of taxes currently payable on earnings and changes in deferred tax balances, excluding those changes related to business acquisitions. Income tax expense is recognized in net earnings except to the extent that it relates to items recognized either in other comprehensive income (loss) or directly in equity, in which case it is recognized in other comprehensive income (loss) or in equity respectively.

Current tax expense is comprised of the tax payable on the taxable income for the current financial year using tax rates enacted or substantively enacted at the reporting date, and any adjustment to income taxes payable in respect of previous years.

Deferred tax is recognized using the balance sheet method in respect of taxable temporary differences arising from differences between the carrying amount of assets and liabilities for tax purposes and their carrying amounts in the financial statements. Deferred tax is calculated at the tax rates that are expected to apply to temporary differences in the year they are expected to reverse and are based on the tax legislation that has been enacted or substantively enacted by the reporting date. Deferred tax is not recognized for the following temporary differences: the initial recognition of goodwill and the initial recognition of assets or liabilities in a transaction that is not a business acquisition and that affects neither accounting nor taxable earnings; and, differences relating to investments in subsidiaries to the extent that it is probable that they will not reverse in the foreseeable future. Deferred tax assets and liabilities are offset if there is a legally enforceable right to offset the recognized amounts and the Company intends to settle on a net basis or to realize the asset and settle the liability simultaneously.

A deferred tax asset is recognized to the extent that it is probable that future taxable earnings will be available against which the temporary difference can be utilized. Deferred tax assets are reviewed at each reporting date and are reduced to the extent that it is no longer probable that all or part of the related tax benefit will be realized.

(h) Earnings per Common Share

The Company presents basic and diluted earnings per share ("EPS") amounts for its common shares. Basic EPS is calculated by dividing the net earnings attributable to common shareholders of the Company by the weighted average number of common shares outstanding during the period. Diluted EPS is determined by dividing the net earnings attributable to common shareholders of the Company by the weighted average number of common shares outstanding after adjusting both amounts for the effects of all potential dilutive common shares, which are comprised of share options granted to employees. Anti-dilutive options are not included in the calculation of diluted EPS.

(i) Financial Instruments

(i) Classification of Financial Instruments

Financial instruments are recognized when the Company becomes a party to the contractual provisions of a financial instrument. Financial instruments are classified into one of the following categories: held for trading, held-to-maturity investments, loans and receivables, available-for-sale financial assets or financial liabilities. The classification determines the accounting treatment of the instrument. The classification is determined by the Company when the financial instrument is initially recorded, based on the underlying purpose of the instrument.

Notes to the Consolidated Financial Statements (continued)
December 31, 2011 and January 1, 2011 (in thousands of Canadian dollars, except per share data)

3. SIGNIFICANT ACCOUNTING POLICIES (continued)

(ii) Transaction Costs

Transaction costs are added to the initial fair value of financial assets and liabilities when those financial assets and liabilities are not measured at fair value subsequent to initial measurement. Transaction costs are amortized to net earnings, within finance expenses, using the effective interest method.

(iii) Derivative Financial Instruments and Hedge Accounting

The Company is exposed to fluctuations in interest rates by virtue of its borrowings under its bank credit facilities, commercial paper program and financing programs available to its Associates. Increases and decreases in interest rates will negatively or positively impact the financial performance of the Company. The Company may use, from time to time, interest rate derivatives to manage this exposure. The earnings or expense arising from the use of these instruments is recognized within finance expenses for the financial year.

The Company uses cash-settled equity forward agreements to limit its exposure to future price changes in the Company's share price for share unit awards under the Company's long-term incentive plan ("LTIP") and restricted share unit plan ("RSU Plan"). The earnings or expense arising from the use of these instruments is included in other comprehensive income (loss) and in operating and administrative expenses, based on the amounts considered to be a hedge or a derivative, respectively, for the financial year. See Note 26 to these consolidated financial statements for further discussion of the LTIP and RSU Plan.

The Company formally identifies, designates and documents all relationships between hedging instruments and hedged items, as well as its risk assessment objective and strategy for undertaking various hedge transactions. The Company assesses, both at the inception of the hedge and on an ongoing basis, including on re-designation, whether the derivatives that are used in hedging transactions are highly effective in offsetting changes in fair values or cash flows of hedged items. When such derivative instruments cease to exist or to be effective as hedges, or when designation of a hedging relationship is terminated, any associated deferred gains or losses are recognized in earnings in the same period as the corresponding gains or losses associated with the hedged item. When a hedged item ceases to exist, any associated deferred gains or losses are recognized in earnings in the period the hedged item ceases to exist.

(iv) Embedded Derivatives

Embedded derivatives (elements of contracts whose cash flows move independently from the host contract) are required to be separated and measured at their respective fair values unless certain criteria are met. The Company does not have any significant embedded features in contractual arrangements that require separate accounting or presentation from the related host contracts.

(v) Share Capital

Common Shares Common shares issued by the Company are recorded in the amount of the proceeds received, net of direct issue costs.

Repurchase of Share Capital The Company, from time to time, will repurchase its common shares under a Normal Course Issuer Bid. When common shares are repurchased, the amount of the consideration paid which includes directly attributable costs and is net of any tax effects, is recognized as a deduction from share capital. Any repurchased common shares are cancelled. The premium paid over the average book value of the common shares repurchased is charged to retained earnings. At the end of a reporting period, if there are shares that have not yet been cancelled, they are recognized as treasury shares at the purchase price of the transaction.

(j) Business Combinations

The Company applies the acquisition method in accounting for business combinations.

On acquisition, the assets, including intangible assets, and any liabilities assumed are measured at their fair value. Purchase price allocations may be preliminary when initially recognized and may change pending finalization of the valuation of the assets acquired. Purchase price allocations are finalized within one year of the acquisition and prior periods are restated to reflect any adjustments to the purchase price allocation made subsequent to the initial recognition.

The determination of fair values, particularly for intangible assets, is based on management's estimates and includes assumptions on the timing and amount of future cash flows. The Company recognizes as goodwill the excess of the purchase price of an acquired business over the fair value of the underlying net assets, including intangible assets, at the date of acquisition. Transaction costs are expensed as incurred. The date of acquisition is the date on which the Company obtains control over the acquired business.

(k) Inventory

Inventory is comprised of merchandise inventory, which includes prescription inventory, and is valued at the lower of cost and estimated net realizable value. Cost is determined on the first-in, first-out basis. Cost includes all direct expenditures and other appropriate costs incurred in bringing inventory to its present location and condition. The Company classifies rebates and other consideration received from a vendor as a reduction to the cost of inventory unless the rebate relates to the reimbursement of a selling cost or a payment for services.

Net realizable value is the estimated selling price in the ordinary course of business, less the estimated selling expenses.

(l) Property and Equipment and Investment Property

(i) Recognition and Measurement

Items of property and equipment are carried at cost less accumulated depreciation and any recognized impairment losses (see (p) Impairment).

Cost includes expenditures that are directly attributable to the acquisition of the asset. The cost of self-constructed assets includes the cost of materials and direct labour, any other costs directly attributable to bringing the assets to a working condition for their intended use, and, where applicable, the costs of dismantling and removing the items and restoring the site on which they are located. Borrowing costs are recognized as part of the cost of an asset, where appropriate.

Purchased software that is integral to the functionality of the related equipment is capitalized as part of that equipment.

When components of property and equipment have different useful lives, they are accounted for as separate items of property and equipment.

Gains and losses on disposal of an item of property and equipment are determined by comparing the proceeds from disposal with the carrying amount of property and equipment and are recognized net, within operating and administrative expenses, in net earnings.

Fully-depreciated items of property and equipment that are still in use continue to be recognized in cost and accumulated depreciation.

(ii) Subsequent Costs

The cost of replacing part of an item of property and equipment is recognized in the carrying amount of the item if it is probable that the future economic benefits embodied within the part will flow to the Company and its cost can be measured reliably. The carrying amount of the replaced part is de-recognized. The costs of repairs and maintenance of property and equipment are recognized in earnings as incurred.

Notes to the Consolidated Financial Statements (continued)
December 31, 2011 and January 1, 2011 (in thousands of Canadian dollars, except per share data)

3. SIGNIFICANT ACCOUNTING POLICIES (continued)

(ii) Depreciation

Depreciation is recognized in earnings on a straight-line basis over the estimated useful lives of each component of an item of property and equipment. Land is not depreciated. The Company commences recognition of depreciation in earnings when the item of property and equipment is ready for its intended use.

The estimated useful lives for the current and comparative periods are as follows:

Buildings and their components	10 to 40 years
Equipment and fixtures	3 to 10 years
Computer equipment	2 to 10 years
Leasehold improvements	Lesser of term of the lease and useful life
Assets under financing leases	Lesser of term of the lease and useful life

Depreciation methods and useful lives are reviewed at each reporting date.

(iv) Investment Property

Investment property is carried at cost less accumulated depreciation and any recognized impairment losses.

(m) Goodwill

(i) Recognition and Measurement

The Company recognizes goodwill as the excess amount of the purchase price of an acquired business over the fair value of the underlying net assets, including intangible assets, at the date of acquisition. Goodwill is not amortized but is tested for impairment on an annual basis or more frequently if there are indicators that goodwill may be impaired (see (p) impairment).

(ii) Acquisitions Prior to January 3, 2010

As described in Note 30 to these consolidated financial statements, as part of its transition to IFRS, the Company elected to apply IFRS 3, "Business Combinations" ("IFRS 3"), only to those business combinations that occurred on or after January 3, 2010. In respect of acquisitions prior to January 3, 2010, goodwill represents the amount recognized under previous Canadian GAAP.

(iii) Subsequent Measurement

Goodwill is measured at cost less any accumulated impairment losses.

(n) Intangible Assets

(i) Computer Software

The Company acquires computer software through purchases from vendors and internal development. Computer software that is an integral part of computer equipment is presented in property and equipment. All other computer software is treated as an intangible asset. The Company includes computer software under development in intangible assets. The assessment of whether computer software is an integral part of computer hardware is made when the software development project is complete and placed into use. Costs for internally developed computer software include directly attributable costs including direct labour and overheads associated with the software development project. Expenditures on research activities as part of internally developed computer software are recognized in earnings when incurred.

(ii) Other Intangible Assets

Other intangible assets that are acquired by the Company, other than as a result of a business acquisition, which have finite useful lives, are measured at cost less accumulated amortization and any accumulated impairment losses (see (p) impairment). Other intangible assets that are acquired by the Company as a result of a business acquisition are measured at their fair values as at the date of acquisition.

(iii) Amortization

Amortization is recognized in earnings on a straight-line basis over the estimated useful lives of intangible assets from the date that they are available for their intended use. The estimated useful lives are as follows:

Prescription files	7 to 12 years
Customer relationships	5 to 25 years
Computer software	3 to 10 years
Other	Term of the lease or 3 years

Computer software under development is not amortized. Amortization methods and useful lives are reviewed at each reporting date.

(o) Leases

The Company leases most of its store locations and office space. Terms vary in length and typically permit renewal for additional periods. Leases for which substantially all the benefits and risks of ownership are transferred to the Company based on certain criteria are recorded as financing leases and classified as property and equipment, accounts payable and accrued liabilities and other long-term liabilities. All other leases are classified as operating leases under which minimum rent, including scheduled escalations, is expensed on a straight-line basis over the term of the lease, including any rent-free periods. Landlord inducements are deferred and amortized as reductions to rent expense on a straight-line basis over the same period.

In the normal course of business, the Company sells certain real estate properties and enters into leaseback arrangements for the area occupied by the Associate-owned stores. The leases are assessed as financing or operating in nature as applicable, and are accounted for accordingly. The gains realized on the disposal of the real estate properties related to sale-leaseback transactions, which are financing in nature, are deferred and amortized on a straight-line basis over the shorter of the lease term and the estimated useful life of the leased asset. The gains realized on the disposal of real estate properties related to sale-leaseback transactions, which are transacted at fair value and are operating in nature, are recognized within operating and administrative expenses in the consolidated statements of earnings. In the event the fair value of the asset at the time of the sale-leaseback transaction is less than its carrying value, the difference would be recognized within operating and administrative expenses in the consolidated statements of earnings.

Leases may include additional payments for real estate taxes, maintenance and insurance. These amounts are expensed in the period to which they relate.

(p) Impairment

(i) Financial Assets

A financial asset is assessed at each reporting date to determine whether there is any objective evidence that it is impaired. A financial asset is considered to be impaired if objective evidence indicates that one or more events, which have a negative effect on the estimated future cash flows of that asset, have occurred.

An impairment loss in respect of a financial asset measured at amortized cost is calculated as the difference between its carrying amount and the present value of the estimated future cash flows, discounted at the original effective interest rate.

Individually significant financial assets are tested for impairment on an individual basis. The remaining financial assets are assessed collectively in groups that share similar credit risk characteristics.

All impairment losses are recognized in the consolidated statements of earnings.

An impairment loss is reversed if the reversal can be objectively related to an event occurring after the impairment loss was recognized. For financial assets measured at amortized cost, the reversal is recognized in earnings.

Notes to the Consolidated Financial Statements (continued)
December 31, 2011 and January 1, 2011 (in thousands of Canadian dollars, except per share data)

3. SIGNIFICANT ACCOUNTING POLICIES (continued)

(ii) Property and Equipment and Intangible Assets with Finite Useful Lives

The carrying amount of property and equipment and intangible assets with finite useful lives is reviewed at each reporting date to determine whether there are any indicators of impairment. If any such indicators exist, then the recoverable amount of the asset is estimated as the higher of the fair value of the asset less costs to sell, or value-in-use. An impairment loss is recognized in net earnings for the amount by which the carrying amount of the asset exceeds its recoverable amount. For the purposes of assessing impairment, when an individual asset does not generate cash flows in and of itself, assets are then grouped and tested at the lowest level for which there are separately identifiable cash flows, called a cash-generating unit. The Company has determined that its cash generating units are primarily its retail stores.

(iii) Goodwill and Intangible Assets with Indefinite Useful Lives

For goodwill and intangible assets that have indefinite useful lives or that are not yet available for use, the carrying value is reviewed for impairment on an annual basis, or more frequently if there are indicators that impairment may exist.

Goodwill is allocated to cash-generating units expected to benefit from the synergies created from a business combination and to the lowest level at which management monitors goodwill. To review for impairment, the recoverable amount of each cash-generating unit to which goodwill is allocated is compared to its carrying value, including goodwill.

(iv) Recoverable Amount

The recoverable amount of an asset or cash-generating unit is the greater of its value-in-use and its fair value less costs to sell. In assessing value-in-use, the estimated future cash flows are discounted to their present value using a pre-tax discount rate that reflects current market assessments of the time value of money and the risks specific to the asset.

(v) Impairment Losses

An impairment loss is recognized if the carrying amount of an asset or its cash-generating unit exceeds its estimated recoverable amount. Impairment losses are recognized in operating and administrative expenses in the consolidated statements of earnings. Impairment losses recognized in respect of cash-generating units and, then, to reduce the carrying amount of any goodwill allocated to the cash-generating units and, then, to reduce the carrying amounts of the other assets in the cash-generating unit (group of cash-generating units) on a pro rata basis.

An impairment loss in respect of goodwill is not reversed. In respect of other assets, impairment losses recognized in prior periods are assessed at each reporting date for any indicators that the loss has decreased or no longer exists. An impairment loss is reversed if there has been a change in the estimates used to determine the recoverable amount. An impairment loss is reversed only to the extent that the carrying amount of the asset does not exceed the carrying amount that would have been determined, net of depreciation or amortization, if no impairment loss had been recognized.

(q) Bank Indebtedness

Bank indebtedness is comprised of corporate bank overdraft balances, corporate and Associate-owned store bank lines of credit and outstanding cheques.

(r) Employee Benefits

(i) Defined Benefit Plans

The Company maintains registered defined benefit pension plans under which benefits are available to certain employee groups. The Company also makes supplementary retirement benefits available to certain employees under a non-registered defined benefit pension plan.

The Company accrues for its defined benefit plans under the following policies:

* The cost of pensions and other retirement benefits earned by employees is actuarially determined using the projected unit credit method (also known as the projected benefit method pro-rated on service) and management's best estimate of expected plan investment performance, salary escalation, retirement ages of employees and their expected future longevity.

* For the purposes of calculating the expected return on plan assets, those assets are valued at fair value.

* The Company recognizes actuarial gains and losses in other comprehensive income (loss) in the period in which those gains and losses occur.

The pension plans are funded through contributions based on actuarial cost methods as permitted by applicable pension regulatory bodies. Benefits under these plans are based on the employees' years of service and final average earnings.

(ii) Defined Contribution Plans

The Company maintains a defined contribution plan for a small number of employees. Required contributions are recognized as an expense when the employees have rendered service.

(iii) Other Long-term Employee Benefits

The Company maintains post-retirement benefit plans, other than pensions, covering benefits such as health and life insurance for certain retirees. The cost of these plans is charged to earnings as benefits are earned by employees on the basis of service rendered.

(s) Share-based Payment Transactions

The grant date fair value of stock options granted to employees is recognized as employee compensation expense, with a corresponding increase in equity, over the period that the employees become unconditionally entitled to the options. Fair value is measured using the Black-Scholes option-pricing model. If the Company can reasonably estimate forfeitures of vested options, the amount expensed is adjusted for estimated forfeitures. For amounts that have been recognized related to options not yet vested that are subsequently forfeited, the amounts recognized as expenses and equity are reversed.

The fair value of the amount payable to employees in respect of cash-settled share-based payments is recognized as an expense, with a corresponding increase in liabilities, over the period that the employees become unconditionally entitled to payment. The fair value of the amount payable is re-measured at each reporting date and at settlement date. Any changes in the fair value of the liability are recognized within operating and administrative expenses in the consolidated statements of earnings.

(t) Provisions

Provisions are recognized when there is a present legal or constructive obligation as a result of a past event, it is probable that an outflow of economic benefits will be required to settle the obligation and that obligation can be measured reliably. If the effect of the time value of money is material, provisions are discounted using a current pre-tax rate that reflects the risks specific to the liability. Provisions are reviewed on a regular basis and adjusted to reflect management's best current estimates. Due to the judgmental nature of these items, future settlements may differ from amounts recognized. Provisions are comprised of estimated insurance claims, litigation settlements and store closing costs.

(i) Insurance Claims

The insurance claim provision is management's best estimate of future payments for current insurance claims that are below the Company's deductible limits and is based on determinations made by an independent insurance adjuster. The timing of utilization of the provision will vary according to the individual claims.

(ii) Litigation Claims

A provision for legal claims is recognized when it is probable that a settlement will be made in respect of a claim.

(iii) Store Closing Costs

The Company records a provision for store closings when it vacates current leased-store locations and relocates.

Notes to the Consolidated Financial Statements (continued)
December 31, 2011 and January 1, 2011 (in thousands of Canadian dollars, except per share data)

3. SIGNIFICANT ACCOUNTING POLICIES (continued)

(u) Associate Interest

Associate interest reflects the investment the Associates have in the net assets of their businesses. Under the terms of the Company's agreements with Associates (the "Associate Agreements"), the Company agrees to purchase the assets that the Associates use in store operations, primarily at the carrying value to the Associate, when Associate Agreements are terminated by either party.

(v) New Standards and Interpretations Not Yet Adopted

A number of new standards, amendments to standards and interpretations have been issued but are not yet effective for the financial year ended December 31, 2011, and accordingly, have not been applied in preparing these consolidated financial statements:

(i) Financial Instruments – Disclosures

The IASB has issued an amendment to IFRS 7, "Financial Instruments: Disclosures" ("IFRS 7 amendment"), requiring incremental disclosures regarding transfers of financial assets. This amendment is effective for annual periods beginning on or after July 1, 2011. The Company will apply the amendment at the beginning of its 2012 financial year and does not expect the implementation to have a significant impact on the Company's disclosures.

(ii) Deferred Taxes – Recovery of Underlying Assets

The IASB has issued an amendment to IAS 12, "Income Taxes" ("IAS 12 amendment"), which introduces an exception to the general measurement requirements of IAS 12 in respect of investment properties measured at fair value. The IAS 12 amendment is effective for annual periods beginning on or after January 1, 2012. The Company will apply the amendment at the beginning of its 2012 financial year and does not expect the implementation to have a significant impact on its results of operations, financial position and disclosures.

(iii) Financial Instruments

The IASB has issued a new standard, IFRS 9, "Financial Instruments" ("IFRS 9"), which will ultimately replace IAS 39, "Financial Instruments: Recognition and Measurement" ("IAS 39"). The replacement of IAS 39 is a multi-phase project with the objective of improving and simplifying the reporting for financial instruments and the issuance of IFRS 9 is part of the first phase of this project. IFRS 9 uses a single approach to determine whether a financial asset or liability is measured at amortized cost or fair value, replacing the multiple rules in IAS 39. For financial assets, the approach in IFRS 9 is based on how an entity manages its financial instruments in the context of its business model and the contractual cash flow characteristics of the financial assets. IFRS 9 requires a single impairment method to be used, replacing multiple impairment methods in IAS 39. For financial liabilities measured at fair value, fair value changes due to changes in an entity's credit risk are presented in other comprehensive income. IFRS 9 is effective for annual periods beginning on or after January 1, 2015 and must be applied retrospectively. The Company is assessing the impact of the new standard on its results of operations, financial position and disclosures.

(iv) Fair Value Measurement

The IASB has issued a new standard, IFRS 13, "Fair Value Measurement" ("IFRS 13"), which provides a standard definition of fair value, sets out a framework for measuring fair value and provides for specific disclosures about fair value measurements. IFRS 13 applies to all International Financial Reporting Standards that require or permit fair value measurements or disclosures. IFRS 13 defines fair value as the price that would be received to sell an asset or paid to transfer a liability in an orderly transaction between market participants at the measurement date. IFRS 13 is effective for annual periods beginning on or after January 1, 2013 and must be applied retrospectively. The Company is assessing the impact of IFRS 13 on its results of operations, financial position and disclosures.

(v) Consolidated Financial Statements

The IASB has issued a new standard, IFRS 10, "Consolidated Financial Statements" ("IFRS 10"), which establishes the principles for the presentation and preparation of consolidated financial statements when an entity controls one or more other entities. IFRS 10 establishes control as the basis for consolidation and defines the principle of control. An investor controls an investee if the investor has power over the investee, exposure or rights to variable returns from its involvement with the investee and the ability to use its power over the investee to affect the amount of the investor's returns. IFRS 10 was issued as part of the IASB's broader project on interests in all types of entities. This project also resulted in the issuance of additional standards as described in (vi) to (ix) below. IFRS 10 is effective for annual periods beginning on or after January 1, 2013 and must be applied retrospectively. The Company is assessing the impact of IFRS 10 on its results of operations, financial position and disclosures.

(vi) Joint Arrangements

The IASB has issued a new standard, IFRS 11, "Joint Arrangements" ("IFRS 11"), which establishes the principles for financial reporting by parties to a joint arrangement. IFRS 11 supersedes IAS 31, "Interests in Joint Ventures" and SIC Interpretation 13, "Jointly Controlled Entities – Non-Monetary Contributions by Venturers". The standard defines a joint arrangement as an arrangement where two or more parties have joint control, with joint control being defined as the contractually agreed sharing of control where decisions about relevant activities require unanimous consent of the parties sharing control. The standard classifies joint arrangements as either joint operations or joint investments and the classification determines the accounting treatment. IFRS 11 is effective for annual periods beginning on or after January 1, 2013 and must be applied retrospectively. The Company is assessing the impact of IFRS 11 on its results of operations, financial position and disclosures.

(vii) Disclosure of Interests in Other Entities

The IASB has issued a new standard, IFRS 12, "Disclosure of Interests in Other Entities" ("IFRS 12"), which integrates and provides consistent disclosure requirements for all interests in other entities such as subsidiaries, joint arrangements, associates and unconsolidated structured entities. IFRS 12 is effective for annual periods beginning on or after January 1, 2013 and must be applied retrospectively. The Company is assessing the impact of IFRS 12 on its disclosures.

(viii) Separate Financial Statements

The IASB has issued a revised standard, IAS 27, "Separate Financial Statements" ("IAS 27"), which contains the accounting and disclosure requirements for investments in subsidiaries, joint ventures and associates when an entity prepares separate (non-consolidated) financial statements. IAS 27 is effective for annual periods beginning on or after January 1, 2013 and must be applied retrospectively. IAS 27 will not have an impact on the Company's consolidated results of operations, financial position and disclosures.

(ix) Investments in Associates and Joint Ventures

The IASB has issued a revised standard, IAS 28, "Investments in Associates and Joint Ventures" ("IAS 28"), which prescribes the accounting for investments in associates and sets out the requirements for the application of the equity method when accounting for investments in associates and joint ventures. IAS 28 is effective for annual periods beginning on or after January 1, 2013 and must be applied retrospectively. The Company is assessing the impact of IAS 28 on its results of operations, financial position and disclosures.

(x) Presentation of Financial Statements – Other Comprehensive Income

The IASB issued an amendment to IAS 1, "Presentation of Financial Statements" (the "IAS 1 amendment") to improve consistency and clarity of the presentation of items of other comprehensive income. A requirement has been added to present items in other comprehensive income grouped on the basis of whether they may be subsequently reclassified to earnings in order to more clearly show the effects the items of other comprehensive income may have on future earnings. The IAS 1 amendment is effective for annual periods beginning on or after July 1, 2012 and must be applied retrospectively. The Company is assessing the impact of the IAS 1 amendment on its presentation of other comprehensive income.

Notes to the Consolidated Financial Statements (continued)
December 31, 2011 and January 1, 2011 (in thousands of Canadian dollars, except per share data)

3. SIGNIFICANT ACCOUNTING POLICIES (continued)

(xi) Post-Employment Benefits

The IASB has issued amendments to IAS 19, "Employee Benefits" ("IAS 19"), which eliminates the option to defer the recognition of actuarial gains and losses through the "corridor" approach, revises the presentation of changes in assets and liabilities arising from defined benefit plans and enhances the disclosures for defined benefit plans. IAS 19 is effective for annual periods beginning on or after January 1, 2013 and must be applied retrospectively. The Company is assessing the impact of IAS 19 on its results of operations, financial position and disclosures.

4. DETERMINATION OF FAIR VALUES

A number of the Company's accounting policies and disclosures require the determination of fair value, for both financial and non-financial assets and liabilities. Fair values have been determined for measurement and/or disclosure purposes based on the following methods. When applicable, further information about the assumptions made in determining the fair values is disclosed in the notes specific to that asset or liability.

(a) Non-derivative Financial Assets

The fair values of cash, accounts receivable and deposits approximate their carrying values due to their short-term maturities. The fair values of long-term receivables approximate their carrying values due to their current market rates. Long-term receivables are recognized within other assets in the consolidated balance sheets.

(b) Property and Equipment Acquired in a Business Combination

The fair values of property and equipment recognized as a result of a business combination are based on the amount for which an item of property and equipment could be exchanged on the date of valuation between knowledgeable, willing parties in an arm's length transaction.

(c) Investment Property

The fair value of investment property is determined by comparison to comparable properties or recent nearby sale transactions as well as a review of recent property tax assessments.

(d) Intangible Assets Acquired in a Business Combination

The fair values of prescription files and customer relationships acquired in a business combination are based on the discounted cash flows that the prescription files and customer relationships, respectively, are expected to generate using an estimated rate of return.

The fair values of other intangible assets acquired in a business combination are based on external valuations, discounted cash flows expected to be derived from the use and eventual sale of these assets, or other methods appropriate to the nature of the assets.

(e) Derivatives

The fair value of the interest rate derivative was valued using the one-month Reuters Canadian Dealer Offered Rate Index as the Company's interest rate derivative agreement had a reset term of one month. The primary valuation input for the determination of the fair values of the equity forward derivatives is the Company's common share price.

(f) Non-derivative Financial Liabilities

The fair values of bank indebtedness, commercial paper, accounts payable and accrued liabilities and dividends payable approximate their carrying values due to their short-term maturities. The fair values of the revolving term facility and other long-term liabilities approximate their carrying values due to the current market rates associated with those instruments. The fair values of medium-term notes are determined by discounting the associated future cash flows using current market rates for items of similar risk.

(g) Share-based Payment Transactions

The grant-date fair values of employee stock options granted to employees are measured using the Black-Scholes option-pricing model (the "model"). Measurement inputs to the model include share price on measurement date, exercise price of the instruments, expected volatility, weighted average expected life of the instruments (based on historical experience and general option holder behaviour), expected dividends and the risk-free interest rate (based on government bonds). The fair value of the amount payable to employees in respect of cash-settled share-based payments is measured based on the Company's common share price.

5. FINANCIAL RISK MANAGEMENT OBJECTIVES AND POLICIES RELATED TO FINANCIAL INSTRUMENTS

Financial Risk Management Objectives and Policies

In the normal course of business, the Company is exposed to financial risks that have the potential to negatively impact its financial performance. The Company may use derivative financial instruments to manage certain of these risks. The Company does not use derivative financial instruments for trading or speculative purposes. These risks are discussed in more detail below.

Interest Rate Risk

Interest rate risk is the risk that fair value or future cash flows associated with the Company's financial assets or liabilities will fluctuate due to changes in market interest rates.

The Company, including its Associate-owned store network, is exposed to fluctuations in interest rates by virtue of its borrowings under its bank credit facilities, commercial paper program and financing programs available to its Associates. Increases or decreases in interest rates will positively or negatively impact the financial performance of the Company.

The Company monitors market conditions and the impact of interest rate fluctuations on its fixed and floating rate debt instruments on an ongoing basis and may use interest rate derivatives to manage this exposure. Until December 2010, the Company used interest rate derivatives to manage a portion of the interest rate risk on its commercial paper. The Company was party to an agreement converting an aggregate notional principal amount of $50,000 of floating rate commercial paper debt into fixed rate debt at a rate of 4.18%, which expired in December 2010. Throughout 2011, the Company no longer had interest rate derivative agreements to convert its floating rate debt into fixed rate debt. See Note 18 to these consolidated financial statements for further discussion of the derivative agreement.

As at December 31, 2011, the Company had $166,592 (2010: $304,410) of unhedged floating rate debt. During the current financial year, the Company's average outstanding unhedged floating rate debt was $386,193 (2010: $538,243). Had interest rates been higher or lower by 50 basis points during the current financial year, net earnings for the financial year would have decreased or increased, respectively, by approximately $1,396 (2010: $1,885) as a result of the Company's exposure to interest rate fluctuations on its unhedged floating rate debt.

Credit Risk

Credit risk is the risk that the Company's counterparties will fail to meet their financial obligations to the Company, causing a financial loss.

Accounts receivable arise primarily in respect of prescription sales billed to governments and third-party drug plans and, as a result, collection risk is low. There is no concentration of balances with debtors in the remaining accounts receivable. The Company does not consider its exposure to credit risk to be material.

Notes to the Consolidated Financial Statements (continued)—
December 31, 2011 and January 1, 2011 (in thousands of Canadian dollars, except per share data)

5. FINANCIAL RISK MANAGEMENT OBJECTIVES AND POLICIES RELATED TO FINANCIAL INSTRUMENTS (continued)

Liquidity Risk

Liquidity risk is the risk that the Company will be unable to meet its obligations relating to its financial liabilities.

The Company prepares cash flow budgets and forecasts to ensure that it has sufficient funds through operations, access to bank facilities and access to debt and capital markets to meet its financial obligations, capital investment program requirements and fund new investment opportunities or other unanticipated requirements as they arise. The Company manages its liquidity risk as it relates to financial liabilities by monitoring its cash flow from operating activities to meet its short-term financial liability obligations and planning for the repayment of its long-term financial liability obligations through cash flow from operating activities and/or the issuance of new debt or equity.

The contractual maturities of the Company's financial liabilities in the consolidated balance sheet as at December 31, 2011 are as follows:

	Carrying Amount	Payments Due in the Next 90 Days	Payments Due Between 90 Days and Less Than a Year	Payments Due Between 1 Year and Less Than 2 Years	Payments Due After 2 Years	Total Contractual Cash Flows
Bank indebtedness	$ 172,262	$ 172,262	$ –	$ –	$ –	$ 172,262
Accounts payable and accrued liabilities	1,055,891	1,032,431	23,460	–	–	1,055,891
Derivatives	915		793	122	–	915
Dividends payable	53,119	53,119	–	–	–	53,119
Medium-term notes	945,494	262,488	28,943	474,202	256,487	1,022,120
Revolving-term debt	152				152	152
Other long-term liabilities	231,970			18,478	213,492	231,970
Total	**$ 2,459,803**	**$ 1,520,300**	**$ 53,196**	**$ 492,802**	**$ 470,131**	**$ 2,536,429**

The contractual maturities of the Company's financial liabilities in the consolidated balance sheet as at January 1, 2011, were as follows:

	Carrying Amount	Payments Due in the Next 90 Days	Payments Due Between 90 Days and Less Than a Year	Payments Due Between 1 Year and Less Than 2 Years	Payments Due After 2 Years	Total Contractual Cash Flows
Bank indebtedness	$ 209,013	$ 209,013	$ –	$ –	$ –	$ 209,013
Commercial paper	127,828	128,000	–	–	–	128,000
Accounts payable and accrued liabilities	930,910	920,384	10,526	–	–	930,910
Derivatives	2,257		674	1,583	–	2,257
Dividends payable	48,927	48,927	–	–	–	48,927
Medium-term notes	946,641	12,488	34,943	291,430	730,690	1,069,551
Other long-term liabilities	167,709		19,207	148,502		167,709
Total	**$ 2,433,285**	**$ 1,318,812**	**$ 46,143**	**$ 312,220**	**$ 879,192**	**$ 2,556,367**

The accounts payable and accrued liabilities and other long-term liabilities amounts exclude certain liabilities that are not considered financial liabilities. The medium-term note amounts, which are recognized within long-term debt in the consolidated balance sheets, include principal and interest liabilities.

6. CAPITAL MANAGEMENT

The Company's primary objectives when managing capital are to profitably grow its business while maintaining adequate financing flexibility to fund attractive new investment opportunities and other unanticipated requirements or opportunities that may arise. Profitable growth is defined as earnings growth commensurate with the additional capital being invested in the business in order that the Company earns an attractive rate of return on that capital. The primary investments undertaken by the Company to drive profitable growth include additions to the selling square footage of its store network via the construction of new, relocated and expanded stores, including related leasehold improvements and fixtures and the purchase of sites as part of a land bank program, as well as the acquisition of independent drug stores or their prescription files. In addition, the Company makes capital investments in information technology and its distribution capabilities to support an expanding store network. The Company also provides working capital to its Associates via loans and/or loan guarantees. The Company largely relies on its cash flow from operations to fund its capital investment program and dividend distributions to its shareholders. This cash flow is supplemented, when necessary, through the borrowing of additional debt. No changes were made to these objectives during the financial years ended December 31, 2011 and January 1, 2011.

The Company considers its total capitalization to be bank indebtedness, commercial paper, long-term debt (including the current portion thereof), financing lease obligations and shareholders' equity, net of cash. The Company also gives consideration to its obligations under operating leases when assessing its total capitalization. The Company manages its capital structure with a view to maintaining investment grade credit ratings from two credit rating agencies. In order to maintain its desired capital structure, the Company may adjust the level of dividends paid to shareholders, issue additional equity, repurchase shares for cancellation or issue or repay indebtedness. The Company has certain debt covenants and was in compliance with those covenants as at December 31, 2011, January 1, 2011 and January 3, 2010.

The Company monitors its capital structure principally through measuring its net debt to shareholders' equity and net debt to total capitalization ratios, and ensures its ability to service its debt and meet other fixed obligations by tracking its financing and other fixed charges coverage ratios.

The following table provides a summary of certain information with respect to the Company's capital structure and financial position at the end of the periods indicated.

	December 31, 2011	January 1, 2011	January 3, 2010
Cash	$ (118,566)	$ (64,354)	$ (44,391)
Bank indebtedness	172,262	209,013	270,332
Commercial paper	–	127,828	260,386
Current portion of long-term debt	249,971	–	–
Long-term debt	695,675	943,412	946,098
Financing lease obligations	120,810	79,031	56,670
Net debt	1,120,152	1,294,930	1,489,095
Shareholders' equity	4,267,830	4,102,635	3,711,884
Total capitalization	$ 5,387,982	$ 5,397,565	$ 5,200,979
Net debt:Shareholders' equity	0.26:1	0.32:1	0.40:1
Net debt:Total capitalization	0.21:1	0.24:1	0.29:1
EBITDA:Cash interest expense[1][2]	18.73:1	18.62:1	19.59:1

[1] For the purposes of calculating the ratios, earnings before interest, taxes, depreciation and amortization ("EBITDA") is comprised of EBITDA for the 52 week periods ended December 31, 2011 and January 1, 2011. The EBITDA for the 52 week period ended January 3, 2010 has not been adjusted for the impact of adopting IFRS. EBITDA is not addressed in IFRS. Such financial measures do not have standardized meanings prescribed by IFRS and therefore may not be comparable to similar measures presented by other reporting issuers.

[2] Cash interest expense is also not addressed in IFRS. Cash interest expense is comprised of finance expense for the 52 week periods ended December 31, 2011 and January 1, 2011. It excludes finance income, finance expenses associated with financing leases and the amortization of deferred financing costs and includes capitalized interest. The cash interest expense for the 52 week period ended January 3, 2010 has not been adjusted for the impact of adopting IFRS.

Funds Held in Escrow

As at January 1, 2011, the Company had amounts held in escrow of $105 with respect to a number of offers to acquire certain pharmacies. These amounts were recognized within the prepaid expenses and deposits balance in the consolidated balance sheets.

9. COST OF GOODS SOLD

During the current financial year, the Company recorded $39,943 (2010: $37,884) as an expense for the write-down of inventory as a result of net realizable value being lower than cost in cost of goods sold in the consolidated statements of earnings.

During the financial years ended December 3:, 2011 and January 1, 2011, the Company did not reverse any significant inventory write-downs recognized in previous years.

10. OPERATING AND ADMINISTRATIVE EXPENSES

During the financial year ended January 1, 2011, the Company recognized an expense of $10,282 in operating and administrative expenses related to the settlement of a long-standing legal dispute related to a commercial arrangement with one of the Company's ancillary businesses.

11. EMPLOYEE BENEFITS EXPENSE

Employee benefits expense, recognized within operating and administrative expenses, is as follows:

	Note	2011	2010
Wages and salaries		$ 1,391,430	$ 1,325,489
Statutory deductions		164,528	155,721
Expense related to pension and benefits	21	6,130	6,059
Share-based payment transactions	26	2,135	12,618
		$ 1,564,223	$ 1,499,887

12. FINANCE EXPENSES

The components of the Company's finance expenses are as follows:

	2011	2010
Finance expense on bank indebtedness	$ 5,907	$ 5,642
Finance expense on commercial paper	1,702	4,269
Finance expense on long-term debt	52,626	50,961
Finance expense on financing leases	6,859	4,757
	67,094	65,629
Finance expense capitalized	(3,056)	(4,996)
	$ 64,038	$ 60,633

The amount of finance expense capitalized is based on the Company's weighted average cost of borrowing and is attributed to those items of property and equipment which meet the definition of a qualifying asset. A qualifying asset is defined as an asset that requires a substantial period of time to get ready for its intended use or sale.

Notes to the Consolidated Financial Statements (continued)
December 31, 2011 and January 1, 2011 (in thousands of Canadian dollars, except per share data)

6. CAPITAL MANAGEMENT (continued)

As measured by the ratios set out above, the Company maintained its desired capital structure and financial position during the financial year.

The following table provides a summary of the Company's credit ratings at December 31, 2011:

	Standard & Poor's	DBRS Limited
Corporate credit rating	BBB+	A (low)
Senior unsecured debt	BBB+	–
Commercial paper	–	R-1 (low)

There were no changes to the Company's credit ratings during the financial years ended December 31, 2011 and January 1, 2011.

On April 8, 2010, DBRS Limited placed the short and long-term ratings of the Company under review with negative implications. The rating action was in response to the Ontario Ministry of Health and Long-Term Care's April 7, 2010 announcement with respect to further drug reform in the province. On July 30, 2010, DBRS Limited confirmed the short and long-term ratings of the Company and changed the ratings trend from under review with negative implications to stable.

7. ACCUMULATED OTHER COMPREHENSIVE LOSS

	December 31, 2011	January 1, 2011	January 3, 2010
Unrealized loss on the interest rate derivative (net of tax of $nil, $nil and $525, respectively)	$ –	$ –	$ (1,120)
Unrealized loss on equity forward derivatives (net of tax of $44, $195 and $2, respectively)	(121)	(493)	(5)
Actuarial losses on retirement benefit obligations (net of tax of $10,338, $2,905 and $nil, respectively)	(30,093)	(8,150)	–
Accumulated other comprehensive loss	$ (30,214)	$ (8,643)	$ (1,125)

During the current financial year, amounts previously recorded in accumulated other comprehensive loss related to the equity forward derivatives of $411 (2010: $33) were recognized in net earnings in the consolidated statements of earnings.

8. BUSINESS ACQUISITIONS

In the normal course of business, the Company acquires the assets or shares of pharmacies. The total cost of these acquisitions during the financial year ended December 31, 2011 of $10,496 (2010: $11,779) was allocated primarily to goodwill and other intangible assets based on their fair values. The goodwill acquired represents the benefits the Company expects to receive from the acquisitions. See Note 16 to these consolidated financial statements for further details on goodwill. The Company expects $814 (2010: $8,258) of acquired goodwill will be deductible for tax purposes.

The values of assets acquired and liabilities assumed have been valued at the acquisition date using fair values. See Note 4 to these consolidated financial statements for the methods used in determining fair values, except as shown below. The intangible assets acquired are composed of prescription files. In determining the fair value of prescription files acquired, the Company applied a pre-tax discount rate of 9 percent (2010: 8 percent) to the estimated expected future cash flows.

The Company did not incur any acquisition related costs for acquisitions during the financial year end December 31, 2011 (2010: $38 relating primarily to legal fees). Acquisition-related costs were recognized within operating and administrative expenses in the Company's consolidated statement of earnings for the financial year ended January 1, 2011.

The operations of the acquired pharmacies have been included in the Company's results of operations from the date of acquisition.

Notes to the Consolidated Financial Statements (continued)

December 31, 2011 and January 1, 2011 (in thousands of Canadian dollars, except per share data)

13. DEPRECIATION AND AMORTIZATION EXPENSE

The components of the Company's depreciation and amortization expense, recognized within operating and administrative expenses, are as follows:

	Note	2011	2010
Property and equipment	15	$ 250,965	$ 238,008
Investment property	15	325	420
Intangible assets	17	46,392	43,077
		$ 297,682	$ 281,505

These amounts include net gains and losses on the disposition of property and equipment and intangible assets and any impairment losses recognized by the Company. During the financial year ended December 31, 2011, the Company recognized a net loss of $1,498 (2010: a net gain of $6,818) on the disposal of property and equipment and a net loss of $24 (2010: $9) on the disposition of intangible assets. During the financial year ended December 31, 2011, the Company did not recognize any impairment losses on property and equipment. During the financial year ended January 1, 2011, the Company recognized an impairment loss on store assets in property and equipment of $10,338. During the financial years ended December 31, 2011 and January 1, 2011, the Company did not recognize any impairment losses on intangible assets.

14. INCOME TAX EXPENSE AND DEFERRED TAX ASSETS AND LIABILITIES

	2011	2010
Current income tax expense		
Current period	$ 201,905	$ 239,379
Adjustment for prior periods	6,791	(600)
	208,696	238,779
Deferred income tax expense		
Origination and reversal of temporary differences	26,843	3,303
Reduction in tax rate	1,834	1,969
Adjustment for prior periods	(4,440)	787
	24,237	6,059
Total income tax expense	$ 232,933	$ 244,838

The effective income tax rate is comprised of the following:

	2011	2010
Net earnings for the financial year	$ 613,934	$ 591,851
Total income tax expense	232,933	244,838
Earnings before income tax expense	$ 846,867	$ 836,689
Income tax using the Combined Canadian federal and provincial statutory tax rate	$ 229,738 27.13%	$ 240,992 28.80%
Reduction in tax rate	1,834 0.22%	1,969 0.24%
Non-deductible expenses	(990) (0.12%)	1,690 0.20%
Adjustments for prior periods	2,351 0.28%	187 0.02%
Effective income tax rate	$ 232,933 27.51%	$ 244,838 29.26%

The effective income tax rate for the financial year ended December 31, 2011 declined from the prior financial year due to reductions in statutory income tax rates.

Movement in Deferred Tax Assets (Liabilities) Related to Temporary Differences during the Financial Year

	Balance, January 1, 2011	Recognized in Earnings	Recognized in Equity	Acquired in Business Combinations (Note 8)	Balance, December 31, 2011
Deferred revenue	$ 6,746	$ (26,840)	$ —	$ —	$ (20,094)
Deferred rent obligations	33,585	1,489	(151)	—	35,074
Derivatives	195	—	—	—	44
Property and equipment and investment property	(59,710)	5,241	—	—	(54,469)
Goodwill and intangible assets	(19,968)	1,122	—	(305)	(19,151)
Retirement benefit obligations	3,876	(1,566)	7,433	—	9,743
Provisions	12,822	(572)	—	—	12,250
Non-capital loss carryforwards	17,645	(5,691)	—	—	11,954
Capital loss carryforwards	5,151	192	—	—	5,343
Other items	(685)	2,388	—	—	1,703
Deferred tax assets (liabilities)	$ (343)	$ (24,237)	$ 7,282	$ (305)	$ (17,603)

	Balance, January 3, 2010	Recognized in Earnings	Recognized in Equity	Acquired in Business Combinations (Note 8)	Balance, January 1, 2011
Deferred revenue	$ 5,346	$ 1,400	$ —	$ —	$ 6,746
Deferred rent obligations	30,859	2,726	—	—	33,585
Derivatives	527	—	(332)	—	195
Property and equipment and investment property	(50,450)	(9,260)	—	—	(59,710)
Goodwill and intangible assets	(21,562)	1,688	—	(94)	(19,968)
Retirement benefit obligations	3,070	(2,099)	2,905	—	3,876
Provisions	11,156	1,666	—	—	12,822
Non-capital loss carryforwards	19,784	(2,139)	—	—	17,645
Capital loss carryforwards	5,215	(64)	—	—	5,151
Other items	(708)	23	—	—	(685)
Deferred tax assets (liabilities)	$ 3,237	$ (6,059)	$ 2,573	$ (94)	$ (343)

Deferred tax assets are recognized for non-capital loss carryforwards to the extent that the realization of the related tax benefit through future profits is probable and for capital loss carryforwards to the extent that the Company can realize capital gains on the sale of assets.

Notes to the Consolidated Financial Statements (continued)
December 31, 2011 and January 1, 2011 (in thousands of Canadian dollars, except per share data)

15. PROPERTY AND EQUIPMENT AND INVESTMENT PROPERTY

	Properties Under Development	Land	Buildings	Equipment, Fixtures and Computer Equipment	Leasehold Improvements	Assets Under Financing Leases (Note 23)	Total
Cost							
Balance at January 1, 2011	$72,035	$70,411	$206,472	$1,135,805	$1,179,795	$83,082	$2,747,600
Additions:							
– Asset acquisitions	9,979	—	—	—	—	43,952	53,931
– Development	9,990	3,688	25,738	168,204	131,667	—	339,287
Transfers	(20,662)	6,147	8,791	752	320	—	(4,652)
Computer software transfers from intangible assets	—	—	—	1,330	—	—	1,330
Disposals	—	(14,768)	(26,958)	(23,563)	(20,337)	—	(85,626)
Retirements	—	—	—	534	—	—	534
Balance at December 31, 2011	$71,342	$65,478	$214,043	$1,283,062	$1,291,445	$127,034	$3,052,404
Depreciation							
Balance at January 1, 2011	—	—	$16,102	$655,467	$355,523	$11,446	$1,038,538
Depreciation for the financial year	—	—	11,542	140,537	92,423	4,965	249,467
Transfers	—	—	(216)	375	(123)	—	36
Computer software transfers from intangible assets	—	—	—	(18)	—	—	(18)
Disposals	—	—	(3,103)	(19,792)	(11,807)	—	(34,702)
Retirements	—	—	—	(182)	—	—	(182)
Balance at December 31, 2011	$—	$—	$24,325	$776,387	$436,016	$16,411	$1,253,139
Impairment losses							
Balance at January 1, 2011	—	—	—	$16,257	$15,465	—	$31,722
Impairment loss	—	—	—	—	—	—	—
Balance at December 31, 2011	$—	$—	$—	$16,257	$15,465	$—	$31,722
Net book value							
At December 31, 2011	$71,342	$65,478	$189,718	$490,418	$839,964	$110,623	$1,767,543

	Properties Under Development	Land	Buildings	Equipment, Fixtures and Computer Equipment	Leasehold Improvements	Assets Under Financing Leases (Note 23)	Total
Cost							
Balance at January 3, 2010	$113,478	$57,683	$144,515	$1,048,056	$1,022,868	$59,382	$2,445,982
Additions:							
– Asset acquisitions	11,139	531	695	—	—	23,700	36,065
– Development	94,745	327	5,206	135,454	166,986	—	402,718
Transfers	(143,302)	27,880	97,365	(1,223)	11,943	—	(7,337)
Computer software transfers from intangible assets	—	—	—	1,395	—	—	1,395
Disposals	(4,025)	(16,010)	(41,309)	(45,515)	(22,002)	—	(128,861)
Retirements	—	—	—	(2,362)	—	—	(2,362)
Balance at January 1, 2011	$72,035	$70,411	$206,472	$1,135,805	$1,179,795	$83,082	$2,747,600
Depreciation							
Balance at January 3, 2010	—	—	$24,412	$561,691	$288,519	$8,135	$882,757
Depreciation for the financial year	—	—	8,759	136,933	85,487	3,311	234,490
Transfers	—	—	732	(439)	(293)	—	—
Disposals	—	—	(17,801)	(41,255)	(18,190)	—	(77,246)
Retirements	—	—	—	(1,463)	—	—	(1,463)
Balance at January 1, 2011	$—	$—	$16,102	$655,467	$355,523	$11,446	$1,038,538
Impairment losses							
Balance at January 3, 2010	—	—	—	$10,502	$10,882	—	$21,384
Impairment loss	—	—	—	5,755	4,583	—	10,338
Balance at January 1, 2011	$—	$—	$—	$16,257	$15,465	$—	$31,722
Net book value							
At January 1, 2011	$72,035	$70,411	$190,370	$464,081	$808,807	$71,636	$1,677,340
At January 3, 2010	$113,478	$57,683	$120,103	$475,863	$723,467	$51,247	$1,541,841

During the financial year ended December 31, 2011, the Company recognized depreciation expense of $249,467 (2010: $234,490), an impairment loss on store assets of $nil (2010: $10,338) and a loss on disposal of property and equipment of $1,498 (2010: a net gain of $6,818) within operating and administrative expenses in the consolidated statements of earnings.

Impairment Loss

During the financial year ended December 31, 2011, the Company reviewed its long-lived assets for indicators of impairment at the cash-generating unit level and determined that an impairment test was not necessary.

During the financial year ended January 1, 2011, the Company reviewed its long-lived assets for indicators of impairment at the cash-generating unit level and determined that a test for impairment was necessary on certain of its store assets. This resulted in the identification of an impairment charge of $7,554, which is net of taxes of $2,784. The impaired assets consist primarily of equipment, fixtures, computer equipment and leasehold improvements at certain of the Company's newer stores. The recoverable amount of the impaired assets was determined through a value-in-use methodology using a pre-tax discount rate of 8 percent.

During the financial years ended December 31, 2011 and January 1, 2011, the Company did not record any reversals of previously recorded impairment charges.

Property under Development

During the financial year ended December 31, 2011, the Company acquired properties with the intention of developing retail stores on the sites. The cost of acquisition was $9,979 (2010: $11,139).

Notes to the Consolidated Financial Statements (continued)
December 31, 2011 and January 1, 2011 (in thousands of Canadian dollars, except per share data)

15. PROPERTY AND EQUIPMENT AND INVESTMENT PROPERTY (continued)

Investment Property

	2011			2010		
	Land	Building	Total	Land	Building	Total
Cost						
Balance, beginning of financial year	$ 8,084	$ 5,995	$ 14,079	$ 3,729	$ 3,044	$ 6,773
Transfers	4,325	327	4,652	4,386	2,951	7,337
Disposals	(723)	(2)	(725)	(31)	–	(31)
Balance, end of financial year	$ 11,686	$ 6,320	$ 18,006	$ 8,084	$ 5,995	$ 14,079
Amortization						
Balance, beginning of financial year	$ –	$ 1,309	$ 1,309	$ –	$ 889	$ 889
Amortization for the financial year	–	325	325	–	420	420
Transfers	–	–	–	–	–	–
Balance, end of financial year	$ –	$ 1,634	$ 1,634	$ –	$ 1,309	$ 1,309
Net book value			$ 16,372			$ 12,770
Net book value at January 3, 2010						$ 5,884

The fair value of investment property approximates its carrying value.

16. GOODWILL

	Note	2011	2010
Cost			
Balance, beginning of the financial year		$ 2,493,108	$ 2,483,430
Additions			
– business acquisitions	8	10,496	11,779
Transfers		(3,882)	(2,101)
Balance, end of the financial year		$ 2,499,722	$ 2,493,108

During the financial year ended December 31, 2011, the Company transferred $3,882 (2010: $2,101) from goodwill related to business acquisitions transacted during the financial year to prescription files, which are recognized within intangible assets, net of deferred taxes.

Impairment Testing of Goodwill

For the purpose of impairment testing, goodwill is allocated to the group of cash-generating units which represent the lowest level within the group at which the goodwill is monitored for internal management purposes.

The aggregate carrying amounts of goodwill allocated to each unit are as follows:

	December 31, 2011	January 1, 2011	January 3, 2010
Goodwill allocated to the store network	$ 2,474,540	$ 2,467,926	$ 2,458,248
Goodwill allocated to Shoppers Home Health Care®	25,182	25,182	25,182
	$ 2,499,722	$ 2,493,108	$ 2,483,430

During the financial years ended December 31, 2011 and January 1, 2011, the Company performed impairment testing of goodwill in accordance with the Company's accounting policy. No impairment was identified.

The Company uses the value-in-use method for determining the recoverable amount of the group of cash-generating units to which goodwill is allocated. The values assigned to the key assumptions represent management's assessment of future trends in the retail and drug industry and are based on both external sources and internal sources (historical data). Key assumptions include comparable store sales growth, gross margin rates, changes in employee wages and benefits, occupancy cost changes and other operating expense changes. The Company has projected cash flows based on the most recent three-year budgets and forecasts. For the purposes of the impairment test, the Company has adjusted budgets and forecasts to reflect a zero growth assumption at the time the test was performed. Years four and five of the projection continue to reflect a zero growth rate and terminal value growth of two percent after the fifth year is used for the present value calculation.

The Company has used a pre-tax discount rate of 9 percent (2010 – 8 percent), which is based on the Company's weighted average cost of capital with appropriate adjustments for the risks associated with the group of cash-generating units to which goodwill is allocated and market data from a comparable industry grouping. Cash flow projections are discounted over a five-year period.

The above estimates are particularly sensitive in the following areas:

* An increase in one percentage point in the discount rate used would have decreased the excess of fair value over the carrying value of goodwill by approximately $1,600 (2010: $1,300).

* A 10 percent decrease in future planned revenues would have decreased the excess of fair value over the carrying value of goodwill by approximately $1,200 (2010: $900).

17. INTANGIBLE ASSETS

	Note	Prescription Files	Customer Relationships	Computer Software	Computer Software Under Development	Other	Total
Cost							
Balance at January 1, 2011		$ 129,803	$ 43,600	$ 211,162	$ 52,412	$ 8,824	$ 445,801
Additions							
– purchases		–	7,136	1,381	–	696	9,213
– development		–	–	–	44,624	–	44,624
– business acquisitions	8,15	4,184	–	–	–	–	4,184
Transfers	16	–	–	74,260	(75,337)	(253)	(1,330)
Disposals		–	–	–	–	(24)	(24)
Balance at December 31, 2011		$ 133,987	$ 50,736	$ 286,803	$ 21,675	$ 9,267	$ 502,468
Amortization							
Balance at January 1, 2011		$ 49,675	$ 9,959	$ 108,463	$ –	$ 5,487	$ 173,584
Amortization for the financial year		14,697	3,732	27,932	–	804	47,165
Transfers		–	11	–	–	(29)	(18)
Balance at December 31, 2011		$ 64,372	$ 13,691	$ 136,406	$ –	$ 6,262	$ 220,731
Net book value							
At December 31, 2011		$ 69,615	$ 37,045	$ 150,397	$ 21,675	$ 3,005	$ 281,737

Notes to the Consolidated Financial Statements (continued)
December 31, 2011 and January 1, 2011 (in thousands of Canadian dollars, except per share data)

17. INTANGIBLE ASSETS (continued)

	Note	Prescription Files	Customer Relationships	Computer Software	Computer Software Under Development	Other	Total
Cost							
Balance at January 3, 2010		$ 127,701	$ 43,600	$ 170,285	$ 39,639	$ 7,274	$ 388,499
Additions							
– purchases		–	–	10,963	–	–	10,963
– development		–	–	44,112	–	1,550	45,662
– business acquisitions	8,15	1,577	–	–	–	–	1,577
Transfers	15,16	525	–	29,944	(31,339)	–	(870)
Disposals		–	–	(30)	–	–	(30)
Balance at January 1, 2011		$ 129,803	$ 43,600	$ 211,162	$ 52,412	$ 8,824	$ 445,801
Amortization							
Balance at January 3, 2010		$ 34,288	$ 6,448	$ 84,639	$ –	$ 4,358	$ 129,733
Amortization for the financial year		15,387	3,511	23,845	–	1,129	43,872
Disposals		–	–	(21)	–	–	(21)
Balance at January 1, 2011		$ 49,675	$ 9,959	$ 108,463	$ –	$ 5,487	$ 173,584
Net book value							
At January 1, 2011		$ 80,128	$ 33,641	$ 102,699	$ 52,412	$ 3,337	$ 272,217
At January 3, 2010		$ 93,413	$ 37,152	$ 85,646	$ 39,639	$ 2,916	$ 258,766

During the financial year ended December 31, 2011, the Company recognized amortization expense of $46,368 (2010: $43,068), operating expense of $797 (2010: $804) and a pre-tax loss on disposal of intangible assets of $24 (2010: $9) within operating and administrative expenses in the consolidated statements of earnings.

Impairment Loss

During the financial years ended December 31, 2011 and January 1, 2011, the Company reviewed its definite life intangible assets for indicators of impairment at the cash-generating unit level and determined that an impairment test was not necessary. An impairment loss and any subsequent reversals, if any, are recognized within operating and administrative expenses in the consolidated statements of earnings.

18. FINANCIAL INSTRUMENTS

See Note 5 to these consolidated financial statements for a discussion of the Company's exposure to risks from its use of financial instruments.

Interest Rate Derivatives

Until December 2010, the Company used interest rate derivatives to manage a portion of the interest rate risk on its commercial paper. The Company was party to an agreement converting an aggregate notional principal amount of $50,000 of floating rate commercial paper debt into fixed rate debt at a rate of 4.18%, which expired in December 2010. The Company recorded a net loss of $3,766 over the life of the agreement that expired in 2010 as finance expense on commercial paper. As at January 1, 2011, the Company no longer had any interest rate derivative agreements to convert its floating rate debt into fixed rate debt and the Company did not enter into any new interest rate derivative agreements during the financial year ended December 31, 2011.

Based on the market value of the interest rate derivative agreement at January 3, 2010, the Company recognized a liability of $1,645, all of which was presented in accounts payable and accrued liabilities. During the financial year ended January 1, 2011, the Company assessed that the interest rate derivative was an effective hedge for the floating interest rates on the associated commercial paper debt.

Equity Forward Derivatives

The Company uses cash-settled equity forward agreements to limit its exposure to future price changes in the Company's share price for share unit awards under the Company's LTIP and RSU Plan. The earnings or expense arising from the use of these instruments is recognized within operating and administrative expenses on the consolidated statements of earnings for the financial year.

Based on the market values of the equity forward agreements at December 31, 2011, the Company recognized a liability of $916 (2010: $2,257), of which $794 (2010: $674) is presented in accounts payable and accrued liabilities and $122 (2010: $1,583) is presented in other long-term liabilities. Based on the market values of the equity forward agreements at January 3, 2010, the Company recognized a net liability of $910, of which $286 was presented in other assets and $1,196 was presented in accounts payable and accrued liabilities. During the financial years ended December 31, 2011 and January 1, 2011, the Company assessed that the percentages of the equity forward derivatives in place related to unearned units under the LTIP and RSU Plan were effective hedges for its exposure to future changes in the market price of its common shares in respect of the unearned units.

Fair Value of Financial Instruments

The fair value of financial assets and financial liabilities measured at fair value in the consolidated balance sheet as at December 31, 2011 is as follows:

	Level 1	Level 2	Level 3	Total
Equity forward derivatives	$ –	$ (916)	$ –	$ (916)
Total	$ –	$ (916)	$ –	$ (916)

The fair value of financial assets and financial liabilities measured at fair value in the consolidated balance sheet at January 1, 2011 is as follows:

	Level 1	Level 2	Level 3	Total
Equity forward derivatives	$ –	$ (2,257)	$ –	$ (2,257)
Total	$ –	$ (2,257)	$ –	$ (2,257)

The fair value of financial assets and financial liabilities measured at fair value in the consolidated balance sheet at January 3, 2010 is as follows:

	Level 1	Level 2	Level 3	Total
Interest rate derivative	$ –	$ (1,645)	$ –	$ (1,645)
Equity forward derivatives	$ –	$ (910)	$ –	$ (910)
Total	$ –	$ (2,555)	$ –	$ (2,555)

The fair values of the interest rate derivative and equity forward derivatives are determined based on current market rates and on information received from the Company's counterparties to the agreements. The interest rate derivative was valued using the one-month Reuters Canadian Dealer Offered Rate Index. The primary valuation input for the equity forward derivatives is the Company's common share price.

For financial assets and liabilities that are valued at other than fair value on the consolidated balance sheets: cash, accounts receivable, deposits, bank indebtedness, commercial paper, accounts payable and accrued liabilities and dividends payable, fair values approximate their carrying values at December 31, 2011, January 1, 2011 and January 3, 2010 due to their short-term maturities. The fair values of long-term receivables, revolving term facility and other long-term liabilities approximate their carrying values at December 31, 2011, January 1, 2011, and January 3, 2010 due to the current market rates associated with these instruments. The fair value of the medium-term notes at December 31, 2011 was approximately $984,442 (2010: $997,345, 2009: $1,007,522) compared to a carrying value of $950,000 (2010 and 2009: $950,000) (excluding transaction costs) due to decreases in market interest rates for similar instruments.

Notes to the Consolidated Financial Statements (continued)
December 31, 2011 and January 1, 2011 (in thousands of Canadian dollars, except per share data)

19. BANK INDEBTEDNESS AND COMMERCIAL PAPER

Bank Indebtedness

The Associate-owned stores borrow under their bank line of credit agreements guaranteed by the Company. The Company has entered into agreements with banks to guarantee a total of $520,000 (2010 and 2009: $520,000) of lines of credit. At December 31, 2011, the Associate-owned stores utilized $166,592 (2010: $176,410, 2009: $254,332) of the available lines of credit.

Commercial Paper

Commercial paper is issued with maturities from overnight to 90 days at floating interest rates based on bankers' acceptance rates. Until December 2010, the Company used interest rate derivative agreements to manage a portion of the interest rate risk on its commercial paper. The Company was party to an agreement converting an aggregate notional principal amount of $50,000 of floating rate commercial paper debt into fixed rate debt at a rate of 4.18%, which expired in December 2010. The Company recorded a net loss of $3,766 over the life of the agreement that expired in 2010 as finance expense on commercial paper in the consolidated statement of earnings. As at January 1, 2011, the Company no longer had any interest rate derivative agreements to convert its floating rate debt into fixed rate debt. During the financial year ended December 31, 2011, the Company did not enter into any interest rate derivative agreements to convert its floating rate debt into fixed rate debt. See Notes 5 and 18 to these consolidated financial statements for further discussion of the derivative agreement.

20. LONG-TERM DEBT

	Face Value as at December 31, 2011	Maturity	December 31, 2011	January 1, 2011	January 3, 2010
Medium-term notes					
Series 2 Notes – 4.99%	$ 450,000	June 2013	$ 449,298	$ 448,704	$ 447,977
Series 3 Notes – 4.80%	250,000	January 2012	249,971	249,305	248,640
Series 4 Notes – 5.19%	250,000	January 2014	249,081	248,632	248,183
			948,350	946,641	944,800
Less: current portion of long-term debt			(249,971)		
			698,379	946,641	944,800
Revolving term facility	$ 725,000	December 2015	152		1,298
Less: financing costs			(2,856)	(3,229)	
			(2,704)	(3,229)	1,298
Total long-term debt			$ 695,675	$ 943,412	$ 946,098

As at December 31, 2011, $9,598 (2010: $137,053) of the $725,000 (2010: $750,000) revolving term facility was utilized as follows: drawings on the revolving term facility $152 (2010: $nil), $9,446 (2010: $9,053) relating to letters of credit and trade finance guarantees and $nil (2010: $128,000) relating to commercial paper issued by the Company. As at January 3, 2010, the revolving term facility was $800,000 and was utilized as follows: $8,322 related to letters of credit and trade finance guarantees and $261,000 relating to commercial paper issued by the Company.

2011 Debt Refinancing Transactions

On October 27, 2011, the Company amended its previously existing $750,000 revolving term credit facility that was to mature on December 10, 2014. The credit facility was amended to reduce the size of the credit facility to $725,000, to extend the maturity date by one year to December 10, 2015, reduce the applicable stamping fee on bankers' acceptance borrowings from 150 basis points per annum to 100 basis points per annum and reduce the applicable commitment fee rate on undrawn amounts to 20 basis points per annum from 37.5 basis points per annum. The consolidated net debt position of the Company remained substantially unchanged as a result of this refinancing. The new credit facility is available for general corporate purposes, including backstopping the Company's $500,000 commercial paper program. The Company recognized financing costs related to the credit facility of $575, the unamortized portion of which was netted against the long-term debt balance on the consolidated balance sheets.

2010 Debt Refinancing Transactions

On December 10, 2010, the Company entered into a $750,000 revolving term credit facility. This credit facility, which was to mature on December 10, 2014, replaced the Company's previously existing $800,000 revolving term credit facility that was to mature on June 6, 2011. The credit facility, as was the case with the credit facility it replaced, was available for general corporate purposes, including backstopping the Company's $500,000 commercial paper program. The Company recognized financing costs related to the credit facility of $3,281, the unamortized portion of which was netted against the long-term debt balance on the consolidated balance sheets.

Minimum Repayments

Future minimum required repayments of long-term debt are as follows:

Medium-term notes	
2012 – Series 3	$ 250,000
2013 – Series 2	450,000
2014 – Series 4	250,000
	$ 950,000

See Note 31 Subsequent Events for additional discussion of long-term debt transactions.

21. RETIREMENT BENEFIT OBLIGATIONS

	Note	December 31, 2011	January 1, 2011	January 3, 2010
Present value of defined benefit obligation for unfunded plans		$ (6,380)	$ (5,750)	$ (5,172)
Present value of defined benefit obligation for partially funded plans		(140,340)	(110,774)	(90,138)
Total present value of defined benefit obligations		(146,720)	(116,524)	(95,310)
Fair value of plan assets		108,616	106,040	85,199
Defined benefit liability included in other long-term liabilities	23	$ (38,104)	$ (10,484)	$ (10,111)

Information about the Company's pension and other post-retirement benefit plans is as follows:

	2011		2010	
	Pension Plans	Other Benefit Plans	Pension Plans	Other Benefit Plans
Fair value of plan assets				
Fair value of plan assets, beginning of the financial year	$ 106,040	$ –	$ 85,199	$ –
Expected return on plan assets	6,718	–	5,659	–
Actuarial gains/(losses)	(7,588)	–	2,161	–
Company contributions	7,262	625	16,230	510
Plan participants' contributions	1,292	–	1,237	–
Benefits paid	(5,108)	(625)	(4,446)	(510)
Fair value of plan assets, end of the financial year	$ 108,616	$ –	$ 106,040	$ –
Present value of the defined benefit obligation				
Defined benefit obligation, beginning of the financial year	$ 110,774	$ 5,750	$ 90,138	$ 5,172
Current service cost	6,200	306	5,936	287
Interest cost	6,044	298	5,200	295
Plan participants' contributions	1,292	–	1,237	–
Actuarial losses	21,138	651	12,709	506
Benefits paid	(5,108)	(625)	(4,446)	(510)
Present value of the defined benefit obligations, end of the financial year	$ 140,340	$ 6,380	$ 110,774	$ 5,750
Net defined benefit liability	$ 31,724	$ 6,380	$ 4,734	$ 5,750

Right sheet (page 99)

The experience adjustments are as follows:

	2011		2010	
	Pension Plans	Other Benefit Plans	Pension Plans	Other Benefit Plans
Asset experience adjustments				
Asset (gain)/loss during the financial year	$ 7,588	$ -	$ (2,161)	$ -
Liability experience adjustments				
Liability loss during the financial year	$ -	$ -	$ -	$ -
Liability assumptions				
Liability loss during the financial year	$ 21,138	$ 651	$ 12,709	N/A

The components of the Company's pension and other post-retirement benefit plans expense are as follows:

	2011		2010	
	Pension Plans	Other Benefit Plans	Pension Plans	Other Benefit Plans
Current service costs	$ 6,200	$ 306	$ 5,936	$ 287
Interest on obligation	6,044	298	5,200	295
Expected return on plan assets	(6,718)	-	(5,659)	-
Expense recognized in operating and administrative expenses	$ 5,526	$ 604	$ 5,477	$ 582

The actual loss on plan assets for the financial year was $870 (2010: gain of $7,820).

The Company recognized the following actuarial losses for the financial year in other comprehensive income (loss):

	2011		2010	
	Pension Plans	Other Benefit Plans	Pension Plans	Other Benefit Plans
Cumulative amount, beginning of the financial year	$ (10,548)	$ (506)	$ -	$ -
Recognized during the financial year	(28,726)	(651)	(10,548)	(506)
Cumulative amount, end of the financial year	$ (39,274)	$ (1,157)	$ (10,548)	$ (506)

Cash payments for employee future benefits, which consist of the Company's contributions to the pension plans and cash payments made directly to beneficiaries of the other benefit plans, totalled $7,887 (2010: $16,740). The Company expects to make contributions to the pension plans and cash payments to beneficiaries of the other benefit plans of $6,302 in 2012.

The assets of the registered pension plans consist of cash, contributions receivable and investments held in a Master Trust for the benefit of the Company's pension plans. The assets held by the Master Trust are invested in a limited number of pooled funds, based on market values as at November 30, 2011, 2010 and 2009, respectively, as follows:

	December 31, 2011	January 1, 2011	January 3, 2010
Equity	57%	60%	61%
Fixed income	42%	39%	39%
Cash and cash equivalents	1%	1%	-
	100%	100%	100%

There were no significant changes in the assets held by the Master Trust between November 30, 2011 and December 31, 2011, between November 30, 2010 and January 1, 2011 and between November 30, 2009 and January 3, 2010.

Left sheet (page 98)

Notes to the Consolidated Financial Statements (continued)

December 31, 2011 and January 1, 2011 (in thousands of Canadian dollars, except per share data)

21. RETIREMENT BENEFIT OBLIGATIONS (continued)

The significant actuarial assumptions adopted are as follows:

	2011			2010		
	Registered Pension Plans	Non-registered Pension Plans	Other Benefit Plans	Registered Pension Plans	Non-registered Pension Plans	Other Benefit Plans
Defined benefit obligations, end of the financial year						
Discount rate	4.25%	4.25%	4.25%	5.25%	5.00%	5.00%
Rate of compensation increase	4.00%	4.00%	4.00%	4.00%	4.00%	4.00%
Net benefit expense for the financial year						
Discount rate	5.25%	5.00%	5.00%	6.00%	5.75%	5.25%
Expected rate of return on plan assets	7.50%	3.75%	N/A	7.50%	3.75%	N/A
Rate of compensation increase	4.00%	4.00%	4.00%	4.00%	4.00%	4.00%

The discount rate is based on current market interest rates at the end of the Company's fiscal year, assuming a portfolio of corporate AA rated bonds with terms to maturity that, on average, match the terms of the accrued retirement benefit obligations. A 1.0% increase in the assumed discount rate would decrease the amount of the Company's accrued retirement benefit obligations and retirement benefit expense in respect of its registered and non-registered defined benefit plans by $23,049 and $1,843, respectively. Conversely, a 1.0% decrease in the assumed discount rate would increase the amount of the Company's accrued retirement benefit obligations and retirement benefit expense in respect of its registered and non-registered defined benefit plans by $27,318 and $1,933, respectively.

The expected long-term rate of return on plan assets is based on the asset mix of invested assets and historical returns. A 1.0% increase in the assumed long-term rate of return on plan assets would decrease the amount of the Company's retirement benefit expense in respect of its registered and non-registered defined benefit plans by $928. Conversely, a 1.0% decrease in the assumed long-term rate of return on plan assets would increase the amount of the Company's retirement benefit expense in respect of its registered and non-registered defined benefit plans by $928.

A 1.0% increase in the assumed rate of compensation increase would increase the amount of the Company's accrued retirement benefit obligations and retirement benefit expense in respect of its registered and non-registered defined benefit plans by $4,414 and $708, respectively. Conversely, a 1.0% decrease in the assumed rate of compensation increase would decrease the amount of the Company's accrued retirement benefit obligations and retirement benefit expense in respect of its registered and non-registered defined benefit plans by $4,214 and $732, respectively.

The expected health care cost trend rate is based on historical trends and external data. The health care cost trend rate used was 8.0% for 2011 (2010: 8.0%), with 8.0% being the trend rate for 2012. The trend rate is then reduced by 0.5% in each of the following years until reaching the ultimate trend rate of 5.0% for 2018 and later years. A 1.0% change in the assumed health care cost trend rate would result in an impact of $639 (2010: $570) on the retirement benefit obligation and a pre-tax impact of $38 (2010: $30) on the benefits expense recognized in earnings.

Assumptions regarding future mortality are based on published statistics and mortality tables. The current longevities underlying the values of the liabilities in the defined benefit plans as at December 31, 2011 and January 1, 2011 are as follows:

	Males	Females
Longevity at age 65 for current pensioners	19.7	22.1
Longevity at age 65 for current member aged 45	21.2	22.9

The calculation of the defined benefit obligation is sensitive to the mortality assumptions set out above. As the actuarial estimates of mortality continue to be refined, an increase of one year in the lives shown above is considered reasonably possible in the next financial year.

Notes to the Consolidated Financial Statements (continued)
December 31, 2011 and January 1, 2011 (in thousands of Canadian dollars, except per share data)

21. RETIREMENT BENEFIT OBLIGATIONS (continued)

The assets of the non-registered plan consist of investments and refundable tax on account with Canada Revenue Agency. The investments are in pooled funds with an allocation of 59% equities, 40% bonds and 1% cash and cash equivalents based on market values as at November 30, 2011. The investments were in pooled funds with an allocation of 61% equities, 38% bonds and 1% cash and cash equivalents as at November 30, 2010 and 60% equities, 39% bonds and 1% cash and cash equivalents based on market values as at November 30, 2009. There were no significant changes in the allocation of investments between November 30, 2011 and December 31, 2011, between November 30, 2010 and January 1, 2011 and between November 30, 2009 and January 3, 2010.

22. PROVISIONS

	2011	2010
Balance, beginning of the financial year	$ 14,414	$ 12,071
Provisions made	8,980	12,341
Provisions used	(9,907)	(9,817)
Provisions reversed	(192)	(306)
Unwind of discount	430	125
Balance, end of the financial year	$ 13,725	$ 14,414

	2011	2010
Balance, end of the financial year, presented as follows:		
Current liabilities	$ 12,024	$ 12,562
Long-term liabilities	1,701	1,852
	$ 13,725	$ 14,414

The Company has been served with a Statement of Claim in a proposed class proceeding that has been filed in the Ontario Superior Court of Justice by two of its licensed Associate-owners, claiming various declarations and damages of $1,000,000 on behalf of a proposed class comprised of all of its current and former licensed Associate-owners resident in Canada, other than in Quebec. The claim alleges, among other things, that Shoppers Drug Mart and two of its affiliates breached contractual and other duties to its Associate-owners by collecting, receiving and/or retaining funds and/or benefits that are in excess of those permitted to be collected, received and/or retained by the applicable agreements. The Company believes that the claim is without merit and will vigorously defend the claim. However, there can be no assurance that the outcome of this claim will be favourable to the Company or that it will not have a material adverse impact on the Company's financial position. The amount payable, if any, is not reasonably determinable at this time.

In addition, the Company is involved in certain legal claims arising in the normal course of business. In the opinion of the Company's management, the eventual settlement of such claims will not have a significant effect on the Company's financial position or results of operations. Management has recorded a provision for these claims based on its best estimate of the final settlements.

23. OTHER LONG-TERM LIABILITIES

The components of the Company's other long-term liabilities are as follows:

	Note	December 31, 2011	January 1, 2011	January 3, 2010
Deferred rent obligations		$ 338,721	$ 330,295	$ 300,826
Retirement benefit obligations	21	38,104	10,484	10,111
Deferred gains on sale-leaseback transactions on financing leases		12,525	7,769	6,754
Financing lease obligations	15, 28	117,911	76,918	55,500
Long-term incentive plan and restricted share unit plan	26	8,134	11,900	4,531
Unrealized loss on derivatives	18	122	1,583	—
Other		4,671	3,175	8,540
		$ 520,188	$ 442,124	$ 386,262

Deferred Rent Obligations

The deferred rent obligations represent the difference between rent expense and cash rent payments and the deferral of landlord inducements.

Sale-leaseback Transactions

During the financial year ended December 31, 2011, the Company sold certain real estate properties for net proceeds of $54,210 (2010: $57,307) and entered into lease agreements for the area used by the Associate-owned stores. The leases have been accounted for as operating or financing leases as appropriate. During the financial year ended December 31, 2011, the Company recognized gains on disposal of $9,935 (2010: $14,182), of which $5,250 (2010: $1,597) were deferred under financing lease treatment. The deferred gains are presented in other long-term liabilities on the consolidated balance sheets and are being amortized over lease terms of 15-20 years.

24. SHARE CAPITAL

Share Capital and Contributed Surplus

Authorized

Unlimited number of common shares

Unlimited number of preferred shares, issuable in series without nominal or par value

Outstanding

	2011		2010	
	Number of Common Shares	Stated Value	Number of Common Shares	Stated Value
Beginning balance	217,452,068	$ 1,520,558	217,431,898	$ 1,519,870
Shares issued for cash	109,729	1,220	20,170	491
Shares repurchased in cash	(5,086,200)	(35,576)	—	—
Repayment of share purchase loans	—	7	—	33
Exercise of share options	—	246	—	164
Ending balance	212,475,597	$ 1,486,455	217,452,068	$ 1,520,558

The Company also has issued share options. See Note 26 to these consolidated financial statements for further details on the Company's issued share options.

Individual shareholder agreements address matters related to the transfer of certain shares issued to the Company's management and Associates, including shares issued under certain options granted to management. In particular, each provides, subject to certain exceptions, for a general prohibition on any transfer of a member of management's or Associate's shares for a period of five years from the date that the individual entered into the shareholder agreement.

The holders of common shares are entitled to receive dividends as declared from time to time and are entitled to one vote per share at meetings of the Company.

Normal Course Issuer Bid

On February 10, 2011, the Company implemented a normal course issuer bid to repurchase, for cancellation, up to 8,700,000 of its common shares, representing approximately 4.0% of the Company's then outstanding common shares. Repurchases will be effected through the facilities of the Toronto Stock Exchange (the "TSX") and may take place over a 12-month period ending no later than February 14, 2012. Repurchases will be made at market prices in accordance with the requirements of the TSX.

From February 10, 2011 to December 31, 2011, the Company purchased and cancelled 5,086,200 common shares under the normal course issuer bid at a cost of $206,779. The premium paid over the average book value of the common shares repurchased of $171,203 has been charged to retained earnings. The Company purchased an additional 115,900 shares at the end of the financial year at a cost of $4,735. These shares were cancelled subsequent to the end of the financial year. The cost of this latter purchase is recorded as treasury shares in Shareholders' Equity as at December 31, 2011.

Notes to the Consolidated Financial Statements (continued)
December 31, 2011 and January 1, 2011 (in thousands of Canadian dollars, except per share data)

24. SHARE CAPITAL (continued)

Dividends

The following table provides a summary of the dividends declared by the Company:

Declaration Date	Record Date	Payment Date	Dividend per Common Share
February 10, 2011	March 31, 2011	April 15, 2011	$ 0.250
April 27, 2011	June 30, 2011	July 15, 2011	$ 0.250
July 21, 2011	September 30, 2011	October 14, 2011	$ 0.250
November 9, 2011	December 30, 2011	January 13, 2012	$ 0.250
February 11, 2010	March 31, 2010	April 15, 2010	$ 0.225
April 28, 2010	June 30, 2010	July 15, 2010	$ 0.225
July 22, 2010	September 30, 2010	October 15, 2010	$ 0.225
November 9, 2010	December 31, 2010	January 14, 2011	$ 0.225

On February 9, 2012, the Board of Directors declared a dividend of 26.5 cents per common share payable April 13, 2012 to shareholders of record as of the close of business on March 30, 2012.

25. EARNINGS PER COMMON SHARE

Basic Net Earnings per Common Share

The calculation of basic net earnings per common share at December 31, 2011 was based on net earnings for the financial year of $613,934 (2010: $591,851) and a weighted average number of shares outstanding (basic) of 216,420,096 (2010: 217,435,868). The weighted average number of shares outstanding (basic) is calculated as follows:

Weighted Average Shares Outstanding (Basic)

	Note	2011	2010
Issued shares, beginning of the financial year	24	217,452,068	217,431,898
Effect of share options exercised		52,350	8,094
Effect of shares repurchased		(1,082,326)	
Effect of share purchase loans		(1,996)	(4,124)
Weighted average number of shares outstanding (basic), end of the financial year		216,420,096	217,435,868

Diluted Net Earnings per Common Share

The calculation of diluted net earnings per common share at December 31, 2011 was based on net earnings for the financial year of $613,934 (2010: $591,851) and a weighted average number of shares outstanding, after adjustment for the effects of all potentially dilutive shares, of 216,504,784 (2010: 217,537,709). The weighted average number of shares outstanding (diluted) is calculated as follows:

Weighted Average Shares Outstanding (Diluted)

	2011	2010
Weighted average number of shares outstanding (basic), end of the financial year	216,420,096	217,435,868
Potentially dilutive share options	84,688	101,841
Weighted average number of shares outstanding (diluted), end of the financial year	216,504,784	217,537,709

The average market value of the Company's shares for purposes of calculating the effect of dilutive share options was based on quoted market prices for the period that the stock options were outstanding. Anti-dilutive stock options have been excluded.

26. SHARE-BASED PAYMENTS

The Company established stock option plans for certain employees and its Board of Directors, as described below, and has reserved 20,000,000 common shares for issuance under the plans. Effective February 2007, non-employee directors are no longer eligible to participate in the stock option plans. The Company established deferred share unit plans for its Chief Executive Officer and non-employee directors, which are described below. The Company uses the fair value method to account for stock options issued under employee and director stock option programs. The fair value of each option is established on the date of the grant using the Black-Scholes options-pricing model.

The Company recognized the following compensation expense or reversal of compensation expense associated with stock options issued under the employee plan ("share plan") and the director stock option plan in the financial years ended December 31, 2011 and January 1, 2011:

	Note	2011	2010
Options granted in 2006		$ (921)	$ 395
Options granted in 2010		(637)	1,197
Options granted in 2011		348	–
Total net (reversal of) expenses recognized in operating and administrative expenses	11	$ (1,210)	$ 1,592

During the financial year ended December 31, 2011, the Company recognized compensation expense of $505 (2010: $1,592) associated with the stock options outstanding and reversed compensation expense of $1,715 (2010: $nil), the latter as a result of the departure of certain management personnel.

Employee Stock Option Plan

Options issued to certain employees have an exercise price per share of no less than the fair market value on the date of the option grant. These options include awards for shares that vest based on the passage of time, performance criteria, or both.

The following is a summary of the status of the share plan and changes during the current and prior financial years:

	2011		2010	
	Options on Common Shares	Weighted Average Exercise Price Per Share	Options on Common Shares	Weighted Average Exercise Price Per Share
Outstanding, beginning of the financial year	803,492	$ 39.53	541,542	$ 36.59
Granted	253,186	41.80	282,120	44.09
Exercised	(109,729)	12.15	(20,170)	24.54
Forfeited/cancelled including repurchased	(566,072)	45.38		
Outstanding, end of the financial year	380,877	$ 40.23	803,492	$ 39.53
Options exercisable, end of the financial year	88,917	$ 33.47	451,372	$ 35.62

	2011 Outstanding Options			2011 Exercisable Options	
Range of Exercise Price	Number of Options Outstanding	Weighted Average Contractual Life (Years)	Weighted Average Exercise Price Per Share	Number of Exercisable Options	Weighted Average Exercise Price Per Share
$23.48 – $26.57	32,390	0.61	$ 23.68	32,388	$ 23.68
$29.30 – $36.41	29,253	2.68	34.39	29,253	34.39
$40.81 – $44.09	319,234	6.29	42.43	27,276	44.09
	380,877	5.53	$ 40.23	88,917	$ 33.47

Notes to the Consolidated Financial Statements (continued)
December 31, 2011 and January 1, 2011 (in thousands of Canadian dollars, except per share data)

26. SHARE-BASED PAYMENTS (continued)

Options Granted Prior to the Company's 2010 Financial Year

Time-based options are exercisable 20% per year on the anniversary of the grant date in each of the five subsequent years.

Performance-based options are exercisable 20% per year on the anniversary of the grant date in each of the five subsequent years, provided that the Company achieves specified earnings-based performance targets. As at December 31, 2011, all performance targets have been achieved.

Upon the termination of an option holder's employment, all unexercisable options expire immediately and exercisable options expire within 180 days of the date of termination. The share plan provides that the Company may pay, in cash, certain terminated option holders the appreciated value of the options to cancel exercisable options.

Subject to certain prior events of expiry, such as the termination of employment for cause, all exercisable options expire on the tenth anniversary of the date of grant.

Options Granted During the Company's 2010 and 2011 Financial Years

In February 2011 and 2010, the Company granted awards of time-based options under the share plan in respect of the Company's 2010 and 2009 financial years, respectively, to certain senior management, with one-third of such options vesting each year.

In November 2011, the Company granted an award of time-based options under the share plan to the Company's Chief Executive Officer, with one-fourth of such options vesting each year.

The following assumptions were used in the Black-Scholes option-pricing model to calculate the fair value for those options granted during the financial years ended December 31, 2011 and January 1, 2011:

	November 2011	February 2011	2010
Fair value per unit at grant date	$ 5.89	$ 6.32	$ 6.94
Share price	$ 42.28	$ 40.81	$ 44.09
Exercise price	$ 42.28	$ 40.81	$ 44.09
Valuation assumptions:			
Expected life	5 years	5 years	5 years
Expected dividends	2.37%	2.45%	2.10%
Expected volatility (based on historical share price volatility)	19.86%	19.32%	18.70%
Risk-free interest rate (based on government bonds)	1.39%	2.63%	2.54%

Upon the termination of an option holder's employment, all unexercisable options expire immediately and exercisable options expire within 180 days of the date of termination. The share plan provides that the Company may pay, in cash, certain terminated option holders the appreciated value of the options to cancel exercisable options.

Subject to certain prior events of expiry, such as termination of the employment for cause, all exercisable options expire on the seventh anniversary of the date of grant.

Director Stock Option Plan

Prior to February 2007, under the Company's director stock option plan, participating directors were issued time-based options to purchase 60,000 common shares. The options have an exercise price per share at fair market value on the date of the option grant, which is normally the date the option holder becomes a director. One-third of the options become exercisable in each of the following three years on the anniversary of the date of grant. Unexercisable options expire upon the option holder ceasing to be a director. Exercisable options expire on the earlier of (i) depending on the circumstances of the option holder ceasing to be a director and the determination of the Human Resources and Compensation Committee, 180 or 365 days of the option holder ceasing to be a director or (ii) the expiry date of the options, which is on the tenth anniversary of the date of grant.

A summary of the status of the director stock option plan and changes during the financial years ending December 31, 2011 and January 1, 2011 is presented below:

	2011		2010	
	Options on Common Shares	Weighted Average Exercise Price Per Share	Options on Common Shares	Weighted Average Exercise Price Per Share
Outstanding, beginning of the financial year	346,000	$ 40.38	346,000	$ 40.38
Exercised	-	-	-	-
Forfeited/cancelled including repurchased	-	-	-	-
Outstanding, end of the financial year	346,000	$ 40.38	346,000	$ 40.38
Options exercisable, end of the financial year	346,000	$ 40.38	346,000	$ 40.38

2011 Outstanding and Exercisable Options

Exercise Price	Number of Options Outstanding	Weighted Average Contractual Life (Years)	Weighted Average Exercise Price Per Share
$26.95	60,000	1.8	$ 26.95
$41.80	106,000	3.6	41.80
$44.02	180,000	4.1	44.02
	346,000	3.5	40.38

Deferred Share Unit Plan for Non-employee Directors

The Company maintains a deferred share unit ("DSU") plan to provide non-employee directors with the option to elect to receive DSUs in lieu of cash payment for all or a portion of their director fees. When such an election is made, the Company credits to the account of each non-employee director a number of DSUs (each equivalent in value to a common share) equal to the amount of fees divided by the fair market value of the common shares. The directors' accounts are credited with dividend equivalents in the form of additional DSUs if and when the Company pays dividends on the common shares. Upon the director ceasing to be a member of the Board of Directors, the director shall receive a cash amount equal to the number of DSUs in his or her account multiplied by the fair market value of the common shares on the date the director ceases to be a member of the Board of Directors or on a later date selected by the director, which shall in any event be a date prior to the end of the following calendar year. During the current financial year, the Company recorded $1,487 (2010: $801) in director fee compensation, which is included in operating and administrative expenses in the consolidated statements of earnings.

Non-employee directors who are not holders of unvested stock options to purchase common shares of the Company are eligible to receive an annual award of DSUs in the amount of up to $60.

The non-executive Chair of the Board of Directors receives an annual fee of $120 in addition to the director fees and annual award of DSUs, one-half of which the Chair may elect, in whole or in part, to be received in DSUs and the other half of which is payable in DSUs.

During the current financial year, the Company issued an aggregate of 31,039 DSUs (2010: 30,569 DSUs) at a weighted average grant date fair value of $40.70 (2010: $41.34). During the financial year ended December 31, 2011, no director (2010: one director) ceased being a member of the Board of Directors and thus, the Company did not make any cash payments (2010: $147 cash payment which was the equivalent of 3,926 DSUs). As at December 31, 2011, there were 128,995 DSUs (2010: 97,956 DSUs) outstanding.

Notes to the Consolidated Financial Statements (continued)
December 31, 2011 and January 1, 2011 (in thousands of Canadian dollars, except per share data)

26. SHARE-BASED PAYMENTS (continued)

Chief Executive Officer Deferred Share Unit Plan

In November 2011, the Company established a deferred share unit plan for its Chief Executive Officer ("CEO DSU Plan") and granted time-based deferred share units ("DSUs") under the CEO DSU Plan, which vest 100% after three years. At the award date, the Company converted compensation awarded to the Chief Executive Officer into a number of DSUs based on the weighted average fair value at the award date. The Company records the compensation expense related to the granted DSUs evenly over the vesting period.

In addition, the Human Resource and Compensation Committee of the Board of Directors can mandate that all or a specified percentage of the Chief Executive Officer's short-term incentive compensation in respect of a calendar year be paid in the form of DSUs. Subject to any such determination, the Human Resource and Compensation Committee may permit the Chief Executive Officer to elect to receive an additional percentage of the Chief Executive Officer's short-term incentive compensation in respect of any calendar year in the form of DSUs. If such a mandate or election is made, the Company will credit to the amount account of the Chief Executive Officer a number of DSUs (each equivalent in value to a common share) equal to the amount of short-term incentive compensation divided by the fair value of the common shares. The date the short-term incentive compensation is payable is the award date of the DSUs, which will be fully vested at that time. The Chief Executive Officer's account is credited with dividend equivalents in the form of additional DSUs if and when the Company pays dividends on its common shares.

Upon the termination of employment, the Company will arrange to purchase shares, equal to the number of Chief Executive Officer DSUs on account of the Chief Executive Officer, on the secondary market. These shares will be held on behalf of the Chief Executive Officer for a one-year period.

Long-term Incentive Plan

Prior to 2010, the Company maintained a long-term incentive plan ("LTIP") pursuant to which certain employees were eligible to receive an award of share units equivalent in value to common shares of the Company ("share units"). Awards of share units under the LTIP were made in February of the financial year immediately following the year in respect of which the award was earned.

During the financial years ended December 31, 2011 and January 1, 2011, the Company did not award any share units under the Company's LTIP. During the financial years ended December 31, 2011 and January 1, 2011, the Company paid out the fully-vested awards granted in 2009 and 2008, respectively.

During the current financial year, the Company cancelled 18,289 share units (2010: nil) under the LTIP as a result of the departure of certain management personnel.

During the current financial year, the Company recognized compensation expense of $337 (2010: $2,221) associated with the LTIP share units outstanding and reversed compensation expense of $537 (2010: $nil), the latter as a result of the cancellation of previously granted share units under the LTIP.

As at December 31, 2011, there were no share units (2010: 148,086 share units) outstanding under the LTIP and the Company did not have any liability associated with the share units earned by the employees under the LTIP (2010: the liability associated with the share units earned by the employees under the LTIP was recognized within accounts payable and accrued liabilities in the consolidated balance sheet and was carried at the market value of the Company's shares at the end of the financial year).

In December 2011, the Company's cash-settled equity forward agreement, which related to the share units granted in 2009 under the LTIP, matured. Until December 2011, a percentage of the equity forward derivatives, which related to unearned share units under the LTIP, was designated as a hedge. As at December 31, 2011, the Company no longer has any cash-settled equity forward agreements related to the share units granted under the LTIP.

Restricted Share Unit Plan

In February 2011 and 2010, the Company made grants of restricted share units ("RSUs"), in respect of the 2010 and 2009 financial years under the Company's restricted share unit plan ("RSU Plan") and, for certain senior management, grants of RSUs, combined with grants of stock options under the Company's share plan.

During the current financial year, the Company awarded 193,474 RSUs (2010: 350,384 RSUs) at a grant-date fair value of $40.81 (2010: $44.09), which vest 100% after three years. Full vesting of RSUs will be phased in for employees who received an award under the Company's LTIP in respect of a financial year prior to the Company's 2009 financial year.

During the current financial year, the Company cancelled 80,537 RSUs (2010: nil) as a result of the departure of certain management personnel.

As at December 31, 2011, there were 381,380 RSUs (2010: 326,117 RSUs) outstanding.

During the financial year ended December 31, 2011, the Company recognized compensation expense of $4,973 (2010: $8,804) associated with the RSUs granted during the financial year and reversed compensation expense of $1,428 (2010: $nil), the latter as a result of the cancellation of previously granted RSUs.

As at December 31, 2011 and January 1, 2011, the liability associated with the RSUs is recognized within accounts payable and accrued liabilities and other long-term liabilities in the Company's consolidated balance sheets and is carried at the market value of the Company's shares at the end of the respective financial year.

The Company entered into cash-settled equity forward agreements to limit its exposure to future price changes in the Company's share price for the Company's RSUs. These agreements mature in December 2012 and December 2013.

A percentage of the equity forward derivatives, related to unearned RSUs, has been designated as a hedge.

27. NET CHANGE IN NON-CASH WORKING CAPITAL BALANCES

	2011	2010
Accounts receivable	$ (36,242)	$ 38,846
Inventory	(84,242)	(103,749)
Prepaid expenses	32,759	4,218
Accounts payable and accrued liabilities	119,891	25,861
	$ 32,166	$ (34,824)

Notes to the Consolidated Financial Statements (continued)
December 31, 2011 and January 1, 2011 (in thousands of Canadian dollars, except per share data)

28. CONTINGENCIES, COMMITMENTS AND GUARANTEES

Obligations under Operating Leases

As at December 31, 2011, the minimum lease payments (exclusive of taxes, insurance and other occupancy charges) on a calendar year basis under long-term leases for store locations and office space are as follows:

	2012	2013	2014	2015	2016	Thereafter	Total
Minimum lease payments	$ 406,831	$ 408,198	$ 397,259	$ 382,422	$ 369,568	$ 2,335,088	$ 4,299,366
Less: sub-lease revenue	3,409	2,756	2,046	1,707	1,317	3,316	14,551
Total operating lease obligations	$ 403,422	$ 405,442	$ 395,213	$ 380,715	$ 368,251	$ 2,331,772	$ 4,284,815

Obligations under Financing Leases

As at December 31, 2011, the minimum lease payments on a calendar year basis for the Company's assets under financing leases are as follows:

	2012	2013	2014	2015	2016	Thereafter	Total
Minimum lease payments	$ 11,583	$ 11,634	$ 11,811	$ 11,943	$ 12,268	$ 161,549	$ 220,788
Less: financing expenses included in minimum lease payments	8,684	8,479	8,254	8,000	7,717	58,844	99,978
Total financing lease obligations	$ 2,899	$ 3,155	$ 3,557	$ 3,943	$ 4,551	$ 102,705	$ 120,810

The Company has financing lease obligations for buildings. The leases have an average interest rate of 7% (2010: 8 percent) and an average remaining term of approximately 17 years (2010: 17 years).

Distribution Services

The Company has entered into an agreement with a third party to provide inventory distribution services to the Company's locations to December 31, 2012. Under the terms of this agreement, the third party will charge the Company specified costs incurred to provide the distribution services, plus an annual management fee.

Information Services

The Company has entered into agreements with several third parties to provide information services to the Company. These agreements have terms of 5 years. The Company has committed to annual payments over the next five years as follows:

	Minimum commitment
2012	$ 8,952
2013	7,050
2014	6,665
2015	4,066
2016	1,744
Total	$ 28,477

Litigation

See Note 22 to these consolidated financial statements for a discussion of the Company's exposure to litigation claims.

Other

In the normal course of business, the Company enters into significant commitments for the purchase of goods and services, such as the purchase of inventory or capital assets, most of which are short-term in nature and are settled under normal trade terms.

The Company is involved in and could potentially be subject to various claims by third parties arising out of its business including, but not limited to, contract, product liability, labour and employment, regulatory and environmental claims. In addition, the Company is subject to regular audits from federal and provincial tax authorities relating to income, capital and commodity taxes, and as a result of these audits, may receive reassessments. While income, capital and commodity tax filings are subject to audits and reassessments, management believes that adequate provisions have been made for all income and other tax obligations. However, changes in the interpretations or judgements may result in an increase or decrease in the Company's income, capital, or commodity tax provisions in the future. The amount of any such increase or decrease cannot be reasonably estimated.

29. RELATED PARTY TRANSACTIONS

Key Management Personnel Compensation

Key management personnel are those individuals having authority and responsibility for planning, directing and controlling the activities of the Company including the Company's Board of Directors. The Company considers key management to be the members of the Board of Directors and the Chief Executive Officer.

Key management personnel may also participate in the Company's stock-based compensation plans and the Company's LTIP and RSU Plan. See Note 26 to these consolidated financial statements for further details on the Company's share-based payment plans.

Key management personnel compensation is comprised of:

	2011	2010
Salaries and directors' fees	$ 5,134	$ 1,638
Statutory deductions	104	105
Expense related to pension and benefits	293	1,745
Share-based payment transactions	(734)	5,120
	$ 4,797	$ 8,608

Key management personnel may purchase goods for personal and family use from the Company on the same terms as those available to all other employees of the Company.

Principal Subsidiaries

All of the Company's subsidiaries are wholly-owned. Intra-company balances and transactions and any unrealized earnings and expenses arising from intra-company transactions are eliminated in preparing the consolidated financial statements. Principal subsidiary companies as at December 31, 2011 were as follows:

Shoppers Home Health Care (Canada) Inc.
Shoppers Drug Mart Specialty Health Network Inc.
MediSystem Technologies Inc.
Shoppers Drug Mart Inc.
Shoppers Drug Mart (London) Limited
Pharmaprix Inc.
911979 Alberta Ltd.
Shoppers Realty Inc.
Sanis Health Inc.

The list excludes non-trading companies that have no material effect on the accounts of the Company.

The Associate-owned stores are each operated through a corporation owned by the Associates. See Note 3(a)(ii) to these consolidated financial statements for a further discussion.

Notes to the Consolidated Financial Statements (continued)
December 31, 2011 and January 1, 2011 (in thousands of Canadian dollars, except per share data)

30. EXPLANATION OF TRANSITION TO IFRS

As stated in Note 2(a) to these consolidated financial statements, these are the Company's first consolidated financial statements prepared in accordance with IFRS. Prior to the adoption of IFRS, the Company prepared its financial statements in accordance with Canadian Generally Accepted Accounting Principles ("previous GAAP").

The accounting policies set out in Note 3 to these consolidated financial statements have been applied in preparing the financial statements for the financial year ended December 31, 2011, the comparative information presented in these financial statements for the financial year ended January 1, 2011 and in the preparation of an opening IFRS balance sheet at January 3, 2010 (the Company's date of transition).

In preparing its opening IFRS balance sheet, the Company has adjusted amounts reported previously in financial statements prepared in accordance with previous GAAP based on IFRS 1, "First-time Adoption of International Financial Reporting Standards" ("IFRS 1"), elections and exceptions and IFRS policy choices. An explanation of how the transition from previous GAAP to IFRS has affected the Company's financial performance, financial position and cash flows is set out in the following tables and the notes that accompany the tables.

31. SUBSEQUENT EVENTS

Subsequent to the end of the financial year, on January 6, 2012, the Company filed with the securities regulators in each of the provinces of Canada, a final short form base shelf prospectus (the "Prospectus") for the issuance of up to $1,000,000 of medium-term notes. Subject to the requirements of applicable law, medium-term notes can be issued under the Prospectus for up to 25 months from the date of the final receipt. No incremental debt was incurred by the Company as a result of this filing.

On January 20, 2012, $250,000 of three-year medium-term notes (the "Series 3 Notes"), were repaid in full, along with all accrued and unpaid interest owing on the final semi-annual interest payment. The repayment was financed through the combination of available cash and commercial paper issued under the Company's commercial paper program. The net debt position of the Company remained substantially unchanged as a result of these refinancing activities.

On February 9, 2012, the Board of Directors declared a dividend of 26.5 cents per common share payable April 13, 2012 to shareholders of record as of the close of business on March 30, 2012.

The consolidated financial statements were authorized for issue by the Board of Directors on February 9, 2012.

Quiz

Note: All assignment material with an asterisk (*) relates to Appendix 5A.

Brief Exercises

(LO 1) BE5-1 Larsen Corporation is a popular clothing retailer with 15 stores located across Canada. After five consecutive years of increasing sales, Larsen would like to expand operations by adding 10 stores within the next three years. To help fund the expansion, Larsen is seeking a loan from its bank. As Larsen's bank manager, discuss the usefulness of (a) the statement of financial position and (b) the statement of cash flows, in evaluating Larsen's operations.

(LO 1) BE5-2 Gator Printers Incorporated is an on-line retailer of printing services, reaching thousands of customers across North America every year. The company was founded 15 years ago as a university campus copy shop, and has reported consistent year-over-year sales growth every year since, with a fast-growing base of individual customers, as well as large corporate accounts. Two years ago, the company issued shares to the general public through a highly publicized and successful initial public offering. Gator is currently considering expanding to South America, and issuing bonds to fund the expansion. Identify the users of Gator Printers' statement of cash flows and how they are likely to use the statement.

(LO 2) BE5-3 One of the weaknesses or limitations of the statement of financial position is that it leaves out financial statement elements if they cannot be objectively recorded. Name three examples of items that are omitted because of this limitation.

(LO 3) BE5-4 Kahnert Corporation's adjusted trial balance contained the following asset accounts at December 31, 2014: Cash $3,000; Treasury Bills (with original maturity of three months) $4,000; Land $40,000; Intangible Assets—Patents $12,500; Accounts Receivable $90,000; Prepaid Insurance $5,200; Inventory $30,000; Allowance for Doubtful Accounts $4,000; FV-NI (Fair Value—Net Income Investments) $11,000. Prepare the current assets section of the statement of financial position, listing the accounts in proper sequence. Identify which items are monetary.

(LO 3) BE5-5 The following accounts are in Tan Limited's December 31, 2014 trial balance: Prepaid Rent $1,300; Fair Value—OCI Investments $62,000; Unearned Revenue $7,000; Land Held for Investment $139,000; and Long-Term Receivables $45,000. Prepare the long-term investments section of the statement of financial position. Identify which items are financial instruments.

(LO 3) BE5-6 Lowell Corp.'s December 31, 2014 trial balance includes the following accounts: Inventory $120,000; Buildings $207,000; Accumulated Depreciation—Equipment $19,000; Equipment $190,000; Land Held for Investment $46,000; Accumulated Depreciation—Buildings $45,000; Land $71,000; Machinery Under Capital Leases $229,000; and Accumulated Depreciation—Capital Leases $103,000. Prepare the property, plant, and equipment section of the statement of financial position.

(LO 3) BE5-7 Pine Corporation's adjusted trial balance contained the following asset accounts at December 31, 2014: Prepaid Rent $12,000; Goodwill $50,000; Franchise Fees Receivable $2,000; Intangible Assets—Franchises $47,000; Intangible Assets—Patents $33,000; and Intangible Assets—Trademarks $10,000. Prepare the intangible assets section of the statement of financial position.

(LO 3) BE5-8 Included in Cellin Limited's December 31, 2014 trial balance are the following accounts: Accounts Payable $251,000; Obligations Under Capital Leases $175,000; Discount on Bonds Payable $142,000; Unearned Revenue $141,000; Bonds Payable $600,000; Salaries and Wages Payable $127,000; Interest Payable $42,000; Income Tax Payable $9,000; and Notes Payable $97,000 (due on March 31, 2015). On January 31, 2015, Cellin finalized refinancing of the notes payable with a new note payable due on March 31, 2016. The financial statements were issued on February 28, 2015.

(a) Prepare the current liabilities section of the statement of financial position if Cellin prepares financial statements in accordance with IFRS, and identify which items are monetary.

(b) Explain how your answer to part (a) would be different if Cellin prepares financial statements in accordance with ASPE.

(LO 3) BE5-9 Use the information presented in BE5-8 for Cellin Limited to prepare the non-current liabilities section of the statement of financial position in accordance with (a) IFRS and (b) ASPE.

(LO 3) BE5-10 Hawthorn Corporation's adjusted trial balance contained the following accounts at December 31, 2014: Retained Earnings $120,000; Common Shares $700,000; Bonds Payable $100,000; Contributed Surplus $200,000; Preferred Shares $50,000; Goodwill $55,000; and Accumulated Other Comprehensive Income (Loss) ($150,000). Prepare the shareholders' equity section of the statement of financial position.

(LO 7) BE5-11 What is the purpose of the statement of cash flows? How does it differ from a statement of financial position and an income statement?

(LO 8) BE5-12 Healey Corporation's statement of financial position as at December 31, 2014, showed the following amounts: Cash $100; Accounts Receivable $600; Land $1,000; Accounts Payable $300; Bonds Payable $500; Common Shares $400; and Retained Earnings $500. Healey's statement of financial position as at December 31, 2013, showed the following amounts: Cash $150; Accounts Receivable $450; Land $800; Accounts Payable $700; Common Shares $400; and Retained Earnings $300. Assume that no dividends were declared or paid in 2014. Calculate the net cash provided (used) by operating activities for the year ended December 31, 2014.

(LO 8) BE5-13 Ames Company reported 2014 net income of $151,000. During 2014, accounts receivable increased by the $13,000 and accounts payable increased by $9,500. Depreciation expense was $44,000. Prepare the cash flows from operating activities section of the statement of cash flows.

(LO 8) BE5-14 Mills Corporation engaged in the following cash transactions during 2014:

Sale of land and building	$196,000
Repurchase of company's own shares	25,000
Purchase of land	43,000
Payment of cash dividend	58,000
Purchase of equipment	35,000
Issuance of common shares	140,000
Retirement of bonds payable	200,000

Mills prepares financial statements in accordance with IFRS. Calculate the net cash provided (used) by investing activities.

(LO 8) BE5-15 Use the information from BE5-14 for Mills Corporation. (a) Calculate the net cash provided (used) by financing activities, if dividends paid are treated as operating activities. (b) Explain how your answer to part (a) would be different if Mills prepares financial statements in accordance with ASPE.

(LO 9, 10, 12) BE5-16 Use the information from BE5-14 for Mills Corporation. Determine Mills's free cash flow, assuming that it reported net cash provided by operating activities of $400,000.

(LO 8, 9, 12) BE5-17 Midwest Beverage Company reported the following items in the most recent year:

Net income	$40,000
Dividends paid	5,000
Increase in accounts receivable	10,000
Increase in accounts payable	7,000
Purchase of equipment	8,000
Depreciation expense	4,000
Issue of notes payable for cash	20,000

(a) Calculate net cash provided (used) by operating activities, the net change in cash during the year, and free cash flow. Dividends paid are treated as financing activities. (b) Assuming Midwest had 100,000 common shares outstanding for the entire year, calculate cash flow per share to be included in the financial statements if Midwest follows IFRS and chooses to disclose the ratio. (c) How would your answer to part (b) change if Midwest follows ASPE?

Exercises

(LO 3) E5-1 (Statement of Financial Position Classifications) Several statement of financial position accounts of Greenspoon Inc. follow:

1. FV—OCI Investments
2. Common Shares
3. Dividends Payable
4. Accumulated Depreciation—Equipment
5. Construction in Process (Warehouse)
6. Petty Cash
7. Interest Payable

8. Deficit
9. FV—NI Investments
10. Income Tax Payable
11. Unearned Subscriptions Revenue
12. Work-in-Process Inventory—Direct Materials
13. Salaries and Wages Payable
14. Unearned Revenue

Instructions

For each account, indicate the proper statement of financial position classification. In the case of borderline items that could be classified in more than one category, indicate the additional information that would be required to determine the proper classification. (Refer to Illustration 5-1 as a guideline.) Also identify which items are monetary and which are financial instruments (or both).

(LO 3) E5-2   (Classification of Statement of Financial Position Accounts) The classifications on Chesapeake Limited's statement of financial position are as follows:

1. Current assets
2. Long-term investments
3. Property, plant, and equipment
4. Intangible assets
5. Other assets
6. Current liabilities
7. Non-current liabilities
8. Capital shares
9. Contributed surplus
10. Retained earnings
11. Accumulated other comprehensive income

Instructions

Indicate by number where each of the following accounts would be classified:

(a) Preferred Shares
(b) Intangible Assets—Franchises
(c) Salaries and Wages Payable
(d) Accounts Payable
(e) Buildings
(f) FV—NI Investments
(g) Current Portion of Long-Term Debt
(h) Premium on Bonds Payable
(i) Allowance for Doubtful Accounts
(j) Accounts Receivable
(k) Bonds Payable (maturing in two years)
(l) Notes Payable (due next year)
(m) Office Supplies
(n) Mortgage Payable
(o) Land
(p) Bond Sinking Fund Investment
(q) Inventory
(r) Prepaid Insurance
(s) Bonds Payable (maturing next year)
(t) Income Tax Payable
(u) Unrealized Gain or Loss—OCI

(LO 3) E5-3   (Classification of Statement of Financial Position Accounts) Plato Inc. prepares financial statements in accordance with IFRS and uses the following headings on its statement of financial position:

1. Current assets
2. Long-term investments
3. Property, plant, and equipment
4. Intangible assets
5. Other assets
6. Current liabilities
7. Long-term liabilities
8. Capital shares
9. Contributed surplus
10. Retained earnings
11. Accumulated other comprehensive income

Instructions

Indicate by number how each of the following should usually be classified. If an item need not be reported at all on the statement of financial position, use the letter X. Also indicate also whether an item is monetary and/or represents a financial instrument.

(a) Prepaid insurance
(b) Investment in associate
(c) Unearned subscriptions revenue
(d) Advances to suppliers
(e) Unearned rent revenue
(f) Copyrights
(g) Petty cash

(h) Sales tax payable

(i) Accrued interest on notes receivable

(j) Twenty-year issue of bonds payable that will mature within the next year (no sinking funds exist, and refunding is not planned)

(k) Machinery retired from use and reclassified as held for sale

(l) Fully depreciated machine still in use

(m) Investment in bonds that will be held until maturity in two years

(n) Accrued interest on bonds payable

(o) Salaries that the company budget shows will be paid to employees within the next year

(p) Accumulated depreciation related to equipment

(q) Accumulated unrealized gains on securities accounted for under the fair value through OCI model

(r) Bank demand loan

(s) Land held for speculation

(LO 3, 4, 12)   **E5-4**   **(Preparation of Corrected Statement of Financial Position)** Bruno Corp. has decided to expand its operations. The bookkeeper recently completed the following statement of financial position in order to obtain additional funds for expansion:

BRUNO CORP.
Statement of Financial Position
For the Year Ended December 31, 2014

Current assets	
Cash (net of bank overdraft of $30,000)	$260,000
Accounts receivable (net)	340,000
Inventory at the lower of cost and net realizable value	401,000
FV-NI investments (at cost—fair value $120,000)	140,000
Property, plant, and equipment	
Building (net)	570,000
Equipment (net)	160,000
Land held for future use	175,000
Intangible assets	
Goodwill	80,000
Investment in bonds to be held until maturity, at amortized cost	90,000
Prepaid expenses	12,000
Current liabilities	
Accounts payable	195,000
Notes payable (due next year)	125,000
Pension obligation	82,000
Rent payable	49,000
Premium on bonds payable	53,000
Long-term liabilities	
Bonds payable	500,000
Shareholders' equity	
Common shares, unlimited authorized, 290,000 issued	290,000
Contributed surplus	180,000
Retained earnings	?

Instructions

(a) Prepare a revised statement of financial position using the available information. Assume that the bank overdraft relates to a bank account held at a different bank than the account with the cash balance. Assume that the accumulated depreciation balance for the buildings is $160,000 and that the accumulated depreciation balance for the equipment is $105,000. The allowance for doubtful accounts has a balance of $17,000. The pension obligation is considered a long-term liability.

Digging Deeper   *(b) What effect, if any, does the classification of the bank overdraft have on the working capital and current ratio of Bruno Corp.? What is the likely reason that the bank overdraft was given that particular classification?

(LO 3, **E5-5** **(Correction of Statement of Financial Position)** The bookkeeper for Garfield Corp. has prepared the fol-
4, 12) lowing statement of financial position as at July 31, 2014:

GARFIELD CORP.
Statement of Financial Position
As at July 31, 2014

Cash	$ 69,000	Notes and accounts payable	$ 44,000
Accounts receivable (net)	40,500	Long-term liabilities	75,000
Inventory	60,000	Shareholders' equity	155,500
Equipment (net)	84,000		$274,500
Patents	21,000		
	$274,500		

The following additional information is provided:

1. Cash includes $1,200 in a petty cash fund and $12,000 in a bond sinking fund.

2. The net accounts receivable balance is composed of the following three items: (a) accounts receivable debit balances $52,000; (b) accounts receivable credit balances $8,000; (c) allowance for doubtful accounts $3,500.

3. Inventory costing $5,300 was shipped out on consignment on July 31, 2014. The ending inventory balance does
not include the consigned goods. Receivables of $5,300 were recognized on these consigned goods.

4. Equipment had a cost of $112,000 and an accumulated depreciation balance of $28,000.

5. Income Tax Payable of $9,000 was accrued on July 31. Garfield Corp., however, had set up a cash fund to meet this
obligation. This cash fund was not included in the cash balance, but was offset against the income tax payable
account.

Instructions

(a) Use the information available to prepare a corrected classified statement of financial position as at July 31, 2014.
(Adjust the account balances based on the additional information.)

***(b)** What effect, if any, does the treatment of the credit balances in accounts receivable of $8,000 have on the working
capital and current ratio of Garfield Corp.? What is likely the reason that the credit balances in accounts receivable
were given that particular classification? What is likely the cause of the credit balances in accounts receivable?

Digging
Deeper

(LO 4) **E5-6** **(Preparation of Classified Statement of Financial Position)** Assume that Iris Inc. has the following accounts
at the end of the current year:

1. Common Shares	11. Accumulated Depreciation—Buildings
2. Raw Materials	12. Restricted Cash (for plant expansion)
3. FV—OCI Investments	13. Land Held for Future Plant Site
4. Unearned Rent Revenue	14. Allowance for Doubtful Accounts
5. Work-in-Process Inventory	15. Retained Earnings
6. Intangible Assets—Copyrights	16. Unearned Subscriptions Revenue
7. Buildings	17. Accounts Receivable—Officers (due in one year)
8. Notes Receivable (due in three months)	18. Finished Goods Inventory
9. Cash	19. Accounts Receivable
10. Salaries and Wages Payable	20. Bonds Payable (due in four years)

Instructions

Prepare a classified statement of financial position in good form (no monetary amounts are necessary).

(LO 4) **E5-7** **(Current versus Long-Term Liabilities)** Samson Corporation is preparing its December 31, 2014 statement
of financial position. The following items may be reported as either current or long-term liabilities:

1. On December 15, 2014, Samson declared a cash dividend of $2.50 per share to shareholders of record on
December 31. The dividend is payable on January 15, 2015. Samson has issued one million common shares.

2. Also on December 31, Samson declared a 10% stock dividend to shareholders of record on January 15, 2015. The dividend will be distributed on January 31, 2015. Samson's common shares have a market value of $54 per share.

3. At December 31, bonds payable of $100 million is outstanding. The bonds pay 7% interest every September 30 and mature in instalments of $25 million every September 30, beginning on September 30, 2015.

4. At December 31, 2013, customer advances were $12 million. During 2014, Samson collected $40 million of customer advances, and advances of $25 million were earned.

5. At December 31, 2014, retained earnings set aside for future inventory losses is $22 million.

6. At December 31, 2014, Samson has an operating line of credit with a balance of $3.5 million. For several years now, Samson has successfully met all the conditions of this bank loan. If Samson defaults on any of the loan conditions in any way, the bank has the right to demand payment of the loan.

Instructions

(a) For each item above, indicate the dollar amounts to be reported as a current liability and as a long-term liability, if any.

Digging
Deeper

(b) Referring to the definition of a liability (discussed in Chapter 2), explain the accounting treatment of item 4 above.

(LO 4) E5-8 (Preparation of Statement of Financial Position) The trial balance of Zeitz Corporation at December 31, 2014, follows:

Digging
Deeper

	Debits	Credits
Cash	$ 205,000	
Sales revenue		$ 7,960,000
FV-NI investments (at fair value)	153,000	
Cost of goods sold	4,800,000	
Bond investment at amortized cost	299,000	
FV—OCI investments (fair value $345,000)	277,000	
Notes payable (due in six months)		98,000
Accounts payable		545,000
Selling expenses	1,860,000	
Unrealized gain or loss (on investments)		63,000
Land	260,000	
Buildings	1,040,000	
Commission payable		136,000
Accrued liabilities		96,000
Accounts receivable	515,000	
Accumulated depreciation—buildings		152,000
Allowance for doubtful accounts		25,000
Administrative expenses	900,000	
Interest expense	211,000	
Inventory	687,000	
Unusual gain		160,000
Correction of prior year's error	140,000	
Notes payable (due in five years)		900,000
Equipment	600,000	
Bonds payable		1,000,000
Accumulated depreciation—equipment		60,000
Intangible assets—franchises	160,000	
Common shares		809,000
Intangible assets—patents	195,000	
Retained earnings		218,000
Accumulated other comprehensive income		80,000
Totals	$12,302,000	$12,302,000

Instructions

(a) Prepare a classified statement of financial position as at December 31, 2014. Ignore income taxes.

(b) Is there any situation where it would make more sense to have a statement of financial position that is not classified?

(LO 4, 5) E5-9   (Current Liabilities) Chelsea Smith is the controller of Lincoln Corporation and is responsible for the preparation of the year-end financial statements on December 31. Lincoln prepares financial statements in accordance with ASPE. The following transactions occurred during the year:

1. On December 20, 2014, an employee filed a legal action against Lincoln for $100,000 for wrongful dismissal. Management believes the action to be frivolous and without merit. The likelihood of payment to the employee is remote.

2. Bonuses to key employees based on net income for 2014 are estimated to be $150,000.

3. On December 1, 2014, the company borrowed $900,000 at 8% per year. Interest is paid quarterly.

4. Credit sales for the year amounted to $10 million. Lincoln's expense provision for doubtful accounts is estimated to be 2% of credit sales.

5. On December 15, 2014, the company declared a $2.00 per share dividend on the 40,000 shares of common shares outstanding, to be paid on January 5, 2015.

6. During the year, customer advances of $160,000 were received; $50,000 of this amount was earned by December 31, 2014.

Instructions

For each item above, indicate the dollar amount to be reported as a current liability. If a liability is not reported, explain why.

(LO 4, 5, 6) E5-10   (Current Assets Section of Statement of Financial Position) Selected accounts follow of Aramis Limited at December 31, 2014:

Finished Goods Inventory	$ 52,000	Cost of Goods Sold	$2,100,000
Unearned Revenue	90,000	Notes Receivable	40,000
Bank Overdraft	8,000	Accounts Receivable	161,000
Equipment	253,000	Raw Materials	187,000
Work-in-Process Inventory	34,000	Supplies Expense	60,000
Cash, R.M. Bank	50,000	Allowance for Doubtful Accounts	12,000
FV-NI Investments	31,000	Intangible Assets—Trade Names	18,000
Interest Payable	36,000	Contributed Surplus	88,000
Restricted Cash (for Plant Expansion)	50,000	Common Shares	22,000

The following additional information is available:

1. Inventory is valued at lower of cost and net realizable value using FIFO.

2. Equipment is recorded at cost. Accumulated depreciation, calculated on a straight-line basis, is $50,600.

3. The fair value—net income investments have a fair value of $29,000.

4. The notes receivable are due April 30, 2015, with interest receivable every April 30. The notes bear interest at 6%. (*Hint*: Accrue interest due on December 31, 2014.)

5. The allowance for doubtful accounts applies to the accounts receivable. Accounts receivable of $50,000 are pledged as collateral on a bank loan.

6. Intangible Assets—Trade Names are recorded net of accumulated amortization of $14,000.

Instructions

(a) Prepare the current assets section of Aramis Limited's statement of financial position as at December 31, 2014, with appropriate disclosures.

(b) Outline the other ways or methods that can be used to disclose the details that are required for the financial statement elements in part (a).

(LO 4, 8) E5-11   (Preparation of Statement of Financial Position) Zezulka Corporation's statement of financial position at the end of 2013 included the following items:

Current assets	$1,105,000	Current liabilities	$1,020,000
Land	30,000	Bonds payable	1,100,000
Building	1,120,000	Common shares	180,000
Equipment	320,000	Retained earnings	174,000
Accumulated depreciation—building	(130,000)	Total	$2,474,000
Accumulated depreciation—equipment	(11,000)		
Intangible assets—patents	40,000		
Total	$2,474,000		

The following information is available for 2014:

1. Net income was $391,000.

2. Equipment (cost of $20,000 and accumulated depreciation of $8,000) was sold for $10,000.

3. Depreciation expense was $4,000 on the building and $9,000 on equipment.

4. Patent amortization expense was $3,000.

5. Current assets other than cash increased by $229,000. Current liabilities increased by $213,000.

6. An addition to the building was completed at a cost of $31,000.

7. A fair value—OCI investment in shares was purchased for $20,500 at the end of the year.

8. Bonds payable of $75,000 were issued.

9. Cash dividends of $180,000 were declared and paid. Dividends paid are treated as financing activities.

Instructions

(a) Prepare a statement of financial position as at December 31, 2014. (*Hint:* You may need to adjust the December 31, 2014 amount of current assets to ensure it balances.)

(b) Prepare a statement of cash flows for the year ended December 31, 2014.

(LO 4, 12) E5-12 (Current Assets and Current Liabilities) The current assets and current liabilities sections of the statement of financial position of Agincourt Corp. are as follows:

AGINCOURT CORP.
Statement of Financial Position (partial)
December 31, 2014

Cash		$ 40,000	Accounts payable	$ 61,000
Accounts receivable	$89,000		Notes payable	67,000
Allowance for doubtful accounts	7,000	82,000		$128,000
Inventory		171,000		
Prepaid expenses		9,000		
		$302,000		

The following errors have been discovered in the corporation's accounting:

1. January 2015 cash disbursements that were entered as at December 2014 included payments of accounts payable in the amount of $35,000, on which a cash discount of 2% was taken.

2. The inventory included $27,000 of merchandise that was received at December 31 but with no purchase invoices received or entered. Of this amount, $10,000 was received on consignment; the remainder was purchased f.o.b. destination, terms 2/10, n/30.

3. Sales for the first four days in January 2015 in the amount of $30,000 were entered in the sales book as at December 31, 2014. Of these, $21,500 were sales on account and the remainder were cash sales.

4. Cash, not including cash sales, collected in January 2015 and entered as at December 31, 2014, totalled $35,324. Of this amount, $23,324 was received on account after cash discounts of 2% had been deducted; the remainder was proceeds on a bank loan.

Instructions

(a) Restate the statement of financial position's current assets and liabilities sections. (Assume that both accounts receivable and accounts payable are recorded gross.)

*(b) Calculate the current ratio before and after the corrections prepared in part (a). Did the restatement improve or worsen this ratio?

(c) State the net effect of your adjustments on Agincourt Corp.'s retained earnings balance.

(d) Assume that in February 2015, Agincourt approaches its bank for another bank loan, based on its restated statement of financial position as at December 31, 2014. Also assume that the terms of the new bank loan would require that Agincourt maintain a current ratio of 1.5. As Agincourt's bank manager, discuss the importance of recording the adjustments above and restating the statement of financial position as at December 31, 2014.

Digging Deeper

(LO 5) E5-13 (Supplemental Disclosures) It is February 2015 and Janix Corporation is preparing to issue financial statements for the year ended December 31, 2014. To prepare financial statements and related disclosures that are faithfully representative, Janix is reviewing the following events in 2014:

1. In August 2014, Maddux Incorporated filed a lawsuit against Janix for alleged patent infringement, claiming $1.3 million in damages. In the opinion of Janix's management and legal counsel, it is not likely that damages will be awarded to Maddux.

2. In January 2015, there was a significant decline in the fair value of Janix's FV-NI (fair value—net income) investments, resulting in an unrealized holding loss of $720,000.

3. In January 2015, a customer filed a lawsuit against Janix for alleged breach of contract related to services provided in 2014. The customer is seeking damages of $950,000. Janix's legal counsel believes that Janix will likely lose the lawsuit and have to pay between $850,000 and $950,000.

4. In August 2014, Janix signed a contract to purchase 200,000 inventory units in August 2015 for a price of $12 per unit. According to the supplier's price list at December 31, 2014, the price per inventory unit had decreased to $10 per unit.

5. At December 31, 2014, Janix has a $1.1-million demand loan outstanding. The terms of the demand loan restrict Janix's payment of dividends to $2 per share.

6. On January 31, 2015, Janix issued 100,000 new common shares, raising $2 million in new capital.

Janix prepares financial statements in accordance with IFRS.

Instructions

For each item above, indicate whether the event relates to a provision, contingency, commitment, or subsequent event, and explain the appropriate accounting treatment. If no adjustment or disclosure is required, explain why.

(LO 6, **E5-14** **(Prepare Statement of Cash Flows)** A comparative statement of financial position for Carmichael Industries
8, 9) Inc. follows:

**CARMICHAEL
INDUSTRIES INC.**
Statement of Financial Position

	December 31	
Assets	2014	2013
Cash	$ 21,000	$ 34,000
Accounts receivable	104,000	54,000
Inventory	220,000	189,000
Land	71,000	110,000
Equipment	260,000	200,000
Accumulated depreciation—equipment	(69,000)	(42,000)
Total	$607,000	$545,000
Liabilities and Shareholders' Equity		
Accounts payable	$ 52,000	$ 59,000
Bonds payable	150,000	200,000
Common shares	214,000	164,000
Retained earnings	91,000	22,000
Accumulated other comprehensive income	100,000	100,000
Total	$607,000	$545,000

Additional information:

1. Net income for the fiscal year ending December 31, 2014, was $129,000.

2. Cash dividends of $60,000 were declared and paid. Dividends paid are treated as financing activities.

3. Bonds payable amounting to $50,000 were retired through issuance of common shares.

4. Land was sold at its carrying amount.

5. No equipment was sold during the year.

Instructions

(a) Prepare a statement of cash flows using the indirect method for cash flows from operating activities.

(b) Comment in general on the results reported in the statement of cash flows.

(LO 7) E5-15 (Statement of Cash Flows—Classifications) The major classifications of activities reported in the statement of cash flows are operating, investing, and financing. For this question, assume the following:

1. The direct method is used.

2. The indirect method is used.

Instructions

Assume that the statement of cash flows is being prepared in accordance with ASPE. Classify each of the transactions in the lettered list that follows as:

1. Operating activity
2. Investing activity

3. Financing activity
4. Not reported as a cash flow

Transactions

(a) Issuance of common shares

(b) Purchase of land and building

(c) Redemption of bonds

(d) Proceeds on sale of equipment

(e) Depreciation of machinery

(f) Amortization of patent

(g) Issuance of bonds for plant assets

(h) Payment of cash dividends

(i) Exchange of furniture for office equipment

(j) Loss on sale of equipment

(k) Increase in accounts receivable during year

(l) Decrease in accounts payable during year

(m) Payment of interest

(n) Receipt of dividend revenue

(LO 8) E5-16 (Prepare Partial Statement of Cash Flows—Operating Activities) The income statement of Kneale Transport Inc. for the year ended December 31, 2014, reported the following condensed information:

KNEALE TRANSPORT INC.
Income Statement
Year Ended December 31, 2014

Sales revenue		$545,000
Operating expenses		370,000
Income from operations		175,000
Other revenues and expenses		
Gain on sale of equipment	$25,000	
Interest expense	10,000	15,000
Income before income taxes		190,000
Income tax expense		42,000
Net income		$148,000

Kneale's statement of financial position contained the following comparative data at December 31:

	2014	2013
Accounts receivable	$50,000	$60,000
Prepaid insurance	8,000	5,000
Accounts payable	30,000	41,000
Interest payable	2,000	750
Income tax payable	8,000	4,500
Unearned revenue	10,000	14,000

Additional information:

Operating expenses include $70,000 in depreciation expense. The company follows IFRS. Assume that interest is treated as an operating activity for purposes of the cash flow statement.

Instructions

(a) Prepare the operating activities section of the statement of cash flows for the year ended December 31, 2014, using the indirect method.

(b) Prepare the operating activities section of the statement of cash flows for the year ended December 31, 2014, using the direct method.

Digging Deeper

(c) From the perspective of a user of Kneale Transport's financial statements, discuss the usefulness of the statement of cash flows prepared using the indirect method versus the direct method.

(LO 8, 9) E5-17   (Prepare Statement of Cash Flows) The comparative statement of financial position of Marubeni Corporation for the fiscal year ending December 31, 2014, follows:

MARUBENI CORPORATION
Statement of Financial Position
December 31

	December 31	
Assets	2014	2013
Cash	$ 53,000	$ 13,000
Accounts receivable	91,000	88,000
Equipment	27,000	22,000
Less: Accumulated depreciation	(10,000)	(11,000)
Total	$161,000	$112,000
Liabilities and Shareholders' Equity		
Accounts payable	$ 20,000	$ 15,000
Common shares	100,000	80,000
Retained earnings	41,000	17,000
Total	$161,000	$112,000

Net income of $37,000 was reported and dividends of $13,000 were paid in 2014. New equipment was purchased, and equipment with a carrying value of $5,000 (cost of $12,000 and accumulated depreciation of $7,000) was sold for $8,000.

Instructions

Prepare a statement of cash flows using the indirect method for cash flows from operating activities. Assume that Marubeni prepares financial statements in accordance with ASPE.

(LO 12) *E5-18   (Analysis) Use the information in E5-17 for Marubeni Corporation.

Instructions

(a) Calculate the current ratio and debt to total assets ratio as at December 31, 2013 and 2014. Calculate the free cash flow for December 31, 2014.

(b) Based on the analysis in (a), comment on the company's liquidity and financial flexibility.

(LO 12) *E5-19   (Analysis) Use the information in E5-14 for Carmichael Industries.

Instructions

(a) Calculate the current and acid test ratios for 2013 and 2014.

(b) Calculate Carmichael's current cash debt coverage ratio for 2014.

(c) Based on the analyses in (a) and (b), comment on Carmichael's liquidity and financial flexibility.

Problems

P5-1   A list of accounts follows:

Accounts Receivable	Pension Obligation, non-current
Land	Premium on Bonds Payable
Salaries and Wages Payable	Bonds Payable
Land Held for Future Plant Site	Prepaid Rent
Accumulated Depreciation—Buildings	Buildings
Loss—Other	Purchase Returns and Allowances
Accumulated Depreciation—Equipment	Cash
Notes Payable (due in six months)	Purchases
Accumulated Other Comprehensive Income	Restricted Cash
Intangible Assets—Patents (net of accumulated amortization)	Notes Receivable (due in five years)
	Commission Expense
Advances to Employees	Retained Earnings

Advertising Expense	Common Shares
Petty Cash	Sales Revenue
Allowance for Doubtful Accounts	Intangible Assets—Copyrights (net of accumulated
Preferred Shares	amortization)
Fair Value—OCI Investments	Sales Discounts
Equipment	Dividends Payable
Income Tax Payable	Selling Expenses
Gain on Sale of Equipment	Inventory
FV-NI (Fair Value—Net Income) Investments	Unearned Subscriptions Revenue
Interest Receivable	Unrealized Holding Gain or Loss—OCI

The Loss—Other account contains a loss due to a flood during the year.

Instructions

Prepare a classified statement of financial position in good form, without monetary amounts.

Digging Deeper

P5-2 Statement of financial position items for Montoya Inc. follow for the current year, 2014:

Goodwill	$ 125,000	Accumulated depreciation—equipment	$ 292,000
Payroll taxes payable	177,591	Inventory	239,800
Bonds payable due 2019	300,000	Rent payable	45,000
Discount on bonds payable	15,000	Income tax payable	98,362
Cash	360,000	Rent payable (long-term)	480,000
Land	480,000	Common shares (20,000 shares issued)	200,000
Notes receivable	445,700	Preferred shares (15,000 shares issued)	150,000
Notes payable	265,000	Prepaid expenses	87,920
Accounts payable	490,000	Equipment	1,470,000
Retained earnings	?	FV-NI investments	121,000
Income taxes receivable	97,630	Accumulated depreciation—building	270,200
Notes payable (due in five years)	1,600,000	Building	1,640,000

Instructions

(a) Prepare a classified statement of financial position in good form. The numbers of authorized shares are as follows: 400,000 common and 20,000 preferred. Assume that income tax accounts, notes receivable and notes payable are short-term, unless stated otherwise, and that the fair value—net income investments are stated at fair value.

(b) What additional disclosures would you expect to provide for the rental obligation?

P5-3 The trial balance of Eastwood Inc. and other related information for the year 2014 follows:

EASTWOOD INC.
Trial Balance
December 31, 2014

	Debits	Credits
Cash	$ 41,000	
Accounts receivable	163,500	
Allowance for doubtful accounts		$ 8,700
Prepaid insurance	5,900	
Inventory	208,500	
Fair value—OCI investments	339,000	
Land	85,000	
Construction in progress	124,000	
Intangible assets—patents	36,000	
Equipment	400,000	
Accumulated depreciation—equipment		240,000
Accounts payable		148,000
Accrued liabilities		49,200
Notes payable		94,000
Bonds payable, net of discount		180,000
Common shares		500,000
Accumulated other comprehensive income		45,000
Retained earnings		138,000
	$1,402,900	$1,402,900

Additional information:

1. The inventory has a net realizable value of $212,000. The FIFO method of inventory valuation is used.

2. The fair value—OCI investments' fair value is $478,000.

3. The amount of the Construction in Process account represents the costs to date on a building in the process of construction. (The company is renting factory space while waiting for the new building to be completed.) The land that the building is being constructed on cost $85,000, as shown in the trial balance.

4. The company purchased the patents at a cost of $40,000 and are being amortized on a straight-line basis.

5. Of the $20,000 discount on bonds payable, $2,000 will be amortized in 2015.

6. The notes payable represent bank loans that are secured by fair value—OCI investments carried at $120,000. These bank loans are due in 2015.

7. The bonds payable bear interest at 11% payable every December 31, and are due January 1, 2025.

8. For common shares, 600,000 are authorized and 500,000 are issued and outstanding.

Instructions

(a) Prepare a statement of financial position as at December 31, 2014, ensuring that all important information is fully disclosed.

Digging Deeper

(b) From the perspective of a potential creditor, discuss the importance of proper classification of Eastwood's Construction in Process account.

P5-4 The statement of financial position of Delacosta Corporation as of December 31, 2014, is as follows:

DELACOSTA CORPORATION
Statement of Financial Position
December 31, 2014

Assets

Goodwill (Note 2)	$ 70,000
Buildings (Note 1)	1,640,000
Inventory	312,100
Investments—trading (Note 4)	100,000
Land	950,000
Accounts receivable	170,000
Investments in shares (fair value through OCI) (Note 4)	87,000
Cash	175,900
Assets allocated to trustee for plant expansion	
Cash	120,000
Treasury notes, at cost and fair value	138,000
	$3,763,000

Equities

Notes payable (Note 3)	$ 600,000
Common shares, unlimited authorized, 1,000,000 issued	1,150,000
Retained earnings	706,000
Accumulated other comprehensive income	252,000
Appreciation capital (Note 1)	570,000
Income tax payable	75,000
Reserve for depreciation of building	410,000
	$3,763,000

Note 1: Buildings are stated at cost, except for one building that was recorded at its appraised value as management determined the building to be worth more than originally paid at acquisition. The excess of the appraisal value over cost was $570,000. Depreciation has been recorded based on cost.

Note 2: Goodwill in the amount of $70,000 was recognized because the company believed that the carrying amount of assets was not an accurate representation of the company's fair value. The gain of $70,000 was credited to Retained Earnings.

Note 3: Notes payable are long-term except for the current instalment due of $100,000.

Note 4: Investments—trading are fair value—net income investments and have a fair value of $75,000. Investments in shares (fair value through OCI) have a fair value of $200,000. Both investments are currently recorded at cost.

Digging
Deeper

Instructions

(a) Prepare a corrected classified statement of financial position in good form. The notes above are for information only. Assume that you have decided not to use the revaluation model for property, plant, and equipment.

(b) From the perspective of a user of Delacosta's statement of financial position, discuss the importance of proper accounting of goodwill.

P5-5 Lydia Trottier has prepared baked goods for sale since 1998. She started a baking business in her home and has been operating in a rented building with a storefront since 2003. Trottier incorporated the business as MLT Inc. on January 1, 2014, with an initial share issue of 1,000 common shares for $2,500. Lydia Trottier is the principal share-holder of MLT Inc.

Sales have increased by 30% annually since operations began at the present location, and additional equipment is needed for the continued growth that is expected. Trottier wants to purchase some additional baking equipment and to finance the equipment through a long-term note from a commercial bank. Woodslee Bank & Trust has asked Trottier to submit an income statement for MLT Inc. for the first five months of 2014 and a statement of financial position as at May 31, 2014.

Trottier assembled the following information from the corporation's cash basis records to use in preparing the financial statements that the bank wants to see:

1. The bank statement showed the following 2014 deposits through May 31:

Sale of common shares	$ 2,500
Cash sales	22,770
Rebates from purchases	130
Collections on credit sales	5,320
Bank loan proceeds	2,880
	$33,600

2. The following amounts were disbursed through May 31, 2014:

Baking materials	$14,400
Rent	1,800
Salaries and wages	5,500
Maintenance	110
Utilities	4,000
Insurance premium	1,920
Equipment	3,600
Principal and interest payment on bank loan	298
Advertising	424
	$32,052

3. Unpaid invoices at May 31, 2014, were as follows:

Baking materials	$256
Utilities	270
	$526

4. Accounts receivable records showed uncollected sales of $4,336 at May 31, 2014.

5. Baking materials costing $2,075 were on hand at May 31, 2014. There were no materials in process or finished goods on hand at that date. No materials were on hand or in process and no finished goods were on hand at January 1, 2014.

6. The note for the three-year bank loan is dated January 1, 2014, and states a simple interest rate of 8%. The loan requires quarterly payments on April 1, July 1, October 1, and January 1. Each payment is to consist of equal principal payments plus accrued interest since the last payment.

7. Lydia Trottier receives a salary of $750 on the last day of each month. The other employees have been paid through May 25, 2014, and are due an additional $270 on May 31, 2014.

8. New display cases and equipment costing $3,600 were purchased on January 2, 2014, and have an estimated useful life of five years. These are the only fixed assets that are currently used in the business. Straight-line depreciation is used for book purposes.

9. Rent was paid for six months in advance on January 2, 2014.

10. A one-year insurance policy was purchased on January 2, 2014.

11. MLT Inc. is subject to an income tax rate of 20%.

12. Payments and collections from the unincorporated business through December 31, 2013, were not included in the corporation's records, and no cash was transferred from the unincorporated business to the corporation.

Instructions

Digging
Deeper

(a) Using the accrual basis of accounting, prepare an income statement for the five months ended May 31, 2014.

(b) Using the accrual basis, prepare a statement of financial position as at May 31, 2014.

*(c) Assume the role of a bank manager at Woodslee Bank & Trust. Based only on MLT's current ratio as a measure of liquidity, and times interest earned ratio as a measure of coverage, would you recommend extending a long-term note for financing of MLT's purchase of additional baking equipment?

(CMA adapted. Used with permission.)

P5-6   In an examination of Wirjanto Corporation as at December 31, 2014, you have learned about the following situations. No entries have been made in the accounting records for these items.

1. The corporation erected its present factory building in 1998. Depreciation was calculated using the straight-line method, based on an estimated life of 35 years. Early in 2014, the board of directors conducted a careful survey and estimated that the factory building had a remaining useful life of 25 years as at January 1, 2014.

2. An additional assessment of 2013 income taxes was levied and paid in 2014.

3. When calculating the accrual for officers' salaries at December 31, 2014, it was discovered that the accrual for officers' salaries for December 31, 2013, had been overstated.

4. On December 15, 2014, Wirjanto Corporation declared a common shares dividend of $1 per share on its issued common shares outstanding, payable February 1, 2015, to the common shareholders of record on December 31, 2014.

5. Wirjanto Corporation, which is on a calendar-year basis, changed its inventory cost flow formula as at January 1, 2014. The inventory for December 31, 2013, was costed by the weighted average method, and the inventory for December 31, 2014, was costed by the FIFO method.

6. On January 15, 2015, Wirjanto's warehouse containing raw materials was damaged by a flash flood.

7. During December 2014, the former president retired and a new president was appointed.

Instructions

Describe fully how each item above should be reported in the financial statements of Wirjanto Corporation for the year 2014.

P5-7   Aero Inc. had the following statement of financial position at the end of operations for 2013:

AERO INC.
Statement of Financial Position
December 31, 2013

Cash	$ 20,000	Accounts payable	$ 30,000
Accounts receivable	21,200	Bonds payable	41,000
Investments—trading	32,000	Common shares	100,000
Equipment (net)	81,000	Retained earnings	23,200
Land	40,000		
	$194,200		$194,200

During 2014, the following occurred:

1. Aero liquidated its investment portfolio at a loss of $5,000. The investments were fair value—net income investments.

2. A parcel of land was purchased for $38,000.

3. An additional $30,000 worth of common shares was issued.

4. Dividends totalling $10,000 were declared and paid to shareholders.

5. Net income for 2014 was $35,000, including $12,000 in depreciation expense.

6. Land was purchased through the issuance of $30,000 in additional bonds.

7. At December 31, 2014, Cash was $70,200; Accounts Receivable was $42,000; and Accounts Payable was $40,000.

Instructions

(a) Prepare the statement of financial position as it would appear at December 31, 2014.

(b) Prepare a statement of cash flows for the year ended December 31, 2014. Assume dividends paid are treated as financing activities.

*(c) Calculate the current and acid test ratios for 2013 and 2014.

*(d) Calculate Aero's free cash flow and the current cash debt coverage ratio for 2014.

(e) What is the cash flow pattern? Discuss the sources and uses of cash.

(f) Use the analysis of Aero to illustrate how information in the statement of financial position and statement of cash flows helps the user of the financial statements.

P5-8 Jia Inc. applies ASPE and had the following statement of financial position at the end of operations for 2013:

JIA INC.
Statement of Financial Position
December 31, 2013

Cash	$ 20,000	Accounts payable	$ 30,000
Accounts receivable	21,200	Notes payable	41,000
FV-NI investments	32,000	Common shares	100,000
Equipment (net)	81,000	Retained earnings	23,200
Land	40,000		
	$194,200		$194,200

During 2014, the following occurred:

1. Jia Inc. sold some of its fair value—net income investment portfolio for $19,000. This transaction resulted in a gain of $3,400 for the firm. At December 31, 2014, the remaining fair value—net income investments in the portfolio had fair value of $16,400 and original cost of $13,000. No investments were purchased in 2014.

2. A tract of land was purchased for $18,000 cash.

3. Long-term notes payable in the amount of $17,000 were retired before maturity by paying $17,000 cash.

4. An additional $26,000 in common shares was issued.

5. Dividends totalling $9,200 were declared and paid to shareholders.

6. Net income for 2014 was $32,000 after allowing for depreciation of $12,000.

7. Land was purchased through the issuance of $30,000 in bonds.

8. At December 31, 2014, cash was $41,000; accounts receivable was $41,600; and accounts payable remained at $30,000.

Instructions

(a) Prepare a statement of cash flows for the year ended December 31, 2014.

(b) Prepare the statement of financial position as it would appear at December 31, 2014.

(c) How might the statement of cash flows help the user of the financial statements?

*(d) Calculate the following ratios:
  1. Free cash flow
  2. Current cash debt coverage ratio
  3. Cash debt coverage ratio

(e) What is Jia's cash flow pattern? Discuss any areas of concern.

Digging
Deeper

P5-9 The statement of financial position of Sargent Corporation follows for the current year, 2014:

SARGENT CORPORATION
Statement of Financial Position
December 31, 2014

Current assets	$ 485,000	Current liabilities	$ 380,000
Investments	640,000	Long-term liabilities	1,000,000
Property, plant, and equipment	1,720,000	Shareholders' equity	1,770,000
Intangible assets	305,000		$ 3,150,000
	$3,150,000		

The following additional information is available:

1. The current assets section includes the following: cash $150,000; accounts receivable $170,000, less $10,000 allowance for doubtful accounts; inventory $180,000; and unearned revenue $5,000. The cash balance is composed of $190,000, less a bank overdraft of $40,000. Inventory is stated at the lower of FIFO cost and net realizable value.

2. The investments section includes the following: note receivable from a related company, due in 2020, $40,000; fair value—net income investments in shares, $80,000 (fair value $80,000); fair value—OCI investments in shares, $125,000 (fair value $155,000); bond sinking fund $250,000; and patents $115,000, net of accumulated amortization.

3. Property, plant, and equipment includes buildings $1,040,000, less accumulated depreciation $360,000; equipment $450,000, less accumulated depreciation $180,000; land $500,000; and land held for future use $270,000.

4. Intangible assets include the following: franchise, net of accumulated amortization $165,000; goodwill $100,000; and discount on bonds payable $40,000.

5. Current liabilities include the following: accounts payable $140,000; notes payable, short-term $80,000, long-term $120,000; and income tax payable $40,000.

6. Long-term liabilities are composed solely of 7% bonds payable due in 2022.

7. Shareholders' equity has 70,000 preferred shares (200,000 authorized), which were issued for $450,000, and 100,000 common shares (400,000 authorized), which were issued at an average price of $10 per share. In addition, the corporation has retained earnings of $290,000 and accumulated other comprehensive income of $30,000.

Instructions

(a) Prepare a statement of financial position in good form (adjust the amounts in each statement of financial position classification based on the additional information).

Digging
Deeper

(b) What makes the condensed format of the original statement of financial position inadequate in terms of the amount of detail that needs to be disclosed under IFRS and ASPE?

P5-10 The statement of financial position of Rodges Corporation follows (in thousands):

RODGES CORPORATION
Statement of Financial Position
December 31, 2014

Assets		
Current assets		
Cash	$26,000	
Investments—trading (fair value through net income)	18,000	
Accounts receivable	25,000	
Inventory	20,000	
Supplies	4,000	
Investment in subsidiary company	20,000	$113,000
Investments		
Investments in shares		25,000
Property, plant, and equipment		
Buildings and land	91,000	
Less: Reserve for depreciation	31,000	60,000
Other assets		
Investment in bonds to be held to maturity (at cost)		19,000
		$217,000

Liabilities and Equity

Current liabilities

Accounts payable	$22,000	
Reserve for income taxes	15,000	
Customer accounts with credit balances	1	$ 37,001

Deferred credits

Unamortized premium on bonds payable	2,000

Long-term liabilities

Bonds payable	60,000
Total liabilities	99,001

Shareholders' equity

Common shares issued	85,000	
Earned surplus	24,999	
Cash dividends declared	8,000	117,999
		$217,000

Instructions

Evaluate the statement of financial position. Briefly describe the proper treatment of any item that you find incorrect. Assume the company follows IFRS.

P5-11 A comparative statement of financial position for Spencer Corporation follows:

SPENCER CORPORATION
Statement of Financial Position

	December 31	
Assets	2014	2013
Cash	$ 65,000	$ 29,000
Accounts receivable	87,000	59,000
Inventory	233,000	181,000
Investments in shares (fair value through OCI)	63,000	84,000
Land	65,000	103,000
Equipment	390,000	430,000
Accumulated depreciation—equipment	(117,000)	(86,000)
Goodwill	124,000	173,000
Total	$910,000	$973,000
Liabilities and Shareholders' Equity		
Accounts payable	$ 12,000	$ 51,000
Dividends payable	15,000	32,000
Notes payable	320,000	435,000
Common shares	265,000	125,000
Retained earnings	288,000	284,000
Accumulated other comprehensive income	10,000	46,000
Total	$910,000	$973,000

Additional information:

1. Net income for the fiscal year ending December 31, 2014, was $19,000.

2. In March 2014, a plot of land was purchased for future construction of a plant site. In November 2014, a different plot of land with original cost of $86,000 was sold for proceeds of $95,000.

3. In April 2014, notes payable amounting to $140,000 were retired through issuance of common shares. In December 2014, notes payable amounting to $25,000 were issued.

4. Fair value—OCI investments were purchased in July 2014 for a cost of $15,000. By December 31, 2014, the fair value of Spencer's portfolio of fair value—OCI investments decreased to $63,000. No fair value—OCI investments were sold in the year.

5. On December 31, 2014, equipment with an original cost of $40,000 and accumulated depreciation to date of $12,000 was sold for proceeds of $21,000. No equipment was purchased in the year.

6. Dividends on common shares of $32,000 and $15,000 were declared in December 2013 and December 2014, respectively. The 2013 dividend was paid in January 2014 and the 2014 dividend was paid in January 2015. Dividends paid are treated as financing activities.

7. Goodwill impairment loss was recorded in the year to reflect a decrease in the recoverable amount of goodwill. No goodwill was purchased or sold in the year.

Digging Deeper

Instructions

(a) Prepare a statement of cash flows using the indirect method for cash flows from operating activities.

(b) From the perspective of a shareholder, comment in general on the results reported in the statement of cash flows.

Cases

Refer to the Case Primer to help you answer these cases.

Real World Emphasis

CA5-1   In the late 1990s, **CIBC** helped **Enron Corporation** structure 34 "loans" that appeared in the financial statements as cash proceeds from sales of assets. Enron subsequently went bankrupt in 2001 and left many unhappy investors and creditors with billions of dollars lost. In December 2003, CIBC settled four regulatory investigations with the U.S. Securities and Exchange Commission, U.S. Federal Reserve, U.S. Justice Department, and Canadian Office of the Superintendent of Financial Institutions. The settlement, which amounted to U.S. $80 million, was then one of the largest regulatory penalties against a Canadian bank. The regulatory authorities felt that CIBC had aided Enron in boosting its earnings and hiding debt. CIBC set aside a $109-million reserve in early 2003 in preparation for this settlement. No additional reserves were set aside.

As part of the settlement, CIBC agreed to get rid of its structured financing line of business (where all of these "loans" were created). Bank management noted that the decision to get rid of the structured financing business would reduce annual earnings by 10 cents a share. The bank had previously reported annual earnings of $5.21 per share. In addition, the bank had to accept the appointment of an outside monitor whose role, among other things, would be to review the bank's compliance with the settlement. Strategically, the bank had already reduced its emphasis on corporate lending (having suffered heavy losses in 2002) in favour of an increased focus on earnings from branch banking operations.

At the end of 2003, CIBC was still owed $213 million by Enron. There were many additional Enron-related lawsuits pending against the bank, but the bank announced that the lawsuits were without merit. The bank had insurance against many of these claims and noted that it planned to vigorously defend itself.

In 2005, the bank settled a lawsuit with institutional investors, paying $2.4 billion, again setting a standard for the size of the settlement. Then in 2009, the Canada Revenue Agency (CRA) challenged the bank regarding the tax deductibility of the payment. If CRA is successful in arguing that the payment is non-deductible, CIBC will have to pay just under $1 billion in taxes. As of 2012, the case with CRA is still ongoing.

Instructions

Discuss any financial reporting issues relating to CIBC's 2003 and 2009 financial statements. Use the conceptual framework noted in Chapter 2 for the analysis.

Ethics

CA5-2   Hastings Inc. (HI) is a manufacturer that produces stainless steel car parts. It began as a family business several years ago and all shares are owned by the Hastings family. The company's main assets are its manufacturing facility and surrounding land. The property was purchased many years ago and the carrying value reflects only a fraction of the asset's cost.

The company currently follows ASPE and is wondering what the impact would be of switching to IFRS. Several of the Hastings family members would like to take the company public in the next five to 10 years.

Because of the recent dip in the economy, the company has suffered losses over the past three years. However, as the economy has recently begun picking up, management is confident that this year will be a profitable one.

Instructions

Adopt the role of the company's auditors and discuss any financial reporting issues. Use the conceptual framework noted in Chapter 2 for the analysis.

Integrated Case

(*Hint*: If there are issues here that are new, use the conceptual framework to help you support your analysis with solid reasoning.)

IC5-1   Franklin Drug Ltd. (FDL) is a global public company that researches, develops, markets, and sells prescription drugs. Revenues and net income are down this year, partly because one of the company's competitors, Balogun Drug

Inc. (BDI), has created and is selling generic versions of two of FDL's best selling drugs. The drugs, known as FD1 and FD2, are still protected by patents that will not expire for another three years. Normally, when a drug is patented, other drug companies are not legally allowed to sell generic versions of the drug. This practice of patenting new drugs allows the companies that develop the drugs enough time to recover their large investment in research and development of the drugs.

In recent years, however, generic drug companies have become more aggressive in producing and selling generic copies of drugs before patents expire. FDL refers to this practice as "launching the generic products at risk" because, legally, the competitors are not allowed to sell them while the patent is still in force. Currently, FDL has about $2 million in development costs capitalized on the balance sheet. It has launched a lawsuit against BDI, ordering it to cease and desist selling the generic drugs. These types of lawsuits are usually long and very expensive. By the time the lawsuit is settled one way or the other, the patents will have expired. So far, legal costs incurred for the lawsuit are $300,000.

During the year, the patent on a third drug, FD3, expired and several competitor drug companies began actively marketing generic replacements. FDL still has $500,000 worth of FD3 development costs on the balance sheet. Although the increased competition may result in this asset being impaired, FDL feels that it can hold its market share based on FD3's past success in treating patients. So far, sales of FD3 have declined only 3%. On the other hand, the company's share price has declined significantly because of the uncertainty surrounding future sales. Company management is not happy with the drop in share price, because a significant portion of their remuneration is based on stock options.

The company gives volume rebates to some of its larger customers. Under the terms of the sales agreements, the more purchases that a customer makes in a certain time frame, the larger the rebate percentage is on these purchases. The length of the time frame varies. Three large contracts are currently outstanding at year end with new customers. The time frames on these contracts extend beyond year end. FDL must estimate the volume rebates by considering what the total sales will be under these contracts. The company always bases this estimate on past experience.

It is now early January and the auditors are coming in for an audit planning meeting.

Instructions

In preparation for the meeting, you, as audit senior on the job, have done some preliminary research on the company. Write a memo that outlines the potential financial reporting issues.

Writing Assignments

WA5-1 The partner in charge of the Spencer Corporation audit comes by your desk and leaves a letter he has started to the CEO and a copy of the statement of cash flows for the year ended December 31, 2014. Because he must leave on an emergency, he asks you to finish the letter by explaining (1) the difference between the net income and cash flow amounts, (2) the importance of operating cash flow, (3) the sustainable source(s) of cash flow, and (4) possible suggestions to improve the cash position.

Cash flows from operating activities		
Net income		$ 100,000
Adjustments to reconcile net income to net cash provided by operating activities:		
Depreciation expense	$ 11,000	
Loss on sale of fixed assets	5,000	
Increase in accounts receivable (net)	(40,000)	
Increase in inventory	(35,000)	
Decrease in accounts payable	(41,000)	(100,000)
Net cash provided by operating activities		–0–
Cash flows from investing activities		
Sale of plant assets	25,000	
Purchase of equipment	(100,000)	
Purchase of land	(200,000)	
Net cash used by investing activities		(275,000)
Cash flows from financing activities		
Payment of dividends	(10,000)	
Redemption of bonds	(100,000)	
Net cash used by financing activities		(110,000)
Net decrease in cash		(385,000)
Cash balance, January 1, 2014		400,000
Cash balance, December 31, 2014		$ 15,000

Date
James Spencer III, CEO

James Spencer Corporation
125 Bay Street
Toronto, ON

Dear Mr. Spencer:

I have good news and bad news about the financial statements for the year ended December 31, 2014. The good news is that net income of $100,000 is close to what we predicted in the strategic plan last year, indicating strong performance this year. The bad news is that the cash balance is seriously low. Enclosed is the Statement of Cash Flows, which best illustrates how both of these situations occurred at the same time...

Instructions

Complete the letter to the CEO, including the four elements that the partner asked for.

Ethics

WA5-2 The ethical accountant for Khouri Industries, is trying to decide how to present property, plant, and equipment in the notes to the balance sheet. She realizes that the statement of cash flows will show that the company made a significant investment in purchasing new equipment this year, but overall she knows the company's plant assets are rather old. She feels that she can disclose one amount for the title "Property, plant, and equipment, net of depreciation," and the result will be a low figure. However, it will not disclose the assets' age. If she chooses to show the cost less accumulated depreciation, the assets' age will be visible. She proposes the following:

Property, plant, and equipment, net of depreciation	$10,000,000

rather than

Property, plant, and equipment	$50,000,000
Less: Accumulated depreciation	(40,000,000)
Net book value	$10,000,000

Instructions

Discuss the financial reporting issues, including any ethical issues.

WA5-3 Brookfield Properties Corporation reported net income of $1,896 million for the year ended December 31, 2011, which is up 12.5% from the prior year. The company owns, develops, and manages North American office properties and its shares trade on both the New York and Toronto stock exchanges. The company takes pride in its strong financial position and in providing a foundation for growth. Obtain the Consolidated Balance Sheets for 2011 and 2008, which can be found on the company website or on Sedar (www.sedar.com).

Instructions

Many companies in the real estate business choose not to use a classified balance sheet. For example, if you compare the 2008 balance sheet with the 2011 balance sheet of Brookfield Properties, you will notice that they previously did not use a classified balance sheet. Compare the two forms of balance sheet presentation and discuss the advantages and disadvantages of the classified balance sheet.

WA5-4 In determining if a contingent liability should be recognized or not on the balance sheet at the report date, management must decide if there is a present obligation or a contingent obligation or both. Only a present obligation would be recorded under IFRS.

Instructions

For each of the following cases, determine if there is a present obligation and/or a contingent obligation, giving support for your answer assuming the company follows IFRS.

(a) Food for Thought is a restaurant that held a Christmas party in early December for a customer. During the party, 30 people became violently ill, possibly from food poisoning, and had to be hospitalized. Two months later, there are still lingering effects from this illness. The restaurant is now being sued for damages. However, Food for Thought disputes the charges and does not believe that the food it served is to blame. The year-end report is just being finalized for December 31. The entity's lawyers believe that it is unlikely that the restaurant will be found liable.

(b) Encor Oil is an oil company, operating in Country A and Country B, that has caused contamination at all of its oil production sites. Encor only cleans up when it is required to do so by the country's laws. In Country A, the laws have just been amended, on December 31, 2014, to require companies to clean up any environmental contamination that they have caused in the past and, of course, any new contamination done going forward. In Country B, although new legislation is being considered with respect to environmental cleanup, nothing yet has been legislated.

(c) A manufacturer provides a three-year warranty to repair or replace any defective products that have been sold. It also, in the past, has replaced parts for some key customers where the defect was found four years after the date of sale. The company decided to replace these goods in order to maintain good relations with these customers.

WA5-5 Write a brief essay highlighting the differences between IFRS and accounting standards for private enterprises noted in this chapter, discussing the conceptual justification for each.

RESEARCH AND FINANCIAL ANALYSIS

RA5-1 Shoppers Drug Mart Corporation

Real World Emphasis

The financial statements of **Shoppers Drug Mart Corporation** for the year ended December 31, 2011 appear in Appendix 5B.

Instructions

(a) What alternative formats could the company have used for its balance sheet? Which format did it adopt?

(b) Identify the various techniques of disclosure that the company could have used to disclose additional financial information that is pertinent. Which techniques does it use in its financials?

(c) Which presentation method does the company use for its statement of cash flows (direct or indirect method)? What were the company's cash flows from its operating, investing, and financing activities for the year ended December 31, 2011? What were its trends in net cash provided by operating activities for the periods ended December 31, 2010, and 2011? Is the cash generated from operating activities significantly different from net earnings in both periods? Suggest why this might happen.

(d) Calculate the company's (1) current cash debt coverage ratio, (2) cash debt coverage ratio, and (3) free cash flow for the years ended December 31, 2011, and January 1, 2011. What do these ratios indicate about the company's financial condition?

RA5-2 Bombardier Inc.

Real World Emphasis

The financial statements for **Bombardier Inc.** for the year ended December 31, 2011, can be found on the company's website or at www.sedar.com.

Instructions

(a) What form of presentation has the company used in preparing its balance sheet?

(b) Calculate the ratios identified in Appendix 5A for both years that are presented in the financial statements. Make note of any ratios that cannot be calculated and why.

(c) Comment on the company's liquidity, solvency, and profitability.

(d) Review the cash flow patterns on the statements of cash flows and comment on where the company is getting its cash from and where it is spending it.

(e) Perform a "vertical analysis" of the assets. (Calculate each asset as a percentage of total assets.) How has this result changed from year to year?

RA5-3 Maple Leaf Foods Inc.

The financial statements for **Maple Leaf Foods Inc.** may be found on the company's website or at www.sedar.com.

Instructions

(a) Calculate the liquidity and coverage (solvency) ratios identified in Appendix 5A for both years that are presented in the financial statements.

(b) Comment on the company's financial flexibility.

(c) Review the cash flow patterns on the statements of cash flows and comment on where the company is getting its cash from and where it is spending it. (*Hint:* Identify the cash flow pattern and explain what information the pattern provides.)

(d) Perform a "horizontal analysis" for working capital. How has this result changed from year to year and what are the implications for the company's financial health?

RA5-4 Goldcorp Inc.

Real World Emphasis

Obtain the 2001 and 2011 annual reports for **Goldcorp Inc.** (from SEDAR www.sedar.com). Read the material leading up to the financial statements and answer the following questions:

(a) Explain how the company's business changed from 2000 to 2001. What significant events occurred?

(b) What was the impact on key ratios of the event(s) identified in part (a)? Include in these ratios the cash cost to produce an ounce of gold and the average selling price of gold. (This information can be found in the Management Discussion and Analysis part of the annual report.)

(c) Examine and calculate the same key ratios for 2011. Do you notice any differences 10 years later? What are some of the reasons for the changes?

RA5-5 Quebecor Inc. and Thomson Reuters Corporation

Real World Emphasis

The financial statements for **Quebecor Inc.** and **Thomson Reuters Corporation** may be found on SEDAR (www.sedar.com) or the companies' websites.

Instructions

(a) What business is Quebecor Inc. in? Is Thomson Reuters Corporation a good benchmark for comparing against? Explain.

(b) Identify three other companies that might be used for comparisons.

(c) Calculate industry averages for these five companies for the current and debt to total assets ratios.

(d) Based on this very brief analysis, is Quebecor or Thomson Reuters in better shape in terms of liquidity and solvency? How do these companies compare with the other three companies?

(e) Review the statements of cash flows for Quebecor and Thomson Reuters for the last two years. Describe the cash flow patterns for each company.

(f) Comment on these cash flow patterns, noting changes over the past two to three years.

RA5-6 IASB's Discussion Paper: Preliminary Views on Financial Statement Presentation

Real World Emphasis

From the International Accounting Standards Board website (www.iasb.co.uk), access the Discussion Paper: Preliminary Views on Financial Statement Presentation dated October 2008 (or if out in Exposure Draft, the most updated version).

Instructions

(a) What is the proposed new format for the Statement of Financial Position? Explain the different classification and categories that will be used. Identify the types of assets and liabilities to be included in each section.

(b) Why has the IASB determined that a new format is required for the presentation of a company's financial position?

(c) Discuss the advantages and disadvantages of this new presentation.

ENDNOTES

1 Risk means the unpredictability of the enterprise's future events, transactions, circumstances, and results.

2 The formulas for these ratios and other ratios are summarized in Appendix 5A.

3 Liquidity measures are important inputs to bankruptcy prediction models, such as those developed by Altman and others. See G. White, A. Sondhi, and D. Fried, *The Analysis of Financial Statements* (New York: John Wiley & Sons, 2003), Chapter 18.

4 "Reporting Income, Cash Flows, and Financial Position of Business Enterprises," *Proposed Statement of Financial Accounting Concepts* (Stamford, Conn.: FASB, 1981), par. 25.

5 Several of these omitted items (such as internally generated goodwill and certain commitments) are discussed in later chapters.

6 While the term "capitalize" is often used in the context of recording costs as assets, it is sometimes used differently: in the context here, it means recognizing the liabilities on the balance sheet.

7 *CICA Handbook–Accounting*, Part II, Section 3831.05.

8 *CICA Handbook–Accounting*, Part II, Section 3831.05.

9 See *CICA Handbook–Accounting*, Part II, Section 3856.05 for definition of financial instrument. Markets often exist or can be created for these instruments because of their nature and measurability. Liabilities are included because they represent the other side of an asset contract; for example, accounts payable to one company represents accounts receivable to another. Accounts receivable contracts or pools are often bought and sold.

10 See *CICA Handbook–Accounting*, Part II, Section 3856, IAS 32, and IAS 39 for more complete definitions.

11 This type of comparison is done by performing a **vertical analysis,** which calculates the percentage that a specific asset represents when divided by total assets. This number may then be compared with the same percentage from past years. The latter comparison is generally called **horizontal** or **trend analysis.** Horizontal and vertical analyses are discussed further on the Student Website under Financial Statement Analysis.

12 *CICA Handbook–Accounting*, Part II, Section 1510.01 and IAS 1.66.

13 The real estate industry is an example of an industry that does not follow this approach. This is because the industry feels that a more meaningful presentation results when the most important assets are presented first. In most real estate development companies, the most important and largest asset is investment properties. This asset includes hotels, shopping centres, leased buildings, and so on that generate revenue or profits for the company. **Brookfield Office Properties Inc.** records this asset first on its balance sheet. On the liabilities side, the corresponding debt related to the properties is recorded. For Brookfield, this asset represents over 80% of total assets. Many real estate companies follow specialized industry accounting principles (REALpac *IFRS Handbook*) as published by the Real Properties Association of Canada or REALpac (see www.realpac.ca).

14 *CICA Handbook–Accounting*, Part II, Section 1540.06 and IAS 7.6.

15 The identification and measurement of related parties and related-party transactions will be covered in Chapter 23.

16 *CICA Handbook–Accounting*, Part II, Section 3031.07 and IAS 2.6. Copyright © 2012 IFRS Foundation. All rights reserved. Reproduced by Wiley Canada with the permission of the IFRS Foundation ®. No permission granted to third parties to reproduce or distribute.

17 *CICA Handbook–Accounting*, Part II, Section 1510.08 and IAS 1.69.

18 In Chapter 13, there is a more detailed discussion of debt.

19 The rights and privileges of the various securities that are outstanding (both debt and equity) are usually explained in the notes to the financial statements. Examples of information that should be disclosed are dividend and liquidation preferences, participation rights, call prices and dates, conversion or exercise prices or rates and pertinent dates, sinking fund requirements, unusual voting rights, and significant terms of contracts to issue additional shares.

20 In Canada, under the Canada Business Corporations Act, shares that are reacquired must be cancelled. However, some provincial jurisdictions and other countries (such as the United States) still allow treasury shares to exist.

21 *CICA Handbook–Accounting*, Part II, Section 3290.05. The IFRS definition differs somewhat (see IAS 37.10). In short, under IFRS, provisions are required for situations such as lawsuits where it is more likely than not that a present obligation exists (these are considered liabilities under IFRS, not contingencies). However, provisions are not required for loss contingencies for items like lawsuits

where it is more likely than not that no obligation exists at the date of the financial statements. These are "possible obligations" whose existence will only be confirmed by uncertain future events. The differences in the definitions are examined in more detail in Chapter 13.

[22] IAS 37.27 to IAS 37.35 and *CICA Handbook*, Part II, Section 3290.08 to 3290.24.

[23] *CICA Handbook–Accounting*, Part II, Section 1508 and various other sections.

[24] *CICA Handbook–Accounting*, Part II, Section 3280 and various other sections.

[25] IAS 10 and *CICA Handbook–Accounting*, Part II, Section 3820.

[26] According to the *CICA Handbook–Accounting*, Part II, Section 1540.03 and IAS 7.1, the cash flow statement should be presented as an integral part of the financial statements.

[27] *CICA Handbook–Accounting*, Part II, Section 1540.01 and IAS 7.4.

[28] *CICA Handbook–Accounting*, Part II, Section 1540.06 and IAS 7.6.

[29] In determining free cash flow, some companies do not subtract dividends, because they believe these expenditures are discretionary.

[30] "Air Canada Reports Second Quarter 2011 Results: Operating Income Improvement of $26 Million to $73 Million," company news release, August 4, 2011.

[31] Air Canada Pension Plan Funding Regulations, 2009, available at http://www.gazette.gc.ca/rp-pr/p2/2009/2009-08-05/html/sor-dors211-eng.html.

[32] For further details, see the financial statement presentation project page on the IASB website at http://www.ifrs.org/Current+Projects/IASB+Projects/Financial+Statement+Presentation/Financial+Statement+Presentation.htm.

[33] This is a brief overview only. It is meant to link risk with the business model and with the use of financial statements in communicating information about risk management. A thorough review of risk models and risk management is beyond the scope of this text.

Cumulative Coverage: Chapters 3 to 5

Musical Notes Incorporated is a company involved in two different aspects of the music business. It has a chain of three stores in southwestern Ontario that sell and repair musical instruments, and another single store that sells CDs, DVDs, and other consumer entertainment products. All four stores are in leased space, and the main office is located in the largest of the three stores selling musical instruments. The company has been in business for many years, and you have just been hired as the new controller. The previous controller had been in the job since the company first opened, and had been ill for a few years, and away from the office for the past six months. As a result, the books need a thorough review in order to straighten out a few errors that have developed over the past fiscal year. The fiscal year ends January 31, 2014, and you will need to correct the errors and draft financial statements using ASPE in preparation for the annual visit of the auditors. The following information has been gathered for you to work with.

The trial balance at January 31, 2014, before any adjustments are made is as follows:

Account Description	Debit	Credit
Cash	$ 53,265	
Accounts receivable	251,000	
Allowance for doubtful cccounts		$ 7,200
Inventory—instruments	8,000,000	
Inventory—CDs, DVDs, and other entertainment products	200,000	
Prepaid insurance	5,000	
Equipment—instrument division	500,000	
Accumulated depreciation—equipment instrument division		350,000
Accounts payable		100,000
Notes payable		100,000
Income tax payable		23,000
Unearned revenue		60,000
Common shares (10,000 shares issued and outstanding)		100
Retained earnings		7,453,565
Sales revenue—instrument division		2,500,000

Account Description	Debit	Credit
Cost of goods sold—instrument division	1,200,000	
Operating expenses—instrument division	150,000	
Bad debt expense—instrument division	5,000	
Insurance expense—instrument division	6,600	
Sales revenue—CD division		250,000
Cost of goods sold—CD division	350,000	
Operating expenses—CD division	100,000	
Income tax expense	23,000	

Your search through the company files has led you to the following information, which may require adjustments:

1. The CD division store is located in a shopping mall in an area of town where a number of factories have closed. The mall is virtually empty. This area of the business has been struggling for a few years due to the availability of downloadable music and movies off the Internet and recent changes to the local economy. This has resulted in a decision to close this store. It is unlikely that a buyer can be found, and the store will be closed on March 31, 2014. The only asset of this division is the inventory, and all attempts will be made to sell this by the closing date. It is expected that the company will recover the book value of the inventory as it is being carried at its current fair value. There are no liabilities related to this division.

2. The company's income tax rate is normally 20%. When the income tax was paid for 2013, the payment was debited to income tax expense.

3. The company paid a dividend of $25,000 to its shareholders in December 2013. This amount was incorrectly recorded as an operating expense of the instrument division.

4. Accounts payable at year end, which had not been recorded, were a total of $20,000 of operating expenses for the instrument division. Last year's accounts payable had been paid and were all related to operating expenses: $65,000 for the instrument division and the remaining $35,000 for the CD division. When paid, operating expense accounts had been debited.

5. During the year, one accounts receivable invoice in the amount of $5,000 for a violin had become uncollectible and was written off to bad debt expense. The company follows a policy of recording 1% of its year-end accounts receivable as an allowance for doubtful accounts. The CD division has cash sales, whereas the sales of the instrument division are 100% on credit.

6. The equipment is being amortized using the straight-line method over 10 years, assuming no residual value. Depreciation has not been recorded for the current year.

7. Insurance is paid each November 30, and covers a 12-month period. When the invoice was paid on November 30, 2013, it was debited to insurance expense. The 2012 invoice was for $6,000.

8. Inventory listings have been provided by the store staff that indicate the inventory has been properly accounted for at year end.

9. The instrument repair department forgot to credit a customer who had paid a deposit of $500 on a repair to a bassoon. The customer invoice for $750 is included in accounts receivable.

10. The note payable is due in two equal instalments of $50,000 each, plus interest, on January 30, 2015, and 2016. The annual interest rate is 5%, and the note has been outstanding since August 1, 2013.

Instructions

Prepare the journal entries required to correct the accounts at year end. Post these journal entries to the trial balance using a 10-column work sheet, and complete the other columns of the work sheet in good form. Prepare the January 31, 2014 statement of financial position and combined income statement and statement of retained earnings for Musical Notes Incorporated for the year ended January 31, 2014.

AP–Charles Rex Arbogast/The Canadian Press

E-Commerce Transactions Bring Accounting Challenges

MILLIONS OF PEOPLE AROUND THE WORLD have used an on-line coupon site like Groupon but have probably never wondered how these sites make money. They use a business model that was not easily possible before the dawn of e-commerce.

Groupon, which had the largest share of the on-line coupon market in Canada as of April 2010, offers up to 90% off local and national products and services—everything from cupcakes to car repairs—via daily e-mails to subscribers. Once a certain number of people have signed up for the coupon, the deal goes ahead. Groupon collects money upfront from customers for the goods and services. It keeps a portion of the money as a commission and then passes on the rest of the payments to the merchants.

Customers spread the word of the deals via e-mail and social networks. The merchants set the terms on the quantity of coupons available, how the coupons will be redeemed, and when they'll expire. Groupon provides the advertising and a worldwide customer base of some 150 million to the merchants, who then hope for repeat business after the deals expire.

How does the accounting work for such a company? Groupon used to consider its gross billings—the gross amount it collects from customers for coupons sold—as revenue. But after filing with the U.S. Securities and Exchange Commission in 2011 to become a publicly traded company, the regulators required Groupon to change its accounting practice so that only the net amount it keeps after paying merchants is counted as revenue. Its refiled documents showed net revenues about half what they were under the previous practice of gross billings.

An important part of Groupon's business model is to refund money to any dissatisfied customers. In that way, the company is not always assured of being able to keep all of its net revenues and it is difficult to predict how many customers will ask for their money back. For example, in the fourth quarter of 2011, Groupon's loss was U.S. $22.6 million larger than initially reported.

Groupon CEO Andrew Mason says the company's initial focus was gaining subscribers and merchants. "We believe that the most important thing for us to be focused on is growing the business, building something that our consumers and our merchant partners love. And when you focus on those inputs, revenue and profitability is the output and it follows naturally."

Sources: Groupon Investor Presentation, December 2011; Associated Press, "Groupon Says 4th-quarter Was Weaker than Reported," *Canadian Business*, March 30, 2012; Shayndi Raice, "Groupon and Its 'Weird' CEO," *The Wall Street Journal*, January 31, 2012; Alistair Barr and Clare Baldwin, "Groupon's IPO Biggest by U.S. Web Company Since Google," Reuters, November 4, 2011.

Revenue Recognition

LEARNING OBJECTIVES

After studying this chapter, you should be able to:

1. Understand the economics and legalities of selling transactions from a business perspective.

2. Analyze and determine whether a company has earned revenues.

3. Discuss issues relating to measurement and measurement uncertainty.

4. Understand how to account for sales where there is collection uncertainty.

5. Prepare journal entries for consignment sales and long-term contracts.

6. Understand how to present sales transactions in the income statement and prepare basic disclosures.

7. Discuss current trends in standard setting for revenue recognition including the contract-based approach.

8. Identify differences in accounting between ASPE and IFRS.

When should revenue be recognized? What is considered revenues and how do you measure them? As mentioned in the opening vignette on Groupon Inc., it often depends on the nature of the business arrangement and whether the entity is providing a service or selling products. Accounting for revenue is a complex issue, but the answer can be found by analyzing the earnings process. This chapter presents the general principles that are used in recognizing revenues for most business transactions.

The chapter is organized as follows:

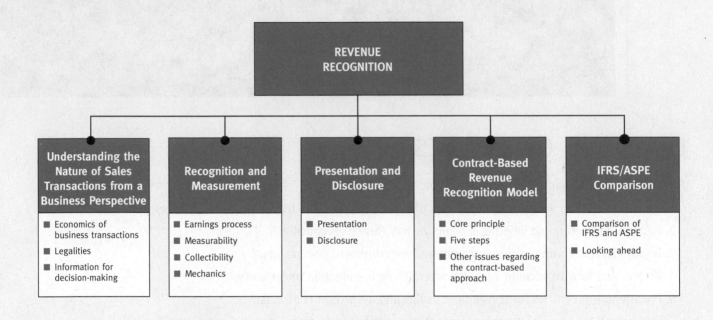

UNDERSTANDING THE NATURE OF SALES TRANSACTIONS FROM A BUSINESS PERSPECTIVE

Objective 1
Understand the economics and legalities of selling transactions from a business perspective.

Much of the complexity of accounting for revenues comes from the way sales transactions are structured. It is critical to understand from a **business perspective** what is being given up in the transaction and what is being received. Business people are not necessarily accountants, yet they generally understand how to price their products and services in order to make a profit and what they need to do to make a sale. In most selling transactions, an entity gives up one asset (for instance, inventory) in exchange for another (for instance, cash). The process of capturing this information for financial reporting purposes involves deciding when to recognize the transaction (on both the statement of financial position and income statement) and how to measure and present it. Accountants must therefore understand the business an entity is engaged in, in order to account for transactions properly.[1]

Let's go a little deeper and examine the economics and the legalities of a sales transaction.

Economics of Business Transactions

Certain economic attributes underlie most business transactions. We will discuss some of these below. The accounting and journal entries for the examples that follow will be covered in Illustration 6-6 or in the following section entitled "Mechanics."

Basics—Are We Selling Goods, Services, or Both? What Is the Physical Nature of the Transaction?

Selling transactions involves an entity transferring goods or services to its customers. The goods or services are often referred to as deliverables. It is important to focus on whether goods or services (or both) are being transferred.

Why Does this Matter for Accounting Purposes?
Sales of goods and of services are different.

Goods are tangible assets. As a result, there is a definite point in time when control over the goods or the item being sold passes to the buyer. Control of an asset means that the entity has access to the benefits provided by the asset where others do not. This normally coincides with the transfer of risks and rewards as indicated by **possession** and **legal title**. Normally this would be a point in time but may span several periods, such as in a construction contract.

Services are not tangible assets and therefore the concepts of possession and legal title are irrelevant. Service contracts may be completed in one period but often span more than one period. Therefore, there is the added complexity of how much, if any, revenue is earned in any given period. Many contracts involve both goods and services (referred to as **multiple deliverables** or **bundled sales**), and this complicates the accounting when the goods and services are sold together as a bundle for one price. This is because possession and legal title to goods might pass before, after, or during the time when the services are rendered. Example 1 looks at a bundled sale.

EXAMPLE 1

A manufacturing company sells cameras and provides a warranty for a total of $100. Under the terms of the warranty, the company promises to fix the camera should it break over the next year. Thus, the company has contracted to provide not only the camera (goods) but also a service (under the warranty). The value of the camera is estimated at $80 and the warranty at $20. The company also sells warranties separately.

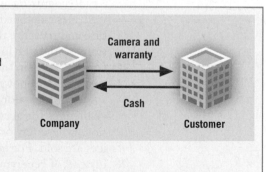

Understanding what the company is selling will help to determine when to recognize revenues. Care should be taken to identify the terms of the transaction, whether it be documented in one or more agreements or not at all. When products and services are sold and priced together as one package, as in Example 1, this creates complexities in terms of determining how much revenue to recognize and when. How much should be attributed to the sale of the camera and how much to the warranty service? Obligations to deliver something in the future can increase measurement uncertainty because we do not always know what will happen in the future.

Reciprocal Nature—What Is Being Received?

Most business transactions are **reciprocal**; that is, the entity gives something up and receives something in return. In addition to assessing what we are giving up, we should determine what we are getting back. **Consideration** is what the entity receives in return for the provision of goods or services. Is the consideration cash or cash-like or is it another good or service?

Why Does the Reciprocal Nature of Transactions Matter for Accounting Purposes?

If we assume that the transactions are at **arm's length**—that is, they are between unrelated parties—then we may assume that the value of what is given up usually approximates the value of what is received in the transaction. Unless otherwise noted, we will generally assume that transactions are at arm's length and reciprocal. Example 2 illustrates this.

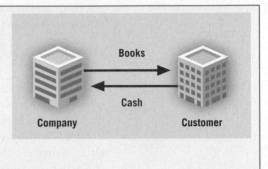

EXAMPLE 2

A retail company sells books for $100 cash. If the company and customer are unrelated, both of them will want to give up and receive things that have the same value. Therefore, it is reasonable to assume that the books have a fair value equal to the cash consideration. If the parties are related, there might be other reasons (such as tax or legal purposes) to transfer something that has a different value from the consideration received.

Sales agreements normally specify what is being given up and what is being acquired as follows:

- **Acquired:** Consideration or rights to the consideration. The amount, nature, and timing of what the customer agrees to pay are normally agreed upon.

- **Given up:** Goods/services (now or in the future). Details regarding delivery (quantities, nature of goods/services, timing, shipping terms) are agreed upon.

Recognizing and focusing on the reciprocal and arm's-length nature of transactions, as well as the detailed agreement between the customer and vendor, allows us to better capture and measure the economics of transactions in the financial statements. Just as obligations to deliver in the future create measurement uncertainty, so do rights to receive consideration in the future. For instance, if the entity sells on credit, there is a risk that the customer will not pay. (This is known as **credit risk**.)

Consideration that is non-monetary[2] (as with **barter** transactions) presents greater challenges for accounting purposes. **Barter** or **nonmonetary transactions** are transactions where few or no monetary assets are received as consideration when goods or services are sold. For instance, a computer manufacturing company might sell a computer, but instead of receiving cash as consideration, the company might receive another type of asset, such as office furniture. From a business perspective, is this still a sale? How should it be measured?

Generally, a barter transaction is seen as a sale if the transaction has **commercial substance**. What does "commercial substance" mean? It means that the transaction is a **bona fide**—or legitimate—purchase and sale and that the entity has entered into the transaction for business purposes, exchanging one type of asset or service for a different type of asset or service. After the transaction, the entity will be in a different position and its future cash flows are expected to change significantly as a result of the transaction in terms of timing, amount, and/or riskiness.

When a reciprocal transaction occurs, the entity's risk profile changes. For instance, in Example 3 below, before the sale, the company did not know how much it would eventually sell the gold for[3] or how much it would realize on the sale. The risk that the price of an asset will change is referred to as a **price risk**. Once the sale occurs, the company gets rid of the price risk of the gold. However, if it sells gold and receives electricity as consideration, as in Example 3, the company gets rid of the price risk on the gold but has taken on a price risk related to the electricity.

Underlying Concept

The representational faithfulness concept supports full disclosure of risks and changes in risk, as they affect the entity's ability to generate future cash flows.

EXAMPLE 3

A resource company sells gold bars (which it has mined and refined) to its customers in exchange for electricity. It uses the electricity immediately in its production operations. If the gold were sold for cash, it would be easy to measure the transaction. However, if it is sold in exchange for another product or service, such as electricity in this case, the company must measure the value of the electricity. Assume a market exists for buying and selling electricity and that the value is estimated at $100. If no market exists (which is often the case when the consideration is a used or unique asset), then the transaction is more difficult to measure.

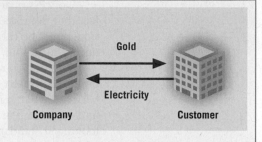

Sometimes, it is common in the industry for companies to swap inventory in order to facilitate a sale. For instance, oil Company A may ask oil Company B to ship oil to A's customer, who might be geographically located close to B. In this way, A's customer receives the oil faster. A would then repay B with the oil at a later date. B would not treat this as a sale as it is not a bona fide sale to B. After the transaction is complete, it is in exactly the same situation as before; that is, it has oil. Non-monetary transactions will be discussed further in Chapter 10.

Concessionary Terms—Are the Terms of Sale Normal or Is this a Special Deal?

In some cases, one party is in a better bargaining position than the other. This might occur, for instance, where supply exceeds demand. In this case, the buyer in the transaction may be able to negotiate a better deal than normal because there are many sellers who want to sell their products and few buyers. **Concessionary terms** are terms negotiated by a party to the contract that are more favourable than normal.

Examples of concessionary terms are as follows:

The selling price is deeply discounted.

The entity agrees to a more **lenient return or payment policy** (including paying in instalments over an extended term or using consignment sales).

The entity loosens its **credit policy**.

The entity transfers legal title but allows the customer to take delivery at a later date (sometimes referred to as "**bill and hold**").

The goods are shipped subject to **customer acceptance conditions**. Extended trial periods would be an example.

The entity agrees to provide **ongoing or additional services** beyond the main goods/services agreed to in order to make the sale. This might include, for example, installation of an asset, ongoing servicing, or continuing fees, such as in a franchise agreement.

The **seller continues to have some involvement**, including a guarantee of resale (or permission to return) or guarantee of profit.

Why Does this Matter for Accounting Purposes? Care must be taken to identify concessionary (or abnormal) terms in any deal as they may complicate the accounting. Concessionary terms are terms that are more lenient than usual and are meant to induce sales.

Concessionary or abnormal terms may create additional obligations or may reflect the fact that the risks and rewards or control has not yet passed to the customer. These situations must be carefully analyzed as they create additional recognition and measurement uncertainty. They may even indicate that no sale has taken place at all.

The question that should be asked is whether the selling terms are normal business practices for the company or are special or unusual in some way. There is a fine line between what is normal and what is abnormal. In order to do this analysis properly, an understanding must be obtained of normal business practices (this can be evidenced by looking at standard documentation of selling transactions such as contracts and/or history of past transactions).

Illustration 6-1 helps differentiate between normal selling terms and abnormal concessionary terms. The normal selling terms are examples of the standard terms that many companies use.

Illustration 6-1

Normal versus Concessionary Terms

	Examples of Normal Selling Terms	Examples of Concessionary Selling Terms
Selling price	Selling price reflects a normal profit margin for the company for that product.	Selling price is deeply discounted.
Payment terms	Sell for cash or on credit. If credit, payment is usually expected within 30 to 60 days.	Any terms that are more lenient than this; for example, • selling on credit where the buyer does not have to pay for 90 days or more, or • instalment sales where these are not normal industry practice.
Extension of credit	Sell to customers that are creditworthy.	Sell to customers that are riskier than the existing customer base.
Shipping terms	Ship when ordered and ready to ship.	Ship at a later date; for example, the entity may hold the inventory in its warehouse for an extended period.
Other terms	Once shipped and legal title passes, no continuing involvement except for normal rights of return and/or standard warranties.	Extended right of return/warranty period, cash flow guarantee on future rental of building sold, profit guarantees on future resale or buyback provisions.

Example 4 illustrates a contract with concessionary terms.

EXAMPLE 4

A merchandising company sells inventory to a customer for $100 cash. Legal title passes when the cash is paid. The merchandise is stored in the warehouse for a few days until after year end. Is this a sale at year end or not? It is not clear. Normally, delivery to the customer would accompany the sales order and payment. However, the merchandising company is agreeing to a non-standard selling term (that is, to store the goods) in order to make the sale more attractive. This might mean revenue cannot be recognized until it is delivered to the customer or that the company is selling both the inventory as well as a storage service.

One last thought on the topic of normal business practices. Note that many companies continue to change their product mix and selling terms in an effort to provide maximum value to customers and shareholders. This is a completely normal part of evolving the business and dealing with changes that may be happening in the industry. For instance, a company that usually sells a product to ensure a certain profit margin may sell the product at a deep discount in order to achieve market penetration and get customers using the product.

What Do the Numbers Mean?

Real World Emphasis

Research In Motion (RIM) did this in 2011 with its BlackBerry PlayBook tablet. Hoping to get customers using the PlayBook instead of the very popular iPad, RIM offered the PlayBook at a deeply discounted price of $199. This was about $300 less than the original suggested retail price. The company hoped that by getting a significant number of PlayBooks into the hands of users, it would encourage software developers to create new applications. In this case, the selling price was well received by the market and the sales were recognized as revenues since all revenue recognition criteria were met and there were bona fide business reasons for changing the selling terms. Because of the deep discount, however, the company took an inventory writedown of $485 million in the third quarter of 2011 related to the PlayBooks.

Source: Jared Newman, "BlackBerry PlayBook: $199 Yet Again," *PCWorld*, February 2, 2012; "Research In Motion Announces Third Quarter Provision Related To PlayBook Inventory and Confirms Commitment to Tablet Market; Provides Update to Q3 and Fiscal 2012 Guidance," company news release, December 2, 2011; Matt Hartley, "RIM Offering Discounted PlayBooks at Several Retailers," *Financial Post*, September 26, 2011.

Legalities

Underlying Concept

Any promise that is enforceable under law and any obligation that is imposed by law should be included in the statements under the full disclosure and transparency principles assuming that they are material.

Companies operate within environments governed by law, including contract law, common law, and securities law. Laws exist to protect the rights of individuals and legal entities. It is important to understand the legal environment because rights and obligations often arise from the operation of the law.

Contract Law

When an entity sells something, both the entity and the customer enter into a contract. A contract with customers is an agreement that creates enforceable obligations and establishes the terms of the deal.[4] The contract may be written or verbal or may be evidenced by, for instance, a cash register receipt. The important thing is that two parties have promised to exchange assets and this creates a contract. There is a promissor (the seller), a promissee (the customer), and an agreement. Thus, the act of entering into a sales agreement creates legal rights and obligations.

In addition, the contract establishes the point in time when **legal title** passes (entitlement and ownership under law). When the customer takes physical **possession** of the goods straight away, legal title would normally pass at this point. If the goods are shipped, the point at which legal title passes is often indicated by the shipping terms as follows:

FOB shipping point: title passes at the point of shipment.

FOB destination: title passes when the asset reaches the customer.

Why Does this Matter for Accounting Purposes? As noted above, if the entity has promised to provide goods and/or services now or in the future, the contract binds it and can be enforced. It creates contractual rights and obligations that may meet the definition of assets and liabilities. The contract also establishes the substantive terms of the deal, which need to be analyzed when determining if revenue has been earned. If, for instance, the contract stipulates that customers must sign invoices as evidence that they are satisfied with the goods, it may mean that no revenue may be recognized until this is done.

Constructive Obligation

Performance obligations may arise even if not stated in a contract. In many cases, an entity may have an implicit obligation even if it is not explicitly noted in a selling contract. This is referred to as a **constructive obligation**. A constructive obligation is an obligation that is created through past practice or by signalling something to potential customers. Constructive obligations are often enforceable under common or other law. Example 5 illustrates the concept of a constructive obligation.

EXAMPLE 5

A clothing company sells goods worth $100 with a standard return policy. The policy states that the customer may return the goods within 30 days of purchase if defective. This policy is stated on the bill of sale and creates a contractual obligation. In practice, the company advertises that it stands behind its products 100%. Furthermore, it has a past history and a customary business practice of accepting all returns for any reason and even after the 30-day period. The company may have a constructive obligation regarding these returns. In other words, it effectively has an obligation to accept customer returns for any reason at any time beyond the 30-day contractual obligation because it has created an expectation.

Why Does this Matter for Accounting Purposes?   Any enforceable promise that results from the sale (whether implicit or explicit) may create a performance obligation that needs to be recognized in the statement of financial position. This includes both contractual and other promises.

Information for Decision-Making

Ethics

Although the revenue number is used in several key ratios, the most important revenue analysis is normally a trend analysis showing changes in revenues from year to year. Due to the sensitivity and high profile of the revenues number on the income statement, there is a lot of pressure to report biased revenue numbers. Biased reporting is possible under both a principles-based accounting standards system (because there is less specific guidance) and a rules-based accounting standards system (by finding loopholes in the rules). Revenues are a key number used to judge management's job performance and they are a signal in the marketplace of sustainable growth potential. The value of firms in certain industries, such as Internet companies, is often based on revenues, since many of these firms do not generate profits in their early years.

Theory

Revenue recognition is one of the main areas of misrepresentation in financial statements. It is often difficult to spot such misrepresentations, since the note disclosures are often very general. It is therefore important to carefully understand the company's underlying business and business model and to ensure that any changes in the business model are reflected appropriately in the statements. Care should also be taken to ensure that large and unusual transactions are entered into for bona fide business reasons (for example, to add value for the shareholders) rather than to make the company's performance look better than it really is.

RECOGNITION AND MEASUREMENT

Now that we understand selling transactions from a business perspective, let's look at how to account for sales transactions.

Real World Emphasis

Revenue is defined as an **inflow of economic benefits** (cash, receivables, or other consideration) arising from **ordinary activities**.

Ordinary activities are the entity's day-to-day business activities. For instance, for **Magnotta Winery Corporation**, the ordinary activities are the production and sale of wine. Revenues are **realized** when goods and services are exchanged for cash. **Realization** is the process of converting noncash resources and rights into money. As noted earlier, this is referred to as the cash-to-cash cycle. Now let's take a look at when revenues are **recognized**.

From an **accounting perspective**, there are two conceptual views of how to account for revenues:

1. earnings approach and

2. contract-based approach.

The **earnings approach** focuses on the earnings process and how a company adds value for its customers. The **contract-based approach** focuses on the contractual rights and obligations created by sales contracts. In all cases, in order to properly account for the transaction, there should be persuasive evidence of the sales arrangement. This is important so that we know a transaction has occurred and what the terms are. Evidence might consist of a contract (written or verbal), an invoice, or other documents depending on what are considered normal business practices for the company. The contract-based approach is currently the subject of an IASB Revised Exposure Draft and is discussed later in the chapter.

The earnings approach is currently in place under ASPE and IFRS.[5] It is seen primarily as an income statement approach to accounting for revenues, and so the focus is essentially on measuring revenues and costs and recognizing revenues when earned. Recall that the matching principle requires recognition of costs in the period that the related revenues are recognized. Let's look at the general revenue recognition principle first.

Under the earnings approach, revenues for **sale of goods** and related costs are recognized when:[6]

- the **risks and rewards** of ownership are transferred to the customer;

- the vendor has **no continuing involvement in, nor effective control over**, the goods sold;

- costs and revenues can be **measured reliably**; and

- **collectibility** is probable.[7]

If the company cannot measure the transaction, then either there is too much uncertainty surrounding the transaction (for instance, where there are abnormal concessionary terms), or the company has not completed all that it has to do to earn the revenues.

Earnings Process

What does the company do to create valuable products or services that customers will pay for? How does it add value? **Earnings process** is a term that refers to the actions that a company takes to add value. It is an important part of the business model as it focuses on operating activities. The earnings process is unique to each company and each industry. Different industries add value in different ways. For example, companies that sell goods that they manufacture have vastly differing earnings processes than those that sell goods that they buy wholesale and sell retail. In addition, companies that are in the biotechnology business have models that are different from real estate companies. For this reason, it is important to begin with an understanding of the earnings process.

On February 1, 2012, **Facebook Inc.** filed documents with the U.S. Securities and Exchange Commission in the process of going public. The company was started up by Mark Zuckerberg and was incorporated in July 2004. Its mission, described as a "social mission" by Mr. Zuckerberg, is to make the world more open and connected. According to the registration statement, there are over 845 million active monthly users (which had risen to over 1 billion in 2012). Users upload pictures and other personal information and interact with each other. The company notes that it creates value for all of its stakeholders including its users, application developers, and advertisers.

In 2011, the company reported revenues of U.S. $3.7 billion, up from U.S. $777 million in 2009. Approximately 85% of these revenues are generated through advertising. The rest is generated by a commission that Facebook earns on any applications that are sold through Facebook (including games). What are the ordinary activities of

Facebook? Who are the customers? If its customers are its users, then any activities related to users are considered "ordinary" activities. On the other hand, if its customers are the advertisers, then any activities related to maximizing advertising exposures are considered "ordinary" activities.

Most companies sell products or services to their customers, who pay them for these items. Facebook has a different model. It provides services to its users for free and finances this through advertising dollars. This creates an interesting business model triangle (company, user, and advertiser). If we view this from a more traditional approach, we might argue that the real business is selling advertising. The users provide a very rich database of information that can be mined to determine user preferences. Facebook then matches the advertisers with the users who are most likely to use them. Is the company using advertising dollars to facilitate the process of connecting people or is it using the process of connecting people to generate advertising dollars? This is an interesting question.

Facebook notes that privacy is a big risk factor in this type of business and takes all precautions to ensure user privacy. As accountants, it is important to understand the business model so that the financial statements are transparent. In his letter to potential investors, Mr. Zuckerberg noted the following:

> Simply put: we don't build services to make money; we make money to build better services.

> And we think this is a good way to build something. These days I think more and more people want to use services from companies that believe in something beyond simply maximizing profits.

In conclusion, Facebook is a prime example of how Internet-based companies all have unique business models that are changing all the time.

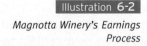
Real World Emphasis

Source: S-1 Registration Statement filed by Facebook with the SEC in February 2012; Erik Sherman, "Facebook vs. Twitter: Old-School Business Models Still Rule," *Inc.*, March 12, 2012; Shayndi Raice and Randall Smith, "Facebook Targeting May IPO," *Wall Street Journal*, March 28, 2012.

Selling Goods

When an entity sells goods, there is often one main act or **critical event** in the earnings process that signals **substantial completion or performance**. At this point, although some uncertainty remains, its level is acceptable and revenues can be recognized under accrual accounting. In businesses that sell goods, substantial completion normally occurs at the **point of delivery**. This is generally when the risks and rewards of ownership (including legal title and possession) pass. If the earnings process has a critical event, it is often referred to as a **discrete earnings process**.

As an example, Magnotta Winery Corporation makes wine (among other products). Its business involves the steps shown in Illustration 6-2.

Magnotta Winery's Earnings Process

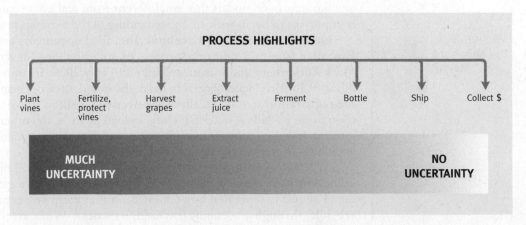

PROCESS HIGHLIGHTS

Plant vines → Fertilize, protect vines → Harvest grapes → Extract juice → Ferment → Bottle → Ship → Collect $

MUCH UNCERTAINTY .... **NO UNCERTAINTY**

Magnotta must perform all of the acts in the illustration in order to make a profit from the sale of its wine. The entity starts with cash, invests it in inventory, sells the inventory at a price that is higher than its cost, and collects cash. At the early points of the earnings process, there is significant uncertainty about how much product will be produced and its quality. What if the vines get diseased? What if temperatures are too low or it rains too much? What if there is no market for the product? Moving along the earnings process timeline (from left to right), the conditions creating the uncertainty resolve themselves. At the far right-hand side of the earnings process, once the product is shipped and paid for, all uncertainty is eliminated about creation of the product itself, the measurability of both its costs and revenues, and the collectibility of those revenues.

The concept of **risks and rewards (benefits) of ownership** is a core concept in the earnings approach to revenue recognition. It helps to establish ownership and to indicate when ownership passes from one party to another. As a general rule, the entity that has the risks and rewards treats the goods as an asset.[8]

Illustration 6-3 presents some of the risks and rewards associated with the sale of wine at Magnotta.

Illustration **6-3**	Risks	Rewards
Risks and Rewards of Ownership—Case of Wine	— wine will age poorly and therefore decline in value — wine will be stolen/vandalized — wine will be stored improperly	— wine will age well and appreciate in value — wine can be consumed by owner or buyer — wine inventory may be used as collateral for bank loan — wine may be sold for cash

In determining who has the risks and rewards of ownership and, therefore, whether a sale has occurred at the point of delivery, it is important to look at who has **possession** of

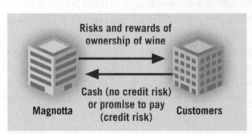

the goods and who has **legal title**. The risks and rewards usually stem from these two factors. For example, Magnotta is not entitled to sell inventory or pledge it as collateral (that is, to reap the rewards) unless it has legal title to it. Legal title and possession expose Magnotta to risk of loss.

The principle is quite general and, therefore, there are a wide range of practical applications. Different companies interpret these principles in different ways.[9] Inventory will be more fully discussed in Chapter 8.

What about recognizing income *before* possession and legal title to goods pass to a customer? Is there ever a situation whereby revenue might be recognized before this critical event? In some cases, revenue may be recognized even before there is a specific customer. Examples of such situations can be found in the forestry and agricultural industries when some products have assured prices and ready markets. Revenue is recognized over time as the assets mature. The critical event is the appreciation in value of the asset.[10]

Selling Services

The focus is different when determining the earnings process for services. When services are provided, the focus is on **performance of the service**. An example of an earnings process for a service that is a discrete earnings process is a maintenance inspection on a car. The service is offered on the spot and is completed in a very short time. The critical event is when the mechanic hands over the inspected car and the bill.

The accounting is more complex where the earnings process has **numerous significant events (continuous earnings process)**. Example 6 illustrates this.

Law

Often a contract to set the terms of the relationship or engagement is signed upfront. This contract establishes the nature of the services to be provided and their value, among other things. It also lays out the parties' rights and obligations. Illustration 6-4 depicts the earnings process for an engineering firm.

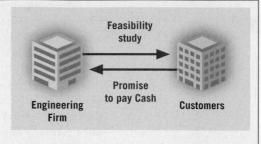

EXAMPLE 6

An engineering firm accepts a contract to provide a long-term feasibility study to determine the feasibility of building a new road. The earnings process is noted in Illustration 6-4. When does performance occur in the earnings process? Should the company wait until the study is complete (at the end of the contract) before recognizing the revenue? There is no easy answer. If this is seen as a **continuous earnings process** with many significant events, it might make sense to recognize revenues bit by bit as each significant event is performed (as long as the revenue is collectible). Judgement is required.

Illustration 6-4

Earnings Process of Engineering Firm Providing Long-Term Feasibility Study

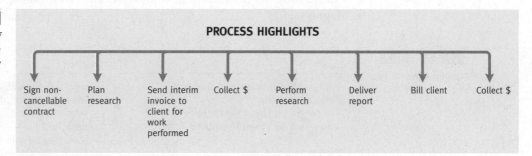

Long-Term Contracts

Accounting gets more complex where the contract is a long-term contract that involves providing a service to develop an asset. Is the company providing a service or an asset or both? Examples include contracts for the development of buildings, military and commercial aircraft, weapons delivery systems, and space exploration hardware. These contracts frequently provide that the seller (builder) may invoice the purchaser at intervals, as various points in the project are reached. This feature provides the seller (builder) with financing so that it covers its costs during construction. These invoices are referred to as **billings**.

Two methods of accounting for long-term construction and other service contracts are generally recognized under ASPE. Either you recognize the revenues over the life of the contract or at the end. These approaches are noted below:[11]

1. **Percentage-of-completion method**: Revenues and gross profit are recognized each period based on progress made to a specific point in time. This makes the most sense in long-term service contracts when it is the service that is being provided to build something or work on something that is owned by the customer (numerous significant events). For instance, Bombardier accounts for revenues of its specially designed products such as railway vehicles under this method.

2. **Completed-contract method**: Revenues and gross profit are recognized only when the contract is completed. It may make sense to use this method as a default method when there are measurement problems, as discussed below. This method might also be used where performance consists of one significant act. For instance, a home builder who pre-sells houses from standard floor plans and then builds them would recognize the revenues at the end of the contract when legal title to the house passes to the buyer.

The method that **best matches the revenues to be recognized to the work performed** should be used.[12] In other words, if performance requires many ongoing acts (in other words, it is a **continuous earnings process**), the percentage-of-completion method should be used as long as the company is able to **measure** the transaction. Alternatively, the completed-contract method should be used when performance consists of a single act (a **discrete earnings process**) or should be the default method when there is a **continuous earnings process but the progress toward completion is not measurable**.

IFRS only mentions the percentage-of-completion method; however, it does not prevent recognition of revenue at the end of the contract if that is appropriate. IAS 18.25 notes that when a specific act is much more significant than other acts, revenue recognition is postponed until that significant act is completed. For instance, Bombardier signs contracts with airlines in advance for construction of aircraft. Revenues from these contracts are recognized when the aircraft is delivered and other recognition criteria are met. IFRS allows earlier recognition of recoverable revenues equal to costs incurred where the outcome is not reliably measurable. This is sometimes referred to as the **zero-profit method**.

Law

Under many of these contracts, an asset is being built for a customer and the buyer and seller have obtained **enforceable rights**. The buyer has the legal right to require specific performance on the contract; the seller has the right to require progress payments that may provide evidence of the buyer's ownership interest.

IFRS deals with this very fundamental issue when accounting for construction of real estate.[13] Where the buyer is able to specify major structural elements before and/or during construction, the business arrangement is seen as a provision of a service. If the buyers only have limited ability to dictate changes and influence design, it is seen as a sale of goods. ASPE does not provide this explicit guidance. Example 7 illustrates this.

> **EXAMPLE 7**
>
> A construction company signs a contract to build a shopping centre. The complex is expected to take three years to complete. Is the company selling a good (the shopping centre) or a service (construction services)? This is an excellent question. One might argue that this is very similar to producing inventory and that therefore it is a sale of goods. This might be the case if title to the shopping centre does not pass until completion. Others might argue that it is the service of constructing the centre that is being provided. This might be the case if the customer has legal title to the asset as it is being constructed.
>
>
>
> To help determine whether the company is selling a good or service, the transaction's economics and legalities should be carefully analyzed. Who has the risks and rewards and/or control over the asset? When does legal title pass? The use of professional judgement also assists in determining this. The contract itself should state clearly what is being given up and received and when legal title passes.

The mechanics of these methods will be discussed later in the chapter.

Measurability

Objective 3
Discuss issues relating to measurement and measurement uncertainty.

The general revenue recognition principle notes that revenue should only be recognized if the transaction is measurable. Sales are generally measured at fair value, which is represented by the value of the consideration received or receivable. Where the sale is on credit and the repayment term extends over a longer period (and the receivable is non–interest-bearing or the interest rate is below market rate), the receivable should be discounted to reflect the time value of money.[14] IFRS gives explicit guidance on how to calculate the interest rate. IFRS notes that the discount rate should be whichever of the following is more clearly determinable: (1) the prevailing rate for a similar note receivable or (2) the imputed rate that discounts the cash flows to the current cash selling price of the item sold.

For instance, assume that an entity sells inventory for $200 (including $100 upfront). The remaining amount is payable in two years. The entity estimates that the interest rate for a similar financing arrangement would be between 9 and 10%. The inventory normally

Finance

sells for $180. In order to calculate the selling price, the entity has to either rely on the estimated borrowing rate (between 9 and 10%) or the cash selling price ($180). The present value of the cash flows using both 9 and 10% would result in a selling price greater than the cash selling price (using present value factors of .82645 for 10% and .84168 for 9%). Because of this, it may be more prudent to use the cash selling price and impute the interest rate. In addition, the company regularly sells the item for $180. If we calculate the discount rate required to equate the present value of the cash flows with the cash selling price, we see that the rate is 12% [$100 + ($100 × .79719)].

For barter transactions, if the fair value of the consideration is not available, the fair value of the product or service sold is used as long as the sale has commercial substance and is reciprocal, as discussed earlier.[15]

Measurement uncertainty results from an inability to measure the transaction or parts of the transaction. This might arise for the following and other reasons:

- the inability to reasonably estimate the consideration (such as barter transactions, price protection clauses, or sales returns provisions on new products);[16]

- the inability to reasonably estimate related costs (such as costs to complete the contract or warranty costs); or

- the inability to measure the outcome of the transaction itself (for example, where the sales are contingent upon a future event, the terms of the transaction are not sufficiently solidified, or the customer may cancel the contract during the trial period).

Earlier in the chapter, we discussed the issue of concessionary terms. Concessionary terms generally make it more difficult to measure the transaction. This is the case because concessionary terms often involve longer time horizons, are unique or one-time, and include more lenient return and other policies. In addition, there is often no history of similar transactions to assist in measuring the uncertain items. Care should be taken to analyze external factors such as obsolescence, business or economic cycles, the financial health of customers, and the arrival of a competitor's products that may cause the company's products to become obsolete.

What Do the Numbers Mean?

Real World Emphasis

Ethics

In 2005, the U.S. Securities and Exchange Commission (SEC) released a statement noting an enforcement action against **Coca-Cola**. The company settled the proceedings without admitting or denying the findings. No fine was paid. In question was a selling practice known as "channel stuffing" or "gallon pushing." According to the statement, the company offered extended credit terms to certain of its bottlers to induce them to purchase additional flavour concentrates. This was done at or near the end of each reporting period in 1997, 1998, and 1999.

The SEC noted that the accounting treatment regarding the revenues was fine but that the company should have disclosed this practice in the interest of transparency. This raises an interesting question relating to these types of concessionary terms. Should the more lenient credit terms have caused the company to account for the sales differently? In all likelihood, the goods were shipped and not subsequently returned so the sales likely met the revenue recognition criteria. However, by purchasing more inventory before year end, the bottlers did not purchase this inventory in the following period. Therefore, the practice resulted in moving sales from a future period to the prior period. Without the additional disclosures, would financial statement users be able to assess the impact, if any, on future revenues and earnings?

It is interesting to note that the SEC was concerned not about the recognition and measurement accounting practices or the alleged channel stuffing but rather the disclosure of the enhanced sales terms.

Source: "The Coca-Cola Company Settles Antifraud and Periodic Reporting Charges Relating to its Failure to Disclose Japanese Gallon Pushing," SEC news release, April 18, 2005; Coca-Cola Settles SEC Investigation, Isdell Sends Memo," *Atlanta Business Chronicle*, April 18, 2005; Siobhan Hughes, "Coca-Cola Settles Charges Tied to 'Gallon Pushing,'" Dow Jones Newswires, April 18, 2005.

Two alternative revenue recognition treatments are available where there is measurement uncertainty.

1. Do not record a sale if it is not measurable.

2. Record the sale, but attempt to measure and accrue an amount relating to the uncertainty as a cost or reduced revenues. For example, sales returns and allowances may be treated as contra sales accounts.

The second treatment is preferred under accrual accounting. Measurement models should be used to help quantify risks and uncertainties.

Measuring Parts of a Sale

Sales involving more than one product or service create additional measurement challenges. Recall that sales of products are dealt with differently than sales of services for revenue recognition purposes. Different services may also be accounted for differently depending on when the related revenues are earned. In order to accommodate this, the sale needs to be **bifurcated**, or divided up, into separate units or components. For instance, a cellular telephone company might sell a phone plus a monthly service to provide airtime. The phone and the access are separate units for accounting purposes.

Once we establish whether there are separate units, we then allocate the overall price to each unit. Ideally, the **relative fair value method** would be used. In this method, the fair value of each item (sometimes referred to as the stand-alone value) is determined and then the purchase price is allocated based on the relative fair values. Alternatively, the **residual value method** could be used. In this method, the fair value of the **undelivered** item is subtracted from the overall purchase price. The residual value is then used to value the delivered item (in this case the telephone). Example 8 illustrates how to measure parts of a sale. Where stand-alone values are estimated, the estimate should maximize the use of observable inputs.

EXAMPLE 8

Assume that Jason Inc. sells a phone and access service for two years bundled together. Assume further that the separate deliverables meet the GAAP criteria for treatment as separate units. The fair value of the phone is $100 and the fair value of the service is $200. In order to make the sale, Jason Inc. sold the bundle at a discount for $250. Under the fair value method, the amount that is allocated to the product would be $83.33 and the value attributed to the service would be $166.67. If the residual value method is used, the service would be valued at $200 and the product at $50. The table below shows the calculations.

	Fair value method calculation	Fair value method allocation	Residual method calculation	Residual method allocation
Product	[$100 ÷ ($100 + $200) × $250]	$ 83.33	($250 − $200)	$ 50
Service	[$200 ÷ ($100 + $200) × $250]	$166.67	($250 − $50)	$200
Total		$250.00		$250

Once we allocate the purchase price to each unit, we then follow GAAP (ASPE or IFRS) to see if the revenue for each unit should be recognized. The revenue for the phone would be recognized upon delivery, and the revenue for the airtime would be recognized as the service is provided (or the airtime is used up). For instance, in the above example, assuming a fair value allocation, the following journal entry would be recorded at the time of sale:

A = L + SE			
Accounts Receivable		250	
Sales Revenue			83
Unearned Revenue			167

A   =   L   +   SE
+250   +167   +83

Cash flows: No effect

Care should be taken to consider the economic value of the services, which may change over time. For example, under warranty contracts, the company may have to provide more services toward the end of the period.

Accounting for bundled sales is a highly complex area requiring much judgement.

Onerous Contracts

Sometimes contracts become **onerous**, which means that the contract is no longer profitable to the company. Where this is the case, consideration should be given to remeasuring the contract and reflecting a loss in the income statement. We will look at an example of this shortly when we review losses on long-term contracts.

Payments to Customers

Normally, the company sells products or services to its customers and receives monetary consideration. However, sometimes, the company pays its customers. Why would it do this? There are many business reasons, including the following:

- Volume rebates: These payments are made to encourage customers to buy more. The more they buy, the lower the price per unit.

- Reimbursement of costs: These payments occur when the customer incurs a cost such as advertising that benefits both the customer and the company. If both parties have agreed to share the cost, then the vendor may pay the customer its share of the expenses incurred by the customer.

- Acquisition of assets to facilitate sales: These payments may be made to acquire assets from the customer that are needed to sell the products. For instance, the company may purchase a refrigeration display unit that will be kept at the customer's location to display the vendor's product.

Accounting for these payments to customers (often referred to as promotional payments) has been very controversial over the past few years, with some customers recognizing these amounts as revenues or income when received. Chapter 8 will revisit this issue, but the accounting is generally as noted in Illustration 6-5.

Ethics

Illustration 6-5

Accounting for Payments to Customers

Transaction	Vendor Accounting (IAS 18.10 and ASPE 3400.28)	Customer Accounting (IAS 2.11; ASPE 3031.12 and 3400.25)

	Dr. Appropriate account
	   Cr. Cash
		Dr. Cash
		   Cr. Appropriate account

Volume rebates	Debit is **Revenue**	Credit is **Inventory**
Cost reimbursements	Debit is **Expense** as long as the vendor receives an identifiable benefit in exchange for the payment (such as advertising)	Credit is **Expense** as long as the payment received is a reimbursement for costs incurred by the customer to sell the vendor's product (such as advertising)

On August 4, 2010, the SEC filed a report alleging that **Navistar International Corp.** engaged in fraudulent accounting activities. The document alleges that during the period 2001 to 2004, Navistar expanded its production, which resulted in the company buying more inventory from its suppliers. Navistar negotiated vendor rebates with 35 of its suppliers. These rebates were identified as volume rebates and signing bonuses for the additional business that Navistar was bringing to its suppliers. Thirty of the rebates were booked by Navistar as revenues and resulted in restatements of pre-tax income in 2003 (2.7% of pre-tax income) and 2004 (27.7%).

The question is whether these rebates should have been booked as revenues or reductions in inventory. As evidence for booking as revenues, the company allegedly referred to a form letter or contract that stated that the rebates were for past purchases. The SEC alleged that in some instances, the company also had verbal and/or written side arrangements noting that the payments were contingent upon future purchases, that the vendor could recover the payments if those future purchases were not made, and that the vendor could inflate future prices to recover the rebates.

The complaint was subsequently settled, with the SEC noting that the restatements resulted from a deficient system of internal controls rather than fraudulent activity. As part of the settlement, the company was required to hire additional accounting employees and a new corporate compliance officer.

Sources: "Navistar Settles with Commission over Certain Restated 2002-2005 Financial Results," SEC litigation release, August 5, 2010; Stephen Taub, "SEC Settles Charges Against Six Former Navistar Finance Execs," CFOZone.com, August 6, 2010; Dan Leone, "Navistar Execs Must Return Bonus Pay, SEC Says," *Transport Topics*, August 6, 2010.

Collectibility

At the point of sale, if it is reasonably sure that the receivable will ultimately be collected (or it is probable that economic benefits will flow to the entity), revenues are recognized.[17] Note that, as long as it is possible to estimate uncollectible amounts at the point of sale (perhaps based on historical data), the sale is booked and the potential uncollectible amount is accrued.

Alternatively, when **collectibility** cannot be reasonably assured, revenues cannot be recognized. In these cases, it is presumed that if collectibility is not established at the time of sale, then in substance no real sale has been made. Why would a company sell something to a customer who will not be able to pay for the goods? This would not make economic sense. The accounting would default to a cash basis (that is, income is recognized when cash is received). In the past, two methods—the instalment sales method and the cost recovery method—have been included in many accounting texts. Discussion of these can be found on the expanded discussion area on the text's companion website and in *WileyPLUS*.

Real-World Examples

Let's revisit the examples looked at so far and examine the accounting treatment for revenue recognition and measurement using real-world examples in Illustration 6-6. IFRS has been used since the companies referred to are public companies.

Example Number	Facts from Examples	Accounting Treatment	Alternate Accounting Treatment
1	A manufacturing company sells cameras and provides a warranty (for total cash of $100). The warranty is sold separately for $20.	The warranty is a separate service being offered and is therefore treated as unearned revenue. Cash 100 Sales Revenue 80 Unearned Warranty Revenue 20 For instance, **Best Buy** records unearned revenues from extended warranties.	Note that when the warranty is not sold separately, it is often accounted for as an expense and liability (measured at the estimated cost). This usually reflects the fact that the warranties exist to ensure that inventories sold are defect free. Cash 100 Sales Revenue 100 Warranty Expense 15 Warranty Liability 15 (Assume estimated cost of fixing the cameras is $15) For instance, **EADS** and **Sunpower** expense their warranty costs.
2	A retail company sells books for $100 cash. The companies are not related.	The revenues are booked at the cash consideration, which reflects the fair value of the books. Cash 100 Sales Revenue 100 Cost of Goods Sold 60 Inventory 60 (Assume the cost of the inventory is $60)	Where the parties are related to each other (for instance, where the companies are owned by the same shareholder), the cash consideration may not reflect fair value and special accounting may apply. This will be covered in Chapter 23.
3	A resource company sells gold bars (which it has mined and refined) to its customers in exchange for electricity (fair value $100).	The transaction is measured at the fair value of the consideration (the electricity) unless the fair value of the gold is more readily available. Utiltiies Expenses 100 Cost of Good Sold 60 Sales Revenue 100 Inventory 60 (Assume the cost of the gold is $60 and that inventory is valued at cost)	Where the goods exchanged are similar in nature and the exchange is made to facilitate a sale to a customer, the transaction is not treated as a sale. This is often the case with commodities like oil where suppliers swap the oil in various locations to fulfill customer demand. In a swap situation such as this, there would be no journal entry and therefore no sale. For example, **Imperial Oil** measures these transactions at book value.
4	A merchandising company sells inventory to a customer for $100 cash (legal title passes at this point). The merchandise is stored in the warehouse for a few days until after year end.	IFRS allows revenue recognition in limited situations where delivery to the customer is delayed at the customer's request. The sale must be probable, inventory must be on hand and ready for delivery, and payment terms must be normal. Cash 100 Sales Revenue 100 Many companies wait until the customer receives the goods. For instance, **Best Buy** defers revenue recognition for on-line sales until the customer receives the goods. Customers may pick the goods up or have them shipped (for a fee).	Assume the terms of the contract specify that the goods are to be stored for the customer because the goods need to be temperature controlled. This may be seen as a bundled sale. The storage service revenues would be recognized separately depending on the length of time stored. Cash 100 Unearned Revenue 10 Sales Revenue 90 (Assuming that the fair value of the storage service is $10) **Trenton Cold Storage Transportation and Logistics** transports and stores inventory needing temperature control as a service to its customers.

Illustration 6-6

Accounting Treatment for Previously Discussed Examples

(continued)

Example Number	Facts from Examples	Accounting Treatment	Alternate Accounting Treatment

5	A clothing company sells goods for $100 with a standard return policy. The policy states that the customer may return the goods within 30 days of purchase if defective.	Assume that the company only honours returns for the stated 30-day period and that it estimates the value of the returns to be $5 at time of sale. The $5 would be recorded as a sales return and allowance.
		
		Cash 100
		Sales Returns and Allowances 5
		   Sales Revenue 100
		   Allowance for Sales Returns and Allowances 5
		
		Best Buy estimates sales returns and allowances based on historical return rates.
			Assume that the company honours returns for the stated 30-day period. In addition, the company has a past practice of honouring returns beyond the stated period. It estimates the value of the returns to be $10 at time of sale with $5 of this amount estimated for returns beyond the 30-day period. The $10 represents partly a contractual obligation and partly a constructive obligation (the additional $5 estimated liability for the period beyond the 30 days). The $10 would be recorded as a sales return and allowance.
			
			Cash 100
			Sales Returns and Allowances 10
			   Sales Revenue 100
			   Allowance for Sales Returns and Allowances 10

6	An engineering company accepts a contract to complete a long-term feasibility study.	The revenue on the contract would be recognized when the first part of the work is done and the customer is invoiced for the first instalment. This example assumes that revenues of $100 are billed as earned.
		
		Accounts Receivable 100
		   Service Revenue 100
			Some companies recognize the contract upon signing (prior to invoicing or incurring costs) as long as the company is legally entitled to receive cash.
			
			Accounts Receivable 100
			   Unearned Revenue 100
			
			For instance, for certain contracts, **EADS** recognizes a financial asset when it has an unconditional right to receive cash.

7	A construction company signs a contract to build a shopping centre. The centre is expected to take three years to complete.	Use the percentage-of-completion method assuming that the contract is signed upfront and that legal title to the shopping centre rests with the customer as it is being built. Assume further that the customer has control over the construction and any changes made to the building. The percentage of completion method is examined in the next section in more detail.
		
		For instance, **Bombardier** and **SNC Lavalin** use the percentage-of-completion method for certain types of contracts.
			If no contract is signed upfront, the centre may be treated like inventory or a self-constructed asset until the end and then accounted for as a sale of a building or inventory (depending on the seller's normal business). Assume amounts as noted.
			
			Accounts Receivable/ Cash 100
			Cost of Goods Sold 50
			   Sales Revenue 100
			   Inventory 50
			
			Sunpower treats costs related to construction of solar power systems as non-current assets while building and then transfers them to Prepaid and other current assets once a customer contract is signed. The costs are treated as expense when the project is completed and delivered.

8	A telecommunications company sells a phone and access service for two years bundled together.	Treat the phone and services as separate units and record revenues for the phone and unearned revenue for the services. The journal entries were presented in the earlier discussion. For instance, **Telus** and **Rogers** allocate revenues on multiple element arrangements using relative fair values.	The residual method could be used to allocate the revenues.

Mechanics

Objective 5
Prepare journal entries
for consignment sales
and long-term contracts.

This section deals with the calculations and journal entries for several of the more complex topics discussed in the chapter to this point.

Consignment

In some distribution arrangements, the vendor **retains legal title** to the goods. In such cases, the point of delivery is therefore not proof of full performance. This specialized method of marketing for certain types of products uses what is known as a **consignment**. Under this arrangement, the **consignor** (such as a manufacturer) ships merchandise to the **consignee** (such as a dealer), who acts as an agent for the consignor in selling the merchandise. Both consignor and consignee are interested in selling. The consignor wants to make a profit or develop a market, while the consignee wants to make a commission on the sales. Example 9 explains consignment accounting in greater detail.

EXAMPLE 9

To illustrate consignment accounting entries, assume that Sunshine Manufacturing Corp. ships merchandise costing $36,000 on consignment to Lebel Stores. Sunshine pays $3,750 of freight costs and Lebel pays $2,250 for local advertising costs that are reimbursable by Sunshine. By the end of the period, two thirds of the consigned merchandise has been sold for $40,000 cash. Lebel notifies Sunshine of the sales, retains a 10% commission, and remits the cash due to Sunshine. The journal entries in Illustration 6-7 would be made by the consignor (Sunshine) and the consignee (Lebel).

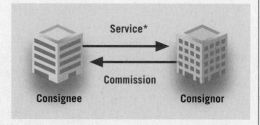

Why would companies use consignment to sell their goods? The company selling the goods will often use this type of distribution mechanism to maximize sales. By using the distribution channels and networks of an existing retailer, a consignor can avoid having to incur the set-up costs related to creating its own retail distribution system. Under the consignment arrangement, the manufacturer (consignor) retains the risk that the merchandise might not sell and frees the dealer (consignee) from having to commit part of its working capital to inventory. Presumably, if the products sell very well to third parties, the consignor could push for the consignee to actually purchase the goods outright. A variety of different systems and account titles are used to record consignments, but they all share the common goal of postponing the recognition of revenue until it is known that a sale to a third party (the customer) has occurred.

The consignee accepts the merchandise and agrees to exercise due diligence (or care) in looking after the inventory and selling it. When the merchandise is sold, cash received from customers is then remitted to the consignor by the consignee, after deducting a sales commission and any chargeable expenses. Revenue is recognized by the consignor only after it receives notification of the sale. For the entire time of the consignment, the merchandise is carried as the consignor's inventory and is separately classified as Merchandise on Consignment. It is not recorded as an asset on the consignee's books.

Upon sale of the merchandise, the consignee has a liability for the net amount that it must remit to the consignor. The consignor periodically receives from the consignee a report that shows the merchandise received, merchandise sold, expenses chargeable to the consignment, and cash remitted.

Sunshine Mfg. Corp. (Consignor)		Lebel Stores (Consignee)	
Shipment of consigned merchandise			
Inventory on Consignment	36,000	No entry (record memo of	
Finished Goods Inventory	36,000	merchandise received).	
Payment of freight costs by consignor			
Inventory on Consignment	3,750	No entry.	
Cash	3,750		
Payment of advertising by consignee			
No entry until notified.		Accounts Receivable	2,250
		Cash	2,250
Sales of consigned merchandise			
No entry until notified.		Cash	40,000
		Accounts Payable	40,000
Notification of sales and expenses and remittance of amount due			
Cash	33,750	Accounts Payable	40,000
Advertising Expense	2,250	Accounts Receivable	2,250
Commission Expense	4,000	Revenue from Consignment	
Revenue from Consignment		Sales	4,000
Sales	40,000	Cash	33,750
Adjustment of inventory on consignment for cost of sales			
Cost of Goods Sold	26,500	No entry.	
Inventory on Consignment	26,500		
[²/₃ ($36,000 + $3,750) = $26,500]			

Illustration 6-7

Entries for Consignment Sales

Long-Term Contracts

Percentage-of-Completion Method. **The percentage-of-completion method recognizes revenues, costs, and gross profit as progress is made toward completion on a long-term contract.** If recognition of these items were deferred until the entire contract was complete, the efforts (costs) and accomplishments (revenues) of the interim accounting periods would be misrepresented. In order to apply the percentage-of-completion method, however, there has to be a basis or standard for measuring the progress toward completion at particular interim dates.

Measuring progress toward completion requires significant judgement. Costs, labour hours worked, tonnes produced, and other such measures are often used. The various measures are identified and classified as either input or output measures. **Input measures** (costs incurred, labour hours worked) measure the efforts that have been devoted to a contract. **Output measures** (tonnes produced, storeys of a building completed, kilometres of a highway completed) measure results. Neither of these measures can be applied to all long-term projects; instead, the measure needs to be carefully tailored to the circumstances, which means that judgement is essential.

Whichever method is used, there are some disadvantages with input and output measures. Input measures are based on an established relationship between a unit of input and productivity. If inefficiencies cause the productivity relationship to change, inaccurate measurements result. Another potential problem, called front-end loading, produces higher estimates of completion because significant costs are incurred upfront. Some early-stage construction costs should therefore be ignored if they do not relate directly to the

Underlying Concept

Both input and output measures have measurement uncertainty.

actual performance of the contract; these include, for example, the costs of uninstalled materials or the costs of subcontracts that have not yet been performed.

Output measures can also result in inaccurate measures if the units that are used are not comparable in time, effort, or cost to complete. For example, using storeys completed can be deceiving; completing the first storey of an eight-storey building may require more than one eighth of the total cost because of the substructure and foundation construction.

One of the more popular input measures used to determine the progress toward completion is cost, sometimes referred to as the **cost-to-cost basis**. Under the cost-to-cost basis, the percentage of completion is measured by comparing costs incurred to date with the most recent estimate of the total costs to complete the contract. The formula for this is shown in Illustration 6-8.

Illustration 6-8

Formula for Percentage of Completion, Cost-to-Cost Basis

$$\frac{\text{Costs incurred to date}}{\text{Most recent estimate of total costs}} = \text{Percent complete to date}$$

The percentage of costs incurred out of total estimated costs is then applied to the total revenue or the estimated total gross profit on the contract to arrive at the revenue or the gross profit amounts to be recognized to date. Illustration 6-9 shows this formula.

Illustration 6-9

Formula for Total Revenue to Be Recognized to Date

Percent complete to date	×	Estimated total revenue (or gross profit)	=	Revenue (or gross profit) to be recognized to date

To find the amount of revenue and gross profit that will be recognized in each period, we would need to subtract the total revenue or gross profit that has been recognized in prior periods, as shown in Illustration 6-10.

Illustration 6-10

Formula for Amount of Current Period Revenue, Cost-to-Cost Basis

Revenue (or gross profit) to be recognized to date	−	Revenue (or gross profit) recognized in prior periods	=	Current period revenue (or gross profit)

Illustration of Percentage-of-Completion Method, Cost-to-Cost Basis.

To illustrate the percentage-of-completion method, assume that Hardhat Construction Ltd. has a contract starting in July 2014 to construct a $4.5-million bridge that is expected to be completed in October 2016, at an estimated cost of $4 million. Illustration 6-11 shows the data for the entire construction period. (Note that by the end of 2015 the estimated total cost has increased from $4 million to $4,050,000.) Assume that the customer has control over the asset and can make major changes to the project during construction (therefore there is a continuous transfer of assets).

Illustration 6-11

Application of Percentage-of-Completion Method, Cost-to-Cost Basis

	2014	2015	2016
Costs to date	$1,000,000	$2,916,000	$4,050,000
Estimated costs to complete	3,000,000	1,134,000	—
Progress billings during the year	900,000	2,400,000	1,200,000
Cash collected during the year	750,000	1,750,000	2,000,000

The percent complete is calculated as follows.

(continued)

	2014	2015	2016
Contract price	$4,500,000	$4,500,000	$4,500,000
Less estimated cost:			
Costs to date	1,000,000	2,916,000	4,050,000
Estimated costs to complete	3,000,000	1,134,000	
Estimated total costs	4,000,000	4,050,000	4,050,000
Estimated total gross profit	$ 500,000	$ 450,000	$ 450,000
Percent complete[a]	$1,000,000	$2,916,000	$4,050,000
	$4,000,000	$4,050,000	$4,050,000
	= 25%	= 72%	= 100%

Illustration 6-11

Application of Percentage-of-Completion Method, Cost-to-Cost Basis (continued)

[a]Assume that this percentage represents a reasonable proxy of the amount of goods and services passed on to the customer.

Based on the data above, the entries in Illustration 6-12 would be prepared to record (1) the costs of construction, (2) progress billings, and (3) collections. These entries appear as summaries of the many transactions that would be entered individually as they occur during the year.

Illustration 6-12

Journal Entries—Percentage-of-Completion Method, Cost-to-Cost Basis

	2014		2015		2016	
1. *To record cost of construction:*						
Construction in Process	1,000,000		1,916,000		1,134,000	
Materials, Cash, Payables, etc.		1,000,000		1,916,000		1,134,000
2. *To record progress billings:*						
Accounts Receivable	900,000		2,400,000		1,200,000	
Billings on Construction in Process		900,000		2,400,000		1,200,000
3. *To record collections:*						
Cash	750,000		1,750,000		2,000,000	
Accounts Receivable		750,000		1,750,000		2,000,000

The estimated revenue and gross profit to be recognized for each year are calculated in Illustration 6-13.

Illustration 6-13

Percentage of Completion, Revenue, and Gross Profit by Year

	2014	2015	2016
Revenue recognized in:			
2014 $4,500,000 × 25%	$1,125,000		
2015 $4,500,000 × 72%		$3,240,000	
Less: Revenue recognized in 2014		1,125,000	
Revenue in 2015		$2,115,000	

(continued)

Illustration 6-13
Percentage of Completion, Revenue, and Gross Profit by Year (continued)

2016 $4,500,000 × 100%		$4,500,000
Less: Revenue recognized in 2014 and 2015		3,240,000
Revenue in 2016		$1,260,000
Gross profit recognized in:		
2014 $500,000 × 25%	$ 125,000	
2015 $450,000 × 72%	$ 324,000	
Less: Gross profit recognized in 2014	125,000	
Gross profit in 2015	$ 199,000	
2016 $450,000 × 100%		$ 450,000
Less: Gross profit recognized in 2014 and 2015		324,000
Gross profit in 2016		$ 126,000

The entries to recognize revenue and gross profit each year and to record the completion and final approval of the contract are shown in Illustration 6-14.

	2014		2015		2016	
4. *To recognize revenue and gross profit:*						
Construction in Process	125,000		199,000		126,000	
Construction Expenses	1,000,000		1,916,000		1,134,000	
Revenue from Long-Term Contracts		1,125,000		2,115,000		1,260,000
5. *To record completion of the contract:*						
Billings on Construction in Process					4,500,000	
Construction in Process						4,500,000

Illustration 6-14
Journal Entries to Recognize Revenue and Gross Profit and to Record Contract Completion—Percentage-of-Completion Method, Cost-to-Cost Basis

Note that the gross profit that was calculated above is debited to Construction in Process, while Revenue from Long-Term Contracts is credited for the amounts calculated above. The difference between the amounts that are recognized each year for revenue and gross profit is debited to Construction Expenses (similar to Cost of Goods Sold in a manufacturing enterprise), which is reported in the income statement. That amount (the difference) is usually the actual cost of construction incurred in that period. For example, for Hardhat Construction the actual costs of $1 million in 2014 are used to calculate both the gross profit of $125,000 and the percent complete (25%).

Costs continue to be accumulated in the Construction in Process account so that there is a record of total costs incurred (plus recognized profit) to date. The Construction in Process account represents the value of the service earned to date and would include the summary entries over the term of the construction project that are shown in Illustration 6-15.

Construction in Process

2014 construction costs	$1,000,000	12/31/16	to close	
2014 recognized gross profit	125,000		completed	
2015 construction costs	1,916,000		project	$4,500,000
2015 recognized gross profit	199,000			
2016 construction costs	1,134,000			
2016 recognized gross profit	126,000			
Total	$4,500,000		Total	$4,500,000

The Hardhat illustration contains a change in estimate in the second year, 2015, when the estimated total costs increased from $4 million to $4,050,000. By adjusting the percent completed to the new estimate of total costs, and then deducting the amount of revenues and gross profit that has been recognized in prior periods from revenues and gross profit calculated for progress to date, the change in estimate is accounted for in a cumulative catch-up manner. That is, the change in estimate is accounted for in the period of change so that the SFP at the end of that period and the accounting in subsequent periods are the same as if the revised estimate had been the original estimate.

Financial Statement Presentation—Percentage-of-Completion Method. The Construction in Process and Billings accounts are presented on a net basis in the financial statements. They represent the difference between the amount that has been earned versus the amount billed. When the amount in the Construction in Process account is more than the amount in the Billings account, this excess is reported as a current asset (or noncurrent if the contract is a longer-term contract) entitled "Recognized Revenues in Excess of Billings." The unbilled portion of the revenue recognized to date can be calculated at any time by subtracting the billings to date from the revenue recognized to date, as shown for 2014 for Hardhat in Illustration 6-16.

Illustration 6-16

Calculation of Unbilled Contract

Amount of unbilled revenue at Dec. 31, 2014

Contract revenue recognized to date: $4,500,000 \times \dfrac{\$1,000,000}{\$4,000,000} = \$1,125,000$

Billings to date	900,000
Unbilled revenue	$ 225,000

When the billings are more than the costs incurred and gross profit to date, this excess is reported as a liability entitled "Billings in Excess of Recognized Revenues." The excess signifies that the company has billed more than it has earned. Separate disclosures of the dollar amounts of billings and costs are preferred, rather than a summary presentation of the net difference.

Using data from the previous illustration, Hardhat would report the status and results of its long-term construction activities under the percentage-of-completion method as in Illustration 6-17.

HARDHAT CONSTRUCTION LTD.

Income Statement	2014	2015	2016
Revenue from long-term contracts	$1,125,000	$2,115,000	$1,260,000
Construction expenses	1,000,000	1,916,000	1,134,000
Gross profit	$ 125,000	$ 199,000	$ 126,000

(continued)

Statement of Financial Position (12/31)		2014	2015
Current assets			
Accounts receivable		$ 150,000	$ 800,000
Inventories			
Construction in process	$1,125,000		
Less: Billings	900,000		
Recognized revenues in excess of billings		$ 225,000	
Current liabilities			
Billings ($3,300,000) in excess of recognized revenues ($3,240,000)			$ 60,000

Note 1. Summary of significant accounting policies.

LONG-TERM CONSTRUCTION CONTRACTS. The company recognizes revenues and reports profits from long-term construction contracts, its principal business, under the percentage-of-completion method of accounting. These contracts generally extend for periods in excess of one year. The amounts of revenues and profits that are recognized each year are based on the ratio of costs incurred to the total estimated costs. Costs included in construction in process include direct materials, direct labour, and project-related overhead. Corporate general and administrative expenses are charged to the periods as incurred and are not allocated to construction contracts.

Completed-Contract Method

In the completed-contract method, revenue and gross profit are recognized when the contract is completed. Costs of long-term contracts in process and current billings are accumulated, but there are no interim charges or credits to income statement accounts for revenues, costs, and gross profit.

The main advantage of the completed-contract method is that reported revenue is based on final results rather than on estimates of unperformed work. Its major disadvantage is that it does not reflect current performance when the period of a contract is longer than one accounting period. Although operations may be fairly steady during the contract period, revenue is not reported until the year of completion, which distorts earnings.

The annual entries to record costs of construction, progress billings, and collections from customers would be identical to those illustrated under the percentage-of-completion method, but with the very important exclusion of the recognition of revenue and gross profit. For Hardhat Construction's bridge project illustrated on the preceding pages, the following entries are made in 2016 under the completed-contract method to recognize revenue and costs and to close out the inventory and billing accounts:

A   = L +   SE
+$450,000   +$450,000

Cash flows: No effect

Billings on Construction in Process	4,500,000	
Revenue from Long-Term Contracts		4,500,000
Construction Expenses	4,050,000	
Construction in Process		4,050,000

Illustration 6-18 compares how Hardhat would have recognized gross profit on the same bridge project under the percentage-of-completion and completed-contract methods.

	Percentage-of-Completion	Completed-Contract
2014	$125,000	$ 0
2015	199,000	0
2016	126,000	450,000
	450,000	450,000

Hardhat would report its long-term construction activities as shown in Illustration 6-19.

Illustration 6-19

Financial Statement Presentation—Completed-Contract Method—Earnings Approach

HARDHAT CONSTRUCTION LTD.

Income Statement	2014	2015	2016
Revenue from long-term contracts	—	—	$4,500,000
Construction expenses	—	—	4,050,000
Gross profit	—	—	450,000

Statement of Financial Position (12/31)		2014	2015
Current assets			
Accounts receivable		$150,000	$800,000
Construction in process	$1,000,000		
Less: Billings	900,000		
Unbilled contract costs		$100,000	
Liabilities			
Billings ($3,300,000) in excess			
of contract costs ($2,916,000)			$384,000

Note 1. Summary of significant accounting policies.

LONG-TERM CONSTRUCTION CONTRACTS. The company recognizes revenues and reports profits from long-term construction contracts, its principal business, under the completed-contract method. These contracts generally extend for periods in excess of one year. Contract costs and billings are accumulated during the periods of construction, but no revenues or profits are recognized until contract completion. Costs included in construction in process include direct material, direct labour, and project-related overhead. Corporate general and administrative expenses are charged to the periods as incurred and are not allocated to construction contracts.

Zero-Profit Method

In the above Hardhat example, an additional complexity may arise where the outcome of the contract is not determinable. This might occur, for example, at the beginning of the contract where it might be difficult to estimate costs to completion and therefore the percentage complete. In this case, as noted earlier, recoverable revenues equal to costs incurred would be recognized under IFRS. Under ASPE, if the outcome were not determinable, the accounting would default to the completed contract method.

Illustration 6-20 shows the revenue-related journal entries for 2014, comparing the accounting under IFRS and ASPE where the outcome is not determinable. In addition to the journal entries in Illustration 6-12, the following entry would be booked under IFRS in 2014. Assume that the entity is reasonably assured that it will be able to recover its $1 million construction costs incurred to date.

Illustration 6-20

Accounting when the Outcome of the Contract Is Not Reasonably Determinable

IFRS			ASPE
Construction Expenses	1,000,000		No JE; the completed contract method would
Revenue from			dictate that no revenue or expense be
Long-Term Contracts		1,000,000	recognized until the end of the contract.

Losses on Long-Term Contracts

Two types of losses can occur under long-term contracts:

1. **Loss in current period on a profitable contract:** This condition occurs when there is a significant increase in the estimated total contract costs during construction but

the increase does not eliminate all profit on the contract. Under the percentage-of-completion method only, the increase in the estimated cost requires an adjustment in the current period for the excess gross profit that was recognized on the project in prior periods. This adjustment is recorded as a loss in the current period because it is a change in accounting estimate (discussed in Chapter 21).

2. **Loss on an unprofitable contract:** Cost estimates at the end of the current period may indicate that a loss will result once the contract is completed. Under both the percentage-of-completion and completed-contract methods, the entire loss that is expected on the contract must be recognized in the current period.

Loss in Current Period.　To illustrate a loss in the current period on a contract that is expected to be profitable upon completion, assume that on December 31, 2015, Hardhat estimates the costs to complete the bridge contract at $1,468,962 instead of $1,134,000. Assuming all other data are the same as before, Hardhat would calculate the percent complete and recognize the loss as shown in Illustration 6-21. Compare these calculations with those for 2015 in Illustration 6-11. The percent complete has dropped from 72% to $66\frac{1}{2}\%$ due to the increase in estimated future costs to complete the contract.

<table>
<tr><td>Cost to date (12/31/15)</td><td>$2,916,000</td></tr>
<tr><td>Estimated costs to complete (revised)</td><td>1,468,962</td></tr>
<tr><td>Estimated total costs</td><td>$4,384,962</td></tr>
<tr><td></td><td></td></tr>
<tr><td>Percent complete ($2,916,000 ÷ $4,384,962)</td><td>66½%</td></tr>
<tr><td>Revenue recognized in 2015</td><td></td></tr>
<tr><td>($4,500,000 × 66½%) − $1,125,000</td><td>$1,867,500</td></tr>
<tr><td>Costs incurred in 2015</td><td>1,916,000</td></tr>
<tr><td></td><td></td></tr>
<tr><td>Loss recognized in 2015</td><td>($ 48,500)</td></tr>
</table>

Illustration 6-21

Calculation of Recognizable Loss, 2015—Loss in Current Period

The loss of $48,500 in 2015 is a cumulative adjustment of the excessive gross profit that was recognized on the contract in 2014. Instead of restating the prior period, the prior period misstatement is absorbed entirely in the current period. In this illustration, the adjustment was large enough to result in recognition of a loss.

Hardhat would record the loss in 2015 as follows:

A	=	L	+	SE
−48,500				−48,500

Cash flows: No effect

Construction Expenses	1,916,000	
Construction in Process		48,500
Revenue from Long-Term Contracts		1,867,500

The loss of $48,500 will be reported on the 2015 income statement as the difference between the reported revenues of $1,867,500 and the costs of $1,916,000.[18] Under the completed-contract method, no loss is recognized in 2015, because the contract is still expected to result in a profit that will be recognized in the year of completion.

Loss on an Unprofitable Contract.　To illustrate the accounting for an overall loss on a long-term contract, assume that at December 31, 2015, Hardhat estimates the costs to complete the bridge contract at $1,640,250 instead of $1,134,000. Revised estimates on the bridge contract appear as follows:

	2014 Original Estimates	2015 Revised Estimates
Contract price	$4,500,000	$4,500,000
Estimated total cost	4,000,000	4,556,250[a]
Estimated gross profit	$ 500,000	
Estimated loss		$ (56,250)

[a]($2,916,000 + $1,640,250)

Under the percentage-of-completion method, $125,000 of gross profit was recognized in 2014 (see Illustration 6-14). This $125,000 must be offset in 2015 because it is no longer expected to be realized. In addition, the total estimated loss of $56,250 must be recognized in 2015 since losses must be recognized as soon as they can be estimated. Therefore, a total loss of $181,250 ($125,000 + $56,250) must be recognized in 2015.

Illustration 6-22 shows the calculation for the revenue to be recognized in 2015.

Illustration 6-22

Calculation of Revenue Recognizable, 2015— Unprofitable Contract

Revenue recognized in 2015		
Contract price		$4,500,000
Percent complete		× 64%[a]
Revenue recognizable to date		2,880,000
Less: Revenue recognized prior to 2015		1,125,000
Revenue recognized in 2015		$1,755,000
Cost to date (12/31/15)	$2,916,000	
Estimated cost to complete	1,640,250	
Estimated total costs		$4,556,250

[a]Percent complete: $2,916,000 ÷ $4,556,250 = 64%

To calculate the construction costs to be expensed in 2015, we add the total loss to be recognized in 2015 ($125,000 + $56,250) to the revenue to be recognized in 2015.

This calculation is shown in Illustration 6-23.

Illustration 6-23

Calculation of Construction Expense, 2015— Unprofitable Contract

Revenue recognized in 2015 (calculated above)		$1,755,000
Total loss recognized in 2015:		
Reversal of 2014 gross profit	$125,000	
Total estimated loss on the contract	56,250	181,250
Construction cost expensed in 2015		$1,936,250

Hardhat would record the long-term contract revenues, expenses, and loss in 2015 as follows:

A = L + SE
−181,250   −181,250

Cash flows: No effect

Construction Expenses	1,936,250	
Construction in Process		181,250
Revenue from Long-Term Contracts		1,755,000

As Illustration 6-24 shows, Construction in Process has a balance of $2,859,750 at the end of 2015.[19]

Illustration 6-24

Content of Construction in Process Account at End of 2015—Unprofitable Contract

Construction in Process			
2014 Construction costs	$1,000,000		
2014 Recognized gross profit	125,000		
2015 Construction costs	1,916,000	2015 Recognized loss	$181,250
Balance	2,859,750		

Under the completed-contract method, the contract loss of $56,250 is also recognized in the year in which it first became evident. The following entry is therefore made in 2015:

A   = L +   SE
−56,250   −56,250

Cash flows: No effect

Loss from Long-Term Contracts	56,250	
Construction in Process		56,250

Just as the Billings for Construction in Process account balance cannot be higher than the contract price, neither can the balance in Construction in Process exceed the contract price. In circumstances where the Construction in Process balance is more than the Billings for Construction in Process amount, the recognized loss may be deducted on the statement of financial position from the construction costs that have accumulated in Construction in Process. That is, under both the percentage-of-completion and completed-contract methods, the provision for the loss (the credit) may be combined with Construction in Process, thereby reducing the balance. In circumstances where the billings are more than the accumulated costs (as in the 2015 illustration above), the amount of the estimated loss must be reported separately on the statement of financial position as a current liability. That is, under both the percentage-of-completion and completed-contract methods, the amount of the loss of $56,250, as estimated in 2015, would be taken from the Construction in Process account and reported separately as a current liability entitled Estimated Liability from Long-Term Contracts.

PRESENTATION AND DISCLOSURE

Presentation

We have looked at some specific presentation issues related to long-term contracts. Let's look at general presentation issues related to revenues in this next section.

Revenues versus Gains

What about sales of assets other than the entity's inventory? The principles discussed above do not apply only to sales of inventory, as in the case of Magnotta's wine inventory. They also apply to items that are disposed of through sales that are not part of the normal earnings process, such as sales of income-producing or capital assets. In these cases, a gain[20] is generated (instead of revenues). It is important to carefully establish that, in substance, a disposition has actually occurred. In certain cases, a company may sell a fixed asset and receive a note receivable that is secured by the asset itself. If very little other consideration is received, has the asset really been sold? Have the risks and rewards really passed?

Net Income versus Other Comprehensive Income

In some cases, income is generated when assets are revalued. Consider the case of investments and property, plant, and equipment measured and carried at fair value on the SFP. Should these gains and losses be recognized in the income statement, in other comprehensive income, or not at all? We will revisit this issue in subsequent chapters.

Gross versus Net Revenues

Objective 6
Understand how to present sales transactions in the income statement and prepare basic disclosures.

Although net income does not change if a company chooses to report revenues as the **gross** amount billed to the customer (as well as the related cost of goods sold) instead of the **net** amount retained, the revenue number changes. Since revenue is the focus of many financial statement users, this is an important issue.

In analyzing this issue (which is essentially a **presentation** issue), consider whether the company:

- acts as a **principal** in the transaction or an **agent or broker** (who is buying and selling an item for commission),
- takes **title to the goods** being sold, and
- has the **risks and rewards of ownership** of the goods being sold.

Real World Emphasis

For example, a real estate agent acts as a **broker** or **agent**, finding a house for a customer and then taking a **commission** on the sale. The agent does not take **title** to the house nor does he or she have the **risks and rewards** associated with ownership of the house. Revenues associated with the sale of a house would be recorded net as commissions. On the other hand, a company such as **Mattamy Homes Limited**, which builds houses and then sells them to customers, acts as a **principal**. It has the risks and rewards of ownership of the house before selling it (including legal title). When Mattamy sells a house, it would record the house's market value as revenue and the cost to build it as cost of goods sold.

What Do the Numbers Mean?

Consider **Priceline.com**, the U.S. company that allows you to "name your own price" for airline tickets and hotel rooms. In its 2010 annual report, Priceline recognized revenues of U.S. $3 billion, including "merchant revenues," which made up 55% of this number. The other 45% was made up of "agency" and other revenues. What is the difference between Priceline's merchant and agency revenues?

Ethics

According to Priceline, merchant revenues include the full amount that customers paid for tickets, hotel rooms, and rental cars (gross revenues). Traditional travel agencies call that amount "gross bookings," not revenues. And much like regular travel agencies, Priceline keeps only a small portion of gross bookings—namely, the spread between the customers' accepted bids and the price it paid for the merchandise. Agency revenues are essentially net revenues, which represent commissions (more like traditional travel agencies).

Why does Priceline book some revenues gross and some net? Priceline notes that for the merchant revenues it is the merchant of record and as such it selects suppliers and determines prices that it will accept from the customer. Thus it is acting as the principal in the transaction as opposed to the agent.

As referred to in the opening story, this same issue arose when Groupon went public. It initially filed its financial statements with the SEC showing gross billings as revenues. The SEC objected and the company subsequently refiled its statements showing net revenues (which represented its commission on transactions).

Source: Jeremy Kahn, "Presto Chango! Sales Are Huge," *Fortune* (March 20, 2000), p. 44; Priceline 2010 Annual Report; Thomas J. Phillips, Michael S. Luehlfing, and Cynthia M. Daily, "The Right Way to Recognize Revenue," *Journal of Accountancy*, June 2001; "Groupon Says 4th-quarter Was Weaker than Reported," *Canadian Business*, March 30, 2012.

Disclosure

IFRS requires the following disclosures:

1. accounting policies, including methods to determine stage of completion;

2. amount of significant categories of revenues recognized; and

3. amount of revenues arising from exchange of goods and services.

ASPE has similar requirements.

CONTRACT-BASED REVENUE RECOGNITION MODEL

Objective 7
Discuss current trends in standard setting for revenue recognition including the contract-based approach.

The IASB and FASB are currently studying a new model for revenue recognition. A Revised Exposure Draft (RED) was issued in 2011 and the standard had not been finalized at the time of writing this chapter. That proposed model, known as the contract-based model, applies to contracts with customers and is discussed below. The standard defines a contract as an agreement between parties that creates enforceable rights and obligations. The contract may be written, oral, or implied by customary business practices. For instance, a sales invoice may be evidence of a contract.

Core Principle

The core principle of the contract-based model as noted in the RED[21] is as follows:

> the entity should recognize revenue to depict the transfer of promised goods or services to customers in an amount that reflects the consideration to which the entity expects to be entitled...

Five Steps

Significant Change

Under the proposed standard, the following steps should be followed in determining when and how to recognize revenues using the contract-based model.

1. Identify the contract(s) with the customer.

2. Identify the separate performance obligations in the contract.

3. Determine the transaction price.

4. Allocate the transaction price.

5. Recognize revenue when a performance obligation is satisfied.

The standard applies where the contact has commercial substance, is approved by both parties, and rights and obligations including payment terms are identified. The standard does not apply to contracts that may be terminated by either party at no cost if both the following criteria are met:

1. goods/services have not been transferred and

2. payment has not been received and no entitlement to receive payment exists.

The approach is a balance sheet approach, as compared with the current earnings approach, which is an income statement approach. As a balance sheet approach, there is greater emphasis on looking at contractual rights and performance obligations created by the contract with the customer. Although at first glance much of the substance of the new standard looks similar, the detailed accounting will likely change a fair amount.

Let's look at each of the five steps of the contract-based model.

Identify the Contract(s) with the Customer

The first step involves determining the business transaction: What have both parties agreed to? This refers to essentially what we have already discussed earlier; that is, the economics and legalities of the transactions.

The RED gives the following as examples of deliverables under sales contracts:

- Goods produced for sale (manufacturer)

- Goods purchased for resale (retailer)

- Providing the service of arranging for another party to transfer goods/services (agent)

- Stand-ready obligations to provide goods or services (online software platforms)

- Construction services on behalf of a customer (service)

Identify Separate Performance Obligations

Enforceable obligations under the contract are referred to as **performance obligations**. These obligations represent what the company has agreed to sell or do under the contract. For instance, as noted above, the company might agree to sell inventory or provide on-line access to a software platform. If the performance obligations are **distinct** then they should be accounted for as separate performance obligations. Under the RED, **distinct** refers to a good or service that is either sold separately on a regular basis or provides a separate benefit to the customer. Contracts with multiple distinct performance obligations represent bundled sales, as discussed earlier in the chapter.

Looking at a more complex scenario, assume that a company ships goods to its customer FOB shipping point via an independent shipping company. Note further that the company assumes responsibility for any damage during the shipping (notwithstanding the fact that it is shipped FOB shipping point). This represents two distinct performance obligations: (1) the obligation to provide the inventory and (2) the obligation to cover the risk of loss or damage while being shipped. Revenues would be recognized when each performance obligation was satisfied. The obligation to provide inventory would be satisfied when goods were shipped but the obligation to cover risk of loss or damage would not be satisfied until the goods were received in satisfactory condition.

Where goods and services are **highly interrelated**, then they are not separated out as distinct or separate performance obligations and the whole contract is accounted for together. Goods and services would be highly interrelated where the company has to provide a significant service to integrate the goods/services into a combined item or where the goods/services are significantly modified or customized. Items are grouped together until distinct.

For instance, assume a construction company has contracted to build a new shopping centre for a customer. The contract involves designing the building, obtaining planning permissions, buying raw materials, and building the shopping centre. This represents a performance obligation in which provision of the goods (the building) and services (the construction) are highly interrelated because the company is providing a significant service (the construction) to integrate the goods (the building supplies) into a combined item: the shopping centre. In addition, the building materials are significantly modified in that they are converted from raw materials to a building. The revenue would be recognized over time.

Determine the Transaction Price

Next, the transaction has to be measured. The entity must consider the following:

- Variable consideration such as discounts, rebates, refunds, credits, incentives, performance bonuses, penalties, contingencies, and price concessions: The company may use the expected value of the consideration (sum of the probability weighted amounts) or the most likely amount. If the entity expects to refund a portion of the consideration, this is set up separately as a refund liability.

- Time value of money (where significant and the contract exceeds one year): The discount rate should reflect the customer's credit risk and may be calculated using the rate needed to equate the payments required under the contract to the present cash selling price of the goods.

- Noncash consideration: The transaction would be measured at the fair value of the noncash consideration unless it was not reasonably estimable, in which case the company would use the fair value of the goods/services delivered to the customer.

- Consideration payable to a customer: This would be accounted for as a reduction of the selling price unless it was for a separate good or service.

Customer credit risk must be measured and presented separately on the income statement as a separate line item, not as part of revenues. The amount of the estimated loss would be presented as a contra account to Revenues (as a reduction of Revenues). The credit would be booked to the Allowance for Doubtful Accounts. The entity would use the Financial Instruments standards to measure impairment. The net amount should not exceed the amount that the entity is reasonably assured to be entitled to.

As an example of variable consideration, consider a contract where a company sells 1,000 units for $1 each and gives the customer a right of return. The units cost $0.90 each. The company estimates that out of the $1,000 selling price, $30 will be refunded to the customer for returns based on history. Assume that the company would record the following journal entry:

Cash	1,000	
Sales Revenue		970
Contract Liability		30
Contract Asset	27	
Cost of Goods Sold	873	
Inventory		900
If there are no returns, the company would record the following entry:		
Cost of Goods Sold	27	
Contract Liability	30	
Contract Asset		27
Sales Revenue		30

Allocate the Transaction Price

This step is important where there is more than one performance obligation. The transaction price is allocated based on the relative stand-alone selling price of each distinct good or service. The best evidence of the stand-alone selling price is an observable price in the market. For instance, if the company sells a product on its own, this would be good evidence to support the stand-alone selling price. Where the selling price is not available, the company should try to estimate it. It could estimate it using a residual value technique, as discussed earlier in the chapter.

Where the total stand-alone selling prices add up to more than the transaction price, the discount is allocated using a relative fair value basis. (This method was discussed earlier in the chapter.) The entity may allocate the discount to one deliverable in certain cases.

Recognize Revenue when a Performance Obligation Is Satisfied

The last step of the contract-based model involves recognizing the revenues. The entity recognizes revenue when it satisfies the performance obligation. This occurs when the customer obtains control over the good or service. Revenue is either recognized at a point in time or over time. In recognizing whether control passes at a point in time, consider:

- Right to payment
- Legal title
- Possession
- Significant risks and rewards of ownership
- Customer acceptance

In order to recognize the revenues over time, one of the following criteria must be met:

1. The activities related to satisfying the performance obligation create or enhance an asset that is controlled by the customer.

2. The activities do not create an asset that has an alternative use to the entity (for example, the entity could not sell it to someone else under the terms of the contract or the asset is so customized that it is only useful to the customer) and one of the following criteria is met:

   (a) The customer receives and consumes the benefits from the activities during the performance period.

   (b) Another entity would not need to substantially re-perform the work the entity has completed to date.

   (c) The entity has a right to payment for performance completed to date.

   If revenue is recognized over time, the entity must be able to measure its progress and may use an appropriate measure of progress. Input and output measures may be used to estimate the progress to date. If the entity is not able to measure the progress toward completion, it may recognize revenues equal to costs incurred as long as it expects to recover those costs.

   In our earlier example where the company is hired to build a shopping centre, the revenue may be recognized over time. This is because the shopping mall is controlled by the customer since it owns the land and has control over the building design and specifications. In other words, the company is building a unique asset for the customer.

Other Issues Regarding the Contract-Based Approach

The IASB and FASB Revised Exposure Draft proposes increased disclosures that will help users understand the nature, amount, timing, and uncertainty of revenues and related cash flows. It also proposes standards for accounting for costs relating to obtaining or fulfilling the contract.

Accounts receivable are recognized as assets where the company has an unconditional right to receive the benefits. A contract asset is recognized when the right to payment is contingent upon future performance. A contract liability is recognized when payment is received in advance. Onerous contracts must be recognized as a loss and liability.

The following are some areas where there may be differences from current practice:

- There is a presumption that revenues and related costs are measurable and thus, measurability is not a specific revenue recognition criterion. Note that it remains a general recognition criterion.

- Measurement uncertainty is embedded in the calculation of the transaction price through the use of the "expected value" and "most likely" methods. As a general rule the RED provides more measurement guidance.

- The transaction price is measured at the amount the entity expects to receive. As such the entity may have to set up a liability for funds that it expects to refund; for instance, for merchandise returns. The entity must also account for the time value of money where it is significant.

- Customer credit risk is measured upon initial recognition of the revenue and is recorded in a separate account on the income statement, which would be presented just beneath Revenues.

- Warranties will be treated as quality assurance warranties (Dr. Expense and Cr. Liability) or insurance type warranties (separate performance obligations). A warranty is treated as a separate performance obligation (Dr. Cash and Cr. Unearned Revenue) where it is sold separately. Basically, a quality assurance warranty is a promise that the goods sold are in good working order when they are first sold. An insurance type warranty is a promise to fix any problems that arise subsequent to the sale. Although this treatment is generally followed under existing GAAP, practice may vary.

- Contract assets are recognized upon signing where contracts are non-cancellable.

IFRS/ASPE COMPARISON

Objective 8
Identify differences in accounting between ASPE and IFRS.

A Comparison of IFRS and ASPE

Illustration 6-25 presents a comparison of IFRS and ASPE related to revenue recognition.

	Accounting Standards for Private Enterprises (ASPE)—*CICA Handbook*, Part II, Section 3400	IFRS—IAS 11, 18, and 41	IASB Proposed Model	References to related illustrations and select brief exercises
Recognition	The earnings approach requires recognition when performance is achieved, that is, when risks and rewards have passed and services are rendered, measurable, and collectible.	Earnings approach requires recognition when risks and rewards passed and services are rendered, there is no continuing involvement, and services are measurable and collectible.	Contract-based approach consists of five steps: 1. Identify contract. 2. Identify separate performance obligations. 3. Determine transaction price. 4. Allocate transaction price. 5. Recognize revenue when performance obligation is satisfied (when control passes). Collectibility and measurability are not considered specific recognition criteria. Credit risk is assessed and accounted for when revenue is first recognized (recognized separately from revenues). Provision is recorded separately from sales.	Existing ASPE and IFRS are essentially the same.
	Percentage-of-completion and completed-contract methods allowed for long-term contracts.	More detailed guidance is given regarding construction accounting, including percentage-of-completion method.	Recognize revenue at a point in time or over time. Percentage of completion and zero profit methods are acceptable.	Illustration 6-20 BE 6-18, BE 6-19, BE 6-23, and BE 6-24

(continued)

	Accounting Standards for Private Enterprises (ASPE)— *CICA Handbook*, Part II, Section 3400	IFRS—IAS 11, 18, and 41	IASB Proposed Model	References to related illustrations and select brief exercises
		Zero-profit method is used where the outcome is not determinable. Clear direction is given regarding whether to account for long-term real estate contracts as sale of service or goods.	May recognize revenue over time if (1) the customer controls the asset being constructed or (2) an asset is created that does not have an alternate use and certain criteria are met. If providing goods and services together, must consider if performance obligations are interrelated. (If they are, treat as one performance obligation.)	
	Warranty costs have historically accrued as costs/obligation when revenues recognized. More recently, these may have been accounted for as bundled sales (unearned revenues).	Warranty costs have historically accrued as costs/obligation when revenues recognized. More recently, these may have been accounted for as bundled sales (unearned revenues).	Quality assurance type warranties are accrued as costs/liabilities and insurance type warranties are treated as separate performance obligations resulting in recording Unearned Revenue (if sold separately).	Existing ASPE and IFRS are essentially the same.
Measurement	At transaction or consideration price, which is generally assumed to be fair value. Where payment is received over time, ASPE notes that the amount should be discounted using a prevailing market rate.	At fair value, which is assumed to be transaction price unless onerous contract. Where payment is received over time, IAS 18 provides specific guidance as to how to calculate the discount rate.	Transaction price is the amount that the entity expects to receive. Where the contract is onerous, must recognize. Greater emphasis is on using measurement models to quantify risk/uncertainty. Guidance is provided as to how to calculate discount rate.	Existing ASPE and IFRS are essentially the same.
	Barter transactions are measured at fair value when transaction has commercial substance.	Barter transactions are measured at fair value when products/services exchanged are dissimilar.	Measure at fair value of consideration (or of goods and services provided as a default).	Existing ASPE and IFRS are essentially the same.
	Accounting for biological assets is not explicitly discussed.	Biological assets (living animals or plants) are valued at fair value less costs to sell under IAS 41 (even before they are sold).	IAS 41 still stands since the proposed standard does not cover these areas.	Illustration 8-27 (Chapter 8)
	Bundled sales are bifurcated using relative fair value or residual value method.	Bundled sales are bifurcated using relative fair value or residual value method.	Bundled sales are bifurcated using relative fair value (estimate where not available and may use residual method to estimate).	Existing ASPE and IFRS are essentially the same.

Illustration 6-25

IFRS and ASPE Comparison Chart (continued)

Looking Ahead

The IASB and FASB proposal to use the contract-based revenue recognition model was covered earlier in the chapter in the section Contract-Based Revenue Recognition Model and is summarized in Illustration 6-25 in the column "IASB Proposed Model." The new standard is expected to be issued in 2013 and although the mandatory adoption date has not been set, it would likely be 2014 or 2015. In addition, the IASB is beginning to study the issue of biological assets and whether "bearer" biological assets such as grape vines should be accounted differently from consumable biological assets such as wheat.

SUMMARY OF LEARNING OBJECTIVES

1 Understand the economics and legalities of selling transactions from a business perspective.

It is critical to understand a transaction from a business perspective before attempting to account for it. The analysis should begin with what is being sold to the customer (goods or services) and note also the nature and amount of the consideration. When one party is in a better bargaining position than the other, it may be able to negotiate concessions such as more lenient payment terms. These concessions often complicate the accounting as they introduce measurement uncertainty in many cases.

Selling transactions are based on contractual arrangements between a buyer and a seller. Contracts create rights and obligations under law that must be considered when accounting for the transactions. In addition to contractual law, rights and obligations may exist under other forms of the law, such as common law or contract law. These should also be considered.

2 Analyze and determine whether a company has earned revenues.

Under current accounting standards, the revenues are earned when the risks and rewards of ownership are passed or when the company has done what it said it would do to be entitled to the revenues. Where sale of goods are involved, legal title and possession provide evidence of this. The accounting is more complex when the contract is a long-term contract and when it involves both goods and services. The percentage-of-completion method is commonly used for long-term contracts. The completed contract method is used under ASPE and although IFRS does not mention this method, it is acceptable to recognize revenues at the end of a contract if there is one significant event. IFRS requires the zero-profit method where the outcome is not determinable.

3 Discuss issues relating to measurement and measurement uncertainty.

Under accrual accounting, revenue may only be recognized when reliably measurable. There are many reasons that measurement uncertainty exists including inability to reliably measure the revenue itself (for example, barter transactions or price protection clauses) and inability to measure costs or uncertainty relating to the outcome of the contract itself (contingencies). In the latter case, extreme uncertainty may indicate that the contract or business deal has not yet been completed. Where the sale involves more than one element (such as goods and services), then the selling price must be allocated to the respective parts of the sale using an allocation method such as the relative fair value method or residual method.

4 Understand how to account for sales where there is collection uncertainty.

Collectibility issues also create measurement uncertainty and must be considered when recognizing and measuring sales transactions. When collectibility cannot be assured and/or the related revenue is not measurable in terms of collection or credit risk, then no sale is booked.

5 Prepare journal entries for consignment sales and long-term contracts.

Under consignment sales, the risks and rewards remain with the seller and, therefore, revenues are not recognized until the goods are sold to a third party. Special accounts separate inventory on consignment.

To apply the percentage-of-completion method to long-term contracts, a basis is needed for measuring the progress toward completion at particular interim dates. One of the most popular input measures that is used to determine the progress toward completion is the cost-to-cost basis. Using this basis, the percentage of completion is measured by comparing costs incurred to date with the most recent estimate of the total costs to complete the contract. The percentage of the total estimated costs that the costs incurred amount to is applied to the total revenue or the estimated total gross profit on the contract to arrive at the revenue or the gross profit amounts to be recognized to date.

Under the completed contract method, revenue and gross profit are recognized only when the contract is completed. Costs of long-term contracts in process and current billings are accumulated, but there are no interim charges or credits to income statement accounts for revenues, costs, and gross profit. The annual entries to record costs of construction, progress billings, and collections from customers would be identical to those for the percentage-of-completion method, with one significant exception: revenue and gross profit are not recognized until the end of the contract. The zero-profit method (IFRS) is used when the outcome of the contract is not determinable. Recoverable revenues equal to cost are recognized.

6 Understand how to present sales transactions in the income statement and prepare basic disclosures.

Transactions where the seller is acting as a principal in the sale should be accounted for on a gross basis.

Where the seller is acting as an agent (putting buyers and sellers together), the transaction should be booked on a net basis. Consideration should be given to whether the seller has the risks and rewards of ownership of the product being sold.

Transactions are treated as revenues when they relate to the entity's ordinary activities. They are treated as gains when they deal with ancillary activities. In general, revenues and gains are booked to net income except in very limited circumstances.

7 Discuss current trends in standard setting for revenue recognition including the contract-based approach.

IASB and FASB are currently studying a new model for revenue recognition: the contract-based model, which is felt to be conceptually superior.

8 Identify differences in accounting between ASPE and IFRS.

The main differences are identified in the chart in Illustration 6-25.

KEY TERMS

arm's length, p. 318	credit risk, p. 318	output measures, p. 335
barter transactions, p. 318	critical event, p. 324	percentage-of-completion method, p. 326
billings, p. 326	discrete earnings process, p. 324	
bundled sales, p. 317	distinct, p. 347	performance obligations, p. 347
commercial substance, p. 318	earnings approach, p. 323	point of delivery, p. 324
completed-contract method, p. 326	earnings process, p. 323	possession, p. 321
concessionary terms, p. 319	FOB destination, p. 321	price risk, p. 318
consideration, p. 317	FOB shipping point, p. 321	reciprocal, p. 317
consignment, p. 334	input measures, p. 335	relative fair value method, p. 329
constructive obligation, p. 321	legal title, p. 321	residual value method, p. 329
continuous earnings process, p. 325	measurement uncertainty, p. 328	revenue, p. 322
contract-based approach, p. 323	multiple deliverables, p. 317	risks and rewards (benefits) of ownership, p. 325
control, p. 317	nonmonetary transactions, p. 318	
cost-to-cost basis, p. 336	onerous, p. 330	zero-profit method, p. 327

Quiz

Brief Exercises

(LO 1) BE6-1   Explain the basic economics of what is being received and what is being given up in each of the following business transactions.

(a) A company sells packaging material to another company. The terms of sale require full payment upon delivery.

(b) A company sells packaging material to another company. The terms of sale require payment over one year with interest.

(c) A law firm provides legal services to an accounting firm. In lieu of payment, the accounting firm provides accounting services to the law firm.

(d) A company sells telecommunications equipment for a set fee that includes delivery, installation, a 60-day trial period, a three-year maintenance package (often sold separately), and a one-year manufacturer's warranty (often sold separately). Payment will be received over one year without interest.

(LO 1) BE6-2   Explain the rights and obligations created in the following transactions.

(a) A manufacturer sells goods with terms FOB shipping point.

(b) A manufacturer sells goods with terms FOB destination point.

(c) A manufacturer sells goods with terms FOB shipping point, but routinely replaces products lost or damaged during shipping.

(LO 2) BE6-3   XYZ Company has manufactured a new product that will be marketed and sold during the current year. To encourage distributors to carry the product, XYZ will not require payment until the distributor receives the final payment from its customers. This is not a normal business practice for XYZ Company. Should XYZ record revenue of the new product upon delivery to its distributors? Why or why not?

(LO 2) BE6-4   What is the earnings process for each of the following scenarios?

(a) A manufacturer makes and sells farm equipment. The customer picks up the equipment upon purchase. In addition, there is a one-year warranty that will be honoured by another company.

(b) A company sells books on-line and ships to the customer. Payment is made via credit cards and the company does not accept any product returns.

(c) A company provides cable television services for residential customers. The customer signs a three-year contract. The wiring was already in place from the prior homeowner.

(LO 2) BE6-5   For each of the scenarios noted in BE6-4 above, when would revenue be recognized under the earnings approach?

(LO 2, **BE6-6**   For each of the following scenarios, how will these circumstances affect the recognition of revenue under the
3, 7)   earnings approach and under the contract-based approach?

(a) The anticipated revenues on a contract are $10 million but the associated costs cannot be estimated.

(b) There is a 60-day price protection clause requiring the seller to provide a cash refund to the buyer if the purchase price goes down.

(c) A new product is launched for which the manufacturer will allow unlimited returns.

(LO 2) BE6-7   Mackenzie Construction Services Ltd. has entered into a contract to construct an office building for Designers Corporation. Mackenzie prepares financial statements in accordance with IFRS. Explain how Mackenzie should recognize revenue under the earnings approach in each of the following scenarios:

(a) Designers Corp. has control over the asset being constructed and can make major structural changes during its construction.

(b) Designers Corp. does not have control over the asset being constructed and title only passes at the end of the contract.

(LO 3) BE6-8   How should revenue be measured in each business transaction described in BE6-1? Assume that each company recognizes revenue under the earnings approach.

(LO 3) BE6-9   Adventurers Inc. sold a mountain bike to a customer for $1,000 including a two-year annual maintenance package. The fair value of the mountain bike is $1,100 and the fair value of the maintenance package is $100. Calculate the allocation of revenue for each unit using (a) the relative fair value method and (b) the residual value method. For the residual value method calculation, assume that only the fair value of the maintenance package is known.

(LO 3) BE6-10 Alpha Corp. is a major supplier to Beta Corp. To encourage Beta to buy more, Alpha offers Beta an annual volume rebate of 1% of total invoiced purchases exceeding $100,000. Beta's invoiced purchases in 2014 totalled $110,000. Prepare the journal entry to record the volume rebate for 2014 in the books of (a) Alpha and (b) Beta.

(LO 3) BE6-11 Gardi Inc. sold a unit of inventory to a buyer for $1,000 payable in one year. Gardi estimates that the interest rate for a similar financing arrangement would be 8%. The unit of inventory normally sells for $900. Calculate the discount rate to be applied in calculating the cash selling price of the unit of inventory. Gardi prepares financial statements in accordance with IFRS.

(LO 3) BE6-12 Massey Ltd., an equipment manufacturer, sold and delivered a piece of equipment to a buyer for $100,000, with 50% payable in one year and the remaining 50% payable in two years from the date of sale. Massey estimates that the interest rate for a similar financing arrangement would be 12%. Calculate the amount of revenue that Massey should recognize on the date of sale.

(LO 4) BE6-13 Storage Services Corporation recognizes revenue under the earnings approach. Explain how uncertainty about collectibility would affect revenue recognition if Storage prepares financial statements in accordance with (a) ASPE or (b) IFRS.

(LO 4) BE6-14 Eastern Chemicals Corp. produces a chemical compound at its plant in Halifax, Nova Scotia, and Western Polymers Inc. produces the same chemical compound at its plant in Kelowna, British Columbia. Both companies have manufacturing facilities across Canada, which require the chemical compound as an input in production of industrial adhesives. For more efficient production cycles, and to save on freight costs, Eastern and Western have a swap agreement in place. Eastern has shipped some of the chemical compound from its inventory to Western's manufacturing facility located in Beresford, New Brunswick, according to an order placed by Western. The quantity of chemical compound shipped would normally be sold for $150, and the inventory cost of the chemical compound is $100. According to the swap agreement, Western will repay Eastern with the chemical compound at a later date. Prepare the journal entry to record the transaction in the books of Eastern, if any (assuming that Eastern recognizes revenue under the earnings approach).

(LO 4) BE6-15 Builder Corp. is constructing a warehouse that is expected to take two years to complete. Builder prepares financial statements in accordance with IFRS. Explain how Builder should recognize revenue under the earnings approach, in each of the following scenarios:

(a) Builder signs a contract upfront to construct the warehouse for a specific buyer. Legal title rests with the buyer as the warehouse is being built. The buyer has control over the construction and can require major structural changes during construction.

(b) No contract is signed upfront. Builder normally constructs building structures for sale upon completion.

(LO 5) BE6-16 Finch Industries shipped $550,000 of merchandise on consignment to Royal Crown Company. Finch paid freight costs of $5,000. Royal Crown Company paid $1,500 for local advertising, which is reimbursable from Finch. By year end, 75% of the merchandise had been sold for $618,750. Royal Crown notified Finch, retained a 10% commission, and remitted the cash due to Finch. Prepare all of the journal entries required by Finch for this transaction under the earnings approach.

(LO 5) BE6-17 On August 15, 2014, Japan Ideas consigned 500 electronic play systems, costing $100 each, to YoYo Toys Company. The cost of shipping the play systems amounted to $1,250 and was paid by Japan Ideas. On December 31, 2014, an account sales summary was received from the consignee, reporting that 420 play systems had been sold for $160 each. Remittance was made by the consignee for the amount due, after deducting a 20% commission. Calculate the following at December 31, 2014:

(a) The inventory value of the units unsold in the hands of the consignee.

(b) The profit for the consignor for the units sold.

(c) The amount of cash that will be remitted by the consignee.

(LO 5) BE6-18 Pennfield Construction Corp. began work on a $5,020,000 construction contract in 2014. During 2014, the company incurred costs of $1,600,000, billed its customer for $1,750,000, and collected $1,500,000. At December 31, 2014, the estimated future costs to complete the project total $2,500,000. Assume that Pennfield uses the percentage-of-completion method. Prepare all journal entries required for the year ended December 31, 2014, under the earnings approach.

(LO 5) BE6-19 Using the data from BE6-18, assume that Pennfield cannot reliably measure the outcome of the contract. Explain how this transaction would be accounted for under each scenario:

(a) if Pennfield Construction Corp. is reporting under current IFRS (IAS 11 and 18).

(b) if Pennfield Construction Corp. is reporting under ASPE.

(LO 5) BE6-20 Tampa Inc. began work on an $11.5-million contract in 2014 to construct an office building. During 2014, Tampa Inc. incurred costs of $3.3 million, billed its customers for $5.1 million, and collected $2.9 million. At December 31, 2014, the estimated future costs to complete the project total $6.0 million. Assuming that Tampa uses the completed-contract method, prepare the journal entries for 2014 under the earnings approach.

(LO 5) BE6-21 Inexperienced construction company ABC Corp. signed a risky contract to build a research facility at a fixed contract amount of $2 million. The work began in early 2014 and ABC incurred costs of $900,000. At December 31, 2014, the estimated future costs to complete the project totalled $900,000. During 2015, ABC ran into trouble with weather conditions and incurred the expected costs of $900,000 and estimated that it would need to spend an additional $300,000 to complete the project. During 2016, ABC reluctantly completed the project, incurring further costs of $400,000.

Assuming that ABC uses the percentage-of-completion method and the earnings approach, prepare a schedule to calculate the amount of revenues and gross profit or loss to be recognized by ABC Corp. during the three years of the contract. Provide all journal entries.

(LO 5) BE6-22 Using the information provided in BE6-21, assume instead that ABC uses the completed-contract method and the earnings approach. Prepare a schedule to calculate the amount of revenues and gross profit or loss to be recognized by ABC Corp. during the three years of the contract and provide the journal entry for 2015.

(LO 5) BE6-23 Lombardo Construction Corp. began work on a $100-million construction contract in 2014 to build a luxury hotel to be completed in 2016. During 2014, Lombardo incurred costs of $42 million, billed its customer for $38 million, and collected $35 million. In 2014, the construction industry also experienced significant expansion, rendering construction materials and labour more costly than originally estimated. At December 31, 2014, Lombardo has determined that it is difficult to estimate the costs to complete construction and therefore difficult to estimate the percent complete. Determine the amount of revenue that would be recognized in 2014 under current IFRS (IAS 11 and 18) and the zero-profit method. Lombardo believes it can recover at least the amount of costs incurred to date.

(LO 5) BE6-24 Using the information provided in BE6-23, assume instead that Lombardo prepares financial statements in accordance with ASPE. Determine the amount of revenue that would be recognized in 2014 under the completed-contract method.

(LO 6) BE6-25 Rancourt Corp. is a real estate company. Approximately 50% of sales are properties that Rancourt owns. In the remaining 50%, Rancourt brokers the transactions by finding buyers for property owned by other companies. Explain how Rancourt should present the revenues from both of these operations.

(LO 7) BE6-26 Discuss how the contract-based approach to revenue recognition is consistent with the definition of revenues in the conceptual framework discussed in Chapter 2. Explain the main concepts of the earnings approach and the contract-based approach. What are the conceptual differences between the two approaches?

(LO 8) BE6-27 Compare the accounting for long-term contracts under ASPE and under IFRS.

Exercises

(LO 1) E6-1 (Economics of the Transaction—Various Consumer Industries) The following are independent situations that require professional judgement for determining when to recognize revenue from the transactions.

1. Costco sells you a one-year membership with a single, one-time upfront payment. This non-refundable fee is paid at the time of signing the contract, and entitles you to shop at Costco for one year.

2. DOT Home and Patio sells you patio furniture on a "no money down, no interest, and no payments for one year" promotional deal. The furniture is delivered to your home the same day.

3. The Toronto Blue Jays sell season tickets on-line to games in the Rogers Centre. Fans can purchase the tickets at any time, although the season does not officially begin until April 1. The season runs from April 1 through October each year. Payment is due in full at the time of purchase.

4. CIBC lends you money in August. The loan and interest are repayable in full in two years.

5. Students pre-register for fall classes at Seneca College in August. The fall term runs from September through December.

6. Sears sells you a sweater. In August, you place the order using Sears' on-line catalogue. The sweater is shipped and arrives in September and you charge it to your Sears credit card. In October, you receive the Sears credit card statement and pay the amount due.

7. In March, Hometown Appliances sells a washing machine with an extended warranty plan for five years. The washing machine will not be delivered to the customer until June. Payment is due upon delivery. The extended warranty plans are normally sold separately.

8. Premier Health Clubs sells you a membership with an initiation fee (which covers a medical assessment) and an ongoing monthly fee. The initiation fee is payable at the time of the medical assessment and approximates the cost of the medical assessment.

Instructions

For each scenario, identify what is being "sold": goods, services, or a combination.

(LO 2) E6-2 (Revenue Recognition Under Earnings Approach—Various Consumer Industries)

Instructions

(a) Explain the principles and criteria for revenue recognition under the earnings approach.

(b) For each scenario noted in E6-1, discuss when revenue should be recognized under the earnings approach. Provide the journal entries that would be recorded to recognize the revenue under the earnings approach.

(LO 1) E6-3 (Transactions with Customer Acceptance Provisions Under Earnings Approach) Consider the following unrelated situations:

1. Book of the Week Limited sends books out to potential customers on a trial basis. If the customers do not like the books, they can return them at no cost.

2. Sea Clothing Company Inc. has a return policy that allows customers to return merchandise in good order for a full refund within 30 days of purchase.

3. Shivani Inc. sells machinery to manufacturers. Customers have the right to inspect the equipment upon delivery and may return it if certain customer-specific requirements for size and weight are not met.

Instructions

(a) Explain the implications of customer acceptance provisions for revenue transactions.

(b) Indicate the point at which these transactions may be recognized as sales under the earnings approach.

(c) Using the information provided in scenario 2, assume Sea Clothing Company Inc. advertises that "customer satisfaction is guaranteed," and assume the role of a customer of Sea Clothing Company Inc. Has the company's advertised statement created an expectation that returns will be accepted at any time, perhaps even beyond the 30-day refund period? Discuss the implications of this expectation on Sea Clothing Company's books, if any.

Digging Deeper

(LO 2) E6-4 (Bill and Hold Transaction Under Earnings Approach) Dave Scotland Inc. (DSI) sold inventory to a new customer, Jamali Ltd., on December 20, 2014. Jamali was given a significant discount to entice it to switch from its regular supplier. Jamali asked DSI not to ship the inventory until January 2, 2015, because Jamali's warehouse was shutting down for the holidays. DSI agreed and decided to leave the inventory on its warehouse shelves with unsold inventory. DSI felt that the shipment would be in the way if it was left on the shipping docks and that the shipping department could easily get the inventory ready for shipment on January 2.

Instructions

(a) Discuss whether the transaction should be booked as a sale on the December 31, 2014 financial statements under the earnings approach if DSI prepares financial statements in accordance with ASPE.

(b) Discuss whether the transaction should be booked as a sale on the December 31, 2014 financial statements under the earnings approach, if DSI prepares financial statements in accordance with IFRS.

(LO 2) E6-5 (Revenue Recognition on Sales with Discounts) Seaport Marina has 500 slips (boat docks) that rent for $1,000 per season. Payments must be made in full at the start of the boating season, April 1. Slips may be reserved for the next season if they are paid for by December 31. Under a new policy, if payment is made by December 31, a 5% discount is allowed. The boating season ends on October 31, and the marina has a December 31 year end. To provide cash flow for major dock repairs, the marina operator is also offering a 25% discount on the fees for a second season if the second season is also paid for before December 31 of the current year.

For the fiscal year ended December 31, 2014, all 500 slips were rented at full price. Two hundred slips were reserved and paid for in advance of the 2015 boating season, and 160 slips were reserved and paid for in advance of the 2016 boating season.

Instructions

(a) Explain how revenue would be recorded for the 2015 and 2016 sales in fiscal 2014 under the earnings approach.

(b) Prepare the appropriate journal entries for fiscal 2014.

(c) If Seaport Marina had not offered a discount of 25% for the 2016 boating season, it would have received the annual fee of $1,000 per slip on April 1, 2016. Calculate the real cost of the discount given by Seaport Marina. Express the cost as an annual percentage so that it can be compared fairly with alternative sources of financing.

(LO 3) E6-6   (Bundled Sales Under Earnings Approach) Louis Manufacturing Inc. (LMI) purchased some telecommunications equipment in January of the current year. The equipment normally sells for $2,300. In order to entice LMI to close the deal, the salesperson offered LMI related services that normally sell for $1,000. The services allow LMI to access the Internet for the next year. The equipment and services were bundled together and LMI was charged $2,700 for the whole thing—a great deal. There is a general right of return but LMI has already taken delivery of the equipment and has started using it. All is working well and LMI is very happy with the service.

Instructions

(a) Explain how bundled sales are accounted for under the earnings approach.

(b) Calculate how revenue would be allocated to the separate units in the transaction under the relative fair value method.

(c) Calculate how revenue would be allocated to the separate units in the transaction under the residual value method, assuming:

1. the value of the equipment is known but the value of the Internet service is unknown.

2. the value of the Internet service is known but the value of the equipment is unknown.

(LO 1, E6-7   (Revenue Recognition—Measurement and Collection Uncertainty) Genesis Corporation is an equipment
4, 7) manufacturing company.

Instructions

(a) How should revenue be recorded under the earnings and contract-based approaches if Genesis has a normal business practice of offering customers a one-year payment term?

(b) How would your response to (a) change if Genesis were a new company?

(c) How would your response to (a) change if Genesis started offering deep discounts and extending payment terms to five years?

(LO 5) E6-8   (Consignment Calculations Under Earnings Approach) On May 3, 2014, Brown Motors Limited consigned 80 motorcycles, costing $25,000 each, to Mississauga Motors Inc. The total cost of shipping the motorcycles was $5,800 and was paid by Brown Motors. On December 30, 2014, an account sales report was received from the consignee, reporting that 37 motorcycles had been sold for $33,500 each. A remittance was made by the consignee for the amount due, after deducting a commission of 6%, advertising costs of $3,200, and total inspection costs of $4,200 on the motorcycles sold. Assume that Brown Motors recognizes revenue under the earnings approach.

Instructions

(a) Calculate the inventory value of the unsold units that are in the hands of the consignee.

(b) Calculate the consignor's profit on the units sold.

(c) Calculate the amount of cash that will be remitted by the consignee.

(LO 5) E6-9   (Consignment Sales) Chang Industries ships merchandise costing $120,000 on consignment to XYZ Inc. Chang pays the freight of $5,000. XYZ Inc. is to receive a 15% commission upon sale and a 5% allowance to offset its advertising expenses. At the end of the period, XYZ notifies Chang that 75% of the merchandise has been sold for $160,000.

Instructions

Record the entries required by the two companies under the earnings-based approach.

(LO 5) E6-10   (Analysis of Percentage-of-Completion Method Financial Statements) In 2014, Aldcorn Construction Corp. began construction work on a three-year, $10-million contract. Aldcorn uses the percentage-of-completion method for financial accounting purposes. The income to be recognized each year is based on the proportion of costs incurred out of the total estimated costs for completing the contract. The financial statement presentations for this contract at December 31, 2014, are as follows:

Balance Sheet		
Accounts receivable—construction contract billings		$996,500
Construction in process	$2,015,000	
Less contract billings	1,236,500	
Cost of uncompleted contract in excess of billings		778,500
Income Statement		
Income (before tax) on the contract recognized in 2014		$863,629

Instructions

Under the earnings approach:

(a) How much cash was collected in 2014 on this contract?

(b) What was the initial estimated total gross profit before tax on this contract?

(c) What is the relationship between the balances in the Construction in Process and Contract Billings accounts during the contract? Is one always more than the other? Is there a predictable ratio between the two account balances during the progress of the contract?

(AICPA adapted)

(LO 5) E6-11 (Gross Profit on Uncompleted Contract) On April 1, 2014, Lisboa Limited entered into a cost-plus-fixed-fee contract to manufacture an electric generator for Martinez Corporation. At the contract date, Lisboa estimated that it would take two years to complete the project at a cost of $6.5 million. The fixed fee that is stipulated in the contract is $1.5 million. Lisboa chooses appropriately to account for this contract under the percentage-of-completion method. During 2014, Lisboa incurred costs of $2.7 million related to the project. The estimated cost at December 31, 2014, to complete the contract is $4.9 million. Martinez was billed $600,000 under the contract.

Instructions

Under the earnings approach, prepare a schedule to calculate the amount of gross profit that Lisboa should recognize under the contract for the year ended December 31, 2014. Show supporting calculations in good form.

(AICPA adapted)

(LO 5) E6-12 (Recognition of Profit—Percentage-of-Completion Method) In 2014, Ronaldo Construction Inc. agreed to construct an apartment building at a price of $10 million. Information on the costs and billings for the first two years of this contract is as follows:

	2014	2015
Costs incurred in the period	$2,180,000	$3,100,000
Estimated costs yet to be incurred	4,300,000	1,700,000
Customer billings in the period	3,000,000	4,000,000
Collection of billings in the period	2,000,000	2,000,000

Instructions

Assume the earnings approach is used. Round the percentage complete to two decimal places.

(a) For the percentage-of-completion method, (1) calculate the amount of gross profit to be recognized in 2014 and 2015, and (2) prepare the journal entries for 2014 and 2015.

(b) For 2014 and 2015, show how the details related to this construction contract would be disclosed on the balance sheet and on the income statement.

(LO 5) E6-13 (Recognition of Profit on Long-Term Contracts and Entries) During 2014, Antoinette started a construction job with a contract price of $2.5 million. The job was completed in 2016 and information for the three years of construction is as follows:

	2014	2015	2016
Costs incurred to date	$1,050,000	$1,555,000	$1,785,000
Estimated costs to complete	850,000	175,000	–0–
Billings to date	1,000,000	1,900,000	2,500,000
Collections to date	770,000	1,810,000	2,500,000

Instructions

Under the earnings approach:

(a) Calculate the amount of gross profit that should be recognized each year under the percentage-of-completion method. Round the percentage complete to two decimal places.

(b) Prepare all necessary journal entries for 2014, 2015, and 2016, including closing the contract accounts upon completion of the contract, assuming the percentage-of-completion method is used.

(c) Calculate the amount of gross profit that should be recognized each year under the completed-contract method.

(d) Prepare the necessary journal entry in 2016 to close the contract accounts and to recognize the revenues and costs upon completion, assuming the completed-contract method is used.

(e) Assume that Antoinette cannot reliably measure the outcome of the contract. Explain how this transaction would be accounted for:

1. if Antoinette is reporting under current IFRS (IAS 11 and 18).

2. if Antoinette is reporting under ASPE.

(LO 5) E6-14   (Recognition of Gross Profit on Long-Term Contract with Loss and Entries) During 2014, Darwin Corporation started a construction job with a contract price of $4.2 million. Darwin ran into severe technical difficulties during construction but managed to complete the job in 2016. The following information is available:

	2014	2015	2016
Costs incurred to date	$ 600,000	$2,100,000	$4,100,000
Estimated costs to complete	3,150,000	2,100,000	–0–

Instructions

Under the earnings approach:

(a) Calculate the amount of gross profit that should be recognized each year under the percentage-of-completion method.

(b) Prepare the journal entries for 2015 to recognize the revenue from the contract, assuming the percentage-of-completion method is used. Explain the treatment of losses under the earnings approach for percentage-of-completion.

(c) Calculate the amount of gross profit or loss that should be recognized each year under the completed-contract method. Explain the treatment of losses under the earnings approach for completed-contract.

(d) Prepare the necessary journal entry in 2016 to close the contract accounts and to recognize the revenues and costs upon completion, assuming the completed-contract method is used.

(LO 5) E6-15   (Recognition of Profit and Balance Sheet Amounts for Long-Term Contracts) Venetian Construction Corp. began operations on January 1, 2014. During the year, Venetian entered into a contract with Ravi Corp. to construct a manufacturing facility. At that time, Venetian estimated that it would take five years to complete the facility at a total cost of $7.6 million. The total contract price to construct the facility is $11.9 million. During the year, Venetian incurred $3,648,000 in construction costs on the project. The estimated cost to complete the contract is $4,452,000. Venetian billed Ravi for 30% of the contract price and Ravi paid the amount.

Instructions

Assuming that Venetian Construction Corp. uses the earnings approach, prepare schedules to calculate the amount of gross profit to be recognized and the amount to be shown as cost of uncompleted contract in excess of related billings or billings on uncompleted contract in excess of related costs for fiscal 2014, under each of the following methods:

(a) completed-contract method.

(b) percentage-of-completion method.

Show supporting calculations in good form.

(AICPA adapted)

(LO 5) E6-16   (Long-Term Contract Reporting) Vaneeta Construction Ltd. began operations in 2014. Construction activity for the first year follows. All contracts are with different customers, and any work remaining at December 31, 2014, is expected to be completed in 2015.

Project	Total Contract Price	Billings through 12/31/14	Cash Collections through 12/31/14	Contract Costs Incurred through 12/31/14	Estimated Additional Costs to Complete
1	$3,360,000	$2,260,000	$2,040,000	$2,450,000	$1,070,000
2	2,670,000	1,220,000	1,210,000	1,126,000	504,000
3	750,000	750,000	500,000	435,000	–0–
	$6,780,000	$4,230,000	$3,750,000	$4,011,000	$1,574,000

Instructions

Under the earnings approach, prepare a partial income statement and balance sheet to indicate how the above information would be reported in the financial statements. Assume that Vaneeta Construction uses the completed-contract method.

(LO 5) E6-17 (Recognition of Revenue on Long-Term Contract and Entries) Van Horn Construction Corp. uses the percentage-of-completion method of accounting. In 2014, Van Horn began work under contract #SG-OO1, which provided for a contract price of $5.2 million. Other details follow:

	2014	2015
Costs incurred during the year	$1,750,000	$1,315,000
Estimated costs to complete, as at December 31	1,050,000	–0–
Billings during the year	3,420,000	1,780,000
Collections during the year	3,350,000	1,850,000

Instructions

Under the earnings approach:

(a) What portion of the total contract price would be recognized as revenue in 2014? In 2015?

(b) Assuming the same facts as those above except that the company uses the completed-contract method of accounting, what portion of the total contract price would be recognized as revenue in 2015?

(c) Prepare a complete set of journal entries for 2014 and 2015 under the percentage-of-completion method, including the entries for closing the contract.

(d) Prepare a complete set of journal entries for 2014 and 2015 under the completed-contract method.

E6-18 (Recognition of Profit and Balance Sheet Amounts—Zero-Profit Method and Completed-Contract Method) On January 1, 2014, Stephenson Corporation agreed to construct a community centre for the Town of Tuason at a price of $4.5 million. At that time, Stephenson estimated that it would take two years to complete the community centre for a total cost of $3.3 million. During 2014, Stephenson incurred $1,574,000 in construction costs on the project, and halted construction on August 31, 2014, when the company's construction workers went on strike after failed union negotiations for increased wages. The company's construction workers were still on strike on September 30, 2014, Stephenson's financial statement date. It became clear to management that with ongoing negotiations for higher wages, it would be difficult to estimate the costs to complete construction of the community centre. As of September 30, 2014, Stephenson has billed the Town of Tuason a total of $1.5 million and collected 80% of the amount billed. Stephenson prepares financial statements in accordance with IFRS. The company believes that it will be able to collect any amounts owing under the contract for work performed.

Instructions

Assume the earnings approach is used.

(a) Calculate the amount of revenue and gross profit to be recognized in 2014.

(b) Prepare all necessary journal entries for 2014.

(c) Show how the details related to this construction contract would be disclosed on the 2014 statement of financial position and income statement.

(d) Assume that construction is completed on September 15, 2015, and that between September 30, 2014, and completion of construction, Stephenson incurred $3,025,000 in construction costs. As of September 30, 2015, Stephenson has billed the Town of Tuason a total of $4.5 million and collected 90% of the amount billed. Show how the details related to this construction contract would be disclosed on the 2015 statement of financial position and income statement.

(e) Repeat parts (a) through (d) assuming that Stephenson prepares financial statements in accordance with ASPE.

Problems

P6-1 Soorya Enterprises sells a corporate monitoring system that includes the hardware, software, and monitoring services and annual maintenance for three years for a fixed price of $750,000. The new controller would like to understand the accounting for this transaction under both the contract-based approach and the earnings approach.

Instructions

(a) Explain the principles for recognizing revenues under the earnings and contract-based approaches. Be sure to focus on the areas of difference between the two approaches.

(b) Explain the impact of collection and measurement uncertainty for revenue recognition under the earnings and contract-based approaches.

(c) Explain how this transaction should be accounted for under the earnings and contract-based approaches.

(d) Calculate how much revenue would be recorded under the following independent assumptions, rounding any percentages to two decimal places.

1. The fair values of the items are known and are as follows: hardware and software are approximately $650,000; monitoring services are $150,000 for the three-year period; and the maintenance is $75,000 for the three-year period.

2. The fair value of hardware and software is not determinable but the fair value of the monitoring services is $150,000 for the three-year period and the fair value of the maintenance is $75,000 for the three-year period.

3. The fair value of the hardware and software is approximately $650,000, but the fair value of the monitoring and annual maintenance cannot be established.

4. Soorya offers a delayed payment program under which payments may be made over the three-year service period of the contract.

Digging Deeper

(e) From the perspective of a potential investor in Soorya, consider the recognition of revenue in scenario 2 of part (d) above. Soorya estimates that for the three-year period, the fair value of the monitoring services is $100,000 and the fair value of the maintenance is $50,000. Meanwhile, its competitors are offering similar services valued at $150,000 and $75,000, respectively. What would be the impact of the company's revenue recognition policy on your decision to invest in the company?

P6-2 Daisy Construction Ltd. has entered into a contract beginning January 1, 2014, to build a parking complex. It has estimated that the complex will cost $8 million and will take three years to construct.

The complex will be billed to the purchasing company at $11 million. The details are as follows:

	2014	2015	2016
Costs to date	$3,060,000	$6,435,000	$ 9,300,000
Estimated costs to complete	4,595,000	2,656,000	–0–
Progress billings to date	4,000,000	6,300,000	11,000,000
Cash collected to date	3,500,000	5,000,000	11,000,000

Instructions

Under the earnings approach:

(a) Using the percentage-of-completion method, calculate the estimated gross profit that would be recognized during each year of the construction period. Round percentages to two decimal places.

(b) Prepare all necessary journal entries for 2014 to 2016, including the entries for closing the contract accounts upon completion, assuming the percentage-of-completion method is used.

(c) Prepare a partial comparative income statement for the fiscal years ending December 31, 2014 and 2015.

(d) Prepare a balance sheet at December 31, 2014 and 2015, that shows the accounts related to the contract and includes their classifications assuming the percentage-of-completion method is used.

(e) Calculate the estimated gross profit that would be recognized during each year of the construction period if the completed-contract method is used. Prepare a partial income statement for the fiscal year ending December 31, 2016.

(f) Prepare the necessary entries in 2016 to close the contract accounts and to recognize the revenues and costs upon completion, assuming the completed-contract method is used.

(g) Prepare a balance sheet at December 31, 2014 and 2015, that shows the accounts related to the contract and includes their classifications assuming the completed-contract method is used.

(h) Assume that Daisy Construction cannot reliably measure the outcome of the contract. Explain how this transaction would be accounted for:

Digging Deeper

1. if Daisy is reporting under current IFRS (IAS 11 and 18).

2. if Daisy is reporting under ASPE.

(i) From the perspective of a creditor, evaluate Daisy's liquidity based on the financial statements prepared under the percentage-of-completion method versus the completed-contract method.

P6-3 Granite Engineering Ltd. has entered into a contract beginning January 1, 2013, to build a bridge in Tuktoyuktuk Shores. It estimates that the bridge will cost $14.8 million and will take three years to construct.

The bridge will be billed to the municipality at $15.5 million. The following data are for the construction period:

	2014	2015	2016
Costs to date	$ 4,500,000	$13,790,000	$15,700,000
Estimated costs to complete	10,500,000	1,934,000	–0–
Progress billings to date	4,600,000	10,000,000	15,500,000
Cash collected to date	3,000,000	9,000,000	15,500,000

Instructions

Under the earnings approach:

(a) Using the percentage-of-completion method, calculate the estimated gross profit or loss that would be recognized during each year of the construction period. Round percentages to two decimal places.

(b) Prepare all necessary journal entries for 2014 to 2016, including the entries for closing the contract accounts upon completion, assuming the percentage-of-completion method is used.

(c) Prepare a partial comparative income statement for the fiscal years ending December 31, 2014 and 2015.

(d) Prepare a balance sheet at December 31, 2014 and 2015, that shows the accounts related to the contract and includes their classifications assuming the percentage-of-completion method is used.

(e) Calculate the estimated gross profit or loss that would be recognized during each year of the construction period under the completed-contract method. Prepare any necessary entries to accrue contract losses (note the year the entry would be made). Prepare partial income statements for the fiscal years ending December 31, 2015 and 2016.

(f) Prepare the necessary entry in 2016 to close the contract accounts and to recognize the revenues and costs upon completion, assuming the completed-contract method is used.

Digging Deeper

(g) Prepare a balance sheet at December 31, 2014 and 2015, that shows the accounts related to the contract and includes their classifications assuming the completed-contract method is used.

(h) If in 2015 estimated cost to complete construction is $1,700,000 instead of $1,934,000, what would be the effect on Granite's financial statements in 2015? As a potential investor in Granite, what would be the impact of Granite's estimate on your decision to invest in the company?

P6-4 Vaughan Construction Ltd. has entered into a contract beginning in February 2014 to build two warehouses for Atlantis Structures Ltd. The contract has a fixed price of $9.5 million. The following data are for the construction period:

	2014	2015	2016
Costs for the year	$3,825,000	$4,675,000	$1,300,000
Estimated costs to complete	4,675,000	1,270,000	–0–
Progress billings to date	3,500,000	7,600,000	9,500,000
Cash collected to date	3,100,000	7,250,000	9,350,000

Instructions

Under the earnings approach:

(a) Using the percentage-of-completion method, calculate the estimated gross profit that should be recognized during each year of the construction period.

(b) Prepare all necessary journal entries for 2014 to 2016, including the entries to close the contract accounts upon completion, assuming the percentage-of-completion method is used.

(c) Prepare a partial comparative income statement for the fiscal years ending December 31, 2014 to 2016, assuming the percentage-of-completion method is used.

(d) Prepare a balance sheet at December 31, 2014 and 2015, that shows the accounts related to the contract and includes their classifications, assuming the percentage-of-completion method is used.

(e) Calculate the estimated gross profit or loss that should be recognized during each year of the construction period, assuming the completed-contract method is used. Prepare any necessary entries to accrue contract losses (note the year the entry would be made). Prepare a partial income statement for the fiscal year ending December 31, 2016.

(f) Prepare the necessary entry in 2016 to close the contract accounts and to recognize the revenues and costs upon completion, assuming the completed-contract method is used.

Digging Deeper

(g) Prepare a balance sheet at December 31, 2014 and 2015 that shows the accounts related to the contract and includes their classifications, assuming the completed-contract method is used.

(h) If in 2015 estimated cost to complete construction is $400,000 instead of $1,270,000, what would be the effect on Vaughan's financial statements in 2015? As a potential investor in Vaughan, what would be the impact of Vaughan's estimate on your decision to invest in the company?

P6-5 Unique Construction Inc. entered into a firm fixed-price contract with A-One Clinic on July 1, 2014, to construct a multi-storey medical office. At that time, Unique Construction estimated that it would take between two and three years to complete the project. The total contract price is $5.5 million. Unique Construction chooses appropriately to account for this contract under the completed-contract method in its financial statements and for income tax reporting. The building was deemed substantially completed on December 31, 2016.

The estimated percentage of completion, accumulated contract costs incurred, estimated costs to complete the contract, and accumulated billings to the clinic under the contract were as follows:

	Dec. 31, 2014	Dec. 31, 2015	Dec. 31, 2016
Percentage complete	30%	71.14%	100%
Contract costs incurred to date	$1,140,000	$4,055,000	$5,800,000
Estimated costs to complete the contract	$2,660,000	$1,645,000	–0–
Billings to A-One Clinic	$1,500,000	$2,500,000	$5,500,000

Instructions

Under the earnings approach:

(a) Prepare schedules to calculate the amount to be shown as "cost of uncompleted contract in excess of related billings" or "billings on uncompleted contract in excess of related costs" at December 31, 2014, 2015, and 2016. Ignore income taxes. Show supporting calculations in good form.

(b) Prepare schedules to calculate the profit or loss that should be recognized from this contract for the years ended December 31, 2014, 2015, and 2016. Ignore income taxes. Show supporting calculations in good form.

(c) Assume a construction company had all of the information that it required to use the percentage-of-completion method for construction contracts. Why would this company want to account for contracts using the completed-contract method?

(AICPA adapted.)

P6-6 Jupiter Inc. was established in 1985 by Joyce Fukomoto and initially operated under contracts to build highly energy-efficient, customized homes. In the 1990s, Joyce's two daughters joined the firm and expanded the company's activities into the high-rise apartment and commercial markets. When the company's long-time financial manager retired, Joyce's daughters hired Jean-Guy Beaulieu as controller. Jean-Guy, a former university friend of Joyce's daughters, had been working for a public accounting firm for the last four years.

When he reviewed the company's accounting practices, Jean-Guy noticed that the company followed the completed-contract method of revenue recognition, as it always had since the years when individual home building was the company's main focus. Several years ago, most of the company's activities shifted to the high-rise and commercial building areas. From land acquisition to the completion of construction, most building contracts now cover several years. Under the circumstances, Jean-Guy believes that the company should follow the percentage-of-completion method of accounting. From a typical building contract, Jean-Guy developed the following data:

JUPITER INC.

Contract price: $10,000,000

	2014	2015	2016
Estimated costs for the year	$2,010,000	$4,015,000	$1,675,000
Progress billings for the year	2,000,000	2,500,000	5,500,000
Cash collections for the year	1,800,000	2,300,000	5,900,000

Instructions

Under the earnings approach:

(a) Explain the difference between completed-contract revenue recognition and percentage-of-completion revenue recognition.

(b) Using the data provided for Jupiter Inc. and assuming the percentage-of-completion method of revenue recognition is used, calculate the company's revenue and gross profit for 2014 to 2016, under each of the following circumstances. Round all percentages to two decimal places.

1. Assume that all costs are incurred, all billings to customers are made, and all collections from customers are received within 30 days of billing as planned.

2. The company came across unexpected local bylaws that it had to comply with. The building site is in a wetlands area and it had to overcome environmental barriers to construction. As a result, the company had cost overruns of $1.2 million in 2014 to pay for changes to the site.

3. Further assume that, in addition to the cost overruns of $1.2 million for this contract, inflation was greater than expected when the original contract cost was set and caused an additional cost overrun of $1,240,000 in 2015. No cost overruns are expected to occur in 2016.

(CMA adapted. Used with permission.)

P6-7 On March 1, 2014, Wilma Limited signed a contract to build a factory for Slate Construction Manufacturing Inc. for a total contract price of $9.4 million. The building was completed by October 31, 2016. The annual contract costs that were incurred, the estimated costs to complete the contract, and the accumulated billings to Slate Construction were as follows:

	2014	2015	2016
Contract costs incurred during the year	$1,600,000	$5,000,000	$2,200,000
Estimated costs to complete the contract at Dec. 31	4,800,000	2,084,000	–0–
Billings to Slate Construction during the year	2,000,000	5,100,000	2,300,000
Cash collections from Slate Construction during the year	1,950,000	4,900,000	2,550,000

Instructions

Under the earnings approach:

(a) Using the percentage-of-completion method, prepare schedules to calculate the profit or loss that should be recognized from this contract for the years ended December 31, 2014 to 2016.

(b) Using the completed-contract method, prepare schedules to calculate the profit or loss that should be recognized from this contract for the years ended December 31, 2014 to 2016.

(c) Prepare all necessary journal entries for 2014 to 2016, including the entries to close the contract accounts upon completion, assuming the completed-contract method is used.

P6-8 You have been engaged by Ashely Corp. to advise it on the proper accounting for a series of long-term contracts. Ashely began doing business on January 1, 2014, and its construction activities for the first year of operations are shown below. All contract costs are with different customers, and any work that remains to be done at December 31, 2014, is expected to be completed in 2015.

Project	Total Contract Price	Billings through 12/31/14	Cash Collections through 12/31/14	Contract Costs Incurred through 12/31/14	Estimated Additional Costs to Complete
A	$ 300,000	$200,000	$180,000	$248,000	$ 67,000
B	350,000	110,000	105,000	67,800	271,200
C	280,000	280,000	255,000	186,000	–0–
D	200,000	35,000	25,000	123,000	87,000
E	240,000	205,000	200,000	185,000	15,000
	$1,370,000	$830,000	$765,000	$809,800	$440,200

Instructions

Assuming that Ashely Corp. uses the earnings approach:

(a) Using the percentage-of-completion method, prepare a schedule to calculate gross profit or loss to be reported, unbilled contract costs and recognized profit, and billings in excess of costs and recognized profit.

(b) Prepare a partial income statement and balance sheet to show how the information would be reported for financial statement purposes.

(c) Repeat the requirements for part (a) under the completed-contract method.

(d) Using information from your answers to the previous questions, prepare a brief report that compares the conceptual features (both positive and negative) of the two revenue recognition methods.

Cases

Refer to the Case Primer to help you answer these cases.

CA6-1 *Cutting Edge* is a monthly magazine that has been on the market for 18 months. It is owned by a private company and has a circulation of 1.4 million copies. Negotiations are underway to obtain a bank loan in order to update its facilities. It is producing close to capacity and expects to grow at an average of 20% per year over the next three years.

After reviewing the financial statements of *Cutting Edge*, Gary Hall, the bank loan officer, said that a loan could only be offered to *Cutting Edge* if it could increase its current ratio and decrease its debt-to-equity ratio to a specified level. Alexander Pang, the marketing manager of *Cutting Edge*, has devised a plan to meet these requirements. Pang indicates that an advertising campaign can be used to immediately increase circulation. The potential customers would be contacted after purchasing another magazine's mailing list. The campaign would include:

1. An offer to subscribe to *Cutting Edge* at three-quarters the normal price

2. A special offer to all new subscribers to receive the most current world atlas whenever requested at a guaranteed price of $2.00

3. An unconditional guarantee of a full refund for any subscriber who is dissatisfied with the magazine

Although the offer of a full refund is risky, Pang claims that few people will ask for a refund after receiving half of their subscription issues. Pang notes that other magazine companies have tried this sales promotion technique and experienced great success. Their average cancellation rate was 25%. On average, each company increased its initial circulation threefold and in the long run increased circulation to twice the level that it was before the promotion. In addition, 60% of the new subscribers are expected to take advantage of the atlas premium. Pang feels confident that the increased subscriptions from the advertising campaign will increase the current ratio and decrease the debt-to-equity ratio.

In addition to the above, Pang has just signed a large deal with a newly opened store to take delivery of the current edition of the magazine. The new customer has asked that the magazines be held by *Cutting Edge* for a couple of weeks to a month.

Instructions

Assume the role of the controller and discuss the financial reporting issues assuming that *Cutting Edge* uses ASPE.

CA6-2   Nimble Health and Racquet Club (NHRC) is a public company that operates eight clubs in a large city and offers one-year memberships. The members may use any of the eight facilities but must reserve racquetball court time and pay a separate fee before using the court. As an incentive to new customers, NHRC advertised that any customers who are not satisfied for any reason can receive a refund of the remaining portion of their unused membership fees. Membership fees are due at the beginning of the individual membership period; however, customers are given the option of financing the membership fee over the membership period at a 15% interest rate.

In the past, some customers had said they would like to take only the regularly scheduled aerobic classes and not pay for a full membership. During the current fiscal year, NHRC began selling coupon books for aerobic classes only to accommodate these customers. Each book is dated and contains 50 coupons that may be redeemed for any regularly scheduled aerobic class over a one-year period. After the one-year period, unused coupons are no longer valid.

During 2014, NHRC expanded into the health equipment market by purchasing a local company that manufactures rowing machines and cross-country ski machines. These machines are used in NHRC's facilities and are sold through the clubs and mail-order catalogues. Customers must make a 20% down payment when placing an equipment order. Delivery is in 60 to 90 days after an order is placed. The machines are sold with a two-year unconditional guarantee. Based on experience, NHRC expects the costs to repair machines under guarantee to be 4% of sales.

Ethics

NHRC is in the process of preparing financial statements as at May 31, 2014, the end of its fiscal year. James Hogan, corporate controller, expressed concern over the company's performance for the year and decided to review the preliminary financial statements prepared by Magda Bambenek, NHRC's assistant controller, for the company's bankers. After reviewing the statements, Hogan proposed that the following changes be reflected in the May 31, 2014 published financial statements:

1. Membership revenue should be recognized when the membership fee is collected.

2. Revenue from the coupon books should be recognized when the books are sold.

3. Down payments on equipment purchases and expenses associated with the guarantee on the rowing and cross-country machines should be recognized when they are paid.

Bambenek told Hogan that the proposed changes are not in accordance with IFRS, but Hogan insisted that the changes be made. Bambenek believes that Hogan wants to manipulate income to delay any potential financial problems and increase his year-end bonus. At this point, Bambenek is unsure what action to take.

Instructions

Discuss the financial reporting issues and how any ethical issues should be handled.

(CMA adapted. Used with permission.)

Integrated Cases

(*Hint*: If there are issues that are new, use the conceptual framework to help support your analysis with solid reasoning.)

IC6-1   Treetop Pharmaceuticals (TP) researches, develops, and produces over-the-counter drugs. During the year, it acquired 100% of the net assets of Treeroot Drugs Limited (TDL) for $200 million. The fair value of the identifiable assets at the time of purchase was $150 million (which included $120 million for patents). The company plans to sell the patents to a third party at the end of seven years even though, at that time, the remaining legal life of the patents will be five years. TP already has a commitment from a specific third party that has agreed to pay $50 million for the patents (in seven years).

In January, in an unrelated deal, the company acquired a trademark that has a remaining legal life of three years. The trademark is renewable every 10 years at little cost. TP is unsure if it will renew the trademark or not.

Because of the two acquisitions, TP was short of cash and entered into an arrangement with Drug Development Corporation (DDC) whereby DDC paid $30 million to TP upfront when the contract was signed. Under the terms, the money is to be used to develop drugs and new distribution channels. TP has already spent a considerable portion of this money. TP agreed that it will pay DDC 2% of the revenues from the subsequent sale of the drugs (which are now close to the point of commercial production).

Because of the cash shortage, the company entered into negotiations with its bank to increase its line of credit. The bank is concerned about the company's liquidity. TP's top management has graciously agreed to take stock options instead of any bonuses or raises for the next two years in order to reduce cash flow constraints.

It is now year end and TP is preparing its financial statements. It is concerned because one of its major competitors has just come out with several new drugs that will compete directly with the drugs that TDL sells. Management is worried that this may erode the market for TDL's products. In fact, TP is considering selling TDL and has contacted a consultant to help find a buyer.

Jacinthe Kimble, the controller, is preparing for a planning meeting with TP's auditors. The auditors are analyzing TP's draft financial statements to identify critical and high-risk areas. The draft financial statements show the company as barely breaking even. The CFO has commented that the company's share price is likely to "take a tumble" since the company has always been profitable in past years and its competitors seem to be doing well. Kimble is also debating the latest news from TP's lawyers—apparently, the company is being sued in a class action lawsuit (by a significant number of people) for an illness that was allegedly caused by one of TP's main pharmaceutical products. The claim is for an amount equal to revenues from last year. At this point, the lawyers are concerned that the case against TP may be successful and they are trying to estimate the potential loss to the company.

Instructions

Adopt the role of the controller and prepare an analysis of all the financial reporting issues that TP is facing.

IC 6-2 Stock Car Auto Inc. (SCA) is a promoter and sponsor of motor-sport activities. Its shares trade on the Toronto Stock Exchange. The company owns two racing tracks where it hosts races (including those sponsored by NASCAR—the National Association for Stock Car Auto Racing) and operates a driving school. In between races, it rents the facilities out.

SCA operates like a club. An upfront fee is charged, which gives the individual the right to belong to the club for his or her lifetime. SCA owns a fleet of high-performance stock cars that members may "adopt." All members adopt a car as this is a main reason for joining the club. Under the adoption agreement, individuals pay a monthly fee for access to the stock car and the rights to race the car on the race tracks for a certain number of hours a week (including unlimited gas). Individuals must get insurance in order to adopt a car but this is provided by SCA, which has a master insurance plan. Race car driving is risky and insurance premiums are very high (as is the injury and mortality rate). The master insurance plan is negotiated by SCA with an outside insurance company and covers all club members. The monthly fee covers the insurance. Adoptions are annual and individuals often switch cars each year. The company just completed a membership drive and has signed up 100 new members at $20,000 each. This amount has been paid upfront and received prior to year end. It is non-refundable. In order to become a member, individuals had to earn the rights to join by proving that they were capable of driving race cars safely. To this end, all members must take a two-week racing course and qualify for the company's stringent insurance program. All new members had completed the requirements by year end.

Last year, oil and gas prices began to skyrocket. Given that the company uses a lot of oil and gas in its business, Sam Stock (the president and CEO of the company) decided to strategically diversify the company's operations into the oil and gas sector. Sam hired two additional traders to deal with this part of the business. At first, they were entering into advance gas purchase commitments to secure a steady supply of gas at a fixed price. However, the traders soon found that they were able to create profits by trading in the gas contracts. As a matter of fact, half of the company's net income for the current year came from trading gains. As part of their activities, the traders have purchased shares in three oil and gas companies. They have not decided whether they will keep these shares for the longer term. It really depends on the markets. Sam is currently in discussions with the traders as to what their job is supposed to be. Even though he likes the profits, he is not convinced that he likes the additional risk that this activity is exposing the company to. The company has a major shareholder who has declared that SCA should only be in the business of racing cars and nothing else.

The company is being sued by the surrounding community for alleged pollution from the racing activities. Apparently, the racing cars produce a fair amount of airborne toxins, which settle in the surrounding area. Unknown to SCA, the nearby city had passed a bylaw stating that companies must clean up any pollution that they are responsible for. SCA's lawyers have argued on a preliminary basis that the alleged pollution in the surrounding area is due to the nearby superhighway and airport and that it is not possible to prove that SCA is the cause of the pollution. Even if they were responsible for a small fraction of it, it would be very difficult to determine just what that fraction was. The lawyers are therefore denying that SCA has any responsibility with respect to cleanup. The lawyers for the surrounding community have asked for the financial statements of SCA to determine whether the company is profiting at their expense.

Instructions

Assume the role of the auditors and discuss the financial reporting issues.

Ethics

IC6-3 Comminc Industries (CI) is a leader in delivering communications technology that powers global commerce and secures the world's most critical information. Its shares trade on the Canadian and U.S. national stock exchanges. The company had been experiencing unprecedented growth, but then, in 2011, industry demand for the company's services and products declined dramatically due to an industry realignment, an economic downturn, and a tightening in global capital and product markets. By the end of 2013, the industry stabilized and the company began to enter a turn-around period after significant downsizing.

In 2013, employee morale was very low because of all the downsizing. Many employees were being actively recruited away from CI. Management decided to set up bonus programs for employees who stayed to see the company through the difficult times and back to profitability. Under one plan, every employee would receive a bonus in the first quarter that the company achieved enough profit to cover the bonus costs. In order to help achieve profitability, the CFO met with the managers of his divisions and established profitability targets and what he referred to as "roadmaps" that showed how these targets could be achieved. The roadmaps included statements that the profits could only be achieved through the release from the statement of financial position of excess provisions (that is, provisions for obsolete inventory and bad debts). The provisions had been overprovided for in earlier years in an effort to "manage" profits.

In 2014, the company came under scrutiny from the securities regulators. The government notified it of a criminal investigation into alleged accounting irregularities. In addition, there were several class action lawsuits outstanding against the company by shareholders alleging that CI had provided misleading information to them in the financial statements for 2012 and 2013. Once news of this was released, credit rating agencies significantly downgraded their ratings of CI's securities. As a result of this negative activity, the company had not released its financial statements for 2014 and was now in breach of the stock exchange requirements to file financial statements. Although the stock exchanges had not done so, they now had the power to delist CI's shares.

The controller of CI must now finalize the financial statements and has come across the following information.

1. During the year, the company signed contracts to sell optical products, which included software. Before year end, the company shipped out what it called an "interim product solution"—in other words, the optical product ordered by the company was not yet ready in its final form so the company shipped a beta or draft version of it. This interim product would then be followed shortly by the final version. Revenues were recognized upon shipment of the interim product solution as it was felt that the final version just needed minor refinements. The customers generally paid more than half of what was owed under the contract when they received the interim product solution. It was rare that customers backed out of this type of contract for any reason.

2. In 2013, CI had purchased a subsidiary of ABC Inc. and agreed to pay additional future consideration for the purchase (the consideration would take the form of additional CI shares). The additional consideration was a function of the profitability of the subsidiary. The more profitable the subsidiary, the more shares that CI would issue as consideration. Given that CI's shares are highly volatile, CI and ABC agreed that the number of shares to be issued should be based on the average price per share in the three months prior to the future issuance date of the shares. So far, the subsidiary has been performing above expectations.

3. By the end of 2014, CI was still restructuring to streamline its core operations and activities. Part of the restructuring included abandoning its voice-over fibre operations. The operations would be closed down in early 2015, and this would involve workforce reductions and abandonment of plant and equipment.

Instructions

Adopt the role of controller and analyze the financial reporting issues.

Writing Assignments

WA6-1 The Comfort-Zone Company installs heating, ventilation, and air conditioning in large buildings such as domed stadiums, military bases, airports, and highrises. Its contracts usually take two to three years to complete. At any fiscal year end, this work-in-process (WIP) inventory is a sizable percentage of its assets. The company is privately held and has a senior management group whose compensation is based almost entirely on the earnings results for the year. As the ethical accountant (who is also the CFO), you have been reviewing the year-end WIP figures, which have been estimated using the percentage-of-completion method. These estimates have been provided to you by the project managers responsible for the completion of the various contracts.

This year has not been as successful or as active as previous ones and the company's two senior founders have asked you to bring in a net income figure at least equal to the last couple of years. In your mind, you know that the project managers' estimates are somewhat fluid and you have been considering making the requested adjustments.

Instructions

Ethics   How would you handle the two senior founders' request?

WA6-2   Franchise contracts are complex contractual arrangements with many parts.

Instructions

Access the Accounting Guideline (AcG) 2 *Franchise Fee Revenue* from the Canadian Institute of Chartered Accountants Standards and Guidance Collection, Accounting Handbook, Accounting Guidelines. (This guideline can be accessed through Knotia, available through your school's library database.) Answer the following questions.

(a) What is a franchise?

(b) Using the information provided in the guideline, compare the accounting guidance given in this guideline for reporting and measuring the franchisee fee revenue with the general principles for revenue recognition. Address each issue separately, highlighting similarities and differences between the guidance and application of the general revenue principles.

WA6-3   The IASB was considering additional guidance on reporting revenues when other parties are involved in providing goods and services to a company's customer. The Board has been debating the conditions that must be present for a company to record revenue at the gross amount collected from the customer or the net amount the company keeps after reimbursing the other party for any related goods or services.

Instructions

Answer the following questions with respect to the gross versus net revenue issue.

(a) How can the contract-based model be applied to determine whether the revenues charged to customers should be at the gross amount collected from the customer or the net amount the company keeps after reimbursing the other party for any goods or services?

(b) What indicators might be used to signify that a company should record the revenue at the gross amount?

(c) What indicators might be used to signify that a company should record the revenue at the net amount?

(d) Apply the above discussions to the following scenario to determine if the company should report at gross or net revenue:

Office Supply Co. sells office supplies and office furniture. The company keeps catalogues from five different furniture suppliers on hand and customers make their orders from these catalogues. Once the order is received from the supplier, Office Supply Co. takes title of the goods, and records the amount as inventory until shipped to the customer. There is no other inventory kept on hand. Office Supply Co. invoices the customer, and the customer must pay within 60 days of delivery and installation of the furniture. At the point of delivery to the customer's premises, the customer takes title to the furniture. The supplier sets the selling price to the customer, as detailed in the catalogue. Office Supply Co. is allowed to keep 25% of the sale price and remits the difference to the supplier. Office Supply Co. also charges for installation, and keeps this full amount. Office Supply Co. must pay the supplier for the furniture even if the customer has not yet paid. At the time of the sale, the customer is told that if there are any issues that arise after the sale dealing with damage, quality, wrong colour, wrong size, and so on, they may contact Office Supply Co., which will, in turn, contact the supplier to resolve the problem.

WA6-4   The IASB exposure draft (ED) and re-exposure draft (RED) on revenue recognition discuss how onerous contracts should be reported and measured.

Instructions

Refer to the IASB's ED and RED "Revenue Recognition in Contracts with Customers" from June 2010 and November 2011, respectively, available on the IASB website at www.ifrs.org. Answer the following questions with respect to onerous contracts.

(a) What is an onerous contract? What is its significance to revenue recognition?

(b) For each of the following examples, assess whether the contracts have become onerous.

1. A construction contract has customer consideration totalling $500,000. The company had originally estimated costs to perform under the contract to be $425,000, resulting in profits of $75,000. However, during the contract, material costs increased substantially, so that the current total expected costs of the contract are now $460,000.

2. A gold producer has entered into a contract to sell 1,000 ounces of gold (originally over a two-year period) to a customer at a price of $600 per ounce. Currently, the selling price of gold has risen to $850 per ounce. The costs to produce the gold are $250 per ounce.

WA6-5

Instructions

Write a brief essay highlighting the differences between IFRS and ASPE noted in this chapter, discussing the conceptual justification for each.

RESEARCH AND FINANCIAL ANALYSIS

RA6-1 Shoppers Drug Mart

Shoppers Drug Mart's financial statements can be found in Appendix 5B.

Instructions

Refer to the company's financial statements and accompanying notes to answer these questions.

(a) What were the company's gross revenues for the fiscal years 2011 and 2012? What is the percentage change? Why has the company seen this result?

(b) Based on your findings in (a), comment on the company's net income/loss over the period.

(c) Review the notes to the financial statements to determine the company's revenue recognition policy. Discuss the policy, considering the nature of the business and the industry.

(d) On transition to IFRS from Canadian GAAP, adjustments to revenues were required to restate revenue. Explain why the company had to make these adjustments and the amounts required.

RA6-2 BCE Inc. and TELUS Corporation

Access **BCE Inc.**'s financial statements for the year ended December 31, 2011, from either the company's website or SEDAR (www.sedar.com). Access **TELUS Corporation**'s financial statements for the year ended December 31, 2011, from either the company's website or SEDAR.

Instructions

Using the annual reports for BCE Inc. and TELUS, answer the following.

(a) What types of revenue does BCE have and how are they recognized?

(b) What types of revenue does TELUS have and how are they recognized?

(c) Are there any examples of when either company would report revenue on a net basis? What factors does the company consider?

(d) Explain the types of contracts where the companies have multiple deliverables. How does each company allocate the revenues on these types of contracts?

(e) Telus has a unique accounting policy for dealing with revenues in non–high-cost serving areas. Review the accounting policy note and page 76 of the annual report for details. Explain the business reason for the transaction and comment on the appropriateness of the accounting.

(f) Do you find one company's disclosure on revenue recognition better than another? Why?

RA6-3 EADS N.V.

Access the financial statements for **EADS N.V.** (European Aeronautic Defence and Space Company) for its year ended December 31, 2011, from the company's website (www.eads.com).

Instructions

Answer the following questions with respect to EADS N.V.

(a) What business is EADS in?

(b) Explain how the revenue related to the construction contracts is recorded. How does the company determine when revenue should be recognized on these contracts?

(c) How does the company treat probable losses on existing contracts?

(d) What are the balance sheet amounts related to this revenue recognition? What was the aggregated amount of costs and profits recognized to date? What was the gross amount due to customers and due from customers at December 31, 2011? What do these amounts represent? (*Hint*: See Note 19.)

ENDNOTES

1 Recall that a view of the business model was presented in Chapters 4 and 5.

2 Monetary consideration includes anything that is cash or measured in terms of cash such as a receivable. Nonmonetary consideration includes other types of assets such as other inventory or fixed assets.

3 Where the asset being sold is a commodity, prices fluctuate since they are based on supply and demand.

4 IASB, *Preliminary Views on Revenue Recognition in Contracts with Customers*. Discussion Paper, December 2008, par. S10.

5 *CICA Handbook–Accounting*, Part II, Section 3400.04 and IAS 11 and 18.

6 Recognition is the process of including an item in the financial statements. Recognition is not the same as realization, although the two terms are sometimes used interchangeably in accounting literature and practice.

7 *CICA Handbook–Accounting*, Part II, Section 3400.04 and IAS 11 and 18. ASPE groups the criteria into two parts: performance (which includes the first three bulleted items) and collectibility. In addition, the wording of the revenue recognition standard under ASPE is slightly different. Copyright © 2012 IFRS Foundation. All rights reserved. Reproduced by Wiley Canada with the permission of the IFRS Foundation®. No permission granted to third parties to reproduce or distribute.

8 In order to recognize an asset on the balance sheet, a company must prove that it has control over substantially all of the risks and rewards of ownership. If these have been passed on to another party, a disposition has occurred.

9 Because of this, and in part also because of the increased profile of revenue recognition issues with the securities commissions, companies are required to disclose the revenue recognition method in the notes to their financial statements.

10 IAS 41 deals with biological assets and produce up to the point of harvest. It requires that these assets be measured at fair value less estimated point-of-sale costs. This topic is discussed in greater detail in Chapter 8 in the context of measuring inventories.

11 *CICA Handbook–Accounting*, Part II, Section 3400.06. *Accounting Trends and Techniques—2010* reports that, of the 86 of its 500 sample companies that referred to long-term construction contracts, 63 used the percentage-of-completion method and 20 used the completed-contract method.

12 *CICA Handbook–Accounting*, Part II, Section 3400.06 and IAS 18.20.

13 IFRIC 15 *Agreements for the Construction of Real Estate*.

14 *CICA Handbook–Accounting*, Part II, Section 3856.A8 and IAS 18.11.

15 *CICA Handbook–Accounting*, Part II, Section 3831.06 and IAS 18.12. IFRS looks at whether the goods are dissimilar or not as a test for commercial substance.

16 Price protection clauses state that if the purchase price goes down before the customer has resold the product, the vendor will provide a cash refund. They are included to stop the customer from returning the product and repurchasing it at the lower price.

17 *CICA Handbook–Accounting*, Part II, Section 3400.19 and IAS 18.20.

18 In 2016, Hardhat will recognize the remaining 33½% of the revenue ($1,507,500), with costs of $1,468,962 as expected, and report a gross profit of $38,538. The total gross profit over the three years of the contract would be $115,038 [$125,000 (2014) − $48,500 (2015) + $38,538 (2016)], which is the difference between the total contract revenue of $4,500,000 and the total contract costs of $4,384,962.

19 If the costs in 2016 are $1,640,250 as projected, at the end of 2016 the Construction in Process account will have a balance of $1,640,250 + $2,859,750, or $4,500,000, which is equal to the contract price. When the revenue remaining to be recognized in 2016 of $1,620,000 [$4,500,000 (total contract price) − $1,125,000 (2014) − $1,755,000 (2015)] is matched with the construction expense to be recognized in 2016 of $1,620,000 [total costs of $4,556,250 less the total costs recognized in prior years of $2,936,250 (2014, $1,000,000; 2015, $1,936,250)], a zero-profit results. Thus, the total loss has been recognized in 2015, the year in which it first became evident.

20 Gains (as contrasted with revenues) commonly result from transactions and other events that do not involve an earnings process. For gain recognition, being earned is generally less important than being realized or realizable.

21 *Revenue from Contracts with Customers*

Collecting from Incommunicado Clients

TELEPHONE, INTERNET, AND TV SERVICE COMPANY Bell Aliant is one of North America's largest land-line communications and Internet service providers. With a staff of approximately 7,000, the company earns revenue of $2.8 billion a year under the brands Bell Aliant in Atlantic Canada and Bell in Ontario and Quebec, as well as Télébec, Northern Tel, and Kenora Municipal Telephone Services.

Bell Aliant's main sources of revenue are fees for local and long-distance phone services, high-speed Internet, and television services. It also receives revenue from equipment rentals and value-added technology business solutions for large enterprises.

"Our total receivables balance is typically around $370 million at any one month end," says Eleanor Marshall, Vice-President and Treasurer at Bell Aliant. On the balance sheet, under IFRS, this amount includes accounts receivable the company has pledged as part of its securitization program. The proceeds from the securitized receivables are reflected as short-term borrowing.

Certain of Bell Aliant's billing terms are regulated by the Canadian Radio-television and Telecommunications Commission (CRTC). The company bills monthly for services in arrears, and payments are due within 21 days of the billing date, which results in receivables being about 31 to 35 days outstanding, Ms. Marshall explains.

Even though the bills are due within 21 days of billing date, late payment charges begin to accrue at 30 days from the billing date. "Late payment charges are intended to be punitive. Since we primarily bill monthly recurring charges, we really want customers to pay on time, so they do not get behind," Ms. Marshall explains. "As such, these charges are currently set at 3% per month."

If the bill does not get paid on time, Bell Aliant will start making calls, sending reminder notices and perhaps negotiating new payment terms that might include stripping down the account to basic services. If there is still no payment, the company will suspend the account for 21 days, then reconnect for one day, and contact the client again. If there is still no payment, it will permanently disconnect the customer. The company then sends two notices to the client, and finally the bill goes to a collection agency.

"We establish provisions for bad debts long before it gets to this point," Ms. Marshall adds. Receivables are assigned to aging categories, and certain percentages, which are based on past experience, apply to each category to estimate the amount of uncollectible accounts. The company recognizes bad debt expense, which is typically just under 1% of revenue, each month.

Cash and Receivables

LEARNING OBJECTIVES

After studying this chapter, you should be able to:

1. Understand cash and accounts receivable from a business perspective.
2. Define financial assets, and identify items that are considered cash and cash equivalents and how they are reported.
3. Define receivables and identify the different types of receivables from an accounting perspective.
4. Account for and explain the accounting issues related to the recognition and measurement of accounts receivable.
5. Account for and explain the accounting issues related to the impairment in value of accounts receivable.
6. Account for and explain the accounting issues related to the recognition and measurement of short-term notes and loans receivable.
7. Account for and explain the accounting issues related to the recognition and measurement of long-term notes and loans receivable.
8. Account for and explain the basic accounting issues related to the derecognition of receivables.
9. Explain how receivables and loans are reported and analyzed.
10. Identify differences in accounting between accounting standards for private enterprises (ASPE) and IFRS, and what changes are expected in the near future.

After studying Appendix 7A, you should be able to:

11. Explain common techniques for controlling cash.

PREVIEW OF CHAPTER 7

As our opening story implies, estimating the collectibility of accounts receivable has important implications for accurate reporting of operating profits, net income, and assets. In this chapter, we discuss cash and receivables—two assets that are important to companies as diverse as giant BCE (the parent company of Bell Aliant) and small owner-operated private operations. The chapter is organized as follows:

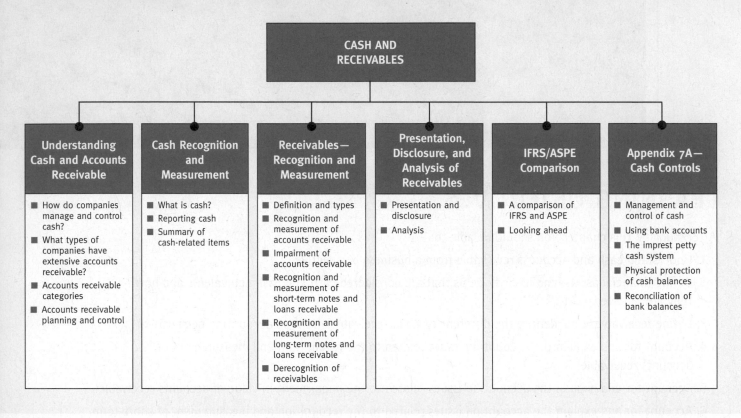

CASH AND RECEIVABLES					
Understanding Cash and Accounts Receivable	**Cash Recognition and Measurement**	**Receivables—Recognition and Measurement**	**Presentation, Disclosure, and Analysis of Receivables**	**IFRS/ASPE Comparison**	**Appendix 7A—Cash Controls**
■ How do companies manage and control cash? ■ What types of companies have extensive accounts receivable? ■ Accounts receivable categories ■ Accounts receivable planning and control	■ What is cash? ■ Reporting cash ■ Summary of cash-related items	■ Definition and types ■ Recognition and measurement of accounts receivable ■ Impairment of accounts receivable ■ Recognition and measurement of short-term notes and loans receivable ■ Recognition and measurement of long-term notes and loans receivable ■ Derecognition of receivables	■ Presentation and disclosure ■ Analysis	■ A comparison of IFRS and ASPE ■ Looking ahead	■ Management and control of cash ■ Using bank accounts ■ The imprest petty cash system ■ Physical protection of cash balances ■ Reconciliation of bank balances

UNDERSTANDING CASH AND ACCOUNTS RECEIVABLE

Objective 1
Understand cash and accounts receivable from a business perspective.

It is important to understand the business of the company when considering issues relating to cash and accounts receivable. How do companies manage and control cash? What types of companies are more likely to carry significant accounts receivable balances? What are the different types of accounts receivable? What aspects of accounts receivable must be managed and how do companies do this? Lastly, what information do financial statement users need to assess a company's management of receivables? These questions will be addressed below.

How Do Companies Manage and Control Cash?

Cash management and control is a key issue for many companies, including retailers that have significant cash sales. Businesses rely on cash flow budgets to help anticipate cash needs and minimize borrowing requirements. Generally, companies with surplus cash try to minimize "idle" cash by putting extra cash resources into short-term deposits. Banks and other financial institutions take this to the extreme with very short-term borrowing and lending in the overnight money market where borrowed funds plus interest must be repaid at the start of the next business day. For companies without surplus cash, management must still carefully manage its cash resources to minimize any bank loans and other borrowings. The control of cash includes implementing internal control over physical custody of cash on hand and preparation of regular bank reconciliations. Control of cash is of such importance that we devote an entire appendix to it at the end of this chapter, where we discuss it in much more detail.

What Types of Companies Have Extensive Accounts Receivable?

Real World Emphasis

As a general rule, manufacturers and wholesalers often have a significant amount of accounts receivable. For instance, **Magna International Inc.**, a large Canadian automobile supplier, reported accounts receivable of U.S. $4,398 million (or over 50% of current assets) at the end of 2011. This was Magna's largest current asset and it reflected an increase of 24% from 2010 to 2011. An increase in accounts receivable might be cause for concern for some companies, when it indicates an inability to collect receivables on a timely basis. However, Magna also showed a very significant (22.5%) increase in sales that year. Magna adopted U.S. generally accepted accounting principles in 2011, and uses the U.S. dollar as its functional currency. Therefore its Canadian accounts receivable are translated into U.S. dollars on its balance sheet.

On the other hand, retailers such as **Sears Canada Inc.** often have relatively low accounts receivable due to customers' use of major credit cards (like Visa) and debit cards for payments. For example, at the end of the 2011–2012 fiscal year, Sears had accounts receivable of only $116.2 million (or less than 9% of current assets). Of that $116.2 million balance, the company reported that 26.5% of its receivables were from just one party, which likely makes monitoring of collection issues less difficult.

Accounts Receivable Categories

Real World Emphasis

Manufacturers and wholesalers have accounts receivable relating to their sales transactions, as discussed in Chapter 6. For instance, **Suncor Energy**—a major Canadian integrated energy company with operations including oil sands development, retail operations (such as products marketed under the PetroCanada brand), and wholesale operations—had accounts receivable of $5,412 million at the end of 2011 (or 13.6% of revenues). These receivables represented Suncor's largest current asset. Large accounts receivable balances are typical in the oil and gas industry, in part due to extended payment terms which can stretch from 30 to 60 days. For most companies, typical accounts receivable related categories include trade receivables, loans receivable, and nontrade receivables (including items like interest receivable, amounts due from officers, and advances to employees). However, there are more complicated items sometimes included in accounts receivable. For example, Suncor includes the fair value of its interest rate swaps as part of its accounts receivable balance. These swaps relate to Suncor's fixed rate debt, and the fair value of the swaps included in receivables was $8 million at the end of 2010; there were no swaps outstanding at the end of 2011. Interest rate swaps generally involve one party that was making payments based on a fixed interest rate, and another that was making payments based on a floating rate, agreeing to swap or exchange their payment streams. Swaps are discussed in more detail in Chapter 16, as part of Complex Financial Instruments.

Accounts Receivable Planning and Control

For many reasons, it is important for management to carefully consider how to manage and control its accounts receivable balances. Of course accounts receivable are directly related to sales, and if the sales department is overly aggressive with its credit policy, it could result in significant increases in bad debts and uncollectible accounts. Companies will typically assess the creditworthiness of new customers and grant them a credit limit accordingly. Established customers' track records and payment history will also impact how credit limits change over time.

Receivables management can be a delicate balancing act. If credit policies are too "tight" or restrictive, potential sales could be lost to competitors. On the other hand, if the credit policy is too "loose" or flexible, an aggressive sales team might enter into contracts with higher risk customers, resulting in collectibility difficulties. Some companies offer discounts to encourage faster payment of outstanding balances. These discounts are popular with customers, as the savings from early payment are much better than the interest that could be earned on short-term investments. However, the costs to the company offering the discount must also be considered.

Companies also need to monitor outstanding accounts receivable balances. An important tool for management to monitor outstanding accounts receivable is to conduct an aged accounts receivable analysis, discussed in the section "Impairment of Accounts Receivable" later in this chapter. Companies that do not regularly assess and follow up on overdue accounts receivable may find that some of their customers take advantage of the situation. In particular, customers that are facing cash flow difficulties may be influenced regarding which companies they pay first by the number of phone calls and follow-up letters they receive from collection departments. (After all, it is easier to "oil the squeaky wheel" than to listen to it!) Discussions with tardy customers may result in a schedule of payments that is beneficial to both the seller and customer.

Companies should therefore monitor accounts receivable levels carefully to:

- minimize the stress on working capital and related bank debt, while

- encouraging prompt payment from their customers.

What Do the Numbers Mean?

As noted above, companies should monitor their accounts receivable balances carefully and may want to take a variety of actions to speed up collections. For example, **Bell Aliant** uses late payment charges and follow-up letters to help encourage prompt payment. The opening story to this chapter provides other details of how the company moves from encouraging payment to the use of a collection agency as a last resort in the collection process.

Other companies may sell accounts receivable to factors to convert the receivables into cash more quickly, rather than waiting for customers to pay. These services tend to be used more by small and medium-sized businesses that may not have the cash resources to wait for payment (or the credit history to allow them to obtain a bank loan at a better interest rate). Alternatively, larger companies may rely on securitization of pools of accounts receivables, where the receivables are grouped together and turned into securities for sale to investors. The use of these asset-backed securities by large companies to raise funds and improve cash flow is discussed in more detail as part of the section on sales of receivables later in this chapter.

CASH RECOGNITION AND MEASUREMENT

Objective 2

Define financial assets, and identify items that are considered cash and cash equivalents and how they are reported.

We now begin our detailed study of statement of financial position accounts and the recognition and measurement concepts that apply to the different categories of assets, liabilities, and shareholders' equity. The first assets we cover are highly liquid, and they are considered financial assets. A **financial asset** is any asset that is:

(i) cash;

(ii) a contractual right to receive cash or another financial asset from another party;

(iii) a contractual right to exchange financial instruments with another party under conditions that are potentially favourable to the entity; or

(iv) an equity instrument of another entity.[1]

Financial assets are covered in several chapters of this text. Chapter 7 deals with cash and cash equivalents, and with accounts, notes, and loans receivable. Chapter 9 covers other major categories of financial assets—mainly investments in the debt and equity instruments of other companies. The financial assets in these two chapters fit parts (i), (ii), and (iv) of the definition. Chapter 9 highlights the profession's recent move away from the long-standing transactions-based historical cost model toward one that relies more on fair values. Chapter 2 includes a discussion of what fair value is and how it is measured. Coverage of the more complex instruments that fit part (iii) of the definition, such as derivatives, along with financial liabilities and equity, is found in Chapter 16 of Volume 2.

What Is Cash?

Cash is the most liquid asset and is the standard medium of exchange and the basis for measuring and accounting for all other items. It meets the definition of a financial asset, and is generally classified as a current asset.

Cash consists of coins, currency, and other available funds that are on deposit at a bank. Negotiable instruments such as money orders, certified cheques, cashier's cheques, personal cheques, and bank drafts are also viewed as cash. Although a company's bank may have a legal right to demand advance notice before it allows a withdrawal from a savings account, banks rarely ask for this notice and savings accounts are therefore also usually classified as cash.

It is more appropriate to classify money-market funds, certificates of deposit, and similar types of deposits and "short-term paper" that allow investors to earn interest as **cash equivalents** or **short-term investments** than as cash. The reason is that there are usually restrictions, or penalties, on these securities if they are converted to cash prior to maturity. Money-market funds that give chequing account privileges, however, are usually classified as cash.

Certain items present classification problems: for example, postdated cheques from customers and IOUs are treated as receivables. It is proper to treat travel advances granted to employees as receivables if the advances are to be collected from the employees or deducted from their salaries. Otherwise, it is more appropriate to classify the travel advance as a prepaid expense. Postage stamps on hand are classified as part of office supplies inventory or as a prepaid expense. Petty cash funds and change funds are included in current assets as cash because these funds are used to meet current operating expenses and to liquidate current liabilities.

Reporting Cash

Although the reporting of cash is fairly straightforward, there are some issues that need special attention. They concern the reporting of:

- Restricted cash
- Cash in foreign currencies
- Bank overdrafts
- Cash equivalents

Restricted Cash

Petty cash (see Appendix 7A) and special payroll, and dividend bank accounts are examples of cash that has been set aside for a particular purpose. In most situations, these balances are not material and therefore are not segregated from cash when it is reported in the financial statements. When an amount is material, restricted cash is segregated from regular cash for reporting purposes. The **restricted cash** is separately disclosed and reported in the Current Assets section or is classified separately in the Long-Term Assets section, depending on the date of availability or of the expected disbursement.[2] In general, it should not be classified in current assets if there are restrictions that prevent it from being used for current purposes, unless the restricted cash offsets a current liability. Cash that is classified in the long-term section has often been set aside for investment or financing purposes, such as for a plant expansion, long-term debt retirement, or as collateral for a long-term loan.

Some lending institutions require customers who borrow money from them to keep minimum cash balances in their chequing or savings accounts. These minimum balances are called **compensating balances** and are defined as the portion of any demand deposit (or any time deposit or certificate of deposit) that a corporation keeps as support for its existing or maturing obligations with a lending institution.[3] By requiring a compensating balance, the bank gets an effective interest rate on its loan that is higher than the stated rate because it can use the restricted amount that must remain on deposit. In the United States, where banks more often require compensating balances, the accounting practice is to report in current assets any legally restricted deposits that are held as compensating balances against short-term borrowing arrangements.

Law

To ensure that investors are not misled about the amount of cash that is available to meet recurring obligations, legally restricted balances have to be reported separately in current assets or non-current assets, as appropriate. In practice, many companies report this through note disclosure.

Cash in Foreign Currencies

Underlying Concept

When entities have cash accounts in more than one currency, they are remeasured using the rate at the date of the statement of financial position into a common monetary unit, typically Canadian dollars. Some Canadian companies, however, identify the U.S. dollar as their functional currency and present their statements in this unit instead.

Many companies have bank accounts in other countries, especially if they have recurring transactions in that country's currency. The foreign currency is translated into Canadian dollars at the exchange rate on the date of the statement of financial position. In situations where there is no restriction on the transfer of those funds to the Canadian company, it is included as cash in current assets. If there are restrictions on the flow of capital out of a country, the cash is reported as restricted. The classification of the cash as current or non-current is based on the circumstances and, in extreme cases, restrictions may be so severe that the foreign balances do not even qualify for recognition as assets.

Bank Overdrafts

Bank overdrafts occur when cheques are written for more than the amount in the bank account. Overdrafts are reported in the Current Liabilities section, and companies sometimes do this by adding the amount to what is reported as accounts payable. If the overdraft amount is material, it should be disclosed separately either on the face of the statement of financial position or in the related notes.

In general, bank overdrafts should not be offset against the Cash account. A major exception is when there is available cash in another account at the same bank as the overdraft. Offsetting in this case is appropriate.

Cash Equivalents

IFRS
ASPE

Cash is often reported with the asset category called cash equivalents. **Cash equivalents** are defined as "short-term, highly liquid investments that are readily convertible to known amounts of cash and which are subject to an insignificant risk of changes in value."[4] Companies usually hold cash equivalents for meeting upcoming cash requirements. Generally, only investments with **maturities of three months or less** when acquired qualify under the definition. While equity investments are excluded from the ASPE definition of cash equivalents, IFRS allows preferred shares that are acquired close to their maturity date to qualify. Examples of cash equivalents are investments in treasury bills, commercial paper, and money-market funds.

In some circumstances, bank overdrafts may be deducted when the amount of cash and cash equivalents is being determined. If overdrafts are part of the firm's cash management activities, if they are repayable on demand, and if the bank balance fluctuates often between a positive and negative balance, the overdrafts may be considered part of cash and cash equivalents.

Because some companies report investments that qualify as cash equivalents in other categories of current assets, such as short-term or trading investments, it is important for entities to disclose their reporting policy in a note to the financial statements. Investments that are classified as cash equivalents are held to be sold in the very short term. These are generally reported at fair value. Their fair values at acquisition plus accrued interest to the date of the statement of financial position often approximate fair value at the date of the statement of financial position.

Illustration 7-1 shows the information that Ottawa-based **Zarlink Semiconductor Inc.** reports in its financial statements for the year ended March 25, 2011. Zarlink was subsequently acquired by **Microsemi Corporation** in October 2011.

Real World Emphasis

Illustration 7-1

Reporting of Cash and Cash Equivalents—Zarlink Semiconductor Inc.

	March 25, 2011	March 26, 2010
ASSETS		
Current assets:		
Cash and cash equivalents	$128,197	$74,369
Restricted cash and cash equivalents	—	15,720

2. ACCOUNTING POLICIES

(D) CASH, CASH EQUIVALENTS

All highly liquid investments with original maturities of three months or less are classified as cash and cash equivalents. The fair value of cash equivalents approximates the amounts shown in the financial statements.

(E) RESTRICTED CASH AND CASH EQUIVALENTS

Restricted cash and cash equivalents consist of cash and cash equivalents used as security pledges against liabilities or other forms of credit.

Summary of Cash-Related Items

Cash and cash equivalents include currency and most negotiable instruments. If the item cannot be converted to coin or currency on short notice, it is classified separately as an investment, receivable, or prepaid expense. Cash that is not available for paying liabilities that are currently maturing is classified in the long-term assets section. The chart below summarizes the classification of cash-related items. Appendix 7A provides further details on the control of cash.

Classification of Cash, Cash Equivalents, and Noncash Items		
Item	**Classification**	**Comment**
Cash	Cash	Report it as cash. If restricted, identify and report it separately as a current or noncurrent asset.
Petty cash	Cash	Report as cash.
Short-term paper	Cash equivalents	Classify as cash equivalents if investments have a maturity of three months or less when acquired.

(continued)

Item	Classification	Comment
Short-term paper	Short-term investments	Classify as short-term investments if investments have a maturity of 3 to 12 months when acquired.
Postdated cheques and IOUs	Receivables	Classify as receivables if they are considered to be collectible.
Travel advances	Receivables or prepaid expenses	Classify as receivables or prepaid expenses if they are collectible from employees or to be spent on travel in the future, respectively.
Postage on hand (as stamps or in postage meters)	Prepaid expenses	These may alternatively be classified as office supplies inventory.
Bank overdrafts	Current liability	If there is a right of offset, report as a reduction of cash.
Compensating balances	Classified separately as a deposit that is maintained as a compensating balance	Classify as current asset in the statement of financial position. Disclose details of the arrangement.

RECEIVABLES—RECOGNITION AND MEASUREMENT

We now turn to the second type of asset that is important to companies: receivables.

Definition and Types

Objective 3
Define receivables and identify the different types of receivables from an accounting perspective.

In general, receivables are claims that a company has against customers and others, usually for specific cash receipts in the future. As we saw in the introduction to this chapter, when the claim is a **contractual** right to receive cash or other financial assets from another party, the receivable is a financial asset. On a classified statement of financial position, receivables are either current (short-term) or non-current (long-term). Current receivables are expected to be realized (converted to cash) within a year or during the current operating cycle, whichever is longer. All other receivables are classified as non-current.

These financial assets are generally referred to in a more specific way as loans or receivables, with loans being a type of receivable.[5] **Loans and receivables** result from one party delivering cash (or other assets or services) to a borrower in exchange for a promise to repay the amount on a specified date or dates, or on demand, along with interest to compensate for the time value of money and the risk of non-payment. They are not usually acquired to be held as a cash equivalent or temporary investment of excess cash. Investments in government debt, corporate bonds, convertible debt, commercial paper, and other securities, while similar, are not loans and receivables. They are traded in an active market, while loans and receivables are not.

Finance

Trade receivables are amounts owed by customers to whom the company has sold goods or services as part of its normal business operations; that is, they are amounts that result from operating transactions. They can be either open accounts receivable or notes receivable. Open accounts receivable are short-term extensions of credit that are based on a purchaser's **verbal** promise to pay for goods and services that have been sold. They are normally collectible within 30 to 60 days, but credit terms may be longer—or shorter—depending on the industry. **Notes receivable** are **written** promises to pay a certain amount of money on a specified future date. They may arise from sales of goods and services, or from other transactions.

As the term "loan" suggests, **loans receivable** are created when one party advances cash or other assets to a borrower and receives a promise to be repaid later. Loans tend to result from financing transactions by borrowers and investing transactions by lenders. When there is a written document that gives the terms and conditions of the loan receivable, the loan is then also called a note receivable.

Nontrade receivables are created by a variety of transactions and can be written promises either to pay cash or to deliver other assets. Examples of nontrade receivables include the following:

- Advances to officers and employees, or to subsidiaries or other companies

- Amounts owing from a purchaser on the sale of capital assets or investments where delayed payment terms have been agreed on

- Amounts receivable from the government: income taxes paid in excess of the amount owed, GST/HST payments recoverable, investment tax credits, or other tax rebates receivable

- Dividends and interest receivable

- Claims against insurance companies for losses the company has suffered; against trucking companies or railways for damaged or lost goods; against creditors for returned, damaged, or lost goods; or against customers for returnable items (crates, containers, etc.)

Real World Emphasis

Because of their special nature, nontrade receivables are generally classified and reported as separate items in the statement of financial position or in a note that is cross-referenced to the statement. Illustration 7-2 shows the balance sheet and separate reporting of the cash and cash equivalents and receivables on the financial statements of Nova Scotia–based **Empire Company Limited** for its year ended May 7, 2011.

Illustration 7-2

Receivables Reporting— Empire Company Limited

CONSOLIDATED BALANCE SHEETS

(in millions)	May 7, 2011	May 1, 2010
Assets		
Current		
Cash and cash equivalents	$616.9	$401.0
Receivables	346.6	336.9
Income taxes receivable	0.3	—
Loans and other receivables (Note 6)	81.7	105.8
Loans and other receivables (Note 6)	68.8	79.2

Note 6 Loans and Other Receivables

	May 7, 2011	May 1, 2010
Loans and mortgages receivable	$109.2	$110.5
Notes receivable and other	41.3	74.5
	150.5	185.0
Less amount due within one year	81.7	105.8
	$ 68.8	$ 79.2

Another type of receivable, loans and mortgages receivable, represent long-term financing by Empire to certain retail associates. These loans are primarily secured by inventory, fixtures, and equipment; bear various interest rates; and have repayment terms up to 10 years. The carrying amount of the loans receivable approximates fair value based on the variable interest rates charged on the loans and the operating relationship of the associates with the company.

Note that the following discussion of **accounts and notes receivable** assumes that they are short-term trade receivables, and that the discussion of **loans receivable** is based on long-term nontrade loans or notes. In addition, it is assumed that they all are financial assets. The basic accounting issues are discussed in the following sections: **recognition and measurement**, **impairment**, and **derecognition**.

Recognition and Measurement of Accounts Receivable

Objective 4
Account for and explain the accounting issues related to the recognition and measurement of accounts receivable.

The general accounting standards for the recognition and initial measurement of accounts receivable are as follows:

- recognize an account receivable when the entity becomes a party to the contractual provisions of the financial instrument;

- measure the receivable initially at its fair value;[6] and

- after initial recognition, measure receivables at amortized cost.

The entity becomes a party to the contractual provisions of the financial instrument only when it has a legal claim to receive cash or other financial assets. While a commitment to sell goods or services to a customer might be made when a customer's order is received, there is usually no legal claim until one of the parties to the contract has performed under the agreement. Therefore the timing of recognition of accounts receivable is intertwined with the recognition of revenue, which was discussed in Chapter 6. Typically, when the sale is recognized, either cash is received (realized) or an account receivable is recognized.

Recognizing receivables initially at their fair value is not as straightforward as it might seem. This is because fair value may not be the same as the exchange price that the parties agree on. The **exchange price**, **the amount due** from the customer or borrower, is generally indicated on a business document, usually an invoice. Two factors can make measuring the fair value of short-term receivables more complicated: (1) the availability of discounts (trade and cash discounts) and (2) the length of time between the sale and the payment due date (the interest element).

Trade Discounts

Customers are often quoted prices based on list or catalogue prices that may have trade or quantity discounts. **Trade discounts** are used to avoid frequent changes in catalogues, to quote different prices for different quantities purchased, or to hide the true invoice price from competitors.

Trade discounts are commonly quoted in percentages. For example, if your textbook has a list price of $90 and the publisher sells it to college and university bookstores for list less a 30% trade discount, the receivable recorded by the publisher is $63 per textbook. The normal practice is simply to deduct the trade discount from the list price and recognize the net amount as the receivable and revenue.

Cash Discounts (Sales Discounts)

Cash discounts or **sales discounts** are offered to encourage fast payment. They are expressed in specific terms: for example, 2/10, n/30 means there is a 2% discount if the invoice is paid within 10 days and that the gross amount is due in 30 days; while 2/10, E.O.M., n/30, means there is a 2% discount if the invoice is paid before the 10th day of the following month, with full payment due by the 30th of the following month.

Companies that buy goods or services but fail to take sales discounts are usually not using their money as effectively as they could. An enterprise that receives a 1% reduction in the sales price for paying within 10 days when the total payment is due within 30 days is basically earning 18.25% interest (1.0% divided by 20/365) because of the discount—or, more technically, it is at least avoiding that rate of interest included in the undiscounted invoice price. For this reason, companies usually take the discount unless their cash is severely limited.[7]

In theory, the receivable and the associated sale should both be recognized at the net amount or fair value; that is, the present value of the future cash flows. Under this approach, sales to customers who pay within the discount period are reported at the cash price; for customers who pay after the discount period expires, the company separately reports Sales Discounts Forfeited, similar to interest income earned.

The most commonly used method of recording short-term receivables and related sales, however, is to **record the gross amounts of the receivable and sale; that is, at the full amount assuming no discount will be taken**. Under this method, sales discounts are recognized in the accounts only when payment is received within the discount period. Sales discounts are then shown in the income statement as a deduction from sales to arrive at net sales.

The entries in Illustration 7-3 show the difference between the gross and net methods.

	Gross Method			Net Method		
Illustration 7-3						
Entries under Gross and Net Methods of Recording Cash (Sales) Discounts						

Gross Method

Sales of $10,000, terms 2/10, n/30:

Accounts Receivable	10,000	
Sales Revenue		10,000

Payment on $4,000 of sales received within discount period:

Cash	3,920	
Sales Discounts	80	
Accounts Receivable		4,000

Payment on $6,000 of sales received after discount period:

Cash	6,000	
Accounts Receivable		6,000

Net Method

Sales of $10,000, terms 2/10, n/30:

Accounts Receivable	9,800	
Sales Revenue		9,800

Payment on $4,000 of sales received within discount period:

Cash	3,920	
Accounts Receivable		3,920

Payment on $6,000 of sales received after discount period:

Accounts Receivable	120*	
Sales Discounts Forfeited		120
Cash	6,000	
Accounts Receivable		6,000*

*One net entry could be made:

Cash	6,000	
Accounts Receivable		5,880
Sales Discounts Forfeited		120

If the **gross method** is used, proper asset valuation requires that a reasonable estimate be made of discounts that are expected to be taken after the date of the statement of financial position and that the amount be recorded if it is material. Allowance for Sales Discounts, a contra account to Accounts Receivable on the statement of financial position, is credited for such amounts and the Sales Discounts account on the income statement is increased (debited). If the **net method** is used, the receivables are already at their realizable value so no further adjustment is needed. The Sales Discounts Forfeited account is recognized as an item of "Other revenue" on the income statement.

Although the net method is theoretically preferred, it is rarely used. This is because it requires more bookkeeping for the additional adjusting entries after the discount period has passed. Using the gross method, along with the added requirement to estimate and record discounts that are expected to be taken after the date of the statement of financial position, results in the same effect on the statement of financial position and income statement.

Sales Returns and Allowances

To properly measure **sales revenues** and **receivables**, allowance accounts are normally used. Probable sales returns and price reductions are estimated and deducted as contra accounts against sales on the income statement and accounts receivable on the statement of financial position. This results in net sales and the net estimated amount of accounts receivable being properly reported on the financial statements.

This procedure is followed so that the sales returns or price allowances (called **sales returns and allowances**) are reported in the same period as the sales that they relate to. If this adjustment is not made, however, the amount of mismatched returns and allowances is usually not material as long as the items are handled consistently from year to year. The situation changes when a company completes a few special orders for large amounts near the end of its accounting period: in this case, sales returns and allowances should be anticipated and recognized in the period of the sale to avoid distorting the current period's income statement. There are some companies that by their nature have significant returns and therefore usually have an allowance for sales returns.

As an example, assume that Astro Corporation estimates that approximately 5% of its $1 million of trade receivables outstanding will be returned or some adjustment will be made to the sales price. Leaving out a $50,000 charge could have a material effect on net income for the period. The entry to show expected sales returns and allowances is:

A   = L +   SE
−50,000   −50,000

Cash flows: No effect

| Sales Returns and Allowances | 50,000 | |
| Allowance for Sales Returns and Allowances | | 50,000 |

The account Sales Returns and Allowances is reported as a deduction from Sales Revenue in the income statement. Allowance for Sales Returns and Allowances is an asset valuation account (contra asset) that is deducted from total accounts receivable. It is similar to the Allowance for Doubtful Accounts discussed below.

Nonrecognition of Interest Element

Ideally, receivables should be measured initially at their fair value, represented by their present value; that is, the amount of cash that would be required at the date of the sale to satisfy the outstanding claim. As mentioned in the previous section, this is equivalent to the discounted value of the cash that will be received in the future. When a company has to wait for the cash receipts, the receivable's face amount is not a precise measure of its fair value.

To illustrate, assume that a company makes a sale on account for $1,000. The applicable annual interest rate is 12%, and cash is to be received at the end of four months. The receivable's present value is not $1,000 but $961.56 ($1,000 × 0.96156, Table A-2 n = 1, i = 4%).[8] In other words, $1,000 to be received in four months is equivalent to $961.56 received today.

In theory, the discounted amount of $961.56 is the fair value of the receivable and sales revenue, and any additional amount received after the sale is interest revenue. **In practice, accountants generally ignore this for accounts receivable because the discount amount is not usually material when compared with the net income for the period.**

Both ASPE and IFRS support measuring financial assets at the **present value of the cash that is expected to be received**, and both allow net realizable value to approximate the present value for short-term trade receivables because the effect of the time value of money is immaterial.

Measurement of Accounts Receivable after Acquisition

Accounts receivable are measured in subsequent accounting periods at amortized cost. Where there is no interest element recognized, as discussed above, there is nothing to

Underlying Concept

Materiality means that an amount in question would make a difference to a decision-maker. Standard setters believe that interest and present value concepts do not need to be strictly applied if omitting them results in financial statements that are not materially different.

amortize, so amortized cost and cost are the same thing. For notes and loans receivable that have an interest component, the asset's carrying amount is amortized as described later in this chapter.

Impairment of Accounts Receivable

Objective 5
Account for and explain the accounting issues related to the impairment in value of accounts receivable.

The goal in valuing accounts receivable on the statement of financial position is to report them at no more than the benefits they will ultimately provide to the entity. Because of this, in addition to reductions for expected returns, allowances, or cash discounts that will be granted, all receivables have to be assessed for indications of uncollectibility or impairment. Loans and receivables are impaired if there has been a "significant adverse change" in either the expected timing of the future cash flows or in the amount expected to be repaid. Impaired trade receivables are usually referred to as **bad debts** or **uncollectible accounts**.

Estimating Uncollectible Trade Accounts Receivable

As one accountant so aptly noted, the credit manager's idea of heaven would probably be a place where everyone (eventually) paid his or her debts.[9] Except in some segments of the retail sector, the usual method of conducting business is through extending credit to customers. This means that most companies are exposed to varying levels of **credit risk**: the likelihood of loss because of the failure of the other party to fully pay the amount owed. Except for cash sales, it is possible that the full amount of the sale will never be collected. Many companies set their credit policies to allow for a certain percentage of uncollectible accounts. In fact, some feel that if the percentage is not reached, it may indicate sales being lost because of credit policies that are too strict.

The **accounting issue**, therefore, is ensuring that a reasonable estimate is made of the amount of the Accounts Receivable that is unlikely to be collected. An allowance for this amount is then deducted from the receivables reported on the statement of financial position. If there are only a few relatively large accounts, an analysis of each separate account can be made; but most companies have large numbers of similar accounts with smaller balances in each. How does management estimate how much may be uncollectible?

The single most important indicator used to identify impaired accounts receivable is the age of the accounts; that is, how long the amounts owed have been outstanding, especially beyond their due dates. Other factors that are taken into account include the company's past loss experience and current economic conditions. Accounts are also analyzed by grouping those with similar credit risk characteristics—perhaps by geographic location or type of industry. If one area of the country is experiencing high unemployment and depressed economic conditions, this may affect the ability of debtors in that area to pay their accounts. Or a particular industry, such as forestry or real estate, may be going through a low in the business cycle with a higher than usual incidence of tight cash, or receivership or bankruptcy.

One common method used by most companies to estimate how much of their total Accounts Receivable is probably uncollectible is the **aging method**. This approach allows a company to use its past experience to estimate the percentage of its outstanding receivables that will become uncollectible, without identifying specific accounts. This is referred to as the **percentage-of-receivables approach**. Its objective is to report receivables on the statement of financial position at their **net realizable value**, this being the net amount expected to be received in cash. The percentage that is used in this approach may be a combined rate that reflects an overall estimate of the uncollectible receivables. A better approach is to set up an **aging schedule**, which is more sensitive to the actual status of the accounts receivable. This approach determines the age of each account receivable and applies a different percentage to each of the various age categories, based on past experience. Aging schedules are often used because they show which accounts need special attention by highlighting how long various accounts receivable have been outstanding. The schedule of Wilson & Co. in Illustration 7-4 is an example.

Illustration 7-4

Accounts Receivable Aging Schedule

WILSON & CO.
Aging Schedule

Name of Customer	Balance Dec. 31	Under 60 days	61–90 days	91–120 days	Over 120 days
Atlantic Stainless Steel Corp.	$ 9,800	$ 7,000	$ 2,800		
Brockville Steel Company	34,000	34,000			
Cambridge Sheet & Tube Co.	4,500				$ 4,500
Eastern Iron Works Ltd.	7,200	6,000		$ 1,200	
Other individual customers	491,500	413,000	15,200	12,800	50,500
	$547,000	$460,000	$18,000	$14,000	$55,000

Summary

Age	Amount	Percentage Estimated to Be Uncollectible	Estimate of Uncollectible Accounts
Under 60 days old	$460,000	4%	$18,400
61–90 days old	18,000	15%	2,700
91–120 days old	14,000	20%	2,800
Over 120 days	55,000	25%	13,750
Year-end balance of Allowance for Doubtful Accounts should =			$37,650

Allowance Method

This analysis indicates that Wilson & Co. expects to receive $547,000 less $37,650, or $509,350 net cash receipts from the December 31 amounts owed. That is, $509,350 is the Accounts Receivable's estimated net realizable value. The **allowance method** is used to account for this estimate of impairment. On Wilson & Co.'s December 31 statement of financial position, a **contra account**, Allowance for Doubtful Accounts (or Allowance for Uncollectible Accounts) of $37,650, is reported, as indicated in Illustration 7-5. A contra account is used because the Accounts Receivable account is supported by a subsidiary ledger of each customer's balance owing and management does not know yet which specific accounts will result in non-collection and bad debt losses.

WILSON & CO. STATEMENT OF FINANCIAL POSITION
December 31

Current Assets		
Accounts receivable		$547,000
Less: Allowance for doubtful accounts		37,650
		$509,350

The ending balance in the allowance account should be $37,650. The appropriate entry, therefore, depends on what the balance is in the account before making the adjusting entry. Assume this is Wilson's first year of operations and that there is **no previous balance in the allowance account before this adjustment.** In this case, the entry to record the impairment for the current year is:

A = L + SE
−37,650   −37,650
Cash flows: No effect

Bad Debt Expense	37,650	
Allowance for Doubtful Accounts		37,650

To change the illustration slightly, assume that **the allowance account already has a credit balance of $18,800 before adjustment**. In this case, the amount to be added to the account is $18,850 ($37,650 − $18,800). This will bring the balance in the allowance account to $37,650. The following entry is made:

A   = L +   SE
−18,850   −18,850

Cash flows: No effect

Bad Debt Expense	18,850	
Allowance for Doubtful Accounts		18,850

If instead the **balance in the allowance account before adjustment is a debit balance of $200**, then the amount to bring the allowance account to the correct credit balance of $37,650 is $37,850 ($37,650 desired credit balance + $200 debit balance). When using the allowance procedure, the balance that is already in the allowance account before the adjusting entry is made **cannot be ignored**; it has to be considered to calculate the amount needed for the adjustment.

Bad Debt Expense and the Allowance Account.   So far, we have focused on the balance in the Allowance for Doubtful Accounts. The reason for this is the emphasis in our current accounting model on ensuring good measurements of assets and liabilities. The model assumes that if assets and liabilities are measured properly, the related revenues and expenses will be as well. Let's turn now to bad debt expense.

The allowance method reports receivables at their estimated realizable value and recognizes bad debt losses as an expense in the same accounting period as when the sales on account are made. The allowance method accomplishes two things: a proper carrying amount for receivables on the statement of financial position, and the resulting matching of expenses and revenues in the same period. Using the allowance method, companies typically follow one of two accounting procedures, both of which result in the same ending balances in the Allowance and Bad Debt Expense accounts.

1. **Allowance procedure only:** At the end of every month, management carries out an analysis of the Accounts Receivable balances and makes an assessment of the estimated uncollectible accounts. An accounting entry is prepared, as illustrated above for Wilson & Co., adjusting the Allowance for Doubtful Accounts to its correct balance. The Bad Debt Expense account is debited or credited as necessary and at the end of the fiscal year, the total of all the entries to the expense account during the year is the bad debt expense for the year. The balance in the Allowance account is an appropriate amount because all entries were based on an analysis of the receivables.

2. **Mix of procedures:** At the end of every month, management estimates the company's **bad debt expense** for that month. This estimate is based on a percentage of the sales reported, and therefore is called the **percentage-of-sales approach**. If there is a fairly stable relationship between previous years' credit sales and bad debts, then that relationship can be turned into a percentage and used to estimate any period's bad debt expense. Because the amount of sales is known, this is a **fast and simple way** to estimate the expense each period. Each month, the Bad Debt Expense is debited and the Allowance for Doubtful Accounts is credited.

At the end of the fiscal year, however, when financial statements are issued, management still has to assess the year-end receivables to ensure that the balance in the Allowance account is appropriate. If necessary, an adjustment is then made to the Allowance account to bring it to the necessary balance, with the offsetting debit or credit made to Bad Debt Expense.

As an example, assume that every month, Dockrill Corp. estimates from past experience that about 2% of net credit sales will become uncollectible. If Dockrill Corp. has net credit sales of $400,000 in 2014, the entries made through the year to record bad debt expense in 2014 can be summarized in one entry as follows:

Underlying Concept

The percentage-of-sales approach is a good illustration of using the matching concept, which relates expenses to revenues earned. The final adjustment based on the net realizable value of the receivables, however, supports the primacy of asset measurement in the model.

A	=	L	+	SE
−8,000				−8,000

Cash flows: No effect

Bad Debt Expense (2% × $400,000)	8,000	
Allowance for Doubtful Accounts		8,000

At year end, management prepares an analysis of receivables and estimates that $9,900 will not be collectible. Therefore, the balance in the Allowance account **after adjustment** must be a credit of $9,900. The correct adjusting entry depends on the balance in the Allowance account before the adjustment is made. The balance is not likely to be a credit of $8,000, the amount of the credits to the account during the year. The Allowance is a statement of financial position account and therefore would have had an opening balance, and entries to record accounts written off (as explained below) would also have been made to the account during the current year.

Assuming the balance in the Allowance for Doubtful Accounts before adjustment is $7,500 credit, then the following adjusting entry is needed:

A	=	L	+	SE
−2,400				−2,400

Cash flows: No effect

Bad Debt Expense	2,400	
Allowance for Doubtful Accounts		2,400
($9,900 − $7,500 = $2,400)		

Either approach can be used. Many companies use the percentage-of-sales method for internal reporting through the year because of its ease of use, and make an adjustment at year end based on receivable balances at the date of the statement of financial position for their external financial statements.

Accounts Written Off and the Allowance Account

Accounts Receivable Written Off.   Under the allowance method, after all efforts have been made to collect a **specific account** and it is determined to be uncollectible, its balance is removed from Accounts Receivable and the Allowance for Doubtful Accounts is reduced. For example, assuming the account of Brown Ltd. of $550 is considered uncollectible, the writeoff entry is as follows:

A	=	L	+	SE
0		0		0

Cash flows: No effect

Allowance for Doubtful Accounts	550	
Accounts Receivable		550

Note that there is no effect on the income statement **from writing off an account**, nor should there be. This is because the associated bad debt expense was **previously** recognized as an estimate **in the period of the sale**. There is also no effect on the net amount of the receivables because Accounts Receivable and its contra account are **both** reduced by equal amounts.

Collection of an Account Previously Written Off.   If a collection is made on a receivable that was previously written off, the procedure is to first re-establish the receivable by reversing the writeoff entry, and **then** recognize the cash inflow as a regular receipt on account. To illustrate, assume that Brown Ltd. eventually remits $300, and indicates that this is all that will be paid. The entries to record this transaction are as follows:

A	=	L	+	SE
0		0		0

Cash flows: No effect

Accounts Receivable	300	
Allowance for Doubtful Accounts		300
(To reinstate the account written off and now determined to be collectible)		

A = L + SE	Cash 300
0 0 0	Accounts Receivable 300
Cash flows: ↑ 300 inflow	(To record the receipt of cash on account from Brown Ltd.)

Effects on Accounts

Illustration 7-6 provides a summary of the transactions and events that affect the accounts related to accounts receivable.

Accounts Receivable		Allowance for Doubtful Accounts	
Opening balance			Opening balance
1. Credit sales	2. Cash received on account		3. Bad debt expense recognized
5. Reinstatement of accounts previously written off	4. Accounts written off	4. Accounts written off	5. Reinstatement of accounts previously written off
		6. Year-end adjustment to reduce balance in allowance account	7. Year-end adjustment to increase balance in allowance account

Bad Debt Expense		Sales	
3. Bad debt expense recognized			1. Credit sales
7. Year-end adjustment to increase balance in allowance account	6. Year-end adjustment to reduce balance in allowance account		

Illustration 7-6

Effects on Related Accounts

The ending balance of the Accounts Receivable account represents the total of all amounts owed to the company at the date of the statement of financial position, except those accounts written off, of course. This amount is backed up by a subsidiary ledger of the individual customers and the amount owed by each. The ending balance of the allowance account represents management's estimate of the total accounts receivable that will not be collected. When reported together, the net amount is the estimate of the net realizable value of the total amount owed.

The allowance for doubtful accounts as a percentage of receivables varies considerably, depending on the industry and recent economic conditions. **Stantec Inc.**, a professional engineering services firm, for example, reported an allowance for doubtful accounts of 4% of its accounts receivable at December 31, 2011, down considerably from the 10% reported six years earlier, while **Potash Corporation of Saskatchewan Inc.**, an integrated fertilizer and related industrial and feed products company, reported an allowance of less than 1% of its trade receivables.

Real World Emphasis

What Do the Numbers Mean?

In its 2011 Annual Report, **Canadian Tire Corporation**'s results for the Financial Services Division are influenced in large part by growth in gross average receivables (GAR), which drives interest revenue. The key indicators of performance in the Financial Services segment are the size, profitability and quality of the total managed portfolio of receivables. Growth in the total managed portfolio of receivables is measured by growth in the average number of accounts and growth in the average account balance. A key profitability measure the company tracks is the return on the average total managed portfolio (also referred to as "return on receivables" or "ROR"), which is calculated by dividing income before tax and gain/loss on disposal of property and equipment by the average total managed portfolio over a 12-month period. The quality of the portfolio is reflected in the rolling 12-month net writeoff rate, the aging of the portfolio, and the allowance rate. A continuity schedule from Canadian Tire's 2011 Annual Report shows its **allowance for credit losses**:

(C$ in millions)	Trade and other receivables		Loans receivable[1,2]		Total	
	2011	2010	2011	2010	2011	2010
Balance, beginning of year	$ 7.7	$ 3.6	$ 117.7	$ 127.4	$ 125.4	$ 131.0
Impairment for credit losses	5.0	4.3	302.0	300.7	307.0	305.0
Recoveries	0.1	0.2	50.0	46.2	50.1	46.4
Write-offs	(0.6)	(0.4)	(351.0)	(356.6)	(351.6)	(357.0)
Balance, end of year	$ 12.2	$ 7.7	$ 118.7	$ 117.7	$ 130.9	$ 125.4

[1] Loans include credit card loans, personal loans and lines of credit loans.
[2] No allowances for credit losses have been made with respect to Franchise Trust loans receivable.

The Company's aging of the trade and other receivables and loans receivable that are past due, but not impaired is as follows:

(C$ in millions)	2011			2010		
	0-90 days	> 90 days	Total	0-90 days	> 90 days	Total
Trade and other receivables	$ 27.0	$14.1	$ 41.1	$ 16.5	$10.2	$ 26.7
Loans receivable[1]	94.0	69.2	163.2	93.7	64.8	158.5
Total	$121.0	$83.3	$204.3	$110.2	$75.0	$185.2

[1] No past due loans for Franchise Trust.

A loan is considered past due when the counterparty has not made a payment by the contractual due date. Credit card and line of credit loan balances are written off when a payment is 180 days in arrears. Line of credit loans are considered impaired when a payment is over 90 days in arrears and are written off when a payment is 180 days in arrears. Personal loans are considered impaired when a payment is over 90 days in arrears and are written off when a payment is 365 days in arrears. No collateral is held against loans receivable.

The increase in Canadian Tire's allowance for credit losses relates primarily to an increase in the allowance for credit losses for "Trade and other receivables" which increased from $7.7 million to $12.2 million. "Trade and other receivables" on Canadian Tire's Balance Sheet increased by 23% (from $673.9 million to $829.3 million) while Loans receivable were quite stable (up less than 1% from 2010 to 2011). Similarly, increases in the amounts past due over 90 days are most noticeable for "Trade and other receivables."

Direct Writeoff Method

Some cash-based businesses, such as corner grocery stores, do not extend credit often and therefore have very few credit transactions and small accounts receivable balances. For such businesses, **where the effect of not applying the allowance method is highly immaterial**, the simpler **direct writeoff method** is sometimes used. No estimates are made in advance and no allowance account is used. Instead, when an account is determined to be uncollectible, the specific account receivable is written off with the debit recognized as bad debt expense:

A   =   L   +   SE
−$$ 0   −$$
Cash flows: No effect

Bad Debt Expense	$$	
Accounts Receivable		$$

If amounts are later collected on an account that was previously written off, a notation is made in the customer's record, and the amount collected is recognized through entries to Cash and a revenue account entitled Uncollectible Amounts Recovered.

<table>
<tr><td>A = L + SE
+$$ 0 +$$
Cash flows: ↑ $$ inflow</td><td>Cash
    Uncollectible Amounts Recovered</td><td align="right">$$</td><td align="right">$$</td></tr>
</table>

Recognition and Measurement of Short-Term Notes and Loans Receivable

Objective 6
Account for and explain the accounting issues related to the recognition and measurement of short-term notes and loans receivable.

A note receivable is similar to an account receivable, with one difference: the note is supported by a formal **promissory note**, which is a **written** promise to pay a specific sum of money at a specific future date, and this makes a note receivable a negotiable instrument.

The note is signed by a **maker** in favour of a designated **payee** who can then legally and readily sell or transfer the note to others. **Notes always contain an interest element** because of the time value of money, but they may be classified as interest-bearing or non–interest-bearing. **Interest-bearing notes** have a stated rate of interest that is payable in addition to the face value of the note; **zero-interest-bearing notes** (or **non–interest-bearing notes**) also include interest, but it is equal to the difference between the amount that was borrowed (the proceeds) and the higher face amount that will be paid back. The rate may not be stated explicitly.

Companies often accept notes receivable from customers who need to extend the payment period of an outstanding account receivable. Notes are also sometimes required from high-risk or new customers. In addition, they are often used in loans to employees and subsidiaries and in sales of property, plant, and equipment. In some industries (such as the pleasure and sport boat industry), all credit sales are supported by notes. Most notes, however, are created by lending transactions. The basic issues in accounting for notes receivable are the same as those for accounts receivable: recognition, measurement, impairment, and disposition. This section discusses only the recognition and measurement of **short-term** notes or loans. Longer-term instruments are covered in the next section.

To illustrate the accounting for notes or loans receivable, assume that on March 14, 2014, Prime Corporation agreed to allow its customer, Gouneau Ltd., to substitute a six-month note for the account receivable of $1,000 that Gouneau was unable to pay when it came due for payment. This means that Gouneau is basically borrowing $1,000 from Prime for six months. It was agreed that the note would bear interest at a rate of 6%. Prime's entries to record the substitution and payment of the note are as follows:

<table>
<tr><td>A = L + SE
0 0 0
Cash flows: No effect</td><td colspan="3" align="center">**March 14, 2014**</td></tr>
<tr><td></td><td>Notes Receivable
    Accounts Receivable</td><td align="right">1,000</td><td align="right">
1,000</td></tr>
<tr><td></td><td colspan="3" align="center">**September 14, 2014**</td></tr>
<tr><td>A = L + SE
+30 0 +30
Cash flows: ↑ 1,030 inflow</td><td>Cash
    Notes Receivable
    Interest Income
*$1,000 × .06 × $^{6}/_{12}$</td><td align="right">1,030</td><td align="right">
1,000
30*</td></tr>
</table>

Alternatively, a note could be accepted in exchange for lending money to an employee or subsidiary company; for example, in a **non–interest-bearing note** situation. In this case, the interest is the difference between the amount of cash that is borrowed and the face or maturity value of the note receivable. Assume that the president of Ajar Ltd. borrowed money from the company on February 23, 2014, and signed a promissory note for

$5,000 repayable in nine months' time. Assume an interest rate of 8% is appropriate for this type of loan. Instead of borrowing $5,000 and repaying this amount with 8% interest added at the maturity date, the president receives only $4,717 on February 23. The $283 difference between the $4,717 borrowed and the $5,000 repaid represents interest for the nine-month period that the note is outstanding: $4,717 × 8% × 9/12 = $283. Ajar's entries are as follows:[10]

A   =   L   +   SE
0   0   0

Cash flows: ↓ 4,717 outflow

February 23, 2014		
Notes Receivable	4,717	
Cash		4,717

A   =   L   +   SE
+283   +283

Cash flows: ↑ 5,000 inflow

November 23, 2014		
Cash	5,000	
Notes Receivable		4,717
Interest Income		283*

*4,717 × .08 × 9/12

In both examples provided, if financial statements are prepared while the note receivable is still outstanding, interest is accrued to the date of the statement of financial position.

Recognition and Measurement of Long-Term Notes and Loans Receivable

Objective 7

Account for and explain the accounting issues related to the recognition and measurement of long-term notes and loans receivable.

Since some form of **promissory note** is often the proof that a loan exists, the above explanation of notes receivable applies equally well to loans receivable. The examples of loans receivable that are illustrated below assume that a note is the basis for each transaction. What changes as we move from short-term to long-term notes and loans is the length of time to maturity and the importance of interest in measuring and accounting for the financial asset.

The accounting standards for the recognition and measurement of loans receivable are the same as those identified above for accounts receivable.

- Recognize a loan receivable when the entity becomes a party to the contractual provisions of the financial instrument.

- When recognized initially, measure the loan receivable at its fair value.

- After initial recognition, measure loans receivable at amortized cost.

- Recognize bad debt losses on the loans receivable when they are deemed to be impaired.[11]

Finance

The **fair value** of a note or loan receivable is measured as **the present value of the cash amounts that are expected to be collected in the future, with the amounts discounted at the market rate of interest that is appropriate for a loan with similar credit risk and other characteristics.** When the interest stated on an interest-bearing note is the same as the effective (market) rate of interest, the note's fair value is equal to its face value.[12] When the stated rate is not the same as the market rate, the note's **fair value** (its **present value**) is different from the note's **face value**. The difference between the price for the note now and its maturity value—resulting in either a discount or a premium—is then amortized over the note's life, affecting the amount of interest income that is reported. Under **IFRS**, the **effective interest method of amortization** is required, while under **ASPE**, the **amortization method is not specified**. The effective interest method is illustrated further below.

Transaction costs that are incurred in acquiring a loan or note receivable, such as commissions, can be treated in one of two ways:

1. They can be recognized as an expense when they are incurred.

2. They can be added to the fair value of the instrument, which then increases the original amount that is recognized as its "cost" at acquisition. In this case, the transaction costs are an adjustment to the discount or premium that will be amortized over the life of the loan, requiring the effective rate of interest to be recalculated.

Both ASPE and IFRS agree that transaction costs associated with financial assets that are carried at amortized cost should be accounted for as explained in the second treatment above.

Under ASPE, loans and receivables are accounted for at amortized cost. **Amortized cost** is the amount that was recognized when the instrument was acquired, reduced by any principal payments received, and adjusted for the amortization of any discount or premium, if appropriate, and writedowns for impairment. Under IFRS, the same accounting applies provided the note or loan has basic loan features and is managed on a contractual yield basis.[13] **Basic loan features** means that the instrument has contractual terms that result in cash flows that are payments of principal and interest. Management on a **contractual yield basis** refers to a company's business model of holding the instruments for their principal and interest flows. Let's see how this works.

Notes Issued at Face Value

To illustrate an interest-bearing note issued at face value, assume that Bigelow Corp. lends Scandinavian Imports $10,000 in exchange for a $10,000, three-year note bearing interest at 10% payable annually. The market rate of interest for a note of similar risk is also 10%. The first step is always to identify the amounts and timing of the cash flows. For our example, the following diagram shows both the interest and principal cash flows:

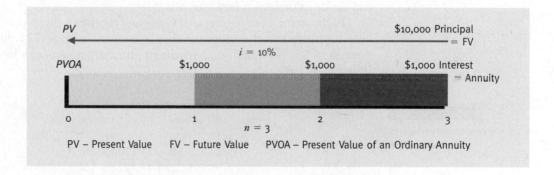

The note's present value and exchange price is calculated in Illustration 7-7.

Illustration 7-7
Present Value of Note—Stated and Market Rates the Same

Face value of the note		$10,000
Present value of the lump sum principal:		
$10,000 (PVF*~3, 10%~) = $10,000 (0.75132) (Table A-2)	$7,513	
Present value of the ordinary interest annuity:		
$1,000 (PVFOA~3, 10%~) = $1,000 (2.48685) (Table A-4)	2,487	
Present value of the note		10,000
Difference		$ –0–

*Present Value Factors (PVF) found in Tables A1 to A5

In this case, the note's fair value, present value, and face value are the same ($10,000) **because the effective and stated interest rates are the same**. Bigelow Corp. records its acquisition of the note as follows:

A = L + SE
0   0   0

Cash flows: ↓ 10,000 outflow

| Notes Receivable | 10,000 | |
| Cash | | 10,000 |

Bigelow Corp. later recognizes the interest earned each year ($10,000 × 0.10) as follows:

A = L + SE
+1,000   +1,000

Cash flows: ↑ 1,000 inflow

| Cash | 1,000 | |
| Interest Income | | 1,000 |

Notes Issued at Other than Face Value

Not all notes are issued at market rates of interest. Sometimes companies issue non-interest bearing notes or notes with interest rates below market rates to encourage sales or to facilitate intercompany transactions.

Finance

Zero-Interest-Bearing Notes.   If a zero-interest-bearing note is received in exchange for cash, its present value is usually the cash paid to the issuer. Because both the note's future amount and present value are known, the interest rate can be calculated; in other words, it is implied. The **implicit interest rate** is the rate that equates the cash paid with the amounts receivable in the future. The difference between the future (face) amount and the present value (cash paid) is a discount and this amount is amortized to interest income over the life of the note. In most cases, the implicit interest rate is the market rate. This is because the transaction is usually carried out between two parties who are at arm's length and acting in their own best interests.[14]

To illustrate, assume Jeremiah Company receives a three-year, $10,000 zero-interest-bearing note, and the present value is known to be $7,721.80. The implicit rate of interest of 9% (assumed to approximate the market rate) can be calculated as shown in Illustration 7-8.

Illustration **7-8**

Determination of Implicit Interest Rate

PV of note = PV of future cash flows
PV of note = FV of note × $PVF_{3,\ ?\%}$ (Table A-2)
$7,721.80 = $10,000 × $PVF_{3,\ ?\%}$
$$PVF_{3,\ ?\%} = \frac{\$7,721.80}{\$10,000}$$
$PVF_{3,\ ?\%}$ = 0.77218

Table A-2: Where $n = 3$ and PVF = 0.77218, $i = 9\%$

Thus, the implicit rate that makes the total cash to be received at maturity ($10,000) equal to the present value of the future cash flows ($7,721.80) is 9%. Note that if any two of the three variables on the second line of the equation in Illustration 7-8 are known, the third variable can be determined. For example, if the note's maturity value **(face value)** and **present value factor (i and n)** are known, the note's **present value** can be calculated.

The time diagram for the single cash flow of Jeremiah's note is as follows:

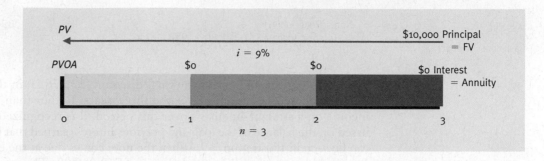

The entry to record the transaction is:

A = L + SE
0   0   0

Cash flows: ↓ 7,721.80 outflow

Notes Receivable	7,721.80	
Cash		7,721.80

Effective Interest Method of Amortization. Under IFRS, and as applied by many private enterprises, the discount (that is, the $2,278.20 difference between the $7,721.80 provided as a loan and the $10,000 that will be repaid) is amortized each year using the **effective interest method** to recognize the interest income. This method requires that the effective interest or yield rate be calculated at the time when the investment is made. This rate is then later used to calculate interest income by applying it to the carrying amount (book value) of the investment for each interest period. The note's carrying amount changes as it is increased by the amount of discount amortized. **Thus, the net carrying amount is always equal to the present value of the note's remaining cash flows (principal and interest payments) discounted at the market rate at acquisition.** Jeremiah's three-year discount amortization and interest income schedule is shown in Illustration 7-9.

Illustration 7-9

Discount Amortization Schedule—Effective Interest Method

SCHEDULE OF NOTE DISCOUNT AMORTIZATION
Effective Interest Method
0% Note Discounted at 9%

	Cash Received	Interest Income	Discount Amortized	Carrying Amount of Note
Date of issue				$ 7,721.80
End of year 1	$ –0–	$ 694.96[a]	$ 694.96[b]	8,416.76[c]
End of year 2	–0–	757.51	757.51	9,174.27
End of year 3	–0–	825.73[d]	825.73	10,000.00
	$ –0–	$2,278.20	$2,278.20	

[a] $7,721.80 × 0.09 = $694.96
[b] $694.96 − 0 = $694.96
[c] $7,721.80 + $694.96 = $8,416.76 or $10,000 − ($2,278.20 − $694.96) = $8,416.76
[d] $0.05 adjustment for rounding

Interest income at the end of the first year using the effective interest method is recorded as follows:

<table>
<tr><td>A = L + SE
+694.96 +694.96

Cash flows: No effect</td><td>Notes Receivable
   Interest Income ($7,721.80 × 9%)</td><td>694.96

694.96</td></tr>
</table>

Note that the amount of the total discount, $2,278.20 in this case, represents the interest income on the note over the three years. Rather than recognize it as interest income on a straight-line basis over this period, it is recognized in increasing amounts based on the balance of the loan and previous interest earned that is still outstanding. This can be seen in Illustration 7-9. When the note comes due at the end of Year 3, the Notes Receivable account will have a balance of $10,000.00. Therefore, Jeremiah Company makes the following entry:

<table>
<tr><td>A = L + SE
0   0   0

Cash flows: ↑ 10,000 inflow</td><td>Cash
   Notes Receivable</td><td>10,000

10,000</td></tr>
</table>

Straight-Line Method of Amortization. Some private entities that follow ASPE prefer to use the **straight-line method** of amortizing discounts and premiums because of its simplicity. For example, in the Jeremiah Company example above, the total discount of $2,278.20 is amortized over the three-year period in equal amounts each year. Therefore, the annual amortization is $2,278.20 ÷ 3 or $759.40 each year. The entry to record the annual interest for years 1 and 2 under the straight-line method is compared with the effective interest method below:

Straight-line
A = L + SE
+759.40 +759.40

Cash flows: No effect

	Effective interest		Straight-line	
Notes Receivable (Year 1)	694.96		759.40	
Interest Income		694.96		759.40
Notes Receivable (Year 2)	757.51		759.40	
Interest Income		757.51		759.40

At the end of Year 3, the Notes Receivable's balance is $10,000 and the same entry is made to record the receipt of the cash.

While easier to apply, the results of using straight-line amortization do not reflect the economic reality of a loan. That is, in Year 3 Jeremiah should be reporting more interest income than in Year 1 because of the interest that also accrues on the accumulating and unpaid interest for Years 1 and 2. Under the straight-line method, equal amounts of income are reported each period.

Underlying Concept

Using a simpler method that gives similar results to the effective interest method is an application of the materiality concept.

Interest-Bearing Notes. A note's stated rate and its effective rate are often different, as they were in the zero-interest-bearing case above. To illustrate a different situation, assume that Morgan Corp. makes a loan to Marie Co. and receives in exchange a $10,000, three-year note bearing interest at 10% annually. The market rate of interest for a note of similar risk is 12%. The time diagram for all cash flows is as follows:

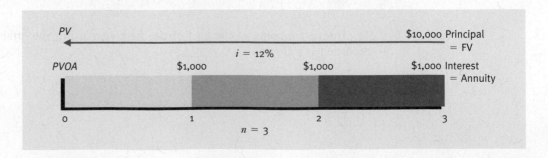

Note that the **interest cash flows are dictated by the stated rate** (10%) but that **all cash flows are discounted at the market rate** (12%) in determining the note's present value. The present value ($9,520) of the two streams of cash is calculated in Illustration 7-10.[15]

Illustration 7-10

Calculation of Present Value—Effective Rate Different from Stated Rate

Face value of the note		$10,000
Present value of the principal:		
$10,000 (PVF*$_{3, 12\%}$) = $10,000 (0.71178)	$7,118	
Present value of the interest:		
$1,000 (PVFOA**$_{3, 12\%}$) = $1,000 (2.40183)	2,402	
Present value of the note		9,520
Difference		$ 480

*Present Value Factor
**Present Value Factor Ordinary Annuity

Because the **effective interest rate** or market interest rate (12%) is higher than the rate that the note actually pays (10%), you would expect the note's present value (also its fair value) to be less than its face value; that is, the note would be exchanged at a **discount**. This makes intuitive sense. If you were to invest in a note that promises 10% when you could get 12% elsewhere in the market at the same level of risk, you would not be willing to pay face value for the 10% note.

The receipt of the note in exchange for cash equal to its fair value is recorded by Morgan as follows:

$$\begin{array}{ccc} A & = & L & + & SE \\ 0 & & 0 & & 0 \end{array}$$

Cash flows: ↓ 9,520 outflow

Notes Receivable	9,520	
Cash		9,520

Over the term of the note, Morgan will receive $1,000 interest each year (a rate of 10%) and at maturity get $480 more than the cash originally loaned. This $480 (the discount) effectively increases the return on the investment from 10% to 12%. It is amortized each period and the amount of interest income that is recognized is greater than the $1,000 received each year. Morgan's three-year discount amortization and interest income schedule using the effective interest method is shown in Illustration 7-11.

Illustration 7-11

Discount Amortization Schedule—Effective Interest Method

SCHEDULE OF NOTE DISCOUNT AMORTIZATION
Effective Interest Method
10% Note Discounted at 12%

	Cash Received	Interest Income	Discount Amortized	Carrying Amount of Note
Date of issue				$ 9,520
End of year 1	$1,000[a]	$1,142[b]	$142[c]	9,662[d]
End of year 2	1,000	1,159	159	9,821
End of year 3	1,000	1,179	179	10,000
	$3,000	$3,480	$480	

[a] $10,000 × 10% = $1,000
[b] $9,520 × 12% = $1,142
[c] $1,142 − $1,000 = $142
[d] $9,520 + $142 = $9,662 or $10,000 − ($480 − $142) = $9,662

On the date of issue, the note has a present value of $9,520. Its unamortized discount—the interest income that will be spread over the three-year life of the note—is $480.

At the end of Year 1, Morgan receives $1,000 in cash, but the interest income under the effective interest method is based on the note's carrying amount and effective interest rate: $1,142 ($9,520 × 12%). The difference between $1,000 and $1,142 is the discount to be amortized, $142, and it is amortized directly to the Notes Receivable account. Morgan records the annual interest received at the end of the first year as follows:

A = L + SE
+1,142   +1,142

Cash flows: ↑ 1,000 inflow

Cash	1,000	
Notes Receivable	142	
Interest Income		1,142

The note's carrying amount has now been increased to $9,662 ($9,520 + $142). This process is repeated until the end of Year 3.

Under the **straight-line method**, the initial discount of $480 is amortized at a rate of $480 ÷ 3 = $160 each year with the following entry. The same entry is made each year.

A = L + SE
+1,160   +1,160

Cash flows: ↑ 1,000 inflow

Cash	1,000	
Notes Receivable	160	
Interest Income		1,160

When the stated rate is higher than the effective interest rate, the note's fair value (its present value) is more than its face value and the note is exchanged at a **premium**. The premium on a note receivable is recognized by recording the Note Receivable at its higher initial present value. The excess is amortized over the life of the note by crediting the Note Receivable and reducing (debiting) the amount of interest income that is recognized.

Notes Received for Property, Goods, or Services

When property, goods, or services are sold and a long-term note is received as the consideration instead of cash or a short-term receivable, there may be an issue in determining the selling price. If an appropriate market rate of interest is known for the note, or for a note of similar risk, there is no problem. The sale amount is the present value of the cash flows promised by the note, discounted at the market rate of interest. Remember that **if the stated rate and market rate are the same**, **the note's face value and fair value are the same**. It is when the two rates are different that the note's fair value has to be calculated by discounting the cash flows at the market rate. What if you don't know what the market rate is? In this case, one of two approaches can be used.

1. The fair value of the property, goods, or services that are given up can be used as an estimate of the fair value of the note received. In this case, because we have an estimate of the note's present value, the actual cash flow amounts, and the timing of the cash flows are all known, the market or yield interest rate can be calculated. This is needed in order to apply the effective interest method.

2. An appropriate interest rate can be imputed. **Imputation** is the process of determining an appropriate interest rate, and the resulting rate is called an **imputed interest rate**. The objective for calculating the appropriate interest rate is to approximate the rate that would have been agreed on if an independent borrower and lender had negotiated a similar transaction. The choice of a rate is affected by the prevailing rates for similar instruments of issuers with similar credit ratings. It is also affected by such factors as restrictive covenants, collateral, the payment schedule, and the existing prime interest rate.

To illustrate, assume that Oasis Corp. sold land in exchange for a five-year note that has a maturity value of $35,247 and no stated interest rate. The property originally cost Oasis $14,000. What are the proceeds on disposal of the land; that is, what selling price should be recognized in this transaction?

Situation 1: Assume that the market rate of interest of 12% is known. In this case, the proceeds from the sale are equal to the present value of the note, which we calculate (below) to be $20,000. This is a non–interest-bearing note, so the only cash flow is the $35,247 received in five periods' time: $35,247 × .56743 (Table A-2) = $20,000. The entry to record the sale is:

A = L + SE	
+6,000 +6,000	
Cash flows: No effect	

Notes Receivable	20,000	
Land		14,000
Gain on Sale of Land ($20,000 − $14,000)		6,000

Situation 2: Assume that the market rate of interest is unknown, but the land has been appraised recently for $20,000 and the future cash flow amount is known to be $35,247. In this case, the property's fair value determines the amount of the proceeds and the note's fair value. The entry is the same as in Situation 1. To amortize the discount using the effective interest method, however, the implicit interest rate must be determined. This is done by finding the interest rate that makes the present value of the future cash flow amount of $35,247 equal to its present value of $20,000. The procedure is as follows. First the present value factor is calculated: $20,000 ÷ $35,247 = .5674241. Table A-2 then identifies the interest rate for five periods and a factor of .56743 as 12%.

Situation 3: Assume that neither the market rate nor the land's fair value is known. In this case, a market rate must be imputed and then used to determine the note's present value. It will also be used to recognize the effective interest income over the five years and amortize the discount. If a 12% rate is estimated based on prevailing interest rates for companies similar to the one purchasing the land, and the future cash flow amount is $35,247, then the entry will be the same as in Situation 1. If a different rate results, the note and the gain on sale will both be different as well.

Fair Value Not Equal to Cash Consideration

Accountants need to be alert when recognizing and measuring loans receivable. Sometimes, the cash that is exchanged when the loan is made may not be the same as the fair value of the loan. In this situation, the substance of the transaction has to be determined and accounted for. Imagine a situation where a company advances $20,000 to an officer of the company, charges no interest on the advance, and makes it repayable in four years. Assuming a market rate of 6%, the fair value of the loan receivable is $15,842 ($20,000 × .79209, the PV factor for $n = 4$ and $i = 6$). Although the loan's fair value is $15,842, the officer of the company actually received $20,000. This $4,158 difference must then be recognized and accounted for according to its nature—in this case, it is likely for additional compensation. It is required to be recognized immediately as an expense unless it qualifies to be reported as an asset. The entry to record this transaction is as follows.

A = L + SE	
−4,158 −4,158	
Cash flows: ↓ 20,000 outflow	

Notes Receivable	15,842	
Salaries and Wages Expense	4,158	
Cash		20,000

Derecognition of Receivables

In the normal course of events, accounts and notes receivable are collected when they are due and then removed from the books, or **derecognized**. However, as credit sales and

Objective 8

Account for and explain the basic accounting issues related to the derecognition of receivables.

Real World Emphasis

receivables have grown in size and significance, this normal course of events has evolved. **In order to receive cash more quickly from receivables, owners now often transfer accounts or loans receivable to another company for cash.**

There are various reasons for this early transfer. First, for competitive reasons, providing sales financing for customers is almost mandatory in many industries. In the sale of durable goods, such as automobiles, trucks, industrial and farm equipment, computers, and appliances, a large majority of sales are on an instalment contract basis. This means that the seller is financing the purchase by allowing the buyer to pay for it over time, usually in equal periodic payments or instalments. Many major companies in these and other industries have created wholly owned subsidiaries that specialize in receivables financing. For example, **Canadian Tire Corporation, Limited**'s Financial Services segment incorporated a federally regulated bank, **Canadian Tire Bank**. This wholly owned subsidiary manages and finances Canadian Tire's MasterCard and retail credit card and personal loan portfolios, as well as other finance-related products.

Second, the **holder** may sell receivables because money is tight and access to normal credit is not available or is far too expensive, or because the holder wants to accelerate its cash inflows. A firm may have to sell its receivables, instead of borrowing, to avoid violating the terms of its current borrowing agreements. In addition, the billing and collecting of receivables is often time-consuming and costly. Credit card companies, such as MasterCard and Visa, and other finance companies take over the collection process and provide merchants with immediate cash in exchange for a fee to cover their collection and bad debt costs. There are also **purchasers** of receivables who buy the receivables to obtain the legal protection of ownership rights that are given to a purchaser of assets, instead of the lesser rights that an unsecured creditor like Visa or MasterCard has. In addition, banks and other lending institutions may be forced to purchase receivables because of legal lending limits; that is, they may not be allowed to make any additional loans but still are able to buy receivables and charge a fee for this service.

Receivables can be used to generate immediate cash for a company in two ways. Often referred to as **asset-backed financing**, these ways are:

1. secured borrowings and

2. sales of receivables.

Secured Borrowings

Like many other assets, receivables are often used as collateral in borrowing transactions. A creditor may require that the debtor assign or pledge receivables as security for a loan, but leave the receivables under the control of the borrowing company. The note or loan payable, a liability, is reported on the statement of financial position and, if it is not paid when it is due, the creditor has the right to convert the collateral to cash; that is, to collect the receivables. Canadian banks commonly use receivables as collateral under lending agreements.

A company accounts for the collateralized assets in a **secured borrowing in the same way as it did before the borrowing**, and it accounts for the liability according to accounting policies for similar liabilities. The debtor thus recognizes interest expense on the borrowed amount, and may have to pay an additional finance charge, which is expensed. Each month, the proceeds from collecting accounts receivable are used to retire the loan obligation.

Sales of Receivables

The selling of receivables has increased significantly in recent years. One common type is a sale to a factor. **Factors** are financial intermediaries, such as finance companies, that buy receivables from businesses for a fee and then collect the amounts owed directly from the customers. **Factoring receivables** was traditionally associated with the garment trade in Montreal, but it is now common in other industries as well, such as furniture, consumer electronics, and automotive aftermarkets. Illustration 7-12 shows a factoring arrangement.

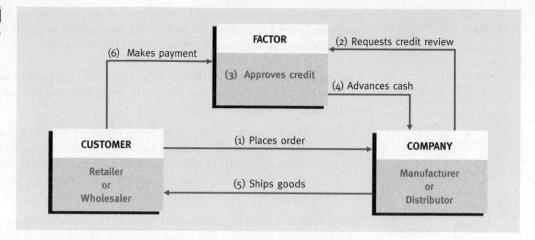

Illustration 7-12

Basic Procedures in Factoring

It is common today for larger companies to **transfer receivables** through a process known as **securitization**. Securitization is the process by which interests in financial assets are sold to a third party. It is the transformation of financial assets such as loans and receivables into securities, which are then referred to as **asset-backed securities**. The process takes a pool of assets that produces interest and principal payments, such as credit card receivables, mortgage receivables, or car loan receivables, and issues debt and equity interests in these pools. The resulting securities are backed by pools of assets. Almost every asset that has a payment stream (that is, it produces payments) and has a long-term payment history is a candidate for securitization.

For example, **Canadian Tire Corporation, Limited**'s 2011 Annual Report indicates that instead of owning all of its receivables throughout the collection period, it sells interests in its customer credit card loans receivable to **Glacier Credit Card Trust**. Glacier Credit Card Trust was formed to handle receivables portfolios and is financed by the issue of debt securities to third-party investors. By this process, the receivables are transformed into securities being held by a **special purpose entity (SPE)**, the trust.

The arrangements that are made in a securitization transaction differ from company to company. Canadian Tire, for example, sells pools of these receivables for cash and retains interest in some components of the receivables. The components it gets back typically include the right to the interest portion of the receivables (but not the principal), a subordinated interest in the accounts sold, and a securitization reserve along with a servicing liability. Canadian Tire continues to service the receivables; that is, it manages the accounts, including the responsibility to collect the amounts due.

Real World Emphasis

What Do the Numbers Mean?

What is the motivation for this type of transaction? Basically, it is a financing transaction that gives companies a more attractive way to raise funds than by issuing a corporate bond or note. The credit risk for a bond or note issued by a company is higher than the credit risk of a special purpose entity that holds the company's receivables. For example, **Sears Canada Inc.**'s annual report recently reported a credit rating of AAA and R-1 (High) **for its trust securitized debt issues and commercial paper**, respectively, which are the highest possible ratings for these debt classifications. Compare these with BBB and BBB (High) ratings at the same time for Sears' **senior unsecured debt**. The higher credit rating is due to the fact that receivables transferred to an SPE are often credit enhanced[16] and the cash flows to the SPE are much more predictable than the cash flows to the operating company because there are no operating risks for an SPE. When the risk is less, the cost of financing is also less. The net result is that the company that transfers its receivables gets access to lower-cost financing that it can then use to pay off debt that has a higher interest rate.

The differences between factoring and securitization are that **factoring** usually involves a sale to only one company, fees are relatively high, the quality of the receivables may be lower, and the seller does not usually service the receivables afterward. In a **securitization**, many investors are involved, margins are tight, the receivables are generally of higher quality, and the seller usually continues to service the receivables. When the company making the transfer continues to be involved in some way with the transferred assets, and measurement of the underlying transaction amounts involves some uncertainty, many disclosures are required in the financial statements.

Underlying Principles.   Before identifying the criteria that need to exist for a transaction to be treated as a sale, it is important to understand two basic concepts that underlie the decisions of standard setters.

1. The first concept, which is the focus under IFRS, is that an entity (the transferor) should derecognize the financial asset from its financial statements only when it transfers substantially all of the risks and rewards of ownership of that financial asset. (However, the transferor would recognize separately as assets or liabilities any rights and obligations created or retained in the transfer.)

2. Where it cannot be determined whether the risks and rewards have been transferred, then IFRS considers the second concept of control. When assessing control, if the transferee can sell the entire asset to an unrelated party, and can make that decision on its own and without imposing further restrictions on the transfer, then the transferor has not retained control. If the transferor has not retained control, it would derecognize the financial asset (and recognize separately as assets or liabilities any rights and obligations created or retained in the transfer). If the transferee cannot sell the entire asset to an unrelated party or cannot make the decision to sell an asset on its own without any further restrictions, then the transferor has retained control. If the transferor has retained control, it will continue to recognize the financial asset.

As this text went to print, accounting standards governing the derecognition of financial assets differed somewhat between ASPE and IFRS. For example, as discussed above, the initial focus under IFRS is the first concept of whether the risks and rewards have been transferred, whereas the focus under ASPE is the second concept of whether the entity retains control of the financial assets. In many cases, change in control and transfer of the risks and rewards occur at the same time (see, for example, BCE Inc. in Illustration 7-17 later in this chapter). However, the treatment under IFRS and ASPE often differs. For example, under IFRS, Canadian Tire Corporation, Limited noted in its 2011 annual report that "Since 1995, the Company has securitized credit card receivables ... Under previous GAAP, the Company recorded a gain/loss on sale and derecognized the credit card receivables. Under IFRS, an entity may not derecognize an asset when it maintains the majority of the risks and rewards associated with the asset. Therefore, the securitization transactions no longer qualify for derecognition under IFRS and the Company must recognize the receivables in the Consolidated Balance Sheets. Accordingly, the gain/loss on the sale of the receivables was reversed."[17]

The following discussion illustrates the key concepts involved, with some illustrative examples that would apply under ASPE and IFRS.

Criteria for Treatment as a Sale.   Not long ago, companies tended to account for many transactions as sales of receivables, even when they had a major continuing interest in and control over the transferred receivables. Doing this resulted in derecognizing accounts receivable (that is, removing them from the statement of financial position), reporting no additional debt but often recording a gain on sale. The major challenge for accounting standards is to identify when a transfer of receivables qualifies for **being treated as a sale** (derecognition), and when it is merely a **secured borrowing**. Most managers would prefer to have the transaction treated as a sale for accounting purposes because this results in not having to record additional debt on the statement of financial position.

In general, standard setters have concluded that the receivable or component parts of the receivable should be derecognized when the risks and rewards have been transferred (IFRS) or when control over the accounts receivable has been surrendered (ASPE). This is problematic in situations when the company "selling" the receivables has a continuing involvement in the asset. Currently there are disagreements as to how to interpret and apply the control criteria and the retention of partial interests. The accounting issues are important because of a company's ability to remove significant assets from the statement of financial position, and not report liabilities when substantial risks have been retained.

The discussion below illustrates standards set out in IAS 39 and IFRS 9. The following conditions are used to indicate whether the receivables have actually been transferred by an entity, supporting treatment as a sale. The entity transfers a financial asset, such as accounts receivable, if the entity:

1. transfers the contractual rights to receive cash flows from the accounts receivable; or

2. retains the contractual rights to receive cash flows from the accounts receivable, but has a contractual obligation to pay the cash flows to one or more recipients. Three additional conditions also must be met:

   (a) The entity has no obligation to pay amounts to the eventual recipient unless it collects equivalent amounts from the original receivable.

   (b) The entity is prohibited by the terms of the transfer contract from selling or pledging the original asset other than as security to the eventual recipients for the obligation to pay them cash flows.

   (c) The entity has an obligation to remit any cash flows it collects on behalf of the eventual recipients without material delay.

Accounting for transfers of receivables under ASPE also focuses on whether a company has retained or given up control of the receivables. Under ASPE, if all three conditions set out in Illustration 7-13 do not apply, the transferring company records the transfer as a secured borrowing. **Only when all three conditions are satisfied** is control over the assets assumed to be given up, and the transaction accounted for as a sale. If accounting for the transaction as a sale is appropriate but there is continuing involvement, the specific asset components retained need to be identified, as well as any liability components that were assumed. This approach is depicted in a decision tree format in Illustration 7-13.

Illustration 7-13

Accounting for Transfers of Receivables—ASPE

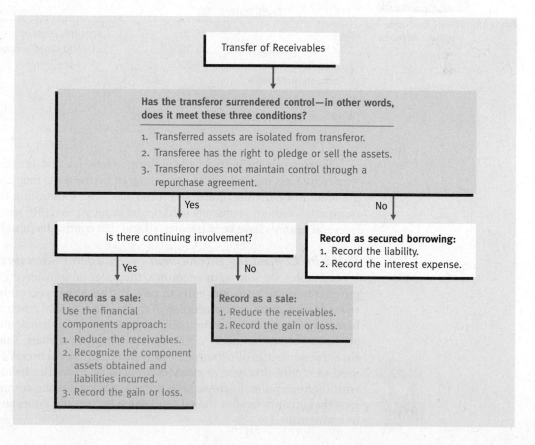

These transactions become more complex because of specialized contracts with different terms and conditions between companies, the securitization of receivables, and special purpose entities. The illustrations that follow are somewhat simplified to make the basic process of accounting for such transactions easier to follow.

Sale with No Continuing Involvement by Transferor. The most straightforward transaction is when the receivables are sold outright to another unrelated party, such as a factor, and they are sold without recourse. In this situation, it is apparent that the risks and rewards have been transferred to the other party (the factor) as the company is no longer exposed to risk associated with variability in the amounts and timing of cash flows from the factored/transferred accounts receivable.

When receivables are sold **without recourse**, the purchaser assumes the risk of collection and absorbs any credit losses.[18] Such a transfer is an outright sale of the receivables both in form (the title is transferred) and substance (control is transferred). In nonrecourse transactions, as in any sale of assets, Cash is debited for the proceeds. Accounts Receivable is credited for the receivables' face value. The difference, reduced by any provision for probable adjustments (such as discounts, returns, and allowances), is recognized in the account Gain or Loss on the Sale of Receivables. When appropriate, the seller uses a Due from Factor account (reported as a receivable) to account for the proceeds that are retained by a factor in order to cover probable sales discounts, sales returns, and sales allowances.

To illustrate, Crest Textiles Ltd. factors $500,000 of accounts receivable with Commercial Factors, Inc. on a **without recourse** basis. The receivables records are transferred to Commercial Factors, which takes over full responsibility for the collections. Commercial Factors assesses a finance charge of 3% of the amount of accounts receivable and withholds an initial amount equal to 5% of the accounts receivable for returns and allowances. Illustration 7-14 shows the journal entries for both Crest Textiles and Commercial Factors for this receivables transfer without recourse.

Illustration 7-14

Entries for Sale of Receivables without Recourse

Crest Textiles Ltd.			Commercial Factors, Inc.		
Cash	460,000		Accounts Receivable	500,000	
Due from Factor	25,000[a]		Due to Crest Textiles		25,000
Loss on Sale of Receivables	15,000[b]		Finance Revenue		15,000
Accounts Receivable		500,000	Cash		460,000

[a](5% × $500,000)
[b](3% × $500,000)

To recognize the outright sale of the receivables, Crest Textiles records a loss of $15,000. The factor's net income will be the difference between the financing revenue of $15,000 and the amount of any uncollectible receivables. The accounting treatment for a transfer of receivables without recourse would be the same under IFRS and ASPE, assuming that the risks and rewards have been transferred and that control has also been transferred.

Sale with Continuing Involvement by Transferor—Recourse Component Retained. If receivables are sold **with recourse**, the seller or transferor guarantees payment to the purchaser if the customer fails to pay. In this situation, under IFRS, if the risks and rewards have not been transferred to the factor company, then the transaction would not be treated as a sale (and the secured borrowing treatment discussed earlier could be applied). However, under ASPE, the accounting treatment would be based on the decision tree set out in Illustration 7-13. Specifically, a **financial components approach** is used to record this type of transaction because the seller has a continuing involvement with the receivable. Each party to the sale recognizes the components (assets and liabilities) that it controls after the sale and derecognizes the assets and liabilities that were sold or extinguished.

To illustrate, assume the same information as in Illustration 7-14 for Crest Textiles and Commercial Factors except that the receivables are sold **with recourse**. Crest Textiles estimates that the recourse obligation (a liability) has a fair value of $6,000. This is the company's estimate of the cost of its agreement in the contract to pay the amount of any receivables that debtors fail to pay. To determine the loss on the sale of Crest Textiles' receivables, the net proceeds from the sale are calculated and compared with the carrying amount of the assets that were sold, as shown in Illustration 7-15. Net proceeds are cash or other assets received in a sale less any liabilities incurred.

Illustration 7-15

Calculation of Net Proceeds and Loss on Sale

Calculation of net proceeds:

Cash received (an asset)	$460,000	
Due from factor (an asset)	25,000	$485,000
Less: Recourse obligation (a liability)		6,000
Net proceeds		$479,000

Calculation of loss on sale:

Carrying amount of receivables	$500,000
Net proceeds	479,000
Loss on sale of receivables	$ 21,000

Illustration 7-16 shows the journal entries for both Crest Textiles and Commercial Factors for the receivables sold with a recourse component being retained.

Illustration 7-16

Entries for Sale of Receivables with Recourse Component Retained

Crest Textiles Ltd.			Commercial Factors, Inc.		
Cash	460,000		Accounts Receivable	500,000	
Due from Factor	25,000		Due to Crest Textiles		25,000
Loss on Sale of Receivables	21,000		Finance Revenue		15,000
Accounts Receivable		500,000	Cash		460,000
Recourse Liability		6,000			

In this case, Crest Textiles recognizes a loss of $21,000. In addition, it records a liability of $6,000 to indicate the probable payment to Commercial Factors for uncollectible receivables. If all the receivables are collected, Crest Textiles would eliminate its recourse liability and increase income. Commercial Factors' net income is the financing revenue of $15,000 because it will have no bad debts related to these receivables.

What about servicing? Often, the transferor in a securitization will retain the responsibility for servicing the receivables. This usually includes collecting the principal and interest, monitoring slow-paying accounts, and remitting cash to those who hold **beneficial interests** in the receivables. It may also include other specified services. If the transferor receives no reimbursement for these activities or receives less than the estimated cost of carrying them out, a **servicing liability component** is recorded. This decreases the net proceeds on disposal. Alternatively, a **servicing asset component** is recognized if the benefits of servicing (such as servicing fees under contract or late charges recovered from customers) are greater than the estimated cost.

Most of the complications associated with the accounting for the disposition of accounts receivable are related to situations when the transferor continues to have some involvement with those assets.

Disclosure

The need for transparency requires significant disclosures for securitized receivables that are accounted for as sales. The goal is to inform readers about the fair value measurements and key assumptions that were used, the characteristics of the securitizations, cash flows between the special purpose entity and the transferor, and the balances and risk of servicing the assets and liabilities. Illustration 7-17 in the next section of the chapter gives an example of the main securitization disclosures made by BCE Inc. for its year ended December 31, 2011.

PRESENTATION, DISCLOSURE, AND ANALYSIS OF RECEIVABLES

Presentation and Disclosure

Objective 9
Explain how receivables and loans are reported and analyzed.

When financial statements are prepared, the presentation of and disclosures related to receivables have to be addressed. The objective is to allow users to be able to evaluate the significance of these financial assets to the entity's financial position and performance and to allow users to assess the nature and extent of the associated risks. Aside from providing information about the accounting policies applied, entities are required to present the following data associated with loans and receivables, with more information required under IFRS than ASPE:

1. The segregation and separate reporting of ordinary trade accounts, amounts owing by related parties, prepayments, and other significant amounts

2. An indication of the amounts and, where practicable, the maturity dates of accounts with a maturity of more than one year

3. Separate reporting of receivables that are current assets from those that are non-current

4. Separate reporting of any impaired balances, and the amount of any allowance for credit losses with, under IFRS, a reconciliation of the changes in the allowance account during the accounting period

5. Disclosure on the income statement of the amounts of interest income, impairment losses, and any reversals associated with such losses

Major disclosures are also required about the securitization or transfers of receivables, whether derecognized or not. Users are particularly interested in the risks to which the entity is exposed in general, and as a result of such transactions. Credit risk is the major concern associated with loans and receivables, so extensive qualitative and quantitative information is required under IFRS about the entity's situation, as is fair value information about loans and receivables, except for short-term trade accounts. Far less information about risk exposures and fair values is required under ASPE.

Extensive excerpts from the December 31, 2011 statement of financial position of the well-known Canadian communications company **BCE Inc.** along with the notes cross-referenced to its statement of financial position are presented in Illustration 7-17. These disclosures are based on IFRS, the first annual financial statements prepared under IFRS by BCE.

Real World Emphasis

Illustration 7-17

BCE Inc., Disclosures of Receivables and Loans

Consolidated Statements of Financial Position

AT DECEMBER 31 (in $ millions)	NOTE	2011	2010
ASSETS			
Current assets			
Cash		130	129
Cash equivalents		45	642
Trade and other receivables	11	3,119	2,885
Current tax receivable		43	139

(continued)

		2011	2010
Inventory	12	427	431
Prepaid expenses		262	224
Other current assets		152	205
Total current assets		4,178	4,655
Other non-current assets	15	629	652

NOTE 1: SIGNIFICANT ACCOUNTING POLICIES (Extracts)

Cash Equivalents
Cash equivalents are comprised mainly of highly liquid investments with original maturities of three months or less from the date of purchase.

Securitization of Trade Receivables
Proceeds on the securitization of trade receivables are recognized as collateralized borrowing as we do not transfer control and substantially all of the risks and rewards of ownership to another entity.

NOTE 11: TRADE AND OTHER RECEIVABLES

AT DECEMBER 31	2011	2010
Trade receivables	3,069	2,620
Allowance for doubtful accounts	(105)	(95)
Allowance for revenue adjustments	(74)	(89)
Investment tax credits	176	306
Other accounts receivable	53	143
Total trade and other receivables	3,119	2,885

NOTE 15: OTHER NON-CURRENT ASSETS

AT DECEMBER 31	NOTE	2011	2010
Employee benefit plans assets	20	31	33
AFS publicly-traded and privately-held securities	22	41	272
Long-term notes and other receivables		49	51
Long-term asset held for sale	8	57	—
Derivative assets	22	203	87
Other		248	209
Total other non-current assets		629	652

NOTE 22: FINANCIAL AND CAPITAL MANAGEMENT (Extracts)

FINANCIAL MANAGEMENT
Management's objectives are to protect BCE and its subsidiaries on a consolidated basis against material economic exposures and variability of results against various financial risks that include credit risk, liquidity risk, interest rate risk, foreign currency risk and equity price risk.

DERIVATIVES
We use derivative instruments to manage our exposure to foreign currency risk, interest rate risk and changes in the price of BCE common shares under our share-based payment plans. We do not use derivative instruments for speculative purposes, as such we are not exposed to any significant liquidity risks relating to them.

The following derivative instruments were outstanding at December 31, 2011, December 31, 2010 and January 1, 2010:
- cross-currency swaps and foreign currency forward contracts that hedge foreign currency risk on a portion of our long-term debt
- foreign currency forward contracts that manage the foreign currency risk of certain purchase commitments
- interest rate swaps that hedge interest rate risk on a portion of our long-term debt
- forward contracts on BCE common shares that mitigate the cash flow exposure related to share-based payment plans.

For fair value hedges, the gains recognized on the hedging instruments were $36 million and $5 million in 2011 and 2010, respectively, and the losses recognized on the positions hedged were $42 million and $9 million in 2011 and 2010, respectively.

CREDIT RISK
We are exposed to credit risk from operating activities and certain financing activities, the maximum exposure of which is represented by the carrying amounts reported on the statements of financial position.

We are exposed to credit risk if counterparties to our trade receivables and derivative instruments are unable to meet their obligations. The concentration of credit risk from our customers is minimized because we have a large and diverse customer base. We regularly monitor our credit risk and credit exposure. There was minimal credit risk relating to derivative instruments at December 31, 2011, December 31, 2010 and January 1, 2010. We deal with institutions that have strong credit ratings and as such we expect that they will be able to meet their obligations.

The following table provides the change in allowance for doubtful accounts for trade accounts receivable.

(continued)

Illustration 7-17

BCE Inc., Disclosures of Receivables and Loans (continued)

AT DECEMBER 31	**2011**	2010
Balance, beginning of the year	**(95)**	(105)
Additions	**(105)**	(20)
Use	**100**	30
Acquisition through business combinations	**(5)**	
Balance, end of the year	**(105)**	(95)

For many of our customers, trade receivables are written off directly to bad debt expense if the account has not been collected after a pre-determined period of time.

The following table provides further details on trade receivables not provisioned.

	DECEMBER 31, 2011	DECEMBER 31, 2010	JANUARY 1, 2010
Trade receivables not past due	**2,170**	1,945	1,890
Trade receivables past due and not provisioned			
Under 60 days	**361**	284	216
60 to 120 days	**390**	196	209
Over 120 days	**43**	100	129
Trade receivables, net of allowance for doubtful accounts	**2,964**	2,525	2,444

Analysis

Analysts often calculate financial ratios to evaluate the liquidity of a company's accounts receivable. To assess the receivables' liquidity, the **receivables turnover ratio** is used. This ratio measures the number of times, on average, that receivables are collected during the period. The ratio is calculated by dividing net sales by average receivables (net) outstanding during the year. Theoretically, the numerator should include only credit sales, but this information is often not available. As long as the relative amounts of credit and cash sales stay fairly constant, however, the trend indicated by the ratio will still be valid. Average receivables outstanding can be calculated from the beginning and ending balances of net trade receivables unless seasonal factors are significant. If significant, as they often are for many retail enterprises, using an average of the year's opening balance and the amounts at the end of each quarter will be more representative.

Real World Emphasis

To illustrate, we use the 2011 accounts of **Canadian Utilities Limited**, a Canadian-based company in the power generation, transmission, and distribution business. Canadian Utilities reported 2011 revenue of $2,999 million and accounts receivable balances at December 31, 2010 and 2011, of $357 million and $421 million, respectively. Its accounts receivable turnover ratio is calculated in Illustration 7-18.

Illustration 7-18

Calculation of Accounts Receivable Turnover

$$\text{Accounts Receivable Turnover} = \frac{\text{Net Sales/Revenue}}{\text{Average Trade Receivables (net)}}$$

$$= \frac{\$2,999}{(\$357 + \$421)/2}$$

$$= 7.7 \text{ times, or every } 47.4 \text{ days}$$

$$(365 \text{ days} \div 7.7 = 47.4)[19]$$

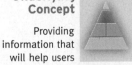

Underlying Concept

Providing information that will help users assess an enterprise's current liquidity and potential future cash flows is one of the main objectives of accounting.

The results give information about the quality of the receivables. They also give an idea of how successfully the firm collects its outstanding receivables, particularly when compared with prior periods, industry standards, the company's credit terms, or internal targets. Management would also prepare an aging schedule to determine how long specific receivables have been outstanding. It is possible that a satisfactory receivables turnover may have resulted because certain receivables were collected quickly although others have been outstanding for a relatively long time. An aging schedule would reveal such patterns.

Theory

Because the estimated expense for uncollectible accounts is subject to a degree of judgement, there is always some concern that companies can use this judgement to manage earnings. By overestimating the amount of uncollectible loans in a good earnings year, a bank, for example, can "save for a rainy day." In future less profitable periods, the bank will then be able to reduce its overly conservative allowance for its loan loss account and increase earnings as a result.[20] Remember, though, that reversals of such impairment losses should be based on specific events and circumstances occurring after the original bad debt loss was recognized.

Further analysis is often carried out on changes in the basic related accounts. Ordinarily, sales, accounts receivable, and the allowance for doubtful accounts should all move in the same direction. Higher sales should generate more receivables and an increased allowance. If sales have increased as well as receivables, but the allowance has not increased proportionately, the reader should be alert to the possibility of earnings management. If the allowance grows faster than receivables, particularly when sales have not increased, this could indicate deterioration in credit quality. Alternatively, perhaps the company has built up its allowance account so that there is a cushion for poorer performing years ahead. The answers are not always obvious, but this type of analysis can identify concerns.

With the increased practice of selling receivables through securitization transactions, especially where a company retains servicing (such as collection) responsibilities, the financial ratios have to be calculated and interpreted carefully. Consider the following:

- It is not appropriate to directly compare the turnover ratio of a company that securitizes or factors its receivables with another company that does not. This financing comes at a cost, but should provide cash flow for other value-adding purposes. Therefore, each company's situation has to be analyzed separately.

- Growth in a company's sales and growth in its receivables generally go hand in hand, but will not for a company involved in selling its receivables. Any company that begins such a program in the year should notice a significant change in the key account receivable ratios due to the lower receivable balances.

- Securitization is "off–balance sheet" because the receivables sold are removed from the current assets and because the amount "borrowed" is not reported in a company's liabilities. This affects liquidity ratios such as the current and quick ratios. Even though the same dollar amount is missing from the assets and liabilities, the ratios can be significantly affected.

Securitization transactions can be complex, making it necessary to be very cautious when interpreting financial statement ratios. Companies are increasingly required by regulators to provide a full discussion in the MD&A of critical issues like liquidity, especially if the company depends on such off–balance sheet financing arrangements.

IFRS/ASPE COMPARISON

Objective 10

Identify differences in accounting between accounting standards for private enterprises (ASPE) and IFRS, and what changes are expected in the near future.

A Comparison of IFRS and ASPE

From an intermediate accounting perspective, the general approaches explained in the chapter are expected to continue, although the standards may evolve to have more specific application guidance. ASPE is designed to eliminate much of the complexity in pre-2011 financial instrument standards, and IFRS has a similar goal.

Illustration 7-19 presents the more important differences that are expected to continue.

	Accounting Standards for Private Enterprises (ASPE)—*CICA Handbook*, Part II, Sections 1510 and 3856	IAS 1, 32, 39 and IFRS 7	References to Related Illustrations and Select Brief Exercises
Cash and cash equivalents	Cash equivalents are non-equity short-term, highly liquid investments that are readily convertible to known amounts of cash with a negligible risk of change in value.	IFRS also allows preferred shares that are acquired close to their maturity date to qualify as a cash equivalent.	BE 7-3
Receivables: Recognition and measurement	The standard does not require use of the effective interest method of recognizing interest income and amortizing any discounts or premiums; therefore, either the straight-line method or the effective interest method may be used.	The effective interest method is required for recognizing interest income and amortizing discounts and premiums.	Illustrations 7-9 to 7-11 and related examples BE 7-15 and BE 7-16.
Derecognition	To determine whether a financial asset should be derecognized, ASPE considers whether control of receivables has been retained or given up.	To determine whether a financial asset asset should be derecognized, IFRS considers whether the risks and rewards of ownership have been transferred.	Illustrations 7-13 to 7-14. More detailed analysis is beyond the scope of this text. BE 7-18 and BE 7-19
Disclosures	Basic disclosures are required related to the significance of receivables to the entity's financial position and financial performance, and the financial risks to which it is exposed.	Detailed quantitative and qualitative disclosures are required about the receivables, interest income, related risks, and sensitivity analysis linked to the measurements made. IFRS has detailed disclosure requirements for transferred financial assets that are either partly or entirely derecognized.	N/A

Illustration 7-19

ASPE and IFRS Comparison Chart

Looking Ahead

ASPE

While most requirements set out in generally accepted accounting principles for private enterprises are not likely to change in the short term, one area that is open to change is that of the derecognition (transfer) of receivables. The Accounting Standards Board has indicated that changes may be made to ASPE after the IASB and FASB develop final standards on derecognition of financial assets, which are now largely complete. Also, as discussed earlier in this chapter, the IASB has indicated that there may not be general support for some of its proposed changes regarding impairment. However, while the IASB redeliberates the proposals in prior exposure drafts to address the comments received from respondents, changes in ASPE are unlikely.

The approach taken in this chapter relative to these unresolved issues has been to discuss the general approaches and not the detailed requirements.

IFRS

The IASB has been working, along with the FASB, to simplify aspects of the accounting for and reporting of financial instruments. Because FASB's proposed financial instruments standard differs from IFRS 9, the IASB has agreed to consider some amendments to IFRS 9. The IASB and FASB have also been working toward a new model for impairments and have proposed the use of the expected loss approach. However, comment letters received by the IASB indicate that there may not be general support for some of its proposed changes regarding impairment, so the board was re-deliberating the proposals in the exposure draft to address the comments received from respondents, an expert advisory panel, and others. The issues relating to impairment are discussed further in Chapter 9. In addition, the accounting treatment for receivables transferred to a special purpose entity that the transferring entity continues to have an interest in may change significantly. A major issue was whether or not the financial statements of the special purpose entity should be consolidated with those of the transferor.

In December 2011, the IASB amended IFRS 9 to require application of the new standard for annual periods beginning on or after January 1, 2015, and not to require the restatement of comparative-period financial statements when the new standard is adopted.

SUMMARY OF LEARNING OBJECTIVES

1 Understand cash and accounts receivable from a business perspective.

Companies often have a significant amount of accounts receivable, which requires time and effort to manage and control. Companies strive to ensure that their collection policy is restrictive enough to minimize large losses in the form of uncollectible accounts receivable, while not being so restrictive that it interferes with the ability to attract new customers. Typical accounts receivable related categories include trade receivables, loans receivable, and nontrade receivables (including items like interest receivable, amounts due from officers and advances to employees).

2 Define financial assets, and identify items that are considered cash and cash equivalents and how they are reported.

Financial assets are a major type of asset defined as cash, a contractual right to receive cash or another financial asset, an equity holding in another company, or a contractual right to exchange financial instruments under potentially favourable conditions. To be reported as cash, an asset must be readily available to pay current obligations and not have any contractual restrictions that would limit how it can be used in satisfying debts. Cash consists of coins, currency, and available funds on deposit at a bank. Negotiable instruments such as money orders, certified cheques, cashier's cheques, personal cheques, and bank drafts are also viewed as cash. Savings accounts are usually classified as cash. Cash equivalents include highly liquid short-term investments (that is, those maturing three months or less from the date of purchase) that can be exchanged for known amounts of cash and have an insignificant chance of changing in value. Examples include treasury bills, commercial paper, and money-market funds. In certain circumstances, temporary bank overdrafts may be deducted in determining the balance of cash and cash equivalents.

Cash is reported as a current asset in the statement of financial position, with foreign currency balances reported at their Canadian dollar equivalent at the date of the statement of financial position. The reporting of other related items is as follows: (1) Restricted cash: Legally restricted deposits that are held as compensating balances against short-term borrowing are stated separately in Current Assets. Restricted deposits held against long-term borrowing arrangements are separately classified in non-current assets either in Investments or Other Assets. (2) Bank overdrafts: These are reported in the Current Liabilities section and may be added to the amount reported as accounts payable. (3) Cash equivalents: This item is often reported together with cash as "cash and cash equivalents."

3 Define receivables and identify the different types of receivables from an accounting perspective.

Receivables are claims held against customers and others for money, goods, or services. Most receivables are financial assets. The receivables are described in the following ways: (1) current or non-current; (2) trade or nontrade; and (3) accounts receivable or notes or loans receivable.

4 Account for and explain the accounting issues related to the recognition and measurement of accounts receivable.

The entity becomes a party to the contractual provisions of the accounts receivable financial instrument only when it has a legal claim to receive cash or other financial assets. Therefore the timing of recognition of accounts receivable is intertwined with the timing of recognition of revenue as was discussed in Chapter 6. For most companies when the sale is recognized, either cash is received (realized) or an account receivable is recognized.

Two issues that may complicate the measurement of accounts receivable are (1) the availability of discounts (trade and cash discounts) and (2) the length of time between the sale and the payment due dates (the interest element). Ideally, receivables should be measured initially at their fair value, which is their present value (discounted value of the cash to be received in the future). Receivables that are created by normal business transactions and are due in the short term are excluded from present value requirements.

5 Account for and explain the accounting issues related to the impairment in value of accounts receivable.

Short-term receivables are reported at their net realizable value—the net amount that is expected to be received in cash, which is not necessarily the amount that is legally receivable. Determining net realizable value requires estimating uncollectible receivables and any future returns or allowances and discounts that are expected to be taken. The adjustments to the asset account also affect the income statement amounts of bad debt expense, sales returns and allowances, and sales discounts. The assessment of impairment is usually based on an aged accounts receivable report, with higher percentages of uncollectible accounts indicated for older amounts outstanding. Even if a company estimates bad debt expense each period as a percentage of sales, the accounts receivable at the date of the statement of financial position are analyzed to ensure the balance in the allowance account is appropriate.

6 Account for and explain the accounting issues related to the recognition and measurement of short-term notes and loans receivable.

The accounting issues related to short-term notes receivable are similar to those of accounts receivable. However, because notes always contain an interest element, interest income must be properly recognized. Notes receivable either bear interest on the face amount (interest-bearing) or have an interest element that is the difference between the amount lent and the maturity value (non–interest-bearing).

7 Account for and explain the accounting issues related to the recognition and measurement of long-term notes and loans receivable.

Long-term notes and loans receivable are recognized initially at their fair value (the present value of the future cash flows) and subsequently at their amortized cost. Transaction costs are capitalized. This requires amortizing any discount if the item was issued at less than its face value, or any premium if it was issued for an amount greater than its face value, using the effective interest method. The straight-line method may be used under ASPE. Amortization of the premium (or discount) results in a reduction of (or increase in) interest income below (or above) the cash amount received.

8 Account for and explain the basic accounting issues related to the derecognition of receivables.

To accelerate the receipt of cash from receivables, the owner may transfer the receivables to another entity for cash. The transfer of receivables to a third party for cash may be done in one of two ways: (1) Secured borrowing: the creditor requires the debtor to designate or pledge receivables as security for the loan. (2) Sale (factoring or securitization) of receivables: Factors are finance companies or banks that buy receivables from businesses and then collect the remittances directly from the customers. Securitization is the transfer of receivables to a special purpose entity that is mainly financed by highly rated debt instruments. In many cases, transferors have some continuing involvement with the receivables they sell. For the transfer to be recorded as a sale, IFRS focuses on whether the risks and rewards of ownership have been transferred to the transferee. ASPE focuses on whether the transferor has surrendered control and has continued involvement with the receivables.

9 Explain how receivables and loans are reported and analyzed.

Disclosure of receivables requires that valuation accounts be appropriately offset against receivables, that the receivables be appropriately classified as current or non-current, and that pledged or designated receivables be identified. As financial instruments, specific disclosures are required for receivables so that users can determine their significance to the company's financial position and performance and can assess the nature and extent of associated risks and how these risks are managed and measured. Private entities require less disclosure than those reporting under IFRS. Receivables are analyzed in terms of their turnover and age (number of days outstanding), and in terms of relative changes in the related sales, receivables, and allowance accounts.

10 Identify differences in accounting between accounting standards for private enterprises (ASPE) and IFRS, and what changes are expected in the near future.

The two sets of standards are very similar, with minor differences relating to what is included in cash equivalents. ASPE does not require use of the effective interest method, whereas IFRS does for financial asset investments that are not held for trading purposes. Impairment provisions is one issue that remains under study by IFRS; the eventual resolution may generate additional differences between IFRS and ASPE.

KEY TERMS

aging method, p. 385
aging schedule, p. 385
allowance method, p. 386
amortized cost, p. 393
asset-backed financing, p. 400
asset-backed securities, p. 401
bad debts, p. 385
bank overdrafts, p. 378
basic loan features, p. 393
beneficial interest, p. 405
cash, p. 377
cash discounts, p. 382
cash equivalents, p. 378
compensating balances, p. 378
contra account, p. 386
contractual yield basis, p. 393
coupon rate, p. 444
credit risk, p. 385
derecognized, p. 399
direct writeoff method, p. 390
discount, p. 397

effective interest method, p. 392
effective interest rate, p. 397
face rate, p. 444
face value, p. 392
factoring receivables, p. 400
fair value, p. 392
financial asset, p. 376
financial components approach, p. 404
implicit interest rate, p. 394
imputed interest rate, p. 398
interest-bearing notes, p. 391
loans and receivables, p. 380
loans receivable, p. 381
market rate, p. 444
net realizable value, p. 385
non-interest-bearing notes, p. 391
nontrade receivables, p. 381
notes receivable, p. 380
percentage-of-receivables approach, p. 385
percentage-of-sales approach, p. 387

premium, p. 398
promissory note, p. 392
receivables turnover ratio, p. 408
restricted cash, p. 378
sales discounts, p. 382
sales returns and allowances, p. 384
secured borrowing, p. 400
securitization, p. 401
servicing asset component, p. 405
servicing liability component, p. 405
stated interest rate, p. 444
straight-line method, p. 396
trade discounts, p. 382
trade receivables, p. 380
with recourse, p. 404
without recourse, p. 404
yield rate, p. 444
zero-interest-bearing notes, p. 391

APPENDIX 7A

CASH CONTROLS

Management and Control of Cash

Objective 11
Explain common techniques for controlling cash.

Of all assets, cash is at the greatest risk of being used or diverted improperly. Management must overcome two problems in accounting for cash transactions: (1) it must establish proper controls to ensure that no unauthorized transactions are entered into by officers, employees, or others; and (2) it must ensure that the information that is needed in order to properly manage cash on hand and cash transactions is made available. Yet even with sophisticated control devices, errors can and do happen. *The Wall Street Journal* once ran a story entitled "A $7.8 Million Error Has a Happy Ending for a Horrified Bank," which described how **Manufacturers Hanover Trust Co.** mailed about $7.8 million too much in cash dividends to its shareholders. As the headline suggests, most of the money was eventually returned.

To safeguard cash and ensure the accuracy of the accounting records for this asset, companies need effective **internal control** over cash. There are new challenges to maintaining control over liquid assets as more and more transactions are done with the swipe of a debit or credit card or through the unregulated electronic payment services like PayPal. Canadians are among the highest users of debit and credit cards in the world. The shift from hard cash to digital cash brings new challenges for the internal control systems that are designed to control this asset. The purpose of this appendix is to identify some of the basic controls related to cash.

Using Bank Accounts

Even with the increased use of electronic banking, a company may use different banks in different locations and different types of bank accounts. For large companies that operate in multiple locations, the location of bank accounts can be important. Having collection accounts in strategic locations can speed up the flow of cash into the company by shortening the time between a customer's payment mailing and the company's use of the cash. Multiple collection centres are generally used to reduce the size of a company's **collection float**, which is the difference between the amount on deposit according to the company's records and the amount of collected cash according to the bank record.

The **general chequing account** is the main bank account in most companies and often the only bank account in small businesses. Cash is deposited in and disbursed from this account as all transactions are cycled through it. Deposits from and disbursements to all other bank accounts are made through the general chequing account.

Imprest bank accounts are used to make a specific amount of cash available for a limited purpose. The account acts as a clearing account for a large volume of cheques or for a specific type of cheque. The specific and intended amount to be cleared through the imprest account, such as for a payroll, is deposited by transferring that amount from the general chequing account or other source. Imprest bank accounts are also used for disbursing dividend cheques, commissions, bonuses, confidential expenses (such as officers' salaries), and travel expenses, although increasingly these payments are being made in electronic form.

Lockbox accounts are often used by large companies with multiple locations to make collections in cities where most of their customer billing occurs. The company rents a local post office box and authorizes a local bank to pick up the remittances mailed to that box number. The bank empties the box at least once a day and immediately credits the company's account for collections. The greatest advantage of a lockbox is that it accelerates the availability of collected cash. Generally, in a lockbox arrangement, the bank microfilms the cheques for record purposes and provides the company with a deposit slip, a list of collections, and any customer correspondence. If the control over cash is improved and if the income generated from accelerating the receipt of funds is more than what the lockbox system costs, it is considered worthwhile to use it.

Companies continue to increase their use of systems that electronically transfer funds from customers and to suppliers. While these advances will make many of the controls in a paper cheque-based system obsolete, companies will still always need to improve the effectiveness of the controls that are part of their information and processing systems.

The Imprest Petty Cash System

Almost every company finds it necessary to pay small amounts for a great many things, such as employee lunches, taxi fares, minor office supplies, and other miscellaneous expenses. It is usually impractical to require that such disbursements be made by cheque, but some control over them is important. A simple method of obtaining reasonable control, while following the rule of disbursement by cheque, is the **petty cash** system, particularly an imprest system.

This is how the system works.

1. Someone is designated as the petty cash custodian and given a small amount of currency from which to make small payments. The transfer of funds from the bank account to petty cash is recorded as follows, assuming a $300 transfer:

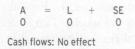

A   =   L   +   SE
0   0   0

Cash flows: No effect

| Petty Cash | 300 | |
| Cash | | 300 |

2. As payments are made out of this fund, the petty cash custodian gets signed receipts from each individual who receives cash from the fund. If possible, evidence of the

disbursement should be attached to the petty cash receipt. Petty cash transactions are not recorded in the accounts until the fund is reimbursed, and they are recorded by someone other than the petty cash custodian.

3. When the cash in the fund runs low, the custodian presents to the controller or accounts payable cashier a request for reimbursement that is supported by the petty cash receipts and other disbursement evidence. In exchange for these, the custodian receives a company cheque to replenish the fund. At this point, transactions are recorded in the accounting system based on the petty cash receipts. For example:

A   = L +   SE
−173   −173

Cash flows: ↓ 173 outflow

Office Expense	42	
Postage Expense	53	
Entertainment Expense	76	
Cash Over and Short	2	
Cash		173

4. If it is decided that the fund's balance is too high, an adjustment may be made and the surplus amount is then deposited back into the bank account. The following adjustment is made to record the reduction in the fund balance from $300 to $250:

A   =   L +   SE
0   0   0

Cash flows: No effect

Cash	50	
Petty Cash		50

Note that **only** entries to increase or decrease the size of the fund are made **to the Petty Cash account**.

A **Cash Over and Short** account is used when the cash in the petty cash fund plus the dollar amount of the receipts does not add up to the imprest petty cash amount. When this occurs, it is usually due to an error, such as a failure to provide correct change, overpayment of an expense, or a lost receipt. If cash is short (in other words, the sum of the receipts and cash in the fund is less than the imprest amount), the shortage is debited to the Cash Over and Short account. If there is more cash than there should be, the overage is credited to Cash Over and Short. Cash over and short is left open until the end of the year, when it is closed and generally shown on the income statement as part of "other expense or revenue."

Unless a reimbursement has just been made, there are usually expense items in the fund. This means that, if accurate financial statements are wanted, the fund needs to be reimbursed at the end of each accounting period in addition to when it is nearly empty.

Under an **imprest system**, the petty cash custodian is responsible at all times for the amount of the fund on hand, whether the amount is in cash or signed receipts. These receipts are the evidence that the disbursing officer needs in order to issue a reimbursement cheque. Two additional procedures are followed to obtain more complete control over the petty cash fund.

1. Surprise counts of the fund are made from time to time by a superior of the petty cash custodian to determine that the fund is being accounted for satisfactorily.

2. Petty cash receipts are cancelled or mutilated after they have been submitted for reimbursement so that they cannot be used again.

Physical Protection of Cash Balances

It is not only cash receipts and cash disbursements that need to be safeguarded through internal control measures. Cash on hand and in banks must also be protected. Because receipts become cash on hand and disbursements are made from the cash in banks, adequate control of receipts and disbursements is part of protecting cash balances. Certain other procedures, therefore, are also carried out.

The physical protection of cash is such an elementary necessity that it requires little discussion. Every effort should be made to minimize the cash on hand in the office. A petty cash fund, the current day's receipts, and perhaps funds for making change should be the only funds on hand at any time. As much as possible, these funds should be kept in a vault, safe, or locked cash drawer. Each day's receipts should be transmitted intact to the bank as soon as is practical. Intact means that the total receipts are accounted for together and no part of the amount is used for other purposes. This leaves a clear trail from the receipts activity to the bank.

Every company has a record of cash received and disbursed, and the cash balance. Because of the many cash transactions, however, errors or omissions can occur in keeping this record. It is therefore necessary to periodically prove the balance shown in the general ledger. Cash that is actually present in the office—petty cash, funds kept for making change, and undeposited receipts—can be counted and compared with the company records. Cash on deposit is not available for count so it is proved by preparing a bank reconciliation, which is a reconciliation of the company's record and the bank's record of the company's cash.

Reconciliation of Bank Balances

At the end of each calendar month, the bank sends each customer a bank statement (a copy of the bank's account with the customer) together with the customer's cheques that were paid by the bank during the month, or a list of the company's payments that have been presented to and cleared by the bank during the month.[21] Less and less hard copy is being returned as banks provide companies with electronic access to this information. If no errors were made by the bank or the customer, if all deposits made and all cheques drawn by the customer reached the bank within the same month, and if no unusual transactions occurred that affected either the company's or the bank's record of cash, the balance of cash reported by the bank to the customer will be the same as the balance in the customer's own records. This rarely occurs, because of one or more of the following:

RECONCILING ITEMS

1. **Deposits in transit:** End-of-month deposits of cash that are recorded on the depositor's books in one month are received and recorded by the bank in the following month.

2. **Outstanding cheques:** Cheques written by the depositor are recorded when they are written but may not be recorded by (or "clear") the bank until the next month.

3. **Bank charges:** Charges are recorded by the bank against the depositor's balance for such items as bank services, printing cheques, **not-sufficient-funds (NSF) cheques**, and safe-deposit box rentals. The depositor may not be aware of these charges until the bank statement is received.

4. **Bank credits:** Collections or deposits by the bank for the depositor's benefit may not be known to the depositor until the bank statement is received. These are reconciling items as long as they have not yet been recorded on the company's records. Examples are note collections for the depositor, interest earned on interest-bearing accounts, and direct deposits by customers and others.

5. **Bank or depositor errors:** Errors by either the bank or the depositor cause the bank balance to disagree with the depositor's book balance.

For these reasons, differences between the depositor's record of cash and the bank's record are usual and expected. The two records therefore need to be reconciled to determine the reasons for the differences between the two amounts.

A **bank reconciliation** is a schedule that explains any differences between the bank's and the company's records of cash. If the difference results only from transactions not yet recorded by the bank, the company's record of cash is considered correct. But if some part of the difference is due to other items, the bank's records or the company's records must be adjusted.

Two forms of bank reconciliation can be prepared. One form reconciles from the bank statement balance to the book balance or vice versa. The other form reconciles both the bank balance and the book balance to a correct cash balance. This latter form is more popular. A sample of this form and its common reconciling items is shown in Illustration 7A-1.

Illustration 7A-1			

Bank Reconciliation Form and Content

Balance per bank statement (end of period)			$$$
Add: Deposits in transit		$$	
Undeposited receipts (cash on hand)		$$	
Bank errors that understate the bank statement balance		$$	$$
			$$$
Deduct: Outstanding cheques		$$	
Bank errors that overstate the bank statement balance		$$	$$
Correct cash balance			$$$
Balance per company's books (end of period)			$$$
Add: Bank credits and collections not yet recorded in the books		$$	
Book errors that understate the book balance		$$	$$
			$$$
Deduct: Bank charges not yet recorded in the books		$$	
Book errors that overstate the book balance		$$	$$
Correct cash balance			$$$

This form of reconciliation has two sections: (1) the "Balance per bank statement" and (2) the "Balance per company's books." Both sections end with the same correct cash balance. The correct cash balance is the amount that the books must be adjusted to and is the amount reported on the statement of financial position. **Adjusting journal entries are prepared for all the addition and deduction items that appear in the "Balance per company's books" section**, and the bank should be notified immediately about any errors that it has made.

To illustrate, Nugget Mining Company's books show a cash balance at the Ottawa National Bank on November 30, 2014, of $20,502. The bank statement covering the month of November shows an ending balance of $22,190. An examination of Nugget's accounting records and the November bank statement identified the following reconciling items.

1. A deposit of $3,680 was taken to the bank late on November 30 but does not appear on the bank statement.

2. Cheques written in November but not charged to (deducted from) the November bank statement are:

Cheque #7327	$ 150
#7348	4,820
#7349	31

3. Nugget has not yet recorded the $600 of interest collected by the bank on November 20 on Sequoia Co. bonds held by the bank for Nugget.

4. Bank service charges of $18 are not yet recorded on Nugget's books.

5. A $220 cheque for Nugget from a customer was returned with the bank statement and marked "NSF." The bank, having originally recognized this as part of one of Nugget's deposits, now deducted this bad cheque as a disbursement from Nugget's account.

6. Nugget discovered that cheque #7322, written in November for $131 in payment of an account payable, had been incorrectly recorded in its books as $311.

7. A cheque written on Nugent Oil Co.'s account for $175 had been incorrectly charged to Nugget Mining and was included with the bank statement.

Illustration 7A-2 shows the reconciliation of the bank and book balances to the correct cash balance of $21,044.

Illustration 7A-2

Sample Bank Reconciliation

NUGGET MINING COMPANY
Bank Reconciliation
Ottawa National Bank, November 30, 2014

Balance per bank statement, November 30/14			$22,190
Add: Deposit in transit	(1)	$3,680	
Bank error—incorrect cheque charged to account by bank	(7)	175	3,855
			26,045
Deduct: Outstanding cheques	(2)		5,001
Correct cash balance, November 30/14			$21,044
Balance per books, November 30/14			$20,502
Add: Interest collected by the bank	(3)	$ 600	
Error in recording cheque #7322	(6)	180	780
			21,282
Deduct: Bank service charges	(4)	18	
NSF cheque returned	(5)	220	238
Correct cash balance, November 30/14			$21,044

The journal entries to adjust and correct Nugget Mining's books in early December 2014 are taken from the items in the "Balance per books" section and are as follows:

Cash	600	
Interest Income		600
(To record interest on Sequoia Co. bonds, collected by bank)		
Cash	180	
Accounts Payable		180
(To correct error in recording amount of cheque #7322)		
Office Expense—Bank Charges	18	
Cash		18
(To record bank service charges for November)		
Accounts Receivable	220	
Cash		220
(To record customer's cheque returned NSF)		

A	=	L	+	SE
+762		+180		+582

Cash flows: ↑ 542 inflow

Quiz

Alternatively, one summary entry could be made with a net $542 debit to Cash, which is the difference between the balance before adjustment of $20,502 and the correct balance of $21,044. When the entries are posted, Nugget's cash account will have a balance of $21,044. Nugget should return the Nugent Oil Co. cheque to Ottawa National Bank, informing the bank of the error.

SUMMARY OF LEARNING OBJECTIVE FOR APPENDIX 7A

11 Explain common techniques for controlling cash.

The common techniques that are used to control cash are as follows: (1) Using bank accounts: A company can vary the number and location of banks and the types of accounts to meet its control objectives. (2) The imprest petty cash system: It may be impractical to require small amounts of various expenses to be paid by cheque, yet some control over them is important. (3) Physical protection of cash balances: Adequate control of receipts and disbursements is part of protecting cash balances. Every effort should be made to minimize the cash on hand in the office. (4) Reconciliation of bank balances: Cash on deposit is not available for counting and is proved by preparing a bank reconciliation.

KEY TERMS

bank reconciliation, p. 417

deposits in transit, p. 416

imprest system, p. 415

not-sufficient-funds (NSF) cheques, p. 416

outstanding cheques, p. 416

petty cash, p. 414

Note: All assignment material with an asterisk (*) relates to the appendix to the chapter.

Brief Exercises

(LO 1) BE7-1 Creative Corporation is a manufacturer of children's toys. Creative has significant debt outstanding that has been used to purchase equipment and inventory used in its manufacturing process. Creative has positive cash from operating activities during the holiday season (November and December), but negative cash from operating activities during the months preceding the holiday season. Meanwhile, Technology Inc. is a mature, successful software development company with no debt outstanding and very few non-current assets. Which company requires a higher amount of cash on hand? Discuss, in general terms, how much cash each firm should have on hand for effective cash management.

(LO 1) BE7-2 Topaz Inc. has accounts receivable terms of 2/10, n/30. In the past, 50% of Topaz's customers have taken advantage of the discount and paid within 10 days of the invoice date, and the remaining 50% of customers have paid in full within 30 days of the invoice date. However, due to an economic recession this year, 30% of customers have paid within 10 days, 60% of customers have paid within 30 days, and the remaining 10% of customers have paid within 40 days. What steps might Topaz consider to speed up collection of its accounts receivable?

(LO 2) BE7-3 Stowe Enterprises owns the following assets at December 31, 2014:

Cash in bank savings account	48,500	Chequing account balance	30,500
Cash on hand	14,800	Postdated cheque from Yu Co.	450
Cash refund due (overpayment of income taxes)	31,400	Cash in a foreign bank (CAD equivalent)	90,000
Preferred shares acquired shortly before their		Debt instrument with a maturity date of	
fixed maturity date	15,500	three months from the date acquired	12,000

If Stowe follows ASPE, what amount should be reported as cash and cash equivalents? Explain how your answer would differ if Stowe followed IFRS.

(LO 3) BE7-4 Staj Co., a clothing manufacturer, is preparing its statement of financial position at December 31, 2014. For each of the following amounts as of December 31, 2014, indicate whether the amount is (a) current or non-current and (b) a trade receivable, a nontrade receivable, or not a receivable. If the amount is not a receivable, indicate its correct statement of financial position classification.

1. Cheque received from a customer for $1,200, dated January 1, 2015

2. Bank overdraft balance of $50,000

3. Income taxes recoverable of $14,000

4. $10,300 owing from a customer (now 10 days overdue), exchanged for a two-year note bearing interest at 8% payable annually

5. Staj sold a piece of machinery to Marus Company this past year. As part of the sale transaction, $20,000 is owing from Marus, due to be received on January 31, 2016

(LO 4) BE7-5   Boyko Company received an order from Lister Inc. on May 15, 2014, valued at $2,200. Boyko shipped the goods to Lister on May 31, 2014, with terms f.o.b. shipping point, and credit terms 2/10, n/30. Assuming Boyko uses the gross method of recording sales, prepare the required journal entries for Boyko on May 15, 2014, and May 31, 2014 (if any).

(LO 4) BE7-6   Civic Company made sales of $40,000 with terms 1/10, n/30. Within the discount period, it received a cash payment on $35,000 of the sales from customers; after the discount period, it received $5,000 in payments from customers. Assuming Civic uses the gross method of recording sales, prepare journal entries for the above transactions.

(LO 4) BE7-7   Use the information for Civic Company in BE7-6, but assume instead that Civic uses the net method of recording sales. Prepare the journal entries for the transactions.

(LO 4) BE7-8   Yoshi Corp. uses the gross method to record sales made on credit. On June 1, the company made sales of $45,000 with terms 1/15, n/45. On June 12, Yoshi received full payment for the June 1 sale. Prepare the required journal entries for Yoshi Corp.

(LO 4) BE7-9   Use the information from BE7-8, assuming Yoshi Corp. uses the net method to account for cash discounts. Prepare the required journal entries for Yoshi Corp.

(LO 5) BE7-10   Battle Tank Limited had net sales in 2014 of $1.1 million. At December 31, 2014, before adjusting entries, the balances in selected accounts were as follows: Accounts Receivable $250,000 debit; Allowance for Doubtful Accounts $2,800 credit. Assuming Battle Tank has examined the aging of the accounts receivable and has determined the Allowance for Doubtful Accounts should have a balance of $30,000, prepare the December 31, 2014 journal entry to record the adjustment to Allowance for Doubtful Accounts.

(LO 5) BE7-11   Use the information for Battle Tank Limited in BE7-10 and assume instead that the unadjusted balance in Allowance for Doubtful Accounts is a debit balance of $3,000. Based on this, prepare the December 31, 2014 journal entry to record the adjustment to Allowance for Doubtful Accounts.

(LO 6) BE7-12   Emil Family Importers sold goods to Acme Decorators for $20,000 on November 1, 2014, accepting Acme's $20,000, six-month, 6% note. (a) Prepare Emil's November 1 entry, December 31 annual adjusting entry, and May 1 entry for the collection of the note and interest. (b) Assume instead that Emil uses reversing entries. Prepare any appropriate reversing entry at January 1, 2015, and the May 1, 2015 entry for the collection of the note and interest.

(LO 6) BE7-13   Aero Acrobats lent $47,573 to Afterburner Limited, accepting Afterburner's $49,000, three-month, zero-interest-bearing note. The implied interest is approximately 12%. Prepare Aero's journal entries for the initial transaction and the collection of $49,000 at maturity.

(LO 7) BE7-14   Lin Du Corp. lent $30,053 to Prefax Ltd., accepting Prefax's $40,000, three-year, zero-interest-bearing note. The implied interest is 10%. (a) Prepare Lin Du's journal entries for the initial transaction, recognition of interest each year assuming use of the effective interest method, and the collection of $40,000 at maturity. (b) Use time value of money tables, a financial calculator, or Excel functions to prove that the note will yield 10%.

(LO 7) BE7-15   Bartho Products sold used equipment with a cost of $15,000 and a carrying amount of $2,500 to Vardy Corp. in exchange for a $5,000, three-year non–interest-bearing note receivable. Although no interest was specified, the market rate for a loan of that risk would be 9%. Assume that Bartho follows IFRS. Prepare the entries to record (a) the sale of Bartho's equipment and receipt of the note, (b) the recognition of interest each year, and (c) the collection of the note at maturity.

(LO 7) BE7-16   Use the information for Bartho Products in BE7-15 and assume instead that Bartho follows ASPE. Prepare the entries to record (a) the sale of Bartho's equipment and receipt of the note, (b) the recognition of interest each year if Bartho uses the straight-line method, and (c) the collection of the note at maturity.

(LO 8) BE7-17   On October 1, 2014, Alpha Inc. assigns $2 million of its accounts receivable to Alberta Provincial Bank as collateral for a $1.6-million loan evidenced by a note. The bank's charges are as follows: a finance charge of 4% of the assigned receivables and an interest charge of 13% on the loan. Prepare the October 1 journal entries for both Alpha and Alberta Provincial Bank.

(LO 8) BE7-18   Landstalker Enterprises sold $750,000 of accounts receivable to Leander Factors, Inc. on a without recourse basis under IFRS, as the risks and rewards have been transferred to Leander. The transaction meets the criteria for a sale, and no asset or liability components of the receivables are retained by Landstalker. Leander Factors assesses a finance charge of 4% of the amount of accounts receivable and retains an amount equal to 5% of accounts receivable. Prepare journal entries for both Landstalker and Leander.

(LO 8) BE7-19 Use the information for Landstalker Enterprises in BE7-18 and assume instead that the receivables are sold with recourse. Prepare the journal entry for Landstalker to record the sale, assuming the recourse obligation has a fair value of $9,000 and that Landstalker follows ASPE.

(LO 8) BE7-20 Keyser Woodcrafters sells $600,000 of receivables with a fair value of $620,000 to Keyser Trust in a securitization transaction that meets the criteria for a sale. Keyser Woodcrafters receives full fair value for the receivables and agrees to continue to service them, estimating that the fair value of this service liability component is $26,000. Prepare the journal entry for Keyser Woodcrafters to record the sale.

(LO 9) BE7-21 The financial statements of **Magnotta Winery Corporation** report net sales of $23,223,804 for its year ended January 31, 2011. Accounts receivable are $616,797 at January 31, 2011, and $590,322 at January 31, 2010. Calculate the company's accounts receivable turnover ratio and the average collection period for accounts receivable in days.

(LO 9) BE7-22 The financial statements of **BCE Inc.** report net sales of $19,497 million for its year ended December 31, 2011, and $18,069 million for its year ended December 31, 2010. Accounts receivable (net) was $2,964 million at December 31, 2011, $2,525 million at December 31, 2010, and $1,140 at December 31, 2009. Calculate the company's accounts receivable turnover ratio for 2010. Did it improve in 2011?

(LO 11) *BE7-23 Genesis Ltd. designated Alexa Kidd as petty cash custodian and established a petty cash fund of $400. The fund is reimbursed when the cash in the fund is at $57. Petty cash receipts indicate that funds were disbursed for $174 of office supplies and $167 of freight charges on inventory purchases. Genesis uses a perpetual inventory system. Prepare journal entries for the establishment of the fund and the reimbursement.

(LO 11) *BE7-24 Use the information in BE7-23. Assume that Genesis decides (a) to increase the size of the petty cash fund to $600 immediately after the reimbursement, and (b) to reduce the size of the petty cash to $250 immediately after the reimbursement. Prepare the entries that are necessary to record the (a) and (b) transactions.

(LO 11) *BE7-25 Jaguar Corporation is preparing a bank reconciliation and has identified the following potential reconciling items. For each item, indicate if it is (a) added to the balance per bank statement, (b) deducted from the balance per bank statement, (c) added to the balance per books, (d) deducted from the balance per books, or (e) not needed for the reconciliation.

1. Deposit in transit of $5,500
2. Previous month's outstanding cheque for $298 cleared the bank in the current month
3. Interest credited to Jaguar's account of $31
4. Bank service charges of $20
5. Outstanding deposit from previous month of $876 shown by bank as deposit of current month
6. Outstanding cheques of $7,422
7. NSF cheque returned of $260, and related service charge of $20

(LO 11) *BE7-26 Use the information for Jaguar Corporation in BE7-25. Prepare any entries that are necessary to make Jaguar's accounting records correct and complete.

Exercises

(LO 2) E7-1 **(Determining Cash Balance)** The controller for Eastwood Co. is trying to determine the amount of cash to report on the December 31, 2014 statement of financial position. The following information is provided:

1. A commercial savings account with $600,000 and a commercial chequing account balance of $900,000 are held at First National Bank. There is also a bank overdraft of $35,000 in a chequing account at the Royal Scotia Bank. No other accounts are held at the Royal Scotia Bank.
2. Eastwood has agreed to maintain a cash balance of $100,000 at all times in its chequing account at First National Bank to ensure that credit is available in the future.
3. Eastwood has a $5-million investment in a Commercial Bank of Montreal money-market mutual fund. This fund has chequing account privileges.
4. There are travel advances of $18,000 for executive travel for the first quarter of next year (employees will complete expense reports after they travel).

5. A separate cash fund in the amount of $1.5 million is restricted for the retirement of long-term debt.

6. There is a petty cash fund of $3,000.

7. A $1,900 IOU from Marianne Koch, a company officer, will be withheld from her salary in January 2015.

8. There are 20 cash floats for retail operation cash registers: 8 at $475, and 12 at $600.

9. The company has two certificates of deposit, each for $500,000. These certificates of deposit each had a maturity of 120 days when they were acquired. One was purchased on October 15 and the other on December 27.

10. Eastwood has received a cheque dated January 12, 2015, in the amount of $25,000 from a customer owing funds at December 31. It has also received a cheque dated January 8, 2015, in the amount of $11,500 from a customer as an advance on an order that was placed on December 29 and will be delivered February 1, 2015.

11. Eastwood holds $2.1 million of commercial paper of Rocco Leone Co., which is due in 60 days.

12. Currency and coin on hand amounted to $7,700.

13. Eastwood acquired 1,000 shares of Sortel for $3.90 per share in late November and is holding them for trading. The shares are still on hand at year end and have a fair value of $4.10 per share on December 31, 2014.

Instructions

Digging Deeper

(a) Calculate the amount of cash to be reported on Eastwood's statement of financial position at December 31, 2014.

(b) Indicate the proper way to report items that are not reported as cash on the December 31, 2014 statement of financial position.

(c) Referring to item 2 above, why would First National Bank require Eastwood to maintain a cash balance of $100,000 at all times in its chequing account?

(d) From the perspective of a potential lender to Eastwood, discuss the importance of proper reporting of item 5.

(LO 2) E7-2 (Determining Cash Balance) Several independent situations follow.

1. Chequing account balance $625,000; certificate of deposit $1.1 million; cash advance to subsidiary $980,000; utility deposit paid to gas company $180.

2. Chequing account balance $500,000; overdraft in special chequing account at same bank as normal chequing account $17,000; cash held in bond sinking fund $200,000; petty cash fund $300; cash on hand $1,350.

3. Chequing account balance $540,000; postdated cheque from customer $11,000; cash restricted to maintain compensating balance requirement $100,000; certified cheque from customer $9,800; postage stamps on hand $620.

4. Chequing account balance at bank $57,000; money-market balance at mutual fund (has chequing privileges) $38,000; NSF cheque received from customer $800.

5. Chequing account balance $700,000; cash restricted for future plant expansion $500,000; short-term (60-day) treasury bills $180,000; cash advance received from customer $900 (not included in chequing account balance); cash advance of $7,000 to company executive, payable on demand; refundable deposit of $26,000 paid to federal government to guarantee performance on construction contract.

Instructions

For each situation above, determine the amount that should be reported as cash. If the item(s) is (are) not reported as cash, explain why.

(LO 3, 9) E7-3 (Financial Statement Presentation of Receivables) Thériault Inc. shows a balance of $420,289 in the Accounts Receivable account on December 31, 2014. The balance consists of the following:

Instalment accounts due in 2015	$ 48,000
Instalment accounts due after 2015	44,000
Overpayments to creditors	12,640
Due from regular customers, of which $40,000 represents accounts pledged as security for a bank loan	165,000
Advances to employees	49,649
Advance to subsidiary company (made in 2009)	101,000
	$420,289

Instructions

Show how the information above should be presented on the statement of financial position of Thériault Inc. at December 31, 2014.

(LO 4, 11) E7-4 (Determining Ending Accounts Receivable) Your accounts receivable clerk, Mitra Adams, to whom you pay a salary of $1,500 per month, has just purchased a new Cadillac. You have decided to test the accuracy of the accounts receivable balance of $86,500 shown in the general ledger.

The following information is available for your first year in business:

1. Collections from customers are $198,000.

3. Ending merchandise inventory is $99,000.

2. Merchandise purchased totalled $320,000.

4. Goods are marked to sell at 40% above cost.

Instructions

(a) Estimate the ending balance of accounts receivable from customers that should appear in the ledger and any apparent shortages. Assume that all sales are made on account.

(b) Discuss cash controls that can be implemented to prevent theft in this situation. Also discuss a cash control that can be implemented to detect any differences between the company's records of cash collected and cash actually received by the company.

(LO 4) E7-5 (Recording Sales Transactions) Information from Salini Computers Ltd. follows:

July	1	Sold $82,000 of computers to Robertson Corp., terms 2/15, n/30.
	5	Robertson Corp. returned for full credit one computer with an invoice price of $6,200.
	10	Salini received payment from Robertson for the full amount owed from the July transactions.
	17	Sold $160,000 in computers and peripherals to Nawaz Store, terms 2/10, n/30.
	26	Nawaz Store paid Salini for half of its July purchases.
Aug.	30	Nawaz Store paid Salini for the remaining half of its July purchases.

Instructions

(a) Prepare the entries for Salini Computers Ltd., assuming the gross method is used to record sales and cash discounts.

(b) Prepare the entries for Salini Computers Ltd., assuming the net method is used to record sales and cash discounts.

(LO 4) E7-6 (Recording Sales Gross and Net) On June 3, Arnold Limited sold to Chester Arthur merchandise having a sale price of $3,000 with terms 3/10, n/60, f.o.b. shipping point. A $90 invoice, terms n/30, was received by Chester on June 8 from John Booth Transport Service for the freight cost. When it received the goods on June 5, Chester notified Arnold that $500 of the merchandise contained flaws that rendered it worthless; the same day Arnold Limited issued a credit memo covering the worthless merchandise and asked that it be returned to them at their expense. The freight on the returned merchandise was $25, which Arnold paid on June 7. On June 12, the company received a cheque for the balance due from Chester Arthur.

Instructions

(a) Prepare journal entries on Arnold Limited's books assuming that:

1. Sales and receivables are entered at gross selling price.

2. Sales and receivables are entered net of cash discounts.

(b) Prepare the journal entry under assumption 2, if Chester Arthur did not pay until July 29.

(c) From Chester Arthur's perspective, calculate the implied annual interest rate on accounts receivable not paid to Arnold within the discount period. Chester Arthur has a line of credit facility with its bank at 10%.

Digging Deeper

(LO 4, 5, 8) E7-7 (Journalizing Various Receivable Transactions) Information on Janut Corp. follows:

July	1	Janut Corp. sold to Harding Ltd. merchandise having a sales price of $9,000, terms 3/10, net/60. Janut records its sales and receivables net.
	3	Harding Ltd. returned defective merchandise having a sales price of $700.
	5	Accounts receivable of $19,000 (gross) are factored with Jackson Credit Corp. without recourse at a financing charge of 9%. Cash is received for the proceeds and collections are handled by the finance company. (These accounts were subject to a 2% discount and were all past the discount period.)
	9	Specific accounts receivable of $15,000 (gross) are pledged to Landon Credit Corp. as security for a loan of $11,000 at a finance charge of 3% of the loan amount plus 9% interest on the outstanding balance. Janut will continue to make the collections. All the accounts receivable pledged are past the discount period and were originally subject to a 2% discount.
Dec.	29	Harding Ltd. notifies Janut that it is bankrupt and will be able to pay only 10% of its account. Give the entry to write off the uncollectible balance using the allowance method. (Note: First record the increase in the receivable on July 11 when the discount period passed.)

Instructions

Prepare all necessary journal entries on Janut Corp.'s books.

(LO 5) E7-8   (Recording Bad Debts) At the end of 2013, Perez Corporation has accounts receivable of $1.2 million and an allowance for doubtful accounts of $80,000. On January 16, 2014, Perez determined that its $16,000 receivable from Morganfield Ltd. will not be collected, and management has authorized its writeoff. On January 31, 2014, Perez received notification that the company will be receiving $0.10 for every $1.00 of accounts receivable relating to McKinley Ltd. The company had previously written off 100% of the amount due from McKinley ($60,000).

Instructions

(a) Prepare the journal entry for Perez Corporation to write off the Morganfield receivable and any journal entry necessary to reflect the notice regarding McKinley Ltd.

(b) What is the estimated net realizable value of Perez's accounts receivable before and after the entries in (a)? What is the book value of Perez's accounts receivable before and after the entries in (a)?

(LO 5) E7-9   (Calculating Bad Debts) At January 1, 2014, the credit balance of Andy Corp.'s Allowance for Doubtful Accounts was $400,000. During 2014, the bad debt expense entry was based on a percentage of net credit sales. Net sales for 2014 were $80 million, of which 90% were on account. Based on the information available at the time, the 2014 bad debt expense was estimated to be 0.8% of net credit sales. During 2014, uncollectible receivables amounting to $500,000 were written off against the allowance for doubtful accounts. The company has estimated that at December 31, 2014, based on a review of the aged accounts receivable, the allowance for doubtful accounts would be properly measured at $525,000.

Instructions

Prepare a schedule calculating the balance in Andy Corp.'s Allowance for Doubtful Accounts at December 31, 2014. Prepare any necessary journal entry at year end to adjust the allowance for doubtful accounts to the required balance.

(LO 5) E7-10   (Reporting Bad Debts) The chief accountant for Dickinson Corporation provides you with the following list of accounts receivable that were written off in the current year:

Date	Customer	Amount
Mar. 31	Eli Masters Ltd.	$ 7,700
June 30	Crane Associates	6,800
Sept. 30	Annie Lowell's Dress Shop	12,000
Dec. 31	Vahik Uzerian	6,830

Dickinson Corporation follows the policy of debiting Bad Debt Expense as accounts are written off. The chief accountant maintains that this procedure is appropriate for financial statement purposes.

All of Dickinson Corporation's sales are on a 30-day credit basis, and the accounts written off all related to current year sales. Sales for the year total $3.2 million, and your research suggests that bad debt losses approximate 2% of sales.

Instructions

(a) Do you agree with Dickinson Corporation's policy on recognizing bad debt expense? Why?

(b) By what amount would net income differ if bad debt expense was calculated using the allowance method and percentage-of-sales approach?

(c) Under what conditions is using the direct writeoff method justified?

(LO 5) E7-11   (Calculating Bad Debts and Preparing Journal Entries) The trial balance before adjustment of Chloe Inc. shows the following balances:

	Dr.	Cr.
Accounts receivable	$105,000	
Allowance for doubtful accounts	1,950	
Sales revenue (all on credit)		$684,000
Sales returns and allowances	30,000	

Instructions

(a) Give the entry for bad debt expense for the current year assuming:

1. The allowance should be 4% of gross accounts receivable.

2. Historical records indicate that, based on accounts receivable aging, the following percentages will not be collected:

	Balance	Percentage Estimated to Be Uncollectible
0–30 days outstanding	$36,000	1%
31–60 days outstanding	48,000	5%

	Balance	Percentage Estimated to Be Uncollectible
61–90 days outstanding	12,200	12%
Over 90 days outstanding	8,800	18%

3. Allowance for Doubtful Accounts is $1,950 but it is a credit balance and the allowance should be 4% of gross accounts receivable.

4. Allowance for Doubtful Accounts is $1,950 but it is a credit balance and historical records indicate that the same percentages in (b) are to be used to determine the Allowance for Doubtful Accounts.

Digging Deeper

(b) From the perspective of an independent reviewer of Chloe's trial balance, comment on the unadjusted debit balance in Chloe's allowance for doubtful accounts at year end.

(LO 5) E7-12 **(Bad Debts—Aging)** Lenai Co. has the following account among its trade receivables:

			Hopkins Co.				
1/1	Balance forward	$ 850		1/28	Cash (#1710)		1,100
1/20	Invoice #1710	1,100		4/2	Cash (#2116)		1,350
3/14	Invoice #2116	1,350		4/10	Cash (1/1 Balance)		155
4/12	Invoice #2412	2,110		4/30	Cash (#2412)		1,000
9/5	Invoice #3614	490		9/20	Cash (#3614 and part of #2412)		790
10/17	Invoice #4912	860		10/31	Cash (#4912)		860
11/18	Invoice #5681	2,000		12/1	Cash (#5681)		1,250
12/20	Invoice #6347	800		12/29	Cash (#6347)		800

Instructions

Age the Hopkins Co. account at December 31 and specify any items that may need particular attention at year end.

(LO 6) E7-13 **(Interest-Bearing and Non–Interest-Bearing Notes)** Little Corp. was experiencing cash flow problems and was unable to pay its $105,000 account payable to Big Corp. when it fell due on September 30, 2014. Big agreed to substitute a one-year note for the open account. The following two options were presented to Little by Big Corp.:

Option 1: A one-year note for $105,000 due September 30, 2015. Interest at a rate of 8% would be payable at maturity.

Option 2: A one-year non–interest-bearing note for $113,400. The implied rate of interest is 8%.

Assume that Big Corp. has a December 31 year end.

Instructions

(a) Assuming Little Corp. chooses Option 1, prepare the entries required on Big Corp.'s books on September 30, 2014, December 31, 2014, and September 30, 2015.

(b) Assuming Little Corp. chooses Option 2, prepare the entries required on Big Corp.'s books on September 30, 2014, December 31, 2014, and September 30, 2015.

(c) Compare the amount of interest income earned by Big Corp. in 2014 and 2015 under both options. Comment briefly.

Digging Deeper

(d) From management's perspective, does one option provide better liquidity for Big at December 31, 2014? Does one option provide better cash flows than the other?

(LO 6) E7-14 **(Non–Interest-Bearing Note)** On September 1, 2014, Myo Inc. sold goods to Khin Corporation, a new customer. Prior to shipment of the goods, Myo's credit and collections department conducted a procedural credit check and determined that Khin is a high credit risk customer. As a result, Myo did not provide Khin with open credit by recording the sale as an account receivable; instead, Myo required Khin to provide a non–interest-bearing promissory note for $35,000 face value, to be repaid in one year. Khin has a credit rating that requires it to pay 12% interest on borrowed funds. Myo pays 10% interest on a loan recently obtained from its local bank. Myo has a December 31 year end.

Instructions

(a) Prepare the entries required on Myo's books to record the sale, annual adjusting entry, and collection of the full face value of the note.

(b) Assume that on the note's maturity date, Khin informs Myo that it is having cash flow problems and can only pay Myo 80% of the note's face value. After extensive discussions with Khin's management, Myo's credit and collections department considers the remaining balance of the note uncollectible. Prepare the entry required on Myo's books on the note's maturity date.

(c) What else could have been done by Myo to decrease collection risk related to the sale to Khin?

(LO 7) E7-15 **(Notes Receivable with Zero and Unrealistic Interest Rates)** On July 1, 2014, Agincourt Inc. made two sales:

1. It sold excess land in exchange for a four-year, non–interest-bearing promissory note in the face amount of $1,101,460. The land's carrying value is $590,000.

2. It rendered services in exchange for an eight-year promissory note having a face value of $400,000. Interest at a rate of 3% is payable annually.

The customers in the above transactions have credit ratings that require them to borrow money at 12% interest. Agincourt recently had to pay 8% interest for money it borrowed from British National Bank.

3. On July 1, 2014, Agincourt also agreed to accept an instalment note from one of its customers in partial settlement of accounts receivable that were overdue. The note calls for four equal payments of $20,000, including the principal and interest due, on the anniversary of the note. The implied interest rate on this note is 10%.

Digging
Deeper

Instructions

(a) Prepare the journal entries to record the three notes receivable transactions of Agincourt Inc. on July 1, 2014.

(b) Prepare an effective-interest amortization table for the instalment note obtained in partial collection of accounts receivable. From Agincourt's perspective, what are the advantages of an instalment note compared with a non–interest-bearing note?

(LO 7, 9) E7-16 **(Notes Receivable with Zero Interest Rate)** By December 31, 2013, Clearing Corp. had performed a significant amount of environmental consulting services for Rank Ltd. Rank was short of cash, and Clearing agreed to accept a $200,000, non–interest-bearing note due December 31, 2015, as payment in full. Rank is a bit of a credit risk and typically borrows funds at a rate of 12%. Clearing is much more creditworthy and has various lines of credit at 9%.

Instructions

(a) Prepare the journal entry to record the transaction on December 31, 2013, for Clearing Corp.

(b) Assuming Clearing's fiscal year end is December 31, prepare the journal entry required at December 31, 2014.

(c) Assuming Clearing's fiscal year end is December 31, prepare the journal entry required at December 31, 2015.

(d) What are the amount and classification of the note on Clearing Corp.'s statement of financial position as at December 31, 2014?

(e) If an appropriate market rate of interest for the note receivable is not known, how should the transaction be valued and recorded on December 31, 2013?

(LO 8) E7-17 **(Assigning Accounts Receivable)** On April 1, 2014, Ibrahim Corporation assigns $400,000 of its accounts receivable to First National Bank as collateral for a $200,000 loan that is due July 1, 2014. The assignment agreement calls for Ibrahim to continue to collect the receivables. First National Bank assesses a finance charge of 3% of the accounts receivable, and interest on the loan is 10%, a realistic rate for a note of this type.

Instructions

(a) Prepare the April 1, 2014 journal entry for Ibrahim Corporation.

(b) Prepare the journal entry for Ibrahim's collection of $350,000 of the accounts receivable during the period April 1 to June 30, 2014.

(c) On July 1, 2014, Ibrahim paid First National Bank the entire amount that was due on the loan.

(LO 8) E7-18 **(Journalizing Various Receivable Transactions)** The trial balance before adjustment for Sinatra Company shows the following balances.

	Dr.	Cr.
Accounts receivable	$82,000	
Allowance for doubtful accounts	1,750	
Sales revenue		$430,000

The following cases are independent:

1. To obtain cash, Sinatra factors without recourse $20,000 of receivables with Stills Finance. The finance charge is 10% of the amount factored.

2. To obtain a one-year loan of $55,000, Sinatra assigns $65,000 of specific accounts receivable to Ruddin Financial. The finance charge is 8% of the loan; the cash is received.

3. The company wants to maintain the Allowance for Doubtful Accounts at 5% of gross accounts receivable.

4. The company wishes to increase the allowance account by 1½% of sales.

Instructions

Using the data above, prepare the journal entries to record each of the above cases.

(LO 8, 9) E7-19 (Transfer of Receivables with Recourse) Chessman Corporation factors $600,000 of accounts receivable with Liquidity Financing, Inc. on a with recourse basis. Liquidity Financing will collect the receivables. The receivable records are transferred to Liquidity Financing on August 15, 2014. Liquidity Financing assesses a finance charge of 2.5% of the amount of accounts receivable and also reserves an amount equal to 5.25% of accounts receivable to cover probable adjustments. Chessman prepares financial statements under ASPE.

Instructions

(a) According to ASPE, what conditions must be met for a transfer of receivables to be accounted for as a sale?

(b) Assume the conditions from part (a) are met. Prepare the journal entry on August 15, 2014, for Chessman to record the sale of receivables, assuming the recourse obligation has a fair value of $6,000.

(c) What effect will the factoring of receivables have on calculating the accounts receivable turnover for Chessman? Comment briefly.

(d) Assume that Chessman is a private enterprise and prepares financial statements under IFRS. What conditions must be met for the transfer of receivables to be accounted for as a sale?

(LO 8, 9) E7-20 (Transfer of Receivables with Servicing Retained) Lute Retail Ltd. follows ASPE, it transfers $355,000 of its accounts receivable to an independent trust in a securitization transaction on July 11, 2014, receiving 96% of the receivables balance as proceeds. Lute will continue to manage the customer accounts, including their collection. Lute estimates this obligation has a liability value of $12,500. In addition, the agreement includes a recourse provision with an estimated value of $9,900. The transaction is to be recorded as a sale.

Instructions

(a) Prepare the journal entry on July 11, 2014, for Lute Retail Ltd. to record the securitization of the receivables.

(b) What effect will the securitization of receivables have on Lute Retail Ltd.'s accounts receivable turnover? Comment briefly.

(LO 9) E7-21 (Analysis of Receivables) Information follows for Patuanak Company:

1. The beginning of the year Accounts Receivable balance was $25,000.

2. Net sales for the year were $410,000. (Credit sales were $200,000 of the total sales.) Patuanak does not offer cash discounts.

3. Collections on accounts receivable during the year were $140,000.

Instructions

(a) Prepare summary journal entries to record the items noted above.

(b) Calculate Patuanak Company's accounts receivable turnover ratio for the year. How old is the average receivable?

(c) Use the turnover ratio calculated in (b) to analyze Patuanak Company's liquidity. The turnover ratio last year was 4.85.

(LO 9) E7-22 (Receivables Turnover) The **Becker Milk Company Limited**, a real estate and investment management company, reports the following information in its financial statements for the years ended April 30, 2011, 2010, and 2009:

Accounts receivable, net of allowance for doubtful accounts	April 30, 2011	$ 146,753
	April 30, 2010	90,137
	April 30, 2009	63,669
Revenue (note 8), year ended	April 30, 2011	3,893,667
	April 30, 2010	3,918,790
	April 30, 2009	3,859,039

Note 8: Revenue
As of April 30, 2011, the company's largest single tenant, Alimentation Couche-Tard Inc., accounted for 86% of the revenue. It accounted for 84% of the revenue in 2010.

Real World Emphasis

Digging Deeper

Instructions

(a) Calculate the accounts receivable turnover and days sales outstanding (or average collection period of accounts receivable in days) for the two most recent years provided.

(b) Comment on your results.

(c) Why do you think the information in Note 8 was provided by the company?

(LO 11) *E7-23   (Petty Cash) Kali Corp. established a petty cash fund early in 2014 to increase the efficiency of accounting for small cash transactions and to improve control over many of the small expenditures it makes. The company decided to set up the imprest fund at $200 and a cheque was issued for this amount and given to the petty cash custodian.

During January, the petty cash custodian made the following disbursements and placed a receipt for each in the cash box provided.

Tim Hortons coffee order for a management meeting	$ 18.62
Office supplies purchased	9.50
Courier charges paid	25.00
Travel advance to employee	100.00
Card, wrapping paper for gift for employee in hospital	9.40

The petty cash was replenished on January 22 when the amount of cash in the fund was $36.40. In June, after six months' experience with the fund, management decided to increase the imprest fund to $300.

Instructions

(a) Prepare the journal entries to establish the petty cash fund, to reimburse it on January 22, and to increase the fund in June.

(b) Describe where the petty cash will be reported on Kali Corp.'s financial statements.

(c) Explain briefly why many companies have a policy of reimbursing the petty cash fund on each balance sheet date.

(LO 11) *E7-24   (Bank Reconciliation and Adjusting Entries) Ling Corp. deposits all receipts intact and makes all payments by cheque. The following information is available from the cash records:

April 30 Bank Reconciliation

Balance per bank	$ 7,120
Add: Deposits in transit	1,540
Deduct: Outstanding cheques	(2,000)
Balance per books	$ 6,660

Month of May Results

	Per Bank	Per Books
Balance on May 31	$8,760	$9,370
May deposits	5,000	5,810
May cheques	4,000	3,100
May note collected (not included in May deposits)	1,000	—
May bank service charge	25	—
May NSF cheque from a customer, returned by the bank (recorded by the bank as a charge)	335	—

Instructions

(a) Keeping in mind the time lag between deposits and cheques being recorded in the books and when they are recorded by the bank, determine the amount of outstanding deposits and outstanding cheques at May 31.

(b) Prepare a May 31 bank reconciliation showing balance per bank statement and balance per books and correct cash balance.

(c) Prepare the journal entry or entries to correct the Cash account at May 31.

(LO 11) *E7-25   (Bank Reconciliation and Adjusting Entries) Eli Corp. has just received its August 31, 2014 bank statement, which is summarized as follows:

Provincial Bank of Manitoba	Disbursements	Receipts	Balance
Balance, August 1			$ 9,369
Deposits during August		$32,200	41,569
Note collected for depositor, including $40 interest		1,040	42,609
Cheques cleared during August	$34,500		8,109
Bank service charges	20		8,089
Balance, August 31			8,089

The general ledger Cash account contained the following entries for the month of August:

Cash			
Balance, August 1	10,050	Disbursements in August	34,903
Receipts during August	35,000		

Deposits in transit at August 31 are $3,800, and cheques outstanding at August 31 total $1,050. Cash currently on hand at August 31 is $310 and there were postdated cheques from customers (for September 1) in the amount of $540. The bookkeeper improperly entered one cheque in the books at $146.50. The cheque was actually written for $164.50 for supplies (expense) and cleared the bank during the month of August.

Instructions

(a) Prepare a bank reconciliation dated August 31, 2014, proceeding to a correct balance.

(b) Prepare any entries that are needed to make the books correct and complete.

(c) What amount of cash should be reported on the August 31 statement of financial position?

Problems

P7-1 Dev Equipment Corp. usually closes its books on December 31, but at the end of 2014 it held its cash book open so that a more favourable statement of financial position could be prepared for credit purposes. Cash receipts and disbursements for the first 10 days of January were recorded as December transactions. The company uses the gross method to record cash discounts.

The following information is given:

1. January cash receipts recorded in the December cash book totalled $38,900. Of that amount, $25,300 was for cash sales and $13,600 was for collections on account for which cash discounts of $630 were given.

2. January cash disbursements that were recorded in the December cheque register were for payments on account totalling $24,850 of accounts payable on which discounts of $520 were taken.

3. The general ledger has not been closed for 2014.

4. The amount shown as inventory was determined by a physical count on December 31, 2014.

Instructions

(a) Prepare any entries that you consider necessary to correct Dev Equipment Corp.'s accounts at December 31.

(b) To what extent was Dev Equipment Corp. able to show a more favourable statement of financial position at December 31 by holding its cash book open? (Use ratio analysis.) Assume that the statement of financial position that was prepared by the company showed the following amounts prior to any required adjustments:

	Debit	Credit
Cash	$39,000	
Accounts Receivable	42,000	
Inventory	67,000	
Accounts payable		$45,000
Accrued liabilities		14,200

(c) Discuss the ethical implications of holding the cash book open and showing a more favourable statement of financial position.

P7-2 A series of unrelated situations follow:

1. Atlantic Inc.'s unadjusted trial balance at December 31, 2014, included the following accounts:

	Debit	Credit
Allowance for doubtful accounts	$ 8,000	
Sales revenue		$1,980,000
Sales returns and allowances	60,000	
Sales discounts	4,400	

2. An analysis and aging of Central Corp.'s accounts receivable at December 31, 2014, disclosed the following:

Amounts estimated to be uncollectible	$ 160,000
Accounts receivable	1,790,000
Allowance for doubtful accounts (per books)	125,000

3. Western Co. provides for doubtful accounts based on 4.5% of credit sales. The following data are available for 2014:

Credit sales during 2014	$3,200,000
Allowance for doubtful accounts 1/1/14	37,000
Collection of accounts written off in prior years	
(customer credit was re-established)	18,000
Customer accounts written off as uncollectible during 2014	36,000

4. At the end of its first year of operations, on December 31, 2014, Pacific Inc. reported the following information:

Accounts receivable, net of allowance for doubtful accounts	$950,000
Customer accounts written off as uncollectible during 2014	24,000
Bad debt expense for 2014	92,000

5. The following accounts were taken from Northern Inc.'s unadjusted trial balance at December 31, 2014:

	Debit	Credit
Sales revenue (all on credit)		$950,000
Sales discounts	$ 21,400	
Allowance for doubtful accounts	34,000	
Accounts receivable	610,000	

Instructions

(a) For situation 1, Atlantic estimates its bad debt expense to be 1.5% of net sales. Determine its bad debt expense for 2014.

(b) For situation 2, what is the net realizable value of Central Corp.'s receivables at December 31, 2014?

(c) For situation 3, what is the balance in Allowance for Doubtful Accounts at December 31, 2014?

(d) For situation 4, what is the balance in accounts receivable at December 31, 2014, before subtracting the allowance for doubtful accounts?

(e) For situation 5, if doubtful accounts are 7% of accounts receivable, what is the bad debt expense amount to be reported for 2014?

P7-3 Fortini Corporation had record sales in 2014. It began 2014 with an Accounts Receivable balance of $475,000 and an Allowance for Doubtful Accounts of $33,000. Fortini recognized credit sales during the year of $6,675,000 and made monthly adjusting entries equal to 0.5% of each month's credit sales to recognize bad debt expense. Also during the year the company wrote off $35,500 of accounts that were deemed to be uncollectible, although one customer whose $4,000 account had been written off surprised management by paying the amount in full in late September. Including this surprise receipt, $6,568,500 cash was collected on account in 2014.

In preparation for the audited year-end financial statements, the controller prepared the following aged listing of the receivables at December 31, 2014:

Days Account Outstanding	Amount	Probability of Collection
Less than 16 days	$270,000	97%
Between 16 and 30 days	117,000	92%
Between 31 and 45 days	80,000	80%
Between 46 and 60 days	38,000	70%
Between 61 and 75 days	20,000	50%
Over 75 days	25,000	0%
	$550,000	

Instructions

(a) Reconcile the 2014 opening balance in Accounts Receivable to the $550,000 ending balance on the controller's aged listing.

(b) Prepare the adjusting entry to bring the Allowance for Doubtful Accounts to its proper balance at year end.

(c) Show how accounts receivable would be presented on the December 31, 2014 statement of financial position.

(d) What is the dollar effect of the year-end bad debt adjustment on the before-tax income?

P7-4 From its first day of operations to December 31, 2014, Campbell Corporation provided for uncollectible accounts receivable under the allowance method: entries for bad debt expense were made monthly based on 2.5% of credit sales, bad debts that were written off were charged to the allowance account, recoveries of bad debts previously written off were credited to the allowance account, and no year-end adjustments were made to the allowance account. Campbell's usual credit terms were net 30 days, and remain unchanged.

The balance in Allowance for Doubtful Accounts was $184,000 at January 1, 2014. During 2014, credit sales totalled $9.4 million, interim entries for bad debt expense were based on 2.5% of credit sales, $95,000 of bad debts were written off, and recoveries of accounts previously written off amounted to $15,000. Campbell upgraded its computer facility in November 2014, and an aging of accounts receivable was prepared for the first time as at December 31, 2014. A summary of the aging analysis follows:

Classification by Month of Sale	Balance in Each Category	Estimated % Uncollectible
November–December 2014	$1,080,000	8%
July–October 2014	650,000	12.5%
January–June 2014	420,000	20%
Before January 1, 2014	150,000	60%
	$2,300,000	

Based on a review of how collectible the accounts really are in the "Before January 1, 2014" aging category, additional receivables totalling $69,000 were written off as at December 31, 2014. The 60% uncollectible estimate therefore only applies to the remaining $81,000 in the category. Finally, beginning with the year ended December 31, 2014, Campbell adopted a new accounting method for estimating the allowance for doubtful accounts: it now uses the amount indicated by the year-end aging analysis of accounts receivable.

Instructions

(a) Prepare a schedule that analyzes the changes in Allowance for Doubtful Accounts for the year ended December 31, 2014. Show supporting calculations in good form. (*Hint:* In calculating the allowance amount at December 31, 2014, subtract the $69,000 writeoff of receivables.)

(b) Prepare the journal entry for the year-end adjustment to the Allowance for Doubtful Accounts balance as at December 31, 2014.

(AICPA adapted)

P7-5 The following information relates to Shea Inc.'s Accounts Receivable for the 2014 fiscal year:

1. An aging schedule of the accounts receivable as at December 31, 2014, is as follows:

Age	Net Debit Balance	% to Be Applied after Writeoff Is Made
Under 60 days	$172,342	1%
61–90 days	136,490	3%
91–120 days	39,924*	7%
Over 120 days	23,644	$4,200 definitely uncollectible; 20% of remainder is estimated uncollectible
	$372,400	

*The $2,740 writeoff of receivables (see item 4 below) is related to the 91–120-day category.

2. The Accounts Receivable control account has a debit balance of $372,400 on December 31, 2014.

3. Two entries were made in the Bad Debts Expense account during the year: (1) a debit on December 31 for the amount credited to Allowance for Doubtful Accounts, and (2) a credit for $2,740 on November 3, 2014, and a debit to Allowance for Doubtful Accounts because of a bankruptcy.

4. Allowance for Doubtful Accounts is as follows for 2014:

Allowance for Doubtful Accounts				
11/3 Uncollectible accounts written off	2,740	1/1	Beginning balance	8,750
		12/31	5% of $372,400	18,620

5. There is a credit balance in Accounts Receivable (61–90 days) of $4,840, which represents an advance on a sales contract.

Instructions

Assuming that the books have not been closed for 2014, make the necessary correcting entries.

P7-6 The statement of financial position of Reynolds Corp. at December 31, 2013, includes the following:

Notes receivable	$ 26,000	
Accounts receivable	182,100	
Less: Allowance for doubtful accounts	(17,300)	$190,800

Transactions in 2014 include the following:

1. Accounts receivable of $138,000 were collected. This amount includes gross accounts of $40,000 on which 2% sales discounts were allowed.

2. An additional $6,700 was received in payment of an account that was written off in 2014.

3. Customer accounts of $19,500 were written off during the year.

4. At year end, Allowance for Doubtful Accounts was estimated to need a balance of $21,000. This estimate is based on an analysis of aged accounts receivable.

Instructions

Prepare all necessary journal entries to reflect the information above.

(AICPA adapted)

P7-7   On October 1, 2014, Healy Farm Equipment Corp. sold a harvesting machine to Homestead Industries. Instead of a cash payment, Homestead Industries gave Healy Farm Equipment a $150,000, two-year, 10% note; 10% is a realistic rate for a note of this type. The note required interest to be paid annually on October 1, beginning October 1, 2015. Healy Farm Equipment's financial statements are prepared on a calendar-year basis.

Instructions

(a) Assuming that no reversing entries are used and that Homestead Industries fulfills all the terms of the note, prepare the necessary journal entries for Healy Farm Equipment Corp. for the entire term of the note.

(b) Repeat the journal entries under the assumption that Healy Farm Equipment Corp. uses reversing entries.

P7-8   On December 31, 2014, Zhang Ltd. rendered services to Beggy Corp. at an agreed price of $91,844.10. In payment, Zhang accepted $36,000 cash and agreed to receive the balance in four equal instalments of $18,000 that are due each December 31. An interest rate of 11% is applicable.

Instructions

(a) Prepare the entries recorded by Zhang Ltd. for the sale and for the receipts including interest on the following dates:

1. December 31, 2014
2. December 31, 2015
3. December 31, 2016
4. December 31, 2017
5. December 31, 2018

Digging Deeper

(b) From Zhang Ltd.'s perspective, what are the advantages of an instalment note compared with a non–interest-bearing note?

P7-9   Desrosiers Ltd. had the following long-term receivable account balances at December 31, 2013:

Notes receivable	$1,800,000
Notes receivable—Employees	400,000

Transactions during 2014 and other information relating to Desrosiers' long-term receivables were as follows:

1. The $1.8-million note receivable is dated May 1, 2013, bears interest at 9%, and represents the balance of the consideration received from the sale of Desrosiers' electronics division to New York Company. Principal payments of $600,000 plus appropriate interest are due on May 1, 2014, 2015, and 2016. The first principal and interest payment was made on May 1, 2014. Collection of the note instalments is reasonably assured.

2. The $400,000 note receivable is dated December 31, 2013, bears interest at 8%, and is due on December 31, 2016. The note is due from Marcia Cumby, president of Desrosiers Ltd., and is secured by 10,000 Desrosiers common shares. Interest is payable annually on December 31, and the interest payment was made on December 31, 2014. The quoted market price of Desrosiers' common shares was $45 per share on December 31, 2014.

3. On April 1, 2014, Desrosiers sold a patent to Pinot Company in exchange for a $200,000 non–interest-bearing note due on April 1, 2016. There was no established exchange price for the patent, and the note had no ready market. The prevailing rate of interest for a note of this type at April 1, 2014, was 12%. The present value of $1 for two periods at 12% is 0.79719 (use this factor). The patent had a carrying amount of $40,000 at January 1, 2014, and the amortization for the year ended December 31, 2014, would have been $8,000. The collection of the note receivable from Pinot is reasonably assured.

4. On July 1, 2014, Desrosiers sold a parcel of land to Four Winds Inc. for $200,000 under an instalment sale contract. Four Winds made a $60,000 cash down payment on July 1, 2014, and signed a four-year, 11% note for the $140,000 balance. The equal annual payments of principal and interest on the note will be $45,125, payable on July 1, 2015, through July 1, 2018. The land could have been sold at an established cash price of $200,000. The cost of the land to Desrosiers was $150,000. Collection of the instalments on the note is reasonably assured.

Instructions

(a) For each note:

    1. Describe the relevant cash flows in terms of amount and timing.

    2. Determine the amount of interest income that should be reported in 2014.

    3. Determine the portion of the note and any interest that should be reported in current assets at December 31, 2014.

    4. Determine the portion of the note that should be reported as a long-term investment at December 31, 2014.

(b) Prepare the long-term receivables section of Desrosiers' statement of financial position at December 31, 2014.

(c) Prepare a schedule showing the current portion of the long-term receivables and accrued interest receivable that would appear in Desrosiers' statement of financial position at December 31, 2014.

(d) Determine the total interest income from the long-term receivables that would appear on Desrosiers' income statement for the year ended December 31, 2014.

P7-10   Logo Limited follows ASPE. It manufactures sweatshirts for sale to athletic-wear retailers. The following summary information was available for Logo for the year ended December 31, 2013:

Cash	$20,000
Accounts receivable	40,000
Inventory	85,000
Accounts payable	65,000
Accrued liabilities	15,000

Part 1

During 2014, Logo had the following transactions:

    1. Total sales were $465,000. Of the total sales amount, $215,000 was on a credit basis.

    2. On June 30, a $50,000 account receivable of a major customer was settled, with Logo accepting a $50,000, one-year, 11% note, with the interest payable at maturity.

    3. Logo collected $160,000 on accounts receivable during the year.

    4. At December 31, 2014, Cash had a balance of $15,000, Inventory had a balance of $80,000, Accounts Payable was $70,000, and Accrued Liabilities was $16,000.

Instructions

(a) Prepare summary journal entries to record the items noted above.

(b) Calculate the current ratio and the receivables turnover ratio for Logo at December 31, 2014. Use these measures to assess Logo's liquidity. The receivables turnover ratio last year was 4.75.

Part 2

Now assume that at year end 2014, Logo enters into the following transactions related to the company's receivables:

    1. Logo sells the note receivable to Prairie Bank for $50,000 cash plus accrued interest. Given the creditworthiness of Logo's customer, the bank accepts the note without recourse and assesses a finance charge of 3.5%. Prairie Bank will collect the note directly from the customer.

    2. Logo factors some accounts receivable at the end of the year. Accounts totalling $40,000 are transferred to Primary Factors, Inc., with recourse. Primary Factors retains 6% of the balances and assesses a finance charge of 4% on the transfer. Primary Factors will collect the receivables from Logo's customers. The fair value of the recourse obligation is $4,000.

Instructions

(c) Prepare the journal entry to record the transfer of the note receivable to Prairie Bank.

(d) Prepare the journal entry to record the sale of receivables to Primary Factors.

(e) Calculate the current ratio and the receivables turnover ratio for Logo at December 31, 2014. Use these measures to assess Logo's liquidity. The receivables turnover ratio last year was 4.85.

(f) Discuss how the ratio analysis in (e) would be affected if Logo had transferred the receivables in secured borrowing transactions.

(g) From Prairie Bank's perspective, what is the total effect on its net income as a result of purchasing the note receivable without recourse?

Digging Deeper

(h) From Primary Factors' perspective, what is the total effect on its net income as a result of purchasing the accounts receivable with recourse?

P7-11   In 2014, Ibran Corp. required additional cash for its business. Management decided to use accounts receivable to raise the additional cash and has asked you to determine the income statement effects of the following transactions:

1. On July 1, 2014, Ibran assigned $600,000 of accounts receivable to Provincial Finance Corporation as security for a loan. Ibran received an advance from Provincial Finance of 90% of the assigned accounts receivable less a commission of 3% on the advance. Before December 31, 2014, Ibran collected $220,000 on the assigned accounts receivable, and remitted $232,720 to Provincial Finance. Of the latter amount, $12,720 was interest on the advance from Provincial Finance.

2. On December 1, 2014, Ibran sold $300,000 of accounts receivable to Wunsch Corp. for $275,000. The receivables were sold outright on a without recourse basis and Ibran has no continuing interest in the receivables.

3. On December 31, 2014, an advance of $120,000 was received from First Bank by pledging $160,000 of Ibran's accounts receivable. Ibran's first payment to First Bank is due on January 30, 2015.

Instructions

Prepare a schedule showing the income statement effects of these transactions for the year ended December 31, 2014.

P7-12   The Cormier Corporation sells office equipment and supplies to many organizations in the city and surrounding area on contract terms of 2/10, n/30. In the past, over 75% of the credit customers have taken advantage of the discount by paying within 10 days of the invoice date. However, the number of customers taking the full 30 days to pay has increased within the last year. It now appears that less than 60% of the customers are taking the discount. Bad debts as a percentage of gross credit sales have risen from the 1.5% of past years to about 4% in the current year.

The controller responded to a request for more information on the deterioration in collections of accounts receivable by preparing the following report:

THE CORMIER CORPORATION
Finance Committee Report–Accounts Receivable Collections
May 31, 2014

The fact that some credit accounts will prove uncollectible is normal. Annual bad debt writeoffs have been 1.5% of gross credit sales over the past five years. During the last fiscal year, this percentage increased to slightly less than 4%. The current Accounts Receivable balance is $1.6 million. The condition of this balance in terms of age and probability of collection is as follows:

Proportion of Total (%)	Age Categories	Probability of Collection (%)
68	not yet due	99
15	less than 30 days past due	96.5
8	30 to 60 days past due	95
5	61 to 120 days past due	91
2.50	121 to 180 days past due	70
1.50	more than 180 days past due	20

Allowance for Doubtful Accounts had a credit balance of $43,300 on June 1, 2013. The Cormier Corporation has provided for a monthly bad debt expense accrual during the current fiscal year based on the assumption that 4% of gross credit sales will be uncollectible. Total gross credit sales for the 2013–14 fiscal year amounted to $4 million. Writeoffs of bad accounts during the year totalled $145,000.

Instructions

(a) Prepare an accounts receivable aging schedule for the Cormier Corporation using the age categories identified in the controller's report to the finance committee. Show (1) the amount of accounts receivable outstanding for each age category and in total, and (2) the estimated amount that is uncollectible for each category and in total.

(b) Calculate the amount of the year-end adjustment that is needed to bring Allowance for Doubtful Accounts to the balance indicated by the aging analysis. Then prepare the necessary journal entry to adjust the accounting records.

(c) Assuming that the economy is currently in recession, with tight credit and high interest rates:
   1. Identify steps that the Cormier Corporation might consider to improve the accounts receivable situation.
   2. Evaluate each step you identify in terms of the risks and costs that it involves.

(CMA adapted)

P7-13   The Patchwork Corporation manufactures sweaters for sale to athletic-wear retailers. The following information was available on Patchwork for the years ended December 31, 2013, and 2014:

	12/31/13	12/31/14
Cash	$ 20,000	$ 15,000
Accounts receivable	90,000	?
Allowance for doubtful accounts	8,500	?
Inventory	85,000	80,000
Current liabilities	80,000	86,000
Total credit sales	600,000	550,000
Collections on accounts receivable	440,000	500,000

During 2014, Patchwork had the following transactions:

1. On June 1, 2014, sales of $80,000 to a major customer were settled, with Patchwork accepting an $80,000, one-year note bearing 7% interest that is payable at maturity. The $80,000 is not included in the total credit sales amount above.

2. Patchwork factors some accounts receivable at the end of the year. Accounts totalling $60,000 are transferred to Primary Factors Inc., with recourse. Primary Factors retains 5% of the balances, and will receive the collections directly from Patchwork's customers. Patchwork is assessed a finance charge of 6% on this transfer. The fair value of the recourse obligation is $7,000.

3. Patchwork wrote off $3,200 of accounts receivable during 2014.

4. Based on the latest available information, the 2014 allowance for doubtful accounts should have a balance of $12,000 at December 31, 2014.

Additional information:

Included in the cash balance at December 31, 2014, are the following: a chequing account with a balance of $9,600, postage stamps of $100, petty cash of $300, coins and currency on hand of $3,000, and postdated cheques from customers of $2,000. Patchwork is a private company that follows ASPE.

Instructions

(a) Prepare the journal entry for the factoring of the accounts receivable to Primary Factors Inc.

(b) Based on the above transactions and additional information, determine the balances of Accounts Receivable and Bad Debt Expense at December 31, 2014.

(c) Prepare the current assets section of Patchwork's statement of financial position at December 31, 2014.

(d) Calculate the current ratios for Patchwork for 2013 and 2014.

(e) Calculate the receivables turnover ratio for Patchwork for 2014. Patchwork's receivables turnover ratio for 2013 was 3.8 times.

(f) Comment on Patchwork's liquidity and ability to collect accounts receivable. Comment also on the improvement or deterioration of the current and accounts receivable turnover ratios.

Digging Deeper

(g) Discuss the effect on the current and accounts receivable turnover ratios if Patchwork had decided to assign $40,000 of accounts receivable instead of factoring them to Primary Factors Inc. Recalculate the ratios to support your conclusions.

*P7-14 Joseph Kiuvik is reviewing the cash accounting for Connolly Corporation, a local mailing service. Kiuvik's review will focus on the petty cash account and the bank reconciliation for the month ended May 31, 2014. He has collected the following information from Connolly's bookkeeper:

Petty Cash

1. The petty cash fund was established on May 10, 2014, in the amount of $400.

2. Expenditures from the fund as at May 31, 2014, were supported by approved receipts for the following:

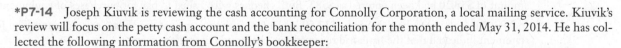

Postage expense	$63.00
Envelopes and other supplies	25.00
In-house business lunch provided	99.50
Donation to local charity	35.00
Shipping charges, for goods to customers	48.50
Newspaper advertising	22.80
Taxi for sales manager to attend meeting downtown	18.75
Freight paid on incoming purchases	37.70

3. On May 31, 2014, the petty cash fund was replenished and increased to $500; currency and coin in the fund at that time totalled $47.10.

Bank Reconciliation

SCOTIA IMPERIAL BANK
Bank Statement

	Disbursements	Receipts	Balance
Balance, May 1, 2014			$9,019
Deposits		$28,000	
Note payment, direct from customer (interest of $30)		930	
Cheques cleared during May	$31,100		
Bank service charges	37		
Balance, May 31, 2014			6,812

Connolly's general ledger Cash account had a balance of $9,300 on May 1. During the month, the company deposited $31,000 in the bank and wrote cheques in payment of accounts payable and the payroll for $31,685. Deposits in transit at the end of the month are determined to be $3,000, cash still on hand with the company cashier is $246 (besides petty cash), and cheques outstanding at May 31 total $550.

Instructions

(a) Prepare the journal entries to record the transactions related to the petty cash fund for May.

(b) Prepare a bank reconciliation dated May 31, 2014, proceeding to a correct balance, and prepare the journal entries to make the books correct and complete.

(c) What amount of cash should be reported in the May 31, 2014 statement of financial position?

*P7-15   The cash account of Villa Corp. shows a ledger balance of $3,969.85 on June 30, 2014. The bank statement as at that date indicates a balance of $4,150. When the statement was compared with the cash records, the following facts were determined:

1. There were bank service charges for June of $25.00.

2. A bank memo stated that Bao Dai's note for $900 and interest of $36 had been collected on June 29, and the bank had made a charge of $5.50 on the collection. (No entry had been made on Villa's books when Bao Dai's note was sent to the bank for collection.)

3. Receipts for June 30 of $2,890 were not deposited until July 2.

4. Cheques outstanding on June 30 totalled $2,136.05.

5. On June 29, the bank had charged Villa Corp.'s account for a customer's uncollectible cheque amounting to $453.20.

6. A customer's cheque for $90 had been entered as $60 in the cash receipts journal by Villa Corp. on June 15.

7. Cheque no. 742 in the amount of $491 had been entered in the cashbook as $419, and cheque no. 747 in the amount of $58.20 had been entered as $582. Both cheques were issued to pay for purchases of equipment.

8. In May 2014, the bank had charged a $27.50 Wella Corp. cheque against the Villa Corp. account. The June bank statement indicated that the bank had reversed this charge and corrected its error.

Instructions

(a) Prepare a bank reconciliation dated June 30, 2014, proceeding to a correct cash balance.

(b) Prepare any entries that are needed to make the books correct and complete.

*P7-16   Information related to Bonzai Books Ltd. is as follows: balance per books at October 31, $41,847.85; November receipts, $173,528.91; November disbursements, $166,193.54; balance per bank statement at November 30, $56,270.20. The following cheques were outstanding at November 30:

#1224	$1,635.29	#1232	3,625.15
#1230	2,468.30	#1233	482.17

Included with the November bank statement and not recorded by the company were a bank debit memo for $31.40 covering bank charges for the month, a debit memo for $572.13 for a customer's cheque returned and marked NSF, and a credit memo for $1,400 representing bond interest collected by the bank in the name of Bonzai Books Ltd. Cash on hand at November 30 that had been recorded and was not yet deposited amounted to $1,920.40.

Instructions

(a) Prepare a bank reconciliation proceeding to the correct balance at November 30 for Bonzai Books Ltd.

(b) Prepare any journal entries that are needed to adjust the Cash account at November 30.

*P7-17 Information follows for Quartz Industries Ltd.:

QUARTZ INDUSTRIES LTD.
Bank Reconciliation
May 31, 2014

Balance per bank statement		$30,928.46
Less: Outstanding cheques		
No. 6124	$2,125.00	
No. 6138	932.65	
No. 6139	960.57	
No. 6140	1,420.00	5,438.22
		25,490.24
Add deposit in transit		4,710.56
Balance per books (correct balance)		$30,200.80

CHEQUE REGISTER–JUNE

Date	Payee	No.	Invoice Amount	Discount	Cash
June 1	Bren Mfg.	6141	$ 237.50		$ 237.50
1	Stempy Mfg.	6142	915.00	$ 9.15	905.85
8	Regent Co., Inc.	6143	122.90	2.45	120.45
9	Bren Mfg.	6144	306.40		306.40
10	Petty Cash	6145	89.93		89.93
17	Pretty Babies Photo	6146	706.00	14.12	691.88
22	Hey Dude Publishing	6147	447.50		447.50
23	Payroll Account	6148	4,130.00		4,130.00
25	Dragon Tools, Inc.	6149	390.75	3.91	386.84
28	Be Smart Construction	6151	2,250.00		2,250.00
29	M M T, Inc.	6152	750.00		750.00
30	Lasso Co.	6153	400.00	8.00	392.00
			$10,745.98	$37.63	$10,708.35

PROVINCIAL BANK
Bank Statement
General Chequing Account of Quartz Industries–June 2014

Date	Debits			Credits	Balance
					$30,928.46
June 1	$2,125.00	$ 237.50	$ 905.85	$4,710.56	32,370.67
12	932.65	120.45		1,507.06	32,824.63
23	1,420.00	447.50	306.40	1,458.55	32,109.28
26	4,130.00	11.05[a]			27,968.23
28	89.93	2,250.00	1,050.00[b]	4,157.48	28,735.78

[a]Bank service charges

[b]Bank debit memo for $1,050.00 for a customer's cheque returned and marked NSF was included with the June bank statement. Cash received on June 30 and put in the bank's night deposit box on the evening of June 30 was recorded by the bank in the general chequing account on July 2 for the amount of $4,607.96. Because the Cash account balance at June 30 is not given, it must be calculated based on other information in the problem.

Instructions

Prepare a bank reconciliation to the correct balance as at June 30, 2014, for Quartz Industries.

Cases

Refer to the Case Primer to help you answer these cases.

CA7-1   Hanley Limited manufactures camera equipment. The company plans to list its shares on the Venture Exchange. To do so, it must meet all of the following initial listing requirements (among others):

1. Net tangible assets must be at least $500,000.

2. Pre-tax earnings must be $50,000.

3. The company must have adequate working capital.

Ethics

Hanley has experienced significant growth in sales and is having difficulty estimating its bad debt expense. During the year, the sales team has been extending credit more aggressively in order to increase commission revenues. Under the percentage-of-receivables approach using past percentages, the estimate is $50,000. Hanley has performed an aging and estimates the bad debts at $57,000. Finally, using a percentage of sales, the expense is estimated at $67,000. Before booking the allowance, net tangible assets are approximately $550,000. The controller decides to accrue $50,000, which results in pre-tax earnings of $60,000.

Instructions

Adopt the role of the Venture Exchange staff and decide whether the company meets the financial aspects of the initial requirements for listing on the Venture Exchange.

CA7-2   TELUS Corporation is one of Canada's largest telecommunications companies and provides both products and services. Its shares are traded on the Toronto and New York stock exchanges. The credit facilities contain certain covenants relating to the amount of debt the company is allowed to hold.

**Real World
Emphasis**

The following are selected excerpts from the 2011 Annual Report:

Note 18 - SHORT-TERM BORROWINGS - Review of short-term borrowings and related disclosures

On July 26, 2002, TELUS subsidiary TELUS Communications Inc. (see Note 23(a)) entered into an agreement with an arm's-length securitization trust associated with a major Schedule I bank under which TELUS Communications Inc. is able to sell an interest in certain of its trade receivables up to a maximum of $500 million (December 31, 2010 – $500 million; January 1, 2010 – $500 million). This revolving-period securitization agreement's current term ends August 1, 2014. TELUS Communications Inc. is required to maintain at least a BBB (low) credit rating by Dominion Bond Rating Service or the securitization trust may require the sale program to be wound down prior to the end of the term.

When the Company sells its trade receivables, it retains reserve accounts, which are retained interests in the securitized trade receivables, and servicing rights. As at December 31, 2011, the Company had transferred, but continued to recognize, trade receivables of $456 million (December 31, 2010 – $465 million; January 1, 2010 – $598 million). Short-term borrowings of $400 million (December 31, 2010 – $400 million; January 1, 2010 – $500 million) are comprised of amounts loaned to the Company from the arm's-length securitization trust pursuant to the sale of trade receivables.

The balance of short-term borrowings (if any) comprised amounts drawn on the Company's bilateral bank facilities.

Note 25 – EXPLANATION OF TRANSITION TO IFRS-IASB

Previously, Canadian GAAP de-recognized trade receivables sold to the arm's-length securitization trust with which the Company transacts. IFRS-IASB does not de-recognize the trade receivables sold to the arm's-length securitization trust with which the Company transacts and considers the sale proceeds to be short-term borrowings of the Company.

Instructions

Adopt the role of the controller of TELUS and discuss the differing accounting treatment regarding the securitization transactions under IFRS and pre-changeover GAAP. (Since ASPE is very similar to pre-changeover GAAP for securitizations, use ASPE for the analysis.)

Integrated Cases

(Hint: If there are issues here that are new, use the conceptual framework to help you support your analysis with solid reasoning.)

IC7-1 Fritz's Furniture (FF) is a mid-sized owner-operated business that was started 25 years ago by Fred Fritz. The retail furniture business is cyclical, with business dropping off in times of economic downturn, as is the case currently. In order to encourage sales, the store offers its own credit cards to good customers. FF has run into a bit of a cash crunch and is planning to go to the bank to obtain an increase in its line of credit in order to replenish and expand the furniture stock. At present, the line of credit is limited to 70% of the credit card receivables and inventory. The receivables and inventory have been pledged as security for the loan.

Fred has identified two possible sources of the cash shortage: outstanding credit card receivables and a buildup in old inventory. He has come up with two strategies to deal with the problem:

1. Credit card receivables: For the existing receivables, Fred has found the company Factors Inc., which will buy the receivables for 93% of their face value. The two companies are currently negotiating the terms of the deal. So far, FF has agreed to transfer legal title to the receivables to Factors Inc., and FF will maintain and collect the receivables. The one term that is still being discussed is whether Factors Inc. will have any recourse to FF if the amounts become uncollectible.

2. Excess inventory: A new sales promotion has been advertised in the newspaper for the past two months. Under the terms of the promotion, customers do not pay anything up front and will be able to take the furniture home and begin payments the following year. Response to the advertisement has been very good and a significant amount of inventory has been moved to date, leaving room for new inventory once the bank financing comes through.

Instructions

Assume the role of FF's bookkeeper and advise Fred about the impact of the strategies on the company's financial reporting. The company follows ASPE.

IC7-2 Bowearth Limited (BL) is in the lumber business. The company sells pulp and paper products as well as timber and lumber. It has over 500,000 hectares of timberland that it either owns or leases. The company's shares trade on the public stock exchange. Net income for the past few years has been positive and increasing, and it has averaged approximately $1 million over the past five years. This year, however, due to various factors, the company is expecting to just break even.

During the year, BL announced an exclusive licensing agreement with Lindor Inc. (LI), an unrelated company. Under the terms of the agreement, BL will have exclusive sales and distribution rights for LI's technology and products. In return, it will pay LI royalties. The technology and products target the pulp and paper industry. During the first five years of the agreement, royalty payments that BL must pay to LI are 3% of sales in the first year, 2% in the second, and 1% thereafter. A minimum royalty of $500,000 must be paid regardless of the level of sales. LI has been in business many years and the technology is proven and in great demand. It is therefore very likely that BL will have to pay.

The U.S. government has recently levied anti-dumping fees of 8% on all softwood lumber shipped to the United States. Anti-dumping fees are levied on foreign imports that a government thinks are being sold below fair market value. The U.S. government has also imposed countervailing duties of 20% on Canadian lumber. Counterveiling duties are meant to counteract imported goods that are subsidized by their home countries. The amounts must be paid by the company to the U.S. government in order to continue to sell in the United States. The Canadian government has challenged the right of the U.S. government to charge these duties and has appealed to the World Trade Organization. Canada feels that under the North American Free Trade Agreement (NAFTA), such charges cannot be legally levied. In the meantime, BL has been accruing and setting the amounts aside in cash deposits with the bank just in case the appeal is unsuccessful. The amounts accrued and set aside to date are approximately $3 million. The U.S. government is continuing to allow the company to ship lumber as long as the cash is set aside in the bank. To date, the appeal process is going well and the Canadian government feels that the duties will at least be reduced significantly, if not completely eliminated. There are rumours that the duties may be cancelled next year.

In addition, BL is currently being sued by a former major shareholder for providing misleading financial statements. The lawsuit alleges that net income was materially misstated. The case has not yet gone to court. BL feels that the case is not very strong but has nonetheless fired the president, William Chesiuk, to be on the safe side. As a result, BL is also being sued for wrongful dismissal by its former president. Chesiuk is suing for a lost bonus of $300,000 as well as lost future income in the amount of $10 million. BL is investigating the claim of overstated net income and, to date, has not found anything that indicates a material misstatement.

BL's controller, Youssef Haddad, is unsure of how to book all of the above in the financial statements (or if he even should). He has a meeting with the bank next week to discuss increasing the company's line of credit. He is hopeful that once the ruling comes down from the World Trade Organization, the increased line of credit will not be needed. In the meantime, the bank has signalled that it will be looking at the company's liquidity very closely. The auditors will also be coming in to review the statements in the next month.

Instructions

Adopt the role of Youssef Haddad and discuss the financial reporting issues.

IC7-3 Creative Choice Corporation (CC) is a publicly traded company that has been providing traditional mortgage loans for the past 10 years. In an effort to grow its business, it has decided to build another 5 banking service locations across the country. The expected cost of construction is around $10 million. The company contracted to build the new banks requires a $2 million retainer upfront before it begins construction.

To accelerate cash flow, CC pooled outstanding mortgage loans for a value of $2 million and transferred them to a newly created special purpose entity (the trust). The trust in turn has sold mortgage-backed securities to third-party investors for cash. CC will continue to service and manage the mortgage receivables sold, including collecting the principal and interest payments from customers and remitting cash to the trust for payment to investors. An annual fee of $25,000 will be earned by CC for servicing and collecting the mortgage receivables. The fee will be paid as a reduction of the returns earned on the securities.

As part of the agreement, CC is still responsible to pay the full payment to investors even when a customer defaults on a mortgage payment. This recourse obligation, or the liability that CC may be at risk of incurring as a result of any mortgage payments not collected, has an estimated fair value of 2% of the mortgage receivables. This is based on CC's historical payment defaults. The majority of pooled mortgage receivables sold have adjustable rates after five years, meaning the interest rate charged on the mortgage may increase if there is an overall increase in interest rates.

At the beginning of the year, CC loaned $133,500 to a smaller independent bank in exchange for a two-year, $150,000 non–interest-bearing note. The note's present value is $133,500. CC has recorded the note receivable at $150,000. No interest has been recorded in relation to the note receivable.

In the last quarter, customer defaults have increased by 1%. Interest rates are expected to increase by 1 percentage point over the next quarter. As a result, CC expects a further increase of 1% in defaults next quarter.

An excerpt of the note for the mortgage receivables is provided below.

Mortgage Loans (pooled and sold)	$ 2,000,000
Mortgage Loans, net of allowance	45,700,000
Mortgage servicing asset	0
Accrued interest receivable	15,000

CC uses credit lines from a larger independent bank to finance the majority of its mortgage lending practice. Given the recent changes in economic conditions, the bank has been monitoring CC's liquidity. As such, CC is subject to certain covenants including a debt to equity ratio of no more than 2 to 1. Prior to pooling the mortgage receivables the debt to equity ratio was 1.8 to 1. The majority of mortgage loans that remain on the balance sheet have also been pledged as collateral to the bank.

Instructions

It is now the week after month end and you are reviewing the current-year results. Assume the role of the controller and discuss the financial reporting issues. Provide journal entries when appropriate.

Writing Assignments

WA7-1   The trial balance of Imotex Ltd. contains the following accounts:

1. Accounts receivable, trade

2. Accounts receivable, related company

3. Accounts receivable, to be exchanged for shares in another company

4. Note receivable, receivable in grams of a precious metal

5. Cash

6. Investment in Royal Bank common shares (long-term investment)

7. Income taxes receivable

8. Interest rate swap: contract to receive fixed rate (at 8%) and to pay variable rate (current rates are 6%) on debenture debt

9. U.S. dollar cash holdings in a U.S. subsidiary's bank account

Instructions

For 1 to 9, indicate whether the item is or is not a financial asset. Give an explanation for each of your choices.

WA7-2   IFRS provides guidance on impairment testing—in particular, what is supportable evidence of impairment of loans and receivables.

Instructions

Read IAS 39, paragraphs 58 to 64, and answer the following questions.

(a) When is a financial asset tested for impairment?

(b) What are examples of "objective evidence" that might indicate impairment?

(c) What evidence, by itself, does not indicate impairment?

(d) Are loans and receivables treated individually or as a group?

WA7-3   Soon after beginning the year-end audit work on March 10 for the 2014 year end at Arkin Corp., the auditor has the following conversation with the controller:

Controller: The year ending March 31, 2014, should be our most profitable in history and, because of this, the board of directors has just awarded the officers generous bonuses.

Auditor: I thought profits were down this year in the industry, at least according to your latest interim report.

Controller: Well, they were down, but 10 days ago we closed a deal that will give us a substantial increase for the year.

Auditor: Oh, what was it?

Controller: Well, you remember a few years ago our former president bought shares of Hi-Tek Enterprises Ltd. Because he had those grandiose ideas about becoming a conglomerate? They cost us $3 million, which is the current carrying amount. On March 1, 2014, we sold the shares to Campbell Inc., an unrelated party, for $4 million. So, we'll have a gain of $686,000, which results from $1 million pre-tax minus a commission of $20,000 for legal fees and taxes at 30%. This should increase our net income for the year to $5.2 million, compared with last year's $4.8 million. The transaction fees were higher than normal due to the setting up of the note receivable. As far as I know, we'll be the only company in the industry to register an increase in net income this year. That should help the market value of our shares!

Auditor: Do you expect to receive the $4 million in cash by March 31, your fiscal year end?

Controller: No. Although Campbell Inc. is an excellent company, they're a little tight for cash because of their rapid growth. We have a $4-million non–interest-bearing note with $400,000 due each year for the next 10 years, which Campbell signed. The first payment is due March 1 of next year and future payments are due on the same date every year thereafter.

Auditor: Why is the note non–interest-bearing? I thought the market rate of interest was closer to 8%?

Controller: Because that's what everybody agreed to. Since we don't have any interest-bearing debt, the funds invested in the note don't cost us anything, and we weren't getting any dividends on the Hi-Tek shares.

Instructions

Prepare the auditor's written report to the controller on how this transaction should be accounted for, and how any corrections that are necessary will affect the reported results for the current year ending March 31, assuming that the company reports under IFRS. Make assumptions where required and make the appropriate journal entries at March 1 and March 31, 2014. What is the revised net income for the company for the year ending March 31? What changes would be necessary if the company reported under ASPE? (Assume that Arkin records the investment in Hi-Tek as an FV-NI Investment under both IFRS and ASPE, and that in all prior years fair value equalled cost).

Ethics

WA7-4   Rudolph Corp. is a subsidiary of Huntley Corp. The ethical accountant, working as Rudolph's controller, believes that the yearly charge for doubtful accounts for Rudolph should be 2% of net credit sales. The president, nervous that the parent company might expect the subsidiary to sustain its 10% growth rate, suggests that the controller increase the charge for doubtful accounts to 3% yearly. The supervisor thinks that the lower net income, which reflects a 6% growth rate, will be a more sustainable rate for Rudolph.

Instructions

(a) Should the controller be concerned with Rudolph Corp.'s growth rate in estimating the allowance? Explain.

(b) Does the president's request pose an ethical dilemma for the controller? Why or why not?

WA7-5   Who would have thought that musicians David Bowie and James Brown had anything to do with accounting? Asset- or artist-backed financing vehicles have been used by these performers and others as a means of securitizing royalties and rights to other intellectual property.

Instructions

Perform an Internet search on "Bowie bonds" or on David Pullman, who created them. Write a brief report explaining how this securitization works and what similarities it has to accounts receivable securitization.

WA7-6   Write a brief essay highlighting the differences between IFRS and ASPE noted in this chapter, discussing the conceptual justification for each.

RESEARCH AND FINANCIAL ANALYSIS

RA7-1 Maple Leaf Foods Inc.

Access the annual financial statements for **Maple Leaf Foods Inc.** for the year ended December 31, 2011. These statements are available from the company's website or from SEDAR (www.sedar.com).

Instructions

(a) Explain the securitization that the company is involved in (see Note 4).

(b) Calculate the accounts receivable turnover for 2011 and 2010 and the average age of the accounts receivable at December 31, 2011, and 2010, without taking the additional securitized receivables into account. Comment on your results. For the calculation of average age, use the closing balance of accounts receivable in the formula:

$$(\text{Year-end accounts receivable} / \text{sales}) \times 365$$

(c) Calculate the percentage growth in sales and accounts receivable in 2011 and 2010 without taking the securitized receivables into account. Comment on your results.

(d) Explain how the securitized receivables should be taken into account in the calculations in (a) and (b) above, or not taken into account at all. Recalculate your ratios and percentages. Did the securitizations have an effect on your assessment of the company? Explain.

RA7-2 Canadian Tire Corporation, Limited

Canadian Tire Corporation, Limited is one of Canada's best-known retailers. The company operates 488 "hard-goods" retail stores through associate dealers, and a total of 385 corporate and franchise stores under its subsidiary Mark's Work Wearhouse, and has almost 290 independently operated gasoline sites and 87 PartSource stores. It offers financial services through its branded credit cards and now provides personal loans and a variety of insurance and warranty products.

Instructions

Access the financial statements of Canadian Tire Corporation, Limited for its year ended December 31, 2011, either on the company's website or the SEDAR website (www.sedar.com). Refer to these financial statements and their accompanying notes to answer the following questions.

(a) How does Canadian Tire define cash and cash equivalents on its statement of financial position?

(b) What criteria does the company use to determine what short-term investments to include in this category?

(c) Review the financial statements and notes and identify the assets reported by Canadian Tire that qualify as loans and receivables. Does the company disclose the amount of its allowance for doubtful accounts? What was the amount of impairment for credit losses for the year? How does the company determine allowance for impairment? Be specific. What were the amounts for the writeoffs, recoveries, and impairment for credit losses for the year?

(d) When is a loan impaired? How is an impaired loan valued by Canadian Tire? Be specific.

(e) Accounting standards require companies to disclose information about their exposure to credit risk. What is credit risk? What does Canadian Tire report? What is your assessment of its exposure to credit risk?

(f) Canadian Tire uses its accounts receivable to generate cash before the receivables are due via securitization. Briefly describe the forms of "secuitization" activities that the company uses. Does Canadian Tire have a continuing relationship with the accounts? Is the accounting different under IFRS than it was prior to the adoption of IFRS for Canadian Tire?

RA7-3 Loblaw Companies Limited and Empire Company Limited

Real World Emphasis

Instructions

From SEDAR (www.sedar.com), or the company websites, access the financial statements of **Loblaw Companies Limited** for its year ended December 31, 2011, and of **Empire Company Limited** for its year ended May 5, 2012. Review the financial statements and answer the following questions.

(a) What businesses are the companies in?

(b) Compare how the two companies report cash and cash equivalents on the statement of financial position. What is included in the cash and cash equivalents of each and what are the amounts of these? Is any restricted cash reported by either company?

(c) What types of receivables do Loblaw and Empire have and what was the reported amount for each? How does each type of receivable arise? Which types are similar or different between the companies? How are the loans and receivables reported?

(d) Explain the type of credit risk that the companies have and how this risk is managed. What was the allowance for doubtful accounts at the end of year? What percentages of the accounts receivable were past due? How was the allowance for doubtful accounts determined for each company? How does the company test for impairment? What was the bad debts expense for the year? Is the allowance adequate?

(e) Does either company dispose of receivables before their due date to generate cash? Comment on how this is done and what the company has retained.

(f) Can an accounts receivable turnover ratio be determined for either company? Why or why not?

RA7-4 Research Case

The IASB issued the discussion paper "Preliminary Views on Financial Statement Presentation" in October 2008, which discusses the treatment of cash equivalents, among other things. This was followed up in July 2010 with a "Staff Draft of Exposure Draft IFRS X: Financial Statement Presentation."

Instructions

From the IASB website (www.ifrs.org), access the discussion paper and the staff draft of the exposure draft. Paragraph 3.14 of the discussion paper proposes that cash equivalents be "presented and classified in a manner similar to other short-term investments, not as part of cash." Similarly, paragraph 118 of the staff draft of the exposure draft on financial statement presentation suggests that cash should "not include short-term investments regardless of their liquidity or nearness to maturity." Why are cash equivalents currently grouped with cash on the statement of financial position? Why is the IASB proposing to segregate cash from cash equivalents? Do you agree or disagree with this proposed treatment? Why or why not?

ENDNOTES

[1] Based on *CICA Handbook–Accounting*, Part II, Section 3856 *Financial Instruments*. The IFRS definition in IAS 32 introduces additional complexity beyond the scope of this text related to when the entity enters into a contract that will be settled with its own shares. ASPE excludes from its definition the entity's costs of rights to reacquire its own equity instruments.

[2] Under IFRS, if current and non-current asset classifications are not used on the balance sheet, separate disclosure is required of the amounts to be recovered within 12 months and more than 12 months after the balance sheet date.

[3] *Accounting Series Release No. 148*, "Amendments to Regulations S-X and Related Interpretations and Guidelines Regarding the Disclosure of Compensating Balances and Short-Term Borrowing Arrangements," Securities and Exchange Commission, November 13, 1973.

[4] *CICA Handbook–Accounting*, Part II, Section 1540.06(b) and IAS 7.6. Copyright © 2012 IFRS Foundation. All rights reserved. Reproduced by Wiley Canada with the permission of the IFRS Foundation ®. No permission granted to third parties to reproduce or distribute.

[5] Some receivables are not financial assets. They are excluded when the claim does not result from a contractual commitment, such as income taxes receivable, which result from government legislation, or when the claim is not for cash or another financial asset.

[6] Receivables that are created by related party transactions may be an exception. Chapter 23 discusses the issues underlying related party transactions.

[7] Note that 18.25% is the stated annual rate. If the compounded, or effective, rate of interest is required, the following formula is used: Rate $= [1/(1 - .01)]^{365/(30-10)} - 1$. This results in an effective annual rate of 20.13%. See David B. Vicknair, "The Effective Annual Rate on Cash Discounts: A Clarification," *Journal of Accounting Education* 18 (2000), pp. 55–62.

[8] Present and future value tables are provided immediately following Chapter 12.

[9] William J. Vatter, *Managerial Accounting* (Englewood Cliffs, N.J.: Prentice-Hall, 1950), p. 60.

[10] Alternatively, the entries could initially recognize the note's maturity value in Notes Receivable and the discount in Discount on Notes Receivable, a contra account to Notes Receivable:

Feb. 23	Notes Receivable	5,000	
	Cash		4,717
	Discount on Notes Receivable		283
Nov. 23	Cash	5,000	
	Notes Receivable		5,000
	Discount on Notes Receivable	283	
	Interest Income		283

[11] Impairment of long-term loans is discussed in Chapter 9 along with the impairment of other financial asset investments.

[12] The **stated interest rate,** also referred to as the **face rate** or the **coupon rate,** is the rate that is part of the note contract. The **effective interest rate,** also referred to as the **market rate** or the **yield rate,** is the rate that is used in the market to determine the note's value; that is, the discount rate that is used to determine its present value.

[13] IFRS also allows a "fair value option" for loans and receivables in restricted circumstances and ASPE provides the same option for any financial instrument. These are explained in more detail in Chapter 9.

[14] There may be situations when the implicit interest rate is not the market rate; that is, when the fair value of the loan differs from the cash consideration. This circumstance is dealt with later in this chapter.

[15] Be alert to the fact that "n" equals the number of interest periods, **not one year,** and that "i" is the interest rate **for the period defined by** n. If interest were paid semi-annually in this example, n would be 6, not 3, and i would be 6%, not 12%, and these would be used to discount both the maturity amount **and** the interest flows. The interest cash flow used in the present value calculation would be $500, not $1,000.

[16] Credit enhancements include guaranteeing payment through recourse to the company selling the receivables or third-party guarantee provisions, the use of cash reserve accounts, or overcollateralization (providing security with a greater fair value than the amount that is at risk).

[17] In 2009, the IASB fast-tracked a replacement standard for IAS 39 *Financial Instruments—Recognition and Measurement*. This included the adoption of IFRS 9 to reduce the number of classifications and accounting methods for financial assets. In June 2010 the IASB decided to retain the existing requirements from IAS 39 for the derecognition of financial assets and financial liabilities, while

improving related disclosure requirements. (The original requirements for derecognition were carried forward from IAS 39 to IFRS 9.) For further discussion of the status of expected changes to IFRS, see Learning Objective 10.

[18] Recourse is defined as "the right of a transferee of receivables to receive payment from the transferor of those receivables for failure of debtors to pay when due, the effects of prepayments, or adjustments resulting from defects in the eligibility of the transferred receivables" (*CICA Handbook–Accounting*, Part II, Section 3856 *Financial Instruments*, Appendix B, Transfers of Receivables).

[19] Often the receivables turnover is converted to "days to collect accounts receivable" or "days sales outstanding"; that is, to an average collection period. In this case, 7.7 is divided into 365 days to obtain 47.4 days. Several figures other than 365 could be used here; a common alternative is 360 days because it is divisible by 30 (days) and 12 (months). Please use 365 days in any assignment calculations.

[20] Recall from the earnings management discussion in Chapter 4 that increasing or decreasing income through management manipulation reduces the quality of financial reports.

[21] Use of paper cheques continues to be a popular means of payment. However, easy access to desktop publishing software and hardware has created new opportunities for cheque fraud in the form of duplicate, altered, or forged cheques. At the same time, new fraud-fighting technologies, such as ultraviolet imaging, high-capacity bar codes, and biometrics are being developed. These technologies convert paper documents into document files that are processed electronically, thereby reducing the risk of fraud.

Sales Signals

TECHNOLOGIES SUCH AS barcode scanners at checkouts and electronic security tags have drastically changed retail operations in the last two decades. Now, more retailers are using radio-frequency identification (RFID), which involves putting special tags on merchandise with antennas and computer chips that track their movement through radio signals.

RFID began as a way to speed up inventory counting. "Counting inventory is something that retailers used to do once or twice a year because it was so laborious," says Bill Hardgrave, former director of the University of Arkansas's RFID research laboratory and now dean of the College of Business at Auburn University in Alabama. Because at least two people must be physically present to count inventory, it's also expensive, costing some large department stores millions of dollars every year. Inventory was usually counted just for accounting purposes, so companies could assign a value to what they had on hand at year end.

RFID makes it easier for retailers to switch to a perpetual inventory system, since the tags can keep a constant count of items. It's also transforming inventory cost formulas, helping stores move to a specific identification method for goods that typically had to be valued based on their average cost. With an RFID tag, "every single item has a unique identifier. Now when I sell this pair of jeans, I can see I paid $8 for this pair and sold it for $20," Dr. Hardgrave says. "I know my precise profit for that item. We've never, ever been able to do that before."

RFID goes "way beyond" its initial use as an accounting tool, Dr. Hardgrave says. Whereas traditional inventory counting can be less than 50% accurate, RFID can increase inventory accuracy to over 95%, which significantly reduces stockouts (what happens when an item runs out of stock). It's estimated that retailers typically lose about 4% of their sales each year to stockouts. RFID also reduces the carrying costs of having too much inventory. "Inventory accuracy is the silver bullet for retailers," says Dr. Hardgrave. RFID also helps retailers locate products on shelves, in the backroom, and in warehouses.

What's next for RFID? It's expected that more manufacturers will tag their items so retailers won't have to. The technology will extend to canned food as the metal tins become antennas to transmit signals. RFID will help improve food safety and quality. And retailers will use RFID data to learn more about consumers' buying habits to enhance their shopping experience. "That's the next big thing in retail," Dr. Hardgrave says.

CHAPTER

8 | Inventory

LEARNING OBJECTIVES

After studying this chapter, you should be able to:

1. Understand inventory from a business perspective.

2. Define inventory from an accounting perspective.

3. Identify which inventory items should be included in ending inventory.

4. Identify the effects of inventory errors on the financial statements and adjust for them.

5. Determine the components of inventory cost.

6. Distinguish between perpetual and periodic inventory systems and account for them.

7. Identify and apply GAAP cost formula options and indicate when each cost formula is appropriate.

8. Explain why inventory is measured at the lower of cost and market, and apply the lower of cost and net realizable value standard.

9. Identify inventories that are or may be valued at amounts other than the lower of cost and net realizable value.

10. Apply the gross profit method of estimating inventory.

11. Identify how inventory should be presented and the type of inventory disclosures required by ASPE and IFRS.

12. Explain how inventory analysis provides useful information and apply ratio analysis to inventory.

13. Identify differences in accounting between ASPE and IFRS, and what changes are expected in the near future.

After studying Appendices 8A and 8B, you should be able to:

14. Apply the retail method of estimating inventory.

15. Identify other primary sources of GAAP for inventory.

This chapter introduces the basic issues related to the recognition, measurement, and reporting of inventory on the statement of financial position and income statement. Appendix 8A explains how to determine inventory cost using the retail inventory method. Accounting for long-term construction contract inventories, a closely related topic, was examined in Chapter 6.

The chapter is organized as follows:

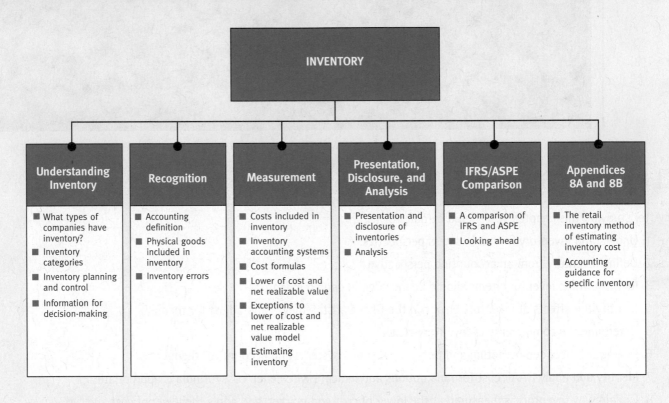

INVENTORY					
Understanding Inventory	**Recognition**	**Measurement**	**Presentation, Disclosure, and Analysis**	**IFRS/ASPE Comparison**	**Appendices 8A and 8B**
■ What types of companies have inventory? ■ Inventory categories ■ Inventory planning and control ■ Information for decision-making	■ Accounting definition ■ Physical goods included in inventory ■ Inventory errors	■ Costs included in inventory ■ Inventory accounting systems ■ Cost formulas ■ Lower of cost and net realizable value ■ Exceptions to lower of cost and net realizable value model ■ Estimating inventory	■ Presentation and disclosure of inventories ■ Analysis	■ A comparison of IFRS and ASPE ■ Looking ahead	■ The retail inventory method of estimating inventory cost ■ Accounting guidance for specific inventory

UNDERSTANDING INVENTORY

Objective 1
Understand inventory from a business perspective.

It is important to understand the business of the company before thinking about issues relating to inventory. What types of companies carry significant amounts of inventory? What are the different types of inventory? What aspects of inventory must be managed and how is this done? Finally, what information do financial statement users need? These questions will be addressed below.

Underlying Concept

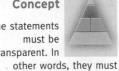

The statements must be transparent. In other words, they must represent the underlying business. Therefore, accountants need to understand a company's underlying business model.

What Types of Companies Have Inventory?

As a general rule, companies in industries such as manufacturing, retail, and wholesale often have a significant amount of inventories. For instance, **European Aeronautic Defence and Space Company EADS N.V.** ("EADS") manufactures commercial aircraft, civil and military helicopters, commercial space launch vehicles, missiles, military aircraft, satellites, defence systems, and defence electronics. Inventories make up approximately 25% of its total assets. Similarly, **Shoppers Drug Mart Corporation** operates full-service

Real World Emphasis

drug stores across Canada (through its associate-owners). Inventories make up approximately 27% of its total assets.

Some companies, such as **Dell Inc.**, follow a strategy of producing inventories on a "just-in-time" basis. This means they wait until a customer orders a product and then they arrange with other companies to actually manufacture the product. Thus their inventories are only about 3% of total assets.

Inventory Categories

Real World Emphasis

Retailers and wholesalers have inventory that is ready for sale. For instance, **RONA Inc.**, a major Canadian distributor and retailer of hardware, home renovation, and garden products, reported over $840 million of inventory at the end of 2011. This accounted for 30% of total assets. Like other **merchandising concerns**, RONA purchases most of its merchandise in a form that is ready for sale, and unsold units left on hand at each reporting date are usually referred to as **merchandise inventory**.

Manufacturing companies, on the other hand, have inventories in various states of completion. **Potash Corporation of Saskatchewan Inc.**, one of Canada's most profitable companies, is an integrated fertilizer and related industrial and feed products company. It is a manufacturer. At December 31, 2011, Potash Corporation reported inventories amounting to 30.4% of its current assets. Although the products manufacturers produce can be quite different, they normally have three types of inventory accounts: Raw Materials, Work in Process, and Finished Goods. Amounts for goods and materials that are on hand but have not yet gone into production are reported as **raw materials inventory**. Raw materials include the wood to make a baseball bat, for example, or the steel to make a car. These materials can be traced directly to the end product. At any point in a continuous production process, some units are not completely processed. The cost of the raw material on which production has started but is not yet complete, plus the direct labour cost applied specifically to this material and its applicable share of manufacturing overhead costs, make up the **work-in-process inventory**. The costs associated with the completed but still unsold units on hand are reported as **finished goods inventory**. Finished goods made up 47.7% of the total inventory for Potash Corporation as at December 31, 2010.

Inventory Planning and Control

How much and what types of inventories should be on hand and how does a company control inventories so that it can maximize profits? For many reasons, management is vitally interested in inventory planning and control.

Inventory management is a double-edged sword. On the one hand, management wants to have a wide variety and sufficient quantities on hand so that customers have the greatest selection and always find what they want in stock. On the other hand, such a policy may result in excessive carrying costs (for example, in investment, storage, insurance, taxes, obsolescence, risk of theft, and damage). The higher the levels of inventories held, the higher the costs of looking after them. For instance, most companies that sell in retail markets have a significant risk of theft and so must incur costs to reduce this risk, such as insurance and theft deterrent equipment. Low inventory levels generally have lower carrying costs, but this may lead to running out of specific products (called stockouts), lost sales, and unhappy customers.

Inefficient purchasing procedures, faulty manufacturing techniques, or inadequate sales efforts may leave management with excessive and unusable inventories. All of this reduces profits.

Companies must therefore monitor inventory levels carefully to:

• minimize carrying costs, and

• meet customer demands.

Whether a company manufactures or merchandises goods, it needs an accurate accounting system with up-to-date records.

As noted above, companies must monitor the quantity and quality of inventories on hand. **Eli Lilly and Company** actually goes one step further and also monitors inventory levels of its wholesale customers for significant products that it supplies. The company develops, manufactures, and distributes drugs, primarily through wholesalers or major retail chains. According to the company's annual report, Eli Lilly's management tries to keep wholesaler inventory levels at an average of one month's supply. They monitor unusual wholesaler buying patterns to determine the impact on future sales and demand for product. The company notes that the production processes are complex and highly regulated, varying from product to product. Unusual demand could result in an interruption of supply, which is undesirable. It could also signal potential problems with a drug (if there is a significant decrease in demand, for instance).

Information for Decision-Making

Just as management is interested in monitoring and controlling inventory, users of financial statements such as creditors and investors are also interested in this information. While management has access to all types of information regarding inventory that is generated by internal management information systems, external users of financial statements often look to the statements as a significant source of information. Therefore, they also want to know how management is controlling and managing its inventory in order to maximize profits. Information about inventory must therefore be presented so that it is transparent to the nature of the business. The **existence** of various types of inventory that the company owns must be clearly represented and information as to **how this inventory has been measured** must also be disclosed. The rest of the chapter will look at how inventory is accounted for, including how it is recognized, measured, presented, and disclosed in the statements.

Because the goods that are sold or used during an accounting period almost never correspond exactly with the goods that were bought or produced during that period, the physical inventory of items either increases or decreases. In addition, the cost of the number of items could be higher or lower at the end of the period than at the beginning. The cost of all the goods that are available for sale or use has to be allocated between the goods that were sold or used and those that are still on hand. The **cost of goods available for sale or use** is the total of (1) the cost of the goods on hand at the beginning of the period and (2) the cost of the goods acquired or produced during the period. The **cost of goods sold** is the difference between those available for sale during the period and those on hand at the end of the period, as shown in Illustration 8-1.

Illustration 8-1

Calculation of Cost of Goods Sold

Beginning inventory, Jan. 1	$100,000
Cost of goods acquired or produced during the year	800,000
Total cost of goods available for sale	**900,000**
Ending inventory, Dec. 31	200,000
Cost of goods sold during the year	**$700,000**

Calculating the cost of ending inventory takes several steps. It can be a complex process that requires answers to each of the following questions:

1. **Which physical goods should be included as part of inventory?** Who owns inventory still in transit at the statement of financial position (SFP) date, or inventory on consignment? What about inventory under special sales agreements?

2. **What costs should be included as part of inventory cost?** Consider purchase discounts and vendor rebates, product versus period costs, capacity considerations in allocating overhead, and standard costs.

3. **What cost formula should be used?** Consider specific identification, average cost, or FIFO.

Determining the final value that should be reported on the statement of financial position requires one additional question to be answered:

4. **Has there been an impairment in value of any of the inventory items?** Inventory cannot be reported on the statement of financial position at more than the net cash amount that is expected to be recovered from its sale or use.

We will now explore these and other basic issues one at a time.

RECOGNITION

Which items should be recognized as inventory in the financial statements and at what point should they be recognized? In order to make this decision, we need to have a common understanding of what inventory is.

Inventory comes in many forms. Securities held by an investment dealer, land and other property held by developers for resale, unbilled employee and partner time spent on client files in a law office or professional accounting practice, grain in silos, salmon in a fish farming operation, and long-term construction projects are all items of inventory. Some of these are not covered by the basic accounting standards for inventories: *CICA Handbook* Section 3031 under ASPE or IAS 2 under IFRS. These standards exclude some inventories entirely, and exclude others from only the measurement requirements of the standards.

In general, inventories of financial instruments, construction in progress, biological assets and agricultural products, mineral products, and inventories held by producers of agricultural and forest producers and by commodity broker-traders may have special requirements. Appendix 8B summarizes where the accounting guidance is found for these forms of inventory.

Accounting Definition

Objective 2
Define inventory from an accounting perspective.

For accounting purposes, **inventories** are defined as:

"assets

(a) held for sale in the ordinary course of business;

(b) in the process of production for such sale; or

(c) in the form of materials or supplies to be consumed in the production process or in the rendering of services."[1]

Recall the definition of an asset as previously discussed in Chapter 2. As assets, inventories represent a **future benefit**, which the entity has **control over or access to**. The inventory purchase is the **transaction** that gives rise to the recognition of an inventory asset.

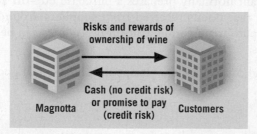

An inventory purchase is the opposite side of a sales transaction. The diagram here was taken from Chapter 6 and was used there to illustrate a basic sale of wine transaction.

Just as accountants recognize a sale when the risks and rewards of ownership are passed to the purchaser, the purchaser can use the same "risks and rewards" test to determine when the inventory should be recognized. Once the risks and rewards pass, the inventory meets the definition of an asset for the purchaser (it is no longer an asset for the vendor). Recall Illustration 6-3 from

Chapter 6, which lists the risk and rewards of ownership for wine. This has been reproduced below in Illustration 8-2.

Risks	Rewards
— wine will age poorly and therefore decline in value — wine will be stolen/vandalized — wine will be stored improperly	— wine will age well and appreciate in value — wine can be consumed by owner or buyer — wine inventory may be used as collateral for bank loan — wine may be sold for cash

Physical Goods Included in Inventory

Objective 3
Identify which inventory items should be included in ending inventory.

When substantially all risks and rewards of ownership have passed to the purchaser, inventory is recognized. Legal title and possession help make this determination. Usually purchased goods would be included as inventory when legal title passes. In practice, however, acquisitions are often recorded when the goods are received (possession) because it may be difficult for the buyer to identify the exact time when the legal title passes to the buyer for every purchase. At the point when the goods are received, the entity has control over and access to the future benefits. As a general rule, legal title has often passed by then as well.

Both legal title and possession are important factors as they give rise to risks and rewards. For instance, possession allows the owner to use the inventory and legal title allows the owner to sell the inventory or pledge it to obtain a loan. It is important to use professional judgement to decide when the inventory should be recognized as an asset, since legal title and possession do not always pass to the purchaser at the same time. Let's analyze some specific transactions in a little more detail.

Goods in Transit

Law

Underlying Concept

It is important to look at the terms of the transaction to identify when legal title passes. If there is some doubt about whether or not title has passed, in coming to a conclusion, the accountant considers other evidence, such as the sales agreement's intent, past transactions, the policies of the parties involved, and industry practices.

Sometimes purchased goods are in transit—that is, not yet received—at the end of a fiscal period. Although the company does not yet have possession, we may look to the legal title to determine whether the goods should be recognized as inventory. The legal title is determined by the shipping terms that have been agreed upon between the buyer and the seller. If the goods are shipped **FOB shipping point**, the legal title passes to the buyer when the seller delivers the goods to the common carrier (transporter), who then acts as an agent for the buyer. (The abbreviation "FOB" stands for "free on board.") If the goods are shipped **FOB destination**, legal title passes when the goods reach the destination. "Shipping point" and "destination" are often indicated by naming a specific location; for example, FOB Regina.[2] Once legal title passes, it is argued that the purchaser has the risks of ownership. For instance, if something happened to the inventory while in transit for goods shipped FOB shipping point, it would be the purchaser's loss.

Goods in transit at the end of a fiscal period that were sent FOB shipping point are recorded by the buyer as purchases of the period and should be included in ending inventory. If these purchases are not recognized, the result is **understated** inventories and accounts payable in the statement of financial position and **understated** purchases and ending inventories when calculating the cost of goods sold for the income statement.

The accountant normally prepares a purchase **cut-off schedule** for the end of a period to ensure that goods received from suppliers around the end of the year are recorded in the appropriate period. Cut-off procedures can be extensive and include the following controls:

• Curtailing and controlling the receipt and shipment of goods around the time of the count

- Marking freight and shipping documents as "before" and "after" the inventory count
- Ensuring that receiving reports on goods received before the count are linked to invoices that are also recorded in the same period

Because goods that are bought FOB shipping point may still be in transit when a period ends, the cut-off schedule is not completed until a few days after the period's end since this gives time for goods in transit at year end to be received.

Consigned Goods

Accounting for the sale of consigned goods was covered in Chapter 6. In terms of accounting for inventory, it is important to recognize that goods out on consignment remain the consignor's property. They are included in the consignor's inventory at their purchase price or production cost plus the cost of handling and shipping the goods to the consignee. In this case, even though possession rests with the consignee, legal title is held by the consignor. The consignor essentially has the risks and rewards of ownership. For instance, if the inventory becomes obsolete while held by the consignee, it is the consignor that suffers the loss. When the consignee sells the **consigned goods**, the revenue, less a selling commission and expenses incurred in accomplishing the sale, is remitted to the consignor.

Occasionally, the inventory out on consignment is shown as a separate item or there are additional disclosures in the notes, but unless the amount is large, there is little need for this. For the consignee, no entry is made to adjust its Inventory account for the goods it received, because the goods remain the consignor's property. In addition, the consignee should be extremely careful not to include any consigned goods in its inventory count.

Sales with Buyback Agreements

Sometimes an enterprise uses its inventory to obtain financing without reporting either the liability or the inventory on its SFP. This approach—often referred to as a product financing arrangement—usually involves a transfer of the inventory with either a real or

EXAMPLE 1

Company A needs financing but is unable to borrow funds from traditional sources (such as the bank) because the bank believes the loan would be too risky. The company therefore enters into an agreement with Company B to obtain the funds. A's inventory is used to support the value of the loan and legal title is transferred to B. At the same time, both parties agree to transfer the same inventory back to A at the end of 30 days for $1,010.

Note that the risks and rewards have not transferred in this example when you look at two transactions as one (even though the legal title and possession are transferred in the first part of the transaction). To illustrate, if the value of the inventory declines over the 30-day period, Company A still has to pay $1,010 to buy it back. Company A therefore retains the risk that the inventory will decline in value. (This is sometimes referred to as **price risk**.)

implied "buyback" agreement. Under the terms of these types of arrangements, the purchaser agrees to buy the inventory and then sell it back later to the same supplier. These are sometimes called "parking transactions" because the seller simply "parks" the inventory on another company's statement of financial position for a short period of time, agreeing to repurchase it in the future. **If the risks and rewards of ownership have not been transferred, the inventory should remain on the seller's books.**

Sales with High Rates of Return

There are often formal or informal agreements in such industries as book and magazine publishing, music, toys, and sporting goods that allow a buyer to return inventory for a full or partial refund. Essentially, the vendor retains the risks and rewards for those items expected to be returned. This does not necessarily prevent the vendor from recognizing a sale nor the purchaser from recognizing the inventory as an asset. **If a reasonable prediction of the returns can be established**, then the goods may be considered sold by the vendor and **an allowance for returns should be estimated and recognized.**

Conversely, if the returns are unpredictable, the sale is not recognized and the goods are not removed from the Inventory account. In this case, because the company is unable to determine which inventory will be returned, or how much, it cannot conclude that the risks and rewards have been passed on to the purchaser. Note disclosure would be important in this case.

Sales with Delayed Payment Terms

Underlying Concept

Revenues should be recognized in this situation because they have been earned and are reasonably estimable. Substantially all risks and rewards of ownership have been transferred. Collection is not the most critical event and bad debts can be reasonably estimated. The purchaser recognizes the inventory as an asset.

Because the risk of loss due to uncollectible accounts is higher in delayed payment sales than in other sales transactions, the seller often retains legal title to the merchandise until all payments have been received. Should the inventory be considered sold, even though legal title has not passed? If the risk of loss due to failure to collect (that is, the bad debts) **can be reasonably estimated and therefore accrued**, then the answer is yes—the sale is recorded and the goods are removed from the seller's inventory.

Purchase Commitments

In many lines of business, it is common for a company to agree to buy inventory weeks, months, or even years in advance. Such arrangements may be made based on either estimated or firm sales commitments from the company's customers. Generally, title to the merchandise or materials described in these **purchase commitments** does not pass to the buyer until delivery. Indeed, when the commitment is made, the goods may exist only as natural resources or, in the case of commodities, as unplanted seed, or in the case of a product, as work in process.

Ordinary orders, where the prices are determined at the time of shipment and **the buyer or seller can still cancel the order**, do not represent either an asset or a liability to the buyer. They are therefore not recorded in the books or reported in the financial statements.

Even with formal, **non-cancellable purchase contracts**, no asset or liability is recognized on the date when the contract takes effect, because it is an **executory contract**. In other words, neither party has performed (or fulfilled) its part of the contract.[3] However, if the amounts are abnormal in relation to the entity's normal business operations or financial position, the contract details should be disclosed in the notes to the buyer's financial statements. This is shown in Illustration 8-3 for **Cameco Corporation**, a Canadian-based uranium producer, in its 2010 financial statements.

If the unavoidable costs of completing the contract are higher than the benefits expected from receiving contracted goods or services, a loss provision is recognized according to IAS 37 *Provisions, Contingent Liabilities, and Contingent Assets*. This is known as

Illustration 8-3

*Disclosure of Purchase
Commitments—Cameco
Corporation*

24. Commitments and Contingencies

(f) At December 31, 2010, Cameco's purchase commitments, the majority of which are fixed price uranium and conversion purchase arrangements, were as follows:

	(Millions (US))
2011	$267
2012	226
2013	397
2014	114
2015	60
Thereafter	6
Total	**$1,070**

an **onerous contract**. Although ASPE has no similar requirement, Canadian practice has historically been to recognize the loss and liability as well. Under ASPE, if the loss was likely and measurable, the loss would be recognized.

EXAMPLE 2

Company A signs purchase contracts in 2013. Under the terms of the contract, Company A will take delivery of the inventory in 2014 and pay a price of $640,000 to Company B. The fair value of the inventory at the company's December 31, 2013 year end is $500,000. Company A does not expect to be able to recover its additional costs. Assume that the fair value remains at $500,000 until the goods are delivered.

Upfront, in 2013:

No exchange. Terms of agreement are finalized and contract may be signed.

In 2014:

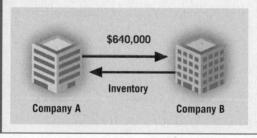

The following entry is made on December 31, 2013:

A = L + SE
  +140,000 −140,000

Cash flows: No effect

Loss on Purchase Contracts	140,000	
Liability for Onerous Contracts		140,000

When the goods are delivered in 2014, the entry is:

A = L + SE
+500,000 +500,000

Cash flows: No effect

Inventory	500,000	
Liability for Onerous Contracts	140,000	
Accounts Payable		640,000

If the price has partially or fully recovered before the inventory is received, the Liability for Onerous Contracts amount is reduced. A resulting gain (Recovery of Loss) is

Underlying Concept

Reporting the loss reflects the risks associated with locking into the contract at a fixed price in advance. However, reporting the decline in market price is debatable because no asset is recorded and the accrued liability on purchase contracts is not a present obligation. If the fair value changes again, the value might recover before the purchase takes place. This area demonstrates the need for good definitions of assets and liabilities.

then reported in the period of the price increase for the amount of the partial or full recovery. This accounting treatment is very similar to recognizing an impairment in inventory value by recording inventories at the lower of cost and net realizable value.

Accounting for purchase commitments (indeed, for all commitments) is unsettled and controversial. Some argue that these contracts should be reported as assets and liabilities when the contract is signed; others believe that recognition at the delivery date is more appropriate. As work proceeds on the IFRS conceptual framework, this debate is likely to be resolved.[4]

Summary of When to Recognize Inventory Based on Risks and Rewards

Illustration 8-4 summarizes various purchase transactions in terms of the risks and rewards test and inventory recognition. Note that in cases where the legal title is held by one party and the other party has possession, increased judgement is required to determine whether risks and rewards of ownership have passed. Even where the same party has legal title and possession, care should be taken to analyze the underlying substance of the transaction.

Transaction	Who has legal title?	Who has possession?	Have substantially all risks and rewards passed?	Who recognizes inventory?
Goods in transit shipped FOB shipping point	Purchaser	Shipping company	Yes	Purchaser
Consignment sale	Consignor	Consignee	No	Consignor
Sale with buyback (same goods, fixed buyback price that includes a charge for carrying costs)	Purchaser	Purchaser	No (where it is essentially a financing transaction)	Vendor
Sales with high rates of return where returns estimable	Purchaser	Purchaser	Yes	Purchaser
Sales with delayed payment terms where vendor retains title until consideration collected (bad debts are estimable)	Vendor	Purchaser	Yes	Purchaser
Purchase commitments (non-cancellable)	Vendor (assuming the inventory exists)	Vendor (assuming the inventory exists)	No but may have to accrue losses if onerous contract	Vendor (assuming the inventory exists)

Illustration 8-4

Determining When to Recognize Inventory Based on Risks and Rewards

Flow of Costs

As Illustration 8-5 shows, the flow of costs for merchandising and manufacturing companies is different. The **cost of goods manufactured** referred to in Illustration 8-5 represents the product costs of goods that are completed and transferred to Finished Goods Inventory. You are probably familiar with a statement of cost of goods manufactured that summarizes all the product costs incurred during the period that resulted in finished goods. (You may want to refer to a managerial accounting text for an example.) A cost of goods manufactured statement is far more detailed than information found in published financial statements. Note that **the cost of goods manufactured during the year is similar to the cost of goods purchased in a merchandising company**. Each is the source of the cost of goods available for sale in the period.

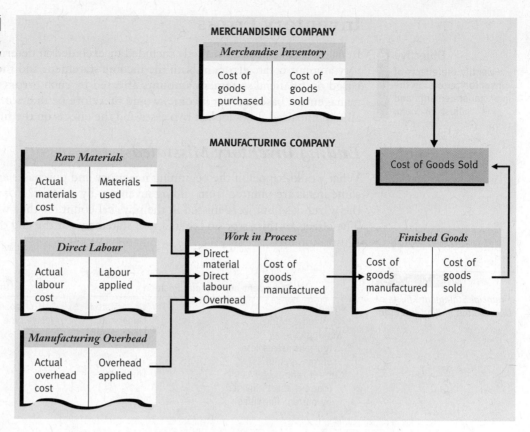

What Do the Numbers Mean?

Real World Emphasis

Before we move on to the next section, it is important to look at changing business models and how they might affect which assets are included in inventory on the statement of financial position. Consider **Indigo Books & Music Inc.** Indigo is the largest book retailer in Canada and operates under the names of Chapters, Indigo, World's Biggest Book Store, Coles, SmithBooks, as well as others. In 2009, the company launched a new business called Shortcovers. Shortcovers provided online access to books and other print materials. In December 2009, Indigo transferred the net assets of Shortcovers to a newly created company called Kobo Inc. Indigo described 2010 as a "tipping point," a year when reading digitally went mainstream. Indigo now had two quite differing business segments: one selling hard copy books and one selling online access to books.

While we would generally agree that the hard copy books are inventory to Indigo, what about the e-books? In essence Indigo is in the business of selling books, whether hard copies or e-books, so shouldn't they both appear as inventory on the balance sheet? Not necessarily. Selling access to an e-book represents a very different business model than selling an actual hard copy of a book. With paper books, the company has to purchase the books, merchandise them, and hopefully sell them. One might argue that it has the risks and rewards of ownership. In other words, if a book sells, the company profits, but if it does not sell, unless it can be returned to the publisher, the company suffers a loss. With an e-book, all the company needs is an agreement that allows it to sell or distribute access to the e-books. For this, the company likely earns some sort of percentage of the revenues. This relationship is more of an agency relationship: the company is acting as a selling agent and essentially earning a commission.

In November 2011, Indigo announced that it had entered a deal to sell Kobo to Rakuten Inc., a large Japanese e-commerce company. Indigo still sells Kobo e-reader devices as well as e-books. It will be interesting to see how Indigo's balance sheet changes as more and more e-books are sold instead of hard copy books.

Sources: Sunny Freeman, The Canadian Press, "Indigo Books and Music Sells Kobo Ereader to Rakuten in US$315 Million Deal," *Canadian Business*, November 8, 2011; Indigo Books & Music Inc., 2010-2011 annual report; and "Indigo Spins off Shortcovers to Launch Kobo," company news release, December 15, 2009.

Inventory Errors

Objective **4**
Identify the effects of
inventory errors on the
financial statements and
adjust for them.

Items that have been incorrectly included or excluded in determining the ending inventory amount create errors in both the income statement and the SFP. Decisions that are based on financial statement amounts affected by such errors (such as bonuses paid to management based on net income) would therefore be in error and comparability would also be impaired. Let's look at two cases and the effects on the financial statements.

Ending Inventory Misstated

What would happen if the beginning inventory and purchases are recorded correctly, but some items are omitted from ending inventory by mistake? For example, if items were in the warehouse but were missed in the physical count, or they were out on consignment? The effects of this error on the financial statements at the end of the period are shown in Illustration 8-6.

Illustration 8-6

*Financial Statement Effects of
Understated Ending Inventory*

Statement of Financial Position		Income Statement	
Inventory	Understated	Cost of goods sold	Overstated
Retained earnings	Understated	Net income	Understated
Working capital	Understated		
(current assets less current liabilities)			
Current ratio	Understated		
(current assets divided by current liabilities)			

Working capital and the current ratio are understated because a portion of the ending inventory is omitted. Net income is understated because cost of goods sold is overstated.

To illustrate the effect on net income over a two-year period, assume that the 2014 ending inventory of Wei Ltd. is understated by $10,000 and that all other items are stated correctly. The effect of this error is an understatement of net income in the current year and an overstatement of net income in the following year. The error affects the following year because the beginning inventory of that year is understated, which causes net income to be overstated. Both net income figures are misstated, but the total for the two years is correct as the two errors will be counterbalanced (or offset), as shown in Illustration 8-7.

**Underlying
Concept**

When inventory
is misstated, the
asset reported
lacks faithful representation.

Illustration 8-7

*Effect of Ending Inventory
Error on Two Periods*

	WEI LTD.			
	Incorrect Recording		Correct Recording	
	2014	2015	2014	2015
Revenues	$100,000	$100,000	$100,000	$100,000
Cost of goods sold				
Beginning inventory	25,000	20,000	25,000	30,000
Purchased or produced	45,000	60,000	45,000	60,000
Goods available for sale	70,000	80,000	70,000	90,000
Less: Ending inventory*	20,000	40,000	30,000	40,000
Cost of goods sold	50,000	40,000	40,000	50,000
Gross profit	50,000	60,000	60,000	50,000
Administrative and selling expenses	40,000	40,000	40,000	40,000
Net income	$ 10,000	$ 20,000	$ 20,000	$ 10,000
	Total income for two years = $30,000		Total income for two years = $30,000	

*Ending inventory understated by $10,000 in 2014; correct amount is $30,000.

If the error is discovered in 2014 just before the books are closed, the correcting entry in 2014 would be:

A   = L +   SE
+10,000   +10,000

Cash flows: No effect

Inventory	10,000	
Cost of Goods Sold		10,000

If the error is not discovered until 2015, after the books are closed for 2014, the correcting entry in 2015 would be:

A   = L +   SE
+10,000   +10,000

Cash flows: No effect

Inventory	10,000	
Retained Earnings		10,000

If the error is discovered after the books for 2015 are closed, **no entry is required as the error is self-correcting over the two-year period.** The inventory on the statement of financial position at the end of 2015 is correct, as is the total amount of retained earnings. **However, whenever comparative financial statements are prepared that include 2014 or 2015, the inventory and net income for those years are restated and reported at the correct figures.**

If ending inventory is **overstated** at the end of 2014, the reverse effect occurs. Inventory, working capital, current ratio, and net income are overstated and cost of goods sold is understated in 2014. The error's effect on net income will be counterbalanced in the next year, but both years' net income figures are incorrect, which distorts any analysis of trends in earnings and ratios.

Purchases and Inventory Misstated

Suppose that certain goods that the company owns are **not recorded as a purchase** and are **not counted in ending inventory.** Illustration 8-8 shows the effect on the financial statements, assuming this is a purchase on account.

Illustration 8-8

Financial Statement Effects of Understated Purchases and Inventory

Statement of Financial Position		Income Statement	
Inventory	Understated	Purchases	Understated
Retained earnings	No effect	Ending inventory	Understated
Accounts payable	Understated	Cost of goods sold	No effect
Working capital	No effect	Net income	No effect
Current ratio	Overstated		

Omitting both the purchase of goods and the inventory results in understated inventory and accounts payable on the statement of financial position, and understated purchases and ending inventory on the income statement. **Net income for the period is not affected by omitting such goods, because purchases and ending inventory are both understated by the same amount; that is, the error offsets itself in cost of goods sold.**[5] Total working capital is unchanged, but the **current ratio** is overstated (assuming it was greater than 1 to 1) because equal amounts were omitted from inventory and accounts payable.

To illustrate the effect on the current ratio, assume that a company understates its accounts payable and ending inventory by $40,000. The understated and correct data are shown in Illustration 8-9.

Illustration 8-9

Effects of Purchases and Ending Inventory Errors

Purchases and Ending Inventory Understated		Purchases and Ending Inventory Correct	
Current assets	$120,000	Current assets	$160,000
Current liabilities	$ 40,000	Current liabilities	$ 80,000
Current ratio	3 to 1	Current ratio	2 to 1

The correct current ratio is 2 to 1 rather than 3 to 1. Thus, understating accounts payable and ending inventory can lead to a "window dressing" of the current ratio. In other words, it can appear better than it really is.

If purchases (on account) and ending inventory are both overstated, then the effects on the statement of financial position are exactly the reverse. That is, inventory and accounts payable are overstated, and the current ratio is understated, even though the dollar amount of working capital is not affected. Cost of goods sold and net income are also unaffected because the errors offset each other. The preceding examples show some of the errors that can occur and their consequences, but there are many other types of possible errors. These include not recording a purchase but counting the new inventory, not recording a sale in the current period although the items have been delivered, omitting the adjusting entry to update the account Allowance for Sales Returns and Allowances in situations where the sales are known to have a high rate of return, and failing to adjust inventory to the lower of cost and net realizable value.

Ethics

Determining correct amounts for purchases, sales, and inventory in the correct accounting period is a critical step in preparing reliable financial statements. We only have to read the financial press to learn how misstating inventory can generate high income numbers. For example, in the past some Canadian farm equipment manufacturers treated deliveries to dealers as company sales (which reduced their inventory), even though sales to the ultimate consumer did not occur as quickly as the deliveries to the dealers. The result was a significantly inflated reported income for the manufacturers.

As Chapter 5 showed, when an error from a prior period is corrected, it is accounted for retroactively as an adjustment to retained earnings. Full disclosure requires a description of the error and a statement of the effect on the current and prior-period financial statements.

MEASUREMENT

Costs Included in Inventory

Objective 5
Determine the components of inventory cost.

After deciding what items are to be included in the ending inventory, the next step in accounting for inventory is to determine its cost. As mentioned previously, most inventories—like other non-financial assets—are generally recognized initially on the basis of cost. How is cost determined, and what should be included in "cost"?

Both IFRS and ASPE indicate that inventory cost is made up of "all costs of purchase, costs of conversion and other costs incurred in bringing the inventories to their present location and condition."[6] This includes transportation and handling costs and other direct costs of acquisition, such as non-recoverable taxes and duties.

Purchase Discounts

Suppliers often offer cash discounts to purchasers for prompt payment. There are two possible methods to account for the purchases and discounts: the gross method and the net method. Under the **gross method**, both the purchases and payables are recorded at **the gross amount of the invoice**, and any **purchase discounts** that are later taken **are**

credited to a Purchase Discounts account. This account is reported as a contra account to Purchases, as a reduction in the cost of the period's purchases.

The alternative approach, called the **net method**, records the purchases and accounts payable initially at an amount **net of the cash discounts.** If the account payable is paid within the discount period, the cash payment is exactly equal to the amount originally set up in the payable account. **If the account payable is paid after the discount period** is over, the discount that is lost is recorded in a **Purchase Discounts Lost account.** Recording the loss allows the company to assign responsibility for the loss to a specific employee. This treatment is considered more theoretically appropriate because it (1) provides a correct reporting of the asset cost and related liability,[7] and (2) makes it possible to measure the inefficiency of financial management if the discount is not taken.

Assume Company A purchases goods for $10,000 with terms 2/10, net 30. Company A pays for $4,000 of this amount within the discount period and the rest after the discount period. Illustration 8-10 illustrates the difference between the gross and net methods.

Illustration 8-10

Entries Under Gross and Net Methods

Gross Method			Net Method		
Purchase cost of $10,000, terms 2/10, net 30:					
Purchases	10,000		Purchases	9,800	
Accounts Payable		10,000	Accounts Payable		9,800
Invoices of $4,000 are paid within discount period:					
Accounts Payable	4,000		Accounts Payable	3,920	
Purchase Discounts		80	Cash		3,920
Cash		3,920			
Invoices of $6,000 are paid after discount period:					
Accounts Payable	6,000		Accounts Payable	5,880	
Cash		6,000	Purchase Discounts Lost	120	
			Cash		6,000

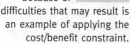

Underlying Concept

Not using the net method because of difficulties that may result is an example of applying the cost/benefit constraint.

Under the gross method, purchase discounts are deducted from purchases in determining cost of goods sold. If the net method is used, purchase discounts not taken are considered a financial expense and are reported in the income statement's Other Expenses section. Many believe that the difficulty of using the more complicated net method outweighs its benefits. This may explain why the less theoretically correct, but simpler, gross method is so popular.

Vendor Rebates

Assume that Johnston Corp., with a June 30 year end, has been purchasing more and more inventory from Roster Limited in recent years. Roster offers its customers a special **vendor rebate** of $0.10 per unit on each unit purchased, if the customer buys more than 100,000 units in the calendar year (from January 1 to December 31). This year, for the first time, Johnston management expects to exceed the 100,000-unit volume. It has purchased 60,000 units in the first six months of the current year and its forecast purchases for the next six months are over 50,000 units. Should Johnston recognize the anticipated rebate in its current year ended June 30? If so, how much should be recognized, and how does this affect the financial statements?

Cash rebates are generally a reduction of the purchase cost of inventory. If the "rebate receivable" meets both the definition of an asset and its recognition criteria, the rebate is recognized before it is received. In general:

- If the rebate is discretionary on the part of the supplier, no rebate is recognized until it is paid or the supplier becomes obligated to make a payment.

- If the rebate is **probable** and the amount can be **reasonably estimated**, the asset recognition criteria are met and the receivable can be recorded.[8] In this case, it is recognized as a reduction in the cost of purchases for the period. The amount receivable is allocated between the goods remaining in inventory, and the goods sold.

- The amount of the receivable recognized is based on the proportion of the total rebate that is expected relative to the transactions to date.

If the rebate offered by Roster Limited is not discretionary, and if it is probable that Johnston will purchase 110,000 units by December 31, and if management is able to make a reasonable estimate of the total rebate for the calendar year, Johnston recognizes the rebate as follows for its current year ended June 30. The entry assumes only 5,000 units are still on hand at year end.

A   = L +   SE
+5,500   +5,500

Cash flows: No effect

Rebate Receivable	6,000	
Inventory (5,000 units)		500
Cost of Goods Sold (55,000 units)		5,500

110,000 units × $0.10 = $11,000; 60,000/110,000 × $11,000 = $6,000
or 60,000 units × $0.10 = $6,000

Offering promotional payments is very common in the world of retail. Eager to meet their sales targets or promote their products through shelf placements and in-store advertisements, suppliers have been happy to boost sales with rebates, allowances, and price breaks. The question is, how should retailers account for these payments? For a while, a variety of methods were used, but some questionable practices changed that.

At one point, the Securities and Exchange Commission in the United States sued three executives of **Kmart Holding** and some Kmart vendors for their role in a $24-million accounting fraud that booked vendor allowances early as income. The scheme apparently allowed some Kmart managers to meet internal profit-margin targets. Similarly, **Royal Ahold**, a large Dutch supermarket operator, discovered that its U.S. Foodservice unit had improperly accounted for vendor payments, resulting in overstated earnings of at least $500 million (later revised upward to $800 million). Other subsidiaries were also found to have inflated profits for similar reasons.

Not surprisingly, standard setters issued guidelines to curb the previous flexibility in accounting for these promotional payments. As noted earlier, IFRS and ASPE require that trade discounts, rebates, and similar items be deducted in arriving at the cost of the purchase.

Sources: C. Schneider, "Retailers and Vendor Allowances," CFO.com, August 13, 2003; "SEC Charges Kmart's Former CEO and CFO with Financial Fraud," Securities and Exchange Commission news release, August 23, 2005; and Dean Starkman, "Ahold Settles Lawsuit for $1.1 Billion," *Washington Post*, November 29, 2005.

Illustration 8-11 provides an excerpt from the financial statement notes for **OfficeMax Incorporated**.

Vendor Rebates and Allowances

We participate in volume purchase rebate programs, some of which provide for tiered rebates based on defined levels of purchase volume. We also participate in programs that enable us to receive additional vendor subsidies by promoting the sale of vendor products. Vendor rebates and allowances are accrued as earned. Rebates and allowances received as a result of attaining defined purchase levels are accrued over the incentive period based on the terms of the vendor arrangement and estimates of qualifying purchases during the rebate program period. These estimates are reviewed on a quarterly basis and adjusted for changes in anticipated product sales and expected purchase levels. Vendor rebates and allowances earned are recorded as a reduction in the cost of merchandise inventories and are included in operations (as a reduction of cost of goods sold) in the period the related product is sold.

Product Costs

Product costs are costs that "attach" to inventory and are recorded in the inventory account. That is, they are capitalized. These costs are directly connected with bringing goods to the buyer's place of business and converting them to a saleable condition. They include freight charges on goods purchased, other direct costs of acquisition, and labour and other production costs that are incurred in processing the goods up to the time they are ready for sale. Under IFRS, product costs also include any eventual decommissioning or restoration costs incurred as a result of production, even though the related expenditures may not be incurred until far into the future. Under ASPE, such costs are generally added to the cost of the related property, plant, and equipment. Such **asset retirement costs** are discussed more fully in Chapters 10 and 13.

How should taxes be accounted for? Taxes that cannot be recovered from the government by the purchaser, such as some provincial sales taxes that are paid on goods that are purchased for resale or manufacturing purposes, are a cost of inventory. Taxes that can be recovered from the government, such as the federal Goods and Services Tax and the Harmonized Sales Tax charged in many provinces, are not included as part of the inventory's cost. Chapter 13 discusses this type of tax in more detail.

Conversion costs include direct labour and an allocation of the fixed and variable production overhead costs that are incurred in processing direct materials into finished goods. The allocation of fixed production costs is based on the company's **normal production capacity**.[9] In this way, costs of idle capacity or low production levels do not end up in inventory, but instead are charged to expense as they are incurred. However, if production levels are abnormally high, the fixed costs are spread out over the larger number of units that are produced so that inventory is not measured at an amount higher than its cost. Actual production levels can be used if they are close to normal levels. Actual levels are also used to charge variable costs to production.

It is theoretically correct to allocate a share of any buying costs to inventory, or expenses of a purchasing department, insurance costs in transit, or other costs that are incurred in handling the goods before they are ready for sale. This is because such costs are incurred to bring the inventories "to their present location and condition." However, on a cost/benefit basis, these items are not ordinarily included in inventory cost.

Borrowing Costs. If interest costs are incurred to finance activities that help bring inventories to a condition and place ready for sale, they are considered by many to be as much a cost of the asset as materials, labour, and overhead.[10] Under IFRS, interest costs incurred for an inventory item that takes an extended period of time to produce or manufacture are considered **product costs.** However, if the financing relates to inventories that are manufactured or produced in large quantities and on a repetitive basis, companies can choose whether to capitalize them or not.[11] Under ASPE, the only requirement is that **if interest is capitalized**, this policy and the amount that is capitalized in the current period must be **disclosed.**

Standard Costs. A company that uses a **standard cost system** predetermines the unit costs for material, labour, and manufacturing overhead. Usually the standard costs are based on the costs that should be incurred per unit of finished goods when the plant is operating at normal levels of efficiency and capacity. When actual costs are not the same as the standard costs, the differences are recorded in variance accounts that management can examine and follow up on by taking appropriate action to achieve greater control over costs. For financial statement purposes, **reporting inventories at standard cost is acceptable only as long as the results approximate actual cost.** Unallocated overheads are **expensed** as they are incurred.

Cost of Service Providers' Work in Process. Companies that provide services rather than manufacture products may accumulate significant costs of work-in-process inventories. These, too, are measured at their production costs. For service providers, the major "production" costs are for service personnel and overhead costs associated with this "direct labour." Supervisory costs and other overheads are allocated using the same principles as for manufactured products.

Costs Excluded from Inventory.   Some costs are closely related to acquiring and converting a product, but they are not considered to be product costs. An example is storage costs, unless they are necessary because the product must be held before the next stage of production, such as in wine production. Other examples are abnormal spoilage or wastage of materials, labour, or other production costs; and interest costs when inventories that are ready for use or sale are purchased on delayed payment terms.

Selling expenses and, under ordinary circumstances, **general and administrative expenses** are not considered directly related to the acquisition or conversion of goods and, therefore, are not considered a part of inventory. Such costs are **period costs**. Why are these costs not considered part of inventory? Selling expenses are generally more directly related to the cost of goods sold than to the unsold inventory. In most cases, these costs are so unrelated or indirectly related to the actual production process that any allocation would be completely arbitrary.

"Basket" Purchases and Joint Product Costs.   A special problem occurs when a group of units with different characteristics is purchased at a single lump-sum price, in what is called a **basket purchase**. Assume that Woodland Developers purchases land for $1 million and it can be subdivided into 400 lots. These lots are of different sizes and shapes but can be roughly sorted into three groups, graded A, B, and C. The purchase cost of $1 million must be allocated among the lots so that the cost of the lots that are later sold (cost of goods sold) and those remaining on hand (ending inventory) can be calculated.

It is inappropriate to use the average lot cost of $2,500 (the total cost of $1 million divided by the 400 lots) because the lots vary in size, shape, and attractiveness. When this kind of situation occurs—and it is not at all unusual—the most reasonable practice is to allocate the total cost among the various units **based on their relative sales value**. For our example, the cost allocation is shown in Illustration 8-12.

Lots	Number of Lots	Sales Price Per Lot	Total Sales Value	Relative Sales Value	Total Cost	Cost Allocated to Lots	Cost Per Lot
A	100	$10,000	$1,000,000	100/250	$1,000,000	$ 400,000	$4,000
B	100	6,000	600,000	60/250	1,000,000	240,000	2,400
C	200	4,500	900,000	90/250	1,000,000	360,000	1,800
			$2,500,000			$1,000,000	

This method, the **relative sales value method**, is rational, can be applied consistently, and is commonly used whenever there is a **joint cost** that needs to be allocated. Other examples include when two or more products are produced at the same time and the costs for each product cannot be distinguished. The petroleum industry uses it to value (at cost) the many products and by-products obtained from a barrel of crude oil, as does the food processing industry, where different cuts of meat of varying value are "split off" from one animal carcass. When the value of a by-product is relatively minor, it is often measured at its net realizable value and deducted from the cost of the major product.

Objective 6
Distinguish between perpetual and periodic inventory systems and account for them.

Inventory Accounting Systems

Technology has played an important role in the development of inventory systems. As mentioned in the opening story, radio-frequency identification data communications systems for warehouses, for example, have helped companies increase the accuracy of their inventory information and the efficiency and productivity of their inventory management activities.

Management is well aware that the level of inventory can materially affect the amount of current assets, total assets, net income, and therefore, retained earnings. These amounts, or totals that include them, are used to calculate ratios that allow users to evaluate management's performance (for use in calculation of bonuses) and adherence to debt restrictions (for calculation of the debt-to-total-asset ratio or dividend payout ratio).

For these and other reasons, companies are very interested in having an inventory accounting system that gives accurate, up-to-date information. One of two systems is commonly used for maintaining accurate inventory records: a perpetual system or a periodic system.

Recall the opening vignette regarding the use of radio-frequency data identification (RFID). This technology has allowed more and more companies to reduce the costs of tracking inventory. In 2004, **The Boeing Company** began using the technology for raw materials needed to build its planes including aluminum plates. The company attaches the small RFID identification tags to the side of the carts used to unload the plates at its manufacturing facility. When the plates are received at Boeing's factory and pass through the loading dock doors, scanners on the loading dock are able to identify the time of unloading and the nature of the specific raw materials. The material is automatically logged by the computer, which triggers a payment to the supplier.

Before this system, it would take seven Boeing employees to unload, check, and input data into the computer. This is now all done by one person, so the savings are tremendous. In addition, the RFID tags allow the company to keep track of those specific aluminum plates at all times. Boeing and **Airbus** are working to adopt common standards for use of RFID and are now delivering aircraft to customers with parts carrying electronic histories of their own.

Sources: Bradley Perret, "Boeing Looking at RFID on Production Aircraft," *Aviation Week*, November 10, 2011; Olga Kharif, "RFID's Second Wave," *Business Week*, August 9, 2005; and Phil Hochmuth, "Boeing Turns to Wireless LAN when a Key Part Goes Missing," *Network World*, May 1, 2006, Vol. 23, No. 17.

Perpetual System

A **perpetual inventory system** continuously tracks changes in the Inventory account. This means that the cost of all purchases and the cost of the items sold (or issued out of inventory) are recorded directly in the Inventory account as the purchases and sales occur. The accounting features of a perpetual inventory system are as follows.

1. Purchases of merchandise for resale or raw materials for production are debited to Inventory rather than to Purchases.

2. Freight-in is debited and purchase returns and allowances and purchase discounts are credited to Inventory instead of being accounted for in separate accounts.

3. The cost of the items sold is recognized at the time of each sale by debiting Cost of Goods Sold and crediting Inventory.

4. Inventory is a control account that is supported by a subsidiary ledger of individual inventory records. The subsidiary records show the quantity and cost of each type of inventory on hand.

The perpetual inventory system provides a continuous record of the balances in both the Inventory account and the Cost of Goods Sold account. In a computerized record-keeping system, changes in these accounts can be recorded almost instantaneously. The popularity and affordability of computerized accounting software have made the perpetual system cost-effective for many kinds of businesses. It is now common for most retail stores, big or small, to use optical scanners at the cash register that record reductions in inventory as it is sold as part of the store's perpetual inventory system.

Periodic System

In a **periodic inventory system**, the quantity of inventory on hand is determined, as the name implies, only **periodically**. Each acquisition of inventory during the accounting period is recorded by a debit to the Purchases account. The total in the Purchases account at the end of the accounting period is added to the cost of the inventory on hand at the beginning of the period to determine the total cost of the goods available for sale during the period. The cost of ending inventory is subtracted from the cost of goods available for sale to calculate the cost of goods sold.

Note that under a periodic inventory system, the **cost of goods sold** is a **residual amount that depends on first calculating the cost of the ending inventory.** The cost of the ending inventory can be determined by physically counting and costing it. This process is referred to as "taking a physical inventory." Companies that use the periodic system take a physical inventory at least once a year.

Comparing Perpetual and Periodic Systems

To illustrate the difference between a perpetual and a periodic system, assume that Fesmire Limited had the following balances and transactions during the current year:

Beginning inventory	100 units at $ 6 = $ 600
Purchases	900 units at $ 6 = $5,400
Defective units returned to the supplier	50 units at $ 6 = $ 300
Sales	600 units at $12 = $7,200
Ending inventory	350 units at $ 6 = $2,100

The entries to record these transactions during the current year are shown in Illustration 8-13.

Illustration 8-13

*Comparative Entries—
Perpetual Versus Periodic*

Perpetual Inventory System			Periodic Inventory System		
1. Beginning Inventory, 100 units at $6:					
The inventory account shows the inventory on hand at $600.			The inventory account shows the inventory on hand at $600.		
2. Purchase 900 units at $6:					
Inventory	5,400		Purchases	5,400	
Accounts Payable		5,400	Accounts Payable		5,400
3. Return 50 defective units:					
Accounts Payable	300		Accounts Payable	300	
Inventory		300	Purchase Returns and Allowances		300
4. Sale of 600 units at $12:					
Accounts Receivable	7,200		Accounts Receivable	7,200	
Sales Revenue		7,200	Sales Revenue		7,200
Cost of Goods Sold	3,600				
(600 at $6)					
Inventory		3,600	(No entry)		
5. End-of-period entries for inventory accounts, 350 units at $6 = $2,100:					
No entry necessary.			Purchase Returns		
The account, Inventory, shows the ending			and Allowances	300	
balance of $2,100			Inventory ($2,100 − 600)	1,500	
($600 + $5,400 − $300 − $3,600).			Cost of Goods Sold	3,600	
			Purchases		5,400

When a **perpetual inventory system** is used and there is a difference between the perpetual inventory record and the physical inventory count, a separate entry is needed to adjust the perpetual Inventory account. To illustrate, assume that at the end of the reporting period, the perpetual Inventory account reported a balance of $4,000, but a physical count indicated $3,800 was actually on hand. The adjusting entry is:

A   = L + SE
−200   −200

Cash flows: No effect

| Inventory Over and Short | 200 | |
| Inventory | | 200 |

The overage or shortage may be due to normal and expected shrinkage, breakage, shoplifting, or record-keeping errors, and is usually recognized as an adjustment of Cost of Goods Sold. Alternatively, the Loss on Inventory account is sometimes reported in the "Other revenues and gains" or "Other expenses and losses" section of the income statement. When this is done, the gross profit percentage is not affected by the costs of shrinkage, breakage, and theft.

In a **periodic inventory system**, there is no separate account to track these inventory losses. This is because there is no up-to-date inventory account that can be compared with the physical count. The amount of any inventory overage or shortage is therefore included in cost of goods sold.

Supplementary System—Quantities Only

In a perfect world, companies would like a continuous record of inventory levels, their cost, and the cost of goods sold. However, even with advances in technology, it may not be cost-effective to have a complete perpetual inventory system that keeps track of both inventory quantities and their cost. Because management needs current information about inventory levels to avoid stockouts and overpurchasing, to respond to customer queries, and to help prepare monthly or quarterly financial data, many companies use a **quantities only system**. This system provides detailed inventory records of increases and decreases **in quantities only**—not dollar amounts. This memorandum record is not part of the double-entry accounting system; therefore, the company would need to use a periodic system in its main accounts.

Whether a company maintains a perpetual inventory in quantities and dollars, in quantities only, or no perpetual inventory record at all, it usually takes a physical inventory once a year. No matter what type of inventory records are used or how well controlled the procedures for recording purchases and requisitions are, the dangers of loss and error are always present. Waste, breakage, theft, improper entry, failure to prepare or record requisitions, and similar possibilities may cause the inventory records to be different from the actual inventory on hand. Therefore, all companies need periodic verification of the inventory records by actual count, weight, or measurement, with the **counts compared with the detailed records.** The **records are then corrected** so that they agree with the quantities actually on hand.

As far as possible, the physical inventory should be taken near the end of a company's fiscal year so that correct inventory quantities are used in preparing annual accounting reports and statements. Because this is not always possible, physical inventories that are taken within two or three months of the year end are considered satisfactory as long as the **internal controls** indicate that the detailed inventory records are maintained with a fair degree of accuracy.[12]

Cost Formulas

Objective 7
Identify and apply GAAP cost formula options and indicate when each cost formula is appropriate.

Two main issues have now been addressed in determining inventory cost: which inventory items to include, and which costs to include in, or exclude from, the product's cost. The next issue is this: if inventories need to be priced at cost and many purchases have been made at **different unit costs, which of the various cost prices should be assigned to Inventory** on the statement of financial position and **which costs should be charged to Cost of Goods Sold** on the income statement?

Conceptually, **identifying the specific costs** of the actual items sold and those unsold seems ideal, but doing this is often too expensive or simply impossible to achieve. Consequently, companies must choose another acceptable inventory cost formula. A **cost formula** is a method of assigning inventory costs incurred during the accounting period to inventory that is still on hand at the end of the period (ending inventory) and to inventory that was sold during the period (cost of goods sold).

Illustration 8-14 provides data to use in the discussion of the cost formula choice. The data summarize the inventory-related activities of Call-Mart Inc. for the month of March. Note that the company experienced increasing unit costs for its purchases throughout the month.

CALL-MART INC.

Date	Purchases	Sold or Issued	Balance
Mar. 1	(beginning inventory)		
	500 @ $3.80		500 units
Mar. 2	1,500 @ $4.00		2,000 units
Mar. 15	6,000 @ $4.40		8,000 units
Mar. 19		4,000	4,000 units
Mar. 30	2,000 @ $4.75		6,000 units
	10,000	4,000	

From this information, we see that there were 10,000 units available for sale, made up of 500 units in opening inventory and 9,500 units purchased during the month. Of the 10,000 available, 4,000 were sold, leaving 6,000 units in ending inventory.

The **cost of goods available for sale** is calculated as follows:

500 units @ $3.80 =	$ 1,900
1,500 units @ $4.00 =	6,000
6,000 units @ $4.40 =	26,400
2,000 units @ $4.75 =	9,500
10,000 units	$43,800

Having this information, the question now is: **which price or prices should be assigned to the 6,000 units still in inventory and which to the 4,000 units sold?** The answer depends on which cost formula is chosen.

Both IFRS and ASPE recognize three acceptable cost formulas:

1. Specific identification
2. Weighted average cost
3. First-in, first-out (FIFO)

Specific Identification

When using the **specific identification** cost formula, each item that is sold and each item in inventory needs to be identified. The costs of the specific items that are sold are included in the cost of goods sold, and the costs of the specific items on hand are included in the ending inventory. This method is appropriate and required for goods that are not ordinarily interchangeable, and for goods and services that are produced and segregated for specific projects. It is used most often in situations involving a relatively small number of items that are costly and easily distinguishable by such things as their physical characteristics, serial numbers, or special markings. In the retail trade, this includes some types of jewellery, fur coats, automobiles, and furniture. In manufacturing, it includes special orders and many products manufactured under a job cost system.

To illustrate this method, assume that Call-Mart Inc.'s inventory items are distinguishable and that the 6,000 units of ending inventory consist of 100 units from the opening inventory, 900 from the March 2 purchase, 3,000 from the March 15 purchase, and 2,000 from the March 30 purchase. The ending inventory and cost of goods sold are calculated as shown in Illustration 8-15.

Illustration 8-15

Specific Identification Cost Formula

Units from	No. of Units	Unit Cost	Total Cost
Beginning inventory	100	$3.80	$ 380
March 2 purchase	900	4.00	3,600
March 15 purchase	3,000	4.40	13,200
March 30 purchase	2,000	4.75	9,500
Ending inventory	**6,000**		**$26,680**
Cost of goods available for sale (beginning inventory + purchases)	$43,800		
Deduct: Ending inventory	26,680		
Cost of goods sold	**$17,120**		

Conceptually, this method appears ideal because actual costs are matched against actual revenue, and ending inventory items are reported at their specific cost. In fact, the requirement that this method **only be used for goods that are not ordinarily interchangeable** is an attempt to make sure this benefit is achieved and to prevent management from manipulating the amount of net income.

Consider what might happen if businesses were allowed to use this method more generally. Assume, for instance, that a wholesaler purchases identical plywood early in the year at three different prices. When the plywood is sold, the wholesaler can choose either the lowest or the highest price to charge to expense simply by choosing which plywood is delivered to the customer. This means that a manager can manipulate net income simply by delivering to the customer the higher- or lower-priced item, depending on whether lower or higher reported income is wanted for the period.

Another problem with the broader use of the specific identification cost formula is that allocating certain costs can become arbitrary when the inventory items are interchangeable. In many circumstances, **it is difficult to directly relate shipping charges, storage costs, discounts, and other blanket charges to a specific inventory item**. The only option, then, is to allocate these costs somewhat arbitrarily, which eliminates some of the benefits offered by the specific identification method.[13]

Weighted Average Cost

As its name implies, an average cost formula prices inventory items based on the average cost of the goods that are available for sale during the period. The **weighted average cost formula** takes into account that the volume of goods acquired at each price is different. Assuming that Call-Mart Inc. uses a periodic inventory method, the ending inventory and cost of goods sold are calculated as indicated in Illustration 8-16.

Note that the beginning inventory units and cost are both included in calculating the average cost per unit.

Another weighted-average cost method is the **moving-average cost formula**. This method is used with **perpetual** inventory records that are **kept in both units and dollars.** Use of the moving-average cost method for full perpetual records is shown in Illustration 8-17.

Illustration 8-16

Weighted Average Cost Formula—Periodic Inventory

	Date	No. of Units	Unit Cost	Total Cost
Inventory	Mar. 1	500	$3.80	$ 1,900
Purchases	Mar. 2	1,500	4.00	6,000
Purchases	Mar. 15	6,000	4.40	26,400
Purchases	Mar. 30	2,000	4.75	9,500
Total goods available		10,000		$43,800

Weighted average cost per unit $\dfrac{\$43,800}{10,000} = \$4.38$

Ending inventory in units   6,000
Cost of ending inventory   6,000 × $4.38 = **$26,280**

Cost of goods available for sale $43,800
Deduct ending inventory   26,280

Cost of goods sold $17,520   (= 4,000 × $4.38)

Illustration 8-17

Moving-Average Cost Formula—Full Perpetual Inventory

Date	Purchased	Sold or Issued	Balance*
Mar. 1	Beginning inventory		(500 @ $3.80) $ 1,900
Mar. 2	(1,500 @ $4.00) $ 6,000		(2,000 @ $3.95) 7,900
Mar. 15	(6,000 @ $4.40) 26,400		(8,000 @ $4.2875) 34,300
Mar. 19		(4,000 @ $4.2875) $17,150	(4,000 @ $4.2875) 17,150
Mar. 30	(2,000 @ $4.75) 9,500		(6,000 @ $4.4417) 26,650

*Calculation of moving-average cost per unit:
After March 2 purchase
= Cost of units available / Units available
= [$1,900 + (1,500 × $4.00)] / (500 + 1,500)
= ($1,900 + $6,000) / 2,000
= $7,900 / 2,000
= $3.95

After March 15 purchase
= [$7,900 + (6,000 × $4.40)] / (2,000 + 6,000)
= $34,300 / 8,000
= $4.2875

After March 30 purchase
= [17,150 + (2,000 × $4.75)] / (4,000 + 2,000)
= $26,650 / 6,000
= $4.4417

In this method, a **new average unit cost is calculated each time** a purchase is made. This is **because the cost of goods sold at the updated average cost has to be recognized at the time of the next sale.** On March 15, after 6,000 units are purchased for $26,400, 8,000 units with a total cost of $34,300 ($7,900 plus $26,400) are on hand. The average unit cost is $34,300 divided by 8,000, or $4.2875. This unit cost is used in costing withdrawals of inventory until another purchase is made, when a new average unit cost is calculated. Accordingly, the cost of each of the 4,000 units withdrawn on March 19 is shown at $4.2875, which makes a total cost of goods sold of $17,150. On March 30, following the purchase of 2,000 units for $9,500, the total inventory cost of the 6,000 units is $26,650. The new unit cost is now $4.4417.

Justification for using the average cost method is that the costs it assigns to inventory and cost of goods sold closely follow the actual physical flow of many inventories that are interchangeable. While it is impossible to measure the specific physical flow of inventory, it is reasonable to cost items based on an average price. There are also practical reasons that support this method. It is simple to apply, objective, and not very open to income manipulation. This argument is particularly persuasive when the inventory involved is relatively homogeneous in nature. In terms of achieving financial statement objectives, an average cost method results in an average of costs being used to determine both the cost of goods sold in the income statement and ending inventory in the statement of financial position.

First-In, First-Out (FIFO)

The **first-in, first-out (FIFO) cost formula** assigns costs based on the assumption that goods are used in the order in which they are purchased. In other words, it assumes that **the first items purchased are the first ones used** (in a manufacturing concern) **or sold** (in a merchandising concern). The inventory remaining, therefore, must come from the most recent purchases.

To illustrate, assume that Call-Mart Inc. uses a periodic inventory system, where the inventory cost is calculated only at the end of the month. **The ending inventory's cost for the 6,000 units remaining is calculated by taking the cost of the most recent purchase and working back until all units in the ending inventory are accounted for.** The ending inventory and cost of goods sold are calculated as shown in Illustration 8-18.

Illustration 8-18

*FIFO Cost Formula—
Periodic Inventory*

Date	No. of Units	Unit Cost	Total Cost
Mar. 30	2,000	$4.75	$ 9,500
Mar. 15	4,000	4.40	17,600
Ending inventory	6,000		$27,100
Cost of goods available for sale	$43,800		
Deduct: Ending inventory	27,100		
Cost of goods sold	$16,700		

If a full perpetual inventory system **in quantities and dollars** is used, a cost figure is attached to each withdrawal from inventory when the units are withdrawn and sold. In the example, the cost of the 4,000 units removed on March 19 is made up first from the items in the beginning inventory, then the items purchased on March 2, and finally some from the March 15 purchases. The inventory recorded under FIFO and **a perpetual system** for Call-Mart Inc. is shown in Illustration 8-19, which also results in an ending inventory of $27,100 and a cost of goods sold of $16,700.

Illustration 8-19

*FIFO Cost Formula—
Perpetual Inventory*

Date	Purchased	Sold or Issued	Balance	
Mar. 1	Beginning inventory		500 @ $3.80	$ 1,900
Mar. 2	(1,500 @ $4.00) $ 6,000		500 @ 3.80 ⎱ 1,500 @ 4.00 ⎰	7,900
Mar. 15	(6,000 @ $4.40) 26,400		500 @ 3.80 ⎱ 1,500 @ 4.00 ⎰ 6,000 @ 4.40 ⎰	34,300
Mar. 19		500 @ $3.80 ⎱ 1,500 @ 4.00 ⎰ 2,000 @ 4.40 ⎰ **$16,700**	4,000 @ 4.40	17,600
Mar. 30	(2,000 @ $4.75) 9,500		4,000 @ 4.40 ⎱ 2,000 @ 4.75 ⎰	**27,100**

Notice that in these two FIFO examples, the cost of goods sold and ending inventory are the same. **In all cases where FIFO is used, the inventory and cost of goods sold are the same at the end of the period whether a perpetual or periodic system is used.** This is true because the same costs will always be first in and, therefore, first out, whether cost of goods sold is calculated as goods are sold throughout the accounting period (the perpetual system) or based on what remains at the end of the accounting period (the periodic system).

One objective of FIFO is to roughly follow the actual physical flow of goods. When the physical flow of goods really is first-in, first-out, the FIFO method approximates the use of specific identification. At the same time, it does not permit manipulation of income because the enterprise is not free to choose a certain cost to be charged to expense.

Another advantage of the FIFO method is that the ending inventory is close to its current cost. Because the costs of the first goods in are transferred to cost of goods sold, the ending inventory is made up of the cost of the most recent purchases. This approach generally provides a cost that is close to the replacement cost for inventory on the statement of financial position particularly when the inventory turnover is rapid or price changes have not occurred since the most recent purchases.

The FIFO method's basic disadvantage is that current costs are not matched against current revenues on the income statement. The oldest costs are charged against current revenue, which can lead to distortions in gross profit and net income when prices are changing rapidly.

Choice of Cost Formula

The inventory standards limit the ability of preparers to choose a cost formula. Specific identification is required when inventory is made up of goods that are not ordinarily interchangeable, and when goods and services are produced and segregated for specific projects. Otherwise, the choice is between a weighted average method and FIFO. The choice is further restricted by the requirement that companies apply the same inventory cost formula to all inventories of a similar nature and use.

The overriding objectives that underlie the inventory standards and guide management are as follows.

1. Choose an approach that corresponds as closely as possible to the physical flow of goods.

2. Report an inventory cost on the statement of financial position that is representative of the inventory's recent cost.

3. Use the same method for all inventory assets that have similar economic characteristics for the entity.

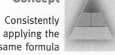

Underlying Concept

Applying the standards results in statement of financial position and income statement amounts that faithfully represent the asset's cost and the cost of the inventory that was sold, respectively.

These requirements are consistent with standard setters' emphasis on an asset and liability approach to the accounting model, as explained in Chapter 2. That is, assets and liabilities are the fundamental building blocks whose definition and measurement underlie the amounts and timing of revenues and expenses.

Income taxes are also a consideration. Methods that permit a lower ending inventory valuation result in lower income and reduced cash outflows for taxes. Compared with the FIFO cost formula, an average cost formula results in recent costs being reflected more in the cost of goods sold and older costs in ending inventory. In a period of rising prices, there may be tax advantages to the average cost formula.

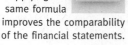

Underlying Concept

Consistently applying the same formula improves the comparability of the financial statements.

If companies were permitted to switch from one inventory costing method to another, this would adversely affect the comparability of financial statements. Therefore, companies choose the costing formula that is most suitable to their particular circumstances and, once selected, apply it consistently from then on. If conditions indicate that another accounting policy would result in a reliable and more relevant presentation in the financial statements, a change may be made. Such a change is unusual, but is accounted for retroactively and its effect is clearly disclosed in the financial statements.

Last-In, First-Out (LIFO)

The **last-in, first-out (LIFO) cost formula** is no longer permitted under ASPE and IFRS. LIFO assigns costs based on the assumption that the cost of the most recent purchase is the first cost to be charged to cost of goods sold. The cost assigned to the inventory remaining therefore comes from the earliest acquisitions (those that are "first-in, still-here") and is made up of the oldest costs.

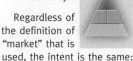
This method is no longer permitted for the following reasons.

1. In almost all situations, LIFO does not represent the actual flow of costs.

2. The statement of financial position cost of ending inventory is not a fair representation of the recent cost of inventories on hand.

3. Use of LIFO can result in serious distortions of reported income, especially when old inventory costs are expensed in the period. This happens when old, low-cost inventory gets charged to cost of goods sold due to a reduction in base inventory levels.

Because the Canada Revenue Agency has never allowed companies to use LIFO to calculate their income for tax purposes, this method was not widely used in Canada. However, it is permitted under U.S. GAAP, and allowed for tax purposes there if a company also uses the method for financial reporting purposes. Canadian public companies that are listed on a U.S. stock exchange as well as a Canadian exchange are permitted to prepare their financial statements under U.S. GAAP, so it is likely that LIFO-based inventories will continue to be seen in Canada for a while yet.

Lower of Cost and Net Realizable Value

Rationale for Lower of Cost and Net Realizable Value (LC&NRV)

So far in the chapter, we have learned how to calculate the cost of ending inventory at the statement of financial position date, determining: (1) the goods to include in ending inventory, (2) the costs to capitalize in inventory cost, and (3) the cost formulas available to allocate costs to ending inventory. The last step in applying this cost-based model is to decide whether cost is appropriate for reporting inventory on the statement of financial position.

A departure from reporting inventory at cost makes sense if the value of inventory to the entity falls below its cost. This reduction in value may be due to the inventory itself (if, for example, the goods are obsolete or damaged), a reduction in selling prices, or an increase in the costs to complete and dispose of the inventory. **Cost is not appropriate if the asset's value (its ability to generate net cash flows) is now less than its carrying amount.** Inventories therefore are valued at the **lower of cost and net realizable value**.

This departure from cost is justified for two main reasons. First, readers presume that **current assets can be converted into at least as much cash as the amount reported on the statement of financial position** and second, **a loss of utility should be deducted from (matched with) revenues in the period in which the loss occurs,** not in the period when the inventory is sold.

For many years, inventory was valued in the cost-based system at the lower of cost and market (LCM), and there were a variety of alternative definitions of "market." The term **market** in LCM valuation could mean replacement cost, net realizable value, or net realizable value less a normal profit margin. Under U.S. GAAP, all these terms are still incorporated in a rule that is applied to calculate market and therefore to measure inventory on the statement of financial position.

The option of choosing a meaning of "market" has been eliminated in Canada and under IFRS. The phrase **lower of cost and market** is no longer part of GAAP in Canada, and market is now strictly defined as **net realizable value (NRV)**: the estimated selling price less the estimated costs to complete and sell the goods. Why has there been such support for this concept of market?

The use of a "replacement cost" definition of market is based on the assumption that a decline in an item's replacement cost results in a decline in its selling price. While replacement cost may be appropriate in a few specific circumstances, it is not reasonable to assume that prices will fall in the same proportion as input costs fall, or that they will fall below inventory cost, or that such market conditions exist for all products. Also, the use of a "net realizable value less a normal profit margin" definition of market value has the effect of arbitrarily shifting profits from one period to another. In effect, a very large writedown may be taken in the year the inventory's value drops, so that a normal profit can be reported in the period in which it is later sold.

If inventory is written down only to its net realizable value, a lower loss is recognized in the current period and, if the estimates are correct, the company breaks even on the sale of the item. Although the net result is the same when you add the two periods together, there is little justification for the arbitrary shifting of profit into a future period as happens when the NRV is further reduced by the profit margin. Therefore, ASPE and IFRS both require the use of NRV as "market."

What Is Net Realizable Value?

Net realizable value is an estimate. Unlike inventory cost, which usually remains at a determined value, net realizable value changes over time for a variety of reasons. Inventory may deteriorate or become obsolete with time; selling prices fluctuate with changes in supply and demand; substitute products become available; and input costs to complete and sell, liquidate, or otherwise dispose of the product vary with conditions and the specific markets that the inventory is sold into.

Estimates of NRV are based on the best evidence available at and shortly after the statement of financial position date. The objective is to determine the most likely (net) realizable value of the product on hand at the end of the accounting period given the specific circumstances of the particular entity. A new assessment is required at each statement of financial position date. If economic circumstances change and the estimate of the net realizable value changes from the previous estimate, the revised amount is used in determining the lower of cost and NRV at the end of the next period.

Application of Lower of Cost and Net Realizable Value

The **lower of cost and net realizable value (LC&NRV) standard** requires that inventory be valued at cost unless NRV is lower than cost, in which case the inventory is valued at NRV. To apply this:

1. Determine the cost.

2. Calculate the net realizable value.

3. Compare the two.

4. Use the lower value to measure inventory for the statement of financial position.

To demonstrate, consider the information in Illustration 8-20 for the inventory of Regner Foods Limited.

Illustration 8-20

Applying the Lower of Cost and NRV

Food	Cost	Net Realizable Value	LC&NRV
Spinach	$ 80,000	$120,000	$ 80,000
Carrots	100,000	100,000	100,000
Cut beans	50,000	40,000	40,000
Peas	90,000	72,000	72,000
Mixed vegetables	95,000	92,000	92,000
Final inventory value at LC&NRV			$384,000

To establish the LC&NRV of each item of inventory, compare the net realizable value in the middle column of Illustration 8-20 with cost. The lower of the two values is then chosen. Cost is the lower amount for spinach; net realizable value is lower for cut beans, peas, and mixed vegetables; and cost and NRV are identical for carrots. The inventory amount reported on Regner Foods' statement of financial position is therefore $384,000.

This analysis is usually only applied to losses in value that occur in the normal course of business from such causes as style changes, a shift in demand, or regular shop wear. Damaged or deteriorated goods are reduced directly to net realizable value. If the amount is significant, such goods may be carried in separate inventory accounts.

In Illustration 8-20 for Regner Foods, we assumed that the lower of cost and net realizable value rule is applied to each separate item of food. Indeed, **the accounting standards specify that the comparison is usually applied on an item-by-item basis.** However, the standards recognize that it may be appropriate in some circumstances to group similar or related items and then compare their cost and NRV as a group. Grouping inventory for this purpose may be appropriate, for example, for inventory items relating to the same product line in the following situations:

1. They are closely related in terms of their end use.

2. They are produced and marketed in the same geographical area.

3. They cannot be evaluated separately from other items in the product line in a practical or reasonable way.[14]

Grouping all finished goods inventory, or all products within a geographic area, or all inventory that is specific to an industry, is **not** considered appropriate.

The extent to which inventory items are grouped and their subtotals of cost and net realizable value are compared can affect the amount of inventory that is reported on the statement of financial position. To illustrate, assume that Regner Foods separates its food products into "frozen" and "canned" categories.

As indicated in Illustration 8-21, if the lower of cost and NRV rule is applied to the **subtotals** of these groups, the valuation of inventory is $394,000; if it is applied to individual items, it is $384,000. The reason for the difference is that individual realizable values lower than cost are offset against realizable values higher than cost when categories are used. For example, the lower NRVs for cut beans, peas, and mixed vegetables are partially offset by the higher NRV for spinach. **The item-by-item approach** is always the more conservative (that is, lower asset cost) method because net realizable values above cost are never included in the calculations.[15]

Illustration 8-21

Grouping Inventory Categories

	Cost	NRV	Lower of Cost and NRV by: Individual Items	Lower of Cost and NRV by: Related Products
Frozen				
Spinach	$ 80,000	$120,000	$ 80,000	
Carrots	100,000	100,000	100,000	
Cut beans	50,000	40,000	40,000	
Total frozen	230,000	260,000		$230,000
Canned				
Peas	90,000	72,000	72,000	
Mixed vegetables	95,000	92,000	92,000	
Total canned	185,000	164,000		164,000
Total			$384,000	$394,000

Recording the Lower of Cost and Net Realizable Value

Two different methods are used for **recording** inventory at the lower market amount. The **direct method** records the NRV of the inventory directly in the Inventory account at the reporting date if the amount is lower than cost. No loss is reported separately in the income statement because the loss is buried in cost of goods sold. The other method does not change the Inventory account itself. Instead it keeps the Inventory account at cost and establishes a separate contra asset account to Inventory on the statement of financial position. (This is very similar to Accounts Receivable and the Allowance for Doubtful Accounts.) A loss account is recognized in the income statement to record the writeoff. This second approach is referred to as the **indirect method** or **allowance method**.

The following data are the basis for Illustrations 8-22 and 8-23, which show the entries under both methods:

Inventory	At Cost	At NRV
Beginning of the period	$65,000	$65,000
End of the period	82,000	70,000

The entries in Illustration 8-22 assume the use of a **periodic** inventory system. Those in Illustration 8-23 assume a **perpetual** inventory system.

Illustration 8-22

Accounting for the Reduction of Inventory to NRV—Periodic Inventory System

Ending Inventory Recorded at NRV (Direct Method)			Ending Inventory Recorded at Cost and Reduced to NRV Using an Allowance		
To transfer out beginning inventory balance:					
Cost of Goods Sold	65,000		Cost of Goods Sold	65,000	
Inventory		65,000	Inventory		65,000
To record ending inventory:					
Inventory	70,000		Inventory	82,000	
Cost of Goods Sold		70,000	Cost of Goods Sold		82,000
To write down inventory to lower NRV:					
No entry			Loss on Inventory Due to Decline in NRV*	12,000	
			Allowance to Reduce Inventory to NRV		12,000

*A debit to Cost of Goods Sold is also acceptable.

Illustration 8-23

Accounting for the Reduction of Inventory to NRV— Perpetual Inventory System

Direct Method			Indirect or Allowance Method		
To reduce inventory from cost to NRV:					
Cost of Goods Sold	12,000		Loss on Inventory Due to Decline in NRV*	12,000	
Inventory		12,000	Allowance to Reduce Inventory to NRV		12,000

*A debit to Cost of Goods Sold is also acceptable.

The advantage of identifying the loss due to the decline in net realizable value separately is that it may be reported separately. It thus clearly discloses the loss resulting from the market decline in inventory prices instead of burying it in the cost of goods sold. The advantage of using an allowance account is that inventory cost numbers are retained in both the Inventory control and subsidiary ledger accounts.

Although using an allowance account makes it possible to disclose the inventory at cost and at the lower of cost and NRV on the statement of financial position, it raises the problem of how to dispose of the new account balance in the following period. If the particular merchandise is still on hand, the allowance account should be retained. Otherwise, beginning inventory and cost of goods available for sale will be overstated. But **if the goods have been sold,** then the account should be closed. A new allowance account balance is then established for any decline in inventory value that exists at the end of the next accounting period.

Many accountants leave the allowance account on the books and merely adjust its balance at the next reporting date to agree with the difference between cost and

the lower of cost and NRV at that time. If prices are falling, a loss is recorded. If prices are rising, a loss recorded in prior years is recovered and a gain (which is not really a gain, but **a recovery of a previously recognized loss**) is recorded, as shown in Illustration 8-24. The recovery amount is ordinarily recognized as a reduction in the cost of goods sold.

Date	Inventory at Cost	Inventory at NRV	Amount Required in Allowance Account	Allowance Account before Adjustment	Adjustment of Allowance Account Balance	Effect on Net Income
Dec. 31/13	$188,000	$176,000	$12,000 cr.	$ –0–	$12,000 increase	Loss
Dec. 31/14	194,000	187,000	7,000 cr.	12,000 cr.	5,000 decrease	Gain
Dec. 31/15	173,000	174,000	–0–	7,000 cr.	7,000 decrease	Gain
Dec. 31/16	182,000	180,000	2,000 cr.	–0–	2,000 increase	Loss

Any net "gain" can be thought of as the excess of the credit effect of closing the beginning allowance balance over the debit effect of setting up the current year-end allowance account. Recovering the loss up to the original cost is permitted, **but it may not exceed the original cost**. That is, the Allowance account cannot have a debit balance.

Evaluation of the Lower of Cost and Net Realizable Value Rule

Measuring inventories at the LC&NRV has some conceptual and practical deficiencies. Recognizing net realizable values only when they are lower than cost is an inconsistent treatment that can lead to distortions in reported income. The accounting values that are reported are not neutral and unbiased measures of income and net assets. Also, because NRV is an estimate, company management has the opportunity to over- or underestimate realizable values, depending on the results it would like to report for the period. Others feel that any accounting method that arbitrarily transfers income from one period to another reduces the quality of earnings.

On the other hand, many financial statement users appreciate the lower of cost and net realizable value requirement because they know that inventory and income are not overstated. Supporters contend that accounting measurement has not reached a level of sophistication that enables us to provide acceptably reliable (that is, verifiable) fair values for inventory above cost.

Exceptions to Lower of Cost and Net Realizable Value Model

Inventories Measured at Net Realizable Value

Objective 9
Identify inventories that are or may be valued at amounts other than the lower of cost and net realizable value.

For most companies and in most situations, inventory is reported at the lower of cost and net realizable value. Some critics believe that inventory should always be valued at its **net realizable value** because that is the net amount that will be collected in cash from the inventory in the future. In certain restricted circumstances, it is possible to record inventory at its net realizable value even if that amount is above cost. The following criteria have to be met to value inventory above cost and for revenue to be recognized before the point of sale:

1. The sale is assured or there is an active market for the product and minimal risk of failure to sell.

2. The costs of disposal can be estimated.

Inventories of certain minerals (rare metals especially) are sometimes reported at NRV because there is often a controlled market without significant costs of disposal. A

Real World Emphasis

similar treatment may be used for agricultural produce after harvest and inventories of agricultural and forest products. When such inventories are measured at NRV in accordance with accounting policies common in the industry, measurement at NRV is GAAP. Changes in net realizable value are recognized in net income each period. **Viterra Inc.**, with operations in grain handling, agri-products, and agri-food processing, among others, reports such a policy in the notes to its 2010 financial statements. The note is shown in Illustration 8-25.

Illustration 8-25

Inventory Valued at Net Realizable Value— Viterra Inc.

---

e) INVENTORIES

Grain inventories include both hedgeable and non-hedgeable commodities. Grain inventories are valued on the basis of closing market quotations less freight and handling costs. Agri-products inventories are valued at the lower of cost and net realizable value where cost is determined on a first-in, first-out basis. Processing inventories are valued at the lower of cost and net realizable value where cost is determined using the weighted average method.

Measurement at net realizable value may also be used when cost figures are too difficult to obtain. In some cases, minor marketable by-products are produced where the costs are indistinguishable. Instead of the company attempting a costly exercise of arbitrary cost allocation, the by-products are measured at the selling price of the by-product less any costs to bring them to market.

Inventories Measured at Fair Value Less Costs to Sell

Inventories of Commodity Broker-Traders.   Another exception to the lower of cost and net realizable value measurement standard is the inventory of commodity broker-traders who measure their inventories at **fair value less costs to sell**.[16] This inventory consists of such items as grain and livestock futures contracts. Changes in the fair value less costs to sell the inventory items are recognized in net income in the period of the change.

Biological Assets and Agricultural Produce at Point of Harvest.   There is often confusion about what is a biological asset, agricultural produce, and a product that results from processing after harvest. The following excerpt of examples in Illustration 8-26, reproduced from IAS 41 *Agriculture*, helps to clarify what is included as each type of asset.

Illustration 8-26

Examples of Agricultural Activity Assets

Biological Assets	Agricultural Produce	Products that Result from Processing after Harvest
Sheep	Wool	Yarn, carpet
Trees in a plantation forest	Felled trees	Logs, lumber
Dairy cattle	Milk	Cheese
Pigs	Carcass	Sausages, cured hams
Vines	Grapes	Wine
Fruit trees	Picked fruit	Processed fruit

ASPE.   Inventories of biological assets (living plants and animals) and products of the entity's biological assets (agricultural produce) at the point of harvest are excluded from the **measurement** requirements of ASPE for inventories, but they are included for the **expense recognition** and **disclosure** requirements. This means that there is no specific guidance on how such assets should be measured. A review of the financial statements of many Canadian companies with such assets indicates that they tend to follow a lower of cost and net realizable value approach. This is reasonable considering that this valuation corresponds closely to what is the **primary source of GAAP** for similar assets.

Regardless, products resulting from further processing after harvest have to meet all the requirements of the inventory standard. They are measured at the lower of cost and NRV with whatever value they were assigned at the point of harvest recognized as their deemed cost.

IFRS. Under IFRS, accounting for biological assets and agricultural produce at the point of harvest is covered in a separate standard: IAS 41 *Agriculture.* This is a specialized industry, so at an intermediate accounting level, it is enough to know that these inventories are measured at fair value less costs to sell. For produce at the point of harvest, such as grapes or picked fruit, the "fair value less costs to sell" measure is deemed to be the inventory's "cost" for purposes of subsequent accounting (and further processing, if applicable) under IAS 2 *Inventories.*

Basic entries to account for this measurement model are set out in Illustration 8-27.[17] Assume that the enterprise is a farm that raises sheep for their wool. The sheep are biological assets, lambs born into the existing flock are biological assets, and the wool is an agricultural product.

Illustration 8-27

Accounting for Inventories at Fair Value Less Costs to Sell (IFRS Versus ASPE)

	IFRS		ASPE*	
To record the birth of a lamb (fair value $500):			NA	
Biological Assets	500			
Unrealized Gain or Loss		500		
To record general farm expenditures of $200:				
Expenses	200		200	
Cash/Accounts Payable		200		200
To record an increase in value of lambs and other sheep of $700:				
Biological Assets	700			
Unrealized Gain or Loss		700	NA	
To record the wool inventory produced from the sheep (valued at $100):				
Inventory	100			
Biological Assets		100	NA	
To record the immediate sale of wool produced for $100:				
Cash/Accounts Receivable	100		100	
Inventory		100		
Unrealized Gain or Loss	100			
Realized Gain or Loss		100		100

*ASPE does not offer any guidance. Therefore as long as the accounting policy choice is supportable under the conceptual framework, companies following ASPE might use the same accounting as IFRS or perhaps use the historical cost as a default. The above-noted accounting uses historical cost and recognizes gains/profits when realized (that is, when the wool is sold). The flock would have to be tested for impairment. In other words, how long will the sheep produce wool? Some interesting questions arise. If one animal dies, should we write off part of the flock? Alternatively, given that the flock is likely replenishing itself because new lambs are born as old animals die, is there a need to write anything down? Finally, it may be argued that direct costs of maintaining the sheep could be capitalized. If this were done, we would have to be careful to set a limit on the total carrying value. In addition, if this were the case, we would likely have to recognize some costs when sold.

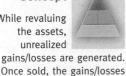

Underlying Concept

While revaluing the assets, unrealized gains/losses are generated. Once sold, the gains/losses become realized. This is an important distinction and should be disclosed under the full disclosure principle.

Note that the costs to raise or produce the lambs may be capitalized to the Biological Asset account.[18] If these costs are capitalized as an accounting policy choice, direct costs would be included whereas more general costs would be expensed. In this manner, when revalued to fair value less cost to sell, the unrealized gain for instance will be net of the direct costs. The account Biological Asset, representing the fair value less selling costs of the sheep, seems to have some of the characteristics of both inventory and plant and equipment assets. However, biological assets are classified as neither. They require separate disclosure on the statement of financial position.

Nutreco N.V. is a public company with operations in 30 countries. The company is in the animal nutrition and fish feed business. Illustration 8-28 is taken from the notes to the 2011 financial statements.

19 BIOLOGICAL ASSETS

(EUR x million)	2011	2010
Balance at 1 January	**127.8**	**104.9**
Expenses capitalised	745.1	671.2
Decrease due to sales	-186.4	-165.5
Decrease due to harvest	-543.4	-484.6
Change in fair value	0.3	1.0
Reclassification to assets held for sale	-2.9	—
Effect of movement in foreign exchange rates	—	0.8
BALANCE AT 31 DECEMBER	**140.5**	**127.8**

The increase of biological assets is mainly due to the increase in the number of pigs in Spain. Furthermore, the average weight of these pigs has increased by 16 kilo due to the demand for heavier pigs.

At balance sheet date, Nutreco has biological assets in Spain, Canada and the Netherlands related to pig livestock, poultry livestock, hatching eggs and a small amount of animals used for research purposes. In Spain, the poultry business is integrated whereby the fattened broilers are transferred from the fattening farm to our processing facility. The decrease of biological assets due to harvest as shown in the above movement schedule refers to these transfers. The poultry livestock in all other countries and the fattening pigs in Spain are sold externally which is reflected by the decrease due to sales.

As you can see in the Nutreco note, expenses are capitalized.

Estimating Inventory

The Need for Estimates

Objective 10

Apply the gross profit method of estimating inventory.

Recall that the basic purpose of taking a physical inventory is to verify the accuracy of the perpetual inventory records or, if there are no perpetual records, to arrive at an inventory amount. Sometimes, taking a physical inventory is impractical or impossible. In such cases, estimation methods are used to approximate inventory on hand. One such method is called the gross profit, or gross margin, method. This method is used in situations where only an estimate of inventory is needed (for example, preparing interim reports or testing the reasonableness of the cost calculated by some other method) or where inventory has been destroyed by fire or some other catastrophe. It may also be used to provide a rough check on the accuracy of a physical inventory count. For example, the estimated amount is compared with the physical count amount to see if they are reasonably close; if they are not, the reason for the difference is investigated.

Another method that is widely used with retail inventories is the retail inventory method. Like the gross profit method, it depends on establishing a relationship between selling (retail) prices and cost. Appendix 8A discusses the retail inventory method in detail.

Applying the Gross Profit Method

The **gross profit method** is based on three premises:

1. The beginning inventory plus purchases equals the **cost of goods available for sale**.

2. Goods not included in cost of goods sold must be on hand **in ending inventory**.

3. When an estimate of cost of goods sold is deducted from the cost of goods available for sale, the result is an estimate of ending inventory.

To illustrate, assume that a company has a beginning inventory of $60,000 and purchases of $200,000, both at cost. Sales at selling price amount to $280,000. The gross profit on the selling price is 30%. Illustration 8-29 walks you through the gross profit method of estimating ending inventory.[19]

Beginning inventory (at cost)		$ 60,000
Purchases (at cost)		200,000
Goods available for sale (at cost)		260,000
Sales (at selling price)	$280,000	
Less: Gross profit (30% of $280,000)	84,000	
Sales at cost = Estimated cost of goods sold		196,000
Estimated inventory (at cost)		$ 64,000

Note that the estimated cost of goods sold could also have been calculated directly as 70% of sales; that is, 100% less 30%. **The cost of goods sold percentage is always the complement of the gross profit percentage.**

All the information needed to estimate the inventory at cost, except for the gross profit percentage, is available in the current period's accounting records. The gross profit percentage is determined by reviewing company policies and the records of prior periods. The percentage is adjusted if the prior periods are not considered representative of the current period.

Gross Profit Percentage Versus Markup on Cost

In most situations, the **gross profit percentage** is used and it is the gross profit as a percentage of the selling price. The previous illustration, for example, used a 30% gross profit on sales. Gross profit on selling price is the common method for quoting the profit for several reasons.

1. Most goods are stated on a retail basis, not a cost basis.

2. A profit quoted on the selling price is lower than one based on cost, and this lower rate gives a favourable impression to the consumer.

3. The gross profit based on selling price can never exceed 100%.[20]

In the previous example, the percentage was given to you. But how was that figure derived? To see how a gross profit percentage is calculated, assume that an article cost $15.00 and sells for $20.00, a gross profit of $5.00. This markup of $5.00 is one quarter or 25% of the selling (or retail) price but is one third or $33^{1}/_{3}$% of cost (see Illustration 8-30).

$$\frac{\text{Gross profit}}{\text{Selling price}} = \frac{\$5.00}{\$20.00} = 25\% \text{ of selling price} \qquad \frac{\text{Gross profit}}{\text{Cost}} = \frac{\$5.00}{\$15.00} = 33^{1}/_{3}\% \text{ of cost}$$

Although gross profit is based on sales, you should understand the relationship between this ratio and the percentage of **markup on cost**.

For example, assume that you were told that the **markup on cost** for a specific item is 25%. What, then, is the **gross profit on selling price?** To find the answer, assume that the item's selling price is $1.00. In this case, the following formula applies:

$$\begin{aligned} \text{Cost} + \text{Gross profit} &= \text{Selling price} \\ C + .25C &= \$1.00 \\ 1.25C &= \$1.00 \\ C &= \$0.80 \end{aligned}$$

The amount of gross profit is $0.20 ($1.00 − $0.80), and the rate of gross profit on selling price is 20% ($0.20/$1.00).

Alternatively, assume that you know that the **gross profit on selling price** is 20%. What is the **markup on cost?** To find the answer, again assume that the selling price is $1.00. The same formula can be used:

$$
\begin{aligned}
\text{Cost} + \text{Gross profit} &= \text{Selling price} \\
C + .20\,(\$1.00) &= \$1.00 \\
C + \$0.20 &= \$1.00 \\
C &= \$0.80
\end{aligned}
$$

Here, as in the example above, the amount of the markup or gross profit is $0.20 ($1.00 − $0.80), and the percentage markup on cost is 25% ($0.20/$0.80). Retailers use the formulas in Illustration 8-31 to express these relationships.

Illustration 8-31

Formulas Relating to Gross Profit

$$
1.\ \text{Percent gross profit on selling price} = \frac{\text{Percent markup on cost}}{100\% + \text{Percent markup on cost}}
$$

$$
2.\ \text{Percent markup on cost} = \frac{\text{Percent gross profit on selling price}}{100\% - \text{Percent gross profit on selling price}}
$$

Using the Results

What are the disadvantages of using the gross profit method? One is that **it provides an estimate** only. Second, the gross profit method uses **past percentages** in determining the markup. Although the future may repeat the past, a current rate is usually more appropriate. Whenever fluctuations in the rate of profit occur, the percentage must be adjusted appropriately. Third, **it may be inappropriate to apply a single gross profit rate.** Often, a store or department handles merchandise with very different rates of gross profit. In these situations, the gross profit method may have to be applied by type of merchandise, or by combining merchandise with similar profit margins.

Because the result is only an estimate, the gross profit method is **not normally acceptable for financial reporting purposes.** A physical inventory is needed as an additional verification that the inventory indicated in the records is actually on hand. Nevertheless, the gross profit method is used to estimate ending inventory for **interim** (monthly and quarterly) **reporting** and for **insurance purposes** (such as fire losses). Note that the results of applying the gross profit method will reflect the inventory method that is used (specific identification, FIFO, or average cost) because this method is based on historical records.

PRESENTATION, DISCLOSURE, AND ANALYSIS

Presentation and Disclosure of Inventories

Objective 11

Identify how inventory should be presented and the type of inventory disclosures required by ASPE and IFRS.

Sometimes there is a fine line between what is considered to be inventory and what is better classified as property, plant, and equipment. Minor spare parts and servicing equipment, for example, are usually classified as inventory. Major spare parts and standby equipment, on the other hand, are recognized as capital assets if they are expected to provide benefits beyond the current accounting period. The classification issue often requires the exercise of professional judgement.

Inventories are one of the most significant assets of manufacturing and merchandising companies, and of many service enterprises. For this reason, companies are required to disclose additional information about these resources.

Some disclosures are similar to the ones required for other SFP items:

- the choice of accounting policies adopted to measure the inventory;
- the carrying amount of the inventory in total and by classification (such as supplies, material, work in process, and finished goods);
- the amount of inventories recognized as an expense in the period, including unabsorbed and abnormal amounts of production overheads; and
- the carrying amount of inventory pledged as collateral for liabilities.

The amount of inventory recognized as an expense is usually reported according to its function—as cost of goods sold. However, a company that chooses to present its expenses according to the nature of its costs instead of by function would present expenses for raw materials and consumables used, labour costs, and other expenses along with the change in inventories for the period.

Additional disclosures are required for inventories **under IFRS.** These include the carrying amount of inventory carried at fair value less costs to sell, and details about inventory writedowns and reversals of writedowns, such as information about what led to the reversal of any writedowns. Considerable information is required in addition for biological assets and agricultural produce at the point of harvest, such as a reconciliation of opening to ending account balances.

The excerpts in Illustration 8-32 are taken from the 2010 financial statements of **MEGA Brands Inc.**, a Canadian company that designs, manufactures, and markets toys, stationery, and activity products in over 100 countries. The excerpts illustrate the company's disclosure of its accounting policy choices for determining inventory cost including the cost formula used, the basis of valuation on the statement of financial position the carrying value of major categories making up the total inventory, and the cost of goods sold. In addition, the company reports its accounting policy for vendor rebates.

Real World Emphasis

The MEGA Brands Inc. disclosures exceed those now required under ASPE, and meet the requirements for disclosures under IFRS.

Illustration 8-32

Inventory Disclosures—MEGA Brands Inc. (numbers in 000's unless noted)

Vendor allowance

Cash considerations received from vendors are deemed a reduction of the prices of the vendors' products or services and are accounted for as a reduction of cost of sales and related inventory when recognized in the Corporation's consolidated statement of earnings and consolidated balance sheet.

Inventories

Inventories are stated at the lower of cost and net realizable value. Cost is established based on the first-in, first-out method and, as appropriate, includes material, labour and manufacturing overhead costs.

	2010 $	2009 $
Raw materials and supplies	2,662	2,594
Work in progress	12,302	10,169
Finished goods	36,211	33,484
	51,135	46,247

As at December 31, 2010, the Corporation had provided for writedowns of $3.5 million of inventories (2009 – $5.3 million).

The cost of inventories recognized as expense in 2010 included in cost of sales amounts to $199.8 million (2009 – $194.2 million).

Analysis

Objective 12
Explain how inventory analysis provides useful information and apply ratio analysis to inventory.

Financial ratios can be used to help management make decisions about how much and what types of inventory to carry and to help investors assess management's performance in terms of controlling inventory to maximize profits. Common ratios that are used to evaluate inventory levels are the inventory turnover and a related measure, average days to sell (or average age of) the inventory.

The **inventory turnover ratio** measures the number of times on average that the inventory was sold during the period. This ratio helps to measure the liquidity of the investment in inventory because the faster the turnover, the sooner the company generates cash inflows from this asset. A manager may use past turnover experience to determine how long the inventory now in stock will take to be sold. This ratio is calculated by dividing the cost of goods sold by the average inventory on hand during the period.

Average inventory can be calculated from the beginning and ending inventory balances.[21] For example, MEGA Brands Inc. reported beginning inventory of $46.2 million, ending inventory of $51.1 million, and cost of goods sold of $221.7 million for its 2010 fiscal year. The calculation of MEGA Brands' 2010 inventory turnover is shown in Illustration 8-33.

Illustration 8-33

Inventory Turnover Ratio

$$\text{Inventory Turnover} = \frac{\text{Cost of Goods Sold}}{\text{Average Inventory}}$$

$$= \frac{\$221,692}{(\$51,135 + \$46,247)/2}$$

$$= 4.55 \text{ times}$$

A closely related ratio is the **average days to sell inventory**, which represents the average age of the inventory on hand or the number of days it takes to sell inventory after it is acquired. For example, if MEGA Brands' inventory turns over 4.55 times per year, that means it takes, on average, 365 days divided by 4.55 or approximately 80 days to sell its investment in inventory.

Is this a good turnover ratio? If the company sells fresh fruit and vegetables, you would know that this is not a good number. However, for other products, it is not as easy to come to a firm conclusion. For example, MEGA Brands designs and manufactures a broad line of toys, stationery, and activity products, so you might expect that it would move its inventory out faster than only every three months. Each industry has its norms, however, so the industry average is one standard that the company's ratio can be compared against. Because the choice of inventory cost formula may affect the inventory reported on the statement of financial position and the cost of goods sold, these differences make adjustments necessary in any inter-company comparisons. This is true not only for turnover ratios but for any analysis that includes inventory: the amount of working capital, the working capital ratio, and the gross profit percentage, for example. Internally, company management compares these numbers with its goals and objectives for the year.

There is no absolute standard of comparison for most ratios, but generally speaking, companies that are able to keep their inventory at lower levels with higher turnovers than those of their competitors, and still satisfy customer needs, are the most successful.

What Do the Numbers Mean?

Real World Emphasis

Managers and analysts closely follow gross profits. A small change in the gross profit rate can significantly affect the bottom line. For example, at one time, **Apple Computer** suffered a textbook case of shrinking gross profits. In response to pricing wars in the personal computer market, Apple had to quickly reduce the price of its signature Macintosh computers—reducing prices more quickly than it could reduce its costs. As a result, its gross profit rate fell from 44% in 1992 to 40% in 1993. Though the drop of 4 percentage points seems small, its impact on the bottom line caused Apple's share price to drop from $57 per share to $27.50 in just six weeks. As another example, **Debenham**, the second largest department store in the United Kingdom, experienced a 14 percentage share price decline. The cause? Markdowns on slow-moving inventory reduced its gross margin. On the positive side, an increase in the gross profit rate provides a positive signal to the market. For example, just a 1 percentage point boost in **Dr. Pepper**'s gross profit rate cheered the market, indicating the company was able to avoid the squeeze of increased commodity costs by raising its prices.

Sources: Alison Smith, "Debenham's Shares Hit by Warning," *Financial Times*, July 24, 2002, p. 21; D. Kardous, "Higher Pricing Helps Boost Dr. Pepper Snapple's Net," *Wall Street Journal Online*, June 5, 2008; and Barry Cooper, "Apple Continues to Fight Back with New Series, Lower Price," *Orlando Sentinel*, October 24, 1993.

IFRS/ASPE COMPARISON

A Comparison of IFRS and ASPE

Objective 13
Identify differences in accounting between ASPE and IFRS, and what changes are expected in the near future.

Because *CICA Handbook*, Part II, Section 3031 *Inventories* is converged with IAS 2 *Inventories*, there are few differences in the recognition and measurement standards for most inventories. The most significant difference relates to the fact that there is a separate international standard (IAS 41) covering biological assets and agricultural produce at the point of harvest, and these assets are not specifically covered by ASPE. Illustration 8-34 identifies the differences between ASPE and IFRS.

	Accounting Standards for Private Enterprises (ASPE)—*CICA Handbook*, Part II, Sections 3031 and 3850	IFRS—IAS 2, 11, 23, and 41	References to Illustrations and Select Brief Exercises
Scope	There is no primary source of GAAP covering biological assets and agricultural produce at the point of harvest.	IAS 41 provides standards for biological assets and agricultural produce at the point of harvest.	Illustration 8-27
Measurement	Asset retirement and decommissioning costs arising from production activities are added to the carrying amount of the PP&E asset.	Asset retirement and decommissioning costs arising from production activities are added to the cost of the inventory.	Discussed in further detail in Chapter 10.
	Companies may choose a policy of capitalizing interest or a policy of expensing the costs. No guidance is provided on what is a qualifying asset.	Interest costs directly attributable to the acquisition, construction, or production of qualifying inventory are capitalized. Such costs may be expensed for inventory measured at fair value and for qualifying inventory produced in large quantities on a repetitive basis.	BE8-22
	No guidance is provided for onerous contractual obligations such as may occur with purchase commitments	A liability and loss are required to be recognized for onerous contracts if the unavoidable costs exceed the benefits from receiving the contracted goods or services.	Illustration 8-3 and subsequent discussion.
	No guidance is provided for measuring biological assets and agricultural produce prior to and at the point of harvest. After harvest, its carrying amount becomes the inventory's deemed cost, and subsequently it is accounted for at the lower of (the deemed) cost and NRV.	Biological assets and agricultural produce at the point of harvest are measured at fair value less costs to sell. At harvest, this becomes the inventory's deemed cost, and subsequently it is accounted for at the lower of cost and NRV.	Illustration 8-27 BE8-21
Presentation and disclosure	Limited disclosures are required.	Additional disclosures are required, particularly about writedowns and any reversals. In addition, significant information is required about biological assets and agricultural produce.	

Illustration 8-34

IFRS and ASPE Comparison Chart

Looking Ahead

No major changes are expected in the general inventory standards in the near future. However, the IASB issued a Discussion Paper in 2010 on extractive activities related to the search for, discovery of, and extraction of minerals and oil and gas. This project is expected to result in new standards for the associated reserves and resources and therefore inventories in these industries. A final standard will take a number of years to develop.

SUMMARY OF LEARNING OBJECTIVES

1 Understand inventory from a business perspective.

It is important to understand the nature of the various types of businesses that have significant inventory as well as the different types of inventory. Retailers, manufacturers, and wholesalers generally carry significant amounts of inventory. However, different companies have different business models. For example, some manufacturers follow a just-in-time strategy and carry very little inventory on hand. Only one inventory account, Merchandise Inventory, appears in the financial statements of a merchandising concern. A manufacturer normally has three inventory accounts: Raw Materials, Work in Process, and Finished Goods. There may also be an inventory account for factory or manufacturing supplies. Management must manage inventory levels in order to ensure sufficient choice and quantities to meet customer needs yet keep costs to a minimum. The financial statements need to provide information about all of this.

2 Define inventory from an accounting perspective.

Differing companies have different types of inventories including securities, land for development, work in progress, grain, and other. For accounting purposes, inventory is defined as an asset that is held for sale in the ordinary course of business or for the production of such inventory (including raw materials, work in process, and supplies). Special guidance and/or industry practice exists for inventories of financial instruments, construction in progress, biological assets, agricultural products, mineral products, inventories held by producers of agricultural and forest producers, and inventories held by commodity broker-traders.

3 Identify which inventory items should be included in ending inventory.

Inventory is included on the SFP of the entity that has substantially all of the risks and rewards of ownership, which is generally the company that has possession and legal title to the goods. Professional judgement must be used to determine whether substantially all of the risks and rewards have passed. For instance, consigned goods remain the property of the consignor. Purchase commitments are generally not recognized unless onerous.

4 Identify the effects of inventory errors on the financial statements and adjust for them.

If the ending inventory is misstated, (1) the inventory, retained earnings, working capital, and current ratio in the SFP will be incorrect; and (2) the cost of goods sold and net income in the income statement will be incorrect. If purchases and inventory are misstated, (1) the inventory, accounts payable, and current ratio will be incorrect; and (2) purchases and ending inventory will be incorrect.

5 Determine the components of inventory cost.

Inventory costs include all costs of purchase, conversion, and other costs incurred in bringing the inventories to the present location and condition necessary for sale. Such charges include freight charges on goods purchased, other direct costs of acquisition, and labour and other direct production costs incurred in processing the goods up to the time of sale. Manufacturing overhead costs are allocated to inventory based on the normal capacity of the production facilities. Interest and asset retirement costs may be included as part of the cost of inventory in some circumstances.

6 Distinguish between perpetual and periodic inventory systems and account for them.

Under a perpetual inventory system, a continuous record of changes in inventory is maintained in the Inventory account. That is, all purchases into and transfers of goods out of the account are recorded directly in the Inventory account as they occur. No such record is kept under a periodic inventory system. Under the periodic system, year-end inventory is determined by a physical count, and the amount of ending inventory and cost of goods sold is based on this count. Even under the perpetual system, an annual count is needed to test the accuracy of the records.

7 Identify and apply GAAP cost formula options and indicate when each cost formula is appropriate.

The specific identification method is used to assign costs for items of inventory that are not ordinarily interchangeable or that are produced for specific projects. The weighted-average or first-in, first-out cost formula is used to assign costs to other types of inventory. All inventory items that have a similar nature and use to the entity apply the same cost formula.

8 Explain why inventory is measured at the lower of cost and market, and apply the lower of cost and net realizable value standard.

Current assets should not be reported on the SFP at a higher amount than the net cash that is expected to be generated from their use or sale. When this amount is less than "cost," inventory is written down and the loss in value is recognized in the same period as the decline. Net realizable value is the estimated selling price in the ordinary course of business reduced by the expected costs to complete and sell the goods. Ordinarily, each item's cost and NRV are compared and the lower value is chosen. However, items that are related to each other and have similar purposes, that are produced and marketed in the same geographical area, and that cannot be evaluated separately from other items may be grouped and the lower of the group's cost and net realizable value is chosen.

9 Identify inventories that are or may be valued at amounts other than the lower of cost and net realizable value.

Inventories of financial instruments, construction contract work in process, biological assets related to agricultural activity, agricultural produce at the point of harvest and after harvest, inventories held by producers of agricultural and forest producers, mineral products, and inventories of commodity broker-traders all may be accounted for at other than the lower of cost and net realizable value.

10 Apply the gross profit method of estimating inventory.

Ending inventory is determined by deducting an estimate of cost of goods sold from the actual cost of goods available for sale. Cost of goods sold is estimated by multiplying net sales by the percent-

age of cost of goods sold to sales. This percentage is derived from the gross profit percent: 100% – gross profit percentage = cost of goods sold percentage.

11 Identify how inventory should be presented and the type of inventory disclosures required by ASPE and IFRS.

ASPE requires disclosure of how cost is determined, inventory that is pledged as security, the amount charged to the income statement as expense in the period, and the inventories' carrying value by category. Additional information is required by IFRS, including details about inventory impairment writedowns and any recoveries, the circumstances responsible for these, and the carrying amounts and reconciliations of items measured at NRV or fair value. Biological assets must be presented separately on the statement of financial position under IFRS. In general, cost of sales is presented on the income statement under both IFRS and ASPE unless expenses are grouped by nature.

12 Explain how inventory analysis provides useful information and apply ratio analysis to inventory.

Common ratios that are used in the management and evaluation of inventory levels are the inventory turnover and a related measure, average days to sell the inventory, often called the average age of inventory. This is useful information as excessive investment in inventory is expensive to carry, yet too little inventory results in lost sales and dissatisfied customers.

13 Identify differences in accounting between ASPE and IFRS, and what changes are expected in the near future.

ASPE and IFRS are substantially harmonized. IFRS has specific guidance on the measurement of agricultural and construction inventories, the capitalization of borrowing costs on qualifying assets, and on onerous contracts. Asset retirement obligations may be treated differently under IFRS. No major changes are expected in the near future.

KEY TERMS

allowance method, p. 476
asset retirement costs, p. 463
average days to sell inventory, p. 484
basket purchase, p. 464
consigned goods, p. 453
conversion costs, p. 463
cost formula, p. 468
cost of goods available for sale or use, p. 450

cost of goods manufactured, p. 456
cost of goods sold, p. 450
current ratio, p. 459
cut-off schedule, p. 452
direct method, p. 475
executory contract, p. 454
finished goods inventory, p. 449
first-in, first-out (FIFO) cost formula, p. 471

FOB (free on board) destination, p. 452
FOB (free on board) shipping point, p. 452
gross method, p. 460
gross profit method, p. 480
gross profit percentage, p. 481
indirect method, p. 476
inventories, p. 451
inventory turnover ratio, p. 484

joint cost, p. 464

last-in, first-out (LIFO) cost formula, p. 472

lower of cost and market, p. 473

lower of cost and net realizable value, p. 473

lower of cost and net realizable value (LC&NRV) standard, p. 474

market, p. 473

markup on cost, p. 481

merchandise inventory, p. 449

moving-average cost formula, p. 469

net method, p. 461

net realizable value (NRV), p. 473

normal production capacity, p. 463

onerous contract, p. 455

period costs, p. 464

periodic inventory system, p. 466

perpetual inventory system, p. 465

price risk, p. 453

product costs, p. 463

purchase commitments, p. 454

purchase discounts, p. 460

quantities only system, p. 467

raw materials inventory, p. 449

relative sales value method, p. 464

specific identification, p. 468

standard cost system, p. 463

vendor rebate, p. 461

weighted average cost formula, p. 469

work-in-process inventory, p. 449

APPENDIX 8A

The Retail Inventory Method of Estimating Inventory Cost

Objective 14
Apply the retail method of estimating inventory.

Accounting for inventory in a retail operation presents several challenges. Some retailers can use the specific identification method to value their inventories. As explained in the chapter, this approach makes sense when individual inventory units are significant, such as automobiles, pianos, or fur coats. However, imagine attempting to use such an approach at The Bay or Sears—high-volume retailers that have many different types of merchandise at relatively low unit costs! It would be difficult to determine the cost of each sale, to enter cost codes on the tickets, to change the codes to reflect declines in value of the merchandise, to allocate costs such as transportation, and so on. An alternative is to estimate inventory cost when necessary by taking a physical inventory at retail prices. Also, to avoid misstating the inventory, especially in retail operations where losses due to shoplifting and breakage are common, periodic inventory counts are made at retail prices and are then converted to cost. Differences between the records and the physical count require an adjustment to make the records agree with the count.

In most retail businesses, there is an observable pattern between cost and selling prices. Retail prices can be converted to cost simply by multiplying them by the cost-to-retail ratio. This method, called the **retail inventory method, requires that the following information be available:**

1. **the total cost and retail value of the goods purchased,**

2. **the total cost and retail value of the goods available for sale, and**

3. **the sales for the period.**

Real World Emphasis

Here is how it works. The sales for the period are deducted from the retail value of the goods available for sale. The result is an estimate of the ending inventory at retail (selling prices). The ratio of cost to retail for all goods is calculated by dividing the total goods available for sale at cost by the total goods available for sale at retail. The ending inventory valued at selling prices is then converted to the ending inventory at cost by applying the **cost-to-retail ratio.** Use of the retail inventory method is very common. For example, **Hart Stores Inc.** and **Reitmans (Canada) Limited** both report using the retail inventory method in determining inventory cost. Hart Stores' note disclosure of its policy for the year ended January 31, 2011, is shown in Illustration 8A-1.

Illustration 8A-1

Example of Retail Inventory Method Note—Hart Stores Inc.

Inventory

Inventory is valued at the lower of cost and net realizable value. Cost is net of cash consideration received from vendors and includes the cost of making goods available for sale such as freight and duty expenses. Costs such as storage costs, administrative overhead and selling costs are specifically excluded from the cost of inventory. Cost is determined using the retail method.

An example of how the retail inventory method works is shown in Illustration 8A-2.

Illustration 8A-2

Retail Inventory Method

	Cost	Retail
Beginning inventory	$14,000	$ 20,000
Purchases	63,000	90,000
Goods available for sale	$77,000	110,000
Deduct: Sales		85,000
Ending inventory, at retail		$ 25,000
Ratio of cost to retail ($77,000 ÷ $110,000)		70%
Ending inventory at cost (70% of $25,000)		$ 17,500

The retail method is approved by various retail associations and the accounting profession under both ASPE and IFRS, and is allowed by the Canada Revenue Agency. **One advantage of the retail inventory method is that the inventory balance can be approximated without a physical count.** This makes the method particularly useful when preparing interim reports. Insurance adjusters use this approach to estimate losses from fire, flood, or other types of casualty.

This method also **acts as a control device** because any deviations from a physical count at year end have to be explained. In addition, the retail method **speeds up the physical inventory count at year end.** The crew taking the inventory only needs to record the retail price of each item, which is often done using a scanner. There is no need to determine each item's invoice cost, thus saving time and expense.

Retail Method Terminology

The amounts shown in the Retail column of Illustration 8A-2 represent the original retail or selling prices (cost plus an original markup or mark-on), assuming no price changes.

Sales prices, however, are often marked up or down from the original sales price. For retailers, the term **markup** means an increase in the price above the original sales price. **Markup cancellations** are decreases in merchandise prices that had been marked up above the original retail price. Markup cancellations cannot be greater than markups. **Net markups** refer to markups less markup cancellations.

Markdowns are reductions in price below the original selling price. They are a common phenomenon and occur because of a decline in general price levels, special sales, soiled or damaged goods, overstocking, and competition. **Markdown cancellations** occur when the markdowns are later offset by increases in the prices of goods that had been marked down, such as after a one-day sale. A markdown cancellation cannot exceed the original markdown. Markdowns less markdown cancellations are known as **net markdowns**.

To illustrate these different concepts, assume that Designer Clothing Store recently purchased 100 dress shirts from a supplier. The cost for these shirts was $1,500, or $15 a shirt. Designer Clothing established the selling price on these shirts at $30 each. The manager noted that the shirts were selling quickly, so she added $5 to the price of each shirt. This markup made the price too high for customers and sales lagged. The manager then responded by reducing the price to $32. To this point, there has been a **markup of $5** and a **markup cancellation of $3** on the original selling price of a shirt. When the major marketing season ended, the manager set the price of the remaining shirts at $23. This price change constitutes a **markup cancellation of $2** and a **$7 markdown.** If the shirts are later priced at $24, a **markdown cancellation of $1** occurs.

Retail Inventory Method with Markups and Markdowns— Conventional Method

To determine the ending inventory figures, a decision must be made on the treatment of markups, markup cancellations, markdowns, and markdown cancellations **when calculating the ratio of cost to retail.**

To illustrate the different possibilities, consider the data for In-Fashion Stores Inc., shown in Illustration 8A-3. In-Fashion's ending inventory at cost can be calculated under two different cost-to-retail ratios.

Ratio A: Reflects a cost percentage that includes net markups but excludes net markdowns.

Ratio B: Reflects a cost ratio that incorporates both net markups and net markdowns.

Illustration **8A-3**

Retail Inventory Method with Markups and Markdowns— In-Fashion Stores Inc.

Information in Records

	Cost	Retail
Beginning inventory	$ 500	$ 1,000
Purchases (net)	20,000	35,000
Markups		3,000
Markup cancellations		1,000
Markdowns		2,500
Markdown cancellations		2,000
Sales (net)		25,000

Retail Inventory Method

	Cost		Retail	
Beginning inventory	$ 500		$ 1,000	
Purchases (net)	20,000		35,000	
Merchandise available for sale	20,500		36,000	
Add:				
Markups		$ 3,000		
Less: Markup cancellations		(1,000)		
Net markups				2,000
	20,500		38,000	
Cost-to-retail ratio $\dfrac{\$20,500}{\$38,000}=53.9\%$				(A)
Deduct:				
Markdowns		2,500		
Less: Markdown cancellations		(2,000)		
Net markdowns				500
	$20,500		37,500	
Cost-to-retail ratio $\dfrac{\$20,500}{\$37,500}=54.7\%$				(B)
Deduct: Sales (net)			25,000	
Ending inventory at retail			$12,500	

The calculations to determine the cost of ending inventory for In-Fashion Stores are therefore:

Ending inventory at retail × Cost ratio = Ending inventory, at cost
Under **(A)**: $12,500 × 53.9% = $6,737.50
Under **(B)**: $12,500 × 54.7% = $6,837.50

Which percentage should be used to calculate ending inventory? The answer depends on whether you are trying to determine inventory "cost" or a more conservative lower of cost and market figure.

The conventional retail inventory method uses the cost-to-retail ratio that includes net markups but excludes net markdowns, as shown in the calculation of **ratio A.** It is designed to approximate **the lower of average cost and market,** with market being defined as **net realizable value less a normal profit margin.** To understand why net markups but not net markdowns are included in the cost-to-retail ratio, we must understand how a retail outlet operates. When a company has a net markup on an item, this normally indicates that the item's market value has increased. On the other hand, if the item has a net markdown, this means that the item's utility has declined. Therefore, to approximate the lower of cost and market, net markdowns are considered a current loss and are not included in calculating the cost-to-retail ratio. **This makes the denominator a larger number and the ratio a lower percentage.** With a lower cost-to-retail ratio, the result approximates a lower of cost and market amount.

To make this clearer, assume two different items were purchased for $5 each, and the original sales price was established at $10 each. One item was then marked down to a selling price of $2. Assuming no sales for the period, if markdowns are included in the cost-to-retail ratio (**ratio B** above), the ending inventory is calculated as shown in Illustration 8A-4.

Markdowns Included in Cost-to-Retail Ratio

	Cost	Retail
Purchases	$10.00	$20.00
Deduct: Markdowns		8.00
Ending inventory, at retail		$12.00

Cost-to-retail ratio $\dfrac{\$10.00}{\$12.00} = 83.3\%$

Ending inventory at average cost ($12.00 × .833) =		$10.00

This approach results in ending inventory at the average cost of the two items on hand without considering the loss on the one item.

If markdowns are excluded from the ratio (**ratio A** above), the result is ending inventory at the lower of average cost and market. The calculation is shown in Illustration 8A-5.

Markdowns Not Included in Cost-to-Retail Ratio

	Cost	Retail
Purchases	$10.00	$20.00

Cost-to-retail ratio $\dfrac{\$10.00}{\$20.00} = 50\%$

Deduct: Markdowns	8.00
Ending inventory, at retail	$12.00
Ending inventory at lower of average cost and market ($12 × .50) =	$6.00

The $6 inventory valuation includes two inventory items: one inventoried at $5 (its cost) and the other at $1 (its NRV less a normal profit margin of 50%). For the item with the market decline, the price was reduced from $10 to $2 and the cost was reduced from $5 to $1. Therefore, to approximate the lower of average cost and market, the cost-to-retail ratio is established by dividing the cost of goods available by the sum of the original retail price of these goods plus the net markups; the **net markdowns are excluded** from the ratio.

Many possible cost-to-retail ratios could be calculated. The schedule below summarizes how including or excluding various items in the cost-to-retail ratio relates to specific inventory valuation methods. Note that net purchases are always included in the ratio:

Beginning Inventory	Net Markups	Net Markdowns	Inventory Cost Formula and Valuation Method Approximated
Include	Include	Include	Average cost
Include	Include	Exclude	Lower of average cost and market (conventional method)
Exclude	Include	Include	FIFO cost
Exclude	Include	Exclude	Lower of FIFO cost and market

Using the FIFO cost formula, the estimated ending inventory (and its cost) will, by definition, come from the purchases of the current period. **Therefore, the opening inventory, at cost and retail, is excluded in determining the cost ratio.** The retail price of the opening inventory is then added to determine the total selling price of goods available for the period.

CICA Handbook Section 3031 and IAS 2 are clear that, for purposes of determining inventory **cost,** markdowns below the original sales price are included in calculating the ratio. This means that a separate adjustment has to be made to get a **lower of cost and NRV** valuation. Why not just exclude the markdowns from the cost-to-retail ratio? As mentioned above, this results in a lower of cost and market value where market represents NRV less a normal profit margin. This concept of market is not permitted by either ASPE or IFRS.

Special Items

The retail inventory method becomes more complicated when such items as freight-in, purchase returns and allowances, and purchase discounts are involved. In the retail method, we treat such items as follows:

- **Freight costs** are treated as a part of the purchase cost.

- **Purchase returns** are ordinarily considered a reduction of the cost price and retail price.

- **Purchase allowances** are considered a reduction of the purchase cost column only unless normal selling prices are adjusted because of the allowance.

- **Purchase discounts** are usually considered a reduction of the purchase cost only.

In short, the treatment for the items affecting the cost column of the retail inventory approach follows the calculation of cost of goods available for sale.

Note also that it is considered proper to treat **sales returns and allowances** as adjustments to gross sales; **sales discounts to customers,** however, are not recognized when sales are recorded gross. If the Sales Discount account were adjusted in such a situation, the ending inventory figure at retail would be overvalued.

In addition, a number of special items require careful analysis.

- **Transfers-in** from another department are reported in the same way as purchases from an outside enterprise.

- **Normal shortages** (breakage, damage, theft, shrinkage) are deducted in the retail column because these goods are no longer available for sale. These costs are reflected in the selling price because a certain amount of shortage is considered normal in a retail enterprise. As a result, this amount is not considered in calculating the cost-to-retail percentage. Rather, it is shown as a deduction, similar to sales, to arrive at ending inventory at retail.

- **Abnormal shortages** are deducted from both the cost and retail columns before calculating the cost-to-retail ratio and are reported as a special inventory amount or as a loss. To do otherwise distorts the cost-to-retail ratio and overstates ending inventory.

- **Employee discounts** (given to employees to encourage loyalty, better performance, and so on) are deducted from the retail column in the same way as sales. These discounts should not be considered in the cost-to-retail percentage because they do not reflect an overall change in the selling price.

Illustration 8A-6 shows some of these concepts in more detail, using the conventional retail inventory method to determine the ending inventory at the lower of average cost and market.

Illustration 8A-6

Conventional Retail Inventory Method— Special Items Included

	Cost		Retail
Beginning inventory	$ 1,000		$ 1,800
Purchases	30,000		60,000
Freight-in	600		–0–
Purchase returns	(1,500)		(3,000)
Totals	30,100		58,800
Net markups			9,000
Abnormal shrinkage	(1,200)		(2,000)
Totals	$28,900		65,800
Deduct:			
Net markdowns			1,400
Sales		$36,000	
Sales returns		(900)	35,100
Employee discounts			800
Normal shrinkage			1,300
Ending inventory at retail			$27,200

Cost-to-retail ratio $\dfrac{\$28,900}{\$65,800} = 43.9\%$

Ending inventory, lower of average cost and market (43.9% × $27,200) =	$11,940.80

Evaluation of Retail Inventory Method

The retail inventory method of calculating inventory is used for these reasons:

1. To permit the calculation of net income without a physical count of inventory
2. As a control measure in determining inventory shortages
3. To control quantities of merchandise on hand
4. As a source of information for insurance and tax purposes

One characteristic of the retail inventory method is that it **has an averaging effect for varying rates of gross profit.** When it is used in a business where rates of gross profit vary among departments, the method should be refined by calculating inventory separately by departments or by classes of merchandise with similar rates of gross profit. This method's reliability rests on the assumption that the mix of inventory items is similar to the mix in the total goods available for sale.

SUMMARY OF LEARNING OBJECTIVE FOR APPENDIX 8A

14 Apply the retail method of estimating inventory.

The retail inventory method is based on converting the retail price of ending inventory by a cost-to-retail percentage, which is derived from information in the accounting and supplementary records. To use this method, records must be kept of the costs and retail prices for beginning inventory, net purchases, and abnormal spoilage, as well as the retail amount of net markups, net markdowns, and net sales. Which items go into the numerator and denominator of the cost-to-retail ratio depends on the type of inventory valuation estimate that is wanted.

KEY TERMS

conventional retail inventory method, p. 491

cost-to-retail ratio, p. 488

markdown, p. 489

markdown cancellations, p. 489

markup, p. 489

markup cancellations, p. 489

net markdowns, p. 489

net markups, p. 489

retail inventory method, p. 488

APPENDIX 8B

Accounting Guidance for Specific Inventory

Objective 15

Identify other primary sources of GAAP for inventory.

Illustration 8B-1 summarizes the primary sources of GAAP for most types of inventory.

Illustration 8B-1

Inventory—Primary Sources of GAAP

Form of Inventory	ASPE Source of Guidance	IFRS Source of Guidance
Most inventories apply a lower of cost and net realizable value model	*CICA Handbook–Accounting,* Part II, Section 3031 *Inventories*	IAS 2 *Inventories*
Excluded from Section 3031 and IAS 2 but Covered by Other Primary Sources of GAAP		
Financial instruments	*CICA Handbook–Accounting,* Part II, Section 3856 *Financial Instruments*	IAS 32 *Financial Instruments: Presentation,* and IAS 39 *Financial Instruments: Recognition and Measurement*
Construction contract work in process		IAS 11 *Construction Contracts*
All contracts accounted for using the percentage-of-completion method, including construction work in process	*CICA Handbook–Accounting,* Part II, Section 3400 *Revenue*	
Biological assets related to agricultural activity, and agricultural product at the point of harvest	See below	IAS 41 *Agriculture*
Industry-Specific Exclusions, from Only the Measurement Provisions of Section 3031 and IAS 2 (All disclosure requirements still apply.)		
Inventory held by producers of agricultural and forest products, agricultural produce after harvest, and mineral and mineral products	Excluded from the measurement provisions of Section 3031 if measured at net realizable value in accordance with established industry practice; otherwise, apply Section 3031	Excluded from the measurement provisions of IAS 2 if measured at net realizable value in accordance with established industry practice; otherwise, apply IAS 2
Inventory held by commodity broker-traders	Excluded from the measurement provisions of Section 3031 if measured at fair value less costs to sell; otherwise apply Section 3031	Excluded from the measurement provisions of IAS 2 if measured at fair value less costs to sell; otherwise apply IAS 2
Biological assets and harvested agricultural produce	Excluded from the measurement provisions of Section 3031. Not covered by any specific primary source of GAAP.	See above

Note: All assignment material with an asterisk (*) relates to the appendices to the chapter.

Brief Exercises

(LO 1, 13) BE8-1 Indicate whether the following would be considered inventory for a public company like **Toyota Motor Corporation**. If so, indicate the inventory category to which that item would belong.

(a) Engines purchased to make the Toyota Corolla

(b) Nuts and bolts purchased to attach the engine to the car body

(c) Spare parts purchased for the manufacturing equipment

(d) Standby equipment in case a machine breaks down

(e) Wages paid to assembly-line employees

(f) Rent for manufacturing facility

(g) Wages paid to supervisor

(h) Toyota Corolla ready to be shipped to the dealer

(i) Manufacturing plant

How would your responses change if the manufacturer followed ASPE?

(LO 2) BE8-2 Betadyne Corp. is a public company that manufactures and sells medical equipment. What kind of information would be useful for users of the company's financial statements?

(LO 3, 6) BE8-3 Hare Ltd. had beginning inventory of 50 units that cost $100 each. During September, the company purchased 200 units on account at $100 each, returned 6 units for credit, and sold 150 units at $200 each.

(a) Journalize the September transactions assuming that Hare Ltd. uses a perpetual inventory system.

(b) Journalize the September transactions assuming that Hare Ltd. uses a periodic inventory system.

(c) Assume that Hare uses a periodic system and prepares financial statements at the end of each month. An inventory count determines that there are 94 units of inventory remaining at September 30. Prepare the necessary adjusting entry at September 30.

(LO 5, 13) BE8-4 Serafina Corp. purchases inventory costing $4,000 on July 11 on terms 3/10, n/30, and pays the invoice in full on July 15.

(a) Prepare the required entries to record the two transactions assuming Serafina uses (1) the gross method of recording purchases, and (2) the net method of recording purchases. Assume the periodic method is used.

(b) Journalize the two transactions under (1) the gross method and (2) the net method, assuming the invoice was paid on July 31 instead of July 15.

(c) Assuming that Serafina is a private company reporting under ASPE, can interest costs incurred to finance inventory be added to the cost of the inventory?

(d) Assuming that Serafina is a public company following IFRS, under what circumstances can interest costs incurred to finance inventory be added to the cost of the inventory?

(LO 3) BE8-5 Mayhelm Ltd. took a physical inventory on December 31 and determined that goods costing $2,000 were on hand. This amount included $500 of goods held on consignment for Delhi Corporation. Not included in the physical count were $400 of goods purchased from Taylor Corporation, FOB shipping point, and $180 of goods sold to Mount Pilot Ltd. for $300, FOB destination. Both the Taylor purchase and the Mount Pilot sale were in transit at year end. What amount should Mayhelm report as its December 31 inventory?

(LO 5, 6) BE8-6 Doors Unlimited Ltd. purchases units of wood frames that have manufacturer's rebates from Traders Inc. The rebate requires Doors Unlimited to purchase a minimum number of units in a calendar year. The initial unit cost of each wood frame is $2.50 before any rebate. If more than 3,500 units are purchased, the rebate is $0.25 per unit for all units purchased beyond the base amount of 3,500 units. Doors Unlimited Ltd. has a June 30 fiscal year end. By June 30, 2014, Doors Unlimited had purchased 3,000 wood frames for the six-month period from January 1, 2014, to June 30, 2014. Doors Unlimited estimates that an additional 3,000 wood frames will be purchased from July 1, 2014, to December 31, 2014. Doors Unlimited's management is very confident that this estimate will be confirmed by future purchases from Traders.

(a) Explain the conceptual principles involved in determining if an accrual should be made for the volume rebate from Traders. Under what circumstances would an accrual not be permissible?

(b) Calculate the amount of any rebate that Doors Unlimited should accrue at June 30, 2014, assuming the rebate cannot be cancelled by Traders.

(c) Calculate the unit cost that Doors Unlimited should use in the costing of wood frames using the perpetual inventory system. (Round to four decimal places.)

(LO 4) BE8-7 Angus Enterprises Ltd. reported cost of goods sold for 2014 of $2.4 million and retained earnings of $4.2 million at December 31, 2014. Angus later discovered that its ending inventories at December 31, 2013 and 2014 were overstated by $155,000 and $45,000, respectively. Determine the correct amounts for 2014 cost of goods sold and December 31, 2014 retained earnings.

(LO 5) BE8-8 Gamers' World buys 1,000 computer game CDs from a distributor that is discontinuing those games. The purchase price for the lot is $7,500. Gamers' World will group the CDs into three price categories for resale, as follows:

Group	No. of CDs	Price per CD
1	100	$ 5
2	800	10
3	100	15

Determine the cost per CD for each group, using the relative sales value method.

(LO 7) BE8-9 Moorea Corp. uses a periodic inventory system. On June 24, the company sold 600 units. The following additional information is available:

	Units	Unit Cost	Total Cost
June 1 inventory	200	$12	$ 2,400
June 15 purchase	400	14	5,600
June 23 purchase	400	15	6,000
	1,000		$14,000

(a) Calculate the June 30 inventory and the June cost of goods sold using the weighted average cost formula.

(b) Calculate the June 30 inventory and the June cost of goods sold using the FIFO formula.

(c) Assume that 200 units sold on June 24 had a unit cost of $12; 300 had a unit cost of $14; and the remaining 100 units had a unit cost of $15. Calculate the June 30 inventory and the June cost of goods sold using the specific identification method.

(LO 6, 7) BE8-10 Canali Corporation uses a perpetual inventory system. On November 19, the company sold 600 units. The following additional information is available:

	Units	Unit Cost	Total Cost
Nov. 1 inventory	250	$12	$ 3,000
Nov. 15 purchase	400	14	5,600
Nov. 23 purchase	350	15	5,250
	1,000		$13,850

Calculate the November 30 inventory and the November cost of goods sold using

(a) the moving average cost formula, and

(b) the FIFO cost formula.

(LO 7, 8, 13) BE8-11 Antimatter Corporation has the following four items in its ending inventory:

Item	Cost	Estimated Selling Price	Estimated Disposal Costs
Neutrinos	$1,820	$2,100	$100
Ocillinos	5,000	4,900	100
Electrons	4,290	4,625	200
Protons	3,200	4,210	100

(a) Assume that Antimatter is a public company using IFRS. Determine the total value of ending inventory using the lower of cost and net realizable value model applied on an individual item basis.

(b) Would there be any difference in accounting if Antimatter were a private entity using ASPE?

(LO 6, 8) BE8-12   Bluebell Enterprises Ltd.'s records reported an inventory cost of $55,600 and a net realizable value of $54,000 at December 31, 2012. At December 31, 2013, the records indicated a cost of $68,700 and a net realizable value of $61,625. All opening inventory had been sold during the year.

(a) Assuming that Bluebell Enterprises uses a perpetual inventory system, prepare the necessary December 31, 2013 entry under (1) the direct method and (2) the indirect method.

(b) Assume that at December 31, 2014, the records indicate inventory with a cost of $60,000 and a net realizable value of $60,900. Prepare the necessary December 31, 2014 entry under (1) the direct method and (2) the indirect method. Explain why a "gain" is reported under the indirect method of accounting.

(LO 3, 5, 13) BE8-13   Beaver Corp., public company using IFRS, signed a long-term non-cancellable purchase commitment with a major supplier to purchase raw materials at an annual cost of $2 million. At December 31, 2013, the raw materials to be purchased in 2014 have a market price of $1,965,000.

(a) Prepare any necessary December 31, 2013 entry.

(b) In 2014, Beaver receives the raw materials and pays the required $2 million. The raw materials now have a market value of $1,915,000. Prepare the entry to record the purchase.

(c) Explain how the accounting treatment under (a) compares with the accounting treatment for private companies under ASPE.

(LO 9, 13) BE 8-14

(a) Briefly explain the criteria that have to be met for inventory to be recorded at an amount greater than cost.

(b) Briefly explain the accounting for the following inventory items under ASPE:

1. Sheep   2. Wool   3. Carpet

(c) Briefly explain the accounting for the items in (b) under IFRS.

(LO 10) BE 8-15   Great Balls of Fire Inc.'s April 30 inventory was destroyed by an explosion of an underground oil tank. January 1 inventory was $310,000 and purchases for January through April totalled $780,000. Sales for the same period were $1.1 million. Great Balls of Fire's normal gross profit percentage is 31%. Using the gross profit method, estimate the amount of Great Balls of Fire's April 30 inventory that was destroyed.

(LO 12) BE8-16   **Kraft Foods Inc.** reported inventory of $5,706 million at the end of its 2011 fiscal year and $5,310 million at the end of its 2010 fiscal year. It reported cost of goods sold of $35,350 million for the fiscal year 2011 and net sales of $54,365 million for fiscal year 2011. Calculate Kraft's inventory turnover and the average days to sell inventory for the fiscal year 2011.

(LO 14) *BE8-17   Feretti Inc. had beginning inventory of $22,000 at cost and $30,000 at retail. Net purchases were $157,500 at cost and $215,000 at retail. Net markups were $10,000, net markdowns were $7,000, and sales were $184,500. Calculate the ending inventory at cost using the conventional retail method. Round the cost-to-retail percentage to one decimal place.

(LO 2) BE8-18   Which of the following would be included in inventory? For any amount not included in inventory, explain where the amount would be recorded.

(a) Raw materials costs of leather, to a manufacturer of leather furniture

(b) Cost of cans of corn held on the shelves of a grocery store

(c) The cost of a truck in the process of being manufactured by an automobile manufacturer

(d) The cost of land being held for development to a property developer

(e) The cost of a van being used as a courtesy vehicle to an automobile service centre

(f) The costs of construction for a home being built for a specific customer, to a builder

(g) The cost of soap and paper towels for the washrooms of a restaurant

(LO 1) *BE8-19   **Walmart** uses a just-in-time inventory system to reduce its costs, allowing it to sell goods at lower prices to its customers. What are the benefits of a good inventory management system? What are the risks associated with a very tight inventory control system?

(LO 15) BE8-20   What are the primary sources of GAAP relating to inventory

(a) under IFRS?   (b) under ASPE?

(LO 9) BE8-21   Farmer John Industries Inc. is in the business of producing organic foods for sale to restaurants and in local markets. The company uses IFRS and has a June 30 fiscal year end.

As an experiment, the company has decided to attempt raising organic free-range chickens. On May 1, 2014, Farmer John purchased 100 new hatchlings for cash at a total cost of $1,000. The company incurs feed and labour costs of $150 per month to look after the chicks. Their (acceptable) accounting policy is to capitalize these costs.

On June 30, the company estimated that the chickens would mature in mid-October. At year end they have a fair value of $1,800 and the company would have to transport the chickens to their customers at an average cost of $3 per chicken.

On October 30, all 100 chickens had matured and the company sold and shipped 50 of the chickens to one of its key customers for $30 per chicken. Transportation costs were $3 per chick, as expected.

(a) Prepare the journal entries to record the inventory activity relating to the chickens for the month of May.

(b) Prepare the journal entries to record the inventory activity relating to the chickens for the month of June, including any year-end adjustments required under IAS 41.

(c) How would the result be different if the company used ASPE?

(LO 5) BE8-22   Sunny Valley Limited produces wine. Certain vintage wines take more than one year to age. The company has borrowed funds to cover the costs of this aging process. The company meets the interest capitalization criteria under IFRS. Capitalizable interest under IFRS is $100.

(a) Prepare the journal entry to record the $100 interest under IFRS.

(b) Show the possible journal entries under ASPE.

Exercises

(LO 6, 7) E8-1   (Periodic Versus Perpetual Entries) Ruggers Corporation sells one product, with information for July as follows:

July	1	Inventory	100 units at $15.00 each
	4	Sale	80 units at $18.00 each
	11	Purchase	150 units at $16.50 each
	13	Sale	120 units at $18.75 each
	20	Purchase	160 units at $17.00 each
	27	Sale	100 units at $20.00 each

Ruggers uses the FIFO cost formula. All purchases and sales are on account.

Instructions

(a) Assume Ruggers uses a periodic system. Prepare all necessary journal entries, including the end-of-month adjusting entry to record cost of goods sold. A physical count indicates that the ending inventory for July is 110 units.

(b) Calculate gross profit using the periodic system.

(c) Assume Ruggers uses the periodic system, and a count on July 31 reports only 102 units in ending inventory. How would your entries in (a) change, if at all? Explain briefly.

(d) Assume Ruggers uses a perpetual system. Prepare all July journal entries.

(e) Calculate gross profit using the perpetual system.

(f) Assume Ruggers uses the perpetual system, and a count on July 31 reports only 102 units in ending inventory. How would your entries in (d) change, if at all? Explain briefly.

(LO 6) E8-2   (Determining Merchandise Amounts—Periodic) Two or more items are omitted in each of the following tabulations of income statement data. Fill in the amounts that are missing.

	2013	2014	2015
Sales	$290,000	$_____	$410,000
Sales returns	6,000	13,000	
Net sales	_____	347,000	_____
Beginning inventory	20,000	32,000	_____
Ending inventory	_____		_____
Purchases	_____	260,000	298,000

	2013	2014	2015
Purchase returns and allowances	5,000	8,000	10,000
Transportation-in	8,000	9,000	12,000
Cost of goods sold	238,000		303,000
Gross profit on sales	46,000	91,000	97,000

(LO 1, 5) E8-3   (Purchases Recorded—Gross Method and Net Method) Transactions follow for Whitehall Limited:

> March 10   Purchased goods billed at $25,000, terms 3/10, n/60.
>   11   Purchased goods billed at $26,575, terms 1/15, n/30.
>   19   Paid invoice of March 10.
>   24   Purchased goods billed at $11,500, terms 3/10, n/30.

Instructions

(a) Prepare general journal entries for the transactions above, assuming that purchases are to be recorded at net amounts after cash discounts and that discounts lost are to be treated as a financial expense. Assume a periodic inventory system.

(b) Assuming there are no purchase or payment transactions other than the ones mentioned above, prepare the adjusting entry required on March 31 if financial statements are to be prepared as at that date.

(c) Prepare general journal entries for the transactions above, assuming that purchases are to be recorded using the gross method. Assume a periodic inventory system.

(d) Indicate whether there are entries required at March 31 in addition to those in (c) if financial statements are to be prepared. Explain.

(e) Which method would provide the general manager of Whitehall with better information for managing the business?

(LO 3, 5, 13) E8-4   (Inventoriable Costs) In an annual audit of Solaro Company Limited, you find that a physical inventory count on December 31, 2014, showed merchandise of $441,000. You also discover the following items were excluded from the $441,000.

1. Merchandise of $61,000 is held by Solaro on consignment from BonBon Corporation.

2. Merchandise costing $33,000 was shipped by Solaro FOB destination to XYZ Ltd. on December 31, 2014. This merchandise was accepted by XYZ on January 6, 2015.

3. Merchandise costing $46,000 was shipped FOB shipping point to ABC Company on December 29, 2014. This merchandise was received by ABC on January 10, 2015.

4. Merchandise costing $73,000 was shipped FOB destination from Wholesaler Inc. to Solaro on December 30, 2014. Solaro received the items on January 8, 2015.

5. Merchandise costing $51,000 was shipped by Distributor Ltd. FOB shipping point on December 30, 2014, and received at Solaro's office on January 2, 2015.

6. Solaro had excess inventory and incurred additional $1,500 in storage costs due to delayed shipment in transaction (3) above.

7. Solaro incurred $2,000 for interest expense on inventory it purchased through delayed payment plans in fiscal 2014.

Instructions

(a) Based on the information provided above, calculate the amount of inventory that should appear on Solaro's December 31, 2014 balance sheet.

(b) Under what circumstances can a private company reporting under ASPE capitalize interest costs incurred to finance inventory?

(c) Under what circumstances can a public company reporting under IFRS capitalize interest costs incurred to finance inventory?

(LO 3, 4) E8-5   (Inventoriable Costs—Perpetual) The Motuto Equipment Corporation maintains a general ledger account for each class of inventory, debiting the individual accounts for increases during the period and crediting them for decreases. The transactions that follow are for the Raw Materials inventory account, which is debited for materials purchased and credited for materials requisitioned for use.

1. An invoice for $8,100, terms FOB destination, was received and entered on January 2, 2015. The receiving report shows that the materials were received on December 28, 2014.

2. Materials costing $7,300 were returned to the supplier on December 29, 2014, on FOB shipping point terms. The returns were entered into Motuto's general ledger on December 28 even though the returned items did not arrive at the vendor's office until January 6, 2015.

3. Materials costing $28,000, shipped FOB destination, were not entered by December 31, 2014, because they were in a railroad car on the company's siding on that date and had not been unloaded.

4. An invoice for $7,500, terms FOB shipping point, was received and entered on December 30, 2014. The receiving report shows that the materials were received on January 4, 2015, and the bill of lading shows that they were shipped on January 2, 2015.

5. Materials costing $19,800 were received on December 30, 2014. No entry was made for them as of that date, because they were ordered with a specified delivery date of no earlier than January 10, 2015.

6. Materials costing $20,000 were received on December 29, 2014. The supplier's warehouse was full and the supplier asked Motuto to hold these items on its behalf and has also insured these items for the period that Motuto will be holding them. The purchase terms indicate that the supplier will purchase these items back from Motuto Equipment in early January 2015 at $20,000 plus storage fees.

7. Materials costing $5,500 were received on December 20, 2014, that are on consignment from Able Company.

Instructions

Ethics

(a) Prepare any correcting journal entries that are required at December 31, 2014, assuming that the books have not been closed. Also indicate which entries must be reversed after closing so that the next period's accounts will be correct.

(b) Are there any ethical concerns raised by these transactions? How should Motuto deal with this situation?

(LO 3, 4) E8-6 (Inventoriable Costs—Error Adjustments) Jaeco Corporation asks you to review its December 31, 2014 inventory values and prepare the necessary adjustments to the books. The following information is given to you.

1. Jaeco uses the periodic method of recording inventory. A physical count reveals $234,890 of inventory on hand at December 31, 2014, although the books have not yet been adjusted to reflect the ending inventory.

2. Not included in the physical count of inventory is $10,420 of merchandise purchased on December 15 from Shamsi. This merchandise was shipped FOB shipping point on December 29 and arrived in January. The invoice arrived and was recorded on December 31.

3. Included in inventory is merchandise sold to Sage on December 30, FOB destination. This merchandise was shipped after it was counted. The invoice was prepared and recorded as a sale on account for $12,800 on December 31. The merchandise cost $7,350, and Sage received it on January 3.

4. Included in the count of inventory was merchandise received from Dutton on December 31 with an invoice price of $15,630. The merchandise was shipped FOB destination. The invoice, which has not yet arrived, has not been recorded.

5. Not included in inventory is $8,540 of merchandise purchased from Growler Industries. This merchandise was received on December 31 after the inventory had been counted. The invoice was received and recorded on December 30.

6. Included in inventory was $10,438 of inventory held by Jaeco on consignment from Jackel Industries.

7. Included in inventory is merchandise sold to Kemp, FOB shipping point. This merchandise was shipped after it was counted on December 31. The invoice was prepared and recorded as a sale for $18,900 on December 31. The cost of this merchandise was $11,520, and Kemp received the merchandise on January 5.

8. Excluded from inventory was a carton labelled "Please accept for credit." This carton contains merchandise costing $1,500, which had been sold to a customer for $2,600. No entry had been made to the books to record the return, but none of the returned merchandise seemed damaged.

9. Jaeco has sold $12,500 of inventory to Simply Corp. on December 15, 2014. These items were shipped FOB shipping point. The terms of sale indicate that Simply Corp. will be permitted to return an unlimited amount until May 15, 2015. Jaeco has never provided unlimited returns in the past and is not able to estimate the amount of any potential returns that Simply may make.

Instructions

(a) Determine the proper inventory balance for Jaeco Corporation at December 31, 2014.

(b) Prepare any adjusting correcting entries necessary at December 31, 2014. Assume the books have not been closed.

(LO 3, 4, **E8-7** **(Inventoriable Costs)** The following is a list of items that may or may not be reported as inventory in Keesa
5, 13) Corp.'s December 31 balance sheet:

1. Goods out on consignment at another company's store

2. Goods sold on an instalment basis

3. Goods purchased FOB shipping point that are in transit at December 31

4. Goods purchased FOB destination that are in transit at December 31

5. Goods sold to another company, with Keesa having signed an agreement to repurchase the goods at a set price that covers all costs related to the inventory

6. Goods sold where large returns are predictable

7. Goods sold FOB shipping point that are in transit at December 31

8. Freight charges on goods purchased

9. Freight charges on goods sold

10. Factory labour costs incurred on goods that are still unsold

11. Interest costs incurred for inventories that are routinely manufactured in large quantities

12. Costs incurred to advertise goods held for resale

13. Materials on hand and not yet placed into production by a manufacturing firm

14. Office supplies

15. Raw materials on which a manufacturing firm has started production, but which are not completely processed

16. Factory supplies

17. Goods held on consignment from another company

18. Goods held on consignment by another company

19. Costs identified with units completed by a manufacturing firm, but not yet sold

20. Goods sold FOB destination that are in transit at December 31

21. Temporary investments in shares and bonds that will be resold in the near future

22. Costs of uncleared land to be developed by a property development company

23. Cost of normal waste or spoilage of raw materials during production

24. Cost of waste and spoilage experienced above normal levels; that is, abnormal levels of waste of raw materials

25. Costs to store excess materials inventory for a manufacturer

26. Costs to store wine as it ages for a wine producer

27. Decommissioning costs incurred as a part of the extraction of minerals

Instructions

(a) Assuming that ASPE is followed, indicate which of these items would typically be reported as inventory in the financial statements. If an item should not be reported as inventory, indicate how it should be reported in the financial statements.

(b) How would your response to (a) change under IFRS?

(LO 4) **E8-8** **(Inventory Errors—Periodic)** Salamander Limited makes the following errors during the current year. Each error is an independent case.

1. Ending inventory is overstated by $1,020, but purchases are recorded correctly.

2. Both ending inventory and a purchase on account are understated by the same amount. (Assume this purchase of $1,500 was recorded in the following year.)

3. Ending inventory is correct, but a purchase on account was not recorded. (Assume this purchase of $850 was recorded in the following year.)

Instructions

Indicate the effect of each error on working capital, current ratio (assume that the current ratio is greater than 1), retained earnings, and net income for the current year and the following year.

(LO 4) E8-9 (Inventory Errors) Eureka Limited has a calendar-year accounting period. The following errors were discovered in 2014.

1. The December 31, 2012 merchandise inventory had been understated by $51,000.

2. Merchandise purchased on account in 2013 was recorded on the books for the first time in February 2014, when the original invoice for the correct amount of $2,400 arrived. The merchandise had arrived on December 28, 2013, and was included in the December 31, 2013 merchandise inventory. The invoice arrived late because of a mix-up by the wholesaler.

3. Inventory, valued at $1,000, held on consignment by Eureka was included in the December 31, 2013 count.

Instructions

(a) Calculate the effect of each error on the 2013 net income.

(b) Calculate the effect, if any, that each error had on the related December 31, 2013 statement of financial position items.

(LO 4) E8-10 (Inventory Errors) The net income per books of Lyondell Industries Limited was determined without any knowledge of the following errors. The 2008 year was Lyondell's first year in business. No dividends have been declared or paid.

Year	Net Income per Books	Error in Ending Inventory	
2008	$50,000	Overstated	$ 5,000
2009	52,000	Overstated	9,000
2010	54,000	Understated	11,000
2011	56,000	No error	
2012	58,000	Understated	2,000
2013	60,000	Overstated	10,000

Instructions

(a) Prepare a work sheet to show the adjusted net income figure for each of the six years after taking into account the inventory corrections.

(b) Prepare a schedule that indicates both the original retained earnings balance reported at the end of each year and the corrected amount.

Ethics

(c) Consider the trends in the increase in income from 2008 to 2013 as originally reported and as revised after the corrections. Would you suspect that the income is being manipulated by adjusting the ending balance in the inventory account?

(LO 4, 8, E8-11 (Lower of Cost and Net Realizable Value—Effect of Error) Iqbal Corporation uses the lower of FIFO cost
12, 13) and net realizable value method on an individual item basis, applying the direct method. The inventory at December 31, 2014, included product AG. Relevant per-unit data for product AG follow:

Estimated selling price	$50
Cost	45
Replacement cost	51
Estimated selling expense	19
Normal profit	14

There were 1,000 units of product AG on hand at December 31, 2014. Product AG was incorrectly valued at $35 per unit for reporting purposes. All 1,000 units were sold in 2015.

Instructions

Assume that Iqbal follows the reporting under ASPE and answer the following questions.

(a) Was net income for 2014 overstated or understated? By how much (ignore income tax aspects)?

(b) Was net income for 2015 overstated or understated? By how much?

(c) Indicate whether the current ratio, inventory turnover ratio, and debt-to-total-assets ratio would be overstated, understated, or not affected for the years ended December 31, 2014, and December 31, 2015. Explain briefly.

(d) Assume that management did not discover the error in inventory until after the end of the fiscal year but before the closing entries were made and the financial statements were released. Should the adjustment be recorded? How would the error be treated if it were discovered after the financial statements were released?

(e) How would your responses above change if Iqbal followed the reporting under IFRS?

(LO 5) E8-12   (Relative Sales Value Method) In fiscal 2014, Ivanjoh Realty Corporation purchased unimproved land for $55,000. The land was improved and subdivided into building lots at an additional cost of $34,460. These building lots were all the same size but, because of differences in location, were offered for sale at different prices as follows:

Group	No. of Lots	Price per Lot
1	9	$3,500
2	15	4,500
3	17	2,400

Operating expenses that were allocated to this project totalled $18,200 for the year. At year end, there were also unsold lots remaining, as follows:

Group 1	5 lots
Group 2	7 lots
Group 3	2 lots

Instructions

Determine the year-end inventory and net income of Ivanjoh Realty Corporation. Round all amounts to the nearest dollar. Ignore income taxes.

(LO 6, 8) E8-13   (Cost Allocation and Lower of Cost and NRV) During 2014, Jinnah Furniture Limited purchased a railway carload of wicker chairs. The manufacturer of the chairs sold them to Jinnah for a lump sum of $59,850 because it was discontinuing manufacturing operations and wanted to dispose of its entire stock. Three types of chairs are included in the carload. The three types and the estimated selling price for each are as follows:

Type	No. of Chairs	Estimated Selling Price per Chair
Lounge chairs	400	$95
Armchairs	300	85
Straight chairs	700	55

Jinnah estimates that the costs to sell this inventory would amount to $2 per chair. During 2014, Jinnah sells 350 lounge chairs, 210 armchairs, and 120 straight chairs, all at the same prices as estimated. At December 31, 2014, the remaining chairs were put on sale: the lounge chairs at 25% off the regular price, the armchairs at 30% off, and the straight chairs at 40% off. All were expected to be sold at these prices.

Instructions

(a) Rounding percentages to one decimal place and all other amounts to two decimal places, what is the total cost of the chairs remaining in inventory at the end of 2014 using the relative sales value method?

(b) What is the net realizable value of the chairs remaining in inventory?

(c) What is the appropriate inventory value to be reported on the December 31, 2014 statement of financial position assuming the lower of cost and NRV is applied on an individual item basis?

(LO 6, 7) E8-14   (FIFO and Weighted Average) Aquind Corporation is a multi-product firm. The following information concerns one of its products, the Trinton:

Date	Transaction	Quantity	Price/Cost
Jan. 1	Beginning inventory	1,000	$12
Feb. 4	Purchase	2,000	18
Feb. 20	Sale	2,500	30
Apr. 2	Purchase	3,000	23
Nov. 4	Sale	2,000	33

Instructions

Calculate cost of goods sold, assuming Aquind uses:

(a) A periodic inventory system and FIFO cost formula

(b) A periodic inventory system and weighted average cost formula

(c) A perpetual inventory system and moving average cost formula

(LO 7) **E8-15** **(Alternative Inventory Methods)** Schonfeld Corporation began operations on December 1, 2014. The only inventory transaction in 2014 was the purchase of inventory on December 10, 2014, at a cost of $20 per unit. None of this inventory was sold in 2014. Relevant information for fiscal 2015 is as follows:

Ending inventory units:		
December 31, 2014		100
December 31, 2015, by purchase date		
—Dec. 2, 2015	100	
—July 20, 2015	30	130

During 2015, the following purchases and sales were made:

Purchases		Sales	
Mar. 15	300 units at $24	Apr. 10	200
July 20	300 units at $25	Aug. 20	300
Sept. 4	200 units at $28	Nov. 18	170
Dec. 2	100 units at $30	Dec. 12	200

The company uses the periodic inventory method.

Instructions

Determine ending inventory under (1) specific identification, (2) FIFO, and (3) weighted average cost.

(LO 6, 7, 12) **E8-16** **(Calculate FIFO, Weighted Average Cost—Periodic)** The following information is for the inventory of mini kettles at Funnell Company Limited for the month of May:

Date	Transaction	Units In	Unit Cost	Total	Units Sold	Unit Price	Total
May 1	Balance	100	$4.10	$ 410			
6	Purchase	800	4.20	3,360			
7	Sale				300	$7.00	$ 2,100
10	Sale				300	7.30	2,190
12	Purchase	400	4.50	1,800			
15	Sale				200	7.40	1,480
18	Purchase	300	4.60	1,380			
22	Sale				400	7.40	2,960
25	Purchase	500	4.58	2,290			
30	Sale				200	7.50	1,500
Totals		2,100		$9,240	1,400		$10,230

Instructions

(a) Assuming that the periodic inventory method is used, calculate the inventory cost at May 31 under each of the following cost flow formulas:

1. FIFO

2. Weighted average (round the weighted average unit cost to the nearest one tenth of one cent)

(b) Which method will yield the higher current ratio or gross profit?

(LO 6, 7) **E8-17** **(Calculate FIFO, Moving Average Cost—Perpetual)** Information is presented in E8-16 on the inventory of mini kettles at Funnell Company Limited for the month of May.

Instructions

(a) Assuming that the perpetual inventory method is used, calculate the inventory cost at May 31 under each of the following cost flow formulas:

1. FIFO

2. Moving average (round all unit costs to the nearest one tenth of one cent)

(b) Indicate where the inventory costs that were calculated in this exercise are different from the ones in E8-16 and explain the possible reasons why.

(LO 6, 8, 12) **E8-18** **(Lower of Cost and Net Realizable Value, Periodic Method—Journal Entries)** As a result of its annual inventory count, Tarweed Corp. determined its ending inventory at cost and at lower of cost and net realizable value at December 31, 2014, and December 31, 2015. This information is as follows:

	Cost	Lower of Cost and NRV
Dec. 31, 2014	$321,000	$283,250
Dec. 31, 2015	385,000	351,250

Instructions

(a) Prepare the journal entries required at December 31, 2014 and 2015, assuming that the inventory is recorded directly at the lower of cost and net realizable value and a periodic inventory system is used. Assume that cost was lower than NRV at December 31, 2013.

(b) Prepare the journal entries required at December 31, 2014 and 2015, assuming that the inventory is recorded at cost and an allowance account is adjusted at each year end under a periodic system.

(c) Which of the two methods above provides the higher net income in each year?

(LO 8) **E8-19** **(Lower of Cost and NRV Valuation Account)** The following information is for Takin Enterprises Ltd.:

	Jan. 31	Feb. 28	Mar. 31	Apr. 30
Inventory at cost	$25,000	$25,100	$29,000	$23,000
Inventory at the lower of cost				
and net realizable value	24,500	17,600	22,600	17,300
Purchases for the month		20,000	24,000	26,500
Sales for the month		29,000	35,000	40,000

Instructions

(a) Using the above information, prepare monthly income statements (as far as the data permit) in columnar form for February, March, and April. Show the inventory in the statement at cost; show the gain or loss due to fluctuations in NRV separately. Takin uses the indirect or allowance method.

(b) Prepare the journal entry that is needed to establish the valuation account at January 31 and the entries to adjust it at the end of each month after that.

(LO 3, 13) **E8-20** **(Purchase Commitments)** At December 31, 2014, Ichor Ltd. has outstanding non-cancellable purchase commitments for 45,500 litres of raw material at $3.25 per litre. The material will be used in Ichor's manufacturing process, and the company prices its raw materials inventory at cost or NRV, whichever is lower.

Instructions

(a) Explain the accounting treatment for purchase commitments under ASPE and IFRS.

(b) Assuming that the market price as at December 31, 2014, is $3.55 per litre, how would this commitment be treated in the accounts and statements? Explain.

(c) Assuming that the market price as at December 31, 2014, is $2.60 per litre instead of $3.55, how would you treat this commitment in the accounts and statements?

(d) Prepare the entry for January 15, 2015, when the entire shipment is received, assuming that the situation in (c) existed at December 31, 2014, and that the market price in January 2015 is $2.60 per litre. Explain your treatment.

(e) Why would users of the financial statements want to see disclosure about purchase commitments? Is it ever ethical for a company to decide not to disclose this information?

(LO 10) **E8-21** **(Gross Profit Method)** Furlana Company Limited uses the gross profit method to estimate inventory for monthly reports. Information follows for the month of May:

Inventory, May 1	$360,000	Sales	$1,200,000
Purchases	700,000	Sales returns	70,000
Freight-in	50,000	Purchase discounts	12,000

Instructions

(a) Calculate the estimated inventory at May 31, assuming that the gross profit is 25% of sales.

(b) Calculate the estimated inventory at May 31, assuming that the markup on cost is 25%. Round the gross profit percentage to two decimal places.

(LO 4, 10) E8-22 (Gross Profit Method) Linsang Corporation's retail store and warehouse closed for the entire weekend while the year-end inventory was counted. When the count was finished, the controller gathered all the count books and information from the clerical staff, completed the ending inventory calculations, and prepared the following partial income statement for the general manager for Monday morning:

Sales		$2,750,000
Beginning inventory	$ 650,000	
Purchases	1,550,000	
Total goods available for sale	2,200,000	
Less ending inventory	650,000	
Cost of goods sold		1,550,000
Gross profit		$1,200,000

The general manager called the controller into her office after quickly reviewing the preliminary statements. "You've made an error in the inventory," she stated. "My pricing all year has been carefully controlled to provide a gross profit of 35%, and I know the sales are correct."

Instructions

(a) How much should the ending inventory have been?

(b) If the controller's ending inventory amount was due to an error, suggest where the error might have occurred.

(LO 12) E8-23 (Analysis of Inventories) The financial statements of Trifolium Corporation for fiscal 2012 to fiscal 2014 are as follows (in thousands):

	Fiscal 2014	Fiscal 2013	Fiscal 2012
Inventory	$ 291,497	$ 319,445	$ 302,207
Sales	1,346,758	1,331,009	1,263,955
Gross margin	483,519	478,401	451,592
Net income	29,325	47,451	35,217

Instructions

(a) Calculate Trifolium's (1) inventory turnover and (2) average days to sell inventory for each of the two years ending in 2014 and 2013.

(b) Calculate Trifolium's gross profit percentage and percentage markup on cost for each fiscal year.

(c) Is the growth in inventory levels over the last year consistent with the increase in sales? Explain your answer.

(LO 12) E8-24 (Ratios) Partial information follows for a Canadian manufacturing company:

	Year 10	Year 9	Year 8	Year 7
Sales	$401,244	$_____	$344,759	
Cost of goods sold	_____	286,350	263,979	
Gross margin	95,086	87,957	_____	
Ending inventory	34,511	_____	34,750	36,750
Gross profit percentage	_____	23.5%	_____	
Inventory turnover	_____	8.19 times	_____	
Days sales in inventory	_____	44.57 days	_____	

Instructions

(a) Enter the missing amounts where indicated for years 8, 9, and 10 in the above schedule.

(b) Comment on the profitability and inventory management trends, and suggest possible reasons for these results.

(LO 14) *E8-25 (Retail Inventory Method) The records of Monde Menswear report the following data for the month of September:

Sales	$118,500	Purchases (at cost)	$ 59,500
Sales returns	2,500	Purchases (at sales price)	112,600
Additional markups	10,500	Purchase returns (at cost)	2,500
Markup cancellations	1,500	Purchase returns (at sales price)	3,500
Markdowns	9,300	Beginning inventory (at cost)	32,000
Markdown cancellations	2,800	Beginning inventory (at sales price)	48,500
Freight on purchases	3,600		

Instructions

(a) Estimate the ending inventory using the conventional retail inventory method.

(b) Assuming that a physical count of the inventory determined that the actual ending inventory at retail prices at the end of September was $42,000, estimate the loss due to shrinkage and theft.

(c) Identify four reasons why the estimate of inventory may be different from the actual inventory at cost.

(LO 9, 13) E8-26 (Biological Inventory Assets) Nicholas's Christmas Tree Farm Ltd. grows pine, fir, and spruce trees. The farm cuts and sells trees during the Christmas season and exports most of the trees to the United States. The remaining trees are sold to local tree lot operators.

It normally takes 12 years for a tree to grow to a suitable size and the average selling price of a tree is $24. The biggest costs to the business are pest control, fertilizer, and pruning trees over the 12-year period. These costs average $12 per tree (assume these are incurred evenly over the 12-year growing cycle).

Instructions

(a) How should this inventory be recorded under ASPE?

(b) How should the costs of pest control, fertilizer, and pruning be recognized under IFRS?

(c) Assume that the fair value of each tree at the end of 2014 is $8 and the opening value was $5. Prepare the journal entries if the costs are *capitalized* each year.

(d) Assume that the fair value of each tree at the end of 2014 is $8 and the opening value was $5. Prepare the journal entries if the costs are *expensed* each year.

(LO 15) *E8-27 (Primary Sources of GAAP) There are a few primary sources of GAAP for inventory under both ASPE and IFRS. List the sources of guidance in the table below.

Type of Inventory	Primary Guidance under ASPE	Primary Guidance under IFRS
Equipment manufactured		
Financial derivatives held by a financial institution		
Biological assets at the point of harvest		
Harvested agricultural produce		

Problems

P8-1 The following independent situations relate to inventory accounting:

1. Draper Co. purchased goods with a list price of $175,000 and a trade discount of 20% based on the quantity purchased, with terms 2/10, net 30.

2. Assayer Company's inventory of $1.1 million at December 31, 2014, was based on a physical count of goods priced at cost and before any year-end adjustments relating to the following items.

   (a) Goods shipped FOB shipping point on December 24, 2014, from a vendor at an invoice cost of $69,000 to Assayer Company were received on January 4, 2015.

   (b) The physical count included $29,000 of goods billed to Makee Corp., FOB shipping point, on December 31, 2014. The carrier picked up these goods on January 3, 2015.

   (c) Goods shipped FOB destination received by Assayer on January 5, 2015. The invoiced amount was $77,000.

   (d) Goods shipped FOB destination received by Assayer on December 25, 2014, that are on consignment. The value of the goods is $83,500 and they have not been included in the physical inventory count.

3. Alidade Corp. had 1,500 units on hand of part 54169 on May 1, 2014, with a cost of $21 per unit. Alidade uses a periodic inventory system. Purchases of part 54169 during May were as follows:

	Units	Unit Cost
May 9	2,000	$22.00
17	3,500	23.00
26	1,000	24.00

   A physical count on May 31, 2014, shows 2, units of part 54169 on hand.

4. Galane Ltd., a retail store chain, had the following information in its general ledger for the year 2014:

Merchandise purchased for resale	$909,400
Interest on notes payable to vendors for the purchase of inventory	8,700
Purchase returns	16,500
Freight-in	22,000
Freight-out	17,100
Cash discounts on purchases	6,800
Storage costs incurred when warehouse became full	8,300

Instructions

Answer the following questions for the situations above and explain your answer in each case:

(a) For situation 1, how much should Draper Co. record as the purchase cost of these goods on the date of purchase assuming the company uses (i) the gross method and (ii) the net method?

(b) For situation 2, what should Assayer Company report as its inventory amount on its 2014 balance sheet?

(c) For situation 3, using the FIFO method, what is the inventory cost of part 54169 at May 31, 2014? Using the weighted average cost formula, what is the inventory cost?

(d) For situation 4, assume that Galane Ltd. is a private company reporting under ASPE. What is Galane's inventoriable cost for 2014? Explain any items that are excluded.

(e) How would your answer to part (d) differ if Galane used IFRS? Which of these standards provides the most useful information to users: ASPE or IFRS? Why?

P8-2 On February 1, 2014, Quass Ltd. began selling electric scooters that it purchased exclusively from Ionone Motors Inc. Ionone Motors offers vendor rebates based on the volume of annual sales to its customers, and calculates and pays the rebates at its fiscal year end, December 31. Quass has a September fiscal year end and uses a perpetual inventory system. The rebate offer that Quass received is for a $75 rebate on each scooter that is purchased in excess of 150 units in the calendar year ending December 31. An additional rebate of $30 is given for all units purchased in excess of 175 units in the same year. By September 30, 2014, Quass had purchased 190 units from Ionone Motors and had sold all but 35. Although it only made its first purchase on February 1, 2014, Quass expects to purchase a total of 250 electric scooters from Ionone Motors by December 31, 2014. Before arriving at the estimate of 250 electric scooters, Quass's management looked carefully at trends in purchases by its competitors and the strong market for sales of electric scooters in the coming months; sales are especially strong among environmentally conscious customers in suburban areas. Management is very confident the 250 electric scooters will be purchased by December 31, 2014.

Instructions

Assuming that Quass follows the reporting requirements under ASPE, answer the following questions.

(a) Based on the conceptual framework, discuss the reasoning that Quass should use in how it treats the rebate that it expects to receive from Ionone Motors.

(b) Would your opinion change if the rebate that is expected from Ionone Motors had been discretionary?

(c) Discuss some of the factors that management should consider in arriving at a reasonable estimate of its amount of purchases to December 31, 2014.

(d) Calculate the amount of any accrued rebate to be recorded by Quass at September 30, 2014, assuming that the rebate is not discretionary and that management has a high degree of confidence in its estimate of the amount of purchases that will occur by December 31, 2014.

(e) Record the accruals that are necessary at Quass's fiscal year end of September 30, 2014.

(f) How would your response change if Quass followed the reporting requirements of IFRS?

P8-3 Ianthe Limited, a manufacturer of small tools, provided the following information from its accounting records for the year ended December 31, 2014:

Inventory at December 31, 2014 (based on physical count of goods in Ianthe's plant, at cost, on December 31, 2014)	$1,720,000
Accounts payable at December 31, 2014	1,300,000
Total current assets	2,680,000
Total current liabilities	1,550,000
Net sales (sales less sales returns)	8,550,000

Additional information:

1. Included in the physical count were tools billed to a customer FOB shipping point on December 31, 2014. These tools had a cost of $37,000 and were billed at $57,000. The shipment was on Ianthe's loading dock waiting to be picked up by the common carrier.

2. Goods were in transit from a vendor to Ianthe on December 31, 2014. The invoice cost was $51,000, and the goods were shipped FOB shipping point on December 29, 2014. Ianthe will sell these items in 2015 for $87,500. These were excluded from the inventory count.

3. Work-in-process inventory costing $38,000 was sent to an outside processor for plating on December 30, 2014. This was excluded from the inventory count.

4. Tools that were returned by customers and awaiting inspection in the returned goods area on December 31, 2014, were not included in the physical count. On January 8, 2015, these tools, costing $38,000, were inspected and returned to inventory. Credit memos totalling $48,000 were issued to the customers on the same date.

5. Tools shipped to a customer FOB destination on December 26, 2014, were in transit at December 31, 2014, and had a cost of $21,000. When it was notified that the customer received the goods on January 2, 2014, Ianthe issued a sales invoice for $42,000. These were excluded from the inventory count.

6. Goods with an invoice cost of $27,000 that were received from a vendor at 5:00 p.m. on December 31, 2014, were recorded on a receiving report dated January 2, 2015. The goods were not included in the physical count, but the invoice was included in accounts payable at December 31, 2014.

7. Goods that were received from a vendor on December 26, 2014, were included in the physical count. However, the vendor invoice of $56,000 for these goods was not included in accounts payable at December 31, 2014, because the accounts payable copy of the receiving report was lost.

8. On January 3, 2015, a monthly freight bill in the amount of $7,000 was received. The bill specifically related to merchandise purchased in December 2014, and half of this merchandise was still in the inventory at December 31, 2014. The freight charges were not included in either the inventory account or accounts payable at December 31, 2014.

Instructions

(a) Using the format shown below, prepare a schedule of adjustments to the initial amounts in Ianthe's accounting records as at December 31, 2014. Show separately the effect, if any, of each of the eight transactions on the December 31, 2014 amounts. If the transaction has no effect on the initial amount that is shown, write "NONE."

Digging Deeper

	Inventory	Accounts Payable	Net Sales
Initial amounts	$1,720,000	$1,300,000	$8,550,000
Adjustments—increase (decrease)			
Total adjustments	_____	_____	_____
Adjusted amounts	$ _____	$ _____	$ _____

(b) After you arrive at the adjusted balance for part (a) above, determine if the following ratios have improved or if they have deteriorated:

1. Working capital   3. Gross profit
2. Current ratio   4. Profit margin

(AICPA adapted)

P8-4   Halm Skidoos Limited, a private company that began operations in 2010, always values its inventories at their current net realizable value. The company uses ASPE. Its annual inventory figure is arrived at by taking a physical count and then pricing each item in the physical inventory at current resale prices. The condensed income statements for the company's past four years are as follows:

	2010	2011	2012	2013
Sales	$850,000	$880,000	$950,000	$990,000
Cost of goods sold	560,000	590,000	630,000	650,000
Gross profit	290,000	290,000	320,000	340,000
Operating expenses	190,000	180,000	200,000	210,000
Income before taxes	$100,000	$110,000	$120,000	$130,000

Instructions

(a) Comment on the procedures that Halm uses for valuing inventories.

(b) Prepare corrected condensed income statements using an acceptable method of inventory valuation, assuming that the inventory at cost and as determined by the corporation (using net realizable value) at the end of each of the four years is as follows:

Year	At Cost	Net Realizable Value
2010	$150,000	$160,000
2011	147,000	160,000
2012	178,000	170,000
2013	175,000	189,000

(c) Compare the trend in income for the four years using the corporation's approach to valuing ending inventory and using a method that is acceptable under GAAP.

(d) Calculate the cumulative effect of the difference in the valuation of inventory on the ending balance of retained earnings from 2010 through 2013.

(e) Comment on the differences that you observe after making the corrections to the inventory valuation over the four years.

P8-5 Some of the transactions of Spandrel Corp. during August follow. Spandrel uses the periodic inventory method.

Aug. 10	Purchased merchandise on account, $12,000, terms 2/10, n/30.
13	Returned $1,200 of the purchase of August 10 and received a credit on account.
15	Purchased merchandise on account, $16,000, terms 1/10, n/60.
25	Purchased merchandise on account, $20,000, terms 2/10, n/30.
28	Paid the invoice of August 15 in full.

Instructions

(a) Assuming that purchases are recorded at gross amounts and that discounts are to be recorded when taken:
   1. Prepare general journal entries to record the transactions.
   2. Describe how the various items would be shown in the financial statements.

(b) Assuming that purchases are recorded at net amounts and that discounts lost are treated as financial expenses:
   1. Prepare general journal entries to enter the transactions.
   2. Prepare the adjusting entry that is necessary on August 31 if financial statements are prepared at that time.
   3. Describe how the various items would be shown in the financial statements.

(c) Which method results in a higher reported gross profit ratio? Explain.

(d) Which of the two methods do you prefer and why?

P8-6 Lupulin Limited stocks a variety of sports equipment for sale to institutions. The following stock record card for basketballs was taken from the records at the December 31, 2014 year end:

Date	Invoice Number	Terms	Units Received	Unit Invoice Cost	Gross Invoice Amount
Jan. 1	balance	Net 30	100	$20.00	$2,000.00
15	10624	Net 30	60	20.00	1,200.00
Mar. 15	11437	1/5, net 30	65	16.00	1,040.00
June 20	21332	1/10, net 30	90	15.00	1,350.00
Sept. 12	27644	1/10, net 30	84	12.00	1,008.00
Nov. 24	31269	1/10, net 30	76	11.00	836.00
	Totals		475		$7,434.00

A physical inventory on December 31, 2014, reveals that 100 basketballs were in stock. The bookkeeper informs you that all the discounts were taken. Assume that Lupulin Limited uses a periodic inventory system and records purchases at their invoice price less discounts. During 2014, the average sales price per basketball was $22.25.

Instructions

(a) Calculate the December 31, 2014 inventory using the FIFO formula.

(b) Calculate the December 31, 2014 inventory using the weighted average cost formula. (Round unit costs to the nearest cent.)

(c) Prepare income statements for the year ended December 31, 2014, as far as the "gross profit" line under each of the FIFO and weighted average methods, and calculate the gross profit rate for each. Explain the difference in the gross profit under the two methods.

(d) If the selling prices for the basketballs that were sold follow the same pattern as their wholesale prices from the supplier, might this have an effect on the inventory cost that is reported on the December 31, 2014 balance sheet? (*Hint*: Review your answers to parts [a] to [c].)

P8-7   The summary financial statements of KwikMart Ltd. on December 31, 2014, are as follows:

KWIKMART LTD.
Balance Sheet, December 31, 2014
Assets

Cash	$ 5,000
Accounts and notes receivable	39,000
Inventory	79,000
Property, plant, and equipment (net)	125,000
	$248,000

Liabilities and Shareholders' Equity

Accounts and notes payable	$ 75,000
Long-term debt	62,000
Common shares	60,000
Retained earnings	51,000
	$248,000

The following errors were made by the inexperienced accountant on December 31, 2013, and were not corrected.

1. The inventory was overstated by $13,000.

2. A prepaid expense of $2,400 was omitted (it was fully expensed in 2013).

3. Accrued revenue of $2,500 was omitted. (It was recognized when cash was received in 2014.)

4. A supplier's invoice for $1,700 for purchases made in 2013 was not recorded until 2014.

On December 31, 2014, there were further errors:

5. The inventory was understated by $17,000.

6. A prepaid expense of $750 was omitted.

7. Accrued December 2014 salaries of $1,800 were not recognized.

8. Unearned income of $2,300 was recorded in the 2014 revenue.

9. In addition, it was determined that $20,000 of the accounts payable were long-term, and that a $500 dividend was reported as dividend expense and deducted in calculating net income.

The net income reported on the books for 2014 was $53,000.

Instructions

(a) Calculate the working capital, current ratio, and debt-to-equity ratio for KwikMart Ltd. based on the original balance sheet information provided above.

(b) Calculate the corrected net income for 2014.

(c) Prepare a corrected balance sheet at December 31, 2014.

(d) Using the corrected data, recalculate the ratios in part (a). Explain the resulting differences in the ratios as a result of the use of the corrected data.

P8-8   Astro Languet established Languet Products Co. as a sole proprietorship on January 5, 2014. At the company's year end of December 31, 2014, the accounts had the following balances (in thousands):

Current assets, excluding inventory	$ 10
Other assets	107
Current liabilities	30
Long-term bank loan	50
Owner's investment (excluding income)	40

Purchases during year	
Jan. 2: 5,000 @ $11	55
June 30: 8,000 @ $12	96
Dec. 10: 6,000 @ $16	96
	247
Sales	284
Other expenses	40

A count of ending inventory on December 31, 2014, showed there were 4,000 units on hand.

Astro is now preparing financial statements for the year. He is aware that inventory may be costed using the FIFO or weighted average cost formula. He is unsure of which one to use and asks for your assistance. In discussions with Astro, you learn the following.

1. Suppliers to Languet Products provide goods at regular prices as long as Languet Products' current ratio is at least 2 to 1. If this ratio is lower, the suppliers increase their price by 10% in order to compensate for what they consider to be a substantial credit risk.

2. The terms of the long-term bank loan include the bank's ability to demand immediate repayment of the loan if the debt-to-total-assets ratio is greater than 45%.

3. Astro thinks that, for the company to be a success, the rate of return on total assets should be at least 30%.

4. Astro has an agreement with the company's only employee that, for each full percentage point above a 25% rate of return on total assets, she will be given an additional one day off with pay in the following year.

Instructions

(a) Prepare an income statement and a year-end balance sheet assuming the company applies:
   1. The FIFO cost formula
   2. The weighted average cost formula

(b) Identify the advantages of each formula in (a).

(c) Identify the disadvantages of each formula in (a).

(d) Which method do you recommend? Explain briefly.

Digging Deeper

(e) Considering the choice of inventory cost formulas that are available, do the ratios noted above adequately measure the financial performance of Languet Products from the perspective of the users?

P8-9 Schonfeld Company determined its ending inventory at cost and at lower of cost and net realizable value at December 31, 2012, 2013, and 2014, as follows:

	Cost	Lower of Cost and Net Realizable Value
Dec. 31, 2012	$720,000	$720,000
Dec. 31, 2013	980,000	918,400
Dec. 31, 2014	950,000	880,000

Instructions

(a) Prepare the journal entries that are required at December 31, 2013 and 2014, assuming that a periodic inventory system and the direct method of adjusting to NRV are used.

(b) Prepare the journal entries that are required at December 31, 2013 and 2014, assuming that a periodic inventory system is used, with inventory recorded at cost and reduced to NRV through the use of an allowance account.

P8-10 Reena Corp. lost most of its inventory in a fire in December just before the year-end physical inventory was taken. The corporation's books disclosed the following:

Beginning inventory	$440,000	Sales	$1,350,000
Purchases for the year	850,000	Sales returns	50,000
Purchase returns	55,000	Gross margin on sales	40%

Merchandise with a selling price of $42,000 remained undamaged after the fire. Damaged merchandise with an original selling price of $30,000 had a net realizable value of $10,600.

Instructions

(a) Calculate the amount lost due to the fire, assuming that the corporation had no insurance coverage.

(b) Prepare the journal entry to record the loss and account for the damaged inventory in a separate Damaged Inventory account. In the same entry, record cost of goods sold for the year ended December 31.

(c) How would the loss be classified on the income statement of Reena Corp.?

(d) While the gross profit percentage has averaged 40% over the past five years, it has been as high as 42% and as low as 37.5%. Given this information, should a range of possible loss amounts be provided instead of a single figure? Explain.

P8-11 Sube Specialty Corp., a division of FH Inc., manufactures three models of gearshift components for bicycles that are sold to bicycle manufacturers, retailers, and catalogue outlets. Since beginning operations in 1969, Sube has used normal absorption costing and has assumed a first-in, first-out cost flow in its perpetual inventory system. Except for overhead, manufacturing costs are accumulated using actual costs. Overhead is applied to production using prede-termined overhead rates. The balances of the inventory accounts at the end of Sube's fiscal year, September 30, 2014, follow. The inventories are stated at cost before any year-end adjustments.

Finished goods	$757,000
Work in process	192,500
Raw materials	300,000
Factory supplies	69,000

The following information relates to Sube's inventory and operations:

1. The finished goods inventory consists of these items:

	Cost	Net realizable value
Down tube shifter		
Standard model	$ 97,500	$ 67,000
Click adjustment model	94,500	87,000
Deluxe model	108,000	110,000
Total down tube shifters	300,000	264,000
Bar end shifter		
Standard model	133,000	120,050
Click adjustment model	79,000	108,150
Total bar end shifters	212,000	228,200
Head tube shifter		
Standard model	128,000	103,650
Click adjustment model	117,000	145,300
Total head tube shifters	245,000	248,950
Total finished goods	$757,000	$741,150

2. Half of the finished goods inventory of head tube shifters is at catalogue outlets on consignment.

3. Three-quarters of the finished goods inventory of bar end shifters has been pledged as collateral for a bank loan.

4. Half of the raw materials balance is for derailleurs acquired at a contracted price that is 20% above the current market price. The net realizable value of the rest of the raw materials is $135,500.

5. The total net realizable value of the work-in-process inventory is $105,500.

6. Included in the cost of factory supplies are obsolete items with a historical cost of $4,200. The net realizable value of the remaining factory supplies is $65,900.

7. Sube applies the lower of cost and net realizable value method to each of the three types of shifters in finished goods inventory. For each of the other three inventory accounts, Sube applies the lower of cost and net realizable value method to the total of each inventory account.

8. Consider all of the amounts presented above as being material amounts in relation to Sube's financial statements as a whole.

Instructions

(a) Assuming that ASPE is followed, prepare the inventory section of Sube's statement of financial position as at September 30, 2014, including any required note(s).

(b) Regardless of your answer to (a), assume that the net realizable value of Sube's inventories is less than cost. Explain how this decline would be presented in Sube's income statement for the fiscal year ended September 30, 2014, under ASPE.

(c) Assume that Sube has a firm purchase commitment for the same type of derailleur that is included in the raw materials inventory as at September 30, 2014, and that the purchase commitment is at a contracted price that is 15% higher than the current market price. These derailleurs are to be delivered to Sube after September 30, 2014. Discuss the impact, if any, that this purchase commitment would have on Sube's financial statements prepared for the fiscal year ended September 30, 2014, under ASPE.

(d) How would your response to (c) change under IFRS?

(e) Explain and compare the disclosure requirements under ASPE and IFRS.

(CMA adapted. Used with permission.)

P8-12 The Eserine Wood Corporation manufactures desks. Most of the company's desks are standard models that are sold at catalogue prices. At December 31, 2014, the following finished desks appear in the company's inventory:

Finished Desks	Type A	Type B	Type C	Type D
2014 catalogue selling price	$460	$490	$890	$1,040
FIFO cost per inventory list, Dec. 31, 2014	410	450	830	960
Estimated current cost to manufacture (at Dec. 31, 2014 and early 2015)	460	440	790	1,000
Sales commissions and estimated other costs of disposal	40	65	95	130
2015 catalogue selling price	575	650	780	1,420
Quantity on hand	15	117	113	110

The 2014 catalogue was in effect through November 2014, and the 2015 catalogue is effective as of December 1, 2014. All catalogue prices are net of the usual discounts. Generally, the company tries to obtain a 20% gross margin on the selling price and it has usually been successful in achieving this.

Instructions

(a) Assume that the company has adopted a lower of FIFO cost and net realizable value approach for the valuation of inventories and applies it on an individual inventory item basis. At what total inventory value will the desks appear on the company's December 31, 2014 balance sheet?

(b) Explain the rationale for using the lower of cost and market rule for inventories.

(c) Explain the impact if inventory was valued at lower of cost or net realizable value on a total basis.

*P8-13 The records for the Clothing Department of Ji-Woon's Department Store are summarized as follows for the month of January:

1. Inventory, January 1: at retail, $28,000; at cost, $18,000
2. Purchases in January: at retail, $147,000; at cost, $110,000
3. Freight-in: $6,000
4. Purchase returns: at retail, $3,500; at cost, $2,700
5. Purchase allowances: $2,200
6. Transfers in from suburban branch: at retail, $13,000; at cost, $9,200
7. Net markups: $8,000
8. Net markdowns: $4,000
9. Inventory losses due to normal breakage, etc.: at retail, $400
10. Sales at retail: $121,000
11. Sales returns: $2,400

Instructions

(a) Estimate the inventory for this department as at January 31 at (1) retail and (2) the lower of average cost and market. Round the cost-to-retail ratio to two decimal places.

(b) Assume that a physical inventory count taken at retail prices after the close of business on January 31 indicated an inventory amount that is $450 less than what was estimated in (a) part (1). What could have caused this discrepancy?

P8-14 Some of the information found on a detailed inventory card for Soave Stationery Ltd. for May is as follows:

	Received		Issued	Balance
Date	No. of Units	Unit Cost	No. of Units	No. of Units
May 1 (opening balance)	1,150	$2.90		1,150
2	1,050	3.00		2,200
7			700	1,500
10	600	3.20		2,100
13			500	1,600
18	1,000	3.30	300	2,300
20			1,100	1,200
23	1,300	3.40		2,500
26			800	1,700
28	1,500	3.60		3,200
31			1,300	1,900

Instructions

(a) From the above data, calculate the ending inventory based on each of the following cost formulas. Assume that perpetual inventory records are kept in units only and average cost is calculated monthly at each month end. Carry unit costs to the nearest cent and ending inventory to the nearest dollar.

   1. First-in, first-out (FIFO)   **2.** Weighted average cost

(b) Based on your results in part (a), and assuming that the average selling price per unit during May was $7.25, prepare partial income statements up to the "gross profit on sales" line. Calculate the gross profit percentage under each inventory cost formula. Comment on your results.

(c) Assume the perpetual inventory record is kept in dollars, and costs are calculated at the time of each withdrawal. Recalculate the amounts under this revised assumption, carrying average unit costs to four decimal places. Would the ending inventory amounts under each of the two cost formulas above be the same? Explain.

Cases

Refer to the Case Primer to help you answer these cases.

CA8-1 Tobacco Group Inc. (TGI) is in the consumer packaged goods industry. Its shares are widely held and key shareholders include several very large pension funds.

In the current year, 59% of the net revenues and 61% of operating income came from tobacco product sales. Because of the health risks related to the use of tobacco products, the industry is increasingly regulated by government and the company is implicated in substantial tobacco-related litigation.

During the past three years, the company entered into agreements with the government to settle asserted and unasserted health-care recovery costs and other claims. The agreements, known as the Government Settlement Agreements, call for payments by the domestic tobacco industry into a fund in the following amounts:

Current Year	$10.9 billion
Following four years	$8 billion each year
Thereafter	$9 billion each year

The fund will be used to settle claims and aid tobacco growers. Each company's share of these payments is based on its market share and TGI records its portion of the settlement costs as cost of goods sold upon shipment. These amounts may increase based on several factors, including inflation and industry volume. In the past three years, the company accrued costs of more than $5 billion each year.

Another significant lawsuit, the class action, is still in process. Last year, the jury returned a verdict assessing punitive damages against various defendants, and TGI was responsible for $74 billion. The company is contesting this and the lawsuit continues. As a result of preliminary judicial stipulations, the company has placed $500 million into a separate interest-bearing escrow account. This money will be kept by the court and distributed to the plaintiffs regardless of the outcome of the trial. The company also placed $1.2 billion into another escrow account, and this amount will be returned to the company if it wins the case.

Instructions

Assume the role of a financial analyst and discuss the related financial reporting issues. Specifically, note alternative accounting treatments for each issue and recommend how each issue should be treated in the financial statements.

CA8-2 Findit Gold Inc. (FGI) was created in 2005 and is 25% owned by Findit Mining Corporation (FMC). FGI's shares trade on the local exchange and its objective is to become a substantial low-cost mineral producer in developing countries. FMC has provided substantial financial support to FGI when FGI was in the exploration stage.

Over the most-recent five-year period, FGI carried its gold bullion inventory at net realizable value and recognized revenues on the gold produced (net of refining and selling costs) at net realizable value, when the minerals were produced. Gold is a commodity that trades actively and whose price fluctuates according to supply and demand.

Instructions

Assume the role of the controller of FMC and assess the financial reporting policies relating to inventory valuation and revenue recognition.

Integrated Case

(*Hint:* If there are issues here that are new, use the conceptual framework to help you support your analysis with solid reasoning.)

IC8-1 Grappa Grapes Inc. (GGI) grows grapes and produces fine champagne. The company is located in a very old area of town with easy access to fertile farmland that is excellent for growing grapes. It is owned by the Grappa family. The company has been in operation for 100 years and a large part of its success lies in the excellent vineyards and unique process for producing vintage wines. The winery sits at the edge of a range of hills that are composed of chalk. GGI has dug "caves" into the side of the hills at a significant cost and the chalk caves provide the perfect temperature and humidity for the maturing wines. All of the vintage wines are produced, aged, and stored in these chalk caves. People come from all over the country to visit the "caves." As a matter of fact, 25% of the company's revenues are from winery tours.

The company has had three years where it has managed to produce vintage wines. Vintage wines are of higher quality and sell for a higher price. In addition, they contribute to the prestige of the winery. Because of this success, GGI has started to sell wine "futures." Under the terms of the contract, large wholesalers pay GGI upfront and agree to take delivery of a certain number of bottles in two years at 20% off the pre-determined future price. A market for trading these contracts now exists for the buyers of the futures.

During the year, in anticipation of increasing costs, the entity placed a purchase order for a significant number of oak barrels from France. The barrels are used to age the wines. Due to the declining value of the dollar during a current economic recession and the demand for wines in general over the past year, the value of the barrels has actually declined below the price locked in under the purchase commitments. The supplier is confident that this is only a temporary decline in value and that the price of the barrels will increase within the next couple of months. GGI may get out of the purchase commitment either by taking delivery of the barrels at the agreed-upon price or by settling net in cash for the difference between the agreed-upon price and the market price (times the number of barrels ordered).

The year has been a very rainy one and some of the very old chalk caves have begun to leak and deteriorate. One of the caves holding a large number of vintage wines collapsed. It is unclear whether the wine is salvageable. The company's insurance will not cover the expected loss, although GGI has hired its lawyers to challenge this as it feels that the insurance company should cover the loss. GGI has decided to follow GAAP for the current year's financial statements as it is planning to go to the bank for a loan.

Instructions

Assume the role of the controller and analyze the financial reporting issues.

Writing Assignments

WA8-1 Jack McDowell, the controller for McDowell Lumber Corporation, has recently hired you as assistant controller. He wishes to determine your expertise in the area of inventory accounting and therefore asks you to answer the following unrelated questions.

Instructions

Write a memo to him that answers each of his questions.

(a) A company is involved in the wholesaling and retailing of automobile tires for foreign cars. Most of the inventory is imported, and it is valued on the company's records at the actual inventory cost plus freight-in. At year end, the warehousing costs are prorated over cost of goods sold and ending inventory. Are warehousing costs considered a product cost or a period cost?

(b) A certain portion of a company's inventory consists of obsolete items. Should obsolete items that are not currently consumed in the production of goods or services to be available for sale be classified as part of inventory?

(c) A company purchases airplanes for sale to others. However, until they are sold, the company charters and services the planes. What is the proper way to report these airplanes in the company's financial statements?

(d) A company wants to buy coal deposits but does not want the financing for the purchase to be reported on its financial statements. The company therefore establishes a trust to acquire the coal deposits. The company agrees to buy the coal over a certain period of time at specified prices. The trust is able to finance the coal purchase and then pay off the loan when it is paid by the company for the minerals. How should this transaction be reported?

WA8-2   Local Drilling Inc. is a Canadian drilling-site company. All of the company's drilling material is purchased by the head office and stored at a local warehouse before being shipped to the drilling sites. The price of drilling material has been steadily decreasing over the past few years. The drilling material is sent to various sites upon request of the site manager, where it is stored and then used in drilling. When the material is sent, managers are charged the inventory cost based on the cost assigned to the item in the head office records. At any particular time, it is estimated that about one half of the company's drilling material inventory will be at the local warehouse. Part of each site manager's performance evaluation is based on the net income reported for the site.

Instructions

Answer the following questions by choosing among the specific identification, FIFO, and moving-average cost formulas and use of a perpetual inventory system.

(a) Which costing method would you, as a site manager, want to see used? Why?

(b) If FIFO were used, what could you, as a site manager, do that would help your performance evaluation when you request inventory? Why, and what might the implications be for the company as a whole?

(c) As the decision-maker at head office, which method would you recommend if you wanted the results to be fair for all site managers? Why?

(d) Which method would you recommend for determining the company's taxable income? Why?

(e) Which method would you recommend for financial statement purposes? Why?

WA8-3   PERO Lumber Limited is a private company. It operates in the forestry sector and owns timber lots. The company produces and sells specialty lumber to distributors and retailers. The company has a management bonus plan, which is based on net earnings and gross profits. In the past, the company has estimated decommissioning costs related to its sawmill facility and recorded them as a liability with an offsetting increase to the cost of the plant. Since the production period can be fairly long, including the curing and special treatments applied to the lumber, the company has had to borrow to finance this production process. However, historically, it has expensed this interest. Finally, the owners explained that they did have a purchase commitment to buy a minimum amount of specialty resins used to treat the lumber. This is a five-year contract at a fixed price. At the time, they were very excited about it, but now they are in the fourth year of the contract and realize that the company will not need the volumes that it committed to buy. They have now developed a new technique that is cheaper and uses a different solution to treat the wood. In fact, it looks as though the company will have to pay for items that will not be required. The owners are trying to decide whether or not to break the contract or remain with the contract and just pay for the items but not take delivery. The company has two years still remaining on this contract.

Instructions

PERO Lumber Limited has just hired you as its new controller. It is trying to decide whether to adopt IFRS or report under ASPE. Provide the owners with a report that details the impact of reporting under IFRS on the company's financial results and management bonus plan, giving consideration to the issues indicated above.

*WA8-4   There are many forms of inventory that are not covered under the basic accounting standards for inventory: *CICA Handbook*, Part II, Section 3031 (ASPE) and IAS 2 for IFRS.

Instructions

For each of the following forms of inventory, briefly explain how the inventory would be reported and where guidance would be found under ASPE and IFRS. Explain the impact on the balance sheet and the income statements that would result.

(a) Securities held by an investment company

(b) Unbilled work in progress for a legal firm (that is, employee and partner time spent on client work not yet billed)

(c) Milk from dairy cattle

(d) Sheep that are kept for wool production

(e) Construction contracts in progress

(f) Nickel resources not yet mined

WA8-5   Write a brief essay highlighting the differences between IFRS and ASPE noted in this chapter, discussing the conceptual justification for each.

WA8-6   Consider a large dairy farming company that reports under IFRS. Beyond manufacturing, farm property, and equipment, the farm's main assets are the dairy cows and the milk that they produce. Describe how these assets may be presented on the financial statements. Additionally, discuss the accounting treatments of the following events:

(a) A new dairy cow is bought by the farm

(b) A cow owned by the farm loses its ability to produce milk

How would this differ if the farm reported under ASPE? Comment on which standard you believe provides better presentation of the assets and why.

WA8-7   IFRS requires greater disclosure for inventory compared with ASPE. List the additional requirements and explain what benefit each one might serve for the users of the financial statements.

Ethics

WA8-8   Assume the role of the ethical accountant. The company you work for manufactures pharmaceuticals and has a large stock of inventory for a new drug as the fiscal year end approaches. The company has a compensation system that relies partially on individual performance and partially on the company's net income for the year. A large contract with a nearby hospital was recently cancelled after production of the drugs had been completed. The shelf life of those drugs that are included in inventory is three months, while there are six months of sales being held as a result of the contract loss. In discussion with the CEO, she indicates that the inventory is measured at cost as required by IFRS so she sees no problem with the assets recorded on the statement of financial position. She further explains that there has been no damage to the inventory and it is all fully saleable at year end so the net realizable value still exceeds its cost.

Instructions

Address the CEO's comments and explain how ethical issues may impact decision-making in terms of accounting for inventory. What steps have accounting standards taken to avoid this type of situation?

RESEARCH AND FINANCIAL ANALYSIS

RA8-1 Shoppers Drug Mart

Real World Emphasis

Shoppers Drug Mart, as described in Note 1 to its financial statements, is a "licensor of 1,199 Shoppers Drug Mart®/Pharmaprix® full-service retail drug stores across Canada." Shoppers' financial statements for its annual period ended December 31, 2011, are in Appendix 5B.

Instructions

(a) How much inventory does Shoppers have at December 31, 2011, and January 1, 2011? Identify the types of inventory that Shoppers reports on its December 31, 2011 balance sheet. How much was recognized as an expense in the year? What comments can you make about the inventory held at the end of the reporting period?

(b) Describe the accounting policies for inventory. Is there any additional information you would like to know? Were there any adjustments required to inventory on conversion to IFRS from Canadian GAAP?

RA8-2 Stora Enso Oyj

Stora Enso Oyj describes its business in its annual report as the "global rethinker of the biomaterials, paper, packaging and wood products industry."

Real World Emphasis

Instructions

Access the financial statements of Stora Enso Oyj for the year ended December 31, 2011, from the company's website. Using the financial statements, answer the following questions.

(a) Describe the accounting policies that the company uses for reporting inventories. What types of expenses are included in costs? Is interest included in inventory costs?

(b) What different components are there in inventory and what is the percentage of each to the total for 2011 and 2010? Which items represent a high percentage of the inventory? How has this changed over the years? Is there any cause for concern? What was the amount reported on the income statement related to inventory items? Is it possible to calculate the days in inventory ratio?

(c) How are the inventories of the standing trees measured and reported? What types of assumptions are used to determine the reported amount of these assets? Where are these assets located? How much was harvested this year? What other changes occurred in the statement of financial position and what were changes related to in 2011? How are the changes in these amounts reported and what are the impacts on earnings for the current year and previous year?

(d) Does the company use the allowance method or the direct method to record writedowns to the inventory? What were these related amounts at the 2011 year end? Were there any amounts reversed during the year?

(e) Is this disclosure useful to the reader? Is there any other information you would like to have?

RA8-3 Canadian Tire Corporation, Limited

Real World Emphasis

Refer to the 2011 annual report of **Canadian Tire Corporation, Limited** available on SEDAR (www.sedar.com) or the company's website (www.canadiantire.ca). Note that the company provides a 10-year financial review at the end of its annual report. This summary gives relevant comparative information that is useful for determining trends and predicting the company's future results and position.

Instructions

Prepare three graphs covering the 2007 to 2011 period (express all amounts in $000). The first graph is for net earnings from continuing operations over this five-year period, the second for working capital, and the third for the current ratio. Based on the graphs, predict the values you might expect for the next fiscal period.

RA8-4 Research: Inventory Management Systems

Real World Emphasis

Many companies, such as **HydroMississauga** and **Matsushita Electric of Canada Ltd.**, have invested in technology to improve their inventory management systems.

Instructions

Research the topic of improvements to inventory management systems, and focus in particular on two examples where companies have been able to change the way they manage this critical asset. You may choose any companies you like. Identify what improvements the companies have made. How do these efficiencies affect the statement of financial position and income statement, if at all? Be specific.

RA8-5 Andrew Peller Limited

Real World Emphasis

Access the annual financial statements of **Andrew Peller Limited** for the year ended March 31, 2012, on SEDAR (www.sedar.com), or the company's website (www.andrewpeller.com).

Instructions

Refer to these financial statements and the accompanying notes to answer the following questions.

(a) How significant are the inventories relative to total current assets? What categories of inventory does Andrew Peller Limited report?

(b) Identify all the accounting policies that are the basis for the inventory values reported on the March 31, 2012 balance sheet.

(c) Which category of inventory represents the highest percentage? Is this what you would expect?

(d) What was the amount recognized in expense related to inventory for 2012 and 2011? Were there any writedowns of inventory or reversals of writedowns for 2011 or 2012?

(e) What was Andrew Peller's inventory turnover ratio for the year ended March 31, 2012? What is the average age of the inventory? Comment briefly.

(f) Compare the gross profit ratios for the two most recent years that are reported. Comment briefly on why there might be changes from year to year.

(g) Until 2012, the company reported under Canadian GAAP. The company moved to IFRS in fiscal 2012. What was the impact of the move to IFRS on vineyard and grape assets? What was the impact on the balance sheet? On the income statement?

RA8-6 Loblaw Companies Limited and Empire Company Limited

Instructions

Real World Emphasis

From SEDAR (www.sedar.com), or the company websites, access the financial statements of **Loblaw Companies Limited** for its year ended December 31, 2011, and of **Empire Company Limited** for its year ended May 5, 2012. Review the financial statements and answer the following questions.

(a) Describe the business that Loblaw and Empire operate in.

(b) What is the amount of inventory reported by Loblaw at December 31, 2011, and by Empire at May 5, 2012? What percent of total assets is invested in inventory by each company? How does this compare with the previous year?

(c) Identify the inventory policies for each company that support the inventory values reported on their respective balance sheets.

(d) How much did each company report for inventory expenses in the current and previous year? What was the writedown (or reversal of writedowns) related to inventories for the current and previous year for each company?

(e) How do the companies account for vendor allowances? Is this the appropriate treatment? How might this change if proposed changes in the framework are adopted?

(f) Calculate and compare the inventory turnover ratios and days to sell inventory for the two companies for the most current year.

(g) Comment on the results of your calculations in (f) above. Would any differences identified in any of the earlier analyses above help explain differences in the ratios between the two companies? What might be some reasons for the differences between the two companies?

RA8-7 Research: Manufacturing Inventory

Identify a company in your local community that develops a product through some form of manufacturing process. Consider a farming operation, bakery, cement supplier, or other company that converts or assembles inputs to develop a different product.

Instructions

Write a report on the company's inventory. Suggestions: Visit the manufacturing site, view a video of the operation, or speak to company management. Identify what types of costs are incurred in the manufacturing process. Determine which costs are included in inventory cost in the accounting records, and explain why some may be treated as period costs. Does the company use a periodic or a perpetual system? What cost formula does the company use? How does the company determine NRV, or does it?

ENDNOTES

1 *CICA Handbook–Accounting*, Part II, Section 3031.07 and IAS 2.6. Copyright © 2012 IFRS Foundation. All rights reserved. Reproduced by Wiley Canada with the permission of the IFRS Foundation®. No permission granted to third parties to reproduce or distribute.

2 Terms other than "FOB shipping point" or "FOB destination" (for example, "CIF" for "cost, insurance, freight") are often used to identify when legal title passes. The FOB terms are used in this text to reflect that an agreement on when title passes must be reached between the buyer and seller in the purchase–sale contract. In a particular situation, the terms of the sale contract are examined to determine when the risks and rewards of ownership pass from the seller to the buyer.

3 With the conceptual framework moving toward a more contract-based definition of assets and liabilities, there may be upcoming changes in this approach.

4 Purchase commitments sometimes have the characteristics of derivatives. Derivatives are generally recognized and valued at fair value on an ongoing basis. Should purchase commitments be accounted for as derivatives? This topic will be revisited in Chapter 16.

5 To correct the error in the same year before the books are closed, and assuming inventories are adjusted before the closing entries, the following entries are needed depending on whether the periodic or perpetual methods are used. We will come back to these two methods later in the chapter.

Periodic Method			Perpetual Method		
Purchases	$x		Inventory	$x	
Accounts Payable		$x	Accounts Payable		$x
Inventory	$x				
Cost of Goods Sold		$x			

6 *CICA Handbook–Accounting*, Part II, Section 3031.11 and IAS 2.10.

7 Both *CICA Handbook–Accounting*, Part II, Section 3031 and IAS 2 indicate that trade discounts are deducted in determining the costs of purchase. They also indicate that, to the extent the purchase arrangement contains a financing element, the amount paid in excess of the amount payable under normal credit terms is recognized as interest expense over the period when the payable is outstanding.

8 As indicated in Chapter 2, as work progresses on a revised conceptual framework, it is likely that the "probable" criterion of the asset definition will be removed. Instead, probability will be taken into account in the measurement of the asset.

9 Normal capacity is "the production expected to be achieved on average over a number of periods or seasons under normal circumstances, taking into account the loss of capacity resulting from planned maintenance" (*CICA Handbook–Accounting*, Part II, Section 3031.14 and IAS 2.13). Copyright © 2012 IFRS Foundation. All rights reserved. Reproduced by Wiley Canada with the permission of the IFRS Foundation®. No permission granted to third parties to reproduce or distribute.

10 The reporting rules on interest capitalization have their greatest impact in accounting for property, plant, and equipment and, therefore, are discussed in detail in Chapter 10.

11 IAS 23.7 and 8 as well as IAS 23.4. This option also exists for qualifying inventory items measured at fair value, such as biological assets.

12 In recent years, some companies have developed methods of determining inventories, including statistical sampling, that are sufficiently reliable to make an annual count of each item of inventory unnecessary.

13 A good illustration of the cost allocation problem occurs in the motion picture industry. Often actors and actresses receive a percentage of net income for a particular movie or television program. Some actors who have had these arrangements have alleged that their programs have been extremely profitable to the motion picture studios but they have received little in the way of profit-sharing. Actors contend that the studios allocate additional costs to successful projects to ensure that there will be no profits to share. Such contentions illustrate the type of problem that can emerge when contracts are based on accounting numbers that include arbitrary allocations. One way to help overcome such problems is to establish specific measurement rules on how the accounting numbers are to be determined. This should be done before the contract is signed so that all parties clearly understand what they are getting into.

14 *CICA Handbook–Accounting*, Part II, Section 3031.28 and IAS 2.29.

[15] The Canada Revenue Agency dictates that, in determining the lower of cost and NRV, the comparison should be made separately and individually in respect of each item in the inventory (or each usual class of items if specific items are not readily distinguishable). Comparing total cost and total market is only permitted when the cost of the specific items (using specific identification, FIFO, or average cost) is not known and only an average cost is available (*CRA Interpretation Bulletin*—473R, December 21, 1998, on "Inventory Valuation," par. 3).

[16] While fair value less costs to sell appears to be the same as net realizable value (selling price less costs to sell), it is different. NRV is an entity-specific value, whereas fair values reflect a market-based valuation. IFRS has a new standard on fair value measurement (IFRS 13).

[17] The entries to account for inventories carried at net realizable value are similar to those for assets carried at fair value less costs to sell. The changes in NRV are recognized in the Inventory account and in income in the period the NRV changes.

[18] IAS 41.B61 notes that the standard does not prescribe how to account for expenditures related to biological assets. Therefore there is a choice to capitalize or expense. In addition, there is judgement involved in determining which costs should be capitalized if this option is used. Inventory accounting would generally support direct costs and a reasonable allocation of overhead.

[19] An alternative approach to estimating inventory using the gross profit percentage, considered by some to be less complicated than the method in Illustration 8-29, uses the standard income statement format as follows (assume the same data as in Illustration 8-29):

Sales		$280,000	$280,000
Cost of goods sold			
Beginning inventory	$ 60,000		$ 60,000
Purchases	200,000		200,000
Goods available for sale	260,000		260,000
Ending inventory	(3) ?		(3) 64,000 Est.
Cost of goods sold		(2) ?	(2) 196,000 Est.
Gross profit on sales (30%)		(1) ?	(1)$ 84,000 Est.

Calculate the unknowns as follows: first the gross profit amount, then cost of goods sold, and then the ending inventory.

(1) $280,000 \times 30\% = \$84,000$ (gross profit on sales)

(2) $\$280,000 - \$84,000 = \$196,000$ (cost of goods sold)

(3) $\$260,000 - \$196,000 = \$64,000$ (ending inventory)

[20] The terms "gross profit percentage," "gross margin percentage," "rate of gross profit," and "rate of gross margin" mean the same thing: they all reflect the relationship of gross profit to the selling price. The terms "percentage markup" or "rate of markup" are used to describe the relationship of gross profit to cost. It is very important to understand the difference.

[21] Some seasonal variation is common in most companies. Fiscal year ends are usually chosen at a low activity point in the year's operations, which means that inventories in the annual financial statements are at their lowest levels in the year. Management can make adjustments to use the average monthly inventory level. External users, however, are limited to using the average between the opening and closing annual inventory balances. Public companies are required to issue quarterly reports, so external users can base the average on five inventory amounts through the year.

Banking on Investments

AS YOU PROBABLY KNOW if you have a student loan or a credit card, banks earn interest-based revenue from borrowing and loaning money to individuals and businesses—what's known as the "spread." "The spread is simply the difference between the interest a bank earns on loans extended to customers and the interest paid to depositors for the use of their money," explains Terry Campbell, President of the Canadian Bankers Association (CBA), which represents the banking industry.

Banks also earn interest income from investing in securities, such as treasury bills or bonds. In 2011, 55% of bank revenues came from interest income. Roughly another 45% was non-interest income from providing services such as trading securities, helping companies issue new equity financing, and earning commissions on securities and wealth management, according to the CBA.

There are more than 75 banks operating in Canada—23 of them are domestic. They are governed under the federal Bank Act and its regulations. Banks have two main regulators: the Office of the Superintendent of Financial Institutions (OSFI), which monitors the banks' financial strength and stability, and the Financial Consumer Agency of Canada, which oversees banks' compliance with federal consumer protection regulations.

According to previous international regulations, banks had to maintain at least a 4% Tier 1 capital ratio (the ratio of a bank's common equity plus preferred shares and others, known as Tier 1 capital, to its total assets, as weighted by the riskiness of those assets) and at least an 8% total capital ratio (the ratio of all capital to its risk-weighted assets). Canada's OFSI, meanwhile, required banks operating in Canada to have Tier 1 and total capital ratios of at least 7% and 10%, respectively. At the end of the third quarter of 2012, Canada's six largest banks exceeded these standards with an average Tier 1 capital ratio of 12.8% and a total capital ratio of 15.6%.

The global financial crisis of 2008 did not begin in Canada, but banks around the world were impacted. To help avoid another similar crisis, a subcommittee of the Bank for International Settlements, an international organization that "acts as a bank for central banks," is phasing in new requirements from 2013 to 2019, although OSFI required full adoption of these new international rules as of January 1, 2013. These requirements increase both the quality and quantity of capital.

In addition to credit risk, "banks face a wide variety of risks, including liquidity risk, financing risk, operational risk, and economic risk," Mr. Campbell says. OSFI oversees Canadian banks' risk management practices, which Mr. Campbell describes as strong. "This is evident in the fact that Canada's banks avoided the difficulties that banks in other countries experienced during the global financial crisis of 2008," he says.

CHAPTER
9 | Investments

LEARNING OBJECTIVES

After studying this chapter, you should be able to:

1. Understand the nature of investments including which types of companies have significant investments.

2. Explain and apply the cost/amortized cost model of accounting for investments.

3. Explain and apply the fair value through net income model of accounting for investments.

4. Explain and apply the fair value through other comprehensive income model of accounting for investments.

5. Explain and apply the incurred loss, expected loss, and fair value loss impairment models.

6. Explain the concept of significant influence and apply the equity method.

7. Explain the concept of control and when consolidation is appropriate.

8. Explain how investments are presented and disclosed in the financial statements noting how this facilitates analysis.

9. Identify differences in accounting between IFRS and ASPE, and what changes are expected in the near future.

PREVIEW OF CHAPTER 9

This chapter focuses on the different types of financial asset investments in equity and debt instruments, and the various models used to account for them. The nature of the investment and the company's business model help determine how investments are accounted for and reported. This chapter covers a variety of investments, from those held for short-term profit-taking to those held for longer term strategic purposes. Accounting for investments in loans and receivables, also financial assets, was covered in Chapter 7. Accounting for investments in nonmonetary assets such as land and investment properties is covered in Chapter 10.

The problems with the historical cost model have been recognized for a long time, especially in accounting for financial instruments. Because of this, accounting for such instruments has been on the agendas of standard-setting bodies around the world for many years. Standard setters have put accounting standards in place that require many of these assets to be accounted for at fair value, but financial reporting under these standards has its problems. Because only some of the instruments are recognized at fair value, the standards are unnecessarily complicated. While many of the problems are related to more complex issues, accounting for ordinary investments in other companies' debt and equity instruments continues to be controversial.

The IASB has issued comprehensive guidance on how to measure fair values, as discussed in Chapter 2, as well as a new standard dealing with investments (IFRS 9). The mandatory implementation date for IFRS 9 has been pushed back to 2015. This will allow the IASB to work to minimize the differences between IFRS 9 and the proposed U.S. standard. Until then, IAS 39 deals with accounting for investments unless companies make a decision to adopt IFRS 9 early. Once IFRS 9 is fully implemented, IAS 39 will disappear. New guidance under ASPE became effective in 2011 (Section 3856). Because of the various models, this chapter focuses on the basics, including measurement and recognition of income.

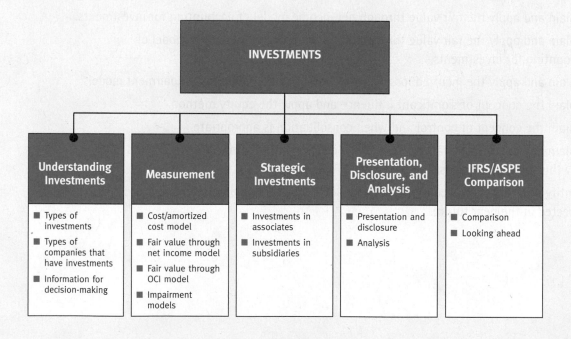

INVESTMENTS				
Understanding Investments	**Measurement**	**Strategic Investments**	**Presentation, Disclosure, and Analysis**	**IFRS/ASPE Comparison**
■ Types of investments ■ Types of companies that have investments ■ Information for decision-making	■ Cost/amortized cost model ■ Fair value through net income model ■ Fair value through OCI model ■ Impairment models	■ Investments in associates ■ Investments in subsidiaries	■ Presentation and disclosure ■ Analysis	■ Comparison ■ Looking ahead

UNDERSTANDING INVESTMENTS

Types of Investments

As a general rule, investments are held for capital appreciation purposes or to earn dividends and/or income. Companies that invest in **debt instruments** of another entity are creditors of the issuing company. Debt instruments include **debt securities**, whose prices are normally quoted in an active market, such as investments in government and corporate bonds, convertible debt, and commercial paper. Debt instruments generally have contractual requirements regarding repayment of principal and payment of interest. The rights depend on the specific debt instrument. As shown in the transaction box, when a company invests in debt instruments, it usually pays cash up front and receives the rights to receive interest and the return of principal at a later date.

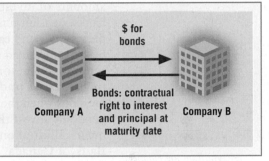

Company A buys bonds from Company B. The bonds carry with them contractual rights to annual interest and repayment of principal in 10 years. Bonds may also be purchased through intermediaries.

Law

Equity instruments, on the other hand, represent ownership interests. Typical examples are common, preferred, or other capital stock or shares. They also include rights to acquire or dispose of ownership interests at an agreed-upon or determinable price, such as warrants, rights, and call or put options. An equity instrument is any contract that is evidence of a residual interest in the assets of an entity after deducting all of its liabilities. Equity instruments generally do not have a maturity date and pay dividends (instead of interest). The holder of the share is entitled to certain rights depending on the nature of the instrument. As shown in the transaction box, when a company purchases equity instruments, it pays cash up front and receives various rights, which may include rights to dividends, voting rights and rights to residual assets upon liquidation.

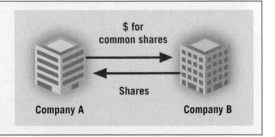

Company A invests in common shares of Company B. The shares carry with them contractual rights to declared dividends, voting rights, and rights to residual assets upon windup of the company.

This chapter will deal with investments in equity and debt instruments, both temporary and long term. Chapter 16 will discuss the more complex financial instruments such as stock options and other derivatives.

Types of Companies That Have Investments

Before looking at how to account for investments, we address the **different motivations that companies have for investing** in debt and equity instruments issued by other companies. One motivation is **the returns provided by investments** through interest, dividends, or capital appreciation (an increase in the underlying value of the investment). Note that some types of investments provide guaranteed returns (such as term deposits), while others are riskier (such as investments in shares of other companies). Managers may invest for **short-term returns** or **longer term returns,** depending on their business and whether, and when, they need the cash for other purposes.

Another reason for investing in equity instruments such as common shares has more to do with **corporate strategy** than returns. Companies may invest in common shares of other companies because they want to have a special relationship with a supplier or customer, such as being able to access certain distribution channels or a supply of raw materials. Other investments are made so that the **investor** can exercise its rights to influence or control the operations of the other company, the **investee.** The intent with these strategic investments is usually to establish a long-term operating relationship between the two entities.

Not all companies invest in other companies. It depends on the nature of the business model and the industry that they operate in. Examples of companies that carry significant amounts of investments in financial instruments include financial institutions such as banks, pension funds, and insurance companies. Banks add value by investing other people's money and earning a return that is higher than their cost of capital. Their expertise lies in understanding how and when to buy and sell shares and debt instruments in order to maximize profits. They often buy and sell investments over the short term for profit (referred to as **trading**). Pension plans collect money from employees and pay out funds as pensions when the employees retire. In order to maximize the payout on retirement, they generally invest the money in the interim and try to maximize the value of the investments. Illustration 9-1 shows the significance of investments in securities for the **Royal Bank of Canada**. Investments in securities represent just under 24% of total assets with their trading portfolio accounting for most of the investments.

Real World Emphasis

Illustration 9-1

Excerpt from the Financial Statements of the Royal Bank of Canada (2011)

Consolidated Balance Sheets		
As of October 31 (C$ millions)	2011	2010 (1)
Assets		
Cash and due from banks	$ 13,247	$ 8,440
Interest-bearing deposits with banks	12,181	13,254
Securities (Note 3)		
Trading	145,274	144,925
Available-for-sale	34,284	38,594
	179,558	183,519
Assets purchased under reverse repurchase agreements and securities borrowed	84,947	72,698
Loans (Note 4 and 5)		
Retail	228,484	214,937
Wholesale	69,758	60,107
	298,242	275,044
Allowance for loan losses	(1,958)	(2,038)
	296,284	273,006
Other		
Customers' liability under acceptances	7,689	7,371
Derivatives (Note 7)	100,013	106,155
Premises and equipment, net (Note 8)	2,490	2,139
Goodwill (Note 10)	7,703	6,660
Other intangibles (Note 10)	2,115	1,710
Assets of discontinued operations (Note 11)	27,143	34,364
Other assets (Note 12)	18,332	16,890
	165,485	175,289
	$751,702	$726,206

(1) Comparative information has been restated to reflect the presentation of discontinued operations. Refer to Notes 1 and 11.

Illustration 9-2 is an excerpt from the financial statements of **Canada Life**, an insurance company. Note that insurance companies sell coverage against risk of loss. They charge their customers insurance premiums up front in return for assuming the risk of loss. If an insured loss occurs in future, they have to pay out a settlement to the insured party. In the meantime, they invest the premiums in order to maximize their value. Investments in bonds and stocks represent 44% of the total assets of Canada Life. In addition, the segregated funds are primarily investments in stocks and bonds, so when we adjust for this, the percentage is actually approximately 73%.

Illustration 9-2

*Excerpt from the Financial
Statements of Canada Life
(2011)*

**Real World
Emphasis**

CONSOLIDATED BALANCE SHEETS
(in Canadian $ millions)

	December 31 2011	December 31 2010	January 1 2010
Assets			
Cash and cash equivalents (note 5)	$ 1,353	$ 1,167	$ 2,655
Bonds (note 6)	43,525	40,013	37,939
Mortgage loans (note 6)	5,712	5,362	6,189
Stocks (note 6)	1,612	1,611	1,503
Investment properties (note 6)	2,436	2,231	2,002
Loans to policyholders	875	868	884
	55,513	51,252	51,172
Funds held by ceding insurers (note 7)	9,576	9,537	10,574
Goodwill (note 11)	259	256	293
Intangible assets (note 11)	58	62	58
Derivative financial instruments (note 29)	494	544	420
Owner occupied properties (note 12)	151	152	154
Fixed assets (note 12)	17	15	19
Reinsurance assets (note 15)	4,116	4,571	4,996
Other assets (note 13)	1,928	1,986	1,669
Deferred tax assets (note 27)	31	11	212
Segregated funds for the risk of unitholders (note 14)	29,452	28,739	27,522
Total assets	**$101,595**	**$97,125**	**$97,089**

Note the diversity in presentation in these two illustrations. Sometimes the investments are labelled for the nature of the instruments, such as bonds or stocks, and sometimes they are labelled with accounting labels, such as **available for sale** or **held for trading**.[1] Many companies use different labels so it is important to recognize which items represent investments.

A quick look at the level of investments in other industries, such as the airline, resort, and retail industries, shows that very few, if any, investments are generally reported on the statement of financial position. Examples include Air Canada, ClubLink, Sobeys, and Indigo Books & Music. Why don't they have significant amounts of investments? This is a good question. The answer lies in the fact that these companies' business models do not require investments to be held. Excess cash is normally used to reinvest in the business, pay down loans, or pay dividends. These companies make their income in other ways, such as selling airline tickets, golf club memberships, groceries, and books.

Information for Decision-Making

Because the nature and risk of various investments are different, it is useful to provide this information in the financial statements. It is also important to show how significant the investments are, including how much income is being earned (both realized and unrealized). In order to be transparent, financial reporting should therefore present this information, either in the notes or on the face of the statement of financial position. For this reason, disclosure and presentation requirements for investments are significant.

MEASUREMENT

How investments are accounted for can depend on **the type of instrument, management's intent,** company **strategy,** and the **ability to reliably measure the investment's fair value**.

The next section of this chapter explains the accounting models generally applied in accounting for straightforward investments in other companies' debt and equity instruments—situations where the investment does not result in the investor having significant influence or control over the other company. After these models are explained, the chapter turns to investments where the investor can exercise significant influence over or control the strategic decisions of the investee company. For these investments, the investor's ownership interest is usually large enough to give the investor a substantial voice at the investee's boardroom table in decisions about the entity's operations, investments, and financing. This, in turn, affects how these investments are accounted for and reported.

Accounting for investments usually requires them to be recognized and measured initially at their fair value at acquisition. Recall that Chapter 2 discusses what is meant by fair value and identifies various ways that fair value can be measured. Chapter 2 also indicates that some methods of measuring fair value are preferred over others, with prices in an active market being the best evidence of the value we are trying to capture. We saw in previous chapters that unless there is evidence to the contrary, the price paid to acquire an asset is usually considered to be its fair value.

The price of a **debt** instrument is quoted as a percentage of its par or face value. For example, if a $25,000 face value bond is priced at 99, this means that its fair value is 99% of $25,000, or $24,750. If it is priced at 103.5, it will sell for 103.5% of $25,000, or $25,875. **Shares** that are traded on a stock exchange are usually quoted at the market price per share in dollars and cents.

Finance

Investments in shares may be acquired **on margin**. This means that the investor pays only part of the purchase price to acquire the shares. The rest is financed by the broker. Since the shares legally belong to the investor, the asset is recorded at the full share price and a liability to the broker for the amount that was financed is also recognized.

If financial assets are measured initially at their fair value, how should **transaction costs** that are directly related to the acquisition—such as fees, commissions, or transfer taxes—be accounted for?[2] The obvious choices are to expense these amounts immediately or to add them to the cost of the assets acquired. The answer is—it depends.[3] It is logical to capitalize the transaction costs associated with any investment that is accounted for using a cost-based model because transaction costs are a necessary cost of acquiring the asset. Alternatively, for assets accounted for using a fair value model, it makes more sense to expense the transaction costs because the fair value of an asset is its market price. Regardless of how transaction costs are accounted for at acquisition, they are **not included** in the fair value amount at later statement of financial position dates.

When a financial instrument is measured at fair value after acquisition, changes in its fair value carrying amount are called **unrealized holding gains or losses**. The change in value is unrealized because it has not been converted to cash or a claim to cash—the asset is still held by the entity. Such gains and losses are only **realized** when the asset is disposed of. Unrealized holding gains and losses may be separately identified from realized gains and losses on the financial statements.[4]

With this brief introduction of basics, let's turn to the specific accounting models for a variety of investments in debt and equity securities. This next section of the chapter identifies and explains three major models of accounting for investments:

1. Cost/amortized cost model

2. Fair value through net income model (FV-NI)

3. Fair value through other comprehensive income model (FV-OCI)

These models are summarized in Illustration 9-3.

Illustration 9-3

Application of Accounting Models

	Cost/Amortized Cost Model	Fair Value through Net Income Model (FV-NI)	Fair Value through OCI Model (FV-OCI)
At acquisition, measure at:	Cost (equal to fair value + transaction costs)	Fair value	Fair value
At each reporting date, measure at:	Cost or amortized cost	Fair value	Fair value
Report unrealized holding gains and losses (changes in fair value):	N/A	In net income	In OCI
Report realized holding gains and losses:	In net income	In net income	Transfer total realized gains/losses to net income (recycling) or directly to retained earnings (no recycling)

Note that there are only two choices when it comes to measuring investments: cost/amortized cost and fair value. Note further that where fair value is used, the unrealized gains and losses are either booked to net income or OCI. It is easier to think about how to account for investments using this simple framework rather than focusing on the labels and various definitions that the different standard setters use for investments.

Cost/Amortized Cost Model

Objective 2
Explain and apply the cost/amortized cost model of accounting for investments.

The accounting standards do not always differentiate between the cost and the amortized cost models, referring to them both as amortized cost. The amortized cost model applies only to investments in debt instruments and long-term notes and loans receivable, while the cost model may be applied to investments in equity instruments (shares) of other companies. Regardless, they are both cost-based methods.

Investments in Shares of Other Entities

Application of the **cost model** to the investment one company makes in another entity's shares is straightforward:

1. Recognize the cost of the investment at the fair value of the shares acquired (or the fair value of what was given up to acquire them, if more reliable). Add to this any direct transaction costs (such as commissions) incurred to acquire the shares.

2. Unless impaired, report the investment at its cost at each statement of financial position date.

3. Recognize dividend income when the entity has a claim to the dividend.

4. When the shares are disposed of, derecognize them and report a gain or loss on disposal in net income. The gain or loss is the difference between the investment's carrying amount and the net proceeds on disposal.

To illustrate, assume that Kiwan Corp. (KC) purchases 1,000 shares of Hirj Co. at $4.25 per share on March 8, 2014. A 1.5% commission is charged on the transaction. On December 15, 2014, Hirj Co. directors declare a dividend of $0.10 per share to shareholders of record on December 31, 2014, payable on January 15, 2015. On July 11, 2015, KC sells 800 of the Hirj Co. shares for $5.08 per share and pays a 1.5% commission on the sale. KC has a December 31 year end. KC's entries to record these transactions and events are as follows:

March 8, 2014		
Other Investments	4,314	
Cash		4,314
(1,000 × \$4.25) + (1,000 × \$4.25 × .015)		

A = L + SE
0   0   0
Cash flows: ↓ 4,314 outflow

December 31, 2014		
Dividend Receivable	100	
Dividend Revenue		100
(1,000 × \$0.10)		

A = L + SE
+100   +100
Cash flows: No effect

January 15, 2015		
Cash	100	
Dividend Receivable		100

A = L + SE
0   0   0
Cash flows: ↑ 100 inflow

July 11, 2015		
Cash	4,003	
Other Investments		3,451
Gain on Sale of Investments		552
(800 × \$5.08) − (800 × \$5.08 × .015) = \$4,003		
\$4,314 × 800/1,000 = \$3,451		
\$4,003 − \$3,451 = \$552		

A = L + SE
+552   +552
Cash flows: ↑ 4,003 inflow

When shares of a company have been purchased at various times and at various costs and only a portion of the holdings are sold, use of an average carrying value for the disposal is logical. This is specifically required under ASPE.

Investments in Debt Securities of Other Entities

When the cost model is applied to an investment in debt securities (and long-term notes and loans receivable), it is referred to as the **amortized cost model**. This is because any difference between the acquisition cost recognized and the face value of the security is amortized over the period to maturity.[5] Amortized cost is the amount recognized at acquisition minus principal repayments, where applicable, plus or minus the cumulative amortization of any discount or premium; that is, amortization of the difference between the initial amount recognized and the maturity value. Impairment charges, discussed later in the chapter, also reduce the amortized cost. The following statements describe this method.

1. Recognize the cost of the investment at the fair value of the debt instrument acquired (or the fair value of what was given up to acquire it, if more reliable a measure). Add to this any direct transaction costs, such as commissions, incurred to acquire the investment.

2. Unless impaired, report the investment at its amortized cost as well as any outstanding interest receivable at each statement of financial position date.

3. Recognize interest income as it is earned, amortizing any discount or premium at the same time by adjusting the carrying amount of the investment.

4. When the investment is disposed of, first bring the accrued interest and discount or premium amortization up to date. Derecognize the investment, reporting any gain or

loss on disposal in net income. The gain or loss is the difference between the proceeds received for the security and the investment's amortized cost at the date of disposal.

Accounting for investments in debt securities using the amortized cost method should be familiar to you. The procedures are the same as accounting for long-term notes and loans receivable, and you may find it useful to review this section of Chapter 7 before continuing. One complication is added in this chapter: the acquisition and disposal of investments between interest payment dates.

Finance

Income under the Amortized Cost Model. Income from debt investments is usually in the form of interest. It can be received in one of two ways, depending on whether the investment is interest-bearing or non–interest-bearing. If it is **interest-bearing,** the party holding the investment on the interest payment date receives all the interest since the last interest payment date. Because debt securities can be bought and sold throughout the year, practice has developed for the purchaser to pay the seller an amount equal to the accrued interest since the last interest payment date. This interest is paid to the seller over and above the agreed exchange price for the investment. If the instrument is **non–interest-bearing,** the price of the bond or other instrument is equal to its present value at the date of the transaction.

The total income from this type of investment is the net cash flow over the time that the investment is held. In the case of investments that are held until they mature, the total income is the difference between the principal amount that is received at maturity plus all periodic interest that is received, and the amount paid to acquire the investment including the accrued interest. Because the decision to acquire and hold the investment is usually based on its yield on the date when it is purchased, the yield rate is also the most appropriate rate to measure periodic income over the term that the investment is held.

To illustrate, assume that on January 1, 2014, Robinson Limited pays $92,278 to purchase $100,000 of Chan Corporation 8% bonds.[6] Robinson accounts for this investment at amortized cost. The bonds mature on January 1, 2019, and interest is payable each July 1 and January 1. The lower-than-face-value purchase price of $92,278 provides an effective interest rate of 10%. This is a combination of the 8% interest received in cash each year and the benefit of the $7,722 discount on the bond ($100,000 – $92,278). Note that the bond is acquired on an interest payment date and there is therefore no accrued interest for Robinson to pay on January 1. Assume Robinson Limited has an August 31 year end.

Cash principal received on maturity of bond	$100,000
Add cash interest to be received:	
($100,000 × 0.08)/2 × 10 payments	40,000
Less cash paid to acquire the bond	(92,278)
Less cash paid for accrued interest when purchased	–0–
Total income to be recognized	$ 47,722

Because Robinson decided to purchase the bond based on its yield, the amount of income that is recognized each period should ideally reflect the yield rate. The **effective interest method**, required under IFRS unless the investment is held for trading purposes, results in recognizing interest income at a constant yield rate on the investment each period. The straight-line method of recognizing interest and amortizing the discount or premium, permitted under ASPE, was explained in Chapter 7 and is briefly reviewed again below. Note that ASPE does not specify a method and so either the effective interest method or straight-line method would be acceptable.

Illustration 9-4 shows the application of the effective interest method to Robinson's investment in the Chan bonds. The original discount is fully amortized by the date the bond matures.

Illustration 9-4

Schedule of Interest Income and Bond Discount Amortization—Effective Interest Method

8% Bonds Purchased to Yield 10%

Date	Cash Received	Interest Income	Bond Discount Amortization	Amortized Cost of Bonds
1/1/14				$ 92,278
7/1/14	$ 4,000ᵃ	$ 4,614ᵇ	$ 614ᶜ	92,892ᵈ
1/1/15	4,000	4,645	645	93,537
7/1/15	4,000	4,677	677	94,214
1/1/16	4,000	4,711	711	94,925
7/1/16	4,000	4,746	746	95,671
1/1/17	4,000	4,783	783	96,454
7/1/17	4,000	4,823	823	97,277
1/1/18	4,000	4,864	864	98,141
7/1/18	4,000	4,907	907	99,048
1/1/19	4,000	4,952	952	100,000
	$40,000	$47,722	$7,722	

ᵃ $4,000 = $100,000 × 0.08 × 6/12
ᵇ $4,614 = $92,278 × 0.10 × 6/12
ᶜ $614 = $4,614 − $4,000
ᵈ $92,892 = $92,278 + $614

The entry to record the purchase of the investment is:

A = L + SE
0   0   0

Cash flows: ↓ 92,278 outflow

Jan. 1/14	Bond Investment at Amortized Cost	92,278
	Cash	92,278

In practice, and as illustrated, **the discount or premium on a bond investment is not usually recognized and reported separately**.

If Robinson Limited follows ASPE, it may decide to use **straight-line amortization** instead of the effective interest method. If so, the original discount of $7,722 ($100,000 − $92,278) is amortized to interest income in equal amounts from the date of acquisition to maturity, a period of 60 months. For each month of interest income recognized, 1/60 of $7,722 or $128.70 of discount is amortized. Under this approach, a constant **amount** of interest income is recognized each period instead of a constant **rate** of interest. All the other entries that involve interest income and the carrying amount of the investment will be affected in the same way when the straight-line method is used.

The journal entry to record the receipt of the first semi-annual interest payment on July 1, 2014, is:

A   = L +   SE
+4,614   +4,614

Cash flows: ↑ 4,000 inflow

A   = L +   SE
+4,772   +4,772

Cash flows: ↑ 4,000 inflow

IFRS: effective interest method (allowed under ASPE as well)			ASPE: may use straight-line method since no specific method is mandated		
July 1/14			July 1/14		
Cash	4,000		Cash	4,000	
Bond Investment at Amortized Cost	614		Bond Investment at Amortized Cost (6 × $128.70)	772	
Interest Income		4,614	Interest Income		4,772

At its year end on August 31, 2014, Robinson recognizes the interest income that has accrued since July 1 and amortizes the discount for the two-month period:

A   = L +   SE
+1,548   +1,548

Cash flows: No effect

IFRS: effective interest method (allowed under ASPE as well)		ASPE: may use straight-line method since no specific method is mandated	
August 31/14		August 31/14	
Interest Receivable	1,333	Interest Receivable	1,333
($4,000 × 2/6)			
Bond Investment at		Bond Investment at	
Amortized Cost	215	Amortized Cost	257
($645 × 2/6)		(2 × $128.70)	
Interest Income	1,548	Interest Income	1,590
($4,645 × 2/6)			

A   = L +   SE
+1,590   +1,590

Cash flows: No effect

When the interest payment is received on January 1, 2015, the following entry is made, assuming that Robinson does not use reversing entries:

A   = L +   SE
+3,097   +3,097

Cash flows: ↑ 4,000 inflow

IFRS: effective interest method (allowed under ASPE as well)		ASPE: may use straight-line method since no specific method is mandated	
January 1/15		January 1/15	
Cash	4,000	Cash	4,000
Bond Investment at		Bond Investment at	
Amortized Cost	430	Amortized Cost	515
($645 × 4/6)		(4 × $128.70)	
Interest Receivable	1,333	Interest Receivable	1,333
Interest Income	3,097	Interest Income	3,182
($4,645 × 4/6)			

A   = L +   SE
+3,182   +3,182

Cash flows: ↑ 4,000 inflow

Sale of Investments.   Assume that Robinson Limited sells its investment in the Chan Corporation bonds on November 1, 2018, at 99.75% plus accrued interest. Remember that interest receivable of $1,333 (2/6 × $4,000) and discount amortization of $317 (2/6 × $952) were recognized at the company's August 31, 2018 year end. The following entry is then made on November 1, 2018, to accrue an additional two months' interest (September and October), to amortize the discount from September 1 to November 1, and bring the investment to its correct carrying amount at the date of disposal. The discount amortization for this two-month period is $317 (2/6 × $952). Assume the effective interest method is used.

A   = L +   SE
+1,650   +1,650

Cash flows: No effect

Nov. 1/18	Interest Receivable (2/6 × $4,000)	1,333	
	Bond Investment at Amortized Cost	317	
	Interest Income (2/6 × $4,952)		1,650

The calculation of the realized gain on the sale is explained in Illustration 9-5.

Illustration 9-5

Calculation of Gain on Sale of Bonds

Selling price of bonds ($100,000 × .9975)		$99,750
Less: Carrying amount of bonds on November 1, 2018:		
Amortized cost, July 1, 2018 (see amortization schedule)	$99,048	
Add: Discount amortized for the period July 1, 2018, to November 1, 2018 ($317 to August 31 + $317 from September 1 to November 1)	634	99,682
Gain on sale of bonds		$ 68

The entry to record the sale of the bonds is:

<table>
<tr><td>A = L + SE
+68   0   +68

Cash flows: ↑ 102,416 inflow</td><td>Nov. 1/18   Cash
Interest Receivable
Bond Investment at Amortized Cost
Gain on Sale of Investments</td><td>102,416</td><td>
2,666
99,682
68</td></tr>
</table>

The credit to Interest Receivable is for the four months of accrued interest from July 1 to November 1, all of which the purchaser pays in cash to Robinson. The debit to Cash is made up of the selling price of the bonds, $99,750, plus the four months of accrued interest, $2,666. The credit to the Bond Investment at Amortized Cost account is the bonds' carrying amount on the sale date, and the credit to Gain on Sale of Investments is the excess of the selling price over the bonds' carrying amount.

Fair Value through Net Income (FV-NI) Model

Objective 3
Explain and apply the fair value through net income model of accounting for investments.

The **fair value through net income (FV-NI)** model, referred to as **fair value through profit or loss (FVTPL)** under IFRS, is required today for many financial assets and liabilities, including many investments in other entities' debt and equity securities. When investments to be accounted for at FV-NI are acquired, they are recognized at their fair value. Consistent with measurement at fair value, transaction costs incurred in acquiring such assets are expensed as incurred. The name of the method—fair value through net income—is very descriptive of how the accounting works! The carrying amount of each FV-NI investment is adjusted to its current fair value at each reporting date. All resulting holding gains and losses are reported in net income along with any dividends or interest income earned.

Income from Investments

As explained for investments carried at amortized cost, the total income on the investment is the net cash flow from the investment: the gain or loss on the instrument itself plus any interest or dividend return. Accounting for income on an investment is the art of allocating the total income to specific accounting periods.

For FV-NI investments, periodic income is a combination of the change in an investment's carrying amount plus the interest or dividend income that has been received or is receivable for the period. For FV-NI investments in general, and especially those that are held for trading purposes—that is, they are held to sell in the near term or to generate a profit from short-term fluctuations in price—it may not be important to report interest and dividend income separately from the holding gains or losses. Under IFRS, both types of income may be accounted for and reported together because this tends to mirror how such investments are managed.[7] ASPE requires separate reporting of interest income and net gains or losses recognized on financial instruments. Note that many companies may wish to report dividends and interest separately for tax purposes and since the financial statements provide the basis for the tax returns, it may be worthwhile to show these items separately in the financial statements as well. Let's look at an example showing both separate and combined reporting of the income.

The reporting entity may need or want to keep track of holding gains and losses separately from interest and dividend income whether it is required or for additional transparency and decision-making. Accounting for dividend income separately from holding gains and losses is straightforward.

• When a dividend is received (or receivable), it is recognized as Dividend Revenue.

• When the investment is adjusted to its fair value at each reporting date, the change in value is recognized in a separate account, such as Unrealized Gain or Loss.

It is now easier for the entity to report the dividend income separately from the fair value changes because the information has been captured in two different accounts.

Recognizing interest income under the effective interest method (or even the straight-line method) separately requires more complex entries than described above. This is because **any discount or premium must be amortized before the change in fair value is recognized.** Amortizing the discount or premium changes the investment's carrying amount. Therefore, the subsequent adjustment to bring the investment to its new fair value has to take this interest adjustment into account. Two sets of information have to be kept to make this work: a schedule of the investment's amortized cost, for purposes of interest income calculations; and information on its fair value, in order to report the asset at the appropriate amount.

The bookkeeping can be handled in at least two different ways. One method keeps the investment in the accounts at its amortized cost and uses a separate valuation allowance account to bring it to its fair value at each statement of financial position date. Alternatively, the investment account itself is maintained at fair value and the necessary amortized cost information is kept in records that are supplementary to the accounts. In this chapter, for purposes of explanation, the second approach is used. The authors prefer this method because it emphasizes the use of fair value measurement rather than an adjusted cost-based measure. In short, the entries are as follows.

- Recognize interest income in an account such as Interest Income on FV-NI Investments as it is earned, adjusting the investment's book value by the amount of any discount or premium amortization.

- When the investment is adjusted to its current fair value at each reporting date, the change in value is recognized in a separate account such as Unrealized Gain or Loss on FV-NI debt investments.

The following illustrates the accounting for an investment in a debt instrument at FV-NI using the effective interest method. Assume that a company purchases $100,000, 10%, five-year bonds of Graff Corporation on January 1, 2014, with interest payable on July 1 and January 1. The bond sells for $108,111, resulting in a bond premium of $8,111 and an effective interest rate of 8%. The entry to record the purchase of the bonds is:

A = L + SE
0   0   0

Cash flows: ↓ 108,111 outflow

Jan. 1/14	FV NI Investments	108,111	
	Cash		108,111

Illustration 9-6 shows the effect that the premium amortization has on the interest income that is reported each period. The process is identical to the amortization of debt investments explained earlier in this chapter, except this situation involves a premium instead of a discount.

Illustration **9-6**

Schedule of Interest Income and Bond Premium Amortization—Effective Interest Method

10% BONDS PURCHASED TO YIELD 8%

Date	Cash Received	Interest Income	Bond Premium Amortization	Amortized Cost of Bonds
1/1/2014				$108,111
7/1/2014	$ 5,000[a]	$ 4,324[b]	$ 676[c]	107,435[d]
1/1/2015	5,000	4,297	703	106,732
7/1/2015	5,000	4,269	731	106,001
1/1/2016	5,000	4,240	760	105,241
7/1/2016	5,000	4,210	790	104,451
1/1/2017	5,000	4,178	822	103,629
7/1/2017	5,000	4,145	855	102,774
1/1/2018	5,000	4,111	889	101,885

(continued)

Illustration 9-6

Schedule of Interest Income and Bond Premium Amortization—Effective Interest Method (continued)

Date	Cash Received	Interest Income	Bond Premium Amortization	Amortized Cost of Bonds
7/1/2018	5,000	4,075	925	100,960
1/1/2019	5,000	4,040	960	100,000
	$50,000	$41,889	$8,111	

^a $5,000 = $100,000 \times 0.10 \times 6/12$
^b $4,324 = $108,111 \times 0.08 \times 6/12$
^c $676 = $5,000 - $4,324$
^d $107,435 = $108,111 - 676

The entries to record interest income on the first interest date and at the December 31 year end are:

IFRS
A　=　L　+　SE
+5,000　　　　+5,000

Cash flows: ↑ 5,000 inflow

ASPE
A　=　L　+　SE
+4,324　　　　+4,324

Cash flows: ↑ 5,000 inflow

IFRS: no requirement to report interest separately under FV-NI			ASPE: requirement to report interest separately (including amortization of premiums and discounts)		
July 1/14			July 1/14		
Cash	5,000		Cash	5,000	
Investment Income			FV-NI Investments		676
or Loss		5,000	Interest Income		4,324

IFRS
A　=　L　+　SE
+5,000　　　　+5,000

Cash flows: No effect

ASPE
A　=　L　+　SE
+4,297　　　　+4,297

Cash flows: No effect

IFRS: no requirement to report interest separately			ASPE: requirement to report interest separately (including amortization of premiums and discounts)		
December 31/14			December 31/14		
Interest Receivable	5,000		Interest Receivable	5,000	
Investment Income			FV-NI Investments		703
or Loss		5,000	Interest Income		4,297

Assume that at December 31, 2014, the fair value of the Graff Corporation bonds is $105,000. Their carrying amount at this time is $106,732 (assuming that we have amortized the premium) and the adjustment needed to bring the Investment account to fair value is $1,732:

Original cost and carrying amount of bonds		$108,111
Entries made to Investment in Graff Corp. Bonds account during year when recognizing interest income:		
July 1, 2014	$676 credit	
Dec. 31, 2014	703 credit	(1,379)
Carrying amount before fair value adjustment		106,732
Fair value, December 31, 2014		105,000
Fair value adjustment needed		$ 1,732 credit

If we have not amortized the discount, the carrying amount would still be $108,111 and the adjustment amount would be $108,111 − $105,000 = $3,111. The entry to adjust the investment to its fair value at December 31, 2014, is:

IFRS

A	=	L	+	SE
−3,111				−3,111

Cash flows: No effect

ASPE

A	=	L	+	SE
−1,732				−1,732

Cash flows: No effect

IFRS: no requirement to report interest separately		ASPE: requirement to report interest separately (including amortization of premiums and discounts)	
December 31/14		December 31/14	
Investment Income		Unrealized Gain	
or Loss	3,111	or Loss	1,732
FV-NI Investments	3,111	FV-NI Investments	1,732

The impact on net income is the same under both methods noted above. However, it is presented differently, with ASPE showing interest (including the bond amortization) separately.

For a **non–interest-bearing debt investment** that is held for short-term trading, the investment income that is earned is the difference between the instrument's purchase price and its maturity value or the proceeds on its disposal. Treasury bills, for example, are usually traded in non–interest-bearing form. Assume that Investor Inc. pays $19,231 on March 15 for a $20,000 six-month treasury bill that matures on September 15. The investment, purchased to yield an 8% return, is designated as an FV-NI investment. Illustration 9-7 shows how to account for the investment income, assuming that interest income is not reported separately.

Illustration 9-7

Income on a Non–Interest-Bearing Debt Instrument Accounted for at FV-NI, Interest Income Not Reported Separately

Mar. 15	FV-NI Investments		19,231	
	Cash			19,231
	(To record purchase of a $20,000, six-month treasury bill)			
Sept. 15	Cash		20,000	
	FV-NI Investments			19,231
	Investment Income or Loss			769
	(To record the proceeds on maturity of a $20,000 treasury bill)			

Note that the investment income, which consists entirely of interest in this case, is equal to an 8% yield on the amount paid for the investment: $19,231 × 8% × 6/12 = $769. If Investor Inc. needed cash prior to September 15 and sold the investment before maturity, the investment income reported is the difference between its carrying amount and the proceeds on disposal.

Investments in **equity securities** that are held for short-term trading profits may pay dividends. If the company does not report interest income separately, it is unlikely that it would report dividend income separately, either. Because the holder of the shares on the date of record is entitled to the dividend and this date is generally a few weeks before the dividend is paid, a dividend receivable and the related income may be recognized before the cash is received. As an FV-NI investment, the shares are remeasured to their fair value at each statement of financial position date with the change in fair value also recognized in the Investment Income or Loss account. When the investment is sold, its carrying amount is removed from the investment account and investment income is recognized.

To demonstrate the accounting for a portfolio of temporary investments accounted for at FV-NI with no separate reporting of interest and dividend income, assume that on December 31, 2014, Western Publishing Corporation provides the information shown in Illustration 9-8 about its investments portfolio. Assume that all investments were acquired in 2014. The investments were recorded at their fair value at acquisition in an account entitled FV-NI Investments, and this value is their **carrying amount** on the books before any adjustment.

Illustration 9-8

Calculation of Fair Value Adjustment—Investments Portfolio, December 31, 2014

FV-NI INVESTMENTS PORTFOLIO
December 31, 2014

Investments	Carrying Amount	Fair Value
Burlington Corp. shares	$ 43,860	$ 51,500
Genesta Corp. 8% bonds	184,230	175,200
Warner Ltd. shares	86,360	91,500
Total portfolio	$314,450	$318,200

Adjustment needed to the portfolio to bring it to fair value at
December 31, 2014: $318,200 − $314,450 = $3,750 debit

At December 31, an adjusting entry is made to bring the investments portfolio to its year-end fair value and to record the holding gain. This entry assumes that Western Publishing has one control account in its general ledger for the entire portfolio. It would be equally correct to make a separate entry for each of the three different investments.

A = L + SE
+3,750   +3,750

Cash flows: No effect

| Dec. 31/14 | FV-NI Investments | 3,750 | |
| | Investment Income or Loss | | 3,750 |

The Investment Income or Loss account is included in net income on the income statement, and the fair values of the investments at December 31, 2014, now become the carrying amounts on the books. With a fair value measurement approach, the original cost or fair value at acquisition is not relevant.[8]

Now assume that the Genesta Corp. bonds are sold for $174,000 on February 4, 2015, their interest payment date, and that 1,000 shares of Next Ltd. are acquired for their fair value of $49,990 on September 21, 2015. The entries to record the February 4 and September 21 transactions follow. Note that the bond's carrying amount before the sale is $175,200, its fair value at the last statement of financial position date.

A = L + SE
−1,200   −1,200

Cash flows: ↑ 174,000 inflow

Feb. 4/15	Cash	174,000	
	Investment Income or Loss	1,200	
	FV-NI Investments		175,200

A = L + SE
0   0   0

Cash flows: ↓ 49,990 outflow

| Sept. 21/15 | FV-NI Investments | 49,990 | |
| | Cash | | 49,990 |

Because the gains and losses on FV-NI investments are reported in net income, the distinction between the portions that are realized and unrealized is blurred. This is not usually an issue, however, particularly for trading securities that are acquired for short-term profit-taking.

Illustration 9-9 indicates the carrying amounts and fair values of the investments portfolio at December 31, 2015. As Western Publishing prepares financial statements only once a year, the carrying amounts of the Burlington and Warner shares that are still on hand are the fair values reported at December 31, 2014. The carrying amount of the Next Ltd. shares acquired during the year is their fair value at acquisition.

Illustration 9-9

*Fair Value Adjustment—FV-NI
Investments Portfolio,
December 31, 2015*

FV-NI INVESTMENTS PORTFOLIO
December 31, 2015

Investments	Carrying Amount	Fair Value
Burlington Corp. shares	$ 51,500	$ 50,500
Warner Ltd. shares	91,500	90,100
Next Ltd. shares	49,990	50,600
Total portfolio	$192,990	$191,200

Adjustment needed to bring the portfolio to fair value at
December 31, 2015: $192,990 − $191,200 = $1,790 credit

At December 31, an adjusting entry is made to bring the investments to their year-end fair values.

A	= L +	SE
−1,790		−1,790

Cash flows: No effect

| Dec. 31/15 | Investment Income or Loss | 1,790 | |
| | FV-NI Investments | | 1,790 |

The investment loss is included in the 2015 income statement, added to the loss recognized on February 4.

Fair Value through Other Comprehensive Income (FV-OCI) Model

Objective 4

Explain and apply the fair value through other comprehensive income model of accounting for investments.

The concept of other comprehensive income was explained in Chapter 4. It is an income statement account and is closed out to an account called Accumulated Other Comprehensive Income.[9]

Illustration 9-10 shows how these financial statement categories are related.

Illustration 9-10

*A Review of How Net Income,
Other Comprehensive Income,
and Accumulated Other
Comprehensive Income
are Related*

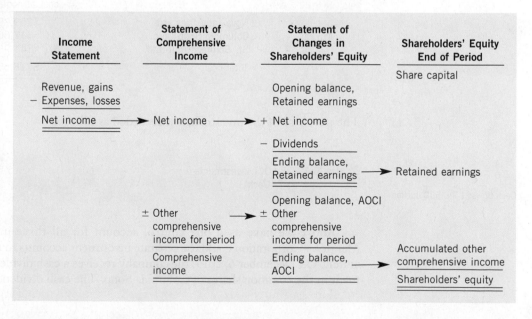

Income Statement	Statement of Comprehensive Income	Statement of Changes in Shareholders' Equity	Shareholders' Equity End of Period
			Share capital
Revenue, gains − Expenses, losses		Opening balance, Retained earnings	
Net income →	Net income →	+ Net income	
		− Dividends	
		Ending balance, Retained earnings →	Retained earnings
		Opening balance, AOCI	
	± Other comprehensive income for period →	± Other comprehensive income for period	
	Comprehensive income	Ending balance, AOCI →	Accumulated other comprehensive income
			Shareholders' equity

Investments accounted for at **fair value through other comprehensive income (FV-OCI)** are recognized at acquisition at their fair value. However, unlike the FV-NI model, the transaction costs tend to be added to the carrying amount of the investment. When the investment is adjusted to its fair value at the first reporting date, the transaction costs automatically end up as part of the holding gain or loss recognized in OCI at that time.

Income from FV-OCI Investments

Underlying Concept

Recycling supports the continued use of net income as the main performance measure, while not recycling supports the concept that comprehensive income is the appropriate measure of performance.

At each reporting date, the carrying amount of each FV-OCI investment is adjusted to its current fair value. As the name of the model implies, the changes in fair value—the holding gains and losses—are recognized in other comprehensive income. The dividend income from these investments is reported separately from the holding gains and losses because the dividend income is reported in net income, while the unrealized holding gains and losses are captured in OCI, net of income tax.[10] There are two different versions of the FV-OCI model, however. The difference between them relates to how they treat the holding gains and losses once they are realized:

1. FV-OCI with recycling, and

2. FV-OCI without recycling.

Under the **FV-OCI model with recycling,** when the investments are disposed of and converted to cash or a claim to cash, the previously unrealized holding gains or losses to the date of disposal are transferred or "recycled" into net income.[11] Under the **FV-OCI model without recycling,** the realized gains and losses do not get recycled through net income, but are transferred directly into retained earnings.[12] Aside from this, both versions of the FV-OCI model are the same. Under the current IFRS 9, FV-OCI investments are **limited to equity investments** in other companies.[13] Therefore, the following illustration is limited to this type of investment.

Assume that on November 3, 2013, Manitoba Corporation purchases common shares of three companies, with the investments to be accounted for at FV-OCI. The purchases are as follows:

	Fair value and cost at acquisition
Nova Industries Ltd.	$259,700
Columbia Soup Corp.	317,500
St. Boniface Pulp Ltd.	141,350
Total cost	$718,550

The purchase of the investments is recorded as follows:

A = L + SE
0   0   0

Cash flows: ↓ 718,550 outflow

| Nov. 3/13 | FV-OCI Investments | 718,550 | |
| | Cash | | 718,550 |

Above we have used one control account for all three investments. Alternatively, Manitoba Corporation could use separate investment accounts to track each investment separately. On December 6, 2013, the company receives a cash dividend of $4,200 on its investment in the common shares of Columbia Soup. The cash dividend is recorded as follows:

A = L + SE
+4,200   +4,200

Cash flows: ↑ 4,200 inflow

| Dec. 6/13 | Cash | 4,200 | |
| | Dividend Revenue | | 4,200 |

Illustration 9-11 indicates the carrying amounts (and cost), fair values, and unrealized gains and losses at December 31, 2013, for Manitoba's FV-OCI investments.

FV-OCI EQUITY INVESTMENTS PORTFOLIO
December 31, 2013

Investments	Carrying Amount	Fair Value	Holding Gain (Loss) for Period
Nova Industries Ltd.	$259,700	$275,000	$ 15,300
Columbia Soup Corp.	317,500	304,000	(13,500)
St. Boniface Pulp Ltd.	141,350	104,000	(37,350)
Total of portfolio	$718,550	$683,000	$(35,550)

For Manitoba's portfolio, the gross holding gains are $15,300, and the gross holding losses are $50,850 ($13,500 + $37,350), resulting in a net unrealized loss of $35,550. The portfolio's fair value is $35,550 less than its carrying amount (and cost, in this first accounting period). The unrealized gains and losses are recorded in a Holding Gain or Loss account and are reported as part of other comprehensive income assuming that the investments are not impaired. The carrying amount of the investments is adjusted in the following entry to their fair value at the statement of financial position date.

A = L + SE
−35,550   −35,550

Cash flows: No effect

Dec. 31/13		
Unrealized Gain or Loss—OCI	35,550	
FV-OCI Investments		35,550

Sale of FV-OCI Investments

We carry on our example to show how to account for the sale of FV-OCI investments. Now assume that Manitoba sells all of its Nova Industries Ltd. common shares on January 23, 2014, receiving proceeds of $287,220. This is $12,220 more than the current carrying amount of the Investment in Nova Industries in the accounts.

While it is possible to record this event using different combinations of entries, the following series of three entries clearly accomplishes what is needed:

(a) The **first entry** adjusts the investment's carrying amount to its fair value at the date of disposal and captures the holding gain up to that date in OCI.

(b) The **second entry** removes the investment's carrying amount from the asset account and records the proceeds on disposal.

(c) The **third entry** is a **reclassification adjustment** that transfers the holding gain that is now realized out of OCI and into (i) net income (if FV-OCI with recycling) or (ii) retained earnings (if FV-OCI without recycling).

A = L + SE
+12,220   +12,220

Cash flows: ↑ 287,220 inflow

Jan. 23/14	(a) FV-OCI Investments	12,220	
	Unrealized Gain or Loss—OCI		12,220
	($287,220 − $275,000)		
	(b) Cash	287,220	
	FV-OCI Investments		287,220
	($275,000 + $12,220)		
	(c) (i) if FV-OCI with recycling:		
	Unrealized Gain or Loss—OCI	27,520	
	Gain on Sale of Investments		27,520
	or (c) (ii) if FV-OCI without recycling:		
	Unrealized Gain or Loss—OCI	27,520	
	Retained Earnings		27,520
	($287,220 − $259,700) or ($15,300 + $12,220)		

The amount either recycled through OCI to net income or transferred to retained earnings is the difference between the investment's original cost and the proceeds on disposal ($287,220 – $259,700). It is also the sum of all prior entries to OCI for the Nova Industries shares: a $15,300 gain on December 31, 2013, and a $12,220 gain on January 23, 2014, for a total of $27,520. All that remains in accumulated other comprehensive income now is the unrealized net holding gains/losses on the remaining investments.

To continue with this example, assume that the information in Illustration 9-12 is provided for Manitoba's FV-OCI portfolio at December 31, 2014.

<table>
<tr><td>Illustration 9-12

Calculation of Holding Gain/Loss for Period—FV-OCI Equity Investments Portfolio (2014)</td><td colspan="5">

FV-OCI INVESTMENTS PORTFOLIO
December 31, 2014

Investments	Cost	Carrying Amount	Fair Value	Holding Gain (Loss) for Period
Columbia Soup Corp.	$317,500	$304,000	$362,550	$58,550
St. Boniface Pulp Ltd.	141,350	104,000	139,050	35,050
Total of portfolio	$458,850	$408,000	$501,600	$93,600

</td></tr>
</table>

The entry to bring the investments to their fair value at December 31, 2014, is:

A = L + SE
+93,600   +93,600

Cash flows: No effect

Dec. 31/14		
FV-OCI Investments	93,600	
Unrealized Gain or Loss—OCI		93,600

Now that the three common methods of accounting for financial instruments have been explained and illustrated, how does a company decide which method is accepted under accounting standards for a particular investment? The correct answer is, "It depends on when you are asking." Illustration 9-13 summarizes how the three measurement models are used by IFRS and ASPE.

Measurement models	ASPE (in effect since 2011)	IFRS 9 (effective 2015 but may adopt early)	IAS 39 (currently in effect)
Cost/Amortized Cost	All investments except where they are equity instruments that are quoted in an active market or derivatives	Debt investments that are managed on a contractual yield basis where the business model requires the entity to hold the investments to maturity	**Held to maturity** including debt investments where the company has the ability and intent to hold the debt instrument to maturity.
FV-NI	Equity investments that are quoted in an active market and derivatives Companies may make an accounting policy choice and elect to account for investments using FV-NI **(fair value option)**	Equity instruments not accounted for under FV-OCI model Debt instruments not accounted for using the amortized cost model Derivatives May elect to account for investments under this model (fair value option) as long as certain conditions are met (for example, to avoid an	**Held for trading** including debt and equity investments (including derivatives) that are held for short-term profit-taking and are bought and sold on a regular basis May elect to account for investments using FV-NI (fair value option) as long as certain conditions are met

(continued)

Measurement models	ASPE (in effect since 2011)	IFRS 9 (effective 2015 but may adopt early)	IAS 39 (currently in effect)
FV-OCI	N/A	accounting mismatch where offsetting economic gains and losses on instruments managed using fair value do not otherwise offset in the statements) May elect to classify certain equity investments here (where no significant influence or control and not trading investments) No recycling but dividend income recognized in net income unless it is deemed to be a return of capital	**Available for sale** including debt and equity investments that are not **held to maturity** or **held for trading**. Use cost as a default measure where unable to estimate fair value Use recycling where there is objective evidence of impairment or investments are sold
Notes	Interest must be disclosed or presented separately	Interest must be disclosed or presented separately if FV-NI model not used	Interest must be disclosed or presented separately if FV-NI model not used
Reclassifications between categories	Not addressed specifically	Not permitted unless change in business model	Reclassifications permitted in very limited situations

Illustration 9-13

Classification of Investments Under IFRS and ASPE (Where no Significant Influence or Control) (continued)

Objective 5

Explain and apply the incurred loss, expected loss, and fair value loss impairment models.

Impairment Models

Financial asset investments are reviewed for possible impairment for the same reasons that non-financial assets are: the SFP value for any asset cannot be more than the future benefits the asset can bring to the organization. Since financial assets measured at fair value are already measured at their current fair value amount, it is usually only those measured at cost or amortized cost that need a method of accounting for impairment.

Both IFRS and ASPE require that entities adjust for impairment at each reporting date. To the extent possible, this review is carried out at the level of individual assets. However, sometimes the information is not available on a timely basis to do this on each specific asset, so investments with similar characteristics are grouped. Even if assets are assessed for impairment on an individual basis, they should also be assessed for impairment as a group where they share similar risk characteristics. For instance, a portfolio of loans to a certain industry that is experiencing an economic downturn should be assessed as a group as well as individually. If an instrument, or portfolio of instruments, is determined to be impaired, the amount of the impairment loss is calculated and recognized. There are differences of opinion, however, on how such a loss should be determined and reported. Three different impairment models are explained next: an incurred loss model, an expected loss model, and a full fair value model. We will then summarize which models are used under IFRS and ASPE and when.

Incurred Loss Model

Under the **incurred loss impairment model**, investments are recognized as impaired when there is no longer reasonable assurance that the future cash flows associated with them will be either collected in their entirety or when due. Entities look for objective evidence that there has been a significant adverse change in the period in the expected amount of future cash flows or in the timing of those cash flows. These events are called **trigger events or loss events**. Examples of situations that might indicate impairment include the fact that the entity that issued the debt or equity instrument:

- is experiencing significant financial difficulties,
- has defaulted on or is late making interest or principal payments,
- is likely to undergo a major financial reorganization or enter bankruptcy, or
- is in a market that is experiencing significant negative economic change.

If such evidence exists, the next step is to measure the investment's estimated realizable amounts. This is calculated as the present value of the revised amounts and timing of the future cash flows, discounted at the interest rate originally used to measure the instrument when it was first recognized if IFRS or at the current market rate if ASPE. Alternatively, if the revised amount and timing of the cash flows cannot be reasonably determined, the realizable amount can be calculated as the current market price for the instrument, or the fair value of the net proceeds the entity would get on liquidating any collateral it is entitled to. The **impairment loss** is the difference between this revised present value calculation and the instrument's carrying amount.

After the impairment is recorded, interest income is recognized based on the revised cash flow estimates and the **discount rate that was used to determine the present value of those flows**. Any further change in the investment's realizable value related to an event occurring after the original impairment is recognized as an adjustment of the impairment loss. It could be a further decline in value (an increased loss) or a recovery of part or all of the previous estimated impairment loss.

This impairment method is described as an **incurred loss impairment model** because it captures only credit losses that were triggered by events that occurred by the SFP date. Notice also that this model retains its cost basis when the original discount rate continues to be used to calculate the recoverable amount, but moves to a partial fair value measurement when a current interest rate is used to discount the impaired cash flows.

Expected Loss Model

Under an **expected loss impairment model**, estimates of future cash flows used to determine the present value of the investment are made on a **continuous basis** and do not rely on a triggering event to occur. Even though there may be no objective evidence that an impairment loss has been incurred, revised cash flow projections may indicate changes in credit risk associated with the issuer of the instrument. Under the expected loss model, these revised expected cash flows are discounted at the same effective interest rate used when the instrument was **first acquired,** therefore retaining a cost-based measurement.

Again similar to the incurred loss approach, the expected impairment loss is the difference between the revised present value calculation and the instrument's carrying amount. After the impairment is recognized, interest income continues to be recognized based on the continuously revised cash flow estimates and the original discount rate. Changes in the investment's realizable value from one period to the next are recognized as adjustments of the impairment loss. This could be an improvement and a reversal of a previous loss, or an increase in the amount already recognized.

Because the impairment loss under this model reflects both incurred losses to date and future expected credit losses, it results in earlier recognition of such losses in net income. This model is more difficult to apply, especially in continually estimating the amounts of the expected future cash flows.

To illustrate, assume that Xia Ltd. has an investment in a $100,000 face value bond of Chan Corp. with a carrying amount of $98,900 on an amortized cost basis. All payments of interest and principal have been received on a timely basis and there are no indicators that the investment is impaired. Chan's credit rating has been reduced recently, although it is still at an acceptable level. With the reduction in credit quality, the estimate of future defaults on the bond's cash flows has increased. If discounting the revised future cash flows at the original discount rate results in a valuation of $97,200, an impairment loss of $1,700 ($98,900 − $97,200) is recognized.

Underlying Concept

The expected loss model provides more objective information since the assessment of a trigger or loss event can be very subjective. This may be offset by the fact that it is not easy to measure the fair value of many instruments where they are not traded in an active market.

Fair Value Loss Model

Under the **fair value loss impairment model**, the impairment loss is the difference between the asset's fair value and its current carrying amount, assuming the fair value is less than the carrying amount. Fair value is calculated using all current information including revised cash flows, current interest rates, and market values. Refer back to Chapter 2 for a discussion regarding calculating fair values. Interest income recognized after the impairment is calculated using the revised discount rate that determined the instrument's fair value. For investments valued using FV-NI, there is no need to be concerned about doing a separate impairment test. This is because the FV-NI model requires that all changes in fair value, whether they are gains or losses, be recognized in net income.

Illustration 9-14 summarizes the various impairment models under ASPE and IFRS.

Illustration 9-14

Summary of Impairment Models

Impairment Models	ASPE	IAS 39	IFRS 9
Incurred loss	Used for all investments measured at cost/amortized cost Reduce carrying value to the higher of the discounted cash flow (DCF; discounted using the market interest rate) and net realizable value (either through sale or by exercising the entity's rights to collateral) May use an allowance account or reduce carrying value directly Impairment losses may be reversed	Used for all investments measured using cost/amortized cost Reduce carrying value to DCF (discounted using historic interest rate for debt instruments and market interest rate for equity instruments measured at cost) May use an allowance account or reduce carrying value directly Used for FV-OCI investments where a loss/trigger event has occurred Reduce carrying value to fair value and book loss through net income Impairment losses may be reversed for debt instruments only	Used for all investments measured using cost/amortized cost Reduce carrying value to DCF (discounted using historic interest rate) May use an allowance account or reduce carrying value directly Impairment losses may be reversed for debt instruments only
Expected loss	N/A	N/A	N/A
Fair value	Used for equity investments (where active market) and derivatives No need to do a separate impairment test since the assets are continually revalued to fair value with gains and losses booked to net income	Used for all investments that are accounted for as FV-NI No need to do a separate impairment test since the assets are continually revalued to fair value with gains and losses booked to net income	Used for all investments that are accounted for as FV-NI No need to do a separate impairment test since the assets are continually revalued to fair value with gains and losses booked to net income

Illustration 9-15 looks at how to account for impairment under ASPE and IFRS.

Assume a company purchased an investment in AB Ltd. bonds for $100,000 at par value at the beginning of the year. The bonds pay interest on December 31 each year. AB Ltd. is experiencing financial difficulties. The company determines that the existence of financial difficulties provides objective evidence of impairment and represents a triggering or loss event.

IFRS ↑↓ ASPE

The present value of the discounted revised cash flows is $80,000 using the original effective interest rate and $70,000 using the current market interest rate (which is higher). The market value of the bonds is $70,000 less commissions.

This situation would be reflected in the financial statements as shown in Illustration 9-15 under the various models and considering ASPE versus IFRS.

	ASPE	IAS 39	IFRS 9
Amortized Cost Must be a triggering event. If there is no triggering event, no loss would be recognized under ASPE or IFRS.	Loss on Impairment 30,000 Bond Investment at Amortized Cost 30,000 ($100,000 − $70,000, which represents the higher of the DCF at the current interest rate and the NRV)	Loss on Impairment 20,000 Bond Investment at Amortized Cost 20,000 ($100,000 − $80,000, which represents the DCF using the historic or original interest rate)	Loss on Impairment 20,000 Bond Investment at Amortized Cost 20,000 ($100,000 − $80,000, which represents the DCF using the historic or original interest rate)
FV-NI Need not be a triggering event	Loss on Impairment 30,000 FV-NI Investments 30,000 (revalue to FV without any adjustment for transactions costs)	Loss on Impairment 30,000 FV-NI Investments 30,000 (revalue to FV without any adjustment for transactions costs)	Loss on Impairment 30,000 FV-NI Investments 30,000 (revalue to FV without any adjustment for transactions costs)
FV-OCI Must be a triggering event to recognize impairment loss in net income	N/A: FV-OCI category not used under ASPE	Loss on Impairment 30,000 FV-OCI Investments 30,000 (revalue to FV without any adjustment for transactions costs)	N/A: FV-OCI category only used for certain equity investments (not debt investments)

Illustration 9-15

Accounting for Impairment under ASPE and IFRS

STRATEGIC INVESTMENTS

Accounting for investments in the common shares of another corporation after acquisition depends mostly on the relationship that exists between the investor and the investee. Relationships are classified by the level of influence that is exercised by the investor and this, in turn, is generally related to the degree of share ownership. In other words, more shares usually mean more influence. When the investment is made for strategic purposes, management usually wants to influence or control the investee's policies. Therefore, the investor is more likely to acquire a higher percentage of the outstanding voting shares.

The levels of influence and types of investment are summarized in Illustration 9-16 with reference to the percentage of ownership. Note that the percentages given are guidelines only.

Illustration 9-16

Levels of Influence and Types of Investment

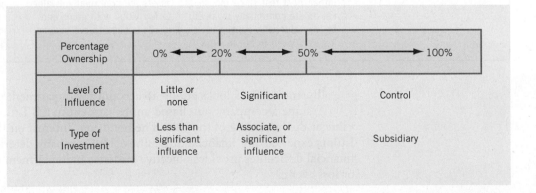

Investments in Associates

The accounting standards and reporting for equity investments depend on the level of influence that dictates what type of investment a particular holding is.[14] The first part of this chapter covers how to account for investments where the investor is not able to exercise significant influence, let alone control of the investee company. Although some of those investments could have been made for strategic purposes, it was assumed earlier in the chapter that the required level of **significant influence** was not reached.

Significant Influence

When an investor has an interest of less than 20%, **it is presumed that the investor has little or no influence over the investee**. This may not be the case, however. For example, a 16% interest may allow an investor to very significantly influence decisions if the remaining shares are widely held. Alternatively, ownership of 30% of a company's shares may not give an investor company any influence at all if a 70% majority shareholder does not permit any.

Although an equity interest of less than 50% of an investee corporation does not give an investor **legal control**, it might give an investor significant influence over the strategic policies of the investee. To provide guidance, the IASB defines **significant influence** as "the power to participate in the financial and operating policy decisions" of an entity, but not control over those policies.[15] This is similar to the ASPE concept, and both indicate that an ability to exercise influence at a significant level over another company's operating, investing, and financing activities may be indicated in several ways. Examples include the following: representation on the board of directors, participation in policy-making processes, material inter-company transactions, interchange of managerial personnel, or provision of technical information.[16] Under IFRS specifically, and in general, the term **associate** is used to refer to the entity that the investor has significant influence over, provided it is neither a subsidiary nor a joint venture.

To ensure that the significant influence criterion is applied in a reasonably consistent manner, the standard setters concluded that an investment (direct or indirect) of 20% or more of the voting shares of another company should lead to a presumption that, unless there is evidence to the contrary, an investor has the ability to exercise significant influence over an investee. With less than a 20% voting interest, the assumption is that the investor cannot exercise the required degree of influence, unless the ability to influence is clearly shown. If the investor holds potential voting rights that can be exercised or converted currently, these also should be considered in deciding whether or not it has the power to exercise significant influence.

As indicated above, the extent of influence dictates the type of investment, and this, in turn, dictates the appropriate method of accounting. For investments in associates, **IFRS** requires the investor to use the equity method of accounting.[17] **ASPE** allows investors to choose the equity method or the cost method in accounting for this type of investment, but the investor must choose one method for all "significant influence" investments. However, if the associate's shares are quoted in an active market, the cost method cannot be used. Instead, the fair value approach, with gains and losses being recognized in income, can be chosen. Both the cost and FV-NI models are explained earlier in this chapter, so we turn next to how the equity method works.

Equity Method Basics

Under the **equity method**, the investment is initially recorded at the cost of the acquired shares. After this, its carrying amount is adjusted each period for the investor's proportionate share of the changes in the investee's net assets. The equity method sounds complex at first, but it is basically **the accrual basis of accounting applied to investment income**.

Under this method, **the investor recognizes investment income as the investee earns income** by debiting the Investment account and crediting Investment Income. When cash is received from the investment (that is, the investee pays a dividend on the

Alternative Terminology

Under ASPE, Investments in Associates are often labelled Significant Influence Investments.

Illustration 9-17

Application of the Equity Method Basics (in $ooo's)

shares), this converts an asset that has already been recognized—the Investment—to cash. Therefore, Cash is debited and the Investment account is credited.

As indicated, the Investment account under the equity method changes to mirror the increases and decreases in the investee's book value:

- **When the associate's net assets increase** because it earns income, **the investor increases the carrying amount of its investment** for its proportionate share of the associate's increase in net assets and also **reports its share of the associate's income as investment income.**

- **When the associate's net assets decrease** because the company pays a dividend, **the investor recognizes the cash received and decreases the carrying amount of the investment** by its share of the decrease in the associate's net assets.

To illustrate the basics of the equity method, assume that Maxi Corp. purchases a 20% interest in Mini Corp. and has the ability to exercise significant influence over Mini's financial and operating policies. The entries are shown in Illustration 9-17. Note the effects on the Investment account and on the income statement.

	IFRS/ASPE Equity Method ($000)		ASPE FV-NI (may use where traded in an active market) ($000)		ASPE Cost Model (may use except where shares are traded in an active market) ($000)	

On January 2, 2013, Maxi Corp. acquires 48,000 shares (20% of Mini Corp. common shares) at a cost of $10 a share.	Investment in Associate 480
	  Cash
		480	FV-NI Investments 480
			  Cash
				480	Other Investments 480
					  Cash
						480

For the year 2013, Mini Corp. reports net income of $200,000; Maxi Corp.'s share is 20%, or $40,000.	Investment in Associate 40 Investment Income or Loss*	40	N/A		N/A	
At December 31, 2013, the 48,000 shares of Mini Corp. have a fair value of $12 a share, or $576,000.	N/A		FV-NI Investments 96 Unrealized Gain or Loss	96	N/A	

On January 28, 2014, Mini Corp. announces and pays a cash dividend of $100,000; Maxi Corp. receives 20%, or $20,000.	Cash 20
	  Investment in Associate
		20	Cash 20
			  Investment Income or Loss
				20	Cash 20
					  Investment Income or Loss
						20

For the year 2014, Mini Corp. reports a net loss of $50,000; Maxi Corp.'s share is 20%, or $10,000.	Investment Income or Loss* 10 Investment in Associate	10	N/A		N/A	
At December 31, 2014, the 48,000 Mini Corp. shares have a fair value of $11 a share, or $528,000. The investment value is not considered impaired.	N/A		Unrealized Gain or Loss 48 FV-NI Investments	48	N/A	

*This entry is sometimes referred to as the **equity pickup**. The term refers to the fact that the investor is picking up its share of income or loss under the equity method. Another commonly used account title is Equity in Earnings of Associate Company.

Under the equity method, **the accrual basis of accounting** is applied. Maxi Corp. therefore reports investment income as Mini Corp. earns income. Revenue recognition is permitted before receiving a dividend, because of the degree of influence that the investor has over the investee's decisions, including dividend decisions. If the investee company suffers a loss, as Mini Corp. did in 2014, the investor accrues its share of the loss and reduces the carrying amount of its investment.

One of the benefits of this method is that the investor's income statement reports the economics of the situation: if the associate performs well, the investor's income statement reflects positive investment income. If the associate incurs losses, the investor's income statement reflects its share of the loss. In addition, when the equity method is used, the investor cannot manipulate its own income by influencing the timing of a dividend from the associate.

Expanded Illustration of the Equity Method

There are two more complexities in applying the equity method:[18]

1. Differences between what was originally paid for the investment and the investor's share of the associate's book value need to be identified and accounted for according to the reason for the extra payment.

2. The major classifications of the income reported by the associate are retained and reported in the same way on the investor's income statement.

The first item requires an understanding of what the cost of the investment represents. It is unusual for the investor to pay an amount for the investment that is exactly equal to its share of the other company's book value. The excess payment (usually it is extra) could be due to several reasons: there may be unrecorded assets; there may be assets whose fair value is greater than the carrying amount on the associate's books, or liabilities whose fair value is less than book value; there may be intangibles, such as goodwill, that the associate has but that are not recognized in its books; and so on. **Any payment in excess of (or less than) the investor's share of book value is part of the cost of the investment, and after acquisition, it has to be accounted for appropriately.**

If the difference is caused by long-lived assets with fair values that are greater than book value, the amount above the asset's book value must be amortized. If it relates to inventory with a fair value in excess of its carrying amount on the associate's books, it will be recognized as an increased expense as the inventory is sold. There may also be assets with fair values that are lower than book value or liabilities with present values higher than book value. **None of these differences are on the associate's books, but they are captured as part of the purchase cost of the investment,** so it is the investment account itself and the investment income or loss that need to be adjusted over time.

Because the equity method recognizes and reports the investor's share of the associate's income, **the type of income that is reported should remain the same.** That is, the portion that is the investor's share of the associate's discontinued operations is reported separately from the investor's share of income before discontinued operations. The same principle applies to the investor's portion of the associate's other comprehensive income, changes in accounting policy reported in retained earnings, and capital charges. The investor reports its share of all of these in the appropriate place in its financial statements.

To illustrate, assume that on January 1, 2014, Investor Company purchases 250,000 of Investee Company's one million outstanding common shares for $8.5 million. Investor has therefore acquired a 25% interest in Investee. The book value (net assets) of Investee Company on this date is $30 million and Investor's proportionate share is 25% of this, or $7.5 million. Investor Company therefore has paid $1 million in excess of its share of the book value ($8,500,000 – $7,500,000).

Why did Investor pay $1 million more than its share of Investee's book value? Assume that part of the reason is because Investee's depreciable assets **are undervalued on the books** by $2.4 million. This explains $600,000 ($2,400,000 × 25%) of the excess, because

Investor would only pay more in proportion to its ownership interest. Investor Company estimates the remaining life of the depreciable assets to be eight years, so the $600,000 excess payment included in the Investment account will have to be amortized over this future period.

The remaining $400,000 is unexplained and therefore is determined to be unrecorded goodwill. Investor will have to assess the carrying amount of the balance of the Investment account each year to determine whether there has been any impairment in its value. This purchase is analyzed in Illustration 9-18.

Illustration 9-18

Analysis of Acquisition of Associate Company

Cost of 25% investment in Investee Co. shares	$8,500,000
25% of book value of Investee Co. represented by investment	
25% × $30,000,000	7,500,000
Payment in excess of share of book value	1,000,000
Fair value allocation to depreciable assets	
25% × $2,400,000	600,000
Unexplained excess assumed to be goodwill	$ 400,000
Annual amortization of excess payment for capital assets	
$600,000/8-year life	$ 75,000

Investee Company later reports net income of $2.8 million for its 2014 fiscal year, including a loss on discontinued operations of $400,000. **Income before discontinued operations,** therefore, is $3.2 million. Dividends of $1.4 million are declared and paid by Investee Company on December 31, 2014. To record these transactions and events, Investor Company makes the following 2014 entries.

A = L + SE
0   0   0
Cash flows: ↓ 8,500,000 outflow

Jan. 1/14	Investment in Associate	8,500,000	
	Cash		8,500,000
	(To record the acquisition of 25% of Investee Co.)		

A = L + SE
0   0   0
Cash flows: ↑ 350,000 inflow

Dec. 31/14	Cash	350,000	
	Investment in Associate		350,000
	(To record the dividend from Investee Co. [$1,400,000 × 0.25])		

On December 31, Investor Company recognizes its 25% share of Investee Company's net income. Because its associate's income includes both continuing and discontinued operation components, 25% of each amount is reported separately by Investor Company. The account Investment in Associate is increased by 25% of the increase in Investee's net assets from earning net income (25% × $2,800,000). Furthermore, Investor Company paid more than book value for Investee Company's net assets and a portion of the excess amount relates to assets that are depreciable. The "extra cost" of the depreciable assets to Investor has not been recognized on the associate's books, nor has the additional depreciation. As a result, the investment income needs to be adjusted for this additional expense.

A = L + SE
+700,000   +700,000
Cash flows: No effect

Dec. 31/14	Investment in Associate	700,000	
	Loss from Discontinued Operations	100,000	
	Investment Income or Loss		800,000
	(To record the investment income from Investee Co. [Investee Co. income × 0.25])		

A = L + SE		
−75,000		−75,000

Cash flows: No effect

Dec. 31/14	Investment Income or Loss	75,000	
	Investment in Associate		75,000
	(Amortization of fair value difference, depreciable assets)		

Illustration 9-19 shows the calculation of the investment in Investee Company that is presented on Investor Company's December 31, 2014 statement of financial position.

Illustration 9-19

Calculation of Investment Carrying Amount

Acquisition cost, January 1, 2014	$8,500,000
Add: 25% of increase in Investee's net assets from earning net income	700,000
Less: 25% of decrease in Investee's net assets from declaration/payment of dividend	(350,000)
Less: Amortization of fair value difference related to capital assets	(75,000)
Investment in Investee Co., Dec. 31, 2014, at equity	$8,775,000

Impairment in Value, Equity Method

Under both **IFRS** and **ASPE,** an investment that results in significant influence is assessed at each statement of financial position date to determine if there are any indications that the investment may be impaired. If there are, its carrying amount is compared with the investment's **recoverable amount:** the higher of its value in use and fair value less costs to sell, both of which are discounted cash flow concepts.[19] If the carrying amount is more than the investment's recoverable amount, an impairment loss equal to the difference is recognized in net income and the investment is written down directly. This loss may be reversed if future events indicate that the recoverable amount has improved.

Disposal of Investment in Associate

When the investment in the associate is sold, the statement of financial position Investment in Associates account and the Investment Income or Loss account are first brought up to date as at the date of sale. This involves adjusting these accounts for the investor's share of the associate's earnings and changes in book value since the last reporting date. Then the investment's carrying value is removed from the accounts and the difference between this and the proceeds on disposal is recognized in income as a gain or loss.

Continuing with the example in Illustrations 9-18 and 9-19, assume that Investor Company sells its investment in Investee Company on January 2, 2015, for $9 million. Because the accounts are already up to date in this case, the entry to record the sale is:

A = L + SE		
+225,000		+225,000

Cash flows: ↑ 9,000,000 inflow

Cash	9,000,000	
Investment in Associate		8,775,000
Gain on Sale of Investments		225,000

Summary of Accounting Standards for Associates

The equity method is also known as "one-line consolidation" and is applied in ways that are related to how consolidation principles are applied. In fact, the equity method "investment income" is the same amount that is needed to increase or decrease the investor's income to the amount that would be reported if the investor had consolidated the results of the investee with those of the investor, with possible exceptions related to goodwill and investment impairment. Given this similarity, other complexities that result from such investments are left for an advanced accounting course that covers inter-corporate investments.

Illustration 9-20 summarizes the accounting for investments in the equity instruments of companies in which the investor has significant influence.

Illustration 9-20

Accounting for Associates

	IFRS	ASPE		
Measurement after recognition	Equity method	Equity method is used for all or the cost method is used for all. If shares are quoted in an active market, cannot use cost method. May use FV-NI where traded in an active market.		
		Equity method	**Cost method**	**FV-NI model**
Unrealized holding gains/losses	Not recognized	Not recognized	Not recognized	Recognized in net income
Investment income	Percentage of associate's income, adjusted for differences between cost and share of book value and inter-company profits	Percentage of associate's income, adjusted for differences between cost and share of book value and inter-company profits	Dividends received or receivable	Dividends received or receivable
Impairment, when assessment indicates possibility	Loss = carrying amount less recoverable amount (higher of value in use and fair value less costs to sell)	Loss = carrying amount less recoverable amount (higher of value in use and fair value less costs to sell)	Loss = carrying amount less recoverable amount (higher of DCF and NRV; essentially the same as the value in use and fair value less costs to sell)	N/A
Impairment reversal	Permitted	Permitted	Permitted	N/A

Investments in Subsidiaries

Objective 7
Explain the concept of control and when consolidation is appropriate.

When one corporation acquires control of another entity, the investor corporation is referred to as the **parent** and the investee corporation as the **subsidiary**. Control is assumed when the investor owns 50% or more of the voting shares of another company. This is because it holds a majority of the votes at the board of directors meetings of the investee company, and therefore, the investor's management controls all the subsidiary's net assets and operations.

Standard setters have wrestled for many years with the best way to explain what **control** really is. They acknowledge that sometimes, an entity with less than 50% of the voting shares can have control, while an entity with more than 50% sometimes may not have control. According to **ASPE**, control is the continuing power to determine the strategic operating, financing, and investing policies of another entity without the co-operation of others. Under **IFRS**, a new definition has been put forward that would allow control to extend to a broader range of investments. This definition indicates that an investor controls another if it has the power to direct the activities of the other entity to generate returns, either positive or negative, for the investor. Similar to previous descriptions, the "power to direct the activities of another" means that an investor can determine the other entity's strategic operating and financing policies. The differences in the definitions are subtle, but real, and they will become more apparent in an advanced accounting course that deals with inter-corporate investments.

An investment in the common shares of a subsidiary is presented as a long-term investment on the separate financial statements of the parent, usually accounted for by either the equity or cost method. When preparing **IFRS** statements, however, an investor with subsidiaries is required to present consolidated financial statements for the group of companies under its control; that is, it **eliminates the investment account** and instead **reports all the assets and liabilities of the subsidiary on a line-by-line basis**. Under **ASPE**, this is a **permitted**, but **not required**, option. A parent company can choose to:

1. consolidate all its subsidiaries, or

2. present all of its subsidiaries under either the equity method or cost model.

The same choice is applied to all subsidiaries, although investments in shares that are quoted in an active market are not permitted to be accounted for using the cost model. They may instead be measured and reported at FV-NI. You can see here the similarities between ASPE for associates and subsidiary companies. Separate reporting on the balance sheet is required for subsidiaries accounted for using the equity method and for those using the cost method. The income statement also reports the income from each group of subsidiaries accounted for on a different basis.

Because we have already covered the cost, equity, and FV-NI methods and models, the emphasis now is on understanding **consolidation**. In place of the one-line long-term investment in subsidiary, the parent reports 100% of each of the assets and liabilities over which it has control. Instead of reporting investment income on the income statement, 100% of each of the revenues and expenses reported by the subsidiary is reported on a line-by-line basis with those of the parent company. That is, the parent presents **consolidated financial statements**. This method of reporting an investment in a controlled company is much more informative to the parent company's shareholders than a single-line statement of financial position and a single-line income statement account.

The requirement to include 100% of the assets and liabilities and 100% of the revenues, expenses, gains, and losses under the parent's control even when the ownership is less than 100% leads to the recognition of unique statement of financial position and income statement accounts. These **noncontrolling interest** accounts (sometimes referred to as **minority interest**), represent the portion of the net assets **not** owned and the portion of the consolidated net income of the entity that does **not** accrue to the parent company's shareholders. These claims to net assets and net income are **equity claims** because they represent the interests of the noncontrolling **shareholders** of the subsidiary companies.

Real World Emphasis

Illustration 9-21, taken from the 2011 annual report of **Indigo Books & Music Inc.**, shows extracts from the consolidated (group) statement of comprehensive income and balance sheet.

Illustration 9-21

Minority (Noncontrolling) Interests on the Statement of Comprehensive Income and Balance Sheet

(thousands of dollars, except per share data)	52-week period ended April 2, 2011	53-week period ended April 3, 2010
Revenues	1,017,325	968,927
Cost of sales, operations, selling and administration (notes 10 and 18)	991,155	895,930
	26,170	72,997
Depreciation of property, plant and equipment	19,311	19,682
Amortization of intangible assets	10,679	8,326
Write-off of capital assets (note 6)	—	1,086
	29,990	29,094
Earnings (loss) before the undernoted items	(3,820)	43,903
Interest on long-term debt and financing charges	212	214
Interest income on cash and cash equivalents	(567)	(333)
Dilution gain on reduction of ownership in subsidiary (notes 17 and 18)	(3,915)	(3,019)
Deemed disposition of goodwill (note 17)	—	891
Earnings before income taxes and non-controlling interest	450	46,150
Income tax expense (note 7)		
Current	1,237	1,481
Future	1,445	11,056
	2,682	12,537
Earnings (loss) before non-controlling interest	(2,232)	33,613
Non-controlling interest (notes 17 and 18)	(13,578)	(1,310)
Net earnings and comprehensive earnings for the period	11,346	34,923

(continued)

Illustration 9-21

*Minority (Noncontrolling)
Interests on the Statement of
Comprehensive Income and
Balance Sheet
(continued)*

Net earnings per common share (note 8)		
Basic	$0.46	$1.42
Diluted	$0.45	$1.39

See accompanying notes

	As at April 2, 2011	As at April 3, 2010
LIABILITIES AND SHAREHOLDERS' EQUITY		
Current		
Accounts payable and accrued liabilities (notes 11, 13 and 18)	**224,959**	229,920
Deferred revenue	**11,528**	12,882
Income taxes payable	**657**	—
Current portion of long-term debt (notes 13 and 19)	**1,290**	1,863
Total current liabilities	**238,434**	244,665
Long-term accrued liabilities (note 13)	**6,284**	8,203
Long-term debt (notes 13 and 19)	**1,995**	1,174
Total liabilities	**246,713**	254,042
Non-controlling interest (notes 17 and 18)	**6,347**	6,831
Shareholders' equity		
Share capital (note 8)	**202,196**	198,635
Contributed surplus (note 9)	**5,039**	4,670
Retained earnings	**55,885**	55,664
Total shareholders' equity	**263,120**	258,969
Total liabilities and shareholders' equity	**516,180**	519,842

Underlying Concept

The consolidation of the financial results of different companies follows the economic entity assumption. It disregards the legal boundaries between entities. The key objective is to provide useful information to financial statement users about all the resources under the control of parent company management.

What Do the Numbers Mean?

Real World Emphasis

Consolidated financial statements disregard the distinction between separate legal entities and treat the parent and subsidiary corporations as an economic unit—an **economic entity.** After acquisition, this means that all inter-company balances and unrealized intercompany gains and losses are eliminated for reporting purposes. An entity cannot report sales or make a profit selling to itself. The preparation of consolidated financial statements is discussed in detail in advanced financial accounting.

The rules for consolidation seem very straightforward: If a company owns more than 50% of another company, it generally should be consolidated. If it owns less than 50%, it generally is not consolidated. However, with complex modern business relationships, standard setters realize that this test is too artificial, and that determining who really has control is often based on factors other than share ownership.

In fact, specific guidelines have been developed that force consolidation even though share ownership is not above 50%. For example, the well-known **Enron Corporation** failure to consolidate three special-purpose entities that were effectively controlled by Enron led to a U.S. $569-million overstatement of income and a U.S. $1.2-billion overstatement of equity. In these three cases, the new accounting standards would have led to consolidation. That is, the following factors indicate that consolidation should have occurred: the majority owner of the shares of the special-purpose entity made only a modest investment, Enron received the primary economic benefits from the activities of the entity, and the substantive risks and rewards related to the special entity's assets and debt rested directly or indirectly with Enron.

These arrangements were not unique to Enron! Many companies used non-consolidated special-purpose entities to "window dress" or make their financial statements look better than they really were. Such actions caused the standard setters to issue separate guidance on the consolidation of variable interest entities (VIEs) where control is achieved in ways other than through ownership of voting interests. The guideline, harmonized with FASB's approach, requires a company to consolidate a **variable interest entity** when the company is the primary beneficiary of such an entity; that is, when it will absorb a majority of a VIE's expected losses, receive a majority of its expected residual returns, or both. As this text went to print, the IASB was in the process of issuing a revised standard to change its definition of control so that if an investor meets the new definition, it will account for VIEs under its regular consolidation standards.

PRESENTATION, DISCLOSURE, AND ANALYSIS

Objective 8
Explain how investments are presented and disclosed in the financial statements noting how this facilitates analysis.

Where should a company report investments on its statement of financial position? What types of disclosures are necessary for transparency? Finally, what information is important for users when analyzing financial statements? These questions will be answered in this section of the chapter.

Presentation and Disclosure

First, let's take a look at presentation and disclosure issues. For purposes of this discussion, investments are subdivided into two groups – those where the investor has no significant influence or control and those where the investor has significant influence.

Investments without Significant Influence or Control

Should investments that the investor cannot exercise significant influence over or control be reported as current or long-term assets? The requirements for presentation of an investment as a current asset are the same as for other assets. In general, those classified as current are continuously turning over or affecting working capital. As indicated in Chapter 5, **IFRS** specifies that if an investment has any one of the following characteristics, it is classified as current:

- It is expected to be sold or otherwise realized within the entity's normal operating cycle or within 12 months from the statement of financial position date.

- It is held primarily for trading purposes.

- It is a cash equivalent.

Under **ASPE,** the conditions are similar: an investment is classified as a current asset only if it is usually realizable within 12 months from the balance sheet date (or normal operating cycle, if longer) and it can be converted to cash relatively quickly.

This means that debt and equity investments measured at cost or amortized cost and those at FV-NI could be either current or long-term assets, depending on the specific situation. Debt instruments are likely to be classified as current only if they are held to be traded, or expected to mature or be sold, within the following year. Equity instruments will be current only if they are marketable and are expected to be converted to cash that can be used for current purposes. Under the revised IFRS 9, investments carried at FV-OCI are most likely non-current assets: they are held for longer term strategic purposes, and not for current trading.

The **objective of the disclosures** required for financial assets that are investments in debt and equity instruments is generally the same under both ASPE and IFRS: to provide information that allows users to assess the following:

- how significant these financial assets are to an entity's financial position and performance,

- the nature and extent of risks that the entity faces as a result of these assets, and

- how the entity manages these risks.

The specific standards are the best source of the many required disclosures for financial asset investments. The following section is meant to provide you with an understanding of the **types of information** that are required to be made available to users of the financial statements. Understanding the goal of the disclosures is helpful in determining and even predicting what information is reported.

- Disclose the **carrying amount of investments** in debt instruments carried at amortized cost, in equity instruments carried at cost, and in equity instruments carried using FV-NI. Also disclose the carrying amount of any investments accounted for using FV-OCI. The carrying amount of any impaired investments and related allowances for impairment, by type (method of accounting for the assets), is also separately reported.

- To enable readers to relate the **income statement effects** to the investments on the statement of financial position disclose the following:
  - net gains or losses recognized (by method of accounting),
  - total interest income (under IFRS, include only interest income calculated using the effective interest method for financial assets except for those at FV-NI),
  - interest income on impaired investments (IFRS), and
  - impairment losses and reversals.

- For each type of **financial risk** that results from the investments, disclose what the risk exposures are, how they arise, any changes over the accounting period, and information about any concentrations of risk such as those that arise from significant investment in particular industries or foreign currency. IFRS requires additional information, such as how risks are managed, credit risk by classification of instrument, past due and impaired investments, and sensitivity analyses for each type of market risk to which the entity is exposed.[20]

Finance

- Under IFRS, in addition to providing such qualitative disclosures, entities also provide quantitative measures of their risk exposures and concentrations, as well as specific information that management uses internally to manage each major type of risk.

Real World Emphasis

Refer back to Illustration 9-2, which shows the balance sheet of Canada Life. Illustration 9-22 provides additional excerpts from the financial statements, including the statement of earnings, additional details regarding what is included as investments, and information about how fair valued is assessed. The bulk of the investments are in bonds and are carried at fair value using either FV-NI (fair value through profit or loss) or FV-OCI (available for sale). You can see from the statement of earnings the significance of the income from investments (which make up 57% of total income).

Illustration 9-22

Excerpts from the Statement of Earnings and Selected Notes for Canada Life

CONSOLIDATED STATEMENTS OF EARNINGS
(in Canadian $ millions except per share amounts)

Income	For the years ended December 31	
	2011	2010
Premium income		
Gross premiums written	**$ 9,214**	$ 9,587
Ceded premiums	**(5,278)**	(5,195)
Total net premiums	**3,936**	4,392
Net investment income (note 6)		
Regular net investment income	**3,097**	3,183
Changes in fair value through profit or loss	**2,923**	2,215
Total net investment income	**6,020**	5,398
Fee and other income	**652**	692
	$10,608	$10,482

(continued)

Selected excerpts from notes to the financial statements:

Fair Value Measurement

Financial instrument carrying values necessarily reflect the prevailing market liquidity and the liquidity premiums embedded within the market pricing methods the Company relies upon.

The following is a description of the methodologies used to value instruments carried at fair value:

Bonds—Fair Value Through Profit or Loss and Available for Sale

Fair values for bonds classified as fair value through profit or loss or available for sale are determined with reference to quoted market bid prices primarily provided by third party independent pricing sources. Where prices are not quoted in a normally active market, fair values are determined by valuation models. The Company maximizes the use of observable inputs and minimizes the use of unobservable inputs when measuring fair value. The Company obtains quoted prices in active markets, when available, for identical assets at the balance sheet date to measure bonds at fair value in its fair value through profit or loss and available for sale portfolios.

The Company estimates the fair value of bonds not traded in active markets by referring to actively traded securities with similar attributes, dealer quotations, matrix pricing methodology, discounted cash flow analyses and/or internal valuation models. This methodology considers such factors as the issuer's industry, the security's rating, term, coupon rate and position in the capital structure of the issuer, as well as, yield curves, credit curves, prepayment rates and other relevant factors. For bonds that are not traded in active markets, valuations are adjusted to reflect illiquidity, and such adjustments generally are based on available market evidence. In the absence of such evidence, management's best estimate is used.

Stocks—Fair Value Through Profit or Loss and Available for Sale

Fair values for public stocks are generally determined by the last bid price for the security from the exchange where it is principally traded. Fair values for stocks for which there is no active market are determined by discounting expected future cash flows. The Company maximizes the use of observable inputs and minimizes the use of unobservable inputs when measuring fair value. The Company obtains quoted prices in active markets, when available, for identical assets at the balance sheet date to measure stocks at fair value in its fair value through profit or loss and available for sale portfolios.

Mortgages and Bonds—Loans and Receivables

Market values for bonds and mortgages classified as loans and receivables are determined by discounting expected future cash flows using current market rates.

Investment Properties

Market values for investment properties are determined using independent qualified appraisal services and include management adjustments for material changes in property cash flows, capital expenditures or general market conditions in the interim period between appraisals.

Impairment

Investments are reviewed regularly on an individual basis to determine impairment status. The Company considers various factors in the impairment evaluation process, including, but not limited to, the financial condition of the issuer, specific adverse conditions affecting an industry or region, decline in fair value not related to interest rates, bankruptcy or defaults and delinquency in payments of interest or principal. Investments are deemed to be impaired when there is no longer reasonable assurance of timely collection of the full amount of the principal and interest due. The market value of an investment is not a definitive indicator of impairment, as it may be significantly influenced by other factors including the remaining term to maturity and liquidity of the asset. However market price must be taken into consideration when evaluating impairment.

For impaired mortgages and bonds classified as loans and receivables, provisions are established or write-offs made to adjust the carrying value to the net realizable amount. Wherever possible the fair value of collateral underlying the loans or observable market price is used to establish net realizable value. For impaired available for sale bonds, recorded at fair value, the accumulated loss recorded in accumulated other comprehensive income (AOCI) is reclassified to net investment income. Impairments on available for sale debt instruments are reversed if there is objective evidence that a permanent recovery has occurred. All gains and losses on bonds classified or designated as fair value through profit or loss are already recorded in income, therefore a reduction due to impairment of these assets will be recorded in income. As well, when determined to be impaired, interest is no longer accrued and previous interest accruals are reversed.

6. Portfolio Investments

(a) Carrying values and estimated market values of portfolio investments are as follows:

	December 31, 2011		December 31, 2010		January 1, 2010	
	Carrying value	Market value	Carrying value	Market value	Carrying value	Market value
Bonds						
Designated fair value through profit or loss (1)	**$32,592**	**$32,592**	$29,904	$29,904	$28,546	$28,546

(continued)

Illustration 9-22

Excerpts from the Statement of Earnings and Selected Notes for Canada Life (continued)

	December 31, 2011		December 31, 2010		January 1, 2010	
	Carrying value	Market value	Carrying value	Market value	Carrying value	Market value
Classified as fair value through profit or loss (1)	12	12	22	22	11	11
Available for sale	2,849	2,849	2,677	2,677	1,620	1,620
Loans and receivables	8,072	8,579	7,410	7,720	7,762	7,896
	43,525	44,032	40,013	40,323	37,939	38,073
Mortgage loans						
Residential	1,382	1,527	1,178	1,279	1,394	1,464
Non-residential	4,330	4,578	4,184	4,363	4,795	4,802
	5,712	6,105	5,362	5,642	6,189	6,266
Stocks						
Designated fair value through profit or loss (1)	1,503	1,503	1,453	1,453	1,307	1,307
Available for sale	109	109	144	144	196	196
Other	—	—	14	14	—	—
	1,612	1,612	1,611	1,611	1,503	1,503
Investment Properties	2,436	2,436	2,231	2,231	2,002	2,002
	$53,285	$54,185	$49,217	$49,807	$47,633	$47,844

(1) Investments can be fair value through profit or loss in two ways: designated as fair value through profit or loss at the option of management; or, classified as fair value through profit or loss if they are actively traded for the purpose of earning investment income.

Investments in Associates

As a general rule, the significance of an investment to the investor's financial position and performance generally determines how much disclosure is required. Investments in associates are classified as non-current assets (unless they are held for sale), and income from these significantly influenced companies is reported as income before discontinued operations, discontinued operations, or other comprehensive income, according to its nature in the associate's financial statements. Management reports the following for associates accounted for using the equity method:

1. Separate disclosure of the investment category on the statement of financial position or in the notes to the financial statements, and the method of accounting used

2. The fair value of any of these investments that has a price quoted in an active market

3. Separate disclosure of the income from investments that are accounted for using the equity method

4. Information about associates' year ends that are different from the investors' year end

Under **IFRS,** additional information is required, such as summarized financial information about the associates' assets, liabilities, revenue, and net income, and any relevant contingent liabilities that may affect the investor. Under **ASPE,** the information required to be provided is a list of any significant investments, including a description of the investment, the names, carrying amounts, and percentage ownership held. Because private enterprises are allowed to use methods other than the equity method, they are also required to separately report the carrying amount of investments in companies subject to significant influence accounted for at cost, as well as the amount of investment income reported from these investments.

Analysis

To effectively analyze a company's performance and position, it is essential to understand the accounting and reporting for the entity's investments. Some of the key aspects that analysts watch for include the following:

1. Separation of investment results from operating results (although where the management of investments is a key part of operations, such as for financial institutions, this is not as relevant)

2. The relationship between the investment asset and related returns (income)

3. Information that is lost in the process of consolidation

4. Risks related to the investments and how they are managed

Because the income statement reports on management's performance in operating the company's assets, it is important to separate the results of active operating income from the investment returns, where management's role is often more passive. As gains or losses on sales of investments or special dividends can obscure a company's operating performance, these must be separately identified and assessed.

Accounting standards require disclosures that make it possible for a reader to relate the investment category on the SFP to the investment income reported on the income statement, and to the holding gains and losses in other comprehensive income.

Understanding the effects of the accounting methods that are used for different categories of investments is a key requirement for the analyst. If an entity has significant investments in companies that are accounted for by the equity method, for example, the analyst needs to be aware that some information is not available because the one-line investment account hides the debt and risk characteristics of the investee company that the entity is exposed to.

Consolidation of subsidiary companies also presents problems. While the financial statements reflect the combined operations of the economic entity, important information is lost through aggregating the parent's results with those of its subsidiaries. This is why segmented information, discussed in Chapter 23, has to be separately reported in the notes. Analysts also watch for major acquisitions during the current or previous year. The statement of financial position contains all the assets of the subsidiary, but the income statement includes only the income earned by the subsidiary after it was acquired by the parent. Any analysis that looks at relationships between income and assets has to adjust for major acquisitions in the period(s) being examined.

IFRS/ASPE COMPARISON

Objective 9
Identify differences in accounting between IFRS and ASPE, and what changes are expected in the near future.

As indicated earlier, accounting for financial assets in general is in the midst of change.

A Comparison of IFRS and ASPE

Illustration 9-23 sets out the major differences between IFRS and ASPE concerning accounting for investments.

	Accounting Standards for Private Enterprises (ASPE)— CICA Handbook, Part II, Sections 1582, 1601, 1602, 3051, and 3856	IFRS—IAS 1, 27, 28, 32, and 39; IFRS 3 and 7	IFRS 7 and 9 (mandatory adoption in 2015 but may adopt early)	References to Related Illustrations and Select Brief Exercises
Investments— no significant influence or control: Measurement models	Permits only two measurement models: FV-NI (for equity investments that trade in an active market, derivatives, and those accounted for under the fair value option), and cost/amortized cost (everything else).	Permits three measurement models: amortized cost (held to maturity investments), FV-NI (trading, derivatives, and other instruments accounted for under the fair value option) and FV-OCI with recycling (available for sale investments).	Permits three measurement models: amortized cost (for debt instruments where the business model requires holding to maturity), FV-OCI with no recycling (for certain equity instruments only), and FV-NI for everything else.	Illustration 9-13 BE9-15
Fair value option	FV-NI can be designated on initial recognition.	FV-NI can be designated on initial recognition if it reduces or eliminates an accounting mismatch.	FV-NI can be designated on initial recognition if it reduces or eliminates an accounting mismatch.	N/A
Interest and dividend income	Use either straight-line or effective interest method when applicable; all interest and dividends to net income. Must show interest separately.	Use effective interest method when interest income is required to be reported separately; all interest and dividends to net income except for those at FV-OCI where dividends that are a return of investment are recognized in OCI. Where using FV-NI, may show investment income combined (no need to show interest separately).	Use effective interest method when interest income is required to be reported separately; all interest and dividends to net income except for those at FV-OCI where dividends that are a return of investment are recognized in OCI. Where using FV-NI, may show investment income combined (no need to show interest separately).	Illustrations 9-4 and 9-6 and subsequent journal entries BE9-4, BE9-5, and BE9-6
Realized gains and losses	Recognize in net income.	Recognize in net income including those accounted for at FV-OCI (recycling).	Recognize in net income, except for those accounted for at FV-OCI (no recycling).	Illustration 9-11 and subsequent journal entries
Reclassifications	FV option designation is irrevocable; otherwise this issue is not addressed.	Reclassification permitted in certain very limited circumstances (for instance, if no longer held for trading or entity no longer intends or is able to hold investment to maturity).	No reclassification is permitted between measurement models unless there is a rare occurrence of a change in the entity's business model.	N/A
Impairment	Use the incurred loss model with a market discount rate to measure revised DCF; reversals are permitted if due to a specific subsequent event. New carrying value is higher of DCF and NRV through sale or by exercising right to collateral.	Use incurred loss model for cost/amortized cost investments. New carrying value is based on revised DCF for debt instruments using historic interest rate and for equity instruments carried at cost, revised DCF using market interest rate.	Use incurred loss model for cost/amortized cost investments (new carrying value is based on revised DCF using historic interest rate). May reverse impairment losses.	Illustrations 9-14 and 9-15 BE9-16 and BE9-17

Illustration 9-23

IFRS and ASPE Comparison Chart

(continued)

	Accounting Standards for Private Enterprises (ASPE)— *CICA Handbook*, Part II, Sections 1582, 1601, 1602, 3051, and 3856	IFRS—IAS 1, 27, 28, 32, and 39; IFRS 3 and 7	IFRS 7 and 9 (mandatory adoption in 2015 but may adopt early)	References to Related Illustrations and Select Brief Exercises
		Use also for FV-OCI investments where trigger event has occurred. New carrying value of FV-OCI investment is fair value and loss is booked to net income. May reverse impairment losses for debt instruments only.		
Investments— in associates/ significant influence: Method of accounting	Allows an accounting policy choice of the equity method or the cost method. If shares are quoted in an active market, cannot use cost model; may use FV-NI.	Requires the equity method.	N/A – covered by IAS 28	Illustrations 9-17 and 9-20 BE9-19 and BE9-20
Investments— in subsidiaries: Control	Has a narrower definition of control that relies more strongly on holding more than 50% of the voting interests in another entity.	Has a new definition that expands the meaning of control. Emphasis is on the power to direct another entity's activities to generate returns for the Investor.	N/A – covered by IAS 28	BE9-21
Method of reporting	Allows an accounting policy choice of consolidation or presenting all subsidiaries using the equity method or the cost method. If shares are quoted in an active market, cannot use cost model; may use FV NI.	Use consolidation.	N/A – covered by IAS 28	N/A – covered in advanced accounting courses
Disclosures	Uses the same financial reporting objectives as IFRS, but more limited disclosures are required.	Requires more extensive disclosures.	Requires more extensive disclosures.	BE9-22

Illustration 9-23

IFRS and ASPE Comparison Chart (continued)

Looking Ahead

As indicated in this chapter, the IASB has been working, along with the FASB, to simplify the accounting for and reporting of financial instruments. Because the proposed financial instruments standard under FASB differs from IFRS 9, the IASB has agreed to consider some amendments to IFRS 9 including allowing debt instruments to be classified as FV-OCI. The IASB is also working toward a new model for impairments and has proposed the use of the expected loss approach where investments are divided into three categories for impairment assessment. These categories are general, group or portfolio of investments with similar risk, and individual investments. In the longer run, the FASB and IASB are also working together on revisions to their conceptual frameworks. Phase D of this project relates to how the reporting entity should be defined and therefore accounted for.

Quiz

SUMMARY OF LEARNING OBJECTIVES

1 Understand the nature of investments including which types of companies have significant investments.

This chapter deals with investments in basic debt and equity instruments of other companies. Debt instruments such as bonds generally carry contractual rights to receive principal and interest payments. Equity instruments such as shares may carry contractual rights to receive dividends (depending on the type of share) and may also carry voting rights and /or rights to receive residual assets upon windup of a company. Care must be taken to determine exactly what rights the investments entitle the holder to as this will help determine the accounting. Not all companies carry significant investments. It depends on the business model. Examples of types of companies that generally carry significant investments are financial institutions, insurance companies, and pension funds.

2 Explain and apply the cost/amortized cost model of accounting for investments.

At acquisition, the cost of the investment is recognized as its fair value plus transaction costs. If the investment is a debt instrument, any premium or discount is amortized to interest income. Holding gains are recognized only when realized, as are holding losses, unless the investment is impaired. The investment is reported at its cost or amortized cost as either a current asset or a long-term investment, depending on its maturity and management's intention to hold it. ASPE uses this model for most investments excluding equity investments where an active market exists for trading the shares and derivatives. IAS 39 uses this model for debt investments where the entity has the intent and ability to hold the investment to maturity. It is also used for equity investments where the entity is unable to measure fair value. IFRS 9 uses this model for debt instruments where the entity's business model is to hold the investments to maturity.

3 Explain and apply the fair value through net income model of accounting for investments.

At acquisition, the investment is recognized at its fair value, with transaction costs being expensed. At each reporting date, the investment is revalued to its current fair value, with holding gains and losses recognized in net income. Dividend and interest income is also recognized in net income. If the investment is not held for trading purposes, any interest income is reported separately and is adjusted for discount or premium amortization. If held for trading or other current purposes, the investment is reported as a current asset. ASPE uses this for equity instruments where there is an active market and derivatives. IAS 39 uses this for held for trading securities including derivatives. IFRS 9 uses this model for all investments not accounted for under the cost/amortized cost model or the FV-OCI model. ASPE and IFRS both allow any investment to be accounted for using FV-NI under the fair value option.

4 Explain and apply the fair value through other comprehensive income model of accounting for investments.

At acquisition, the investment is recognized at fair value plus transaction costs. At each reporting date, the investment is revalued to its current fair value, with the holding gains or losses reported in other comprehensive income. On disposal, the accumulated holding gains or losses are either recycled to net income (IAS 39) or transferred directly to retained earnings (IFRS 9). Investments are reported as current or long-term assets, depending on marketability and management intent. ASPE does not allow this method. IAS 39 allows this method for available for sale investments. IFRS 9 allows this method for certain equity investments.

5 Explain and apply the incurred loss, expected loss, and fair value loss impairment models.

The three impairment loss models differ in the timing of the recognition of impairment losses and the discount rate used. Under the incurred loss approach, a triggering event is required before a loss is recognized and measured, and the revised cash flows are discounted using either the historical or a current market rate. Under the expected loss approach, no triggering event is required, and revised cash flows and impairment losses are determined on a continual basis. The discount rate is the historical/original rate. Using the fair value loss model, the asset is written down to fair value taking into account market information (refer back to Chapter 2). ASPE and IFRS use the incurred loss model for all cost/amortized cost investments, although the post-impairment carrying values are measured differently. IAS 39 uses the incurred loss model for FV-OCI investments once a trigger or loss event has occurred and any resulting impairment loss is recognized in net income. Under IFRS 9, impairment losses on FV-OCI investments are not recognized in net income. Where the FV-NI model is used, there is no need to specifically assess impairment because the investment is continually revalued to fair value and any gains or losses are booked to income.

6 Explain the concept of significant influence and apply the equity method.

Significant influence is the ability to have an effect on strategic decisions made by an investee's board of directors, but not enough to control those decisions. The equity method, sometimes referred to as one-line consolidation, is used because income is recognized by the investor as it is earned. The investor's income statement will reflect the performance of the investee company. Under this method, the investment account is adjusted for all changes in the investee's book value and for the amortization of any purchase discrepancy. IFRS requires use of the equity method for its associates (investees a company can significantly influence). ASPE provides a policy choice: either the equity method or the cost method, except that associates with a quoted price in an active market cannot be accounted for at cost. Instead, the FV-NI model can be used.

7 Explain the concept of control and when consolidation is appropriate.

Control relates to the ability to direct the strategic decisions of another entity and to generate returns for your own benefit or loss. When one company controls another, it controls all the net assets of that entity and is responsible for all its revenues and expenses. Therefore, all of the subsidiary's assets and liabilities, and revenues and expenses, are reported by the parent investor on a line-by-line basis in consolidated financial statements. The interests of the noncontrolling shareholders in the subsidiary company are reported separately as noncontrolling interest. Under IFRS, all subsidiaries are consolidated. ASPE, on the other hand, allows consolidation or a choice of the equity or cost method. Investments in companies with shares traded in an active market cannot be reported using the cost method, but may use FV-NI.

8 Explain how investments are presented and disclosed in the financial statements noting how this facilitates analysis.

The objectives of disclosure are to provide information so users can assess the significance of the financial asset investments to the entity's financial position and performance, the extent of risks to which the company is exposed as a result, and how those risks are managed. As a result, the investments are identified on the statement of financial position according to how they are classified for accounting purposes, with the income statement reporting information on the returns by method of classification. Extensive disclosure is required, particularly under IFRS, on the entity's risk exposures and how it manages those risks.

9 Identify differences in accounting between IFRS and ASPE, and what changes are expected in the near future.

The differences are noted in Illustrations 9-13, 9-14, and 9-23. There are significant differences because there are two standards currently in effect under IFRS (IAS 39 and IFRS 9) and because the standards are currently in transition. It is expected that IFRS 9 will change in order to align more closely with the proposed U.S. standard. In addition, both the IASB and FASB are looking at a new impairment model.

KEY TERMS

amortized cost model, p. 532
associate, p. 549
available for sale investments, p. 545
consolidation, p. 555
control, p. 554
cost model, p. 531
debt securities, p. 527
effective interest method, p. 533
equity instruments, p. 527
equity method, p. 549
equity pickup, p. 550
expected loss impairment model, p. 546

fair value loss impairment model, p. 547
fair value option, p. 544
fair value through net income (FV-NI), p. 536
fair value through other comprehensive income (FV-OCI), p. 542
fair value through profit or loss (FVTPL), p. 536
held for trading, p. 544
held to maturity, p. 544
incurred loss impairment model, p. 545
joint ventures, p. 592

minority interest, p. 555
noncontrolling interest, p. 555
on margin, p. 530
realized, p. 530
regular-way purchase or sale, p. 592
significant influence, p. 549
straight-line amortization, p. 534
subsidiary, p. 554
trading, p. 528
transaction costs, p. 530
unrealized holding gains or losses, p. 530

Brief Exercises

(LO 1) BE9-1 Bali Corp. has $10,000 surplus funds to invest and is considering investing in either Company A or Company B. Company A promises to return the $10,000 original amount invested in three years' time and pay a 2% annual return on the principal amount. Company B does not promise to repay the original amount invested, but indicates that it is likely that the $10,000 investment will be worth more than $10,000 if Company B is profitable. Whether Bali will receive an annual return on the investment depends on Company B's cash flows and whether Company B's board of directors votes to distribute the cash. (a) Identify whether the potential investments are investments in debt or in equity securities and (b) explain how you determined your answer.

(LO 1) BE9-2 Jax Taylor has the financial statements of an old established university, a manufacturing company, an insurance company, a real estate developer, a major retail enterprise, and a pension plan. (a) Identify the organizations whose statements of financial position are most likely to report a significant proportion of investments. (b) For those identified, what types of investments would you expect to find?

(LO 2) BE9-3 Eastwind Corporation purchased 400 common shares of Ditch Inc. for $13,200 on February 21. Eastwind paid a 1% commission on the share purchase and, because the shares were not publicly traded, decided to account for them using the cost/amortized cost method. On June 30, Ditch declared and paid a cash dividend of $1.50 per share. Prepare Eastwind Corporation's journal entries to record (a) the purchase of the investment, (b) the dividends received, and (c) the sale of the Ditch Inc. shares in early January the following year for $15,100 less a 1% commission paid on the sale.

(LO 2) BE9-4 Beta Corp. invested in a three-year, $100 face value 8% bond, paying $95.03. At this price, the bond will yield a 10% return. Interest is payable annually. (a) Prepare a bond discount amortization table for Beta Corp. assuming Beta uses the effective interest method required by IFRS. (b) Prepare journal entries to record the initial investment, the receipt of interest, and recognition of interest income in each of the three years, and the maturity of the bond at the end of the third year. (c) Assuming Beta Corp. applies ASPE and has chosen to use the straight-line method of amortization, determine the amount of discount that is amortized each year. (d) Under the assumption in (c), prepare journal entries to record the initial investment, the receipt of interest and recognition of interest income in each of the three years, and the maturity of the bond at the end of the third year. (e) Compare the total interest income under the two methods over the three-year period.

(LO 2) BE9-5 Gamma Corp. invested in a three-year, $100 face value 6% bond, paying $105.55. At this price, the bond will yield a 4% return. Interest is payable annually. (a) Prepare a bond premium amortization table for Gamma Corp. assuming Gamma uses the effective interest method required by IFRS. (b) Prepare journal entries to record the initial investment, the receipt of interest and recognition of interest income in each of the three years, and the maturity of the bond at the end of the third year. (c) Assuming Gamma Corp. applies ASPE and has chosen to use the straight-line method of amortization, determine the amount of premium that is amortized each year. (d) Under the assumption in (c), prepare journal entries to record the initial investment, the receipt of interest and recognition of interest income in each of the three years, and the maturity of the bond at the end of the third year. (e) Compare the total interest income under the two methods over the three-year period.

(LO 2) BE9-6 Carras Corporation purchased $60,000 of five-year, 6% bonds of Hu Inc. for $55,133 to yield an 8% return, and classified the purchase as an amortized cost method investment. The bonds pay interest semi-annually. (a) Assuming Carras Corporation applies IFRS, prepare its journal entries for the purchase of the investment and the receipt of semi-annual interest and discount amortization for the first two interest payments that will be received. Round amounts to the nearest dollar. (b) Assuming Carras applies ASPE and has chosen the straight-line method of discount amortization, prepare the same three entries requested in part (a), rounding amounts to the nearest dollar.

(LO 2) BE9-7 On September 1, Louisa Ltd. purchased $80,000 of five-year, 9% bonds for $74,086, resulting in an effective (yield) rate of 11%. The bonds pay interest each March 1 and September 1. Louisa Ltd. applies ASPE, accounts for the investment under the amortized cost approach using the effective interest accounting policy, and has a December 31 year end. The following March 1, after receiving the semi-annual interest on the bonds, Louisa sells the bonds for $75,100. Prepare Louisa's journal entries for (a) the purchase of the investment, (b) any adjusting entry(ies) needed at December 31, (c) the receipt of interest on March 1, and (d) the sale of the bond investment on March 1. Round amounts to the nearest dollar.

(LO 3) BE9-8 Abdul Corporation purchased 400 common shares of Sigma Inc. for trading purposes for $13,200 on September 8 and accounted for the investment under ASPE at FV-NI. In December, Sigma declared and paid a cash dividend of $1.75 per share. At year end, December 31, Sigma shares were selling for $35.50 per share. In late January, Abdul sold the Sigma shares for $34.95 per share. Prepare Abdul Corporation's journal entries to record (a) the purchase of the investment, (b) the dividends received, (c) the fair value adjustment at December 31, and (d) the January sale of the investment.

(LO 3) BE9-9 On October 1, Qilan Ltd. purchased 7% bonds with a face value of $1,000 for trading purposes, accounting for the investment at fair value through net income. The bonds were priced at 1.044 to yield Qilan 6%, and pay interest annually each October 1. Qilan has a December 31 year end, and at this date, the bonds' fair value was $1,055. Assuming Qilan applies IFRS and follows a policy of not reporting interest income separately from other investment income, prepare Qilan's journal entries for (a) the purchase of the investment, (b) the December 31 interest accrual, and (c) the year-end fair value adjustment. Assuming Qilan applies ASPE, uses the effective interest method, and follows a policy of reporting interest income separately, prepare Qilan's journal entries for (d) the December 31 interest accrual, and (e) the year-end fair value adjustment. Round amounts to two decimal places.

(LO 3) BE9-10 On March 31, Ramesh Corp. invests in a $1,000, 6% bond to be held for short-term trading purposes, and accounts for this investment using the FV-NI method. The bond's fair value when acquired was $970, but an additional $10 was paid (and debited to Interest Receivable) representing the interest accrued since the annual interest payment date of February 1. Ramesh applies IFRS, does not report interest separately from other investment income, and prepares financial statements each December 31. The fair value of the bond on December 31 is $963, and on February 1 when Ramesh sells the bond, is $961. Prepare journal entries to record (a) the purchase of the bond, (b) any December 31 adjustments needed, (c) the receipt of interest on February 1, and (d) the sale of the bond on February 1. Ramesh Corp. does not use reversing entries.

(LO 4) BE9-11 Alaska Corporation purchased 300 common shares of Burke Inc. for $23,400 and accounted for them using the fair value through other comprehensive income model. During the year, Burke paid a cash dividend of $3.25 per share. At year end, Burke shares had a fair value of $74.50 per share. Prepare Alaska's journal entries to record (a) the purchase of the investment, (b) the dividends received, and (c) the fair value adjustment.

(LO 4) BE9-12 Early in its 2014 fiscal year (December 31 year end), Hayes Company purchased 10,000 shares of Kenyon Corporation common shares for $26.18 per share, plus $1,800 in brokerage commissions. These securities were accounted for at FV-OCI (with recycling) and transaction costs are capitalized. In September, Kenyon declared and paid a dividend of $1.02 per share, and on December 31, 2014, the fair value of these shares was $271,500. On April 13, 2015, Hayes sold all the Kenyon shares at a price of $28.10 each, incurring $1,925 in brokerage commissions on the sale. Prepare the entries to record (a) the purchase of the Kenyon shares, (b) the receipt of the dividend, (c) the fair value adjustment at December 31, 2014, and (d) all entries associated with the disposal of the investment on April 13, 2015. (*Hint*: In part [d], first bring the investment to its April 13 fair value net of the brokerage commission.)

(LO 4) BE9-13 Using the information presented in BE9-12, assume instead that Hayes follows a policy of accounting for its investment in Kenyon shares at FV-OCI without recycling. Prepare all entries associated with the disposal of the investment on April 13, 2015. (*Hint*: First bring the investment to its April 13 fair value net of the brokerage commission.)

(LO 4) BE9-14 The following information relates to Cortez Corp. for 2014: net income of $672,683; unrealized loss of $20,830 related to investments accounted for at fair value through other comprehensive income during the year; and accumulated other comprehensive income of $37,273 on January 1, 2014. Determine (a) other comprehensive income for 2014, (b) comprehensive income for 2014, and (c) accumulated other comprehensive income at December 31, 2014.

(LO 2, 3, 4, 9) BE9-15 A review of the financial statements of private and publicly accountable enterprises may result in finding the following measurement approaches used for their non-strategic investments: (1) cost/amortized cost, (2) FV-NI (or FVTPL), (3) FV-OCI (with recycling), and (4) FV-OCI (without recycling). Indicate by number (1, 2, 3, or 4) which methods are permitted for enterprises applying (a) ASPE, (b) IAS 39, and (c) IFRS 9.

(LO 5) BE9-16 The standard setters identify three approaches to accounting for the impairment of financial asset investments: an incurred loss model, an expected loss model, and a fair value model. Identify which models are required to be used by enterprises applying (a) ASPE, (b) IAS 39, and (c) IFRS 9. If more than one model is used under each of (a), (b), and (c), identify when each model would be applied.

(LO 5) BE9-17 Ramirez Company has an investment in 6%, 10-year bonds of Soto Company. The investment was originally purchased at par for $100 in 2013 and it is accounted for at amortized cost. Early in 2014, Ramirez recorded an impairment on the Soto investment due to Soto's financial distress. At that time, the present value of the cash flows discounted using the original effective interest rate was $90, and the present value of the cash flows using the then current market rate was $91. In 2015, Soto returned to profitability and the Soto investment was no longer considered impaired. Prepare the entries Ramirez would make in 2014 and 2015 under (a) ASPE, (b) IAS 39, and (c) IFRS 9.

(LO 6) BE9-18 Poot Corporation purchased a 40% interest in Moss, Inc. for $100. This investment gave Poot significant influence over Moss. During the year, Moss earned net income of $15 and paid dividends of $5. Assuming the purchase price was equal to 40% of Moss's net carrying amount when it was acquired, prepare Poot's journal entries related to this investment using the equity method. Poot applies IFRS.

(LO 6) BE9-19 Julip Corporation purchased a 25% interest in Krov Corporation on January 2, 2014, for $1,000. At that time, the carrying amount of Krov's net assets was $3,600. Any excess of the cost of the investment over Julip's share of Krov's carrying amount can be attributed to unrecorded intangibles with a useful life of 20 years. Krov declared and paid a dividend of $12 and reported net income of $60 for its year ended December 31, 2014. Prepare Julip's 2014 entries to record all transactions and events related to the investment in its associate. Assume Julip is a publicly accountable enterprise that applies IFRS.

(LO 6) BE9-20 Use the information from BE9-19 except that Julip Corporation is a private enterprise that applies ASPE. Prepare Julip's 2014 entries to record all transactions and events related to its significant influence investment in Krov Corporation assuming (a) Krov's shares are traded in an active market, Julip applies the FV-NI approach, the fair value of Julip's share of Krov Corp. at December 31, 2014, is $1,020 and (b) Julip applies the cost method to account for its investment in Krov.

(LO 7) BE9-21 Beckett Corp. is facing a decision of whether to purchase 40% of Kyla Corp.'s shares for $1.6 million cash, giving Beckett significant influence over the investee company, or 60% of Kyla's shares for $2.4 million cash, making Kyla a subsidiary company. The book value of Kyla's net assets is $4 million (assets are $10 million and liabilities are $6 million). How will this investment affect Beckett's GAAP statement of financial position if Beckett acquires (a) a 40% interest and (b) a 60% interest, assuming Beckett applies IFRS? That is, for each of (a) and (b), indicate the immediate effect on Beckett's total assets, total liabilities, and shareholders' equity, assuming Beckett applies IFRS.

(LO 8) BE9-22 Both ASPE and IFRS require disclosures about an enterprise's investments that include the carrying amount of each type of investment by the accounting method used and the income, gains, or losses classified in a similar way. Identify the disclosure objective for financial assets that this information is intended to help meet.

Exercises

(LO 1, 2, 3, 4) E9-1 (Investment Classifications) Each of the following investments is independent of the others.

1. A bond that will mature in four years was bought one month ago when the price dropped. As soon as the value increases, which is expected next month, it will be sold.

2. Ten percent of the outstanding shares of Farm Corp. were purchased. The company is planning on eventually getting a total of 30% of the outstanding shares.

3. Ten-year bonds were purchased this year. The bonds mature on January 1 of next year.

4. Bonds that will mature in five years are purchased. The company would like to hold them until they mature, but money has been tight recently and the bonds may need to be sold.

5. A bond that matures in 10 years was purchased with money that the company has set aside for an expansion project that is planned for 10 years from now.

6. Preferred shares were purchased for their consistent dividend. The company is planning to hold the preferred shares for a long time.

7. Common shares of a distributor are purchased to meet a regulatory requirement for doing business in the distributor's region. The investment is expected to be held indefinitely.

Instructions

Identify the best accounting model classification(s) for each of the investments described above under (a) ASPE, (b) IAS 39, and (c) IFRS 9.

(LO 2) E9-2 (Entries for Cost/Amortized Cost Investments) On January 1, 2014, Kenn Corp. purchased at par 10% bonds having a maturity value of $300,000. They are dated January 1, 2014, and mature on January 1, 2019, with interest receivable on December 31 of each year. The bonds are accounted for using the amortized cost model.

Instructions

(a) Prepare the journal entry to record the bond purchase.

(b) Prepare the journal entry to record the interest received for 2014.

(c) Prepare the journal entry to record the interest received for 2015.

(d) Prepare the journal entry to record the redemption of the bond at maturity.

(LO 2) E9-3 (Entries for Cost/Amortized Cost Investments) On January 1, 2014, Mustafa Limited paid $537,907.40 for 12% bonds with a maturity value of $500,000. The bonds provide the bondholders with a 10% yield. They are dated January 1, 2014, and mature on January 1, 2019, with interest receivable on December 31 of each year. Mustafa accounts for the bonds using the amortized cost approach, applies ASPE using the effective interest method, and has a December 31 year end.

Instructions

(a) Prepare the journal entry to record the bond purchase.

(b) Prepare a bond amortization schedule, rounding to two decimal places.

(c) Prepare the journal entry to record interest received and interest income for 2014.

(d) Prepare the journal entry to record interest received and interest income for 2015.

(e) Prepare the journal entry to record the redemption of the bond at maturity.

(f) If Mustafa used the straight-line method of discount/premium amortization, prepare the journal entry to record interest received and interest income the company would make each year.

(g) Compare the total interest income reported over the five-year period under the effective interest method and the straight-line method. What can you conclude?

Digging Deeper

(h) Why might a reader of the financial statements find the effective interest method more relevant than the straight-line method?

(LO 2) E9-4 (Cost/Amortized Cost Investments) On January 1, 2014, Phantom Corp. acquires $300,000 of Spider Products, Inc. 9% bonds at a price of $278,384. The interest is payable each December 31, and the bonds mature on December 31, 2016. The investment will provide Phantom Corp. with a 12% yield. Phantom Corp. applies IFRS and accounts for this investment using the amortized cost model.

Instructions

(a) Prepare a three-year bond amortization schedule, rounding to the nearest dollar.

(b) Prepare the journal entry to record interest received and interest income on December 31, 2015.

(c) Prepare the journal entries to record interest received and interest income on December 31, 2016, and the maturity of the bond.

(d) If Phantom sold the bond on December 31, 2015, for $285,270 instead of holding it to maturity, prepare the entry for the disposal of the investment. Assume 2015 interest received and interest income have already been recorded.

(LO 3) E9-5 (Fair Value through Net Income Investment in Bonds) Refer to the information in E9-3, except assume that Mustafa hopes to make a gain on the bonds as interest rates are expected to fall. Mustafa accounts for the bonds at fair value with changes in value taken to net income, and separately recognizes and reports interest income. The fair value of the bonds at December 31 of each year end is as follows:

2014	$534,200	2017	$507,000
2015	$515,000	2018	$500,000
2016	$513,000		

Instructions

(a) Prepare the journal entry at the date of the bond purchase.

(b) Prepare the journal entries to record interest income and interest received, and recognition of fair value at December 31, 2014, 2015, and 2016.

Digging Deeper

(c) Did market interest rates fall as expected? Explain briefly.

(LO 2, 3) E9-6 (Amortized Cost and Fair Value-NI Investments in Bonds Purchased between Interest Payment Dates) The following information relates to the debt investments of Wildcat Inc. during a recent year:

1. On February 1, the company purchased Gibbons Corp. 10% bonds with a face value of $300,000 at 100 plus accrued interest. Interest is payable on April 1 and October 1.

2. On April 1, semi-annual interest is received on the Gibbons bonds.

3. On June 15, Sampson Inc. 9% bonds were purchased. The $200,000 par-value bonds were purchased at 100 plus accrued interest. Interest dates are June 1 and December 1.

4. On August 31, Gibbons Corp. bonds with a par value of $60,000 purchased on February 1 were sold at 99 plus accrued interest.

5. On October 1, semi-annual interest is received on the remaining Gibbons Corp. bonds.

6. On December 1, semi-annual interest is received on the Sampson Inc. bonds.

7. On December 31, the fair values of the bonds purchased on February 1 and June 15 are 98.5 and 101, respectively.

Assume the investments are accounted for under the recognition and measurement requirements of IFRS 9 *Financial Instruments.*

Instructions

(a) Prepare all journal entries that you consider necessary, including December 31 year-end entries, assuming these investments are accounted for at fair value through net income, and interest income is not reported separately from other related investment gains and losses.

(b) Assume instead that Wildcat manages these investments based on their yield to maturity. Prepare all journal entries you consider necessary, including December 31 adjusting entries.

Digging Deeper

(c) Briefly explain what it means to manage an investment on the basis of yield to maturity and why the recommended accounting method is reasonable in such a situation.

(LO 3) E9-7   (Fair Value through Net Income Equity Investments) On December 31, 2013, Zurich Corp. provided you with the following pre-adjustment information regarding its portfolio of investments held for short-term profit-taking:

	December 31, 2013	
Investments	Carrying Amount	Fair Value
Moonstar Corp. shares	$20,000	$19,000
Bilby Corp. shares	10,000	9,000
Radius Ltd. shares	20,000	20,600
Total portfolio	$50,000	$48,600

During 2014, Bilby Corp. shares were sold for $9,500. The fair values of the securities on December 31, 2014, were as follows: Moonstar Corp. shares $19,300 and Radius Ltd. shares $20,500. Dividends and other investment income and losses are all reported in one investment income account.

Instructions

(a) Prepare the adjusting journal entry needed on December 31, 2013.

(b) Prepare the journal entry to record the sale of the Bilby Corp. shares during 2014.

(c) Prepare the adjusting journal entry needed on December 31, 2014.

(LO 3) E9-8   (Investment in Debt Instruments Held for Trading Purposes, Accounted for Using FV-NI) NB Corp. purchased a $100,000 face-value bond of Myers Corp. on August 31, 2013, for $104,490 plus accrued interest. The bond pays interest annually each November 1 at a rate of 9%. On November 1, 2013, NB Corp. received the annual interest. On December 31, 2013, NB's year end, *The Globe and Mail* newspaper indicated a fair value for these bonds of 103.2. NB sold the bonds on January 15, 2014, for $102,900 plus accrued interest. Assume NB Corp. follows IFRS and does not report interest income separately from gains and losses on these investments.

Instructions

(a) Prepare the journal entries to record the purchase of the bond, the receipt of interest, any adjustments required at year end, and the subsequent sale of the bonds.

(b) How many months were the bonds held by NB Corp. in 2013? Based on this, how much of the income reported on these bonds should be for interest received? Verify that your answer fits with the income that is reported.

(c) How would the accounting and reporting change if NB Corp. applied accounting standards for private enterprises?

Digging Deeper

(d) If these bonds were acquired to earn a return on excess funds, did the company meet its objective? If yes, how much return did NB Corp. earn while the bonds were held? If not, why not?

(LO 3) E9-9   (Fair Value through Net Income Equity Investment Entries) Activet Corporation, a Canadian-based international company that follows IFRS, including IAS 39, has the following securities in its portfolio of investments acquired for trading purposes and accounted for using the fair value through net income method on December 31, 2013:

Investments	Carrying Amount (before adjustment)	Fair Value
1,500 shares of David Jones Inc., common	$ 71,500	$ 69,000
5,000 shares of Hearn Corp., common	180,000	175,000
400 shares of Alessandro Inc., preferred	60,000	61,600
	$311,500	$305,600

In 2014, Activet completed the following securities transactions:

Mar. 1   Sold the 1,500 shares of David Jones Inc. common at $45 per share, less fees of $500.
Apr. 1   Bought 700 shares of Oberto Ltd. common at $75 per share, plus fees of $1,300.

Activet Corporation's portfolio of trading securities appeared as follows on December 31, 2014:

Investments	Original Cost	Fair Value
5,000 shares of Hearn Corp., common	$180,000	$175,000
700 shares of Oberto Ltd., common	52,500	50,400
400 shares of Alessandro Inc., preferred	60,000	58,000
	$292,500	$283,400

Instructions

Prepare the Activet Corporation general journal entries for the following assuming the company does not recognize and report dividends and other components of investment gains and losses separately:

(a) The December 31, 2013 adjusting entry

(b) The sale of the David Jones Inc. shares

(c) The purchase of the Oberto Ltd. shares

(d) The December 31, 2014 adjusting entry

(LO 3, 4) **E9-10**   **(Entries for FV-NI and FV-OCI Equity Investments)** The following information is available about Kao Corp.'s investments at December 31, 2014. This is the first year Kao has purchased securities for investment purposes.

Securities	Cost	Fair Value
3,000 shares of Petra Corporation common shares	$40,000	$46,000
1,000 shares of Dugald Inc. preferred shares	25,000	22,000
	$65,000	$68,000

Assume that Kao Corp. follows IFRS and applies IAS 39.

Instructions

(a) Prepare the adjusting entry(ies), if any, at December 31, 2014, assuming the investments are acquired for trading purposes and accounted for using the fair value through net income model with no separate reporting of dividends and other types of FV-NI investment income and losses.

(b) Prepare the adjusting entry(ies), if any, at December 31, 2014, assuming the investments are accounted for using the fair value through other comprehensive income model.

(c) Discuss how the amounts reported in the financial statements are affected by the choice of accounting method.

(d) Would any of your answers to (a) to (c) change if Kao Corp. had adopted IFRS 9? Explain briefly.

(LO 3, 4) **E9-11**   **(Equity Investment Entries—FV-NI and FV-OCI)** Arantxa Corporation made the following purchases of investments during 2014, the first year in which Arantxa invested in equity securities:

1. On January 15, purchased 9,000 shares of Nirmala Corp.'s common shares at $33.50 per share plus commission of $1,980.

2. On April 1, purchased 5,000 shares of Oxana Corp.'s common shares at $52.00 per share plus commission of $3,370.

3. On September 10, purchased 7,000 shares of WTA Corp.'s preferred shares at $26.50 per share plus commission of $2,910.

On May 20, 2014, Arantxa sold 3,000 of the Nirmala common shares at a market price of $35 per share less brokerage commissions of $2,850. The year-end fair values per share were as follows: Nirmala $30; Oxana $55; and WTA $28. The chief accountant of Arantxa tells you that Arantxa Corporation holds these investments with the intention of selling them in order to earn short-term profits from appreciation in their prices and accounts for them using the fair value though net income model, with no separate reporting of dividends and other types of FV-NI investment income and losses.

Assume that Arantxa Corporation follows IFRS, and specifically IAS 39.

Instructions

(a) Prepare the journal entries to record the three investments.

(b) Prepare the journal entry(ies) for the sale of the 3,000 Nirmala shares on May 20.

(c) Prepare the adjusting entries needed on December 31, 2014.

(d) Repeat parts (a) to (c), assuming the investments are accounted for using the fair value through other comprehensive income model with recycling. Arantxa's policy is to capitalize transaction costs on the acquisition of FV-OCI investments and reduce the proceeds on disposal.

(e) How would your entries in (d) change, if at all, if Arantxa adopted IFRS 9 in 2014 to account for its financial asset investments?

(LO 4) E9-12   (Fair Value through Other Comprehensive Income Investment Entries and Financial Statement Presentation) At December 31, 2014, the equity investments of Wang Inc. that were accounted for using the fair value through other comprehensive income model without recycling (application of IFRS 9) were as follows:

Investment	Cost and Carrying Amount	Fair Value	Unrealized Gain (Loss)
Ahn Inc.	$175,200	$150,000	$(25,200)
Burnham Corp.	121,500	140,600	19,100
Chi Ltd.	73,000	75,500	2,500
Total	$369,700	$366,100	$ (3,600)

Because of a change in relationship with Ahn Inc., Wang Inc. sold its investment in Ahn for $153,300 on January 20, 2015. No other investments were acquired or sold during 2015; however, a dividend of $1,300 was received from Burnham Corp. in June. At December 31, 2015, the fair values of Burnham and Chi shares were $153,750 and $72,600, respectively.

Instructions

(a) Prepare the entry to adjust the portfolio of investments to fair value at December 31, 2014.

(b) Prepare the presentation of all investment-related accounts on the statement of financial position at December 31, 2014.

(c) Indicate what accounts and amounts would be reported on the statement of comprehensive income for the year ended December 31, 2014, and where each would be reported.

(d) Prepare the journal entries for the 2015 sale of the investment in Ahn Inc. and for the dividend received from Burnham Corp.

(e) Prepare the journal entry required at December 31, 2015, to adjust the investments to fair value.

(LO 4) E9-13   (Fair Value through Other Comprehensive Income Investments—Entries) Niger Corp. provided you with the following information about its investment in Fahad Corp. shares purchased in May 2014 and accounted for using the FV-OCI method:

Cost	$39,900
Fair value, December 31, 2014	$41,750
Fair value, December 31, 2015	$32,200
Fair value, December 31, 2016	$36,400

Instructions

(a) Prepare the adjusting journal entries needed on December 31, 2014, 2015, and 2016.

(b) Determine the balance in accumulated other comprehensive income on the statement of financial position on each of December 31, 2014, 2015, and 2016.

(c) Assume Niger sold its investment in Fahad Corp. on February 13, 2017, for $38,000. Prepare the journal entry(ies) needed on this date if (1) the FV-OCI method required recycling, and (2) the FV-OCI method did not require recycling.

(LO 2, 3, 4, 8, 9) E9-14   (Entry and Financial Statement Comparison of Cost, FV-NI, and FV-OCI Approaches) In early 2014, for the first time, HTSM Corp. invested in the common shares of another Canadian company. It acquired 5,000 shares of Toronto Stock Exchange–traded Bayscape Ltd. at a cost of $68,750. Bayscape is projected to reach a value of $15.50 per share by the end of 2014 and $17.00 by the end of 2015, and has consistently paid an annual dividend of $0.90 per share. HTSM is also a Canadian public corporation with a December 31 year end.

The controller of HTSM is uncertain about which accounting method to use. The company is interested in establishing a closer relationship with Bayscape, but if that fails, HTSM considers the investment a good opportunity to make a gain on its sale in the future. The controller has been advised that the investment could be accounted for at cost or at fair value. If at fair value, a decision would have to be made about whether to put the changes in fair value through net income or into other comprehensive income. As one step in making a decision, the controller would like to know what the effect would be on total assets and net income in each of 2014 and 2015 if the predictions about Bayscape's share prices and dividends actually occur. Assume there would be no recycling of realized investment gains and losses.

Instructions

(a) Prepare and complete a table with a column for each of the three accounting alternatives indicated and rows for journal entries to recognize each of the following: (1) the 2014 dividend, (2) any December 31, 2014 adjustments, (3) the 2015 dividend, and (4) any December 31, 2015 adjustments.

(b) Based on the table in (a), prepare a summary comparison of each accounting method, indicating the effect of applying each of the three accounting methods on: (1) total assets at December 31, 2014, (2) 2014 net income, (3) total assets at December 31, 2015, and (4) 2015 net income.

(c) Determine the effect on net income for the year ended December 31, 2016, under each of the accounting method options assuming the investment in Bayscape was sold in early 2016 for $17.00 per share.

(d) If HTSM applied ASPE instead of IFRS, identify the accounting policy choices that would be available to the controller, and when each would be appropriate.

(LO 5) E9-15 (Impairment of Debt Investment and Subsequent Recovery in Value) Tsui Corporation owns corporate bonds at December 31, 2014, accounted for using the amortized cost model. These bonds have a par value of $800,000 and an amortized cost of $788,000. After an impairment review was triggered, Tsui determined that the discounted impaired cash flows are $737,500 using the current market rate of interest, but are $734,000 using the market rate when the bonds were first acquired. The company follows a policy of directly reducing the carrying amount of any impaired assets.

Instructions

(a) Assuming Tsui Corporation is a private enterprise that applies ASPE, prepare any necessary journal entry(ies) related to (1) the impairment at December 31, 2014, and (2) a December 31, 2015 fair value of $760,000 and an adjusted carrying amount at that date of $741,500.

(b) Assuming Tsui Corporation applies IFRS using IAS 39, prepare any necessary journal entry(ies) related to (1) the impairment at December 31, 2014, and (2) a December 31, 2015 fair value of $760,000 and an adjusted carrying amount at that date of $741,500.

(c) Assuming Tsui Corporation applies IFRS and has adopted IFRS 9, prepare any necessary journal entry(ies) related to (1) the impairment at December 31, 2014, and (2) a December 31, 2015 fair value of $760,000 and an adjusted carrying amount at that date of $741,500.

(d) Assume that Tsui is a private enterprise under the situation described in part (a), and that the company uses a valuation allowance instead of directly reducing the carrying amount of the investment. Prepare the entries required in part (a) for (1) the impairment and (2) the subsequent increase in fair value.

(LO 2, E9-16 (Impairment of FV-NI Investment and Subsequent Recovery in Value) On January 1, 2012, Mamood **3, 5)** Ltd. paid $322,744.44 for 12% bonds of Variation Ltd. with a maturity value of $300,000. The bonds provide the bondholders with a 10% yield. They are dated January 1, 2012, mature on January 1, 2018, and pay interest each December 31. Mamood acquired the bond investment as part of its portfolio of trading securities. It accounts for the bonds at FV-NI and reports interest income separately from other investment gains and losses. At December 31, 2012, Mamood's year end, the bonds had a fair value of $320,700. Mamood applies IFRS.

During 2013, the economic outlook related to Variation Ltd.'s primary business took a major downturn, so that Variation's debt was downgraded. By the end of 2013, the bonds were priced at 85.5, and at December 31, 2014, they were selling in the market at 87. Conditions reversed in 2015 and the outlook for Variation Ltd. significantly improved, leaving their bonds with a fair value at December 31, 2015, of 99.5.

Instructions

(a) Prepare the entries to record Mamood's purchase of the bonds on January 1, 2012, the recognition of interest income and interest received on December 31, 2012, and the fair value adjustment required at December 31, 2012.

(b) Prepare all entries required for 2013, including recognition of the impairment in value if necessary, and for 2014.

(c) Prepare all entries required for 2015, including recognition of the recovery of the impairment in value, if necessary.

(d) Identify the impairment loss model applied in this situation. If Mamood had accounted for this investment at amortized cost, identify and briefly describe the impairment model the company would have used if Mamood applied (1) IFRS using IAS 39, (2) IFRS using IFRS 9, and (3) ASPE.

(LO 2, 3, 4, 5)   E9-17   (Investment in Shares, Impairment, and Subsequent Recovery) Weekly Corp., a December 31 year-end company that applies IFRS, acquired an investment in 1,000 shares of Credence Corp. in mid-2010 for $29,850. Between significant volatility in the markets and in the business prospects of Credence Corp., the accounting for this investment presented a challenge to Weekly. Toward the end of 2014, Credence discontinued the small annual dividend of $0.50 per share it had been paying, and announced that a major patent responsible for 50% of its income had lost most of its value due to a technological improvement by a competitor.

Situation 1: Credence Corp. is a private company and the shares were acquired in a private transaction between the principals of the two companies. Because the shares were not actively traded, Weekly applies the cost method to account for this investment. In late 2013, Weekly determined that its value had probably fallen marginally to approximately $26,000. In 2014, Weekly became increasingly concerned and, at year end, carried out a thorough analysis of the present value of the likely cash flows to be derived from this investment and estimated an amount of $12,400.

Situation 2: Credence Corp. is a publicly traded company on the Toronto Stock Exchange, and Weekly has opted to account for its investment at fair value through net income. By the end of 2013, the price of Credence shares had fallen to $26.50 per share from $29.00 the previous year, and by the end of 2014 was trading at $11.10.

Situation 3: Credence Corp. is a private enterprise owned by a group of 20 investors, and is a supplier of materials to Weekly. Weekly purchased the shares to cement the relationship between the two companies and has opted to account for its investment at fair value through OCI. In late 2013, Weekly was beginning to worry about its investment and determined that its value had probably fallen marginally to approximately $26,000 from $27,000 the previous year. In 2014, Weekly was more concerned and, at year end, carried out a thorough analysis of the present value of the likely cash flows to be derived from this investment and estimated an amount of $12,400.

Weekly Corp. adjusts the carrying amount of its investments directly when recognizing an impairment loss, and each type of investment income is accounted for and reported separately.

Instructions

(a) For each situation, identify the impairment model that Weekly should apply assuming it applies IFRS using IAS 39.

(b) Assuming Weekly applies IFRS using IAS 39, prepare the appropriate journal entries at December 31, 2013, and December 31, 2014, under each situation presented.

(c) If Weekly is a private company that applies ASPE, prepare the appropriate journal entries at December 31, 2013, and December 31, 2014, under situations 1 and 2.

(LO 2, 3, 6)   E9-18   (GAAP Accounting Methods with and without Significant Influence under ASPE) Holmes, Inc. purchased 30% of Nadal Corporation's 30,000 outstanding common shares at a cost of $15 per share on January 3, 2014. The purchase price of $15 per share was based solely on the book value of Nadal's net assets. On September 21, Nadal declared and paid a cash dividend of $39,000. On December 31, Holmes's year end, Nadal reported net income of $85,000 for the year. Nadal shares had a fair value of $14.75 per share at December 31. Holmes, Inc., a private Canadian corporation, applies ASPE.

Instructions

(a) Under the assumption that the 30% holding of Nadal does not give Holmes significant influence over Nadal, identify the possible accounting methods Holmes could use under ASPE to account for its investment. Prepare all required 2014 journal entries under each acceptable method.

(b) Under the assumption that the 30% holding of Nadal gives Holmes significant influence over Nadal, prepare all required 2014 journal entries assuming Holmes uses the equity method of accounting.

(c) Indicate the other possible accounting methods, if any, that Holmes could have chosen under the assumption in (b) above.

(d) From the perspective of a financial analyst, why might the equity method be considered a more informative presentation when the investor has significant influence?

(LO 6)   E9-19   (Equity Method) Fox Ltd. invested $1 million in Gloven Corp. early in the current year, receiving 25% of its outstanding shares. At the time of the purchase, Gloven Corp. had a carrying amount of $3.2 million. Gloven Corp. pays out 35% of its net income in dividends each year. Assume that Fox Ltd. applies IFRS and that the 25% holding of Gloven shares is sufficient to enable Fox to significantly influence the operating, investing, and financing decisions of Gloven.

Instructions

Use the information in the following T account for the investment in Gloven to answer the following questions:

Exercises   575

Investment in Gloven Corp.	
1,000,000	
110,000	
	38,500
	14,000

(a) How much was Fox Ltd.'s share of Gloven Corp.'s net income for the year?

(b) How much was Fox Ltd.'s share of Gloven Corp.'s dividends for the year?

(c) How much was Fox Ltd.'s annual depreciation of the excess payment for capital assets?

(d) What was Gloven Corp.'s total net income for the year?

(e) What were Gloven Corp.'s total dividends for the year?

(f) Assuming that depreciable assets had a remaining useful life of 10 years when Fox acquired its investment in Gloven, how much of the payment in excess of carrying amount was assigned to goodwill?

(LO 4, 6, 8) E9-20 (Fair Value-OCI and Equity Method Compared) Harnish Inc. acquired 25% of the outstanding common shares of Gregson Inc. on December 31, 2013. The purchase price was $1,250,000 for 62,500 shares, and is equal to 25% of Gregson's carrying amount. Gregson declared and paid a $0.75 per share cash dividend on June 15 and again on December 15, 2014. Gregson reported net income of $520,000 for 2014. The fair value of Gregson's shares was $21 per share at December 31, 2014. Harnish is a public company and applies IFRS.

Instructions

(a) Prepare the journal entries for Harnish for 2013 and 2014, assuming that Harnish cannot exercise significant influence over Gregson. The investment is accounted for using the fair value through other comprehensive income model.

(b) Prepare the journal entries for Harnish for 2013 and 2014, assuming that Harnish can exercise significant influence over Gregson.

(c) What amount is reported for the investment in Gregson shares on the December 31, 2014 statement of financial position under each of these methods in (a) and (b), and where is the investment reported on this statement?

(d) What amount is reported on Harnish's statement of comprehensive income in 2014 under each of these methods, and where are the amounts reported?

(LO 3, 5, 6) E9-21 (Long-Term Equity Investments, Equity Method, and Impairment) On January 1, 2014, Rae Corporation purchased 30% of the common shares of Martz Limited for $196,000. Martz Limited shares are not traded in an active market. The carrying amount of Martz's net assets was $520,000 on that date. Any excess of the purchase cost over Rae's share of Martz's carrying amount is attributable to unrecorded intangibles with a 20-year life. During the year, Martz earned net income and comprehensive income of $75,000 and paid dividends of $15,000. The investment in Martz had a fair value of $201,000 at December 31, 2014. During 2015, Martz incurred a net loss and comprehensive loss of $80,000 and paid no dividends. At December 31, 2015, the fair value of the investment was $140,000 and the recoverable amount was $149,000. Assume that Rae follows IFRS.

Instructions

(a) Prepare all relevant journal entries related to Rae's investment in Martz for 2014 and 2015, assuming this is its only investment and Rae cannot exercise significant influence over Martz's policies. Rae accounts for this investment using the fair value through net income model and separately records and reports each type of income (loss) separately. Illustrate how the statement of comprehensive income is affected in 2014 and 2015.

(b) Prepare all relevant journal entries related to Rae's investment in Martz for 2014 and 2015, assuming this is its only investment and Rae exercises significant influence over its associates' policies. Illustrate how the statement of comprehensive income is affected in 2014 and 2015. Briefly explain.

(c) How would your answer to part (b) be different if you were told that Martz's 2014 statement of comprehensive income included a loss from discontinued operations of $20,000 (net of tax)?

(LO 4, 6, 8) E9-22 (Determine Proper Income Reporting) The following are two independent situations.

Situation 1: Lauren Inc. received dividends from its common share investments during the year ended December 31, 2014, as follows:

- A cash dividend of $12,250 is received from Peel Corporation. Lauren owns a 1.2% interest in Peel.

- A cash dividend of $68,000 is received from Vonna Corporation. Lauren owns a 30% interest in Vonna and a majority of Lauren's directors are also directors of Vonna Corporation.

• A cash dividend of $172,000 is received from Express Inc., a subsidiary of Lauren.

Situation 2: On April 11, 2014, Chad Corp. purchased as a long-term investment (accounted for using fair value through other comprehensive income without recycling) 6,000 common shares of Roddy Ltd. for $76 per share, which represents a 2% interest. On December 31, 2014, the shares' market price was $81 per share. On March 3, 2015, Chad sold all 6,000 shares of Roddy for $94 per share.

Assume that all companies follow IFRS.

Instructions

(a) For situation 1, determine how much dividend income Lauren should report on its 2014 consolidated statement of comprehensive income.

(b) For situation 2, determine the amount of the gain or loss on disposal that should be included in Chad's net income in 2015 and in its other comprehensive income. The investment in Roddy Ltd. was Chad Corp.'s only investment.

(LO 5, 6, 8) E9-23 **(Equity Method with Cost in Excess of Share of Carrying Amount, Impairment)** On January 3, 2014, Mego Limited purchased 3,000 shares (30%) of the common shares of Sonja Corp. for $438,000. The following information is provided about the identifiable assets and liabilities of Sonja at the date of acquisition:

	Carrying Amount	Fair Value
Assets not subject to depreciation	$ 550,000	$ 550,000
Assets subject to depreciation (10 years remaining)	760,000	880,000
Total identifiable assets	1,310,000	1,430,000
Liabilities	110,000	110,000

During 2014, Sonja reported the following information on its statement of comprehensive income:

Income before discontinued operations	$200,000
Discontinued operations (net of tax)	(50,000)
Net income and comprehensive income	150,000
Dividends declared and paid by Sonja, November 15, 2014	110,000

Assume that the 30% interest is sufficient to make Sonja an associate of Mego, and that Mego is required to apply IFRS for its financial reporting. The fair value of Sonja's shares at December 31, 2014, is $147 per share.

Instructions

(a) Prepare the journal entry to record Mego's purchase of the Sonja shares on January 3, 2014. (*Hint*: Any unexplained payment represents unrecognized goodwill of Sonja.)

(b) Prepare all necessary journal entries associated with Mego's investment in Sonja for 2014. Depreciable assets are depreciated on a straight-line basis.

(c) Would any of your entries in (b) change if you were informed that Mego's long-term business prospects had deteriorated and that the most Mego could expect to recover in the future or to sell its investment in Sonja for at December 31, 2014, is $115 per share? If so, prepare the entry and explain briefly.

(LO 6, 8) E9-24 **(ASPE, Significant Influence, Equity Method with Cost in Excess of Carrying Amount, Alternative Methods)** In early January 2014, Chi Inc., a private enterprise that applies ASPE, purchased 40% of the common shares of Washi Corp. for $410,000. Chi was now able to exercise considerable influence in decisions made by Washi's management. Washi Corp.'s statement of financial position reported the following information at the date of acquisition:

Assets not subject to being amortized	$205,000
Assets subject to amortization (10 years average life remaining)	620,000
Liabilities	115,000

Additional information:

1. Both the carrying amount and fair value are the same for assets that are not subject to amortization and for the liabilities.

2. The fair value of the assets subject to amortization is $750,000.

3. The company amortizes its capital assets on a straight-line basis.

4. Washi reported net income of $163,000 and declared and paid dividends of $112,000 in 2014.

Instructions

(a) Prepare the journal entry to record Chi's investment in Washi Corp. Assume that any unexplained payment is goodwill.

(b) Assuming Chi applies the equity method to account for its investment in Washi, prepare the journal entries to record Chi's equity in the net income and the receipt of dividends from Washi Corp. in 2014.

(c) Assume the same facts as above and in part (b), except that Washi's net income included a loss on discontinued operations of $38,000 (net of tax). Prepare the journal entries necessary to record Chi's equity in the net income of Washi for 2014.

(d) Assume that Chi is a publicly accountable enterprise that applies IFRS and therefore also applies the equity method to account for its associate. In addition to the information in parts (a) and (b), you are told that Washi also reports an unrealized gain of $45,000 on investments accounted for using FV-OCI. If Chi Inc. reports net income of $172,400 and an unrealized gain in OCI of $10,000 on its own financial statements before including the results of its investment in Washi, determine Chi Inc.'s net income, other comprehensive income, and comprehensive income reported on its 2014 statement of comprehensive income. Both Chi and Washi follow a policy of reclassifying realized gains and losses on FV-OCI investments to net income.

Problems

P9-1 MacAskill Corp. has the following portfolio of securities acquired for trading purposes and accounted for using the fair value through net income model at September 30, 2014, the end of the company's third quarter:

Investment	Cost	Fair Value
50,000 common shares of Yuen Inc.	$215,000	$200,000
3,500 preferred shares of Monty Ltd.	135,000	140,000
2,000 common shares of Oakwood Inc.	180,000	179,000

On October 8, 2014, the Yuen shares were sold for $4.30 per share. On November 16, 2014, 3,000 common shares of Patriot Corp. were purchased at $44.50 per share. MacAskill pays a 1% commission on purchases and sales of all securities. At the end of the fourth quarter, on December 31, 2014, the fair values of the shares held were as follows: Monty $106,000; Patriot $122,000; and Oakwood $203,000. MacAskill prepares financial statements every quarter. Assume MacAskill follows IFRS 9 and does not recognize dividends and other investment income accounts separately.

Instructions

(a) Prepare the journal entries to record the sale, purchase, and adjusting entries related to the portfolio for the fourth quarter of 2014.

(b) Indicate how and where the investments would be reported on the December 31, 2014 statement of financial position.

Digging Deeper

(c) Under what conditions might you recommend that the portfolio accounted for at FV-NI be reported somewhere other than where you indicated in part (b)?

P9-2 The following information relates to the 2014 debt and equity investment transactions of Wildcat Ltd., a publicly accountable Canadian corporation. All of the investments were acquired for trading purposes and accounted for using the fair value through net income model with all transaction costs being expensed. No investments were held at December 31, 2013, and the company prepares financial statements only annually, each December 31, following IFRS 9. Dividend and interest income are not recorded or reported separately from other investment income accounts.

1. On February 1, the company purchased Williams Corp. 12% bonds, with a par value of $500,000, at 106.5 plus accrued interest to yield 10%. Interest is payable April 1 and October 1.

2. On April 1, semi-annual interest was received on the Williams bonds.

3. On July 1, 9% bonds of Saint Inc. were purchased. These bonds, with a par value of $200,000, were purchased at 101 plus accrued interest to yield 8.5%. Interest dates are June 1 and December 1.

4. On August 12, 3,000 shares of Scotia Corp. were acquired at a cost of $59 per share. A 1% commission was paid.

5. On September 1, Williams Corp. bonds with a par value of $100,000 were sold at 104 plus accrued interest.

6. On September 28, a dividend of $0.50 per share was received on the Scotia Corp. shares.

7. On October 1, semi-annual interest was received on the remaining Williams Corp. bonds.

8. On December 1, semi-annual interest was received on the Saint Inc. bonds.

9. On December 28, a dividend of $0.52 per share was received on the Scotia Corp. shares.

10. On December 31, the following fair values were determined: Williams Corp. bonds 101.75; Saint Inc. bonds 97; and Scotia Corp. shares $60.50.

Instructions

(a) Prepare all 2014 journal entries necessary to properly account for the investment in the Williams Corp. bonds.

(b) Prepare all 2014 journal entries necessary to properly account for the investment in the Saint Inc. bonds.

(c) Prepare all 2014 journal entries necessary to properly account for the investment in the Scotia Corp. shares.

(d) Assume that there were trading investments on hand at December 31, 2013, accounted for using the fair value through net income model, and that they consisted of shares with a cost of $400,000 and a fair value of $390,000. These non–dividend-paying shares were sold early in 2014 and their original cost was recovered exactly. What effect would this transaction have on 2014 net income?

(e) Assume that the interest income on the Saint Inc. bonds that were purchased on July 1, 2014, was separately tracked and reported. Prepare the entries that are required on July 1, December 1, and December 31, 2014, to account for this investment.

P9-3   The following amortization schedule is for Flagg Ltd.'s investment in Spangler Corp.'s $100,000, five-year bonds with a 7% interest rate and a 5% yield, which were purchased on December 31, 2013, for $108,660:

	Cash Received	Interest Income	Bond Premium Amortized	Amortized Cost of Bonds
Dec. 31, 2013				$108,660
Dec. 31, 2014	$7,000	$5,433	$1,567	107,093
Dec. 31, 2015	7,000	5,354	1,646	105,447
Dec. 31, 2016	7,000	5,272	1,728	103,719
Dec. 31, 2017	7,000	5,186	1,814	101,905
Dec. 31, 2018	7,000	5,095	1,905	100,000

The following schedule presents a comparison of the amortized cost and fair value of the bonds at year end:

	Dec. 31, 2014	Dec. 31, 2015	Dec. 31, 2016	Dec. 31, 2017	Dec. 31, 2018
Amortized cost	$107,093	$105,447	$103,719	$101,905	$100,000
Fair value	$106,500	$107,500	$105,650	$103,000	$100,000

Assume that Flagg Ltd. follows IFRS 9 and reports interest income separately from other investment income except for trading investments accounted for at FV-NI.

Instructions

(a) Prepare the journal entry to record the purchase of these bonds on December 31, 2013, assuming the bonds are accounted for using the amortized cost model.

(b) Prepare the journal entry(ies) related to the bonds accounted for using the amortized cost model for 2014.

(c) Prepare the journal entry(ies) related to the bonds accounted for using the amortized cost model for 2016.

(d) Prepare the journal entry(ies) to record the purchase of these bonds, assuming they are held for trading purposes and accounted for using the FV-NI model.

(e) Prepare the journal entry(ies) related to the trading bonds accounted for using the FV-NI model for 2014.

(f) Prepare the journal entry(ies) related to the trading bonds accounted for using the FV-NI model for 2016.

Digging Deeper

(g) As a member of Flagg's management, suggest a reason why you might have a different policy related to the reporting of interest income (separately versus combined with other investment income) that depends on the accounting measurement method chosen.

P9-4   Pascale Corp. has the following securities (all purchased in 2014) in its investment portfolio on December 31, 2014: (1) 2,500 Anderson Corp. common shares, which cost $48,750; (2) 10,000 Munter Ltd. common shares, which cost $580,000; and (3) 6,000 King Corp. preferred shares, which cost $255,000. Their fair values at the end of 2014 were as follows: Anderson Corp. $49,580; Munter Ltd. $569,500; and King Corp. $254,400.

In 2015, Pascale completed the following transactions:

1. On January 15, sold 2,500 Anderson common shares at $21 per share less fees of $2,150.

2. On April 17, purchased 1,000 Castle Ltd. common shares at $33.50 per share plus fees of $1,980.

The company adds transaction costs to the cost of acquired investments and deducts them from cash received on the sale of investments. On December 31, 2015, the fair values per share of the securities were as follows: Munter $61; King $40; and Castle $29. Pascale's accounting supervisor tells you that all these securities have fair values that can be readily determined, but the company is not likely to actively trade them. Management accounts for them using the fair value through other comprehensive income method without recycling.

Instructions

(a) Prepare the entries for the sale of the Anderson Corp. investment on January 15, 2015.

(b) Prepare the entry to record the Castle Ltd. share purchase on April 17, 2015.

(c) Calculate the unrealized gains or losses and prepare any required adjusting entry(ies) for Pascale Corp. on December 31, 2015.

(d) Indicate how all amounts will be reported on Pascale's statement of financial position, statement of comprehensive income, and the changes in the accumulated other comprehensive income portion of the statement of changes in shareholders' equity for 2015.

Digging Deeper

(e) Pascale Corp.'s shareholders carefully watch the company's reported earnings per share (EPS). If Pascale used an accounting policy of FV-OCI with recycling and the company had 10,000 shares outstanding, would this make the EPS any different than it would be with the policy indicated above? If not, why not? If so, by what amount per share?

P9-5 Castlegar Ltd. had the following investment portfolio at January 1, 2014:

Investment	Quantity	Cost per Share	Fair Value at Dec. 31, 2013
Earl Corp.	1,000	$15.00	$11.50
Josie Corp.	900	20.00	16.50
Asher Corp.	500	9.00	7.20

During 2014, the following transactions took place:

1. On March 1, Josie Corp. paid a $2 per share dividend.

2. On April 30, Castlegar sold 300 shares of Asher Corp. for $10 per share.

3. On May 15, Castlegar purchased 200 more Earl Corp. shares at $16 per share.

4. At December 31, 2014, the shares had the following market prices per share: Earl Corp. $17; Josie Corp. $19; and Asher Corp. $8.

During 2015, the following transactions took place:

5. On February 1, Castlegar sold the remaining Asher Corp. shares for $7 per share.

6. On March 1, Josie Corp. paid a $2 per share dividend.

7. On December 21, Earl Corp. declared a cash dividend of $3 per share to be paid in the next month.

8. At December 31, 2015, the shares had the following market prices per share: Earl Corp. $19; and Josie Corp. $21.

Instructions

(a) Assuming that Castlegar Ltd. is a publicly accountable enterprise that applies IFRS using IAS 39 and accounts for its investment portfolio at FV-OCI (with recycling), prepare journal entries to record all of the 2014 and 2015 transactions and year-end events.

(b) Prepare the relevant parts of Castlegar Ltd.'s 2015 and 2014 comparative statements of financial position, statements of comprehensive income, and statements of changes in shareholders' equity (accumulated other comprehensive income portion), where applicable, to show how the investments and related accounts are reported.

Digging Deeper

(c) Assume Castlegar Ltd. is a private enterprise that applies ASPE and accounts for its investment portfolio at cost (that is, the securities do not have actively traded market prices). Determine the amount by which the company's 2014 net income and 2015 net income would differ from the amounts reported under the assumptions in parts (a) and (b). Explain your results.

(d) Refer to your answers to parts (b) and (c). From an investor's perspective, what additional relevant information, if any, is provided in the financial statements under part (b) that would not be available in financial statements prepared under the method used in part (c)?

P9-6 On December 31, 2013, Nodd Corp. acquired an investment in GT Ltd. bonds with a nominal interest rate of 10% (received each December 31) and the controller produced the following bond amortization schedule based on an effective rate of approximately 15%. The bonds mature on December 31, 2016. The company prepares financial statements each December 31 following IFRS and has adopted the provisions of IFRS 9. Management is in the process of determining whether to hold these bonds for their future cash flows in order to repay debt that is also maturing at the end of 2016, or whether they will hold them for trading purposes.

	Dec. 31, 2013	Dec. 31, 2014	Dec. 31, 2015	Dec. 31, 2016
Amortized cost of GT Ltd. bonds	$487,214	$505,296	$526,090	$550,000
Fair value at each year end	487,214	499,000	523,000	550,000

Instructions (Round amounts to the nearest dollar.)

(a) Assume that management determines these bonds will be held until the end of 2016 with the proceeds being used to retire maturing debt. Prepare all journal entries required at December 31, 2013, 2014, 2015, and 2016, including the recognition of interest income and the bonds' ultimate redemption.

(b) Assume that management determines the investment in the bonds is speculative in nature and will be held for trading purposes. If Nodd continues to hold the GT Ltd. bonds until maturity, prepare all journal entries required at December 31, 2013, 2014, 2015, and 2016, including the receipt of interest each year and the bonds' ultimate redemption. Nodd will not recognize interest separately from other investment income.

(c) Instead of the situation and fair values described above, now assume that GT Ltd. experienced financial difficulties during 2015, and in late December 2015 informed Nodd that it expected to be able to pay only half the contracted 2016 interest in one year's time. In addition, GT asked Nodd to agree to a $50,000 reduction in the principal amount owed. The full interest for 2015 was paid on time. The market reacted to this news by downgrading the bonds' fair value immediately to $487,800 at December 31, 2015. Prepare the entries required under the measurement method used in part (a) at December 31, 2015, and at December 31, 2016, acknowledging this impairment and that GT's reduced payments of principal and interest were made as indicated.

(d) Using the information about impairment in part (c), prepare the entries required under the measurement method used in part (b) at December 31, 2015, and at December 31, 2016, acknowledging this impairment and that GT's reduced payments of principal and interest were made as indicated.

(e) Assume that Nodd Corp. is a private corporation that applies ASPE, and you are the company's controller. What method of accounting are you most likely to use in accounting for the investment in the GT bonds? Explain briefly. Under the method you identify, would you expect the impairment and subsequent entries to be the same as those in (c) or in (d)? If not, explain what would be required in the case of impairment.

Digging Deeper

P9-7 Octavio Corp. prepares financial statements annually on December 31, its fiscal year end. At December 31, 2014, the company has the account Investments in its general ledger that contains the following debits for investment purchases, and no credits:

Feb. 1, 2014	Chiang Corp. common shares, no par value, 200 shares	$ 37,400
April 1	Government of Canada bonds, 6%, due April 1, 2024, interest payable April 1 and October 1, 100 bonds of $1,000 par value each	100,000
July 1	Monet Corp. 12% bonds, par $50,000, dated March 1, 2014, purchased at 108 plus accrued interest to yield 11%, interest payable annually on March 1, due on March 1, 2034	56,000
Nov. 1	$60,000, six-month non–interest-bearing note that matures on May 1, 2015, bought to yield 10%	57,143

The fair values of the individual securities on December 31, 2014, were:

Chiang Corp. common shares (active stock market price)	$ 33,800
Government of Canada bonds	105,900
Monet Corp. bonds	55,600
Note receivable	58,350

Instructions (Round amounts to the nearest dollar.)

(a) Prepare the entries necessary to correct any errors in the Investments account, assuming that the Government of Canada bonds were being managed for their yield to maturity, and that the Monet bonds were acquired with the hope of gaining from falling interest rates. The Chiang Corp. shares were acquired with the hope of ensuring the supply of raw materials from this company in the future. Octavio has adopted the recognition and measurement standards of IFRS 9 and tracks interest income only for investments accounted for at cost/amortized cost.

(b) Prepare the entries required to record any accrued interest, amortization of any premium or discount, and recognition of fair values on December 31, 2014.

(c) During 2015, the following transactions took place:

1. The note was sold on February 1, 2015, for $59,600.

2. The Government of Canada bonds were sold on July 1, 2015, for $109,200 plus accrued interest. Prepare entries to record these transactions.

(d) Using the information from parts (a) and (b), assume that the note was not sold on February 1, 2015, but instead was held until it matured. Provide the proper entry to record the disposal of the note at maturity.

(e) Assume that Octavio Corp. is a private entity and applies ASPE. Identify which, if any, of your answers to parts (a) to (d) would change under this assumption. Explain briefly.

Digging Deeper

(f) Can Octavio management choose which standards to follow, or is it restricted by the type of company it is? Explain.

P9-8 Brooks Corp. is a medium-sized corporation that specializes in quarrying stone for building construction. The company has long dominated the market, and at one time had 70% market penetration. During prosperous years, the company's profits and conservative dividend policy resulted in funds becoming available for outside investment. Over the years, Brooks has had a policy of investing idle cash in equity instruments of other companies. In particular, Brooks has made periodic investments in the company's main supplier, Norton Industries Limited. Although Brooks currently owns 18% of the outstanding common shares of Norton, it does not yet have significant influence over the operations of this investee company. Brooks accounts for its investment in Norton using IFRS 9 and the fair value through other comprehensive income model without recycling.

Yasmina Olynyk has recently joined Brooks as assistant controller, and her first assignment is to prepare the 2014 year-end adjusting entries. Olynyk has gathered the following information about Brooks's relevant investment accounts:

1. In 2014, Brooks acquired shares of Delaney Motors Corp. and Isha Electric Ltd. for short-term trading purposes. Brooks purchased 100,000 shares of Delaney Motors for $1.4 million and the shares currently have a fair value of $1.6 million. Brooks's investment in Isha Electric has not been profitable: the company acquired 50,000 shares of Isha at $20 per share and they currently have a fair value of $720,000.

2. Before 2014, Brooks had invested $22.5 million in Norton Industries and, at December 31, 2013, the investment had a fair value of $21.5 million. While Brooks did not sell or purchase any Norton shares this year, Norton declared and paid a dividend totalling $2.4 million on all its common shares, and reported 2014 net income of $13.8 million. Brooks's 18% ownership of Norton Industries has a December 31, 2014 fair value of $22,225,000.

Instructions

(a) Prepare the appropriate adjusting entries for Brooks as at December 31, 2014.

(b) For both categories of investments, describe how the results of the valuation adjustments made in (a) would appear in the body of and/or notes to Brooks's 2014 financial statements.

(c) Prepare the dividend and adjusting entries for the Norton investment, assuming that Brooks's 18% interest results in significant influence over Norton's activities.

(d) If Brooks Corp. were a private enterprise and followed ASPE, identify how your answers to parts (a), (b), and (c) above would differ.

Digging Deeper

(e) Could an 18% ownership interest actually result in Brooks having significant influence? Could Brooks have a 45% ownership interest and yet not have significant influence? Explain your answers.

P9-9 Harper Corporation has the following portfolio of investments at December 31, 2014, that qualify and are accounted for using the fair value through other comprehensive income (FV-OCI) method:

	Quantity	Percent Interest	Cost per Share	Fair Value per Share
Frank Inc.	2,000 shares	8%	$11	$16
Ellis Corp.	5,000 shares	14%	23	19
Mendota Ltd.	4,000 shares	2%	31	24

Early in 2015, Harper sold all the Frank Inc. shares for $17 per share, less a 1% commission on the sale. On December 31, 2015, Harper's portfolio consists of the following common shares:

	Quantity	Percent Interest	Cost	Fair Value per Share
Ellis Corp.	5,000 shares	14%	$23	$28
Mendota Ltd.	4,000 shares	2%	31	23
Kaptein Inc.	2,000 shares	1%	25	22

Assume Harper reports net income of $158,300 for its year ended December 31, 2015, and the company follows a policy of capitalizing transaction costs and of transferring realized gains and losses from accumulated other comprehensive income directly to retained earnings.

Instructions

(a) What should be reported on Harper's December 31, 2014 statement of financial position for this long-term portfolio?

(b) What should be reported on Harper's December 31, 2015 statement of financial position for these investments?

(c) What should be reported on Harper's 2015 statement of comprehensive income for the investments accounted for using the FV-OCI model? Prepare a partial 2015 statement of comprehensive income for Harper.

(d) Assuming that comparative financial statements for 2014 and 2015 are presented in 2015, draft the footnote that is necessary for full disclosure of Harper's transactions and investments.

Digging
Deeper

(e) As a potential investor in Harper Corporation, explain what information the other comprehensive income portion of the statement of comprehensive income provides to you.

P9-10   Fellows Inc., a publicly traded manufacturing company in the technology industry, has a November 30 fiscal year end. The company grew rapidly during its first 10 years and made three public offerings during this period. During its rapid growth period, Fellows acquired common shares in Yukasato Inc. and Admin Importers.

In 2003, Fellows acquired 25% of Yukasato's common shares for $588,000 and accounts for this investment using the equity method. The book value of Yukasato's net assets at the date of purchase is $1.8 million. The excess of the purchase price over the book value of the net assets relates to assets that are subject to amortization. These assets have a remaining life of 20 years. For its fiscal year ended November 30, 2014, Yukasato Inc. reported net income of $250,000 and paid dividends of $100,000.

In 2005, Fellows acquired 10% of Admin Importers' common shares for $204,000 and accounts for this investment as a financial asset at fair value through other comprehensive income (FV-OCI).

Fellows also has a policy of investing idle cash in equity securities to generate short-term profits. The following data are for Fellows' trading investment portfolio:

TRADING INVESTMENTS (USING THE FV-NI MODEL)
at November 30, 2013

	Cost	Fair Value
Craxi Electric	$326,000	$314,000
Renoir Inc.	184,000	181,000
Seferis Inc.	95,000	98,500
Total	$605,000	$593,500

INVESTMENTS (USING THE FV-OCI MODEL)
at November 30, 2013

Admin Importers	$204,000	$198,000

TRADING INVESTMENTS (USING THE FV-NI MODEL)
at November 30, 2014

	Cost	Fair Value
Craxi Electric	$326,000	$323,000
Renoir Inc.	184,000	180,000
Mer Limited	105,000	108,000
Total	$615,000	$611,000

INVESTMENTS (USING THE FV-OCI MODEL)
at November 30, 2014

Admin Importers	$204,000	$205,000

On November 14, 2014, Ted Yan was hired by Fellows as assistant controller. His first assignment was to prepare the entries to record the November activity and the November 30, 2014 year-end adjusting entries for the current trading investments and the investment in common shares of Admin Importers. Using Fellows' ledger of investment transactions and the data given above, Yan proposed the following entries and submitted them to Julie O'Brien, controller, for review:

ENTRY 1 (NOVEMBER 8, 2014)

Cash	99,500	
FV-NI Investments		98,500
Investment Income or Loss		1,000

(To record the sale of Seferis Inc. shares for $99,500)

ENTRY 2 (NOVEMBER 26, 2014)

FV-NI Investments	105,000	
Cash		105,000

(To record the purchase of Mer common shares for $102,200 plus brokerage fees of $2,800)

ENTRY 3 (NOVEMBER 30, 2014)

Investment Income or Loss	3,000	
Allowance for Investment Impairment		3,000

(To recognize a loss equal to the excess of cost over fair value of equity securities)

ENTRY 4 (NOVEMBER 30, 2014)

Cash	38,500	
Investment Income or Loss		38,500

(To record the following dividends received from investments: Yukasato Inc. $25,000; Admin Importers $9,000; and Craxi Electric $4,500)

ENTRY 5 (NOVEMBER 30, 2014)

Investment in Associate	62,500	
Investment Income or Loss		62,500

(To record share of Yukasato Inc. income under the equity method, $250,000 × 0.25)

Instructions

(a) The journal entries proposed by Ted Yan will establish the value of Fellows' equity investments to be reported on the company's external financial statements. Review each journal entry and indicate whether or not it is in accordance with the applicable accounting standards, assuming the company has adopted the recognition and measurement standards of IFRS 9 *Financial Instruments*. If an entry is incorrect, prepare the correct entry(ies) that should have been made.

Digging Deeper

(b) Because Fellows owns more than 20% of Yukasato Inc., Julie O'Brien has adopted the equity method to account for this investment. Under what circumstances would it be inappropriate to use the equity method to account for a 25% interest in the common shares of Yukasato Inc.? If the equity method is not appropriate in this case, what method would you recommend? Why?

(c) Are there any differences between the characteristics of trading investments accounted for using the FV-NI model and investments accounted for using the FV-OCI model in general? Explain. Are there any differences in the specific case of Fellows Inc.'s investments?

P9-11 On January 1, 2014, Melbourne Corporation, a public company, acquired 15,000 of the 50,000 outstanding common shares of Noah Corp. for $25 per share. The statement of financial position of Noah reported the following information at the date of the acquisition:

Assets not subject to depreciation	$290,000
Assets subject to depreciation	860,000
Liabilities	150,000

Additional information:

1. On the acquisition date, the fair value is the same as the carrying amount for the assets that are not subject to depreciation and for the liabilities.

2. On the acquisition date, the fair value of the assets that are subject to depreciation is $960,000. These assets had a remaining useful life of eight years at that time.

3. Noah reported 2014 net income of $100,000 and paid dividends of $5,000 in December 2014.

4. Noah's shares are not actively traded on the stock exchange, but Melbourne has determined that they have a fair value of $24 per share on December 31, 2014.

Melbourne Corporation accounts for its FV-NI and FV-OCI investments under the provisions of IFRS 9.

Instructions

(a) Prepare the journal entries for Melbourne Corporation for 2014, assuming that Melbourne cannot exercise significant influence over Noah and accounts for the investment at fair value through other comprehensive income.

(b) Prepare the journal entries for Melbourne Corporation for 2014, assuming that Melbourne can exercise significant influence over Noah's operations.

(c) How would your answers to parts (a) and (b) change if Melbourne had acquired the Noah shares on July 2 instead of January 1?

(d) Prepare the 2014 journal entries if Melbourne Corporation were a private company applying ASPE, clearly identifying the methods of accounting you have chosen.

(e) For your answers to (d), prepare a table of the investment amount reported on the statement of financial position and the amount reported on the income statement under each approach identified. As a shareholder of Melbourne Corporation, which method of accounting do you think provides better information? Explain briefly.

Digging Deeper

P9-12   On December 31, 2013, Acker Ltd. reported the following statement of financial position.

ACKER LTD.
Statement of Financial Position
As at December 31, 2013

Assets		Equity	
FV-OCI investments	$240,000	Contributed capital	$260,000
Cash	50,000	Accumulated other comprehensive income	30,000
Total	$290,000		$290,000

The accumulated other comprehensive income was related only to the company's non-traded equity investments. The fair value of Acker Ltd.'s investments at December 31, 2014, was $185,000 and their cost was $140,000. No investments were purchased during 2014. Although Acker is a private company, it applies IFRS and recycles OCI gains and losses to net income when realized.

Acker Ltd.'s statement of net income for 2014 was as follows, ignoring income taxes.

ACKER LTD.
Statement of Net Income
Year ended December 31, 2014

Dividend income	$ 5,000
Gain on sale of equity investments	30,000
Net income	$35,000

Instructions

Assuming all transactions during the year were for cash and that no dividends were declared or paid:

(a) Prepare the journal entries related to the sale of the equity investments in 2014. (*Hint:* First identify what the balance of the accumulated other comprehensive income account represents.)

(b) Prepare a statement of comprehensive income for 2014.

(c) Prepare a statement of financial position as at December 31, 2014.

(d) Assume that Acker Ltd. applies ASPE and management had identified the equity investment as an FV-NI investment when first acquired. Identify and explain any differences in the opening balance sheet at December 31, 2013, the 2014 statement of net income, and the closing balance sheet at December 31, 2014, when the FV-NI method is used instead of the method used under the original IFRS assumption.

Digging Deeper

P9-13   Minute Corp., a Canadian public corporation, reported the following on its December 31, 2013 statement of financial position:

	$
Investment in Hysenaj Ltd. shares, at fair value through net income: 6,400 shares, original cost of $251,540	316,300
Investment in Growthpen Corp. shares, at fair value through OCI, without recycling: 4,000 shares, original cost of $28,800	26,100
Investment in Metal Corp. bonds, at amortized cost: $500,000 face value, 6% bonds, due November 1, 2018, interest paid each May 1 and November 1 to yield 5% (See Note 1)	521,227
Interest receivable on Metal Corp. bonds	5,000
Shareholders' equity	
Accumulated other comprehensive income: unrealized loss on Growthpen Corp. shares	2,700

Additional information:

1. The bond amortization table used by Minute Corp. for this bond indicated the following for the November 1, 2013 interest received and interest income:

Date	Interest Received	Interest Income	Premium Amortization	Balance, Bond Carryng Amount
Nov. 1/13	15,000	13,095	1,905	521,878

Hint: On December 31, 2013, Minute's accountant pencilled in the following numbers below the November 1, 2013 line:

Date	Interest Received	Interest Income	Premium Amortization	Balance, Bond Carryng Amount
Dec. 31/13 adjustment	5,000	4,349	651	521,227

2. Minute Corp. follows the provisions of IFRS 9 for its FV-NI and FV-OCI investments, using the FV-NI method for investments acquired for trading purposes, and the FV-OCI method for investments that it intends to hold for their growth potential. For the FV-OCI investments, transaction costs are capitalized, and when gains and losses are realized, they are reclassified to retained earnings. Interest and dividends are not reported separately from other investment income for investments held for trading and accounted for at FV-NI.

The following transactions and events took place during the company's year ending December 31, 2014:

Jan.   2 Sold 1,000 Growthpen shares for $8.50 per share less a $300 commission. (*Hint:* Remember that only 25% of the holdings have been sold.)

Jan.   3 Purchased 3,600 of the 12,000 outstanding shares of Lloyd Corp. for $234,000. Minute Corp. and Lloyd Corp. managements have worked together on joint projects in the past and Lloyd often asks Minute management for advice on operational and financing issues that Lloyd faces. A review of Lloyd's financial statements on the date these shares were acquired indicated total assets of $1.4 million and total liabilities of $750,000. In addition, the company has an internally developed patent that has a fair value of $60,000, but which is unrecorded in the accounts. The patent is likely to have value to Lloyd for another six years.

Mar. 18 Received a $1 per share dividend on Growthpen shares and a $3 per share dividend on Hysenaj shares.

May   1 Received the semi-annual interest on the Metal Corp. bonds.

June 30 Sold the Metal Corp. bonds for 102 plus accrued interest. (*Hint:* Start by making an entry to accrue the interest income on the bonds to June 30, then make an entry to record the cash received.)

Sept. 17 Sold all the shares of Hysenaj for $58 per share. Paid a 1% commission.

Oct. 15 Received a dividend of $1 per share on the Lloyd Corp. shares.

Dec. 31 Lloyd Corp. management reported that the company earned a net income of $48,000 for its year ended December 31, 2014.

Dec. 31 The fair values of the remaining investments are: Growthpen Corp. $7 per share; Lloyd Corp. $217,800.

Instructions

(a) Showing all calculations, prepare all required entries during 2014 and at December 31, 2014, if necessary, for the transactions and adjustments relating to the investments in the Hysenaj Corp. shares, the Growthpen Corp. shares, the Metal Corp. bonds, and the Lloyd Corp. shares.

(b) Determine the December 31, 2014 balances in each asset account related to the investments and in accumulated other comprehensive income. Prepare a partial statement of financial position, indicating where and how each of the investments and AOCI would be reported.

Digging Deeper

(c) Determine the December 31, 2014 balances in each income and OCI account related to the investments. Assuming Minute Corp. reports a net income of $1,422,600, including all revenue, expense, gain, and loss accounts that are correctly included in net income, prepare a statement of comprehensive income for Minute's year ended December 31, 2014.

(d) After Minute Corp.'s December 31, 2014 financial statements were released, the members of an investment club met to look at Minute as a possible investment. The club members were not familiar with the term "accumulated other comprehensive income" that they saw on the statement of financial position. Explain what the balance in this account represents using terms the club members would understand.

Cases

Refer to the Case Primer on the student website and in *WileyPLUS* to help you answer these cases.

CA9-1   Investment Company Limited (ICL) is a private company owned by 10 doctors. The company's objective is to manage the doctors' investment portfolios. It actually began as an investment club 10 years ago. At that time, each doctor invested equal amounts of cash and the group met every other week to determine where the money should be invested. Eventually, they decided to incorporate the company and each doctor now owns one tenth of the voting shares. The company employs two managers who look after the business full-time and make the investment decisions with input from the owners. Earnings per year after taxes now average $1.5 million. During the year, the following transactions took place:

Investment A (IA): Purchased common shares of IA for $1 million. IA allows researchers to use expensive lab equipment (which is owned by the company) on a pay-per-use basis. These shares represent 15% of the total outstanding common shares of the company. Because of its percentage ownership, ICL is allowed to appoint one member of IA's board of directors. There are three members on the board. One of the ICL owners has also been hired as a consultant to the company to advise on equipment acquisitions. The company is unsure of how long it will keep the shares. At least two of the company owners are interested in holding on to the investments for the longer term as they use the services of IA. The fair value of the shares of IA is determined annually by a valuations expert.

Investment B (IB): Purchased preferred shares of IB representing 25% of the total outstanding shares. The shares will likely be resold within two months, although no decision has yet been made. The fair value of this investment is known.

Investment C (IC): Purchased 25% interest in voting common shares of IC for $1 million two years ago. The current carrying amount is $950,000 since the company has been in the drug development stage. IC develops drug delivery technology. In the past week, a major drug on which the company has spent large amounts (approximately $10 million) for research and development was declined by the Food and Drug Administration for sale in the United States. Most of the $10 million had previously been capitalized in the financial statements of IC. This is a significant blow to IC as it had been projecting that 50% of its future revenues would come from this drug. IC does not produce financial statements until two months after ICL's year end.

Although the investments have been mainly in private companies so far, the doctors are thinking of revising their investment strategy and investing in more public companies. They feel that the stock market is poised for recovery, and are therefore planning to borrow some funds for investment. The accountant is currently reviewing the above transactions in preparation for a meeting with the bank. The company has never prepared GAAP statements before but is considering doing so. The company has not made a decision as to which GAAP to follow (IFRS or ASPE). They are not planning to early adopt IFRS 9.

Instructions

Adopt the role of the company's accountant and analyze the financial reporting issues.

CA9-2   Cando Communications (CC) is a public company that owns and operates 10 broadcast television stations and several specialty cable channels, 10 newspapers (including the *International Post*), and many other non-daily publications. It has a 57.6% economic interest in AustraliaTV (in Australia), and a 29.9% interest in UlsterTV (in Northern Ireland).

According to the notes to the annual financial statements, the company owns approximately 15% of the shares and all of the convertible and subordinated debentures of AustraliaTV. The convertible debentures are convertible into shares that would represent 50% of the company's total issued shares at the time of conversion. In total, including the debentures, the investment in AustraliaTV yields a distribution that is equivalent to 57.5% of all distributions paid by AustraliaTV. CC has a contractual right to be represented on the board of directors and has appointed three of the board's 12 members.

Although the company has made an attempt to influence the decisions made by UlsterTV management, it has been unsuccessful and does not have any representation on the board of directors.

Investments represent approximately $150 million (about 5% of total assets). Even though revenues were up by 15%, net income was only $8 million for the year end, down from $50 million the prior year. Assume that the company will not early adopt IFRS 9.

Instructions

Adopt the role of a financial analyst and analyze the financial reporting issues.

CA9-3 Impaired Investments Limited (IIL) is in the real estate industry. Last year, the company divested itself of some major investments in real estate and invested the funds in several instruments as follows:

1. Investments in 5% bonds: currently carried at amortized cost

2. Investments in common shares (no significant influence or control and not held for trading)—Company A: currently carried at fair value with gains and losses booked to income

3. Investments in common shares—Company B: currently carried at fair value with gains and losses booked to other comprehensive income

During the current year, similar bonds available in the marketplace are yielding 6%. Although the company is not certain, the controller feels this may be due to greater perceived risk associated with changes in the economy and specifically the real estate industry. The investment in Company A shares is significantly below cost at year end according to market prices at year end (Company A's shares trade on a stock exchange). The investment in Company B shares is also below cost but the controller feels that this is just a temporary decline and not necessarily an impairment. The shares of Company B also trade on a stock exchange.

IIL is currently a private entity but has recently considered going public, perhaps in the next five years, and plans to adopt IFRS this year. It will also adopt IFRS 9.

Instructions

Adopt the role of the controller and discuss the financial reporting issues related to the IIL financial statements.

Integrated Case

IC9-1 EMI Inc. is a public company that operates numerous movie theatres in Canada. Historically, it operated as a trust and its business model consisted of distributing all of its earnings to shareholders through dividends. As a result of tax changes two years ago, it converted to a corporation and adopted a strategy of using its excess cash to invest in short-term and strategic investments. Some of EMI's investment transactions for 2014 are identified below.

In the last quarter of 2013, EMI purchased 40% of the outstanding voting shares of ABC. ABC is a movie distributor and has a contract with EMI whereby it pays management fees to EMI for two of EMI's executives to participate in its strategic committee. Also, as part of the investment, one member from EMI's board of directors is eligible to participate as a member on ABC's board of 12 executive members. Just before year end, EMI signed as a guarantor for ABC's newly issued debt, which it will use to build new movie theatres. EMI agreed to the arrangement provided it could use ABC's existing movie theatres as future collateral. ABC is also a public company and of the remaining 60% of shares, no individual shareholder holds more than 1% of outstanding shares. EMI is unsure of how to treat this strategic investment.

At the beginning of the year, EMI invested some of its excess money in corporate bonds with a face value of $100,000, for $94,758. The bonds pay a 6% semi-annual interest rate and provide an effective interest rate of 8% over three years. The bonds mature on January 1, 2017. Management has purchased similar corporate bonds in the past for short-term profits and continues to do so with its existing bonds. However, in the annual board meeting, management had stated its intent of holding these particular corporate bonds as an investment for earning income. EMI has the ability to hold the investment to maturity. EMI is unsure of how to record the investment upon inception and the initial subsequent semi-annual interest payment.

EMI also invested funds into two stock portfolios, A and B. Management's intention for the investment is unclear; however, in the past, similar stock portfolios were purchased with the intention of holding only to generate a short-term gain. Portfolio A consists of a 5% ownership of shares in a publicly traded company, Masrani Corp., for a total investment of $25,000. Portfolio B consists of a 3% ownership in another private movie theatre, for a total investment of $15,000. Transaction costs for both portfolios were 2% of the purchase price. At year end, the fair value of portfolio A had dropped to $19,222. EMI is unsure of the method of measurement for each portfolio investment.

As EMI's shares are trading on the capital market, its financial information and filings are tracked by an equity analyst who produces quarterly analyst reports. These reports are used by shareholders and future investors as an independent review of EMI's results. It is now year end and management is preparing for a meeting with its equity analyst to review its accounting policies. The board of directors is expected to approve the financial statements after the meeting with the analyst.

An excerpt from EMI's 2014 financial statements is below.

Consolidated Balance Sheet

As of December 31, 2014

Assets

Cash and cash equivalents (Note 1)	$1,890,877
Accounts receivable	567,321
Inventory	36,455
Securities	
Bonds—FVTPL, available for sale, and held to maturity (Note 2)	756,210
Portfolio investments (FVTPL, available for sale) (Note 3)	899,321
Total Current Assets	4,150,184
Fixed Assets	
Property, plant, and equipment	
Accumulated depreciation	12,321,888
Net fixed assets	(3,490,211)
Long-term investments	8,831,677
Deferred tax assets	21,999
Goodwill	563,422
Total Assets	**22,398,959**

Instructions

Assume the role of EMI's equity analyst and complete an analysis of EMI's required application of accounting policies for investments. Discuss any choices and differences between IFRS and ASPE. Assume that EMI will not early adopt IFRS 9.

Writing Assignments

WA9-1   Fran Song looked at the consolidated financial statements of Vixen Manufacturing Limited and shook her head. "I was asked to look at the accounting for Vixen's investments," she said, "but I can't find any investments listed on the balance sheet!" Fran has just begun her work term with Potts and Palmer, a CGA firm in public practice, and she has approached you for help.

Instructions

(a) Explain to Fran what type of investments Vixen likely holds and how they have been accounted for.

(b) Explain the rationale for the reporting standards for this type of investment.

(c) Identify what other evidence there might be on the financial statements that would indicate the existence of this type of investment.

WA9-2   Addison Manufacturing holds a large portfolio of debt securities as an investment. The fair value of the portfolio is greater than its original cost, even though some securities have decreased in value. Ted Abernathy, the financial vice-president, and Donna Nottebart, the controller, are in the process of classifying this securities portfolio in accordance with the new IFRS standard (IFRS 9) for the first time. Abernathy wants to classify all investments that have increased in value during the period as fair value through net income in order to increase net income this year. He wants to account for all the securities that have decreased in value at amortized cost.

Nottebart disagrees. She tells Abernathy that there are no options now under IFRS. Depending on certain criteria, the debt instruments must be classified into the amortized cost category or the fair value through net income category. Assume the role of the ethical accountant. You work for Addison Manufacturing and Abernathy and Nottebart have asked for your advice regarding the application of IFRS 9.

Ethics

Instructions

In your role as the ethical accountant, respond to the following questions assuming that the company has no issues related to accounting mismatches.

(a) Is Nottebart correct in that there are no choices for the classification of debt instruments?

(b) For each of the following types of debt instruments, determine, by referring to the newly issued IFRS 9, if the debt security would be measured at amortized cost or fair value.

    1. A debt instrument has a variable rate of interest and matures in 2015. The variable rate is based on the prime bank lending rate and pays 2% above prime. The company has, in the past, bought and sold these bonds and not held them until maturity.

    2. A 5% bond, issued by Exnon Inc., is convertible into equity at the holder's option. If Addison decides to receive shares rather than cash, the conversion rate to be used is a price of $50 per share of Exnon Inc. Addison will likely request to convert to shares when the share price of Exnon is over $55 per share or more.

3. A corporate bond pays interest that is linked to an inflation index. The company expects to hold on to this bond until it matures.

4. A perpetual bond (meaning it has no maturity date), issued by Resource Inc., can be called at any point by the issuer. If the bond is called, Addison will receive the face value of the bond plus any accrued interest. In addition, interest can only be paid on the bond if Resource Inc. meets certain solvency tests, before and after the payment of the interest. The company plans to hold this debt investment in perpetuity.

WA9-3 It is July 31, 2013, and you have just started working for Andrelli Corp. as part of the controller's group involved in current financial reporting problems. Kameela Franklin, controller for Andrelli, is interested in your accounting background because the company has several different types of investments and is wondering how to report them. The company is currently a private entity but is thinking of adopting IFRS. The following are the investments for which the controller is trying to determine what the appropriate accounting treatment would be under ASPE or the IFRS 9 standard, which the company would adopt early.

Situation 1
The company invests excess cash in term deposits that mature in six months and bear interest at 1%. The company holds on to these investments until maturity to receive the cash flows at the maturity date.

Situation 2
Andrelli has an investment in shares of Warren Corp. in which it owns 10% of the voting shares. Warren Corp. is a private company and therefore the shares are not publicly traded.

Situation 3
A corporate bond investment will come due in 2019 and pays interest at a fixed rate of 8%. The company's intention is to hold this until maturity and use the cash flows from the interest payments to help fund operations.

Situation 4
The company invests in money market funds, again using excess cash. The company cashes in these investments as cash is required.

Situation 5
The company has purchased 20% of the common shares of a supplier and has been able to get three of its nominees elected to the supplier's 10-person board of directors. The supplier reported record earnings of $100,000 this year, but unfortunately was not able to pay out a dividend.

Instructions

(a) Under ASPE, what is the effect on the balance sheet and earnings of each of the independent situations above?

(b) Under IFRS 9, what is the effect on the statement of financial position and earnings of each of the independent situations above?

WA9-4 On July 1, 2014, Munns Corp. purchased for cash 25% of the outstanding shares of Huber Corporation. Both Munns and Huber have a December 31 year end. Huber Corporation, whose common shares are actively traded on the Toronto Stock Exchange, paid a cash dividend on November 15, 2014, to Munns Corp. and its other shareholders. Huber also reported net income for 2014 of $920,000.

Instructions

(a) Assuming that Munns Corp. follows IFRS, prepare a one-page memorandum on how Munns Corp. should report the above facts on its December 31, 2014 statement of financial position and its 2014 income statement, and also state what additional disclosure might be required in the notes to the financial statements. In your memo, identify and describe the method of valuation that you recommend. If additional information is needed, identify what other information would be necessary or useful. Address your memo to the chief accountant at Munns Corp. and provide reasons for your choices as much as possible.

(b) If Munns reported under ASPE, what other alternatives would be available?

WA9-5 The International Accounting Standards Board (IASB) is proposing the use of the expected loss model to determine impairment losses for financial assets measured using the cost or amortized cost basis. Currently, the incurred loss model is used under IFRS and ASPE.

An entity has made an investment in a debt instrument that is for $1 million and will pay interest at 5% for the next five years until 2019. The investment is bought at par, and the effective interest rate is 5%, assuming no future credit losses. In determining expected future credit losses, the effective interest rate incorporating these future expected credit losses is only 4.2%.

Instructions

Using the facts from the example above, compare and contrast the expected loss model and the incurred loss model with respect to the following issues:

(a) How is the debt investment initially recorded and the effective rate of interest determined?

(b) When is the impairment loss measured?

(c) How is the revised carrying amount measured? Where is the impairment loss recorded?

(d) When are reversals of the impairment determined and reported?

WA9-6   Write a brief essay highlighting the differences between IFRS and ASPE noted in this chapter, discussing the conceptual justification for each.

WA9-7   Write a short essay (one or two pages) describing the incurred loss model and the expected loss model of impairment. Summarize each model and compare the two models, indicating the potential benefits and drawbacks of each. Which model do you think provides the more transparent information to users?

WA9-8   Discuss the three objectives of disclosure of financial instruments under ASPE and IFRS. In your discussion explain how specific disclosure requirements meet these objectives.

WA9-9   Consider the following types of investments and explain whether they are debt or equity instruments. Provide one or two reasons for each as to why a company might choose this investment.

(a) 10,000 Class A voting shares in One Corp. with a market value of $225,500. The shares pay a 4% annual dividend.

(b) A loan to Two Inc. for $2 million with 8% interest payable semi-annually and the principal to be repaid in 10 years

(c) A loan to Three Company for $500,000 that is due in five years, with 5% interest due annually. The loan can be converted into 5,000 common shares of Three Company at any time during the five-year loan period.

RESEARCH AND FINANCIAL ANALYSIS

RA9-1 Shoppers Drug Mart

Real World Emphasis

Refer to the annual financial statements of **Shoppers Drug Mart** for its fiscal year ended December 31, 2011, found in Appendix 5B.

Instructions

(a) Review Shoppers Drug Mart's balance sheet. Identify all financial investments that are reported. You may need to read the notes to the financial statements to get the necessary details.

(b) Does Shoppers Drug Mart have any investments in subsidiary companies? Does it own 100% of all its subsidiaries? Can you tell this by looking at the balance sheet? At the income statement? What information is disclosed about these subsidiaries?

(c) Did Shoppers acquire any companies during the year? Explain the process you undertook to determine the answer to this question.

RA9-2 Royal Bank of Canada

Real World Emphasis

Refer to the 2011 financial statements and accompanying notes of **Royal Bank of Canada** (RBC) that are found on the company's website (www.royalbank.ca) or www.sedar.com.

Instructions

(a) What percentage of total assets is held in investments (2011 versus 2010)? Note that RBC holds a significant loan portfolio also. What is the business reason for holding loans versus securities? Comment on how the investments are classified and presented on the balance sheet.

(b) What percentage of total interest income comes from securities (2011 versus 2010)? Are there any other lines on the income statement relating to securities? What percentage of net income relates to securities (2011 versus 2010)? Calculate an approximate return on the investments in securities. Comment on the return, while looking at the nature of the securities that are being invested in.

(c) Read the notes to the financial statements that are about securities and note the valuation method.

RA9-3 Research Issue—Variable Interest Entities

Variable interest entities (VIEs) is a very complex topic and continues to be high on the agendas of the accounting standard-setting communities around the world. Part of the recent global credit crisis, as well as the fall of Enron, was a result of the use and non-consolidation of variable interest entities.

Instructions

Research and write a one- to two-page report on variable interest entities. What is a VIE? What is the accounting issue that needs resolution? How is the International Accounting Standards Board proposing to deal with this issue? Identify at least one company that has a VIE and discuss how the investment was reported.

RA9-4 Potash Corporation of Saskatchewan

Instructions

Real World Emphasis

Gain access to the 2011 financial statements of **Potash Corporation of Saskatchewan** from the company's website (www.potashcorp.com) or www.sedar.com.

(a) Based on the information contained in these financial statements, determine each of the following for Potash:

1. Cash used in (for) investing activities during 2011 and 2010 (from the statement of cash flows)

2. Cash used for purchases of long-term investments during 2011 and 2010

3. Total investment in unconsolidated affiliates (or investments and other assets) at December 31, 2011 and 2010

(b) What conclusions about the management of investments can be drawn from the data in part (a)?

(c) Briefly identify from the notes Potash's investments reported under the equity method. Describe these investments, the amount of voting control, and the fair value of each investment. How much cash was received from dividends and how much was reported as Potash's portion of the investee's net income? Where is this income reported?

(d) Describe each investment and the amount of voting control of the other types of investments in long-term investments. What method of accounting has the company used for these?

(e) Explain the impairment assessment that is discussed in the notes by Potash for 2011 and explain the event that triggered this impairment assessment discussion and what other factors Potash considered in its conclusion.

ENDNOTES

[1] IAS 39 introduces the labels "held to maturity," "available for sale," and "held for trading." These are defined terms for investments under the standard. Although the standard notes that the labels do not need to be used, many companies do indeed use these labels. We will define these labels later in the chapter.

[2] Brokerage commissions are usually incurred when buying and selling most securities. Commissions vary with the share value and the number of shares/units purchased, but they are often between 1% and 3% of the trade value for smaller trades. For larger trades, the commissions are often substantially lower as a percentage. Discount brokerages offer significant discounts even on smaller trades. Transactions involving mutual funds may have no commission attached to them (no-load funds) but a commission may be charged when the funds are redeemed (back-end commission).

[3] Companies also have a choice of when to recognize (and derecognize) the financial asset. This could be on the trade date, when the commitment is made to buy or sell, or on the settlement date, when the asset is delivered and title is transferred—usually a short time thereafter. When the period between these dates is the standard term for the instrument and the market—termed a **regular-way purchase or sale**—either trade-date or settlement-date accounting may be used. Canadian equities settle in three business days. The same policy is applied consistently to all purchases and sales that belong to the same category of financial asset and the policy that is chosen is disclosed. This chapter's illustrations assume that trade and settlement dates are the same.

[4] It is interesting to note how accounting for investments at fair value may have influenced the proposed revenues and lease standards. Accounting for financial instruments such as investments and derivatives reflects a contract-based approach, which is the approach currently under discussion for revenues and leases. In addition, the accounting standards for financial instruments have also helped move our thinking forward regarding embracing fair value as opposed to historical cost for measurement purposes.

[5] If the instrument's "cost" and face value are the same, the method is applied in the same way as for an investment in shares except that interest income is recognized instead of dividend income.

[6] As previously indicated, the value is determined by the investment community and is equal to the present value (PV) of the cash inflows of principal and interest payments on the bond, discounted at the market rate. This is relatively straightforward if the bond is bought or sold on its issue date or on an interest payment due date. At other times, a bond's purchase price can be estimated as follows:

PV of cash flows on the immediately preceding interest payment date	= $x
Add the increase in PV to date of sale or purchase at yield rate:	
$x × annual yield rate × portion of year since interest payment date	= y
Deduct the cash interest earned since last interest payment date:	
Face value × annual stated rate × portion of year since last interest date	= (z)
Purchase price of a bond bought or sold between interest payment dates:	x + y − z

[7] IFRS 7 *Financial Instruments: Disclosures* indicates in paragraph B5(e) that entities may disclose whether the net gains or losses on financial assets measured at fair value through profit or loss (FV-NI) and reported on the income statement include interest and dividend income. ASPE, on the other hand, requires separate reporting (*CICA Handbook–Accounting*, Part II, Section 3856.52).

[8] Certainly management's ability to earn a return and realize gains on the investments is relevant. In addition, the entity has to keep track in its files of the securities' original cost because only realized gains and losses are taxable or deductible for tax purposes.

[9] ASPE does not make use of OCI.

[10] Intraperiod tax allocation requires that the unrealized holding gains and losses be recognized in other comprehensive income, net of tax. This is explained more fully in Chapter 18. The illustrations that follow do not include the related taxes to simplify the examples.

[11] Under IAS 39, changes in fair value that represent an impairment loss were transferred out of OCI and into net income. IFRS 9 does not recognize these revaluations as impairment losses.

[12] The FV-OCI model with no recycling argues that the gains and losses need only be recognized once and that is in other comprehensive income. There is no need to recognize realized gains and losses through net income.

[13] IAS 39 also allows debt securities to be accounted for using the FV-OCI model. In that case, interest is recognized in net income (including amortization of premiums and discounts per IAS 39.55).

[14] Joint ventures are another type of equity investment. Since they can be incorporated companies, they can issue shares. **Joint ventures** are characterized by joint control (versus unilateral control). This is

usually shown through a contractual agreement that states that the venturers (investors) must share key decision-making.

[15] IAS 28 *Investments in Associates*, para. 3.

[16] *CICA Handbook–Accounting*, Part II, Section 3051.04.

[17] IAS 28 identifies some exceptions. These include investments in associates that are held for sale and those reported by a parent that is not required to prepare consolidated financial statements.

[18] A third aspect involves eliminating the effects of unrealized inter-company gains and losses. This issue and situations where investors pay less for the shares than their proportionate interest in the identifiable net assets of the associate (that is, "negative goodwill") are topics for an advanced accounting course.

[19] **Value in use** refers to the present value of the cash flows expected to be generated from holding the investment, discounted at an appropriate current market rate of interest.

[20] The types of risk that are associated with financial assets in general—credit, liquidity, and market risk—are discussed more fully in Chapter 16.

Cumulative Coverage: Chapters 6 to 9

Posh Hotels Ltd. (PHL) is a small boutique hotel that provides 38 suites that can be rented by the day, week, or month. Food service is available through room service as well. In addition, there are two suites that have been rented on a long-term basis to corporate tenants, who have access to their suite anytime throughout the year without making a reservation. The company has a December 31 year end, and you are preparing the year-end financial statements using ASPE.

The following issues require your consideration:

1. Cash
   - The hotel keeps a significant amount of euro currency on hand to meet the needs of its guests. At year end, there was € 12,000 on hand. The year-end exchange rate was $1.35, and the average rate for the year was $1.42.
   - The bank statement balance at December 31 was $158,293. There were outstanding cheques of $52,375 and an outstanding deposit of $15,487. Bank charges per the bank statement were $65 for the month of December and have been recorded.

2. Accounts receivable and allowance for doubtful accounts
   - The hotel charges $150 per night for accommodation in one of the rental suites, and guests pay at the end of their stay, with daily revenue being accrued as it is earned. At December 31, the amount outstanding from short-term guests was $10,500. At year end, management expects to be unable to collect an amount equal to 5% of the outstanding receivables for this type of suite. During the year, sales amounted to $1,750,000, and the balance in Allowance for Doubtful Accounts at the end of the previous year was $15,000. During the year, $32,000 in accounts was written off.
   - The two corporate suites are rented for $45,000 per year. The payment for these longer term rentals is due in advance each July 1 for the following 12 months. One of these corporate suites has been in use for part of the year, but the corporate tenant went bankrupt, and was unable to pay the $45,000 fee. Hotel management had hoped the tenant would eventually be able to pay, and it allowed the company to use the suite until the end of October. Since then, the hotel has been in negotiations with the bankruptcy accountant, and expects to eventually receive a settlement of $10,000. The balance will become uncollectible; no allowance for doubtful accounts has been recorded with respect to these suites as there have never been collection problems in the past.

3. Inventory
   - PHL follows a policy of FIFO costing, and values items at the lower of cost and market based on an individual item basis.
   - The hotel has a standing weekly order at set prices with a local catering firm. If the food is not eaten before the next delivery is received, it is donated to the local women's shelter. This ensures that all meals are of appropriate quality for the hotel guests.
   - On December 31, the following items were delivered:

Item	Unit Cost	Net Realizable Value
40 chicken dinners	$5	$12
35 beef dinners	$6	$15
75 frozen vegetable servings	$1	$ 2
75 units of fresh fruit	$1	$ 2
100 desserts	$3	$ 5

   - The invoice for the food delivery on December 31 included an additional delivery charge of $0.10 per item, totalling $32.50.
   - Overnight on December 31, an ice storm resulted in a loss of electricity to the hotel building. As a result, 20 chicken and 10 beef dinners thawed, and were unusable.
   - The hotel also maintains an inventory of white terry cloth bathrobes and towels that are available for sale to their clients. At December 31, the following information is available:

Product	Quantity	Cost/unit	Selling price/unit
Bathrobes, assorted sizes	40	$49.50	$85.00
Towels, extra-large	25	$19.30	$18.00*
Towels, large	20	$15.00	$28.00

*The extra-large towels are no longer popular and management has decided to discontinue them. It offers the hotel staff a 20% commission for all extra-large towels they sell at the sale price of $18.00.

4. Investments

- On December 1, PHL purchased a $100,000, 90-day Canadian government treasury bill for $98,039 to yield 8%.

- During the year, PHL purchased 30% of the shares in Western Hotel Company, a company that owns a similar hotel property in a nearby city, for $5 million, a price corresponding to 30% of its book value. Subsequently, Western Hotel Company paid a dividend totalling $100,000 and earned income of $250,000. PHL management has decided to use the equity method to account for this investment.

- PHL also purchased common shares of Dufort Corp. as a temporary investment for $48,000. At the end of the year, these shares had a fair value of $47,000, according to its December 31 closing price on the Toronto Stock Exchange. A dividend of $500 was received during the year.

Instructions

(a) Determine the amount to be disclosed on the balance sheet under the following headings:

    1. Cash and cash equivalents

    2. Accounts receivable

    3. Allowance for doubtful accounts

    4. Inventory

    5. Investment in Dufort Corp.

    6. Investment in Western Hotel Company

    7. Unearned revenue

    8. Investment income

    9. Bad debt expense

(b) What other specific note disclosures will be required based on the information provided?

Moving to Fair Value

TORONTO, ONT. – Toronto-based Brookfield Asset Management Inc. is a global alternative asset manager with over $150 billion in assets under management. The company has over a 100-year history of owning and operating assets with a focus on property, renewable power, infrastructure, and private equity in Canada and around the world.

With so much property, plant, and equipment (PP&E) under management, asset valuations are a critical component of Brookfield's business model. The company has always internally measured the fair value of its PP&E, so management would know how much Brookfield's assets were actually worth. But it reported these balances under its previous accounting framework, Canadian GAAP, using the historical cost method, which depreciated PP&E based on their actual cost, over a number of years. For example, "we have owned some of our power plants for over 50 years. Under Canadian GAAP, we had fully depreciated some of these assets and the amount of financing placed on the assets has increased to reflect their current value, resulting in a negative net asset value," says Derek Gorgi, Brookfield's Senior Vice President Finance.

IFRS, however, allows public companies to utilize the fair value method for PP&E. Partly because of this, Brookfield adopted IFRS one year earlier than required. "We elected to use the fair value method because, in our perspective, it provides shareholders better information about the value of our assets," Mr. Gorgi says.

The move to IFRS and fair value for reporting for the company's PP&E had a material impact on Brookfield's financial statements. For example, when it accounted for its power assets at fair value, "we recognized approximately a $5-billion fair value adjustment to record these assets at their current values from increases in the value of the assets since acquisition and the fact that we had depreciated them," he says. All told, the move to fair value under IFRS from Canadian GAAP doubled the common equity reported on Brookfield's consolidated balance sheet to $11.3 billion.

While the company feels the move to IFRS was overall very positive, the international standards do present some challenges. For example, Brookfield's different asset classes are treated differently for valuation and recognition purposes. Its commercial (office and retail) properties are considered investment properties, and its timber assets are considered biological assets. Both of these asset classes are fair valued through net income; they are not depreciated. On the other hand, its power plants and infrastructure are considered to be PP&E. These assets are recorded at fair value (because the company elects to do so) annually via other comprehensive income but depreciated quarterly through net income. Furthermore, other asset classes are carried at historical cost. "Net income only includes certain of our asset revaluations, while others are recorded through other comprehensive income or not at all," Mr. Gorgi says.

Property, Plant, and Equipment: Accounting Model Basics

LEARNING OBJECTIVES

After studying this chapter, you should be able to:

1. Understand the importance of property, plant, and equipment from a business perspective.

2. Identify the characteristics of property, plant, and equipment assets.

3. Identify the recognition criteria for property, plant, and equipment.

4. Identify the costs to include in the measurement of property, plant, and equipment assets at acquisition.

5. Determine asset cost when the transaction has delayed payment terms or is a lump-sum purchase, a nonmonetary exchange, or a contributed asset.

6. Identify the costs included in specific types of property, plant, and equipment.

7. Understand and apply the cost model.

8. Understand the revaluation model and apply it using the asset adjustment method.

9. Understand and apply the fair value model.

10. Explain and apply the accounting treatment for costs incurred after acquisition.

11. Identify differences in accounting between ASPE and IFRS, and what changes are expected in the near future.

After studying Appendix 10A, you should be able to:

12. Calculate the amount of borrowing costs to capitalize for qualifying assets.

After studying Appendix 10B, you should be able to:

13. Apply the revaluation model using the proportionate method.

PREVIEW OF CHAPTER 10

This chapter is the first of three chapters that explain the accounting, reporting, and disclosure requirements for an entity's investment in long-lived non-financial assets. Chapter 10 introduces investments in property, plant, and equipment assets and how they are accounted for at acquisition. It then sets out and explains three different accounting models that are used to measure such assets, and the accounting treatment for costs incurred after acquisition. This chapter, like those preceding it, finishes by summarizing significant differences between IFRS and ASPE requirements.

Chapter 11 continues the coverage of tangible long-lived assets by explaining how these assets are accounted for after acquisition (depreciation), when their capacity to generate future cash flows is reduced (impairment), and when they are disposed of (derecognition). This chapter also addresses significant presentation and disclosure requirements. Chapter 12 zeroes in on recognition and measurement issues related to intangible long-lived assets and goodwill.

The chapter is organized as follows:

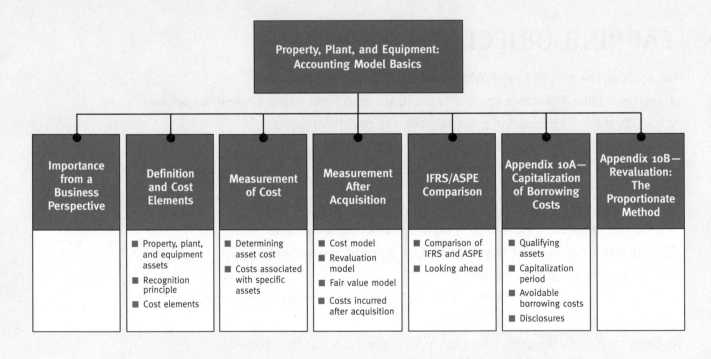

THE IMPORTANCE OF PROPERTY, PLANT, AND EQUIPMENT FROM A BUSINESS PERSPECTIVE

Objective 1
Understand the importance of property, plant, and equipment from a business perspective.

Almost every enterprise, whatever its size or activity, invests in long-lived assets. Such long-term resources include both those that are physical assets—property, plant, and equipment—and those that are intangible, such as patents. Long-lived assets are particularly important for manufacturers because these assets allow them to produce goods and/or provide services. Too much investment in long-lived assets results in costly overcapacity, and too little investment means lost opportunities for profits and future cash flows. Both situations lower the company's rate of return. To properly assess an enterprise's potential for future cash flows, users need a solid understanding of its investment in long-term productive assets, the extent to which this investment has changed in the period, and the accounting policies applied.

It is not just companies, however, that need to focus on investment in long-lived assets. Local and municipal governments often have a significant stock of long-lived assets, including buildings, roads, public transit vehicles, fleets of trucks and other vehicles used for servicing parks and open spaces, and water and sewage infrastructure. The Public Sector Accounting Board of the Canadian Institute of Chartered Accountants (CICA) has provided some guidance for municipalities and local governments as they struggle to maintain and revitalize their long-lived assets. They draw on the accounting requirements set out in the CICA's *Public Sector Accounting Handbook* and research reports on infrastructure in the public sector.[1] The federal government's Infrastructure Canada is helping to develop a long-term infrastructure plan for the federal government, provinces, territories, and municipalities.[2] While in this chapter, and the next two, we concentrate on accounting for long-lived assets by companies and the requirements of IFRS and ASPE, keep in mind that many of the issues faced by businesses also need to be considered by governments as they struggle with infrastructure renewal over the next decade and beyond.

DEFINITION AND COST ELEMENTS

Property, Plant, and Equipment Assets

Objective 2
Identify the characteristics of property, plant, and equipment assets.

Property, plant, and equipment (PP&E) include long-term resources such as office, factory, and warehouse buildings; investment property; equipment (machinery, furniture, tools); and mineral resource properties. PP&E is also commonly referred to as **tangible capital assets**, **plant assets**, or **fixed assets**.

Consistent with the terminology in IFRS, the term "depreciation" is used in this and other chapters to refer specifically to the amortization of property, plant, and equipment; "depletion" is used for the amortization of mineral resource properties; and "amortization" is used for intangibles. In addition, the term **amortization** may be used in a general sense to refer to the allocation of the cost of any long-lived asset to different accounting periods.

Let's begin by defining the types of assets dealt with in this chapter. **Property, plant, and equipment** is defined in both IAS 16 *Property, Plant, and Equipment* and in the standards that apply to private enterprises, *CICA Handbook*, Part II, Section 3061, as assets that have the following characteristics:

1. **They are held for use in the production of goods and services, for rental to others, or for administrative purposes.** They are not intended for sale in the ordinary course of business.

2. **They are used over more than one accounting period** and are usually depreciated. Property, plant, and equipment provide services over many years. Through periodic depreciation charges, the cost of the investment in these assets, with the usual exception of land, is assigned to the periods that benefit from using them.

3. **They are tangible.** These assets have a physical existence or substance, which makes them different from intangible assets such as patents or goodwill.

At times there is a fine line between what is categorized as a capital asset and what is categorized as a supply inventory. Assume, for example, that a company has a substantial fleet of trucks (capital assets) and a variety of assets related to the trucks: spare tires, major motor parts, oil and grease, and truck cleaning equipment. What type of asset is each of these? The general approach is to include any items that have multiple uses and are regularly used and replaced within the accounting period as **inventory**. Major spare parts and standby or servicing equipment used only with a specific capital asset and useful for more than one period are classified as items of **property, plant, and equipment**.

What about agricultural assets, such as trees in an apple orchard, grapevines in a vineyard, or livestock held to produce milk, wool, or additional livestock? These **biological assets**—living plants and animals—have all the characteristics necessary to be items of PP&E. Entities with such assets apply the same accounting principles used for other items of property, plant, and equipment if they report under ASPE. However, companies applying IFRS are required to follow specific standards for biological assets that are set out in IAS 41 *Agriculture*. These are briefly described later in this chapter. Biological assets were also discussed in Chapters 6 and 8.

Recognition Principle

Objective 3

Identify the recognition criteria for property, plant, and equipment.

Underlying Concept

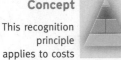

This recognition principle applies to costs incurred when an asset is first acquired and later when incurring costs to upgrade, replace, or service the asset.

Entities incur many costs, but how do they know which ones should be recognized as an item of PP&E? Assuming the resulting item meets the definition of property, plant, and equipment, accounting standards require that the following two recognition criteria be satisfied:

1. It is probable that the item's associated future economic benefits will flow to the entity.

2. Its cost can be measured reliably.

If both are met, the item is **capitalized** (included in the asset's cost) and recognized as a PP&E asset. Some costs, such as those for government-imposed pollution reduction equipment, may not appear to generate any net future cash inflows (future economic benefits), but are still recognized as property, plant, and equipment. This is because these expenditures are necessary in order to obtain the economic benefits from other assets.

If costs are incurred but recognition criteria are **not met**, the costs are recognized as an expense, such as when repair and ongoing maintenance expenditures are made.

Asset Components

While the recognition principle is clear, the standards do not specify what level of asset should be recognized. This is referred to as a **unit of measure** issue. For example, if you buy or construct a building, what items should be recognized? Should it be one asset—"building"—or should each component be recognized as a separate asset, such as the foundation and frame, roof, windows, and elevators? Alternatively, can a number of smaller items, such as individual tools, be aggregated and recognized as a single asset?

The degree of **componentization** is left up to professional judgement. A primary consideration is the **significance of the individual parts** to the "whole" asset. On a cost-benefit basis, an entity would only separate out components that make up a relatively significant portion of the asset's total cost. As explained in the depreciation discussion in Chapter 11, other factors include whether items have **differing useful lives** and/or **different patterns of delivering economic benefits** to the company, making alternative depreciation methods appropriate. The significance of the items and the similarity of their life and use are also considerations in deciding whether to aggregate smaller items into a single larger asset component. While both IFRS and ASPE speak to the need to recognize components, the discussion and application under IFRS are more fully developed.

Once an item of property, plant, and equipment meets the definition and recognition criteria, it is recognized at its cost. This raises two issues that need to be addressed:

1. What elements of cost are capitalized?

2. How is cost measured?

These questions are answered in the next two sections.

Cost Elements

In general, the **cost** of an item of property, plant, and equipment includes all expenditures needed to **acquire** the asset and bring it to its **location** and **ready it for use**. Once the item reaches this stage, no further costs are included in the asset's acquisition cost, and capitalization stops. More specifically, costs capitalized include the following:

- The item's purchase price net of trade discounts and rebates, plus any non-refundable purchase taxes (such as many provincial sales taxes) and duties.

- The expenditures necessary to bring the asset to its required location and condition to operate as management intended. These include employee costs needed to acquire or construct the asset; delivery and handling costs; site preparation, installation, and assembly costs; net material and labour costs incurred to ensure it is working properly; and professional fees.

- The estimate of the costs of obligations associated with the asset's eventual disposal. This includes, e.g., some or all of the costs of the asset's decommissioning and site restoration.

Costs that are not capitalized as part of the PP&E asset include initial operating losses, the costs of training employees to use the asset, and costs associated with a reorganization of operations. Also excluded are administration and general overhead costs and the costs of opening a new facility, introducing a new product or service, and operating in a new location.

Although this general principle is the same under both IFRS and ASPE, it is applied somewhat differently under each and this may result in different outcomes. Consider a situation where a company, after clearing land and while waiting for construction to be completed, either incurs net costs or generates net income from using the property as a parking lot. Should these net costs or revenue be added to or deducted from the cost of the building, or should they be recognized immediately in net income? The answer depends on whether the company follows IFRS or ASPE, as shown in Illustration 10-1 below.

IFRS	ASPE
Capitalization of costs stops when the asset is in place and ready to be used as management intended, even if it has not begun to be used or is used at less than a desirable capacity level.	Capitalization of costs stops when an asset is substantially complete and ready for productive use as determined in advance by management in relation to factors such as reaching a given level of productive capacity, occupancy level, period of time, or other industry-specific consideration.
The principle of being a necessary cost to acquire and get in place and ready for use is strictly applied. The temporary use of land as a parking lot and its net cost or revenue is not necessary to develop the asset being constructed; therefore, it cannot be included in the asset cost. The net cost or revenue is recognized in income when incurred or earned.	Any net revenue or expenses generated prior to substantial completion and readiness for use are included in the asset's cost. Therefore, the net parking lot cost or revenue while the asset is being readied for use would be debited or credited to the asset account.
If the rent from parking lot spaces in the basement of the building was $1,000 while the rest of the building was being finished, the following journal entry would be recorded:	If the rent from parking lot spaces in the basement of the building was $1,000 while the rest of the building was being finished, the following journal entry would be recorded:

Cash	$1,000		Cash	$1,000	
Rent revenue		$1,000	Building		$1,000

Three specific cost issues are more fully discussed in this chapter. They are (1) costs incurred when assets are constructed internally rather than purchased outright, (2) associated borrowing costs, and (3) site restoration or asset retirement costs.

Self-Constructed Assets

Often, companies construct their own assets. Even after deciding what components will be separately recognized, determining the cost of **self-constructed assets** such as machinery or buildings can be a challenge. Without a firm purchase or contract price, the company has to review numerous expenditures that were incurred to arrive at its cost.

The costs of materials and direct labour used in construction are not difficult to identify and measure; they can be traced directly to actual work orders and materials used in the constructed assets. However, allocating the indirect costs of manufacturing may create special problems. These indirect costs, called **overhead** or **burden**, include power, heat, light, insurance, property taxes on factory buildings and equipment, factory supervisory labour, depreciation of fixed assets, and supplies. Which of the following accounting choices is appropriate?

1. Assign a portion of all overhead to the construction project.

2. Assign no fixed overhead to the cost of the constructed asset.

Although the standards for manufactured inventories (see Chapter 8) require that a portion of all production overhead costs be applied to an inventory asset, the principle for PP&E assets is different. For these assets, only **directly attributable costs**—costs directly related to the specific activities involved in the construction process—are capitalized. Therefore, no fixed overhead is usually charged to the PP&E asset account.[3] Whether the entity also makes similar assets for resale or uniquely for its own purposes, care has to be taken to ensure that no abnormal amount of wasted inputs and related excess costs were experienced. If so, these are expensed in the period.

Borrowing Costs

Entities often acquire or construct capital assets that take substantial time to get ready for their intended use. To finance any interim expenditures that have to be made, a company may have to increase its bank loans, otherwise borrow money, or use existing company funds that could be used for other purposes. Do the financing or borrowing costs that are incurred for this purpose meet the criteria to be capitalized as part of the asset's cost, or should they be expensed in the period incurred?

Not surprisingly, IAS 23 *Borrowing Costs* requires capitalization of **avoidable** borrowing costs that are directly attributable to the cost of acquiring, constructing or producing qualifying assets that take a substantial period of time to get ready for use, such as manufacturing plants. These costs are therefore added to the cost of the PP&E asset.

Appendix 10A explains how **borrowing costs** are defined, how to determine which are **avoidable**, and how to determine the **amount to capitalize**.

Until Canadian publicly accountable entities adopted IFRS in 2011, they had a choice of whether to capitalize interest for qualifying assets or to report all interest as an expense in the income statement as incurred. Interest capitalization can have a substantial effect on the financial statements, e.g., **TransAlta Corporation** capitalized $31.0 million of interest to property, plant and equipment in 2011 under IFRS (versus $48.0 million in 2010). Because it previously capitalized interest under prior Canadian GAAP, it did not have to change this accounting policy. But what if TransAlta had previously expensed all interest? Earnings per share would have been $0.95 in 2010 if TransAlta had expensed its interest under prior Canadian GAAP, instead of $1.16 per share (a decrease of $0.21 per share). Similarly, EPS would have been $0.14 lower in 2011 if TransAlta had not capitalized any of its interest.*

How can statement users determine the effect of interest capitalization on a company's bottom line? The amount of interest capitalized in the period has to be disclosed in the notes to the financial statements. For example, **ClubLink Corporation**, a major Canadian owner, operator, and developer of golf clubs across the country, once reported $2,391,000 of capitalized interest, an amount equal to 25% of the interest expense deducted on its income statement. The following year's numbers were lower: about 12%.

---

*This calculation is just for illustrative purposes, for example the comparison ignores the impact of depreciation of capitalized interest costs on EPS.

Real World Emphasis

ASPE permits management to choose between a policy of capitalizing interest and expensing such costs. Regardless, the policy chosen and amount capitalized are required to be disclosed. In 2011, **BCE Inc.** capitalized $12.0 million of its interest costs under IFRS (see excerpt below). It had also capitalized interest under Canadian GAAP in prior years.

BCE Inc. Annual Report 2011
NOTES TO CONSOLIDATED FINANCIAL STATEMENTS
NOTE 7
INTEREST EXPENSE

FOR THE YEAR ENDED DECEMBER 31	2011	2010
Interest expense on long-term debt	**(774)**	(687)
Interest expense on other debt	**(80)**	(56)
Capitalized interest	**12**	58
Total interest expense	**(842)**	(685)

Dismantling and Restoration Costs

In some industries, when a company acquires and uses its long-lived assets, it takes on obligations that need to be met when the assets are eventually retired. For example, a nuclear facility must be decommissioned at the end of its useful life, mine sites must be closed and dismantled and the property restored, and landfill sites have significant closure and post-closure costs associated with the end of their operations.

In order to be able to use the long-lived asset, companies often assume responsibility for the costs associated with dismantling the item, removing it, and restoring the site at the end of its useful life. These **asset retirement costs** meet the recognition criteria for capitalization and are added to the PP&E asset cost.

Once again, while this general principle underlies both IFRS and ASPE, it is applied differently under each, as shown in Illustration 10-2. The differences relate to the types of obligations and activities undertaken.

Illustration 10-2

Asset Retirement Costs: IFRS versus ASPE

Law

	IFRS	ASPE
Category of obligations	Recognizes costs of both legal and constructive obligations, such as when an entity creates an expectation in others through its own actions that it will meet this obligation.	Recognizes costs associated with legal obligations only.
Category of activities	Costs include only those related to the acquisition of the asset, not those related to the use of the asset in the production of goods or services (product costs).	Costs include both retirement obligations resulting from the acquisition of the asset and its subsequent use in producing inventory, such as the mining of coal.

Under both IFRS and ASPE, the original cost estimates and any changes in them are capitalized in the asset account and a credit is made to an asset retirement or restoration liability. Because the actual expenditures will often not be incurred for a number of years, the obligation provision and the asset are both measured using the present value of the future costs. There is a fuller discussion of provisions and liability recognition and measurement issues in Chapters 2 and 13, but you should be aware that the cost of property, plant, and equipment will often include such a charge when the asset is acquired.

MEASUREMENT OF COST

Objective 5
Determine asset cost when the transaction has delayed payment terms or is a lump-sum purchase, a nonmonetary exchange, or a contributed asset.

Now that you have a better idea of what is included in "cost," the second step is to determine how it is measured. In general, **cost** is measured by the amount of cash or cash equivalents paid or the fair value of the other consideration given to acquire an asset when it is acquired.[4]

Determining Asset Cost when Cash Is Not Exchanged at Acquisition

Cost is the **cash cost** when the asset is recognized. This amount may not always be obvious. The paragraphs that follow discuss how several common issues are resolved when cash is not exchanged at the date of acquisition:

1. Cash discounts not taken

2. Deferred payment terms

3. Lump-sum purchases

4. Nonmonetary exchanges—share-based payments

5. Nonmonetary exchanges—asset exchanges

6. Contributed assets and government grants

Cash Discounts

When cash discounts for prompt payment are offered on purchases of plant assets, how should the discount be handled? If the discount is taken, it is definitely a reduction in the asset's purchase price. It is not recognized as a purchase discount (see Chapter 8), because purchase discounts relate only to inventory purchases that are included in the cost of goods sold. What is not clear, however, is whether the asset's cost should be reduced even if the discount is not taken. There are two points of view on this matter.

Under one approach, the net-of-discount amount is considered the asset's cost, **regardless of whether the discount is taken or not**. The rationale for this view is that an asset's cost is its cash or cash equivalent price. The discount, if it is lost, is the cost of not paying at an earlier date and should be recognized according to its nature as a financing or interest expense. Supporters of the **other approach** argue that the discount should not always be deducted from the asset's cost, because the terms may be unfavourable or because it might not be prudent for the company to take the discount. Both methods are used in practice. Recognition of the asset at its lower "cash cost" is preferred, at least on conceptual grounds.

Deferred Payment Terms

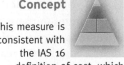

Underlying Concept

This measure is consistent with the IAS 16 definition of cost, which includes the fair value of other consideration given to acquire an asset at the time of its acquisition or construction.

Plant assets are often purchased on long-term credit arrangements through the use of notes, mortgages, bonds, or equipment obligations. The cost of an asset whose payment is deferred beyond normal credit terms is its **cash price equivalent**. Any difference between this fair value and the total payments made is recognized as **interest**. That is, the asset's cost is the **present value of the consideration** that is exchanged at the transaction date.

For example, equipment purchased today in exchange for a $10,000, non–interest-bearing note that is payable four years from now is not recorded at $10,000 because four years before payment far exceeds normal credit terms. Assuming the cash price is not known, the **present value of the note is the transaction's exchange price** and the asset's "cash cost." If 12% is an appropriate interest rate, the equipment is recognized at a cost of $6,355.20 [$10,000 × 0.63552; see Table A-2 for the present value of a single sum, PV = $10,000 $(PVF_{4,12})$].

Finance

When no interest rate is stated, or if the specified rate is unreasonable, an appropriate interest rate is imputed. The objective is to approximate the interest rate that the buyer and seller would negotiate in a similar arm's-length borrowing transaction. Factors to consider in determining an appropriate interest rate are the borrower's credit rating, the note's amount and maturity date, and prevailing interest rates. If the acquired asset's cash exchange price can be determined, it is used as the basis for measuring the asset's cost and identifying the interest element.

To illustrate, assume that Sutter Corporation purchases a specially built robot spray painter for its production line. The company issues a $100,000, five-year, non–interest-bearing note to Wrigley Robotics Ltd. for the new equipment when the prevailing market interest rate for obligations of this nature is 10%. Sutter is to pay off the note in five $20,000 instalments made at the end of each year. Assume that the fair value of this specially built robot cannot readily be determined. Therefore, it has to be approximated by establishing the note's fair value (its present value). This calculation and the entries at the purchase and payment dates are as follows:

A = L + SE
+75,816 +75,816

Cash flows: No effect

At date of purchase		
Equipment	75,816	
Notes Payable		75,816

Present value of note = $20,000 \ (\text{PVFOA}_{5,\ 10\%})$
= $20,000 (3.79079) (Table A-4)
= $75,816

The $24,184 difference between the asset's cash cost of $75,816 and the $100,000 cash that is eventually payable ($20,000 × 5) is the discount or interest on the $75,816 amount borrowed.

A = L + SE
   +7,582 −7,582

Cash flows: No effect

A = L + SE
−20,000 −20,000

Cash flows: ↓ 20,000 outflow

At end of first year		
Interest Expense	7,582	
Notes Payable		7,582
Notes Payable	20,000	
Cash		20,000

Interest expense for the first year under the effective interest method (as required by IFRS and allowed by ASPE) is $7,582 [($75,816) × 10%]. The entries at the end of the second year to record interest and to pay off a portion of the note are as follows:

A = L + SE
   +6,340 −6,340

Cash flows: No effect

A = L + SE
−20,000 −20,000

Cash flows: ↓ 20,000 outflow

At end of second year		
Interest Expense	6,340	
Notes Payable		6,340
Notes Payable	20,000	
Cash		20,000

Interest expense in the second year is calculated by applying the 10% interest rate to the net book value of the outstanding Notes Payable. At the end of the first year, the Notes Payable account was reduced to $63,398 ($75,816 + $7,582 − $20,000) and this was the note's carrying amount throughout the second year. The second year's interest expense is $63,398 × 10%, or $6,340.

If interest is not taken into account in such deferred payment contracts, the asset would be recorded at an amount that is higher than its fair value. In addition, no interest expense would be reported in any of the periods involved.

Lump-Sum Purchases

Underlying Concept

This is the same approach that is applied to a basket purchase of inventory.

There is a special problem in determining the cost of specific capital assets when they are purchased together for a single **lump-sum price**. When this occurs, and it is not at all unusual, the practice is to allocate the total cost among the various assets based on their relative fair values. The assumption is that costs will vary in direct proportion to those values.

To determine the individual fair value of the parts making up the total purchase, any of the following might be used: an appraisal for insurance purposes, the assessed valuation for property taxes, estimates of replacement costs, or simply an independent appraisal by an engineer or other appraiser. Which approach is most appropriate will depend on the information available in the specific situation. When a property is acquired consisting of a building and the land it sits on, the relative property tax value of each is often used. Estimates of replacement cost or independent appraisal might be used to determine the relative values of the components making up the building acquired.

To illustrate, assume that a company decides to purchase several assets of a smaller company in the same business for a total price of $80,000. The assets purchased are as follows:

	Seller's Book Value	Asset Fair Value
Inventory	$30,000	$ 25,000
Land	20,000	25,000
Building	35,000	50,000
	$85,000	$100,000

The allocation of the $80,000 purchase price based on the relative fair values is shown as follows.

		Asset Cost
Inventory	$\dfrac{\$25,000}{\$100,000} \times \$80,000$	$= \$20,000$
Land	$\dfrac{\$25,000}{\$100,000} \times \$80,000$	$= \$20,000$
Building	$\dfrac{\$50,000}{\$100,000} \times \$80,000$	$= \$40,000$
		$\$80,000$

Note that the assets' carrying amounts on the seller's books are not representative of their fair values. **They are irrelevant.** Depending on the situation and the company's accounting policies, the $40,000 cost allocated to the building may have to be further broken down and allocated to more specific components of the building, such as the basic structure, the roof, and the windows. If so, once the relative fair values of each is determined, the process of allocation is carried out using the same approach that is explained above.

Nonmonetary Exchanges

Share-Based Payments. When property, plant, and equipment assets are acquired and the company issues its own shares in payment, the cost of the asset is based either on the fair value of the shares given up or the fair value of the assets acquired. But which should be used?

IFRS 2 *Share-based Payment* indicates that the fair value of the asset acquired should be used to measure its acquisition cost, and it presumes that this value can be determined except in rare cases.[5] If the asset's fair value cannot be determined reliably, then its fair value and cost are determined by using the fair value of the shares given in exchange. If the company shares are widely traded, their fair value should be a good indication of the current cash-equivalent price of the PP&E asset acquired.[6] ASPE is more flexible, indicating only that the more reliable of the fair value of the goods received or the equity instruments given up is the asset cost. As private company shares are not widely traded, the asset fair value is more likely to be used.

To illustrate, assume that a hardware company decides to purchase land next to its current property in order to expand its carpeting and cabinet operation. Instead of paying cash for the land, it issues 5,000 no par value common shares to the seller. Assuming a recent appraisal valued the land at $62,000, the following entry is made:

A	=	L	+	SE
+62,000				+62,000

Cash flows: No effect

Land	62,000	
Common Shares		62,000

If no fair value can be reliably determined for the land, and assuming the company's shares have been recently traded with a fair market value of $12 per share, the land is assigned a cost equal to the estimated fair value of the shares, or 5,000 × $12 = $60,000.

Asset Exchanges. When nonmonetary assets such as property, plant, and equipment are acquired for cash or other monetary assets, the cost of the acquired asset is measured by the fair value (present value) of the cash or other monetary assets that are given up. **Monetary assets** are money or claims to future cash receipts that are fixed or determinable in amount and timing. Cash and accounts and notes receivable are the most common types of monetary assets. **Nonmonetary assets**, on the other hand, are assets that are not claims to fixed or determinable cash flows. Examples include inventory, long-lived plant assets, and equity investments in other companies.

When nonmonetary assets such as property, plant, and equipment **are disposed of and the company receives monetary assets in exchange**, a gain or loss on disposal is recognized in income. The gain is recognized in income because it is realized—that is, it has been converted to cash or a claim to cash—and the entity's economic situation has clearly changed in terms of its future cash flows.

However, when an existing **nonmonetary asset is exchanged for a new nonmonetary asset such as an item of property, plant, and equipment**, the proper accounting is not necessarily obvious. There are two underlying issues:

1. What should be the cost of the nonmonetary asset acquired?

2. Should a gain or loss on disposal be recognized on the nonmonetary asset that was given up?

Some argue that the new asset's cost should be determined by its **fair value**, or by the fair value of the assets given up, and that a **gain or loss should be recognized** on the disposal of the old asset. Others believe that the cost of the new asset should be determined by the **carrying amount** of the assets given up, with **no gain or loss recognized**. Still others favour an approach that would **recognize losses** in all cases, but **defer gains** in special situations.

General Principle—The Fair Value Standard. International and Canadian standard setters have been in agreement for a number of years on the preferred answer to these choices. The general principle is that **nonmonetary transactions are accounted for on**

the same basis as monetary transactions: thus, the cost of the PP&E asset acquired—by giving up a nonmonetary asset or a combination of monetary and nonmonetary assets—is determined by the fair value of the assets given up unless the fair value of the asset received can be more reliably measured. Any gains or losses that result are recognized in income.

Why is the accounting like this? Although cash or a claim to cash is not received or is relatively minor in nonmonetary exchanges, the earnings process related to the "old" asset is usually substantially complete. The specific values to the entity of the assets that are received generally are different from those of the assets that are given up. That is, the company's economic circumstances change as a result of the exchange.

The general standard that **nonmonetary exchanges are measured at fair value** is applied, therefore, **unless one of the following conditions is true**:

1. The transaction lacks commercial substance.

2. Fair values are not reliably measurable.

In these situations, as explained below, the exchange is recorded **at the carrying amount of the asset(s) given up, which is adjusted for the** inclusion of any cash or other monetary assets.

1. **Commercial substance.** In following the general standard, the entity basically derecognizes (takes out of the accounts) the carrying value of the asset(s) given up, recognizes the fair value of the asset(s) received in exchange, and then reports the difference as a gain (or loss) in net income. Because the company's underlying economic situation has changed as a result of the transaction—in other words, the transaction has commercial or economic substance—income is permitted to be reported. However, if the company is in the same economic position after the exchange as it was before, then no gain or loss would be reported as there is little or no justification for reporting increased asset values or income.[7]

   What does **commercial substance** really mean? Simply, it means that there is a **significant change** in the company's expected future cash flows and therefore its value. The exchange transaction has commercial substance if:

   - the amount, timing, or risk of future cash flows associated with the asset(s) received is different from the configuration of cash flows for the asset(s) given up, or

   - the specific value of the part of the entity affected by the transaction has changed as a result. For example, a company may benefit from significant cost savings from economies of scale made possible by acquiring and using the asset.

   In either case, the change must be **significant relative to the fair values of the exchanged assets**. This often requires using professional judgement.

2. **Ability to measure fair values.** As might be expected, the exchange cannot be recorded at fair value if the fair value of neither the asset given up nor the asset received can be reliably measured. Also, this exception helps reduce the risk that entities can assign arbitrarily high values to assets exchanged as a way of engineering and reporting gains.

   An overriding caution: When an asset is acquired, **it cannot be recognized at more than its fair value**. In an exchange when fair values cannot be used, the cost of the new asset is based on the carrying amount of the asset(s) given up. If the carrying amount of the asset(s) given up in the exchange is more than the fair value of the asset(s) received, the new asset has to be recorded at the lower fair value amount and a loss would be recognized.

   Accounting for asset exchanges is summarized in Illustration 10-3. This is followed by examples to illustrate the appropriate entries.

Illustration 10-3

Accounting for Asset Exchanges

Does the exchange meet both criteria? In other words, it has commercial substance, and fair values can be reliably determined.

Yes	No
Apply the fair value standard:	Exception to the fair value standard:
Cost of asset(s) received = fair value of what is given up, or what is acquired, if more reliably measurable.	Cost of asset(s) received = carrying amount of asset(s) given up.
Difference between carrying amount and fair value of asset(s) given up is recognized in income as a gain or loss.	No gain is recognized. Loss is recognized if fair value of asset(s) acquired is less than the carrying amount of the asset(s) given up.

When assets are exchanged or traded in, the transaction often requires a payment or receipt of cash or some other monetary asset. When the transaction's monetary component—or **boot**, as it is sometimes called—is significant, there is less need to question whether the transaction has commercial substance. As the percentage gets smaller, the transaction becomes primarily a nonmonetary exchange and the need to evaluate whether or not the transaction has commercial substance increases.

Asset Exchange—Example 1. Assume that Information Processing, Inc. trades in its used machine for a new model. The machine given up has a book value of $8,000 (original cost of $12,000 less $4,000 accumulated depreciation) and a fair value of $6,000. It is traded for a new model that has a list price of $16,000. In negotiations with the seller, a trade-in allowance of $9,000 is finally agreed on for the used machine.

Note that the amount agreed on as a **trade-in allowance is not necessarily the used asset's fair value**. In many cases, such as with automobiles, the trade-in allowance is essentially used to change the new asset's selling price without reducing its list price.

The cash payment that is needed and the cost of the new machine are calculated in Illustration 10-4. Because the cash paid is significant relative to the fair value of the total consideration, the change in the configuration of the company's future cash flows justifies a conclusion that this transaction has commercial substance.

Illustration 10-4

Calculation of Cost of New Machine

Fair value of assets given up		
Fair value of cash given up = list price less trade-in allowance	$16,000 − $9,000 =	$ 7,000
Fair value of machine given up		6,000
Cost of new machine = fair value of assets given up		$13,000

The journal entry to record this transaction is:

A = L + SE
−2,000   −2,000

Cash flows: ↓ 7,000 outflow

Equipment (new)	13,000	
Accumulated Depreciation (old)	4,000	
Loss on Disposal of Equipment	2,000	
Equipment (old)		12,000
Cash		7,000

The loss on the disposal of the used machine is verified in Illustration 10-5.

Illustration 10-5

*Calculation of Loss on
Disposal of Used Machine*

Fair value of used machine	$6,000
Carrying amount of used machine	8,000
Loss on disposal of used machine	$2,000

Asset Exchange—Example 2. Cathay Corporation exchanges several used trucks plus cash for vacant land that might be used for a future plant site. The trucks have a combined carrying amount of $42,000 (cost of $64,000 less $22,000 of accumulated depreciation). Cathay's purchasing agent, who has had previous dealings in the second-hand market, indicates that the trucks have a fair value of $49,000. In addition to the trucks, Cathay pays $4,000 cash for the land.

This exchange has commercial substance because the pattern and timing of cash flows from the investment in land are very different from those of the trucks. In addition, fair values can be determined. Assuming that the land's fair value is not known, or its fair value is not as reliable as that of the trucks, the cost of the land is calculated as indicated in Illustration 10-6.

Illustration 10-6

*Calculation of Land's
Acquisition Cost*

Cost of land = fair value of assets given up:	
Fair value of trucks exchanged	$49,000
Fair value of cash given up	4,000
Acquisition cost of the land	$53,000

The journal entry to record the exchange is:

A = L + SE
+7,000   +7,000

Cash flows: ↓ 4,000 outflow

Land	53,000	
Accumulated Depreciation—Trucks	22,000	
Trucks		64,000
Cash		4,000
Gain on Disposal of Trucks		7,000

The gain is the difference between the trucks' fair value of $49,000 and their carrying amount of $42,000. Now, if the trucks' fair value was $39,000 instead of $49,000, the land's cost would be $43,000 ($39,000 + $4,000) and a loss on the exchange of $3,000 ($42,000 − $39,000) would be reported.

Asset Exchange—Example 3. Westco Limited owns a number of rental properties in Western Canada as well as a single property in Ontario. Management has decided to concentrate its business in the west and to dispose of its one property outside this area. Westco agrees to exchange its Ontario property for a similar commercial property outside Lethbridge, Alberta, owned by Eastco Limited, a company with many properties east of Manitoba. The two properties are almost identical in size, rentals, and operating costs. Eastco agrees to the exchange but requires a cash payment of $30,000 from Westco to equalize and complete the transaction. Illustration 10-7 sets out information about these two properties.

Illustration 10-7

*Property Exchange—Westco
and Eastco*

	Westco Ltd. Property	Eastco Ltd. Property
Carrying amounts:		
Building	$520,000	$540,000
Accumulated depreciation	100,000	145,000
	$420,000	$395,000

(continued)

	Westco Ltd. Property	Eastco Ltd. Property
Fair value	$615,000	$645,000
Cash paid	$ 30,000	
Cash received		$ 30,000

Assume an evaluation by both Westco and Eastco management indicates that there is an insignificant difference in the configuration of future cash flows and that commercial substance is not indicated. What entry would be made by each company to record this asset exchange? Remember that fair values do not apply in this situation and that the cost of the assets acquired by each company is recognized at the carrying amount of the assets given up by each. Because the companies are recognizing amounts equal to the book value of what is given up, no gain or loss is recorded by either.

Westco Ltd. entry		
Buildings (new)	450,000	
Accumulated Depreciation—Buildings (old)	100,000	
Buildings (old)		520,000
Cash		30,000

A = L + SE
0   0   0

Cash flows: ↓ 30,000 outflow

Eastco Ltd. entry		
Building (new)	365,000	
Accumulated Depreciation (old)	145,000	
Cash	30,000	
Building (old)		540,000

A = L + SE
0   0   0

Cash flows: ↑ 30,000 inflow

Westco recognizes its new asset (the building) at the carrying amount of the assets given up. It gave up cash with a book value of $30,000 and a building with a book value of $420,000, for a total of $450,000. Eastco recognizes its new assets at the carrying amount of what it gave up, which is $395,000. Of this, $30,000 was cash received, leaving $365,000 to be recognized as the new building's cost. As both companies remain in the same economic position after the exchange as before, there is no reason to recognize any change in asset values and related gain or loss on the exchange.

Remember to check whether the fair value of the asset acquired is less than the cost assigned to it. Assets cannot be recognized at more than their fair value, so the asset would have to be recorded at the lower fair value amount and a loss equal to the difference recognized.

Contributed Assets and Government Grants

Companies sometimes receive contributions of assets as donations, gifts, or government grants. Such contributions are referred to as **non-reciprocal transfers** because they are transfers of assets in one direction only—nothing is given in exchange. The grants may be in the form of land, buildings, or equipment, or cash to acquire such assets, or even as the forgiveness of a debt. There are two important accounting issues for non-reciprocal transfers:

1. How should the asset be measured at acquisition?

2. What account should be credited?

When assets are acquired as a donation, a strict cost concept dictates that the asset's acquisition cost is zero. A departure from the cost principle is justified, however, because the only costs that are incurred (legal fees and other relatively minor expenditures) do not form a reasonable basis of accounting for the assets received. To record nothing is to ignore the economic reality of an increase in the entity's resources. Therefore, accounting standards generally require that **the asset's fair value be used to establish its "cost" on the books.**[8]

Having established the asset's acquisition cost, a further question remains about the credit entry in the transaction. Is it income, or is it contributed capital? Two general approaches have been used to record the credit in this type of transaction.

The **capital approach** considers donated assets as contributed capital financing and they are therefore accounted for with a credit directly to Contributed Surplus—Donated Capital. This approach is only appropriate, however, for a donation from an owner, and such donations are rare. The **income approach** reflects contributions in **net income** because the contribution is a non-owner source of the change in net assets.[9]

Accounting standards generally take the position that government assistance should be recognized in income, either as revenue or as a reduction of expense. If the contributed assets are expected to be used over several future periods, as in the case of a grant for a building or equipment, then the effect on income is spread out over the future periods that benefit from having received the grant. When assets or funds to acquire assets are received from federal, provincial, territorial, or municipal governments, GAAP requires that recipients defer and recognize the amount received over the periods that the related assets are used. This is accomplished in one of two ways:

1. by reducing the asset cost and therefore future depreciation by the amount of government assistance received (the **cost reduction method**); or

2. by recording the amount of assistance received as a deferred credit and amortizing it to revenue over the life of the related asset (the **deferral method**).

To illustrate the **cost reduction method**, assume that a company receives a grant of $225,000 from the federal government to upgrade its sewage treatment facility. The entry to record the receipt of the grant under this method is as follows:

A = L + SE
0   0   0
Cash flows: ↑ 225,000 inflow

Cash	225,000	
Equipment		225,000

This results in the equipment being carried on the books **at cost less the related government assistance**. Assuming a 10-year life and straight-line depreciation, the annual depreciation expense for the equipment is reduced by $22,500 and net income therefore is increased by this amount each year.

Alternatively, the **deferral method** credits a deferred revenue account with the grant amount. This amount is then recognized in income each year **on the same basis that is used to amortize the underlying asset**. The entries to record the receipt of the grant and its amortization for the first year under the **deferral method** are as follows:

A = L + SE
+225,000   +225,000
Cash flows: ↑ 225,000 inflow

Cash	225,000	
Deferred Revenue—Government Grants		225,000

A = L + SE
0   −22,500   +22,500
Cash flows: No effect

Deferred Revenue—Government Grants	22,500	
Revenue—Government Grants		22,500

A weakness of the cost reduction method is that it reports assets at less than their fair value to the entity. This issue is resolved if the deferral method is used, but this method also has a weakness. The deferral method is not consistent with the conceptual framework because the Deferred Revenue account does not usually meet the definition of a liability.

Note that a donation **of land** by a government may be deferred and taken into income over future periods because few government grants are provided without some conditions having to be met. If the requirement is to build and operate a manufacturing plant on the land over a specific period of time, then the grant is taken into income over the same period. Only when there is no way to associate the grant with future periods is it taken directly into income when received.

Government grants that are awarded to a company **for incurring certain current expenditures**, such as those related to payroll, are recognized in income in the same period as the related expenses. If grants or donations that have been received have a condition attached to them that requires a future event to occur—such as being required to maintain a specified number of employees on the payroll—the contingency is reported in the notes to the financial statements.

Entities are required to provide extensive disclosure about the amounts, terms and conditions, and accounting treatment they use for government assistance they have received. Readers can then evaluate the effect of such assistance on the entity's financial position and performance.

Costs Associated with Specific Assets

Land

Objective 6
Identify the costs included in specific types of property, plant, and equipment.

Underlying Concept

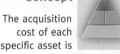

The acquisition cost of each specific asset is determined by applying the recognition and cost principles explained earlier in the chapter.

Land costs typically include (1) the purchase price; (2) closing costs, such as title to the land, legal fees, and recording fees; (3) costs incurred to condition the land for its intended use, such as grading, filling, draining, and clearing; (4) the costs of assuming any liens, such as taxes in arrears or mortgages or encumbrances on the property; and (5) any additional land improvements that have an indefinite life.

When land has been purchased to construct a building, all costs that are incurred up to the excavation for the new building are considered land costs. **Removal of old buildings, clearing, grading, and filling are considered land costs because these costs are necessary to get the land in condition and ready for its intended purpose.** Any proceeds that are obtained in the process of getting the land ready for its intended use—such as amounts received for salvaged materials from the demolition of an old building or the sale of timber that has been cleared—are treated as reductions in the land cost.

Special amounts assessed for local improvements—such as pavements, street lights, and sewers and drainage systems—are usually charged to the Land account because they are relatively permanent and are maintained and replaced by the local government. In addition, it is also proper to charge permanent improvements that are made by the owner, such as landscaping, to the Land account. Improvements with limited lives—such as private driveways, walks, fences, and parking lots—are recorded separately as Land Improvements so they can be amortized over their estimated lives.

Generally, land is considered part of property, plant, and equipment. If the major purpose of acquiring and holding land is for capital appreciation or rentals or an undetermined future use, it is classified as investment property, a special category of PP&E discussed below. If the land is held by a real estate company for resale, or is held by land developers or subdivided, it is classified as inventory.

Buildings

One accounting issue relates to the cost of an old building that is on the site of a planned new building. Is the cost to remove the old building a cost of the land or of the new building? The standards indicate that if land is purchased with an old building on it that will not be used, then the demolition cost less its salvage value is a cost of getting the land ready for its intended use. The costs relate to the land rather than to the new building.

On the other hand, if a company razes (tears down) an old building that it owns and previously used in order to construct a new building on the same land, the costs of the demolition net of any cost recoveries are expensed as disposal costs of the old building. This increases any loss on disposal of the old asset. The remaining book value of the old building is included in depreciation expense in its final year of use.

Under ASPE, an exception is made when a building is torn down to redevelop rental real estate. In this case, the remaining carrying amount of the building and the net costs of removing it can be capitalized as part of the redeveloped property, but only to the extent the costs can be recovered from the project in the future.

Leasehold Improvements

What is the proper accounting for capital expenditures that are made on property that is being leased or rented? Long-term leases ordinarily specify that any **leasehold improvements** revert to the lessor at the end of the lease. If the lessee constructs new buildings on leased land or reconstructs and improves existing buildings, the lessee has the right to use those facilities during the life of the lease, but they become the property of the lessor when the lease expires. The lessee charges the facilities' cost to a separate capital asset account, Leasehold Improvements, and the cost is amortized as an operating expense over the remaining life of the lease or the useful life of the improvements, whichever is shorter.

Equipment

The term "equipment" in accounting includes delivery equipment, office equipment, machinery, furniture and fixtures, furnishings, factory equipment, and similar tangible capital assets. The cost of such assets includes the purchase price, freight and handling charges that are incurred, insurance on the equipment while it is in transit, the cost of special foundations if they are required, assembling and installation costs, testing (less net proceeds of items, such as samples produced and sold during testing), and costs of making any adjustments to the equipment to make it operate as intended. The Goods and Services Tax (GST), Harmonized Sales Tax (HST), or Quebec Sales Tax (QST) that is paid on the acquired assets is a recoverable tax eligible for an input tax credit. It is not included in the asset's acquisition cost.

Investment Property

Investment property, or rental real estate, is a separate category of PP&E that may be accounted for after acquisition in a special way by entities applying international standards. It is defined as property held to generate rentals and/or appreciate in value rather than to sell in the ordinary course of business or to use in production, administration, or supplying goods and services.[10] It includes property that is currently under construction for investment purposes as well.

Investment property, covered in international standards by IAS 40, is different from owner-occupied property, to which IAS 16 *Property, Plant, and Equipment* applies. Complexities arise when one property is used partly as an investment property and is partly owner-occupied. In general, if the two parts could be sold separately (or leased as a finance lease separately), then the two parts should be accounted for separately. Another area of difficulty arises when an owner provides a variety of services in connection with an investment property. If providing the services exposes the owner to the normal risks of running a business (as distinct from investment risk), the classification as an investment property may not be appropriate. Consider a situation where a company rents out office space to tenants and provides furnished units and secretarial support in addition to the space. Judgement is often needed to determine whether the services provided are such a significant component of the arrangement that the property is actually "owner-occupied" space and not investment property.

The cost of investment property under IFRS and ASPE is determined following the same principles as used for PP&E. Also, if the property continues to be accounted for at cost, the components of the property are accounted for separately for purposes of depreciation.

Natural Resource Properties

Mineral resources, sometimes called wasting assets, generally refer to minerals and oil and gas resources that do not regenerate. **Mineral resource properties** are capitalized costs associated with the acquired rights, and the exploration, evaluation, and development of these minerals. Unlike buildings and machinery, natural resource properties are consumed physically over the period of use and do not retain their original physical characteristics. Regardless, many of the accounting problems associated with these assets are similar to those for other capital assets.

How is the acquisition cost of a mineral resource property determined? For example, a company like **Petro-Canada** needs to spend large amounts to find oil and gas reserves, and projects often end in failure. Furthermore, there are long delays between the time it incurs costs and the time it obtains benefits from any extracted resources. The acquisition cost of natural resource property normally includes some costs from each of four stages: (1) acquisition of the property, (2) exploration for and evaluation of reserves, (3) development, and (4) decommissioning and site restoration. In general, the capitalized costs of acquisition, exploration, development, and restoration make up the **depletion base** of the natural resource. As its name implies, the depletion base is the amount that later will be amortized (through a depletion charge) and form a significant portion of the cost of the mined or extracted inventory. Through depletion, the costs of the long-term mineral resource capital asset become part of the cost of the inventory that is produced—very similar to the direct materials cost of a manufactured product.

Accounting for natural resources is a specialized area. Because of the complex nature of this industry, additional coverage is beyond the scope of an intermediate text. It should be noted, however, that many of the issues that need to be resolved are familiar ones: they involve bringing accounting practice into greater consistency with general standards for asset recognition and measurement, cost allocation, and impairment testing. Not surprisingly, these issues are complicated by the uncertainties associated with estimating the volume and fair values of reserves and resources. Differences between IFRS and ASPE exist.

Biological Assets

Under ASPE, the general principles established for PP&E assets are also followed for biological assets. Under IFRS, however, separate standards are set out in IAS 41 *Agriculture* for assets related to agricultural activity. Examples of such assets that are long-lived, tangible, and used in production include fruit trees, grapevines, and livestock held to produce wool, milk, or additional livestock assets. These and other biological assets are measured initially, and at every date of the statement of financial position, at **fair value less costs to sell**, with changes in value recognized in the income statement as the values change. The accounting is similar to the fair value model explained later in this chapter. In the rare situation that no reliable fair value measure can be determined, then the asset is measured at cost less accumulated depreciation and impairment losses.

MEASUREMENT AFTER ACQUISITION

After recognizing the cost of property, plant, or equipment assets at acquisition, companies may have a choice of how to account for them after this point. Three different models have been identified and are currently used: a **cost model** (CM), a **revaluation model** (RM), and a **fair value model** (FVM). However, the GAAP choice of model depends on the type of asset and whether international or private entity standards are being applied. The features of the three models are summarized in Illustration 10-8.

	ASPE			IFRS		
	CM	RM	FVM	CM	RM	FVM
Investment property	✔			✔		✔
Other property, plant, and equipment assets	✔			✔	✔	

Illustration 10-8

Accounting Model Choices

For example, under IFRS, a company must choose whether to measure all of its **investment property** under the cost model or all under the fair value model, with few exceptions. All **other items defined as PP&E** are separated into classes and a decision is made whether to apply the cost model or the revaluation model to each class. The same method must be used for **all assets in each class.** Common classes of assets include:

- Land
- Land and buildings
- Office equipment
- Motor vehicles

- Machinery
- Ships
- Aircraft
- Furniture and fixtures

Not surprisingly, the revaluation model can be applied only to assets whose fair value can be reliably measured. This method is used by relatively few companies, but is included as an IFRS alternative. It tends to be used by companies that operate in countries with relatively high rates of inflation, making the revaluation measure more relevant than historical cost. This leaves the cost model as the most commonly used method under IFRS and the only one acceptable under ASPE. Let us now review how each of these models works.

Cost Model

Objective 7
Understand and apply the cost model.

The **cost model (CM)** is by far the most widely used model to account for PP&E, and you are probably familiar with the basics of how it works from introductory accounting. This model measures property, plant, and equipment assets after acquisition **at their cost less accumulated depreciation and any accumulated impairment losses**. Details about depreciation and impairment are explained in Chapter 11.

Revaluation Model

Objective 8
Understand the revaluation model and apply it using the asset adjustment method.

The choice of a **revaluation model (RM)** is new to most Canadian companies. Under this approach, property, plant, and equipment assets **whose fair value can be measured reliably** are carried after acquisition **at their fair value at the date of the revaluation less any subsequent accumulated depreciation and any subsequent impairment losses**. The discussion of depreciation and impairment under this model is also deferred to Chapter 11.

A revaluation is not required at each reporting date, but must be carried out often enough that the carrying amount reported is not materially different from the assets' fair value. Some assets need to be remeasured only every three years to five years, but for assets whose values change rapidly, an annual revaluation may be needed. Between revaluation dates, **depreciation is taken** on the revalued amount.

What is **fair value**, and how do companies determine this value for their PP&E assets? Fair value is "the price that would be received to sell an asset or paid to transfer a liability in an orderly transaction between market participants at the measurement date."[11] Professional valuators use active market or market-related evidence to the greatest extent possible, but may have to revert to other methods if equipment, for example, is very specialized.[12]

Before walking through an example of how the RM works, one issue needs to be resolved. If you regularly revalue or change the asset's carrying amount, what do you do with the increases and decreases in the carrying amount? The changes are accounted for as follows.

If the asset's carrying amount is increased (debited)	If the asset's carrying amount is decreased (credited)
The amount is recorded as a credit to Revaluation Surplus (OCI), an equity account, unless the increase reverses a revaluation decrease previously recognized in income. If so, recognize the increase in income to the extent of the prior decrease.	The amount is recorded as a debit to Revaluation Surplus (OCI), an equity account, to the extent of any credit balance associated with that asset. This account cannot have a debit (that is, a negative) balance. Any remaining amount is recognized in income.

The amounts debited or credited to the Revaluation Surplus account are reported in the statement of comprehensive income as other comprehensive income (OCI) items. Over the life of the asset, the effect of the treatment described is that there is no **net increase** in net income from revaluing the asset.

When revaluing an asset, two methods of accounting for the balance in the Accumulated Depreciation account are permitted. The account (1) may be adjusted proportionately, or (2) under the Asset Adjustment (or Elimination) method its balance may be eliminated. The proportionate approach adjusts both the carrying amount of the asset and the accumulated depreciation, so that the net balance is the fair value of the asset at the revaluation date.[13] The second method eliminates the balance in the accumulated depreciation account, writing it off against the asset itself. The asset is then adjusted to its new revalued amount. The second, and simpler, method is illustrated in the example that follows. For a similar example using the proportionate method, see Appendix 10B.

Revaluation Model Example

Convo Corp. (CC) purchases a building in early January 2010 and the cost of the basic structure of $100,000 is classified in an account called Buildings. CC accounts for this class of asset using the revaluation model, revalues the class every three years, and uses straight-line depreciation. The building structure is expected to have a useful life of 25 years with no residual value. CC has a December 31 fiscal year end. The asset's fair value at December 31, 2012, is $90,000 and at December 31, 2015, it is $75,000.

Illustration 10-9 walks us through the depreciation for the first three years and the revaluation entries needed at December 31, 2012, assuming the balance in the Accumulated Depreciation account is eliminated.

Illustration 10-9

Convo Corp. 2010 to 2012 and December 31, 2012 Adjustment

A = L + SE
−4,000   −4,000

Cash flows: No effect

Annual depreciation in each of 2010, 2011, and 2012:

Depreciation Expense	4,000	
Accumulated Depreciation—Buildings		4,000

$$\frac{\$100,000 - \$0}{25 \text{ years}} = \$4,000$$

December 31, 2012

	Before Revaluation	Adjustments	After Revaluation
Buildings	$100,000	$(12,000) 2,000	$90,000
Accumulated depreciation $4,000 × 3	(12,000)	12,000	–0–
Carrying amount	$ 88,000	$ 2,000	$90,000

A = L + SE
0   0   0

Cash flows: No effect

Entries, December 31, 2012:

Accumulated Depreciation—Buildings	12,000	
Buildings		12,000
To eliminate the accumulated depreciation.		

A   = L + SE
+2,000   +2,000

Cash flows: No effect

Buildings (90,000 – 88,000)	2,000	
Revaluation Surplus (OCI)		2,000
To adjust the Buildings account to fair value.		

Statement of financial position presentation, December 31, 2012:

Long-term assets:

Buildings	$90,000
Less accumulated depreciation	–0–
	$90,000

Shareholders' equity	
Revaluation surplus (OCI)	$ 2,000

A new depreciation rate needs to be calculated because there has been a change in the asset's carrying amount. This calculation and the revaluation adjustment amounts on December 31, 2015, are provided in Illustration 10-10.

Illustration 10-10

Convo Corp. 2013 to 2015 and December 31, 2015 Adjustment

A   = L + SE
–4,091   –4,091

Cash flows: No effect

Annual depreciation in each of 2013, 2014, and 2015:

Depreciation Expense	4,091	
Accumulated Depreciation—Buildings		4,091

$$\frac{\$90,000 - \$0}{22 \text{ years}} = \$4,091$$

December 31, 2015

	Before Revaluation	Adjustments	After Revaluation
Buildings	$90,000	$(12,273)	$75,000
		(2,727)	
Accumulated depreciation			
$4,091 × 3	(12,273)	12,273	–0–
Carrying amount	$77,727	$ (2,727)	$75,000

A = L + SE
0   0   0

Cash flows: No effect

Entries, December 31, 2015:

Accumulated Depreciation—Buildings	12,273	
Buildings		12,273
To eliminate the accumulated depreciation.		

A   = L + SE
–2,727   –2,727

Cash flows: No effect

Revaluation Surplus (OCI)	2,000	
Revaluation Gain or Loss	727	
Buildings		2,727
To adjust the Buildings account to fair value.		

Statement of financial position presentation, December 31, 2015:

Long-term assets:

Building	$75,000
Less accumulated depreciation	–0–
	$75,000

Notice that the Revaluation Surplus (OCI) account can only be reduced to zero. The remaining loss in value is recognized in the income statement. Once again, the depreciation rate going forward has to be recalculated. The $75,000 carrying amount is now allocated over the remaining 19 years of useful life, so the new rate is $75,000/19 = $3,947 each year.

Revaluation Surplus Account

What happens to the Revaluation Surplus (OCI) account? A company has two choices. One option is to transfer amounts from the account directly into Retained Earnings every period. The amount transferred is the difference between the depreciation expense based on the revalued carrying amount and the expense based on the original cost. Alternatively, the balance in the Revaluation Surplus (OCI) could remain there until the asset is retired or disposed of. At that point, the balance would be transferred directly to Retained Earnings, without going through the income statement.

Notice that the amounts in the Revaluation Surplus (OCI) account are not "recycled" through net income as the asset is depreciated, impaired, or disposed of. The revaluation model, therefore, is closer to a current cost measurement approach, where holding gains and losses are equity adjustments, than to a true fair value model.

Illustration 10-11 provides the accounting entries assuming that Convo Corp. sells the building in the example above on **January 2, 2013**, for $93,000.

<table>
<tr><td>Illustration 10-11</td><td colspan="3"></td></tr>
</table>

Illustration 10-11

Revaluation Surplus Adjustment on Disposal of Asset

A = L + SE
+3,000   +3,000

Cash flows: ↑ 93,000 inflow

A = L + SE
0   0   0

Cash flows: No effect

Cash	93,000	
Buildings		90,000
Gain on Sale of Buildings		3,000
To record the proceeds on sale of the building.		

Revaluation Surplus (OCI)	2,000	
Retained Earnings		2,000
To transfer the Revaluation Surplus in OCI related to the building sold to Retained Earnings.		

Fair Value Model

Objective 9

Understand and apply the fair value model.

As indicated above, investment property is the only tangible capital asset that may be accounted for under the **fair value model (FVM)**. Under this approach, the investment property is recognized on the statement of financial position after acquisition at its fair value. Changes in its value are reported in net income in the period of the change, and no depreciation is recognized over the life of the asset. Once this method is chosen instead of the cost model, the property continues to be measured at fair value until it is disposed of, becomes owner-occupied, or is developed for sale in the ordinary course of business. The example that follows illustrates how the FV model is applied. Note that although biological assets are measured at **fair value less costs to sell** instead of **fair value**, the example provided for investment property below applies also to accounting for the changes in value of biological assets.

Fair Value Model Example

Erican Corp. (EC) acquired a small 10-store shopping mall in eastern Canada for $1 million on February 2, 2014. The mall qualifies as investment property under IAS 40 *Investment Property*. At this time, nine of the stores were leased with remaining lease terms of two to four years. In addition to the purchase price, EC had to pay a $40,000 property transfer fee and legal fees of $3,000, and the company decided to paint the empty store at a cost of $2,000 before advertising it for rent. The acquisition was financed by assuming a $730,000 mortgage from the previous owner, who also turned over $37,000 of tenant damage deposits. The remainder of the transaction was settled in cash. On December 31, 2014, the fair value of the shopping centre property was determined to be $1,040,000; on December 31, 2015, it was $1,028,000, and on December 31, 2016, it had risen to $1,100,000. EC has a December 31 year end and applies the fair value method to all its investment property.

The summary entry to record the acquisition of the property is as follows.

February 2, 2014		
Investment Property	1,043,000	
Maintenance and Repairs Expense	2,000	
Mortgage Payable		730,000
Tenant Deposits Liability		37,000
Cash		278,000

A   =   L   +   SE
+765,000 +767,000   −2,000

Cash flows: ↓ 278,000 outflow

The acquisition cost includes the transfer and legal fees, while the incidental painting is a period expense. The mortgage and the tenant deposits are both liabilities and they reduce the amount of cash EC has to pay on the date of acquisition. Because the building is not being amortized, the land and the building may be reported together, as illustrated in the entry. On each December 31, the investment property is remeasured to its new fair value, with the following entries being made. Note that transaction costs are not included in the asset's fair value.

December 31, 2014		
Loss in Value of Investment Property	3,000	
Investment Property		3,000
($1,043,000 − $1,040,000)		

December 31, 2015		
Loss in Value of Investment Property	12,000	
Investment Property		12,000
($1,040,000 − $1,028,000)		

December 31, 2016		
Investment Property	72,000	
Gain in Value of Investment Property		72,000
($1,100,000 − $1,028,000)		

A   =   L   +   SE
−3,000   −3,000

−12,000   −12,000

+72,000   +72,000

Cash flows: No effect

The gains and losses are recognized directly in income. They are not reported in other comprehensive income.

It is important to recognize that the fair value of investment property must be **disclosed in the financial statements, even if the cost model is used**. Therefore all companies with such properties need to develop appropriate methods to measure fair value.

Costs Incurred after Acquisition

After plant assets are installed and ready for use, additional costs are incurred for anything from ordinary servicing and repairs to periodic overhauls, significant additions, or replacement of components. The major problem is allocating these costs to the proper time periods. Is the cost expensed in the current period, or capitalized and recognized over the future periods benefiting?

Accounting standards take the position that the recognition criteria for these costs should be the same when an asset is acquired and subsequently. If future economic benefits are expected to result from an expenditure, then the cost is capitalized, assuming it can be measured reliably. For a cost after acquisition to be included as part of an asset's cost, the assumption is that there has been **an increase** in the future economic benefits, **not merely a restoration** of the asset to normal operating efficiency.

Day-to-day servicing costs and other maintenance-type expenditures do not meet the asset recognition criteria and are expensed in the period incurred. These costs tend to keep an asset in its proper working condition; they do not add significantly to the asset's future cash-generating ability.

Underlying Concept

Applying the same principle both at acquisition and at a point after acquisition makes for more consistent accounting for similar events.

Underlying Concept

Expensing long-lived staplers, pencil sharpeners, and wastebaskets is an application of the materiality constraint.

It is not uncommon, however, for companies to expense costs below an arbitrary minimum amount even if they meet the capitalization criteria. For example, an entity may adopt a rule that expenditures below, say, $300 or $500 or even higher (depending on the size of the company) are always expensed. Although this treatment may not be correct conceptually, a cost-benefit assessment and materiality justify it.

The distinction between a **capital expenditure** (an asset) and a **revenue expenditure** (an expense) is not always clear-cut, and **this accounting choice can have a significant effect on reported income**. If costs are capitalized as assets on the statement of financial position, the income statement is freed from charges that would otherwise reduce the bottom line and earnings per share in that period.

What Do the Numbers Mean?

Real World Emphasis

The "managing" of earnings has been behind many of the well-publicized accounting scandals of recent years. **WorldCom** executives accounted for billions of dollars of current operating costs as capital additions. **Adelphia Communications Corp.** aggressively deferred operating items as assets on its statement of financial position. Closer to home, **Livent** carried out similar actions in Canada. There is also the case of Toronto-based **Atlas Cold Storage Income Trust**, the second-largest cold storage firm in North America, which announced that expenditures of approximately $3.6 million were inappropriately recorded as additions to capital assets during the previous year. Atlas also adjusted the financial statements of another prior year for an additional $1.6 million of expenditures that had been recognized as assets. While management may set out intentionally to exaggerate profits and mislead investors, decisions are made daily where the distinction between whether an expenditure should be capitalized or expensed is not always clear-cut.

Generally, companies incur four major types of expenditures related to existing assets, as shown below.

MAJOR TYPES OF EXPENDITURES

Additions   Increase or extension of existing assets.

Replacements, major overhauls, and inspections   Substitution of a new part or component for an existing asset, and performing significant overhauls or inspections of assets whether or not physical parts are replaced.

Rearrangement and reinstallation   Movement of assets from one location to another.

Repairs   Servicing expenditures that maintain assets in good operating condition.

Additions

Additions present no major accounting problems. By definition, any **addition to plant assets is capitalized** because a new asset has been acquired. Adding a wing to a hospital or an air conditioning system to an office, for example, increases the service potential of that facility. These costs are capitalized and then recognized as expenses in the future periods that benefit from the asset's use.

One problem that arises in this area is the accounting for any changes related to an existing structure as a result of the addition. Is the cost incurred to tear down an old wall to make room for an addition a cost of the addition or a disposal cost of the portion of the existing asset that is being eliminated? In theory, it is a disposal cost of a part of the existing asset. From a practical standpoint, however, if the wall is a minor portion of the cost of the original asset, most companies would keep the carrying amount of the old wall in the accounts and include the cost to tear down the wall in the cost of the addition.

Replacements, Major Overhauls, and Inspections

Replacements are substitutions of one asset or asset component for another, often resulting from a general policy to modernize or rehabilitate a building, piece of equipment, or interior of an aircraft, for example. Costs of **major overhauls**, reconditioning, or **inspections** are similar to replacements in that they recur and are often needed in order to permit continued use of an asset.

Costs such as those for the replacement of significant parts, or the periodic inspection, overhaul, or reconditioning of major assets, often meet the capitalization criteria. If so, they are, in effect, asset acquisitions. As such, the costs are capitalized and added to the asset's carrying amount. Because it is a replacement of something already incorporated in the asset's cost or of an item recognized as a separate component, the depreciated carrying amount of the original part or inspection is removed. If the original cost of the replaced part or previous overhaul is not known, it has to be estimated. The current cost of the part or overhaul can be used to help estimate the original cost of what is being replaced. Once the original cost is determined, it and the associated accumulated depreciation are both removed from the accounts.

Let's work through the examples described in Illustrations 10-12 and 10-13.

Illustration 10-12

Asset Replacement

Situation 1—Asset Replacement   Ace Manufacturing Ltd. (AML) incurred $27,000 in costs for roofing work on its factory: $26,000 to replace the previous roof installed when the building was first built, and $1,000 to repair and replace a few shingles on the garage extension as a result of a recent storm. The factory building was constructed 15 years ago.

Assumption (a): The original roof was identified as a separate component of the building (Building—Roof) when it was constructed. It cost $16,000 and has been depreciated on a straight-line basis over a 20-year life.

Assumption (b): The original roof was not recognized as a separate component of the building and its original cost is not known. The building has been depreciated on a straight-line basis assuming a 40-year useful life. Construction costs in the area have doubled since the factory was completed 15 years ago.

In **Situation 1(a)**, $26,000 of the roofing costs meets the capitalization criteria and $1,000 does not. The first entry below accounts for the $27,000 expenditure, and the second one removes the original roof's carrying amount and recognizes the associated loss.

A   = L +   SE
−1,000   −1,000

Cash flows: ↓ 27,000 outflow

Maintenance and Repairs Expense	1,000	
Buildings—Roof (new)	26,000	
Cash		27,000

A = L + SE
-4,000   -4,000

Cash flows: No effect

Accumulated Depreciation—Roof (old)	12,000	
Loss on Disposal of Roof	4,000	
Buildings—Roof (old)		16,000
($16,000/20 years × 15 years = $12,000)		

Under **Situation 1(b)**, the exact cost and accumulated depreciation are not known, but can be estimated. If construction costs have doubled in the area since the building was acquired, a reasonable estimate of the roof's original cost might be 50% of $26,000, or $13,000. The first entry below records the $27,000 expenditure assuming the roof is not accounted for after replacement as a separate component. This is a reasonable decision if AML estimates that the new roof will not have to be replaced before the building's useful life is over. If the new roof has a useful life of only 15 years, however, then it should be recognized as a separate asset. The numbers in the second entry below are different than in 1(a) because the old roof was being depreciated over a 40-year life as part of the building.

A = L + SE
-1,000   -1,000

Cash flows: ↓ 27,000 outflow

Maintenance and Repairs Expense	1,000	
Buildings	26,000	
Cash		27,000

A = L + SE
-8,125   -8,125

Cash flows: No effect

Accumulated Depreciation	4,875	
Loss on Disposal of Roof	8,125	
Buildings		13,000
($13,000/40 years × 15 years = $4,875)		

Illustration 10-13

Overhaul Costs

Situation 2—Overhaul Beta Corp. (BC) maintains a fleet of specialized trucks. BC has an operating policy of taking its trucks out of service and giving them a significant overhaul after every 50,000 km of use. The overhaul is a requirement for maintaining the company's insurance coverage. When Truck #B14, acquired two years previously for $63,000, completed its first 50,000 km of service, it was taken off the road and given its first major overhaul. The overhaul cost BC $9,000. When Truck #B14's odometer reading was 92,100 km, the truck was experiencing difficulties and BC management decided to take it in for an early overhaul. This time, the servicing costs totalled $11,000. The useful life of a truck is assumed to be 300,000 km.

Assumption (a): When the truck was acquired, the cost of the benefits to be restored by the overhaul after 50,000 km was estimated to be $8,000, based on current overhaul costs. Therefore the truck was recognized at its cost of $63,000 − $8,000 = $55,000, and the overhaul service component was recognized separately at a cost of $8,000.

Assumption (b): No separate asset components were recognized initially for the truck, but one will be recognized separately when the first full overhaul is carried out.

In **Situation 2(a)**, the same approach is used for the overhaul as for the replacement of the roof in Situation 1(a). The first entry below records the $9,000 overhaul expenditure, and the second one removes the original overhaul component's cost and accumulated depreciation from the accounts. The third entry recognizes the asset cost of the overhaul at 92,100 km, and the fourth entry removes the cost of the first overhaul and its accumulated depreciation to the date of the second one. The first actual overhaul costs of $9,000 were being depreciated at a rate of $9,000 ÷ 50,000 = $0.18 per km. When the truck reached 92,100 km, it had travelled an additional 92,100 − 50,000 = 42,100 km.

A = L + SE
0   0   0

Cash flows: ↓ 9,000 outflow

First overhaul		
Truck Overhaul #B14 (1)	9,000	
Cash		9,000

A = L + SE
0   0   0

Cash flows: No effect

Accumulated Depreciation (old)	8,000	
Truck Overhaul #B14 (old)		8,000
($8,000/50,000 km × 50,000 km = $8,000)		

A = L + SE
0   0   0

Cash flows: ↓ 11,000 outflow

Second overhaul		
Truck Overhaul #B14 (2)	11,000	
Cash		11,000

A = L + SE
−1,422   −1,422

Cash flows: No effect

Accumulated Depreciation (1)	7,578	
Loss on Overhaul	1,422	
Truck Overhaul #B14 (1)		9,000
(42,100 km × $0.18/km = $7,578)		

Under **Situation 2(b)**, because no "overhaul" component was recognized separately when the truck was acquired, a representative cost and the carrying amount have to be determined for it at the time of the 50,000 km servicing. If truck service bay costs have increased 10% over the two-year period since the truck was acquired, this might imply an original cost of $9,000/1.10, or $8,182. The first entry below records the overhaul cost as a separate asset component and the second entry removes the appropriate amount from the truck's book value. It is assumed that the cost of the truck, and therefore any unrecognized overhaul component, was being depreciated over the full useful life of the truck in this situation.

A = L + SE
0   0   0

Cash flows: ↓ 9,000 outflow

First overhaul		
Truck Overhaul #B14 (1)	9,000	
Cash		9,000

A = L + SE
−6,818   −6,818

Cash flows: No effect

Accumulated Depreciation	1,364	
Loss on Overhaul	6,818	
Trucks #B14 (1)		8,182
($8,182/300,000 km × 50,000 km = $1,364)		

Now recognized separately, the Truck Overhaul asset is depreciated over the next 50,000 km at a rate of $9,000/50,000 km, or $0.18 per km. When Truck #B14's odometer reads 92,100 km and it is taken out of service again, the depreciation accumulated on the overhaul service asset is $0.18 × 42,100 km, or $7,578. The two entries required for the second overhaul are exactly the same as under Situation 2(a) above. The first entry below recognizes the cost of the second overhaul and the second entry removes the old overhaul's carrying amount and recognizes a loss.

A = L + SE
0   0   0

Cash flows: ↓ 11,000 outflow

Second overhaul		
Truck Overhaul #B14 (2)	11,000	
Cash		11,000

A = L + SE
−1,422   −1,422

Cash flows: No effect

Accumulated Depreciation (1)	7,578	
Loss on Overhaul	1,422	
Truck Overhaul #B14 (1)		9,000
(42,100 km × $0.18/km = $7,578)		

When an entity uses the revaluation model or the fair value model, the basic principle for replacements and overhauls continues to apply. If the **revaluation model** is used, the cost of the "new" asset component, part, or overhaul is added to the asset's carrying amount, and the carrying amount of the replaced asset component or part is removed, with a gain or loss recognized on disposal. When the **fair value model** is applied to investment property, the property's fair value may already reflect the reduced value of the part to be replaced. This fact may not be known or it may be difficult to reasonably determine the carrying amount of the part being replaced. A practical solution, therefore, is to add the cost of the replacement part or overhaul to the asset and then reassess and adjust the asset to its fair value after the replacement.

Accounting for replacements, and major overhauls or inspections as illustrated in Situations 1 and 2 above, is required by IFRS, with the entries being a direct application of general PP&E principles. ASPE has not required such a strict application of general principles, although this may change.

For now, ASPE removes the net book value of a part and capitalizes the replacement only if the cost and accumulated depreciation of the old part are known. When the carrying amount cannot be determined, and when major overhauls or renovations are carried out, practice differs depending on the circumstances. If the asset's useful life is extended, the Accumulated Depreciation account is often debited, on the basis that the renewal is "recovering" part of the past depreciation. If the quantity or quality of the asset's service potential or productivity is increased, the cost of the improvement is usually capitalized as part of the asset's cost.

Rearrangement and Reinstallation

Rearrangement and reinstallation costs that are intended to benefit future periods are different from additions, replacements, and major overhauls. An example is the rearrangement and reinstallation of a group of machines to facilitate future production. If the original installation cost and the accumulated depreciation taken to date on it can be determined, the rearrangement and reinstallation cost could be handled as a replacement. These amounts, however, are rarely known and may be difficult to estimate. In this case, because the asset's cost at acquisition already includes installation costs, any additional costs incurred to rearrange or reinstall it are recognized as an expense of the current period.

If the amounts are material, ASPE may allow capitalization of such costs on the basis that the original cost of installation is not known, and is likely to have been depreciated to a significant extent.

Repairs

Ordinary repairs are expenditures that are made to maintain plant assets in good operating condition; they are charged to an expense account in the period in which they are incurred, based on the argument that there is no increase in a PP&E asset. Replacing minor parts, the ongoing lubricating and adjusting of equipment, repainting, and cleaning are examples of maintenance charges that occur regularly and are treated as ordinary operating expenses.[14]

Underlying Concept

This is an example of how the asset-liability approach to our accounting model works. If the cost is not an asset, it is an expense.

Real World Emphasis

BP plc, an international integrated oil and gas giant, reported net property, plant, and equipment of U.S. $119,214 million on its December 31, 2011 statement of financial position. Illustration 10-14 includes excerpts from Note 1 to BP's financial statements that explain the acquisition costs of these assets. BP engages in oil and gas exploration and production activities, operates refineries and service stations, and provides a variety of petrochemical products. The company's financial statements are prepared under IFRS.

Illustration 10-14

Property, Plant, and Equipment Accounting Policies

BP Annual Report and Accounts 2011

Notes on financial statements

1. Significant accounting policies

Oil and natural gas exploration, appraisal and development expenditure

Oil and natural gas exploration, appraisal and development expenditure is accounted for using the principles of the successful efforts method of accounting.

Exploration and appraisal expenditure

Geological and geophysical exploration costs are charged against income as incurred. Costs directly associated with an exploration well are initially capitalized as an intangible asset until the drilling of the well is complete and the results have been evaluated. These costs include employee remuneration, materials and fuel used, rig costs and payments made to contractors. If potentially commercial quantities of hydrocarbons are not found, the exploration well is written off as a dry hole. If hydrocarbons are found and, subject to further appraisal activity, are likely to be capable of commercial development, the costs continue to be carried as an asset.

Costs directly associated with appraisal activity, undertaken to determine the size, characteristics and commercial potential of a reservoir following the initial discovery of hydrocarbons, including the costs of appraisal wells where hydrocarbons were not found, are initially capitalized as an intangible asset.

All such carried costs are subject to technical, commercial and management review at least once a year to confirm the continued intent to develop or otherwise extract value from the discovery. When this is no longer the case, the costs are written off. When proved reserves of oil and natural gas are determined and development is approved by management, the relevant expenditure is transferred to property, plant and equipment.

Development expenditure

Expenditure on the construction, installation and completion of infrastructure facilities such as platforms, pipelines and the drilling of development wells, including service and unsuccessful development or delineation wells, is capitalized within property, plant and equipment and is depreciated from the commencement of production as described below in the accounting policy for property, plant and equipment.

Property, plant and equipment

Property, plant and equipment is stated at cost, less accumulated depreciation and accumulated impairment losses.

The initial cost of an asset comprises its purchase price or construction cost, any costs directly attributable to bringing the asset into operation, the initial estimate of any decommissioning obligation, if any, and, for qualifying assets, borrowing costs. The purchase price or construction cost is the aggregate amount paid and the fair value of any other consideration given to acquire the asset. The capitalized value of a finance lease is also included within property, plant and equipment. Exchanges of assets are measured at fair value unless the exchange transaction lacks commercial substance or the fair value of neither the asset received nor the asset given up is reliably measurable. The cost of the acquired asset is measured at the fair value of the asset given up, unless the fair value of the asset received is more clearly evident. Where fair value is not used, the cost of the acquired asset is measured at the carrying amount of the asset given up. The gain or loss on derecognition of the asset given up is recognized in profit or loss.

Expenditure on major maintenance refits or repairs comprises the cost of replacement assets or parts of assets, inspection costs and overhaul costs. Where an asset or part of an asset that was separately depreciated is replaced and it is probable that future economic benefits associated with the item will flow to the group, the expenditure is capitalized and the carrying amount of the replaced asset is derecognized. Inspection costs associated with major maintenance programmes are capitalized and amortized over the period to the next inspection. Overhaul costs for major maintenance programmes, and all other maintenance costs are expensed as incurred.

Objective 11

Identify differences in accounting between ASPE and IFRS, and what changes are expected in the near future.

IFRS/ASPE COMPARISON

A Comparison of IFRS and ASPE

Illustration 10-15 sets out the major differences between ASPE and international accounting standards for publicly accountable enterprises.

	Accounting Standards for Private Enterprises (ASPE)—*CICA Handbook*, Part II, Sections 3061, 3110, 3800, 3831, 3850, and AcG-16	IFRS—IAS 16, 20, 23, 37, and 40; IFRS 6	References to related illustrations and select brief exercises
Scope	The costs of mining and oil and gas properties are considered items of PP&E, with specific application guidance covering the full cost method of accounting in the oil and gas industry covered in AcG-16.	The cost of mineral rights and reserves, including oil, natural gas, and similar non-regenerative resources, are not covered specifically as PP&E in IAS 16; only the costs of the exploration for and evaluation of mineral resources are addressed in IFRS 6.	N/A
	Investment property is considered an item of PP&E and HB 3061 applies.	Investment property is considered an item of PP&E, but a separate IFRS—IAS 40—applies to it. Biological assets are accounted for by standards in IAS 41 for agricultural assets.	BE 10-18 Illustration 10-8 Illustration 8-27 (Chapter 8)
Recognition	Uses general recognition principle in Section 1000 based on measurability and probability of future economic benefits to be received. Less guidance is provided.	Recognition criteria are incorporated in IAS 16 and used for costs both at and after initial recognition—same criteria, based on measurement reliability and probability that associated future economic benefits will flow to the entity.	N/A
Components	Indicates that the costs of significant separable component parts are allocated to those parts when practicable, but practice has not been to carry this out to the same extent as required internationally.	Requires the parts of PP&E with relative significant costs to be depreciated separately. There is no mention made of practicability. Practice under IAS 16 results in more componentization than under HB 3061.	BE10-2
Measurement at recognition	Initial measurement is at cost.	Initial measurement is at cost, but more detail is provided on how cost is measured.	BE10-9
	Any net revenue/expense from using an item of PP&E prior to substantial completion and readiness for use is included in the asset's cost.	Net revenue or expense derived from an item of PP&E prior to its being in place and ready for use as intended is taken into income, on the basis that it was not needed to acquire the asset and bring it to its location and use.	Illustration 10-1 BE10-3
	Capitalization of costs at acquisition stops when the asset is substantially complete and ready for productive use, as predetermined by management with reference to productive capacity, occupancy level, passage of time, or other industry considerations. This is a more flexible approach than under IFRS.	Capitalization of costs in the initial carrying amount stops when the item is in the location and condition necessary for it to be used as management intended, even if it has not begun to be used or is used at less than desired capacity. No initial operating losses or costs of relocation or reorganization of the asset(s) are capitalized.	BE10-4
	Interest costs directly attributable to the acquisition, construction, or development of items of PP&E may be capitalized if that is the accounting policy used by the entity.	Borrowing costs directly attributable to the acquisition, construction, or development of qualifying assets are capitalized under IAS 23.	Illustration 10A-6 BE10-23

(continued)

Illustration 10-15

IFRS versus ASPE Comparison Chart

	Accounting Standards for Private Enterprises (ASPE)—*CICA Handbook*, Part II, Sections 3061, 3110, 3800, 3831, 3850, and AcG-16	IFRS—IAS 16, 20, 23, 37, and 40; IFRS 6	References to related illustrations and select brief exercises
	Only the cost of legal obligations related to asset retirement is capitalized. Changes in the estimate of the cost are also capitalized in the asset.	The cost of legal and constructive obligations related to asset retirement is capitalized, measured under IAS 37 *Provisions, Contingent Liabilities, and Contingent Assets*. Increases in the cost of the obligation related to the production of inventory are specifically excluded.	Illustration 10-2 BE10-16
Measurement after recognition	Only one model—the cost model—applies to all items of PP&E.	All investment property is accounted for either under the cost model or fair value model. Each class of items of other PP&E is accounted for under the cost model or the revaluation model. Companies using the revaluation model have the choice of using the asset adjustment method or the proportionate method. The cost model continues to be used to the greatest extent.	Illustrations 10-9, 10-10, 10-11, 10B-1 and 10B-2 BE10-17
Costs incurred after acquisition	Betterments are capitalized and costs that are incurred to maintain service potential are expensed. Increased service potential means increased physical output or service capacity, lower operating costs, an increase in useful life, or an increase in quality of output. For betterments and major replacements, if the cost of the previous part is known, its carrying amount is removed. If not, and depending on the circumstances, the asset account, its accumulated depreciation, or an expense could be charged with the cost. The redevelopment of rental real estate qualifies as a betterment, with the book value of the existing building included in the cost of the redeveloped property, if recoverable. Overhauls are not specifically addressed and are usually expensed when incurred.	All expenditures that meet the recognition criteria for an item of PP&E are capitalized. Does not specifically refer to betterments, but does refer to replacement parts that meet the recognition criteria. These are capitalized and the replaced part's carrying amount is removed, whether originally recognized as a separate component or not. The carrying amount of the building being redeveloped would not be carried forward as part of the cost of the new asset. Major inspections or overhauls that allow the continued use of an asset are treated similarly to replacements.	BE10-20

Illustration **10-15**

IFRS versus ASPE Comparison Chart (continued)

Looking Ahead

When Canadian publicly accountable entities applied IFRS for the first time, they were permitted to revalue items of PP&E to fair value at the transition date. This amount became the assets' deemed cost at that point. Many Canadian companies took advantage of this transition exemption, even though they were likely to apply the cost model going forward.

An ongoing project related to the IASB's research agenda is particularly important to many companies in Canada. It deals with the development of comprehensive accounting standards for the extractive industries, such as mining and oil and gas. The project's objective is to eventually issue a replacement standard for IFRS 6 *Exploration and Evaluation of Mineral Resources*. The project expects to cover all financial reporting issues associated with upstream extractive activities, reserves, and resources from the exploration for, discovery of, and extraction of minerals and oil and gas. The IASB issued a Discussion Paper on key issues in 2009. In October 2010, IASB staff presented to the Board a summary of comments received on the Discussion Paper on extractive activities prepared for it by national standard setters from Australia, Canada, Norway, and South Africa. The Board plans to use the feedback to help it decide whether to add a project to its active agenda.

Significant Change

A major project that was finalized and issued as a new standard in May 2011 was IFRS 13 *Fair Value Measurement*. It defined fair value, provided a framework for measuring fair value, and detailed required disclosures regarding fair value measurements. It did not introduce any new requirements to measure an asset or a liability at fair value, change what is measured at fair value in IFRS, or address how to present changes in fair value. The new requirements are effective for annual periods beginning on or after January 1, 2013, with earlier application permitted.[15] This standard is discussed in greater detail in Chapter 2.

The IASB has paused a project to update IAS 20 *Accounting for Government Grants and Disclosure of Government Assistance*. It eventually intends to update IAS 20 to improve the information provided to users of financial statements by "eliminating inconsistencies with the Framework, in particular the recognition of a deferred credit when the entity has no liability; and eliminating options that can reduce the comparability of financial statements and understate the assets controlled by an entity." However, the IASB decided to defer work on the project until further progress is made in related projects (such as work on IAS 37 *Provisions, Contingent Liabilities and Contingent Assets* and a separate project clarifying revenue recognition).

SUMMARY OF LEARNING OBJECTIVES

1 Understand the importance of property, plant, and equipment from a business perspective.

Almost every enterprise invests in long-lived assets. These long-term items include both those that are physical assets—property, plant, and equipment—and those that are intangible. Long-lived assets are particularly important for manufacturing companies because they provide the company with the capacity or infrastructure to produce goods and/or provide services. Too much investment in long-lived assets could result in expensive overcapacity, while too little investment could mean lost opportunities for profits and future cash flows. Both situations would lower the company's rate of return.

2 Identify the characteristics of property, plant, and equipment assets.

Property, plant, and equipment assets are tangible assets held for use in the production of goods and services, for rental to others, or for administrative purposes, and have a useful life of more than one accounting period. This type of asset provides an

entity with its operating capacity and infrastructure, but also adds to fixed costs. For this reason, it is important that a company invest enough in PP&E to meet its potential, but not so much that it has to bear the related costs of overcapacity.

3 Identify the recognition criteria for property, plant, and equipment.

PP&E costs that provide probable future economic benefits to the entity and that can be measured reliably are recognized. Asset components should be recognized separately to the extent their costs are significant and/or the related assets have different useful lives or patterns of depreciation.

4 Identify the costs to include in the measurement of property, plant, and equipment assets at acquisition.

Asset costs used when measuring PP&E include all necessary costs directly attributed to acquiring the asset, bringing it to its location, and making it ready for use. These include direct material, direct labour, and variable overhead costs for self-constructed PP&E assets, borrowing costs for those taking substantial time to get ready for use, and dismantling and restoration costs required as a result of the asset's acquisition. Once the asset is in place and ready for use, costs are no longer capitalized.

5 Determine asset cost when the transaction has delayed payment terms or is a lump-sum purchase, a nonmonetary exchange, or a contributed asset.

Cost means the asset's cash equivalent cost. When payment is deferred beyond normal credit terms, the excess paid over cash cost is interest. When a number of assets are acquired in a basket purchase, the cost is allocated based on the relative fair value of each. When PP&E assets are acquired and paid for by issuing the entity's shares, cost is usually determined as the fair value of the asset. When acquired in an exchange of assets, cost is the fair value of the assets given up, unless the fair value of the assets received can be more reliably measured. However, if the transaction lacks commercial substance or fair values cannot be reliably determined, the assets acquired are measured at the book value of the assets given up. This amount cannot exceed the fair value of the assets acquired. Assets contributed to a company are measured at fair value and credited to contributed surplus if donated by a shareholder. This is rare. If contributed by government, the contribution is accounted for under the income approach whereby the amount credited flows through the income statement, usually as the asset is used by the entity.

6 Identify the costs included in specific types of property, plant, and equipment.

Land: Includes all expenditures made to acquire land and to make it ready for use. Land costs typically include the purchase price; closing costs, such as title to the land, legal fees, and registration fees; costs incurred to condition the land for its intended use, such as grading, filling, draining, and clearing; the assumption of any liens, mortgages, or encumbrances on the property; and any additional land improvements that have an indefinite life. Buildings, including investment property: Includes all expenditures related directly to their acquisition or construction. These costs include materials, labour, and direct overhead costs that are incurred during construction and professional fees and building permits. Equipment: Includes the purchase price, freight, and handling charges that are incurred; insurance on the equipment while it is in transit; the cost of special foundations if they are required; assembling and installation costs; and the costs incurred in calibrating the equipment so that it can be used as intended.

Mineral resource properties: Four types of costs may be included in establishing the cost of mineral resource assets. These are (1) acquisition costs, (2) exploration and evaluation costs, (3) development costs, and (4) site restoration and asset retirement costs.

7 Understand and apply the cost model.

The cost model is appropriate for all classes of PP&E, including investment property. Under this model, the assets are carried at cost less accumulated depreciation and any accumulated impairment losses.

8 Understand the revaluation model and apply it using the asset adjustment method.

Under IFRS, the revaluation model may be applied to any class of PP&E except investment property, provided fair value can be measured reliably. Under this model, the assets are carried at their fair value at the revaluation date less any subsequent accumulated depreciation and any subsequent accumulated impairment losses. While held, net increases in fair value are not reported in income, but are accumulated in a Revaluation Surplus (OCI) account in equity. Net losses are reported in income once the revaluation surplus has been eliminated. At the time of revaluation, under this method, the accumulated depreciation account is eliminated (written off against the asset itself). The asset is then adjusted to its new revalued amount.

9 Understand and apply the fair value model.

The fair value model can be applied only to investment property under IFRS, and the choice between cost and fair value must be made for all investment property reported. Under this model, all changes in fair value are recognized in net income. No depreciation is recognized.

10 Explain and apply the accounting treatment for costs incurred after acquisition.

Day-to-day servicing, repair, and maintenance costs, and costs of rearrangement and relocation, are expensed as incurred. PP&E expenditures that provide future economic benefits and whose costs can be reliably measured are capitalized. The cost of additions, replacements, and major overhauls and inspections are capitalized and the carrying amount of the replaced asset or the previous overhaul or inspection is removed from the accounts.

11 Identify differences in accounting between ASPE and IFRS, and what changes are expected in the near future.

In general, the accounting for PP&E assets is very similar under both IFRS and ASPE because the principles underlying both are very similar. However, under IFRS, practice remains closer to the principles identified. This is seen, for example, in accounting for components and major overhauls and inspections, incidental revenues and expenses before asset use, and borrowing costs. IFRS permits application of a revaluation model and a fair value model, neither of which is acceptable under ASPE.

The IASB is researching activities related to the extractive industry with the objective of developing accounting standards to cover the exploration for, and the development and extraction of, minerals and oil and gas resources and assets. In addition, a new IFRS standard on fair value measurement was finalized in May 2011, with an effective date of January 1, 2013.

KEY TERMS

additions, p. 622
asset retirement costs, p. 603
biological assets, p. 600
boot, p. 609
capital approach, p. 612
capital expenditure, p. 621
capitalized, p. 600
commercial substance, p. 608
cost, p. 601
cost model (CM), p. 616
cost reduction method, p. 612
deferral method, p. 612
depletion base, p. 615

fair value, p. 616
fair value model (FVM), p. 619
fixed assets, p. 599
income approach, p. 612
inspections, p. 622
investment property, p. 614
leasehold improvements, p. 614
lump-sum price, p. 606
major overhauls, p. 622
mineral resources, p. 615
mineral resource properties, p. 615
monetary assets, p. 607
nonmonetary assets, p. 607

non-reciprocal transfers, p. 611
ordinary repairs, p. 625
plant assets, p. 599
property, plant, and equipment, p. 599
rearrangement and reinstallation
    costs, p. 625
replacements, p. 622
revaluation model (RM), p. 616
revenue expenditure, p. 621
self-constructed assets, p. 602
tangible capital assets, p. 599
unit of measure, p. 600

APPENDIX 10A

CAPITALIZATION OF BORROWING COSTS

Objective 12
Calculate the amount of borrowing costs to capitalize for qualifying assets.

Chapter 10 introduces some of the issues for the capitalization of borrowing costs, underscoring the underlying principle that borrowing costs that are directly attributable to acquiring, producing or constructing a qualifying asset are included as part of the cost of the asset. Other borrowing costs are expensed. This appendix continues the discussion in more detail and illustrates the recognition guidance in IAS 23 *Borrowing Costs*. Private entities that choose a policy of capitalizing interest costs for relevant PP&E assets are also likely to apply this guidance.

Borrowing costs are made up of interest and related costs that a company incurs related to the borrowing of funds. The cost of equity financing is specifically excluded. Interest and other costs include interest expense that results from applying the effective interest method, finance charges on finance leases, and exchange adjustments on foreign currency borrowings if they are viewed as adjustments to interest costs.

Four issues need to be considered in determining the amount of borrowing costs to be capitalized and how to report them:

1. Which assets qualify?

2. What is the capitalization period?

3. What are the avoidable borrowing costs—the amount eligible to capitalize?

4. What disclosures are needed?

Qualifying Assets

To qualify for inclusion in the cost of an asset, the borrowing costs must:

1. be directly attributable to acquiring, constructing or producing a qualifying asset and

2. meet both recognition criteria—it is probable that associated future economic benefits will flow to the entity, and the cost can be measured reliably.

Qualifying assets must require **substantial time to get ready** for their intended use or sale. This may include inventories; items of property, plant, and equipment; investment properties; or intangible assets.

Borrowing costs for qualifying assets measured at fair value and inventories that are produced in large quantities on a repetitive basis **may be capitalized**, but it is not required.

Examples of assets that **do not qualify**, aside from financial assets, include (1) assets that are already in use or ready for their intended use when acquired; (2) those produced over a short period of time; and (3) assets not undergoing activities necessary to get them ready for use, such as land that is not being developed and assets that are not being used because of obsolescence, excess capacity, or needed repairs.

Capitalization Period

The **capitalization period** is the time over which interest must be capitalized. It **begins** on the **commencement date**, which is when **all three** of the following conditions are met:

1. Expenditures for the asset have been made.

2. Activities that are necessary to get the asset ready for its intended use or sale are in progress, including necessary pre-construction administrative and technical work.

3. Borrowing costs are being incurred.

Capitalization **ends** when substantially all the activities needed to prepare the asset for its intended use or sale are complete. This is usually when the physical activities associated with construction are finished, even if minor matters are still outstanding. If a project is finished in stages so that the parts completed can be used while activities continue on the remainder, capitalization stops on the parts that are substantially complete. If active development of a project is on hold, capitalization of the borrowing costs is **suspended**. Note that this does not refer to temporary delays needed as part of the development process.

Let's apply this to different situations associated with land. What if land was purchased with the intention of developing it for a particular use? If the land is purchased as a site for a structure (such as a plant site), the borrowing costs that are capitalized **during the construction period** are part of the cost of the plant, not of the land. Borrowing costs on the land while held and awaiting the start of construction are expensed. If land is being developed for sale as lots, the borrowing cost is part of the developed land's acquisition cost. However, borrowing costs involved in purchasing land that is held for speculation are not capitalized, because the asset is ready for its intended use.

Avoidable Borrowing Costs

To qualify for capitalization, the costs must be **directly attributable** to a project; in other words, they must be **avoidable borrowing costs**. When an entity borrows funds to finance a specific qualifying asset, the avoidable costs are the actual borrowing costs that would not have been incurred if the expenditures for the qualifying asset had not been made. These costs are reduced by the investment income earned on any temporary investment of these monies.

Avoidable costs are more difficult to calculate when a company's borrowings are not directly related to specific assets or projects. Some companies borrow funds using a variety of debt instruments to support their general financing requirements. In this case, the calculation is not as straightforward and professional judgement is often needed to determine which costs were avoidable.

In general, the following steps are taken to calculate the borrowing costs to capitalize:

1. Determine the expenditures on the qualifying asset.

2. Determine the avoidable borrowing costs on the asset-specific debt.

3. Determine the avoidable borrowing costs on the non–asset-specific debt.

4. Determine the borrowing costs to capitalize.

Step 1: Determine the Expenditures on the Qualifying Asset

The **expenditures on the qualifying asset** means the **weighted-average accumulated expenditures**—the construction expenditures weighted by the amount of time (fraction of a year or accounting period) in which borrowing costs could be incurred. The expenditures include amounts paid for by cash or other asset or an interest-bearing liability, including previously capitalized borrowing costs. The expenditures are reduced by any progress payments received from a customer (in the case of construction of an inventory item) and by any grants received, such as from one or more levels of government.

To illustrate, assume a 17-month bridge construction project with current-year payments to the contractor of $240,000 on March 1, $480,000 on July 1, and $360,000 on November 1. The weighted-average accumulated expenditures for the year ended December 31 are calculated in Illustration 10A-1.

Illustration 10A-1					
Calculation of Weighted-Average Accumulated Expenditures	Expenditures			Capitalization	Weighted-Average Accumulated
	Date	Amount	×	Period*	= Expenditures
	Mar. 1	$ 240,000		10/12	$200,000
	July 1	480,000		6/12	240,000
	Nov. 1	360,000		2/12	60,000
		$1,080,000			$500,000

*Months between the date of expenditure and the date when interest capitalization stops or year end arrives, whichever comes first (in this case, December 31)

The costs incurred are weighted by the amount of time that borrowing costs could have been incurred on each expenditure in the year. For the March 1 expenditure, 10 months of borrowing cost could be associated with the expenditure. For the expenditure on July 1, only 6 months of interest could have been incurred. For the November 1 expenditure, there would only be 2 months.

Step 2: Determine the Avoidable Borrowing Costs on the Asset-Specific Debt

In this example, there is no asset-specific borrowing and therefore, no asset-specific borrowing costs. If there were, remember that the borrowing costs on this debt would have to be reduced by the investment income on any temporary investment of the funds.

Step 3: Determine the Avoidable Borrowing Costs on the Non–Asset-Specific Debt

The next step entails (a) calculating an appropriate **capitalization rate** and (b) applying it to the weighted-average expenditures financed by general debt. The rate is a weighted-average borrowing rate on the general borrowings. Assume that the borrowings identified in Illustration 10A-2 were all outstanding for the full year.

Illustration 10A-2

Calculation of Capitalization Rate

	Principal	Borrowing costs[16]
12%, 2-year note	$ 600,000	$ 72,000
9%, 10-year bonds	2,000,000	180,000
7.5%, 20-year bonds	5,000,000	375,000
	$7,600,000	$627,000

Because each debt instrument was outstanding for the full year, each principal amount is already weighted by 12/12. The interest also represents a full 12 months of borrowing costs. The weighted-average capitalization rate on the general-purpose debt is calculated as follows:

$$\frac{\text{Total borrowing costs}}{\text{Weighted-average principal outstanding}} = \frac{\$627,000}{\$7,600,000} = 8.25\%$$

The avoidable borrowing cost on non-asset-specific debt is the total weighted-average amount of accumulated expenditures (from step 1) reduced by the weighted-average expenditures financed by asset-specific debt from step 2, multiplied by the capitalization rate: ($500,000 − $0) × 8.25% = $41,250.

Step 4: Determine the Borrowing Costs to Capitalize

This step adds the eligible borrowing costs on asset-specific borrowings of $0 (step 2) and those on general borrowings of $41,250 (step 3) for a total of $41,250. This is the amount of cost to capitalize unless the actual borrowing costs incurred in the year are less than this. The lower amount is used.

An example that incorporates both asset-specific and general borrowings is explained next.

Illustration

Assume that on November 1, 2013, Shalla Corporation contracted with Pfeifer Construction Co. Ltd. to have a building constructed for its own use for $1.4 million, on land costing $100,000. The land is acquired from the contractor and its purchase price is included in the first payment. Shalla made the following payments to the construction company during 2014:

January 1	March 1	May 1	December 31	Total
$210,000	$300,000	$540,000	$450,000	$1,500,000

Construction of the building began very early in January and it was completed and ready for occupancy on December 31, 2014. Shalla had the following debt outstanding at December 31, 2014:

Specific Construction Debt	
15%, 3-year note to finance construction of the building, dated December 31, 2013, with interest payable annually on December 31	$750,000
Other Debt	
10%, 5-year note payable, dated December 31, 2011, with interest payable annually on December 31	$550,000
12%, 10-year bonds issued December 31, 2007, with interest payable annually on December 31	$600,000

Step 1. Determine the expenditures on the qualifying asset. The weighted-average accumulated expenditures during 2014 are calculated in Illustration 10A-3.

Illustration 10A-3

Calculation of Weighted-Average Accumulated Expenditures

	Expenditures		Current Year Capitalization		Weighted-Average Accumulated
Date	Amount	×	Period	=	Expenditures
Jan. 1	$ 210,000		12/12		$210,000
Mar. 1	300,000		10/12		250,000
May 1	540,000		8/12		360,000
Dec. 31	450,000		–0–		–0–
	$1,500,000				$820,000

Note that the expenditure made on December 31, the last day of the year, gets a zero weighting in the calculation. It will have no borrowing cost assigned to it.

Step 2. Determine the avoidable borrowing costs on the asset-specific debt. The asset-specific construction debt of $750,000 was outstanding for the full year and is therefore weighted for a full 12 months. Therefore, the avoidable borrowing cost on this debt is $750,000 × 15% = $112,500.

Step 3. Determine the avoidable borrowing costs on the non–asset-specific debt. Illustration 10A-4 shows the calculation of this borrowing cost. It is the weighted-average accumulated expenditures financed by general borrowings multiplied by the capitalization rate.

Illustration 10A-4

Calculation of Avoidable Borrowing Cost on General Debt

Total weighted-average accumulated expenditures	$820,000	
Less financed by specific construction loan	750,000	
Weighted-average accumulated expenditures financed by general borrowings	$ 70,000	
Capitalization rate calculation:	Principal	Borrowing Cost
10%, 5-year note: $550,000 × 12/12	$ 550,000	$ 55,000
12%, 10-year bonds: $600,000 × 12/12	600,000	72,000
	$1,150,000	$127,000

$$\text{Capitalization rate} = \frac{\text{Borrowing cost on general debt}}{\text{Weighted principal outstanding}} = \frac{\$127,000}{\$1,150,000} = 11.04\%$$

Avoidable borrowing cost on general debt: $70,000 × 11.04% = $7,728

Step 4.   Determine the borrowing costs to capitalize. Use the lower of the total avoidable borrowing costs eligible for capitalization (result of 2 and 3 above) and the actual borrowing costs incurred. The calculations are shown in Illustration 10A-5.

Illustration 10A-5
Calculation of Total Avoidable and Actual Borrowing Costs

Avoidable costs on asset-specific debt		$112,500
Avoidable costs on general debt		7,728
Total avoidable borrowing costs		$120,228
Total actual borrowing costs for the period:		
Construction note	$750,000 × 0.15 =	$112,500
5-year note	$550,000 × 0.10 =	55,000
10-year bonds	$600,000 × 0.12 =	72,000
Actual borrowing costs		$239,500

The amount of borrowing costs capitalized, therefore, is $120,228.

The journal entries made by Shalla Company during 2014 are shown in Illustration 10A-6.

Illustration 10A-6
Journal Entries for Recording of Expenditures and Interest Costs

Jan. 1	Land	100,000	
	Buildings (or Construction in Process)	110,000	
	Cash		210,000
Mar. 1	Buildings	300,000	
	Cash		300,000
May 1	Buildings	540,000	
	Cash		540,000
Dec. 31	Buildings	450,000	
	Cash		450,000
Dec. 31	Buildings	120,228	
	Interest Expense		120,228

The capitalized borrowing costs of $120,228 are added to the building's acquisition cost and are amortized as part of its depreciation charge. In other words, under IFRS and ASPE where it is the company's policy to capitalize interest costs, they will be recognized in expense over the useful life of the asset and not over the term of the debt. However, if under ASPE the company's policy is to expense all interest costs, the final journal entry above would not be recorded.

Disclosures

Only two disclosures are required for borrowing costs: the amount capitalized and the capitalization rate.

Illustration 10A-7 provides an example of **BCE Inc.**'s disclosures in its 2011 financial statements. BCE Inc. is one of Canada's leading communications companies.

Illustration 10A-7
Disclosures Related to Borrowing Costs Capitalized

NOTE 7 INTEREST EXPENSE

FOR THE YEAR ENDED DECEMBER 31	2011	2010
Interest expense on long-term debt	(774)	(687)
Interest expense on other debt	(80)	(56)
Capitalized interest	12	58
Total interest expense	(842)	(685)

Real World Emphasis

Included in interest expense on long-term debt is $144 million and $147 million of interest on finance leases for 2011 and 2010, respectively.

Capitalized interest was calculated using an average rate of 5.70% and 7.45% for 2011 and 2010, respectively, which represents the weighted average interest rate on our outstanding long-term debt.

SUMMARY OF LEARNING OBJECTIVE FOR APPENDIX 10A

12 Calculate the amount of borrowing costs to capitalize for qualifying assets.

The avoidable borrowing costs related to the financing of eligible expenditures on qualifying assets are capitalized to the extent they are less than the total borrowing costs incurred in the period.

KEY TERMS

avoidable borrowing costs, p. 632
borrowing costs, p. 631
capitalization period, p. 632

capitalization rate, p. 634
qualifying assets, p. 632

weighted-average accumulated
expenditures, p. 633

APPENDIX 10B

REVALUATION: THE PROPORTIONATE METHOD

Objective 13
Apply the revaluation model using the proportionate method.

Like the asset adjustment method, when using the proportionate method, a revaluation is not necessarily required at each reporting date. However, revaluation should be carried out often enough to ensure the carrying amount reported does not become materially different from fair value. For this example, we will assume that the asset only needs to be remeasured every three years. Between revaluation dates, **depreciation is taken** on the revalued amount that has been increased proportionally. Specifically, on January 1, 2010, Convo Corporation acquires a building at a cost of $100,000. The building is expected to have a 25-year life and no residual value. The asset is accounted for using the proportionate revaluation method and revaluation is carried out every three years. On December 31, 2012, the fair value of the building is appraised at $90,000, and on December 31, 2015, its fair value is $75,000.

Similar to the asset adjustment method, the amounts debited or credited to the Revaluation Surplus account are reported in the statement of comprehensive income as other comprehensive income (OCI) items. Also, over the life of the asset, the effect of the treatment described is that there is no **net increase** in net income from revaluing the asset. However, when revaluing an asset, the account is adjusted proportionately.

Quiz

Specifically, both the asset's carrying amount and its accumulated depreciation are adjusted (upwards if there has been an increase in fair value, or downwards for a decrease in fair value), so that the net balance is the fair value of the asset at the revaluation date. Illustration 10B-1 demonstrates the proportionate method for the building on December 31, 2012 when fair value was $90,000.

Illustration 10B-1

Proportionate Method: Illustration

	Before revaluation		Proportionate amount after revaluation
Buildings	$100,000	× 90/88	$102,273
Accumulated depreciation	12,000	× 90/88	12,273
Carrying amount	$ 88,000	× 90/88	$ 90,000

A   = L +   SE
+2,000   +2,000

Cash flows: No effect

Buildings	2,273	
Accumulated Depreciation—Buildings		273
Revaluation Surplus (OCI)		2,000

Illustration 10B-2 demonstrates the calculations and journal entries for the revaluation adjustment using the proportionate method for 2015 (where $102,273/25 × 6 = $24,546).

Illustration 10B-2

Revaluation Model Using the Proportionate Method: Illustration

	Before revaluation		Proportionate amount after revaluation
Buildings	$102,273	× 75,000/77,727	$98,685
Accumulated depreciation	24,546	× 75,000/77,727	23,685
Carrying amount	$ 77,727	× 75,000/77,727	$75,000

A   = L +   SE
−2,727   −2,727

Cash flows: No effect

Accumulated Depreciation—Buildings	861	
Revaluation Surplus (OCI)	2,000	
Revaluation Gain or Loss	727	
Buildings		3,588

SUMMARY OF LEARNING OBJECTIVE FOR APPENDIX 10B

13 Apply the revaluation model using the proportionate method.

The revaluation model may be applied using the proportionate method, provided fair value can be measured reliably. Similar to the asset adjustment method, the amounts debited or credited to the Revaluation Surplus (OCI) account are reported in the statement of comprehensive income as other comprehensive income (OCI) items. However, when revaluing an asset, the account is adjusted proportionately so that both the carrying amount of the asset and the accumulated depreciation are adjusted (upwards if there has been an increase in fair value, or downwards for a decrease in fair value). After adjustment, the net balance is the fair value of the asset at the revaluation date.

Note: All assignment material with an asterisk (*) relates to the appendices to the chapter.

Brief Exercises

(LO 1) **BE10-1** Caruso Airlines Incorporated is a privately owned commercial airline servicing short-haul routes in Western Canada. Caruso has operated successfully and profitably for five years. It is now considering expanding its fleet of 10 aircraft by adding 15 new aircraft in order to service its existing routes more efficiently. Caruso would pay for the expansion with a combination of internally generated funds and a new bank loan. Discuss the effects of Caruso's expansion on the company's (a) business and operations, (b) financial statements, and (c) rate of return on assets and asset turnover.

(LO 3) **BE10-2** Playtime Corporation purchased a new piece of equipment for production of a new children's toy. According to market research tests, the toy is expected to be very popular among preschool-aged children. The equipment consists of the following significant and separable parts: injection unit (useful life of six years), clamping unit (useful life of six years), and electrical equipment (useful life of three years). The equipment also includes other parts (useful life of five years). Discuss (a) the recognition criteria for recording purchase of the equipment, (b) how the equipment purchase should be recorded if Playtime prepares financial statements in accordance with IFRS, and (c) how the equipment purchase should be recorded if Playtime prepares financial statements in accordance with ASPE.

(LO 4, 6) **BE10-3** Barnet Brothers Inc. purchased land and an old building with the intention of removing the old building and then constructing the company's new corporate headquarters on the land. The land and old building were purchased for $570,000. Closing costs were $6,000. The old building was removed at a cost of $48,000. After readying the land for its intended use, and while waiting for construction to begin, Barnet generated net revenue of $4,000 from using the land as a parking lot. Determine the amount to be recorded as the land cost, and the treatment of the net revenue of $4,000, if Barnet prepares financial statements in accordance with (a) IFRS and (b) ASPE.

(LO 4, 6) **BE10-4** Northern Utilities Corporation incurred the following costs in constructing a new maintenance building during the fiscal period.

   (a) Direct labour costs incurred up to the point when the building is in a condition necessary for use as management intended, but before Northern Utilities begins operating in the building, $73,000

   (b) Additional direct labour costs incurred before Northern begins operating in the building, $6,000

   (c) Material purchased for the building, $82,500

   (d) Interest on the loan to finance construction until completion, $2,300

   (e) Allocation of plant overhead based on labour hours worked on the building, $29,000

   (f) Architectural drawings for the building, $7,500

   (g) Allocation of the president's salary, $54,000

What costs should be included in the cost of the new building if Northern prepares financial statements in accordance with IFRS? With ASPE? (Assume that if there is no specific guidance from GAAP, Northern's management would consider a building ready for productive use when Northern begins operating in the building, and would prefer not to capitalize interest costs directly attributable to the acquisition, construction, or development of property, plant, and equipment.)

(LO 5) **BE10-5** Petri Corporation purchased equipment for an invoice price of $40,000, terms 2/10, n/30. (a) Record the purchase of the equipment and the subsequent payment, assuming the payment was made within the discount period. (b) Repeat (a), but assume the company's payment missed the discount period.

(LO 5) **BE10-6** Chavez Corporation purchased a truck by issuing an $80,000, four-year, non–interest-bearing note to Equinox Inc. The market interest rate for obligations of this nature is 12%. Prepare the journal entry to record the truck purchase.

(LO 5) **BE10-7** Martin Corporation purchased a truck by issuing an $80,000, 12% note to Equinox Inc. Interest is payable annually and the note is payable in four years. Prepare the journal entry to record the truck purchase.

(LO 5) **BE10-8** Hamm Inc. purchased land, a building, and equipment from Spamela Corporation for a cash payment of $306,000. The assets' estimated fair values are land $95,000, building $250,000, and equipment $110,000. At what amounts should each of the three assets be recorded?

(LO 5) **BE10-9** Wizard Corp., a private company, obtained land by issuing 2,000 of its no par value common shares. The land was appraised at $85,000 by a reliable, independent valuator on the date of acquisition. Last year, Wizard sold 1,000 common shares at $41 per share. Prepare the journal entry to record the land acquisition (a) if Wizard elects to prepare financial statements in accordance with IFRS and (b) if Wizard prepares financial statements in accordance with ASPE.

(LO 5) BE10-10 Kristali Corporation traded a used truck (cost $23,000, accumulated depreciation $20,700) for another used truck worth $3,700. Kristali also paid $300 cash in the transaction. Prepare the journal entry to record the exchange, assuming the transaction lacks commercial substance.

(LO 5) BE10-11 Seymour Ltd. traded a used welding machine (cost $9,000, accumulated depreciation $2,000, fair value $3,000) for office equipment with an estimated fair value of $8,000. Seymour also paid $4,000 cash in the transaction. Prepare the journal entry to record the exchange. The equipment results in different cash flows for Seymour, compared with those the welding machine produced.

(LO 5) BE10-12 Spencer Ltd. traded a used truck (cost $30,000, accumulated depreciation $27,000, fair value $2,000) for a new truck worth $35,000. Spencer also made a cash payment of $31,000. Prepare Spencer's entry to record the exchange, and state any assumptions that you have made.

(LO 5) BE10-13 In early January, Swanton Corp. purchased a building to house its manufacturing operations in Moose Jaw for $470,000. The company agreed to lease the land that the building stood on for $14,000 per year from the industrial park owner, and the municipality donated $140,000 to Swanton as an incentive to locate in the area and acquire the building. Prepare entries to record the cash that was exchanged in each of the transactions, assuming the cost reduction method is used.

(LO 5) BE10-14 Use the information for Swanton Corp. in BE10-13. Prepare the entries to record the three cash transactions, assuming the deferral method is used.

(LO 5) BE10-15 Dubois Inc. received equipment as a donation. The equipment has a fair value of $55,000. Prepare the journal entry to record the receipt of the equipment under each of the following assumptions:

(a) The equipment was donated by a shareholder.

(b) The equipment was donated by a retired employee.

(LO 6) BE10-16 Lowell Corporation acquires a gold mine at a cost of $400,000. Development costs that were incurred total $100,000, including $12,300 of depreciation on movable equipment to construct mine shafts. Based on construction to date, the legal obligation to restore the property after the mine is exhausted has a present value of $75,000. Lowell has publicly pledged an additional $20,000 (present value) for improved reclamation of the area surrounding the mine. Prepare the journal entries to record the cost of the natural resource if Lowell prepares financial statements in accordance with (a) IFRS and (b) ASPE.

(LO 8) *BE10-17 Valued Assets Inc., a publicly listed company, has a manufacturing plant with an initial cost of $100,000. At December 31, 2014, the date of revaluation, accumulated depreciation amounted to $55,000. The fair value of the plant, by comparing it with transactions involving similar assets, is assessed to be $65,000. Prepare the journal entries to revalue the plant under the revaluation model using (a) the asset adjustment method and (b) the proportionate method.

(LO 9) BE10-18 TrueValue Investment Properties Inc. and its subsidiaries have provided you with a list of the properties they own:

(a) Land held by TrueValue for undetermined future use

(b) A vacant building owned by TrueValue and to be leased out under an operating lease

(c) Property held by a subsidiary of TrueValue, a real estate firm, in the ordinary course of its business

(d) Property held by TrueValue for use in the manufacturing of products

Advise TrueValue and its subsidiaries as to the proper presentation and measurement options for the above properties under both IFRS and ASPE.

(LO 10) BE10-19 Identify whether the following costs should be treated as a capital expenditure or a revenue expenditure when they are incurred.

(a) $13,000 paid to rearrange and reinstall machinery

(b) $200 paid for a tune-up and oil change on a delivery truck

(c) $200,000 paid for an addition to a building

(d) $7,000 paid to replace a wooden floor with a concrete floor

(e) $2,000 paid for a major overhaul that extends the useful life of a truck

(f) $700,000 paid for relocating company headquarters

(LO 10) BE10-20 Shipper Inc. has acquired a large transport truck at a cost of $90,000 (with no breakdown of the component parts). The truck's estimated useful life is 10 years. At the end of the seventh year, the powertrain requires replacement. It is determined that it is not economical to put any more money or time into maintaining the old powertrain. The remainder of the transport truck is in good working condition and is expected to last for the next three years. The cost of a new powertrain is $40,000. (a) Should the cost of the new powertrain be recognized as an asset or as an expense? (b) How should the transaction be measured and recorded if Shipper prepares financial statements in accordance with IFRS? (c) How should the transaction be measured and recorded if Shipper prepares financial statements in accordance with ASPE?

(LO 4, *BE10-21 Brent Hill Company is constructing a building. Construction began on February 1 and was completed on **12)** December 31. Expenditures were $1.5 million on March 1, $1.2 million on June 1, and $3 million on December 31. Calculate Brent Hill's weighted-average accumulated expenditures that would be used for capitalization of borrowing costs.

(LO 4, *BE10-22 Brent Hill Company (see BE10-21) borrowed $1 million on March 1 on a five-year, 12% note to help **12)** finance the building construction. In addition, the company had outstanding all year a $2-million, five-year, 13% note payable and a $3.5-million, four-year, 15% note payable. Calculate the appropriate capitalization rate on general borrowings that would be used for capitalization of borrowing costs.

(LO 4, *BE10-23 Use the information for Brent Hill Company from BE10-21 and BE10-22. Calculate the company's **12)** avoidable borrowing costs assuming Brent Hill Company follows IFRS. How would your answer change if the company followed ASPE?

Exercises

(LO 2, 3) E10-1 (Cost Elements and Asset Componentization) The following assets have been recognized as items of property, plant, and equipment.

1. Head office boardroom table and executive chairs

2. A landfill site

3. Wooden pallets in a warehouse

4. Forklift vehicles in a manufacturing plant

5. Stand-alone training facility for pilot training, including a flight simulator and classrooms equipped with desks, whiteboards, and electronic instructional aids

6. Large passenger aircraft used in commercial flights

7. Medical office building

8. Computer equipment

Instructions

For each of the items listed:

(a) Identify what specific costs are likely to be included in the acquisition cost.

(b) Explain whether any components of this asset should be given separate recognition, and why.

(LO 4, 5) E10-2 (Purchase and Cost of Self-Constructed Assets) Wen Corp., located in Manitoba, both purchases and constructs various pieces of equipment that it uses in its operations. The following items are for two different pieces of equipment and were recorded in random order during the calendar year 2014:

Purchase	
Cash paid for equipment, including sales tax of $7,000 and recoverable GST of $5,000	$112,000
Freight and insurance cost while in transit	2,000
Cost of moving equipment into place at factory	3,100
Wage cost for technicians to test equipment	4,000
Materials cost for testing	500
Insurance premium paid on the equipment for its first year of operation	1,500
Special plumbing fixtures required for new equipment	8,000
Repair cost on equipment incurred in first year of operations	1,300
Cash received from provincial government as incentive to purchase equipment	25,000

Construction

Material and purchased parts (gross cost $200,000; failed to take 2% cash discount)	$200,000
Imputed interest on funds used during construction (equity/share financing)	14,000
Labour costs	190,000
Overhead costs (fixed $20,000; variable $30,000)	50,000
Profit on self-construction	30,000
Cost of installing equipment	4,400

Instructions

Calculate the total cost for each of these two pieces of equipment. If an item is not capitalized as an equipment cost, indicate how it should be reported.

(LO 4, 5) E10-3   (Entries for Asset Acquisition, Including Self-Construction) The following are transactions related to Producers Limited:

1. The City of Piedmont gives the company five hectares of land as a plant site. This land's fair value is determined to be $92,000.

2. Producers issues 13,000 no par value common shares in exchange for land and buildings. The property has been appraised at a fair value of $1,630,000, of which $407,000 has been allocated to land, $887,000 to the structure of the buildings, $220,000 to the building HVAC heating, ventilation, air conditioning, and $116,000 to the interior coverings in the buildings (such as flooring). Producers' shares are not listed on any exchange, but a block of 100 shares was sold by a shareholder 12 months ago at $57 per share, and a block of 200 shares was sold by another shareholder 18 months ago at $33 per share.

3. No entry has been made to remove amounts for machinery constructed during the year that were charged to the accounts Inventory, Supplies, and Salaries and Wages Expense and should have been charged to plant asset accounts. The following information relates to the costs of the machinery that was constructed:

Construction materials used	$23,000
Direct materials used in calibrating the equipment	625
Factory supplies used	980
Direct labour incurred	56,000
Additional variable overhead (over regular) caused by construction of machinery, excluding factory supplies used (charged to Inventory)	8,700
Fixed overhead rate applied to regular manufacturing operations	70% of direct labour cost
Cost of similar machinery if it had been purchased from outside suppliers	125,000

Instructions

Prepare journal entries on the books of Producers Limited to record these transactions. Assume that Producers Limited prepares financial statements in accordance with IFRS.

(LO 4, 5, 11) E10-4   (Treatment of Various Costs) Farrey Supply Ltd. is a newly formed public corporation that incurred the following costs related to land, buildings, and machinery:

Legal fees for title search		$ 520
Architect's fees		2,800
Cash paid for land and dilapidated building on it		112,000
Removal of old building	$20,000	
Less: Salvage	5,500	14,500
Surveying before construction		370
Interest on short-term loans during construction		7,400
Excavation before construction for basement		19,000
Machinery purchased (subject to 2% cash discount, which was not taken)		65,000
Freight on machinery purchased		1,340
Storage charges on machinery, made necessary because building was still under construction when machinery was delivered		2,180
New building constructed (building construction took six months from date of purchase of land and old building)		485,000
Assessment by city for drainage project		1,600
Hauling charges for delivery of machinery from storage to new building		620
Installation of machinery		2,000
Trees, shrubs, and other landscaping after completion of building (permanent in nature)		5,400
Municipal grant to promote locating building in the municipality		(8,000)

Instructions

Digging Deeper

(a) Determine the amounts that should be included in the cost of land, buildings, and machinery. Indicate how any amounts that are not included in these accounts should be recorded.

(b) Assume that Farrey is not a public company, and that it prepares financial statements in accordance with ASPE. Would the solution provided in part (a) be affected?

(c) From the perspective of a potential investor, what are the financial statement effects of capitalizing borrowing costs related to qualifying assets?

(LO 4, 5, 12) ***E10-5 (Asset Acquisition)** Hayes Industries Corp. purchased the following assets and also constructed a building. All this was done during the current year.

Assets 1 and 2

These assets were purchased together for $100,000 cash. The following information was gathered:

Description	Initial Cost on Seller's Books	Depreciation to Date on Seller's Books	Book Value on Seller's Books	Appraised Value
Machinery	$100,000	$50,000	$50,000	$90,000
Office Equipment	60,000	10,000	50,000	30,000

Asset 3

This machine was acquired by making a $10,000 down payment and issuing a $30,000, two-year, zero-interest-bearing note. The note is to be paid off in two $15,000 instalments made at the end of the first and second years. It was determined that the asset could have been purchased outright for $35,000.

Asset 4

A truck was acquired by trading in an older truck that has the same value in use. The newer truck has options that will make it more comfortable for the driver; however, the company remains in the same economic position after the exchange as before. Facts concerning the trade-in are as follows:

Cost of truck traded	$100,000
Accumulated depreciation to date of sale	40,000
Fair market value of truck traded	80,000
Cash received by Hayes	10,000
Fair market value of truck acquired	70,000

Asset 5

Office equipment was acquired by issuing 100 no par value common shares. The shares are actively traded and had a closing market price the day before the office equipment was acquired of $9.25 per share. Alternatively, the office equipment could have been purchased for a cash price of $900.

Construction of Building

A building was constructed on land that was purchased last year at a cost of $150,000. Construction began on February 1 and was completed November 1. The payments to the contractor were as follows:

Date	Payment
Feb. 1	$120,000
June 1	360,000
Sept. 1	480,000
Nov. 1	100,000

To finance construction of the building, a $600,000, 12% construction loan was taken out on February 1. During the beginning of the project, Hayes invested the portion of the construction loan that was not yet expended and earned investment income of $4,600. The loan was repaid on November 1. The firm had $200,000 of other outstanding debt during the year at a borrowing rate of 8% and a $350,000 loan payable outstanding at a borrowing rate of 6%.

Instructions

Record the acquisition of each of these assets assuming that Hayes prepares financial statements in accordance with IFRS.

(LO 4, 6) **E10-6 (Acquisition Costs of Equipment)** Lili Corporation acquires new equipment at a cost of $100,000 plus 7% provincial sales tax and 5% GST. (GST is a recoverable tax.) The company paid $1,700 to transport the equipment to its plant. The site where the equipment was to be placed was not yet ready and Lili Corporation spent another $500 for one month's storage costs. When installed, $300 of labour and $200 of materials were used to adjust and calibrate the machine to the company's exact specifications. The units produced in the trial runs were subsequently sold to employees for $400. During the first two months of production, the equipment was used only at 50% of its capacity. Labour costs of $3,000 and material costs of $2,000 were incurred in this production, while the units sold generated $5,500 of sales. Lili paid an engineering consulting firm $11,000 for its services in recommending the specific equipment to purchase and for help during the calibration phase. Borrowing costs of $800 were incurred because of the one-month delay in installation.

Instructions

Determine the capitalized cost of the equipment and explain why the remainder of the costs have not been capitalized.

(LO 4, 6) E10-7   (Directly Attributable Costs) DAC Manufacturing Inc. is installing a new plant at its production facility. It has incurred these costs:

Cost of the manufacturing plant (cost per supplier's invoice plus taxes)	$2,500,000
Initial delivery and handling costs	200,000
Cost of site preparation	600,000
Consultants used for advice on the acquisition of the plant	700,000
Interest charges paid to supplier of plant for deferred credit	200,000
Estimated dismantling costs to be incurred after seven years	300,000
Operating losses before commercial production	400,000

Instructions

Determine which costs DAC Manufacturing Inc. can capitalize in accordance with IAS 16.

(LO 4, 6) E10-8   (Acquisition Costs of Realty) The following expenditures and receipts are related to land, land improvements, and buildings that were acquired for use in a business enterprise. The receipts are in parentheses.

1. Money borrowed to pay a building contractor (signed a note), ($275,000)

2. A payment for construction from note proceeds, $275,000

3. The cost of landfill and clearing, $8,000

4. Delinquent real estate taxes on property, assumed by the purchaser, $7,000

5. A premium on a six-month insurance policy during construction, $6,000

6. Refund of one month's insurance premium because construction was completed early, ($1,000)

7. An architect's fee on a building, $22,000

8. The cost of real estate purchased as a plant site (land $200,000; building $50,000), $250,000

9. A commission fee paid to a real estate agency, $9,000

10. The installation of fences around a property, $4,000

11. The cost of razing (demolishing) and removing the building on the plant site (See 8), $11,000

12. Proceeds from the salvage of the demolished building, ($5,000)

13. Interest paid during construction on money borrowed for construction, $13,000

14. The cost of parking lots and driveways, $19,000

15. The cost of trees and shrubbery that were planted (non-permanent in nature, to be replaced every 20 years), $14,000

16. Excavation costs for new building, $3,000

17. The GST on the excavation cost, $150

Instructions

Identify each item by letter and list the items in columnar form, as shown below. Using the column headings that follow, write the number for each item in the first column and its amount under the column heading where it would be recorded. All receipt amounts should be reported in parentheses. For any amounts that should be entered in the Other Accounts column, also indicate the account title.

Item	Land	Land Improvements	Building	Other Accounts

(LO 4, 6) **E10-9** **(Acquisition Costs of Realty)** Glesen Corp. purchased land with two old buildings on it as a factory site for $460,000. The property tax assessment on this property was $350,000: $250,000 for the land and the rest for the buildings. It took six months to tear down the old buildings and construct the factory.

The company paid $50,000 to raze the old buildings and sold salvaged lumber and brick for $6,300. Legal fees of $1,850 were paid for title investigation and drawing up the purchase contract. Payment to an engineering firm was made for a land survey, $2,200, and for drawing the factory plans, $82,000. The land survey had to be made before final plans could be drawn. The liability insurance premium that was paid during construction was $900. The contractor's charge for construction was $3,640,000. The company paid the contractor in two instalments: $1,200,000 at the end of three months and $2,440,000 upon completion. The architects and engineers estimated the cost of the building to be 55% attributable to the structure, 35% attributable to the building HVAC services (heating, ventilation, air conditioning), and the remainder attributable to the roof structure as each of these elements is expected to have a different useful life. Interest costs of $170,000 were incurred to finance the construction.

Instructions

Determine the land and building costs as they should be recorded on the books of Glesen Corp. Assume that the land survey was for the building.

(LO 4, 6) **E10-10** **(Natural Resource—Copper)** Copper Products Limited leases property on which copper has been discovered. The lease provides for an immediate payment of $472,000 to the lessor before drilling has begun and an annual rental of $55,000. In addition, the lessee is responsible for cleaning up the waste and debris from drilling and for the costs associated with reconditioning the land for farming when the mine is abandoned. It is estimated that the legal obligation related to cleanup and reconditioning has a present value of $46,000. Copper Products has publicly pledged an additional $30,000 (present value) to reclaim the area surrounding the mine. Copper Products prepares financial statements in accordance with IFRS.

Instructions

(a) Determine the amount that should be capitalized in the Mineral Resources asset account as a result of the lease agreement.

(b) Would the amount provided in part (a) differ if Copper Products prepares financial statements in accordance with ASPE?

(c) Prior to entering into the lease agreement, assume that Copper Products had total debt of $580,000 and total assets of $1,000,000. Also assume that the immediate payment of $472,000 was paid upfront in cash. From the perspective of a creditor, discuss the effect of the lease agreement on Copper Products' debt to total assets ratio. Assume that Copper Products follows IFRS.

Digging Deeper

(LO 5) **E10-11** **(Acquisition Costs of Trucks)** Jackson Corporation operates a retail computer store. To improve its delivery services to customers, the company purchased four new trucks on April 1, 2014. The terms of acquisition for each truck were as follows:

1. Truck #1 had a list price of $17,000 and was acquired for a cash payment of $15,900.

2. Truck #2 had a list price of $18,000 and was acquired for a down payment of $2,000 cash and a non–interest-bearing note with a face amount of $16,000. The note is due April 1, 2015. Jackson would normally have to pay interest at a rate of 10% for such a borrowing, and the dealership has an incremental borrowing rate of 8%.

3. Truck #3 had a list price of $18,000. It was acquired in exchange for a computer system that Jackson carries in inventory. The computer system cost $13,500 and is normally sold by Jackson for $17,100. Jackson uses a perpetual inventory system.

4. Truck #4 had a list price of $16,000. It was acquired in exchange for 1,000 common shares of Jackson Corporation. The common shares are no par value shares with an active market value of $15 per share.

Instructions

(a) Prepare the appropriate journal entries for Jackson Corporation for the above transactions, assuming that Jackson prepares financial statements in accordance with IFRS. If there is some uncertainty about the amount, give reasons for your choice.

(b) Would the journal entries for transaction 4 provided in part (a) differ if Jackson prepares financial statements in accordance with ASPE?

(LO 5) **E10-12** **(Correction of Improper Cost Entries)** Plant acquisitions for selected companies are as follows:

1. Bella Industries Inc. acquired land, buildings, and equipment from a bankrupt company, Torres Co., for a lump-sum price of $700,000. At the time of purchase, Torres's assets had the following book and appraisal values:

	Book Value	Appraisal Value
Land	$200,000	$150,000
Buildings	250,000	350,000
Equipment	300,000	300,000

To be conservative, Bella Industries decided to take the lower of the two values for each asset it acquired. The following entry was made:

Land	150,000	
Buildings	250,000	
Equipment	300,000	
Cash		700,000

Bella Industries expects the building structure to last another 20 years; however, it expects that it will have to replace the roof in the next five years. Torres Co. indicated that, on initial construction of the building, the roof amounted to 20% of the value of the building. In meetings with contractors, due to the unique design and materials required to replace the roof, the contractors stated that the roof structure is currently worth 15% of the value of the building purchase.

2. Hari Enterprises purchased store equipment by making a $2,000 cash down payment and signing a $23,000, one-year, 10% note payable. The purchase was recorded as follows:

Equipment	27,300	
Cash		2,000
Notes Payable		23,000
Interest Payable		2,300

3. Kim Company purchased office equipment for $20,000, terms 2/10, n/30. Because the company intended to take the discount, it made no entry until it paid for the acquisition. The entry was:

Office Equipment	20,000	
Cash		19,600
Purchase Discounts		400

4. Kaiser Inc. recently received land at zero cost from the Village of Chester as an inducement to locate its business in the village. The land's appraised value was $27,000. The company made no entry to record the land because it had no cost basis.

5. Zimmerman Company built a warehouse for $600,000. It could have contracted out and purchased the building for $740,000. The controller made the following entry:

Buildings	740,000	
Cash		600,000
Profit on Construction		140,000

Instructions

(a) Prepare the entry that should have been made at the date of each acquisition. Round to the nearest dollar.

(b) Prepare the correcting entry that is required in each case to correct the accounts. In other words, do not simply reverse the incorrect entry and replace it with the entry in part (a).

Digging Deeper

(c) List the accounting principle, assumption, or constraint from the conceptual framework that has been violated in each case.

(LO 5) E10-13   (Entries for Equipment Acquisitions) Geddes Engineering Corporation purchased conveyor equipment with a list price of $50,000. Three independent cases that are related to the equipment follow. Assume that the equipment purchases are recorded gross.

1. Geddes paid cash for the equipment 15 days after the purchase, along with 5% GST (recoverable) and provincial sales tax of $3,500, both based on the purchase price. The vendor's credit terms were 1/10, n/30.

2. Geddes traded in equipment with a book value of $2,000 (initial cost $40,000), and paid $40,500 in cash one month after the purchase. The old equipment could have been sold for $8,000 at the date of trade, but was accepted for a trade-in allowance of $9,500 on the new equipment.

3. Geddes gave the vendor a $10,000 cash down payment and a 9% note payable with blended principal and interest payments of $20,000 each, due at the end of each of the next two years.

Digging Deeper

Instructions

(a) Prepare the general journal entries that are required to record the acquisition and the subsequent payment in each of the three independent cases above. Round to the nearest dollar.

(b) Compare the treatment of the cash discount in item 1 above with the accounting for purchase discounts for inventories using the net method in Chapter 8.

(LO 5) E10-14 **(Entries for Acquisition of Assets)** Information for Craig Ltd. follows:

1. On July 6, Craig acquired the plant assets of Desbury Company, which had discontinued operations. The property was appraised by a reliable, independent valuator on the date of acquisition as follows:

Land	$ 550,000
Building—structure	1,500,000
Building—HVAC	175,000
Machinery	725,000
Total	$2,950,000

Craig gave 18,000 of its no par value common shares in exchange. The most recent sale of Craig's common shares took place last month, when 5,000 shares were sold for $180 per share.

2. Craig had the following cash expenses between July 6 and December 15, the date when it first occupied the building:

Repairs to building	$ 98,000
Construction of bases for machinery to be installed later	110,000
Driveways and parking lots	131,000
Remodelling of office space in building, including new partitions and walls	59,000
Special assessment by city on land	16,000

On December 20, Craig purchased machinery for $305,000, subject to a 2% cash discount, and paid freight on the machinery of $14,000. The machine was dropped while being placed in position, which resulted in paying the supplier for repairs costing $12,500. The company paid the supplier within the discount period, and records purchases of machinery using the net method.

Instructions

(a) Prepare the entries for these transactions on the books of Craig Ltd. Craig prepares financial statements in accordance with IFRS.

(b) Would the journal entries for item 1 provided in part (a) differ if Craig prepares financial statements in accordance with ASPE?

(c) Prepare the entry for the purchase and payment of the machinery in item 2, assuming the discount was not taken.

(LO 5) E10-15 **(Purchase of Equipment with Non–Interest-Bearing Debt)** Native Inc. decided to purchase equipment from Central Ontario Industries on January 2, 2014, to expand its production capacity to meet customers' demand for its product. Native issued a $900,000, five-year, non–interest-bearing note to Central Ontario for the new equipment when the prevailing market interest rate for obligations of this nature was 10%. The company will pay off the note in five $180,000 instalments due at the end of each year of the note's life.

Instructions

(Round to nearest dollar in all calculations.)

(a) Prepare the journal entry(ies) at the date of purchase.

(b) Prepare the journal entry(ies) at the end of the first year to record the payment and interest, assuming that the company uses the effective interest method.

(c) Prepare the journal entry(ies) at the end of the second year to record the payment and interest.

(d) Assuming that the equipment has an eight-year life and no residual value, prepare the journal entry that is needed to record depreciation in the first year. (The straight-line method is used.)

(LO 5) E10-16 **(Purchase of Equipment with Debt)** On September 1, 2014, Reta Corporation purchased equipment for $30,000 by signing a two-year note payable with a face value of $30,000 due on September 1, 2016. The going rate of interest for this level of risk was 8%. The company has a December 31 year end.

Instructions

(a) Calculate the cost of the equipment assuming the note is as follows:

1. An 8% interest-bearing note, with interest due each September 1.

2. A 2% interest-bearing note, with interest due each September 1.

3. A non–interest-bearing note.

(b) Record all journal entries from September 1, 2014, to September 1, 2016, for the three notes in (a). Ignore depreciation of the equipment.

(Adapted from CGA-Canada adapted Examination.)

(LO 5) E10-17   (Asset Exchange, Monetary Transaction) Cannondale Company purchased an electric wax melter on April 30, 2014, by trading in its old gas model and paying the balance in cash. The following data relate to the purchase:

List price of new melter	$15,800
Cash paid	10,000
Cost of old melter (five-year life, $700 residual value)	11,200
Accumulated depreciation on old melter (straight-line)	6,300
Market value of old melter in active secondary market	5,200

Instructions

Assuming that Cannondale's fiscal year ends on December 31 and depreciation has been recorded through December 31, 2013, prepare the journal entry(ies) that are necessary to record this exchange. Give reasons for the accounting treatment you used.

(LO 5) E10-18   (Nonmonetary Exchange) Stacey Company Limited exchanged equipment that it uses in its manufacturing operations for similar equipment that is used in the operations of Chokar Company Limited. Stacey also paid Chokar $3,200 in cash. The following information pertains to the exchange:

	Stacey Co.	Chokar Co.
Equipment (cost)	$50,000	$55,000
Accumulated depreciation	31,250	22,000
Fair value of equipment	25,000	28,000
Cash paid	3,200	

Instructions

(a) Prepare the journal entries to record the exchange on the books of both companies assuming the exchange is determined to have commercial substance.

(b) Repeat part (a), assuming the exchange is determined not to have commercial substance.

Digging Deeper

(c) List some of the factors that the accountant would need to consider in order to determine whether the transaction has commercial substance.

(LO 5) E10-19   (Nonmonetary Exchanges) Carver Inc. recently replaced a piece of automatic equipment at a net price of $4,000, f.o.b. factory. The replacement was necessary because one of Carver's employees had accidentally backed his truck into Carver's original equipment and made it inoperable. Because of the accident, the equipment had no resale value to anyone and had to be scrapped. Carver's insurance policy provided for a replacement of its equipment and paid the price of the new equipment directly to the new equipment manufacturer, minus the deductible amount paid to the manufacturer by Carver. The $4,000 that Carver paid was the amount of the deductible that it has to pay on any single claim on its insurance policy. The new equipment represents the same value in use to Carver. The used equipment had originally cost $65,000. It had a book value of $45,000 at the time of the accident and a second-hand market value of $50,800 before the accident, based on recent transactions involving similar equipment. Freight and installation charges for the new equipment cost Carver an additional $1,100 cash.

Instructions

(a) Prepare the general journal entry to record the transaction to replace the equipment that was destroyed in the accident.

(b) Repeat part (a), but assume that the new equipment will result in significant savings to Carver since the new equipment is more efficient and requires less staff time to operate.

(LO 5) E10-20   (Nonmonetary Exchanges) Jamil Jonas is an accountant in public practice. Not long ago, Jamil struck a deal with his neighbour Ralph to prepare Ralph's business income tax and GST returns for 2014 in exchange for Ralph's services as a landscaper. Ralph provided labour and used his own equipment to perform landscaping services for Jamil's personal residence, for which he would normally charge $500. Jamil would usually charge $650 for the number of hours spent completing Ralph's returns but considers the transaction well worth it since he really dislikes doing his own landscaping.

Instructions

How would each party record this transaction? Prepare the journal entries for both Jamil's and Ralph's companies.

(LO 5) E10-21 (Government Assistance) Lightstone Equipment Ltd. wanted to expand into New Brunswick and was impressed by the provincial government's grant program for new industry. After being sure that it would qualify for the grant program, it purchased property in downtown Saint John on June 15, 2014. The property cost $235,000 and Lightstone spent the next two months gutting the building and reconstructing the two floors to meet the company's needs. The building has a useful life of 20 years and an estimated residual value of $65,000. In late August, the company moved into the building and began operations. Additional information follows:

1. The property was assessed at $195,000, with $145,000 allocated to the land.

2. Architectural drawings and engineering fees related to the construction cost $18,000.

3. The company paid $17,000 to the contractor for gutting the building and $108,400 for construction. Lightstone expects that these improvements will last for the remainder of the life of the building.

4. The provincial government contributed $75,000 toward the building costs.

Instructions

(a) Assuming that the company uses the cost reduction method to account for government assistance, answer the following:

1. What is the cost of the building on Lightstone Equipment's statement of financial position at August 31, 2014, its fiscal year end?

2. What is the effect of this capital asset on the company's income statement for the company's year ended August 31, 2015?

(b) Assuming the company uses the deferral method to account for government assistance, answer the following:

1. What is the cost of the building on Lightstone Equipment's statement of financial position at August 31, 2014?

2. What is the effect of this capital asset on the company's income statement for the company's year ended August 31, 2015?

Digging Deeper

(c) Compare the statement of financial position and income statement presentations for the two alternative treatments for government assistance for the fiscal year ended August 31, 2015.

(LO 6) E10-22 (Biological Assets) On March 1 2014, Russell Winery Ltd. purchased a five-hectare commercial vineyard for $1,050,000. The total purchase price was based on appraised market values of the building, grapevines, and equipment ($580,000, $260,000, and $210,000, respectively). Russell Winery incurred the following cash expenditures between March 1 and June 30, the date of Russell Winery's first harvest of the grapevines:

Major repairs to sprayer equipment	$28,000
Grapevine fertilizer	7,000
Phase 1 construction of a new grape trellis system for the grapevines	31,000
Construction of a new custom wine cellar	62,000
Harvesting labour	36,000

The fair value of the grapevines was estimated to have increased to $295,000 by December 31, 2014, the company's fiscal year end, and any sale of vineyard assets would attract a 4% realtor commission. Russell Winery prepares financial statements in accordance with IFRS.

Instructions

(a) What is the carrying amount of the grapevines on the statement of financial position at December 31, 2014? If there are differing accounting treatments of the items involved, discuss the options.

(b) In 2015, Russell Winery incurs $17,000 in costs related to Phase 2 construction of the new grape trellis system for the grapevines, and the fair value of the grapevines increases to $330,000 by December 31, 2015. What is the carrying amount of the grapevines on the statement of financial position at December 31, 2015?

(c) Would the carrying amount of the grapevines provided in part (a) differ if Russell Winery prepares financial statements in accordance with ASPE?

(LO 7, 9) E10-23 (Measurement after Acquisition—Fair Value Model versus Cost Model) Plaza Holdings Inc., a publicly listed company in Canada, ventured into construction of a mega shopping mall in Edmonton, which is rated as the largest shopping mall in North America. The company's board of directors, after much market research, decided that instead of selling the shopping mall to a local investor who had approached them several times with excellent offers that he steadily increased during the year of construction, the company would hold this property for the purposes of capital appreciation and earning rental income from mall tenants. Plaza Holdings retained the services of a real estate company to find and attract many important retailers to rent space in the shopping mall, and within months of completion at the end of 2014, the shopping mall was fully occupied.

According to the company's accounting department, the total construction cost of the shopping mall was $50 million. The company used an independent appraiser to determine the mall's fair value annually. According to the appraisal, the fair values of the shopping mall at the end of 2014 and at each subsequent year end were:

2014	$50 million
2015	$60 million
2016	$63 million
2017	$58 million

The independent appraiser felt that the useful life of the shopping mall was 20 years and its residual value was $5 million.

Instructions

Describe the impact on the company's income statement and prepare the necessary journal entries for 2015, 2016, and 2017 if it decides to treat the shopping mall as an investment property under IAS 40:

(a) Using the fair value model.

(b) Using the cost model.

Note that the mall's rental income and expenses would be the same under both options, and thus can be omitted from the analysis for this exercise.

(LO 7, 9) E10-24   (Measurement after Acquisition—Fair Value Model) Nevine Corporation owns and manages a small 10-store shopping centre and classifies the shopping centre as an investment property. Nevine has a May 31 year end and initially recognized the property at its acquisition cost of $10.8 million on June 2, 2013. The acquisition cost consisted of the purchase price of $10 million, costs to survey and transfer the property of $500,000, and legal fees for the acquisition of the property of $300,000. Nevine determines that approximately 25% of the shopping centre's value is attributable to the land, with the remainder attributable to the building. The following fair values are determined:

Date	Fair Value
May 31, 2014	$10,500,000
May 31, 2015	$10,400,000
May 31, 2016	$11,000,000

Nevine expects the shopping centre building to have a 35-year useful life and a residual value of $1.1 million. Nevine uses the straight-line method for depreciation.

Instructions

(a) Assume that Nevine decides to apply the cost model. What journal entries, if any, are required each year, and how will the investment property be reported on each year-end statement of financial position?

(b) Assume that Nevine decides to apply the fair value model. Prepare the journal entries, if any, required at each year end. In addition, explain how the property would be reported if Nevine prepared a statement of financial position shortly after acquisition in 2013.

(LO 8, *E10-25   (Measurement after Acquisition—Revaluation Model) A partial statement of financial position of
13) Bluewater Ltd. on December 31, 2013, showed the following property, plant, and equipment assets accounted for under the cost model (accumulated depreciation includes depreciation for 2013):

Buildings	$300,000	
Less: accumulated depreciation	100,000	$200,000
Equipment	$120,000	
Less: accumulated depreciation	40,000	80,000

Bluewater uses straight-line depreciation for its building (remaining useful life of 20 years, no residual value) and for its equipment (remaining useful life of eight years, no residual value). Bluewater applies IFRS and has decided to adopt the revaluation model for its building and equipment, effective December 31, 2013. On this date, an independent appraiser assessed the fair value of the building to be $160,000 and that of the equipment to be $90,000.

Instructions

(a) Prepare the necessary general journal entry(ies), if any, to revalue the building and the equipment as at December 31, 2013, using the asset adjustment method.

(b) Prepare the entries to record depreciation expense for the year ended December 31, 2014.

(c) Repeat parts (a) and (b) using the proportionate method to revalue the building and the equipment.

(LO 8, ***E10-26** **(Measurement after Acquisition—Revaluation Model)** On January 1, 2014, ABC Company acquires a
13) building at a cost of $125,000. The building is expected to have a 25-year life and no residual value. The asset is
accounted for under the revaluation model, using the asset adjustment method. Revaluations are carried out every three
years. On December 31, 2016, the fair value of the building is appraised at $120,000, and on December 31, 2019, its fair
value is $90,000. ABC Company applies IFRS.

Instructions

(Round to the nearest dollar in all calculations.)

(a) Prepare the journal entry(ies) required on December 31, 2014.

(b) Prepare the journal entry(ies) required on December 31, 2015.

(c) Prepare the journal entry(ies) required on December 31, 2016.

(d) Prepare the journal entry(ies) required on December 31, 2017.

(e) Prepare the journal entry(ies) required on December 31, 2019.

*(f) Prepare the journal entry required on December 31, 2016, and the journal entry required on December 31, 2019,
to revalue the building, if ABC uses the proportionate method.

Digging
Deeper

(g) From the perspective of an investor in ABC, discuss the financial statement effects of using the revaluation model
to determine the carrying amount of ABC's building.

(LO 10) **E10-27** **(Analysis of Subsequent Expenditures)** On January 1, 2014, the accounting records of Sasseville Ltée
included a debit balance of $15 million in the building account and of $12 million in the related accumulated depreciation account. The building was purchased in January 1974 for $15 million, and was estimated to have a 50-year useful
life with no residual value. Sasseville uses the straight-line depreciation method for all of its property, plant, and equipment. During 2014, the following expenditures relating to the building were made:

1. The original roof of the building was removed and replaced with a new roof. The old roof cost $1 million and the
new roof cost $2.5 million. It is expected to have a 15-year useful life.

2. The ongoing frequent repairs on the building during the year cost $57,000.

3. The building's old heating system was replaced with a new one. The new HVAC cost $700,000 and is estimated to
have a seven-year useful life and no residual value. The cost of the old HVAC is unknown.

4. A natural gas explosion caused $44,000 of damage to the building. This major repair did not change the estimated
useful life of the building.

Instructions

Prepare the journal entries to record the expenditures related to the building during 2014.

(Adapted from CGA-Canada Examination.)

(LO 10) **E10-28** **(Analysis of Subsequent Expenditures)** The following transactions occurred during 2014. Assume that
depreciation of 10% per year is charged on all machinery and 5% per year on buildings, on a straight-line basis, with no
estimated residual value. Assume also that depreciation is charged for a full year on all fixed assets that are acquired during the year, and that no depreciation is charged on fixed assets that are disposed of during the year.

Jan. 30	A building that cost $132,000 in 1997 was torn down to make room for a new building structure. The wrecking contractor was paid $5,100 and was permitted to keep all materials salvaged.
Mar. 10	A new part costing $2,900 was purchased and added to a machine that was purchased in 2012 for $16,000. The new part replaces an original machine part, and does not extend the machine's useful life. The old part's cost was not separable from the original machine's cost.
Mar. 20	A gear broke on a machine that cost $9,000 in 2009, and the gear was replaced at a cost of $85. The replacement does not extend the machine's useful life.
May 18	A special base that was installed for a machine in 2008 when the machine was purchased had to be replaced at a cost of $5,500 because of defective workmanship on the original base. The cost of the machinery was $14,200 in 2008. The cost of the base was $3,500, and this amount was charged to the Machinery account in 2008.
June 23	One of the buildings was repainted at a cost of $6,900. It had not been painted since it was constructed in 2010.

Instructions

(a) Prepare general journal entries for the transactions. (Round to nearest dollar.)

(b) Assume that on March 20, the gear replacement extends the machine's useful life. How would your journal entry change?

(LO 10)   E10-29   (Analysis of Subsequent Expenditures) Plant assets often require expenditures subsequent to acquisition. It is important that they be accounted for properly. Any errors will affect both the statements of financial position and income statements for several years.

Instructions

For each of the following items, indicate whether the expenditure should be capitalized (C) or expensed (E) in the period when it was incurred:

(a) _____ A betterment

(b) _____ Replacement of a minor broken part on a machine

(c) _____ An expenditure that increases an existing asset's useful life

(d) _____ An expenditure that increases the efficiency and effectiveness of a productive asset but does not increase its residual value

(e) _____ An expenditure that increases the efficiency and effectiveness of a productive asset and its residual value

(f) _____ An expenditure that increases a productive asset's output quality

(g) _____ An overhaul to a machine that increases its fair market value and its production capacity by 30% without extending the machine's useful life

(h) _____ Ordinary repairs

(i) _____ A major overhaul

(j) _____ Interest on borrowing that is necessary to finance a major overhaul of machinery that extends its life

(k) _____ An expenditure that results in a 10%-per-year production cost saving

(l) _____ Costs of a major overhaul that brings the asset's condition back to "new," with no change in the estimated useful life

(LO 4,   *E10-30   (Capitalization of Borrowing Costs) On December 31, 2013, Omega Inc. borrowed $3 million at 12%
12) payable annually to finance the construction of a new building. In 2014, the company made the following expenditures related to this building structure (unless otherwise noted): March 1, $360,000; June 1, $600,000; July 1, $1.5 million (of which $400,000 was for the roof); December 1, $1.5 million (of which $700,000 was for the building HVAC including heating, ventilation, air conditioning).

Additional information follows:

1. Other debt outstanding:

   $4-million, 10-year, 13% bond, dated December 31, 2007, with interest payable annually

   $1.6-million, six-year, 10% note, dated December 31, 2011, with interest payable annually

2. The March 1, 2014 expenditure included land costs of $150,000.

3. Interest revenue earned in 2014 on the unused idle construction loan amounted to $49,000.

Instructions

(a) Determine the interest amount that could be capitalized in 2014 in relation to the building construction.

(b) Prepare the journal entry to record the capitalization of borrowing costs and the recognition of interest expense, if any, at December 31, 2014.

(LO 4,   *E10-31   (Capitalization of Borrowing Costs) The following three situations involve the capitalization of borrow-
12) ing costs.

Situation 1

On January 1, 2014, Oksana Inc. signed a fixed-price contract to have Builder Associates construct a major head office facility at a cost of $4 million. It was estimated that it would take three years to complete the project. Also on January 1, 2014, to finance the construction cost, Oksana borrowed $4 million that is repayable in 10 annual instalments of $400,000, plus interest at the rate of 10%. During 2014, Oksana made deposit and progress payments totalling $1.5 million under the contract; and the weighted-average amount of accumulated expenditures was $800,000 for the year. The excess amount of borrowed funds was invested in short-term securities, from which Oksana realized investment income of $25,000.

Situation 2

During 2014, Midori Ito Corporation constructed and manufactured certain assets and incurred the following borrow-ing costs in connection with these activities:

Borrowing Costs Incurred	
Warehouse constructed for Ito's own use	$30,000
Special-order machine for sale to unrelated customer, produced according to customer's specifications	9,000
Inventories routinely manufactured, produced on a repetitive basis, that require many months to complete	8,000

Situation 3

Fleming, Inc. has a fiscal year ending April 30. On May 1, 2014, Fleming borrowed $10 million at 11% to finance construction of its own building. Repayments of the loan are to begin the month after the building's completion. During the year ended April 30, 2015, expenditures for the partially completed structure totalled $7 million. These expenditures were incurred evenly throughout the year. Interest that was earned on the part of the loan that was not expended amounted to $650,000 for the year.

Instructions

(a) For situation 1, what amount should Oksana report as capitalized borrowing costs at December 31, 2014?

(b) For situation 2, assuming the effect of capitalization of borrowing costs is material, what is the total amount of borrowing costs to be capitalized?

(c) For situation 3, how much should be shown as capitalized borrowing costs on Fleming's financial statements at April 30, 2015?

(CPA adapted)

(LO 4, 12) ***E10-32** **(Capitalization of Borrowing Costs)** In early February 2014, Huey Corp. began construction of an addition to its head office building that is expected to take 18 months to complete. The following 2014 expenditures relate to the addition:

Feb. 1	Payment #1 to contractor	$120,000
Mar. 1	Payment to architect	24,000
July 1	Payment #2 to contractor	60,000
Dec. 1	Payment #3 to contractor	180,000
Dec. 31	Asset carrying amount	$384,000

On February 1, Huey issued a $100,000, three-year note payable at a rate of 12% to finance most of the initial payment to the contractor. No other asset-specific debt was entered into. Details of other interest-bearing debt during the period are provided in the table below:

Other debt instruments outstanding—2014	Principal amount
7%, 10-year bonds, Issued June 15, 2008	$500,000
6%, 12-year bonds, issued May 1, 2014	$300,000
9%, 15-year bonds, issued May 1, 1999, matured May 1, 2014	$300,000

Instructions

What amount of interest should be capitalized according to IAS 23?

Problems

P10-1 Adamski Corporation manufactures ballet shoes and is experiencing a period of sustained growth. In an effort to expand its production capacity to meet the increased demand for its product, the company recently made several acquisitions of plant and equipment. Tanya Mullinger, newly hired with the title Capital Asset Accountant, requested that Walter Kaster, Adamski's controller, review the following transactions:

Transaction 1

On June 1, 2014, Adamski Corporation purchased equipment from Venghaus Corporation. Adamski issued a $20,000, four-year, non–interest-bearing note to Venghaus for the new equipment. Adamski will pay off the note in four equal instalments due at the end of each of the next four years. At the transaction date, the prevailing market interest rate for obligations of this nature was 10%. Freight costs of $425 and installation costs of $500 were incurred in completing this transaction. The new equipment qualifies for a $2,000 government grant.

Transaction 2

On December 1, 2014, Adamski purchased several assets of Haukap Shoes Inc., a small shoe manufacturer whose owner was retiring. The purchase amounted to $210,000 and included the assets in the following list. Adamski engaged the services of Tennyson Appraisal Inc., an independent appraiser, to determine the assets' fair values, which are also provided.

	Haukap Book Value	Fair Value
Inventory	$ 60,000	$ 50,000
Land	40,000	80,000
Building	70,000	120,000
	$170,000	$250,000

During its fiscal year ended May 31, 2015, Adamski incurred $8,000 of interest expense in connection with the financing of these assets.

Transaction 3

On March 1, 2015, Adamski traded in four units of specialized equipment and paid an additional $25,000 cash for a technologically up-to-date machine that should do the same job as the other machines, but much more efficiently and profitably. The equipment that was traded in had a combined carrying amount of $35,000, as Adamski had recorded $45,000 of accumulated depreciation against these assets. Adamski's controller and the sales manager of the supplier company agreed that the new equipment had a fair value of $64,000.

Instructions

(a) Tangible capital assets such as land, buildings, and equipment receive special accounting treatment. Describe the major characteristics of these assets that differentiate them from other types of assets.

(b) For each of the three transactions described above, determine the value at which Adamski Corporation should record the acquired assets. Support your calculations with an explanation of the underlying rationale.

(c) The books of Adamski Corporation show the following additional transactions for the fiscal year ended May 31, 2015:

1. Acquisition of a building for speculative purposes

2. Purchase of a two-year insurance policy covering plant equipment

3. Purchase of the rights for the exclusive use of a process used in the manufacture of ballet shoes

For each of these transactions, indicate whether the asset should be classified as an item of property, plant, and equipment. If it should be, explain why. If it should not, explain why not, and identify the proper classification.

(CMA adapted. Used with permission.)

P10-2   At December 31, 2013, certain accounts included in the property, plant, and equipment section of Golden Corporation's statement of financial position had the following balances:

Land	$310,000
Buildings—Structure	883,000
Leasehold Improvements	705,000
Equipment	845,000

During 2014, the following transactions occurred:

1. Land site No. 621 was acquired for $800,000 plus a commission of $47,000 to the real estate agent. Costs of $33,500 were incurred to clear the land. In clearing the land, topsoil and gravel were recovered and sold for $11,000.

2. Land site No. 622, which had a building on it, was acquired for $560,000. The closing statement indicated that the land's assessed tax value was $309,000 and the building's value was $102,000. Shortly after acquisition, the building was demolished at a cost of $28,000. A new building was constructed for $340,000 plus the following costs:

Excavation fees	$38,000
Architectural design fees	15,000
Building permit fee	2,500
"Green roof" design and construction (to be retrofitted every seven years)	36,000
Imputed interest on funds used during construction (share financing)	8,500

The building, completed and occupied on September 30, 2014, is expected to have a 30-year useful life.

3. A third tract of land (No. 623) was acquired for $265,000 and was put on the market for resale.

4. During December 2014, costs of $89,000 were incurred to improve leased office space. The related lease will terminate on December 31, 2016, and is not expected to be renewed.

5. A group of new machines was purchased under a royalty agreement. The terms of the agreement require Golden Corporation to pay royalties based on the units of production for the machines. The machines' invoice price was $111,000, freight costs were $3,300, installation costs were $3,600, and royalty payments for 2014 were $15,300.

Instructions

(a) Prepare a detailed analysis of the changes in each of the following statement of financial position accounts for 2014: Land, Leasehold Improvements, Buildings—Structure, Buildings—Roof, and Equipment. Ignore the related accumulated depreciation accounts.

(b) List the items in the situation that were not used to determine the answer to part (a) above, and indicate where, or if, these items should be included in Golden's financial statements.

(c) Using the terminology from the conceptual framework in Chapter 2, explain why the items in part (b) were not included in the accounts Land, Leasehold Improvements, Buildings (the Structure and Roof accounts), and Equipment.

Digging Deeper

(AICPA adapted)

P10-3 Webb Corporation prepares financial statements in accordance with IFRS. Selected accounts included in the property, plant, and equipment section of the company's statement of financial position at December 31, 2013, had the following balances:

Land	$ 300,000
Land Improvements	140,000
Buildings	1,100,000
Equipment	960,000

During 2014, the following transactions occurred:

1. A tract of land was acquired for $150,000 as a potential future building site.

2. A plant facility consisting of land and a building was acquired from Knorman Corp. in exchange for 20,000 of Webb's common shares. The most recent sale of Webb's common shares took place last month, when 4,000 of Webb's common shares sold for $57 per share. The plant facility was carried on Knorman's books at $110,000 for land and $320,000 for the building at the exchange date. At the exchange date, a reliable, independent valuator determined the fair value of the land and building to be $230,000 and $690,000 respectively.

3. Equipment was purchased for a total cost of $400,000. Additional costs incurred were as follows:

Freight and unloading	$13,000
Sales taxes	28,000
GST	20,000
Installation	26,000

4. Expenditures totalling $95,000 were made for new parking lots, streets, and sidewalks at the corporation's various plant locations. These expenditures had an estimated useful life of 15 years.

5. A piece of equipment that cost $80,000 on January 1, 2006, was scrapped on June 30, 2014. Double-declining-balance depreciation had been recorded based on a 10-year life.

6. A piece of equipment was sold for $20,000 on July 1, 2014. Its original cost was $44,000 on January 1, 2011, and it was depreciated on the straight-line basis over an estimated useful life of seven years, assuming a residual value of $2,000.

Instructions

(a) Prepare a detailed analysis of the changes in each of the following statement of financial position accounts for 2014: Land, Land Improvements, Buildings, and Machinery and Equipment. (*Hint*: Ignore the related accumulated depreciation accounts.)

(b) List the items in the transactions above that were not used to determine the answer to (a), and show the relevant amounts and supporting calculations in good form for each item. In addition, indicate where, or if, these items should be included in Webb's financial statements.

Digging Deeper

(c) How will the land in item 1 be accounted for when it is used as a building site?

(AICPA adapted)

P10-4 Kiev Corp. was incorporated on January 2, 2014, but was unable to begin manufacturing activities until July 1, 2014, because new factory facilities were not completed until that date. The Land and Building account at December 31, 2014, was as follows:

	2014		
	Jan. 31	Land and building	$166,000
	Feb. 28	Cost of removal of building	9,800
	May 1	Partial payment of new construction	60,000
	1	Legal fees paid	3,770
	June 1	Second payment on new construction	40,000
	1	Insurance premium	2,280
	1	Special tax assessment	4,000
	30	General expenses	36,300
	July 1	Final payment on new construction	10,000
	1	Payment for plumbing, furnace, air conditioning system	30,000
	Dec. 31	Asset write-up	43,800
			405,950
	31	Depreciation for 2014 at 1%	4,060
	Account balance		$401,890

The following additional information needs to be considered:

1. To acquire land and a building, the company paid $110,400 cash and 800 of its no par value, $8, cumulative preferred shares. The fair value of each share was estimated at $98 per share; however, Kiev's shares are not actively traded. The land and building were assessed by an independent, reliable valuator to have fair value of $166,000.

2. The costs for removing the building amounted to $9,800, and the demolition company kept all the building materials.

3. Legal fees covered the following:

Cost of organization	$ 610
Examination of title covering purchase of land	1,300
Legal work in connection with construction contract	1,860
	$3,770

4. The insurance premium covered the building for a two-year term beginning May 1, 2014.

5. The special tax assessment covered street improvements that are permanent in nature.

6. General expenses covered the following for the period from January 2, 2014, to June 30, 2014:

President's salary	$32,100
Plant superintendent's wages covering supervision of new building	4,200
	$36,300

7. Because of a general increase in construction costs after entering into the building contract, the board of directors increased the building's value by $43,800. It believed that such an increase was justified to reflect the current market at the time when the building was completed. Retained Earnings was credited for this amount.

8. The estimated life of the building structure is 50 years. The depreciation for 2014 on the building structure was 1% of the asset value (1% of $405,950, or $4,060). The estimated useful life of the building services (heating system, plumbing, air conditioning) is 20 years. No depreciation has been recorded on the building services.

Instructions

Prepare the entries to reallocate the proper balances into the Land, Buildings, and Accumulated Depreciation accounts at December 31, 2014.

(AICPA adapted)

P10-5   On June 28, 2014, in relocating to a new town, Kerr Corp. purchased a property consisting of two hectares of land and an unused building for $225,000 plus property taxes in arrears of $4,500. The company paid a real estate broker's commission of $12,000 and legal fees on the purchase transaction of $6,000. The closing statement indicated that the assessed values for tax purposes were $175,000 for the land and $35,000 for the building. Shortly after acquisition, the building was demolished at a cost of $24,000.

Kerr Corp. then entered into a $1.3-million fixed-price contract with Maliseet Builders, Inc. on August 1, 2014, for the construction of an office building on this site. The building was completed and occupied on April 29, 2015, as was a separate maintenance building that was constructed by Kerr's employees. Additional costs related to the property included:

Plans, specifications, and blueprints	$25,000
Architects' fees for design and supervision	82,000
Landscaping	42,000
Extras on contract for upgrading of windows	46,000
External signage on the property	23,000
Advertisements in newspaper and on television announcing opening of the building	10,600
Gala opening party for customers, suppliers, and friends of Kerr	18,800
Costs of internal direct labour and materials for maintenance building	67,000
Allocated plant overhead based on direct labour hours worked on maintenance building	10,000
Allocated cost of executive time spent on project	54,000
Interest costs on debt incurred to pay contractor's progress billings up to building completion	63,000
Interest costs on short-term loan to finance maintenance building costs	3,200

As an incentive for Kerr to locate and build in the town, the municipality agreed not to charge its normal building permit fees of approximately $36,000. This amount was included in the $1.3-million contract fee. The building and the maintenance building are estimated to have a 40-year life from their dates of completion and will be depreciated using the straight-line method.

Kerr has an April 30 year end, and the company accountant is currently analyzing the new Buildings account that was set up to capture all the expenditures and credits explained above that relate to the property.

Instructions

(a) Prepare a schedule that identifies the costs that would be capitalized and included in the new Buildings account on the April 30, 2015 balance sheet, assuming the accountant wants to comply with ASPE, but tends to be very conservative in nature; in other words, she does not want to overstate income or assets. Briefly justify your calculations. How would your answer change if Kerr were to comply with IFRS?

(b) Prepare a schedule that identifies the costs that would be capitalized and included in the new Buildings account on the April 30, 2015 balance sheet, assuming the accountant wants to comply with ASPE, but is aware that Kerr needs to report increased income to support a requested increase in its bank loan next month. Briefly justify your calculations.

(c) Comment on the difference in results for (a) and (b) above. Calculate the total expenses related to the building under both scenarios. What else should be considered in determining the amount to be capitalized?

P10-6 Vidi Corporation made the following purchases related to its property, plant, and equipment during its fiscal year ended December 31, 2014. The company uses the straight-line method of depreciation for all its capital assets.

1. In early January, Vidi issued 140,000 common shares in exchange for property consisting of land and a warehouse. On the date of acquisition, a reliable, independent appraiser estimated that the fair value of the land and warehouse was $600,000 and $300,000, respectively. The seller had advertised a price of $860,000 or best offer for the land and warehouse in a commercial retail magazine. Vidi paid a local real estate broker a finder's fee of $35,000. The most recent sale of Vidi's shares took place last month when 15,000 common shares were sold for $9 per share.

2. On March 31, the company acquired equipment on credit. The terms were a $7,000 cash down payment plus payments of $5,000 at the end of each of the next two years. The implicit interest rate was 12%. The equipment's list price was $17,000. Additional costs that were incurred to install the equipment included $1,000 to tear down and replace a wall, and $1,500 to rearrange existing equipment to make room for the new equipment. An additional $500 was spent to repair the equipment after it was dropped during installation.

During the year, the following events also occurred:

3. A new motor was purchased for $50,000 for a large grinding machine (original cost of the machine, $350,000; accumulated depreciation at the replacement date, $100,000). The motor will not improve the quality or quantity of production; however, it will extend the grinding machine's useful life from the current eight years to 10 years.

4. On September 30, the company purchased a small building in a nearby town for $125,000 to use as a display and sales location. The municipal tax assessment indicated that the property was assessed for $95,000, which consists of $68,000 for the building and $27,000 for the land. The building had been empty for six months and required considerable maintenance work before it could be used. The following costs were incurred in 2014 prior to moving into the building: previous owner's unpaid property taxes on the property for the previous year, $900; current year's (2014) taxes, $1,000; reshingling of roof, $2,200; cost of hauling refuse out of the basement, $230; cost of spray cleaning the outside walls and washing windows, $750; cost of painting inside walls, $3,170; and incremental fire and liability insurance for 15 months, $940.

5. The company repaired the plumbing system in its factory for $35,000. The original plumbing costs were not known.

6. On June 30, the company replaced a freezer with a new one that cost $20,000 cash (fair value of $21,000 for the new freezer less trade-in value of old freezer). The cost of the old freezer was $15,000. At the beginning of the year, the company had depreciated 60% of the old freezer; that is, 10% per year of use.

7. The company painted the factory exterior at a cost of $12,000.

Instructions

(a) Prepare the journal entries that are required to record the acquisitions and/or costs incurred in the above transactions.

(b) If there are alternative methods to account for any of the transactions, indicate what the alternatives are and your reason for choosing the method that you used.

P10-7 The production manager of Chesley Corporation wants to acquire a different brand of machine by exchanging the machine that it currently uses in operations for the brand of equipment that others in the industry are using. The brand being used by other companies is more comfortable for the operators because it has different attachments that allow the operators to adjust the controls for a variety of arm and hand positions. The production manager has received the following offers from other companies:

1. Secord Corp. offered to give Chesley a similar machine plus $23,000 in exchange for Chesley's machine.

2. Bateman Corp. offered a straight exchange for a similar machine with essentially the same value in use.

3. Shripad Corp. offered to exchange a similar machine with the same value in use, but wanted $8,000 cash in addition to Chesley's machine.

4. The production manager has also contacted Ansong Corporation, a dealer in machines. To obtain a new machine from Ansong, Chesley would have to pay $93,000 and also trade in its old machine.

Chesley's equipment has a cost of $160,000, a net book value of $110,000, and a fair value of $92,000. The following table shows the information needed to record the machine exchange between the companies:

	Secord	Bateman	Shripad	Ansong
Machine cost	$120,000	$147,000	$160,000	$130,000
Accumulated depreciation—machinery	45,000	71,000	75,000	–0–
Fair value	69,000	92,000	100,000	185,000

Instructions

Digging Deeper

(a) For each of the four independent situations, assume that Chesley accepts the offer. Prepare the journal entries to record the exchange on the books of each company. (Round to the nearest dollar.) When you need to make assumptions for the entries, state the assumptions so that you can justify the entries.

(b) Suggest scenarios or situations where different entries would be appropriate. Prepare the entries for these situations.

P10-8 During the current year, Garrison Construction traded in two relatively new small cranes (cranes no. 6RT and S79) for a larger crane that Garrison expects will be more useful for the particular contracts that the company has to fulfill over the next couple of years. The new crane is acquired from Pisani Manufacturing, which has agreed to take the smaller equipment as trade-ins and also pay $17,500 cash to Garrison. The new crane cost Pisani $165,000 to manufacture and is classified as inventory. The following information is available:

	Garrison Const.	Pisani Mfg.
Cost of crane #6RT	$130,000	
Cost of crane #S79	120,000	
Accumulated depreciation, #6RT	15,000	
Accumulated depreciation, #S79	18,000	
Fair value, #6RT	128,000	
Fair value, #S79	87,500	
Fair value of new crane		$185,000
Cash paid		17,500
Cash received	17,500	

Instructions

(a) Assume that this exchange has commercial substance. Prepare the journal entries on the books of (1) Garrison Construction and (2) Pisani Manufacturing. Pisani uses a perpetual inventory system.

(b) Assume that this exchange lacks commercial substance. Prepare the journal entries on the books of (1) Garrison Construction and (2) Pisani Manufacturing. Pisani uses a perpetual inventory system.

(c) Assume that you have been asked to recommend whether it is more appropriate for the transaction to have commercial substance or not to have commercial substance. Develop arguments that you could present to the controllers of both Garrison Construction and Pisani Manufacturing to justify both alternatives. Which arguments are more persuasive?

P10-9 On July 1, 2014, Lucas Ltd., a publicly listed company, acquired assets from Jared Ltd. On the transaction date, a reliable, independent valuator assessed the fair values of these assets as follows:

Manufacturing plant (building #1)	$400,000
Storage warehouse (building #2)	210,000
Machinery (in building #1)	75,000
Machinery (in building #2)	45,000

The buildings are owned by the company and the land that the buildings are situated on is owned by the local municipality and is provided free of charge to the owner of the buildings as a stimulus to encourage local employment.

In exchange for the acquisition of these assets, Lucas issued 156,000 common shares. Lucas's shares are thinly traded, and in the most recent sale of Lucas's shares on the Toronto Stock Exchange, 1,000 shares were sold for $5 per share. At the time of acquisition, both buildings were considered to have an expected remaining useful life of 10 years, the machinery in building #1 was expected to have a remaining useful life of 3 years, and the machinery in building #2 was expected to have a useful life of 9 years. Lucas uses straight-line depreciation.

At December 31, 2014, Lucas's fiscal year end, Lucas recorded the correct depreciation amounts for the six months that the assets were in use. An independent appraisal concluded that the assets had the following fair values:

Manufacturing plant (building #1)	$387,000
Storage warehouse (building #2)	178,000

At December 31, 2015, Lucas once again retained an independent appraiser and determined that the fair value of the assets was:

Manufacturing plant (building #1)	$340,000
Storage warehouse (building #2)	160,000

Instructions

(a) Prepare the journal entries required for 2014 and 2015, assuming that the buildings are accounted for under the revaluation model (using the asset adjustment method), and that the machinery is accounted for under the cost model.

(b) Assume that the asset revaluation surplus for the buildings was prepared based on a class-by-class basis rather than on an individual asset basis as required by IAS 16. Prepare the journal entries required for 2014 and 2015 that relate to the buildings. (Ignore the machinery accounts since they are accounted for using the cost model.)

(c) Comment on the effects on the 2014 income statement with respect to parts (a) and (b).

*P10-10 Camco Manufacturers Inc., a publicly listed company, has two machines that are accounted for under the revaluation model. Technology in Camco's industry is fast-changing, causing the fair value of each machine to change significantly approximately every two years. The following information is available:

	Machine #1	Machine #2
Acquisition date	Jan. 2, 2011	June 30, 2010
Original cost	350,000	540,000
Original estimate of useful life	8 years	12 years
Original estimate of residual value	–0–	–0–
Pattern of depreciation	Straight-line	Straight-line
Fair value at Dec. 31, 2012	225,000	440,000
Balance in Machinery account after proportionate		
method revaluation on Dec. 31, 2012	300,000	555,789
Balance in Accumulated Depreciation account after		
proportionate method revaluation on Dec. 31, 2012	75,000	115,789
Cumulative balance in Revaluation Surplus (OCI)/		
(Revaluation Gain or Loss at Jan. 1, 2014	(37,500)	12,500
Fair value at Dec. 31, 2014	190,000	328,000

Both machines were last revalued on December 31, 2012. Camco has a December 31 year end.

Instructions

(a) Prepare the journal entries required for 2014, using the asset adjustment method.

(b) Prepare the journal entries required for 2014, using the proportionate method.

(c) Comment on the effects on the 2014 statement of comprehensive income with respect to parts (a) and (b).

(d) Comment on the effects on the December 31, 2014 statement of financial position with respect to parts (a) and (b).

Digging Deeper

(e) Would a potential investor prefer Camco to use the asset adjustment method or the proportionate method to apply the revaluation model?

P10-11   On March 1, 2014, Jessi Corp. acquired a 10-unit residential complex for $1,275,000, paid in cash. An independent appraiser determined that 75% of the total purchase price should be allocated to buildings, with the remainder allocated to land. On the date of acquisition, estimated useful life of the building was 25 years, with estimated residual value of $325,000. Jessi estimates that straight-line depreciation would best reflect the pattern of benefits to be received from the building. Fair value of the complex, as assessed by an independent appraiser on each date, is as follows:

Date	Fair Value
December 31, 2014	$1,322,000
December 31, 2015	$1,255,000
December 31, 2016	$1,223,000

The complex qualifies as an investment property under IAS 40 *Investment Property*. Jessi has a December 31 year end.

Instructions

(a) Prepare the journal entries required for 2014, 2015, and 2016, assuming that Jessi applies the fair value model to all of its investment property.

(b) Prepare the journal entries required for 2014, 2015, and 2016, assuming that Jessi applies the cost model to all of its investment property.

(c) Comment on the effects on the 2014 statement of comprehensive income with respect to parts (a) and (b).

(d) Comment on the effects on the December 31, 2014 statement of financial position with respect to parts (a) and (b).

Digging Deeper

(e) From the perspective of an investor in Jessi, discuss the financial statement effects of using the fair value model to determine the property's carrying amount.

P10-12   Donovan Resources Group has been in its plant facility for 15 years. Although the plant is quite functional, numerous repair costs are incurred to keep it in good working order. The book value of the company's plant is currently $800,000, calculated as follows:

Original cost	$1,200,000
Accumulated depreciation	400,000
	$ 800,000

During the current year, the following expenditures were made to the plant:

1. Because of increased demand for its product, the company increased its plant capacity by building a new addition at a cost of $270,000.

2. The entire plant was repainted at a cost of $23,000.

3. The roof was made of asbestos cement slate; for safety purposes, it was removed at a cost of $4,000 and replaced with a wood shingle roof at a cost of $61,000. The original roof's cost had been $40,000 and it was being depreciated over an expected life of 20 years.

4. The electrical system was completely updated at a cost of $22,000. The cost of the old electrical system was not known. It is estimated that the building's useful life will not change as a result of this updating.

5. A series of major repairs was made at a cost of $47,000, because parts of the wood structure were rotting. The cost of the old wood structure was not known. These extensive repairs are estimated to increase the building's useful life.

Instructions

Indicate how each of these transactions would be recorded in the accounting records.

*P10-13   Inglewood Landscaping Corp. began constructing a new plant on December 1, 2014. On this date, the company purchased a parcel of land for $184,000 cash. In addition, it paid $2,000 in surveying costs and $4,000 for title transfer fees. An old dwelling on the premises was demolished at a cost of $3,000, with $1,000 being received from the sale of materials.

Architectural plans were also formalized on December 1, 2014, when the architect was paid $30,000. The necessary building permits costing $3,000 were obtained from the city and paid for on December 1 as well. The excavation work began during the first week in December and payments were made to the contractor as follows:

Date of Payment	Amount of Payment
Mar. 1	$240,000
May 1	360,000
July 1	60,000

The building was completed on July 1, 2015.

To finance the plant construction, Inglewood borrowed $600,000 from a bank on December 1, 2014. Inglewood had no other borrowings. The $600,000 was a 10-year loan bearing interest at 10%.

Instructions

(a) Calculate the balance in each of the following accounts at December 31, 2014, and December 31, 2015. Assume that Inglewood prepares financial statements in accordance with IFRS.

    1. Land

    2. Buildings

    3. Interest Expense

(b) Identify what the effects would be on Inglewood's financial statements for the years ending December 31, 2014 and 2015, if its policy was to expense all borrowing costs as they are incurred.

(c) Discuss the financial statement effects of capitalization of borrowing costs. Contrast the financial statement effects of capitalizing borrowing costs against the financial statement effects of paying for the construction with internally generated funds.

Digging Deeper

*P10-14 Wordcrafters Inc. is a book distributor that had been operating in its original facility since 1988. The increase in certification programs and continuing education requirements in several professions has contributed to an annual growth rate of 15% for Wordcrafters since 2008. Wordcrafters' original facility became obsolete by early 2014 because of the increased sales volume and the fact that Wordcrafters now carries audio books and DVDs in addition to books.

On June 1, 2014, Wordcrafters contracted with Favre Construction to have a new building constructed for $5 million on land owned by Wordcrafters. Wordcrafters made the following payments to Favre Construction:

Date	Amount
July 30, 2014	$1,200,000
Jan. 30, 2015	1,500,000
May 30, 2016	1,300,000
Total payments	$4,000,000

Construction was completed and the building was ready for occupancy on May 27, 2015. Wordcrafters had no new borrowings directly associated with the new building but had the following debt outstanding at May 31, 2015, the end of its fiscal year:

14½%, five-year note payable of $2 million, dated April 1, 2011, with interest payable annually on April 1

12%, 10-year bond issue of $3 million sold at par on June 30, 2007, with interest payable annually on June 30

The company is an international distributor and thus prepares financial statements in accordance with IFRS.

Instructions

(a) Calculate the weighted-average accumulated expenditures on Wordcrafters' new building during the capitalization period.

(b) Calculate the avoidable interest on Wordcrafters' new building.

(c) Wordcrafters Inc. capitalized some of its interest costs for the year ended May 31, 2015:

    1. Identify the item(s) relating to interest costs that must be disclosed in Wordcrafters' financial statements.

    2. Calculate the amount of the item(s) that must be disclosed.

(CMA adapted Used with permission.)

Case

Refer to the Case Primer on the student website and in *WileyPLUS* to help you answer this case.

CA10-1 Real Estate Investment Trust (RE) was created to hold hotel properties. RE currently holds 15 luxury and first-class hotels in Europe. The entity is structured as an investment trust, which means that the trust does not pay income taxes on the earnings from the assets that it holds directly. Instead, income taxes are paid by the unitholders—those who own units in the trust. The other key feature of the trust is that 85% to 90% of the distributable income is required to be paid to unitholders every year. The units of RE trade on the national stock exchange.

Distributable income is calculated as net income (according to GAAP) before special charges less a replacement reserve, which is an amount set aside to refurbish assets. RE distributed 127% and 112% of its distributable income in 2014 and 2013, respectively. Management calculates distributable income since this calculation is not defined by GAAP. As at the end of 2014, property and equipment was $1.7 billion compared with $1.9 billion in total assets. Net income for the year was $55 million.

According to the notes to the financial statements, RE accounts for its property, plant, and equipment at amortized cost.

Instructions

Assume the role of the entity's auditors, and discuss any financial reporting issues.

Integrated Cases

(*Hint*: If there are issues here that are new, use the conceptual framework to help you support your analysis with solid reasoning.)

IC10-1 Iskra Vremec and Colin McFee are experienced scuba divers who have spent many years in the salvage business. About a year ago, they decided to start their own company to recover damaged and sunken vessels and their cargoes off the east coast of Canada. They incorporated Atlantic Explorations Limited (AEL) on February 1, 2013. Iskra (president) and Colin (vice-president) each own 30% of AEL's shares. The remaining 40% of the shares were purchased by a group of 10 investors who contributed $50,000 each so that AEL could acquire the necessary equipment and cover other start-up costs.

AEL carries on two types of activities. The first is a commercial salvage operation. The second is treasure hunting. To date, commercial salvage operations have generated all of AEL's revenues. The demand for these services is strong, and there are few competitors due to the unpredictable nature of the business and the long hours. Colin manages the commercial salvage operations. Customers pay in three instalments, including an upfront fee, a fee payable approximately midway through the contract, and a fee at the end once the items in question have been salvaged (found and brought to land). If the item is never found or AEL cannot bring the item to the surface and to land, then the final payment is not made.

Iskra spends most of her time locating and recovering underwater artifacts and, where possible, sunken treasure. Her research shows that numerous vessels carrying gold, silver, and other valuables to the "Old World" were wrecked off the shores of Nova Scotia. AEL has permits to investigate three target areas. As compensation for the permits, AEL agrees to remit 1% of the fair value of any treasure found. These funds are to be invested in the local economy by AEL (subject to government approval). The company also pays an upfront fee that allows it to search a given area. There has been a discovery in the first of these target areas.

It is now September 5, 2013. AEL has engaged your auditing firm to provide advice on the accounting for the ongoing operations and the discovery that AEL has just made. You (as audit manager) and Alex Green, the partner assigned to the engagement, met with Colin and Iskra.

During your meeting, Iskra said that she believes that finding treasure is like winning a lottery as all revenues would accrue to AEL and thus should be treated accordingly. If this discovery proves to be as substantial as preliminary results suggest, AEL will require additional financing of $1.5 million to acquire the equipment and on-shore laboratory, and lease a specially equipped vessel needed to salvage the wreck and its treasures. The bank has said that it is not willing to advance further funds. However, Iskra and Colin know of other individuals who are interested in investing in AEL.

AEL receives grants from the government to assist in the process of finding treasure and salvaging sunken vessels. Iskra and Colin have just found out that they are likely to receive a grant in connection with the recent discovery.

Instructions

Draft a memo for auditor Alex Green, analyzing all financial reporting issues and providing recommendations.

(CICA adapted)

IC10-2 OG Limited (OG) is in the oil and gas business. It spends quite a bit of money each year exploring for new wells. Currently, it has several wells that are in the production phases. The company's shares trade on the London Stock Exchange. OG is looking to expand its exploration into China and therefore would like to issue more shares next year to fund the exploration. The company's top management is compensated partly with stock options.

One of the company's wells recently exploded, pouring a significant amount of oil into a nearby waterway. It took one month to cap the well, and during that time the company incurred significant costs in capping the well including costs related to many failed attempts. OG has announced that it will clean up the spilled oil and estimates that it will cost between $5 and $10 million to do so. It has also announced that it will act in a responsible manner when dealing with any losses and complaints that the local farmers may have in connection with the spill.

OG is now being sued in a class action suit brought about by the farmers. They are suing for $100 million in compensation for their land, which is now unusable due to the oil. The company's lawyers feel they can settle for 10% of that amount.

The company capitalizes all costs incurred in connection with searching for new oil and gas wells, even when the exploration does not result in a well that has oil in it. They argue that they must incur those costs in order to find a producing well. In many countries where OG explores and operates, there are no legal requirements to restore the land to its original state once the exploration is complete or a well is depleted. The company does, however, state that it considers this an important activity and will make every effort to restore the site.

When excavating one site, OG came across a significant amount of gold. OG is now mining and selling the gold. Currently, it is trying to decide how to account for the gold inventory and is considering valuing the gold at market price once it has been refined, even though it is not yet sold.

Instructions

Assume the role of the company's auditors and analyze the financial reporting issues.

Writing Assignments

WA10-1 Highstreet Inc. is a distributor of electronic equipment. In January 2014, the company purchased a new building for its warehousing and head office requirements for a total cost of $5 million. It is now August 27, 2014, and the company has just completed renovations costing an additional $2 million and will be moving in on August 31. During these eight months, the company was able to rent out a portion of the building to a company next door for storage. Net storage revenue of $100,000 was earned during this renovation period. The elevator has just been inspected for a total cost of $150,000 and the next inspection will occur in five years as required. Based on a property inspection that was completed prior to the purchase, the inspector reported that the roof would likely last another 7 years, and the heating and air conditioning system would likely have to be replaced in 10 years. The company has determined that the roof is worth about 10% of the total original cost of the building and the heating and air conditioning system is worth about 15%. The company expects the building's useful life will be 30 years.

Instructions

(a) Assuming Highstreet follows ASPE, discuss how the costs of the building should be initially recorded. Also discuss how any additional subsequent costs should be recorded and the related depreciation costs.

(b) Assuming Highstreet follows IFRS, discuss how the costs of the building should be initially recorded. Also discuss how any additional subsequent costs should be recorded and the related depreciation.

WA10-2 Gomi Medical Labs, Inc. began operations five years ago producing a new type of instrument it hoped to sell to doctors, dentists, and hospitals. The demand for the new instrument was much higher than had been planned for, and the company was unable to produce enough of them to meet demand. The company was manufacturing its product on equipment that had been built at the start of its operations.

To meet demand, more efficient equipment was needed. The company decided to design and build the equipment because the equipment currently available on the market was unsuitable for producing this product.

In 2014, a section of the plant was devoted to developing the new equipment and special employees were hired. Within six months, a machine, developed at a cost of $714,000, increased production dramatically and reduced labour costs substantially. Thrilled by the new machine's success, the company built three more machines of the same type at a cost of $441,000 each.

Instructions

(a) In general, what costs should be capitalized for self-constructed equipment?

(b) Discuss whether the capitalized cost of self-constructed assets should include the following:

  1. The increase in overhead that results from the company's own construction of its fixed assets

  2. A proportionate share of overhead on the same basis as what is applied to goods that are manufactured for sale

(c) Discuss the proper accounting treatment of the $273,000 cost amount ($714,000 – $441,000) that was higher for the first machine than the cost of the subsequent machines.

WA10-3   Hotel Resort Limited is a company that builds world-class resorts in tourist areas around the globe. When the company decided to build a resort in Yellowknife, the federal government agreed to provide a forgivable loan in the amount of $50 million to help fund the construction of the tourist facilities anticipated to cost about $700 million. The loan will be forgiven provided the tourist facility is operated for at least 15 years. If the resort is closed or sold before 15 years have elapsed, the amount of the loan must be repaid in full, along with interest at the prevailing market rate.

In addition, the federal government also agreed to provide annual funding to cover 70% of the related costs of payroll and room and board for 50 summer students provided the students were hired to work for four full months. The company would receive this annual funding once it proved the costs incurred for these students.

Instructions

Prepare a memo that would be suitable to present to the Hotel Resort Limited board of directors in which you explain how the receipt of the government funding is expected to affect the company's reported total assets and earnings. Also, draft the related note disclosure that would be required.

WA10-4   You have two clients in the construction industry that are considering exchanging machinery with each other. Ames Construction has decided to market its services to clients who need major construction projects, but it has a significant inventory of equipment that is more appropriate for smaller home renovations. Jung Corp.'s strategic plan, on the other hand, has recently changed to focus on home renovations, additions, and repairs. Jung would like to sell off the equipment it used in constructing larger apartment buildings and condominiums over the past few years and acquire equipment that is more suitable for its new strategy. A deal has been reached between the owner-managers of both companies to exchange a group of machinery and equipment. The fair values determined for the equipment are reliable in both cases. The details of the transaction are as follows:

	Ames Construction	Jung Corp.
Original cost	$100,000	$150,000
Accumulated depreciation	40,000	80,000
Market value	85,000	95,000
Cash received (paid)	(10,000)	10,000

Instructions

Write a memo to the accountants of both Ames Construction and Jung Corp. with your recommendation on how this transaction should be recorded on the books of each company. If there are any choices available to them, identify what they are. Be sure to explain the rationale for your recommended treatment.

Ethics

WA10-5   A machine's invoice price is $40,000. Various other costs relating to the acquisition and installation of the machine—including transportation, electrical wiring, a special base, and so on—amount to $7,500. The machine has an estimated life of 10 years, with no residual value at the end of that period.

The owner-manager of the company that you work for as an accountant suggests that the incidental costs of $7,500 be charged to expense immediately for the following reasons:

- If the machine is ever sold, these costs cannot be recovered in the sale price.

- The inclusion of the $7,500 in the machinery account on the books will not necessarily result in a closer approximation of this asset's market price over the years, because demand and supply levels could change.

- Charging the $7,500 to expense immediately will reduce income taxes.

Instructions

Prepare a memo to the owner-manager that addresses each of the issues assuming that the company follows ASPE.

(AICPA adapted)

WA10-6   Write a brief essay highlighting the differences between IFRS and ASPE noted in this chapter, discussing the conceptual justification for each.

RESEARCH AND FINANCIAL ANALYSIS

RA10-1 Magna International Inc.

Access the financial statements of **Magna International Inc.** for the company's year ended December 31, 2011. These are available at www.sedar.com or the company's website. Review the information that is provided and answer the following questions about the company.

Instructions

(a) What business is Magna International in?

(b) What types of tangible capital assets does Magna report? Do these assets form a significant portion of the company's total assets at December 31, 2011?

(c) Identify all the accounting policies disclosed in the notes to the financial statements that explain how the company determines the cost of its property, plant, and equipment.

(d) How much did Magna spend on new capital asset acquisitions in 2010 and 2011 (excluding business acquisitions)? Identify where the company obtained the funds to invest in these additions.

(e) Explain how the company accounts for government assistance.

RA10-2 Stora Enso Oyj

Access the annual financial statements of **Stora Enso Oyj** for the company's year ended December 31, 2011. These are available at the company's website, www.storaenso.com. Review the information that is provided and answer the following questions about the company.

Instructions

(a) What major business(es) is Stora Enso Oyj in?

(b) What type of biological assets does the company have? Identify the accounting policies disclosed in the notes to the financial statements that explain how the company accounts for these assets.

(c) What was the amount in the biological assets account at December 31, 2011, and 2010, owned directly by Stora Enso? What caused this account balance to change from 2010 to 2011? Be specific.

(d) How is fair value of the biological assets determined? What kinds of estimates are required to determine fair value?

(e) What was the impact on the net earnings for 2011 and 2010 related to the biological assets valuation?

RA10-3 Empire Company Limited and Loblaw Companies Limited

Companies in the same line of business usually have similar investments and capital structures, and an opportunity for similar rates of return. One of the key performance indicators that is used to assess the profitability of companies is the return on assets ratio. This ratio results from two key relationships—the profit margin and the total asset turnover—and in general terms can be written as follows:

Return on assets = Total asset turnover (or Sales/Total assets) × Profit margin (or Income/Sales)

This says that profitability depends directly on how many sales dollars are generated for each dollar invested in assets (total asset turnover) and on how costs are controlled for each dollar of sales (profit margin). An increase in either ratio results in an increase in the return on assets. As property, plant, and equipment is often the largest single asset on the balance sheet, companies need to have strategies to manage their investment in such assets.

Instructions

Access the financial statements of two companies that are in the food distribution business: **Empire Company Limited** for the year ended May 5, 2012, and **Loblaw Companies Limited** for the year ended December 31, 2011. These are available at www.sedar.com or each company's website. Review the financial statements and answer the following questions.

(a) At each company's year end, determine the percentage of property, plant, and equipment to total assets.

(b) Calculate each company's fixed asset turnover, total asset turnover, and profit margin (using net income) for the most recent year.

(c) Determine the return on assets for each company. Which company is more profitable?

(d) Which company appears to use its total assets more effectively in generating sales? Its fixed assets?

(e) Are there any differences in accounting policies that might explain the differences in the fixed asset turnover ratios?

(f) Examine the leasing note for each company. How might the amount of assets that are leased impact the above asset turnover ratios?

(g) Which company has better control over its expenses for each dollar of sales? How do you explain the asset turnover ratios and the profit ratio comparisons?

RA10-4 First Capital Realty

Real World Emphasis

First Capital Realty, a Canadian company, reported under Canadian GAAP in 2010 and under IFRS in 2011.

Instructions

Access the financial statements for First Capital Realty for the years ended December 31, 2010, and December 31, 2011, from the company's website, www.firstcapitalrealty.ca. Review the statements that are presented and answer the following questions.

(a) What business is First Capital Realty in?

(b) Identify the single most significant accounting difference between the 2010 results under Canadian GAAP and the 2011 results under IFRS, and indicate the effect that this has on the income statements. Be specific. What is the impact of these differences on the income statement? On the balance sheet?

(c) Which set of financial statements do you think comes closer to meeting the objectives of financial reporting? Discuss briefly.

(d) Using the IFRS-prepared financial statements, explain how the company determined fair values for the investment properties. What methods were used and what were the key assumptions required?

RA10-5 Extractive Industry

Real World Emphasis

Access the financial statements of **BHP Billiton plc** for the company's year ended June 30, 2012. Access the financial statements of **Newfield Exploration Company** for the company's year ended December 31, 2011. These are available at the companies' websites. Review the information that is provided and answer the following questions about the companies.

Instructions

(a) What business is BHP Billiton plc in? What business is Newfield Exploration Co. in?

(b) How does BHP Billiton account for exploration, evaluation, and development expenditures related to its mineral reserves and resources? What specific costs are included?

(c) How does Newfield account for exploration, evaluation, and development expenditures related to its mineral reserves and resources? What specific costs are included?

(d) Using the two companies as examples, discuss the similarities and differences between the successful efforts method and the full cost method.

(e) One method for reporting these assets that is being contemplated by IFRS is the fair value method. What assumptions would be required to determine the fair value of mineral or oil and gas reserves? What are some drawbacks to using the fair value method to value these types of assets?

(f) From a user's perspective, which method(s) discussed above would provide the most faithful presentation and/or relevant information?

ENDNOTES

[1] For details, see "Guide to Accounting for and Reporting Tangible Capital Assets: Guidance for Local Governments and Local Government Entities that Apply the Public Sector Handbook" (available on-line at: http://www.psab-ccsp.ca/other-non-authoritative-guidance/item14603.pdf)

[2] See http://www.infrastructure.gc.ca/plan/plan-eng.html for details.

[3] If a company is involved in a significant amount of self-construction activity, some of its fixed costs may be considered "directly attributable."

[4] Sometimes a standard will specify that another amount will be the asset's **deemed cost.** The deemed cost is the amount recognized under the specific requirements of a particular standard, such as IFRS 2 *Share-based Payment*, for example.

[5] IFRS 2 *Share-based Payment* is considerably more complex than is indicated here. The recognition and measurement guidance depends on what is being acquired as well as whether the payment is in shares directly or in cash with the amount based on the price of the shares, or whether there is a choice of cash-based settlement or settlement in shares.

[6] As detailed in IFRS 13, which was released in 2011, IFRS 2 *Share-based Payment* "uses the term 'fair value' in a way that differs in some respects from the definition of fair value in IFRS 13 Fair Value Measurement. Therefore, when applying IFRS 2 an entity measures fair value in accordance with IFRS 2, not IFRS 13." Copyright © 2012 IFRS Foundation. All rights reserved. Reproduced by Wiley Canada with the permission of the IFRS Foundation®. No permission granted to third parties to reproduce or distribute.

[7] For example, if a company exchanges inventory held for sale for other similar merchandise for sale in order to complete a sale to a customer, it would be difficult to justify the claim that the company's economic position has changed significantly. In fact, private enterprise standards list this situation as a third exception to the use of fair value in a nonmonetary exchange.

[8] IAS 20 *Accounting for Government Grants and Disclosure of Government Assistance* indicates that while government grants in the form of nonmonetary assets are usually measured at their fair value, an entity may record both the asset and the grant at a nominal amount (see IAS 20.23).

[9] While a credit to Other Comprehensive Income (OCI) may seem like a valid option, accounting standards tend to be prescriptive about what can bypass net income and be recognized directly in OCI. This option is not provided in either IFRS or ASPE for government grants.

[10] Investment property includes land or buildings or part of a building or both under IAS 40, and could be property held under a finance lease or directly owned.

[11] IFRS 13 *Fair Value Measurement*, Paragraph 9. Copyright © 2012 IFRS Foundation. All rights reserved. Reproduced by Wiley Canada with the permission of the IFRS Foundation®. No permission granted to third parties to reproduce or distribute.

[12] Chapter 2 includes a discussion of the meaning of fair value and ways in which fair values are determined, and Appendix B of IFRS 13 provides detailed guidance relating to the fair value measurement approach under IFRS.

[13] This method is easy to apply when fair values are based on an index of specific prices, such as a construction price index. It also has the benefit of providing additional information to users about the relative age of the assets because the accumulated depreciation continues.

[14] Note that, to the extent these ordinary expenditures are classified as factory overhead, the costs are included as an inventory (product) cost before being charged to the income statement as an expense—cost of goods sold.

[15] For details see http://www.ifrs.org/Archive/IASB+completed+projects/Completed+projects.htm.

[16] Unlike investment income earned on the temporary investment of asset-specific borrowings, IAS 23 *Borrowing Costs* does not speak to whether investment income earned on general-purpose debt should reduce the borrowing costs eligible to be capitalized or not. The principles set out in this IFRS and the company-specific circumstances would have to be assessed to determine the best approach in each case.

Accounting for Aircraft

WITH OVER $5 BILLION worth of property and equipment, including more than 200 airplanes, Air Canada must carefully account for depreciation of these assets in order to meet financial reporting requirements and for management to get the most accurate picture of their costs.

Its recent move to IFRS caused Canada's largest airline to rethink how it accounts for its aircraft. "Under old Canadian GAAP, an aircraft was recorded as one single asset and then amortized over its estimated useful life, generally 25 years," says Chris Isford, Air Canada's Vice President and Controller. "Under IFRS, the guidance was more explicit. The aircraft needed to be split into its major component parts that have different useful lives. The major components are typically the engines, the airframe or the body of the aircraft, and the interior galley equipment, in-flight entertainment systems and the seats."

The body of the aircraft, referred to as the airframe, its avionics—the navigation and communication systems—and the aircraft's engines all have various maintenance checks performed at varying intervals. In addition, interior components such as in-flight entertainment systems are frequently upgraded. That means that useful lives of different components can vary, along with their maintenance schedules. Routine maintenance is considered an operating cost, but major maintenance events and overhauls, done in accordance with Air Canada's maintenance programs, are considered a capital cost because they increase the service life of the asset, Mr. Isford says.

Air Canada did not consider the move to IFRS to be too onerous. Its accountants did spend time getting a deeper understanding of the aircraft's components and maintenance cycles to assign useful lives, but that has resulted in information that is not only more detailed, but more accurately reflects how and when capital costs are incurred. Under previous Canadian GAAP, "you had new aircraft with very low operating costs from an accounting perspective but older aircraft with high costs given their higher maintenance," Mr. Isford explains. "Now under IFRS, as we are capitalizing these events separately and recognizing them separately over their individual useful lives, you have a better cost recognition stream for the assets."

One practice that did not change with the change in accounting standards is how Air Canada estimates the residual value of its airplanes. Air Canada obtains general aircraft appraisals and considers company specific plans in order to estimate residual values. Residual values are reviewed at least annually and depreciation rates are adjusted accordingly on a prospective basis.

Depreciation, Impairment, and Disposition

LEARNING OBJECTIVES

After studying this chapter, you should be able to:

1. Understand the importance of depreciation, impairment, and disposition from a business perspective.

2. Explain the concept of depreciation and identify the factors to consider when determining depreciation charges.

3. Identify how depreciation methods are selected.

4. Calculate depreciation using the straight-line, decreasing charge, and activity methods and recognize the effects of using each.

5. Explain the accounting issues for depletion of mineral resources.

6. Explain and apply the accounting procedures for partial periods and a change in depreciation rate.

7. Explain the issues and apply the accounting standards for capital asset impairment under both IFRS and ASPE.

8. Explain and apply the accounting standards for long-lived assets that are held for sale.

9. Account for derecognition of property, plant, and equipment.

10. Describe the types of disclosures required for property, plant, and equipment.

11. Analyze a company's investment in assets.

12. Identify differences in accounting between ASPE and IFRS, and what changes are expected in the near future.

After studying Appendix 11A, you should be able to:

13. Calculate capital cost allowance in straightforward situations.

As noted in the opening story, capital assets can be a major investment for companies. It is therefore important that you have a firm understanding of this chapter's topics, given this and other facts. For example, you should be aware of the alternatives that exist for charging these capital costs to operations and the potential for impairment in their values. Some critics argue that financial statement readers do not need to be concerned with non-cash expenses such as depreciation, so it is important to understand the purpose of charging depreciation and the difference between cost allocation and valuation. It is also important to understand rules governing allocation of capital costs for income taxes. The appendix outlines key aspects of the capital cost allowance system that is required for income tax purposes.

The chapter is organized as follows:

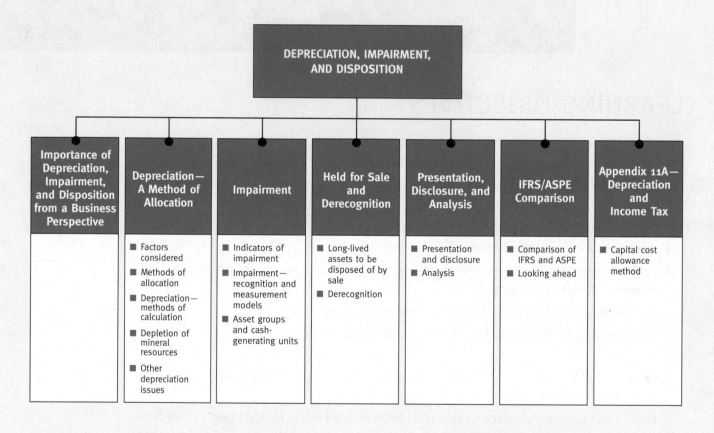

THE IMPORTANCE OF DEPRECIATION, IMPAIRMENT, AND DISPOSITION FROM A BUSINESS PERSPECTIVE

Objective 1
Understand the importance of depreciation, impairment, and disposition from a business perspective.

The economic benefits of property, plant, and equipment (PP&E) are typically consumed as the items are used by the organization. Because PP&E is used over multiple periods, companies must find an appropriate method for allocating the benefits as the assets' capacity and expected output are used up. Businesses usually cannot determine the exact period of time a long-lived asset will be used productively. However, they are generally able to make a reasonable estimate of useful life. Several factors may have an impact on the asset's useful life and residual value. These factors include the asset's planned repairs and maintenance, its expected technical or commercial obsolescence, and legal or other limits on its use (such as lease terms).[1]

By allocating the cost of property, plant, and equipment over its useful life, businesses are better able to match the costs and benefits of the assets to the revenues that they help generate. This also ensures that businesses do not have to record a disproportionate amount of expense in the year the asset is acquired. Similarly, if PP&E is not depreciated or expensed, businesses might need to record large losses in the year of disposition.

What Do the Numbers Mean?

Under IFRS, determining a reasonable basis for depreciation has become even more of a challenge for many businesses. For example, Ontario Power Generation (OPG) had planned to adopt IFRS starting in 2012. The delay to 2012, when most businesses adopted IFRS in 2011, was due partly to the complications involving organizations whose rates are regulated by the government, such as OPG. With its PP&E having a carrying amount of more than $13.6 billion at the end of 2010, OPG had to consider matters such as the impact of IFRS's focus on individual components of PP&E. This affects items such as OPG's nuclear, hydroelectric, and thermal generating stations. The switch to IFRS was to come just a few years after a significant change in the estimated useful life of its Darlington nuclear generating station, which was extended from 2019 to 2051 after the organization announced the station's refurbishment. This change in estimate was largely responsible for a decrease of $62 million in OPG's depreciation expense between 2009 and 2010.[2] Starting in 2012, OPG decided to adopt US GAAP instead of IFRS to minimize the differences from "old" Canadian GAAP, which was followed until 2011.

Depreciation helps businesses ensure that assets are carried at an amount no higher than what is expected to be recoverable for the asset. However, over time, the asset could still end up being carried at too high an amount. If the asset's carrying value exceeds its recoverable amount (due to poor estimates of useful life, residual value, or other factors such as unexpected obsolescence), the carrying amount should be reduced.[3] Companies therefore need to assess their PP&E for indications of impairment. If these indications are present they should re-estimate how much will be recoverable. This should help them better understand their business, along with complying with GAAP.

DEPRECIATION—A METHOD OF ALLOCATION

Many people at one time or another buy and sell a vehicle. The automobile dealer and the buyer typically discuss what the old car's trade-in value is. Also, they may talk about what the new car's trade-in value will be in several years. In both cases, the decline in value is generally referred to as depreciation.

To accountants, however, depreciation is not a matter of valuation (determining an asset's declining value). **Depreciation**—or amortization, as it is also called—**is a means of cost allocation**. It is the process of allocating the depreciable amount of a PP&E asset to expense in a systematic manner to those periods expected to benefit from its use. As explained in this chapter, the depreciable amount is the asset's cost less its residual amount. (There could, however, be a substitute value used instead of cost, such as that used when the revaluation model is applied.)

Underlying Concept

Assessing the fair value of long-lived assets at each reporting date may provide more relevant information to users. However, amortized cost is more reliable and verifiable. So, when evaluated on a cost-benefit basis, most preparers continue to support the use of amortized cost.

It is true that an asset's value changes between the time it is purchased and the time it is sold or scrapped. Most companies use a cost allocation approach rather than a valuation approach, however, because objectively measuring the changes in their assets' values every reporting period is often difficult and usually costly.

As mentioned above, the terms **amortization** and **depreciation** are almost interchangeable. **Amortization** refers to the general process of allocating the carrying amount of any long-lived asset to the accounting periods that benefit from its use. It can also specifically refer to this process for **intangible assets**. The term **depreciation** is reserved for property, plant, and equipment, and **depletion** is used only with natural resource assets.

Factors Considered in the Depreciation Process

Objective 2
Explain the concept of depreciation and identify the factors to consider when determining depreciation charges.

Before calculating the dollar amount of depreciation expense, a company has to answer four basic questions:

1. What asset components are depreciated separately?

2. What is the asset's depreciable amount?

3. Over what period is the asset depreciated?

4. What pattern best reflects how the asset's economic benefits are used up?

As you might expect, judgement and estimates are needed to answer these questions. This means that the resulting **depreciation can only ever be an estimate**. A perfect measure of expense for each period is impossible.

Asset Components

As mentioned in Chapter 10 and in the opening vignette to this chapter, management has to develop a **componentization** policy; that is, a policy to guide decisions on which fixed asset components to recognize separately. What individual parts of multi-component assets, such as a building, should be pulled out and recorded separately? And when should numerous small PP&E assets, such as small tools, be combined and accounted for together? Determining the unit of account is the first step in the depreciation process.

The following principles guide the componentization decision:

- Identify each part of a PP&E asset whose cost is a significant portion of the total asset cost as a separate component.

- Group together significant components with similar useful lives and patterns of providing economic benefits.

- Add together the costs of the remaining parts of the asset, none of which is individually significant. These may be depreciated as a single component, taking into account the nature of the different parts.

- Group together individual minor assets to depreciate as one component based on the similarity of their useful life and pattern of consumption.

Real World Emphasis

British Airways plc reports, for example, that the cabin interior modifications of its aircraft fleet are recognized and depreciated separately from the aircraft itself. **Air Canada** indicates that aircraft reconfiguration costs are separately recognized and depreciated over a much shorter period of time than the aircraft and flight equipment.

Both IFRS and ASPE require entities to recognize separate components for the purpose of depreciation, but the international standards are more fully developed and more strictly applied.

Depreciable Amount

The amount of an asset that is to be depreciated—its **depreciable amount**—is the difference between the asset's cost (or revalued amount, if the revaluation model is being used) and its residual value.[4] The **residual value** is defined as the estimated amount a company would **receive today** if it disposed of the asset, less any related disposal costs, if the asset were at the **same age and condition expected at the end of its useful life**.[5] It is the amount the company depreciates the asset to over its useful life. For example, Illustration 11-1 shows that if an asset has a cost (or net revalued amount) of $10,000 and a residual value of $3,600, only $6,400 of its cost is depreciated.

In some cases, the residual value may be so low as to be immaterial. Some long-lived assets, however, have substantial net realizable values at the end of their useful lives to a specific enterprise. As long as the residual value is less than the asset's carrying amount, depreciation is recognized on the asset. If the residual value increases so it is more than the

Illustration 11-1

Calculation of Amount to Be Depreciated

Original cost (or amount substituted for "cost")	$10,000
Less: residual value	3,600
Depreciable amount	$ 6,400

asset's carrying amount, no depreciation is taken until this situation reverses. It is important that the residual value be reviewed regularly, but particularly whenever changes in the environment occur that might affect its estimate. Under IFRS, this review is required at least at each year end.

A more technical and conservative policy is sometimes required, such as under ASPE where, to ensure that charges to the income statement are adequate, the depreciation charge is based on the higher of two amounts:

1. the cost less salvage value over the life of the asset; and

2. the cost less residual value over the asset's useful life.

The **salvage value** is the estimate of the asset's net realizable value at the end of its life, rather than its value at the end of its useful life to the entity. The salvage value is usually an insignificant amount. In practice, the residual value is most commonly used.

So, for example, if the asset in Illustration 11-1 is a machine with a cost of $10,000, an estimated useful life of eight years, and a residual value of $3,600, its depreciation under IFRS would be $800 if it uses straight-line depreciation. However, if the total expected life of the asset is 10 years with no salvage value, under ASPE the minimum depreciation charge would be $1,000 per year. Journal entries to record the depreciation under IFRS versus ASPE are provided in Illustration 11-2.

Illustration 11-2

Accounting for Depreciation (IFRS versus ASPE)

IFRS
A   = L +   SE
−800   −800

Cash flows: No effect

ASPE
A   = L +   SE
−1,000   −1,000

Cash flows: No effect

To record depreciation of the machine:	IFRS^a		ASPE^b	
Depreciation Expense	800		1,000	
Accumulated Depreciation—Machinery		800		1,000

^aIFRS depreciation ($10,000 − $3,600)/8 = $800
^bASPE depreciation is the greater of ($10,000 − $3,600)/8 = $800 or ($10,000 − $0)/10 = $1,000

Depreciation Period

As indicated above, to calculate depreciation, an estimate of the asset's **useful life** is needed. An asset's useful life is the period during which the asset is expected to be available for use by the entity based on factors such as the asset's expected capacity. Alternatively, useful life can be stated in terms of the number of units of product or service that the asset is expected to produce or provide over this period.

Depreciation begins when the asset is available for use; that is, when it is in place and in the condition necessary for it to be able to operate as management intends. The **depreciation process ends** when the asset is derecognized (removed from the accounts), or when it is classified as held for sale, if earlier. **Depreciation continues** even if the asset is idle or has been taken out of service, unless it is fully depreciated, of course.

Useful or service life and physical life are often not the same. A piece of machinery may be physically capable of producing a specific product for many years past its useful life in a particular organization, but the equipment may not be used for all of those years due to **economic factors** such as obsolescence. The useful lives of Air Canada's aircraft components, described in the opening vignette, are likely determined through discussions with others in the organization such as engineering and manufacturing specialists. New processes or techniques or improved machines may provide the same product or service at lower cost or with higher quality. Changes needed in the product or service itself may shorten an asset's service life. Environmental factors and asset management policies also influence asset retirement decisions.

Physical factors set the outside limit for an asset's service life. Physical factors relate to such things as decay or wear and tear that result from use of the asset and the passage of time. Whenever the asset's physical nature is the main factor that determines its useful life, a company's maintenance policies play a vital role—the better the maintenance, the longer the life of the asset.[6] An asset's **legal life** may also limit its useful life to a specific entity. For example, the benefits of leasehold improvements end when the lease term is over.

To illustrate these concepts, consider a new nuclear power plant. Which is most important in determining its useful life: physical factors, economic factors, or its legal life? The limiting factors seem to be (1) ecological considerations, (2) competition from other power sources, and (3) safety concerns. Physical and legal life do not appear to be primary factors affecting the plant's useful life. While the plant's physical life may be far from over, the plant may be obsolete in 20 years.

The estimate of useful life is often not easy to determine. In some cases, arbitrary lives are selected; in others, sophisticated statistical methods are used. The main basis for estimating an asset's useful life is often judgement and the company's past experience with similar assets. In an industrial economy such as Canada's, where research and innovation are so prominent, economic and technological factors have as much effect on the service lives of tangible assets as do physical factors, if not more.

Underlying Concept

Depreciation is a good example of how the matching concept is applied when there is no direct relationship between revenues and costs.

Methods of Allocation (Depreciation)

Objective 3

Identify how depreciation methods are selected.

The last major issue in the depreciation process is deciding **which depreciation method is most appropriate**. The underlying principle is that the resulting depreciation should reflect the pattern in which the asset benefits are expected to be used up by the entity. This suggests that the concern is with the pattern in which the physical capacity, wear and tear, technical obsolescence, or legal life are used up as the asset provides service to the company. Four possible patterns are identified in Illustration 11-3.

Illustration 11-3

Possible Benefit Patterns for Assets

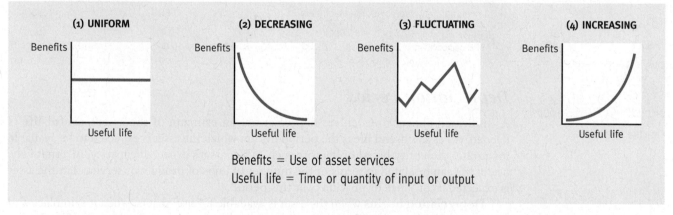

Benefits = Use of asset services
Useful life = Time or quantity of input or output

Underlying Concept

The accounting profession is sometimes criticized for failing to consider the economic consequences that accounting principles have on companies. However, the neutrality concept requires that the statements be free from bias in that methods are not chosen to achieve a predetermined result.

Pattern (1) is for an asset that provides roughly the same level of benefits in each year of its life. A warehouse could be an example. For such assets, a straight-line method is rational because it results in a constant depreciation expense each period. An airplane may be an example of an asset with a decreasing benefit pattern (2). When it is new, it is constantly in service on major routes. As it gets older, its operating efficiency declines—it may be repaired more often and used for less busy routes. Depreciation expense should therefore decline each year. The use of a truck, in terms of kilometres driven, may fluctuate considerably from period to period, yielding a benefit pattern that varies, such as that in pattern (3). An increasing benefit pattern (4) is seldom experienced because few assets provide more service potential or generate higher value cash flows as they age.

Because of the difficulty in some cases in identifying the pattern in which benefits are received, the **simplicity** of each method may be considered. If so, some argue that a straight-line method should be used. However, others may think that the method used for income tax purposes should be used for book purposes **because it eliminates some record-keeping costs**. Canadian companies are required to use the capital cost allowance approach for tax purposes (explained in Appendix 11A), so they may decide to also use this for financial reporting purposes. While this is common for smaller companies, a larger company is more likely to use one method for tax purposes and a different method for financial reporting. This is more reasonable because the objectives of financial reporting differ from those of calculating income tax. One result of using different methods for financial reporting than for taxes is that the entity's financial statement amounts for property, plant, and equipment and for income before taxes will be different from the tax value of capital assets and from taxable income. The financial accounting consequences of such differences are explored in Chapter 18.

Theory

Management sometimes appears to choose a depreciation method based on the **perceived economic consequences** of the amounts that will be reported. Companies that want to appear more profitable change from the declining-balance method to a straight-line approach. Because share value tends to be related to reported income, management feels that such a change favourably affects the firm's market value. In fact, research in this area has found just the opposite, with companies that switch to more liberal accounting policies experiencing declines in share values. One explanation is that changes like this signal that the company is in trouble and also lead to scepticism about management's attitudes and behaviour.

The choice of a depreciation method affects both the statement of financial position (in terms of the carrying amount of property, plant, and equipment) and the income statement (in terms of the depreciation expense). It follows, therefore, that various ratios are affected by the choice that is made. These ratios include the rate of return on total assets, debt-to-total assets, and the total asset turnover. Consequently, contractual commitments based on financial statement ratios, such as agreements related to management compensation plans and bond indentures, are potentially important aspects that tend to be considered when choosing a depreciation method.

Depreciation—Methods of Calculation

Objective 4
Calculate depreciation using the straight-line, decreasing charge, and activity methods and recognize the effects of using each.

How is each of the major depreciation methods applied? Regardless of whether the cost model or the revaluation model is chosen to measure assets after acquisition, the three major systematic methods are:

1. Straight-line method

2. Diminishing balance method

3. Units of production (or activity) method

To illustrate these choices, assume that a company purchases a crane for heavy construction purposes. Illustration 11-4 presents the relevant data on the purchase of the crane.

Illustration 11-4

Data Used to Illustrate Depreciation Methods

Cost of crane	$500,000
Estimated useful life	5 years
Productive life	30,000 hours
Estimated residual value	$ 50,000

Straight-Line Method

Under the **straight-line method**, depreciation is considered **a function of the passage of time**. This is the most widely used method in practice. Not only is it straightforward to apply, it is often the most conceptually appropriate method as well. When creeping obsolescence is the main reason for a limited service life, the decline in usefulness is likely constant from period to period. The depreciation expense for the crane under the straight-line method is calculated in Illustration 11-5.

$$\frac{\text{Cost less residual value}}{\text{Estimated useful life}} = \text{Depreciation charge}$$

$$\frac{\$500,000 - \$50,000}{5 \text{ years}} = \$90,000$$

One objection to the straight-line method is that it relies on two assumptions: (1) that the asset actually does deliver equal economic benefits each year, and (2) that maintenance expense is about the same each period (assuming constant revenue flows). If these assumptions are not valid, some argue that this method will not give a rational matching of expense with the periods that benefit from the asset.

Another issue with this method (and often some of the others) is the distortion that develops in a rate of return analysis (income ÷ assets). Illustration 11-6 indicates how the rate of return increases, assuming constant revenue flows, because the asset's book value decreases. The increasing trend in the rate of return can be very misleading as a basis for evaluating the success of operations because the increase is only due to the accounting method used, and not to improvements in underlying economic performance.

Year	Depreciation Expense	Undepreciated Asset Balance (net book value)	Income (after depreciation expense)	Rate of Return (income ÷ assets)
0		$500,000		
1	$90,000	410,000	$100,000	24.4%
2	90,000	320,000	100,000	31.2%
3	90,000	230,000	100,000	43.5%
4	90,000	140,000	100,000	71.4%
5	90,000	50,000	100,000	200.0%

Diminishing Balance Method

Diminishing balance methods, often called **decreasing charge methods** or **accelerated amortization**, create a higher depreciation expense in the earlier years and lower charges in later periods. The justification for this approach is that many assets offer their greatest benefits in the early years, so that this method best reflects their pattern of use. Another argument is that repair and maintenance costs are often higher in later periods, and an accelerated method therefore provides a fairly constant total expense (for depreciation plus repairs and maintenance). When a diminishing balance approach is used by Canadian companies, it is usually a version of what is called the declining-balance method.[7]

Declining-Balance Method.   The **declining-balance method** uses a depreciation rate (expressed as a percentage and called the declining-balance rate) that stays constant throughout the asset's life, assuming there is no change in estimate. This rate is applied each year to the net book value (cost less accumulated depreciation and any accumulated impairment losses) to calculate depreciation expense. For assets accounted for by the revaluation method, the rate is applied to the revalued asset amount less the total of any accumulated depreciation and accumulated impairment losses.

The rate is usually calculated as a multiple of the straight-line rate.[8] For example, the double-declining-balance rate for an asset with a 10-year life is 20% (the straight-line rate of 100% ÷ 10, or 10%, multiplied by 2). For an asset with a 20-year life, the triple declining-balance rate is 15% (the straight-line rate of 100% ÷ 20, or 5%, multiplied by 3), while the double-declining-balance rate would be 10% (100% ÷ 20, or 5%, multiplied by 2).

Unlike other methods, **the asset's residual value is not deducted** in calculating depreciation expense. Instead, the declining-balance method applies the appropriate rate to the asset's carrying amount at the beginning of each period. Since the asset's book value is reduced each period by the depreciation charge, the rate is applied to a lower and lower carrying amount each period, resulting in a depreciation charge that gets smaller each year. This process continues until the asset's carrying amount is reduced to its estimated residual value. **When the residual value is reached, the asset is no longer depreciated.**

Illustration 11-7 shows how to apply the **double-declining-balance method**, using the crane example.

<table>
<tr><td></td></tr>
</table>

	Illustration 11-7					
	Depreciation Calculation, *Double-Declining-Balance* *Method—Crane Example*					

Year	Book Value of Asset, Beginning of Year	Rate on Declining Balance[a]	Depreciation Expense	Balance of Accumulated Depreciation	Net Book Value, End of Year
1	$500,000	40%	$200,000	$200,000	$300,000
2	300,000	40%	120,000	320,000	180,000
3	180,000	40%	72,000	392,000	108,000
4	108,000	40%	43,200	435,200	64,800
5	64,800	40%	14,800[b]	450,000	50,000

[a] $(100\% \div 5) \times 2$
[b] Limited to $14,800 because the book value is not reduced below the residual value.

Units of Production Method

The **units of production method**, often called the **activity method** or a **variable charge approach**, calculates depreciation **according to usage or productivity** instead of the passage of time. The asset's life is defined in terms of either the output it provides (units produced), or the input required (the number of hours it operates). Conceptually, a better cost association results from using output instead of an input measure such as hours used, but both are widely accepted and used.

The crane's usage in hours is relatively easy to measure. If it is used for 4,000 hours the first year, the depreciation charge is calculated as shown in Illustration 11-8.

	Illustration 11-8
	Depreciation Calculation, *Activity Method—* *Crane Example*

$$\frac{\text{Cost less residual value}}{\text{Total estimated hours}} = \text{Depreciation expense per hour}$$

$$\frac{\$500,000 - \$50,000}{30,000 \text{ hours}} = \$15 \text{ per hour}$$

First year depreciation expense: 4,000 hours $\times$ $15 = $60,000

When the asset's economic benefits are consumed by usage, activity, or productivity, the units of production method results in the best measure of periodic expense. Companies that adopt this approach have low depreciation during periods of low usage, high charges during high usage, and zero depreciation expense when the asset is available, but idle.

This method's major limitation is that it is appropriate in only a few situations. For example, a building usually suffers a great amount of steady deterioration from the weather (a function of time) regardless of how it is used. In addition, when an asset's useful life is affected by economic or functional factors that have nothing to do with its usage, the activity method is not appropriate. If a company is expanding rapidly, a particular building may soon become obsolete for its intended purpose. The level of activity is irrelevant.

One industry where the activity method is particularly relevant is the extractive industry, which includes mining and oil and gas. Accounting for the depletion of natural resources is discussed in the next section.

Other Methods

Sometimes, because of cost-benefit considerations or because the assets have unique characteristics, an entity may choose not to use one of the more common depreciation methods. Instead, it may use the method required by the Canada Revenue Agency for tax purposes as explained in Appendix 11A, or develop its own tailor-made amortization method.

What Do the Numbers Mean?

Some companies try to imply that amortization is not a cost. For example, in their press releases, they often draw more attention to earnings before interest, taxes, depreciation, and amortization (referred to as EBITDA) or pro forma earnings (which may exclude items such as depreciation and restructuring costs) rather than net income as calculated under GAAP.[9] Some companies like the EBITDA figure because it "dresses up" their earnings numbers, and they promote it using the argument that the excluded costs are not operating costs or that amortization and depreciation are non-cash charges. Regardless, when all is said and done, companies must generate enough cash from revenues to cover all their costs, as the amounts they borrow to finance long-term asset acquisitions have to be repaid. Investors need to understand the differences between these various indicators of financial performance.

Real World Emphasis

Consider **Aliant Inc.**'s review of its results for a prior year. EBITDA was reported at $941.6 million, while net income under GAAP amounted to $177.6 million. In the same year, **Hollinger International Inc.** reported EBITDA of U.S. $111.4 million and a GAAP net loss of U.S. $238.8 million! Because of concerns that investors may be confused or misled by non-GAAP earnings measures, the Canadian Securities Administrators, which is the umbrella group for provincial regulators, issued specific guidance for certain disclosures that are associated with non-GAAP earnings measures. These include requiring that entities present a reconciliation of their non-GAAP measure(s) with audited GAAP results.

While reporting EBITDA and other pro forma numbers has not been prohibited, it appears that the new requirements have made some companies less enthusiastic about reporting these results as prominently as they previously did.

Depletion of Mineral Resources

Objective 5
Explain the accounting issues for depletion of mineral resources.

One industry where the activity method is particularly relevant is the extractive industry. Chapter 10 explains that generally the costs of oil and gas reserves and mineral deposits are capitalized into mineral resource assets. The amortization of the cost of these reserves as the wells or ore bodies are put into production is known as **depletion**. The resulting **depletion expense** is a product cost, and therefore is a part of the direct cost of the minerals or petroleum products (inventory) produced during the period.

The accounting issues associated with the depletion of mineral resources are similar to those encountered with the amortization of other types of property, plant, and equipment. They include:

1. determining the pattern of depletion (amortization) to be used and

2. the difficulty in estimating the asset's useful life.

Natural resource companies also have to deal with the associated issue of liquidating dividends, as discussed below.

Pattern of Depletion

Once the company establishes the depletion base—the cost of the mineral resource asset to be amortized—the next step is to determine how these capitalized costs will be allocated to accounting periods. Normally, **depletion is calculated using an activity approach, such as the units of production method**. This approach is used because of the close association of the resulting expense with the asset benefits consumed in the period. Under this method, the cost of the resource asset is divided by the estimated recoverable reserves (the number of units that are estimated to be in the resource deposit) to obtain a cost per unit of production. The cost per unit is then multiplied by the number of units extracted during the period to determine the depletion charge.

For example, assume a mining company acquired the right to use 1,000 hectares of land in the Northwest Territories to mine for gold. The lease cost is $50,000, the related exploration and evaluation costs are $100,000, and development costs incurred in opening the mine are $3,850,000, all of which have been capitalized. Total costs related to the mine before the first ounce of gold is extracted are, therefore, $4 million. The company estimates that the mine will provide approximately 10,000 ounces of gold. The depletion rate is determined in Illustration 11-9.

<table>
<tr><td>

Illustration 11-9

Calculation of Depletion Rate

</td><td>

$$\frac{\text{Total cost} - \text{residual value}}{\text{Total estimated units available}} = \text{Depletion cost per unit}$$

$$\frac{\$4,000,000}{10,000} = \$400 \text{ per ounce}$$

</td></tr>
</table>

If 2,500 ounces are extracted in the first year, the depletion for the year is $1,000,000 (2,500 ounces at $400). The entry to record the depletion is:

<table>
<tr><td>

A = L + SE
0   0   0

Cash flows: No effect

</td><td>

| Inventory | 1,000,000 | |
| Accumulated Depletion | | 1,000,000 |

</td></tr>
</table>

The depletion charge for the extracted resource (in addition to labour and other direct production costs) is initially charged (debited) to inventory. When the resource is sold, the inventory costs are transferred to cost of goods sold and matched with the period's revenue. The remaining mineral resource is reported with property, plant, and equipment as a non-current asset, as follows:

| Gold mine (at cost) | $4,000,000 | |
| Less: Accumulated depletion | 1,000,000 | $3,000,000 |

The equipment used in extracting the resource may also be amortized on a units of production basis, especially if the equipment's benefits and useful life are directly related to the quantity of ore extracted from that specific deposit. If the equipment is used on more than one job and at more than one site, other cost allocation methods may be more appropriate.

Estimating Recoverable Reserves

Companies often change the estimate of the resource's useful life; that is, the amount of the recoverable reserves. This may result from new information or from the availability of more sophisticated production processes. Natural resources such as oil and gas deposits and some rare metals are the greatest challenges. Estimates of these reserves are in large measure "knowledgeable guesses."

Accounting for a change in the estimate of reserves is the same as for a change in the useful life of an item of plant and equipment. The procedure, explained later in this chapter, is to revise the depletion rate by dividing the costs remaining on the books less any residual value by the new estimate of the recoverable reserves. Past depletion is not adjusted. This approach has much merit since the required estimates are so uncertain.

Husky Energy, a Canadian company involved in the oil and gas industry, reports in its 2010 annual report that:

> amounts recorded for depletion, depreciation, amortization of accretion expense, asset retirement obligations, fair value measurements, employee future benefits and amounts used in impairment tests … are based on estimates. These estimates include petroleum and natural gas reserves, future petroleum and natural gas prices, future interest rates and future costs required to develop those reserves as well as other fair value assumptions. By their nature, these estimates are subject to measurement uncertainty and changes in such estimates in future years could require a material change on the financial statements.

This caveat, combined with the Simmons & Company International illustration of the Value Pyramid below, underscores the measurement uncertainty associated with resource quantities and therefore the depletion expenses recognized by companies in the industry.

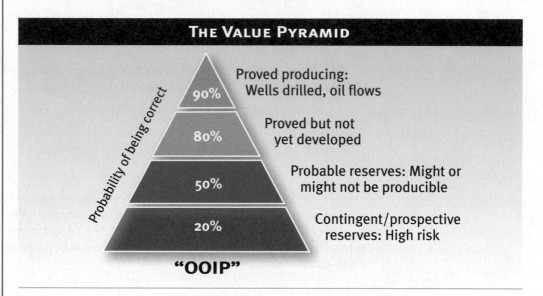

"OOIP" refers to the original oil in place, and determining this is the starting point in the calculation of reserves. After this, the amount of the OOIP that is technically and economically recoverable is then estimated. The percentages indicated in each layer of the pyramid give you some idea of the likelihood of these estimates being correct. The bottom line is that estimating oil and gas reserves may be more an art than a science!

Source: Simmons and Company International. From a presentation given by Matthew R. Simmons to the Standing Group on the Oil Market of the International Energy Agency in Paris, France, March 16, 2004, available at: http://www.simmonsco-intl.com/files/IEA-SOM.pdf, accessed June 2, 2009.

Liquidating Dividends

A company may own a property from which it plans to extract mineral resources, and have this as its only major asset. If the company does not expect to purchase more properties, it may decide to distribute to shareholders a portion or all of their capital investment by paying a **liquidating dividend**, which is a dividend greater than the amount of accumulated net income. These dividends are usually equal to the accumulated amount of net income (after depletion) **plus the amount of depletion that has been charged**.

The major accounting issue is to distinguish between dividends that are a return **of capital** and those that are not. A company issuing a liquidating dividend reduces the appropriate Share Capital account for the portion of the dividend that is related to the original investment instead of reducing Retained Earnings, because the dividend is a return of part of the investor's original contribution.

To illustrate, assume Callahan Mining Corp. has a retained earnings balance of $1,650,000, accumulated depletion on mineral properties of $2.1 million, and common share capital of $5.4 million. Callahan's board declares and pays a dividend of $3 per share on the 1 million shares outstanding. The company records the dividend as follows:

<table>
<tr><td></td><td colspan="2">A = L + SE
−3,000,000   −3,000,000
Cash flows: ↓ 3,000,000 outflow</td><td></td></tr>
</table>

Retained Earnings	1,650,000	
Common Shares	1,350,000*	
Cash		3,000,000
*($3,000,000 − $1,650,000)		

Callahan must inform shareholders that the $3 dividend per share represents a $1.65 ($1,650,000/1,000,000) per share **return on investment** and a $1.35 ($1,350,000/1,000,000) per share liquidating dividend, or **return of capital**.

Other Depreciation Issues

Objective 6

Explain and apply the accounting procedures for partial periods and a change in depreciation rate.

Two additional depreciation issues remain:

1. How should depreciation be calculated for partial periods?

2. How are revisions to depreciation rates made and reported?

Depreciation and Partial Periods

Plant assets arc rarely purchased on the first day of a fiscal period or disposed of on the last day of a fiscal period, except in accounting texts! A practical question therefore is, "How much depreciation should be charged for partial periods?"

Assume, for example, that an automated drill machine with a five-year life is purchased for $45,000 (no residual value) on June 10, 2014. The company's fiscal year ends December 31, and depreciation is charged for $6\frac{2}{3}$ months during the year. The total depreciation for a full year, assuming the straight-line method, is $9,000 ($45,000 ÷ 5). The depreciation for the first, partial year is therefore:

$$\$9,000 \times \frac{6\frac{2}{3}}{12} = \$5,000$$

Rather than making a precise allocation of cost for a partial period, many companies set a policy to simplify the process. One variation is to take no depreciation in the year of acquisition and a full year's depreciation in the year of disposal. For example, depreciation is calculated for the full period on the opening balance in the asset account, and none for acquisitions in the year. Another variation is to charge a full year's depreciation on assets that are used for a full year and charge a half year of amortization in the years of acquisition and disposal. Alternatively, the company may charge a full year's depreciation in the year of acquisition and none in the year of disposal.

Although not conceptually "correct," companies may adopt one of these fractional-year policies in allocating cost to the first and last years of an asset's life if the method is applied consistently and the resulting effect on the financial statements is not material. **Via Rail Canada**, for example, has followed a policy of beginning depreciation in the month after a train is put into service and continuing it up to the month of disposal. For

Real World Emphasis

the illustrations and problem material in this text, depreciation is calculated based on the nearest full month, unless something different is stated. Illustration 11-10 shows depreciation allocated under five different fractional-year policies using the straight-line method on an automated drill machine purchased for $45,000 on June 10, 2014.

Illustration 11-10

Fractional-Year Depreciation Policies, Straight Line Method

Machine Cost = $45,000		Depreciation Allocated Each Year over 5-Year Life (rounded to the nearest dollar)					
Fractional-Year Policy		2014	2015	2016	2017	2018	2019
1. Nearest fraction of a year		$5,000[a]	$9,000	$9,000	$9,000	$9,000	$4,000[b]
2. Nearest full month		5,250[c]	9,000	9,000	9,000	9,000	3,750[d]
3. Half year in period of acquisition and disposal		4,500	9,000	9,000	9,000	9,000	4,500
4. Full year in period of acquisition, none in period of disposal		9,000	9,000	9,000	9,000	9,000	0
5. None in period of acquisition, full year in period of disposal		0	9,000	9,000	9,000	9,000	9,000

[a]6.667/12 ($9,000)   [b]5.333/12 ($9,000)   [c]7/12 ($9,000)   [d]5/12 ($9,000)

The partial period calculation is relatively simple when a company uses the straight-line method. But how is partial period depreciation handled when an accelerated method is used? To illustrate, assume that an asset was purchased for $10,000 on October 1, 2014, with an estimated useful life of five years. The depreciation expense for 2014, 2015, and 2016 using the double-declining-balance method is shown in Illustration 11-11.

Illustration 11-11

Calculation of Partial Period Depreciation, Double-Declining-Balance Method

1st full year	(40% × $10,000) = $4,000
2nd full year	(40% × 6,000) = 2,400
3rd full year	(40% × 3,600) = 1,440
Depreciation October 1, 2014, to December 31, 2014:	3/12 × $4,000 = $1,000
Depreciation for 2015:	9/12 × $4,000 = $3,000
	3/12 × $2,400 = 600
	$3,600
Depreciation for 2016:	9/12 × $2,400 = $1,800
	3/12 × $1,440 = 360
	$2,160

Alternatively:

Depreciation for 2014: (40% × $10,000) × 3/12 = $1,000
    Asset carrying amount now = $10,000 − $1,000 = $9,000

Depreciation for 2015: (40% × $9,000) = $3,600
    Asset carrying amount now = $9,000 − $3,600 = $5,400

Depreciation for 2016: (40% × $5,400) = $2,160
    Asset carrying amount now = $5,400 − $2,160 = $3,240

As you can see, the depreciation amount is identical whether you proceed through yearly "layers" of depreciation or whether you simply apply the rate to the asset's carrying amount at the first of each year.

Revision of Depreciation Rates

When a plant asset is acquired, depreciation rates are carefully determined based on past experience with similar assets and other pertinent information. Depreciation is only an estimate, however, and the estimates of the expected pattern of consumption of the asset's benefits, useful life, and residual value need to be reviewed regularly and at least at each fiscal year end under IFRS. A change in any one of these variables requires that either the depreciation method or the rate also be changed. Unexpected physical deterioration, unforeseen obsolescence, or changes in the extent or way in which the asset is used may make the asset's useful life less than originally estimated. Improved maintenance procedures, a revision of operating policies, or similar developments may prolong its life beyond what was expected.

When a change in estimate takes place, accounting standards **do not permit companies to go back and "correct" the records, nor to make a "catch-up" adjustment** for any accumulated difference. Instead, a company accounts for a change in estimate **prospectively; that is, in the period of change and in the future**, if applicable. This is because estimates are such an inherent part of the accounting process. As new information becomes available, the changes are incorporated into current and future measurements.

For example, assume that machinery that cost $90,000 was estimated originally to have a 20-year life and a $10,000 residual value. It has already been depreciated for eight years. In year nine, the asset's total life is now expected to be 30 years with a residual value of only $2,000. Depreciation has been recorded on the asset at the rate of 1/20 ($90,000 – $10,000), or $4,000 each year, by the straight-line method, but now a new depreciation schedule has to be prepared for the asset. The new schedule uses the undepreciated costs that remain on the books, along with the most recent estimates of the asset's residual value and remaining useful life. If another depreciation method is more appropriate for the current circumstances, then it will be applied going forward.

Continuing with our example, Illustration 11-12 shows the charges for depreciation in the current and subsequent periods based on revised calculations, assuming the straight-line method is still appropriate.

Illustration 11-12

Calculation of Depreciation after Revision of Estimated Life and Residual Value

Machinery cost	$90,000
Less: Accumulated depreciation to date: 8 × $4,000/year	32,000
Carrying amount of machinery at end of 8th year	58,000
Less estimated residual value	2,000
Costs to be depreciated	$56,000

Revised depreciation = $56,000 ÷ (30 – 8) years remaining life = $2,545 per year

The entry to record depreciation in each of the remaining 22 years is:

A = L + SE		
–2,545 –2,545		

Cash flows: No effect

Depreciation Expense	2,545	
Accumulated Depreciation—Machinery		2,545

If the double-declining-balance method had been used initially, the change in estimated life would result in a new depreciation rate to be applied to the book value in the current (ninth) and subsequent years.[10] In this example, a revised remaining life of 22 years results in a revised 100% ÷ 22 or 4.55% straight-line and a 9.09% double-declining rate. As this method initially ignores residual value in determining depreciation expense, a change in residual value is ignored in the revised calculation until such time as book value equals residual value.

TransAlta Corporation, a Canadian power generation and wholesale marketing company operating in Canada, the United States, Mexico, and Australia, recently provided information about a change in the estimated useful life of some of its generating facilities and mining assets. The information, disclosed in Illustration 11-13, also reports the change in its depreciation expense.

Real World Emphasis

Illustration 11-13
Change in Estimate of Useful Life and Depreciation Expense

TransAlta Corporation

Accounting Changes

B. Current Year Accounting Changes

II. Change in Estimate – Useful Lives

In 2010, management initiated a comprehensive review of the estimated useful lives of all generating facilities and coal mining assets, having regard for, among other things, TransAlta's economic lifecycle maintenance program, the existing condition of the assets, progress on carbon capture and other technologies, as well as other market-related factors. Management concluded its review of the coal fleet, as well as its mining assets, and updated the estimated useful lives of these assets to reflect their current expected economic lives. As a result, depreciation was reduced by $26 million for the year ended Dec. 31, 2010 compared to the same period in 2009.

Any other adjustments resulting from the review of the balance of the fleet will be reflected in future periods.

IMPAIRMENT

Objective 7

Explain the issues and apply the accounting standards for capital asset impairment under both IFRS and ASPE.

As indicated in Chapter 10, property, plant, and equipment (PP&E) assets are measured after acquisition by applying the cost model, the revaluation model, or the fair value model. If an **investment property is measured at fair value** and if the asset becomes impaired, the remeasurement of the asset to fair value automatically recognizes this reduction and the associated loss is recognized in income.

Assets measured under the **cost or revaluation model**, however, are not automatically adjusted to fair value. Instead, they are reported at cost (or at fair value at the most recent revaluation date) less accumulated depreciation. Is this amount the appropriate value for the statement of financial position? Or should PP&E assets be valued at **the lower of cost and net realizable value** as most inventory assets are?

It is important to report inventory on the statement of financial position at no more than the net cash the entity expects to receive on its disposal because, as a **current asset**, it is expected to be converted into cash within the operating cycle. Property, plant, and equipment assets, however, are **not held to be directly converted into cash**. They are ordinarily **used in operations over the long term**. For this reason, the same "lower of cost and net realizable value" measure is not appropriate for PP&E assets. However, it is important that any impairment in value be recognized.

What Do the Numbers Mean?

Real World Emphasis

Even when long-lived capital assets become partially obsolete, accountants have been reluctant to reduce their carrying amount. This is because it is often difficult to arrive at a measure for property, plant, and equipment that is not subjective and arbitrary. For example, **Falconbridge Ltd.** at one time had to decide whether all or a part of its property, plant, and equipment in a nickel-mining operation in the Dominican Republic should be written off. The project had been incurring losses because nickel prices were low and operating costs were high. Only if nickel prices increased by about 33% would the project be reasonably profitable. Whether it was appropriate to recognize an impairment loss depended on the future price of nickel. Even if a decision were made to write down the asset, the amount to be written off would not be obvious. This same issue faced most Canadian companies in the oil and gas industry in 2008 and 2009 as the price of a barrel of oil dropped by about 70%.

How do accountants handle this problem? The first step in accounting for **impairments** is for management to be alert to events and circumstances that might indicate that a long-lived asset is **impaired**; in other words, that its carrying amount is higher than its future economic benefits to the company.

Indicators of Impairment

Illustration 11-14 provides examples of possible evidence of impairment.

External Indicators	Internal Indicators
There are observable indications of a significant reduction in the asset's value.	There is evidence of obsolescence or physical damage of the asset.
A significant change in the technological, market, economic, or legal environment has affected or is expected to adversely affect the entity.	Significant changes with adverse effects have taken place or are expected to take place in how the asset is used (for example, the asset becoming idle or subject to plans for early disposition).
Market rates of return have increased, with a negative effect on the asset's value and recoverable amount.	Internal reports about the asset indicate its performance is or will be worse than expected.
The book value of the entity's net assets is more than the company's market capitalization.	Costs incurred for an asset's acquisition or construction significantly exceed the amount originally expected.

Illustration 11-14

Potential Indicators of Impairment (see IAS 36)

There may be other factors that suggest that an asset's carrying amount is overstated. The objective is to be open to the possibility of impairment with changes in the internal and external environment. Even if an impairment loss is not evident, a change may be needed in the estimate of the asset's useful life or residual value, or in the depreciation method applied.

IFRS requires that assets be assessed for indications of impairment at the end of each reporting period, while **ASPE** requires this assessment only when events and changes in circumstances indicate that an asset's carrying amount may not be recoverable. When such an assessment indicates that an asset's carrying amount may not be recoverable, the asset is tested for impairment. Two different approaches to impairment accounting are described next.

Impairment—Recognition and Measurement Models

Just as there are different models for measuring capital assets, there are also different models for measuring impairment losses for these assets. One approach, a **cost recovery impairment model**, concludes that a long-lived asset is impaired only if an entity cannot recover the asset's carrying amount from using the asset and eventually disposing of it. Another approach, a **rational entity impairment model**, assumes that an entity makes rational decisions in managing its long-term assets. A company is likely to continue to use an asset if its use and later disposal earn a higher return than if it is currently disposed of. If current disposal generates a higher return, then management is likely to take this action. This model, therefore, incorporates both these values in the impairment decision.

Cost Recovery Impairment Model

If events or changes in circumstances indicate that an asset's carrying amount may not be recoverable, the cost recovery impairment model uses a **recoverability test** to determine whether an impairment loss needs to be recognized. Two basic assumptions underlie this approach:

1. The asset will continue to be used in operations.

2. As long as the dollars of cost remaining are expected to be recovered by future inflows of dollars, the asset's carrying amount will be recovered and no impairment is evident.

An estimate is made of the future net cash flows that are expected from the use of the asset and its eventual disposal. These cash flows are not discounted. If these **undiscounted future cash flows** are **less than the asset's carrying amount**, the asset is considered impaired. Conversely, if the **undiscounted** future net cash flows are **equal to or greater than the asset's carrying amount**, no impairment has occurred. Essentially, the recoverability test is a screening device to determine whether an asset is impaired.

If the recoverability test indicates that an asset held for use is impaired, an **impairment loss** is calculated. It is the amount by which the asset's carrying amount exceeds its fair value. This is **not the same** as the difference between its carrying amount and its recoverable amount in the recoverability test. **Fair value** under this model is the price that would be agreed upon in an arm's-length transaction between knowledgeable, willing parties who are under no compulsion to act, and by its nature is a discounted or present value measure. It is best measured by quoted market prices in active markets, but if there is no active market—which is often the case—other valuation methods are used.

Example A: Cost Recovery Impairment Model.   Step 1: Because of changes in how equipment is being used, it is reviewed for possible impairment.

Step 2: Based on the possibility of impairment, carry out a **recoverability test**. The asset's carrying amount is $600,000 ($800,000 cost less $200,000 accumulated depreciation). The expected future undiscounted net cash flows from the use of the asset and its later disposal are estimated to be $650,000, and the asset's fair value is $525,000. The recoverability test indicates that the $650,000 of expected net cash flows from the asset exceeds its carrying amount of $600,000. As a result, **no impairment is evident** and no further steps are required.

Example B: Cost Recovery Impairment Model.   Assume the same facts as in Example A above, except that the expected future net cash flows from the equipment are $580,000 instead of $650,000.

Step 1: Because of changes in how equipment is being used, it is reviewed for possible impairment.

Step 2: Based on the possibility of impairment, carry out a recoverability test. The **recoverability test** indicates that the $580,000 of expected net cash flows from the asset is less than its carrying amount of $600,000. Therefore, the asset is considered impaired.

Step 3: Measure and record the impairment loss. If the asset's fair value is $525,000, the impairment loss is calculated as shown in Illustration 11-15.

Illustration 11-15		
Calculation of Impairment Loss—Cost Recovery Impairment Model	Carrying amount of the equipment	$600,000
	Fair value of equipment	525,000
	Impairment loss	$ 75,000

The entry to record the impairment loss is as follows:

A   = L +   SE
−75,000   −75,000

Cash flows: No effect

Loss on Impairment	75,000	
Accumulated Impairment Losses—Equipment		75,000

Notice that the entry credits an Accumulated Impairment Losses account rather than Accumulated Depreciation or the capital asset account itself. Any one of these credits may be and is used in practice. Regardless of which account is credited, the adjusted carrying amount becomes the asset's new "cost" and the writedown is charged to expense. As the asset is considered to have a new cost basis, no reversal of the impairment charge is permitted. After the impairment loss is recorded, the depreciation method chosen for the asset is reviewed, as are the remaining useful life and residual value. Revised depreciation amounts are then calculated.

ASPE uses the cost recovery impairment model.

Rational Entity Impairment Model

Another approach to the recognition and measurement of impairment losses is the **rational entity impairment model**. This approach assumes that an entity makes rational decisions in managing its long-term assets and therefore it compares the asset's book value with a recoverable amount **that differs depending on the circumstances**. If management can earn a higher return from using an asset than from selling it, the company will continue to use it. However, if a higher return is possible from selling the asset, then the rational decision is to sell it. This model, therefore, compares the asset's carrying amount with its **recoverable amount**, defined as the **higher of its value in use and its fair value less costs of disposal**. If the recoverable amount is less than its carrying amount, the impairment loss is equal to the difference. Illustration 11-16 indicates how the loss is calculated.

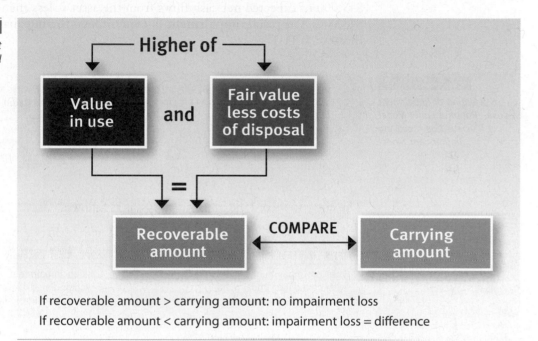

If recoverable amount > carrying amount: no impairment loss

If recoverable amount < carrying amount: impairment loss = difference

Unlike the cost recovery impairment method, there is **no pre-screening test** to determine whether an asset is impaired. Instead, the carrying amount is compared directly with a fair-value-based recoverable amount that is a discounted present value measure.

Value in use is the present value of the future cash flows expected to be derived from the asset's use and subsequent disposal. **Fair value less costs of disposal** is the amount currently expected to be received from the sale of the asset in an orderly transaction between market participants after subtracting incremental costs directly related to the disposal.[11] Disposal costs might include legal costs, transaction taxes, and removal costs, for example, but exclude finance costs and income tax expense. IFRS uses this model.

Example C: Rational Entity Impairment Model.   Step 1: As a result of its annual assessment of property, plant, and equipment for indications of impairment, an entity determines that equipment with a carrying amount of $45,000 (cost of $60,000; accumulated depreciation of $15,000) may be impaired due to technological obsolescence.

Step 2: The entity calculates the asset's recoverable amount to be $47,500. This is the higher of its value in use of $47,500 and its fair value less costs of disposal of $40,000. Because the recoverable amount is more than the asset's book value, there is no impairment loss to be recognized.

Example D: Rational Entity versus Cost Recovery Impairment Model.   Assume the same facts as in Example C, except that the asset's value in use is determined to be

$37,500 and its fair value less costs of disposal (of $2,000) is $40,000. In addition, the expected future undiscounted net cash flows from the use of the asset and its later disposal are estimated to be $43,000. Compare the accounting for impairment under ASPE versus IFRS.

Step 1 (IFRS and ASPE): As a result of its annual assessment of property, plant, and equipment for indications of impairment, an entity determines that equipment with a carrying amount of $45,000 (cost of $60,000; accumulated depreciation of $15,000) may be impaired due to technological obsolescence.

Step 2 (IFRS—Rational Entity Model): The entity calculates the asset's recoverable amount to be $40,000. This is the higher of its value in use of $37,500 and its fair value less costs of disposal of $40,000. Now an impairment loss of $5,000 is indicated, as calculated in Illustration 11-17.

(ASPE—Cost Recovery Impairment Model): The recoverability test indicates that the $43,000 of expected net cash flows from the asset is less than the carrying amount of $45,000. As a result, **impairment is evident**, and the impairment loss is calculated in Illustration 11-17.

	Rational Entity Impairment Model	Cost Recovery Impairment Model
Carrying amount of the equipment	$45,000	$45,000
Recoverable amount (IFRS)/Fair value (ASPE)	40,000	42,000
Impairment loss	$ 5,000	$ 3,000

Illustration 11-17

Calculation of Impairment Loss—Rational Entity Model versus Cost Recovery Impairment Model

The entry to record the impairment loss is as follows:

IFRS
A   = L +   SE
−5,000   −5,000

Cash flows: No effect

ASPE
A   = L +   SE
−3,000   −3,000

Cash flows: No effect

IFRS: Rational Entity Impairment Model			ASPE: Cost Recovery Impairment Model		
Loss on Impairment	5,000		Loss on Impairment	3,000	
Accumulated Impairment Losses—Equipment		5,000	Accumulated Impairment Losses—Equipment		3,000

The loss from the writedown is recognized in net income. However, if the asset is accounted for under the revaluation model, the loss is accounted for on the same basis as a revaluation decrease, explained in Chapter 10: it is charged first through other comprehensive income to any revaluation surplus that exists for that asset, and only the excess is recognized in income. After the impairment loss is recognized, the depreciation method, remaining useful life, and residual value are reviewed, and revised depreciation amounts are determined.

Under the rational entity method, it is important to keep track separately of any impairment losses recognized because, unlike the cost recovery approach, a portion of **the impairment loss may be reversed in the future**. The recoverable amount is considered to be based on estimates that may change in the future. At each reporting date, information that mirrors the original indicators of impairment is assessed to determine whether a previously recognized impairment loss still exists. If the estimates used to determine the asset's value in use and fair value less costs of disposal have changed, then a reversal of the impairment can be recognized.

The reversal amount, however, is limited. The specific asset cannot be increased in value to more than what its book value would have been, net of depreciation, if the original impairment loss had never been recognized.

The method described here as the rational entity model is the one applied under IFRS. What is the core difference between this and the cost recovery impairment method? The IFRS approach better reflects the economic circumstances underlying the asset's usefulness to the entity, capturing both the declines and recoveries in value. The cost recovery approach waits until circumstances indicate that conditions are very bad before recognizing an impairment. It does not take into account the time value of money in the recoverability test and it is not neutral since after recognizing impairment it does not allow for later recognition of any recovery (i.e., no reversals of the impairment loss are permitted).

Asset Groups and Cash-Generating Units

The discussion above assumes that recoverable amounts can be determined for each individual asset. However, many assets do not generate cash flows on their own, but only in combination with other assets. In this case, the cash flows based on a single asset's value in use cannot be independently determined. Instead, the asset has to be identified with an **asset group** or **cash-generating unit (CGU)** and it is the group whose cash flows are tested for impairment. An asset group or CGU is the smallest identifiable group of assets that generates cash inflows that are predominantly independent of the cash flows from other individual assets or other groups of assets.[12] IAS 36 *Impairment of Assets* provides the examples summarized in Illustration 11-18.

Situation	Asset Group or CGU
A mining company owns a private railway to support its mining activities. The railway could be sold for scrap value only. It does not generate cash inflows that are independent of those from the mine's other assets. [IAS 36.67]	It is not possible to estimate the recoverable amount of the private railway alone because its value in use cannot be determined and is probably different from its scrap value. So, the entity should estimate the recoverable amount of the CGU that the private railway belongs to. This is the mine as a whole.
A bus company provides services under contract with a municipality that requires minimum service on each of five separate routes. The assets devoted to each route and the cash flows from each are known. One of the routes operates at a significant loss. [IAS 36.68]	Because the company does not have the option to reduce service on any one bus route, the lowest level of identifiable cash flows that are largely independent of the cash inflows from other assets or groups of assets is represented by the cash flows generated by the five routes together. The CGU for each route is the bus company as a whole.

These examples should help provide a basic understanding of what an asset group or CGU is and how each is generally determined. **Both the cost recovery and the rational entity impairment models are then applied as explained above to the groups of assets rather than individual assets.** Any resulting impairment loss is then allocated proportionally (based on relative carrying amounts) to the long-lived assets in the asset group. However, no individual asset is reduced below its fair value (cost recovery impairment model), or the highest of its fair value less costs of disposal, its value in use, or zero (under the rational entity model). This is illustrated in the following example.

Example E: Asset Group or CGU. Uni Corp. (UC) is a manufacturer that produces parts for residential telephone sets. Recent indications are that the market for this product is likely to decline significantly and UC is testing equipment used in the production process for impairment. The following assets are used only in the manufacture of these parts:

	Cost	Accumulated Depreciation	Carrying Amount
Tools and dies	$1,000	$ 600	$ 400
Specialized equipment	5,000	3,500	1,500
General equipment	3,000	1,800	1,200
	$9,000	$5,900	$3,100

The tools and dies and specialized equipment cannot be used elsewhere and have no resale value, while the general equipment could be sold today for $1,500. UC plans to continue producing the parts for two more years to fill a commitment to its customer. The net future cash flows from the next two years' production of these parts and the disposal of the equipment are estimated to be $3,200, and the present value of these cash flows is $2,600.

Impairment Loss—Cost Recovery Impairment Model.   Because the tools and dies and specialized equipment cannot generate cash flows on their own, they are combined into an asset group with the general equipment. The carrying amount of the asset group is $3,100. The cost recovery impairment model applies a recoverability test to determine if there is impairment. The book value of $3,100 is compared with the undiscounted future cash flows expected from the use and later disposal of the asset group of $3,200. Because the book value can be recovered, there is no impairment, and no loss is recognized. As mentioned above, if an impairment loss is indicated, it is allocated only to the long-lived assets in the group that are held for use. The allocation is based on the assets' relative carrying amounts, although no asset is written down below its fair value, if known.

Impairment Loss—Rational Entity Model.   Under this model, the carrying amount of the cash-generating group of $3,100 is compared with the CGU's recoverable amount. The recoverable amount is $2,600—the higher of the CGU's value in use of $2,600 and its fair value less costs of disposal of $1,500.

Carrying amount of CGU	$3,100
Recoverable amount	2,600
Impairment loss	$ 500

The impairment loss is then allocated to the individual assets in the group, but no individual asset can be reduced below the highest of (1) its value in use, (2) its fair value less costs of disposal, or (3) zero. In this case, the only determinable amount is the general equipment's fair value less costs of disposal of $1,500. Because this asset's book value is already less than this, the $500 loss is therefore allocated only to the tools and dies and specialized equipment.

Allocation:	Carrying Amount	Proportion	Loss Allocation
Tools and dies	$ 400	4/19	$105
Specialized equipment	1,500	15/19	395
Total	$1,900		$500

The entry to record the impairment is:

A   = L   +   SE
−500   −500

Cash flows: No effect

Loss on Impairment	500	
Accumulated Impairment Losses—Tools and Dies		105
Accumulated Impairment Losses—Equipment		395

HELD FOR SALE AND DERECOGNITION

Long-Lived Assets to Be Disposed of by Sale

Objective 8
Explain and apply the accounting standards for long-lived assets that are held for sale.

What happens if a company intends to dispose of its long-lived assets by sale instead of continuing to use them? Because this is relevant information for financial statement readers, such an asset is classified as **held for sale**, is remeasured at the lower of its carrying amount and fair value less costs of disposal, and is reported separately. A "fair value less costs of disposal" measurement is used if this is less than its book value because it corresponds better to the amount of cash a company expects to generate from the asset. The usefulness of this measurement is increased by the strict criteria for classifying a long-lived asset as held for sale, including the requirement that the asset be disposed of within a short period of time. These criteria were presented in Chapter 4 in the section on discontinued operations.

Assets that are held for sale **are not depreciated while they are held**. The reason is that it would be inconsistent to amortize assets that are not in use, that are likely to be sold, and that are carried at the equivalent of the lower of (amortized) cost and net realizable value. In many respects, these assets are closer to inventory than capital assets.

After being classified as a held-for-sale asset, such an asset continues to be carried at the lower of amortized cost and fair value less costs of disposal. Further losses are recognized if the net amount expected from the asset continues to drop. Gains (that is, loss recoveries) are recognized for any increases in net realizable value, but these are limited to the amount of the cumulative losses previously recognized.

How these assets and gains and losses are reported is governed by the need for users to understand the effects of discontinued operations and disposals of non-current assets. If the long-lived asset is a component of an entity that meets the criteria for being reported as a discontinued operation, the losses and any recoveries are reported as part of discontinued operations on the income statement. Otherwise, they are reported in income from continuing operations. Practice differs on how the PP&E assets held for sale are reported on the statement of financial position. ASPE allows these assets to be reclassified as current assets only if they are sold before the financial statements are completed, and the proceeds to be received qualify as a current asset. Otherwise, they are reported separately as non-current assets. Under IFRS, most non-current assets that meet the stringent requirements for classification as held for sale also meet the criteria for recognition as current assets. In all cases, they are reported separately from other assets on the statement of financial position with note disclosure of the major classes of assets making up the total.

Derecognition

Sale of Property, Plant, and Equipment

Objective 9
Account for derecognition of property, plant, and equipment.

Unless an asset has been classified as held for sale, depreciation is taken until the date the asset is **derecognized**; that is, the time when all accounts related to the asset are removed from the accounts. An item of property, plant, and equipment is usually derecognized on the date of disposal, but it could be taken off the books earlier if management thinks it will provide no further economic benefits, from either use or disposal. Ideally, when it is derecognized, the asset's carrying amount would be the same as its disposal value, but this is rarely the case. Therefore, a gain or loss is usually reported.

Under the cost and fair value models, the gain or loss on derecognition is shown on the income statement along with other items that arise from ordinary business activities. However, a gain or loss from the disposal of long-lived assets included in a discontinued business is reported in the discontinued operations section of the statement.

Underlying Concept

The "ideal" treatment of the change in value suggested here is more consistent with a physical concept of capital maintenance.

What happens to the gain or loss on disposal if the asset was accounted for under the revaluation model? Theoretically there would not be a gain or loss on disposal. This is based on the idea that the asset would be revalued to its fair value at the date of disposal with the change in value accounted for in the same way as all previous revaluations. If so, there would be no difference between the proceeds on disposal and the carrying amount to recognize on the income statement. Any remaining balance in the Revaluation Surplus account would be adjusted directly to Retained Earnings. However, IAS 16 *Property, Plant, and Equipment* does not address this issue, stating only that gains or losses on derecognition are reported in income. A company could, then, recognize the difference between the asset's most recent carrying amount and the proceeds of disposal on the income statement.

To illustrate the disposal of an asset that is held for use, assume that a machine costing $18,000 has been used for nine years and depreciated at a rate of $1,200 per year. If the machine is sold in the middle of the tenth year for $7,000, the entry to record the half-year's depreciation up to the sale date is:

```
A    =   L   +   SE
-600              -600

Cash flows: No effect
```

Depreciation Expense	600	
Accumulated Depreciation—Machinery		600

The entry for the asset's sale is:

```
A    =   L   +   SE
+400              +400

Cash flows: ↑ 7,000 inflow
```

Cash	7,000	
Accumulated Depreciation—Machinery	11,400	
[($1,200 × 9) + $600]		
Machinery		18,000
Gain on Sale of Machinery		400

There is a gain on sale because the $7,000 proceeds on disposal is $400 more than the machinery's book value of $6,600 ($18,000 − $11,400).

If an asset is classified as **held for sale**, it is carried at its fair value less costs of disposal. In this case, the net proceeds from sale of the asset should be close to the asset's carrying amount and it is likely that only minor gains or losses would be recognized when the actual disposal occurs.

Involuntary Conversion

Sometimes an asset's service ends through an involuntary conversion, such as fire, flood, theft, or expropriation. When this happens, the gains or losses are calculated in the same way as they are for the sale of an item of property, plant, and equipment. Under U.S. GAAP, the involuntary conversion would be an extraordinary item, but neither IFRS nor ASPE recognizes extraordinary items as a separate section in the income statement.

To illustrate, assume that a company is forced to sell its building that stands directly in the path of a planned major highway. For several years, the provincial government has tried to purchase the land on which the building stands, but the company has always resisted. The government ultimately exercises its right to expropriate and the courts have upheld its actions. In settlement, the company receives $500,000, which is much higher than the $100,000 book value of the building (cost of $300,000 less accumulated depreciation of $200,000) and the $100,000 book value of the land. The following entry is made:

```
A       =   L   +   SE
+300,000          +300,000

Cash flows: ↑ 500,000 inflow
```

Cash	500,000	
Accumulated Depreciation—Buildings	200,000	
Buildings		300,000
Land		100,000
Gain on Disposal of Buildings		300,000

Similar treatment is given to other types of involuntary conversions. The difference between any amount that is recovered, such as through insurance, and the asset's carrying amount is reported as a gain or loss.

Donations of Capital Assets

When a company donates or contributes an asset, the gift is recorded as an expense and is measured at the asset's fair value. The difference between its fair value and its carrying amount is recognized as a gain or loss. To illustrate, assume that Kline Industries donates property with a fair value of $110,000 to the City of Saskatoon for a city park. The land's book and fair value is $30,000 and the small building is carried at its cost of $95,000 and accumulated depreciation to the contribution date of $45,000. The entry to record the donation is:

A = L + SE
−80,000   −80,000

Cash flows: No effect

Contribution Expense	110,000	
Accumulated Depreciation—Buildings	45,000	
Buildings		95,000
Land		30,000
Gain on Disposal of Buildings		30,000

Miscellaneous Issues

If an asset is scrapped or abandoned without any cash recovery, the entity recognizes a loss that is equal to the asset's book value. If the asset can be sold for scrap, the gain or loss is the difference between its scrap value and its book value. If a fully depreciated asset is still used, both the asset and its accumulated depreciation remain on the books.

PRESENTATION, DISCLOSURE, AND ANALYSIS

Presentation and Disclosure

Objective 10
Describe the types of disclosures required for property, plant, and equipment.

A significant amount of information needs to be reported about a company's property, plant, and equipment so that users of financial statements can assess the existence and measurement of, and changes in, such assets. The following is a summary of the types of disclosures that are generally required:[13]

- an entity's investment in property, plant, and equipment, in investment property, and in biological assets;

- changes in that investment and in the accumulated depreciation and impairment;

- the nature and circumstances relating to impairment losses (and any reversal, if applicable);

- how net income is affected by the changes related to depreciation, impairment, and impairment reversals;

- the policies, models, and choices made in measuring PP&E, such as depreciation rates and methods and government grants;

- the existence and amounts of restrictions related to the assets;

- the effects related to each of continuing and discontinued operations;

- changes in assets as a result of fair value remeasurements;

- the carrying amount and other details of capital assets that are not being used because they are under construction or held for sale;

- cash inflows and outflows associated with the exploration and evaluation of mineral resources;

- the fair value of investment property assets;

- assumptions underlying fair-value-related measurements; and

- any outstanding related contingencies.

The requirement for separate disclosure of both the cost and accumulated depreciation gives financial statement readers more information than if only the net book value is disclosed. As an example, consider two companies, each having capital assets with a carrying amount of $100,000. The first company's assets cost $1 million and have accumulated depreciation of $900,000 charged against them. The second company, on the other hand, has assets with a cost of $105,000, and accumulated depreciation of $5,000. With the additional data, information is provided about the size of the original investment in property, plant, and equipment and its relative age. Information about depreciation rates and methods and accounting policy choices are important disclosures as these result in material charges to the income statement, many of which are the largest non-cash expenses recognized by most companies.

Real World Emphasis

Illustration 11-19 provides excerpts from the disclosures for **The Hershey Company**'s property, plant, and equipment, on its December 31, 2011 balance sheet. The company is based in the United States and reports amounts in thousands of U.S. dollars. These disclosures are quite similar to those that would be required in Canada under ASPE. You are probably familiar with some of Hershey's products!

Illustration 11-19

Disclosures for Property, Plant, and Equipment: The Hershey Company

Consolidated Balance Sheets at 31 December 2011

	2011	2010
	000's	000's
Assets		
Property, plant and equipment, net	**1,559,717**	**1,437,702**

1. SUMMARY OF SIGNIFICANT ACCOUNTING POLICIES (excerpts)

Property, Plant and Equipment

Property, plant and equipment are stated at cost and depreciated on a straight-line basis over the estimated useful lives of the assets, as follows: 3 to 15 years for machinery and equipment; and 25 to 40 years for buildings and related improvements. Maintenance and repairs are expensed as incurred. We capitalize applicable interest charges incurred during the construction of new facilities and production lines and amortize these costs over the assets' estimated useful lives. We review long-lived assets for impairment whenever events or changes in circumstances indicate that the carrying amount of such assets may not be recoverable. We measure the recoverability of assets to be held and used by a comparison of the carrying amount of long-lived assets to future undiscounted net cash flows expected to be generated. If these assets are considered to be impaired, we measure impairment as the amount by which the carrying amount of the assets exceeds the fair value of the assets. We report assets held for sale or disposal at the lower of the carrying amount or fair value less cost to sell.

Asset Retirement Obligations

Asset retirement obligations generally apply to legal obligations associated with the retirement of a tangible long-lived asset that result from the acquisition, construction or development and normal operation of a long-lived asset. We assess asset retirement obligations on a periodic basis. We recognize the fair value of a liability for an asset retirement obligation in the period in which it is incurred if a reasonable estimate of fair value can be made. We capitalize associated asset retirement costs as part of the carrying amount of the long-lived asset.

3. BUSINESS REALIGNMENT AND IMPAIRMENT CHARGES

In June 2010, we announced Project Next Century (the "Next Century program") as part of our ongoing efforts to create an advantaged supply chain and competitive cost structure. As part of the program, production will transition from the Company's century-old facility at 19 East Chocolate Avenue in Hershey, Pennsylvania, to an expanded West Hershey facility, which was built in 1992. Production from the 19 East Chocolate Avenue plant, as well as a portion of the workforce, will be fully transitioned to the West Hershey facility primarily during the second quarter of 2012. We now estimate that the Next Century program will incur pre-tax charges and non-recurring project implementation costs of $150 million to $160 million. This estimate includes $130 million to $140 million in pre-tax business realignment and impairment charges and approximately $20 million in project implementation and start-up costs. Total costs of $43.4 million were recorded during 2011 and total costs of $53.9 million were recorded in 2010.

In September 2011, we entered into a sale and leasing agreement for the 19 East Chocolate Avenue manufacturing facility with Chocolate Realty DST, a Delaware Statutory Trust. Chocolate Realty DST is not affiliated with the Milton Hershey School Trust. After manufacturing has fully transitioned to our West Hershey facility we intend to continue leasing a portion of the building for administrative office space. As a result of our continuing involvement and use of the property, we are deemed to be the "owner" of the property for accounting purposes. We received net proceeds of $47.6 million and recorded a lease financing obligation of $50.0 million under the leasing agreement. The initial term of the agreement expires in 2041.[14]

18. SUPPLEMENTAL BALANCE SHEET INFORMATION

Property, Plant and Equipment

The property, plant and equipment balance included construction in progress of $239.9 million as of December 31, 2011 and $179.8 million as of December 31, 2010. Major classes of property, plant and equipment were as follows:

December 31, In thousands of dollars	2011	2010
Land	$ 92,495	$ 71,060
Buildings	895,859	843,094
Machinery and equipment	2,600,204	2,410,609
Property, plant and equipment, gross	3,588,558	3,324,763
Accumulated depreciation	(2,028,841)	(1,887,061)
Property, plant and equipment, net	$1,559,717	$1,437,702

During 2011, we recorded accelerated depreciation of property, plant and equipment of $33.0 million associated with the Next Century program. As of December 31, 2011, certain real estate with a carrying value or fair value less cost to sell, if lower, of $6.9 million was being held for sale. These assets were associated with the closure of facilities as part of our global supply chain transformation program. During 2011, we recorded an adjustment of $5.8 million to reduce the carrying amount of two properties being held for sale due to a decline in the estimated net realizable value of these properties.

Analysis

Objective 11

Analyze a company's investment in assets.

Because property, plant, and equipment and their depreciation are so significant on most companies' statements of financial position and income statements, it is important to understand the nature of these long-lived assets, and to ensure that management is generating an acceptable rate of return on their investment in them.

Depreciation and Replacement of Assets

Depreciation is similar to other expenses in that it reduces net income, but is different in that **it does not involve a current cash outflow**. A common misconception about depreciation is that it provides funds to replace capital assets.

To illustrate that depreciation does not provide funds for replacing plant assets, assume that a business starts operating with plant assets of $500,000 with a useful life of five years. The company's statement of financial position at the beginning of the period is:

Plant assets	$500,000	Owners' equity	$500,000

Now if we assume the company earns no revenue over the five years, the income statements are as follows:

	Year 1	Year 2	Year 3	Year 4	Year 5
Revenue	$ –0–	$ –0–	$ –0–	$ –0–	$ –0–
Depreciation	(100,000)	(100,000)	(100,000)	(100,000)	(100,000)
Loss	$(100,000)	$(100,000)	$(100,000)	$(100,000)	$(100,000)

The statement of financial position at the end of the five years is:

Plant assets	$–0–	Owners' equity	$–0–

This extreme example shows that depreciation in no way provides funds to replace assets. Funds for the replacement of assets usually come from new asset inflows represented by revenues. By setting selling prices high enough to recover out-of-pocket costs plus depreciation expense, companies do generate cash flows to help finance replacements. If management wants to accumulate a replacement fund, however, it has to set aside the cash specifically for this purpose.

Efficiency of Asset Use and Return on Investment

Investors are interested in information that tells them how efficiently management uses the long-lived assets it has invested in. Incurring capital costs provides the company with a certain level of operating capacity, and usually creates the need for significant amounts of fixed costs far into the future.

Which ratios provide information about the usage of the assets? Assets can be analyzed in terms of both activity (turnover) and profitability. How efficiently a company uses its assets to generate revenue is measured by the **asset turnover ratio**. This ratio is calculated by dividing net revenue or sales by average total assets for the period. The resulting number represents the dollars of revenue produced by each dollar invested in assets. **For a given level of investment in assets, a company that generates more revenue per dollar of investment is more efficient and likely to be more profitable.** While this may not be true if the percentage profit on each dollar of revenue is lower than another company's, the asset turnover ratio is one of the key components of return on investment.[15]

To illustrate, the following data are provided from the 2011 financial statements of **Loblaw Companies Limited**. Loblaw is Canada's largest food distributor, with more than 1,000 corporate and franchised stores across the country. Its asset turnover ratio is calculated in Illustration 11-20.

Real World Emphasis

LOBLAW COMPANIES LIMITED	
(in millions)	
Revenues	$31,250
Total assets, December 31, 2011	17,428
Total assets, January 1, 2011	16,841
Net income	769

Illustration 11-20

Asset Turnover Ratio

$$\text{Asset turnover} = \frac{\text{Net revenue}}{\text{Average total assets}}$$

$$= \frac{\$31,250}{\dfrac{\$17,428 + \$16,841}{2}}$$

$$= 1.82$$

The asset turnover ratio shows that Loblaw generated $1.82 of revenue for each dollar invested in assets during 2011. Asset turnover ratios vary considerably among industries. For the same year, **Research in Motion**, a technology company, had a ratio of 1.42 times, and a capital-asset-heavy company like **Canadian Pacific Railway Limited** had a ratio of only 0.37 times.

Using the **profit margin ratio** together with the asset turnover ratio makes it possible to determine another key indicator: the rate of return earned on total assets. By using the Loblaw data shown above, the profit margin ratio and the rate of return on total assets are calculated as in Illustration 11-21.

Illustration 11-21
Profit Margin

$$\text{Profit margin} = \frac{\text{Net income}}{\text{Net revenue}}$$

$$= \frac{\$769}{\$31,250}$$

$$= 2.46\%$$

$$\text{Rate of return on assets} = \text{Profit margin} \times \text{Asset turnover}$$

$$= 2.46\% \times 1.82$$

$$= 4.5\%$$

The profit margin indicates how much is left over from each sales dollar after all expenses are covered. In the Loblaw example, a profit margin of 2.46% indicates that 2.46 cents of profit remained from each $1 of revenue generated. By combining the profit margin with the asset turnover, it is possible to calculate the rate of return on assets for the period. This makes sense. The more revenue that is generated per dollar invested in assets, the better off the company is. Also, the more of each sales dollar that is profit, the better off the company should be. Combined, the ratio provides a measure of the profitability of the company's investment in assets. To the extent that long-lived assets make up a significant portion of total assets, fixed asset management has a definite effect on profitability.

The **rate of return on assets (ROA)** can also be calculated directly by dividing net income by average total assets. Continuing with the same example, Illustration 11-22 shows the calculation of this ratio.

Illustration 11-22
Rate of Return on Assets

$$\text{Rate of return on assets} = \frac{\text{Net income}}{\text{Average total assets}}$$

$$= \frac{\$769}{\dfrac{\$17,428 + \$16,841}{2}}$$

$$= 4.5\%$$

The 4.5% rate of return calculated in this way is the same as the 4.5% rate calculated by multiplying the profit margin by the asset turnover. The rate of return on assets is a good measure of profitability because it combines the effects of cost control (profit margin) and asset management (asset turnover).

A more sophisticated calculation adds back the after-tax interest expense to net income so that the results are not skewed by how the assets are financed. The ratio can then be used more legitimately for inter-company comparisons. An adjustment should also be made when there are significant assets measured at fair values, with the changes in value bypassing the income statement by being reported directly in Other Comprehensive Income (OCI). To be comparable, either the net income should be compared with the reported assets reduced by the related Accumulated OCI, or total comprehensive income should be compared with the total assets as reported.

Care must be taken in interpreting the numbers, however. A manager who is interested in reporting a high return on assets can achieve this in the short run by not investing in new plant and equipment and by cancelling expenditures such as those for research and development and employee training—decisions that may result in lower long-term corporate value. In the short run, the result is a higher return on investment because the net income number (the numerator) will be higher and the total asset number (the denominator) will be lower.

IFRS/ASPE COMPARISON

A Comparison of IFRS and ASPE

Objective 12
Identify differences in accounting between ASPE and IFRS, and what changes are expected in the near future.

In general, the concept of depreciation and how it is applied is almost identical under ASPE and IFRS, and the same is true for non-current assets held for sale. It is also true, however, that there are minor differences not covered in this chapter that require a thorough reading of the specific detailed standards.

The most significant differences between these two sets of GAAP in Chapter 11 relate to the impairment models, as can be seen in Illustration 11-23.

	Accounting Standards for Private Enterprises (ASPE)—*CICA Handbook*, Part II, Sections 1505, 3061, 3063, and 3475	IFRS—IAS 16, 36, 40, and 41; IFRS 5	References to Related Illustrations and Select Brief Exercises
Depreciation process	Practice has been not to recognize asset components to the same extent as under IFRS.	Componentization is more common, with parts of assets recognized separately and depreciated over different periods of time.	BE11-2
	Depreciation is the larger of: (a) cost less salvage value over asset's life, and (b) cost less residual value over asset's useful life.	Depreciation is the allocation of the cost (or other amount) less the residual value over the asset's useful life, including any idle period.	Illustration 11-2 BE11-3 and BE11-4
Impairment	Evaluation of impairment is required only when events and changes in circumstances indicate that the carrying amount may not be recoverable.	In addition, an assessment of indicators of impairment is required at least at each reporting date.	N/A
	Cost recovery approach to impairment is applied. An asset or asset group is impaired only if the entity cannot recover the carrying amount with the net future undiscounted cash flows from use and later disposal.	Rational entity approach is applied. Asset or cash-generating unit is impaired only if the carrying amount is more than the higher of the value in use and the fair value less costs of disposal. These are discounted cash flows.	Illustration 11-17 BE11-15
	"Recoverable test" is based on a comparison of the undiscounted net future cash flows from use and eventual disposal.	"Recoverable amount" is defined as the higher of value in use and the fair value less costs of disposal.	Illustration 11-17 BE11-13
	Once an asset is written down to its impaired value, this becomes the asset's new cost and no reversal of the writeoff is allowed.	An impairment loss is reversed if there is a change in the estimates used to calculate recoverable amount. It is limited in amount.	BE11-12

(continued)

	Accounting Standards for Private Enterprises (ASPE)—*CICA Handbook*, Part II, Sections 1505, 3061, 3063 and 3475	IFRS—IAS 16, 36, 40, and 41; IFRS 5	References to Related Illustrations and Select Brief Exercises
Held for Sale	Long-lived assets classified as held for sale are classified as current only if sold before the date the financial statements are completed and the proceeds will be received within the period defined for an asset to be a current asset.	Non-current assets may be reclassified as current assets only when they meet the criteria to be classified as held for sale (see IFRS 5.3). This requires that the asset (or disposal group) be available for immediate sale in its present condition and its sale must be highly probable.	BE11-16
Disclosure	A reconciliation of the opening to ending balances of the carrying amounts of each class of PP&E asset is not required.	A reconciliation of the opening to ending balances of the carrying amounts of each class of PP&E asset is required, along with the same reconciliation for its associated accumulated depreciation and accumulated impairment losses.	
	Because the cost model is the only accepted model, there are no disclosure requirements related to revaluation and fair value measurement models.	Extensive disclosures are required for investment property measured under the fair value model. Even where the cost model is used for investment property, its fair value must be disclosed.	

Illustration 11-23

IFRS and ASPE Comparison Chart

Looking Ahead

Few changes are expected in the near future to standards covering the majority of property, plant, and equipment. There is one possible exception: accounting standards related to the upstream extractive activities undertaken by companies in the mining and oil and gas industries.

A Discussion Paper based on the IASB's extractive activities research project was released in 2010. In October 2010 the staff presented a summary of the feedback received in response to the discussion paper entitled *Extractive Activities*. The IASB noted that the project's objective was to analyze the unique financial reporting issues regarding extractive activities and to identify a basis for a possible financial reporting model to address these issues. The Board did not add this topic to its active agenda, so it has been put on hold. However, the IASB noted after release of the staff summary that at a future date a possible agenda proposal could be developed. If added to the formal agenda, it would likely take at least two to three years, from the date added, to develop a final standard.

SUMMARY OF LEARNING OBJECTIVES

1 Understand the importance of depreciation, impairment, and disposition from a business perspective.

The economic benefits of property, plant, and equipment are typically consumed as the items are used by the organization. Because the benefits are consumed over multiple periods, companies use depreciation to allocate the benefits of the PP&E to each period as the capacity of the assets is used up. By allocating the cost of property, plant, and equipment over its useful life, businesses are better able to match the costs and benefits of the assets to the revenues that they help generate. Companies also need to assess their PP&E each year under IFRS for indications of impairment, and if these indications are present they should re-estimate how much will be recoverable. Following GAAP should also help companies better understand their business.

2 Explain the concept of depreciation and identify the factors to consider when determining depreciation charges.

Depreciation is the process of allocating the cost of property, plant, and equipment assets in a systematic and rational manner to the periods that are expected to benefit from their use. The allocation of the cost of intangible capital assets is termed "amortization" and the allocation of the costs of mineral resource assets is termed "depletion." Four factors involved in determining depreciation expense are (1) the recognition of the appropriate asset components, (2) the amount to be depreciated (depreciable amount), (3) the estimated useful life, and (4) the pattern and method of depreciation.

3 Identify how depreciation methods are selected.

The depreciation method chosen should amortize an asset in a pattern and at a rate that corresponds to the benefits received from that asset. The choice often involves the use of professional judgement. Tax reporting, simplicity, perceived economic consequences, and impact on ratios are examples of factors that influence such judgements in practice.

4 Calculate depreciation using the straight-line, decreasing charge, and activity methods and recognize the effects of using each.

The straight-line method assumes that an asset provides its benefits as a function of time. As such, cost less residual value is divided by the useful life to determine the depreciation expense per period. The

decreasing charge method provides for a higher depreciation charge in the early years and lower charges in later periods. For this method, a constant rate (such as double the straight-line rate) is multiplied by the net book value (cost less accumulated depreciation and accumulated impairment losses) at the start of the period to determine each period's expense. The main justification for this approach is that the asset provides more benefits in the earlier periods. The activity method assumes that the benefits provided by the asset are a function of use instead of the passage of time. The asset's life is considered in terms of either the output that it provides or an input measure, such as the number of hours it works. The depreciation charge per unit of activity (depreciable amount divided by estimated total units of output or input) is calculated and multiplied by the units of activity produced or consumed in a period to determine the depreciation.

5 Explain the accounting issues for depletion of mineral resources.

After the depletion base has been established through accounting decisions related to the acquisition, exploration and evaluation, development, and restoration obligations associated with mineral resources, these costs are allocated to the natural resources that are removed. Depletion is normally calculated using the units of production method. In this approach, the resource's cost less residual value, if any, is divided by the number of units that are estimated to be in the resource deposit, to obtain a cost per unit of product. The cost per unit is then multiplied by the number of units withdrawn in the period to calculate the depletion.

6 Explain and apply the accounting procedures for partial periods and a change in depreciation rate.

Because all the variables in determining depreciation are estimates—with the exception, perhaps, of an asset's original cost—it is common for a change in those estimates to result in a change in the depreciation amount. When this occurs, there is no retroactive change and no catch-up adjustment. The change is accounted for in the current and future periods.

7 Explain the issues and apply the accounting standards for capital asset impairment under both IFRS and ASPE.

A capital asset is impaired when its carrying amount is not recoverable. The cost recovery method

(ASPE) defines recoverable as the undiscounted cash flows from the asset's use and later disposal. If impaired, the asset is written down to its fair value, and this loss cannot be reversed later if the asset's value recovers. The rational entity model (IFRS) defines recoverable amount as the higher of the asset's value in use and fair value less costs of disposal. Both these values are discounted cash flow amounts. If the recoverable amount subsequently improves, the impairment losses recognized are reversed.

8 Explain and apply the accounting standards for long-lived assets that are held for sale.

Assets held for sale are no longer depreciated. They are remeasured to their fair value less costs of disposal at each statement of financial position date. Recoveries in value may be recognized to the extent of previous losses. Held-for-sale items of property, plant, and equipment are separately reported as non-current assets unless they meet the definition of current assets. Under ASPE, assets held for sale are only permitted to be reported in current assets if sold before the financial statements are completed and the proceeds on sale are expected within 12 months from the date of the statement of financial position (or operating cycle, if longer).

9 Account for derecognition of property, plant, and equipment.

Depreciation continues for PP&E assets until they are classified as held for sale or derecognized. At the date of disposal, all accounts related to the retired asset are removed from the books. Gains and losses from the disposal of plant assets are shown on the income statement in income before discontinued operations, unless the conditions for reporting as a discontinued operation are met. For property, plant, and equipment donated to an organization outside the reporting entity, the donation is reported at its fair value with a gain or loss on disposal recognized.

10 Describe the types of disclosures required for property, plant, and equipment.

The type of information required to be disclosed for property, plant, and equipment is governed by the information needs of users. Because users of private entities' financial information are often able to seek further specific information from a company, there are fewer required disclosures than for public companies reporting under IFRS. The required disclosures under IFRS include those relating to measurement, changes in account balances and the reasons for the changes, information about how fair values are determined, and many others.

11 Analyze a company's investment in assets.

The efficiency of use of a company's investment in assets may be evaluated by calculating and interpreting the asset turnover rate, the profit margin, and the rate of return on assets.

12 Identify differences in accounting between ASPE and IFRS, and what changes are expected in the near future.

In most major ways, international and Canadian accounting standards for the depreciation of property, plant, and equipment are similar. Significant differences do exist, however, in the extent of componentization for depreciation, the impairment models applied, and the extent of disclosure. The impairment differences relate to how it is determined whether an asset is impaired, how the impairment is measured, and the ability to recognize recoveries in value.

KEY TERMS

accelerated amortization, p. 676
activity method, p. 677
amortization, p. 671
asset group, p. 689
asset turnover ratio, p. 696
cash-generating unit (CGU), p. 689
componentization, p. 672
cost recovery impairment model, p. 685
declining-balance method, p. 676
decreasing charge methods, p. 676
depletion, p. 671
depreciable amount, p. 672

depreciation, p. 671
derecognized, p. 691
diminishing balance methods, p. 676
double-declining-balance method, p. 677
fair value, p. 686
impaired, p. 684
impairment loss, p. 686
impairments, p. 684
liquidating dividend, p. 680
profit margin ratio, p. 697
rate of return on assets (ROA), p. 697

rational entity impairment model, p. 685
recoverability test, p. 685
recoverable amount, p. 687
residual value, p. 672
salvage value, p. 673
straight-line method, p. 675
sum-of-the-years'-digits method, p. 732
units of production method, p. 677
useful life, p. 673
value in use, p. 687

APPENDIX 11A

DEPRECIATION AND INCOME TAX

Capital Cost Allowance Method

Objective **13**
Calculate capital cost allowance in straightforward situations.

For the most part, issues related to the calculation of income taxes are not discussed in a financial accounting course. However, because the concepts of tax depreciation are similar to those of depreciation for financial reporting purposes and because the tax method is sometimes adopted for record keeping purposes, an overview of this subject is presented here.

Canadian businesses use the capital cost allowance method to determine depreciation in calculating their taxable income and the tax value of assets, regardless of the method they use for financial reporting purposes. Because companies use this method for tax purposes, some—particularly small businesses—also use it for financial reporting, judging that the benefits of keeping two sets of records are less than the costs of doing this.[16] While keeping only one set of records may be cost-effective, it may not provide a rational measure of expense under GAAP. Therefore, many companies keep a record of capital cost allowance for tax purposes and use another method to determine depreciation for financial reporting purposes.

The capital cost allowance method is similar to the declining-balance approach covered in the chapter, except for the following:

1. Instead of being labelled "depreciation expense," it is called **capital cost allowance (CCA)**.

2. The Income Tax Act (Income Tax Regulations, Schedule II) specifies the rate to be used for an asset class. This rate is called the capital cost allowance or CCA rate. The Income Tax Act identifies several different classes of assets and the maximum CCA rate for each class. To determine which class a particular asset falls into, it is necessary to examine the definition of each asset class and the examples given in the act. Illustration 11A-1 provides examples of various CCA classes, the maximum rate for the class, and the types of assets it includes.

Illustration 11A-1

Examples of CCA Classes

Class	Rate	Examples of Assets Included in the Class
1	4%	• most buildings acquired after 1987, including component parts such as plumbing, elevators, sprinkler systems
8	20%	• manufacturing or processing machinery or equipment not included in other specified classes. Also includes furniture, photocopiers and refrigeration equipment.
10	30%	• automotive equipment, contractor's movable equipment, including portable camp buildings, processing equipment
10.1	30%	• passenger vehicles purchased during a company's 2011 fiscal year or thereafter having a cost of more than $30,000 (the amount that can be used for capital cost purposes is limited to $30,000 plus PST and GST or HST).

Source: Excerpts from CRA - Classes of Depreciable Property

3. CCA is calculated separately for each asset class and can be claimed only on year-end amounts in each class. Assuming there have been no net additions (purchases less proceeds of disposals, if any) to a class during a year, the maximum CCA allowed is the undepreciated capital cost (UCC) at year end multiplied by the CCA rate for the class.

In a year when there is a net addition (regardless of when it occurs), the maximum CCA on the net addition is one half of the allowed CCA rate multiplied by the amount of the net addition. This is often referred to as the **half-year rule**. The CCA for the net addition plus the CCA on the remaining UCC is the total CCA for the asset class. If there is only one asset in a class, the maximum CCA allowed in the acquisition year is the acquisition cost multiplied by one half of the CCA rate, even if the asset was purchased one week before year end. No CCA is allowed in the year of disposal for this single asset, even if it is sold just before year end.

4. The government, through the Income Tax Act, requires that any benefits that a company receives from government grants and investment tax credits for the purpose of acquiring a capital asset reduce the cost basis of the capital asset for tax purposes. For investment tax credits, the capital cost of the asset and the UCC of the class of asset are reduced in the taxation year following the year of acquisition.

5. CCA can be taken even if it results in a UCC balance that is less than the estimated residual value.

6. Companies are not required to take the maximum rate, or even any CCA, in a particular year, although they normally would as long as they have taxable income. If a company takes less than the maximum CCA in a specific year, it cannot add the remainder to the amount claimed in a subsequent year. In any year, the maximum that can be claimed is limited to the UCC times the specified CCA rate.

Basic CCA and UCC Example

To illustrate depreciation calculations under the CCA system, assume the following facts for a company's March 28, 2013 acquisition of manufacturing equipment, its only asset in this CCA class:

Cost of equipment	$500,000	CCA class	Class 8
Estimated useful life	10 years	CCA rate for Class 8	20%
Estimated residual value	$ 30,000		

Illustration 11A-2 shows how to calculate the CCA for the first three years and the UCC at the end of each of the three years.[17]

Illustration 11A-2

CCA Schedule for Equipment

Class 8—20%	CCA	UCC
January 1, 2013		0
Additions during 2013		
Cost of new asset acquisition		$500,000
Disposals during 2013		0
CCA 2013: $500,000 × ½ × 20%	$50,000	(50,000)
December 31, 2013		**$450,000**
Additions less disposals, 2014		0
		$450,000
CCA, 2014: $450,000 × 20%	$90,000	(90,000)
December 31, 2014		**$360,000**
Additions less disposals, 2015		0
		$360,000
CCA, 2015: $360,000 × 20%	$72,000	(72,000)
December 31, 2015		**$288,000**

The **undepreciated capital cost (UCC)** at any point in time is known as the capital asset's **tax value** or **tax basis**. Note that the asset's carrying amount on the statement of financial position will be different from its tax value whenever the depreciation method for financial reporting is not the tax method. The significance of this difference to financial reporting is explained in Chapter 18.

Illustration 11A-3 is a continuation of Illustration 11A-2. It incorporates the following transactions:

1. In 2016, the company bought another Class 8 asset for $700,000.

2. In 2017, the company sold for $300,000 the equipment that it purchased in 2013.

3. In 2018, the company sold the remaining Class 8 asset for $500,000. There are no Class 8 assets remaining.

Illustration 11A-3

CCA Schedule for Class 8

Class 8—20%	CCA	UCC
December 31, 2015		**$288,000**
Additions less disposals, 2016		
Cost of new asset		700,000
CCA, 2016		
$288,000 × 20% =	$57,600	$988,000
$700,000 × ½ × 20% =	70,000	(127,600)
	$127,600	
December 31, 2016		**$860,400**
Additions less disposals, 2017		
Manufacturing equipment		
purchased in 2013 (lesser of		
original cost of $500,000 and		
proceeds of disposal of $300,000)		(300,000)
		$560,400
CCA, 2017: $560,400 × 20% =	$112,080	(112,080)
December 31, 2017		**$448,320**
Additions less disposals, 2018		
2016 asset acquisition (lesser of		
original cost of $700,000 and		
proceeds of disposal of $500,000)		(500,000)
		$ (51,680)
Recaptured CCA, 2018	$ (51,680)	51,680
December 31, 2018		**$ 0**

Additions to an Asset Class

The purchase of another Class 8 asset in 2016 resulted in a **net addition** of $700,000 to the undepreciated capital cost at the end of 2016. Consequently, the balance of the UCC at the end of 2016 prior to calculating CCA is made up of this $700,000 plus the $288,000 UCC of the original equipment. The capital cost allowance for 2016 is therefore 20% of $288,000 ($57,600) plus one half of 20% of the net addition of $700,000 ($70,000) for a total of $127,600.

If a government grant of $35,000 had been received in 2016 to help finance the acquisition of this asset, the addition in 2016 would be reported net of the government grant; that is, at $700,000 − $35,000 = $665,000. If the 2016 acquisition was eligible instead for an investment tax credit (ITC) of $35,000, the tax legislation specifies that the ITC reduces the asset's capital cost and the UCC of the class of assets **in the year following** the year of acquisition.[18] Assuming the Class 8 asset acquired in 2016 in Illustration 11A-3 was eligible for a $35,000 ITC, the $700,000 addition is recognized in 2016, and the UCC is reduced by the $35,000 ITC in 2017 along with the $300,000 proceeds on the original manufacturing equipment. The CCA claimed in 2017 is reduced accordingly.

Retirements from an Asset Class, Continuation of Class

While the CCA class is increased by the cost of additions, it is reduced **by the proceeds on the asset's disposal**, not by the asset's cost. However, if the proceeds on disposal are more than the asset's original capital cost, the class is reduced by the cost only. There is a good reason for this. If the proceeds on disposal are more than the original cost, there is a capital gain on the disposal. Capital gains are taxed differently than ordinary business income; thus, the portion that is a capital gain must be identified as being that. Cost, therefore, is the maximum amount to be deducted from the CCA class. It is not common for most depreciable assets to be sold for more than their cost.

In 2017, the company sells the original manufacturing equipment for $300,000. Since this is less than its $500,000 capital cost, there is no capital gain on disposal. Therefore, Class 8 is reduced by the proceeds on disposal of $300,000, and the CCA for the year is calculated on the remaining balance in the class.

Retirements from an Asset Class, Elimination of Class

When an asset's disposal eliminates the asset class, either because there are no more assets remaining in the class or because the disposal results in the elimination of the UCC balance of the class, the following may result:

1. There may be a recapture of capital cost allowance, with or without a capital gain.

2. There may be a terminal loss, with or without a capital gain. This occurs only when the last asset in the class is disposed of and a UCC balance still exists in the class after deducting the appropriate amount on the asset disposal.

A **recapture** of CCA occurs when, after deducting the appropriate amount from the class on disposal of an asset, a negative amount is left as the UCC balance. The negative balance is the amount of CCA that must be "recaptured" and included in the calculation of taxable income in the year. It is taxed at the normal income tax rates. When this situation occurs, it suggests that too much CCA was deducted throughout the lives of the assets, and the taxing of the recaptured capital cost allowance therefore adjusts for this. This is what occurred in 2018 in our example. When the proceeds of disposal were deducted from the UCC, the UCC became negative. The excess of $51,680 is therefore added back and included in taxable income in 2018.

As indicated above, if an asset is sold for more than its cost, a **capital gain** results. This may occur whether or not the class is eliminated. For tax purposes, a capital gain is treated differently from a recapture of CCA. Essentially, the **taxable** capital gain (that is, the amount subject to tax) is only a portion of the capital gain as defined above.[19] The taxable capital gain is included with other taxable income.

If the Class 8 asset purchased in 2016 had been sold in 2018 for $750,000, a capital gain and a recapture of CCA would have resulted. The capital gain would be $50,000, but only 50% or $25,000 would be the taxable capital gain. In this case, Class 8 would be reduced by $700,000 and the recapture would be $251,680 ($700,000 less the $448,320 UCC).

A **terminal loss** occurs when a positive balance remains in the class after the appropriate reduction is made to the CCA class from the disposal of the last asset. This remaining balance is a terminal loss that is deductible in full when calculating taxable income for the period. If the remaining equipment had been sold in 2018 for $300,000, a terminal loss of $148,320 would have resulted (the UCC of $448,320 less the $300,000 proceeds).

This example illustrating the basic calculations of capital gains, taxable capital gains, recaptured capital cost allowance, and terminal losses has necessarily been simplified. In essence, the tax rate on taxable capital gains is specified by tax law, which may change from time to time and have other implications (such as a refundable dividend tax on hand). Similarly, the tax rate that applies to recaptured CCA is affected by the particular circumstances of the type of taxable income that is being reported, of which the recaptured amount is a component. These and other technical aspects, including definitions, are beyond the scope of this text. You should be warned that specialist knowledge of tax law is often required to determine income taxes payable.

Quiz

SUMMARY OF LEARNING OBJECTIVE FOR APPENDIX 11A

13 Calculate capital cost allowance in straightforward situations.

"Capital cost allowance" (CCA) is the term used for depreciation when calculating taxable income in income tax returns. The CCA method is similar to the declining-balance method except that rates are specified for asset classes and the amount claimed is based on year-end balances. The half-year rule is applied to net additions in the year, which means that only 50% of the normal rate is permitted. For an asset class, retirements are accounted for under specific rules that govern the calculation of taxable income. Capital gains occur if the proceeds on disposal are more than the asset's original cost. When an asset class is eliminated, a terminal loss or recapture of capital cost allowance can occur.

KEY TERMS

capital cost allowance (CCA), p. 702	half-year rule, p. 703	tax value, p. 703
capital cost allowance method, p. 702	recapture, p. 705	terminal loss, p. 705
capital gain, p. 705	tax basis, p. 703	undepreciated capital cost (UCC), p. 703

Note: All assignment material with an asterisk (*) relates to the appendix to the chapter. Unless otherwise indicated, depreciation expense should be calculated to the nearest whole month.

Brief Exercises

(LO 1) BE11-1 Cella Corporation's statement of financial position shows property, plant, and equipment of $100,000. The notes to its financial statements state that the amount is represented by a cost of $600,000, accumulated depreciation of $300,000, and accumulated impairment losses of $200,000. Discuss the usefulness of the information provided, referring to the qualitative characteristics identified in the conceptual framework for financial reporting (discussed in Chapter 2).

(LO 2) BE11-2 On October 1, 2014, Ocean Airways Ltd. purchased a new commercial aircraft for a total cost of $100 million. Included in the total cost are the aircraft's two engines, at a cost of $10 million each, and the aircraft's body, which cost $80 million. The estimated useful life of each of the aircraft's two engines is 10 years, with a residual value of $1 million. The estimated useful life of the aircraft's body is 10 years, with a residual value of $5 million. The entire aircraft's useful life is limited to the life of the aircraft's body. (a) Prepare the journal entries required on October 1, 2014, and December 31, 2014, if Ocean Airways prepares financial statements in accordance with IFRS and uses straight-line depreciation. (b) Explain any differences in the journal entries if Ocean Airways prepares financial statements in accordance with ASPE.

(LO 2) BE11-3 Chong Corp. purchased a machine on July 1, 2014, for $30,000. Chong paid $200 in title fees and a legal fee of $100 related to the machine. In addition, Chong paid $500 of shipping charges for delivery, and paid $400 to a local contractor to build and wire a platform for the machine on the plant floor. The machine has an estimated useful life of 10 years, a total expected life of 12 years, a residual value of $6,000, and no salvage value. Chong uses straight-line depreciation. (a) Calculate the 2014 depreciation expense if Chong prepares financial statements in accordance with IFRS. (b) Calculate the 2014 depreciation expense if Chong prepares financial statements in accordance with ASPE.

(LO 2) BE11-4 Gilles Corp. purchased a piece of equipment on February 1, 2014, for $100,000. The equipment has an estimated useful life of eight years with a residual value of $25,000, and an estimated physical life of 10 years with no salvage value. The equipment was delivered to Gilles's factory floor, installed and in working condition, on March 1, 2014. On April 1, 2014, Gilles's staff used the equipment to produce the first saleable units. (a) Calculate the 2014 depreciation expense if Gilles uses straight-line depreciation and prepares financial statements in accordance with IFRS. (b) Calculate the 2014 depreciation expense if Gilles prepares financial statements in accordance with ASPE.

(LO 3, 4) BE11-5 Odyssey Ltd. purchased machinery on January 1, 2014, for $60,000. The machinery is estimated to have a residual value of $6,000 after a useful life of eight years. (a) Calculate the 2014 depreciation expense using the straight-line method. (b) Calculate the 2014 depreciation expense using the straight-line method, but assuming the machinery was purchased on September 1, 2014.

(LO 3, 4) BE11-6 Use the information for Odyssey Ltd. in BE11-5. (a) Calculate the 2014 depreciation expense using the double-declining-balance method. (b) Calculate the 2015 depreciation expense using the double-declining-balance method, but assuming the machinery was purchased on October 1, 2014. (c) Discuss when it might be more appropriate to use the straight-line method of depreciation and when the declining-balance method is more appropriate.

(LO 3, 4) BE11-7 Use the information for Odyssey Ltd. in BE11-5. (a) Calculate the 2014 depreciation expense using the sum-of-the-years'-digits method. (b) Calculate the 2014 depreciation expense using the sum-of-the-years'-digits method, but assuming the machinery was purchased on April 1, 2014.

(LO 4) BE11-8 Andeo Corporation purchased a truck at the beginning of 2014 for $48,000. The truck is estimated to have a residual value of $3,000 and a useful life of 275,000 km. It was driven for 52,000 km in 2014 and 65,000 km in 2015. Calculate depreciation expense for 2014 and 2015 using the units of production method.

(LO 5) BE11-9 Extract Corporation, a publicly traded mining company, acquires a mine at a cost of $500,000. Capitalized development costs total $125,000. After the mine is depleted, $75,000 will be spent to restore the property, after which it can be sold for $157,500. Extract estimates that 5,000 tonnes of ore can be mined. Assuming that 900 tonnes are extracted in the first year, prepare the journal entry to record depletion.

(LO 6) BE11-10 Chuckwalla Limited purchased a computer for $7,000 on January 1, 2014. Straight-line depreciation is used for the computer, based on a five-year life and a $1,000 residual value. In 2016, the estimates are revised. Chuckwalla now expects the computer will be used until December 31, 2017, when it can be sold for $500. Calculate the 2016 depreciation expense.

(LO 7) BE11-11 Qilin Corp., a small company that follows ASPE, owns machinery that cost $900,000 and has accumulated depreciation of $360,000. The undiscounted future net cash flows from the use of the asset are expected to be $500,000. The equipment's fair value is $400,000. Using the cost recovery impairment model, prepare the journal entry, if any, to record the impairment loss.

(LO 7) BE11-12 Use the information for Qilin Corp. given in BE11-11. By the end of the following year, the machinery's fair value has increased to $490,000. (a) Assuming the machinery continues to be used in production, prepare the journal entry required, if any, to record the increase in its fair value. (b) Explain any differences in your answer to part (a) if Qilin prepares financial statements in accordance with IFRS.

(LO 7) BE11-13 Hambrecht Corp. is preparing its financial statements for the fiscal year ending November 30, 2014. Certain specialized equipment was scrapped on January 1, 2015. At November 30, 2014, this equipment was being used in production by Hambrecht and had a carrying amount of $1 million. As of November 30, 2014, it was estimated that the asset has undiscounted net future cash flows of $1.1 million, value in use of $800,000, and fair value less costs of disposal of $50,000 (scrap value). (a) If Hambrecht prepares financial statements in accordance with IFRS, what is the recoverable amount of the equipment at November 30, 2014? (b) If Hambrecht prepares financial statements in accordance with ASPE, what is the recoverable amount of the equipment at November 30, 2014?

(LO 7) BE11-14 Greentree Properties Ltd. is a publicly listed company following IFRS. Assume that on December 31, 2014, the carrying amount of land on the statement of financial position is $500,000. Management determines that the land's value in use is $425,000 and that the fair value less costs to sell is $400,000. (a) Using the rational entity impairment model, prepare the journal entry required, if any, to record the impairment loss. (b) Due to an economic rebound in the area, by the end of the following year, the land has a value in use of $550,000 and fair value less costs of disposal of $480,000. Prepare the journal entry required, if any, to record the increase in its recoverable amount.

(LO 7) BE11-15 Riverbed Ltd. is a manufacturer of computer network equipment and has just recently adopted IFRS. The wireless division is a cash-generating unit or asset group that has the following carrying amounts for its net assets: land, $20,000; buildings, $30,000; and equipment, $10,000. The undiscounted net future cash flows from use and eventual disposal of the wireless division are $70,000 and the present value of these cash flows is $45,000. The land can be sold immediately for $35,000; however, the buildings and equipment are specialized and cannot be used elsewhere and thus have no resale value. Allocate the impairment loss to the net assets of the wireless division using (a) the cost recovery model under ASPE and (b) the rational entity model under IFRS.

(LO 8) BE11-16 Caley Inc. owns a building with a carrying amount of $1.5 million, as of January 1, 2014. On that date, Caley's management determined that the building's location is no longer suitable for the company's operations and decided to dispose of the building by sale. Caley is preparing financial statements for the fiscal year ending December 31, 2014. As of that date, management had an authorized plan in place to sell the building, the building met all criteria for classification as held for sale, and the building's estimated fair value less costs to sell was $1 million. The building's depreciation expense for 2014 would amount to $200,000. (a) Prepare the journal entry(ies) required on December 31, 2014, if any. (b) Discuss how the building would be classified on the December 31, 2014 statement of financial position if Caley prepared financial statements in accordance with IFRS. (c) Discuss how the building would be classified on the December 31, 2014 statement of financial position if Caley prepared financial statements in accordance with ASPE.

(LO 9) BE11-17 Volumetrics Corporation owns machinery that cost $20,000 when purchased on January 1, 2013. Depreciation has been recorded at a rate of $3,000 per year, resulting in a balance in accumulated depreciation of $6,000 at December 31, 2014. The machinery is sold on September 1, 2015, for $13,500. Prepare journal entries to (a) update depreciation for 2015 and (b) record the sale.

(LO 9) BE11-18 Use the information presented for Volumetrics Corporation in BE11-17, but assume that the machinery is sold for $5,200 instead of $13,500. Prepare journal entries to (a) update depreciation for 2015 and (b) record the sale.

(LO 11) BE11-19 In its 2014 annual report, Winkler Limited reports beginning-of-the-year total assets of $1,923 million, end-of-the-year total assets of $2,487 million, total revenue of $2,687 million, and net income of $52 million. (a) Calculate Winkler's asset turnover ratio. (b) Calculate Winkler's profit margin. (c) Calculate Winkler's rate of return on assets (1) using the asset turnover and profit margin, and (2) using net income.

(LO 13) *BE11-20 Fong Limited purchased an asset at a cost of $45,000 on March 1, 2014. The asset has a useful life of seven years and an estimated residual value of $3,000. For tax purposes, the asset belongs in CCA Class 8, with a rate of 20%. Calculate the CCA for each year, 2014 to 2017, assuming this is the only asset in Class 8.

Exercises

(LO 2, 3) E11-1 (Match Depreciation Method with Assets) The following assets have been acquired by various companies over the past year:

1. Boardroom table and chairs for a corporate head office

2. Dental equipment in a new dental clinic

3. Long-haul trucks for a trucking business

4. Weight and aerobic equipment in a new health club facility

5. Classroom computers in a new community college

Instructions

For each long-lived asset listed above:

(a) Identify the factors to consider in establishing the useful life of the asset.

(b) Recommend the pattern of depreciation that most closely represents the pattern of economic benefits received by the entity that owns the asset.

(c) Discuss how good estimates of asset useful life would help a company manage its assets.

(LO 2, 3, 4) E11-2 (Terminology, Calculations—Straight-Line, Double-Declining-Balance) Diderot Corp. acquired a property on September 15, 2014, for $220,000, paying $3,000 in transfer taxes and a $1,500 real estate fee. Based on the provincial assessment information, 75% of the property's value was related to the building and 25% to the land. It is estimated that the building, with proper maintenance, will last for 20 years, at which time it will be torn down and have zero salvage value. Diderot, however, expects to use it for 10 years only as it is not expected to suit the company's purposes after that. The company should be able to sell the property for $155,000 at that time, with $40,000 of this amount being for the land. Diderot prepares financial statements in accordance with IFRS. Depreciation expense should be calculated to the nearest half month.

Instructions

Assuming a December 31 year end, identify all of the following:

(a) The building's cost

(b) The building's depreciable amount

(c) The building's useful life

(d) Depreciation expense for 2014, assuming the straight-line method

(e) Depreciation expense for 2015, assuming the double-declining-balance method

(f) The building's carrying amount at December 31, 2015, assuming the double-declining-balance method

(g) Depreciation expense for 2014, assuming the straight-line method and assuming Diderot prepares financial statements in accordance with ASPE

(LO 3, 4) E11-3 (Depreciation Calculations—Straight-Line, Double-Declining-Balance; Partial Periods) Gambit Corporation purchased a new plant asset on April 1, 2014, at a cost of $769,000. It was estimated to have a useful life of 20 years and a residual value of $300,000, and a physical life of 30 years and a salvage value of $0. Gambit's accounting period is the calendar year. Gambit prepares financial statements in accordance with IFRS.

Instructions

(a) Calculate the depreciation for this asset for 2014 and 2015 using the straight-line method.

(b) Calculate the depreciation for this asset for 2014 and 2015 using the double-declining-balance method.

(c) Calculate the depreciation for this asset for 2014 and 2015 using the straight-line method, and assuming Gambit prepares financial statements in accordance with ASPE.

(d) Discuss when it might be more appropriate to select the straight-line method, and when it might be more appropriate to select the double-declining-balance method.

(LO 3, 4) E11-4 (Depreciation Calculations—Six Methods; Partial Periods) Jupiter Wells Corp. purchased machinery for $315,000 on May 1, 2013. It is estimated that it will have a useful life of 10 years, residual value of $15,000, production of 240,000 units, and 25,000 working hours. During 2014, Jupiter Wells Corp. used the machinery for 2,650 hours and the machinery produced 25,500 units.

Instructions

From the information given, calculate the depreciation charge for 2014 under each of the following methods, assuming Jupiter has a December 31 year end.

(a) Straight-line

(b) Units-of-production

(c) Working hours

(d) Declining-balance, using a 20% rate

(e) Sum-of-the-years'-digits

(f) CCA at 20%

Digging
Deeper

(g) Assume that Jupiter Wells is a small privately owned company that follows ASPE. From the perspective of a potential investor in Jupiter Wells, discuss the advantages and disadvantages of Jupiter Wells using the capital cost allowance approach to calculate and record depreciation expense for financial reporting purposes.

(LO 3, 4) E11-5 (Different Methods of Depreciation) Jared Industries Ltd. presents you with the following information:

Description	Date Purchased	Cost	Residual Value	Life in Years	Depreciation Method	Accumulated Depreciation to Dec. 31, 2014	Depreciation for 2015
Machine A	Dec. 2, 2013	$142,500	$16,000	10	(a)	$39,900	(b)
Machine B	Aug. 15, 2012	(c)	21,000	5	Straight-line	29,000	(d)
Machine C	July 21, 2011	75,400	23,500	8	Double-declining-balance	(e)	(f)

Instructions

Complete the table for the year ended December 31, 2015. The company depreciates all assets for a half year in the year of acquisition and the year of disposal.

(LO 4) E11-6 (Depreciation Calculations—Straight-Line, Double-Declining-Balance) Jiang Company Ltd. purchases equipment on January 1, 2014, for $387,000 cash. The asset is expected to have a useful life of 12 years and a residual value of $39,000. Jiang prepares financial statements under IFRS.

Instructions

(a) Calculate the amount of depreciation for each of 2014, 2015, and 2016 using the straight-line method.

(b) Calculate the amount of depreciation for each of 2014, 2015, and 2016 using the double-declining-balance method. (In performing your calculations, round percentages to the nearest one-hundredth and round dollar amounts to the nearest dollar.)

(c) Assume that the equipment consists of an input device with a cost of $55,000, residual value of $5,000 and useful life of 5 years; a processor with a cost of $132,000, residual value of $12,000, and useful life of 10 years; and an output device with a cost of $200,000, residual value of $39,000, and useful life of 12 years. Prepare the journal entry to record the purchase on January 1, 2014.

(d) Assume the information given in part (c) above. Also assume that the benefits of the input device and processor are expected to flow to Jiang evenly over time, but that the output device is expected to provide the greatest benefits in the early years. Calculate the amount of depreciation for 2014 using the most appropriate methods.

(LO 4) E11-7 **(Depreciation—Conceptual Understanding)** Hubbub Company Ltd. acquired equipment at the beginning of Year 1. The asset has an estimated useful life of five years. An employee has prepared depreciation schedules for this asset using two different methods to compare the results of using one method with the results of using the other. Assume that the following schedules have been correctly prepared for this asset using (1) the straight-line method and (2) the double-declining-balance method.

Year	Straight-line	Double-Declining-Balance
1	$12,000	$30,000
2	12,000	18,000
3	12,000	10,800
4	12,000	1,200
5	12,000	–0–
Total	$60,000	$60,000

Instructions

(a) What is the cost of the asset that is being depreciated?

(b) What amount, if any, was used in the depreciation calculations for the residual value of this asset?

(c) Which method will produce the higher net income in Year 1?

(d) Which method will produce the higher charge to income in Year 4?

(e) Which method will produce the higher carrying amount for the asset at the end of Year 3?

(f) Which method will produce the higher cash flow in Year 1? In Year 4?

(g) If the asset is sold at the end of Year 3, which method would yield the higher gain (or lower loss) on disposal of the asset?

(LO 4) E11-8 **(Depreciation for Fractional Periods)** On March 10, 2014, Lucas Limited sold equipment that it purchased for $192,000 on August 20, 2007. It was originally estimated that the equipment would have a useful life of 12 years and a residual value of $16,800 at the end of that time, and depreciation has been calculated on that basis. The company uses the straight-line method of depreciation.

Instructions

(a) Calculate the depreciation charge on this equipment for 2007 and for 2014, and the total charge for the period from 2008 to 2013, inclusive, under each of the following six assumptions for partial periods:

1. Depreciation is calculated for the exact period of time during which the asset is owned. (Use 365 days for your base.)

2. Depreciation is calculated for the full year on the January 1 balance in the asset account.

3. Depreciation is calculated for the full year on the December 31 balance in the asset account.

4. Depreciation for a half year is charged on plant assets that are acquired or disposed of during the year.

5. Depreciation is calculated on additions from the beginning of the month following their acquisition and on disposals to the beginning of the month following the disposal.

6. Depreciation is calculated for a full period on all assets in use for over half a year, and no depreciation is charged on assets in use for less than half a year. (Use 365 days for your base.)

(b) Briefly evaluate the above methods in terms of basic accounting theory and how simple the methods are to apply.

(LO 4) E11-9 **(Error Analysis and Depreciation)** Gibbs Inc. purchased a machine on January 1, 2014, at a cost of $60,000. The machine is expected to have an estimated residual value of $5,000 at the end of its five-year useful life. The company capitalized the machine and depreciated it in 2014 using the double-declining-balance method of depreciation. The company has a policy of using the straight-line method to depreciate equipment as this method best reflects the benefits to the company over the life of its machinery. However, the company accountant neglected to follow company policy when he used the double-declining-balance method. Net income for the year ended December 31, 2014, was $53,000 as a result of depreciating the machine incorrectly. Gibbs has not closed its books for 2014 yet.

Digging Deeper

Instructions

(a) Using the method of depreciation that the company normally follows, prepare the correcting entry and determine the corrected net income. Assume the books of account have not yet been closed for 2014, and ignore income taxes.

(b) Discuss the impact on a potential investor if the error was not detected and corrected by Gibbs.

(LO 4) E11-10 (Error Analysis and Depreciation) Wettlauffer Company Ltd. shows the following entries in its Equipment account for 2014. All amounts are based on historical cost.

Equipment					
1/1	Balance	134,750	6/30	Cost of equipment sold	
8/10	Purchases of equipment	32,000		(purchased prior to 2014)	23,000
8/12	Freight on equipment purchased	700			
8/25	Installation costs	2,700			
11/10	Repairs	500			

Instructions

(a) Prepare any correcting entries that are necessary.

(b) Assuming that depreciation is to be charged for a full year based on the ending balance in the asset account no matter when acquired, calculate the proper depreciation charge for 2014 under both methods listed below. Assume an estimated life of 10 years, with no residual value. The machinery included in the January 1, 2014 Equipment balance was purchased in 2012.

   1. Straight-line

   2. Declining-balance (assume twice the straight-line rate)

(LO 5) E11-11 (Depletion Calculations—Timber) Rachel Timber Inc., a small private company that follows Canadian ASPE, owns 9,000 hectares of timberland purchased in 2001 at a cost of $1,400 per hectare. At the time of purchase, the land without the timber was valued at $420 per hectare. In 2002, Rachel built fire lanes and roads, with a physical life of 30 years, at a cost of $84,000 and separately capitalized these costs. Every year, Rachel sprays to prevent disease at a cost of $3,000 per year and spends $7,000 to maintain the fire lanes and roads. During 2003, Rachel selectively logged and sold 700,000 cubic metres of the estimated 3.5 million cubic metres of timber. In 2004, Rachel planted new seedlings to replace the cut trees at a cost of $100,000.

Instructions

(a) Determine the depletion charge and the portion of depletion included in the cost of timber sold for 2003.

(b) Rachel has not logged since 2003. Assume that Rachel logged and sold 900,000 cubic metres of timber in 2014 and the timber cruiser (the appraiser) had estimated a total resource of 5 million cubic metres. Determine the cost of timber sold that relates to the depletion for 2014.

(c) How would Rachel account for the maintenance costs of the fire lanes and roads and the spraying of the timberland?

(d) Discuss the depreciation methods that Rachel could use to depreciate the cost of the fire lanes and roads.

Digging Deeper

(e) Explain how your answers for parts (a) to (d) would differ if Rachel were a public company and followed IFRS.

(LO 5) E11-12 (Depletion Calculations—Oil) Marmon Drilling Limited leases property on which oil has been discovered. Wells on this property produced 21,000 barrels of oil during the current year and it was sold at an average of $85 per barrel. The total oil resources of this property are estimated to be 250,000 barrels.

The lease provided for an immediate payment of $5 million to the lessor (owner) before drilling began and an annual rental of $275,000. Development costs of $6,250,000 were incurred before any oil was produced, and Marmon follows a policy of capitalizing these preproduction costs. The lease also specified that each year the lessor would be paid a premium of 5% of the sales price of every barrel of oil that was removed. In addition, the lessee is to clean up all the waste and debris from drilling and to pay the costs of reconditioning the land for farming when the wells are abandoned. It is estimated that the present value of the obligations at the time of the lease for the cleanup and reconditioning for the existing wells is $300,000.

Instructions

(a) From the information given, provide the journal entry made by Marmon Drilling Limited to record depletion for the current year assuming that Marmon applies ASPE.

(b) Assuming that the oil property was acquired at the beginning of the current year, provide the entry to record the acquisition of the asset and the annual rental payment.

(LO 5) E11-13 **(Depletion Calculations—Minerals)** At the beginning of 2014, Kao Company, a small private company, acquired a mine for $850,000. Of this amount, $100,000 was allocated to the land value and the remaining portion to the minerals in the mine. Surveys conducted by geologists found that approximately 12 million units of ore appear to be in the mine. Kao had $170,000 of development costs for this mine before any extraction of minerals. It also determined that the fair value of its obligation to prepare the land for an alternative use when all of the mineral has been removed was $40,000. During 2014, 2.5 million units of ore were extracted and 2.2 million of these units were sold.

Instructions

Calculate the following information for 2014 (rounding your answers to two decimal places):

(a) The depletion cost per unit

(b) The total amount of depletion for 2014 (and prepare the required journal entry, if any)

(c) The total amount that is charged as an expense for 2014 for the cost of minerals sold during 2014 (and prepare the required journal entry, if any)

(LO 6) E11-14 **(Depreciation—Change in Estimate)** Machinery purchased for $56,000 by Wong Corp. on January 1, 2009, was originally estimated to have an eight-year useful life with a residual value of $4,000. Depreciation has been entered for five years on this basis. In 2014, it is determined that the total estimated useful life (including 2014) should have been 10 years, with a residual value of $4,500 at the end of that time. Assume straight-line depreciation.

Instructions

(a) Prepare the entry that is required to correct the prior years' depreciation, if any.

(b) Prepare the entry to record depreciation for 2014.

Digging Deeper

(c) Repeat part (b) assuming Wong Corp. uses the double-declining-balance method of depreciation.

(LO 6) E11-15 **(Depreciation Calculation—Addition, Change in Estimate)** In 1985, Lincoln Limited completed the construction of a building at a cost of $1.8 million; it occupied it in January 1986. It was estimated that the building would have a useful life of 40 years and a residual value of $400,000.

Early in 1996, an addition to the building was constructed at a cost of $750,000. At that time, no changes were expected in its useful life, but the residual value with the addition was estimated to increase by $150,000. The addition would not be of economic use to the company beyond the life of the original building.

In 2014, as a result of a thorough review of its depreciation policies, company management determined that the building's original useful life should have been estimated at 30 years. The neighbourhood where the building is has been going through a renewal, with older buildings being torn down and new ones being built. Because of this, it is now expected that the company's building and addition are unlikely to have any residual value at the end of the 30-year period.

Instructions

(a) Using the straight-line method, calculate the annual depreciation that was charged from 1986 through 1995.

(b) Calculate the annual depreciation that was charged from 1996 through 2013.

(c) Prepare the entry, if necessary, to adjust the account balances because the estimated useful life was revised in 2014.

(d) Calculate the annual depreciation to be charged beginning with 2014.

Digging Deeper

(e) Comment on the revision of the estimated useful life in 2014, from the perspective of an investor who purchased shares in Lincoln in 2013.

(LO 6) E11-16 **(Depreciation Replacement—Change in Estimate)** Finlay Limited constructed a building at a cost of $2.8 million and has occupied it since January 1994. It was estimated at that time that its life would be 40 years, with no residual value. In January 2014, a new roof was installed at a cost of $370,000, and it was estimated then that the building would have a useful life of 25 years from that date. The cost of the old roof was $190,000 and was capitalized in the Buildings account at that time.

Instructions

(a) What amount of depreciation was charged annually for the years 1994 through 2013? (Assume straight-line depreciation.)

(b) What entry should be made in 2014 to record the roof replacement?

(c) Prepare the entry in January 2014 to record the revision in the building's estimated life, if necessary.

(d) What amount of depreciation should be charged for the year 2014?

(LO 7) E11-17　(Impairment—Cost Recovery Model) The management of Luis Inc., a small private company that uses the cost recovery impairment model, was discussing whether certain equipment should be written down as a charge to current operations because of obsolescence. The assets had a cost of $900,000, and depreciation of $400,000 had been taken to December 31, 2014. On December 31, 2014, management projected the undiscounted future net cash flows from this equipment to be $300,000, and its fair value to be $230,000. The company intends to use this equipment in the future.

Instructions

(a) Prepare the journal entry, if any, to record the impairment at December 31, 2014.

(b) Where should the gain or loss on the impairment, if any, be reported on the income statement?

(c) At December 31, 2015, the equipment's fair value increased to $260,000. Prepare the journal entry, if any, to record this increase in fair value.

(d) Assume instead that as of December 31, 2014, the equipment was expected to have undiscounted future net cash flows of $510,000, and that its fair value was estimated to be $450,000. Prepare the journal entry to record the impairment at December 31, 2014, if any.

(e) Assume instead that as of December 31, 2014, the equipment was expected to have undiscounted future net cash flows of $45,000 per year for each of the next 10 years, and that there is no active market for the equipment. Luis Inc. uses a 10% discount rate in its cash flow estimates. Prepare the journal entry to record impairment at December 31, 2014, if any.

Digging Deeper

(f) Discuss why impairment is tested using undiscounted future cash flows rather than present value of future cash flows.

(LO 7) E11-18　(Impairment—Cash-Generating Units) Perez Corp., a mining company, owns a significant mineral deposit in a northern territory. Included in the asset is a road system that was constructed to give company personnel access to the mineral deposit for maintenance and mining activity. The road system cannot be sold separately. Perez prepares financial statements in accordance with IFRS.

Instructions

How should the road system's recoverable amount be determined?

(LO 7) E11-19　(Impairment—Rational Entity Model and Cash-Generating Units, Cost Recovery Model and Asset Groups) Green Thumb Landscaping Limited has determined that its lawn maintenance division is a cash-generating unit under IFRS. The carrying amounts of the division's assets at December 31, 2014, are as follows:

Land	$ 25,000
Building	50,000
Equipment	30,000
Trucks	15,000
	$120,000

The lawn maintenance division has been assessed for impairment and it is determined that the division's value in use is $108,000, fair value less costs to sell is $75,000, and undiscounted future net cash flows is $144,000.

Instructions

(a) Determine if the cash-generating unit is impaired and prepare the journal entry, if any, to record the impairment at December 31, 2014, assuming that none of the individual assets in the division has a determinable recoverable amount.

(b) Prepare the journal entry, if any, to record the impairment at December 31, 2014, assuming that the division's only individual asset that has a determinable recoverable amount is the building, which has a fair value less costs to sell of $46,000.

(c) Assume that Green Thumb prepares financial statements under ASPE instead, and that the lawn maintenance division is an asset group. Determine if the asset group is impaired and prepare the journal entry, if any, to record the impairment at December 31, 2014, assuming that none of the individual assets in the division has a determinable recoverable amount.

(LO 7) E11-20　(Impairment—Cost Recovery and Rational Entity Models) The information that follows relates to equipment owned by Gaurav Limited at December 31, 2014:

Cost	$9,000,000
Accumulated depreciation to date	1,000,000
Expected future net cash flows (undiscounted)	7,000,000
Expected future net cash flows (discounted, value in use)	6,350,000
Fair value	6,200,000
Costs to sell (costs of disposal)	50,000

Assume that Gaurav will continue to use this asset in the future. As at December 31, 2014, the equipment has a remaining useful life of four years. Gaurav uses the straight-line method of depreciation.

Instructions

(a) Assume that Gaurav is a private company that follows ASPE.

1. Prepare the journal entry at December 31, 2014, to record asset impairment, if any.

2. Prepare the journal entry to record depreciation expense for 2015.

3. The equipment's fair value at December 31, 2015, is $6.5 million. Prepare the journal entry, if any, to record the increase in fair value.

(b) Repeat the requirements in (a) above assuming that Gaurav is a public company that follows IFRS.

(c) Referring to the qualitative characteristics identified in the conceptual framework for financial reporting (discussed in Chapter 2), discuss the differences between the cost recovery impairment model and the rational entity impairment model.

(LO 7, 8) E11-21   (Impairment—Cost Recovery and Rational Entity Models) Assume the same information as in E11-20, except that at December 31, 2014, Gaurav discontinues use of the equipment and intends to dispose of it in the coming year by selling it to a competitor. It is expected that the costs of disposal will total $50,000.

Instructions

(a) Assume that Gaurav is a private company that follows ASPE.

1. Prepare the journal entry at December 31, 2014, to record asset impairment, if any.

2. Prepare the journal entry to record depreciation expense for 2015.

3. Assume that the asset was not sold by December 31, 2015. The equipment's fair value (and recoverable amount) on this date is $6.5 million. Prepare the journal entry, if any, to record the increase in fair value. It is expected that the costs of disposal will total $50,000.

4. Identify where, and at what amount, the asset will be reported on the December 31, 2015 statement of financial position.

(b) Repeat the requirements in (a) above assuming that Gaurav is a public company that follows IFRS, and that the asset meets all criteria for classification as an asset held for sale.

(LO 2, 6, 9) E11-22   (Depreciation Calculation—Replacement, Trade-in) Onkar Corporation bought a machine on June 1, 2010, for $31,800, f.o.b. the place of manufacture. Freight costs were $300, and $500 was spent to install it. The machine's useful life was estimated at 10 years, with a residual value of $1,900.

On June 1, 2011, a part that was designed to reduce the machine's operating costs was added to the machine for a cost of $1,980. On June 1, 2014, the company bought a new machine with greater capacity for a cost of $35,000, delivered. A trade-in value was received on the old machine equal to its fair value of $19,000. The cost of removing the old machine from the plant was $75, and the cost of installing the new machine was $1,300. It was estimated that the new machine would have a useful life of 10 years, with a residual value of $4,000.

Instructions

Assuming that depreciation is calculated on the straight-line basis, determine the amount of any gain or loss on the disposal of the first machine on June 1, 2014, and the amount of depreciation that should be provided during the company's current fiscal year, which begins on June 1, 2014.

(LO 4, 6, 9) E11-23   (Depreciation Calculations—Revaluation Model) Jamoka Corporation is a public company that manufactures farm implements such as tractors, combines, and wagons. Jamoka uses the revaluation model per IAS 16, and records asset revaluations using the elimination method. (This means the balance in the accumulated depreciation account is eliminated against the asset account just prior to revaluation of the asset to fair value.) A piece of manufacturing equipment included in the property, plant, and equipment section on Jamoka's statement of financial position was purchased on December 31, 2013, for a cost of $100,000. The equipment was expected to have a remaining useful life of five years, with benefits being received evenly over the five years. Residual value of the equipment was estimated to be $10,000.

Consider the following two situations:

Situation 1: At December 31, 2014, no formal revaluation is performed as management determines that the carrying amount of the property, plant, and equipment is not materially different from its fair value.

Situation 2: At December 31, 2014, a formal revaluation is performed and the independent appraisers assess the equipment's fair value to be $89,000. During the revaluation process, it is determined that the remaining useful life of the equipment is four years, with residual value of $11,000.

At December 31, 2015, no formal revaluation is performed as management determines that the carrying amount of the property, plant, and equipment is not materially different from its fair value. The equipment is sold on March 31, 2016, for $62,000.

Instructions

(a) Prepare any journal entries required under situation 1 described above for: (1) the fiscal year ended December 31, 2014; (2) the fiscal year ended December 31, 2015; and (3) the disposal of the equipment on March 31, 2016.

(b) Prepare any journal entries required under situation 2 described above for: (1) the fiscal year ended December 31, 2014; (2) the fiscal year ended December 31, 2015; and (3) the disposal of the equipment on March 31, 2016.

(c) Assume that Jamoka uses the proportional method to record asset revaluations under the revaluation model. Prepare any journal entries required under situation 2 described above for: (1) the fiscal year ended December 31, 2014; (2) the fiscal year ended December 31, 2015; and (3) the disposal of the equipment on March 31, 2016.

(LO 9) E11-24 (Entries for Disposition of Assets) Consider the following independent situations for Kwok Corporation. Kwok applies ASPE.

Situation 1: Kwok purchased equipment in 2007 for $120,000 and estimated a $12,000 residual value at the end of the equipment's 10-year useful life. At December 31, 2013, there was $75,600 in the Accumulated Depreciation account for this equipment using the straight-line method of depreciation. On March 31, 2014, the equipment was sold for $28,000.

Situation 2: Kwok sold a piece of machinery for $10,000 on July 31, 2014. The machine originally cost $38,000 on January 1, 2006. It was estimated that the machine would have a useful life of 12 years with a residual value of $2,000, and the straight-line method of depreciation was used.

Situation 3: Kwok sold office equipment that had a carrying amount of $3,500 for $5,200. The office equipment originally cost $12,000 and it is estimated that it would cost $16,000 to replace the office equipment.

Instructions

Prepare the appropriate journal entries to record the disposition of the property, plant, and equipment assets assuming that Kwok's fiscal year end is December 31 and that Kwok only prepares financial statements and adjusts the accounts annually.

(LO 9) E11-25 (Entries for Disposition of Assets) On December 31, 2013, Grey Inc. owns a machine with a carrying amount of $940,000. The original cost and accumulated depreciation for the machine on this date are as follows:

Machine	$1,300,000
Accumulated depreciation	360,000
	$ 940,000

Depreciation is calculated at $60,000 per year on a straight-line basis.

Instructions

A set of independent situations follows. For each situation, prepare the journal entry for Grey Inc. to record the transaction. Ensure that depreciation entries are recorded to update the machine's carrying amount before its disposal.

(a) A fire completely destroys the machine on August 31, 2014. An insurance settlement of $430,000 was received for this casualty. Assume the settlement was received immediately.

(b) On April 1, 2014, Grey sold the machine for $1,040,000 to Dwight Company.

(c) On July 31, 2014, the company donated this machine to the Dartmouth City Council. The machine's fair value at the time of the donation was estimated to be $1.1 million.

(LO 9) E11-26 (Disposition of Assets) On April 1, 2014, Lombardi Corp. was awarded $460,000 cash as compensation for the forced sale of its land and building, which were directly in the path of a new highway. The land and building cost $60,000 and $280,000, respectively, when they were acquired. At April 1, 2014, the accumulated depreciation for the building amounted to $165,000. On August 1, 2014, Lombardi purchased a piece of replacement property for cash. The new land cost $160,000 and the new building cost $410,000. The new building is estimated to have a useful life of 20 years, physical life of 30 years, residual value of $230,000, and salvage value of $75,000. Lombardi prepares financial statements in accordance with IFRS.

Instructions

(a) Prepare the journal entries to record the transactions on April 1 and August 1, 2014.

(b) How would the transactions on April 1 and August 1, 2014, affect the income statement for 2014? Would the effect be different if Lombardi prepared financial statements in accordance with ASPE?

(c) Prepare any journal entries required at December 31, 2014.

(LO 11) E11-27   (Ratio Analysis) The 2014 annual report of Trocchi Inc. contains the following information (in thousands):

	Dec. 31, 2014	Dec. 31, 2013
Total assets	$1,071,348	$ 787,167
Total liabilities	626,178	410,044
Consolidated sales	3,374,463	2,443,592
Net income	66,234	49,062

Instructions

(a) Calculate the following ratios for Trocchi Inc. for 2014:

1. Asset turnover ratio

2. Rate of return on assets

3. Profit margin on sales

(b) How can the asset turnover ratio be used to calculate the rate of return on assets?

(c) Briefly comment on the results for the ratios calculated in part (a).

(LO 3, *E11-28   (Depreciation Calculations—Four Methods; Partial Periods) On August 1, 2014, Iroko Corporation
4, 13) purchased a new machine for its assembly process. The cost of this machine was $136,400. The company estimated that the machine will have a trade-in value of $14,200 at the end of its useful life. Its useful life was estimated to be six years and its working hours were estimated to be 18,000 hours. Iroko's year end is December 31. (Round depreciation per unit to three decimal places.)

Instructions

Calculate the depreciation expense under each of the following:

(a) Straight-line method for 2014

(b) Activity method for 2014, assuming that machine use was 800 hours

(c) Double-declining-balance method for 2014 and 2015

(d) Capital cost allowance method for 2014 and 2015 using a CCA rate of 25%

(LO 13) *E11-29   (CCA) During 2014, Laiken Limited sold its only Class 3 asset. At the time of sale, the balance of the undepreciated capital cost for this class was $37,450. The asset originally cost $129,500.

Instructions

(a) Calculate recaptured CCA, capital gains, and terminal losses, if any, assuming the asset was sold for proceeds of (1) $132,700, (2) $51,000, and (3) $22,000.

**Digging
Deeper**
(b) Assume the tax rates are scheduled to increase for 2014. What strategy could Laiken use to reduce its taxes payable that are due to the recapture on the disposal of the asset?

(LO 13) *E11-30   (Book versus Tax Depreciation) Barnett Inc. purchased computer equipment on March 1, 2014, for $31,000. The computer equipment has a useful life of five years and a residual value of $1,000. Barnett uses a double-declining-balance method of depreciation for this type of capital asset. For tax purposes, the computer is assigned to Class 10 with a 30% rate.

Instructions

(a) Prepare a schedule of depreciation covering 2014, 2015, and 2016 for financial reporting purposes for the new computer equipment purchased. The company follows a policy of taking a full year's depreciation in the year of purchase and none in the year of disposal.

(b) Prepare a schedule of CCA and UCC for this asset covering 2014, 2015, and 2016, assuming it is the only Class 10 asset owned by Barnett.

(c) How much depreciation is deducted over the three-year period on the financial statements? In determining taxable income? What is the carrying amount of the computer equipment on the December 31, 2016 statement of financial position? What is the tax value of the computer equipment at December 31, 2016?

Problems

P11-1 Phoenix Corp. purchased Machine no. 201 on May 1, 2014. The following information relating to Machine no. 201 was gathered at the end of May:

Price	$85,000
Credit terms	2/10, n/30
Freight-in costs	$ 800
Preparation and installation costs	$ 3,800
Labour costs during regular production operations	$10,500

It was expected that the machine could be used for 10 years, after which the residual value would be zero. Phoenix intends to use the machine for only eight years, however, and expects to then be able to sell it for $1,500. The invoice for Machine no. 201 was paid on May 5, 2014. Phoenix has a December 31 year end. Depreciation expense should be calculated to the nearest half month.

Instructions

(a) Calculate the depreciation expense for the years indicated using the following methods. (Round to the nearest dollar.)

  1. Straight-line method for the fiscal years ended December 31, 2014, and 2015

  2. Double-declining-balance method for the fiscal years ended December 31, 2014, and 2015

*(b) Calculate the capital cost allowance for the 2014 and 2015 tax returns, assuming a CCA class with a rate of 25%.

(c) The president of Phoenix tells you that because the company is a new organization, she expects it will be several years before production and sales reach optimum levels. She asks you to recommend a depreciation method that will allocate less of the company's depreciation expense to the early years and more to later years of the assets' lives. Which method would you recommend? Explain.

(d) In your answer to part (c) above, how would cash flows to the new company be affected by the choice of depreciation method? How would current and potential creditors interpret the choice of depreciation method?

Digging Deeper

(e) Assume that Phoenix selects the double-declining-balance method of depreciation. In 2016, demand for the product produced by the machine decreases sharply, due to the introduction of a new and better competing product on the market. On August 15, 2016, the management of Phoenix meets and decides to discontinue manufacturing the product. On September 15, 2016, a formal plan to sell the machine is authorized. On this date, the machine meets all criteria for classification as held for sale, and the machine's fair value less costs to sell is $65,500. Calculate the depreciation expense for 2016.

P11-2 On June 15, 2011, a second-hand machine was purchased for $77,000. Before being put into service, the equipment was overhauled at a cost of $5,200, and additional costs of $400 for direct material and $800 for direct labour were paid in fine-tuning the controls. The machine has an estimated residual value of $5,000 at the end of its five-year useful life. The machine is expected to operate for 100,000 hours before it will be replaced and is expected to produce 1.2 million units in this time. Operating data for the next six fiscal years are provided below. The company has an October 31 fiscal year end. Depreciation expense should be calculated to the nearest half month.

Year	Hours of Operation	Units Produced
2011	10,000	110,000
2012	20,000	270,000
2013	20,000	264,000
2014	20,000	310,000
2015	18,000	134,000
2016	12,000	112,000

Instructions

(a) Calculate the depreciation charges for each fiscal year under each of the following depreciation methods. Where necessary, round depreciation rate per unit to four decimal places.

1. Straight-line method
2. Activity method: based on output
3. Activity method: based on input
4. Double-declining-balance method
*5. CCA, Class 8, 20%

**Digging
Deeper**

(b) What is the carrying amount of the machine on the October 31, 2014 statement of financial position under the first four methods above?

(c) Compare your answers in (b) with the asset's tax value at the same date.

(d) What happens if the actual hours of operation or units produced do not correspond to the numbers that were estimated in setting the rate?

P11-3   Comco Tool Corp. records depreciation annually at the end of the year. Its policy is to take a full year's depreciation on all assets that are used throughout the year and depreciation for half a year on all machines that are acquired or disposed of during the year. The depreciation rate for the machinery is 10%, applied on a straight-line basis, with no estimated scrap or residual value.

The balance of the Machinery account at the beginning of 2014 was $172,300; the Accumulated Depreciation on Machinery account had a balance of $72,900. The machinery accounts were affected by the following transactions that occurred in 2014:

Jan. 15   Machine no. 38, which cost $9,600 when it was acquired on June 3, 2007, was retired and sold as scrap metal for $600.

Feb. 27   Machine no. 81 was purchased. The fair value of this machine was $12,500. It replaced two machines, nos. 12 and 27, which were traded in on the new machine. Machine no. 12 was acquired on February 4, 2002, at a cost of $5,500 and was still carried in the accounts although it was fully depreciated and not in use. Machine no. 27 was acquired on June 11, 2007, at a cost of $8,200. In addition to these two used machines. Comco paid $9,000 in cash.

Apr. 7   Machine no. 54 was equipped with electric controls at a cost of $940. This machine, originally equipped with simple hand controls, was purchased on December 11, 2010, for $1,800. The new electric controls can be attached to any one of several machines in the shop.

     12   Machine no. 24 was repaired at a cost of $720 after a fire caused by a short circuit in the wiring burned out the motor and damaged certain essential parts.

July 22   Machines 25, 26, and 41 were sold for $3,100 cash. The purchase dates and cost of these machines were as follows:

         No. 25   May 8, 2006 $4,000
         No. 26   May 8, 2006   3,200
         No. 41   June 1, 2008   2,800

Instructions

(a) Record each transaction in general journal form.

(b) Calculate and record depreciation for the year. None of the machines currently included in the balance of the account were acquired before January 1, 2006.

P11-4   On January 1, 2012, Dayan Corporation, a small manufacturer of machine tools, acquired new industrial equipment for $1.1 million. The new equipment had a useful life of five years and the residual value was estimated to be $50,000. Dayan estimates that the new equipment can produce 12,000 machine tools in its first year. It estimates that production will decline by 1,000 units per year over the equipment's remaining useful life.

The following depreciation methods may be used: (1) straight-line, (2) double-declining-balance; and (3) units-of-production. For tax purposes, the CCA class is Class 10—30%.

Instructions

(a) Which of the three depreciation methods would maximize net income for financial statement reporting purposes for the three-year period ending December 31, 2014? Prepare a schedule showing the amount of accumulated depreciation at December 31, 2014, under the method you chose.

***(b)** Over the same three-year period, how much capital cost allowance would have been written off for tax purposes?

(c) Which pattern of depreciation do you feel best reflects the benefits that are provided by the new equipment? Explain briefly.

P11-5   The following data relate to the Plant Assets account of Keller Inc. at December 31, 2013:

	A	B	C	D
Original cost	$46,000	$58,000	$68,000	$73,000
Year purchased	2008	2009	2010	2011
Useful life	10 years	17,000 hours	15 years	10 years
Residual value	$3,900	$4,450	$8,000	$4,700
Depreciation method	straight-line	activity	straight-line	double-declining
Accumulated depreciation through 2013[a]	$21,050	$31,600	$12,000	$26,280

[a]In the year an asset is purchased, Keller does not record any depreciation expense on the asset. In the year an asset is retired or traded in, Keller takes a full year's depreciation on the asset.

The following transactions occurred during 2014:

1. On May 5, Asset A was sold for $16,500 cash. The company's bookkeeper recorded this retirement as follows:

Cash	16,500	
Asset A		16,500

2. On December 31, it was determined that Asset B had been used 3,200 hours during 2014.

3. On December 31, before calculating depreciation expense on Asset C, Keller management decided that Asset C's remaining useful life should be nine years as of year end.

4. On December 31, it was discovered that a piece of equipment purchased in 2013 had been expensed completely in that year. The asset cost $31,000 and had a useful life of 10 years when it was acquired and had no residual value. Management has decided to use the double-declining-balance method for this asset, which can be referred to as "Asset E." Ignore income taxes.

Instructions

Prepare any necessary adjusting journal entries required at December 31, 2014, as well as any entries to record depreciation for 2014.

PI1-6 Soon after December 31, 2014, the auditor of Morino Manufacturing Corp. asked the company to prepare a depreciation schedule for semi trucks that showed the additions, retirements, depreciation, and other data that affected the company's income in the four-year period from 2011 to 2014, inclusive. The following data were obtained.

Balance of Trucks account, January 1, 2011:	
Truck no. 1, purchased Jan. 1, 2008, cost	$18,000
Truck no. 2, purchased July 1, 2008, cost	22,000
Truck no. 3, purchased Jan. 1, 2010, cost	30,000
Truck no. 4, purchased July 1, 2010, cost	24,000
Balance, January 1, 2011	$94,000

The account Accumulated Depreciation—Trucks had a correct balance of $30,200 on January 1, 2011. (This includes depreciation on the four trucks from the respective dates of purchase, based on a five-year life, with no residual value.) No charges had been made against the account before January 1, 2011.

Transactions between January 1, 2011, and December 31, 2014, and their record in the ledger were as follows:

July 1, 2011   Truck no. 3 was traded for a larger one (no. 5). The agreed purchase price (fair value) was $34,000. Morino Manufacturing paid the automobile dealer $15,000 cash on the transaction. The entry was a debit to Trucks and a credit to Cash, $15,000.

Jan. 1, 2012   Truck no. 1 was sold for $3,500 cash. The entry was a debit to Cash and a credit to Trucks, $3,500.

July 1, 2013   A new truck (no. 6) was acquired for $36,000 cash and was charged at that amount to the Trucks account. (Assume truck no. 2 was not retired.)

July 1, 2013   Truck no. 4 was so badly damaged in an accident that it was sold as scrap for $700 cash. Morino Manufacturing received $2,500 from the insurance company. The entry made by the bookkeeper was a debit to Cash, $3,200, and credits to Gain on Disposal of Trucks, $700, and Trucks, $2,500.

Entries for depreciation were made at the close of each year as follows: 2011, $20,300; 2012, $21,100; 2013, $24,450; and 2014, $27,800.

Instructions

(a) For each of the four years, calculate separately the increase or decrease in net income that is due to the company's errors in determining or entering depreciation or in recording transactions affecting the trucks. Ignore income tax considerations.

(b) Prepare one compound journal entry as at December 31, 2014, to adjust the Trucks account to reflect the correct balances according to your schedule, and assuming that the books have not been closed for 2014.

P11-7   Linda Monkland established Monkland Ltd. in mid-2013 as the sole shareholder. The accounts on June 30, 2014, the company's year end, just prior to preparing the required adjusting entries, were as follows:

Current assets		$100,000
Capital assets		
Land	$40,000	
Building	90,000	
Equipment	50,000	180,000
Current liabilities		40,000
Long-term bank loan		120,000
Common shares		90,000
Net income prior to depreciation		30,000

All the capital assets were acquired and put into operation in early July 2013. Estimates and usage information on these assets were as follows:

Building: 25-year life, $15,000 residual value

Equipment: Five-year life, 15,000 hours of use, $5,000 residual value. The equipment was used for 1,000 hours in 2013 and 1,400 hours in 2014 up to June 30.

Linda Monkland is now considering which depreciation method or methods would be appropriate. She has narrowed the choices down for the building to the straight-line or double-declining-balance method, and for the equipment to the straight-line, double-declining-balance, or activity method. She has requested your advice and recommendation. In discussions with her, the following concerns were raised:

1. The company acquires goods from suppliers with terms of 2/10, n/30. The suppliers have indicated that these terms will continue as long as the current ratio does not fall below 2 to 1. If the ratio falls lower, no purchase discounts will be given.

2. The bank will continue the loan from year to year as long as the ratio of long-term debt to total assets does not exceed 46%.

3. Linda Monkland has contracted with the company's manager to pay him a bonus equal to 50% of any net income in excess of $14,000. She prefers to minimize or pay no bonus as long as conditions of agreements with suppliers and the bank can be met.

4. In order to provide a strong signal to attract potential investors to join her in the company, Ms. Monkland believes that a rate of return on total assets of at least 5% must be achieved.

Ethics

Instructions

(a) Prepare a report for Linda Monkland that (1) presents tables, (2) analyzes the situation, (3) provides a recommendation on which method or methods should be used, and (4) justifies your recommendation by considering her concerns and the requirement that the method(s) used be considered generally acceptable accounting principle(s).

(b) What other factors should you discuss with Ms. Monkland to help her in choosing appropriate depreciation methods for her business?

Digging Deeper

(c) Do any ethical issues arise if a depreciation method is chosen in order to manipulate the financial results in a way that will satisfy the constraints listed above? Explain.

P11-8   On April 30, 2014, Oceanarium Corporation ordered a new passenger ship, which was delivered to the designated cruise port and available for use as of June 30, 2014. Overall, the cost of the ship was $97 million, with an estimated useful life of 12 years and residual value of $30 million. Oceanarium expects that the new ship, as a whole, will provide its greatest economic benefits in its early years of operation. After further research and discussion with management, it is determined that the ship consists of major parts with differing useful lives, residual values, and patterns of providing economic benefits:

Part	Cost	Useful life	Residual value	Pattern of benefits	Total output (nautical miles)
Engines (6)	$975,000 per engine	8 years	$120,000 per engine	Varies with activity	7.0 million
Hull	$3,350,000	10 years	$502,000	Highest in early years	7.8 million
Body	$87.8 million	15 years	$15.5 million	Evenly over life of body	12.6 million

The ship's first voyage took place on August 1, 2014. The ship sailed a total of 328,000 nautical miles in 2014. Oceanarium prepares financial statements in accordance with IFRS.

Instructions

(a) Identify the factors to consider in determining how to account for the purchase and depreciation of the ship.

(b) Prepare the journal entry to record the purchase of the ship, assuming that Oceanarium paid cash for the purchase.

(c) Prepare the journal entry(ies) to record depreciation expense for 2014.

(d) Explain any differences in part (a) above if Oceanarium prepares financial statements in accordance with ASPE instead of IFRS.

P11-9 Khamsah Mining Ltd. is a small private company that purchased a tract of land for $720,000. After incurring exploration costs of $83,000, the company estimated that the tract will yield 120,000 tonnes of ore having enough mineral content to make mining and processing profitable. It is further estimated that 6,000 tonnes of ore will be mined in the first and last years and 12,000 tonnes every year in between. The land is expected to have a residual value of $30,000.

The company built necessary bunkhouses and sheds on the site at a cost of $36,000. It estimated that these structures would have a physical life of 15 years but, because they must be dismantled if they are to be moved, they have no residual value. The company does not intend to use the buildings elsewhere. Mining machinery installed at the mine was purchased second-hand at a cost of $60,000. This machinery cost the former owner $150,000 and was 50% depreciated when it was purchased. Khamsah Mining estimated that about half of this machinery will still be useful when the present mineral resources are exhausted but that dismantling and removing it would cost about as much as it is worth at that time. The company does not intend to use the machinery elsewhere. The remaining machinery is expected to last until about one half the present estimated mineral ore has been removed and will then be worthless. Cost is to be allocated equally between these two classes of machinery.

Khamsah also spent another $126,400 in opening up the mine so that the ore could be extracted and removed for shipping. The company estimates that the site reclamation and restoration costs that it is responsible for by contract when the mine is depleted have a present value of $53,600. Khamsah follows a policy of expensing exploration costs and capitalizing development costs.

Instructions

(a) As chief accountant for the company, you are to prepare a schedule that shows the estimated depletion and depreciation costs for each year of the mine's expected life.

(b) Prepare the journal entry(ies) to record the transactions for the acquisition of the mining property and related assets during the first year. Also prepare entries to record depreciation and depletion for the first year. Assume that actual production was 5,000 tonnes. Nothing occurred during the year to cause the company engineers to change their estimates of either the mineral resources or the life of the structures and equipment.

(c) Assume that 4,500 tonnes of product were processed and sold during the first year of the mine's expected life. Identify all costs mentioned above that will be included in the first-year income statement of Khamsah Mining Ltd.

P11-10 Conan Logging and Lumber Company, a small private company that follows ASPE, owns 3,000 hectares of timberland on the north side of Mount Leno, which was purchased in 2002 at a cost of $550 per hectare. In 2014, Conan began selectively logging this timber tract. In May of 2014, Mount Leno erupted, burying Conan's timberland under 15 centimetres of ash. All of the timber on the Conan tract was downed. In addition, the logging roads, built at a cost of $150,000, were destroyed, as well as the logging equipment, with a carrying amount of $300,000.

At the time of the eruption, Conan had logged 20% of the estimated 500,000 cubic metres of timber. Prior to the eruption, Conan estimated the land to have a value of $200 per hectare after the timber was harvested. Conan includes the logging roads in the depletion base.

Conan estimates it will take three years to salvage the downed timber at a cost of $700,000. The timber can be sold for pulp wood at an estimated price of $3 per cubic metre. The value of the land is unknown, but must be considered nominal due to future uncertainties.

Instructions

(a) Determine the depletion cost per cubic metre for the timber that was harvested prior to the eruption of Mount Leno.

(b) Prepare the journal entry to record the depletion before the eruption.

(c) Determine the amount of the estimated loss before income taxes and show how the losses of roads, machinery, and timber and the timber salvage value should be reported in Conan's financial statements for the year ended December 31, 2014.

P11-11 Darby Sporting Goods Inc. has been experiencing growth in the demand for its products over the last several years. The last two Olympic Games greatly increased the popularity of basketball around the world. As a result, a European sports retailing consortium entered into an agreement with Darby's Roundball Division to purchase an increasing number of basketballs and other accessories over the next five years.

To be able to meet the quantity commitments of this agreement, Darby had to increase its manufacturing capacity. A real estate firm found an available factory close to Darby's Roundball manufacturing facility, and Darby agreed to purchase the factory and used machinery from Encino Athletic Equipment Company on October 1, 2013. Renovations were necessary to convert the factory for Darby's manufacturing use.

The terms of the agreement required Darby to pay Encino $50,000 when renovations started on January 1, 2014, with the balance to be paid as renovations were completed. The overall purchase price for the factory and machinery was $400,000. The building renovations were contracted to Malone Construction at $100,000. The payments made as renovations progressed during 2014 are shown below. The factory began operating on January 1, 2015.

	Jan. 1	Apr. 1	Oct. 1	Dec. 31
Encino	$50,000	$90,000	$110,000	$150,000
Malone		30,000	30,000	40,000

On January 1, 2014, Darby secured a $500,000 line of credit with a 12% interest rate to finance the purchase cost of the factory and machinery, and the renovation costs. Darby drew down on the line of credit to meet the payment schedule shown above; this was Darby's only outstanding loan during 2014.

Bob Sprague, Darby's controller, will capitalize the maximum allowable interest costs for this project, which he has calculated to be $21,000. Darby's policy regarding purchases of this nature is to use the appraisal value of the land for book purposes and prorate the balance of the purchase price over the remaining items. The factory had originally cost Encino $300,000 and had a carrying amount of $50,000, while the machinery originally cost $125,000 and had a carrying amount of $40,000 on the date of sale. The land was recorded on Encino's books at $40,000. An appraisal, conducted by independent appraisers at the time of acquisition, valued the land at $290,000, the factory at $105,000, and the machinery at $45,000.

Angie Justice, chief engineer, estimated that the renovated factory would be used for 15 years, with an estimated residual value of $30,000. Justice estimated that the productive machinery would have a remaining useful life of five years and a residual value of $3,000. Darby's depreciation policy specifies the 200% declining-balance method for machinery and the 150% declining-balance method for the factory. One half-year's depreciation is taken in the year the factory is placed in service and one half year is allowed when the property is disposed of or retired.

Instructions

(a) Determine the amounts to be recorded on the books of Darby Sporting Goods Inc. as at December 31, 2014, for each of the following properties acquired from Encino Athletic Equipment Company: (1) land, (2) factory, and (3) machinery.

(b) Calculate Darby Sporting Goods Inc.'s 2015 depreciation expense, for book purposes, for each of the assets acquired from Encino Athletic Equipment Company.

(c) Discuss the arguments for and against the capitalization of interest costs.

P11-12 Roland Corporation uses special strapping equipment in its packaging business. The equipment was purchased in January 2013 for $10 million and had an estimated useful life of eight years with no residual value. In early April 2014, a part costing $875,000 and designed to increase the machinery's efficiency was added. The machine's estimated useful life did not change with this addition. By December 31, 2014, new technology had been introduced that would speed up the obsolescence of Roland's equipment. Roland's controller estimates that expected undiscounted future net cash flows on the equipment would be $6.3 million, and that expected discounted future net cash flows on the equipment would be $5.8 million. Fair value of the equipment at December 31, 2014, was estimated to be $5.6 million. Roland intends to continue using the equipment, but estimates that its remaining useful life is now four years. Roland uses straight-line depreciation. Assume that Roland is a private company that follows ASPE.

Instructions

(a) Prepare the journal entry to record asset impairment at December 31, 2014, if any.

(b) Fair value of the equipment at December 31, 2015, is estimated to be $5.9 million. Prepare any journal entries for the equipment at December 31, 2015.

(c) Repeat part (b), assuming that on December 31, 2015, Roland's management decides to dispose of the equipment. As of December 31, 2015, the asset is still in use and not ready for sale in its current state. In February 2016, Roland's management will meet to outline an active program to find a buyer.

(d) Repeat part (b), assuming that the equipment is designated as "held for sale" as of January 1, 2015, and that the equipment was not in use in 2015 but was still held by Roland on December 31, 2015.

Digging Deeper

(e) For each situation in (b), (c), and (d), indicate where the equipment will be reported on the December 31, 2015 balance sheet.

(f) Repeat parts (a) and (b) assuming instead that Roland is a public company that prepares financial statements in accordance with IFRS.

(g) From the perspective of a financial statement user, discuss the importance of frequent impairment testing in producing relevant and faithfully representative financial statements. Do IFRS and ASPE differ in the required frequency? Explain briefly.

P11-13 The following is a schedule of property dispositions for Shangari Corp.:

SCHEDULE OF PROPERTY DISPOSITIONS

	Cost	Accumulated Depreciation	Cash Proceeds	Fair Market Value	Nature of Disposition
Land	$40,000	—	$31,000	$31,000	Expropriation
Building	15,000	—	3,600	—	Demolition
Warehouse	70,000	$16,000	74,000	74,000	Destruction by fire
Machine	8,000	2,800	900	7,200	Trade-in
Furniture	10,000	7,850	—	3,100	Contribution
Automobile	9,000	3,460	2,960	2,960	Sale

The following additional information is available:

Land

On February 15, land that was being held mainly as an investment was expropriated by the city. On March 31, another parcel of unimproved land to be held as an investment was purchased at a cost of $35,000.

Building

On April 2, land and a building were purchased at a total cost of $75,000, of which 20% was allocated to the building on the corporate books. The real estate was acquired with the intention of demolishing the building, which was done in November. Cash proceeds that were received in November were the net proceeds from the building demolition.

Warehouse

On June 30, the warehouse was destroyed by fire. The warehouse had been purchased on January 2, 2011, and accumulated depreciation of $16,000 had been reported. On December 27, the insurance proceeds and other funds were used to purchase a replacement warehouse at a cost of $90,000.

Machine

On December 26, the machine was exchanged for another machine having a fair market value of $6,300. Cash of $900 was also received as part of the deal.

Furniture

On August 15, furniture was contributed to a registered charitable organization. No other contributions were made or pledged during the year.

Automobile

On November 3, the automobile was sold to Jared Dutoit, a shareholder.

Instructions

Prepare the entries to record the transactions and indicate how these items would be reported on the income statement of Shangari Corp. Assume that Shangari follows ASPE, but also indicate if the reporting would be treated differently under IFRS.

(AICPA adapted)

P11-14 Sung Corporation, a manufacturer of steel products, began operations on October 1, 2013. Sung's accounting department has begun preparing the capital asset and depreciation schedule that follows. You have been asked to assist in completing this schedule. In addition to determining that the data already on the schedule are correct, you have obtained the following information from the company's records and personnel:

1. Depreciation is calculated from the first day of the month of acquisition to the first day of the month of disposition.

2. Land A and Building A were acquired together for $820,000. At the time of acquisition, the land had an appraised value of $90,000 and the building had an appraised value of $810,000.

3. Land B was acquired on October 2, 2013, in exchange for 2,500 newly issued common shares. At the date of acquisition, the shares had a fair value of $30 each. During October 2013, Sung paid $16,000 to demolish an existing building on this land so that it could construct a new building.

4. Construction of Building B on the newly acquired land began on October 1, 2014. By September 30, 2015, Sung had paid $320,000 of the estimated total construction costs of $450,000. It is estimated that the building will be completed and occupied by July 2016.

5. Certain equipment was donated to the corporation by a local university. An independent appraisal of the equipment when it was donated estimated its fair value at $30,000 and the residual value at $3,000.

6. Machine A's total cost of $164,900 includes an installation expense of $600 and normal repairs and maintenance of $14,900. Its residual value is estimated at $6,000. Machine A was sold on February 1, 2015.

7. On October 1, 2014, Machine B was acquired with a down payment of $5,740 and the remaining payments to be made in 11 annual instalments of $6,000 each, beginning October 1, 2014. The prevailing interest rate was 8%. The following data were determined from present-value tables and are rounded:

PV of $1 at 8%		PV of an Ordinary Annuity of $1 at 8%	
10 years	0.463	10 years	6.710
11 years	0.429	11 years	7.139
15 years	0.315	15 years	8.559

SUNG CORPORATION
Capital Asset and Depreciation Schedule
For Fiscal Years Ended September 30, 2014, and September 30, 2015

Assets	Acquisition Date	Cost	Residual Value	Depreciation Method	Estimated Life in Years	Depreciation Expense, Year Ended September 30 2014	2015
Land A	Oct. 1, 2013	$ (1)	N/A	N/A	N/A	N/A	N/A
Building A	Oct. 1, 2013	(2)	$40,000	Straight-line	(3)	$17,450	(4)
Land B	Oct. 2, 2013	(5)	N/A	N/A	N/A	N/A	N/A
Building B	Under construction	$320,000 to date	—	Straight-line	30	—	(6)
Donated equipment	Oct. 2, 2013	(7)	3,000	150% declining-balance	10	(8)	(9)
Machine A	Oct. 2, 2013	(10)	6,000	Double-declining-balance	8	(11)	(12)
Machine B	Oct. 1, 2014	(13)	—	Straight-line	20	—	(14)

N/A = Not applicable

Instructions

For each numbered item in the schedule, give the correct amount. Round each answer to the nearest dollar.

P11-15   Consider the following independent situations.

Situation 1: Ducharme Corporation purchased electrical equipment at a cost of $12,400 on June 2, 2011. From 2011 through 2014, the equipment was depreciated on a straight-line basis, under the assumption that it would have a 10-year useful life and a $2,400 residual value. After more experience and before recording 2015's depreciation, Ducharme revised its estimate of the machine's useful life downward from a total of 10 years to eight years, and revised the estimated residual value to $2,000.

On April 29, 2016, after recording part of a year's depreciation for 2016, the company traded in the equipment on a newer model, and received a $4,000 trade-in allowance although its fair value was only $2,800. The new asset had a list price of $15,300 and the supplier accepted $11,300 cash for the balance. The new equipment was depreciated on a straight-line basis, assuming a seven-year useful life and a $1,300 residual value.

Situation 2: Malcolm Limited acquired a truck to deliver and install its specialized products at the customer's site. The vehicle's list price was $45,000, but customization added another $10,000 of costs. Malcolm took delivery of the truck on September 30, 2014, with a down payment of $5,000, signing a four-year, 8% note for the remainder, payable in equal payments of $14,496 beginning September 30, 2015.

Malcolm expected the truck to be usable for 500 deliveries and installations. After that, the product's technology would have changed and made the vehicle obsolete. In late July 2017, the truck was destroyed when a concrete garage collapsed. Malcolm used the truck for 45 deliveries in 2014, 125 in 2015, 134 in 2016, and 79 in 2017. The company received a cheque for $12,000 from the insurance company and paid what remained on the note.

Situation 3: A group of new machines was purchased on February 17, 2015, under a royalty agreement with the following terms: The purchaser, Keller Corp., is to pay a royalty of $1 to the machinery supplier for each unit of product that is produced by the machines each year. The machines are expected to produce 200,000 units over their useful lives. The machines' invoice price was $75,000, freight costs were $2,000, unloading charges were $1,500, and royalty payments for 2015 were $13,000. Keller uses the units of production method to depreciate its machinery.

Situation 4: On March 31, 2011, Wayside Corporation purchased a new piece of manufacturing equipment for a cost of $323,000. At that time, the estimated useful life of the equipment was five years, with residual value of $65,000. On August 1, 2014, due to increased competition causing a decreased selling price for its product, Wayside decided to discontinue manufacturing the product. By December 31, 2014, there was a formal plan in place to sell the equipment, and the equipment qualified for classification as held for sale. At December 31, 2014, the equipment's fair value less costs to sell was $52,000. Due to matters beyond Wayside's control, a potential sale of the equipment fell through in 2015, although consumer confidence in Wayside's product increased significantly due to reported defects in their competitors' products. The equipment remained classified as held for sale at December 31, 2015, when the equipment's fair value less costs to sell increased to $145,000. Wayside uses the straight-line method to depreciate its equipment.

Instructions

(a) For situation 1, determine the amount of depreciation expense reported by Ducharme for each fiscal year for the years ending December 31, 2011, to December 31, 2016.

(b) For situation 2, prepare all entries that are needed to record the events and activities related to the truck, including the depreciation expense on the truck each year. Assume that Malcolm uses an activity approach to depreciate the truck, and bases it on deliveries.

(c) For situation 3, prepare journal entries to record the purchase of the new machines, the related depreciation for 2015, and the royalty payment.

(d) For situation 4, prepare all journal entries required for the years ending December 31, 2014 and December 31, 2015.

*P11-16 Munro Limited reports the following information in its tax files covering the five-year period from 2012 to 2016. All assets are Class 10 with a 30% maximum CCA, and no capital assets had been acquired before 2012.

2012   Purchased assets A, B, and C for $20,000, $8,000, and $1,200, respectively.
2013   Sold asset B for $7,000; bought asset D for $4,800.
2014   Purchased asset E for $5,000; received an investment tax credit of $1,000.
2015   Sold asset A for $9,900 and asset C for $1,800.
2016   Asset D was destroyed by fire and was uninsured; asset E was sold to an employee for $500.

Instructions

(a) Prepare a capital cost allowance schedule for Class 10 assets covering the 2012 to 2016 period.

(b) Identify any capital gains, terminal losses, or recapture of CCA and indicate how each would be taxed.

*P11-17 Kitchigami Limited was attracted to the Town of Mornington by the town's municipal industry commission. Mornington donated a plant site to Kitchigami, and the provincial government provided $180,000 toward the cost of the new manufacturing facility. The total cost of plant construction came to $380,000 and it was ready for use in early October 2014. Kitchigami expects the plant to have a useful life of 15 years before it becomes obsolete and is demolished. The company uses the straight-line method of depreciation for buildings and is required to include the plant in Class 6 (10% rate) for tax purposes.

Instructions

(a) Prepare the entry(ies) that are required in 2014 to record the payment to the contractor for the building and the receipt of the provincial government assistance. Assume that the company treats the assistance as a reduction of the asset's cost. Also prepare any adjusting entries that are needed at the company's year ends, December 31, 2014, and 2015.

(b) Repeat (a), but assume instead that the company treats the government assistance as a deferred credit.

(c) If Kitchigami reports 2015 income of $79,000 before depreciation on the plant and government assistance, what income before tax will the company report assuming (a) above? Assuming (b) above?

(d) What is the building's tax value at December 31, 2015?

Integrated Cases

Refer to the Case Primer to help you answer these cases.

(*Hint*: If there are issues here that are new, use the conceptual framework to help you support your analysis with solid reasoning.)

IC11-1   ClubLoop Corporation (CL) is a large owner, operator, and developer of golf clubs and resorts. The company is privately owned by several wealthy individuals. During the current year, according to the draft financial statements, revenues increased by 7.2% and net operating income increased by 13% to $22.5 million. Net income dropped from $2.9 million to $822,000. The decrease was largely due to two events: a change in accounting policy and costs related to the settlement of a lawsuit.

One of the company's objectives is to always ensure that capital resources are readily available to meet approved capital expenditures and to take advantage of growth opportunities. According to the draft year-end financial statements, the company has current assets of $12 million and current liabilities of $28 million, resulting in a working capital deficit. Included in the current liabilities are long-term debts that are currently due. The company is working with the financial institutions in question to renew or replace these facilities. CL has received unsolicited expressions of interest from several financial institutions concerning these facilities, and management believes that these facilities will be replaced—hopefully before the current financial statements are issued.

The company owns most of the land on which CL's golf courses are developed. Currently, the company follows a rigorous "weed and feed" program in order to keep the grass on the golf courses in top shape. The chemicals in these fertilizers, herbicides, and insecticides are felt by some people in the local community to be toxic to the environment. The company has met with several community groups and has agreed to study the issue further. In a current meeting of the board of directors, the CEO committed the company to spending $1 million to limit any potential damage. As at year end, none of this amount has yet been spent. There is a concern that the community groups are going to launch legal proceedings and the company feels that this move will help CL's position if there ends up being a lawsuit. Part of the money is for landscaping to limit the spread of the sprayed chemicals and part of it is for advertising to promote the company as a good corporate citizen.

The company is currently developing new golf courses. All direct costs related to the acquisition, development, and construction of these properties, including interest and management costs, are capitalized. For one of the new locations, which was just purchased and developed in the current year, the company has run into a small problem. After CL spent several million dollars on development, the planned golf course is being blocked by environmental groups. The costs to develop the land have been capitalized as previously mentioned, on the basis that they would be recoverable from future membership revenues. However, the company has now decided to sell the land to a real estate developer.

CL's stock-based compensation plan consists of stock options. The company does not recognize any expense for this plan when stock options are issued to employees. It has been company policy to repurchase any shares issued under these stock option plans, although this year the company has indicated that it might not do this since it is planning to redesign the stock-based compensation system.

On July 1, the government tax department issued notices of assessment to the company regarding a dispute over the recognition of revenues. Although the outcome of an appeal of the assessment cannot be determined, the company believes that it will owe $8.7 million if its appeal is unsuccessful.

Instructions

Adopt the role of the company's auditor and prepare an analysis of the financial reporting issues.

IC11-2   MA Hydro (MH) is a private company that owns and operates all of Ontario's electricity transmission systems. It is deciding whether it should follow IFRS or ASPE in the upcoming year. The company must choose now and is looking to do an analysis of the impact of following IFRS or ASPE. Each year, MH must prepare and submit audited financial statements to the government.

The company generates and sells electricity to residential and commercial customers. They are committed to the following:

- Identifying and providing innovative solutions that will improve the reliability and efficiency of electrical delivery
- Sustainability (including not only profitability but also environmental sustainability). In this regard, MH has a publicly available environmental policy against which the company is measured by the government.

The company has just finished a new project to install smart meters in all residential houses. The meters allow residents to track usage and power supply and demand. Each unit is very expensive and will likely become technologically obsolete in three years. MH decided to pursue this strategy nonetheless due to its commitment to sustainability. The company wants all customers to think about using electricity wisely and the meters help with this. The company generally requires a security deposit (amounting to the cost of the meter) when a customer signs up to receive electricity or when the meter is first installed. The value of the meter declines over time and after three years is worthless. If a customers cancels their electricity delivery contract early, they get the full amount back once they return the meter. Otherwise, at the end of three years, MH retains the security deposit and has no obligation to return the cash.

MH is rate regulated. This means that it must ask for government approval whenever it wants to raise electricity rates that it charges to customers. Generally, the government allows the company to recover all costs incurred in generating the electricity plus a reasonable profit margin. Therefore, rates are set as being equal to "cost plus reasonable profit margin." This means that once approved, the company is able to charge revenues equal to all costs incurred plus a reasonable profit. Under ASPE, special "rate-regulated accounting" exists. One of the features of this special accounting is that companies following rate-regulated accounting are able to defer any losses that are incurred on disposition of assets, on the basis that they can recover these losses from future revenues. IFRS does not allow this.

Sometimes MH signs supply contract agreements with other suppliers of electricity to ensure that power supplies to MH customers are not disrupted. Under the terms of these contracts, MH locks in the quantity and price of electricity. The contracts do not explicitly include net settlement provisions, however. Because electricity is a commodity, the contracts may be bought and sold on the regional commodities exchange.

MH is concerned about maintaining a consistent supply of electricity to its customers since many of its generating stations are getting very old and the incidence of breakdown and generating station closures due to the age of the equipment is increasing. There is no market for these old generating stations (and MH would probably replace the capacity with newer, greener forms of electricity, such as wind or solar). Often the land that these stations are sitting on is polluted with chemicals. Technically, since this pollution occurred many years ago in most cases, there are no laws in place to force cleanup. Currently, the company is doing a voluntary land assessment and remediation program to identify the extent of this pollution. The company expects that it would recover all of the cleanup costs it might incur from future revenues through increased customer rates. However, there is always the chance that future governments might change the ability to build these costs into the rates charged to customers.

Some of the generating stations are located on lands held by Aboriginals. The company is negotiating to obtain legal title to the lands but understands that it may have to relocate the assets. The assets in question are material.

MH obtains much of its financing through bonds and commercial paper issuances. Therefore, it is important that it retains its good credit ratings. Currently, it has a very good credit rating, awarded by both S&P and Moody's credit rating agencies. This good rating is important in order to keep costs (and therefore customer rates) down. There are debt covenants in the debt agreements that limit the amount of debt as a percentage of total capitalization (total assets). Debt may not exceed 75% of total assets under these covenants. (Currently, the actual debt to total assets ratio is 65%.)

Instructions

Assume the role of an accounting consultant hired to determine which set of accounting standards to follow. Discuss the financial reporting issues relating to the above. Use the case analysis framework presented in class, including an overview, analysis, and recommendations.

Writing Assignments

WA11-1 Prophet Manufacturing Limited was organized on January 1, 2014. During 2014, it used the straight-line method of amortizing its plant assets in its reports to management.

As the company's controller, on November 8 you are having a conference with Prophet's officers to discuss the depreciation method to be used for income tax and for reporting to shareholders. Fred Peretti, president of Prophet, has suggested using a new method that he feels is more suitable than the straight-line method for the company's current needs during what he foresees will be a period of rapid expansion of production and capacity. The following is an example in which the proposed method is applied to a capital asset with an original cost of $248,000, an estimated useful life of five years, and a residual value of approximately $8,000:

Year	Years of Life Used	Fraction Rate	Depreciation Expense	Accumulated Depreciation at Year End	Book Value at Year End
1	1	1/15	$16,000	$ 16,000	$232,000
2	2	2/15	32,000	48,000	200,000
3	3	3/15	48,000	96,000	152,000
4	4	4/15	64,000	160,000	88,000
5	5	5/15	80,000	240,000	8,000
	15				

The president favours the new method because of the following claims that he has heard about it:

1. It will increase the funds that are recovered during the years near the end of the assets' useful life when maintenance and replacement disbursements are high.

2. It will result in increased writeoffs in later years when the company is likely to be in a better operating position.

Instructions

Draft a response to Fred Peretti that explains the purpose of depreciation, and whether the method that has been suggested qualifies as a generally accepted accounting method. Identify the circumstances, if any, that would make using the method reasonable and those, if any, that would make using it unreasonable. Also respond to his statement that depreciation charges recover or create funds.

Ethics

WA11-2 Lian Tang, HK Corporation's controller, is concerned that net income may be lower this year. He is afraid that upper-level management might recommend cost reductions by laying off accounting staff, himself included. Tang knows that depreciation is a major expense for HK. The company currently uses the same method for financial reporting as it uses for tax purposes—that is, a declining-balance method—and he is thinking of changing to the straight-line method.

Tang does not want to draw attention to the increase in net income that would result from switching depreciation methods. He thinks, "Why don't I just increase the estimated useful lives and the residual values of the property, plant, and equipment? They are only estimates anyway. This will decrease depreciation expense and increase income. I may be able to save my job and those of my staff." Tang called his professional accounting body's "Ethics Hotline" and reached the Ethical Accountant for advice.

Instructions

Discuss. Make sure that you, the Ethical Accountant providing advice to Tang, identify the objectives of depreciation, who the stakeholders are in this situation, what disclosures are required, whether any ethical issues are involved, and what Tang should do.

WA11-3 Nickel Strike Mines is a nickel mining company with mines in northern Ontario, Colombia, and Australia. It is a publicly traded company and follows IFRS, and has historically followed industry practice and used units of production as its depreciation policy for all its mines. During 2014, the price of nickel declined significantly, even below the costs of production for the Ontario mines. Consequently, the company has had the Ontario mines closed since early January 2014. It has continued to produce in its Colombian and Australian mines. It is now December 2014 and the controller is trying to decide what accounting issues there are related to the Ontario mines. Since it was a very bad year for the company, and investors are expecting the worst, the controller is considering switching to the declining-balance method of depreciation for the Ontario mine only. This would create a significant depreciation charge for 2014, but in the future, the depreciation costs related to the mine would decrease, resulting in higher net income. In addition, since there were no units produced in the Ontario mine for the year, no depreciation is taken. The controller believes that this is wrong, and that some amount of depreciation should be recorded.

Additionally, the controller is also considering taking as large an impairment loss as possible on all the mines. The controller will do this by assuming a very low nickel price, which will cause the recoverable amounts to be below carrying values for all mines. This impairment loss should likely reverse in the following years, since nickel prices are expected to climb dramatically over the next year, as supplies diminish and as demand from Asian countries increases. With the reversal of the impairment in 2015, this would show a significant improvement in the company's net income.

Instructions

You are a Nickel Strike Mines board member and have just heard the controller's comments on these issues. Comment on the controller's suggestions. Include in your discussion how the impairment test would be completed and the assumptions required. Also discuss the note disclosure that would be required related to all of these issues.

WA11-4 Realtor Inc. is a company that owns five large office buildings that are leased out to tenants. Most of the leases are for 10 years or more with renewal clauses for an additional 5 years. Currently, the company is a private company that follows ASPE. Recently Rita Mendoza was hired as a new controller. Ms. Mendoza has suggested to Habib Ganem, the owner and sole shareholder of the company, that perhaps the company should consider switching to IFRS. She explained that under ASPE, the buildings are recorded at cost and then depreciated and tested for impairment when events occur. However, under IFRS, she explained, the buildings could be classified as investment properties and adjusted to fair value every year. In addition, there is no impact on the income statement since no depreciation is recorded on the investment properties. Finally, Ms. Mendoza stated that there is no impairment testing required for investment properties under IFRS so there would never be any impairment losses to be recognized.

Mr. Ganem was intrigued with this idea. He had just been looking at the calculation of the bank loan covenants and had found that the company's debt to asset ratio was very close to the maximum that would be allowed. He wanted to take this year's annual financial statement, once completed, to the bank and ask for revisions on the covenants, since he was also looking at some new properties to possibly purchase. He particularly liked the idea of no depreciation having to be recorded on these assets, which would also improve the company's times interest earned ratio (calculated as Earnings before taxes and interest / Interest expense). Mr. Ganem decided he might call his banker to discuss this change and get her thoughts.

Instructions

You are the loans officer at the bank. What comments would you make to Mr. Ganem about the controller's suggestions? In particular, explain the impact on the balance sheet and the income statement under both the cost model and the fair value model and the resulting impact on the existing covenants. From a banker's point of view, which method for reporting the investment properties would be most useful? Make a final recommendation to Mr. Ganem.

WA11-5 Puma Paper Company Ltd. operates a 300-tonne per-day kraft pulp mill and four sawmills in New Brunswick. The company is expanding its pulp mill facilities to a capacity of 1,000 tonnes per day and plans to replace three of its older, less efficient sawmills with an expanded facility in three years' time. The fourth mill did not operate for most of 2014 (current year), and there are no plans to reopen it before the new sawmill facility becomes operational. The Board of Directors has approved a plan to sell this mill and is actively seeking a buyer.

In reviewing the depreciation rates and in discussing the residual values of the sawmills that are to be replaced, it was noted that if present depreciation rates were not adjusted, substantial amounts of plant costs on these three mills would not be depreciated by the time the new mill is operational.

Instructions

What is the proper accounting for the four sawmills at the end of 2014 under ASPE? Under IFRS?

WA11-6 Howeven Inc. is a private company that expects to "go public" and become publicly traded soon. Accordingly, it expects to be adopting IFRS by 2014. It is a manufacturing company with extensive investments in property, plant, and equipment. The company currently has a profit sharing plan that is based on 30% of the earnings after depreciation, but before interest and taxes. There is also a debt to fixed asset ratio covenant that must be maintained for the bank loan.

The controller has been learning about IFRS and has determined that there are three different treatments that the property, plant, and equipment can have on the transition to IFRS.

1. The first is to continue using the cost model as the company has been doing. The company currently uses the straight-line method of depreciation for all of its assets.

2. The second option is that the company, on transition at January 1, 2014, can elect to revalue all of its property, plant, and equipment to fair value. This is a one-time increase in value that is allowed for first-time adopters of IFRS. The company would still use the cost model to depreciate this new value (which becomes the deemed cost) in subsequent years.

3. The third option is to adopt the revaluation model for just the "Property and plant" assets. The company would continue to use the cost model for the equipment, as fair market values are not readily available for this type of asset.

The controller has estimated the following numbers at January 1, 2014 (debt is expected to be $1,700 million):

	Remaining Useful Life	Carrying Value	Estimated Fair Value at Jan. 1, 2014
Property and plant	25 years	$2,500 million	$3,250 million
Equipment	10 years	$1,300 million	$1,400 million

Instructions

You are the Vice President Finance and must prepare a memo to the board explaining these options. Using the numbers in the table to assist you, discuss the implications of the three options on the balance sheet, income statement, bonuses, and the debt to fixed asset covenant.

WA11-7 Write a brief essay highlighting the differences between IFRS and ASPE noted in this chapter, discussing the conceptual justification for each.

RESEARCH AND FINANCIAL ANALYSIS

RA11-1 Canadian Tire Corporation, Limited

Real World Emphasis

Canadian Tire Corporation, Limited is one of Canada's best-known retailers. Obtain a copy of Canadian Tire's financial statements for the year ended December 31, 2011, through SEDAR at www.sedar.com or on the company's website. To answer the following questions, you may also want to include the 10-year financial review that is produced as supplementary information in the annual report.

Instructions

(a) How significant is Canadian Tire's investment in property, plant, and equipment compared with its investment in other assets? Compare this with sample companies in other industries, such as financial services, utilities, and technology. Comment.

(b) Calculate the company's total asset turnover for 2011, 2010, and 2009.

(c) Calculate the company's profit margin for the same three years.

(d) Calculate the company's return on assets for the same three years by using the ratios calculated in (b) and (c) above.

(e) Based on your calculations in (d), suggest ways in which Canadian Tire might increase the return that it earns on its investment in assets.

RA11-2 Brookfield Asset Management Inc.

Real World Emphasis

Brookfield Asset Management Inc. is a publicly traded Canadian company that converted to IFRS on January 1, 2010.

Instructions

From the company's website, access the annual report for the year ended December 31, 2009, the last year of reporting under Canadian GAAP. Also obtain the annual report for the year ended December 31, 2011. Review the notes to the statements and answer the following questions.

(a) What business is Brookfield in?

(b) What policies did the company use in 2009 to report commercial properties, power generation, timberlands, utilities, transportation assets, and development and other properties? Include in this discussion the depreciation and impairment testing policies. What is the amount of depreciation expense that is shown on the income statement?

(c) What policies did the company ultimately adopt for each of its capital asset categories (use the 2011 financial statements)? What method and assumptions has the company used to determine fair values for each class of assets?

(d) What other methods are available to determine fair value? Which methods are most reliable from a user's perspective? Review IFRS 13 on fair value measurement to determine what level of fair value measurement the company has used to determine fair values.

RA11-3 Canadian National Railway Company and Canadian Pacific Railway Limited

Real World Emphasis

Two well-known company names in the transportation industry in Canada are **Canadian National Railway Company** and **Canadian Pacific Railway Limited**. Go to either SEDAR (www.sedar.com) or to each company's website to gain access to the financial statements of these companies for their years ended December 31, 2011.

Instructions

(a) How significant are the investments made by these companies in property, plant, and equipment? Express the size of these investments as a percentage of total assets.

(b) Compare the types of property, plant, and equipment that each company reports.

(c) Do the companies follow similar policies in what they capitalize as part of property, plant, and equipment?

(d) What methods of depreciation are used by each company?

(e) For assets that are similar at both companies, compare their useful lives or rates of depreciation. Are these similar or would applying them result in differences in the reported results for each year? Explain briefly.

RA11-4 Lufthansa and Air Canada

Real World Emphasis

Lufthansa and **Air Canada** are both global airline companies. Lufthansa reports under IFRS. Air Canada reported under pre-changeover Canadian GAAP until 2010 and now reports under IFRS. Access the financial statements of Lufthansa for its year ended December 31, 2011, and Air Canada for its years ended December 31, 2011, and December 31, 2010, from the respective company's website.

Instructions

(a) What amounts are reported on the balance sheet for capital assets for Lufthansa and Air Canada at December 31, 2011? What percentage of total assets is invested in these types of assets by each company?

(b) For Lufthansa: What types of capital assets does the company report? What is included in costs? Is interest capitalized? What depreciation methods are used by Lufthansa? How are residual values estimated for aircraft?

(c) For Air Canada: What types of capital assets does the company report in 2010? What is included in costs? Is interest capitalized? What depreciation methods are used by Air Canada? How are residual values estimated for aircraft?

(d) Compare and contrast the above accounting policies for the two companies. Where are there significant differences between the two policies used by Air Canada in 2010 and 2011? What will be the impact on the balance sheet and net earnings based on these differences?

(e) For Lufthansa, how are the assets tested for impairment? Were any impairment losses recorded for the year, and if so, how much? What did these relate to? Was there any reversal of impairment losses from previous years?

(f) For Air Canada, how have the assets been tested for impairment and were there any impairment losses for 2010 and 2011?

(g) Does Lufthansa have assets held for sale? How much has been reclassified to this account and where is it presented on the balance sheet? What does it relate to? Does Air Canada have any assets designated as held for sale?

RA11-5 First Capital Realty

Real World Emphasis

Usually a comparison assignment involves comparing two similar companies that are reporting under different GAAP. Ideally, it would be better to compare the same company's financial reports prepared on two different bases. **First Capital Realty** adopted IFRS in 2011. It is possible to analyze its 2010 results under both bases using the IFRS figures reported in its financial statements for the year ended December 31, 2011 and the ASPE figures reported for year ended December 31, 2010.

Instructions

Access the financial statements for First Capital Realty for the years ended December 31, 2010, and December 31, 2011, from the company's website. Review the statements that are presented and answer the following questions.

(a) What business is First Capital Realty in?

(b) Compare the accounting policies used to report investment properties and development properties under IFRS and ASPE. What are the effects of these differences on the balance sheet, income statement, and statement of cash flows? Be specific.

(c) Calculate the following ratios for the company's year ended December 31, 2010, under both ASPE and IFRS:

1. Total asset turnover

2. Profit margin

3. Return on assets

(d) Comment on the results obtained in part (c). In your opinion, which set of ratios provides a better assessment of the company's profitability? Explain.

(e) Based on your findings, write a short hypothetical memo to the chief financial officer (CFO) of a Canadian company in the same business as First Capital Realty. You need to alert the CFO to the possible effects that the company will experience when adopting IFRS.

RA11-6 Research Topic: Deferred Maintenance

A topic that concerns not-for-profit organizations and relates to their long-lived assets is the matter of "deferred maintenance." Canadian schools and universities in particular are concerned with this issue.

Instructions

(a) Research the topic of deferred maintenance well enough so that you understand the term. Explain the concept in 50 words or less.

(b) Interview the chief financial officer of your college or university or a not-for-profit or government organization to discuss the issue. Can you determine from an organization's financial statements if it has a deferred maintenance problem? Should you be able to? Discuss.

ENDNOTES

[1] See IAS 16, paragraphs 56-57 for further discussion.

[2] Ontario Power Generation 2010 Annual Report, p. 13.

[3] See IAS 36.7-17.

[4] After acquisition, it is the asset's **net carrying amount** and residual value that determine the depreciable amount.

[5] This is the definition in IAS 16 *Property, Plant, and Equipment*. The definition in the *CICA Handbook–Accounting*, Part II, Section 3061 *Property, Plant, and Equipment* refers only to the asset's net realizable value at the end of its useful life to an entity. They are not necessarily inconsistent.

[6] The airline industry illustrates the type of problem found in estimations. In the past, aircraft were assumed not to wear out; they just became obsolete. However, some jets have been in service for as long as 20 years, and maintenance of these aircraft has become increasingly expensive. As a result, some airlines now replace aircraft, not because of obsolescence, but because of physical deterioration.

[7] There is another systematic decreasing charge approach, called the **sum-of-the-years'-digits method**, but it is rarely used in Canada. Under this method, the depreciable amount is multiplied each year by a decreasing fraction. The **denominator** of the fraction equals the sum of the digits of an asset's useful life. For example, the sum of the digits of the life of an asset with a five-year life is $1 + 2 + 3 + 4 + 5 = 15$. The **numerator** decreases year by year and the denominator stays constant. Because this is a decreasing charge approach, depreciation expense is $5/15$ of the depreciable amount in the first year, $4/15$ of the depreciable amount in the second year, $3/15$ in the third, $2/15$ in the fourth, and $1/15$ in the fifth year. At the end of the asset's useful life, its net book value is equal to the estimated residual value. Similarly, for an asset with a 10-year life, the sum of the years' digits, 1 through 10, equals 55. Depreciation in the first year is $10/55$ of the depreciable amount, in the second year it is $9/55$, and so on.

[8] The straight-line rate (%) is equal to 100% divided by the estimated useful life of the asset that is being depreciated. A pure form of the declining-balance method (sometimes called the fixed percentage of book value method) has also been suggested as a possibility, but it is not used very much. This approach finds a rate that depreciates the asset to exactly its residual value at the end of its expected useful life. The formula for determining this rate is as follows:

$$\text{Depreciation rate} = 1 - \sqrt[n]{\frac{\text{Residual value}}{\text{Acquisition cost}}}$$

The life in years is *n*. Once the rate is calculated, it is applied to the asset's declining book value from period to period.

[9] Some critics suggest that pro forma earnings may confuse or mislead users. Investopedia.com notes that one nickname for pro forma earnings is EEBS (earnings excluding bad stuff!).

[10] To determine the undepreciated carrying amount to date when using the double-declining-balance method, the following formula can be used:

Book value = $C(1 - r)^n$, where C = cost of asset; r = depreciation rate; and n = number of full years from the asset's acquisition date. For example, if the machinery in the illustration had been depreciated using the double-declining-balance method instead of the straight-line method, C = $90,000; r = 2 × (100% ÷ 20) = 10%; and n = 8.

The asset's carrying amount at the end of year 8, therefore, is $90,000(1 - 0.10)^8$, or $38,742.

[11] This definition is based on amendments to IAS 36 *Impairment of Assets* after approval of the IASB's *Fair Value Measurement* standard (IFRS 13). The amendments became effective January 1, 2013. Chapter 2 of this text provides a fuller discussion of fair values and how they are measured.

[12] IAS 36.68. This is quite similar to *CICA Handbook–Accounting*, Part II, Section 3063.03. Both ASPE Section 3063 and IAS 36 include liabilities in the asset group if cash flows from the group are the only source of cash to meet the obligation.

[13] Refer to the specific IFRS and ASPE standards for complete coverage of the specific disclosures. Because the users of private entity financial statements can generally request additional information if needed, there are many fewer required disclosures under ASPE than under IFRS.

[14] This represents an extract from the Business Realignment and Impairment Charges note; the full note is available as part of Hershey's annual report available on-line.

[15] The higher the proportion of property, plant, and equipment to total assets, the more this turnover ratio says about the efficiency of capital asset use. Analysts often calculate separate turnover ratios for each major type of asset reported on the balance sheet and analyze each.

[16] The widespread availability of accounting software capable of maintaining detailed records for property, plant, and equipment; the related depreciation expense; and accumulated depreciation under a variety of methods has significantly reduced the cost of record keeping and the possibility of errors.

[17] CCA is subject to rules set by government legislation and can therefore change from time to time. Furthermore, various provincial governments can have different rules for determining CCA for purposes of calculating the income on which provincial taxes are based. The examples in this chapter are based on the federal income tax regulations for 2011.

[18] The rationale is that the ITC is not calculated until after the company's year end, when the tax return is completed and filed.

[19] The percentage of the capital gain that is taxable has varied in recent years. In 2011, the inclusion rate—the taxable portion—was 50%.

Aiming for Brand Loyalty

SHAKESPEARE'S JULIET asked, "What's in a name?," but accountants ask, "How much is in a name?" Companies must decide how to account for intangible assets such as their trade names.

Trade names are important to most companies, but especially to those in the marketing field. This is the case with Montreal-based Aimia Inc., which began life as Aeroplan, the frequent flyer program started in 1984 by Air Canada. In 2002, Aeroplan's popularity had grown to the point where the airline realized the potential to use the brand to create a loyalty program that went beyond rewarding repeat customers with free flights. Air Canada spun off Aeroplan as a separate company that offers members the ability to collect points from retailers and other non-airline partners, and to get non-air travel rewards such as merchandise and store gift cards.

In 2005, Aeroplan became a public company, Groupe Aeroplan Inc., and it rebranded itself as Aimia in 2011.

Growing beyond Canada, Aimia has acquired or partnered with other loyalty programs in 20 countries, including the Nectar program in the United Kingdom. With each acquisition or partnership, the company gains another trade name or access to it that it must assess. Aimia records trade names, which it considers intangible assets with indefinite lives, at cost less accumulated impairment losses. It does not amortize them but instead tests them for impairment each year or more frequently if events warrant. Company management has determined that trade names are intangible assets with an indefinite useful life because there is no foreseeable limit to the period over which the asset is expected to generate cash flows. At December 31, 2011, Aimia reported a net carrying amount for trade names of $389 million.

Trade names also contribute to goodwill—the difference between the amount a company was acquired for and the fair value of its identifiable net assets. For example, goodwill is reflected in the value that Aimia placed on Carlson Marketing. Aimia had purchased Carlson Marketing in 2009 for $188 million as a strategic move to gain a foothold in the U.S. market. Aimia's Chief Financial Officer David Adams said at the time that the acquisition "will be immediately accretive to adjusted net earnings and free cash flow per share as Carlson Marketing is expected to generate positive free cash flow."

However, Aimia stopped using the Carlson Marketing trade name in connection with its loyalty program in the United States when the company rebranded itself as Aimia. That year, it recorded a goodwill impairment charge of $53.9 million related to Carlson Marketing.

Sources: "Group Aeroplan to Acquire Carlson Marketing," company news release, November 3, 2009; "Group Aeroplan Adopts New Name and Global Brand Identity," company fact sheet, October 5, 2011; Aimia 2011 annual report.

CHAPTER 12

Intangible Assets and Goodwill

LEARNING OBJECTIVES

After studying this chapter, you should be able to:

1. Understand the importance of intangible assets and goodwill from a business perspective.

2. Define and describe the characteristics of intangible assets.

3. Identify and apply the recognition and measurement requirements for purchased intangible assets.

4. Identify and apply the recognition and measurement requirements for internally developed intangible assets.

5. Explain how intangible assets are accounted for after initial recognition.

6. Identify and explain the accounting for specific types of intangible assets.

7. Explain and account for impairment of limited-life and indefinite-life intangible assets.

8. Explain the concept of goodwill and how it is measured and accounted for after acquisition.

9. Identify the types of disclosure requirements for intangible assets and goodwill and explain the issues in analyzing these assets.

10. Identify differences in accounting between ASPE and IFRS.

After studying Appendix 12A, you should be able to:

11. Explain and apply basic approaches to valuing goodwill.

As the opening vignette indicates, the valuation of intangible assets is not always clear cut. Because of the difficulty in determining which costs actually result in adding value to an asset such as a "trade name," it is one of the assets whose value is typically recognized only when it is acquired in a purchase and sale transaction. This chapter explains the basic conceptual and reporting issues related to intangible assets and their close relative, goodwill.

The chapter is organized as follows:

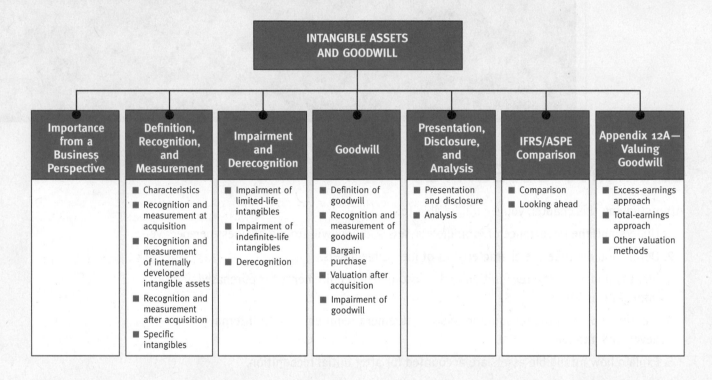

INTANGIBLE ASSETS AND GOODWILL

Importance from a Business Perspective	Definition, Recognition, and Measurement	Impairment and Derecognition	Goodwill	Presentation, Disclosure, and Analysis	IFRS/ASPE Comparison	Appendix 12A— Valuing Goodwill
	■ Characteristics ■ Recognition and measurement at acquisition ■ Recognition and measurement of internally developed intangible assets ■ Recognition and measurement after acquisition ■ Specific intangibles	■ Impairment of limited-life intangibles ■ Impairment of indefinite-life intangibles ■ Derecognition	■ Definition of goodwill ■ Recognition and measurement of goodwill ■ Bargain purchase ■ Valuation after acquisition ■ Impairment of goodwill	■ Presentation and disclosure ■ Analysis	■ Comparison ■ Looking ahead	■ Excess-earnings approach ■ Total-earnings approach ■ Other valuation methods

THE IMPORTANCE OF INTANGIBLE ASSETS AND GOODWILL FROM A BUSINESS PERSPECTIVE

Objective 1
Understand the importance of intangible assets and goodwill from a business perspective.

Lululemon Athletica Inc. and **Roots Canada**'s most important asset is not their store fixtures, it is their brand image. In Lululemon's 2011 Form 10-K Annual Report, the company notes that it is a "designer and retailer of technical athletic apparel ...marketed under the lululemon athletica brand name. We believe consumers associate our brand with innovative, technical apparel products." It discusses the importance of brand awareness, its "branded stores," and the image of its brand. The annual report also states, when discussing the risks that the company faces, that "if we fail to maintain the value and reputation of our brand, our sales are likely to decline." However, if you look at Lululemon's 2011 financial statements, the brand name is not listed as a key part of its $27 million in recorded intangible assets. The company's financial statements list goodwill, non-competition agreements, and reacquired franchise rights as its three most significant intangible assets.

Similarly, the major asset of **Coca-Cola** is not its plant facilities, it's the secret formula for making Coke. **Bell Canada**'s most important asset is not its Internet connection equipment, it's the subscriber base. Our economy is increasingly dominated by information and service providers, and their major assets are often intangible in nature. Identifying and measuring these intangibles is often difficult, and as a result many intangibles have not been captured on companies' statements of financial position. However, intangible assets and goodwill remain a key focus of companies and standard setters around the globe.

DEFINITION, RECOGNITION, AND MEASUREMENT OF INTANGIBLE ASSETS

Characteristics

Objective 2
Define and describe the characteristics of intangible assets.

Law

What are intangible assets? Broadly defined, **intangible assets** are identifiable nonmonetary assets that lack physical substance. Intangible assets must have these three characteristics—**identifiability**, **non-physical existence**, and a **nonmonetary nature**—so that only appropriate assets are recognized as intangibles.

1. **Intangible assets are identifiable.** An asset is **identifiable** if it has at least one of the following characteristics:
   - it results from contractual or other legal rights or
   - it is separable—it can be separated or divided from the entity and sold, transferred, licensed, rented, or exchanged, either by itself or in combination with another contract, identifiable asset, or liability.[1]

   For example, the right to lease space at favourable rates arises from contractual arrangements and the right may or may not be transferable to others. A subscription list of a successful newspaper or magazine has value in contributing to future revenue streams and is saleable. These are examples of identifiable intangibles that are given separate recognition. Note also that in order to recognize these items as assets, the company has to be able to control access to the future benefits and restrict others' access. One way to control access to the benefits is having legally enforceable rights; another is having the ability to enter into exchange transactions related to the intangible.

   Goodwill and some other non-physical items of value, on the other hand, are not separable from the rest of the entity, and control over the future benefits does not result from contractual or legal rights. For example, the synergies of a combined sales force or a superior management team can be identified as having value. However, these items cannot be recognized separately as intangible assets because they cannot be separated from the entity in order to exchange them with others, nor can they be controlled through contractual or other legal rights. They are therefore considered part of goodwill.

   While it is important to distinguish one identifiable intangible from another, financial reporting objectives are not well met if every identifiable intangible is recognized separately. At a minimum, the ones that have similar characteristics (such as continuity, stability, and risk) are grouped and recognized together. Because knowledge-based and high-technology companies with large investments in such "soft" assets are an important part of our modern economy, how accounting treats such intangibles is a major issue.

2. **Intangible assets lack physical substance.** Unlike assets such as property, plant, and equipment (PP&E), the value of intangible assets comes from the rights and privileges that are granted to the company using them. Sometimes it is difficult to tell whether a particular asset is tangible and is therefore an item of PP&E, or whether it is intangible and covered by accounting standards for intangible assets. Consider the example of computer software that is used for the operation of a key piece of equipment on an assembly line. What is the asset? Is it the intangible software, or is it the related tangible asset of equipment? In general, if the intangible component is needed for the

physical component to work, it is treated as an item of PP&E. If the intangible component is not an integral part of the physical object, then it is classified separately as an intangible asset.

3. **Intangible assets are nonmonetary.** Assets such as accounts receivable and long-term loans lack physical substance, but they are not classified as intangible assets. They are **monetary assets** whose value comes from the right (or claim) to receive fixed or determinable amounts of money in the future. Intangible assets do not contain any such right or claim.

In most cases, items that meet the definition of an intangible asset provide **economic benefits** over a period of years. The benefits may be in the form of revenue from selling products or services, a reduction in future costs, or other economies. They are normally classified as long-term assets. Examples include such widely varied assets as patents, copyrights, franchises or licensing agreements, trademarks or trade names, secret formulas, computer software, technological know-how, prepayments, and some development costs. Specific intangibles are discussed later in the chapter.

Recognition and Measurement at Acquisition

Objective 3
Identify and apply the recognition and measurement requirements for purchased intangible assets.

The **recognition criteria** for intangible assets are identical to those for PP&E assets and both are **measured at cost** at acquisition. For example, each type of asset can be recognized only when it meets the same two recognition criteria:

1. It is probable that the entity will receive the expected future economic benefits.

2. The asset's cost can be reliably measured.[2]

In applying these criteria, however, management has to consider that there is often more uncertainty about the future economic benefits associated with intangible assets than with tangible capital assets.

Purchased Intangibles

Underlying Concept

The cost concepts introduced in Chapter 10 for property, plant, and equipment are also appropriate for determining the cost of purchased intangible assets.

Intangible assets may be purchased outright, they can be acquired as part of a business combination, or they can be developed internally.

As indicated above, intangible assets purchased from another party are **measured at cost**. Because the amount paid is based on the company's expectations about receiving future economic benefits from the asset, the "probability" criterion for recognition is met. Cost includes the acquisition cost and all expenditures directly associated with making the intangible ready for its intended use—for example, the purchase price, legal fees, and other direct costs to bring it into working condition. Costs that are **not capitalized** are similar to those for property, plant, and equipment assets: they are those related to product introduction and promotion, conducting business in a new location or with new types of customers, and administration and general overhead. Expenditures incurred after the asset is ready for use as intended and initial operating losses are also excluded.

Similar to other long-lived assets, when direct costs that meet the recognition criteria are incurred after acquisition of the intangible asset, these costs are accounted for as additions or replacements and are capitalized. This is not as common with intangibles, however.

What Do the Numbers Mean?

Canadian-based **Nortel Networks** filed for bankruptcy protection in January 2009. But unlike many bankrupt companies, Nortel still had some valuable assets to sell: its patents. Two and a half years after declaring bankruptcy, Nortel auctioned off approximately 6,000 patents to Apple, Microsoft, Research In Motion, and others for $4.5 billion in cash. The patents included products and processes related to 4G wireless networks, Internet and voice technology, semiconductors, and optical equipment.

Source: Barrie McKenna, "The Ghost of Nortel Continues to Haunt Canada's Tech Sector," *The Globe and Mail,* December 4, 2011; Charles Arthur, "Nortel Patents Sold for $4.5bn," *The Guardian,* July 1, 2011; "Nortel Reports Financial Results for the Fourth Quarter and Full Year 2011," company news release, March 8, 2012.

Cost, as was seen in earlier chapters, is the cash cost.

- If there are **delayed payment terms**, any portion of the payments that represents interest is recognized as a financing expense rather than as part of the asset cost.

- If the intangible asset is **acquired for shares**, cost is the asset's fair value.[3] However, if the fair value of the intangible asset cannot be measured reliably then the shares' fair value is used. ASPE is not as prescriptive. It allows the more reliable of the fair value of the asset or of the shares to be used.

- If the intangible asset is acquired by giving up **nonmonetary assets**, the cost of the intangible is the fair value of what is given up or the fair value of the intangible received, whichever one can be measured more reliably. This assumes that the transaction has **commercial substance** and that fair values can be reliably measured. You may want to review the section in Chapter 10 that discusses this situation and provides examples of transactions and entries for nonmonetary exchanges.

- If the intangible asset is acquired as a government grant, the asset's fair value usually establishes its cost on the books. GAAP does permit a company to recognize a zero or nominal dollar cost in this case. Any other direct costs of acquisition are capitalized into the asset cost, however.

Intangibles Purchased in a Business Combination

When a company purchases an intangible asset as a single asset, such as an acquisition of a specific trademark or patent, the accounting is relatively clear. When several intangibles are bought together in a "basket purchase," the accounting is more complex because the cost has to be allocated to each intangible based on its relative fair value.

A further complication happens when intangibles are acquired in a **business combination**—when one entity acquires control over one or more businesses. This can take place either by directly purchasing the net assets of the business or by acquiring the equity interests (the shares) that control the entity and its net assets. An issue arises because of the variety of assets and liabilities that make up a complete and ongoing business. Even the fact that the business is fully operational instead of being just in the planning stages adds value to it. The entity has to account for all the assets that are acquired, regardless of whether or not they are recognized in the acquired business's accounting records. Many of the assets acquired that contribute to the value of the business are intangible, but only those that are **identifiable** can be separately recognized. Intangibles acquired that are not identifiable assets are considered part of goodwill.

The acquisition cost assigned to each of the identifiable intangible assets acquired as part of a business combination is its fair value.[4] All such assets acquired in this way are recognized, even though they may have been internally generated by the business itself and not eligible for capitalization under the standards for internally generated intangible assets. Examples include brand names, patents, customer relationships, and **in-process research and development (R&D)**. In-process R&D comes about when one company acquires the business of another company, and one of the identifiable assets acquired is the research work and findings of the acquired company. When the research work and findings meet the requirements for reporting as an asset separate from goodwill, they are recognized as an identifiable intangible.

Prepayments

So far we have seen that if expenditures for intangibles do not qualify for recognition as an intangible asset or as part of goodwill in a business combination, they must be recognized as an expense when incurred. In some cases, however, a prepaid asset—a **prepaid expense**—can be recognized initially. A prepayment is recognized as an asset only when an entity pays for **goods** before their delivery (or other right of access) or for **services** before receiving those services. The asset is the right to receive the goods or services. When received, this "right to receive" no longer exists and the costs are expensed.

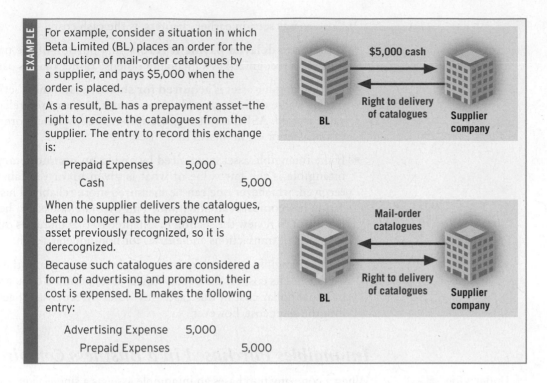

EXAMPLE

For example, consider a situation in which Beta Limited (BL) places an order for the production of mail-order catalogues by a supplier, and pays $5,000 when the order is placed.

As a result, BL has a prepayment asset—the right to receive the catalogues from the supplier. The entry to record this exchange is:

Prepaid Expenses	5,000	
Cash		5,000

When the supplier delivers the catalogues, Beta no longer has the prepayment asset previously recognized, so it is derecognized.

Because such catalogues are considered a form of advertising and promotion, their cost is expensed. BL makes the following entry:

Advertising Expense	5,000	
Prepaid Expenses		5,000

Recognition and Measurement of Internally Developed Intangible Assets

Objective 4
Identify and apply the recognition and measurement requirements for internally developed intangible assets.

It is a more challenging task to decide which costs should be capitalized and recognized as intangible assets when an entity develops such assets internally. The difficulty involves the following recognition and measurement issues.

1. Has an identifiable asset been created that will generate expected future cash flows?

2. What costs should be capitalized? Were the costs incurred just day-to-day operating costs or expenditures related to internally generated goodwill (which are expensed), or were they really additional costs of identifiable assets? How reliably can cost be measured?

Underlying Concept

The Financial Accounting Standards Board (FASB) in the United States has chosen option (b).

How costs associated with internally generated intangible assets should be accounted for has been a controversial issue for many years. The following alternatives have been suggested:

(a) Recognize the costs as internally generated intangible assets when certain criteria are met, and expense all others.

(b) Recognize all costs of internally generated intangible assets as an expense.

(c) Recognize expenditures on all internally generated intangible assets as an expense, with certain specified exceptions.

(d) Allow a choice between the accounting treatments in (a) and (b) above.[5]

The IASB decided on option (a) in IAS 38 *Intangible Assets* while option (d) was selected in *CICA Handbook*, Part II, Section 3064 *Goodwill and Intangible Assets* for private enterprises. Option (a) is illustrated in the next section. Note that the IFRS requirements for recognizing "self-constructed" intangibles are more stringent than those for property, plant, and equipment assets. This is because of the recognition and measurement uncertainties referred to above.

Identifying Research and Development Phase Activities

To deal with the uncertainty of whether an asset should be recognized, the process of generating the intangible is broken down into two parts: a **research phase** and a **development phase**. **Research** is the planned investigation undertaken with the hope of gaining new scientific or technical knowledge and understanding. The investigation may or may not be directed toward a specific practical aim or application. **Development**, on the other hand, is the translation of research findings or other knowledge into a plan or design for new or substantially improved materials, devices, products, processes, systems, or services before starting commercial production or use.[6]

The **research phase** and the **development phase** are interpreted in the accounting standards as broader terms than implied in the definitions of research and development provided. Examples of activities in each of these phases are set out in Illustration 12-1.

Illustration 12-1

Examples of Research Stage Activities and Development Stage Activities

Activities in the Research Stage	Activities in the Development Stage
Obtaining new knowledge	Designing, constructing, and testing prototypes and models prior to production or use
Searching for, evaluating, and selecting ways to use research findings or knowledge in general	Designing tools, jigs, moulds, and dies involving new technology
Investigating possible alternatives for existing materials, products, processes, systems, and services	Designing, constructing, and operating pilot plants that are not economically feasible for commercial production
Formulating, designing, evaluating, and choosing possible alternatives for new or existing materials, products, processes, systems, and services	Designing, constructing, and testing chosen alternatives for new or improved materials, products, processes, systems, and services[7]

If there is uncertainty about which phase a particular activity relates to when internally creating an intangible asset, it is classified as a **research phase** activity.

Accounting for Research Phase Costs

The accounting standards are very clear that no costs incurred on research or during the research phase of an internal project meet the criteria for recognition as an asset. **All such costs are recognized as expenses when they are incurred.** However, if a company has its own research facility consisting of buildings, laboratories, and equipment that are used for general research activities, it accounts for these assets as capitalized property, plant, and equipment. The depreciation and other costs that are related to such facilities are accounted for as research-related expenses.

Sometimes entities conduct research activities for other companies **under a contractual arrangement**. In this case, the contract usually specifies that all direct costs, certain specific indirect costs, and a profit element will be reimbursed to the entity performing the research work. Because reimbursement is expected, such research costs are recorded as inventory or a receivable.

Accounting for Development Phase Costs

An intangible asset can be recognized from the development stage of an internal project, but only when an entity can demonstrate its technical and financial feasibility and the company's intention and ability to generate future economic benefits from it. **All six of the following specific conditions need to be demonstrated** in order to capitalize costs incurred in the development phase:

1. Technical feasibility of completing the intangible asset

2. The entity's intention to complete it for use or sale

3. The entity's ability to use or sell it

4. Availability of technical, financial, and other resources needed to complete it, and to use or sell it

5. The way in which the future economic benefits will be generated; including the existence of a market for the asset if it will be sold, or its usefulness to the entity if it will be used internally

6. The ability to reliably measure the costs associated with and attributed to the intangible asset during its development

Because **all** six criteria must be met, this means that an entity capitalizes development phase costs **only when the future benefits are reasonably certain**. This means that internally generated intangible assets are recognized only in limited situations, and projects may be quite far along in the development stage before all six criteria are met. **Only then do the costs begin to be capitalized.** No expenditures incurred prior to this point and previously expensed are added to the asset's cost, even if the expenditures were in the same accounting period.

Although it is contrary to the usual principles-based approach, several items are specifically identified as not being recognized as internally generated intangible assets. These include brands, mastheads (the front-page or cover banner design of newspapers and magazines), publishing titles, customer lists, and other similar items. They are excluded on the basis that costs incurred to develop them cannot be distinguished from general business development costs.

Costs Included and Excluded

The cost of an internally generated intangible begins to be accumulated at the date when the six criteria in the development process are met. From this point forward, the types of expenditures that are capitalized are familiar: all directly attributable costs needed to create, produce, and prepare the intangible asset to operate in the way intended by management. Examples of such direct costs include:

1. Materials and services used or consumed

2. Direct costs of personnel, such as salaries, wages, payroll taxes, and related employee benefit costs

3. Fees needed to register a legal right

4. Amortization of other intangibles needed to generate the new asset

5. Interest or borrowing costs[8]

Specifically **excluded** as capitalized costs are selling, administrative, and other general overhead costs that cannot be directly linked to preparing the asset for use, costs incurred to train employees, and initial operating losses after the intangible is ready for use.

Generally, the costs of start-up activities such as legal and other costs of incorporation (**organization costs**); pre-opening costs associated with new facilities or businesses; and pre-operating costs for launching new operations, products, or processes are all expensed. Relocation and reorganization costs, and those associated with advertising and promotional activities including mail-order catalogues, are also not capitalized.[9]

To illustrate the accounting treatment of activities associated with intangible items and research and development phases, assume that a company develops, produces, and markets laser machines for medical, industrial, and defence uses. The types of expenditures related to its laser machine activities, along with the recommended IFRS accounting treatment, are listed in Illustration 12-2.

Illustration 12-2

Sample Expenditures and Their Accounting Treatment

Type of Expenditure	Accounting Treatment
1. Construction of long-range research facility (three-storey, 100,000-m² building) for use in current and future projects	Capitalize as PP&E assets; depreciate as a research-type expense.
2. Acquisition of research-related equipment for use on current project only	Capitalize as PP&E asset; depreciate as a research-type expense.
3. Purchase of materials to be used on current and future R&D projects	Capitalize as inventory; expense as a research-type expense as consumed.
4. Salaries of research staff designing new laser bone scanner	Expense immediately as a research-type expense.
5. Research costs incurred under contract for customer and billable monthly	Expense as operating expense in period of related revenue recognition.
6. Material, labour, and overhead costs of prototype laser scanner	Capitalize as intangible asset if development criteria are all met; otherwise expense.
7. Costs of testing prototype and design modifications	Capitalize as intangible asset if development criteria are all met; otherwise expense.
8. Legal fees to obtain patent on new laser scanner	Capitalize as patent (intangible asset) provided asset meets recognition criteria; amortize to cost of goods manufactured as used.
9. Executive salaries	Expense as operating expense (general and administrative).
10. Cost of marketing research related to promotion of new laser scanner	Expense as operating expense (selling).
11. Engineering costs incurred to advance the laser scanner to full production stage	Capitalize as intangible asset if development criteria are all met; otherwise expense.
12. Costs of successfully defending patent on laser scanner	Capitalize as intangible asset (patent); amortize to cost of goods manufactured as used.
13. Commissions to sales staff marketing new laser scanner	Expense as operating expense (selling).

Recognition and Measurement after Acquisition

Objective 5
Explain how intangible assets are accounted for after initial recognition.

Items of property, plant, and equipment commonly have parts added to them or replaced, but most intangible assets do not. The nature of intangibles is such that costs incurred after the asset has been acquired are normally made to maintain the asset's benefits and therefore do not meet the recognition criteria for capitalization. Although there are exceptions, most after-acquisition costs are expensed.

Two models have been put forward for measuring intangible assets after initial recognition: a **cost model (CM)** and a **revaluation model (RM)**. The cost model is the most widely used approach by far, and under ASPE, it is the only method allowed.

Why is the RM not widely used? The reason is simply that it can be applied only to intangible assets that have a fair value determined in an **active market**.[10] This limits its use to situations where the items are homogeneous (interchangeable), there is a good supply of willing buyers and sellers, and the prices are available to the public. An active securities market, such as the Toronto Stock Exchange, exists for equity securities, but active markets do not ordinarily exist for intangible assets. Most intangible assets, such as patents, brands, and trademarks, grant unique rights to the entity that holds them. This results in unique pricing when such assets are bought and sold. There are some exceptions. Examples include the prices of quotas for a variety of agricultural products for which the government sets production limits, such as milk or eggs. The revaluation model could also be used where there are transferable fishing or taxi licences, which are available in some jurisdictions.

When the RM is chosen for an intangible asset, all the assets in the same class must also apply the same method. Examples of classes include copyrights, patents, computer software, secret recipes, and designs. If there is no active market for the other assets in the class, then the cost model is applied to these assets.

Accounting under these two models is the same for intangible assets as for property, plant, and equipment. For both PP&E and intangible assets using the revaluation method, there is no requirement for an annual revaluation, only that the carrying amount reported on the statement of financial position not be materially different from its fair value. Instead of repeating the full coverage of this topic provided in Chapters 10 and 11, the two methods of accounting for limited-life intangible assets are summarized in Illustration 12-3.[11] You may want to review the specific examples in the earlier chapters to reinforce that material.

Illustration 12-3

Cost Model and Revaluation Model for Intangible Assets

Cost Model (CM)	
At acquisition	Recognized and measured at cost.
After acquisition	Carried at cost less accumulated amortization and any accumulated impairment losses.
On disposal	Difference between asset's carrying amount and proceeds on disposal is gain or loss reported in net income.

Revaluation Model (RM)	
At acquisition	Recognized and measured at cost.
After acquisition	Carried at fair value at the date of the revaluation less any subsequent accumulated amortization and any subsequent impairment losses.
Revaluation increase	Record credit to Revaluation Surplus (Other Comprehensive Income) unless this reverses a previous decrease recognized in income. If so, recognize the increase in income to the extent of the prior decrease.
Revaluation decrease	Record debit to Revaluation Surplus (Other Comprehensive Income) to extent there is a balance associated with the same asset. Any remaining amount is recognized in income.
Revaluation	Apply either the **proportional method** (both asset and accumulated amortization balances continue and are adjusted so that net amount is asset's new fair value) or the **asset adjustment method** (accumulated amortization is closed to asset account and begins again at zero; asset is revalued to new amount).
On disposal	Either (a) bring asset to its fair value at the date of disposal, account for the revaluation increase or decrease as above, and recognize no gain or loss on disposal; or (b) recognize a gain or loss on disposal in net income equal to the difference between the proceeds on disposal and the asset's carrying amount on the date of disposal.
Revaluation Surplus account balance	Either transfer amounts directly to Retained Earnings each period (equal to the difference between amortization expense determined on the cost model basis and amortization expense determined on the revaluation model basis), or wait until asset is disposed of and transfer balance remaining in the account directly to Retained Earnings.

As suggested above, intangibles are a diverse mix of assets. Some intangibles have values based on rights that are given legally by contract, statute, or similar means. Examples include a Tim Hortons franchise or licences granted by the federal government to broadcasters. Some of these rights have finite or limited legal lives that can be easily renewed; others have lives that are not renewable, and others are renewable only at a significant cost. Some can be sold while others may not be exchangeable. Internally developed intangibles may have a wide range of useful lives. Other intangibles may be granted in perpetuity and have an indefinite life. An **indefinite life** does not mean "infinite"—that the asset will last forever. Instead, it means that, after looking at all relevant factors, there appears to be no foreseeable limit to how long the asset will generate positive net cash flows to the entity.

Accounting standards used to require all intangible assets to be amortized over a period of not more than 40 years. While this simplified the accounting, the reality is that intangibles are diverse, and the approach to their measurement after acquisition should be based on their specific characteristics. Under current standards, if an intangible asset has a finite, or limited, useful life, it is amortized over that useful life. If instead the intangible has an indefinite life, no amortization is taken. Financial reporting is better served by retaining the asset in the accounts until it is determined to be impaired or its life becomes limited.

Limited-Life Intangibles

An intangible asset with a **finite** or **limited life** is amortized by systematic charges to expense over its useful life whether using the cost model or revaluation model. The factors to consider in determining the useful life are similar to the factors for long-lived property, plant, and equipment, and include:

1. The expected use of the asset by the entity, and the expected useful life of other assets that may affect the useful life of the intangible asset (such as mineral rights for depleting assets).

2. Any legal, regulatory, or contractual provisions that may either limit the useful life or allow renewal or extension of the asset's legal or contractual life without the entity having to pay a substantial cost. (If the renewal cost is significant, then the expenditure for the renewal may be the cost of a new intangible asset.)

3. The effects of obsolescence, demand, competition, and other economic factors. Examples include the stability of the industry, known technological advances, and legislative action that results in an uncertain or changing regulatory environment.

4. The level of maintenance expenditure that is needed to obtain the expected future cash flows from the asset.[12]

Amortization expense for a limited-life asset should ideally reflect the pattern in which the asset's economic benefits are used up, if that pattern can be reliably determined. For example, assume that Second Wave, Inc. has purchased a licence to manufacture a limited quantity of a gene product called Mega. Because the life of the licence is reduced with each unit produced, the cost of the licence is amortized following the pattern of production of Mega—a units of production approach. If the pattern cannot be determined, the straight-line method is used. The amortization charges are usually reported **as expenses**, and the credits are made to **accumulated amortization** accounts. Note that in the Second Wave, Inc. example, the amortization is likely a product cost that is first included in inventory and then expensed on the income statement as part of the cost of goods sold when the product is sold.

The amount to amortize for an intangible asset is its carrying amount less residual value. Uncertainties about residual values for intangibles are greater than they are for items of property, plant, and equipment. Because of this, an intangible asset's residual value is assumed to be zero. This assumption can be overturned only if the asset is expected to be of use to another entity and a third party commits to purchase the asset at the end of its useful life, or if there is an observable market for the asset that is expected to still exist at the end of its useful life to the entity.[13]

There are other similarities between the accounting for limited-life intangibles and property, plant, and equipment assets, as indicated in Illustration 12-4.

Transaction or Event	Accounting Treatment for Intangible Assets with a Limited Life	Same as for Most PP&E Assets?
Amortization begins...	...when the asset is in the location and condition to be able to be used as management intends	Yes
Amortization stops...	...at the earlier of when it is derecognized or classified as held for sale	Yes
Review of useful life and amortization method	ASPE: at least annually	PP&E is reviewed "regularly"
	IFRS: at least at the end of each financial year	Yes
Change in estimate of useful life, residual value, amortization method	Accounted for prospectively—as a change in accounting estimate	Yes

Indefinite-Life Intangibles

An intangible asset with an indefinite life **is not amortized**. For example, assume that Double Clik, Inc. acquires a trademark that is used to distinguish a leading consumer product from other such products. The trademark is renewable every 10 years at minimal cost. After evaluating all relevant factors, the evidence indicates that this trademark product will generate net cash flows for an indefinite period of time. Therefore, it has an indefinite life.

Because of the potential effect on the financial statements, it is important for management to review whether events and circumstances continue to support the assessment of an indefinite life. This is required every accounting period. If the useful life is later considered to be limited instead of indefinite, the change is considered as a change in estimate and past results are not affected. Such an assessment may also indicate that the asset's carrying amount is impaired. The accounting treatment for impairment is discussed later in this chapter.

Specific Intangibles

Objective 6

Identify and explain the accounting for specific types of intangible assets.

The many different types of intangibles are sometimes classified into the following five major categories:[14]

1. Marketing-related intangible assets

2. Customer-related intangible assets

3. Artistic-related intangible assets

4. Contract-based intangible assets

5. Technology-based intangible assets

Marketing-Related Intangible Assets

Marketing-related intangible assets are used mainly in the marketing or promotion of products or services and derive their value from the contractual or legal rights that they contain. Examples are trademarks or trade names, newspaper mastheads, Internet domain names, and non-competition agreements.

Law

A very common form of marketing-related intangible asset is a trademark. A **trademark** or **trade name** is a word, symbol, or design, or combination of these, that is used to distinguish the goods or services of one person or entity from those of others. The terms **brand** and **brand name** are similar but often refer to a group of assets such as a trade name and its related formulas, recipes, and technology. The right to use a trademark, trade name, or brand name in Canada is granted by Industry Canada and the registration system is administered by its Trade-marks Office.[15] In order to obtain and maintain this right, the owner must have made prior and continuing use of it. Trade names like Kraft Dinner, Pepsi-Cola, and Kleenex, and brand names such as President's Choice and Canadian Tire create immediate product recognition in our minds, which makes them more marketable. As indicated in this chapter's opening story, company names themselves may have value and characteristics that companies are willing to spend money on to develop.[16]

If a mark or name is **purchased,** its capitalizable cost is the purchase price and other direct costs of acquisition. If it is **developed** by the enterprise itself and its future benefits to the company are reasonably assured, the costs may be capitalized, but only from the point in time when all six of the required capitalization criteria are met in its development phase. These costs may include lawyers' fees, registration fees, design costs, consulting fees, successful legal defence costs, expenditures related to securing the mark or name, and other direct development costs. When a trademark, trade name, or brand name's total cost is insignificant or all six capitalization criteria have not been met, the costs are expensed.

What Do the Numbers Mean?

Hoping to promote the management of brands in the same financially robust way as other long-term investments, Brand Finance plc published a report entitled the Brand Finance Global 500 in 2011. The study uses a "royalty relief approach" to value the brands of major companies; that is, the authors determine how much a company would have to pay to license the brand from a third party, and the brand's value is the present value of that hypothetical stream of payments.

Real World Emphasis

Google, **Microsoft**, and **Walmart** were ranked as having the three most valuable brands, with Britain's **Vodaphone** being the only non–U.S.-based company in the top 10. In spite of the continued upheaval in global financial services in the 2008 to 2011 period, the most valuable Canadian brand, according to this report, belonged to the **Royal Bank of Canada**, with an estimated worth of almost $7.1 billion. Several other major Canadian banks were also included in the top 500 world brands, together with other well-known companies/brands like **Bombardier**, **Loblaws**, **Research In Motion**'s BlackBerry, Bell Canada, and **Rogers Communications**. The RBC brand, however, does not appear as an asset on the Royal Bank's balance sheet. Why not? Brand value is a function of marketing, advertising, and public relations spending, including customer loyalty and retention programs, which all result in an increased volume of business, retail sales, and shipments. This type of cost is expensed as it is incurred because it cannot be directly related to future benefits.

In an earlier report, Brand Finance contended that "long-term investment decisions about future promotional expenditures, and the host of other activities that combine to build brand value" are better made when management can articulate the arguments in financial terms, as is done for most other investments.

Source: Brand Finance website, http://www.brandfinance.com. Antonia Oprita, "And the World's Most Valuable Brand Is...", CNBC, March 21, 2011; Russ Martin, "RBC Tops Brand Finance List Again," Marketing magazine, August 9, 2012.

Trademark registrations in Canada last for 15 years, and are renewable at a reasonable cost. Although the legal life of such assets **may be unlimited**, in practice they may only provide benefits to the enterprise over a **finite** period. Trademarks can, however, be determined to provide benefits to an enterprise indefinitely. A brand such as Coca-Cola, worth billions of dollars, may reasonably be expected to have an indefinite useful life. In this case, the intangible asset is not amortized.

Customer-Related Intangible Assets

Customer-related intangible assets result from interactions with outside parties and their value may be derived from legal-contractual rights, or because they are separable. Examples include customer lists, order or production backlogs, and customer contracts or non-contractual relationships.

To illustrate, assume that We-Market Inc. acquires the customer list of a large newspaper for $6 million on January 1, 2014. The customer list is a database that includes customer names, contact information, order history, and demographic information.

We-Market expects to benefit from the information on the acquired list for 10 years, and it believes that these benefits will be spread evenly over the 10 years. In this case, assume the customer list is a limited-life intangible that should be amortized on a straight-line basis. The customer list would typically have a limited life due to factors such as people moving into/from the area and competition (from other newspapers and other media sources).

The entries to record the purchase of the customer list and its amortization at the end of each year are as follows:

A = L + SE
0   0   0
Cash flows: ↓ 6,000,000 outflow

January 1, 2014		
Intangible Assets—Customer List	6,000,000	
Cash		6,000,000

A   = L +   SE
−600,000   −600,000

Cash flows: No effect

December 31, 2014 through December 31, 2023		
Amortization Expense	600,000	
Accumulated Amortization—Customer List		600,000

This example assumes that the customer list has no residual value. But what if We-Market determines that it can sell the list for $60,000 to another company at the end of 10 years? In that case, the residual value is subtracted from the cost in order to determine the amortizable amount.

Artistic-Related Intangible Assets

Law

Artistic-related intangible assets involve ownership rights to plays, literary works, musical works, pictures, photographs, and video and audiovisual material. These ownership rights are protected by copyrights and have value because of the legal-contractual nature of the rights.

A **copyright** is the exclusive right to copy a creative work or allow someone else to do so. It is a federally granted right that applies to all original literary, dramatic, musical, and artistic works, whatever the mode or form of expression. A copyright is acquired automatically when an original work is created, but it can also be registered with the federal Copyright Office. The right is granted for the life of the creator plus 50 years, and gives the owner or heirs the exclusive right to reproduce, sell, communicate, or translate an artistic or published work. Copyrights are not renewable. Like trade names, they may be assigned or sold to other individuals.[17] The costs of acquiring and defending a copyright may be capitalized, but research costs that are associated with them are expensed as they are incurred.

Generally, the copyright's useful life is shorter than its legal life. Its useful life depends on the unique facts and circumstances of each case. Consumer habits, market trends, and prior experience all play a part. Because it is so difficult to determine how many periods will benefit from a copyright, companies often choose to write these costs off over a fairly short period of time.

What Do the Numbers Mean?

Copyrights can be valuable. When Michael Jackson died in mid-2009, he was in dire financial trouble. However, he did have one asset that was extremely valuable: a 50% interest in the **Sony Corp./ATV Music Publishing** joint venture set up in 1995. The partnership owns copyrights to the lyrics and music of tens of thousands of songs by such artists as the Beatles, Roy Orbison, Hank Williams, and Jimi Hendrix. The venture is said to have total revenues of approximately $350 million and be worth in excess of $1 billion! Altogether, Sony/ATV Music Publishing owns or administers in excess of 750,000 copyrights for the who's who in the music industry.

Contract-Based Intangible Assets

Contract-based intangible assets are the value of rights that come from contractual arrangements. Examples are licensing arrangements, lease agreements, construction

Law

permits, broadcast rights, and service or supply contracts. A very common form of contract-based intangible asset is a franchise.

When you drive down the street in an automobile purchased from a Toyota dealer, fill your tank at the corner Petro-Canada station, grab a coffee at Tim Hortons, eat lunch at McDonald's, cool off with a Baskin-Robbins cone, work at a Coca-Cola bottling plant, live in a home purchased through a Royal LePage real estate broker, or vacation at a Holiday Inn resort, you are dealing with franchises. A **franchise** is a contractual arrangement under which the franchisor grants the franchisee the right to sell certain products or services, to use certain trademarks, trade names, or brands, or to perform certain functions, usually within a designated geographic area. **Licensing agreements** work in a similar way.

After having developed a unique concept or product, the franchisor protects it through a patent, copyright, trademark, or trade name. The franchisee then acquires the right to take advantage of the franchisor's idea or product by signing a franchise agreement. Another type of franchise is the arrangement that is commonly entered into by a municipality or other government body and a business enterprise that uses public property. In this case, a privately owned enterprise is given permission to use public property in performing its services. Examples are the use of public waterways for a ferry service, the use of public land for telephone or electric lines, the use of city streets for a bus line, or the use of the airwaves for radio or TV broadcasting. Such operating rights are frequently referred to as **licences** or **permits**, and are obtained through agreements with government departments or agencies.

Franchises and licences may be granted for a definite period of time, for an indefinite period of time, or in perpetuity. The enterprise that acquires the franchise or licence recognizes an intangible asset account titled either Franchise or Licence on its books as soon as there are costs (such as a lump-sum payment in advance or legal fees and other expenditures) that are identified with the acquisition of the operating right. The cost of a franchise or licence **with a limited life** is amortized over the lesser of its legal or useful life. A franchise **with an indefinite life, or a perpetual franchise**, is amortized if its **useful life** is deemed to be limited. Otherwise, it is not amortized.

Annual franchise fees paid under a franchise agreement are entered as operating expenses in the period in which they are incurred. They do not represent an asset to the enterprise since they do not relate to future rights.

Another contract-related intangible asset is a **favourable lease**. A **lease** or **leasehold** is a contractual understanding between a lessor (property owner) and a lessee (property renter) that grants the lessee the right to use specific property, owned by the lessor, for a certain period of time in return for specific, usually periodic, cash payments. A lease contract is an intangible asset to the extent that the terms are more favourable than the usual market terms for such an arrangement. It could be an asset to the lessor or the lessee.[18]

Technology-Based Intangible Assets

Law

Technology-based intangible assets relate to innovations or technological advances. Examples include Nortel's patents that were sold in 2011 (as discussed above) and patented technology and trade secrets that are granted by the federal government's Patent Office. Patents are granted for products and processes that are new, workable, and ingenious. A **patent** gives the holder the right to exclude others from making, selling, or using a product or process for a period of 20 years from the date the patent application is filed with the Patent Office. Fortunes can be made by holding patents, as companies such as Research In Motion, Bombardier, **IMAX**, **Polaroid**, and **Xerox** can attest.[19]

If a patent is purchased from an inventor or other owner, the purchase price represents its cost. Other costs that are incurred in connection with securing a patent, including legal fees and unrecovered costs of a successful lawsuit to protect the patent, are capitalized as part of the patent cost. Most research and development costs incurred that result in an internally generated patent are expensed. Only directly attributable costs incurred in the development phase after the six capitalization criteria are met can be included as part of the asset's cost. For this reason, most research and development costs related to developing a product, process, or idea that is subsequently patented are expensed as they are incurred.

The cost of a patent is amortized over its legal life or its useful life to the entity, whichever is shorter. If a patent is owned from the date it is granted, and it is expected to be useful during its entire legal life, it is amortized over 20 years. If it is expected to be useful for a shorter period, its cost is amortized to expense over that shorter period. Changing demand, new inventions replacing old ones, inadequacy, and other factors often limit the useful life of a patent to less than its legal life. For example, the useful life of patents in the pharmaceutical industry is often less than the legal life because of the testing and approval period that follows their issuance. A typical drug patent has five to 11 years knocked off its 20-year legal life. Why? A drug manufacturer spends one to four years on animal tests, four to six years on human tests, and two to three years for government agencies to review the tests—all after the patent is issued but before the product goes on the pharmacist's shelves.

Legal fees and other costs that are associated with a successful defence of a patent are capitalized as part of the asset's cost because lawsuits establish the patent holder's legal rights. Such costs are amortized along with other acquisition costs over the remaining useful life of the patent.

Patent amortization follows a pattern that is consistent with the benefits that are received, if that pattern can be reliably determined. This could be based on time or on units produced. To illustrate, assume that on January 1, 2014, Harcott Ltd. either pays $180,000 to acquire a patent or incurs $180,000 in legal costs to successfully defend an internally developed patent. Further, assume that the patent has a remaining useful life of 12 years and is amortized on a straight-line basis. The entries to record the $180,000 expenditure on January 1, 2014, and the amortization at the end of each year are as follows:

A = L + SE
0   0   0

Cash flows: ↓ 180,000 outflow

A   = L +   SE
−15,000   −15,000

Cash flows: No effect

January 1, 2014		
Intangible Assets—Patents	180,000	
Cash		180,000
December 31, 2014		
Amortization Expense	15,000	
Accumulated Amortization—Patents		15,000

Although a patent's useful life may be limited by its legal life, small modifications or additions may lead to a new patent and an extension of the life of the old patent.[20] In this case, the entity can apply the unamortized costs of the old patent to the new patent if the new patent provides essentially the same benefits. Alternatively, if a patent's value is reduced because, for example, demand drops for the product, the asset is tested for impairment.[21]

Coca-Cola has managed to keep the recipe for the world's best-selling soft drink under wraps for more than 100 years. How has it done so? The company offers almost no information about its lifeblood. The only written copy of the formula is in a vault in the company's own museum in Atlanta, Georgia. This handwritten sheet is not available to anyone except by vote of the Coca-Cola board of directors.

Why is science unable to offer some clues? Coke contains 17 to 18 ingredients. These include the usual caramel colour and corn syrup, as well as a blend of oils known as 7X—rumoured to be a mix of orange, lemon, cinnamon, and others. Distilling natural products like these is complicated since they are made of thousands of compounds. Although the original formula contained trace amounts of cocaine, this is one ingredient that you will not find in today's Coke. When was it removed? That is a secret, too. Some experts indicate that the power of this formula and related brand image account for almost U.S. $65-$75 billion, accounting for a significant portion of the company's market capitalization.

What Do the Numbers Mean?

Real World Emphasis

Sources: Reed Tucker, "How Has Coke's Formula Stayed a Secret?" *Fortune*, July 24, 2000, p. 42; David Kiley, "Best Global Brands," *Business Week*, August 6, 2007, p. 59; and Gavin Allen, "Bad News Pepsi! After 90 Years Coca-Cola's Secret Recipe Is Finally Out of the Bank Vault for Museum Display... But Rivals Still Won't Get a Peek at the Ingredients," *The Daily Mail*, December 9, 2011.

Another common technology-based intangible relates to **computer software costs**, either for internal use or for sale as a product. Costs that are incurred in the development of software as a potential product **for sale** or those directly attributable to the development, betterment, or acquisition of computer software **for internal use** are covered by the same capitalization criteria required for other intangible assets.

IMPAIRMENT AND DERECOGNITION

Objective 7
Explain and account for impairment of limited-life and indefinite-life intangible assets.

Similar to property, plant, and equipment, the carrying amounts of intangible assets and goodwill have to be reviewed to ensure that they do not exceed the economic benefits the assets are expected to provide in the future. If an item is determined to be **impaired**, its carrying amount will have to be written down and an impairment loss recognized.

Impairment of Limited-Life Intangibles

The same impairment models and standards that apply to **long-lived tangible assets** also apply to **limited-life intangibles**.[22] As indicated in Chapter 11, under ASPE, long-lived assets that a company intends to hold and use are assessed for potential impairment whenever events and circumstances indicate the carrying value may not be recoverable. Under IFRS, these assets are **assessed for impairment** at the end of each reporting period.

The internal and external sources of information that may indicate an intangible asset is impaired are the same factors described in Illustration 11-14 in Chapter 11 for items of property, plant, and equipment. Of course, evidence of physical damage would not apply in the assessment of an intangible asset! If an assessment indicates there may be impairment, the asset is formally tested by applying the appropriate impairment model.

A summary of the two models and how they are applied is provided in Illustration 12-5. Remember that the **cost recovery impairment model** is used for **ASPE**, and the **rational entity impairment model** is used for **IFRS**. A review of the section "Impairment—Recognition and Measurement Models" in Chapter 11 might help to reinforce your understanding of the details of each model.

Illustration 12-5

Summary of Impairment Models for Limited-Life Intangible Assets

Cost Recovery Impairment Model	
Concept	Assumes asset will continue to be used; it is impaired only if the asset's carrying amount is not recoverable from the future undiscounted cash flows from use and eventual sale.
Recoverability test	If undiscounted future cash flows ≥ carrying amount, asset is not impaired.
	If undiscounted future cash flows < carrying amount, asset is impaired. Proceed to calculate impairment loss.
Impairment loss	Asset's carrying amount − fair value = impairment loss; fair value is a discounted cash flow, market-based concept.
Entry to record loss	Loss on Impairment $XX Accumulated Impairment Losses $XX
Subsequent amortization	Review carrying amount to be amortized, useful life, and pattern of amortization and determine new periodic rate.
Reversal of impairment loss	Reversal not permitted. The fair value to which the asset is written down becomes the asset's new cost basis.
If no single-asset identifiable cash flows	Combine with other assets into an asset group, test for impairment, and, if impaired, calculate impairment loss using same approach as for an individual asset. Allocate loss only to long-lived assets, based on their relative carrying amounts, within limits.

(continued)

Illustration 12-5

Summary of Impairment Models for Limited-Life Intangible Assets (continued)

Rational Entity Impairment Model	
Concept	Assumes management will use the asset or dispose of it currently, whichever results in a higher return to the entity. It is impaired only if its carrying amount is not recoverable from the more profitable/less costly of the two options.
Recoverability test	No separate test.
Impairment loss	Calculate recoverable amount = **higher of** value in use **and** fair value less costs to sell, both of which are discounted cash flow concepts.
	If recoverable amount ≥ carrying amount, no impairment loss.
	If recoverable amount < carrying amount, impairment loss = the difference.
Entry to record loss under cost model	Loss on Impairment $XX Accumulated Impairment Losses $XX
Subsequent amortization	Review carrying amount to be amortized, useful life, and pattern of amortization and determine new periodic rate.
Reversal of impairment loss	Reversal of loss is required if estimates underlying recoverable amount have changed. Reversal amount is limited.
If no single-asset identifiable cash flows	Combine with other assets into a cash-generating group and calculate impairment loss using same approach as for an individual asset. Allocate loss to assets based on their relative carrying amounts, within limits.

Impairment of Indefinite-Life Intangibles

Accounting for the impairment of intangible assets with an **indefinite life** is a little different than explained above for limited-life intangibles. These differences and the reasons for them are discussed below.

ASPE

An intangible asset with an indefinite life still needs to be tested for impairment only when events and circumstances indicate there might be impairment, but now the test is different. The impairment test for an indefinite-life asset is a **fair value test**. This test compares the **fair value** of the intangible asset with the asset's carrying amount. If its fair value is less than the carrying amount, an impairment loss equal to the difference is recognized.

Why is there a different standard for indefinite-life intangibles? This one-step test is used because it would be relatively easy for many indefinite-life assets to meet the recoverability test. That is, the undiscounted cash flows would extend many years into the future and the total cash to be recovered tends to add up to a large sum. However, the dollars received in periods far into the future have a much lower value today. **As a result, the separate recoverability test is not used**, and the test compares the carrying amount directly with the asset's fair value—a discounted cash flow concept.

To illustrate, assume that Space Corp. (SC) purchases a broadcast licence for $1,150,000, and that the licence is renewable every seven years if the company provides appropriate service and does not violate the rules and regulations of the Canadian Radio-television and Telecommunications Commission (CRTC). The licence is then renewed with the CRTC twice at a minimal cost, and because cash flows are expected to last indefinitely, the licence is reported as an indefinite-life intangible asset. Assume that SC is beginning to question whether the asset might be impaired because advertising revenues are expected to drop with changing demographics in the area covered by the licence. The following information has been gathered about the benefits of the licence:

| Undiscounted future net cash flows expected from its use | $1,800,000 |
| Discounted future net cash flows, or fair value | $ 950,000 |

Is the licence impaired? Yes. Because the carrying amount of $1,150,000 is more than its fair value of $950,000, an impairment loss of $1,150,000 – $950,000 = $200,000 is indicated.

Space Corp. may either set up and credit an accumulated impairment loss account for the licence or credit the asset account itself. The licence is now reported at a net amount of $950,000, and this is its new "cost" for subsequent accounting.

IFRS

There is only a minor difference in the IFRS standard for impairment for indefinite-life intangibles than for those with limited lives. Assets with an indefinite life are **tested for impairment** by comparing their carrying amount and recoverable value **on an annual basis, whether or not there is any indication of impairment**. Why a stronger standard for these assets? The answer lies in the fact that no expense is being charged against income for such assets on a regular basis. For this reason, the assumption of a continuing recoverable value in excess of book value needs to be regularly tested.

Derecognition

An intangible asset is derecognized when it is disposed of or when its continuing use or disposal is not expected to generate any further economic benefits. Similar to property, plant, and equipment assets, a gain or loss is recognized at this time, equal to the difference between the asset's carrying amount and the proceeds on disposal, if any. The gain or loss on disposal is recognized in income in the period of disposal.

GOODWILL

Objective 8
Explain the concept of goodwill and how it is measured and accounted for after acquisition.

While companies capitalize certain costs that are incurred to develop identifiable assets such as patents and copyrights, the amounts that are capitalized are generally not significant. Material amounts of intangible assets are recorded, however, when companies purchase intangible assets. When another business is being purchased in a business combination, goodwill is also often recognized as an asset. In fact, this is the only time that goodwill is ever recognized.

Definition of Goodwill

In a business combination where **one company purchases 100% of another business**, the fair value of what is given up by the acquiring entity (the **acquirer**) is allocated to the various assets and liabilities it receives.[23] All identifiable assets acquired and liabilities assumed (the **identifiable net assets**) are recognized at their fair values at the acquisition date. The difference between the fair value of the consideration transferred to acquire the business and the fair value amounts assigned to the identifiable net assets is the amount recognized as goodwill. This is shown in Illustration 12-6.

Illustration 12-6

Measurement of Goodwill

Fair value of consideration transferred—any one or a combination of cash, other assets, notes payable at a later date, common or preferred shares, or other equity instruments, or contingent consideration

− **Fair value of all identifiable assets acquired and liabilities assumed**, whether or not previously recognized by the acquired entity

= **GOODWILL**

Goodwill is "an asset representing the future economic benefits arising from other assets acquired in a business combination that are not individually identified and separately recognized."[24] As you can tell from Illustration 12-6, it is an unidentified excess or residual amount, and it can only be calculated in relation to the business as a whole. The only way it can be sold is to sell the business.

Recognition and Measurement of Goodwill

Recognition of Internally Generated Goodwill

Goodwill that is generated internally is not capitalized in the accounts. Measuring the components of internally generated goodwill is simply too complex, and associating costs incurred with future benefits is too difficult. In fact, the future benefits of goodwill may have no relationship to the costs that were incurred to develop it. To add to the complexity, goodwill may even exist when there have been no specific expenditures to develop it. In addition, because no transaction has taken place with outside parties, a great deal of subjectivity—even misrepresentation—might be involved in trying to measure it.

Purchased Goodwill

As previously indicated, goodwill is recognized only when a business combination occurs, because the value of goodwill cannot be separated from a business as a whole. The problem of determining the proper values to assign to identifiable intangible assets in a business combination is complex because of the many different types of intangibles that might be acquired. Because goodwill is a residual amount, every dollar that is assigned to other assets, including identifiable intangible assets, is one less dollar assigned to goodwill.

To illustrate, assume that Multi-Diversified, Inc. decides that it needs a parts division to supplement its existing tractor distributorship. The president of Multi-Diversified is interested in buying Tractorling Ltd., a small company near Edmonton that has an established reputation and is looking to sell its business. Illustration 12-7 shows Tractorling's current statement of financial position.

Illustration 12-7

Tractorling Ltd. Statement of Financial Position

TRACTORLING LTD.
Statement of Financial Position
December 31, 2014

Assets		Liabilities and equity	
Cash	$ 25,000	Current liabilities	$ 55,000
Accounts Receivable	35,000	Share capital	100,000
Inventories	42,000	Retained earnings	100,000
Property, plant, and equipment (net)	153,000		
Total assets	$255,000	Total liabilities and equity	$255,000

After considerable negotiation, Tractorling Ltd.'s shareholders decide to accept Multi-Diversified's offer of $400,000. The two companies might agree on a $400,000 cash payment, or $400,000 in value of Multi-Diversified's shares, or on a number of other forms of consideration. How should goodwill, if any, be measured?

The answer is not obvious. The fair values of Tractorling's identifiable assets and liabilities are not disclosed in its cost-based statement of financial position. It is likely, though, that as the negotiations progressed, Multi-Diversified had a detailed investigation done of Tractorling's underlying assets to determine their fair values. Such an investigation may be done through a purchase audit by Multi-Diversified's auditors, or an independent appraisal from some other source. Illustration 12-8 shows the results.

Illustration 12-8

Fair Values of Tractorling Ltd.'s Identifiable Net Assets

Fair Values, December 31, 2014	
Cash	$ 25,000
Accounts Receivable	35,000
Inventories	62,000
Property, plant, and equipment (net)	265,000
Patents	18,000
Liabilities	(55,000)
Fair value of identifiable net assets	$350,000

Differences between the current fair value and carrying amount are more common among long-term assets, although there can also be significant differences in the current asset category. Cash is obviously not a problem in terms of its value. Receivables are normally fairly close to their current valuation, although adjustments do sometimes need to be made because of inadequate bad debt provisions. The fair values of liabilities also are usually close to their recorded book values. However, if interest rates have changed since long-term liabilities were issued, their current value determined using current interest rates may be quite different from their carrying amount. A careful analysis must also be done to ensure that there are no unrecorded liabilities.

Returning to our example, the $20,000 difference between the fair value and carrying amount of Tractorling's inventories ($62,000 – $42,000) could be due to several factors. One explanation might be that Tractorling acquired significant inventories when the prices were lower and uses specific identification or an average cost valuation, in which ending inventory is made up of inventory at older costs.

In many cases, the values of long-lived assets such as property, plant, and equipment and intangibles may have increased substantially over the years. This difference could be due to inaccurate estimates of useful lives, continual expensing of small expenditures (say, amounts less than $500), or substantial increases in replacement costs. Alternatively, there may be assets that have not been recognized in the company's books. In Tractorling's case, land was acquired many years ago and its fair value has increased significantly, and internally developed patents have not been recognized in the accounts, yet they have a fair value of $18,000.

Since the investigation indicates that the fair value of the identifiable net assets is $350,000, why would Multi-Diversified pay $400,000? Tractorling might point to the company's established reputation, good credit rating, top management team, well-trained employees, and so on as factors that make the value of the business as a whole greater than $350,000. Multi-Diversified places a premium on the future earning power of these attributes as well as the company's current basic asset structure. At this point in the negotiations, Tractorling's total fair value, and price, may be due to many factors; the most important may be sheer skill at the bargaining table.

Multi-Diversified labels the difference between the fair value of the consideration paid of $400,000 and the fair value of the identifiable net assets of $350,000 as goodwill.

Goodwill is viewed as the unidentifiable values plus the value of the identifiable intangibles that do not meet the criteria for separate recognition. The procedure for valuation shown in Illustration 12-9 is referred to as a master valuation approach, because goodwill is assumed to cover all the values that cannot be specifically associated with any identifiable tangible or intangible asset. Note that this method of accounting for a business combination is a fair value approach rather than one based on the cost of the acquisition and cost allocation. For example, acquisition-related costs associated with a business combination are expensed as incurred and not capitalized as they would be in a cost-based system.

Fair value of consideration transferred:		$400,000
Fair value of identifiable net assets:		
Cash	$ 25,000	
Accounts Receivable	35,000	
Inventories	62,000	
Property, plant, and equipment	265,000	
Patents	18,000	
Liabilities	(55,000)	350,000
Value assigned to goodwill:		$ 50,000

Illustration 12-9

Determination of Goodwill—Master Valuation Approach

Multi-Diversified's entry to record the purchase of Tractorling's net assets, assuming the consideration is $400,000 cash, is as follows:[25]

Cash	25,000	
Accounts Receivable	35,000	
Inventory	62,000	
Property, Plant, and Equipment	265,000	
Intangible Assets—Patents	18,000	
Goodwill	50,000	
Liabilities		55,000
Cash		400,000

A　=　L　+　SE
+55,000　　+55,000

Cash flows: ↓ 375,000 outflow

Bargain Purchase

A **bargain purchase**, resulting in what is sometimes called **negative goodwill**, arises when the total of the fair value of the identifiable net assets acquired is higher than the fair value of the consideration transferred for those net assets. This situation is a result of market imperfection (a poor decision by the seller) because the seller would be better off to sell the assets individually than in total. However, situations do occur when the value of what is given up is less than the value of the identifiable net assets that are acquired, and this requires accounting for a goodwill "credit."

How should this credit be handled in the accounts? Should it be taken to Retained Earnings directly, to Other Comprehensive Income, to net income in the year of purchase, or amortized to income over a reasonable future period? The accounting standards over the past 40 years or so have taken a variety of approaches to this "bonus," which shows the difficulty there has been in coming to terms with its conceptual nature.

Current standards require the excess to be recognized **as a gain in net income** in the same period that the combination takes place. However, this cannot be done without a thorough reassessment of all the variables, values, and measurement procedures used that resulted in this gain. If a gain still results from the re-examination, then it is recognized in income. While some critics do not agree with the recognition of a gain **on the acquisition of assets**, this treatment is not applied lightly and appears to be a practical approach to a situation that rarely occurs.

Valuation after Acquisition

Once goodwill has been recognized in the accounts, how should it be treated in subsequent periods? Three basic approaches have been suggested:

1. **Charge goodwill immediately to expense.** Supporters of this approach justify an immediate writeoff because the accounting for goodwill is then consistent whether purchased or created internally. Goodwill created internally is not recognized as an asset. Perhaps the best rationale for charging goodwill against income directly is that identifying the periods over which the future benefits are to be received is so difficult that the result is purely arbitrary.

2. **Amortize goodwill over its useful life.** Others believe that goodwill has value when it is acquired, but that its value eventually disappears. Therefore the asset should be charged to expense over the periods that are affected. To the extent that goodwill represents a wasting asset, this method provides a better matching of the costs of the benefits to revenues than other methods, even though the useful life may be difficult to determine.

3. **Retain goodwill indefinitely unless a reduction in value occurs.** Others believe that goodwill can have an indefinite life and should be kept as an asset until a decline in value occurs. Some form of goodwill should always be an asset because the current costs to maintain or enhance the purchased goodwill are being expensed. Also, unless there is strong evidence that a decline in its value has occurred, a writeoff of goodwill is arbitrary and leads to distortions in net income.

Not so long ago, companies were required to amortize goodwill over a period no longer than 40 years. However, goodwill acquired in a business combination **is now considered to have an indefinite life and is no longer amortized**. Although goodwill may decrease over time, predicting the actual life of goodwill and an appropriate pattern of amortization is extremely difficult. Therefore, it is carried on the statement of financial position at the amount originally recognized in the combination less any subsequent impairment losses. **Income statements are not charged with any amounts paid for the goodwill until the asset is considered impaired.**

What Do the Numbers Mean?

Real World Emphasis

The method of accounting for goodwill can have a significant effect on a company's income statement because goodwill is often a major asset on its statement of financial position. **Quebecor Inc.,** for example, reported income of $91.9 million in a recent year. **If the accounting standard for goodwill had not changed,** the company would have had an additional $123.3 million of amortization expense (after tax and noncontrolling interest) related to goodwill. It would have reported a loss of $31.4 million. In addition, because companies were also required to review their existing goodwill and recognize any impairment as an adjustment to their opening balance of retained earnings when the new standard was first applied, Quebecor recognized a goodwill impairment loss of $2.163 billion—a charge that bypassed the income statement completely, and went straight against retained earnings!

Impairment of Goodwill

Goodwill is not an identifiable asset and cannot generate cash flows independently of other assets. Because it can be acquired only in combination with other assets making up a business, it has to be assigned to a reporting or cash-generating unit (CGU) in order to be tested for impairment. Other than this specific feature that focuses on the reporting unit or cash-generating unit, impairment accounting for goodwill is similar to that for intangibles with an indefinite life. Applying the standards in this area can be complex, but a summary of the basic elements is provided in Illustration 12-10.

Illustration 12-10

Summary of Accounting for Impairment of Goodwill

	ASPE	IFRS
Apply impairment test...	...when events or changes in circumstances indicate	...annually, and whenever there is an indication that CGU may be impaired
At acquisition date, assign goodwill...	...to a reporting unit: an operating segment or one level below	...to cash-generating unit: lowest level where goodwill is monitored for management purposes, and no larger than an operating segment
There is an impairment loss...	...when carrying amount of reporting unit including goodwill > fair value of reporting unit. Loss = amount of excess	...when carrying amount of cash-generating unit including goodwill > recoverable amount. Loss = amount of excess. Recoverable amount is the higher of value in use and fair value less costs to sell
Impairment loss is allocated...	...to goodwill as a goodwill impairment loss; impairment test for other assets in group is done before goodwill impairment test	...first to goodwill, then remainder to other assets on a relative carrying amount (proportionate) basis
Goodwill impairment reversal...	...is not permitted	...is not permitted

To illustrate, assume that Coburg Corporation has three divisions. One division, Pritt Products, was purchased four years ago for $2 million and has been identified as a reporting unit. Unfortunately, it has experienced operating losses over the last three quarters and management is reviewing the reporting unit to determine whether there has been an impairment of goodwill. The carrying amounts of Pritt Division's net assets, including the associated goodwill of $900,000, are listed in Illustration 12-11.

Cash	$ 200,000
Receivables	300,000
Inventory	700,000
Property, plant, and equipment (net)	800,000
Goodwill	900,000
Less: Accounts and notes payable	(500,000)
Net assets, at carrying amounts	$2,400,000

Situation 1: The fair value of the Pritt Division reporting unit as a whole is estimated to be $2.8 million. Management determines that the unit's value in use is $2.9 million and that the company would incur direct costs of $50,000 if the unit were sold.

Under **ASPE**, the goodwill is not impaired. The asset group's $2.4-million book value is less than its fair value of $2.8 million. Under **IFRS**, goodwill is not considered impaired either. The recoverable amount of the unit is $2.9 million—the higher of its value in use ($2.9 million) and its fair value less costs to sell ($2.8 million – $50,000)—and this exceeds the unit's carrying amount of $2.4 million.

Situation 2: The fair value of the Pritt Division cash-generating unit as a whole is $1.9 million, its value in use is $2.1 million, and the direct cost of selling the unit is $50,000.

Under **ASPE,** an impairment loss is indicated:

Carrying amount of unit, including goodwil	$2,400,000
Fair value of unit	1,900,000
Goodwill impairment loss	$ 500,000

Under **IFRS**, an impairment loss is also indicated:

Carrying amount of unit, including goodwill		$2,400,000
Recoverable amount of unit: higher of		
Value in use	$2,100,000	
and		(2,100,000)
Fair value less costs to sell	$1,850,000	
Goodwill impairment loss		$ 300,000

The entries to record the loss under ASPE and IFRS are shown in Illustration 12-12.

Illustration 12-12

Entry to Record Impairment of Goodwill under ASPE and IFRS

	ASPE		IFRS	
Loss on Impairment (Goodwill)	500,000		300,000	
Accumulated Impairment		500,000		300,000
Losses (Goodwill)				

Because there is a requirement to report the gross amount of goodwill and accumulated impairment losses at the end of the period, the Accumulated Impairment Losses account is credited instead of the Goodwill account so that the required information is retained. The Goodwill's net carrying amount is now $400,000 (that is, $900,000 − $500,000) under ASPE and $600,000 (that is, $900,000 − $300,000) under IFRS.

Illustration 12-13 summarizes the impairment tests for various intangible assets.

Illustration 12-13

Summary of Intangible Asset Impairment Tests

	Impairment Test	
Type of Asset	**ASPE**	**IFRS**
Limited-life intangible	Recoverability test; if failed, write down to fair value	Compare carrying amount with recoverable amount
Indefinite-life intangible	Compare carrying amount with fair value	Compare carrying amount with recoverable amount
Goodwill	Compare carrying amount of reporting unit with its fair value	Compare carrying amount of CGU with its recoverable amount

PRESENTATION, DISCLOSURE, AND ANALYSIS

Objective 9

Identify the types of disclosure requirements for intangible assets and goodwill and explain the issues in analyzing these assets.

Real World Emphasis

A recent survey indicates that the most common types of intangible assets reported are broadcast rights, publishing rights, trademarks, patents, licences, customer lists, non-competition agreements, franchises, and purchased R&D.[26] These, along with goodwill, have become an increasingly large proportion of companies' reported assets, making intangibles an important contributor to entity performance and financial position. For example, **Corus Entertainment Inc.**, a Canadian-based media and entertainment company, reported indefinite-life broadcast licences and goodwill at August 31, 2011, that amounted to 58.2% of its total assets. There were no write offs for impairment in 2010 or 2011. This represents a nice period of stability for these intangibles, compared to 2009 when the company recognized $175 million of impairment losses on these two classes of assets. This represented about 13% of their opening book value, with the impairment being due, in part, to an unprecedented double-digit decline in radio advertising revenues experienced by Corus in the third quarter of that year.

Presentation and Disclosure

Overview

While there are few required disclosures on the face of the statement of financial position and the statement of comprehensive income, a significant amount of information is required in the notes to the financial statements, particularly those prepared under IFRS. As seen in previous chapters, ASPE disclosures are considerably curtailed on the basis that most users of their financial statements can request additional information as needed. The goal of disclosure for publicly accountable entities is basically to allow readers to understand the significance of intangibles and goodwill to the operations of the business. To that end, this section summarizes some of the major disclosures required.

For each class of intangible asset, and separately for internally generated intangibles and other intangible assets, the following information is required:

- Whether their lives are indefinite or finite (limited), useful life, methods and rates of amortization, and the line where amortization is included on the statement of comprehensive income

- The carrying amount of intangible assets with an indefinite life, and the reasons supporting an assessment of an indefinite life

- A reconciliation of the opening and ending balances of their carrying amount and accumulated amortization and impairment losses, separately identifying each reason for an increase or decrease

- Impairment losses and reversals of impairment losses and where they are reported in the statement of comprehensive income

For each material impairment loss recognized or reversed in the period:

- The circumstances that led to its recognition, the amount recognized, the nature of the asset or cash-generating unit, and information about how the recoverable amount was determined

For each cash-generating unit or group of units that has a significant amount of goodwill or intangible assets with an indefinite life:

- How the unit's recoverable amount was determined, as well as assumptions underlying the calculation of the recoverable amount

For intangible assets measured using the revaluation model:

- Their carrying amount, the carrying amounts if the revaluation model had not been applied, the date of the revaluation, the amount of the associated revaluation surplus and changes in that account, and the methods and assumptions used in estimating fair values

This list identifies only some of the disclosures. The best source of the specific requirements is the standards themselves.

Illustration of Disclosures

Real World Emphasis

Excerpts from the financial statements of Corus Entertainment for its year ended August 31, 2011, are provided in Illustration 12-14. These disclosures are similar to ASPE, as Corus elected to adopt IFRS in its subsequent fiscal year. This Canadian company, reporting in millions of Canadian dollars, operates through two main lines of business: television and radio. Television networks include YTV, Treehouse, W Network, and HBO Canada.

Illustration 12-14

Selected Excerpts: Notes on Intangible Assets, Corus Entertainment

2. Significant accounting policies

The consolidated financial statements have been prepared by management in accordance with Canadian generally accepted accounting principles ("GAAP").

Intangible assets

Intangible assets represent rights acquired from third parties to utilize brand names, trademarks or branded materials exclusively in a licensed territory. The assets and liabilities related to these rights are recorded when the license period has begun and the cost of the rights is known or reasonably determinable. Long-term liabilities related to these rights are recorded at the net present value of future cash flows, using an appropriate discount rate. These costs are amortized over the term of the agreement. Intangible assets are carried at cost less accumulated amortization.

Program rights

Program rights represent contract rights acquired from third parties to broadcast television programs, feature films and radio programs. The assets and liabilities related to these rights are recorded when the license period has begun and all of the following conditions have been met: (i) the cost of the rights is known or reasonably determinable; (ii) the program material is accepted by the Company in accordance with the license agreement; and, (iii) the material is available to the Company for airing. Long-term liabilities related to these rights are recorded at the net present value of future cash flows, using an appropriate discount rate. These costs are amortized over the contracted exhibition period as the programs or feature films are aired. Program and film rights are carried at cost less accumulated amortization. If program rights, feature films or radio programs are not scheduled they are considered impaired and written off.

Amortization of program rights is included in direct cost of sales, general and administrative expenses and has been disclosed separately in the consolidated statements of cash flows.

Broadcast licenses and goodwill

The cost incurred in a business combination is allocated to the fair value of related identifiable tangible and intangible assets acquired. Historically, identifiable intangible assets acquired consist primarily of broadcast licenses. The excess of the cost of acquiring these businesses over the fair value of related net identifiable tangible and intangible assets acquired is allocated to goodwill.

Broadcast licenses are considered to have an indefinite life based on management's intent and ability to renew the licenses without substantial cost and without material modification of the existing terms and conditions of the license.

Broadcast licenses and goodwill are tested for impairment annually or more frequently if events or changes in circumstances indicate that they may be impaired. The Company has selected August 31 as the date it performs its annual impairment test.

Goodwill impairment is determined using a two-step process. The first step of the process is to compare the fair value of a reporting unit with its carrying amount, including goodwill. In performing the first step, the Company determines the fair value of a reporting unit by using various valuation techniques with the primary methods employed being a discounted cash flow ("DCF") analysis and a market-based approach. Determining fair value requires the exercise of significant judgments, including judgments about appropriate discount rates, perpetual growth rates, relevant comparable company earnings multiples and the amount and timing of expected future cash flows. The cash flows employed in the DCF analysis are based on the Company's budgets and business plans, and various growth rates have been assumed for years beyond the long-term business plan period. Discount rate assumptions are based on an assessment of the risks inherent in the future cash flows of the respective reporting units. In assessing the reasonableness of its determined fair values, the Company evaluates its results against other value indicators such as comparable company public trading values, research analyst estimates and values observed in private market transactions. If the fair value of a reporting unit exceeds its carrying amount, goodwill of the reporting unit is considered not to be impaired and the second step of the impairment test is not necessary. If the carrying amount of a reporting unit exceeds its fair value, the second step of the goodwill impairment test is required to be performed to measure the amount of impairment loss, if any. The second step of the goodwill impairment test compares the implied fair value of the reporting unit's goodwill with the carrying amount of that goodwill. The implied fair value of goodwill is determined in the same manner as the amount of goodwill recognized in a business combination. In other

(continued)

words, the estimated fair value of the reporting unit is allocated to all of the assets and liabilities of that unit (including any unrecognized intangible assets) as if the reporting unit had been acquired in a business combination and the fair value of the reporting unit was the purchase price paid. If the carrying amount of the reporting unit's goodwill exceeds the implied fair value of that goodwill, an impairment loss is recognized in an amount equal to that excess.

The impairment test for broadcast licenses consists of comparing the carrying amount of broadcast licenses to their fair values. If the carrying amount exceeds its fair value, an impairment charge is then recognized on the consolidated statements of income. The Company uses a direct method valuation approach known as the Greenfield Income Valuation method in determining fair value. Under this method, the Company projects the cash flows that would be generated by each of its units of accounting as if the unit of accounting were to commence operations in each of its markets at the beginning of the valuation period. This cash flow stream is discounted to arrive at a value for the broadcast license. The Company assumes the competitive situation that exists in each market remains unchanged, with the exception that its unit of accounting was just beginning operations. Major assumptions involved in this analysis include revenue growth rates, profit margin, duration and profile of the start-up period, estimated start-up costs and losses incurred during the build-up period, the risk-adjusted discount rate and terminal values. For its radio stations, the Company has determined the unit of accounting to be all of its stations in a local market. For its television operations, the Company has determined the unit of accounting to be each individual broadcast license.

7. Broadcast licenses and goodwill

Broadcast licenses and goodwill are tested for impairment annually as at August 31 or more frequently if events or changes in circumstances indicate that they may be impaired. At August 31, 2011, the Company performed its annual impairment test for fiscal 2011 and determined that there were no impairments for the year then ended.

The changes in the book value of goodwill, by segment, for the years ended August 31 were as follows:

2011	Opening	Acquisitions	Closing
Radio			
West	129,289	—	129,289
Ontario	103,992	—	103,992
Television			
Kids	143,547	—	143,547
Specialty and Pay	294,999	—	294,999
	671,827	—	671,827

2010	Opening	Acquisitions	Closing
Radio			
West	129,289	—	129,289
Ontario	103,992	—	103,992
Television			
Kids	143,547	—	143,547
Specialty and Pay	273,999	21,000	294,999
	650,827	21,000	671,827

During fiscal 2011, the Company disposed of goodwill in the amount of $23,202 that pertained to the disposal of the Quebec Radio segment (note 16).

The changes in the book value of broadcast licenses, by division, for the years ended August 31, were as follows:

(continued)

2011	Opening	Acquisitions	Disposals	Closing
Radio	**145,997**	—	—	**145,997**
Television	**395,251**	—	—	**395,251**
	541,248	—	—	**541,248**

2010	Opening	Acquisitions	Disposals	Closing
Radio	148,572	—	(2,575)	145,997
Television	372,251	23,000	—	395,251
	520,823	23,000	(2,575)	541,248

During fiscal 2011, the Company disposed of broadcast licenses in the amount of $40,918 that pertained to the disposal of the Quebec Radio Segment (note 16).

Goodwill and broadcast licenses are located primarily within Canada.

The goodwill and intangible asset disclosures in Illustration 12-15 are excerpts from the 2011 financial statements of the **Unilever Group**, an international conglomerate operating in about 100 countries around the world. You may be familiar with many of its brand names, such as Dove, Lipton, Hellmann's, Bertolli, and Knorr—just a few of its products in its broad-based markets. Unilever follows IFRS and reports in euros (€). Intangible assets and goodwill are significant investments to Unilever, which reported €1,009 million in operating costs relating to research and development in 2011!

Illustration 12-15

Excerpts from IFRS Disclosures, Unilever Group

9. Goodwill and Intangible Assets (Excerpts from Note 9)

Goodwill

Goodwill is initially recognised based on the accounting policy for business combinations, see note 21. Goodwill is subsequently measured at cost less amounts provided for impairment.

Goodwill acquired in a business combination is allocated to the Group's cash generating units, or groups of cash generating units, that are expected to benefit from the synergies of the combination. These might not always be precisely the same as the cash generating units that the assets or liabilities of the acquired business are assigned to. Each unit or group of units to which the goodwill is allocated represents the lowest level within the Group at which the goodwill is monitored for internal management purposes, and is not larger than an operating segment.

Intangible assets

Separately purchased intangible assets are initially measured at cost. On acquisition of new interests in group companies, Unilever recognises any specifically identifiable intangible assets separately from goodwill. Intangible assets are initially measured at fair value as at the date of acquisition.

Finite-lived intangible assets mainly comprise patented and non-patented technology, know-how and software. These assets are capitalised and amortised on a straight-line basis in the income statement over the period of their expected useful lives, or the period of legal rights if shorter. None of the amortisation periods exceeds ten years.

Indefinite-lived intangibles mainly comprise trademarks and brands. These assets are capitalised at cost but are not amortised. They are subject to a review for impairment annually, or more frequently if events or circumstances indicate this is necessary. Any impairment is charged to the income statement as it arises.

Research and development

Development expenditure is capitalised only if the costs can be reliably measured, future economic benefits are probable, the product is technically feasible and the Group has the intent and the resources to complete the project. Research expenditure is recognised in profit or loss as incurred.

(continued)

Illustration 12-15

Excerpts from IFRS Disclosures, Unilever Group (continued)

Movements during 2011	€ million Goodwill	€ million Indefinite-lived intangible assets	€ million Finite-lived intangible assets	€ million Software	€ million Total
Cost					
1 January 2011	**14,150**	**4,757**	**644**	**899**	**20,450**
Acquisitions of group companies	**1,677**	**1,935**	**15**	**5**	**3,632**
Disposals of group companies	**(4)**	**(263)**	—	—	**(267)**
Additions	—	**8**	**2**	**260**	**270**
Disposals	—	—	—	**(16)**	**(16)**
Currency retranslation	**106**	**172**	**2**	**4**	**284**
31 December 2011	**15,929**	**6,609**	**663**	**1,152**	**24,353**
Amortisation and impairment					
1 January 2011	**(1,007)**	**(235)**	**(540)**	**(435)**	**(2,217)**
Amortisation for the year	—	—	**(58)**	**(133)**	**(191)**
Disposals	—	—	—	**5**	**5**
Currency retranslation	**(26)**	**(10)**	**(3)**	**2**	**(37)**
31 December 2011	**(1,033)**	**(245)**	**(601)**	**(561)**	**(2,440)**
Net book value					
31 December 2011	**14,896**	**6,364**	**62**	**591**	**21,913**

There are no significant carrying amounts of goodwill and intangible assets that are allocated across multiple cash generating units (CGUs).

Impairment charges in the year

There were no material impairments in 2011, 2010 or 2009.

Significant CGUs

The goodwill and indefinite-lived intangible assets held in the regional Foods CGUs are considered significant in comparison to the total carrying amounts of goodwill and indefinite-lived intangible assets at 31 December 2011. No other CGUs are considered significant in this respect.The goodwill and indefinite-lived intangible assets held in the regional Foods CGUs are:

	€ billion 2011 Goodwill	€ billion 2011 Indefinite-lived intangibles	€ billion 2010 Goodwill	€ billion 2010 Indefinite-lived intangibles
Western Europe	5.2	1.4	5.2	1.4
The Americas	4.1	1.5	4.2	1.5
Asia Africa CEE	2.0	0.6	1.8	0.6

During 2011, the Group conducted an impairment review of the carrying value of these assets. Value in use has been calculated as the present value of projected future cash flows. A pre-tax discount rate of 7.4% was used.

For the regional Foods CGUs, the following key assumptions were used in the discounted cash flow projections:

	Western Europe	Americas	Asia Africa CEE
Longer-term sustainable growth rates	0.2%	1.4%	3.0%
Average near-term nominal growth rates	0.8%	2.9%	7.9%
Average operating margins	19-22%	18-20%	12-14%

The growth rates and margins used to estimate future performance are based on past performance and our experience of growth rates and margins achievable in our key markets.

(continued)

The projections covered a period of five years, as we believe this to be the most appropriate timescale over which to review and consider annual performances before applying a fixed terminal value multiple to the final year cash flows.

The growth rates used are consistent with our annual planning and strategic planning processes.

We have performed sensitivity analyses around the base assumptions and have concluded that no reasonable possible changes in key assumptions would cause the recoverable amount of the regional Foods CGUs to be less than the carrying value.

Analysis

Missing Values

The requirement that most research and development phase costs incurred for internally developed intangibles be expensed immediately is a conservative, practical solution that ensures consistency in practice and uniformity among companies. But the practice of immediately writing off expenditures that are made in the expectation of benefiting future periods cannot always be justified on the grounds that it is good accounting theory.

Since the 1990s, the conventional financial-accounting model has been increasingly criticized for its inability to capture many of the attributes that give a business value. In February 2012, for example, **Apple Inc.** had a total book value of approximately U.S. $80 billion, while its market capitalization (the market value of its outstanding shares) was almost U.S. $470 billion.[27] Why such a significant difference?

The answer is that financial accounting does not capture and report many of the assets that contribute to future cash flows, and this is seen by some critics as the greatest challenge facing the accounting profession today. Many of the missing values belong to unrecognized, internally developed intangible assets known as **knowledge assets** or **intellectual capital**. These include the value of key personnel (not only Tim Cook, the CEO successor to Steve Jobs, but the many creative and technologically proficient employees in general), the investment in products from research and development and their potential, organizational adaptability, customer retention, strategic direction, brands, flexible and innovative management, customer service capability, and effective advertising programs, to name only a few types of knowledge assets. When a company is not allowed to capitalize many of these expenditures, this removes from its statement of financial position what may be its most valuable assets.

These indicators of longer-term value that are created in an organization will ultimately result in realized values through future transactions and, therefore, are relevant information for financial statement readers. Companies increasingly disclose more of this "soft" information in annual reports outside the financial statements, in news releases, and in interviews with market analysts. While some observers believe that standard setters should work to ensure that more of these intangibles are captured on the statement of financial position, others believe that new frameworks for reporting performance need to be developed together with—or that they should even replace—the current financial reporting model.

Our conventional accounting model captures the results of past transactions. This has been considered a very significant benefit as it is what makes it possible to verify the reported measures and therefore add to the reliability of the financial statements. In most cases, the intellectual capital and knowledge assets identified above cannot be measured in financial terms with enough reliability to give them accounting recognition. Some cannot be included as assets because of the enterprise's inability to control access to the benefits. Investments that are made in employee education and development, for example, can walk out the door when employees leave the company to work elsewhere. Others argue that the amount of costs charged to expense in each accounting period is about the same whether there is immediate expensing or capitalization followed by amortization because most companies continuously invest in a variety of research, development, and other activities.

Others opposed to increased capitalization of costs point to the decline in market value of technology shares—in particular, from early 2000 to 2001. Microsoft, a key company in the high-tech-sector, lost over 60% of its value over this period, bringing it much closer to its book value. Some use this as an argument that the historical cost model still has much to recommend it! The "truth," of course, lies somewhere in between. While inflated market values are not reliable enough to support the recognition of previously unrecognized intangible asset value, the historical-cost, transactions-based model certainly fails to capture many of the things that lie at the heart of corporate value. Much research is being carried out in the search for solutions to the discrepancies between what gets reported as having value on the financial statements and what the capital markets perceive as having value and reflect in share prices.

Theory

Comparing Results

Real World Emphasis

When comparing the operating results of companies—either of one company over time or between companies—it is important to pay close attention not only to which set of GAAP each applies, but also to how deferred charges, intangible assets, and goodwill have been accounted for and how any changes in related accounting policies have been handled. This is important because the standards for intangibles have changed significantly in recent years and may continue to change. The Quebecor Inc. example earlier in the chapter showed the effect that one change in accounting principle had on the company's results. The "big bath" writedown that Quebecor took by writing down goodwill that it had previously reported as an asset means that these asset costs will never flow through the company's income statement, and future operating statements are freed from these costs.[28] Care has to be taken when calculating and interpreting any ratios that include earnings and asset numbers, especially when the results of different years are being compared.

IFRS/ASPE COMPARISON

A Comparison of IFRS and ASPE

Objective 10

Identify differences in accounting between ASPE and IFRS.

With a few specific exceptions, accounting for intangible assets and goodwill under IFRS and ASPE is very similar. Illustration 12-16 identifies the relevant standards that apply to intangible assets and goodwill for both and the areas of difference that exist.

	Accounting Standards for Private Enterprises (ASPE)—*CICA Handbook*, Part II, Sections 1582, 3063, 3064, 3475, and 3831	IFRS—IAS 23, 36, and 38; IFRS 3	References to Related Illustrations and Select Brief Exercises
Measurement at acquisition	Interest costs directly attributable to the acquisition, construction, or development of an intangible asset, once it meets the criteria to be capitalized, may be capitalized or expensed, depending on the entity's accounting policy.	Borrowing costs directly attributable to the acquisition, construction, or development of qualifying assets are capitalized.	BE12-3
	Costs associated with the development of internally generated intangible assets that meet the six specific conditions in the development stage may be capitalized or expensed, depending on the entity's accounting policy.	Costs associated with the development of internally generated intangible assets are capitalized when six specific conditions are met in the development stage.	BE12-9

(continued)

	Accounting Standards for Private Enterprises (ASPE)—*CICA Handbook*, Part II, Sections 1582, 3063, 3064, 3475, and 3831	IFRS—IAS 23, 36, and 38; IFRS 3	References to Related Illustrations and Select Brief Exercises
Measurement after acquisition	Intangible assets are accounted for according to the cost model.	Intangible assets are accounted for under the cost model or the revaluation model. The latter is used only when the asset has an active market fair value.	Illustration 12-3 and BE 12-15
Impairment of intangible assets	Test both limited and indefinite-life intangibles for potential impairment whenever events and changing circumstances indicate the carrying value may not be recoverable.	Assess limited-life intangible assets for potential impairment at the end of each reporting period; for those with an indefinite life, this includes calculating the (IFRS) recoverable amount and comparing it with book value.	Illustration 12-5
	For limited-life intangibles, apply the cost recovery impairment model.	For limited-life intangibles, apply the rational entity impairment model.	Illustrations 12-5 and 12-13 BE12-15, BE12-16 and BE12-17
	For indefinite-life intangibles, impairment test is comparison of carrying amount with asset's fair value; loss is equal to the difference when fair value is lower.	For indefinite-life intangibles, apply the rational entity impairment model.	Illustration 12-13 BE12-18
	Impairment losses are not reversed.	Impairment losses are reversed for economic changes.	
Impairment of goodwill	Similar to impairment of indefinite-life intangible assets. See also Illustration 12-10.	Similar to impairment of indefinite-life intangible assets, except that there is no reversal of an impairment loss for goodwill. See also Illustration 12-10.	Illustration 12-10, Illustration 12-12, and Illustration 12-13 BE12-20 and BE12-21
Disclosures	Basic disclosures are required about the balance of intangible assets and goodwill on the balance sheet with additional details by classes and whether or not they are amortized. Details explaining each impairment loss and where each is reported on the income statement are also required.	Significant disclosures are required including detailed reconciliations between opening and ending balances for each type of intangible and goodwill. Considerable information is also required whenever fair values are used to explain how they are determined, as well as background information about impairment losses on goodwill and intangibles.	Illustration 12-14 and Illustration 12-15

Illustration 12-16

IFRS and ASPE Comparison Chart

Looking Ahead

Whether recognized or not, intangible assets are an increasingly important aspect of what gives an entity value, and existing standards do not do a very good job of reporting these assets to users of the financial statements. Current standards significantly restrict the intangibles that can be recognized, and after acquisition only intangibles with fair values determined in an active market can use the revaluation model under IFRS. Also, there are inconsistent treatments of intangible assets developed internally and those acquired in a business combination, as well as for internally developed property, plant, and equipment assets.

The IASB considered a proposal for a joint project with the FASB relating to accounting for identifiable intangible assets, but in December 2007 the IASB decided not to add the project to its agenda. With so many other possible projects competing for time and resources, it is unlikely that there will be changes in the intangible asset standards in the short to medium term.

SUMMARY OF LEARNING OBJECTIVES

1 Understand the importance of intangible assets and goodwill from a business perspective.

We have an economy that is increasingly dominated by information and service providers, and their major assets are often intangible in nature. Identifying and measuring intangible assets tends to be difficult, and as a result many intangibles are not captured on companies' statements of financial position. However, intangible assets and goodwill remain critically important for companies, and are a key focus of standard setters in North America and internationally.

2 Define and describe the characteristics of intangible assets.

Intangible assets have three characteristics: (1) they are identifiable, (2) they lack physical substance, and (3) they are nonmonetary in nature.

3 Identify and apply the recognition and measurement requirements for purchased intangible assets.

A purchased intangible asset is recognized when it is probable that the entity will receive the expected future economic benefits and when its cost can be measured reliably. It is measured initially at cost. When several intangibles, or a combination of intangibles and other assets, are acquired in a business combination, the cost of each intangible asset is its fair value. When acquired in a business combination, the identifiable intangibles are recognized separately from the goodwill component.

4 Identify and apply the recognition and measurement requirements for internally developed intangible assets.

No costs are capitalized unless they meet the general recognition criteria concerning future benefits and measurability. Costs incurred in the research phase of developing an intangible asset internally are expensed. Costs incurred in the development phase of a project are also expensed unless the entity can demonstrate that it meets six stringent criteria. These criteria are designed to provide evidence that the asset is technically and financially feasible and that the company has the intent and ability to generate future economic benefits from it. Under

ASPE, entities have a choice whether to capitalize or expense costs that meet the six criteria.

5 Explain how intangible assets are accounted for after initial recognition.

Under ASPE, intangible assets are accounted for using the cost model, whereas IFRS also allows the revaluation model to be used if the asset's fair value is determined in an active market. This is not often used. An intangible with a finite or limited useful life is amortized over its useful life to the entity. Except in unusual and specific circumstances, the residual value is assumed to be zero. The amount to report for amortization expense should reflect the pattern in which the asset is consumed or used up if that pattern can be reliably determined. Otherwise a straight-line approach is used. An intangible with an indefinite life is not amortized until its life is determined to no longer be indefinite. All intangibles are tested for impairment.

6 Identify and explain the accounting for specific types of intangible assets.

Major types of intangibles include the following: (1) marketing-related intangibles that are used in the marketing or promotion of products or services, (2) customer-related intangibles that result from interactions with outside parties, (3) artistic-related intangibles that involve ownership rights to such items as plays and literary works, (4) contract-related intangibles that represent the value of rights that arise from contractual arrangements, and (5) technology-related intangible assets that relate to innovations or technological advances.

7 Explain and account for impairment of limited-life and indefinite-life intangible assets.

Under ASPE, impairment is determined and applied by using the cost recovery impairment model. Impairment for *limited-life* intangible assets is based first on a recoverability test. If the carrying amount is higher than its net recoverable amount (undiscounted), then an impairment loss must be measured and recognized, based on the asset's fair value. No reversals of such losses are permitted. The procedures are the same as for property, plant, and equipment. *Indefinite-life* intangibles use only a fair value test. Under IFRS, the rational entity impairment model is used. An intangible asset is impaired only if its carrying amount is higher than its recoverable amount. The recoverable amount is defined as the greater of the asset's value in use and its fair value less costs to sell. The impairment loss is the difference between the carrying amount and the recoverable amount, if lower. The loss is reversed subsequently if economic conditions change and the recoverable amount increases. The same approach is used for both limited-life and indefinite-life intangible assets.

8 Explain the concept of goodwill and how it is measured and accounted for after acquisition.

Goodwill is unique because, unlike all other assets, it can be identified only with the business as a whole. It is not an identifiable asset. Goodwill is recorded only when a business is purchased. To calculate goodwill in a 100% acquisition, the fair value of the identifiable assets that are acquired and liabilities that are assumed is compared with the fair value of the consideration transferred for the acquired business. The difference is goodwill. After acquisition, it is not amortized but is regularly assessed for impairment. The goodwill has to be assigned to a cash-generating group or reporting unit and the group is tested for impairment. Under ASPE, a goodwill impairment loss is recognized if the fair value of the asset group is lower than the group's carrying amount, and the loss is equal to the difference. Under IFRS, there is a goodwill impairment loss if the recoverable amount of the cash-generating unit is less than its carrying amount. The loss is equal to the difference and is applied to goodwill first. Under **both**, goodwill impairment losses are not reversed.

9 Identify the types of disclosure requirements for intangible assets and goodwill and explain the issues in analyzing these assets.

Disclosures under ASPE are limited because users can access additional information. Under IFRS, sig-

nificant details are required to be disclosed. The disclosures allow a reader to determine how amounts invested in classes of intangibles (and goodwill) have changed over the period, with substantial information provided when fair values are used, such as under the revaluation model and all impairment calculations. For intangibles that are not amortized, companies must indicate the amount of any impairment losses that have been recognized as well as information about the circumstances that led to the writedown. Goodwill must be separately reported, as are the major classes of intangible assets. Because it is difficult to measure intangibles, some resources, such as intellectual capital and other internally developed intangible assets, do not get captured on the statement of financial position. Other intangibles are recognized, but with a relatively high level of measurement uncertainty. For these reasons and because of recent changes in the accounting policy related to intangibles, care must be taken in the analysis of financial statement information related to earnings and total assets.

10 Identify differences in accounting between ASPE and IFRS.

There are few, but significant, differences between ASPE and IFRS regarding intangible assets and goodwill. One major difference relates to the accounting treatment for costs incurred in the development phase of internally generated intangible assets that meet the six stringent criteria for capitalization. Under ASPE, entities can choose a policy of whether to capitalize these costs or expense all costs associated with internally generated intangibles. Under IFRS, these costs are capitalized. The other major difference relates to the impairment models applied: the cost recovery model for ASPE, and the rational entity model for IFRS.

KEY TERMS

acquirer, p. 753	copyright, p. 748	goodwill, p. 754
active market, p. 743	cost recovery impairment model,	identifiable, p. 737
artistic-related intangible assets,	p. 751	identifiable net assets, p. 753
p. 748	customer-related intangible assets,	impaired, p. 751
bargain purchase, p. 756	p. 747	indefinite life, p. 745
brand, p. 746	development, p. 741	in-process research and development
brand name, p. 746	development phase, p. 741	(R&D), p. 739
business combination, p. 739	economic benefits, p. 738	intangible assets, p. 737
computer software costs, p. 751	favourable lease, p. 749	intellectual capital, p. 765
contract-based intangible assets,	finite life, p. 745	knowledge assets, p. 765
p. 748	franchise, p. 749	lease, p. 749

leasehold, p. 749
licences, p. 749
licensing agreements, p. 749
limited life, p. 745
marketing-related intangible assets, p. 746
monetary assets, p. 738

negative goodwill, p. 756
organization costs, p. 742
patent, p. 749
permits, p. 749
prepaid expense, p. 739
rational entity impairment model, p. 751

research, p. 741
research phase, p. 741
technology-based intangible assets, p. 749
trademark, p. 746
trade name, p. 746

APPENDIX 12A

VALUING GOODWILL

Objective 11
Explain and apply basic approaches to valuing goodwill.

In this chapter, we discussed the method of measuring and recording goodwill when one entity acquires 100% of another business **as the excess of the fair value of the consideration given up by the acquirer over the fair value of the identifiable assets acquired and liabilities assumed in a business acquisition.** Determining the fair value of the consideration transferred and the fair value of the assets and liabilities acquired is an inexact process, and therefore, so is the calculation of the amount of goodwill. As the chapter suggests, it is usually possible to determine the fair value of specifically identifiable assets, but the question remains, "How does a buyer value intangible factors such as superior management, a good credit rating, and so on?"

Excess-Earnings Approach

Finance

One method to estimate the amount of goodwill in a business is the **excess-earnings approach.** This approach works as follows:

1. Calculate the average annual "normalized" earnings that the company is expected to earn in the future.

2. Calculate the annual average earnings that the company would be expected to earn if it generated the same return on investment as the average firm in the same industry. The return on investment is the percentage that results when income is divided by the net assets or shareholders' equity invested to generate that income.

3. Calculate the excess annual earnings: the difference between what the specific company and the average firm in the industry are expected to earn in the future. The ability to generate a higher income indicates that the business has an unidentifiable value that provides this greater earning power. This ability to earn a higher rate of return than the industry is considered to be the heart of what goodwill really is.

4. Estimate the value of the goodwill based on the future stream of excess earnings.

This approach is a systematic and logical way to calculate goodwill because its value is directly related to what makes a company worth more than the sum of its parts. The Tractorling Ltd. example referred to in Illustration 12-8 will be used again now to explain each of the four steps above. As indicated above, we first:

1. **Calculate the average annual "normalized" earnings that the company is expected to earn in the future.** Because the past often provides useful information

about the future, the past earnings are a good place to start in estimating a company's likely future earnings. Going back three to six years is usually adequate.

Assume that Tractorling's net income amounts for the last five years and the calculation of the company's average earnings over this period are as given in Illustration 12A-1.

Illustration 12A-1

Calculation of Average Past Earnings

Earnings History—Tractorling Limited	
2009	$ 60,000
2010	55,000
2011	110,000[a]
2012	70,000
2013	80,000
Total for 5 years	$375,000
Average earnings	$375,000 ÷ 5 years = $75,000

[a]Includes gain on discontinued operation of $25,000

Based on the average annual earnings of $75,000 and the fair value of the company's identifiable net assets of $350,000 from Illustration 12-8, a return on investment of approximately 21.4% is initially indicated: $75,000 ÷ $350,000. Before we go further, however, we need to know whether $75,000 is representative of Tractorling's **future earnings.** A company's past earnings need to be analyzed to determine whether any adjustments are needed in estimating expected future earnings. This process is often called "normalizing earnings" and the income that results is termed **normalized earnings.**

First, **the accounting policies applied should be consistent with those of the purchaser.** For example, assume that the purchasing company measures earnings using the FIFO cost formula rather than average cost, which Tractorling uses. Further assume that the use of average cost had the effect of reducing Tractorling's net income by $2,000 each year below a FIFO-based net income. In addition, Tractorling uses accelerated depreciation while the purchaser uses straight-line. As a result, the reported earnings are $3,000 lower each year than they would have been on a straight-line basis.

Second, because the purchaser will pay current prices for the company, **future earnings should be based on the net assets' current fair values** rather than the carrying amount on Tractorling's books. That is, differences between the assets' carrying amounts and fair values may affect reported earnings in the future. For example, internally developed patent costs of $18,000 not previously recognized as an asset would be recognized on the purchase of Tractorling and are included in the $350,000 fair value of identifiable assets. This asset will need to be amortized, say, at the rate of $1,000 per year.

Finally, because we are trying to estimate future earnings, **amounts that are not expected to recur should be adjusted out of our calculations.** The 2011 gain on discontinued operations of $25,000 is an example of such an item. Illustration 12A-2 shows the analysis that can now be made of what the purchaser expects the annual future earnings of Tractorling to be.

Illustration 12A-2

Calculation of Normalized Earnings

Average past earnings of Tractorling (from Illustration 12A-1)		$75,000
Add		
Adjustment for change from average cost to FIFO	$2,000	
Adjustment for change from accelerated to straight-line depreciation	3,000	5,000
		80,000
Deduct		
Gain on discontinued operation ($25,000 ÷ 5)	5,000	
Patent amortization on straight-line basis	1,000	6,000
Expected future annual earnings of Tractorling		$74,000

Note that it was necessary to divide the gain on the discontinued operation of $25,000 by five years to adjust it correctly. The whole $25,000 was included in the total income earned over the five-year history, but only one fifth of it, or $5,000, is included in the average annual earnings.[29]

2. **Calculate the annual average earnings that the company would be expected to earn if it generated the same return on investment as the average firm in the same industry.** Determining the industry's average rate of return earned on net assets requires an analysis of companies that are similar to the enterprise being examined. An industry average may be determined by examining annual reports or data from statistical services. Assume that a rate of 15% is found to be average for companies in Tractorling's industry. **This is the level of earnings that is expected from a company without any goodwill.** In this case, the estimate of what Tractorling's earnings would be if based on the norm for the industry is calculated in Illustration 12A-3.

Illustration 12A-3

Tractorling's Earnings at the Average Rate for the Industry

Fair value of Tractorling's identifiable net assets	$350,000
Industry average rate of return	15%
Tractorling's earnings if no goodwill	$ 52,500

The net assets' fair value—not their carrying amount—is used to calculate Tractorling's level of earnings at the industry average rate of return. Fair value is used because the cost of the net identifiable assets to any company that is interested in purchasing Tractorling will be their fair value, not their carrying amount on Tractorling's books. This makes fair value the relevant measure.

3. **Calculate the excess annual earnings: the difference between what the specific company and the average firm in the industry are expected to earn in the future.** The next step is to calculate how much of the company's expected earnings exceed the industry norm. This is what gives the company value in excess of the fair value of its identifiable net assets. Tractorling's excess earnings are determined in Illustration 12A-4.

Illustration 12A-4

Calculation of Excess Earnings

Expected future earnings of Tractorling	$74,000
Tractorling's earnings if no goodwill	52,500
Tractorling's excess annual earnings	$21,500

4. **Estimate the value of the goodwill based on the future stream of excess earnings.** Because the excess earnings are expected to continue for several years, they are discounted back to their present value to determine how much a purchaser would pay for them now. A discount rate must be chosen, as well as the length of the discount period.

Discount Rate

The choice of discount rate is relatively subjective.[30] The lower the discount rate, the higher the goodwill value and vice versa. To illustrate, assume that the excess earnings of $21,500 are expected to continue indefinitely. If the excess earnings are capitalized at a rate of 25% in perpetuity, for example, the results are as indicated in Illustration 12A-5.

*Capitalization of Excess
Earnings at 25% in Perpetuity*

Capitalization at 25%

$$\frac{\text{Excess earnings}}{\text{Capitalization rate}} = \frac{\$21,500}{0.25} = \$86,000$$

As indicated in Illustration 12A-6, if the excess earnings are capitalized in perpetuity at a somewhat lower rate, say 15%, a much higher goodwill figure results.[31]

*Capitalization of Excess
Earnings at 15% in Perpetuity*

Capitalization at 15%

$$\frac{\text{Excess earnings}}{\text{Capitalization rate}} = \frac{\$21,500}{0.15} = \$143,333$$

What do these numbers mean? In effect, if a company pays $86,000 over and above the fair value of Tractorling's identifiable net assets because the company generates earnings above the industry norm, and Tractorling actually does generate these excess profits in perpetuity, the $21,500 of extra earnings per year represents a 25% return on the amount invested; that is, there is a $21,500 return on the $86,000 invested.

If the purchaser invests $143,333 for the goodwill, the extra $21,500 represents a 15% return on investment: $21,500 relative to the $143,333 invested.

Because it is uncertain—risky—that excess profits will continue, a conservative or risk-adjusted rate (higher than the normal rate) tends to be used. Factors that are considered in determining the rate are the stability of past earnings, the speculative nature of the business, and general economic conditions.

Discount Period

Determining the period over which excess earnings are expected to continue is perhaps the most difficult problem in estimating goodwill. The perpetuity examples above assume that the excess earnings will last indefinitely. Usually, however, the excess earnings are assumed to last a limited number of years. The earnings are then discounted over the shorter period.

Assume that the company interested in purchasing Tractorling's business believes that the excess earnings will last only 10 years and, because of general economic uncertainty, chooses 25% as an appropriate rate of return. The present value of a 10-year annuity of excess earnings of $21,500 discounted at 25% is $76,766.[32] This is the amount that a purchaser should be willing to pay above the fair value of the identifiable net assets—that is, for goodwill—given the assumptions stated.

Total-Earnings Approach

Another way to estimate goodwill that is similar may help to increase your understanding of the process and resulting numbers. Under this approach—the **total-earnings approach**—the value of the company as a whole is determined, based on the total expected earnings, not just the excess earnings. The fair value of the identifiable net assets is then deducted from the value of the company as a whole. The difference is goodwill. The calculations under both approaches are provided in Illustration 12A-7, assuming the purchaser is looking for a 15% return on the amounts it will invest in Tractorling, and the earnings are expected to continue into perpetuity.

Assumptions:	Expected future earnings		$74,000
	Normal or industry-level earnings		$52,500
	Expected excess future earnings		$21,500
	Discount rate		15%
	Discount period		perpetuity, ∞
Excess-Earnings Approach:	Goodwill	= present value of the annuity of excess future earnings	
		= present value of annuity of $21,500 (n = ∞, i = 0.15)	
		= $\dfrac{\$21{,}500}{0.15}$	= $143,333
Total-Earnings Approach:	Goodwill	= difference between the fair value of the company and the fair value of its identifiable net assets	
	Fair value of company	= present value of the annuity of future earnings	
		= present value of annuity of $74,000 (n = ∞, i = 0.15)	
		= $\dfrac{\$74{,}000}{0.15}$	= $493,333
	Fair value of identifiable net assets	= present value of the annuity of industry-level earnings	
		= present value of annuity of $52,500 (n = ∞, i = 0.15)	
		= $\dfrac{\$52{,}500}{0.15}$	= (350,000)
	Goodwill	=	$143,333

Other Valuation Methods

There are several other methods of valuing goodwill: some are very basic and others are very sophisticated. The methods illustrated here are some of the least complex approaches. Others include simply multiplying excess earnings by the number of years that the excess earnings are expected to continue. One method, often referred to as the **number of years method**, is used to provide a rough measure of goodwill. The approach has the advantage only of simplicity; it does not consider the time value of money because the future cash flows are not discounted.

An even simpler method is one that relies on multiples of average yearly earnings that are paid for other companies in the same industry. If Skyward Airlines was recently acquired for five times its average yearly earnings of $50 million, or $250 million, then Worldwide Airways, a close competitor with $80 million in average yearly earnings, would be worth $400 million.

Finance

Another method (similar to discounting excess earnings) is the **discounted free cash flow method**, which involves projecting the company's free cash flow over a long period, typically 10 or 20 years. The method first projects into the future a dozen or so important financial variables, including production; prices; and noncash expenses such as amortization, taxes, and capital outlays—all adjusted for inflation. The objective is to determine the amount of operating cash flow that will be generated over and above the amount needed to maintain existing capacity. The present value of the free cash flow is then calculated. This amount represents the value of the business.

For example, if Magnaputer Ltd. is expected to generate $1 million a year of free cash flow for 20 years, and the buyer's rate-of-return objective is 15%, the buyer would be willing to pay about $6.26 million for Magnaputer. (The present value of $1 million to be received for 20 years discounted at 15% is $6,259,330.) The goodwill, then, is the difference between the $6.26 million and the fair value of the company's identifiable net assets.

In practice, prospective buyers use a variety of methods to produce a valuation curve or range of prices. But the actual price that ends up being paid may be more a factor of the buyer's or seller's ego and negotiating skill.

Valuation of a business—determining how much to pay for it—and its inherent goodwill is at best a highly uncertain process.[33] The estimated value of goodwill depends on a number of factors, all of which are tenuous and subject to bargaining. It ends up accounted for as the difference between the fair value of what you give up to acquire the business and the fair value of the identifiable net assets acquired.

Quiz

SUMMARY OF LEARNING OBJECTIVE FOR APPENDIX 12A

11 Explain and apply basic approaches to valuing goodwill.

One method of valuing goodwill is the excess-earnings approach. Using this approach, the value of goodwill is based on discounting expected future earnings in excess of the industry average to their present value. Another method involves determining the total value of the business by capitalizing total earnings, and then deducting the fair values of the identifiable net assets. The number of years

method of valuing goodwill simply multiplies the excess earnings by the number of years of expected excess earnings. Another method of valuing goodwill is the discounted free cash flow method, which projects the future operating cash that will be generated over and above the amount needed to maintain current operating levels. The present value of the free cash flows is today's estimate of the firm's value.

KEY TERMS

discounted free cash flow method, p. 774

excess-earnings approach, p. 770

normalized earnings, p. 771

number of years method, p. 774

total-earnings approach, p. 773

Note: All assignment material with an asterisk (*) relates to the appendix to the chapter.

Brief Exercises

(LO 1) **BE12-1**   Wholesome Foods Corporation is a producer of gourmet organic cookies. The company was established three years ago when its founder and president, Martha Spencer, purchased the trademark "Healthy Originals" and its six patented cookie recipes. Martha soon discovered that there was a specialty market for the cookies, and began marketing them as hand-decorated and personalized gourmet organic cookies for special occasions such as birthdays and bridal and baby showers. Nearly all of the company's sales are through the company's internally developed website, where customers can enter personalized orders for batches of individually decorated and wrapped cookies.

(a) Identify any intangible assets that may appear on the company's balance sheet.

(b) Discuss the importance of the intangible assets to the company's business.

(c) Referring to the conceptual framework (discussed in Chapter 2), discuss the importance of recording the intangible assets on the company's balance sheet.

(LO 2, 3, 4) **BE12-2**   For each independent scenario outlined below, discuss whether the three criteria required for an asset to be classified as an intangible are fulfilled:

(a) Software purchased specifically for a manufacturing machine that cannot operate without that software

(b) Software purchased for a hotel reservation system that is not essential to the related ancillary hardware equipment

(c) Software developed internally for eventual sale to customers

(d) Software purchased for eventual resale to customers

(LO 2, 3, 4) **BE12-3**   Brilliant Minds Inc. incurred the following costs associated with its research facilities. Indicate whether these items are capitalized or expensed in the current year:

(a) Executive salaries

(b) Costs of testing prototypes

(c) Market research to prepare for the product launch

(d) Sales commissions

(e) Salaries of research staff investigating alternatives for existing products

(f) Borrowing costs directly attributable to the development of a qualifying intangible asset

(LO 3) **BE12-4**   Azure Industries Ltd. acquired two copyrights during 2014. One copyright was on a textbook that was developed internally at a cost of $18,000. This textbook is estimated to have a useful life of three years from September 1, 2014, the date it was published. The second copyright is for a history research textbook and was purchased from University Press on December 1, 2014, for $29,400. This textbook has an indefinite useful life. How should these two copyrights be reported on Azure's statement of financial position as at December 31, 2014?

(LO 3) **BE12-5**   Sunny Valley Inc. purchased an Internet domain name by issuing a $220,000, five-year, non–interest-bearing note to Ti-Mine Corp. with an effective yield of 12%. The note is repayable in five annual payments of $44,000 each. Prepare the journal entry to record the purchase of the intangible asset.

(LO 3, 4) **BE12-6**   Bountiful Industries Ltd. had one patent recorded on its books as at January 1, 2014. This patent had a book value of $365,000 and a remaining useful life of eight years. During 2014, Bountiful incurred research costs of $140,000 and brought a patent infringement suit against a competitor. On December 1, 2014, Bountiful received the good news that its patent was valid and that its competitor could not use the process Bountiful had patented. The company spent $106,000 to defend this patent. At what amount should the patent be reported on the December 31, 2014 statement of financial position, assuming monthly straight-line amortization of patents?

(LO 3, 4) **BE12-7**   WEBDESIGN Ltd. decided that it needed to update its computer programs for its supplier relationships. It purchased an off-the-shelf program and modified it internally to link it to WEBDESIGN's other programs. The following costs may be relevant to the accounting for the new software:

Net carrying amount of old software	$1,100
Purchase price of new software	5,900
Training costs	4,550
General and administrative costs	3,750
Direct cost of in-house programmer's time spent on conversion	1,720

Prepare journal entries to record the software replacement.

(LO 3, 4) **BE12-8**   Indicate whether the following items are capitalized or expensed in the current year:

(a) The purchase cost of a patent from a competitor

(b) Product research costs

(c) Organization costs

(d) Costs that are incurred internally to create goodwill

(e) Legal costs to successfully support trademark

(f) Pre-operating costs to launch new products

(g) Relocation of manufacturing activities

(h) Corporate reorganization costs

(LO 3, 4, 5, 10) **BE12-9**   Swinson, Inc., a private company that applies ASPE, incurred $15,000 in materials and $12,000 in direct labour costs between January and March 2014 to develop a new product. In May 2014, the criteria required to capitalize development costs were met. A further $45,000 was spent for materials, $15,000 for direct labour costs, $2,000 for borrowing costs, and $72,000 for directly related legal fees. Discuss any options that may be available to Swinson for recording these expenditures. In addition, prepare the appropriate journal entries. How would your answer change if Swinson was a public company following IFRS?

(LO 3, 4, 6)   **BE12-10**   Darrien Corporation purchased a trade name, customer list, and manufacturing equipment for a lump sum of $800,000. The fair market values of each asset are $280,000, $290,000, and $320,000, respectively. There were initial operating losses of $14,500 during the first four months after the assets were put into use. Prepare the journal entry to record the treatment of these costs.

(LO 4)   **BE12-11**   Using the data provided in BE12-10, assume that Darrien also spent $12,500 to promote and launch the product that the manufacturing equipment is used to produce. Explain the accounting for these costs.

(LO 4, 5)   **BE12-12**   Green Earth Corp. has capitalized software costs of $980,000 on a product to be sold externally. During its first year, sales of this product totalled $380,000. Green Earth expects to earn $1,560,000 in additional future revenue from this product, which is estimated to have an economic life of four years. Calculate the amount of software amortization, assuming that amortization is based on the pattern in which Green Earth receives benefits from the software program.

(LO 5)   **BE12-13**   Latupatula Corporation purchased a patent from MaFee Corp. on January 1, 2014, for $87,000. The patent had a remaining legal life of 16 years. Prepare Latupatula's journal entries to record the 2014 patent purchase and amortization.

(LO 3, 4, 5)   **BE12-14**   Use the information in BE12-13 and assume that in January 2016, Latupatula spends $26,000 successfully defending a patent suit. In addition, Latupatula now feels the patent will be useful only for another seven years. Prepare the journal entries to record the 2016 expenditure and amortization.

(LO 4, 5)   **BE12-15**   On December 31, 2014, Convenient Cabs Incorporated was granted 10 taxi licences by the City of Somerdale, at a cost of $1,000 per licence. It is probable that Convenient Cabs will receive the expected future economic benefits of the taxi licences. There is an active market for taxi licences in Somerdale.

    (a) Prepare the journal entry to record the costs incurred.

    (b) Discuss how the licences are accounted for after initial recognition if Convenient Cabs follows ASPE.

    (c) Discuss how the licences are accounted for after initial recognition if Convenient Cabs follows IFRS.

(LO 7, 10)   **BE12-16**   ABC Company has a trademark with a carrying amount of $83,750, and expected useful life of 15 years. As part of an impairment test on December 31, 2014, due to a change in customer tastes, ABC gathered the following data about the trademark for purposes of an impairment test: fair value $45,000; fair value less costs to sell $40,000; value in use $95,200; and undiscounted future cash flows $125,000. Assume that ABC is reporting under ASPE. Determine if the trademark is impaired on December 31, 2014.

(LO 7, 10)   **BE12-17**   Use the data provided in BE12-16. How would your response change if ABC is a public company reporting under IFRS?

(LO 7, 10)   **BE12-18**   Use the data provided in BE12-16, except assume that useful life is expected to be unlimited. How would your response change if ABC reports under (a) ASPE or (b) IFRS?

(LO 8)   **BE12-19**   On September 1, 2014, Luigi Corporation acquired Edinburgh Enterprises for a cash payment of $863,000. At the time of purchase, Edinburgh's statement of financial position showed assets of $900,000, liabilities of $460,000, and owners' equity of $440,000. The fair value of Edinburgh's assets is estimated to be $1,160,000. Calculate the amount of goodwill acquired by Luigi.

(LO 8, 10)   **BE12-20**   Using the data from BE12-19, assume that Luigi Corporation is a public company and that the goodwill was allocated entirely to one cash-generating unit (CGU). Two years later, information about the CGU is as follows: carrying amount $3,925,000; value in use $3,850,000; and fair value less costs to sell $3,450,000. Determine if the goodwill is impaired, and calculate the goodwill impairment loss, if any.

(LO 8, 10)   **BE12-21**   Using the data from BE12-19, assume that Luigi Corporation is a private entity. Explain how goodwill will be tested for impairment. If the unit's carrying amount (including goodwill) is $3,613,000 and its fair value is $3,550,000, determine the amount of impairment loss, if any, under ASPE.

(LO 11)   ***BE12-22**   Nigel Corporation is interested in purchasing Lau Company Ltd. The total of Lau's net income amounts over the last five years is $750,000. During one of those years, Lau reported a gain on discontinued operations of $94,000. The fair value of Lau's net identifiable assets is $690,000. A normal rate of return is 15%, and Nigel wants to capitalize excess earnings at 20%. Calculate the estimated value of Lau's goodwill.

Exercises

E12-1   (Classification Issues—Intangibles) The following is a list of items that could be included in the intangible assets section of the statement of financial position:

1. An investment in a subsidiary company

2. Timberland

3. The cost of an engineering activity that is required to advance a product's design to the manufacturing stage

4. A lease prepayment (six months of rent paid in advance)

5. The cost of equipment obtained under a capital lease

6. The cost of searching for applications for new research findings

7. Costs incurred in forming a corporation

8. Operating losses incurred in the start-up of a business

9. Training costs incurred in the start-up of a new operation

10. The purchase cost of a franchise

11. Goodwill generated internally

12. The cost of testing in the search for product alternatives

13. Goodwill acquired in the purchase of a business

14. The cost of developing a patent

15. The cost of purchasing a patent from an inventor

16. Legal costs incurred in securing a patent

17. Unrecovered costs of a successful legal suit to protect the patent

18. The cost of conceptual formulation of possible product alternatives

19. The cost of purchasing a copyright

20. Product development costs

21. Long-term receivables

22. The cost of developing a trademark

23. The cost of purchasing a trademark

24. The cost of an annual update on payroll software

25. A five-year advertising contract for rights of advertising by a top hockey player in Canada

26. Borrowing costs specifically identifiable with an internally developed intangible asset

Instructions

(a) Indicate which items on the list would be reported as intangible assets on the statement of financial position.

(b) Indicate how, if at all, the items that are not reportable as intangible assets would be reported in the financial statements.

(c) Identify any differences between ASPE and IFRS with respect to capitalization of such items as intangible assets.

E12-2   (Classification Issues—Intangibles) Selected account information follows for Richmond Inc. as at December 31, 2014. All the accounts have debit balances.

Cable Television Franchises	Film Contract Rights
Music Copyrights	Customer Lists Acquired in a Business Combination
Research Costs	Prepaid Expenses
Goodwill	Covenants Not to Compete
Cash	Brand Names
Discount on Notes Payable	Notes Receivable
Accounts Receivable	Investments in Affiliated Companies
Property, Plant, and Equipment	Organization Cost
Leasehold Improvements	Land
Annual Franchise Fee Paid	Excess of Purchase Price over Fair Value of Identifiable
In-Process Research and Development Acquired in a Business Combination	Net Assets, X Corp.

Instructions

Identify which items should be classified as intangible assets. For the items that are not classified as intangible assets, indicate where they would be reported in the financial statements.

(LO 3, 6, 8) **E12-3** **(Classification Issues—Intangibles)** Berrie Inc. has the following amounts included in its general ledger at December 31, 2014:

Organization costs	$ 34,000
Purchased trademarks	17,500
Discount on bonds payable	23,000
Development phase activities (meet all six development phase criteria)	29,000
Deposits with advertising agency for ads to promote goodwill of company	8,000
Excess of cost over fair value of identifiable net assets of acquired subsidiary	81,000
Cost of equipment acquired for research and development projects; the equipment has an alternative future use	125,000
Costs of researching a secret formula for a product that is expected to be marketed for at least 20 years	75,000
Payment for a favourable lease; lease term of 10 years	15,000

Instructions

(a) Based on the information, calculate the total amount for Berrie to report as intangible assets on its statement of financial position at December 31, 2014.

(b) If an item should not be included in intangible assets, explain the proper treatment for reporting it.

(LO 3, 4, 5) **E12-4** **(Intangible Amortization)** Selected information follows for Mount Olympus Corporation for three independent situations:

1. Mount Olympus purchased a patent from Bakhshi Co. for $1.8 million on January 1, 2012. The patent expires on January 1, 2022, and Mount Olympus is amortizing it over the 10 years remaining in its legal life. During 2014, Mount Olympus determined that the patent's economic benefits would not last longer than six years from the date of acquisition.

2. Mount Olympus bought a perpetual franchise from Carmody Inc. on January 1, 2014, for $650,000. Its carrying amount on Carmody's books at January 1, 2014, was $750,000. Assume that Mount Olympus can only provide evidence of clearly identifiable cash flows for 25 years, but thinks the franchise could have value for up to 60 years.

3. On January 1, 2012, Mount Olympus incurred development costs (meeting all required criteria) of $375,000. Mount Olympus is amortizing these costs over five years.

Instructions

(a) In situation 1, what amount should be reported in the statement of financial position for the patent, net of accumulated amortization, at December 31, 2014?

(b) In situation 2, what amount of amortization expense should be reported for the year ended December 31, 2014?

(c) In situation 3, what amount, if any, should be reported as unamortized development costs as at December 31, 2014?

(LO 3, 4, 5) **E12-5** **(Correct Intangible Asset Account)** As the recently appointed auditor for Daleara Corporation, you have been asked to examine selected accounts before the six-month financial statements of June 30, 2014, are prepared. The controller for Daleara Corporation mentions that only one account is kept for intangible assets. The entries in Intangible Assets since January 1, 2014, are as follows:

INTANGIBLE ASSETS

			Debit	Credit	Balance
Jan.	4	Research costs	1,050,000		1,050,000
	5	Legal costs to obtain patent	45,000		1,095,000
	31	Payment of seven months' rent on property leased by Daleara (February to August)	49,000		1,144,000
Feb.	11	Proceeds from issue of common shares		310,000	834,000
Mar.	31	Unamortized bond discount on bonds payable due March 31, 2018	14,000		848,000
Apr.	30	Promotional expenses related to start-up of business	157,000		1,005,000
June	1	Development stage costs (meet all six development stage criteria)	215,000		1,220,000
	30	Operating losses for first six months	316,000		1,536,000

Instructions

Prepare the entry or entries that are necessary to correct this account. Assume that the patent has a useful life of 10 years.

(LO 3, 4, 5, 6) **E12-6   (Recognition and Amortization of Intangibles)** Institute Limited organized late in 2013 and set up a single account for all intangible assets. The following summary shows the entries in 2014 (all debits) that have been recorded in Intangible Assets since then:

Jan. 2	Purchased patent (8-year life)		$ 320,000
Mar. 31	Costs to search for new ways to apply patent that was purchased on Jan. 2		21,000
Apr. 1	Purchased goodwill (indefinite life)		310,000
July 1	Purchased franchise with 10-year life; expiration date July 1, 2024		250,000
1	Promotional costs to increase the future economic benefit of the goodwill that was purchased on Apr. 1		33,000
Aug. 1	Payment for copyright (5-year life)		140,000
1	Purchased trademark (3-year life)		15,000
1	Purchased customer list (2-year life)		10,000
Sept. 1	Research costs		239,000
			$1,338,000

Instructions

(a) Prepare the necessary entries to clear the Intangible Assets account and to set up separate accounts for distinct types of intangibles.

(b) Make the entries as at December 31, 2014, for any necessary amortization so that all balances are accurate as at that date.

(c) Provide the asset amounts reported on the December 31, 2014 statement of financial position.

(LO 3, 4, 5, 6) **E12-7   (Accounting for Trade Name)** In early January 2014, Kara Corporation applied for and received approval for a trade name, incurring legal costs of $45,000. In January 2015, Kara incurred $24,300 of legal fees in a successful defence of its trade name.

Instructions

(a) Management determines that this asset has a limited useful life. Identify the variables that must be considered in determining the appropriate amortization period for this trade name.

(b) Calculate amortization for 2014; carrying amount at December 31, 2014; amortization for 2015; and carrying amount at December 31, 2015, if the company amortizes the trade name over its 15-year legal life.

(c) Repeat part (b), assuming a useful life of five years.

(d) Assume the trade name is assessed as having an indefinite life upon initial acquisition. Explain the accounting implications.

Digging Deeper

(e) Assume the role of a potential investor in Kara. Comment on the estimated useful life of the trade name, and its effects on the company's financial statements.

(LO 4, 5) **E12-8   (Internally Generated Intangibles)** Parastu Corp. incurred the following costs during 2014 in connection with its research and development phase activities:

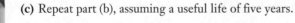

Cost of equipment acquired for use in research and development projects over the next five years (straight-line depreciation used)	$240,000
Materials consumed in research projects	61,000
Materials consumed in the development of a product committed for manufacturing in first quarter 2015	32,000
Consulting fees paid in the last quarter of 2014 to outsiders for research and development projects, including $4,500 for advice related to the $32,000 of materials used above	95,000
Personnel costs of persons involved in research and development projects	108,000
Indirect costs reasonably allocated to research and development projects	25,000
General borrowing costs on the company's line of credit	12,000
Training costs for a new customer service software program	17,500

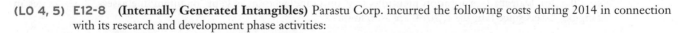

Instructions

(a) Calculate the amount to be reported as research and development expense by Parastu on its income statement for 2014. Assume the equipment is purchased at the beginning of the year.

(b) Explain the treatment of training costs and borrowing costs incurred after the six development phase capitalization criteria are met.

(LO 4, 5, 6) **E12-9** **(Internally Generated Intangibles)** In 2014, Inventors Corp. spent $392,000 on a research project, but by the end of 2014 it was impossible to determine whether any benefit would come from it. Inventors prepares financial statements in accordance with IFRS.

Instructions

(a) What account should be charged for the $392,000, and how should it be shown in the financial statements for fiscal 2014?

(b) The research project is completed in 2015, and a successful patent is obtained. The research phase costs to complete the project are $71,000. The administrative and legal expenses incurred in obtaining patent number 481-761-0092 on January 3, 2015, total $10,000. The patent has an expected useful life of five years. Inventors Corp. will now begin investigating applications that use or apply the knowledge obtained on this project. Record these costs in journal entry form. Also, record patent amortization for a full year in 2015.

(c) In January 2016, the company successfully defended the patent in litigation at a cost of $12,400. The victory extended the patent's life to December 31, 2023. What is the proper way to account for this cost? Also, record patent amortization for a full year in 2016.

(d) By early September 2016, and at an additional cost of $101,000, Inventors Corp. had a product design that was technologically and financially feasible. Additional engineering and consulting costs of $66,000 were incurred in October 2016 to advance the design of the new product to the manufacturing stage. Discuss the proper accounting treatment for the 2016 costs incurred.

(LO 4, 5, 6, 10) **E12-10** **(Accounting for Patents, Franchises, and R&D)** PrideTalk Corp., reporting under ASPE, has provided the following information regarding its intangible assets:

1. A patent was purchased from Marvin Inc. for $1.2 million on January 1, 2013. PrideTalk estimated the patent's remaining useful life to be 10 years. The patent was carried in Marvin's accounting records at a carrying amount of $1,350,000 when Marvin sold it to PrideTalk. On January 1, 2014, because of recent events in the field, PrideTalk estimates that the remaining life of this patent is only five years from January 1, 2014.

2. During 2014, a franchise was purchased from Burr Ltd. for $290,000. As part of the deal, Burr must also be paid 5% of revenue from the franchise operations. Revenue from the franchise for 2014 was $1.4 million. PrideTalk estimates the franchise's useful life to be 10 years and takes a full year's amortization in the year of purchase.

3. PrideTalk incurred the following research costs in 2014:

Materials and equipment	$ 81,000
Personnel	111,000
Indirect costs	55,000
	$247,000

Instructions

(a) Prepare a schedule showing the intangibles section of PrideTalk's balance sheet at December 31, 2014. Show supporting calculations in good form.

(b) Prepare a schedule showing the income statement effect for the year ended December 31, 2014, as a result of the facts above. Show supporting calculations in good form.

(c) Explain how the accounting would differ if PrideTalk is a public company.

(AICPA adapted)

(LO 4, 5, 7, 10) **E12-11** **(Internally Developed Intangibles)** During 2014, Saskatchewan Enterprises Ltd., a private entity, incurred $4.7 million in costs to develop a new software product called Dover. Of this amount, $1.8 million was spent before establishing that the product was technologically and financially feasible. Dover was completed by December 31, 2014, and will be marketed to third parties. Saskatchewan expects a useful life of eight years for this product, with total revenues of $12 million. During 2015, Saskatchewan realized revenues of $2.7 million from sales of Dover.

Instructions

(a) Assuming Saskatchewan reports under ASPE, prepare the journal entries that are required in 2014 to record the above.

(b) Prepare the entry to record amortization at December 31, 2015.

(c) At what amount should the software costs be reported in the December 31, 2015 balance sheet?

(d) Could the net realizable value of this asset at December 31, 2015, affect your answer? Explain how limited-life assets are tested for impairment.

(e) How would your response to (d) change if Saskatchewan Enterprises Ltd. was a public company?

(LO 5, 7) **E12-12   (Revaluation Model)** Safe Ride Incorporated applied for several taxi licences for its taxicab operations in the City of Waterford and, on August 31, 2014, incurred costs of $14,200 in the application process. The outcome of applying for taxi licences in the City of Waterford was uncertain, as the City has been known to limit the number of issued taxi licences in an effort to encourage use of public transportation.

The application was successful and on June 30, 2015, Safe Ride was granted 32 freely transferable taxi licences for a registration fee of $3,500 per licence. According to management, each licence has a useful life of only five years from the date of registration, because demand for taxi services in Waterford is expected to decrease significantly after the city's subway system is expanded. There is an active market for taxi licences in Waterford.

In 2016, in an effort to decrease traffic congestion in the city's downtown, the City did not issue any new taxi licences and the fair value of each taxi licence held by Safe Ride was $4,200 as of December 31, 2016. In 2018, due to a severe shortage of taxis in the city, the City decreased the registration fee and issued many new taxi licences. As of December 31, 2018, each taxi licence had value in use of $6,200, fair value of $1,400, and costs to sell of $200. Safe Ride amortizes intangible assets using the straight-line method, and prepares financial statements in accordance with IFRS.

Instructions

(a) Prepare the entry to record the costs incurred on August 31, 2014.

(b) Prepare the entry to record the costs incurred on June 30, 2015.

(c) Assume that after initial recognition, Safe Ride uses the cost model to measure its intangible assets. Prepare the entries required on December 31, 2016, December 31, 2017, and December 31, 2018, and calculate the carrying amount of the intangible asset, if any, as at December 31, 2018.

(d) Assume that after initial recognition, Safe Ride uses the revaluation model (asset adjustment method) to measure its intangible assets. Prepare the entries required on December 31, 2016, December 31, 2017, and December 31, 2018, and calculate the carrying amount of the intangible asset, if any, as at December 31, 2018. Assume revaluation adjustments are made on December 31, 2016 and December 31, 2018.

Digging Deeper

(e) From the perspective of Safe Ride's auditor, discuss the criteria that must be met for the intangible asset to be measured using the revaluation model.

(LO 7, 10) **E12-13   (Impairment Testing)** At the end of 2014, Dayton Corporation owns a licence with a remaining life of 10 years and a carrying amount of $530,000. Dayton expects undiscounted future cash flows from this licence to total $535,000. The licence's fair value is $425,000 and disposal costs are estimated to be nil. The licence's discounted cash flows (that is, value in use) are estimated to be $475,000. Dayton prepares financial statements in accordance with IFRS.

Instructions

(a) Determine if the licence is impaired at the end of 2014 and prepare any related entries that are necessary.

(b) Assume the recoverable amount is calculated to be $450,000 at the end of 2015. Determine if the licence is impaired at the end of 2015 and prepare any related entries that are necessary.

(c) Explain how the answer to part (b) would change if the licence's fair value is $500,000 at the end of 2015.

(LO 7, 10) **E12-14   (Impairment Testing)**

Instructions

Repeat E12-13, but now assume that Dayton prepares financial statements in accordance with ASPE, and that the recoverable amount under ASPE (undiscounted future cash flows) is calculated to be $500,000 at the end of 2015.

(LO 7, 10) **E12-15   (Impairment Testing)**

Instructions

Repeat E12-13, but now assume that the licence was granted in perpetuity and has an indefinite life.

(LO 7, 10) **E12-16   (Impairment Testing)**

Instructions

Repeat E12-13, but now assume that the licence was granted in perpetuity and has an indefinite life, and that Dayton prepares financial statements in accordance with ASPE.

(LO 7, 10) E12-17   (Intangible Impairment) The following information is for a copyright owned by Venetian Corp., a private entity, at December 31, 2014. Venetian Corp. applies ASPE.

Cost	$4,300,000
Carrying amount	2,150,000
Expected future net cash flows (undiscounted)	2,000,000
Fair value	1,600,000

Assume that Venetian Corp. will continue to use this copyright in the future. As at December 31, 2014, the copyright is estimated to have a remaining useful life of 10 years.

Instructions

Digging Deeper

(a) Prepare the journal entry, if any, to record the asset's impairment at December 31, 2014.

(b) Prepare the journal entry to record amortization expense for 2015 related to the copyright.

(c) The copyright's fair value at December 31, 2015, is $2.2 million. Prepare the journal entry, if any, to record the increase in fair value.

(d) Using the information from part (a), discuss whether the copyright would be amortized in 2014 before the impairment test is conducted. Would the asset be tested for impairment before or after amortizing the copyright in 2014?

(LO 7, 10) E12-18   (Intangible Impairment) Refer to the information provided in E12-17, but now assume that Venetian Corp. is a publicly accountable company. At December 31, 2014, the copyright's value in use is $1,850,000 and its selling costs are $100,000.

Instructions

(a) Prepare the journal entry, if any, to record the asset's impairment at December 31, 2014.

(b) Prepare the journal entry to record amortization expense for 2015 related to the copyright.

(c) The copyright's fair value at December 31, 2015, is $2.2 million. Prepare the journal entry, if any, to record the increase in fair value.

(LO 8) E12-19   (Accounting for Goodwill) Fred Moss, owner of Medici Interiors Inc., is negotiating for the purchase of Athenian Galleries Ltd. The condensed statement of financial position of Athenian follows in an abbreviated form:

ATHENIAN GALLERIES LTD.
Statement of Financial Position
As at December 31, 2014

Assets			Liabilities and Shareholders' Equity		
Cash	$118,000		Accounts payable		$ 92,000
Land	70,000		Long-term notes payable		351,000
Building (net)	244,000		Total liabilities		443,000
Equipment (net)	185,000		Common shares	$200,000	
Copyright (net)	98,000		Retained earnings	72,000	272,000
Total assets	$715,000		Total liabilities and shareholders' equity		$715,000

Medici and Athenian agree that the land is undervalued by $40,000 and the business equipment is overvalued by $12,000. Athenian agrees to sell the business to Medici for $382,000.

Instructions

Prepare the entry to record the purchase of the business's net assets on Medici's books.

(LO 8, 10) E12-20   (Accounting for Goodwill) On July 1, 2014, Zoe Corporation purchased the net assets of Soorya Company by paying $415,000 cash and issuing a $50,000 note payable to Soorya Company. At July 1, 2014, the statement of financial position of Soorya Company was as follows:

Cash	$ 75,000	Accounts payable	$300,000
Accounts receivable	102,000	Soorya, capital	239,000
Inventory	98,000		$539,000
Land	50,000		
Buildings (net)	75,000		
Equipment (net)	90,000		
Trademarks (net)	49,000		
	$539,000		

The recorded amounts all approximate current values except for land (worth $60,000), inventory (worth $125,000), and trademarks (worthless). The receivables are shown net of an allowance for doubtful accounts of $12,000. The amounts for buildings, equipment, and trademarks are shown net of accumulated amortization of $14,000, $23,000, and $47,000, respectively.

Instructions

(a) Prepare the July 1, 2014 entry for Zoe Corporation to record the purchase.

(b) Assume that Zoe is a private entity and tested its goodwill for impairment on December 31, 2015. Management determined that the reporting unit's carrying amount (including goodwill) was $500,000 and that the reporting unit's fair value (including goodwill) was $450,000. Determine if there is any impairment and prepare any necessary entry on December 31, 2015. Zoe applies ASPE.

(c) Repeat part (a), assuming that the purchase price was $204,000, all paid in cash.

(d) Based on part (a), assume now that Zoe is a public entity and tested its goodwill for impairment on December 31, 2015. The cash-generating unit's values (including goodwill) are as follows:

Carrying amount	$500,000
Value in use	475,000
Fair value	450,000
Disposal costs	25,000

Determine if there is any impairment and prepare any necessary entry on December 31, 2015.

Digging Deeper

(e) Based on part (a), discuss factors that Zoe may have considered in deciding to pay total consideration of $465,000 for Soorya.

(LO 8, 10) E12-21 (Goodwill Impairment) The following is net asset information for the Dhillon Division of Klaus, Inc.:

NET ASSETS
as of December 31, 2014
(in millions)

	Book Value	Fair Value Excluding Goodwill
Cash	$ 50	$ 50
Accounts receivable	216	216
Property, plant, and equipment (net)	2,618	2,760
Goodwill	206	
Less: Notes payable	(2,700)	(2,700)
Net assets	$ 390	

The purpose of the Dhillon Division (also identified as a reporting unit or cash-generating unit) is to develop a nuclear-powered aircraft. If successful, travelling delays that are associated with refuelling could be greatly reduced, and operational efficiency would increase significantly.

To date, management has not had much success and is deciding whether a writedown is appropriate at this time. Management has prepared the following estimates for the reporting unit or cash-generating unit:

1. Undiscounted future net cash flows is approximately $400 million.

2. Future value in use is approximately $385 million.

3. Sale of the unit would yield $346 million and selling costs would total $5 million.

Instructions

(a) Under ASPE, determine if there is any impairment and prepare any necessary entry on December 31, 2014.

(b) On December 31, 2015, it is estimated that the reporting unit's fair value has increased to $400 million. Under ASPE, prepare the journal entry, if any, to record the increase in fair value.

(c) Under IFRS, determine if there is any impairment and prepare any necessary entry on December 31, 2014.

(d) On December 31, 2015, it is estimated that the cash-generating unit's fair value has increased to $400 million. Under IFRS, prepare the journal entry, if any, to record the increase in fair value.

(LO 11) ***E12-22** **(Calculate Normalized Earnings)** Rotterdam Corporation's pre-tax accounting income of $725,000 for the year 2014 included the following items:

Amortization of identifiable intangibles	$147,000
Depreciation of building	115,000
Loss from discontinued operations	44,000
Unusual, non-recurring gains	152,000
Profit-sharing payments to employees	65,000

Ewing Industries Ltd. would like to purchase Rotterdam Corporation. In trying to measure Rotterdam's normalized earnings for 2014, Ewing determines that the building's fair value is triple the book value and that its remaining economic life is double the life that Rotterdam is using. Ewing would continue the profit-sharing payments to employees, with the payments being based on income from continuing operations before amortization and depreciation.

Instructions

Calculate the 2014 normalized earnings amount of Rotterdam Corporation that Ewing would use to calculate goodwill.

(LO 11) ***E12-23** **(Calculate Goodwill)** Net income figures for Belgian Ltd. are as follows:

2010—$75,000	2013—$87,000
2011—$53,000	2014—$69,000
2012—$84,000	

Future income is expected to continue at the average amount of the past five years. The company's identifiable net assets are appraised at $460,000 on December 31, 2014. This business is to be acquired by Mooney Corp. in early 2015. The normal rate of return on net assets for the industry is 7%.

Instructions

What amount should Mooney Corp. pay for goodwill, and for Belgian Ltd. as a whole, if:

(a) goodwill is equal to average excess earnings capitalized at 23%?

(b) a perpetual 18% return is expected on any amount paid for goodwill?

(c) goodwill is equal to five years of excess earnings?

(d) goodwill is equal to the present value of five years of excess earnings capitalized at 15%?

(LO 11) ***E12-24** **(Calculate Goodwill)** Aswan Corporation is interested in acquiring Richmond Plastics Limited. Richmond has determined that its excess earnings have averaged approximately $175,000 and feels that such an amount should be capitalized over an unlimited period at a 15% rate. Aswan feels that because of increased competition, the excess earnings of Richmond Plastics will continue for seven years at the most and that a 12% discount rate is appropriate.

Instructions

(a) How far apart are the positions of these two parties?

(b) Is there really a difference in the two approaches being used by the parties to evaluate Richmond Plastics' goodwill? Explain.

(LO 11) ***E12-25** **(Calculate Goodwill)** As the president of Victoria Recording Corp., you are considering purchasing Moose Jaw CD Corp., whose statement of financial position is summarized as follows:

Current assets	$ 400,000		Current liabilities	$ 350,000
Plant and equipment (net)	750,000		Long-term liabilities	600,000
Other assets	325,000		Common shares	425,000
			Retained earnings	100,000
Total	$1,475,000		Total	$1,475,000

The current assets' fair value is $150,000 higher than their carrying amount because of inventory undervaluation. All other assets and liabilities have book values that approximate their fair value. The normal rate of return on net assets for the industry is 15%. The expected annual earnings for Moose Jaw CD Corp. are $125,000.

Instructions

Assuming that the excess earnings are expected to continue for five years, how much would you be willing to pay for goodwill, and for the company? (Estimate goodwill by the present value method.)

(LO 11) *E12-26   (Calculate Fair Value of Identifiable Assets) Louvre Inc. bought a business that is expected to give a 25% annual rate of return on the investment. Of the total amount paid for the business, $75,000 was deemed to be goodwill, and the rest was attributed to the identifiable net assets. Louvre Inc. estimated that the annual future earnings of the new business would be equal to the average ordinary earnings per year of the business over the past three years. The total net income over the past three years was $375,000. This amount included a loss on discontinued operations of $25,000 in one year and an unusual and non-recurring gain of $95,000 in one of the other two years.

Instructions

Calculate the fair value of the identifiable net assets that Louvre Inc. purchased in this transaction.

Problems

P12-1 Guiglano Inc. is a large, publicly held corporation. The following are six selected expenditures that were made by the company during the current fiscal year ended April 30, 2014. The proper accounting treatment of these transactions must be determined in order to ensure that Guiglano's annual financial statements are prepared in accordance with IFRS.

1. Guiglano spent $3 million on a program that is designed to improve relations with its dealers. Dealers responded well to the project and Guiglano's management believes that it will therefore result in significant future benefits. The program was conducted during the fourth quarter of the current fiscal year.

2. A pilot plant was constructed during 2013–14 at a cost of $5.5 million to test a new production process. The plant will be operated for approximately five years. After the five years, the company will make a decision about the economic value of the production process. The pilot plant is too small for commercial production, so it will be dismantled when the test is over.

3. During the year, Guiglano began a new manufacturing operation in Newfoundland, its first plant east of Montreal. To get the plant into operation, the following costs were incurred: (a) $100,000 to make the building fully wheelchair-accessible; (b) $41,600 to outfit the new employees with Guiglano uniforms; (c) $12,700 for the reception to introduce the company to others in the industrial mall where the plant is located; and (d) $64,400 in payroll costs for the new employees while they were being trained.

4. Guiglano purchased Eagle Company for $6 million cash in early August 2013. The fair value of Eagle's net identifiable assets was $5.2 million.

5. The company spent $14 million on advertising during the year. Of that, $2.5 million was spent in April 2014 to introduce a new product to be released during the first quarter of the 2015 fiscal year and $200,000 was used to advertise the opening of the new plant in Newfoundland. The remaining expenditures were for recurring advertising and promotion coverage.

6. During the first six months of the 2013–14 fiscal year, $400,000 was spent on legal work on a successful patent application. The patent became effective in November 2013. The patent's legal life is 20 years and its economic life is expected to be approximately 10 years.

Instructions

For each of the six items presented, determine and justify the following:

(a) The amount, if any, that should be capitalized and included on Guiglano's statement of financial position prepared as at April 30, 2014.

(b) The amount that should be included in Guiglano's statement of income for the year ended April 30, 2014.

(CMA adapted. Used with permission.)

P12-2 Information for Canberra Corporation's intangible assets follows:

1. On January 1, 2014, Canberra signed an agreement to operate as a franchisee of Hsian Copy Service, Inc. for an initial franchise fee of $75,000. Of this amount, $35,000 was paid when the agreement was signed and the balance is payable in four annual payments of $10,000 each, beginning January 1, 2015. The agreement provides that the down payment is not refundable and no future services are required of the franchisor. The present value at January 1, 2014, of the four annual payments discounted at 8% (the implicit rate for a loan of this type) is $33,121. The agreement also provides that 5% of the franchisee's revenue must be paid to the franchisor each year. Canberra's revenue from the franchise for 2014 was $800,000. Canberra estimates that the franchise's useful life will be 10 years. (*Hint*: Refer to Appendix 6A posted to the student website to determine the proper accounting treatment for the franchise fee and payments.)

2. Canberra incurred $45,000 of experimental costs in its laboratory to develop a patent, and the patent was granted on January 2, 2014. Legal fees and other costs of patent registration totalled $13,600. Canberra estimates that the useful life of the patent will be six years.

3. A trademark was purchased from Shanghai Company for $28,600 on July 1, 2011. The legal costs to successfully defend the trademark totalled $8,160 and were paid on July 1, 2014. Canberra estimates that the trademark's useful life will be 15 years from the acquisition date.

Assume that Canberra reports using ASPE.

Instructions

(a) Prepare a schedule showing the intangible assets section of Canberra's statement of financial position at December 31, 2014. Show supporting calculations in good form.

(b) Prepare a schedule showing all expenses resulting from the transactions that would appear on Canberra's income statement for the year ended December 31, 2014. Show supporting calculations in good form.

(c) How would your response change under IFRS?

(AICPA adapted)

P12-3 Gelato Corporation, a private entity reporting under ASPE, was incorporated on January 3, 2013. The corporation's financial statements for its first year of operations were not examined by a public accountant. You have been engaged to audit the financial statements for the year ended December 31, 2014, and your audit is almost complete. The corporation's trial balance is as follows:

GELATO CORPORATION
Trial Balance
December 31, 2014

	Debit	Credit
Cash	$ 57,000	
Accounts receivable	87,000	
Allowance for doubtful accounts		$ 1,500
Inventory	60,200	
Machinery	82,000	
Equipment	37,000	
Accumulated depreciation		26,200
Intangible assets—patents	128,200	
Leasehold improvements	36,100	
Prepaid expenses	13,000	
Goodwill	30,000	
Intangible assets—licensing agreement No. 1	60,000	
Intangible assets—licensing agreement No. 2	56,000	
Accounts payable		93,000
Unearned revenue		17,280
Common shares		300,000
Retained earnings, January 1, 2014		173,020
Sales		720,000
Cost of goods sold	475,000	
Selling expenses	180,000	
Interest expense	29,500	
Totals	$1,331,000	$1,331,000

The following information is for accounts that may still need adjustment:

1. Patents for Gelato's manufacturing process were acquired on January 2, 2014, at a cost of $87,500. An additional $35,000 was spent in July 2014 and $5,700 in December 2014 to improve machinery covered by the patents and was charged to the Intangible Assets—Patents account. Depreciation on fixed assets was properly recorded for 2014 in accordance with Gelato's practice, which is to take a full year of depreciation for property on hand at June 30. No other depreciation or amortization was recorded. Gelato uses the straight-line method for all amortization and amortizes its patents over their legal life, which was 17 years when the patent was granted. Accumulate all amortization expense in one income statement account.

2. At December 31, 2014, management determined that the undiscounted future net cash flows that are expected from the use of the patent would be $80,000, the value in use was $75,000, the resale value of the patent was approximately $55,000, and disposal costs would be $5,000.

3. On January 3, 2013, Gelato purchased licensing agreement no. 1, which management believed had an unlimited useful life. Licences similar to this are frequently bought and sold. Gelato could only clearly identify cash flows from agreement no. 1 for 15 years. After the 15 years, further cash flows are still possible, but are uncertain. The balance in the Licenses account includes the agreement's purchase price of $57,000 and expenses of $3,000 related to the acquisition. On January 1, 2014, Gelato purchased licensing agreement no. 2, which has a life expectancy of five years. The balance in the Licenses account includes its $54,000 purchase price and $6,000 in acquisition expenses, but it has been reduced by a credit of $4,000 for the advance collection of 2015 revenue from the agreement. In late December 2013, an explosion caused a permanent 60% reduction in the expected revenue-producing value of licensing agreement no. 1. In January 2015, a flood caused additional damage that rendered the agreement worthless.

4. The balance in the Goodwill account results from legal expenses of $30,000 that were incurred for Gelato's incorporation on January 3, 2013. Management assumes that the $30,000 cost will benefit the entire life of the organization, and believes that these costs should be amortized over a limited life of 30 years. No entry has been made yet.

5. The Leasehold Improvements account includes the following: (a) There is a $15,000 cost of improvements that Gelato made to premises that it leases as a tenant. The improvements were made in January 2013 and have a useful life of 12 years. (b) Movable assembly-line equipment costing $15,000 was installed in the leased premises in December 2014. (c) Real estate taxes of $6,100 were paid by Gelato in 2014, but they should have been paid by the landlord under the terms of the lease agreement.

   Gelato paid its rent in full during 2014. A 10-year non-renewable lease was signed on January 3, 2013, for the leased building that Gelato uses in manufacturing operations. No amortization or depreciation has been recorded on any amounts related to the lease or improvements.

6. Included in selling expenses are the following costs incurred to develop a new product. Gelato hopes to establish the technical, financial, and commercial viability of this project in fiscal 2015.

Salaries of two employees who spend approximately 50% of their time on research and development initiatives (this amount represents their full salary)	$110,000
Materials consumed	35,000

Instructions

(a) Prepare an eight-column work sheet to adjust the accounts that require adjustment and include columns for an income statement and a statement of financial position. A separate account should be used for the accumulation of each type of amortization. Formal adjusting journal entries and financial statements are not required.

(b) Prepare Gelato's statement of financial position and income statement for the year ended December 31, 2014, in proper form.

(c) Explain how the accounting would differ if Gelato were reporting under IFRS.

(AICPA adapted)

P12-4   Monsecours Corp., a public company incorporated on June 28, 2013, set up a single account for all of its intangible assets. The following summary discloses the debit entries that were recorded during 2013 and 2014 in that account:

INTANGIBLE ASSETS–MONSECOURS

July	1, 2013	8-year franchise; expiration date of June 30, 2021	$ 35,000
Oct.	1	Advance payment on leasehold (2-year lease)	25,000
Dec. 31		Net loss for 2013 including incorporation fee, $1,000; related legal fees of organizing, $5,000; expenses of recruiting and training staff for start-up of new business, $3,800	17,000
Feb.	15, 2014	Patent purchased (10-year life)	65,400
Mar.	1	Direct costs of acquiring a 5-year licensing agreement	86,000
Apr.	1	Goodwill purchased (indefinite life)	287,500
June	1	Legal fee for successful defence of patent (see above)	13,350
Dec. 31		Costs of research department for year	75,000
	31	Royalties paid under licensing agreement (see above)	2,775

The new business started up on July 2, 2013. No amortization was recorded for 2013 or 2014. The goodwill purchased on April 1, 2014, includes in-process development costs that meet the six development stage criteria, valued at $175,000. The company estimates that this amount will help it generate revenues over a 10-year period.

Instructions

(a) Prepare the necessary entries to clear the Intangible Assets account and to set up separate accounts for distinct types of intangibles. Make the entries as at December 31, 2014, and record any necessary amortization so that all balances are appropriate as at that date. State any assumptions that you need to make to support your entries.

(b) In what circumstances should goodwill be recognized? From the perspective of an investor, does the required recognition and measurement of goodwill provide useful financial statement information?

Digging Deeper

P12-5 During 2012, Medicine Hat Tools Ltd., a Canadian public company, purchased a building site for its product development laboratory at a cost of $61,000. Construction of the building was started in 2012. The building was completed in late December 2013 at a cost of $185,000 and placed in service on January 2, 2014. The building's estimated useful life for depreciation purposes is 15 years. The straight-line method of depreciation is used and there is no estimated residual value. After the building went into service, several projects were begun and many are still in process.

Management estimates that about 50% of the development projects will result in long-term benefits (for at least 10 years) to the corporation. The other projects either benefited the current period or were abandoned before completion. A summary of the different projects, their number, and the direct costs that were incurred for development activities in 2014 appears in the table that follows.

Upon recommendation of the research and development group, Medicine Hat Tools Ltd. acquired a patent for manufacturing rights at a cost of $102,500. The patent was acquired on April 1, 2013, and has an economic life of 10 years.

	Number of Projects	Salaries and Employee Benefits	Other Expenses (Excluding Building Depreciation Charges)
Development of viable products (management intent and capability, financial technical and commercial viability criteria were met)	15	$125,000	$ 81,000
Abandoned projects or projects that benefit the current period only	10	87,000	21,000
Projects in process—results uncertain	5	52,500	18,500
Total	30	$264,500	$120,500

Instructions

(a) How should the items above that relate to product development activities be reported under IFRS on the company's income statement and statement of financial position at December 31, 2014? Be sure to give account titles and amounts, and briefly justify your presentation.

(b) Outline the criteria that would have to be met for any development costs to qualify as an intangible asset.

(CMA adapted. Used with permission.)

P12-6 In 2013, Aquaculture Incorporated applied for several commercial fishing licences for its commercial fishing vessels. The application was successful and on January 2, 2014, Aquaculture was granted 22 commercial fishing licences for a registration fee of $18,700 per licence. According to management, each licence had a useful life of eight years from the date of registration. After the eight years, further cash flows might still be possible, but they are uncertain. There is an active market for Aquaculture's licences, which are freely transferable.

In 2015, due to an oil spill in the bordering ocean and severe commercial fishing restrictions, the value of Aquaculture's licences decreased. As of December 31, 2015, each licence had value in use of $9,500, fair value of $8,300, and costs to sell of $200. In 2017, due to much higher demand and restricted issuance of commercial fishing licences, the value of Aquaculture's licences increased. As of December 31, 2017, each licence had value in use of $14,900, fair value of $17,000, and costs to sell of $200. Aquaculture amortizes intangible assets using the straight-line method, revalues the licences at the end of 2015 and 2017, and prepares financial statements in accordance with IFRS.

Instructions

(a) Prepare the entry to record the costs incurred on January 2, 2014.

(b) Assume that after initial recognition, Aquaculture uses the revaluation model (asset adjustment method) to measure its intangible assets. Prepare the entries required on December 31, 2015, December 31, 2016, and December 31, 2017, and calculate the carrying amount of the intangible asset, if any, as at December 31, 2017.

(c) Assume that after initial recognition, Aquaculture uses the revaluation model (proportionate method) to measure its intangible assets. Prepare the entries required on December 31, 2015, December 31, 2016, and December 31, 2017, and calculate the carrying amount of the intangible asset, if any, as at December 31, 2017.

Digging Deeper

(d) Would an investor prefer Aquaculture to use the asset adjustment method or the proportionate method to apply the revaluation model?

P12-7 Meridan Golf and Sports was formed on July 1, 2014, when Steve Powerdriver purchased Old Master Golf Corporation. Old Master provides video golf instruction at kiosks in shopping malls. Powerdriver's plan is to make the instruction business part of his golf equipment and accessory stores. Powerdriver paid $650,000 cash for Old Master. At the time of purchase, Old Master's balance sheet reported assets of $550,000 and liabilities of $100,000 (shareholders' equity was $450,000). The fair value of Old Master's identifiable assets was estimated to be $700,000. Included in the identifiable assets was the Old Master trade name with a fair value of $15,000 and a copyright on some instructional books with a fair value of $25,000. The trade name had a remaining legal life of five years and can be renewed indefinitely at nominal cost. The copyright had a remaining life of 40 years.

Instructions

Assume that Meridan Golf and Sports is a private company reporting under ASPE.

(a) Prepare the intangible assets section of Meridan Golf and Sports at December 31, 2014. How much amortization expense is included in Meridan's income for the year ended December 31, 2014? Show all supporting calculations.

(b) Prepare the journal entry to record the amortization expense for 2015. Prepare the intangible assets section of Meridan Golf and Sports at December 31, 2015. (No impairment needs to be recorded in 2015.)

(c) At the end of 2016, Powerdriver is evaluating the results of the instructional business. Due to fierce competition from Internet sites and television, the Old Master reporting unit has been losing money and has a carrying amount (including goodwill) of $450,000 and fair value (including goodwill) of $430,000.

Powerdriver has collected the following information about the company's intangible assets:

Intangible Asset	Expected Cash Flows (Undiscounted)	Fair Value
Trade name	$11,000	$ 8,000
Copyright	30,000	25,000

Prepare the required journal entries, if any, to record impairment on Meridan's intangible assets. (Assume that amortization for 2016 has been recorded.) Show supporting calculations.

P12-8   Use the data provided in P12-7. Assume instead that Meridan Golf and Sports is a public company. The relevant information for the impairment test on December 31, 2016, is as follows:

	Carrying Amount	Future Net Cash Flows (Undiscounted)	Value in Use	FV – Selling Costs
Trade name	15,000	11,000	7,000	7,500
Copyright	23,438	30,000	27,000	24,000
Cash-generating unit to which goodwill was allocated	450,000	470,000	440,000	420,000

Instructions

Provide the calculations for the impairment test and any associated journal entry.

P12-9   Six examples follow of purchased intangible assets. They are reported on the consolidated statement of financial position of Phelp Enterprises Limited and include information about their useful and legal lives. Phelp prepares financial statements in accordance with IFRS.

Intangible 1(i) is the trade name for one of the company's subsidiaries. The trade name has a remaining legal life of 16 years, but it can be renewed indefinitely at a very low cost. The subsidiary has grown quickly, has been very successful, and its name is well known to Canadian consumers. Phelp management has concluded that it can identify positive cash flows from the use of the trade name for another 25 years, and assumes the cash flows will continue even longer.

Intangible 1(ii) is the trade name as identified in 1(i), but assume instead that Phelp Enterprises expects to sell this subsidiary in three years since the subsidiary operates in an area that is not part of Phelp's core activities.

Intangible 2 is a licence granted by the federal government to Phelp that allows Phelp to provide essential services to a key military installation overseas. The licence expires in five years, but is renewable indefinitely at little cost. Because of the profitability associated with this licence, Phelp expects to renew it indefinitely. The licence is very marketable and will generate cash flows indefinitely.

Intangible 3 is a magazine subscription list. Phelp expects to use this subscriber list to generate revenues and cash flows for at least 25 years. It has determined the cash flow potential of this intangible by analyzing the subscribers' renewal history, the behaviour of the group of subscribers, and their responses to questionnaires.

Intangible 4 is a non-competition covenant. Phelp acquired this intangible asset when it bought out a major owner-managed competitor. The seller signed a contract in which he agreed not to set up or work for another business that was in direct or indirect competition with Phelp. The projected cash flows resulting from this agreement are expected to continue for at least 25 years.

Intangible 5 is medical files. One of Phelp's subsidiary companies owns several dental clinics. A recent purchase of a retiring dentist's practice required a significant payment for the practice's medical files and clients. Phelp considers that this base will benefit the business for as long as it exists, providing cash flows indefinitely.

Intangible 6 is a favourable lease. Phelp acquired a sublease on a large warehouse property that requires an annual rental amount that is 50% below competitive rates in the area. The lease extends for 35 years.

Instructions

For each intangible asset and situation described above, do the following:

(a) Identify the appropriate method of accounting for the asset subsequent to acquisition, and justify your answer.

(b) Provide an example of a specific situation that would cause you to test the intangible asset for impairment.

P12-10   In late July 2014, Mona Ltd., a private company, paid $2 million to acquire all of the net assets of Lubello Corp., which then became a division of Mona. Lubello reported the following statement of financial position at the time of acquisition:

Current assets	$ 415,000	Current liabilities	$ 300,000
Non-current assets	1,335,000	Long-term liabilities	265,000
		Shareholders' equity	1,185,000
	$1,750,000		$1,750,000

It was determined at the date of the purchase that the fair value of the identifiable net assets of Lubello was $1.7 million. Over the next six months of operations, the new division had operating losses. In addition, it now appears that it will generate substantial losses for the foreseeable future. At December 31, 2014, the fair value of the Lubello Division is $1,850,000, and the division reports the following statement of financial position information:

Current assets	$ 462,000
Non-current assets (including goodwill recognized in purchase)	2,400,000
Current liabilities	(703,500)
Long-term liabilities	(530,000)
Net assets	$1,628,500

Assume that Mona Ltd. prepares financial statements in accordance with ASPE.

Instructions

(a) Calculate the amount of goodwill, if any, that should be recognized in late July 2014.

(b) Determine the impairment loss, if any, to be recognized on December 31, 2014.

(c) Assume that the fair value of the Lubello Division on December 31, 2014, is $1.5 million. Determine the impairment loss, if any, that would be recognized.

(d) Prepare the journal entry to record the impairment loss, if any, in (b) and (c) and indicate where the loss would be reported in the income statement.

(e) Explain how the accounting would differ under IFRS.

P12-11   On September 1, 2014, Madonna Lisa Corporation, a public company, acquired Jaromil Enterprises for a cash payment of $763,000. At the time of purchase, Jaromil's statement of financial position showed assets of $850,000, liabilities of $430,000, and owners' equity of $420,000. The fair value of Jaromil's identifiable assets is estimated to be $1,080,000.

Instructions

(a) Calculate the amount of goodwill acquired by Madonna Lisa.

(b) Assume that the goodwill was allocated entirely to one cash-generating unit (CGU) as indicated below. The CGU's value in use at the statement of financial position date was $3,850,000 and the fair value less costs to sell was $4,250,000. Determine if the goodwill is impaired.

	Plant A CGU
Assets (other than goodwill)	$4,500,000
Goodwill	113,000
Total carrying value of CGU	$4,613,000

(c) Explain how a future reversal of impairment is accounted for under IFRS.

*P12-12 Macho Inc. has recently become interested in acquiring a South American plant to handle many of its production functions in that market. One possible candidate is De Fuentes SA, a closely held corporation, whose owners have decided to sell their business if a proper settlement can be obtained. De Fuentes's statement of financial position is as follows:

Current assets	$125,000
Fair value—net income investments	55,000
Buildings (net)	405,000
Total assets	$585,000
Current liabilities	$ 85,000
Notes payable	105,000
Share capital	225,000
Retained earnings	170,000
Total equities	$585,000

Macho has hired Yardon Appraisal Corporation to determine the proper price to pay for De Fuentes SA. The appraisal firm finds that the fair value – net income investments have a fair value of $75,000 and that inventory is understated by $40,000. All other assets and liabilities have book values that approximate their fair values. An examination of the company's income for the last four years indicates that the net income has steadily increased. In 2014, the company had a net operating income of $110,000, and this income should increase by 15% each year over the next four years. Macho believes that a normal return in this type of business is 15% on net assets. The asset investment in the South American plant is expected to stay the same for the next four years.

Instructions

(a) Yardon Appraisal Corporation has indicated that the company's fair value can be estimated in several ways. Prepare estimates of the value of De Fuentes SA, with the value based on each of the following independent assumptions:

  1. Goodwill is based on the purchase of average excess earnings over the next four years.

  2. Goodwill is equal to the capitalization of average excess earnings of De Fuentes SA at 30%.

  3. Goodwill is equal to the present value of the average excess earnings over the next four years discounted at 15%.

  4. The value of the business is based on the capitalization of future excess earnings of De Fuentes SA at 16%.

(b) De Fuentes SA is willing to sell the business for $1 million. What advice should Yardon Appraisal give Macho in regard to this offer?

(c) If Macho were to pay $850,000 to purchase the assets and assume the liabilities of De Fuentes SA, how would this transaction be reflected on Macho's books?

*P12-13 The president of Plain Corp., Joyce Lima, is thinking of purchasing Balloon Bunch Corporation. She thinks that the offer sounds fair but she wants to consult a professional accountant to be sure. Balloon Bunch Corporation is asking for $85,000 in excess of the fair value of the identifiable net assets. Balloon Bunch's net income figures for the last five years are as follows:

2010—$67,000	2013—$80,000
2011—$50,000	2014—$72,000
2012—$81,000	

The company's identifiable net assets were appraised at $400,000 on December 31, 2014.

You have done some initial research on the balloon industry and discovered that the normal rate of return on identifiable net assets is 15%. After analyzing such variables as the stability of past earnings, the nature of the business, and general economic conditions, you have decided that the average excess earnings for the last five years should be capitalized at 20% and that the excess earnings will continue for about six more years. Further research led you to discover that the Happy Balloon Corporation, a competitor of similar size and profitability, was recently sold for $450,000, five times its average yearly earnings of $90,000.

Instructions

(a) Prepare a schedule that includes the calculation of Balloon Bunch Corporation's goodwill and purchase price under at least three methods.

(b) Write a letter to Joyce Lima that includes all of the following:

  1. An explanation of the nature of goodwill.

2. An explanation of the different acceptable methods of determining the fair value of goodwill. (Include with your explanation the rationale for how each method arrives at a goodwill value.)

3. Advice for Joyce Lima on how to determine her purchase price.

Integrated Cases

Refer to the Case Primer to help you answer these cases.

(*Hint*: If there are issues here that are new, use the conceptual framework to help you support your analysis with solid reasoning.)

IC12-1 Dr. Gary Morrow, a former surgeon, is the president and owner of Morrow Medical (MM), a private Ontario company that focuses on the design and implementation of various medical and pharmaceutical products. With the recent success of various products put to market by MM, Dr. Morrow has decided that this would be a good opportunity to sell his company and retire to the Arizona desert. Dr. Morrow has located a potential buyer of the business and an agreement has been put in place that would see MM being sold at five times the December 31, 2013 net income. The potential buyer is extremely interested in an MM product that is currently in the development stage—the MM Surgical Drill.

During 2013, MM launched into production a special latex glove for use during surgery. This glove is laced with a special anti-bacterial agent that significantly reduces the risk of infection during surgery. This product had been in the development phase since 2010, and in early 2012, it was approved by Health Canada for production and use.

Dr. Morrow was pleased with the initial demand for the product after trial runs conducted by surgeons during late 2012. After the success of the trial testing, MM landed contracts with several hospitals in the province and early feedback was favourable. Dr. Morrow was surprised, however, with how small the quantity of orders placed by hospitals actually was. He was certain that hospitals would quickly run out of the gloves and was beginning to fear that they would buy a competitor's product.

Since Dr. Morrow wanted to prevent hospitals from buying elsewhere, as it would result in a loss of sales for MM, for each purchase order received from a hospital, Dr. Morrow shipped several more units than were ordered. He was certain that all of the extra inventory would eventually be consumed and this was MM's way of avoiding the hospitals' running out of inventory. To prevent hospitals from returning the extra inventory, he allowed them eight months to either pay for the entire shipment or return any unused gloves in excess of the initial amount that was ordered. Dr. Morrow's first priority is always getting the product out of the warehouse and into the hospitals. Orders are generally filled and shipped within two days of the receipt of a purchase order. Because MM is dealing with hospitals, there is little concern over collectability.

During 2008, under the supervision of Dr. Morrow, MM began the research and development of a special surgical drill (the MM Surgical Drill mentioned above) that would allow for more precise handling by surgeons than any other drill currently in the market. The development of this product grew from various market surveys conducted in hospitals throughout Ontario that showed that surgeons were unhappy with the drills that were currently available on the market.

The following costs were incurred in 2013:

Cost of setting up production lab	$ 30,000
Testing of Surgical Drill	100,000
Design of the moulds involved in Surgical Drill technology	17,500
Testing to evaluate product alternatives	12,000
Marketing and promotion costs in connection with launching the surgical gloves	15,000

Dr. Morrow intends to capitalize all of these costs for the December 31 year end. In addition, $25,000 of tool design costs that were expensed in 2012 will be capitalized in 2013.

MM has the technical resources available to complete the Surgical Drill project and, since testing to date has been successful, management intends to bring this product to market in early 2015. MM has been faced with cash flow problems in the last few months but hopes that once MM is sold, additional funding will be available to see this product into its production stage.

In early 2013, an engineer testing the Surgical Drill was severely injured as a result of a product malfunction. This glitch was subsequently identified and fixed. MM was recently sued, alleging it was responsible for the engineer's injuries. The claim is for $500,000. MM lawyers' best estimate of what the company will end up paying is $100,000 to $200,000. As the trial does not begin until 2014, MM has no intention of recording this in its December 31, 2013 financial statements.

Instructions

Adopt the role of the auditor hired by MM's potential buyer and analyze the financial reporting issues.

IC12-2   Biofuel Inc. (BI) is a private company that just started up this year. The company's owner, Sarah Biorini, created a process whereby carbon dioxide (CO_2) emissions are converted into biofuel. Specifically, the CO_2 is pumped into a pond where algae is grown. The algae feeds on the CO_2 and releases oxygen. The algae is harvested, dried, and sold as fuel. The fuel is used by cement manufacturing companies to heat their kilns (ovens). Sarah contributed the prototype and idea to the newly formed company in return for common shares. She estimated that the prototype was worth about $500,000. BI spent the first year developing the idea and by year end was producing and selling the fuel to several cement production companies. Cement companies not only produce large amounts of CO_2, but also need large amounts of fuel to heat their kilns.

One of the critical success factors for BI is that the algae-producing pond be close to the source of CO_2. This reduces transportation costs. After much consideration, BI decided to build pipelines to pump CO_2 from the source (the cement company) into an adjacent algae-filled pond. The pond is excavated by BI but it sits on the cement company's land (close to the source of CO_2). Once a month, BI harvests the algae and ships it to its manufacturing plant to process it into biofuel. It then sells the biofuel back to the cement companies.

The cost of constructing the pipelines is funded by the bank, as is the excavation of the ponds. The construction is done by BI and generally takes about three to six months. The finished biofuel made from algae is priced to recover patent costs and the cost of building the pipe and the ponds as well as any other costs. It is sold back to the cement companies. The cement companies are both suppliers of the CO_2 and customers.

The bank is quite happy to continue funding additional projects as long as BI sends its financial statements to the bank every quarter starting next year. In addition, the bank would like to see audited annual financial statements beginning with the current year. The bank and BI have agreed that the debt to equity ratio cannot exceed 3:1, otherwise the loans become immediately due. BI's accountant is looking to produce the annual financial statements for the first year of operations. He has not yet decided whether to follow IFRS or ASPE and is interested in the differences between the two.

Instructions

Assume the role of BI's accountant and discuss the financial reporting issues relating to the above. Use the case analysis framework presented in class, including an overview, analysis, and recommendations.

Writing Assignments

WA12-1   Kolber Manufacturing Limited designs, manufactures, and distributes safety boots. In January 2014, Kolber purchased another business that manufactures and distributes safety shoes, to complement its existing business. The total purchase price was to be $10 million in cash immediately and another $5 million in cash one year from now. The company's current interest cost is 6%. The assets and liabilities purchased included accounts receivable, finished goods inventories, land and plant, manufacturing equipment and office equipment, accounts payable, and a loan that is secured by the manufacturing equipment. In addition, a trademark was purchased (which has six years remaining on its current legal life), as well as existing customer relationships (although there are no outstanding contracts with these customers), and a non-compete agreement with the existing owners that they will not start any similar business for the next five years. The company reports under IFRS.

Instructions

You are the controller of Kolber and have been given the task of recording the purchase in the company's books.

(a) Outline how you might go about determining how to allocate the purchase price to the intangible assets and any goodwill purchased. In addition, consider how each of these assets is subsequently reported and what the impact will be on net earnings in subsequent years given your decisions now.

(b) If this company reported under ASPE, explain how the impairment test for goodwill would differ from the IFRS method.

(To assist you with this question, you may want to read the following article: "From Intangible to Tangible," by Andrew Michelin, *CA Magazine*, June/July 2008.)

(AICPA adapted)

WA12-2   Weaver Limited is a company that is a distributor of hard-to-find computer supplies such as hardware parts and cables. It sells and ships products all over the world. Recently the board of directors approved the plan and a budget for the company to design its own website. The website has two sections. One is for general information and can be accessed by anyone. On this part of the site, the company has information about what it does, and pictures of all the products sold. The other part of the website is only accessible by logging in. There, customers are given passwords to enter the site and can place their orders, which are then reviewed by the order clerks and sent on to shipping. The IT manager has been put in charge of managing the website project, keeping track and approving all the costs incurred.

The company has incurred the following costs to develop the site: the IT manager's salary for the six months required to supervise the project; legal fees to register the domain name; consulting costs for a feasibility study; purchase of the hardware; software developers to develop the code for the application, installation, and testing of the software; graphic artist to design the layout and colour for the web pages; photographers to take pictures of the products to be shown on the site; staff time to upload all the information to the site, including the company and product descriptions; and the data required to place an order, including prices, data entry screens, and shipping options. Finally, the company has incurred costs to train the employees on using the software. Ongoing costs include updating product prices and content, adding new functions, and backing up the data.

Instructions

You are an external auditor and have been hired by Weaver to explain how these costs should be reported. Using IAS 38 and SIC 32 - Intangible Assets - Web Site Costs (an Interpretation under International Financial Reporting Standards that is accessible via an Internet search), discuss the treatment of these costs, referring to the general principles in IAS 38 to support your analysis. Explain how the company must report costs incurred once the website is operating.

WA12-3 On June 30, 2014, your client, Bearcat Limited, was granted two patents for plastic cartons that it had been producing and marketing profitably for the past three years. One patent covers the manufacturing process and the other covers related products.

Bearcat executives tell you that these patents represent the most significant breakthrough in the industry in the past 30 years. The products have been marketed under the registered trademarks Evertight, Duratainer, and Sealrite. Licences under the patents have already been granted by your client to other manufacturers in Canada and abroad and are producing substantial royalties.

On July 1, Bearcat began patent infringement actions against several companies whose names you recognize as substantial and prominent competitors. Bearcat's management is optimistic that these suits will result in a permanent injunction against the manufacture and sale of the infringing products and collection of damages for loss of profits caused by the alleged infringement.

The financial vice-president has suggested that the patents be recorded at the discounted value of expected net royalty receipts.

Instructions

(a) What is the meaning of "discounted value of expected net receipts"? Explain.

(b) How would the value in (a) be calculated for net royalty receipts?

(c) What is the accounting basis of valuation for Bearcat's patents under ASPE? Under IFRS?

(d) The financial VP has suggested the patents be recorded at the discounted value of expected net royalty receipts. Discuss whether or not this would be allowed under IFRS.

(e) Suppose that the VP (Finance) has suggested that an asset be recognized for the infringement litigation in the financial statements. As the ethical accountant, what would you do? What is the appropriate treatment in the financial statements for the year ending September 30, 2014? Discuss.

(AICPA adapted)

Ethics

*WA12-4 Echo Corp., a retail propane gas distributor, has increased its annual sales volume to a level that is three times greater than the annual sales of a dealer that it purchased in 2014 in order to begin operations. The board of directors of Echo Corp. recently received an offer to negotiate the sale of the company to a large competitor. As a result, the majority of the board wants to increase the stated value of goodwill on the balance sheet to reflect the larger sales volume that it developed through intensive promotion and the product's current market price. A few of the board members, however, would prefer to eliminate goodwill from the balance sheet altogether in order to prevent possible misinterpretations. Goodwill was recorded properly in 2014.

Instructions

(a) Discuss the meaning of the term "goodwill."

(b) Why are the book and fair values of Echo Corp.'s goodwill different?

(c) Discuss the appropriateness of each of the following:
 1. Increasing the stated value of goodwill prior to the negotiations
 2. Eliminating goodwill completely from the balance sheet

(AICPA adapted)

WA12-5 Illustrative examples accompanying IAS 38 provide nine examples of acquired intangibles and how their useful lives should be assessed. The examples are as follows:

 1. An acquired customer list

 2. An acquired patent that expires in 15 years

 3. An acquired copyright that has a remaining legal life of 50 years

4. An acquired broadcasting licence that expires in five years

5. A broadcasting licence that is not renewed by the licensing authority

6. An acquired airline route between two European cities that expires in three years

7. An acquired trademark used to identify and distinguish a consumer product that has been a market leader for the last eight years

8. A trademark acquired 10 years ago that distinguishes a leading consumer product

9. A trademark for a line of products that was acquired several years ago in a business combination

Instructions

Take one of the examples above, as assigned by your instructor. Apply the general principles of IAS 38 to support the guidance given. Present your findings to the class.

WA12-6   Write a brief essay highlighting the differences between IFRS and ASPE noted in this chapter, discussing the conceptual justification for each.

RESEARCH AND FINANCIAL ANALYSIS

RA12-1 British Airways

Real World Emphasis

Access the annual report for **British Airways** plc for the year ended December 31, 2011, from the company's website. Use the notes to the financial statements to answer the following questions.

Instructions

(a) Does British Airways plc report any intangible assets in its 2011 financial statements and accompanying notes? Identify all intangibles, describe their nature, their reported balance sheet amounts at December 31, 2011, and the accounting policies that are applied to these assets. Be sure to discuss any changes in these policies and how they were reported and the impact on the 2011 statements. Finally, discuss any discrepancies with IFRS standards.

(b) What additions were made to the landing rights for 2011? How are the identifiable intangible assets tested for impairment?

(c) How is goodwill tested for impairment? Provide details on the methods and key assumptions used by the company. What was the recoverable amount determined? Do these appear reasonable? Were there any impairment losses recorded in 2011? What assumptions would make the recoverable amount equal to the carrying amount for the network airline operations?

(d) Why is the information provided in (c) considered helpful to users?

RA12-2 Rights to Use Sports Celebrities' Names

Real World Emphasis

Since 1996, **Nike, Inc.** has had endorsement contracts with Tiger Woods and some of the world's best known athletes. For example, Nike has been able to gain the rights to use Tiger Woods's name in advertising promotions and on Nike Golf apparel, footwear, golf balls, and golf equipment.

Instructions

Conduct research on the Internet to determine the nature of the endorsement contracts that Nike has with top athletes such as Tiger Woods. How does Nike pay for the rights to use the names of these athletes? Using Nike, Inc.'s most recent financial statements (that can be found in their Form-10K filing), determine how Nike reports the cost of endorsement contracts. Does the cost qualify as an intangible asset under IAS 38?

RA12-3 Comparative Analysis

Real World Emphasis

Instructions

Go to the SEDAR website (www.sedar.com) and choose two companies from each of four different industry classifications. Choose from a variety of industries such as real estate and construction, food stores (under merchandising), biotechnology and pharmaceuticals (under consumer products) or publishing (under communications and media). From the companies' most recent financial statements, identify the intangibles, the total assets, and the accounting policies for each type of intangible that is reported.

(a) What net amounts were reported for intangible assets by each company? What are the amounts of accumulated amortization reported by these companies for the intangible assets? Have any impairment losses been reported in the current period?

(b) What percentage of total assets does each company have invested in intangible assets?

(c) Does the type of intangible assets differ depending on the type of industry? Does the relative size of the investment in this category of asset differ among industries? Comment.

(d) Do the policies differ by type of intangible? By type of industry?

(e) Describe the type of disclosure provided for those companies that reported impairment losses.

RA12-4 L'Oréal

Real World Emphasis

L'Oréal is the world's largest cosmetic company, with brands such as its own name, Redken, Maybelline, Lancome, and Ralph Lauren, just to name a few.

Instructions

Access L'Oréal's annual financial statements for the year ended December 31, 2011, from the company's website and answer the following questions with respect to the intangible assets.

(a) Identify all types of intangibles that are reported by L'Oréal and their related amounts. You may have to refer to the notes to the financial statements to complete your list. How much was added to each intangible asset during the year? Are intangible assets a significant portion of the company's total assets?

(b) For each intangible asset that you identified, indicate the accounting policy that L'Oréal follows.

(c) Describe how L'Oréal's management tests for impairment of intangibles. Be specific on the methods and assumptions used. Are these reasonable? Is there any other information you would like to have as a user? Were any impairment losses reported in 2011?

(d) Does L'Oréal report any R&D assets? Explain. What were the company's expenditures on R&D for its year ended December 31, 2011?

(e) How does L'Oréal account for advertising costs?

(f) Read Note 2 to the financial statements and describe the amounts of the intangible assets acquired.

RA12-5 Regulated Assets

Instructions

Read the article "Recognizing Assets" by John Browne, *CA Magazine*, December 2008. Answer the following questions.

(a) What are regulatory assets? Which types of companies have these assets?

(b) What are the current accounting issues with respect to reporting and measuring these assets?

(c) Do these assets qualify as intangible assets under IAS 38?

ENDNOTES

[1] GAAP for *Business Combinations* in *CICA Handbook–Accounting*, Part II, Section 1582.03(k) and IFRS 3, Appendix A.

[2] IAS 38, paragraph 21 and *CICA Handbook–Accounting*, Part II, Section 3064.21.

[3] IFRS 2 *Share-based Payment* is considerably more complex than is indicated here. In addition, the term "fair value" used in IFRS 2 differs from the definition of fair value in IFRS 13 *Fair Value Measurement*. When applying IFRS 2, an entity measures fair value in accordance with this definition in IFRS 2, not IFRS 13 (see IFRS 2, paragraphs 6A and 16-18).

[4] If control over the assets is acquired through the acquisition of voting shares, the fair value of all the identifiable assets and liabilities (identifiable net assets) is assigned as their cost through the consolidation process. Refer to Chapter 2 for a discussion of how fair values are determined.

[5] IAS 38, *Basis for Conclusions*: BCZ29.

[6] *CICA Handbook–Accounting*, Part II, Section 3064.08.

[7] *CICA Handbook–Accounting*, Part II, Section 3064.39 and .43; IAS 38.56 and .59.

[8] Under ASPE, interest or borrowing costs would be included only if it is the accounting policy chosen by the entity. See Chapter 10 for a fuller discussion of the capitalization of borrowing costs.

[9] Unlike IAS 38 *Intangible Assets*, ASPE does not specifically refer to mail-order catalogues.

[10] See Chapter 2 for a fuller discussion of fair value measurement.

[11] For indefinite-life intangible assets, the same accounting applies except that the amortization amounts would be nil ($0) amounts.

[12] *CICA Handbook–Accounting*, Part II, Section 3064.61.

[13] *CICA Handbook–Accounting*, Part II, Section 3064.59 and IAS 38.100.

[14] This classification framework is used in IFRS 3 *Business Combinations*: Illustrative Examples IE16—IE44 to describe identifiable intangible assets acquired in a business combination. This same classification was previously used in superseded *CICA Handbook–Accounting* Section 1581 *Businesss Combinations*, Appendix A.

[15] Canadian Intellectual Property Office: http://www.cipo.ic.gc.ca.

[16] To illustrate how various intangibles might arise from a specific product, consider what the Canadian creators of the highly successful game Trivial Pursuit did to protect their creation. First, they copyrighted the 6,000 questions that are at the heart of the game. Then they shielded the Trivial Pursuit name by applying for a registered trademark. As a third mode of protection, the creators obtained a design patent on the playing board's design because it represents a unique graphic creation.

[17] Canadian Intellectual Property Office: http://www.cipo.ic.gc.ca.

[18] Accounting for lease contracts themselves is in the midst of change. Under existing standards, a lease that transfers the risks and rewards of ownership to the lessee is usually treated as an item of property, plant, and equipment, not an intangible asset. This may change before long. An exposure draft was issued by the IASB in 2010, and based on comments received, a re-exposure draft was planned for 2013. With a change in concept to a lease being a "right of use" asset being considered, more contracts will likely fall within the intangible asset category.

[19] Consider the opposite result: Sir Alexander Fleming, who discovered penicillin, decided not to use a patent to protect his discovery. He hoped that companies would produce it more quickly to help save sufferers. Companies, however, refused to develop it because they did not have the protection of a patent and, therefore, were afraid to make the investment.

[20] The Canadian Intellectual Property Office website (http://www.cipo.ic.gc.ca) indicates in its "A Guide to Patents, Part 1" that 90% of patents are for improvements to existing patented inventions.

[21] **Eli Lilly's** well-known drug Prozac, which is used to treat depression, accounted for 43% of the company's U.S. sales in 1998. The patent on Prozac expired in 2001 and the company was unable to extend its protection with a second-use patent for the use of Prozac to treat appetite disorders. Sales of Prozac went down substantially in 2001 as generic equivalents entered the market.

[22] *CICA Handbook–Accounting*, Part II, Section 3063 *Impairment of Long-lived Assets* and IAS 36 *Impairment of Assets*.

[23] When less than a 100% interest is acquired or the controlling interest is acquired in stages, the calculation of goodwill is more complex. This is because a choice is permitted in how the noncontrolling shareholders' interest is calculated and prior holdings are revalued. This topic is left to a course in advanced financial accounting.

[24] *CICA Handbook–Accounting*, Part II, 1582.02A(j) and IFRS 3 Appendix A. Copyright © 2012 IFRS Foundation. All rights reserved. Reproduced by Wiley Canada with the permission of the IFRS Foundation®. No permission granted to third parties to reproduce or distribute.

[25] In reality, the Cash amounts would be netted and only $375,000 would be transferred. If Multi-Diversified gained control over Tractorling by purchasing all of that company's shares instead of buying all the individual assets and liabilities making up the business, the entry would be:

Investment in Shares of Tractorling	400,000	
Cash		400,000

When Multi-Diversified prepares consolidated financial statements, the Investment account is removed from the balance sheet and is replaced with the underlying assets and liabilities that the Investment balance represents. Regardless of the transaction's legal form, the goodwill appears on the investor's consolidated GAAP balance sheet.

[26] Nadi Chlala, Diane Paul, Louise Martel, and Andrée Lavigne, *Financial Reporting in Canada, 2007* (CICA, 2007), p. 343, and Clarence Byrd, Ida Chen, and Joshua Smith, *Financial Reporting in Canada, 2005* (CICA, 2005), p. 256.

[27] Based on estimates from Yahoo Finance, which quoted Apple's September 2011 financial statements as compared with its market capitalization on February 17, 2012. Apple's market capitalization continued to rise, exceeding U.S. $600 billion in April 2012, per www.bbc.co.uk.

[28] A "big bath" in accounting refers to a situation when a company decides that if a loss has to be reported, it might as well report a very large loss. Any loss is seen as negative but the advantage of reporting a bigger loss is that fewer costs remain in the accounts to be reported as future expenses.

[29] If you find this unclear, try the following approach: Start with the total earnings of $375,000 over the past five years and make the necessary adjustments. First add $5 \times \$2,000$ for the average cost/FIFO adjustment and $5 \times \$3,000$ for the depreciation, and then deduct $5 \times \$1,000$ for the patent amortization and $25,000 for the gain on discontinued operations. The adjusted total five-year earnings of $370,000 are then divided by 5 to get the expected future annual earnings. The result is $74,000.

[30] The following illustrates how the capitalization or discount rate might be calculated for a small business:

A Method of Selecting a Capitalization Rate

	%
Long-term Canadian government bond rate	4
Add: Average premium return on small company shares over government bonds	5
Expected total rate of return on small publicly held shares	9
Add: Premium for greater risk and illiquidity	6
Total required expected rate of return, including inflation component	15
Deduct: Consensus long-term inflation expectation	3
Capitalization rate to apply to current earnings	12

Adapted from Warren Kissin and Ronald Zulli, "Valuation of a Closely Held Business," *The Journal of Accountancy*, June 1988, p. 42.

[31] Why do we divide by the capitalization or discount rate to arrive at the goodwill amount? Recall that the present value of an ordinary annuity is equal to:

$$P\overline{n}|i = [1 - 1 \div (1 + i)^n] \div i$$

When a number is capitalized in perpetuity, $(1 + i)^n$ becomes so large that $1/(1 + i)^n$ essentially equals zero, which leaves $1/i$ or, as in the case above, $\$21,500/0.25$ or $\$21,500/0.15$.

[32] The present value of an annuity of $1 received in a steady stream for 10 years in the future discounted at 25% is $3.57050. The present value of an annuity of $21,500, therefore, is $21,500 \times 3.57050 = $76,765.75.

[33] Business valuation is a specialist field. The Canadian Institute of Chartered Business Valuators oversees the granting of the specialist designation, Chartered Business Valuator (CBV), to professionals who meet the education, experience, and examination requirements.

Cumulative Coverage: Chapters 10 to 12

Fit Fixtures Incorporated (FFI) is a manufacturer of exercise equipment such as treadmills, stair climbers, and elliptical machines. The company has a December 31 year end and uses ASPE. As at December 31, 2013, the company had the following balances in its capital asset accounts:

Account Title	Description	Cost at December 31, 2013	Accumulated Depreciation/ Amortization at Dec. 31, 2013	Depreciation/ Amortization Method and Rate
Land	Land on which manufacturing facility is located	$1,500,000	$0	Not applicable
Factory building	Manufacturing facility in Ontario	$10,875,000	$1,057,500	Residual value $5,000,000 Straight-line depreciation over 25 years
Equipment	Used in manufacturing	$23,756,000	$17,179,022	Declining-balance, 25%
Office equipment	Used by office staff	$3,000,000	$2,688,960	Declining-balance, 40%
Vehicles	Delivery trucks, vehicles used by sales and office staff	$500,000	$315,680	Declining-balance, 20%
Goodwill	Purchased in 2009 when the company took over the business of its predecessor	$500,000	$0	Not applicable
Customer list	Purchased in 2009 when the company took over the business of its predecessor	$250,000	$112,500	Straight-line over 10 years

The accounting staff member who normally looks after the capital asset accounts was on maternity leave for the year, and the company put all transactions in a temporary account called Asset Additions and Disposals, which has a current balance of $2,844,000. The company policy on calculating depreciation for partial periods of ownership is to take 50% of the normal amount of depreciation in the year of addition and none in the year of disposal. Due to the maternity leave, no depreciation or amortization expense has been taken yet in 2014. FFI does not currently capitalize interest costs.

1. The company completed construction of a new plant in Saskatchewan on December 15, 2014, to help it better meet the needs of its customers west of Ontario. The costs associated with this construction project were as follows:

Land	$ 500,000
Construction contract: building life, 20 years, residual value $50,000	1,500,000
Manufacturing equipment	See point 4.
Office equipment	250,000
Avoidable interest calculated at 8% on financing of project from inception until put in use	75,000

2. FFI purchased a used computer at an auction for $2,500. This purchase included a printer that needed a new drum. The cost of the new drum was $500. The computer was to be used in the

manufacturing plant, and the printer in the office. The used computer's fair market value was $2,000 if purchased separately. The printer was worth $1,000 without a drum and $1,500 with the drum replaced.

3. In June 2014, FFI sold a delivery truck for $10,000. The truck originally cost $25,000, and accumulated depreciation on the truck to December 31, 2013, was $10,000. The sale was recorded as a debit to Cash and a credit to Asset Additions and Disposals.

4. The equipment purchased for the new plant was purchased on a deferred payment contract signed on December 1. FFI issued a $5-million, five-year, non–interest-bearing note payable to the equipment supplier at a time when the annual market rate of interest was 6%. The note will be repaid with five equal payments made on December 1 of each year, beginning in 2015. The equipment's fair market value cannot be readily determined. No entry has been made for the equipment.

5. Due to an office redesign in the Ontario building, FFI traded some old office equipment for different office equipment with a similar life and value in use. The fair value of the equipment disposed of was $5,000. The cost of this equipment was $7,000, and the accumulated depreciation on the equipment at December 31, 2013, was $3,000. This transaction was not recorded in the books of account. No entry was made to record the exchange.

6. Shortly after the new factory was complete, vandals attacked the building and significant damage was done. The costs to correct the damage, which were not covered by insurance, included:

New paint to cover graffiti	$ 4,000
Glass for broken windows	10,000
Improved security system	25,000

7. During the year, the company developed a new piece of exercise equipment that had a built-in video game. It was the policy to amortize development costs on a straight-line basis over three years, with 50% of the normal amount in the year of development. The costs associated with product development included:

Costs to determine how a video game would work with exercise equipment	$ 50,000
Design, testing, and construction of prototype equipment	350,000
Determining the best production process for the new equipment	40,000
Advertising costs to alert customers about the new product	47,000

8. The customer list has lost value and will not provide benefits through to 2019 as was originally predicted. It is now expected to provide undiscounted future cash flows of $50,000 in total over the next two years. There are no estimated costs to sell the list as it will not be sold, and the value in use is $46,000. Goodwill has a recoverable value of $700,000 as at December 31, 2014.

Instructions

It is year end, and you have been asked to assist the company in preparing the financial statements.

(a) Create all necessary journal entries and the Capital Assets section of the statement of financial position at December 31, 2014.

(b) If the company were using IFRS, what changes would be required to your answer?

Table A-1

FUTURE VALUE OF 1

(FUTURE VALUE OF A SINGLE SUM)

$$FVF_{n,\,i} = (1+i)^n$$

(n) periods	2%	2½%	3%	4%	5%	6%	8%	9%	10%	11%	12%	15%
1	1.02000	1.02500	1.03000	1.04000	1.05000	1.06000	1.08000	1.09000	1.10000	1.11000	1.12000	1.15000
2	1.04040	1.05063	1.06090	1.08160	1.10250	1.12360	1.16640	1.18810	1.21000	1.23210	1.25440	1.32250
3	1.06121	1.07689	1.09273	1.12486	1.15763	1.19102	1.25971	1.29503	1.33100	1.36763	1.40493	1.52088
4	1.08243	1.10381	1.12551	1.16986	1.21551	1.26248	1.36049	1.41158	1.46410	1.51807	1.57352	1.74901
5	1.10408	1.13141	1.15927	1.21665	1.27628	1.33823	1.46933	1.53862	1.61051	1.68506	1.76234	2.01136
6	1.12616	1.15969	1.19405	1.26532	1.34010	1.41852	1.58687	1.67710	1.77156	1.87041	1.97382	2.31306
7	1.14869	1.18869	1.22987	1.31593	1.40710	1.50363	1.71382	1.82804	1.94872	2.07616	2.21068	2.66002
8	1.17166	1.21840	1.26677	1.36857	1.47746	1.59385	1.85093	1.99256	2.14359	2.30454	2.47596	3.05902
9	1.19509	1.24886	1.30477	1.42331	1.55133	1.68948	1.99900	2.17189	2.35795	2.55803	2.77308	3.51788
10	1.21899	1.28008	1.34392	1.48024	1.62889	1.79085	2.15892	2.36736	2.59374	2.83942	3.10585	4.04556
11	1.24337	1.31209	1.38423	1.53945	1.71034	1.89830	2.33164	2.58043	2.85312	3.15176	3.47855	4.65239
12	1.26824	1.34489	1.42576	1.60103	1.79586	2.01220	2.51817	2.81267	3.13843	3.49845	3.89598	5.35025
13	1.29361	1.37851	1.46853	1.66507	1.88565	2.13293	2.71962	3.06581	3.45227	3.88328	4.36349	6.15279
14	1.31948	1.41297	1.51259	1.73168	1.97993	2.26090	2.93719	3.34173	3.79750	4.31044	4.88711	7.07571
15	1.34587	1.44830	1.55797	1.80094	2.07893	2.39656	3.17217	3.64248	4.17725	4.78459	5.47357	8.13706
16	1.37279	1.48451	1.60471	1.87298	2.18287	2.54035	3.42594	3.97031	4.59497	5.31089	6.13039	9.35762
17	1.40024	1.52162	1.65285	1.94790	2.29202	2.69277	3.70002	4.32763	5.05447	5.89509	6.86604	10.76126
18	1.42825	1.55966	1.70243	2.02582	2.40662	2.85434	3.99602	4.71712	5.55992	6.54355	7.68997	12.37545
19	1.45681	1.59865	1.75351	2.10685	2.52695	3.02560	4.31570	5.14166	6.11591	7.26334	8.61276	14.23177
20	1.48595	1.63862	1.80611	2.19112	2.65330	3.20714	4.66096	5.60441	6.72750	8.06231	9.64629	16.36654
21	1.51567	1.67958	1.86029	2.27877	2.78596	3.39956	5.03383	6.10881	7.40025	8.94917	10.80385	18.82152
22	1.54598	1.72157	1.91610	2.36992	2.92526	3.60354	5.43654	6.65860	8.14028	9.93357	12.10031	21.64475
23	1.57690	1.76461	1.97359	2.46472	3.07152	3.81975	5.87146	7.25787	8.95430	11.02627	13.55235	24.89146
24	1.60844	1.80873	2.03279	2.56330	3.22510	4.04893	6.34118	7.91108	9.84973	12.23916	15.17863	28.62518
25	1.64061	1.85394	2.09378	2.66584	3.38635	4.29187	6.84847	8.62308	10.83471	13.58546	17.00000	32.91895
26	1.67342	1.90029	2.15659	2.77247	3.55567	4.54938	7.39635	9.39916	11.91818	15.07986	19.04007	37.85680
27	1.70689	1.94780	2.22129	2.88337	3.73346	4.82235	7.98806	10.24508	13.10999	16.73865	21.32488	43.53532
28	1.74102	1.99650	2.28793	2.99870	3.92013	5.11169	8.62711	11.16714	14.42099	18.57990	23.88387	50.06561
29	1.77584	2.04641	2.35657	3.11865	4.11614	5.41839	9.31727	12.17218	15.86309	20.62369	26.74993	57.57545
30	1.81136	2.09757	2.42726	3.24340	4.32194	5.74349	10.06266	13.26768	17.44940	22.89230	29.95992	66.21177
31	1.84759	2.15001	2.50008	3.37313	4.53804	6.08810	10.86767	14.46177	19.19434	25.41045	33.55511	76.14354
32	1.88454	2.20376	2.57508	3.50806	4.76494	6.45339	11.73708	15.76333	21.11378	28.20560	37.58173	87.56507
33	1.92223	2.25885	2.65234	3.64838	5.00319	6.84059	12.67605	17.18203	23.22515	31.30821	42.09153	100.69983
34	1.96068	2.31532	2.73191	3.79432	5.25335	7.25103	13.69013	18.72841	25.54767	34.75212	47.14252	115.80480
35	1.99989	2.37321	2.81386	3.94609	5.51602	7.68609	14.78534	20.41397	28.10244	38.57485	52.79962	133.17552
36	2.03989	2.43254	2.88928	4.10393	5.79182	8.14725	15.96817	22.25123	30.91268	42.81808	59.13557	153.15185
37	2.08069	2.49335	2.98523	4.26809	6.08141	8.63609	17.24563	24.25384	34.00395	47.52807	66.23184	176.12463
38	2.12230	2.55568	3.07478	4.43881	6.38548	9.15425	18.62528	26.43668	37.40434	52.75616	74.17966	202.54332
39	2.16474	2.61957	3.16703	4.61637	6.70475	9.70351	20.11530	28.81598	41.14479	58.55934	83.08122	232.92482
40	2.20804	2.68506	3.26204	4.80102	7.03999	10.28572	21.72452	31.40942	45.25926	65.00087	93.05097	267.86355

Table A-2

PRESENT VALUE OF 1
(PRESENT VALUE OF A SINGLE SUM)

$$PVF_{n,i} = \frac{1}{(1+i)^n} = (1+i)^{-n}$$

(n) periods	2%	2½%	3%	4%	5%	6%	8%	9%	10%	11%	12%	15%
1	.98039	.97561	.97087	.96156	.95238	.94340	.92593	.91743	.90909	.90090	.89286	.86957
2	.96117	.95181	.94260	.92456	.90703	.89000	.85734	.84168	.82645	.81162	.79719	.75614
3	.94232	.92860	.91514	.88900	.86384	.83962	.79383	.77218	.75132	.73119	.71178	.65752
4	.92385	.90595	.88849	.85480	.82270	.79209	.73503	.70843	.68301	.65873	.63552	.57175
5	.90583	.88385	.86261	.82193	.78353	.74726	.68058	.64993	.62092	.59345	.56743	.49718
6	.88797	.86230	.83748	.79031	.74622	.70496	.63017	.59627	.56447	.53464	.50663	.43233
7	.87056	.84127	.81309	.75992	.71068	.66506	.58349	.54703	.51316	.48166	.45235	.37594
8	.85349	.82075	.78941	.73069	.67684	.62741	.54027	.50187	.46651	.43393	.40388	.32690
9	.83676	.80073	.76642	.70259	.64461	.59190	.50025	.46043	.42410	.39092	.36061	.28426
10	.82035	.78120	.74409	.67556	.61391	.55839	.46319	.42241	.38554	.35218	.32197	.24719
11	.80426	.76214	.72242	.64958	.58468	.52679	.42888	.38753	.35049	.31728	.28748	.21494
12	.78849	.74356	.70138	.62460	.55684	.49697	.39711	.35554	.31863	.28584	.25668	.18691
13	.77303	.72542	.68095	.60057	.53032	.46884	.36770	.32618	.28966	.25751	.22917	.16253
14	.75788	.70773	.66112	.57748	.50507	.44230	.34046	.29925	.26333	.23199	.20462	.14133
15	.74301	.69047	.64186	.55526	.48102	.41727.	.31524	.27454	.23939	.20900	.18270	.12289
16	.72845	.67362	.62317	.53391	.45811	.39365	.29189	.25187	.21763	.18829	.16312	.10687
17	.71416	.65720	.60502	.51337	.43630	.37136	.27027	.23107	.19785	.16963	.14564	.09293
18	.70016	.64117	.58739	.49363	.41552	.35034	.25025	.21199	.17986	.15282	.13004	.08081
19	.68643	.62553	.57029	.47464	.39573	.33051	.23171	.19449	.16351	.13768	.11611	.07027
20	.67297	.61027	.55368	.45639	.37689	.31180	.21455	.17843	.14864	.12403	.10367	.06110
21	.65978	.59539	.53755	.43883	.35894	.29416	.19866	.16370	.13513	.11174	.09256	.05313
22	.64684	.58086	.52189	.42196	.34185	.27751	.18394	.15018	.12285	.10067	.08264	.04620
23	.63416	.56670	.50669	.40573	.32557	.26180	.17032	.13778	.11168	.09069	.07379	.04017
24	.62172	.55288	.49193	.39012	.31007	.24698	.15770	.12641	.10153	.08170	.06588	.03493
25	.60953	.53939	.47761	.37512	.29530	.23300	.14602	.11597	.09230	.07361	.05882	.03038
26	.59758	.52623	.46369	.36069	.28124	.21981	.13520	.10639	.08391	.06631	.05252	.02642
27	.58586	.51340	.45019	.34682	.26785	.20737	.12519	.09761	.07628	.05974	.04689	.02297
28	.57437	.50088	.43708	.33348	.25509	.19563	.11591	.08955	.06934	.05382	.04187	.01997
29	.56311	.48866	.42435	.32065	.24295	.18456	.10733	.08216	.06304	.04849	.03738	.01737
30	.55207	.47674	.41199	.30832	.23138	.17411	.09938	.07537	.05731	.04368	.03338	.01510
31	.54125	.46511	.39999	.29646	.22036	.16425	.09202	.06915	.05210	.03935	.02980	.01313
32	.53063	.45377	.38834	.28506	.20987	.15496	.08520	.06344	.04736	.03545	.02661	.01142
33	.52023	.44270	.37703	.27409	.19987	.14619	.07889	.05820	.04306	.03194	.02376	.00993
34	.51003	.43191	.36604	.26355	.19035	.13791	.07305	.05340	.03914	.02878	.02121	.00864
35	.50003	.42137	.35538	.25342	.18129	.13011	.06763	.04899	.03558	.02592	.01894	.00751
36	.49022	.41109	.34503	.24367	.17266	.12274	.06262	.04494	.03235	.02335	.01691	.00653
37	.48061	.40107	.33498	.23430	.16444	.11579	.05799	.04123	.02941	.02104	.01510	.00568
38	.47119	.39128	.32523	.22529	.15661	.10924	.05369	.03783	.02674	.01896	.01348	.00494
39	.46195	.38174	.31575	.21662	.14915	.10306	.04971	.03470	.02430	.01708	.01204	.00429
40	.45289	.37243	.30656	.20829	.14205	.09722	.04603	.03184	.02210	.01538	.01075	.00373

Table A-3

FUTURE VALUE OF AN ORDINARY ANNUITY OF 1

$$FVF-OA_{n,\,i} = \frac{(1+i)^n - 1}{i}$$

(n) periods	2%	2½%	3%	4%	5%	6%	8%	9%	10%	11%	12%	15%
1	1.00000	1.00000	1.00000	1.00000	1.00000	1.00000	1.00000	1.00000	1.00000	1.00000	1.00000	1.00000
2	2.02000	2.02500	2.03000	2.04000	2.05000	2.06000	2.08000	2.09000	2.10000	2.11000	2.12000	2.15000
3	3.06040	3.07563	3.09090	3.12160	3.15250	3.18360	3.24640	3.27810	3.31000	3.34210	3.37440	3.47250
4	4.12161	4.15252	4.18363	4.24646	4.31013	4.37462	4.50611	4.57313	4.64100	4.70973	4.77933	4.99338
5	5.20404	5.25633	5.30914	5.41632	5.52563	5.63709	5.86660	5.98471	6.10510	6.22780	6.35285	6.74238
6	6.30812	6.38774	6.46841	6.63298	6.80191	6.97532	7.33592	7.52334	7.71561	7.91286	8.11519	8.75374
7	7.43428	7.54743	7.66246	7.89829	8.14201	8.39384	8.92280	9.20044	9.48717	9.78327	10.08901	11.06680
8	8.58297	8.73612	8.89234	9.21423	9.54911	9.89747	10.63663	11.02847	11.43589	11.85943	12.29969	13.72682
9	9.75463	9.95452	10.15911	10.58280	11.02656	11.49132	12.48756	13.02104	13.57948	14.16397	14.77566	16.78584
10	10.94972	11.20338	11.46338	12.00611	12.57789	13.18079	14.48656	15.19293	15.93743	16.72201	17.54874	20.30372
11	12.16872	12.48347	12.80780	13.48635	14.20679	14.97164	16.64549	17.56029	18.53117	19.56143	20.65458	24.34928
12	13.41209	13.79555	14.19203	15.02581	15.91713	16.86994	18.97713	20.14072	21.38428	22.71319	24.13313	29.00167
13	14.68033	15.14044	15.61779	16.62684	17.71298	18.88214	21.49530	22.95339	24.52271	26.21164	28.02911	34.35192
14	15.97394	16.51895	17.08632	18.29191	19.59863	21.01507	24.21492	26.01919	27.97498	30.09492	32.39260	40.50471
15	17.29342	17.93193	18.59891	20.02359	21.57856	23.27597	27.15211	29.36092	31.77248	34.40536	37.27972	47.58041
16	18.63929	19.38022	20.15688	21.82453	23.65749	25.67253	30.32428	33.00340	35.94973	39.18995	42.75328	55.71747
17	20.01207	20.86473	21.76159	23.69751	25.84037	28.21288	33.75023	36.97371	40.54470	44.50084	48.88367	65.07509
18	21.41231	22.38635	23.41444	25.64541	28.13238	30.90565	37.45024	41.30134	45.59917	50.39593	55.74972	75.83636
19	22.84056	23.94601	25.11687	27.67123	30.53900	33.75999	41.44626	46.01846	51.15909	56.93949	63.43968	88.21181
20	24.29737	25.54466	26.87037	29.77808	33.06595	36.78559	45.76196	51.16012	57.27500	64.20283	72.05244	102.44358
21	25.78332	27.18327	28.67649	31.96920	35.71925	39.99273	50.42292	56.76453	64.00250	72.26514	81.69874	118.81012
22	27.29898	28.86286	30.53678	34.24797	38.50521	43.39229	55.45676	62.87334	71.40275	81.21431	92.50258	137.63164
23	28.84496	30.58443	32.45288	36.61789	41.43048	46.99583	60.89330	69.53194	79.54302	91.14788	104.60289	159.27638
24	30.42186	32.34904	34.42647	39.08260	44.50200	50.81558	66.76476	76.78981	88.49733	102.17415	118.15524	184.16784
25	32.03030	34.15776	36.45926	41.64591	47.72710	54.86451	73.10594	84.70090	98.34706	114.41331	133.33387	212.79302
26	33.67091	36.01171	38.55304	44.31174	51.11345	59.15638	79.95442	93.32398	109.18177	127.99877	150.33393	245.71197
27	35.34432	37.91200	40.70963	47.08421	54.66913	63.70577	87.35077	102.72314	121.09994	143.07864	169.37401	283.56877
28	37.05121	39.85990	42.93092	49.96758	58.40258	68.52811	95.33883	112.96822	134.20994	159.81729	190.69889	327.10408
29	38.79223	41.85630	45.21885	52.96629	62.32271	73.63980	103.96594	124.13536	148.63093	178.39719	214.58275	377.16969
30	40.56808	43.90270	47.57542	56.08494	66.43885	79.05819	113.28321	136.30754	164.49402	199.02088	241.33268	434.74515
31	42.37944	46.00027	50.00268	59.32834	70.76079	84.80168	123.34587	149.57522	181.94343	221.91317	271.29261	500.95692
32	44.22703	48.15028	52.50276	62.70147	75.29883	90.88978	134.21354	164.03699	201.13777	247.32362	304.84772	577.10046
33	46.11157	50.35403	55.07784	66.20953	80.06377	97.34316	145.95062	179.80032	222.25154	275.52922	342.42945	644.66553
34	48.03380	52.61289	57.73018	69.85791	85.06696	104.18376	158.62667	196.98234	245.47670	306.83744	384.52098	765.36535
35	49.99448	54.92821	60.46208	73.65222	90.32031	111.43478	172.31680	215.71076	271.02437	341.58955	431.66350	881.17016
36	51.99437	57.30141	63.27594	77.59831	95.83632	119.12087	187.10215	236.12472	299.12681	380.16441	484.46312	1014.34568
37	54.03425	59.73395	66.17422	81.70225	101.62814	127.26812	203.07032	258.37595	330.03949	422.98249	543.59869	1167.49753
38	56.11494	62.22730	69.15945	85.97034	107.70955	135.90421	220.31595	282.62978	364.04343	470.51056	609.83053	1343.62216
39	58.23724	64.78298	72.23423	90.40915	114.09502	145.05846	238.94122	309.06646	401.44778	523.26673	684.01020	1546.16549
40	60.40198	67.40255	75.40126	95.02552	120.79977	154.76197	259.05652	337.88245	442.59256	581.82607	767.09142	1779.09031

Table A-4

PRESENT VALUE OF AN ORDINARY ANNUITY OF 1

$$PVF\text{-}OA_{n,\,i} = \frac{1 - \dfrac{1}{(1+i)^n}}{i}$$

(n) periods	2%	2½%	3%	4%	5%	6%	8%	9%	10%	11%	12%	15%
1	.98039	.97561	.97087	.96154	.95238	.94340	.92593	.91743	.90909	.90090	.89286	.86957
2	1.94156	1.92742	1.91347	1.88609	1.85941	1.83339	1.78326	1.75911	1.73554	1.71252	1.69005	1.62571
3	2.88388	2.85602	2.82861	2.77509	2.72325	2.67301	2.57710	2.53130	2.48685	2.44371	2.40183	2.28323
4	3.80773	3.76197	3.71710	3.62990	3.54595	3.46511	3.31213	3.23972	3.16986	3.10245	3.03735	2.85498
5	4.71346	4.64583	4.57971	4.45182	4.32948	4.21236	3.99271	3.88965	3.79079	3.69590	3.60478	3.35216
6	5.60143	5.50813	5.41719	5.24214	5.07569	4.91732	4.62288	4.48592	4.35526	4.23054	4.11141	3.78448
7	6.47199	6.34939	6.23028	6.00205	5.78637	5.58238	5.20637	5.03295	4.86842	4.71220	4.56376	4.16042
8	7.32548	7.17014	7.01969	6.73274	6.46321	6.20979	5.74664	5.53482	5.33493	5.14612	4.96764	4.48732
9	8.16224	7.97087	7.78611	7.43533	7.10782	6.80169	6.24689	5.99525	5.75902	5.53705	5.32825	4.77158
10	8.98259	8.75206	8.53020	8.11090	7.72173	7.36009	6.71008	6.41766	6.14457	5.88923	5.65022	5.01877
11	9.78685	9.51421	9.25262	8.76048	8.30641	7.88687	7.13896	6.80519	6.49506	6.20652	5.93770	5.23371
12	10.57534	10.25776	9.95400	9.38507	8.86325	8.38384	7.53608	7.16073	6.81369	6.49236	6.19437	5.42062
13	11.34837	10.98319	10.63496	9.98565	9.39357	8.85268	7.90378	7.48690	7.10336	6.74987	6.42355	5.58315
14	12.10625	11.69091	11.29607	10.56312	9.89864	9.29498	8.24424	7.78615	7.36669	6.98187	6.62817	5.72448
15	12.84926	12.38138	11.93794	11.11839	10.37966	9.71225	8.55948	8.06069	7.60608	7.19087	6.81086	5.84737
16	13.57771	13.05500	12.56110	11.65230	10.83777	10.10590	8.85137	8.31256	7.82371	7.37916	6.97399	5.95424
17	14.29187	13.71220	13.16612	12.16567	11.27407	10.47726	9.12164	8.54363	8.02155	7.54879	7.11963	6.04716
18	14.99203	14.35336	13.75351	12.65930	11.68959	10.82760	9.37189	8.75563	8.20141	7.70162	7.24967	6.12797
19	15.67846	14.97889	14.32380	13.13394	12.08532	11.15812	9.60360	8.95012	8.36492	7.83929	7.36578	6.19823
20	16.35143	15.58916	14.87747	13.59033	12.46221	11.46992	9.81815	9.12855	8.51356	7.96333	7.46944	6.25933
21	17.01121	16.18455	15.41502	14.02916	12.82115	11.76408	10.01680	9.29224	8.64869	8.07507	7.56200	6.31246
22	17.65805	16.76541	15.93692	14.45112	13.16800	12.04158	10.20074	9.44243	8.77154	8.17574	7.64465	6.35866
23	18.29220	17.33211	16.44361	14.85684	13.48857	12.30338	10.37106	9.58021	8.88322	8.26643	7.71843	6.39884
24	18.91393	17.88499	16.93554	15.24696	13.79864	12.55036	10.52876	9.70661	8.98474	8.34814	7.78432	6.43377
25	19.52346	18.42438	17.41315	15.62208	14.09394	12.78336	10.67478	9.82258	9.07704	8.42174	7.84314	6.46415
26	20.12104	18.95061	17.87684	15.98277	14.37519	13.00317	10.80998	9.92897	9.16095	8.48806	7.89566	6.49056
27	20.70690	19.46401	18.32703	16.32959	14.64303	13.21053	10.93516	10.02658	9.23722	8.45780	7.94255	6.51353
28	21.28127	19.96489	18.76411	16.66306	14.89813	13.40616	11.05108	10.11613	9.30657	8.60162	7.98442	6.53351
29	21.84438	20.45355	19.18845	16.98371	15.14107	13.59072	11.15841	10.19828	9.36961	8.65011	8.02181	6.55088
30	22.39646	20.93029	19.60044	17.29203	15.37245	13.76483	11.25778	10.27365	9.42691	8.69379	8.05518	6.56598
31	22.93770	21.39541	20.00043	17.58849	15.59281	13.92909	11.34980	10.34280	9.47901	8.73315	8.08499	6.57911
32	23.46833	21.84918	20.38877	17.87355	15.80268	14.08404	11.43500	10.40624	9.52638	8.76860	8.11159	6.59053
33	23.98856	22.29188	20.76579	18.14765	16.00255	14.23023	11.51389	10.46444	9.56943	8.80054	8.13535	6.60046
34	24.49859	22.72379	21.13184	18.41120	16.19290	14.36814	11.58693	10.51784	9.60858	8.82932	8.15656	6.60910
35	24.99862	23.14516	21.48722	18.66461	16.37419	14.49825	11.65457	10.56682	9.64416	8.85524	8.17550	6.61661
36	25.48884	23.55625	21.83225	18.90828	16.54685	14.62099	11.71719	10.61176	9.67651	8.87859	8.19241	6.62314
37	25.96945	23.95732	22.16724	19.14258	16.71129	14.73678	11.77518	10.65299	9.70592	8.89963	8.20751	6.62882
38	26.44064	24.34860	22.49246	19.36786	16.86789	14.84602	11.82887	10.69082	9.73265	8.91859	8.22099	6.63375
39	26.90259	24.73034	22.80822	19.58448	17.01704	14.94907	11.87858	10.72552	9.75697	8.93567	8.23303	6.63805
40	27.35548	25.10278	23.11477	19.79277	17.15909	15.04630	11.92461	10.75736	9.77905	8.95105	8.24378	6.64178

Table A-5

PRESENT VALUE OF AN ANNUITY DUE OF 1

$$PVF-AD_{n,\,i}=1+\frac{1-\dfrac{1}{(1+i)^{n-1}}}{i}$$

(n) periods	2%	2½%	3%	4%	5%	6%	8%	9%	10%	11%	12%	15%
1	1.00000	1.00000	1.00000	1.00000	1.00000	1.00000	1.00000	1.00000	1.00000	1.00000	1.00000	1.00000
2	1.98039	1.97561	1.97087	1.96154	1.95238	1.94340	1.92593	1.91743	1.90909	1.90090	1.89286	1.86957
3	2.94156	2.92742	2.91347	2.88609	2.85941	2.83339	2.78326	2.75911	2.73554	2.71252	2.69005	2.62571
4	3.88388	3.85602	3.82861	3.77509	3.72325	3.67301	3.57710	3.53130	3.48685	3.44371	3.40183	3.28323
5	4.80773	4.76197	4.71710	4.62990	4.54595	4.46511	4.31213	4.23972	4.16986	4.10245	4.03735	3.85498
6	5.71346	5.64583	5.57971	5.45182	5.32948	5.21236	4.99271	4.88965	4.79079	4.69590	4.60478	4.35216
7	6.60143	6.50813	6.41719	6.24214	6.07569	5.91732	5.62288	5.48592	5.35526	5.23054	5.11141	4.78448
8	7.47199	7.34939	7.23028	7.00205	6.78637	6.58238	6.20637	6.03295	5.86842	5.71220	5.56376	5.16042
9	8.32548	8.17014	8.01969	7.73274	7.46321	7.20979	6.74664	6.53482	6.33493	6.14612	5.96764	5.48732
10	9.16224	8.97087	8.78611	8.43533	8.10782	7.80169	7.24689	6.99525	6.75902	6.53705	6.32825	5.77158
11	9.98259	9.75206	9.53020	9.11090	8.72173	8.36009	7.71008	7.41766	7.14457	6.88923	6.65022	6.01877
12	10.78685	10.51421	10.25262	9.76048	9.30641	8.88687	8.13896	7.80519	7.49506	7.20652	6.93770	6.23371
13	11.57534	11.25776	10.95400	10.38507	9.86325	9.38384	8.53608	8.16073	7.81369	7.49236	7.19437	6.42062
14	12.34837	11.98319	11.63496	10.98565	10.39357	9.85268	8.90378	8.48690	8.10336	7.74987	7.42355	6.58315
15	13.10625	12.69091	12.29607	11.56312	10.89864	10.29498	9.24424	8.78615	9.36669	7.98187	7.62817	6.72448
16	13.84926	13.38138	12.93794	12.11839	11.37966	10.71225	9.55948	9.06069	8.60608	8.19087	7.81086	6.84737
17	14.57771	14.05500	13.56110	12.65230	11.83777	11.10590	9.85137	9.31256	8.82371	8.37916	7.97399	6.95424
18	15.29187	14.71220	14.16612	13.16567	12.27407	11.47726	10.12164	9.54363	9.02155	8.54879	8.11963	7.04716
19	15.99203	15.35336	14.75351	13.65930	12.68959	11.82760	10.37189	9.75563	9.20141	8.70162	8.24967	7.12797
20	16.67846	15.97889	15.32380	14.13394	13.08532	12.15812	10.60360	9.95012	9.36492	8.83929	8.36578	7.19823
21	17.35143	16.58916	15.87747	14.59033	13.46221	12.46992	10.81815	10.12855	9.51356	8.96333	8.46944	7.25933
22	18.01121	17.18455	16.41502	15.02916	13.82115	12.76408	11.01680	10.29224	9.64869	9.07507	8.56200	7.31246
23	18.65805	17.76541	16.93692	15.45112	14.16300	13.04158	11.20074	10.44243	9.77154	9.17574	8.64465	7.35866
24	19.29220	18.33211	17.44361	15.85684	14.48857	13.30338	11.37106	10.58021	9.88322	9.26643	8.71843	7.39884
25	19.91393	18.88499	17.93554	16.24696	14.79864	13.55036	11.52876	10.70661	9.98474	9.34814	8.78432	7.43377
26	20.52346	19.42438	18.41315	16.62208	15.09394	13.78336	11.67478	10.82258	10.07704	9.42174	8.84314	7.46415
27	21.12104	19.95061	18.87684	16.98277	15.37519	14.00317	11.80998	10.92897	10.16095	9.48806	8.89566	7.49056
28	21.70690	20.46401	19.32703	17.32959	15.64303	14.21053	11.93518	11.02658	10.23722	9.54780	8.94255	7.51353
29	22.28127	20.96489	19.76411	17.66306	15.89813	14.40616	12.05108	11.11613	10.30657	9.60162	8.98442	7.53351
30	22.84438	21.45355	20.18845	17.98371	16.14107	14.59072	12.15841	11.19828	10.36961	9.65011	9.02181	7.55088
31	23.39646	21.93029	20.60044	18.29203	16.37245	14.76483	12.25778	11.27365	10.42691	9.69379	9.05518	7.56598
32	23.93770	22.39541	21.00043	18.58849	16.59281	14.92909	12.34980	11.34280	10.47901	9.73315	9.08499	7.57911
33	24.46833	22.84918	21.38877	18.87355	16.80268	15.08404	12.43500	11.40624	10.52638	9.76860	9.11159	7.59053
34	24.98856	23.29188	21.76579	19.14765	17.00255	15.23023	12.51389	11.46444	10.56943	9.80054	9.13535	7.60046
35	25.49859	23.72379	22.13184	19.41120	17.19290	15.36814	12.58693	11.51784	10.60858	9.82932	9.15656	7.60910
36	25.99862	24.14516	22.48722	19.66461	17.37419	15.49825	12.65457	11.56682	10.64416	9.85524	9.17550	7.61661
37	26.48884	24.55625	22.83225	19.90828	17.54685	15.62099	12.71719	11.61176	10.67651	9.87859	9.19241	7.62314
38	26.96945	24.95732	23.16724	20.14258	17.71129	15.73678	12.77518	11.65299	10.70592	9.89963	9.20751	7.62882
39	27.44064	25.34860	23.49246	20.36786	17.86789	15.84602	12.82887	11.69082	10.73265	9.91859	9.22099	7.63375
40	27.90259	25.73034	23.80822	20.58448	18.01704	15.94907	12.87858	11.72552	10.75697	9.93567	9.23303	7.63805

Glossary

Accelerated amortization A depreciation method that creates a higher depreciation expense in the earlier years and lower charges in the later periods. Also known as *Diminishing balance method*.

Account An individual accounting record of increases and decreases in a specific asset, liability, or shareholders' equity item.

Accounting cycle A series of steps followed by accountants in preparing financial statements.

Accounting information system The system of collecting and processing transaction data and communicating financial information to interested parties.

Accounting Standards Board (AcSB) The group primarily responsible for setting GAAP in Canada and that publishes the *CICA Handbook* and other authoritative documents.

Accounting Standards for Private Enterprises (ASPE) The financial reporting standards applicable to private entities in Canada. Private entities may also use IFRS.

Accounting Standards Oversight Council (AcSOC) The group that provides oversight to AcSB activities such as setting the agenda, reporting to the public, and raising funds for standard setting.

Accrual basis The most commonly used basis of accounting whereby revenue is recognized when it is earned and expenses recognized in the period incurred, without regard to the time of receipt or payment of cash. Also known as "accrual-based accounting."

Accrual-based accounting See *Accrual basis*.

Accrued expenses Expenses incurred, but not yet paid or recorded at the statement date.

Accrued revenues Revenues earned, but not yet received in cash or recorded at the statement date.

Accumulated other comprehensive income The cumulative total of all past charges and credits to OCI up to the statement of financial position date. It is similar to retained earnings, but it is for OCI items.

Acquirer A company that purchases another business.

Active market A level of trading of a particular security or asset where there is a good supply of willing buyers and sellers.

Activity method A method of calculating depreciation whereby depreciation is determined as a function of use or productivity of the asset.

Activity ratios Ratios that measure how effectively a company uses its assets, and the liquidity of certain assets such as inventory and receivables.

Additions Increases or extensions of existing assets.

Adjunct account An account that increases either an asset, a liability, or an owners' equity account.

Adjusted trial balance A list of all open accounts in the ledger and their balances taken immediately after all adjustments have been posted.

Adjusting entries Journal entries made at the end of the accounting period to ensure that the revenue recognition and matching principles are followed.

Adverse selection A result of information asymmetry whereby the capital marketplace may attract the wrong types of companies (that is, those that have the most to gain from having information that others do not).

Aggressive accounting A bias that exists in financial reporting that focuses more on the positive information about a company and its financial position and operations; for example, a company may overstate net income or net assets.

Aging method A method of estimating the percentage of outstanding receivables that will become uncollectible based on past experience using the percentage of receivables approach.

Aging schedule A schedule to organize accounts receivable that indicates which accounts require special attention by providing the age of such accounts receivable.

All-inclusive approach An income measurement approach that indicates that most items, including irregular ones, are recorded in income.

Allowance method A method of estimating uncollectible accounts receivable whereby bad debt expense is recorded in the same period as the sale to obtain a proper matching of expense and revenues, and to achieve a proper carrying value for accounts receivable.

Amortization The process of allocating the cost of an asset to expense over its useful life in a rational and systematic manner. Also known as *Depreciation*.

Amortized cost The acquisition cost adjusted for the amortization of the discount or premium.

Amortized cost model A model applied to investment in debt securities and long-term notes and loans receivable that measures the difference between the initial amount recognized and the maturity value and allocates it to income over time.

Arm's-length transaction A transaction that has been carried out between parties that are not related (resulting in terms that are fairly bargained and represent market terms).

Artistic-related intangible assets Ownership rights over the reproduction of a creative work. They are protected by copyright and have value because of their legal-contractual nature.

Asset group See *Cash-generating unit (CGU)*.

Asset retirement costs Costs recognized at the same time that the liability associated with the retirement of an asset is recognized.

Asset turnover ratio A measurement of how efficiently an entity uses its total assets to generate revenue. It is calculated by dividing net sales by average total assets.

Asset-backed financing The use of receivables as collateral to generate immediate cash for a company, either through secured borrowings or sales of receivables.

Asset-backed securities Securities that represent ownership claims to a pool of individual loans that have been securitized; that is, repackaged into asset pools in which ownership interest has been sold.

Assets Probable future economic benefits obtained or controlled by a particular entity as a result of past transactions or events.

Associate An entity that an investor has significant influence over that is neither a subsidiary nor a joint venture.

Available for sale investments A type of investment that is not otherwise classified under IAS 39 as held to maturity, loans and receivables or at fair value through profit or loss.

Average days to sell inventory A variable of the inventory turnover ratio that represents the average age of the inventory on hand or the number of days it takes to sell inventory once purchased.

Avoidable borrowing costs The actual borrowing costs that would not have been incurred by an entity borrowing funds to finance a specific qualifying asset if the expenditures for the qualifying asset had not been made.

Bad debts Impaired trade receivables. Also known as "uncollectible accounts."

Balance sheet A financial statement that shows an enterprise's financial condition at the end of a period (under ASPE). Also known as *Statement of financial position*.

Bank overdrafts What occurs when cheques are written for more than the amount in the cash account.

Bank reconciliation A schedule explaining any differences between the bank's and the company's records of cash.

Bargain purchase The purchase of an investment at a price that is lower than the fair value of the identifiable net assets acquired. Also known as "negative goodwill."

Barter transactions Transactions where little or no monetary assets are received as consideration when goods or services are purchased or sold. Also known as *Nonmonetary transactions*.

Basic elements Financial reporting terms that constitute the language of accounting and business, such as "assets," "liabilities," and "equity."

Basic loan features Contractual terms that result in cash flows that are payments of principal and interest.

Basket purchase The purchase of a group of units with different characteristics at a single lump-sum price.

Beneficial interest A debt or equity claim to the cash flows of the party that acquired the receivables, arising when a company sells a receivable.

Billings Amounts invoiced (or that may be invoiced) according to long-term contracts such as construction-type contracts.

Biological assets Any living asset, such as livestock or trees.

Book value The amount at which an asset is recognized in the statement of financial position. Also known as *Carrying amount*.

Boot The payment or receipt of a significant amount of cash or other monetary asset when assets are exchanged or traded in.

Borrowing costs Interest and other costs that an entity incurs in connection with the borrowing of funds.

Brand A group of assets such as a trade name and its related formulas, recipes, and technology that are used to distinguish a particular enterprise or product.

Brand name See *Brand*.

Bright-line tests Quantitative thresholds in financial reporting standards that dictate how something is to be accounted for.

Bundled sales Contracts involving the sale of both goods and services for one price. Also known as "multiple deliverables."

Business combination What results when one entity acquires control over the net assets of another business, either by acquiring the net assets directly, or by acquiring the equity interest representing control over the net assets.

Business component A component of an entity being disposed of where the operations, cash flows, and financial elements are clearly distinguishable from the rest of the enterprise.

Business model The manner in which a company adds value. Different business models include manufacturing, retail selling, providing services, exploration and development, and others.

Canadian Institute of Chartered Accountants (CICA) The main professional accounting body for chartered accountants that also has primary responsibility for setting GAAP in Canada through the Accounting Standards Board.

Canadian Public Accountability Board (CPAB) The regulatory oversight body that ensures that certain standards are met regarding quality controls and independence.

Capital allocation The process by which accounting enables investors and creditors to assess the relative returns and risks associated with investment opportunities and thereby channel resources more effectively.

Capital approach A method of accounting for contributions of assets from an owner where the increase in assets is treated as contributed (donated) capital (a Contributed Surplus account) rather than as earned revenue.

Capital cost allowance (CCA) The designation for the allocation of cost in tax returns.

Capital cost allowance method The method used in calculating depreciation for tax purposes and calculating the tax value of an asset by Canadian businesses, regardless of the method used for reporting purposes.

Capital expenditure An expenditure that increases an asset's useful life, increases the quantity of units produced from the asset, or enhances the quality of units produced.

Capital gain What occurs when the proceeds on disposal of a capital asset are greater than the original cost of the asset.

Capital maintenance theory An approach to income measurement whereby income for the period is determined based on the change in equity after adjusting for capital contributions.

Capitalization period The time period during which interest may be capitalized. It begins when three conditions are present: (1) expenditures for the asset have been made, (2) activities that are necessary to get the asset ready for its intended use are in progress, and (3) interest cost is being incurred.

Capitalization rate A weighted-average borrowing rate on general borrowings, used to determine avoidable borrowing costs on non-asset-specific debt.

Capitalized Recorded in asset accounts and then depreciated, as is appropriate for expenditures for items with useful lives greater than one year.

Carrying amount The amount at which an asset is recognized in the statement of financial position. Also known as *Book value*.

Cash Cash on hand and demand deposits.

Cash and cash equivalents Cash, demand deposits, and short-term highly liquid investments that are readily convertible into known amounts of cash and that are subject to insignificant risk of changes in value.

Cash debt coverage ratio A long-run measure of financial flexibility that indicates a company's ability to repay its liabilities from net cash provided by operating activities, without having to liquidate the assets employed in its operations.

Cash discounts Sales discounts that are offered to induce prompt payment.

Cash equivalents Short-term, highly liquid investments that are readily converted to known amounts of cash and are subject to an insignificant risk of change in value.

Cash-generating unit (CGU) The smallest identifiable group of assets that generates cash inflows that are largely independent of the cash flows from other assets or groups of assets. Also known as "asset group."

Change in accounting principle A change that occurs when an accounting principle is adopted that is different from the one previously used.

CICA Handbook A set of principles and guidelines for accounting and assurance.

Closing entries The journal entries that close the temporary accounts in order to start a new financial reporting period. These amounts are posted to retained earnings.

Closing process The procedure generally followed to reduce the balance of temporary accounts to zero in order to prepare the accounts for the next period's transactions.

Commercial substance An exchange of assets where there is a significant change in the company's expected future cash flows relative to the fair values of the assets exchanged.

Comparability What occurs when information that has been measured and reported in a similar manner for different enterprises is considered comparable.

Compensating balances That portion of any demand deposit (or any time deposit or certificate of deposit) maintained by a corporation that constitutes support for existing borrowing arrangements of the entity with a lending institution.

Completed-contract method The revenue recognition method in which revenues and gross profit are recognized only when the contract is completed.

Completeness The quality of accounting information that makes it reliable by including all information necessary to provide an accurate portrayal of events and transactions.

Componentization Decisions regarding which fixed asset components to recognize separately.

Comprehensive income A measure of income under IFRS that includes net income plus other comprehensive income.

Computer software costs A technology-based intangible asset, either developed for internal use or for sale as a product.

Conceptual framework A coherent system of interrelated objectives and fundamentals that can lead to consistent standards and that prescribes the nature, function, and limits of financial accounting and financial statements.

Concessionary terms Terms of a contract that are more lenient than normal arising when one party is in a better bargaining position than the other. Also known as "abnormal terms."

Conservatism A constraint of financial reporting that in doubtful situations, the solution that will least likely overstate assets and income should be chosen.

Conservative accounting A bias that exists in financial reporting that ensures that where uncertainty exists and judgement is needed, net income and/or net assets are understated rather than being overstated.

Consideration In a transaction, the item or rights acquired; can be monetary or nonmonetary.

Consigned goods Goods that are sold on consignment yet remain the consignor's property and therefore must be included in inventory.

Consignment A type of transaction where one party, who does not have legal title to goods, presents them to customers for sale and earns a commission when the customer buys the goods.

Consistency What occurs when an entity applies the same accounting treatment to similar events from period to period.

Consolidation The process of treating both parent and subsidiary companies as a single economic entity.

Constructive obligation A type of performance obligation not stated in a contract that is created through a past practice or by signalling something to potential customers, such as a "100% satisfaction guaranteed" policy.

Contingency "An existing condition or situation involving uncertainty as to a possible gain or loss to an enterprise that will ultimately be resolved when one or more future events occur or fail to occur," as defined under ASPE.

Continuous earnings process A process whereby performance of a sale requires numerous ongoing acts. Also known as "continuous sale."

Contra account An account on the statement of financial position that reduces an asset, a liability, or an owners' equity account.

Contra asset account An account that is offset against an asset account on the statement of financial position.

Contract-based approach An approach to revenue recognition that measures the rights and obligations under sales contracts and recognizes revenues when these rights and obligations change and control over the goods and services passes.

Contract-based intangible assets The value of rights that arise from contractual arrangements, such as licensing agreements, lease agreements, and broadcast rights.

Contractual yield basis A model of managing a long-term receivables contract involving the holding of instruments for their principal and interest flows.

Control Under ASPE, the continuing power to determine the strategic operating, financing, and investing policies of another entity without the cooperation of others. Under IFRS, the power to direct the activities of another entity to generate returns, either positive or negative, for the investor.

Conventional retail inventory method A method to value inventory that uses the cost-to-retail ratio incorporating net markups but excluding net markdowns. This method is designed to approximate the lower of average cost and market.

Conversion costs A type of product cost that includes labour and variable production overhead costs incurred in processing materials into finished goods.

Copyright A federally granted right that all authors, painters, musicians, sculptors, and other artists have in their creations, whatever mode or form of expression. It is an exclusive right to reproduce and sell an artistic or published work.

Cost All expenditures needed to acquire an item of property, plant, and equipment and bring it to its location and ready it for use.

Cost formula A method of assigning inventory costs incurred during the accounting period to inventory that is still on hand at the end of the period. The three acceptable formulas are specific identification; first-in, first-out (FIFO); and weighted average cost.

Cost model (CM) The model that measures property, plant, and equipment assets after acquisition at their cost, less accumulated depreciation and any accumulated impairment losses.

Cost of goods available for sale or use The total of (1) the cost of goods on hand at the beginning of the period and (2) the cost of the goods acquired or produced during the period.

Cost of goods manufactured The total cost of items that have been manufactured including raw materials and related processing costs.

Cost of goods sold The difference between those goods available for sale during the period and those on hand at the end of the period.

Cost recovery impairment model A model of measuring impairment losses whereby a long-lived asset is impaired only if an entity cannot recover the asset's carrying amount from using the asset and eventually disposing of it.

Cost reduction method An income approach method for accounting for government assistance, whereby the asset cost and future depreciation is reduced by the amount of government assistance received.

Cost-benefit relationship A constraint of financial reporting that the costs of obtaining and providing information should not be higher than the benefits that are gained by providing it.

Cost-to-cost basis The process by which the percentage of completion is measured by comparing costs incurred to date with the most recent estimate of the total costs to complete the contract.

Cost-to-retail ratio A ratio used in the retail inventory method determined by dividing goods available for sale at cost, by the goods available for sale at retail.

Coupon rate See *Stated interest rate*.

Coverage ratios Ratios that measure the degree of protection for long-term creditors and investors. Also known as *Solvency ratios*.

Credit The right side of a general ledger account.

Credit risk The likelihood of loss because of the failure of the other party in a transaction to fully pay the amount owed.

Critical event An action or main event in a sales transaction that signifies substantial completion or performance under the terms of the contract, allowing revenues to be recognized under accrual accounting.

Current assets Cash and other assets ordinarily realizable within one year from the date of the balance sheet or within the normal operating cycle where that is longer than a year.

Current cash debt coverage ratio The ratio of net cash provided by operating activities to average current liabilities, indicating how well a company can address its current obligations from internally generated cash flow.

Current liabilities Amounts due within one year from the date of the statement of financial position or within the normal operating cycle, where this is longer than a year.

Current operating performance approach An income measurement approach that argues that the most useful income measure will reflect only regular and recurring revenue and expense elements.

Current ratio The ratio of total current assets to total current liabilities.

Customer-related intangible assets What occur as a result of interactions between company employees and systems with outside parties interested in buying goods and services.

Cut-off schedule A schedule prepared by the accountant for the end of the period to ensure that goods received from suppliers around the end of the year are recorded in the appropriate period.

Debit The left side of a general ledger account.

Debt securities Investments in government and/or corporate bonds.

Decision-usefulness approach Approach to financial reporting whereby the amount and types of information to be disclosed and the format in which information should be presented involves determining which alternate provides the most useful information for decision-making purposes.

Declining-balance method A depreciation method that uses a depreciation rate that remains a constant percentage throughout the asset's useful life and reduces the book value each year to determine depreciation expense.

Decreasing charge method A depreciation method that provides for a higher depreciation expense in the earlier years and lower charges in the later periods on the basis that more depreciation should be charged in earlier years if that is when the asset offers the greatest benefits.

Deferral method The method of recording the amount of government assistance received as a deferred credit, amortizing it to revenue over the life of the related assets.

Deferred income tax assets The future tax consequence due to deductible temporary differences. Also known as *Future income tax assets*.

Deferred income tax liabilities The future tax consequences associated with taxable temporary differences. Also known as *Future income tax liabilities*.

Depletion The amortization of natural resources.

Depletion base A natural resource's capitalized costs of acquisition, exploration, development, and restoration.

Deposits in transit End-of-month deposits of cash recorded in the depositor's books one month and received and recorded by the bank the following month.

Depreciable amount The difference between the asset's cost (or revalued amount, if the revaluation model is being used) and its residual value.

Depreciation The cost of tangible capital assets allocated to the accounting periods benefiting their use; generally used to describe tangible assets. Also known as *Amortization*.

Derecognition The process of removing an item from an entity's statement of financial position or income statements.

Derecognized Describing an asset after all of its related items have been removed from a company's accounts.

Development The translation of research findings or other knowledge into a plan or design for new or substantially improved materials, devices, products, processes, systems, or services prior to the start of commercial production or use.

Development phase A broad category of development activities where costs are capitalized only when future benefits are reasonably certain.

Diminishing balance method A depreciation method that applies a constant percentage rate to net book value to calculate depreciation expense over the useful life of the asset. Also known as *Accelerated amortization*.

Direct method A method of recording inventory used when revaluing inventory to reflect net realizable value under the LC&NRV method where the Inventory account is revalued.

Direct writeoff method A method for recording uncollectible accounts receivable where no entry is made until a specific account has definitely been established as uncollectible.

Discontinued operations The operations of an identifiable business segment that have been sold, abandoned, shut down, or otherwise disposed of, or that is the subject of a formal plan of disposal.

Discount What occurs when a bond sells at less than face value.

Discounted cash flow model A model for measuring fair value that deals with uncertainty and the time value of money. It has two approaches: the traditional approach, and the expected cash flow approach.

Discounted free cash flow method A method to value goodwill that involves a projection of the company's free cash flow over a long period.

Discrete earnings process An earnings process that has a critical event.

Distinct The existence of separate performance obligations, used in revenue recognition. Refers to goods or services that are either sold separately or that provide separate benefits to the customer.

Double-declining-balance method A depreciation method that uses a rate (which is the straight-line rate multiplied by two), which is applied to the net book value every year, resulting in a declining depreciation expense year after year.

Double-entry accounting System of accounting requiring the equality of debits and credits when recording transactions, which helps prove the accuracy of the recorded amounts.

Due process The method used in standard setting in order to ensure that standard-setting bodies operate in full view of the public by giving those that are interested ample opportunity to make their views known.

Earnings approach An approach to revenue recognition whereby revenues are recognized when performance is substantially complete and collection is reasonably assured.

Earnings management The process of targeting certain earnings levels (whether current or future) or desired earnings trends and working backwards to determine what has to be done to ensure that these targets are met.

Earnings per share Net income divided by the number of shares outstanding.

Earnings process The cash-to-cash cycle where goods and services are purchased; when they are sold and converted into cash, or a claim to cash, the earnings process is said to be substantially complete.

Economic benefits Benefits provided by intangible assets, such as increased revenues from sales of products or services and reductions in future costs.

Economic entity assumption An assumption that a company's business activity can be kept separate and distinct from its owners and any other business units. Economic activity can therefore be identified with a particular degree of accountability.

Economic substance The underlying economic reality reported on a representationally faithful document.

Effective interest method A method of amortization whereby the current market rate of interest at the time of investment is used to calculate interest income by applying it to the carrying amount (book value) of the investment for each interest period. The note's carrying amount changes as it is increased by the amount of discount amortized.

Effective interest rate The interest rate actually earned. Also known as *Market rate* or *Yield rate*.

Efficient markets hypothesis A theory that states that if information is available, it will be incorporated into decisions made by market participants.

Elements of financial statements Basic items that are presented in the financial statements.

Entity perspective The viewpoint that companies are viewed as separate and distinct from their owners and therefore financial reporting should focus on the needs of main users and not just the owners.

Equitable obligations Commitments that arise from moral or ethical considerations.

Equity instruments Any contract that evidences a residual interest in the assets of an entity after deducting all of its liabilities; examples are common and certain preferred shares.

Equity method A method of accounting for investments where a substantive economic relationship is acknowledged between the investor and the investee. The investment is originally recorded at its cost, but is subsequently adjusted each period for changes in the investee's net assets.

Equity pickup What occurs when an investor "picks up" its share of income or loss under the equity method.

Equity/net assets The residual interest in the assets of an entity that remains after deducting its liabilities.

Ethical dilemmas Problems where there are no set guidelines to follow in order to resolve a situation. These are the grey areas that one has to ask "Is it right or wrong?"

Event Something of consequence that happens, which is generally the source of changes in asset, liability, and equity balances. An event may be internal or external.

Excess-earnings approach A method used to value goodwill that calculates the "normal" earnings generated by firms in the same industry. If a business earns a higher rate of return than the industry average, this excess is goodwill.

Executory contract An agreement requiring future, continuing performance by both parties.

Exit price A measure of fair value that represents the amount that an entity would receive on selling an asset or transferring a liability.

Expected cash flow approach An approach to the discounted cash flow model where a risk-free discount rate is used to discount cash flows that have been adjusted for uncertainty. The discount rate is the risk-free rate and the cash flow uncertainty is dealt with by using probabilities.

Expected loss impairment model A model of accounting for impairment where estimates of future cash flows used to determine the present value of the investment are made on a continuous basis.

Expenses Decreases in economic resources, either by outflows or reductions of assets or incurrence of liabilities resulting from an entity's ordinary revenue-generating activities.

Face rate See *Stated interest rate.*

Face value The fair value of an interest-bearing note or loan receivable when the stated interest rate is equal to the effective (market) rate.

Factoring receivables What results when a company sells its accounts receivable to banks or finance companies that buy receivables from businesses for a fee and then collects the remittances directly from the customers.

Fair value An estimate of the price an enterprise would have received if it had sold the asset or would have paid, if it had been relieved of the liability, on the measurement date in an arm's-length exchange motivated by normal business considerations.

Fair value loss impairment model A model of impairment whereby the impairment loss is the difference between the asset's fair value and its current carrying amount assuming the fair value is less than the carrying amount.

Fair value model (FVM) A method of accounting for investment property, under which it is recognized on the statement of financial position after acquisition at its fair value.

Fair value option The option given to companies allowing them to use fair value for most financial instruments where certain conditions are met.

Fair value principle The GAAP principle that provides guidance regarding how to measure financial statement elements using best estimates of market values.

Fair value through net income (FV-NI) model A method of measuring the fair value of financial instruments where the carrying amount is adjusted to its current fair value at each reporting date such that all holding gains and losses are reported in net income along with any dividends or interest income earned. Also known as "fair value through profit or loss (FVTPL)."

Fair value through other comprehensive income (FV-OCI) model A model where the carrying amount of each FV-OCI investment is adjusted to its current fair value at each reporting date, and the holding gains and losses are recognized in other comprehensive income.

Fair value through profit or loss (FVTPL) See *Fair value through net income (FV-NI) model.*

Favourable lease A lease that is considered an intangible asset when the terms are more favourable than the usual market terms.

Feedback/confirmatory value The notion that relevant information helps users confirm or correct prior expectations.

Financial accounting The process that culminates in the preparation of financial reports for the enterprise as a whole for use by both internal and external parties. Also known as *Financial reporting.*

Financial Accounting Standards Board (FASB) The major standard-setting body in the United States.

Financial asset A receivable that represents contractual rights to receive cash or other financial assets from another party.

Financial components approach A method of recording a sale of receivables transaction whereby each party to the sale of an account receivable recognizes the components (assets and liabilities) that it controls after the sale and derecognizes the assets and liabilities that were sold or extinguished.

Financial engineering A process whereby a business arrangement or transaction is structured legally such that it meets the company's financial reporting objective (for example, to maximize earnings, minimize a debt-to-equity ratio, or other).

Financial flexibility The measurement of an enterprise's ability to take effective actions to alter the amounts and timing of cash flows so it can respond to unexpected needs and opportunities.

Financial instruments Contracts that give rise to both a financial asset for one party and a financial liability or equity instrument for another.

Financial reporting The process that culminates in the preparation of financial reports for the enterprise as a whole for use by both internal and external parties. Also known as *Financial accounting.*

Financial statements The principal means through which financial information is communicated to those outside an enterprise. They provide a firm's history, quantified in money terms.

Financing activities Activities resulting in changes in the size and composition of the enterprise's equity capital and borrowings.

Finished goods inventory The reporting of the costs associated with the completed but unsold units at the end of the fiscal period.

Finite life A type of asset that has a foreseeable limit to its useful life, and that is amortized by systematic charges to expense over the useful life using the cost model or revaluation model. Also known as "limited life."

First principles Foundational principles from which decisions stem, making all decisions theoretically consistent if they stem from the same foundational reasoning.

First-in, first-out (FIFO) cost formula The method that assigns cost to inventory assuming that goods are used in the order in which they are purchased.

Fixed assets Tangible capital assets that are acquired for use in operations and not for resale, are long-term in nature, and are usually subject to depreciation and possess physical substance. Also known as *Plant assets* or *Property, plant, and equipment.*

FOB destination Shipping designation meaning that the legal title of an asset does not pass to the buyer until the goods reach the customer's location.

FOB shipping point Shipping designation meaning that the legal title of an asset belongs to the buyer when the goods leave the shipping dock.

Franchise A contractual arrangement under which the franchisor grants the franchisee the right to sell certain services, to use certain trademarks or trade names, or to perform certain functions, usually within a designated geographical area. Also known as *Licensing agreement.*

Free cash flow An indicator of financial flexibility that uses information provided on the cash flow statement. Free cash flow is net operating cash flows reduced by the capital expenditures needed to sustain the current level of operations.

Freedom from material error A measure of the reliability of reported information, assuring that the relevant information is accurate and unaffected by the opinions of stakeholders.

Full disclosure principle Financial reporting of any information significant enough to influence the judgement of an informed reader.

Function (of expense) The type of activity, such as cost of goods sold, selling and distribution, and research and development, used as a way of classifying and presenting expenses on the statement of income.

Future income tax assets The future tax consequences due to deductible temporary differences. Also known as *Deferred income tax assets*.

Future income tax liabilities The future tax consequences associated with taxable temporary differences. Also known as *Deferred income tax liabilities*.

GAAP hierarchy Guidance that notes that primary sources of GAAP should be used first, followed by other relevant and reliable sources, including the conceptual framework and professional judgement.

Gains Increases in equity (net assets) from an entity's peripheral or incidental transactions and from all other transactions and other events and circumstances affecting the entity during a period, except those that result from revenues or investments by owners.

General journal A chronological listing of transactions and other events expressed in terms of debits and credits to particular accounts.

General ledger A collection of all asset, liability, shareholders' equity, revenue, and expense accounts and their respective balances.

General-purpose financial statements Basic GAAP financial statements that provide information that meets the needs of external users (normally investors and creditors).

Generally accepted accounting principles (GAAP) The common set of standards and procedures used to prepare financial statements with the expectation that the majority of users' needs will be met.

Going concern assumption The assumption of most accounting methods that the business will have a long life.

Goodwill An asset representing the future economic benefits arising from other assets acquired in a business combination that are not individually identified or separately recognized.

Gross method A method of recording inventory whereby the use of a Purchase Discounts account indicates that the company is reporting its purchases and accounts payable at the gross amount.

Gross profit method A method for estimating inventory where taking a physical count is impractical or impossible. It is based on three assumptions: (1) the beginning inventory plus purchases equal total goods to be accounted for; (2) goods not sold must be on hand; (3) and when the net sales, reduced to cost, are deducted from the total goods to be accounted for, the result is the ending inventory.

Gross profit percentage The gross profit expressed as a percentage of sales.

Half-year rule A requirement of the income tax regulation that in the year a capital asset is acquired, only half the usual capital cost allowance can be claimed for tax purposes.

Held for sale Describing assets where a formal, detailed plan exists to sell the assets, normally within a year.

Held for trading Describing investments that are traded for profit.

Held to maturity Describing investments that are held until they mature.

Highest and best use A concept for valuing assets that assumes the highest value that the market would place on the asset considering uses that are possible, legally permissible, and financially feasible.

Historical cost principle An accounting principle that provides guidance on how to measure transactions and balances on the basis of acquisition price.

Identifiable A characteristic of intangible assets that either results from contractual or other legal rights, or can be separated and divided from the entity and sold, transferred, licensed, rented, or exchanged, either by itself or with another contract, identifiable asset, or liability.

Identifiable net assets What arise when an entity's purchase price is allocated among all the assets and liabilities to which a value can be attributed; refers to all net assets except goodwill.

IFRS Advisory Council A group that provides strategic advice to the IASB.

IFRS Foundation A group that raises finances and provides strategic direction and oversight to the IASB.

Impaired The state of a long-lived asset's carrying amount being higher than its future economic benefits to the company.

Impairment loss The amount by which the asset's carrying amount exceeds its fair value.

Impairments A decrease in the carrying value of a long-term asset to an amount that is less than the amount shown under the cost principle.

Implicit interest rate The discount rate that corresponds to the lessor's internal rate of return on the lease.

Imprest system A petty cash system where the custodian is responsible for the amount of funds on hand at all times, whether the amount is in cash or signed receipts.

Imputed interest rate The actual interest rate realized on a bond, which is different from the stated rate when there is a discount or premium.

In-process research and development (R&D) An identifiable intangible asset involving the research work and findings of a company, acquired when the company purchases another. It must be separable from goodwill to be reported separately.

Income approach A method to account for contributions of assets that requires the amount received to be deferred and recognized over the period that the related assets are employed.

Income statement A report that measures the success of a company's operations used for a specific time period (under ASPE).

Incurred loss impairment model A model where investments are recognized as impaired when there is no longer reasonable assurance that the future cash flows associated with them will be collected in their entirety when due. It accounts for credit losses triggered by specific events that occurred by the balance sheet date.

Indefinite life An asset's useful life where there appears to be no foreseeable limit to how long the asset will generate positive net cash flows to the entity.

Indirect method A method used to revalue inventory to reflect net realizable value under the LC&NRV method whereby a contra Inventory account is used to revalue inventory.

Information asymmetry The state that exists when one party has more information than the other party.

Information overload The phenomenon that too much information may result in a situation where the user is unable to digest or process the information.

Information symmetry The state that exists when both parties have the same information.

Input measures Costs incurred that measure efforts devoted to a contract.

Inspection An organized formal evaluation of property, plant, and equipment that is considered a type of recurring cost after acquisition.

Institutional investors Large corporations or corporate investors such as pension funds or mutual funds.

Intangible assets Nonmonetary assets that lack physical substance and usually have a higher degree of uncertainty concerning their future benefits.

Intellectual capital See *Knowledge assets*.

Interest-bearing notes Notes that have a stated rate of interest that is payable over and above the face value of the note.

International Accounting Standards Board (IASB) The group responsible for setting IFRS with the goal of increasing the transparency of financial reporting by achieving a single, global method of accounting.

International Financial Reporting Interpretation Committee (IFRIC) A committee that studies and provides recommendations on issues not covered by the IASB.

International Financial Reporting Standards (IFRS) The internationally recognized common set of financial reporting standards and procedures.

International Integrated Reporting Committee (IIRC) A group that looks at a broader view of financial reporting that includes management information, governance and compensation, and sustainability reporting.

Intraperiod tax allocation The approach to allocating taxes within the financial statements of the current period.

Inventories Assets that are held for sale in the ordinary course of business.

Inventory turnover ratio A ratio that measures the number of times, on average, the inventory was sold during the period.

Investing activities Activities covering the acquisition and disposal of long-term assets and other investments not included in cash equivalents.

Investment property Property held to generate rentals and/or appreciate in value rather than to sell in the ordinary course of business or to use in production, administration, or in supplying goods and services.

Joint cost A single cost of purchasing or producing multiple items.

Joint ventures A type of equity investment characterized by joint control, rather than unilateral control by one party.

Journal The book of original entry where transactions and selected other events are initially recorded.

Knowledge assets Unrecognized intangible assets related to the creativity and knowledge of key employees that create value for a company. Also known as "intellectual capital."

Laid-down costs Any cost incurred to get the asset in place and ready for use (whether it is for sale or to generate income through use). Also known as "out-of-pocket costs."

Last-in, first-out (LIFO) cost formula A method no longer permitted under ASPE and IFRS that assigns inventory costs on the assumption that the cost of the most recent purchase is the first cost to be charged to cost of goods sold.

Lease A contractual agreement between a lessor (property owner) and a lessee (property renter) that gives the lessee the right to use specific property, owned by the lessor, for a specified time in return for stipulated, and generally periodic, cash payments (rents). Also known as "leasehold."

Leasehold See *Lease*.

Leasehold improvements Improvements made to the leased property by the lessee.

Legal title A right meaning that a good is legally owned; not the same as possession.

Liabilities "Obligations of an enterprise arising from past transactions or events, the settlement of which may result in the transfer of assets, provisions of services or other yielding of economic benefits in the future," as described in the *CICA Handbook*.

Licences Operating rights obtained through agreements with governmental units or agencies, such as the use of airwaves for radio or television broadcasting. Also known as *Permits*.

Licensing agreement A contractual arrangement under which a government body or a business entity grants a business enterprise the right to sell certain services, to use certain trademarks or trade names, or to perform certain functions, usually within a designated geographical area. Also known as *Franchise*.

Limited life See *Finite life*.

Liquidating dividend A dividend greater than accumulated net income, where the dividend is a return of a shareholder's investment rather than profits of the company.

Liquidity A company's ability to convert assets into cash to pay off its current liabilities in the ordinary course of business.

Liquidity ratios Ratios that measure the enterprise's short-run ability to pay its maturing obligations.

Loans and receivables Financial assets that result from the delivery of cash or other assets by a lender to a borrower in return for a promise to pay an amount on specified dates or on demand, usually with interest.

Loans receivable An agreement where one party advances cash or other assets in exchange for a promise to be repaid later.

Long-term liabilities Obligations that are not reasonably expected to be liquidated within the greater of one year or the normal operating cycle, but instead are payable at some date beyond that time.

Losses Decreases in equity (net assets) from an entity's peripheral or incidental transactions and from all other transactions and other events and circumstances affecting the entity during a period, except those that result from expenses or distributions to owners.

Lower of cost and market See *Lower of cost and net realizable value (LC&NRV) standard*.

Lower of cost and net realizable value (LC&NRV) A basis for stating inventory at the lower of its original cost and the net realizable value at the end of the period.

Lower of cost and net realizable value (LC&NRV) standard A principle used for ensuring that inventory is not overstated by comparing carrying cost and the amount that could be received if the inventory were disposed of and measuring the inventory at the lower of the two. Also known as "lower of cost and market."

Lump-sum price When several assets are purchased together for a single price.

Major overhauls Substantial repairs or replacements of equipment, or renovations to property. Treated as recurring component of cost after acquisition.

Management best estimate Assumptions made by management in light of their knowledge and familiarity with the company, the industry, and the economy.

Management bias The presentation by management of information about their company in its best light in order to make their company look as successful as possible.

Managerial accounting The process of identifying, measuring, analyzing, and communicating financial information to internal decision-makers.

Markdown A decrease in price below the original selling price.

Markdown cancellations What occurs when markdowns are offset by the increase in the prices of goods that had been previously marked down.

Market Net realizable value in the context of the LC&NRV principle, as defined by ASPE and IFRS. Can also refer to net realizable value, replacement cost, or net realizable values less a normal profit margin.

Market rate The interest rate actually earned. Also known as *Effective interest rate* or *Yield rate*.

Marketing-related intangible assets Those intangible assets related primarily to the marketing or promotion of products or services.

Markup An increase in the price above the original selling price.

Markup cancellations What occurs when markups are offset by the decrease in the prices of goods that had been previously marked up.

Markup on cost What occurs when the selling price is determined by a rate being equal to the gross profit as a percentage of cost.

Matching The accounting principle that dictates that efforts (expenses) be matched with accomplishments (revenues) whenever reasonable and practicable.

Materiality The constraint that relates to an item's impact on a firm's overall financial operations. An item is material if its inclusion or omission would influence or change the judgement of a reasonable person.

Measurement uncertainty What occurs when there is a variance between the recognized amount and another reasonably possible amount.

Merchandise inventory Inventory purchased in a form ready for sale.

Mineral resource properties Capitalized costs that are associated with the acquired rights, and the exploration, evaluation, and development of these minerals.

Mineral resources Minerals and oil and gas resources that do not regenerate. Also known as "wasting assets."

Minority interest The percentage of the net assets not owned (reported as a liability on the balance sheet), or the percentage of the net income that does not accrue to the parent company (reported as a deduction from the combined net income on the income statement). Also known as *Noncontrolling* interest.

Modified cash basis A mixture of cash basis and accrual basis accounting often followed by professional service firms.

Monetary assets Money or claims to future cash flows that are fixed in amounts and timing by contract or other arrangement.

Monetary unit assumption The assumption that money is the common denominator of economic activity and provides an appropriate basis for accounting measurement and analysis.

Moral hazard The risk that certain parties who have additional information not accessible to others will act in their own self-interest.

Most advantageous market A concept used for measuring fair value that considers the value based on the market that would pay the most for the asset.

Moving-average cost formula An inventory pricing method that prices inventory items based on the moving-average cost of the goods available for sale in the period.

Multiple deliverables See *Bundled sales*.

Multiple-step income statement An income statement format that recognizes a separation between operating transactions and non-operating transactions and matches the relevant costs and expenses with their related revenues.

Nature (of expense) The type of expense, such as payroll, depreciation, and cost of raw materials, as classified and presented on the statement of income.

Negative goodwill See *Bargain purchase*.

Net income Revenues less expenses (including gains and losses) other than those defined under IFRS as other comprehensive income.

Net markdowns Markdowns less markdown cancellations.

Net markups Markups less markup cancellations.

Net method A recording method whereby purchases and accounts payable are recorded at an amount net of cash discounts.

Net realizable value The net amount expected to be received in cash for an asset.

Neutrality The quality of accounting information that makes it reliable by being reasonably free of error and bias.

Non-current investments Long-term investments that will not be realized within one year or during the current operating cycle.

Non-GAAP earnings An adjusted net income number derived from GAAP net income plus or minus any nonrecurring or non-operating items.

Non–interest-bearing notes Notes that include interest, equal to the difference between the amount borrowed (the proceeds) and the face amount paid back. Also known as "zero-interest-bearing notes."

Non-reciprocal transfers Transfers of assets in one direction only, such as donations, gifts, or government grants, where nothing is given in exchange.

Non-sufficient-funds (NSF) cheque A cheque that is written or deposited and the coinciding money for payment does not exist at the time of the deposit.

Noncontrolling interest The percentage of the net assets not owned (reported as a liability on the balance sheet), or the percentage of the net income that does not accrue to the parent company (reported as a deduction from the combined net income on the income statement). Also known as *Minority interest*.

Nonmonetary assets Items whose value in terms of the monetary unit may change over time.

Nonmonetary, non-reciprocal transactions A type of transaction where there is no exchange (such as a donation), making it difficult to determine cost or fair value.

Nonmonetary transactions Transactions where little or no monetary assets are received as consideration when goods or services are purchased or sold. Also known as *Barter transactions*.

Nonmonetary/barter transactions A type of transaction where no cash or monetary consideration is exchanged, making it difficult to determine cost or fair value.

Nontrade receivables Written promises entailing an entity to receive a certain sum of money, arising from a variety of transactions that are not part of normal business operations.

Normal production capacity The usual amount of goods that a company can produce in a year, and the basis for allocating fixed production costs.

Normalized earnings Adjusted past earnings that reflect expected annual future earnings.

Notes receivable Written promises entailing an entity to receive a certain sum of money on a specified future date.

Notes to financial statements Information that is linked to the financial statements that generally amplifies or explains the items presented in the main body of the statements in order to complete the picture of an enterprise's performance and position.

Number of years method A method of valuing goodwill whereby the excess earnings are multiplied by the number of years they are expected to continue.

Objective of financial reporting The goal "to communicate information that is useful to investors, members, contributors, creditors, and other users in making their resource allocation decisions and/or assessing management stewardship," as laid out in the *CICA Handbook*.

On margin Investments in shares where the investor pays only part of the purchase price to acquire the shares, and the broker covers the difference.

Onerous contract A contract where the unavoidable costs of completing the contract are higher than the benefits expected from receiving contracted goods or services. A loss provision is recognized for such a contract under IFRS, though such a provision is not stipulated under ASPE.

Ontario Securities Commission (OSC) A group that regulates companies listed on the TSX by reviewing and monitoring the financial statements with the view to assessing whether the statements present fairly the financial position and results of operations.

Operating activities "The enterprise's principal revenue-producing activities and other activities that are not investing or financing activities," as defined under IFRS and ASPE.

Operating income Income from ongoing revenues after deducting expenses.

Ordinary repairs Expenditures made to maintain plant assets in operating condition, which are charged to an expense account in the period in which they are incurred.

Organization costs Costs incurred in the formation of a corporation.

Other assets Assets that are not included in any other category and are generally not individually material.

Other comprehensive income (OCI) Items of revenues, expenses, gains, and losses that are required by IFRS to be included in comprehensive income, but excluded from net income.

Output measures The output of a contract, or the process that is used to measure results.

Outstanding cheques Cheques written by a depositor and recorded when written but that may not be recorded or cleared by the bank until a following month.

Owners' equity The residual amount, or net assets, of an entity, composed of capital shares, contributed surplus, retained earnings, and accumulated other comprehensive income.

Patent A right to use, manufacture, and sell a product or process for a period of 20 years from the date of application without influence or infringement by others.

Percentage-of-completion method A revenue recognition method that recognizes revenue, costs, and gross profit as progress is made toward completion of a long-term contract.

Percentage-of-receivables approach The process whereby receivables are recorded on the statement of financial position at their net realizable value.

Percentage-of-sales approach The process whereby costs are matched with revenue because it relates to the charge in the period in which the sale is recorded.

Performance obligation An obligation that arises when an entity promises to deliver something or provide a service in the future.

Period costs Costs, such as selling and administrative, that are not considered directly related to the acquisition or production of goods and, therefore, are not considered a part of inventory.

Periodic inventory system The inventory recording system where a Purchases account is used and the Inventory account is unchanged during the period. Cost of goods sold is determined by adding the beginning inventory to the net purchases and deducting ending inventory.

Periodicity assumption The accounting assumption that implies that an enterprise's economic activities can be divided into artificial time periods.

Permanent accounts All of the asset, liability, and equity accounts that appear on the balance sheet. Also known as "real accounts."

Permits Operating rights obtained through agreements with governmental units or agencies. Also known as *Licences*.

Perpetual inventory system The inventory recording system where purchases and sales are recorded in the Inventory account as they occur.

Petty cash A method of keeping cash on hand to cover small amounts where it would not be practical to issue cheques, such as for employee lunches, office supplies, and taxi fares.

Plant assets Tangible capital assets that are acquired for use in operations and not for resale, are long-term in nature, and are usually subject to depreciation and possess physical substance. Also known as *Fixed assets* or *Property, plant, and equipment*.

Point of delivery The point in time when the risks and rewards of ownership pass from the seller to the buyer.

Possession The physical control over a good, but not the legal title to the good.

Post-closing trial balance A trial balance taken immediately after closing entries have been posted.

Posting The process whereby items entered in a general journal must be transferred to the general ledger.

Predictive value A characteristic of accounting information that helps users make predictions about the ultimate outcome of past, present, and future events.

Premium What occurs when a bond sells at more than face value.

Prepaid expenses Expenses paid in cash and recorded as assets before they are used or consumed.

Present economic resources Resources owned by an entity that have economic value and can be sold or used right away.

Price risk The risk that the value of an asset will change due to changes in market conditions.

Principal market The market that the entity normally uses to buy and sell or transfer things, used for measuring fair value.

Product costs Those costs that "attach" to the inventory and are recorded in the Inventory account.

Professional judgement The process by which professional accountants with significant education and experience apply the *CICA Handbook*'s "general principles" appropriately as they see fit, which is important in Canada because IFRS and ASPE are based primarily on general principles rather than specific rules.

Profit margin ratio A ratio that indicates how much is left over from each sales dollar after all expenses are covered.

Profitability ratios Ratios that measure the financial performance of a given enterprise or division for a given period of time.

Promissory note A written promise that supports a note receivable to pay a certain sum of money at a specified future date.

Property, plant, and equipment Tangible capital assets that are acquired for use in operations and not for resale, are long-term in nature, and are usually subject to depreciation and possess physical substance. Also known as *Fixed assets* or *Plant assets*.

Proprietary perspective The viewpoint that financial reporting should focus on the needs of the owners of the company.

Provincial securities commissions The groups that oversee and monitor the provincial capital marketplaces. They ensure that the participants in the capital markets adhere to securities legislation, ensuring that the marketplace is fair.

Public Company Accounting Oversight Board (PCAOB) The regulatory oversight body in the United States that ensures that certain standards are met regarding quality controls and independence.

Purchase commitments Arrangements under which a company agrees to buy inventory weeks, months, or even years in advance.

Purchase discounts A reduction in the price of inventory in order to induce prompt payment.

Qualifying assets Assets that require substantial time to get ready for sale or their intended use.

Qualitative characteristics The characteristics defined by the conceptual framework that distinguish more useful information from less useful information for decision-making purposes.

Quality of earnings The solidity of reported earnings.

Quantities only system A system of tracking inventory that records increases and decreases in quantities only—not dollar amounts.

Rate of return on assets (ROA) Net income expressed as a percentage of average total assets.

Ratio analysis An analysis based on relationships among selected financial statement data.

Rational entity impairment model A model for measuring impairment losses that assumes that an entity makes rational decisions in managing its long-term assets and therefore it compares the asset's book value with a recoverable amount that differs depending on what leads to a higher return for the entity.

Raw materials inventory The costs assigned to goods and materials on hand, but not yet placed into production.

Realizable (revenue) Revenue from assets received or sold that can be readily converted into cash or claims to cash.

Realized (revenue) Revenue from products (goods or services), merchandise, or other assets that are exchanged for cash or claims to cash.

Rearrangement and reinstallation costs Expenditures intended to benefit future periods and to facilitate future production by the movement of assets from one location to another.

Recapture The recovery of capital cost allowance when, after deducting the appropriate amount from the class on disposition of the last asset, a negative amount is left as the UCC balance.

Receivables turnover ratio A ratio calculated to evaluate the liquidity of a company's accounts receivable. It measures the number of times, on average, receivables are collected during the period.

Reciprocal Describing an exchange where an entity gives something up and receives something in return.

Reciprocal exchange A two-way exchange.

Recognition The process of recording a transaction in an entity's statement of financial position or income statement.

Recoverability test A test to determine whether an impairment loss needs to be recognized for a long-lived asset.

Recoverable amount The higher of an asset's value in use and its fair value less costs to sell.

Regular-way purchase or sale A type of sale that occurs when the period between the trade date (the date when the commitment to purchase or sell the security is made) and the settlement date (the date when the delivery occurs and the title is transferred) is short.

Related party transaction A transaction in which one of the transacting parties has the ability to significantly influence the policies of the other, or in which a nontransacting party has the ability to influence the policies of the two transacting parties.

Relative fair value method A method of allocating a price to each unit of a transaction involving multiple units. It involves determining the fair value of each item and allocating the purchase price based on the relative fair values.

Relative sales value method A method used to apportion a total cost or sales amount to individual components using fair values. Commonly used whenever there is a joint product cost that needs to be allocated or in a "basket" purchase or sale.

Relevance A qualitative characteristic of accounting information that indicates that it must make a difference in a decision.

Replacement The substitution of one asset for a similar asset.

Representational faithfulness A qualitative characteristic of accounting information that represents economic reality. It must be transparent, complete, neutral, and free from material error and bias.

Research A planned investigation undertaken with the hope of gaining new scientific or technical knowledge and understanding.

Research phase A broad category of research activities where costs are recognized as expenses when they are incurred.

Residual value An estimate of the amount that a company would obtain from the disposal of an asset at the end of its useful life.

Residual value method A method of allocating a price to each unit of a transaction involving multiple units. It involves determining the fair value of one unit and allocating the purchase price first to this unit with the rest to the remaining units.

Restricted cash Cash that is segregated from "regular" cash for reporting purposes because it needs to be set aside for a particular purpose.

Retail inventory method A method of valuing inventory when necessary, where inventory taken at its selling price (retail) can be converted to inventory at cost by applying the cost-to-retail formula.

Revaluation model (RM) A model for accounting for a long-lived asset that carries the asset at its fair value at the date of revaluation less any subsequent accumulated depreciation and impairment losses.

Revenue expenditure An expenditure where the benefit is in the period in which the expenditure occurred.

Revenue recognition principle The accounting principle that sets guidelines as to when revenue should be reported.

Revenues Increases in economic resources, either by inflows or other enhancements of an entity's assets or settlement of its liabilities resulting from an entity's ordinary activities.

Reversing entries A journal entry made at the beginning of the next accounting period that is the exact opposite of the related adjusting journal entry made in the previous period.

Risk management The identification, assessment, and mitigation of potential risks to a business.

Risk/return tradeoff An economic concept that notes that the higher the risk, the greater the return or compensation that is required to take that risk.

Risks and rewards of ownership A concept of financial reporting that helps establish ownership and when ownership passes from one party to another.

Sales discounts Cash discounts that are offered by the seller to induce prompt payment.

Sales returns and allowances An amount of sales involving large amounts near the end of the accounting period that should be anticipated and recognized in the period of the sale to avoid distorting the current period's income statement.

Salvage value The asset's estimated net realizable value at the end of its life.

Secured borrowing A creditor may require that a debtor designate (assign) or pledge receivables or other assets as security for the loan, but the assets remain under the control of the borrowing company.

Securities and Exchange Commission (SEC) The U.S. counterpart of the OSC, which regulates the capital markets and supports the FASB by indicating that financial statements conforming with FASB standards will be presumed to have substantial authoritative support.

Securitization What occurs when a pool of assets is taken, such as credit card receivables, mortgage receivables, or car loan receivables, and shares are sold in these pools of interest and principal payments. The effect is to create securities backed by these pools of assets.

Self-constructed assets Assets built by a company and assigned all relevant costs to be capitalized.

Servicing asset component An asset that is recognized if the benefits of servicing (such as servicing fees under contract and late charges) are greater than the estimated cost of the obligation.

Servicing liability component An obligation that is recorded if the transferor receives no reimbursements for servicing the receivables, or receives less than the estimated cost of doing so.

Significant influence What an investor has when it owns roughly 20% to 50% of a company and/or there is investor representation on the board of directors, participation in policy-making processes, material intercompany transactions, interchange of managerial personnel, or provision of technical information.

Single-step income statement A simplified income statement that lists all income first followed by all expenses.

Solvency An enterprise's ability to pay its debts and related interest.

Solvency ratios Measures of the degree of protection for long-term creditors and investors or a company's ability to meet its long-term obligations. Also known as *Coverage ratios*.

Special journals Journals that summarize transactions possessing a similar characteristic.

Specific identification A cost formula whereby each inventory item is identified separately, the costs of the specific item sold are included in cost of goods sold, and the cost of the specific items on hand is included in inventory.

Stakeholders Parties who rely on and use financial statements and other financial documents to make decisions.

Stand-ready obligations A type of liability that is unconditional whereby the obligor stands prepared to fulfill the terms of the contract when required, such as an insurance contract or warranty.

Standard cost system A system that predetermines unit costs for material, labour, and manufacturing overhead based on costs that should be incurred at normal levels of efficiency and capacity.

Stated interest rate The interest rate written in terms of the bond indenture. Also known as "coupon rate" or "face rate."

Statement of cash flows A financial statement that provides information about the cash inflows (receipts) and outflows (payments) for a specific period of time. It is divided into operating activities, investing activities, and financing activities, and allows users to assess an enterprise's capacity to generate cash and cash equivalents and its needs for cash resources.

Statement of changes in shareholders' equity The financial statement that reconciles the balance of the retained earnings account, common shares, and other shareholders' equity accounts from the beginning to the end of the period (under IFRS).

Statement of comprehensive income The financial statement that reconciles net income to comprehensive income; reconciling items include unrealized gains and losses on certain financial instruments, and debits/credits from related party or other transactions not recognized in net income (under IFRS). Some companies provide a combined statement of income and comprehensive income.

Statement of financial position The financial statement that shows an enterprise's financial condition at the end of a period. Also known as *Balance sheet*.

Statement of income/earnings The main financial statement that reports a company's financial performance during the period.

Statement of retained earnings The financial statement that reconciles the balance of the retained earnings account from the beginning to the end of the period (under ASPE).

Stewardship Management's responsibility to manage assets with care and trust, which is described as its fiduciary relationship.

Straight-line method A method of depreciation (or amortization) where depreciation is considered a function of the passage of time.

Strict cash basis A basis of reporting whereby revenues and expenses are recorded only when cash is received or paid out.

Subsequent events Events that occur after the balance sheet date, but before the financial statements are issued.

Subsidiary A corporation that is being controlled by another corporation.

Subsidiary ledger A ledger that contains the details related to a given general ledger account.

Sum-of-the-years'-digits method A decreasing charge depreciation method where the depreciable amount is multiplied each year by a decreasing fraction related to the number of years in the asset's useful life.

Supplementary information Information that may include details or amounts that presents a different perspective from that adopted in the financial statements.

T account A convenient method of illustrating the effect of transactions on particular asset, liability, equity, revenue, and expense items.

Tangible capital assets Assets that are acquired for use in operations and not for resale, are long-term in nature, and are usually subject to depreciation and possess physical substance.

Tax basis See *Tax value*.

Tax value The UCC of a capital asset at any point in time. Also known as "tax basis."

Technology-based intangible assets Innovations or technological advances such as patented technology and trade secrets.

Temporary accounts Revenue, expense, and dividend accounts; except for dividends, they appear on the statement of comprehensive income. Temporary accounts are closed at the end of each fiscal year; permanent accounts are left open. Also known as "nominal accounts."

Terminal loss What occurs when the disposition of the last asset in its class results in a positive balance remaining in the CCA class.

Timeliness A characteristic of relevance that states that information must be available for decision-makers before it loses its capacity to influence their decisions.

Toronto Stock Exchange (TSX) The largest stock exchange in Canada.

Total-earnings approach A method of valuing goodwill where the value of the company as a whole is determined based on the total expected earnings, not just the excess earnings.

Trade discounts A reduction in the catalogue price used to avoid frequent changes in catalogues, to quote different prices for different quantities purchased, or to hide the true invoice price from competitors.

Trade name One or more words, or a series of letters or numbers, or a design or shape that distinguishes a particular enterprise or product. Also known as *Trademark*.

Trade receivables Amounts owed by customers for goods and services rendered as part of the normal course of business operations.

Trademark One or more words, or a series of letters or numbers, or a design or shape that distinguishes a particular enterprise or product. Also known as *Trade name*.

Trading The act of buying and selling for profit in the short term.

Traditional discounted cash flow approach An approach to the discounted cash flow model where the discount rate reflects all risks in the cash flows but the cash flows are assumed to be certain. The stream of contracted cash flows is discounted, and the discount rate is adjusted to accommodate their riskiness.

Transaction An external event involving a transfer or exchange between two or more entities or parties.

Transaction costs Costs associated with the acquisition of financial instruments, such as fees, commissions, or transfer taxes.

Transparency A goal of financial reporting such that the information provided reflects the underlying transactions and events and their effects on a company. Is one of the characteristics of *Representational faithfulness*.

Trial balance A list of all open accounts in the ledger and their balances.

Undepreciated capital cost (UCC) The class of assets' cost less total CCA.

Understandability The quality of information that permits reasonably informed users to perceive its significance.

Unearned revenues Revenues received in cash and recorded as liabilities before they are earned.

Unit of measure The level at which an asset such as property, plant and equipment is recognized (that is, the extent to which separate components are measured and recorded).

Units of production method A method of calculating depreciation whereby depreciation is determined as a function of use or productivity of the asset.

Unrealized holding gains or losses The difference between the fair value and cost (carrying amount) of an asset still held (owned) by the investor.

Useful life The term of service provided by a capital asset, often many years long.

Value in use The present value of the future cash flows expected to be derived from an asset's use and subsequent disposal.

Vendor rebate A retroactive discount on goods if the buyer meets certain criteria, such as purchasing a target quantity within a year.

Verifiability The quality of information that demonstrates that independent measurers, using the same measurement methods, obtain similar results.

Weighted average cost formula A cost formula that determines the average cost of inventory weighted by the number of units purchased at each unit cost. It is calculated as the cost of goods available for sale divided by the number of units available for sale.

Weighted-average accumulated expenditures A calculation of construction expenditures that is weighted by the amount of time that interest cost could be incurred on the expenditure.

With recourse Describing receivables sold via a third party, where the transferor guarantees payment to the seller if the customer fails to pay.

Without recourse Referring to receivables sold via a third party, where the buyer assumes the risk of collection and absorbs any credit losses.

Work sheet A spreadsheet that is used to adjust the account balances and prepare the financial statements.

Work-in-process inventory The cost of the raw material on which production has been started but not completed, plus the direct labour cost applied specifically to this material, and an applicable share of manufacturing overhead costs.

Working capital The excess of total current assets over total current liabilities.

Yield rate The interest rate actually earned. Also known as *Effective interest rate* or *Market rate*.

Zero-interest-bearing notes See *Non–interest-bearing notes*.

Zero-profit method A revenue recognition method used when the outcome of a transaction is not determinable whereby recoverable revenues are recognized equal to costs incurred.

Some conventions to note when using this glossary: Terms listed but **not** defined refer to *defined synonyms* as "See…". Terms listed and defined refer to *listed synonyms* as "Also known as" with the synonyms in italics. Terms listed and defined refer to *unlisted synonyms* as "Also known as" with the synonyms in quotation marks.

Company Index

A

Accounting Standards Oversight Council (AcSOC), 14
Adelphia Communications Corp., 621
Aeroplan, 734
Aimia Inc., 734, 734n
Air Canada, 53, 85, 104, 170–172, 224–225, 227–228, 228, 241–242, 251, 529, 668, 672, 673, 731, 734
Air Liquide, 178–179
Airbus Commercial, 180, 465
Aliant Inc., 678
American Accounting Association, 60
American Institute of Certified Public Accountants (AICPA), 60
Andrew Peller Limited, 520
Apple Computer, 484, 738, 765
Arthur Andersen, 4
ASD Specialty Healthcare, Inc., 230
AstraZeneca, 229
Atlanta Business Chronicle, 328n
Atlas Cold Storage Income Trust, 621

B

Bank for International Settlements, 524
Bank of Montreal, 217
Bay Street, 182
BCE Inc., 217–218, 370, 402, 406–407, 421, 603, 636
Bell Aliant, 218, 372, 376
Bell Canada, 372, 736, 747
Bennett Environmental Inc., 82
Best Buy, 165, 332, 333
BHP Biliton plc, 666
Biovail Corporation, 234
The Boeing Company, 465
Bombardier Inc., 309, 333, 747, 749
BP plc, 625, 626
Brand Finance, 747n
Bre-X Minerals (Bre-X), 82
British Airways plc, 227, 672, 796
British Columbia Securities Commission, 16
Brookfield Asset Management Inc., 216, 596, 730
Brookfield Office Properties Inc., 312

C

Cameco Corporation, 168–169, 454, 455
Canada Life, 529, 558–560
Canada Revenue Agency (CRA), 181, 306, 473, 678
Canadian Accounting Standards Board (AcSB), 12, 13, 14, 20, 24, 39, 44, 188
Canadian Bankers Association (CBA), 524
Canadian Business, 314n, 345n
Canadian Coalition for Good Governance, 30

Canadian Institute of Chartered Accountants (CICA), 13, 57, 599
Canadian National Railway Company, 730
Canadian Pacific Railway Limited, 697, 730
Canadian Public Accountability Board (CPAB), 19
Canadian Radio-television and Telecommunications Commission (CRTC), 372, 752
Canadian Securities Administrators (CSA), 19, 88, 217, 678
Canadian Tire Bank, 400
Canadian Tire Corporation, Limited, 389–390, 400, 401, 402, 442, 520, 730
Canadian Utilities Limited, 408
Carlson Marketing, 734
CBC News online, 36n
Cendant, 18
Centerra Gold Inc. (Centerra), 168–169
CGA-Canada, 77n
Chapters, 457
CIBC, 306
ClubLink Enterprises Limited, 233–234, 529, 602
Coca-Cola, 328, 736, 750
Coles, 457
College of Business (Auburn University), 446
Committee of Sponsoring Organizations of the Tredway Commission (COSO), 60, 61n
Competition Bureau of Canada, 171
Corus Entertainment Inc., 759, 760, 761–763

D

Debenham, 484
Dr. Pepper, 484

E

EADS N.V. (European Aeronautic Defence and Space Company), 179–180, 332, 370, 447
ECT Merchant Investments Corp., 44
Eli Lily and Company, 450, 798
Empire Company Limited, 236–237, 381, 443, 521, 665
Enron Corporation, 4, 18, 44, 86, 306, 556
European Commission, 171–172
European Financial Reporting Advisory Group, 20

F

Facebook Inc., 323–324
Falconbridge Ltd., 684
Financial Accounting Foundation, 22n

Financial Accounting Standards Board (FASB), 13, 16, 22, 24, 39, 43, 49, 61, 66, 186, 252–253, 346, 352, 353, 410, 563, 608, 740, 767
Financial Consumer Agency of Canada, 524
Financial Executives International, 60
First Canadian Place, 596
First Capital Realty, 666, 731

G

General Electric Canada Finance Inc., 53
General Electric Capital Canada Inc. (GE), 224
George Weston Limited, 9
Glacier Credit Card Trust, 401
Goldcorp Inc., 310
Google, 747
Groupe Aeroplan Inc., 734, 734n
Groupon, 314, 314n, 345

H

Hart Stores Inc., 488
IIBO Canada, 760
The Hershey Company, 694–695
Hollinger International Inc., 678
Husky Energy, 680
HydroMississauga, 520

I

IFRS Advisory Council, 15
IFRS Foundation, 14
IMAX, 749
Imperial Oil, 332
Indigo Books & Music Inc., 457, 457n, 529
Industry Canada, 746
Institute of Internal Auditors, 60
Institute of Management Accountants, 60
International Accounting Standards Board (IASB), 12, 13, 14–15, 15, 16, 20, 21, 22, 24, 39, 49, 61, 66, 71, 186, 188, 190, 252–253, 254, 310, 323, 346, 351, 352, 353, 410, 411, 485, 526, 549, 557, 563, 629, 631, 699, 740, 767
International Accounting Standards Committee (IASC), 14
International Financial Reporting Interpretation Committee (IFRIC), 14–15, 15, 17
International Integrated Reporting Committee (IIRC), 23

K

Kenora Municipal Telephone Services, 372
Kmart Holding, 462
Kobo Inc., 457
Kraft Foods Inc., 498
Kumtor Gold Company (Kumtor), 169

L

Livent Inc., 18, 42–43, 51, 621
Loblaw Companies Limited, 43, 244, 443, 521, 665, 696, 747
L'Oréal, 797
Lufthana, 731
Lululemon Athletica Inc., 736

M

Macy's, Inc., 159, 160
Magna International Inc., 375, 421, 665
Magnotta Winery Corporation, 322, 324–325
Mainstreet Equity Corp., 216
Manufacturers Hanover Trust Co., 413
Maple Leaf Foods Inc., 309, 442
MasterCard, 400
Matsushita Electric of Canada Ltd., 520
Mattamy Homes Limited, 345
McDonald's, 170, 749
Medi-System Technologies Inc., 259
MEGA Brands Inc., 483–484
Microsemi Corporation, 379
Microsoft, 738, 747, 766
Murale, 259

N

Napster Inc., 165
NASDAQ (National Association of Securities Dealers Automated Quotation), 16, 165
National Association of Accountants, 60
Navistar International Corp., 331
Newfield Exploration Company, 666
Nexen Inc., 157, 158, 159
Nike, Inc., 796
Nortel Networks Inc., 27, 162–163, 738, 738n, 749
Northern Tel, 372
Novartis Ophthalmics (Novartis), 230, 231
Nutreco N.V., 479–480, 480
NYSE (New York Stock Exchange), 16

O

Ontario Power Generation (OPG), 671
Ontario Securities Commission (OSC), 2, 13, 16, 42

P

Petro-Canada, 615, 749
Pharmaprix, 220, 259
Pharmaprix Simplement Santé, 259
Polaroid, 749
Postmedia, 163n
Potash Corporation Saskatchewan Inc., 389, 449, 591

Priceline, 345, 345n
Priority Healthcare Distribution, Inc., 230
Province of Ontario, 19
Public Company Accounting Oversight Board (PCAOB), 19
Public Sector Accounting Board (PSAB), 13, 599

Q

QLT Inc., 230–232, 231
Quebecor Inc., 310, 757, 766

R

Reitmans (Canada) Limited, 488
Research In Motion (RIM), 321, 321n, 697, 738, 747, 749
Rhapsody International Inc., 165
Rite-Aid, 18
Rogers Communications, 333, 747
RONA Inc., 449
Roots Canada, 736
Roxio Inc., 165
Royal Ahold, 462
Royal Bank of Canada (RBC), 216, 217, 220, 220n, 528, 590, 747
Royal LePage, 749

S

Sears Canada Inc., 375, 401
Shoppers Drug Mart Corporation, 151, 216, 220, 220n, 256, 259–287, 309, 370, 447, 519, 590
Shoppers Drug Mart Specialty Health Network Inc., 259
Shoppers Home Health Care, 220
Shoppers Simply Pharmacy, 259
Simmons & Company, 680, 680n
Sino-Forest Corporation, 36, 36n
SmithBooks, 457
SNC Lavalin, 333
Sobeys Inc., 236, 529
Sony Corp./ATV Music Publishing, 748
Sothgobi Resources Ltd., 173
Standard & Poor's, 182
Standards Interpretation Committee (SIC). see International Financial Reporting Interpretation Committee (IFRIC)
Stantec Inc., 389
Stora Enso Oyi, 519, 665
Sunbeam, 18
Suncor Energy, 375
Sunpower, 332, 333

T

Talisman Energy Inc., 237
Teck Resources Limited, 84

Télébec, 372
TELUS Corporation (Telus), 333, 370, 438
Thomson Reuters Corporation, 310
Tim Hortons, 744, 749
Toronto Stock Exchange (TSX), 16, 36, 42, 67–68, 743
Toyota Motor Corporation, 496, 749
TransAlta Corporation, 602, 683, 684
Treehouse, 760
Trenton Cold Storage Transportation and Logistics, 332

U

Unilever Group, 763–765
United States Department of Justice, 171, 306
University of Arkansas, 446
U.S. Federal Reserve, 306
U.S. Justice Department. see United States Department of Justice
U.S. Securities and Exchange Commission (SEC), 13, 16, 18, 22, 60, 61, 162, 306, 314, 323, 328, 328n, 331, 331n, 345, 462, 462n

V

Valeant Pharmaceuticals International, 234–235
Via Rail Canada, 681–682
Visa, 400
Viterra Inc., 478
Vodaphone, 747

W

W Network, 760
The Wallstreet Journal, 413
Walmart Stores Inc., 43, 157, 158, 159, 498, 747
West Jet, 104, 104n
Whitewing, 44
World Financial Center, 596
WorldCom Inc., 4, 31, 621
World's Biggest Book Store, 457

X

Xerox, 749

Y

YTV, 760

Z

Zarlink Semiconductor Inc., 379
Zipcar, 154, 154n

Subject Index

A

abnormal shortages, 493
abnormal terms, 320
accelerated amortization, 676
account, 91
    see also specific types of accounts
    adjunct account, 242
    contra account, 242
    contra asset account, 103
    crediting the account, 92
    debiting the account, 92
account titles, 242
accounting
    accrual-basis accounting, 9–10, 51,
      551
    aggressive accounting, 11
    and capital allocation, 5–6
    challenges and opportunities, 18–23
    conservative accounting, 11
    defined, 5
    double-entry accounting, 92
    essential characteristics of, 5
    financial accounting, 5
    goals and purposes, 39–40
    language of, 45
    managerial accounting, 5
accounting cycle, 94, 95
    adjusted trial balance, 111
    adjustments. *See* adjusting entries
    closing process, 112–115
    identifying and recording transactions
      and other events, 94–96
    journalizing, 96
    post-closing trial balance, 115
    posting, 96–97
    reversing entries, 115
    summary of, 116
    trial balance, 98
accounting data, 91
accounting equation, 92–94
accounting information system, 23, 90
    see also accounting cycle
    accounting equation, 92–94
    basic terminology, 90–91
    debits and credits, 92
accounting oversight board, 19
accounting perspective, 323
accounting policies, 185, 239
accounting standards, 12
    see also Accounting Standards for
      Private Enterprises (ASPE);
      International Financial Reporting
      Standards (IFRS); standard setting
Accounting Standards Board (AcSB), 12,
    13–14, 20
    "component" for discontinued
      operations, 188

conceptual framework, 39
derecognition, 410
Accounting Standards for Private
Enterprises (ASPE), 13
    see also generally accepted accounting
      principles (GAAP); IFRS-ASPE
      comparison
    agricultural produce, 578–579
    amortized cost, 393
    asset retirement costs, 603
    assets held for sale, 167
    associates, investment in, 549, 554,
      560
    biological assets, 578–579, 600, 615
    borrowing costs, 603
    buildings, 614
    changes in accounting principle, 183
    completed-contract method, 326
    comprehensive income and other
      comprehensive income, 48
    control, 49, 554
    cost model, 616
    cost recovery impairment model, 686,
      688, 751
    depreciation, 673
    derecognition, 402, 410
    direct method or indirect method, 248
    discontinued operations, 166
    earnings approach, 323
    and earnings per share, 182
    effective interest method, 605
    equity method, 550
    fair value, 56
    fair value option, 56
    financial assets, 384
    financial instruments, 227
    future income tax assets, 235
    goodwill, 758–759
    held for sale, 691
    impairment, 545
    impairment indicators, 685
    impairment models, 547
    income, 163
    income statement, 172
    incurred loss impairment model, 546
    inventory, 451
    inventory costs, 460
    investment as current asset, 557
    investment disclosures, 557
    investment income, 536
    investment measurement models,
      544–545, 548
    investment property, 614
    liabilities, 239
    long-term construction contracts, 326
    loss provision, 455
    natural resources, 615

    and other comprehensive income, 164
    partial sale of share holdings, 532
    percentage-of-completion method,
      326
    principles-based approach, 21–22, 58
    product costs, 463
    professional judgement, 18
    property, plant, and equipment, 625
    property, plant, and equipment costs,
      601
    real estate construction, 327
    rearrangement and reinstallation,
      625
    receivables, and disclosure, 406
    recognition of components, 600
    retail inventory method, 489
    share-based payments, 607
    significant influence, 549, 553
    statement of retained earnings, 182
    straight-line method, 396, 533
    subsidiaries, 555
    temporary use of land during
      construction, 601
    transaction costs, 393
    transfer of receivables with recourse,
      404
    transfer of receivables without
      recourse, 404
    transfers of receivables, 403
    zero-profit method, 341
Accounting Standards Oversight Council
    (AcSOC), 14
accounting theory, 10
accounts receivable
    see also receivables
    accounts written off, 388–389
    aging method, 385
    aging schedule, 385, 386
    Allowance account, 387–389
    Allowance for Doubtful Accounts,
      386–387
    allowance method, 386–389
    bad debt expense, 387–388
    cash discounts, 382–383
    categories, 375
    collection of account previously
      written off, 388–389
    companies with extensive receivables,
      375
    direct writeoff method, 390–391
    effects on accounts, 389–390
    estimating uncollectible trade
      accounts receivable, 385–386
    impairment, 385–391
    measurement, 382–385
    measurement after acquisition,
      384–385

nonrecognition of interest element, 384

percentage-of-receivables approach, 385

percentage-of-sales approach, 387

planning and control, 375–376

recognition, 382–385

sales discounts, 382–383

sales returns and allowances, 384

trade discounts, 382

accrual basis, 190

accrual-basis accounting, 9–10, 51, 551

accrual basis earnings, 190–194

accruals, 99, 105–108

  accrued expenses, 99, 106–108

  accrued revenues, 99, 105–106

  reversing entries, 124–125

accrued expenses, 99, 106–108

accrued interest, 106–107

accrued revenues, 99, 105–106

accrued salaries, 107–108

accumulated amortization, 745

Accumulated Depreciation account, 625

accumulated other comprehensive income, 111, 184, 237

Accumulated Other Comprehensive Income account, 111, 164

acid-test ratio, 224, 256

acquirer, 753

acquisition cost, 53

acquisition of assets to facilitate sales, 330

AcSB. See Accounting Standards Board (AcSB)

active market, 743

activity approach, 678

activity method, 677

activity ratios, 256, 257

additional services, 319

additions, 621, 622

adjunct account, 242

adjusted trial balance, 91, 111, 117

adjusting entries, 91, 99–100

  accruals, 99, 105–108

  estimated items, 99, 108–111

  prepayments, 99, 100–105

  reclassification adjustment, 543

adjustments columns, 117

administrative expenses, 464

adverse selection, 11, 40

after-closing trial balance, 91

agent, 345

aggressive accounting, 11

aging method, 385

aging schedule, 385, 386

agricultural produce, 478–480

aircraft, 668

all-inclusive approach, 163

allocation technique, 50–51

Allowance account, 387–389, 476

Allowance for Doubtful Accounts, 386–387

allowance for returns, 454

allowance method, 386–389, 476

amortization, 396, 398, 599, 671, 745, 750, 757

see also depreciation; depreciation/amortization

amortized cost, 393

amortized cost model, 532–536

amount due, 382

analysis, 185–186

  depreciation, 695–696

  horizontal analysis, 312

  intangible assets, 765–766

  inventories, 483–485

  investments, 561

  property, plant, and equipment, 695–698

  receivables, 408–409

  revenue analysis, 322

  statement of cash flows, 185

  statement of financial position (balance sheet), 185, 222–223

  transaction, 94

  trend analysis, 312, 322

  vertical analysis, 312

arm's length transaction, 54, 318

artificial time periods, 52

artistic-related intangible assets, 748

ASPE. See Accounting Standards for Private Enterprises (ASPE)

asset account, 92

asset-backed financing, 400

asset-backed securities, 401

asset exchanges, 607–611

asset group, 689–690

asset retirement costs, 463, 603

asset turnover ratio, 257, 696

assets, 46

  see also specific types of assets

  biological assets, 478–480, 600, 615

  classification of, and liquidation approach, 53

  comparison of definitions, 65

  contributed assets, 611–613

  current assets, 228–232

  deferred income tax assets, 235

  disposal of an asset, 166

  donated assets, 611–613

  economic resources, 62–63

  efficiency of asset use, 696–698

  financial assets, 63, 376–377

  function, 226

  future income tax assets, 235

  held for sale, 166, 691

  identifiable, 737

  intangible assets. See intangible assets

  involuntary conversion, 692–693

  long-lived assets, 691

  monetary assets, 226, 607, 738

  net assets, 227

  nonmonetary assets, 226, 607, 739

  other assets, 235

  property, plant, and equipment. See property, plant, and equipment

  proposed definition, 61–63

  qualifying assets, 632

  self-constructed assets, 602

on statement of financial position (balance sheet), 227

tangible nonmonetary assets, 63

associates, 549–554, 560, 563

audit, 6

audit committees, 19

auditors, 6–7

available for sale, 529, 545

average days to sell inventory, 483, 484

avoidable borrowing costs, 602, 632–636

B

bad debt expense, 387–388

bad debts, 99, 109–110, 385–391

balance sheet, 5, 91, 223

  see also statement of financial position (balance sheet)

balance sheet approach, 50

bank accounts, 414

bank charges, 416

bank credits, 416

bank errors, 416

bank overdrafts, 378

bank reconciliation, 416–417

banks, 6, 524

bargain purchase, 756

barter transactions, 54, 318

basic elements, 46

basic loan features, 393

basic terminology, 90–91

basket purchase, 464

beneficial interest, 405

bias

  in financial reporting, 11

  financial reporting bias, 161

  management bias, 11, 20

  motivation to bias information, 11

bifurcated sale, 329–330

bill and hold, 319

billings, 326

biological assets, 478–480, 600, 615

bona fide purchase and sale, 318

bonuses, 19

book value, 103, 551

book value per share, 257

boot, 609

borrowing costs, 463, 602–603, 631–637

brand, 746

brand loyalty, 734

brand name, 746

bright-line tests, 21

broker, 345

budgets, 60

buildings, 613–614

bundled sales, 317

burden, 602

business combination, 739

business component, 165

business environment, 60

business models, 156–159

business perspective

  depreciation, 670–671

  disposition, 670–671

  goodwill, 736–737

impairment, 670–671
  intangible assets, 736–737
  property, plant, and equipment,
    598–599
  sales transaction, 316–322
business transactions, 317–321
buyback agreements, 453–454

C
Canadian Accounting Standards Board
  (AcSB). *See* Accounting Standards Board
  (AcSB)
Canadian Institute of Chartered
  Accountants, 13, 57
Canadian Public Accountability Board
  (CPAB), 19
Canadian Securities Administrators, 19
capital
  allocation of, 5–6
  return of capital, 680
  sources of capital, 6
Capital account, 111
capital allocation, 5
capital allocation process, 5
capital approach, 612
capital cost allowance, 675, 702
capital cost allowance method, 702
capital expenditure, 621
capital gain, 705
capital maintenance theory, 219
capital market risks, 255
capital marketplace
  oversight in, 18–19
  signals to, 56
capital shares, 237
capitalization of borrowing costs, 631–637
capitalization period, 632
capitalization rate, 634
capitalized, 600, 602
carrying amount, 103, 539, 558
cash, 226, 229, 377
  bank overdrafts, 378
  cash equivalents, 377, 378–379
  control of, 374–375, 413
    see also cash controls
  foreign currencies, 378
  IFRS-ASPE comparison, 410
  management, 374–375, 376–380, 413
    see also cash controls
  operating activities, 246, 248
  recognition, 376–380
  reporting cash, 377–379
  restricted cash, 377–378
  summary of cash-related items,
    379–380
cash and cash equivalents, 229
cash basis earnings, 190–194
cash controls
  bank accounts, 414
  imprest petty cash system, 414–415
  internal control, 413
  physical protection of cash balances,
    415–416
  reconciliation of bank balances,

416–418
cash crunch, 249
cash debt coverage ratio, 249–250, 257
cash discounts, 382–383, 604
cash equivalents, 377, 378–379
cash flow patterns, 250
cash flow per share, 252
cash flow statement, 5, 243
  see also statement of cash flows
cash flows
  cash flow patterns, 250
  classification of, 243–244
  discounted, 397
  free cash flow, 250–251
  future cash flows, 63, 226
  interest cash flows, 397
  prospects, 9
cash-generating unit (CGU), 689–690
Cash Over and Short account, 415
cash price equivalent, 604
cause and effect relationship, 50
challenges for accounting profession,
  18–23
changes in accounting principle, 183
checks and balances, 7
cheques
  not-sufficient-funds (NSF) cheques,
    416
  outstanding cheques, 416
CICA Handbook, 13, 17, 451, 492,
  599, 740
  see also Accounting Standards for
    Private Enterprises (ASPE)
classified statement of financial position
  (balance sheet), 228–238
  see also statement of financial position
    (balance sheet)
closing entries, 91, 122
closing process, 112–115
code of ethics, 19
collectibility, 331
collection float, 414
collection of account previously written
  off, 388–389
columnar form, 184
combined statement of income/
  comprehensive income, 173
commencement date, 632
commercial paper, 401
commercial substance, 318, 608
commission, 345
commodity broker-traders, 478
Common Shares account, 111
comparability, 43–44, 59
compensating balances, 378
completed-contract method, 326, 340–341
completeness, 42
componentization, 600, 672
comprehensive income, 47, 48, 163
computer software costs, 751
conceptual framework, 17, 18, 38
  development of, 39–40
  elements of financial statements, 40,
    45–48

expanded conceptual framework, 58
foundational principles, 48–57
objective of financial reporting, 40
overview of, 39–40
proposed financial statement elements
  definitions, 61–65
qualitative characteristics, 40–45
rationale for, 38–39
universally accepted conceptual
  framework, 39
concessionary terms, 319–321, 328
conditional obligation, 63
conditional right, 62
conservatism, 54, 86
conservative accounting, 11
consideration, 317–319, 348
consigned goods, 453
consignee, 334
consignment, 334
consignor, 334
consistency, 45, 59
consolidation, 555
consolidation of financial statements,
  49–50, 555
construction period, 632
constructive obligations, 46, 64, 321–322
contingency, 239
contingent gains, 239
continuing operations, 176
continuous earnings process, 325, 326
contra account, 242, 386
contra asset account, 103
contra items, 242
contract-based approach, 323, 346–350
  allocation of transaction price, 348
  core principle, 346
  determination of transaction price,
    347–348
  five steps, 346–349
  identify contract with customer, 347
  identify separate performance
    obligations, 347
  other issues, 349–350
  recognition of revenue, 348–349
contract-based intangible assets, 748–749
contract law, 321
contractual rights, 226
contractual situations, 240
contractual yield basis, 393
contributed assets, 611–613
contributed surplus, 237
Contributed Surplus account, 111
control, 49, 317, 554
conventional retail inventory method,
  490–492
conversion costs, 463
copyright, 748
corporate scandals, 18
corporate strategy, 528, 530
corporation, 111
cost, 601
  acquisition cost, 53
  amortized cost, 393
  asset retirement costs, 463, 603

avoidable borrowing costs, 602, 632–636
borrowing costs, 463, 602–603, 631–637
computer software costs, 751
conversion costs, 463
development phase costs, 741–742
directly attributable costs, 602
dismantling costs, 603
flow of costs, 456–457
freight costs, 492
historical cost principle, 53, 54
inventory costs. See inventory costs
joint cost, 464
laid-down costs, 54
markup on cost, 482
organization costs, 742
period costs, 51, 464
product costs, 51, 463
property, plant, and equipment, 601–603, 621–626
reimbursement of costs, 330
research phase costs, 741
restoration costs, 603
transaction costs, 393, 530
cost allocation, 671
cost-benefit relationship, 45
cost differentiation strategy, 159
cost formulas, 231, 451, 467–473
    choice of cost formula, 472
    first-in, first-out (FIFO) cost formula, 231, 471–472
    last-in, first-out (LIFO) cost formula, 43, 472–473
    moving-average cost formula, 469
    specific identification, 231, 468–469
    weighted average cost formula, 231, 469–471
cost model (CM), 531–536, 615, 616, 684, 743, 744
cost of goods available for sale or use, 450
cost of goods manufactured, 456
cost of goods sold, 115, 450, 466, 467
cost recovery impairment model, 685–686, 689, 690, 751
cost reduction method, 611
cost-to-cost basis, 336–339
cost-to-retail ratio, 488, 491
coupon rate, 444
coverage (solvency) ratios, 256, 257
credible financial statements, 43
credit, 92
credit extension, 320
credit policy, 319
credit rating agencies, 6
credit risk, 318, 348, 350, 385
crediting the account, 92
creditors, 7
creditworthiness of companies, 223
critical event, 324
cross-references, 242
current assets, 228–232
    cash and cash equivalents, 229
    inventories, 230–232

investments, 557
prepaid expenses, 232
receivables, 230
short-term investments, 229–230
current cash debt coverage ratio, 224, 249, 256
current liabilities, 235–236, 252
current operating performance approach, 163
current ratio, 224, 227, 256, 458, 459
customer acceptance conditions, 319
customer-related intangible assets, 747–748
cut-off schedule, 452

D
debit, 92
debit/credit rules, 93
debiting the account, 92
debt instruments, 527, 530, 563
debt market, 6
debt securities, 527
debt to total assets, 257
decision-making information
    inventory, 450–451
    investments, 529
    sales transactions, 322
decision usefulness, 40
decision-usefulness approach, 9
declining-balance method, 676–677
decreasing charge methods, 676
deferral method, 611
deferred income tax assets, 235
deferred income tax liabilities, 236
deferred payment terms, 604–606
deflation, 52
delayed payment terms, 454, 739
demand deposits, 229
depletion, 671, 678–681
depletion base, 615
depletion expense, 678
depositor errors, 416
deposits in transit, 416
depreciable amount, 672–673
depreciation, 671
    see also amortization
    activity method, 677
    analysis, 695–696
    asset components, 672
    business perspective, 670–671
    capital cost allowance, 675
    declining-balance method, 676–677
    depletion, 671, 678–681
    depreciable amount, 672–673
    depreciation period, 673–674
    diminishing balance methods, 676–677
    double-declining-balance method, 677
    factors considered in depreciation process, 672–674
    IFRS-ASPE comparison, 698
    methods, 674–678
    partial periods, 681–682
    on revalued amount, 616, 637–638
    revision of depreciation rates, 682–683

straight-line method, 675–676
sum-of-the-years'-digits method, 732
units of production method, 677, 678
useful life, 673–674
depreciation/amortization, 102–103
    see also amortization; depreciation
derecognition, 49, 399
    IFRS-ASPE comparison, 410
    intangible assets, 753
    property, plant, and equipment, 691–693
    receivables, 399–406
    sales of receivables, 400–405
    secured borrowings, 400
derecognized, 691
development, 741
development phase, 741
development phase costs, 741–742
diminishing balance methods, 676–677
direct method, 245–248, 475
direct writeoff method, 390–391
directly attributable costs, 602
disclosure
    borrowing costs, 636
    contingent gains, 239
    contra items, 242
    contract-based approach, 349
    cross-references, 242
    date financial statements authorized for issue, 252
    full disclosure principle, 56–57
    goodwill, 760–765
    greater disclosures, 19
    IFRS-ASPE comparison, 410
    increased disclosure under IFRS, 57
    intangible assets, 760–765
    inventories, 482–483
    investment property, fair value of, 620
    investments, 557–560
    Management Discussion and Analysis (MD&A), 57
    material changes, 162
    need for, 12
    non-GAAP earnings, 186
    note disclosures, 5
    notes, 241–242
    notes to financial statements, 185
    parenthetical explanations, 241
    property, plant, and equipment, 693–695
    receivables, 406–408
    restatement of, 19
    revenues, 346
    securitized receivables, 405–406
    supporting schedules, 242
    techniques of disclosure, 240–242
    terminology, 242
discontinued operations, 165–169
    assets held for sale, 166
    formal plan, 166, 168
    measurement, 167–169
    multiple-step income statement, 176
    presentation, 167–169
    separate component, 165–166

discount, 397
discount period, 773
discount rate, 327, 772–773
discounted cash flow model, 70
discounted cash flows, 397
discounted free cash flow method, 774
discounts
    cash discounts, 382–383, 604
    employee discounts, 493
    purchase discounts, 460–461, 493
    sales discounts, 382–383, 493
    trade discounts, 382
discrete earnings process, 324
discussion papers (DPs), 15
dismantling costs, 603
disposal of a component, 166
disposal of an asset, 166
disposition, 670–671
    see also sale
distinct, 347
dividend income, 562
dividends, 680–681
Dividends account, 111
donated assets, 611–613
donations of capital assets, 693
double-declining-balance method, 677
double-entry accounting, 92
Drawings account, 111
due process, 14

E
e-commerce transactions, 314
earnings
    all-inclusive approach, 163
    cash basis *versus* accrual basis earnings, 190–194
    earnings before interest, taxes, depreciation, and amortization (EBITDA), 678
    non-GAAP earnings, 185–186
    normalized earnings, 771
    pro forma earnings, 678
    quality of earnings, 160–161, 223
    retained earnings, 237
earnings approach, 323
earnings before interest, taxes, depreciation, and amortization (EBITDA), 678
earnings management, 162
earnings per share (EPS), 163, 164, 181–182, 257
earnings process, 323–327
    continuous earnings process, 325, 326
    long-term contracts, 326–327
    selling goods, 324–325
    selling services, 325–326
economic activity, 49
economic benefits, 738
economic consequences argument, 43
economic entity, 556
economic entity assumption, 49–50
economic environment, 60
economic factors, 673
economic obligations, 63–64

economic resources, 62–63
economic substance, 42
economic theory, 10
economic value, 62
economics of business transactions, 317–321
effective interest method, 392, 395–396, 533, 605
effective interest rate, 397, 444
efficiency of asset use, 696–698
efficient markets hypothesis, 10
efficient use of resources, 5–6
elements of financial statements, 40, 45–48
    assets, 46
    basic elements, 46
    equity, 47
    expenses, 47
    gains, 47
    liabilities, 46–47
    losses, 47
    proposed financial statement elements definitions, 61–65
    recognition, 48, 94
    revenues, 47
employee discounts, 493
enforceability, 63
enhancing qualitative characteristics, 43–44
entity perspective, 9
entity-specific measure, 55
equipment, 614
equitable obligations, 46
equity, 47, 227
equity claims, 555
equity instruments, 527
equity investments, 226
equity market, 6
equity method, 549–553
equity pickup, 550
equity ratios, 227
equity securities, 539
error
    bank errors, 416
    depositor errors, 416
    freedom from material error, 43
    inventory errors, 458–460
estimated items, 99, 108–111
estimates
    in accrual accounting, 160
    inventories, 480–482, 488–494
    recoverable reserves, 679–680
ethical dilemmas, 19–20
ethical sensitivity, 20
ethics
    biased revenue numbers, 322
    centrality of ethics, 19–20
    code of ethics, 19
    concessionary terms, 328
    contractual situations, 240
    controls and governance structure, 60
    cost deferrals, 51
    and disclosure, 240
    earnings management, 162
    ethical dilemmas, 19–20
    ethical sensitivity, 20

fair values, ability to measure, 608
    gross billings, 345
    principles-based GAAP, 59
    promotional payments, 330
event, 91
    see also transaction
    external event, 95
    identification of, 94–96
    internal event, 95
    loss events, 545
    recording of, 94–96
    subsequent events, 240
    trigger events, 545
excess-earnings approach, 770–773
exchange price, 382
executory contract, 454
exit price, 55
expected cash flow approach, 70
expected loss impairment model, 546, 547
expenditures, 621–626
expense account, 92
expenses, 47, 178
    accrued expenses, 99, 106–108
    administrative expenses, 176, 464
    depletion expense, 678
    general expenses, 176, 464
    nature *versus* function, 178–180
    operating expenses, 193–194
    other expenses and losses, 176
    prepaid expenses, 99, 100–103, 232, 739
    presentation, 178–180
    selling expenses, 176, 464
    single-step income statement, 174
exposure drafts (EDs), 15
extensible business reporting language (XBRL), 23, 88, 152–153
external event, 91, 95
    see also transaction
external users, 5
extractive activities (minerals, oil and gas), 485–486, 629, 699

F
face rate, 444
face value, 392, 393–394
factoring receivables, 400–405
factors, 400
fair value, 392, 596, 616, 686
    active market, 743
    estimate of, 54
    fair value standard, 607–609
    intangible asset, 752
    investment property, 684
    less costs of disposal, 687
    less costs to sell, 478–480
    loans receivable, 392
    not equal to cash consideration, 399
    notes receivable, 392
    recognition at more than fair value, 608
    relative fair value method, 329
fair value hierarchy, 68
fair value loss impairment model, 547–548

fair value method, 233
fair value model (FVM), 615, 619–620, 625
fair value option, 56, 544, 562
fair value principle, 55–56
fair value standard, 607–609
fair value test, 752
fair value through net income (FV-NI), 110, 536–541
fair value through other comprehensive income (FV-OCI), 110, 541–545
fair value through profit or loss (FVTPL), 536
favourable lease, 749
feedback/confirmatory value, 41, 164, 176
financial accounting, 5
Financial Accounting Standards Board (FASB), 13, 16
    common conceptual framework, 61
    conceptual framework, 39
    contract-based approach, 346–350, 352
    debt instruments, 563
    financial instruments, 410–411
    financial statement presentation, 252
    intangible assets, 767–768
    last-in, first-out (LIFO) accounting, 43
    reporting entity, defining, 49
financial analysts, 185
financial assets, 63, 376–377
financial components approach, 404
financial crisis, 8, 18, 524
financial engineering, 59
financial flexibility, 224, 226, 249–250
financial institutions, 6, 8
financial instruments, 226–228
financial market risks, 255
financial obligations, 64
financial reporting, 5
    bias in, 11
    conceptual framework. See conceptual framework
    decision-usefulness approach, 9
    economic or business environment, 60
    entity perspective, 9
    financial engineering, 59
    fraudulent financial reporting, 59–60
    integrated reporting, 23
    issues, 58–61
    objective of financial reporting, 8–10, 58
    other pressures, 60–61
    proprietary perspective, 9
    stakeholders, 6–8
financial reporting bias, 161
financial risk, 558
financial statements, 5, 91
    see also specific types of financial statements
    analysis of, 185
    basic elements, 46
    consolidation, 49–50, 555
    credible financial statements, 43

elements of financial statements, 40, 45–48
general-purpose financial statements, 9, 40
misclassification, and key ratios, 251
note disclosures, 5
notes to financial statements, 56–57, 185
and ownership structure, 111–112
preparation, from work sheet, 119–121
presentation. See presentation
proposed financial statement elements definitions, 61–65
supplementary information, 57
financing activities, 156, 243
finished goods inventory, 449
finite life, 745
first-in, first-out (FIFO) cost formula, 231, 471–472
first principles, 59
fixed assets, 599
    see also property, plant, and equipment
flexibility, 59
flow of costs, 456–457
FOB destination, 321, 452
FOB shipping point, 321, 452
foreign currencies, 378
foundational principles, 48–57
    measurement, 51–56
    presentation and disclosure, 56–57
    recognition and derecognition, 48–51
franchise, 749
fraudulent financial reporting, 59–60
Freakonomics (Levitt and Dubner), 11–12
free cash flow, 250–251
freedom from material error, 43
freight costs, 492
full disclosure principle, 56–57
function, 178, 226
fundamental qualitative characteristics, 41–43
future cash flows, 63, 226
future income tax assets, 235
future income tax liabilities, 236
future performance, 160
future value tables, 802, 804
FV-OCI model. See fair value through other comprehensive income (FV-OCI)
FV-OCI model with recycling, 542
FV-OCI model without recycling, 542

G
GAAP. See generally accepted accounting principles (GAAP)
GAAP hierarchy, 17–18
gains, 47, 170
    contingent gains, 239
    FV-NI investments, 540
    other revenues and gains, 176
    versus revenues, 344
    unrealized holding gain or loss, 99, 110

unrealized holding gain or loss—OCI, 99, 110
unrealized holding gains or losses, 530
general chequing account, 414
general expenses, 464
general journal, 96, 97
general ledger, 91, 96
general-purpose financial statements, 9, 40
generally accepted accounting principles (GAAP), 7, 12
    see also Accounting Standards for Private Enterprises (ASPE)
    in absence of specific GAAP guidance, 59
    application to Canadian entities, 13
    CICA Handbook, 13, 17
    comprehensive income, 163
    conceptual framework, 17
    GAAP hierarchy, 17–18
    not always optimal, 161
    other sources of GAAP, 17
    primary sources, 17, 47, 495
    principles-based approach, 21–22, 59
    principles versus rules, 21–22
    professional judgement, 18
    rational and systematic allocation policy, 50–51
    rules-based approach, 21
    sources of GAAP, 17
    U.S. GAAP, 16, 21, 473
    see also Financial Accounting Standards Board (FASB)
going concern assumption, 53
goods, 317
    consigned goods, 453
    goods in transit, 452–453
    highly interrelated goods and services, 347
    physical goods, 450, 452–457
    sale of goods, 323, 324–325
    see also sales transaction
Goods and Services Tax (GST), 463, 614
goods in transit, 452–453
goodwill, 553, 736–737, 753–759
    amortization, 757
    bargain purchase, 756
    comparing results, 766
    definition, 753–754
    disclosure, 760–765
    discount period, 773
    discount rate, 772–773
    discounted free cash flow method, 774
    excess-earnings approach, 770–773
    IFRS-ASPE comparison, 767
    impairment, 757–759
    internally generated goodwill, 754
    measurement, 754–756
    negative goodwill, 756
    number of years method, 774
    presentation, 760
    purchased goodwill, 754–756
    recognition, 754–756
    total-earnings approach, 773–774
    valuation, 770–775

valuation after acquisition, 757
government grants, 611–613, 629
Great Depression, 12
gross method, 383, 460, 461
gross profit, 494
gross profit method, 480–481
gross profit percentage, 481–482
gross revenues, 345

H
half-year rule, 703
hard numbers, 160
Harmonized Sales Tax (HST), 463, 614
held for sale, 166, 691, 699
held for trading, 529, 544
held to maturity, 544
highest and best use, 67
highly interrelated goods and services, 347
historical cost-based model, 54
historical cost principle, 53, 54
holder, 400
horizontal analysis, 312
hyperinflation, 52

I
IASB. *See* International Accounting
    Standards Board (IASB)
identifiable, 737
identifiable net assets, 753
identifying and recording transactions and
    other events, 94–96
IFRS. *See* International Financial
    Reporting Standards (IFRS)
IFRS Advisory Council, 15
IFRS-ASPE comparison
    see also Accounting Standards for
        Private Enterprises (ASPE);
        International Financial Reporting
        Standards (IFRS)
    accounting changes, 187
    associates, 563
    cash and cash equivalents, 410
    cash flow per share information, 252
    current *versus* non-current liabilities,
        252
    depreciation, 698
    derecognition, 410
    disclosure, 410, 699
    disclosure of date financial statements
        authorized for issue, 252
    discontinued operations, 187
    dividend income, 562
    earnings per share, 187
    expenses, classification of, 187
    fair value option, 562
    goodwill, 767
    held for sale, 699
    impairment, 562–563, 698, 767
    income statement, required
        presentation on face of, 187
    intangible assets, 766–767
    interest income, 562
    inventories, 485
    investment measurement models, 562

investments, 562–563
measurement, 351
other comprehensive income/
    comprehensive income, 187
"probable," and recognition of losses
    and liabilities, 49
property, plant, and equipment,
    626–628, 698–699
realized gains and losses, 562
receivables, 410
reclassifications, 562
recognition, 350–351
statement of cash flow, 252
statement of financial position
    (balance sheet), 252
statement of retained earnings *versus*
    statement of changes in
    shareholders' equity, 187
subsidiaries, 563
IFRS Foundation, 14
impaired, 684, 751
impairment, 684
    accounts receivable, 385–391
    asset group, 689–690
    business perspective, 670–671
    cash-generating unit (CGU), 689–690
    cost recovery impairment model,
        685–686, 689, 690, 751
    equity method, 553
    goodwill, 757–759
    IFRS-ASPE comparison, 562–563,
        698, 767
    impairment loss, 686, 688
    indefinite-life intangibles, 752–753
    indicators of impairment, 684–685
    intangible assets, 751–753
    inventory, 451
    limited-life intangibles, 751–752
    rational entity impairment model,
        685, 687–689, 689, 690, 751, 752
    recognition and measurement models,
        685–689
impairment loss, 686, 688
impairment models, 545–548
    expected loss impairment model, 546,
        547
    fair value loss impairment model,
        547–548
    incurred loss impairment model,
        545–546, 547
implicit interest rate, 394
imprest bank accounts, 414
imprest system, 414–415
imputation, 398
imputed interest rate, 398
in-process research and development
    (R&D), 739
incidental transactions, 47
income
    comprehensive income, 47, 48, 163
    dividend income, 562
    interest income, 536–537, 562
    investment income, 536–541, 542–543
    measurement, 163–165

net income, 52, 112, 163, 345
operating income, 160, 163
other comprehensive income. *See*
    other comprehensive income (OCI)
income approach, 612
income statement, 5, 91, 156
    see also statement of income/
        comprehensive income (income
        statement)
income statement effects, 558
Income Summary account, 112
income taxes column, 119
incurred loss impairment model, 545–546,
    547
indefinite life, 745, 746, 749, 752–753
indirect method, 245–248, 476
industries, 156–159
inflation, 52
information asymmetry, 10–12, 40
    adverse selection, 11, 40
    moral hazard, 11, 40
information overload, 56
information symmetry, 10
input measures, 335
inspections, 621, 622
institutional investors, 10
insurance, 101–102
intangible assets, 63, 234–235, 671, 737
    acquired for shares, 739
    analysis, 765–766
    artistic-related intangible assets, 748
    business perspective, 736–737
    characteristics, 737–738
    comparing results, 766
    contract-based intangible assets,
        748–749
    cost model (CM), 743, 744
    cost recovery impairment model, 751
    customer-related intangible assets,
        747–748
    derecognition, 753
    development phase, 741
    development phase costs, 741–742
    disclosure, 760–765
    fair value, 752
    favourable lease, 749
    finite life, 745
    IFRS-ASPE comparison, 766–767
    impairment, 751–753
    in-process research and development
        (R&D), 739
    included and excluded costs,
        742–743
    indefinite life, 745, 746, 749,
        752–753
    intellectual capital, 765
    internally developed intangible assets,
        740–743
    knowledge assets, 765
    lacking in physical substance, 737
    limited life, 745–746, 749
    long-lived intangible assets, 751
    marketing-related intangible assets,
        746–747

measurement, 738–746
measurement after acquisition, 743–746
measurement at acquisition, 738–740
missing values, 765–766
most common types of, 759
nonmonetary, 738
prepayments, 739
presentation, 760
purchased in business combination, 739
rational entity impairment model, 751, 752
recognition, 738–746
recognition after acquisition, 743–746
recognition at acquisition, 738–740
research phase, 741
research phase costs, 741
revaluation model (RM), 743, 744
technology-based intangible assets, 749–751
integrated reporting, 23
intellectual capital, 765
interest, 604
interest-bearing investment, 533
interest-bearing notes, 391, 396–398
interest cash flows, 397
interest income, 536–537, 562
interest rates
coupon rate, 444
effective interest rate, 397, 444
face rate, 444
implicit interest rate, 394
imputation, 398
imputed interest rate, 398
market rate, 444
stated interest rate, 444
yield rate, 444
internal control, 413
internal control systems, 19
internal event, 95
internal users, 5
internally generated goodwill, 754
International Accounting Standards (IAS), 17
see also International Financial Reporting Standards (IFRS)
biological assets, 600
borrowing costs, 602, 631
fair value through other comprehensive income investments, 164
financial statement presentation, 253
government grants and assistance, 629
hyperinflation, 52
impairment of assets, 689
intangible assets, 740
investment property, 614
long-term contracts, 327
loss provision, 454–455
markdowns, 492
property, plant, and equipment, 599, 614, 692

provisions, contingent liabilities and contingent assets, 629
International Accounting Standards Board (IASB), 12, 14–16, 17, 20–21, 61
see also International Financial Reporting Standards (IFRS)
"component" for discontinued operations, 188
conceptual framework, 39
contract-based approach, 323, 346–350, 352
control, 557
debt instruments, 563
extractive activities (minerals, oil and gas), 485–486, 629, 699
financial instruments, 410–411
financial statement presentation, 252–253
impairments, 563
intangible assets, 740, 767–768
"Performance Reporting" project, 186–188
reporting entity, defining, 49
significant influence, 549
variable interest entity, 557
International Accounting Standards Committee (IASC), 14
International Financial Reporting Interpretation Committee (IFRIC), 14, 17
International Financial Reporting Standards (IFRS), 13, 17–18
see also generally accepted accounting principles (GAAP); IFRS-ASPE comparison; International Accounting Standards (IAS); International Accounting Standards Board (IASB)
accumulated other comprehensive income, 111
agricultural produce, 478–479, 479–480
all-inclusive approach, 163
asset retirement costs, 603
assets held for sale, 167
associates, investment in, 549, 554, 560
balance sheet approach, 50
biological assets, 478–480, 600, 615
Canadian transition to, 2
comprehensive income, 48
control, 49, 554
cost model, 616
depreciation, 671, 673, 683
derecognition, 402
direct method or indirect method, 248
discontinued operations, 166
discount rate, 327
earnings approach, 323
effective interest method, 533, 605
equity method, 550
evolution of a new or revised IFRS, 15

expenses, 178
fair value, 55
fair value measurement, 629
fair value method, 233
fair value option, 56
financial assets, 384
financial instruments, 227, 410–411
goodwill, 758–759
held for sale, 691
impairment, 545
impairment indicators, 685
impairment models, 547
income, 163
increased disclosure, 57
incurred loss impairment model, 546
indefinite-life intangible assets, 752–753, 753
inspections, 625
intangible assets, 767
inventory, 43, 451
inventory costs, 460
inventory disclosures, 483
investment as current asset, 557
investment disclosures, 557, 558
investment income, 536
investment measurement models, 544–545, 548
investment property, 614, 616
liabilities, 239
major overhauls, 625
mineral resources, 629
natural resources, 615
other comprehensive income, 48, 111, 164
percentage-of-completion method, 327
principles-based approach, 21–22, 58
product costs, 463
professional judgement, 18
property, plant, and equipment, 625
property, plant, and equipment costs, 601
purchase commitments, 456
rational entity impairment model, 687, 688, 751, 752
real estate construction, 327
receivables, and disclosure, 406
recognition of components, 600
replacements, 625
research and development costs, 743
retail inventory method, 489
revaluation method, 233
revaluation model, 616, 617
revenues, and disclosure, 346
share-based payments, 607
significant influence, 553
statement of changes in equity, 182, 184
statement of comprehensive income, 172, 173
subsidiaries, 554–555
temporary use of land during construction, 601
transaction costs, 393

transfer of receivables with recourse, 404

transfer of receivables without recourse, 404

United States, and IFRS, 22

zero-profit method, 327, 341

International Integrated Reporting Committee (IIRC), 23

Internet, 12

intraperiod tax allocation, 181

inventories, 451
- accounting definition, 451–452
- agricultural produce, 478–480
- analysis, 483–485
- biological assets, 478–480
- buyback agreements, 453–454
- categories, 449
- closing procedures, 114–115
- commodity broker-traders, 478
- companies with inventory, 446–447
- consigned goods, 453
- cost formulas, 231, 451, 467–473
- cost of goods available for sale or use, 450
- cost of goods sold, 450, 467
- costs. See inventory costs
- decision-making information, 450–451
- disclosure, 482–483
- ending inventory, 471
- estimating inventory, 480–482, 488–494
- exceptions to LC&NRV model, 477–480
- fair value less costs to sell, 478–480
- finished goods inventory, 449
- first-in, first-out (FIFO) cost formula, 231, 471–472
- flow of costs, 456–457
- goods in transit, 452–453
- gross profit method, 480–481
- gross profit percentage, 481–482
- IFRS-ASPE comparison, 485
- impairment, 451
- insurance purposes, 482
- interim reporting, 482
- inventory accounting systems, 464–467
- inventory errors, 458–460
- last-in, first-out (LIFO) cost formula, 43, 472–473
- lower of cost and net realizable value, 473–477
- management, 449–450
- measurement, 460–482
- merchandise inventory, 449
- moving-average cost formula, 469
- nature of, and assessment of value, 231
- net realizable value, 477–478
- periodic inventory system, 115, 466–467
- perpetual inventory system, 114–115, 465, 466–467
- physical count, 114
- physical goods, 450, 452–457
- planning and control, 449–450
- presentation, 482–483
- primary sources of GAAP, 495
- purchase commitments, 454–456
- quantities only system, 467
- raw materials inventory, 449
- recognition, 451–460
- retail inventory method, 488–494
- risk-rewards, and recognition, 456
- sales with delayed payment terms, 454
- sales with high rates of return, 454
- special items, 492–493
- specific identification, 231, 468–469
- specific inventory, 495
- on statement of financial position (balance sheet), 230–232
- supplementary system, quantities only, 467
- understanding inventory, 446–451
- understated inventories, 452
- weighted average cost, 231
- weighted average cost formula, 469–471
- work-in-process inventory, 449

inventory accounting systems, 464–467

inventory costs, 450, 460–464
- basket purchase, 464
- borrowing costs, 463
- conversion costs, 463
- costs excluded from inventory, 464
- joint product costs, 464
- product costs, 463
- purchase discounts, 460–461
- service providers' work in process, 463–464
- standard cost system, 463
- vendor rebates, 461–462

inventory errors, 458–460
- ending inventory misstated, 458–459
- purchases and inventory misstated, 459–460

inventory turnover ratio, 257, 483, 484

investee, 528

investing activities, 157, 243

investment property, 614, 616, 684

investment returns, 528
- longer term returns, 528
- short-term returns, 528

investments
- amortized cost model, 532–536
- analysis, 561
- associates, investments in, 549–554, 560
- available for sale, 529, 545
- carrying amount, 558
- companies that have investments, 527–529
- corporate strategy, 528, 530
- cost/amortized cost model, 531–536
- as current asset, 557
- debt instruments, 527, 530
- in debt securities of other entities, 532–536
- decision-making information, 529
- disclosure, 557–560
- equity instruments, 527
- equity investments, 226
- equity method, 549–553
- equity securities, 539
- expected loss impairment model, 546, 547
- fair value loss impairment model, 547–548
- fair value option, 544
- fair value through net income (FV-NI), 110, 536–541
- fair value through other comprehensive income (FV-OCI), 110, 541–545
- financial risk, 558
- held for trading, 529, 544
- held to maturity, 544
- IFRS-ASPE comparison, 562–563
- impairment models, 545–548
- income from investments, 536–541, 542–543
- income statement effects, 558
- incurred loss impairment model, 545–546, 547
- interest-bearing investment, 533
- interest income, 536–537
- major models of accounting for investments, 530–531
- on margin, 530
- measurement, 530–548
- motivations for investing, 527–528
- non-current investments, 232–233
- non–interest-bearing debt investment, 539
- non–interest-bearing investment, 533
- presentation, 557–560
- recoverable amount, 553
- returns, 528
- sale of investments, 535–536, 543–544
- in shares of other entities, 531–532
- short-term investments, 377
- strategic investments, 548–557
- subsidiaries, investments in, 554–557
- transaction costs, 530
- types of, 527
- understanding investments, 527–529
- without significant influence or control, 557–560

investors, 7, 10, 185, 528

involuntary conversion, 692–693

irregular items, 164

irregular transactions, 177

item-by-item approach, 475

J

joint cost, 464

joint product costs, 464

joint ventures, 549, 592

journal, 91

journalizing, 96

K

knowledge assets, 765

L

laid-down costs, 54
land, 613
language of accounting and business, 45
last-in, first-out (LIFO) cost formula, 43, 472–473
late payment charges, 372
lease, 749
leasehold, 749
leasehold improvements, 614
ledger, 91
legal control, 549
legal entity, 49
legal life, 674
legal title, 317, 321, 325, 334, 345
lenient return or payment policy, 319
liabilities, 46–47
    classification of, and liquidation approach, 53
    comparison of definitions, 65
    current liabilities, 235–236, 252
    deferred income tax liabilities, 236
    future income tax liabilities, 236
    long-term liabilities, 236–237
    non-current liabilities, 252
    proposed definition, 63–64
    recognition, 239
    on statement of financial position (balance sheet), 227
liability account, 92
licences, 749
licensing agreement, 749
limited life, 745–746, 749, 751–752
liquidating dividend, 680
liquidation basis, 53
liquidity, 12, 224, 226, 227, 249
liquidity ratios, 224, 256
loans and receivables, 380
loans receivable, 381, 391–399
    see also notes receivable
    fair value, 392
    long-term loans receivable, 392–399
    short-term loans receivable, 391–392
lockbox accounts, 414
long-lived assets, 691
long-lived intangible assets, 751
long-term contracts, 326–327, 335–344
    completed-contract method, 326, 340–341
    losses on, 341–344
    percentage-of-completion method, 326, 327, 335–340
    zero-profit method, 327, 341
long-term liabilities, 236–237
long-term loans receivable, 392–399
long-term notes receivable, 392–399
loss events, 545
loss provision, 454–455
losses, 47
    FV-NI investments, 540
    impairment loss, 686, 688

on long-term contracts, 341–344
other expenses and losses, 176
profitable contract, 341–342
unprofitable contract, 342–344
unrealized holding gain or loss, 99, 110
unrealized holding gain or loss—OCI, 99, 110
unrealized holding gains or losses, 530
low cost/high volume strategy, 159
lower of cost and market, 473
lower of cost and net realizable value, 473–477
    allowance method, 476
    application of, 474–475
    direct method, 475
    evaluation of, 477
    indirect method, 476
    and markdowns, 492
    net realizable value, 474
    and property, plant, and equipment, 684
    rationale for, 473–474
    recording, 475–477
lower of cost and net realizable value (LC&NRV) standard, 474
loyalty programs, 220
lump-sum price, 606
lump-sum purchases, 606

M

major overhauls, 621, 622
maker, 391
management best estimate, 43
management bias, 11, 20
Management Discussion and Analysis (MD&A), 56, 57
managerial accounting, 5
markdown cancellations, 489, 490
markdowns, 489
market, 473
market-based measure, 55
market rate, 444
market valuation model, 54
market value, 103
marketing-related intangible assets, 746–747
markup, 489
markup cancellations, 489
markup on cost, 481, 482
matching, 50–51, 99
material changes, 162
materiality, 41, 42
MD&A: Guidance on Preparation and Disclosure (CICA), 57
measurement, 51–56
    accounts receivable, 382–385
    of company performance, 5–6
    discontinued operations, 167–169
    entity-specific measure, 55
    fair value principle, 55–56
    going concern assumption, 53
    goodwill, 754–756
    historical cost principle, 54

IFRS-ASPE comparison, 351
and impairment, 685–689
income, 163–165
input measures, 335
intangible assets, 738–746
internally developed intangible assets, 740–743
inventories, 460–482
investments, 530–548
long-term loans receivable, 392–399
long-term notes receivable, 392–399
market-based measure, 55
measurement uncertainty, 52, 54, 185, 328, 349
monetary unit assumption, 52
onerous contracts, 330
output measures, 335
parts of a sale, 329–330
payments to customers, 330–331
periodicity assumption, 52
property, plant, and equipment, after acquisition, 615–626
property, plant, and equipment cost, 604–615
and recognition, 51, 94
revenue recognition, 327–331
short-term loans receivable, 391–392
short-term notes receivable, 391–392
tools, 52
unit of measure, 600
measurement uncertainty, 52, 54, 185, 328, 349
merchandise inventory, 449
merchandising concerns, 449
mineral resource properties, 615
mineral resources, 615, 629, 671, 678–681
minority interest, 555
misclassification, and key ratios, 251
mixed valuation model, 54
modified cash basis, 192
monetary assets, 226, 607, 738
monetary unit assumption, 52
moral hazard, 11, 40
most advantageous market, 67
moving-average cost formula, 469
multiple deliverables, 317
multiple-step income statement, 174–177

N

natural resource properties, 615
natural resources, 36, 615, 679–680
    see also mineral resources
nature, 178
negative goodwill, 756
net assets, 227
net income, 52, 112, 163, 345
net income column, 119
net markdowns, 489, 491, 492
net markups, 489
net method, 383, 461
net realizable value (NVR), 53, 385, 473, 474, 477–478, 491
net revenues, 345
net working capital, 236

neutrality, 42, 59
non-current investments, 232–233
non-current liabilities, 252
non-financial obligations, 64
non-GAAP earnings, 185–186
non–interest-bearing debt investment, 539
non–interest-bearing investment, 533
non–interest-bearing notes, 391
non-operating transactions, 174
non-reciprocal transfers, 611–613
noncash consideration, 348
noncontrolling interest accounts, 555
nonmonetary, non-reciprocal transactions, 54
nonmonetary assets, 226, 607, 739
nonmonetary exchanges, 606–611
nonmonetary transactions, 54, 318, 607–608
nontrade receivables, 381
normal production capacity, 463
normal shortages, 493
normal terms, 320
normalized earnings, 771
not-sufficient-funds (NSF) cheques, 416
note disclosures, 5
notes, 241–242
notes receivable, 380–381, 391–399
    effective interest method, 395–396
    face value, 393–394
    fair value, 392
    fair value not equal to cash
        consideration, 399
    interest-bearing notes, 391, 396–398
    issued at other than face value,
        394–398
    long-term notes receivable, 392–399
    non–interest-bearing notes, 391
    present value, 394
    for property, goods, or services,
        398–399
    short-term notes receivable, 391–392
    straight-line method, 396, 398
    zero-interest-bearing notes, 391, 394
notes to financial statements, 56–57, 185
number of years method, 774

O
objective of financial reporting, 8–10, 40,
    58
obligations, 63
obsolescence, 673
off–balance sheet, 409
on margin, 530
one-line consolidation, 553
onerous contracts, 330, 455
ongoing services, 319
Ontario Securities Commission (OSC), 2,
    13, 16, 186
operating activities, 157, 243, 246, 248
operating cycle, 229
operating expenses, 193–194
operating income, 160, 163
operating items, 164
operating market risks, 255

operating transactions, 174
operations, 160
opportunities, 157
opportunities for accounting profession,
    18–23
ordinary activities, 47, 170–172, 322
ordinary repairs, 625
ordinary revenue-generating activities, 47
ordinary trade accounts, 230
organization costs, 742
other assets, 235
other comprehensive income (OCI), 47,
    48
    accumulated other comprehensive
        income, 111, 237
    fair value through other
        comprehensive income (FV-OCI)
        investments, 110
    under IFRS, 164
    multiple-step income statement, 176
    versus net income, 345
    unrealized holding gain or loss—OCI,
        99, 110
output measures, 335
outstanding cheques, 416
overhead, 602
oversight in capital marketplace, 18–19
owners' equity, 111, 237–238
ownership
    interest, 47
    legal title, 317, 321, 325, 334, 345
    risks and rewards (benefits) of
        ownership, 325, 345
ownership structure, 111–112

P
parent, 554
parenthetical explanations, 241
partial periods, and depreciation, 681–682
partnership, 111
past performance, 160
patent, 749–751
patent amortization, 750
payee, 391
payment terms, 320
payments to customers, 330–331, 348
payout ratio, 257
percentage-of-completion method, 326,
    327, 335–340
percentage-of-receivables approach, 385
percentage-of-sales approach, 387
performance obligations, 63, 347
performance of service, 325
performance reporting
    see also statement of income/
        comprehensive income (income
        statement)
    business models, 156–159
    communication of information about
        performance, 159–160
    future performance, 160
    industries, 156–159
    past performance, 160
    presentation of performance

information, 169
    quality of earnings/information,
        160–161
period costs, 51, 464
periodic inventory system, 115, 466–467
periodicity assumption, 52
peripheral activities, 170–172
peripheral transactions, 47
permanent account, 91
permits, 749
perpetual franchise, 749
perpetual inventory system, 114–115, 465,
    466–467
petty cash, 414–415
Petty Cash account, 415
physical count, 114
physical factors, 674
physical goods, 450, 452–457
physical life, 673
physical protection of cash balances,
    415–416
plant assets, 599
    see also property, plant, and equipment
point of delivery, 324
political environment, standard setting in,
    20–21, 161
possession, 317, 321, 325
post-closing trial balance, 91, 115
posting, 91, 96–97
predictive value, 41, 54, 163, 164, 176
premium, 398
prepaid expenses, 99, 100–103, 232, 739
prepayments, 99, 100–105
    alternative method for adjusting
        prepayments, 105
    intangible assets, 739
    prepaid expenses, 99, 100–103, 739
    reversing entries, 125–126
    unearned revenues, 99, 103–104
present economic resource, 62, 63
present value, 394
present value factor, 394
present value of consideration, 604
present value tables, 803, 805, 806
presentation, 56–57
    discontinued operations, 167–169
    expenses, 178–180
    goodwill, 760
    intangible assets, 760
    inventories, 482–483
    investments, 557–560
    percentage-of-completion method,
        339–340
    of performance information, 169
    property, plant, and equipment,
        693–695
    receivables, 406–408
    revenues, 344–345
    statement of changes in equity, 184
    statement of comprehensive income
        (income statement), 169–182
    statement of retained earnings,
        182–184
price earnings ratio, 257

price-level change, 52
price risk, 318
primary sources of GAAP, 17, 47, 495
principal, 345
principal market, 67
principles-based approach, 21–22, 58–59
principles *versus* rules, 21–22
private entity GAAP. *See* Accounting
    Standards for Private Enterprises
    (ASPE)
pro forma earnings, 678
product costs, 51, 463
product market risks, 255
productivity, 677
professional judgement, 17, 18, 58
profit margin, 491
profit margin on sales, 257
profit margin ratio, 697
profitability, 160
profitability ratios, 256, 257
profitable contract, 341–342
profits, 19
promissory note, 391, 392
promotional payments, 330
property, plant, and equipment, 233–234,
    599
    additions, 621, 622
    analysis, 695–698
    asset exchanges, 607–611
    asset retirement costs, 603
    biological assets, 615
    borrowing costs, 602–603, 631–637
    buildings, 613–614
    business perspective, 598–599
    capital expenditure, 621
    capitalized, 600
    cash discounts, 604
    cash not exchanged at acquisition,
        604–613
    componentization, 600
    contributed assets, 611–613
    cost elements, 601–603
    cost model, 615, 616
    costs incurred after acquisition,
        621–626
    deferred payment terms, 604–606
    definition, 599–600
    depreciation. *See* depreciation
    derecognition, 691–693
    disclosure, 693–695
    dismantling costs, 603
    donated assets, 611–613
    donations of capital assets, 693
    economic benefits, 670
    efficiency of asset use, 696–698
    equipment, 614
    fair value model, 615, 619–620, 625
    fair value standard, 607–609
    government grants, 611–613
    held for sale, 691
    IFRS-ASPE comparison, 626–628,
        698–699
    impairment. *See* impairment
    inspections, 621, 622

investment property, 614, 616
involuntary conversion, 692–693
land, 613
leasehold improvements, 614
lump-sum purchases, 606
major overhauls, 621, 622
measurement after acquisition,
    615–626
measurement of cost, 604–615
natural resource properties, 615
non-reciprocal transfers, 611–613
nonmonetary exchanges, 606–611
presentation, 693–695
proportionate method, 637–638
rearrangement, 621, 625
recognition principle, 600
reinstallation, 621, 625
repairs, 621, 625
replacement of assets, 695–696
replacements, 621, 622–625
restoration costs, 603
return on investment, 696–698
revaluation, 637–638
revaluation model, 615, 616–619, 625
revenue expenditure, 621
sale of, 691–693
self-constructed assets, 602
share-based payments, 606–607
proportionate method, 637–638
proposed financial statement elements
    definitions, 61–65
proprietary perspective, 9
proprietorship, 111
provincial securities commissions, 13,
    16–17
provision, 454–455
Public Company Accounting Oversight
    Board (PCAOB), 19
Public Sector Accounting Handbook (CICA),
    599
purchase allowances, 493
purchase commitments, 454–456
purchase discounts, 460–461, 493
purchase returns, 492
purchasers, 400

Q
qualifying assets, 632
qualitative characteristics, 40–45
    comparability, 43–44
    cost-benefit relationship, 45
    elements of financial statements, 40
    enhancing qualitative characteristics,
        43–44
    fundamental, 41–43
    relevance, 41–42, 45
    representational faithfulness, 41,
        42–43, 45
    timeliness, 44
    trade-offs, 45
    understandability, 44
    verifiability, 44
quality of earnings, 161–162, 223
quantitative data, 52

quantitative factors, 41
quantities only system, 467
Quebec Sales Tax (QST), 614
quick ratio, 224, 256

R
radio-frequency identification (RFID),
    446, 465
rate of return on assets (ROA), 257, 697
rate of return on common share equity,
    257
ratio analysis, 255–258
    acid-test ratio, 224, 256
    activity ratios, 256, 257
    asset turnover ratio, 257, 696
    average days to sell inventory, 483,
        484
    book value per share, 257
    cash debt coverage ratio, 249–250,
        257
    cost-to-retail ratio, 488, 491
    coverage (solvency) ratios, 256, 257
    current cash debt coverage ratio, 224,
        249, 256
    current ratio, 224, 227, 256, 458, 459
    debt to total assets, 257
    earnings per share (EPS), 257
    equity ratios, 227
    inventories, 483–485
    inventory turnover ratio, 257, 483,
        484
    liquidity ratios, 224, 256
    and misclassification, 251
    payout ratio, 257
    price earnings ratio, 257
    profit margin on sales, 257
    profit margin ratio, 697
    profitability ratios, 256, 257
    quick ratio, 224, 256
    rate of return on assets, 257, 697
    rate of return on common share
        equity, 257
    receivables turnover ratio, 257, 408
    short-term liquidity ratios, 224
    summary of financial ratios, 256–257
    times interest earned, 257
    turnover ratios, 224
    types of ratios, 256
rational entity impairment model, 685,
    687–689, 689, 690, 751, 752
ratios. *See* ratio analysis
raw materials inventory, 449
realizable (revenue), 50
realization, 322
realized (gains or losses), 530, 562
realized (revenue), 50, 322
rearrangement, 621, 625
rearrangement and reinstallation costs, 625
reasonable knowledge, 44
rebates, 461–462
recapture, 705
receivables, 230
    see also accounts receivable
    analysis, 408–409

definition, 380–382
derecognition, 399–406
disclosure, 405–406, 406–408
factoring receivables, 400–405
financial components approach, 404
IFRS-ASPE comparison, 410
loans receivable, 381, 391–399
net realizable value, 385
nontrade receivables, 381
notes receivable, 380–381, 391–399
presentation, 406–408
with recourse, 404–405
sales of receivables, 400–405
secured borrowing, 400
trade receivables, 380
transfer of receivables, 401, 403
types of, 380–382
without recourse, 404
receivables management, 376
receivables turnover, 257
receivables turnover ratio, 408
reciprocal, 317–319
reciprocal exchange, 54
reclassification adjustment, 543
recognition, 48–51
    accounts receivable, 382–385
    cash, 376–380
    changes in accounting principle, 183
    control, 49
    economic entity assumption, 49–50
    element, 94
    goodwill, 754–756
    IFRS-ASPE comparison, 350–351
    and impairment, 685–689
    intangible assets, 738–746
    internally developed intangible assets, 740–743
    internally generated goodwill, 754
    inventory, 451–460
    liabilities, 239
    long-term loans receivable, 392–399
    long-term notes receivable, 392–399
    matching principle, 50–51
    and measurement, 51, 94
    property, plant, and equipment, 600
    purchased goodwill, 754–756
    realized and realizable, 50
    revenue recognition. See revenue recognition
    revenue recognition principle, 50
    short-term loans receivable, 391–392
    short-term notes receivable, 391–392
reconciliation of bank balances, 416–418
recording process, 94–98
recoverability test, 685, 686, 752
recoverable amount, 553, 687
recoverable reserves, 679–680
regular-way purchase or sale, 592
reimbursement of costs, 330
reinstallation, 621, 625
related parties, amounts owed by, 230
related party transactions, 54
relative fair value method, 329

relative sales value method, 464
relevance, 41–42, 45
repairs, 621, 625
replacement cost definition of market, 473
replacement of assets, 695–696
replacements, 621, 622–625
reporting entity, 49
representational faithfulness, 41, 42–43, 45
research, 741
research phase, 741
research phase costs, 741
reserves, 162
residual interest, 47
residual value, 668, 671, 672–673, 677
residual value method, 329
resources
    allocation of, 5–6, 40, 44
    economic resources, 62–63
    efficient use of resources, 5–6
    evaluations of alternatives, 44
    extractive activities (minerals, oil and gas), 485–486, 629, 699
    mineral resource properties, 615
    mineral resources, 615, 629, 671, 678–681
    natural resource properties, 615
    natural resources, 615, 679–680
    transfer of, 6
restoration costs, 603
restricted cash, 377–378
retail inventory method, 488–494
    conventional method, 490–492
    special items, 492–493
    terminology, 489–490
retained earnings, 237
Retained Earnings account, 111
retrospective restatement, 183
return on investment, 696–698
returns, investment. See investment returns
returns (sales and purchases), 384, 454, 492
revaluation, 637–638
revaluation method, 233
revaluation model (RM), 615, 616–619, 625, 684, 743, 744
Revaluation Surplus (OCI) account, 619
revenue account, 92
revenue analysis, 322
revenue expenditure, 621
revenue recognition
    accounting perspective, 323
    bifurcated sale, 329–330
    collectibility, 331
    completed-contract method, 326, 340–341
    consignment, 334
    contract-based approach, 323, 346–350
    earnings approach, 323
    earnings process, 323–327
    goods, sale of, 324–325
    long-term contracts, 326–327, 335–344
    measurability, 327–331
    onerous contracts, 330

payments to customers, 330–331
percentage-of-completion method, 326, 327, 335–340
real-world examples, 331–333
revenue recognition principle, 50, 99
services, sale of, 325–326
zero-profit method, 327, 341
revenue recognition principle, 50, 99
revenues, 47, 170, 322
    accrued revenues, 99, 105–106
    disclosure, 346
    versus gains, 344
    gross revenues, 345
    net income versus other comprehensive income, 345
    net revenues, 345
    other revenues and gains, 176
    presentation, 344–345
    realizable (revenue), 50
    realized (revenue), 50, 322
    recognition. See revenue recognition
    sales revenues, 384
    service revenue, 192–193
    single-step income statement, 174
    unearned revenues, 99, 100, 103–104
reversing entries, 91, 115, 124–127
revision of depreciation rates, 682–683
right to access, 62
risk
    credit risk, 318, 348, 350, 385
    financial or capital market risks, 255
    financial risk, 558
    operating or product market risks, 255
    price risk, 318
    and type of activity, 157
risk management, 157
risk/return tradeoff, 157
risks and rewards (benefits) of ownership, 325, 345
rules-based approach, 21

S
sale
    associate, investment in, 553
    delayed payment terms, 454
    of goods, 323, 324–325
    see also sales transaction
    high rates of return, 454
    of investments, 535–536, 543–544
    long-lived assets, 691
    of property, plant, and equipment, 691–693
    of receivables, 400–405
    of services, 325–326
sales discounts, 382–383, 493
sales returns and allowances, 384, 493
sales revenues, 384
sales transaction
    bona fide purchase and sale, 318
    business perspective, 316–322
    concessionary terms, 319–321
    constructive obligation, 321–322
    contract law, 321
    decision-making information, 322

economics of business transactions, 316–322

legalities, 321–322

reciprocal nature, 317–319

revenue recognition. *See* revenue recognition

sale of goods, services or both, 317

salvage value, 673

Sarbanes-Oxley Act (SOX), 18, 19

scarce resources, 5–6

secured borrowing, 400, 402

Securities Act, 19

Securities and Exchange Commission (SEC), 13, 16

securitization, 401, 409

securitization of mortgage assets, 8

securitized debt issues, 401

self-constructed assets, 602

self-interest, 7

selling expenses, 464

selling price, 320

senior unsecured debt, 401

sensitive numbers on financial statements, 41

service life, 673

service providers' work in process, 463–464

service revenue, 192–193

services, 317, 325–326, 347

servicing asset component, 405

servicing liability component, 405

share-based payments, 606–607

shareholders, 555

shipping terms, 320

short-term investments, 229–230, 377

short-term liquidity ratios, 224

short-term notes receivable, 391–392

shortages, 493

significant change, 608

significant influence, 549

single-step income statement, 174

social goals, 154

soft numbers, 160

solvency, 12, 224, 227

solvency ratios, 256

special journals, 96

special purpose entity (SPE), 8, 401, 411

specific identification, 231, 468–469

stakeholders, 6–8

stand-ready obligations, 63

standard cost system, 463

standard setting

Accounting Standards Board (AcSB), 13–14

challenge for, 21–22

and conceptual framework, 38

Financial Accounting Standards Board (FASB), 16

International Accounting Standards Board (IASB), 14–16

need for standards, 12

parties involved in standard setting, 12–13

in political environment, 20–21

provincial securities commissions, 16–17

Securities and Exchange Commission (SEC), 16

standard-setting bodies, 12–13

stated interest rate, 444

statement of cash flows, 91

analysis of, 185

cash flow patterns, 250

caution, 251

content, 243–244

direct method, 245–248

financial flexibility, 249–250

financial liquidity, 249

financing activities, 243

format, 243–244

free cash flow, 250–251

indirect method, 245–248

investing activities, 243

operating activities, 243

perspectives, 250–251

preparation, 245–248

purpose, 243–244

quality of earnings, 223

usefulness of, 222–223, 248–250

statement of changes in equity, 5, 182, 184

see also statement of retained earnings

statement of changes in shareholders' equity, 91, 119, 120

statement of comprehensive income column, 117–118

statement of financial position (balance sheet), 5, 91, 223

accounting policies, 239

additional information reported, 239–240

analysis of, 185, 222–223

assets, 227

cash and cash equivalents, 229

classification, 225–228

classified statement of financial position (balance sheet), 228–238

contingency, 239

contra items, 242

contractual situations, 240

creditworthiness of companies, 223

cross-references, 242

current assets, 228–232

current liabilities, 235–236

elements of, 227

equity/net assets, 227

financial flexibility, analysis of, 224

financial instruments, 226–228

format, 238

intangible assets, 234–235

inventories, 230–232

liabilities, 227

limitations of, 225

liquidity, analysis of, 224

long-term liabilities, 236–237

monetary assets, 226

non-current investments, 232–233

nonmonetary assets, 226

notes, 241–242

other assets, 235

owners' equity, 237–238

parenthetical explanations, 241

prepaid expenses, 232

preparation, 228–238

preparation, from work sheet, 120–121

property, plant, and equipment, 233–234

receivables, 230

short-term investments, 229–230

solvency, analysis of, 224

subsequent events, 240

supplemental statement of financial position, 239

supporting schedules, 242

techniques of disclosure, 240–242

terminology, 242

usefulness of, 222–225

statement of financial position column, 117–118

statement of income/comprehensive income (income statement), 5, 91, 156

see also income statement

basic presentation requirements, 172

business models and industry, 156–159

combined statement of income/comprehensive income, 173

communication of information about performance, 159–160

condensed, 177

continuing operations, 176

discontinued operations, 165–169, 176

earnings per share (EPS), 181–182

expenses (nature *versus* function), 178–180

hard and soft numbers, 160

intraperiod tax allocation, 181

measurement, 163–165

multiple-step income statement, 174–177

ordinary *versus* peripheral activities, 170–172

preparation, from work sheet, 119, 120

presentation, 169–182

sections, 176

shortcomings, 160–161

single-step income statement, 174

statement of income/earnings, 156

see also income statement; statement of income/comprehensive income (income statement)

statement of retained earnings, 5, 91, 182–184

see also statement of changes in equity

stewardship, 11, 40

stock market crash, 12

straight-line amortization, 534

straight-line method, 396, 398, 533, 675–676

strategic investments, 548–557

associates, investments in, 549–554
subsidiaries, investments in, 554–557
strict cash basis, 190
structured financings, 59
subjective values, 54
subprime mortgages, 8
subsequent events, 240
subsidiary, 554–557, 563
subsidiary ledger, 91
substantial completion or performance, 324
sum-of-the-years'-digits method, 732
supplemental statement of financial position, 239
supplementary information, 57
supplementary schedules, 177
supplies, 101
supporting schedules, 242

T

T account, 96
tangible capital assets, 599
  see also property, plant, and equipment
tangible nonmonetary assets, 63
tax basis, 703
tax value, 703
techniques of disclosure, 240–242
technology, impact of, 22–23
technology-based intangible assets, 749–751
temporary account, 91
temporary use of land during construction, 601
10-column work sheet, 116
terminal loss, 705
time value of money, 327, 348
timeliness, 44
times interest earned, 257
Toronto Stock Exchange (TSX), 16
total-earnings approach, 773–774
trade discounts, 382
trade-in allowance, 609
trade name, 746
trade-offs, 45, 157
trade receivables, 380
trademark, 746
trading, 528
traditional discounted cash flow approach, 70
transaction, 91, 95
  see also event
  analysis of, 94
  arm's length transaction, 54, 318
  barter transactions, 54, 318
  business perspective, 316–322
  e-commerce transactions, 314

identification of, 94–96
incidental transactions, 47
irregular transactions, 177
non-operating transactions, 174
nonmonetary, non-reciprocal transactions, 54
nonmonetary transactions, 54, 318, 607–608
operating transactions, 174
peripheral transactions, 47
recording of, 94–96
related party transactions, 54
sales transaction. See sales transaction
transaction costs, 393, 530
transaction price, 347–348, 349
transfer-in, 493
transfer of receivables, 401, 403
transparency, 42
trend analysis, 312, 322
trial balance, 91, 98
  adjusted trial balance, 91, 111, 117
  after-closing trial balance, 91
  columns, 117
  post-closing trial balance, 91, 115
  purpose of, 98
trial balance columns, 117
trigger events, 545
tuition fees, 104
turnover ratios, 224
typical business activities, 170–172

U

uncertainty
  acceptable level of uncertainty, 52
  measurement uncertainty, 52, 54, 185, 328, 349
uncollectible accounts, 385–391
unconditional obligations, 63
unconditional right, 62
undelivered items, 329
undepreciated capital cost (UCC), 703
understandability, 44
understated inventories, 452
unearned revenues, 99, 100, 103–104
unit of accountability, 49
unit of measure, 600
unit of operation, 166
United States, and IFRS, 22
units of production method, 677, 678
unprofitable contract, 342–344
unrealized holding gain or loss, 99, 110
unrealized holding gain or loss—OCI, 99, 110
unrealized holding gains or losses, 530
unusual items of substantial amount, 230
U.S. GAAP, 16, 21, 473

see also Financial Accounting Standards Board (FASB)
U.S. stock markets and exchanges, 16
useful life, 102, 600, 625, 673–674, 749
users of financial information, 5, 6–7, 40

V

value in use, 593, 687
variable interest entity, 556–557
vendor rebates, 461–462
verifiability, 44
vertical analysis, 312
volume rebates, 330

W

warranties, 350
weighted-average accumulated expenditures, 633
weighted average cost formula, 231, 469–471
with recourse, 404–405
withdrawal account, 111
without recourse, 404
work-in-process inventory, 449
work sheet, 116–122
  adjusted trial balance, 117
  adjustments columns, 117
  adjustments entered on, 116–117
  closing entries, 122
  income taxes column, 119
  monthly statements, yearly closing, 122
  net income column, 119
  preparation of financial statements, 119–121
  statement of changes in shareholders' equity, 119, 120
  statement of comprehensive income, 119, 120
  statement of comprehensive income column, 117–118
  statement of financial position, 120–121
  statement of financial position column, 117–118
  10-column work sheet, 116
  trial balance columns, 117
  work sheet columns, 117–119
working capital, 236, 458
written off, 388–389

Y

yield rate, 444

Z

zero-interest-bearing notes, 391, 394
zero-profit method, 327, 341